Fourteenth Edition

ANTHROPOLOGY

THE HUMAN CHALLENGE

WILLIAM A. HAVILAND
Professor Emeritus, University of Vermont

HARALD E. L. PRINS
Kansas State University

DANA WALRATH
University of Vermont

BUNNY McBRIDE
Kansas State University

 **WADSWORTH**
CENGAGE Learning·

Australia • Brazil • Japan • Korea • Mexico • Singapore • Spain • United Kingdom • United States

WADSWORTH
CENGAGE Learning®

Anthropology: The Human Challenge,
Fourteenth Edition
William A. Haviland, Harald E. L. Prins,
Dana Walrath, Bunny McBride

Publisher: Yolanda Cossio

Senior Acquisitions Editor: Aileen Berg

Senior Developmental Editor: Lin Gaylord

Assistant Editor: Margaux Cameron

Editorial Assistant: Victor Luu

Media Editor: John Chell

Senior Brand Manager: Liz Rhoden

Senior Market Development Manager: Michelle Williams

Senior Content Project Manager: Cheri Palmer

Senior Art Director: Caryl Gorska

Manufacturing Planner: Judy Inouye

Rights Acquisitions Specialist: Don Schlotman

Production Service: Joan Keyes, Dovetail Publishing Services

Photo Researcher: Sarah Evertson

Text Researcher: Sarah D'Stair

Copy Editor: Jennifer Gordon

Text Designer: Lisa Buckley

Cover Designer: Larry Didona

Cover Image: Mountain gorillas, Bwindi Impenetrable National Park, Uganda: Paul Souders. / Man engraving a stone for a monastery, Myanmar (Burma): Felix Hug. / Man dressed as monkey god enters into trance, Singapore: Jack Fields. / Skeletons unearthed at ancient mass grave dating to the sixth century AD, Tyre, Southern Lebanon: Hassan Bahsoun. / Globe image: Ocean. / Woman in sari with laptop, Rajasthan: Jami Tarris. / Spacewalk: NASA / Bryan Allen. / Light trails circling stupa at Wat U-Mong, Thailand: Brent T. Madison. / North Pole tourists form a circle and dance through all the time zones: Peter Guttman.

Compositor: PreMediaGlobal

For product information and technology assistance, contact us at
Cengage Learning Customer & Sales Support, 1-800-354-9706.

For permission to use material from this text or product,
submit all requests online at **www.cengage.com/permissions.**
Further permissions questions can be e-mailed to
permissionrequest@cengage.com.

Library of Congress Control Number: 2012949885

Student Edition:
ISBN-13: 978-1-133-94132-3
ISBN-10: 1-133-94132-X

Loose-leaf Edition:
ISBN-13: 978-1-133-94534-5
ISBN-10: 1-133-94534-1

Wadsworth
20 Davis Drive
Belmont, CA 94002-3098
USA

Cengage Learning is a leading provider of customized learning solutions with office locations around the globe, including Singapore, the United Kingdom, Australia, Mexico, Brazil, and Japan. Locate your local office at **www.cengage.com/global.**

Cengage Learning products are represented in Canada by Nelson Education, Ltd.

To learn more about Wadsworth, visit **www.cengage.com/wadsworth.**
Purchase any of our products at your local college store or at our preferred online store **www.CengageBrain.com.**

Printed in the United States of America
1 2 3 4 5 6 7 17 16 15 14 13

DEDICATION

To **Philip Tobias** (1925–2012), South African paleoanthropologist and antiapartheid activist whose integration of scientific and political facts profoundly shaped evolutionary discourse, the social fabric in his beloved homeland, and countless scholars from across the globe and a diverse range of disciplines who were fortunate to call him professor.

And to the applied anthropologists of the world, in particular **Ann Dunham** (1942–1995), a rural Asia development specialist who embraced the common humanity in cultural differences. Born in Kansas, she was a global citizen who committed her scholarship to assisting the poor in adapting to radical change in the Third World. She was the mother of the 44th president of the United States.

Putting the World in Perspective

Although all humans we know about are capable of producing accurate sketches of localities and regions with which they are familiar, **cartography** (the craft of mapmaking as we know it today) had its beginnings in 16th-century Europe, and its subsequent development is related to the expansion of Europeans to all parts of the globe. From the beginning, there have been two problems with maps: the technical one of how to depict on a two-dimensional, flat surface a three-dimensional spherical object, and the cultural one of whose worldview they reflect. In fact, the two issues are inseparable, for the particular projection one uses inevitably makes a statement about how one views one's own people and their place in the world. Indeed, maps often shape our perception of reality as much as they reflect it.

In cartography, a **projection** refers to the system of intersecting lines (of longitude and latitude) by which part or all of the globe is represented on a flat surface. There are more than a hundred different projections in use today, ranging from polar perspectives to interrupted "butterflies" to rectangles to heart shapes. Each projection causes distortion in size, shape, or distance in some way or another. A map that correctly shows the shape of a landmass will of necessity misrepresent the size. A map that is accurate along the equator will be deceptive at the poles.

Perhaps no projection has had more influence on the way we see the world than that of Gerhardus Mercator, who devised his map in 1569 as a navigational aid for mariners. So well suited was Mercator's map for this purpose that it continues to be used for navigational charts today. At the same time, the Mercator projection became a standard for depicting landmasses, something for which it was never intended. Although an accurate navigational tool, the Mercator projection greatly exaggerates the size of landmasses in higher latitudes, giving about two-thirds of the map's surface to the northern hemisphere. Thus the lands occupied by Europeans and European descendants appear far larger than those of other people. For example, North America (19 million square kilometers) appears almost twice the size of Africa (30 million

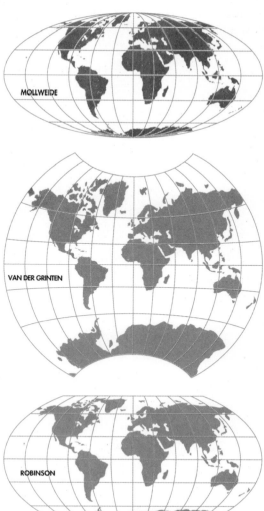

square kilometers), whereas Europe is shown as equal in size to South America, which actually has nearly twice the landmass of Europe.

A map developed in 1805 by Karl B. Mollweide was one of the earlier *equal-area projections* of the world. Equal-area projections portray landmasses in correct relative size, but, as a result, distort the shape of continents more than other projections. They most often compress and warp lands in the higher latitudes and vertically stretch landmasses close to the equator. Other equal-area projections include the Lambert Cylindrical Equal-Area Projection (1772), the Hammer Equal-Area Projection (1892), and the Eckert Equal-Area Projection (1906).

The Van der Grinten Projection (1904) was a compromise aimed at minimizing both the distortions of size in the Mercator and the distortion of shape in equal-area maps such as the Mollweide. Although an improvement, the lands of the northern hemisphere are still emphasized at the expense of the southern. For example, in the Van der Grinten, the Commonwealth of Independent States (the former Soviet Union) and Canada are shown at more than twice their relative size.

The Robinson Projection, which was adopted by the National Geographic Society in 1988 to replace the Van der Grinten, is one of the best compromises to date between the distortions of size and shape. Although an improvement over the Van der Grinten, the Robinson Projection still depicts lands in the northern latitudes as proportionally larger at the same time that it depicts lands in the lower latitudes (representing most Third World nations) as proportionally smaller. Like European maps before it, the Robinson Projection places Europe at the center of the map with the Atlantic Ocean and the Americas to the left, emphasizing the cultural connection between Europe and North America, while neglecting the geographic closeness of northwestern North America to northeastern Asia.

The following pages show four maps that each convey quite different cultural messages. Included among them is the Peters Projection, an equal-area map that has been adopted as the official map of UNESCO (the United Nations Educational, Scientific, and Cultural Organization), and a map made in Japan, showing us how the world looks from the other side.

The Robinson Projection

The map below is based on the Robinson Projection, which is used today by the National Geographic Society and Rand McNally. Although the Robinson Projection distorts the relative size of landmasses, it does so much less than most other projections. Still, it places Europe at the center of the map. This particular view of the world has been used to identify the location of many of the cultures discussed in this text.

SAAMI

RUSSIANS

SLOVAKIANS
TS SERBS   CHECHENS
BOSNIANS
TURKS
KURDS   UZBEK
AWLAD ALI   BAKHTIARI   TAJIK
BEDOUINS   KOHISTANI
BAHREIN   PASHTUN

YUPIK
ESKIMO

MONGOLIANS

UYGHUR

JAPANESE

TIBETANS   HAN CHINESE

NUER   KAREN   MOSUO   TAIWANESE
DINKA   AFAR   TIGREANS   SHAIVITE
AZANDE   SOMALI
                     NAYAR   VEDDA
TURKANA   KOTA AND   TRUK
MBUTI   NANDI   KURUMBA   TODA AND   ACEH
              KIKUYU   MALDIVES   BADAGA
HUTU   MAASAI   MINANGKABAU
AND TUTSI GUSII TIRIKI
HADZA

PINGELAP ISLANDERS

WAPE
KAPAUKU ENGA
              TSEMBAGA
ARAPESH   SOLOMON ISLANDERS
           DOBU TROBRIANDERS

ANSI
MAN

SWAZI
ZULU
BASUTO

BALINESE

ABORIGINAL
AUSTRALIANS

MAORI

TASMANIANS

vii

The Peters Projection

The map below is based on the Peters Projection, which has been adopted as the official map of UNESCO. Although it distorts the shape of continents (countries near the equator are vertically elongated by a ratio of 2 to 1), the Peters Projection does show all continents according to their correct relative size. Though Europe is still at the center, it is not shown as larger and more extensive than the Third World.

Japanese Map

Not all maps place Europe at the center of the world, as this Japanese map illustrates. Besides reflecting the importance the Japanese attach to themselves in the world, this map has the virtue of showing the geographic proximity of North America to Asia, a fact easily overlooked when maps place Europe at their center.

GREENLAND

UNITED
STATES

CANADA

UNITED STATES

MEXICO

THE
BAHAMAS

HAITI
DOMINICAN REPUBLIC

CUBA

JAMAICA

BELIZE
GUATEMALA
EL SALVADOR
HONDURAS
COSTA RICA
PANAMA

NICARAGUA

VENEZUELA

FRENCH GUIANA

COLOMBIA

GUYANA
SURINAM

ECUADOR

BRAZIL

PERU

BOLIVIA

PARAGUAY

CHILE

ARGENTINA

URUGUAY

NEW ZEALAND

ANTARCTICA

The Turnabout Map

The way maps may reflect (and influence) our thinking is exemplified by the Turnabout Map, which places the South Pole at the top and the North Pole at the bottom. Words and phrases such as "on top," "over," and "above" tend to be equated by some people with superiority. Turning things upside-down may cause us to rethink the way North Americans regard themselves in relation to the people of Central America.

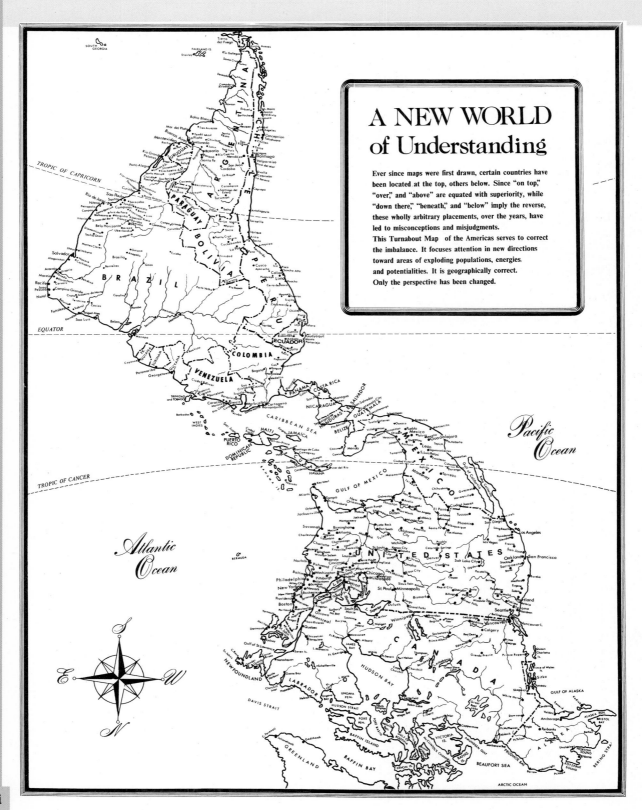

A NEW WORLD of Understanding

Ever since maps were first drawn, certain countries have been located at the top, others below. Since "on top," "over," and "above" are equated with superiority, while "down there," "beneath," and "below" imply the reverse, these wholly arbitrary placements, over the years, have led to misconceptions and misjudgments.

This Turnabout Map of the Americas serves to correct the imbalance. It focuses attention in new directions toward areas of exploding populations, energies and potentialities. It is geographically correct. Only the perspective has been changed.

© Yves Herman/Reuters/Corbis

Chapter 7

Origins of the Genus *Homo* 164

Chapter 8

The Global Expansion of *Homo sapiens* and Their Technology 196

Chapter 9

The Neolithic Revolution: The Domestication of Plants and Animals   224

Chapter 10

The Emergence of Cities and States   248

Chris Trotman/Getty Images

Chapter 11

Modern Human Diversity: Race and Racism   274

Chapter 12
Human Adaptation to a Changing World   298

Chapter 13
Characteristics of Culture   326

Veronique de Viguerie/Getty Images

Chapter 14
Ethnographic Research: Its History, Methods, and Theories   346

Chapter 15

Language and Communication 374

Chapter 16

Social Identity, Personality, and Gender 398

© Harald E. L. Prins

Chapter 20
Kinship and Descent 496

Chapter 21
Grouping by Gender, Age, Common Interest, and Social Status 518

Chapter 22
Politics, Power, War, and Peace 538

Chapter 26

Global Challenges, Local Responses, and the Role of Anthropology   644

Preface

There comes a time when we need to clean out the basement—to sort through the piles clear down to the bottom, to determine what should be kept and what should be tossed, to make room for new things that warrant a place in a limited space. That's what has happened with this edition of *Anthropology: The Human Challenge*—more thoroughly revised than any new edition since Bill Haviland took on coauthors a dozen years ago.

Fueled by our own ongoing research, along with vital feedback from students and anthropology professors who have used and reviewed previous editions, we have scrutinized the archetypal examples of our discipline and weighed them against the latest innovative research methodologies, archaeological discoveries, genetic and other biological findings, linguistic insights, ethnographic descriptions, theoretical revelations, and significant examples of applied anthropology. We believe that these considerations, combined with paying attention to compelling issues in our global theater, have resulted in a lively and relevant textbook that presents both classical and fresh material in ways that stimulate student interest, stir critical reflection, and prompt "ah-ha" moments.

Our Mission

Most students enter an introductory anthropology class intrigued by the general subject but with little more than a vague sense of what it is all about. Thus, the first and most obvious task of our text is to provide a thorough introduction to the discipline—its foundations as a domain of knowledge and its major insights into the rich diversity of humans as a culture-making species. Recognizing the wide spectrum of students enrolled in entry-level anthropology courses, we cover the fundamentals of the discipline in an engaging, illustrative fashion—creating a textbook that establishes a broad platform on which teachers can expand the exploration of concepts and topics in ways that are particularly meaningful to them and their students.

In doing this, we draw from the research and ideas of a number of traditions of anthropological thought, exposing students to a mix of theoretical perspectives and methodologies. Such inclusiveness reflects our conviction that different approaches offer distinctly important insights about human biology, behavior, and beliefs.

If most students start out with only a vague sense of what anthropology is, they often have even less clearly defined—and potentially problematic—views concerning the position of their own species and cultures within the larger world. A second task for this text, then, is to encourage students to appreciate the richness and complexity of human diversity. Along with this goal is the aim of helping them to understand why there are so many differences and similarities in the human condition, past and present.

Debates regarding globalization and notions of progress; the "naturalness" of the mother, father, child(ren) nuclear family; new genetic technologies; and how gender roles relate to biological variation all benefit greatly from the distinct insights gained through anthropology's wide-ranging, holistic perspective. This aspect of the discipline is one of the most valuable gifts we can pass on to those who take our classes. If we as teachers (and textbook authors) do our jobs well, students will gain a wider and more open-minded outlook on the world and a critical but constructive perspective on human origins and on their own biology and culture today. To borrow a favorite line from the famous poet T. S. Eliot, we'll know we've reached the end of our journey when we "arrive where we started/And know the place for the first time" ("Little Gidding" from The Four Quartets).

We have written this text, in large part, to help students make sense of our increasingly complex world and to navigate through its interrelated biological and cultural networks with knowledge and skill, whatever professional path they take. We see the book as a guide for people entering the often-bewildering maze of global crossroads in the 21st century.

A Distinctive Approach

Two key factors distinguish *Anthropology: The Human Challenge* from other introductory anthropology texts: our integrative presentation of the discipline's four fields and a trio of unifying themes that tie the book together.

Integration of the Four Fields

Unlike traditional texts that present anthropology's four fields—physical or biological anthropology, archaeology, linguistics, and cultural or social anthropology—as if they were separate or independent, our book takes an integrative approach. This reflects the holistic character of the discipline in which members of our species are studied in their totality—as social creatures biologically evolved with the inherent capacity for learning and sharing culture by means of symbolic communication. This approach also reflects our collective experience as practicing anthropologists who recognize that we cannot fully understand humanity in all its fascinating complexity unless we see the systemic interplay among environmental, physiological, material, social, ideological, psychological, and symbolic factors, both past and present.

For analytical purposes, however, we discuss physical anthropology as distinct from archaeology, linguistics, and sociocultural anthropology. Accordingly, there are separate chapters that focus primarily on each field, but the links among them are shown repeatedly. Among many examples of this integrative approach, Chapter 11, "Modern Human Diversity— Race and Racism," discusses the social context of race and recent cultural practices that have impacted the human genome. Similarly, material concerning linguistics appears not only in Chapter 15, "Language and Communication," but also in Chapter 4 on primate behavior, Chapter 7 on early *Homo* and the origins of culture, and Chapter 10 on the emergence of cities and states. In addition, nearly every chapter includes a Biocultural Connection feature to further illustrate the interplay of biological and cultural processes in shaping the human experience.

Unifying Themes

In our own teaching, we recognize the value of marking out unifying themes that help students see the big picture as they grapple with the vast array of material involved with the study of human beings. In *Anthropology: The Human Challenge* we employ three such themes.

1. *Systemic adaptation.* We emphasize that every culture, past and present, like the human species itself, is an integrated and dynamic system of adaptation that responds to a combination of internal and external factors, including influences of the environment.
2. *Biocultural connection.* We highlight the integration of human culture and biology in the steps humans take to meet the challenges of survival. The biocultural connection theme is interwoven throughout the text—as a thread in the main narrative and in boxed features that highlight this connection with a topical example for nearly every chapter.
3. *Globalization.* We track the emergence of globalization and its disparate impact on various peoples and cultures around the world. European

colonization was a global force for centuries, leaving a significant and often devastating footprint on the affected peoples in Asia, Africa, and the Americas. Decolonization began about 200 years ago and became a worldwide wave in the mid-1900s. However, since the 1960s, political and economic hegemony has taken a new and fast-paced form: globalization (in many ways a process that expands or builds on imperialism). Attention to both forms of global domination— colonialism and globalization—runs through *Anthropology: The Human Challenge*, culminating in the final chapter where we apply the concept of structural power to globalization, discussing it in terms of hard and soft power and linking it to structural violence.

Pedagogy

Anthropology: The Human Challenge features a range of learning aids, in addition to the three unifying themes described previously. Each pedagogical piece plays an important role in the learning process—from clarifying and enlivening the material to revealing relevancy and aiding recall.

Accessible Language and a Cross-Cultural Voice

In the writing of this text, we consciously cut through unnecessary jargon to speak directly to students. Manuscript reviewers have recognized this, noting that even the most difficult concepts are presented in straightforward and understandable prose for today's first- and second-year college students. Where technical terms are necessary, they appear in bold type with a clear definition in the narrative. The definition appears again in the running glossary at the bottom of our pages, and again in a summary glossary at the end of the book.

To make the narrative more accessible to students, we deliver it in chewable bites—short paragraphs. Numerous subheads provide visual cues to help students track what has been read and what is coming next.

Accessibility involves not only clear writing enhanced by visual cues, but also an engaging voice or style. The voice of *Anthropology: The Human Challenge* is distinct among introductory texts in the discipline because it has been written from a cross-cultural perspective. We avoid the typical Western "we/they" voice in favor of a more inclusive one to make sure the narrative resonates with both Western and non-Western students and professors. Also, we highlight the theories and work of anthropologists from all over the world. Finally, we have drawn the text's cultural examples from industrial and postindustrial societies as well as nonindustrial ones.

Compelling Visuals

The Haviland et al. texts garner praise from students and faculty for having a rich array of visuals, including maps, photographs, and figures. This is important because humans—like all primates—are visually oriented, and a well-chosen image may serve to "fix" key information in a student's mind. Unlike some competing texts, all of our visuals are in color, enhancing their appeal and impact. Notably, all maps and figures are created with a colorblind-sensitive palette.

Photographs

Our pages feature a hard-sought collection of compelling, content-rich photographs. Large in size, many of them come with substantial captions composed to help students do a "deep read" of the image. Each chapter features more than a dozen pictures, including our popular Visual Counterpoints—side-by-side photos that effectively compare and contrast biological or cultural features.

Maps

Map features include our "Putting the World in Perspective" map series, locator maps, and distribution maps that provide overviews of key issues such as pollution and energy consumption. Of special note are the Globalscape maps and stories, described in the boxed features section a bit farther on.

Challenge Issues

Each chapter opens with a Challenge Issue and accompanying photograph, which together carry forward the book's theme of humankind's responses through time to the fundamental challenges of survival within the context of the particular chapter.

Student Learning Objectives, Knowledge Skills, and Chapter Checklist

New to this edition is the set of learning objectives presented at the start of every chapter just after the Challenge Issue and photograph. These objectives focus students on the main goals, identifying the knowledge skills they are expected to have mastered after studying each chapter. The main goals are incorporated in a closing Chapter Checklist, which is also new to this edition.

The Chapter Checklist summarizes the chapter's content in an easy-to-follow format.

Thought-Provoking Questions

Each chapter closes with five Questions for Reflection, including one that relates back to the Challenge Issue introduced in the chapter's opening. Presented right after the Chapter Checklist, these questions ask students to apply the concepts they have learned by analyzing and evaluating situations. They are designed to stimulate and deepen thought, trigger class discussion, and link the material to the students' own lives.

In addition, the Biocultural Connection essay featured in nearly every chapter ends with a probing question designed to help students grapple with and firmly grasp that connection.

Barrel Model of Culture

Past and present, every culture is an integrated and dynamic system of adaptation that responds to a combination of internal and external factors. This is illustrated by a pedagogical device we refer to as the "barrel model" of culture. Depicted in a simple but telling drawing (Figure 13.8), the barrel model shows the interrelatedness of social, ideological, and economic factors within a cultural system along with outside influences of environment, climate, and other societies. Throughout the book examples are linked to this point and this image.

Integrated Gender Coverage

In contrast to many introductory texts, *Anthropology: The Human Challenge* integrates coverage of gender throughout the book. Thus, material on gender-related issues is included in *every* chapter. As a result of this approach, gender-related material in *Anthropology* far exceeds the single chapter that most books devote to the subject.

We have chosen to integrate this material because concepts and issues surrounding gender are almost always too complicated to remove from their context. Spreading this material through all of the chapters has a pedagogical purpose because it emphasizes how considerations of gender enter into virtually everything people do. Gender-related material ranges from discussions of gender roles in evolutionary discourse and studies of nonhuman primates to intersexuality, homosexual identity, same-sex marriage, and female genital mutilation. Through a steady drumbeat of such coverage, this edition avoids ghettoizing gender to a single chapter that is preceded and followed by resounding silence.

Glossary as You Go

The running glossary is designed to catch the student's eye, reinforcing the meaning of each newly introduced term. It is also useful for chapter review, enabling students to readily isolate the new terms from those introduced in earlier chapters. A complete glossary is also included at the back of the book. In the glossaries, each term is defined in clear, understandable language. As a result, less class time is required for going over terms, leaving instructors free to pursue other matters of interest.

Special Boxed Features

Our text includes five types of special boxed features. Nearly every chapter contains a Biocultural Connection, along with two of the following three features: an Original Study, Anthropology Applied, and Anthropologist of Note. In addition, about half of the chapters include a Globalscape. These features are carefully placed and introduced within the main narrative to alert students to their importance and relevance. A complete listing of features is presented just before the detailed table of contents.

Biocultural Connection

Appearing in nearly every chapter, this signature feature of the Haviland et al. textbooks illustrates how cultural and biological processes interact to shape human biology, beliefs, and behavior. It reflects the integrated biocultural approach central to the field of anthropology today. All of the Biocultural Connections include a critical thinking question. For a quick peek at titles, see the listing of features on page xiv.

Original Study

Written expressly for this text, or adapted from ethnographies and other original works by anthropologists, these studies present concrete examples that bring specific concepts to life and convey the passion of the authors. Each study sheds additional light on an important anthropological concept or subject area for the chapter in which it appears. Notably, each Original Study is carefully integrated within the flow of the chapter narrative, signaling students that its content is not extraneous or supplemental. Appearing in twenty-one chapters, Original Studies cover a wide range of topics, evident from their titles (see page xv).

Anthropology Applied

Featured in fourteen chapters, these succinct and fascinating profiles illustrate anthropology's wide-ranging relevance in today's world and give students a glimpse into a variety of the careers anthropologists enjoy (see page xiv for a listing).

Anthropologists of Note

Profiling pioneering and contemporary anthropologists from many corners of the world, this feature puts the work of noted anthropologists in historical perspective and draws attention to the international nature of the discipline in terms of both subject matter and practitioners. This edition highlights twenty-one distinct anthropologists from all four fields of the discipline (see page xiv for a list of the profiles).

Globalscape

Appearing in about half of the chapters, this unique feature charts the global flow of people, goods, and services, as well as pollutants and pathogens. With a map, a story, and a photo highlighting a topic geared toward student interests, every Globalscape shows how the world is interconnected through human activity. Each one ends with a Global Twister—a question that prods students to think critically about globalization. Check out the titles of Globalscapes on page xiv.

Changes and Highlights in the Fourteenth Edition

We have extensively reworked and updated this edition. Definitions of key terms have been honed. Many new visuals and ethnographic examples have been added and others dropped. Every chapter features a new opening photograph and related Challenge Issue that is revised or new. The much-used Questions for Reflection include at least one new question per chapter, plus revisions of effective questions that have been included in previous editions.

As with earlier editions, we further chiseled the writing to make it all the more clear, lively, engaging, and streamlined. On average, chapter narratives have been trimmed by about 10 percent. Also, we have eliminated the chapter "Macroevolution and the Early Primates" by incorporating relevant macroevolutionary material into our chapter on biology, genetics, and evolution (Chapter 2); the primate material from that chapter is now in the chapter on living primates (Chapter 3) and in a new Chapter 6, "From First Primates to First Bipeds." Material on molecular clocks, geologic time, and continental drift is placed in the chapter on methods for studying the past (Chapter 5).

New to this edition is the list of student learning objectives at the start of every chapter, tied to the new Chapter Checklists at the end of every chapter. (Both are described in the pedagogy inventory mentioned earlier.)

In addition to numerous revisions of boxed features, many of these are completely new, including

Biocultural Connections "Bonds Beyond Blood: DNA Testing and Refugee Family Unification," "Chimpanzees in Biomedical Research: Time to End the Practice," "Dogs Get Right to the Point," "Beauty, Bigotry, and the Epicanthic Eyefold of the Beholder," and "Modifying the Human Body"; Original Studies "Disturbing Behaviors of the Orangutan" by Anne Nacey Maggioncalda and Robert M. Sapolsky, "Caveat Emptor: Genealogy for Sale" by Jonathan Marks, and "Can Chantek Talk in Codes?" by H. Lyn White Miles; Anthropology Applied essays "Pre-Columbian Fish Farming in the Amazon" by Clark L. Erickson and "Anthropologist S. Ann Dunham, Mother to a U.S. President" by Nancy I. Cooper; and an Anthropologist of Note profile on shamanic scholar-practitioner Michael Harner.

Finally, we have replaced footnotes with in-text parenthetical citations, making sources and dates more visible and freeing up space for larger visuals. The complete citations appear in the references section at the end of the book.

Beyond these across-the-board changes, significant changes have been made within each chapter.

Chapter 1: The Essence of Anthropology

This chapter gives students a broad-stroke introduction to the holistic discipline of anthropology, the distinct focus of each of its fields, and the common philosophical perspectives and methodological approaches they share. It opens with a new Challenge Issue centered on the mining of coltan—the key component of capacitors in small electronic devices—illustrating our globalized world by revealing the link between the miners and students who use the devices. The lead section on the development of anthropology has been dropped to avoid redundancy with the chapter on ethnographic research. The main narrative now begins with a reworked explanation of the anthropological perspective. As revised, this discussion more carefully contrasts anthropology to other disciplines.

The chapter also offers a brief overview of fieldwork and the comparative method, along with ethical issues and examples of applied anthropology in all four fields, providing a foundation for our two methods chapters—one that explores field methods in cultural anthropology and the other that examines the tools for studying the past shared by archaeology and paleoanthropology. Our presentation of the four fields has been reorganized, starting with cultural anthropology, followed by linguistics, archaeology, and physical or biological anthropology.

This chapter's overview of cultural anthropology has been substantially modified. Changes include a new discussion about how the concept of culture is integral to each of anthropology's four fields. To our narrative on the University of Arizona's modern-day Garbage Project, we added an introductory paragraph about anthropologists studying older garbage dumps, such as shell middens, describing how much these explorations can reveal about everyday life in societies past and present.

The chapter also introduces the concept of ethnocentrism and begins a discussion of globalization that is woven through the text. In addition, this first chapter rejects the characterization of a liberal bias in anthropology, identifying instead the discipline's critical evaluation of the status quo. The ideological diversity among anthropologists is explored while emphasizing their shared methodology that avoids ethnocentrism.

Finally, Chapter 1 introduces the five types of special boxed features that appear in the text, describing the purpose of each, along with an example: a Biocultural Connection on the anthropology of organ transplantation; a Globalscape about the global trafficking of human organs; an Original Study on traditional African healers dealing with HIV/AIDS; an Anthropology Applied about forensic anthropology's role in speaking for the dead; and an Anthropologists of Note profiling two of the discipline's pioneers: Franz Boas and Matilda Coxe Stevenson.

Chapter 2: Biology, Genetics, and Evolution

Covering all the basics of genetics and evolution, this revised chapter's content has been streamlined so that macroevolution, previously covered in a different chapter, can follow right on the heels of our detailed discussion of the microevolutionary process. From a pedagogical standpoint, this helps students make the connections between molecular processes and macroevolutionary change through time.

In order to make the content relevant to students' lives, we emphasize the relationship between culture and science beginning with the new Challenge Issue, featuring a large tattoo of DNA on a freckled upper arm, that illustrates how individuals increasingly turn to DNA to form their identity. A new Biocultural Connection, "Bonds Beyond Blood: DNA Testing and Refugee Family Unification" by Jason Silverstein, likewise shows that the use of genetic testing in isolation does not take into account alternate family structures present in other cultures, particularly those arrangements arising from war and genocide.

A variety of new photos, figures, and content-rich captions reinforce these connections, including a new image of the Great Chain of Being to show the transition from spiritual descriptions of nature toward those with a more scientific basis; a new figure showing Darwin's journey on the HMS *Beagle*; new figures illustrating cladogenesis and anagenesis; new and revised figures on the social consequences of prenatal genetic testing including the use of prenatal testing for sex selection, as well as transnational surrogacy as a social solution to the challenges of infertility for the privileged and wealthy; a new figure illustrating the relation between toxic exposure and mutation; and a revised figure on Darwin's finches that illustrates the connection between gradualism and punctuated equilibria.

Chapter 3: Living Primates

As we trace the basic biology of the living primates, this chapter emphasizes the place of humans within this group, instead of erecting barriers between "us" and "them." A new chapter introduction featuring the early fieldwork of Jane Goodall and a new Challenge Issue on primate conservation set the tone of the chapter.

Biological content is also strengthened through the incorporation of pertinent macroevolutionary concepts such as an expanded comparison of mammalian to reptilian biology that includes a discussion of homeotherms versus isotherms and k-selected versus r-selected species; ancestral and derived characteristics; convergent evolution; preadaptation, adaptive radiation, and ecological niche.

In addition, Michele Goldsmith has updated her exclusive Original Study on ecotourism and primate conservation to illustrate recent changes at her field sites. A new content-rich photo and caption on sexual dimorphism among gorillas expands the discussion of this concept. A new Question for Reflection, comparing mammals and reptiles, prompts students to apply the macroevolutionary concepts of ancestral and derived characteristics.

Chapter 4: Primate Behavior

The new Challenge Issue featuring bonobo sexuality asks students to think about nature versus nurture, a theme that builds throughout the chapter, concluding with our discussion of primate culture.

Frans de Waal's work on reconciliation is now featured in the body of the text to allow for Anne Maggioncalda and Robert Sapolsky's Original Study "Disturbing Behaviors of the Orangutan" on orangutan sexual behavior. Formerly a Biocultural Connection, this reorganization better integrates its content with the text and further develops the theme of how we project our cultural notions onto the study of primates.

A new figure illustrates the various forms of primate social organization, and the text provides more details on marmoset polyandry. We have also augmented our discussion of birth intervals and population size among primates. The chapter closes with an update on NIH policy regarding the use of chimps in biomedical research and a new Biocultural Connection titled "Chimpanzees in Biomedical Research: Time to End the Practice."

Chapter 5: Field Methods in Archaeology and Paleoanthropology

This comprehensive chapter covering methods of investigation opens with the vital question of who owns the past. The Challenge Issue focuses on the current political upheaval in Timbuktu and the potential destruction of monuments, artifacts, and manuscripts in this ancient Muslim city.

Broad chapter changes include moving the material from our old macroevolution chapter on molecular clocks, geologic time, and continental drift into this chapter along with the Anthropologist of Note feature on Allan Wilson. Due to its importance, we moved the material on cultural resource management from a boxed feature into the text proper where students cannot miss it.

Chapter refinements comprise: a revision of the table on dating methods to include more information on process and use of techniques; more emphasis on the human skeleton figure and an insert of the sexually dimorphic pelvis; distinction between frozen remains such as the Ice Man Ötzi and fossil remains; a discussion of the possible deliberate burial at Sima de los Huesos; introduction of the term *archaeological profile*; and a clarified explanation of paleoanthropological and archaeological excavation techniques that avoids suggesting that one is more exacting than the other and that illustrates the laboratory techniques shared by paleoanthropologists, bioarchaeologists, and forensic anthropologists. Finally, a new content-rich photo highlights the difference between looting and real archaeological excavation.

Chapter 6: From First Primates to First Bipeds

Capturing the new inclusion of primate evolution into this chapter, we open with a tightrope-walking chimp from Fongoli to challenge students to think about bipedalism as the defining feature of the hominins. A streamlined introduction to primate evolution follows, including our cladogram illustrating the relationships among the primates, which has been revised to include the chimp–bonobo split.

We also moved the evidence for the earliest potential fossil hominins to this chapter, reorganizing the chapter to make room for this new material. Chapter updates based on recent discoveries include the South African species *Australopithecus sediba*; we both describe and integrate these findings into the discussion about which of these early bipeds led to the human line. We have added thought questions to several figure captions to urge students to participate in the process of paleoanthropological reconstruction. A new photo of reconstructed Laetoli footprints also encourages students to distinguish reenactment based on concrete data from imaginings of the past.

Chapter 7: Origins of the Genus *Homo*

Building on the theme of bringing students into the process of paleoanthropological reconstruction, we open the chapter with paleoartist Elisabeth Daynès bringing a fossil species to life, thus challenging students to think about how to avoid bias. This thread connects to our discussion of Neandertals including a new Visual Counterpoint featuring the varied reenactments that have surrounded their lifeways.

We have dropped "origins of culture" from the chapter title to reflect the current state of primatological research, which has established distinct cultural traditions among our closest relatives. Similarly, this chapter reengages with the notion of purported human uniqueness.

Our section on gender in paleoanthropological reconstructions now includes recent studies on strontium and female dispersal among early hominins. We have tied our discussion on precision grip and cranial capacity back to the previous chapter's discussion of the newly discovered species *Australopithecus sediba*.

Experimental archaeology, a new bolded key term, weaves into our discussion of Oldowan tools and other archaeological assemblages. A photo of the captive bonobo Kanzi making tools helps students visualize the process of reconstructing the past. We have added new material on the potential location of the lost "Peking Man" remains, as well as new evidence for paint fabrication in South Africa 100,000 years ago. Finally, our discussion of the Flores hominins has been placed in this chapter, separating it from the modern human origins controversy.

Chapter 8: The Global Expansion of *Homo sapiens* and Their Technology

To illustrate that paleoanthropology is a science of discovery, we open the chapter with the new, earlier dates for the cave paintings from Spain's El Castillo. This challenges students to consider whether art, once thought to be an accomplishment only of the Cro-Magnons, may have in fact been a part of the Neandertal repertoire. Similarly, our discussion of the recent discoveries related to the Denisovan hominins, and their genetic continuity with extant Asians, shows how paleoanthropologists reshape their understanding of the past as new evidence is discovered.

Our experimental archaeology thread continues in this chapter with a new photo illustrating Upper Paleolithic flint-knapping as well as the content-enriched caption on intricately constructed dwellings made from mammoth bones. We have updated the Biocultural Connection on paleolithic prescriptions for contemporary ailments and made it more relevant to college students by including substances abused today, such as alcohol and tobacco.

The chapter is also enhanced by various other new discoveries including a discussion of the Blombos Cave paint factories, cave flutings by Upper Paleolithic children, as well as new genetic data on peopling of Australia. We have updated our timeline of Upper Paleolithic innovations to include these recent discoveries.

Chapter 9: The Neolithic Revolution: The Domestication of Plants and Animals

This streamlined and updated chapter emphasizes the contemporary relevance of the Neolithic revolution. A new Challenge Issue shows the competition for resources set into motion during the Neolithic, playing out in the context of globalization today as Andean potato farmers battle with industrial asparagus farms that are lowering the aquifers to produce this water-intensive crop for global distribution. The theme of competition for resources threads throughout the chapter.

By incorporating relevant sections of the Biocultural Connection from previous editions on breastfeeding, fertility, and beliefs into the text, we made space for a new Biocultural Connection on the coevolution of humans and dogs featuring the work of evolutionary anthropologist Brian Hare titled "Dogs Get Right to the Point." We have reorganized the heads in the section on why humans became food producers to streamline the content, and we moved the definitions of horticulture and pastoralism to early in the chapter to improve the chapter's conceptual flow. A new Question for Reflection on today's genetically modified crops also drives home the point that today we are still facing challenges introduced during the Neolithic.

Chapter 10: The Emergence of Cities and States

The interrelation of war, power, and monumental structures thematically weaves through this updated chapter. This begins with the new Challenge Issue focusing on the temple at Angkor Wat in Cambodia and the way that the magnificent structure has been the site of violent struggles nearly since its dedication in the 12th century.

An updated introductory section on the interdependence of cities includes Hurricane Katrina, the 2011 Japanese earthquake and tsunami, as well as the role of social media in the Arab Spring of 2011. In a detailed caption, we incorporated key points from the Anthropology Applied feature from previous editions on the U.S. military's employment of archaeologists to train personnel in war zones to preserve archaeological remains. This allowed us to include a new Anthropology Applied feature on rainforest fishing weirs by Clark Erickson titled "Pre-Columbian Fish Farming in the Amazon."

This chapter's rich new visuals include locator maps indicating Mesopotamian sites and the Inca empire; an intriguing photo of a Maya calendar, explaining how it connects to the current doomsday predictions; and a photo of Cairo's "City of the Dead" to illustrate the problems of social stratification today.

Chapter 11: Modern Human Diversity: Race and Racism

Enlivened writing throughout this chapter improves the pedagogy and makes the challenging concepts of race and racism more interesting and accessible for today's students. The new Challenge Issue features NBA star Jeremy Lin to illustrate the social meaning of biological difference.

The chapter now includes the seminal work of Audrey Smedley on the roots of racism in North America, focusing on the English treatment of the Irish along with reference to Bacon's Rebellion. As well, a photo and caption illustrate the Nazi expedition to Tibet in search of the origins of the pure Aryan race.

An updated section includes a discussion of the 2010 census categories of race, and a new footnote to the Tiger Woods story updates the history of African Americans in golf. We also use the families of two U.S. presidents—Thomas Jefferson and Barack Obama—to illustrate cultural beliefs about gene flow.

A new reference to structural violence and race details differences in prison sentences for crack versus powdered cocaine users, a disparity that preferentially privileges the predominantly white users of the more expensive powdered cocaine. Accordingly, we have added the term *structural violence* to the glossary along with the term *genocide*.

Links between Mendel's work on heredity from Chapter 2 strengthen this chapter's discussion of the faults inherent in theories of race and intelligence. The chapter's section on true biological adaptations across populations now includes the work of Gary Nabhan and Laurie Monti on "slow release" foods and activity, instead of the thrifty genotype, and also mentions the rising importance of epigenetics. We moved material on fava beans and G-6-PD to the body of the text to make space for a new Biocultural Connection on ethnic plastic surgery titled "Beauty, Bigotry, and the Epicanthic Eyefold of the Beholder." We are pleased to include as well a new Original Study by Jonathan Marks on the perils and pitfalls of commercial genetic testing titled "Caveat Emptor: Genealogy for Sale."

Chapter 12: Human Adaptation to a Changing World

This chapter provides a broad introduction to human biology and human adaptation, while also reinforcing the powerful influence of culture on all aspects of human biology. The Challenge Issue offers a stunning body map, a life-size depiction of the experience of being an HIV-positive woman in South Africa, to help students see themselves as fully biocultural beings.

A suite of new and revised figures illustrates a variety of biological concepts including a new figure on long bone growth, a new figure on sweat glands, a new figure showing the growth trajectory of different body systems, and a revised figure on human population growth. New figures also help students see the myriad connections between human biology and culture including an intriguing photo of the ship-breaking yards of Bangladesh and a figure on the use of military metaphors in immunology.

We have also expanded our discussion of body fat and fertility globally and added relevant key terms such as *menarche* and *menopause* to the running glossary. As well, our discussion of genetic, developmental, and physiological adaptation has been refined and clarified, again adding the relevant key terms such as *hypoxia* to the glossary.

We close the chapter with new examples of the importance of an integrated anthropological perspective to questions of human health. Among the topics of discussion are the recent appointment of medical anthropologist Jim Yong Kim as the president of the World Bank and ongoing biological evolution as demonstrated in Kenyan sex workers who seem to be HIV-resistant despite constant exposure.

Chapter 13: Characteristics of Culture

This chapter addresses anthropology's core concept of culture, exploring the term and its significance for human individuals and societies. It begins with a new Challenge Issue centered on Kuchi nomads in Afghanistan, easily recognized by their distinctive dress.

As with previous editions, this chapter presents our original "barrel model" illustration, showing the integrative and dynamic nature of culture and introducing the key concepts of the integration of cultural infrastructure, social structure, and superstructure. Subcultures are explored through an ethnographic example of the Amish of North America, and our discussion of ethnicity is illustrated with a map of China's ethnic groups and a photo of the Uyghur. Culture's role in dealing with major issues such as death features a description of cremation rituals in Bali.

As for changes, the section on culture and adaptation has been moved to the beginning of the chapter, setting the foundation for our discussion of culture and its characteristics. As part of the culture and change section, we have added a new discussion distinguishing cultural change from other kinds of change in an individual's life; as well, we have expanded the section on ethnocentrism and reconfigured it into two distinct sections, "Ethnocentrism and Cultural Relativism" and

"Evaluation of Cultures." Striking new photographs have been added, along with captions rich with ethnographic detail: a living root bridge in India, a Sri Lankan father teaching his son to stilt fish, Kapauku villagers and their pigs in New Guinea.

Also new is a Biocultural Connection about human body modifications—from tattoos to circumcision, footbinding, and modern cosmetic surgery. George Esber updated the Anthropology Applied feature about his role in helping to design culturally appropriate homes on the Apache Indian reservation. Finally, the Anthropologist of Note profile on Bronislaw Malinowski has been trimmed in half.

Chapter 14: Ethnographic Research: Its History, Methods, and Theories

This chapter takes a unique approach to discussing ethnographic research. It begins with a historical overview on the subject—from the colonial era and salvage ethnography to acculturation studies, advocacy anthropology, and multi-sited ethnography in the era of globalization. We use the work of numerous anthropologists, past and present, to illustrate this historical journey.

The chapter continues with an overview of research methods—marking out what is involved in choosing a research question and site and how one goes about doing preparatory research and participant observation. This section also covers ethnographic tools and aids, data-gathering methods, fieldwork challenges, and the creation of an ethnography in written, film, or digital formats. Readers will also find an overview of anthropology's theoretical perspectives, along with discussions of the comparative method and the Human Relations Area Files, and the moral dilemmas and ethical responsibilities encountered in anthropological research.

Changes in this chapter include new discussions and photos touching on cyberethnography and dangerous anthropology, and a Visual Counterpoint illustrating multi-sited ethnographic research. Annette Weiner's Original Study on fieldwork in the Trobriand Islands has been shortened.

Chapter 15: Language and Communication

This chapter investigates the nature of language and the three branches of linguistic anthropology—descriptive linguistics, historical linguistics, and the study of language in its social and cultural settings (sociolinguistics and ethnolinguistics). Also found here are sections on paralanguage and tonal languages, an exploration of talking drums and whistled speech. We have retooled the section on language and gender, and we have revised and retitled the body language section to "Nonverbal Communication"

to make it a more fitting header for discussions on proxemics and kinesics.

Our discussion of language loss and revival includes a look at new technology used by linguistic anthropologists collaborating on field research with speakers of endangered Khoisan "click" languages in southern Africa. That section also includes the latest data on the digital divide and its impact on ethnic minority languages, plus an updated chart showing Internet language populations. A historical sketch about writing takes readers from traditional speech performatives and memory devices to Egyptian hieroglyphics to the conception and spread of the alphabet to the 2003 to 2012 Literacy Decade established by the United Nations. A section on literacy and modern telecommunication investigates issues of language in our globalized world.

Boxed features include S. Neyooxet Greymorning's Anthropology Applied essay on language revitalization, a revised Biocultural Connection on the biology of human speech, and a brand-new Original Study and photograph about Lyn Miles's linguistic research with an orangutan.

Chapter 16: Social Identity, Personality, and Gender

Looking at individual identity within a sociocultural context, this chapter surveys the concept of self, enculturation and the behavioral environment, social identity through personal naming, the development of personality, the concepts of group and modal personality, and the idea of national character. It begins with a Challenge Issue about how every society must teach its children the values, social codes, and skills that enable them to become contributing members in the community—illustrated with a new photo of a Khanty mother braiding her daughter's hair inside their tiny wooden home in Siberia.

Our revised investigation of naming practices includes new material on matronyms and teknonyms, the latter illustrated by a striking new photo of a Tuareg naming ceremony. The section on self and the behavioral environment features a new Visual Counterpoint contrasting an Inuit hunter in a sea kayak with an individual navigating cyberspace while waiting to board a plane in a crowded airport.

The heavily reworked discussion of dependence and independence training includes a new narrative and photograph describing interdependence training among the Beng of West Africa. And the section on group personality has a new photo of Yąnomami men with a discussion of their masculine ideal of *waiteri*. The sections on alternative gender models and mental disorders across time and cultures have both been significantly revised and resequenced. For example, the former includes new information about five genders acknowledged by Bugis people of Indonesia, a new paragraph and photo about *hijras* in India, and a new photograph of intersexed Olympian track star Caster Semenya from South Africa.

R. K. Williamson's highly personal Original Study about intersexuality has been streamlined by half. Other special features include an Anthropologist of Note on Ruth Fulton Benedict and a Biocultural Connection about cross-cultural perspectives on psychosomatic symptoms and mental health.

Chapter 17: Patterns of Subsistence

Here we investigate the various ways humans meet their basic needs and how societies adapt through culture to the environment. We begin with a discussion of adaptation, followed by profiles on modes of subsistence in which we look at food-foraging and food-producing societies—pastoralism, crop cultivation, and industrialization. In this edition, chapter headings, along with the narratives they introduce, have been significantly revised to provide greater clarity and a consistent focus on how—across time, space, and cultures—food is obtained, produced, and distributed.

The section on adaptation and cultural evolution includes a new subsection recounting the latest ethnohistorical research on ecosystemic collapse on Rapa Nui, commonly known as Easter Island. A discussion of peasantry leads into an extensive narrative about large-scale industrial food production, using chickens as an example.

The chapter's boxed features include a shortened Original Study on slash-and-burn cultivation in the Amazon basin in Brazil and an Anthropology Applied piece about reviving ancient farming practices in Peru. New visuals accompany the Biocultural Connection on high-altitude subsistence in the Andes and the Globalscape on the international poultry industry. Finally, the conclusion summarizes the pros and cons of new subsistence strategies and technological innovations—how they impact different members of a society in the short and long run.

Chapter 18: Economic Systems

Beginning with a bold, ethnographically rich photo of the open market in Keren, Eritrea, this chapter presents a new, broad-stroke introductory discussion on economic anthropology. The chapter delves into the control of resources (natural, technological, labor) and labor division (by gender or age, through cooperation, or by task specialization). The labor division discussion includes compelling new photographs of child labor and women carrying firewood in Vietnam.

A section on distribution and exchange defines various forms of reciprocity (with a detailed and illustrated description of the Kula ring and a revised definition and new discussion of silent trade), along with redistribution and market exchange. The discussion on leveling mechanisms looks at the potlatch.

Our trimmed concluding section on local economies and global capitalism discusses guest laborers, the global tourism industry, the impact of mobile phones on small producers in remote areas, and genetically modified seeds developed and marketed worldwide—all indicating the economic opportunities and challenges of our era. We also include a new section on the informal economy.

Boxed features in this chapter are a Biocultural Connection on chocolate, Amanda Stronza's Anthropology Applied piece on global ecotourism in Bolivia, and an Anthropologist of Note profile on Rosita Worl, a Tlingit activist.

Chapter 19: Sex, Marriage, and Family

Exploring the inseparable connections among sexual reproductive practices, marriage, family, and household, this chapter opens with a gorgeous new photo of a Muslim bride and her female relatives and friends displaying hands decorated with traditional henna designs. Particulars addressed in this chapter include the incest taboo, endogamy and exogamy, dowry and bridewealth, cousin marriage, same-sex marriage, divorce, residence patterns, and nonfamily households. Up-to-date definitions of *marriage, family, nuclear family*, and *extended family* encompass current real-life situations around the world.

We have reworked and reorganized this chapter's opening paragraphs on marriage and the regulation of sexual relations so they are more logically constructed and easier to follow. A new, recent example of Shariah law as it relates to women and adultery has been added, and the commentary about the relationship between such restrictive rules and the incidence of HIV/AIDS has been nuanced. A short, timely piece on the breakaway Mormon group, the Fundamentalist Church of Jesus of the Latter-Day Saints, has been added to the discussion of polygamy in the United States, along with new data on the decline of polygyny in sub-Saharan Africa.

New visuals include a striking photo of a polyandrous family in Nepal and a vibrant picture of a joyous gay wedding in Connecticut. In the section on residence patterns, we have added brief explanations of ambilocal and avunculocal, and we have fleshed out the section on divorce to clarify its broad impact and the most common reasons for divorce across cultures. Finally, we have revised the chapter's conclusion with new material sketching the impact of global capitalism, electronic communication, and transnationalism on love relations. We have also included new subheads marking the discussions of diversity in families (adoption and new reproductive technologies) and changes in households (migrant workforces).

Boxed features include an Anthropologist of Note box commemorating Claude Lévi-Strauss, Martin Ottenheimer's Biocultural Connection on marriage prohibitions in the United States, a Globalscape chronicling the blessings and issues of transnational adoption, and Serena Nanda's newly illustrated Original Study on arranged marriage in India.

Chapter 20: Kinship and Descent

Beginning with a new photograph showing the opening parade of a clan gathering in Scotland, this chapter marks out the various forms of descent groups and the role descent plays as an integrated feature in a cultural system. We present details and examples concerning lineages, clans, phratries, and moieties (highlighting Hopi Indian matriclans and Scottish highland patriclans, among others), followed by illustrated examples of a representative range of kinship systems and their kinship terminologies. The definition of the term *kinship* itself has been fine-tuned, and the chapter includes an entirely new section on bilateral kinship and the kindred.

This chapter offers ethnographic examples from the Han Chinese, the Maori of New Zealand, and the Canela Indians of Brazil; it also takes a look at diasporic communities in today's globalized world. A section entitled "Making Relatives" explores fictive kin and ritual adoption, illustrating that in cultures everywhere, people have developed ideas about how someone becomes "one of us." Also presented is a discussion of new reproductive technologies, touching on the mind-boggling array of reproductive possibilities and how they are impacting humanity's conceptions of what it means to be biologically related.

Boxed features include an Anthropology Applied piece on resolving Native American tribal membership disputes, a thought-provoking Original Study on honor killings among Turkish immigrants in the Netherlands, and a Biocultural Connection piece about ancient Maori mythical traditions that are now supported by genetic research.

Chapter 21: Grouping by Gender, Age, Common Interest, and Social Status

This much-revised chapter includes discussions of grouping by gender, age, common interest, and social status—starting with a vibrant photograph of Afghan horsemen playing *buzkashi*, their country's fiercely competitive national sport.

The section on age grouping features ethnographic material from the Mundurucu of Brazil and the Tiriki and Maasai of East Africa. Common-interest grouping examples range from the tattooed Yakuzas in Japan to "pink vigilantes" in India and members of the African diaspora in the United States. For the latter, we present new photos and narrative to tell the story of Ashanti migrants, whose locally elected chiefs in major U.S. cities are directly tied to the Ashanti kingdom's confederation in Ghana.

A new subsection titled "Associations in the Digital Age" describes rapid and widespread changes in social networking platforms across the globe. Our reconfigured section on social status indicators has been trimmed in half, and the section on social mobility has a new paragraph leading into a radically revised Globalscape on sports. Changes in our section about grouping by social status include a new paragraph about ethnic minorities in the United States.

Other boxed features include archaeologist Michael Blakey's Biocultural Connection about the African Burial Ground Project in New York City and Susan Lees's Original Study on the Jewish *eruv*.

Chapter 22: Politics, Power, War, and Violence

Another heavily revised chapter, this one opens with a dramatic image of the Nigerian emir of Kano in a military parade during a festival ending the Muslim holy month of Ramadan. The lead paragraphs in the main narrative have been streamlined, defining power and introducing the concept of political organization. Looking at a range of uncentralized and centralized political systems, the chapter explores the question of power, the intersection of politics and religion, and issues of political leadership and gender.

The sections on bands, tribes, chiefdoms, and states have all been significantly revised—reorganized, tightened, and illustrated with adjusted or new ethnographic examples. For example, the Pashtun are now featured in the section on tribes, and the Kpelle chiefdom narrative carries readers from precolonial to contemporary times. The section on state offers a new definition of the term and updated examples. We also improved significantly our discussions and examples of political systems and authority, politics and religion, and politics and gender.

A new section titled "Cultural Controls in Maintaining Order" streamlines our discussion of cultural control and its two forms (self-control/internalized and social control/externalized), each illustrated with ethnographic examples. In a new subsection on social control through sanctions, we discuss informal and formal sanctions, with a simplified conversation about law as a formal sanction. We have also added another new subsection about witchcraft as a cultural control. In another new section, "Holding Trials, Settling Disputes, and Punishing Crimes," we contrast traditional kin-based approaches to those of politically centralized societies, ending with a discussion of restorative justice.

Also new is a section on the evolution of warfare, which looks at its development in chiefdoms and states, up through World War II, the Chinese civil war, and modern inventions in military technology. It features a new photo and substantive caption about drones. Another new section, "Ideologies of Aggression," discusses how religious motivations and ideological justifications are embedded in a society's worldview. Among the ethnographic examples is fresh material on the militant Christian cult in Uganda that led to Joseph Kony's Lord's Resistance Army.

Sections on genocide and today's armed conflicts have been simplified and trimmed by half, making room for a new section on peace through diplomacy. This addition explores sovereignty and diplomatic protocol across time and cultures, including the example of West Papua's independence struggle led by exiled leader Benny Wenda. In another new section we discuss the politics of nonviolence, offering brief profiles of movements led by Gandhi in India and Aung San Suu Kyi in Myanmar.

Boxed features include an Anthropologist of Note on Laura Nader, an Anthropology Applied piece on William Ury's work with dispute resolution, and a newly illustrated and updated Globalscape chronicling the surprising and complex economics behind piracy off the coast of Somalia.

Chapter 23: Spirituality, Religion, and Shamanism

This entirely revised chapter, rich with new visuals, opens with a Challenge Issue concerning humankind's need to make sense of our place in the universe, illustrated with a new photo showing a crowded pilgrimage to the shrine of the Virgin of Guadalupe, patron saint of Mexico.

The chapter narrative begins with a discussion of superstructure and worldview. Noting the distinction between spirituality and religion, we discuss the roles they play and the anthropological approach to studying them. We introduce myths and their role in mapping cosmology. Then we move on to discuss supernatural beings and spiritual forces—from gods and goddesses to ancestral spirits and the concepts of animism and animatism.

Next we mark out religious specialists. Starting with priests and priestesses, we explore spiritual lineages, describing with ethnographic examples four major ways of legitimizing religious leadership. Examples include the election of the Roman Catholic pope and the reincarnation of Buddhist lamas. Continuing our narrative on religious specialists, we discuss shamans and shamanic healing, introducing a new Anthropologist of Note profile on Michael Harner. Other boxed features include Hillary Crane's Biocultural Connection on masculinization of Taiwanese nuns and Bill Maurer's Original Study on Shariah banking.

In our section on ritual performances, we discuss taboos and cleansing ceremonies (noting the use of water, air, fire, and earth), rites of passage (describing the phases of separation, transition, and incorporation), rites of intensification, magic (imitative and contagious), divination (from geomancy to aeromancy, scapulamancy, chiromancy, and necromancy). A section on witchcraft offers a brief cross-cultural overview, followed by a more detailed description of Navajo skin-walkers. Next we explore sacred sites—from shrines to mountains—and the pilgrimages (devotions in motion) they inspire. This includes a subsection on female saints, highlighting Marian devotions and Black Madonnas in particular. It also includes a discussion of desecration, past and present.

In the section on cultural dynamics, we explore religious and spiritual change, including revitalization movements and syncretic religions, focusing on Vodou in Haiti. Next we move on to religious pluralism and secularization, providing an overview of spirituality and religious practices today. The chapter concludes by noting that the anthropological study of religion is crucial to gaining an understanding of today's world.

Chapter 24: The Arts

This chapter begins with a Challenge Issue about articulating ideas and emotions through various art forms, illustrated by an arresting new photograph of Kayapo Indians in artful ceremonial paint and dress heading to a political protest aboard a bus. The chapter explores in detail three key categories of art—visual, verbal, and musical—illustrating what art can reveal and how it functions in societies.

We describe the distinctly holistic approach anthropologists bring to the study of art, noting the range of cultural insights art discloses—from kinship structures to social values, religious beliefs, and political ideas. We also explain the various approaches to analyzing art (such as aesthetic and interpretive) as they are applied to rock art in southern Africa. In the verbal arts section, we offer several ethnographic examples including the Abenaki creation myth of Tabaldak, one of many versions of the classic and culturally widespread father/son/donkey tale, and the popular Thanksgiving legend in the United States.

The section on music begins by stepping back in time to flutes made of bones from 42,000 years ago and whistles unearthed by archaeologists. Then we march forward to Abenaki shamans playing cedar flutes to summon game animals, traditional and new age shamans drumming to evoke trances, laborers on the edge of the Sahara working to the beat of a drum, and West African *griots* who recount their people's history through percussion and lyrics. Beyond such examples, this chapter discusses the elements of music, including tonality, rhythm, and melody.

The chapter includes a Biocultural Connection about the role of peyote in Huichol art, Margo DeMello's newly illustrated Original Study on the modern tattoo community, and a Globalscape on artful West African coffins that are displayed in museums.

Closing out the chapter is Jennifer Sapiel Neptune's moving Anthropology Applied feature. It describes how endangered indigenous groups use aesthetic traditions as part of their cultural and economic survival strategy.

Chapter 25: Processes of Cultural Change

This chapter starts out with a Challenge Issue calling attention to the many changes people must confront, accompanied by a haunting photograph of Nenet reindeer herders in Siberia facing the undoing of their age-old habitat due to the exploration, extraction, and exportation of natural gas.

The themes and terminology of globalization are woven through this chapter, which includes definitions that distinguish *progress* from *modernization, rebellion* from *revolution,* and *acculturation* from *enculturation.* We discuss mechanisms of change—innovation, diffusion, and cultural loss, as well as repressive change. New paragraphs describe the spear-thrower (atlatl) and briefly mention a half-dozen other familiar primary innovations, followed by descriptions of the evolution of firemaking and wheel-and-axle technology. Also new is a discussion about the dynamics that encourage or discourage innovative tendencies, illustrated with brief accounts of findings by Copernicus and Galileo. The discussion on diffusion includes new mention of bagpipes in Bhutan and two new subsections—one on the spread of maize or corn and the other on the metric system.

Our exploration of cultural change and loss covers acculturation and ethnocide, citing a range of examples of repressive change from around the world—including a revised passage on China and Tibet and a new section about Yąnomami ethnocide, which features a photo of Yąnomami shaman and political leader Davi Kopenawa.

A rewritten section on reactions to change includes a subsection on syncretism, highlighting Trobriand cricket, illustrated with a new photo. We cover revitalization movements, describing cargo cults and presenting a new profile on indigenous revitalization in Bolivia, including a new photo illustrating a return to animism. A discussion on rebellion and revolution adds *insurgency* to our list of defined terms (illustrated by the Zapatista Maya Indian insurgency in southern Mexico) and recounts the Muslim fundamentalist toppling of the imperial regime in Iran in 1979.

The chapter also delves into modernization and the issue of self-determination among indigenous peoples. We highlight two contrasting cases, both greatly revised and updated with new visuals: the Sámi reindeer herders living in the Arctic and sub-Arctic tundra of northwest Russia and Scandinavia and the Shuar Indians of Ecuador.

Boxed features include a Biocultural Connection on the emergence of new diseases, an Anthropologist of Note profile on Eric R. Wolf, and an Anthropology Applied piece on development anthropology and dams, with a fascinating satellite image of China's Three Gorges Dam.

Chapter 26: Global Challenges, Local Responses, and the Role of Anthropology

Our final chapter opens with a photo of an Internet café in China, alongside a Challenge Issue about cultural adaptations that have fueled population growth and placed people in closer proximity in countless ways. A new opening section, "Cultural Revolutions: From *Terra Incognita* to Google Earth," offers a 500-year historical overview of technological inventions that have transformed how humans live and how we perceive our place and destiny in the universe. It ends with the first full-view photograph taken of earth, commentary about our ever-growing interconnectedness, and speculations by some that a homogenous global culture is in the making.

A new section on global integration processes marks out the emergence of international organizations. We then consider pluralistic societies and fragmentation, illustrating the push-and-pull aspects of today's world. A new section on global migrations adds to our understanding of that world, noting the number of internal and external migrants, including transnationals working in one country although remaining citizens of another, plus the millions of refugees forced outside their countries. Marking out challenges migrants face, we introduce two new sections: "Migrants and Xenophobia: Violent Conflict in Assam" and "Migrants, Urbanization, and Slums," reporting on the 1 billion people worldwide now living in slums.

We have retained the vital section "Structural Power in the Age of Globalization," with subsections on hard power (economic and military) and soft power (media). But we have reconfigured the section "Problems of Structural Violence," which now features a new section on poverty that introduces students to the UN's Gini income equality index. We have also entirely reworked the section on hunger, obesity, and malnutrition and the section addressing pollution and global warming.

Special box features include a Biocultural Connection about the threat to Arctic cultures from outside contamination; an updated Globalscape on the practice of dumping toxic waste in the Third World, and a new Anthropology Applied piece on Ann Dunham (President Obama's mother), who was a pioneer in microfinancing. The chapter closes with an uplifting Anthropology of Note profile about Paul Farmer and his global Partners in Health work.

Supplements

Anthropology: The Human Challenge comes with a comprehensive supplements program to help instructors create an effective learning environment both inside and outside the classroom and to aid students in mastering the material.

Supplements for Instructors

Online Instructor's Manual and Test Bank

The Instructor's Manual offers detailed chapter outlines, lecture suggestions, key terms, and student activities such as video exercises and Internet exercises. In addition, there are over seventy-five chapter test questions including multiple choice, true/false, fill-in-the-blank, short answer, and essay.

PowerLecture™ with ExamView®

This one-stop class preparation tool contains ready-to-use Microsoft® PowerPoint® slides, enabling you to assemble, edit, publish, and present custom lectures with ease. PowerLecture helps you bring together text-specific lecture outlines and art from Haviland et al.'s text along with videos and your own materials—culminating in powerful, personalized, media-enhanced presentations. Featuring automatic grading, ExamView is also available within PowerLecture, allowing you to create, deliver, and customize tests and study guides (both print and online) in minutes. See assessments onscreen exactly as they will print or display online. Build tests of up to 250 questions using up to twelve question types, and enter an unlimited number of new questions or edit existing questions. PowerLecture also includes the text's Instructor's Resource Manual and Test Bank as Word documents.

WebTutor™ on Blackboard® and WebCT™

Jumpstart your course with customizable, rich, text-specific content within your course management system. Whether you want to web-enable your class or put an entire course online, WebTutor delivers. WebTutor offers a wide array of resources including access to the eBook, glossaries, flash cards, quizzes, videos, and more.

Anthropology Coursereader

Anthropology Coursereader allows you to create a fully customized online reader in minutes. Access a rich collection of thousands of primary and secondary sources, readings, and audio and video selections from multiple disciplines. Each selection includes a descriptive introduction that puts it into context, and the selection is further supported by both critical thinking and multiple-choice questions designed to reinforce key points. This easy-to-use solution allows you to select exactly the content you need for your courses and is loaded with convenient pedagogical features like highlighting, printing, note taking, and downloadable MP3 audio files for each reading. You have the freedom to assign and customize individualized content at an affordable price.

The Wadsworth Anthropology Video Library: Volumes I, II, and III

The Wadsworth Anthropology Video Library (featuring BBC Motion Gallery video clips) drives home the relevance of course topics through short, provocative clips of current and historical events. Perfect for enriching lectures and engaging students in discussion, many of the segments in these volumes have been gathered from the BBC Motion Gallery. Ask your Cengage Learning representative for a list of contents.

AIDS in Africa DVD

Southern Africa has been overcome by a pandemic of unparalleled proportions. This documentary series focuses on the democracy of Namibia and the nation's valiant actions to control HIV/AIDS.

Included in this series are four documentary films created by the Periclean Scholars at Elon University: (1) *Young Struggles, Eternal Faith*, which focuses on caregivers in the faith community; (2) *The Shining Lights of Opuwo*, which shows how young people share their messages of hope through song and dance; (3) *A Measure of Our Humanity*, which describes HIV/AIDS as an issue related to gender, poverty, stigma, education, and justice; and (4) *You Wake Me Up*, a story of two HIV-positive women and their acts of courage helping other women learn to survive.

Cengage/Wadsworth is excited to offer these award-winning films to instructors for use in class. When presenting topics such as gender, faith, culture, poverty, and so on, the films will be enlightening for students and will expand their global perspective of HIV/AIDS.

Online Resources for Instructors and Students

CourseMate

Cengage Learning's Anthropology CourseMate brings course concepts to life with interactive learning, study, and exam preparation tools that support the printed textbook. CourseMate includes an integrated eBook, glossaries, flash cards, quizzes, videos, and more—as well as EngagementTracker, an original tool that monitors student engagement in the course. The accompanying instructor website, available through login.cengage.com, offers access to password-protected resources such as an electronic version of the Instructor's Manual, Test Bank files, and Power-Point® slides. CourseMate can be bundled with the student text. Contact your Cengage sales representative for information on getting access to CourseMate.

Supplements for Students

Telecourse Study Guide

The distance learning course, **Anthropology: The Four Fields**, provides online and print companion study guide options that include study aids, interactive exercises, videos, and more.

Additional Student Resources

Basic Genetics for Anthropology CD-ROM: Principles and Applications (stand-alone version), by Robert Jurmain and Lynn Kilgore

This student CD-ROM expands on such concepts as biological inheritance (genes, DNA sequencing, and so on) and applications of that to modern human populations at the molecular level (human variation and adaptation—to disease, diet, growth, and development). Interactive animations and simulations bring these important concepts to life for students so they can fully understand the essential biological principles required for physical anthropology. Also available are quizzes and interactive flashcards for further study.

Hominid Fossils CD-ROM: An Interactive Atlas, by James Ahern

The interactive atlas CD-ROM includes over seventy-five key fossils important for a clear understanding of human evolution. The QuickTime Virtual Reality (QTVR) "object" movie format for each fossil enables students to have a near-authentic experience of working with these important finds, by allowing them to rotate the fossils 360 degrees.

Unlike some VR media, QTVR objects are made using actual photographs of the real objects and thus better preserve details of color and texture. The fossils used are high-quality research casts as well as actual fossils. Because the atlas is not organized linearly, student are able to access levels and multiple paths, allowing them to see how the fossil fits into the map of human evolution in terms of geography, time, and evolution. The CD-ROM offers students an inviting, authentic learning environment, one that also contains a dynamic quizzing feature that permits students to test their knowledge of fossil and species identification, as well as providing detailed information about the fossil record.

Readings and Case Studies

Classic and Contemporary Readings in Physical Anthropology, edited by M. K. Sandford with Eileen M. Jackson

This highly accessible reader emphasizes science—its principles and methods—as well as the historical development of physical anthropology and the applications of new technology to the discipline. The editors provide an introduction to the reader as well as a brief overview of the article so students know what to look for. Each article also includes discussion questions and Internet resources.

Classic Readings in Cultural Anthropology, 3rd edition, edited by Gary Ferraro

Now in its third edition, this reader includes historical and recent articles that have had a profound effect on the field of anthropology. Organized according to the major topic areas found in most cultural anthropology courses, this reader includes an introduction to the material as well as a brief overview of each article, discussion questions, and InfoTrac College Edition key search terms.

Globalization and Change in Fifteen Cultures: Born in One World, Living in Another, edited by George Spindler and Janice E. Stockard

In this volume, fifteen case study authors write about cultural change in today's diverse settings around the world. Each original article provides insight into the dynamics and meanings of change, as well as the effects of globalization at the local level.

Case Studies in Cultural Anthropology, edited by George Spindler and Janice E. Stockard

Select from more than sixty classic and contemporary ethnographies representing geographic and topical diversity. Newer case studies focus on cultural change and cultural continuity, reflecting the globalization of the world.

Case Studies on Contemporary Social Issues, edited by John A. Young

Framed around social issues, these new contemporary case studies are globally comparative and represent the cutting-edge work of anthropologists today.

Case Studies in Archaeology, edited by Jeffrey Quilter

These engaging accounts of new archaeological techniques, issues, and solutions—as well as studies discussing the collection of material remains—range from site-specific excavations to types of archaeology practiced.

Acknowledgments

In this day and age, no textbook comes to fruition without extensive collaboration. Beyond the shared endeavors of our author team, this book owes its completion to a wide range of individuals, from colleagues in the discipline to those involved in development and production processes. Sincere thanks to colleagues who brought their expertise to bear—as sounding boards and in responding to questions concerning their specializations: Marta P. Alfonso-Durruty, Robert Bailey, Peter Bingham, Frans B. M. de Waal, Jessica Falcone, Michele Goldsmith, John Hawks, Amber Campbell Hibbs, Heather Loyd, Gillian E. Newell, Martin Ottenheimer, Svante Pääbo, Yvette Pigeon, Herbert Prins, and Michael Wesch. We are particularly grateful for the manuscript reviewers listed below, who provided detailed and thoughtful feedback that helped us to hone and re-hone our narrative.

We carefully considered and made use of the wide range of comments provided by these individuals. Our decisions on how to utilize their suggestions were influenced by our own perspectives on anthropology and teaching, combined with the priorities and page limits of this text. Thus, neither our reviewers nor any of the other anthropologists mentioned here should be held responsible for any shortcomings in this book. They should, however, be credited as contributors to many of the book's strengths: Philip Carr, University of South Alabama; Douglas Crews, Ohio State University; William Price, North Country Community College; Frank Salamone, Iona College; David Schwimmer, Columbus State University; and Donna Marshaye White, Webster University.

Thanks, too, go to colleagues who provided material for some of the Original Study, Biocultural Connection, and Anthropology Applied boxes in this text: Michael Blakey, Nancy I. Cooper, Hillary Crane, Margo DeMello, Katherine Dettwyler, Clark L. Erickson, George S. Esber, Anabel Ford, Michele Goldsmith, S. Neyooxet Greymorning, Donna Hart, John Hawks, Michael M. Horowitz, Ann Kendall, Suzanne Leclerc-Madlala, Susan Lees, Roger Lewin, Anne Nacey Maggioncalda, Charles C. Mann, Jonathan Marks, Bill Maurer, H. Lyn White Miles, Serena Nanda, Jennifer Sapiel Neptune, Martin Ottenheimer, Anna Roosevelt, Robert M. Sapolsky, Jason Silverstein, Sherry Simpson, Meredith F. Small, Amanda Stronza, William Ury, Clementine van Eck, Annette B. Weiner, Dennis Werner, and R. K. Williamson.

We have debts of gratitude to office workers in our departments for their cheerful help in clerical matters: Karen Rundquist, Patty Redmond, and Tina Griffiths, along with research librarian extraordinaire Nancy Bianchi. Also worthy of note here are the introductory anthropology teaching assistants at Kansas State University and the College of Medicine and Honors College students at the University of Vermont who, through the years, have shed light for us on effective ways to reach new generations of students. And, finally, we recognize the introductory students themselves, who are at the heart of this educational endeavor and who continually provide feedback in formal and informal ways.

Our thanksgiving inventory would be incomplete without mentioning individuals at Wadsworth/Cengage Learning who helped conceive of this text and bring it to fruition. Of special note is our senior development editor Lin Marshall Gaylord, who has been a shaping force for many generations of the Haviland et al. textbooks. She continues to grace our efforts with vision, resilience, constancy, and anthropological knowledge. We cannot imagine this endeavor without her. Our thanks also go out to Wadsworth's skilled and enthusiastic editorial, marketing, design, and production team: Aileen Berg (senior acquisitions sponsoring editor), Liz Rhoden (senior brand manager), Michelle Williams (senior market development manager), John Chell (media editor), Margaux Cameron (assistant editor), Victor Luu (editorial assistant), as well as Cheri Palmer (content project manager) and Caryl Gorska (art director).

In addition to all of the above, we have had the invaluable aid of several most able freelancers, including veteran photo researcher Sarah Evertson and our alert and artful art team at Graphic World. We are beyond grateful to have once again had the opportunity to work with copy editor Jennifer Gordon and production coordinator Joan Keyes of Dovetail Publishing Services. Consummate professionals and generous souls, both of them keep track of countless details and bring calm efficiency and grace to the demands of meeting difficult deadlines. Their efforts and skills play a major role in making our work doable and pleasurable.

And finally, all of us are indebted to family members and close friends who have not only put up with our textbook preoccupation but cheered us on in the endeavor.

About the Authors

Authors Bunny McBride, Dana Walrath, Harald Prins, and William Haviland

All four members of this author team share overlapping research interests and a similar vision of what anthropology is (and should be) about. For example, all are true believers in the four-field approach to anthropology and all have some involvement in applied work.

WILLIAM A. HAVILAND is professor emeritus at the University of Vermont, where he founded the Department of Anthropology and taught for thirty-two years. He holds a PhD in anthropology from the University of Pennsylvania.

He has carried out original research in archaeology in Guatemala and Vermont; ethnography in Maine and Vermont; and physical anthropology in Guatemala. This work has been the basis of numerous publications in various national and international books and journals, as well as in media intended for the general public. His books include *The Original Vermonters*, coauthored with Marjorie Power, and a technical monograph on ancient Maya settlement. He also served as consultant for the award-winning telecourse *Faces of Culture*, and he is coeditor of the series *Tikal Reports*, published by the University of Pennsylvania Museum of Archaeology and Anthropology.

Besides his teaching and writing, Dr. Haviland has lectured to numerous professional as well as nonprofessional audiences in Canada, Mexico, Lesotho, South Africa, and Spain, as well as in the United States.

A staunch supporter of indigenous rights, he served as expert witness for the Missisquoi Abenaki of Vermont in an important court case over aboriginal fishing rights.

Awards received by Dr. Haviland include being named University Scholar by the Graduate School of the University of Vermont in 1990; a Certificate of Appreciation from the Sovereign Republic of the Abenaki Nation of Missisquoi, St. Francis/Sokoki Band in 1996; and a Lifetime Achievement Award from the Center for Research on Vermont in 2006. Now retired from teaching, he continues his research, writing, and lecturing from the coast of Maine. He serves as a trustee for the Abbe Museum in Bar Harbor, focused on Maine's Native American history, culture, art, and archaeology. His most recent books are *At the Place of the Lobsters and Crabs* (2009) and *Canoe Indians of Down East Maine* (2012).

HARALD E. L. PRINS is a University Distinguished Professor of cultural anthropology at Kansas State University. Academically trained at half a dozen Dutch and U.S. universities, he previously taught at Radboud University (Netherlands), Bowdoin College and Colby College in Maine, and was a visiting professor at the University of Lund, Sweden. Also named a Distinguished University Teaching Scholar, he received numerous honors for his outstanding academic teaching, including the Presidential Award in 1999, Carnegie Professor of the Year for Kansas in 2006, and the AAA/Oxford University Press Award for Excellence in Undergraduate Teaching of Anthropology in 2010.

His fieldwork focuses on indigenous peoples in the western hemisphere, and he has long served as an advocacy anthropologist on land claims and other Native rights. In that capacity, Dr. Prins has been a key expert witness in both the U.S. Senate and Canadian courts. His numerous academic publications appear in seven languages, and his books include *The Mi'kmaq: Resistance, Accomodation, and Cultural Survival*.

Also trained in filmmaking, he was president of the Society for Visual Anthropology, and coproduced award-winning documentaries. He has been the visual anthropology editor of *American Anthropologist*, coprincipal investigator for the U.S. National Park Service, international observer in Paraguay's presidential elections, and a research associate at the National Museum of Natural History, Smithsonian Institution.

DANA WALRATH is assistant professor of family medicine at the University of Vermont and an affiliated faculty member for women's and gender studies. After earning her PhD from the University of Pennsylvania, she taught there and at Temple University. Dr. Walrath broke new ground in medical and biological anthropology through her work on biocultural aspects of childbirth. She has also written on a wide range of topics related to gender in paleoanthropology, the social production of sickness and health, sex differences, genetics, and evolutionary medicine. Her work has appeared in edited volumes and in journals such as *Current Anthropology, American Anthropologist, American Journal of Physical Anthropology*, and *Anthropology Now*. She developed a novel curriculum in medical education at the University of Vermont's College of Medicine that brings humanism, anthropological theory and practice, narrative medicine, and professionalism skills to first-year medical students.

Dr. Walrath also has an MFA in creative writing from Vermont College of Fine Arts and has shown her artwork in galleries throughout the country. Her recent work on Alzheimer's disease combines anthropology with memoir and visual art. Spanning a variety of disciplines, her work has been supported by diverse sources such as the National Science Foundation for the Arts, the Centers for Disease Control, the Health Resources and Services Administration, the Vermont Studio Center, the Vermont Arts Council, and the National Endowment for the Arts. She is currently a Fulbright Scholar at the American University of Armenia and the Institute of Ethnography and Archaeology of the National Academy of Sciences of Armenia, where she is completing a project titled "The Narrative Anthropology of Aging in Armenia."

BUNNY MCBRIDE is an award-winning author specializing in cultural anthropology, indigenous peoples, international tourism, and nature conservation issues. Published in dozens of national and international print media, she has reported from Africa, Europe, China, and the Indian Ocean. Holding an MA from Columbia University, she is highly rated as a teacher, and she has served as visiting anthropology faculty at Principia College and the Salt Institute for Documentary Field Studies. Since 1996 she has been an adjunct lecturer of anthropology at Kansas State University.

Among her many publications are books such as *Women of the Dawn*; *Molly Spotted Elk: A Penobscot in Paris*; *Indians in Eden* (with Harald Prins); and *The Audubon Field Guide to African Wildlife*, which she coauthored. McBride has also authored numerous book chapters. Honors include a special commendation from the state legislature of Maine for significant contributions to Native women's history. As an activist and researcher for the Aroostook Band of Micmacs (1981–1991), she assisted this Maine Indian community in its successful efforts to reclaim lands, gain tribal status, and revitalize cultural traditions.

In recent years, she has served as coprincipal investigator for a National Park Service ethnography project and curated several museum exhibits, including "Journeys West: The David & Peggy Rockefeller American Indian Art Collection" for the Abbe Museum in Bar Harbor, Maine. Her latest exhibit, "Indians & Rusticators," received a 2012 Leadership in History Award from the American Association for State and Local History. Currently, she serves as president of the Women's World Summit Foundation, based in Geneva, Switzerland, and is completing a collection of essays.

© Mark Craemer

Challenge Issue

It is a challenge to make sense of the world and our place in the universe. Who am I and how am I connected to the person in this picture? Why do I look different from so many other people in the world and why are there so many different languages? Who harvested the cotton for my shirt or felled the tree used to build my house? Why are some people immune from a virus that kills others? How is it that many believe in an afterlife but others do not? When did our ancestors first begin to think? What distinguishes us from other animals? Anthropologists take a holistic, integrated approach to such questions, framing them in a broad context and examining interconnections. Our discipline considers human culture and biology, in all times and places, as inextricably intertwined, each affecting the other. This photograph shows the hands of a miner holding coltan, a tarlike mineral mined in eastern Congo. Refined, coltan turns into a heat-resistant powder capable of storing energy. As the key component of capacitors in small electronic devices, it is highly valued on the global market. Coltan mines, enriching the warring Congolese factions that control them, are hellholes for the thousands of people, including children, who work the mines. Bought, transported, and processed by foreign merchants and corporations, small bits of this mineral eventually end up in mobile phones and laptop computers worldwide. Although the link between you and globalization is complex, no more than "six degrees of separation" exist between your hands and those of the miner in the heart of Africa. Anthropology's holistic and integrative perspective will equip you to explore and negotiate today's interconnected and globalized world.

The Essence of Anthropology

1

The Anthropological Perspective

Anthropology is the study of humankind in all times and places. Of course, many other disciplines focus on humans in one way or another. For example, anatomy and physiology concentrate on our species as biological organisms. The social sciences examine human relationships, leaving artistic and philosophical aspects of human cultures to the humanities. Anthropology focuses on the interconnections and interdependence of all aspects of the human experience in all places, in the present and deep into the past, well before written history. This unique, broad **holistic perspective** equips anthropologists to address that elusive thing we call *human nature.*

Anthropologists welcome the contributions of researchers from other disciplines, and in return offer their own findings to these other disciplines. An anthropologist may not know as much about the structure of the human eye as an anatomist or as much about the perception of color as a psychologist. As a synthesizer, however, the anthropologist seeks to understand how anatomy and psychology relate to color-naming practices in different societies. Because they look for the broad basis of human ideas and practices without limiting themselves to any single social or biological aspect, anthropologists can acquire an especially expansive and inclusive overview of human biology and culture.

Keeping a holistic perspective allows anthropologists to prevent their own cultural ideas and values from distorting their research. As the old saying goes, people often see what they believe, rather than what appears before their eyes. By maintaining a critical awareness of their own assumptions about human nature—checking and rechecking the ways their beliefs and actions might be shaping their research—anthropologists strive to gain objective knowledge about human beings. With this

anthropology The study of humankind in all times and places.

holistic perspective A fundamental principle of anthropology: The various parts of human culture and biology must be viewed in the broadest possible context in order to understand their interconnections and interdependence.

in mind, anthropologists aim to avoid the pitfalls of **ethnocentrism**, a belief that the ways of one's own culture are the only proper ones.

To some, an inclusive, holistic perspective that emphasizes the diversity within and among human cultures can be mistaken as shorthand for liberal politics among anthropologists. This is not the case. Anthropologists come from many different backgrounds, and individuals practicing the discipline vary in their personal, political, and religious beliefs (**Figure 1.1**). At the same time, they apply a rigorous methodology for researching cultural practices from the perspective of the culture being studied—a methodology that requires them to check for the influences of their own biases. This is as true for an anthropologist analyzing the culture of the global banking industry as it is for one investigating trance dancing among contemporary hunter-gatherers. We might say that anthropology is a discipline concerned with unbiased evaluation of diverse human systems, including one's own. At times this requires challenging the status quo that is maintained and defended by the power elites of the system under study.

While other social sciences have predominantly concentrated on contemporary peoples living in North American and European (Western) societies, anthropologists have traditionally focused on non-Western peoples and cultures. Anthropologists work with the understanding that to fully access the complexities of human ideas, behavior, and biology, *all* humans, wherever and whenever, must be studied. A cross-cultural and long-term evolutionary perspective distinguishes anthropology from other social sciences. This approach guards against theories about the world and reality that are **culture-bound**—based on the assumptions and values that come from the researcher's own culture.

As a case in point, consider the fact that infants in the United States typically sleep apart from their parents. To people accustomed to multibedroom houses, cribs, and car seats, this may seem normal, but cross-cultural research shows that *co-sleeping,* of mother and baby in particular, is the norm (**Figure 1.2**). Further, the practice of sleeping apart favored in the United States dates back only about 200 years.

Recent studies have shown that separation of mother and infant has important biological and cultural consequences. For one thing, it increases the length of the infant's crying bouts. Some mothers incorrectly interpret crying as an indication that the baby is not receiving sufficient breast milk and consequently switch to using bottled formula, which has been shown to be less healthy. In extreme cases, a baby's cries may provoke physical

© Documentary Educational Resources

Figure 1.1 Anthropologist Jayasinhji Jhala Anthropologists come from many corners of the world and carry out research in a huge variety of cultures all around the globe. Dr. Jayasinhji Jhala, pictured here, hails from the old city of Dhrangadhra in Gujarat, northwestern India. A member of the Jhala clan of Rajputs, an aristocratic caste of warriors, he grew up in the royal palace of his father, the maharaja. After earning a bachelor of arts degree in India, he came to the United States and earned a master's in visual studies from MIT, followed by a doctorate in anthropology from Harvard. Currently a professor and director of the programs of Visual Anthropology and the Visual Anthropology Media Laboratory at Temple University, he returns regularly to India with students to film cultural traditions in his own caste-stratified society.

abuse. But the benefits of co-sleeping go beyond significant reductions in crying: Infants who are breastfed receive more stimulation important for brain development, and they are apparently less susceptible to sudden infant death syndrome (SIDS or "crib death"), which occurs at a higher rate in the United States than in any other country. There are benefits to the mother as well: Frequent nursing prevents early ovulation after childbirth, promotes weight

ethnocentrism The belief that the ways of one's own culture are the only proper ones.
culture-bound A perspective that produces theories about the world and reality that are based on the assumptions and values from the researcher's own culture.

VISUAL COUNTERPOINT

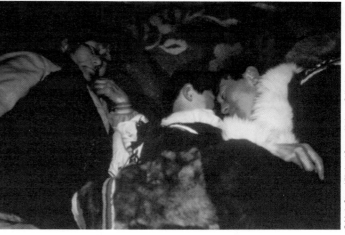

Figure 1.2 Sleeping Habits across Cultures Although infants in the United States typically sleep apart from their parents, cross-cultural research shows that co-sleeping, particularly of mother and baby, is the rule. Without the breathing cues provided by someone sleeping nearby, an infant is more susceptible to sudden infant death syndrome (SIDS), a phenomenon in which a 4- to 6-month-old baby stops breathing and dies while asleep. The highest rates of SIDS are found among infants in the United States. The photo on the right shows a Nenet family sleeping together in their *chum* (reindeer-skin tent). Nenet people are Arctic reindeer pastoralists living in Siberia.

loss to shed pregnancy pounds, and allows nursing mothers at least as much sleep as mothers who sleep apart from their infants (McKenna & McDade, 2005).

Why do so many mothers continue to sleep separately from their infants? In the United States, the cultural values of independence and consumerism come into play. To begin building individual identities, babies are provided with rooms (or at least space) of their own. This room also gives parents a place to stow the toys, furniture, and other paraphernalia associated with good and caring childrearing in the United States.

Although the findings of anthropologists have often challenged the conclusions of sociologists, psychologists, and economists, anthropology is absolutely indispensable to those in other disciplines because it is the only consistent check against culture-bound assertions. In a sense, anthropology is to these disciplines what the laboratory is to physics and chemistry: an essential testing ground for their theories.

Anthropology and Its Fields

Individual anthropologists tend to specialize in one of four fields or subdisciplines: cultural anthropology, linguistic anthropology, archaeology, and physical (biological) anthropology (**Figure 1.3**). Some anthropologists consider archaeology and linguistics to be part of the broader study of human cultures, but archaeology and linguistics also have close ties to physical anthropology. For example, while linguistic anthropology focuses on the social and cultural aspects of language, it has deep connections to the evolution of human language and to the biological basis of speech and language studied within physical anthropology.

Researchers in each of anthropology's fields gather and analyze data to explore similarities and differences among humans, across time and space. Moreover, individuals within

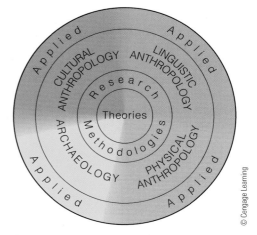

Figure 1.3 The Four Fields of Anthropology Note that the divisions among the fields are not sharp, indicating that their boundaries overlap. Note also that all four include the practice of applied anthropology.

BIOCULTURAL CONNECTION

The Anthropology of Organ Transplantation

In 1954, the first organ transplant occurred in Boston when surgeons removed a kidney from one identical twin to place it inside his sick brother. Today, transplants between unrelated individuals are common, so much so that organs are trafficked in the black market, often across continents from the poor to the wealthy. Though some transplants rely upon living donors, routine organ transplantation depends largely upon the availability of organs obtained from individuals who have died. To reduce illegal traffic, several European countries have enacted policies that assume that any individual who is "brain dead" is automatically an organ donor unless the person has "opted out" ahead of time.

A practice like organ transplantation can exist only if it fits with cultural beliefs about death and the human body. The North American and European view—that the body is a machine that can be repaired much like a car—makes a practice like organ transplantation acceptable. But this is not the view shared by all societies. Anthropologist Margaret Lock has explored differences between Japanese and North American acceptance of the biological state of brain death and how it affects the practice of organ transplantation.

The diagnosis of brain death relies upon the absence of measurable electrical currents in the brain and the inability to breathe without technological assistance. The brain-dead individual, though attached to machines, still seems alive with a beating heart and normal skin coloring. Part of the reason most North Americans find organ transplantation tolerable with the determination of brain death is that personhood and individuality are culturally ascribed to the mind, and thus located in the brain. North Americans' acceptance of brain death has allowed for the "gift of life" through sometimes anonymous organ donation and subsequent transplantation.

By contrast, in Japan, the concept of brain death is hotly contested, and organ transplants are rarely performed. The Japanese idea of personhood does not incorporate a mind–body split; instead, a person's identity is tied to the entire body rather than solely to the brain. Consequently, the Japanese reject that a warm body is a corpse from which organs can be harvested. Further, organs cannot be transformed into "gifts" because anonymous donation is incompatible with Japanese social patterns of reciprocal exchange.

Organ transplantation involves far greater social meaning than the purely biological movement of an organ from one individual to another. Cultural and biological processes are tightly woven into every aspect of this new social practice.

BIOCULTURAL QUESTION

What criteria do you use for death, and is it compatible with the idea of organ donation? Do you think that donated organs are fairly distributed in your society or throughout the globe?

For more on this subject, see Lock, M. (2001). Twice dead: Organ transplants and the reinvention of death. Berkeley: University of California Press.

each of the four fields practice **applied anthropology**, which entails the use of anthropological knowledge and methods to solve practical problems. Most applied anthropologists actively collaborate with the communities in which they work—setting goals, solving problems, and conducting research together. In this book, the Anthropology Applied features spotlight how anthropology contributes to solving a wide range of challenges.

An early example of the application of anthropological knowledge to a practical problem was the international public health movement that began in the 1920s. This marked the beginning of **medical anthropology**—a specialization that brings theoretical and applied approaches from cultural and biological anthropology to the study of human health and disease. The work of medical anthropologists sheds light on the connections between human health and political and economic forces, both locally and globally. Examples of this specialization appear in some of the Biocultural Connections featured in this text, including the one presented on this page, "The Anthropology of Organ Transplantation."

Cultural Anthropology

Cultural anthropology (also called *social* or *socio-cultural anthropology*) is the study of patterns in human behavior, thought, and emotions. It focuses on humans as

applied anthropology The use of anthropological knowledge and methods to solve practical problems, often for a specific client.

medical anthropology A specialization in anthropology that brings theoretical and applied approaches from cultural and biological anthropology to the study of human health and disease.

cultural anthropology The study of patterns in human behavior, thought, and emotions, focusing on humans as culture-producing and culture-reproducing creatures. Also known as *social* or *sociocultural anthropology*.

culture-producing and culture-reproducing creatures. To understand the work of the cultural anthropologist, we must clarify the meaning of **culture**—a society's shared and socially transmitted ideas, values, emotions, and perceptions, which are used to make sense of experience and which generate behavior and are reflected in that behavior. These are the (often unconscious) standards by which societies—structured groups of people—operate. These standards are socially learned, rather than acquired through biological inheritance. The manifestations of culture may vary considerably from place to place, but no individual is "more cultured" in the anthropological sense than any other.

Integral to all the anthropological fields, the concept of culture might be considered anthropology's distinguishing feature. After all, a biological anthropologist is distinct from a biologist *primarily* because he or she takes culture into account. Cultural anthropologists may study the legal, medical, economic, political, or religious system of a given society, knowing that all aspects of the culture interrelate as part of a unified whole. They may focus on divisions in a society—such as by gender, age, or class—factors we will explore in depth later in this text. But it is also worth noting the significance of these same categories to the archaeologist who studies a society through its material remains, to the linguistic anthropologist who examines ancient and modern languages, and to the biological anthropologist who investigates the physical human body.

Cultural anthropology has two main components: ethnography and ethnology. An **ethnography** is a detailed description of a particular culture primarily based on **fieldwork**, which is the term all anthropologists use for on-location research. Because the hallmark of ethnographic fieldwork is a combination of social participation and personal observation within the community being studied and interviews and discussions with individual members of a group, the ethnographic method is commonly referred to as **participant observation** (Figure 1.4). Ethnographies provide the information used to make systematic comparisons among cultures all across the world. Known as **ethnology**, such cross-cultural research allows anthropologists to develop theories that help explain why certain important differences or similarities occur among groups.

Ethnography

Through participant observation—eating a people's food, sleeping under their roof, learning how to speak and behave acceptably, and personally experiencing their habits and customs—the ethnographer seeks to gain the best possible understanding of a particular way of life. Being a participant observer does not mean that the anthropologist must join in battles to study a culture in which warfare is prominent; but by living among a warring people, the ethnographer should be able to understand how warfare fits into the overall cultural framework.

The ethnographer must observe carefully to gain an overview without placing too much emphasis on one

Figure 1.4 Fieldwork in the Arctic British anthropologist Florian Stammler engages in participant observation among Sami reindeer nomads in Siberia. Specializing in Arctic anthropology, particularly in the Russian far north, Stammler coordinates the anthropology research team at the University of Lapland's Arctic Centre. His interests include Arctic economy, human–animal relations, and the anthropology of place and belonging.

cultural feature at the expense of another. Only by discovering how *all* parts of a culture—its social, political, economic, and religious practices and institutions—relate to one another can the ethnographer begin to understand the cultural system. This is the holistic perspective so basic to the discipline.

The popular image of ethnographic fieldwork is that it occurs among hunters, herders, fishers, or farmers who live in far-off, isolated places. To be sure, much ethnographic work has been done in the remote villages of Asia, Africa, or Latin America, islands of the Pacific Ocean, deserts of Australia, and so on. However, as the discipline developed after the mid-1900s with the demise of colonialism, industrialized societies

culture A society's shared and socially transmitted ideas, values, and perceptions, which are used to make sense of experience and which generate behavior and are reflected in that behavior.

ethnography A detailed description of a particular culture primarily based on fieldwork.

fieldwork The term anthropologists use for on-location research.

participant observation In ethnography, the technique of learning a people's culture through social participation and personal observation within the community being studied, as well as interviews and discussion with individual members of the group over an extended period of time.

ethnology The study and analysis of different cultures from a comparative or historical point of view, utilizing ethnographic accounts and developing anthropological theories that help explain why certain important differences or similarities occur among groups.

and neighborhoods in modern cities have also become a significant focus of anthropological study.

Ethnographic fieldwork has transformed from expert Western anthropologists studying people in "other" places to a collaborative approach among anthropologists from all parts of the world and the varied communities in which they work. Today, anthropologists from around the globe employ the same research techniques that were used in the study of non-Western peoples to explore diverse subjects such as religious movements, street gangs, refugee settlements, land rights, conflict resolution, corporate bureaucracies, and health-care systems in Western cultures.

Ethnology

Largely descriptive in nature, *ethnography* provides the raw data needed for *ethnology*—the branch of cultural anthropology that involves cross-cultural comparisons and theories that explain differences or similarities among groups. Intriguing insights into one's own beliefs and practices may come from cross-cultural comparisons. Consider, for example, the amount of time spent on domestic chores by industrialized peoples and traditional food foragers—people who rely on wild plant and animal resources for subsistence.

Anthropological research has shown that food foragers work far less time at domestic tasks and other subsistence pursuits compared to people in industrialized societies. Despite access to "labor-saving" appliances such as dishwashers, washing machines, clothes dryers, vacuum cleaners, food processors, and microwave ovens, urban women in the United States who are not working for wages outside their homes put 55 hours a week into their housework. In contrast, aboriginal women in Australia devoted 20 hours a week to their chores (Bodley, 2008, p. 67). Nevertheless, consumer appliances have become important indicators of a high standard of living in the United States due to the widespread belief that household appliances reduce housework and increase leisure time.

By making systematic comparisons, ethnologists seek to arrive at scientific explanations of cultural features and social practices in all times and places. (The Biocultural Connection you read on page 6 is one of countless examples of anthropological insights gained through comparative research.)

Applied Cultural Anthropology

Today, cultural anthropologists contribute to applied anthropology in a variety of contexts ranging from business to education to health care to governmental interventions to humanitarian aid. For example, anthropologist Nancy Scheper-Hughes has taken her investigative work on the global problem of illegal trafficking of organs and used it to help found Organs Watch, an organization dedicated to solving this human rights issue (see the Globalscape later in this chapter).

Linguistic Anthropology

Perhaps the most distinctive feature of the human species is language. Although the sounds and gestures made by some other animals—especially by apes—may serve functions comparable to those of human language, no other animal has developed a system of symbolic communication as complex as that of humans. Language allows people to create, preserve, and transmit countless details of their culture from generation to generation.

Linguistic anthropology is the branch of anthropology that studies human languages; it investigates their structure, history, and relation to social and cultural contexts. Although it shares data, theories, and methods with the more general discipline of linguistics, it differs in that it includes distinctly anthropological questions, such as, how does language influence or reflect culture? And how does language use differ among distinct members of a society?

In its early years, linguistic anthropology emphasized the documentation of languages of cultures under ethnographic study—particularly those whose future seemed precarious due to colonization, forced assimilation, population decimation, capitalist expansion, or other destructive forces. When the first Europeans began to colonize the world five centuries ago, an estimated 12,000 distinct languages existed. By the early 1900s—when anthropological research began to take off—many languages and peoples had already disappeared or were on the brink of extinction. Sadly this trend continues, with predictions that nearly half of the world's remaining 6,000 languages will become extinct over the next hundred years (Crystal, 2002; Knight, Studdert-Kennedy, & Hurford, 2000).

Linguistic anthropology has three main branches: descriptive linguistics, historical linguistics, and language in relation to social and cultural settings. All three yield valuable information about how people communicate and how they understand the world around them.

Descriptive Linguistics

This branch of linguistic anthropology involves the painstaking work of dissecting a language by recording, delineating, and analyzing all of its features. It leads to a deeper understanding of a language—its structure (including grammar and syntax), its unique linguistic repertoire (figures of speech, word plays, and so on), and its relationship to other languages.

Historical Linguistics

While descriptive linguistics focuses on all features of a particular language at any one moment in time, historical

linguistic anthropology The study of human languages—looking at their structure, history, and relation to social and cultural contexts.

Figure 1.5 Preserving Endangered Languages Linguistic anthropologist David Anderson (right) has devoted his career to documenting and saving indigenous languages. He founded and heads the Living Tongues Institute for Endangered Languages and works throughout the globe to preserve languages that are dying out at a shocking rate of about one every two weeks. Here he is recording for the first time the language of Koro, spoken by some 1,000 people in India's remote northeastern state, Arunachal Pradesh. Situated near India's contested border with China, this region is considered a black hole in the study of languages.

Photo by Chris Rainier/Enduring Voices Project

linguistics deals with the fact that languages change. In addition to deciphering "dead" languages that are no longer spoken, specialists in this field examine interrelationships among different languages and investigate earlier and later forms of the same language. Their findings make significant contributions to our understanding of the human past. By working out relationships among languages and examining their spatial distributions, they may estimate how long the speakers of those languages have lived where they do. By identifying those words in related languages that have survived from an ancient ancestral tongue, they can also suggest not only where, but how, the speakers of the inherited language lived. Such work shows linguistic ties between geographically distant groups such as the Navajo in Arizona's desert and the Gwich'in above the Arctic Circle in Alaska, or between the Magyars in Hungary and the people of Finland.

Language in Its Social and Cultural Settings

Some linguistic anthropologists study the social and cultural contexts of a language. For example, they may research how factors such as age, gender, ethnicity, class, religion, occupation, or financial status affect speech. Because members of any culture may use a variety of different registers and inflections, the ones they choose (often unconsciously) to use at a specific instance convey particular meanings.

Scientists in this branch of linguistics also look into the dynamic relationship between language and culture—investigating to what degree they mutually influence and inform each other. In this vein, they may investigate how a language reflects culturally significant aspects of a people's environment or values.

Linguistic anthropologists may also focus on the socialization process through which an individual becomes part of a culture, moves up in social status, or takes on a new

professional identity. First-year medical students, for example, amass 6,000 new terms and a series of linguistic conventions as they begin to take on the role of a physician. Individuals training for any specialized career, from lawyer to chef, face similar challenges in quickly expanding their vocabularies.

Applied Linguistic Anthropology

Linguistic anthropologists put their research to use in a number of settings. Some, for example, have collaborated with recently contacted cultural groups, small nations (or tribes), and ethnic minorities in the preservation or revival of languages suppressed or lost during periods of oppression by dominant societies. Their work has included helping to create written forms of languages that previously existed only orally. This sort of applied linguistic anthropology represents a trend in mutually useful collaboration that is characteristic of much anthropological research today (**Figure 1.5**).

Archaeology

Archaeology is the branch of anthropology that studies human cultures through the recovery and analysis of material remains and environmental data. Such material products include tools, pottery, hearths, and enclosures that remain as traces of cultural practices in the past, as well as human, plant, and marine remains, some of which date back 2.5 million years. The arrangement of these traces, as much as the traces themselves, reflects specific human ideas and behavior. For example, shallow, restricted concentrations of charcoal that include oxidized earth, bone fragments, and charred plant

---

archaeology The study of cultures through the recovery and analysis of material remains and environmental data.

Figure 1.6 Analyzing Human Remains in a Bioarchaeology Laboratory Bioarchaeology graduate students J. Marla Toyne and Mellisa Lund Valle are conducting a skeletal inventory and checking for pathological conditions in human remains from a 14th-century mass execution and sacrifice site at Punta Lobos in the Huarmey River Valley in northern Peru. Their work is part of a research project directed by Dr. John Verano of Tulane University, New Orleans.

Courtesy of John Verano

remains, located near pieces of fire-cracked rock, pottery, and tools suitable for food preparation, indicate cooking and food processing. Such remains can reveal much about a people's diet and subsistence practices.

In addition to specific questions about a single group of people at a particular place and time, archaeologists use material remains to investigate broad questions, including settlement or migration patterns across vast areas, such as the spread of the earliest humans from Africa or the first peopling of the Americas. Together with skeletal remains, material remains help archaeologists reconstruct the biocultural context of past human lifeways and patterns. Archaeologists organize this material and use it to explain cultural variability and change through time.

Because archaeological research is explicitly tied to unearthing material remains in particular environmental contexts, a variety of innovations in the geographic and geologic sciences have been readily incorporated into archaeological research. Innovations such as geographic information systems (GIS), remote sensing, and ground-penetrating radar (GPR) complement traditional explorations of the past through archaeological digs.

Although archaeologists tend to specialize in particular culture zones or time periods that are connected with particular regions of the world, a number of topical subspecializations also exist. We turn now to these.

historical archaeology The archaeological study of places for which written records exist.

bioarchaeology The archaeological study of human remains—bones, skulls, teeth, and sometimes hair, dried skin, or other tissue—to determine the influences of culture and environment on human biological variation.

Historical Archaeology

Archaeologists can reach back for clues to human behavior far beyond the maximal 5,000 years to which historians are confined by their reliance on written records. Calling this time period "prehistoric" does not mean that these societies were less interested in their history or that they did not have ways of recording and transmitting history. It simply means that written records do not exist.

That said, archaeologists are not limited to the study of societies without written records; they may study those for which historic documents are available to supplement the material remains. **Historical archaeology**, the archaeological study of places for which written records exist, often provides data that differ considerably from the historical record. In most literate societies, written records are associated with governing elites rather than with farmers, fishers, laborers, or slaves, and therefore they include the biases of the ruling classes. In fact, according to James Deetz, a pioneer in historical archaeology of the Americas, in many historical contexts, "material culture may be the most objective source of information we have" (Deetz, 1977, p. 160).

Bioarchaeology

Bioarchaeology is the study of human remains—bones, skulls, teeth, and sometimes hair, dried skin, or other tissue—to determine the influences of culture and environment on human biological variation. Whether mummified (as in the dry deserts of northwestern China, Egypt, or Peru) or not, human remains excavated at archaeological sites provide valuable clues about the lifestyle and health of prehistoric peoples, including information about activity, physiological stress, nutrition, disease, and social rank (**Figure 1.6**).

For example, mummified skeletal remains from the Andean highlands in South America not only reveal this burial practice but also provide evidence of some of the earliest brain surgery ever documented. In addition, these bioarchaeological remains exhibit skull deformation techniques that distinguish nobility from other members of society.

Some archaeologists specialize in *ethnobotany,* studying how people of a given culture made use of indigenous plants. Others specialize in *zooarchaeology,* tracking the animal remains recovered in archaeological excavations. Still others, maritime archaeologists, may research submerged sites or old sailing vessels sunk to the bottom of a sea, lake, or river hundreds or even thousands of years ago.

Contemporary Archaeology

Although most archaeologists concentrate on the past, some study material objects in contemporary settings, and that includes garbage dumps. Just as a 3,000-year-old shell mound (*midden*) on the seacoast of Denmark, New England, or Tiera del Fuego offers significant clues about prehistoric communities living on mussels, oysters, fish, and other natural resources, modern garbage dumps provide evidence of everyday life in contemporary societies. For large cities like New York, the accumulation of daily garbage is staggering. In just a few centuries, millions of inhabitants have dumped so much trash that this urban area has been physically raised 6 to 30 feet—primarily from discarded newspapers and rubble from demolition and building construction, but also from huge amounts of plastic and household and office supplies and equipment (Rathje & Murphy, 2001).

Among the first anthropologists to study modern garbage was William Rathje, who founded the Garbage Project at the University of Arizona in 1973. The project began with a study of household waste of Tucson residents and later expanded to other cities. When surveyed by questionnaires, only 15 percent of households reported consuming beer, and none reported an intake of more than eight cans a week. Analysis of garbage from the same area showed that 80 percent of the households consumed some beer, and 50 percent discarded more than eight cans per week (Rathje & Murphy, 2001).

Beyond providing data on beer consumption, the Garbage Project has tested the validity of research survey techniques, upon which sociologists, economists, other social scientists, and policymakers rely heavily. The tests show a significant difference between what people *say* they do and what the garbage analysis shows they *actually* do.

Applied Archaeology

The Garbage Project also gives us a fine example of applied archaeology producing useful, thought-provoking information about contemporary social issues. Its program of excavating landfills in different parts of North America, initiated in 1987, produced the first reliable data on what materials actually go into landfills and what happens to them there. Again, common beliefs turned out to be at odds with the actual situation. For example, when buried in deep compost landfills, biodegradable materials such as newspapers take far longer to decay than anyone had expected. This kind of information is a vital step toward solving waste disposal problems. The data gathered from the Garbage Project's landfill studies on hazardous wastes and rates of decay of various materials play a major role in landfill regulation and management today (Rathje & Murphy, 2001).

Cultural Resource Management

While archaeology may conjure up images of ancient pyramids and the like, much archaeological fieldwork is carried out as **cultural resource management**. What distinguishes this work from traditional archaeological research is that it is a legally required part of any activity that might threaten important aspects of a country's prehistoric and historic heritage. Many countries, from Chile to China, use archaeological expertise to protect and manage their cultural heritage.

In the United States, for example, if a construction company plans to replace a highway bridge, it must first contract with archaeologists to identify and protect any significant prehistoric or historic resources that might be affected by this new construction. And when cultural resource management work or other archaeological investigation unearths Native American cultural items or human remains, federal laws come into the picture again. The Native American Graves Protection and Repatriation Act (NAGPRA), passed in 1990, provides a process for the return of these remains, especially human bones and burial gifts (such as copper jewelry, weapons, and ceramic bowls), to lineal descendants, culturally affiliated Indian tribes, and Native Hawaiian organizations.

In addition to working in all the capacities mentioned, archaeologists also consult for engineering firms to help them prepare environmental impact statements. Some of these archaeologists operate out of universities and colleges, while others are on the staff of independent consulting firms. When state legislation sponsors any kind of archaeological work, it is referred to as *contract archaeology.*

Physical Anthropology

Physical anthropology, also called *biological anthropology,* focuses on humans as biological organisms. Traditionally, physical anthropologists concentrated on human evolution, primatology, growth and development, human adaptation, and forensics. Today, **molecular anthropology**, or the anthropological study of genes

---

cultural resource management A branch of archaeology concerned with survey and/or excavation of archaeological and historical remains that might be threatened by construction or development; also involved with policy surrounding protection of cultural resources.

physical anthropology The systematic study of humans as biological organisms; also known as *biological anthropology.*

molecular anthropology The anthropological study of genes and genetic relationships, which contributes significantly to our understanding of human evolution, adaptation, and diversity.

and genetic relationships, contributes significantly to our understanding of human evolution, adaptation, and diversity. Comparisons among groups separated by time, geography, or the frequency of a particular gene can reveal how humans have adapted and where they have migrated. As experts in the anatomy of human bones and tissues, biological anthropologists lend their knowledge about the body to applied areas such as gross anatomy laboratories, public health, and criminal investigations.

Paleoanthropology

Dealing with much greater time spans than other branches of anthropology, **paleoanthropology** is the study of the origins, predecessors, and early representatives of the present human species. Focusing on long-time biological changes (evolution) paleoanthropologists seek to understand how, when, and why we became the species we are today. In biological terms, we humans are *Homo sapiens,* a species in the larger order of primates, one of the many kinds of mammals. Because we share a common ancestry with other primates (monkeys and apes), paleoanthropologists look back to the earliest primates (about 65 million years ago, abbreviated mya) or even to the earliest mammals (225 mya) to reconstruct the intricate path of human evolution. At times, paleoanthropologists take a **biocultural** approach, focusing on the interaction of biology and culture.

Paleoanthropologists compare fossilized skeletons of our ancestors to other fossils and to the bones of living members of our species. Combining this knowledge with biochemical and genetic evidence, they strive to scientifically reconstruct the complex course of human evolutionary history. With each new fossil discovery, paleoanthropologists have another piece to add to the puzzle still far from fully solved. Further on in this text, we discuss how, genetic evidence establishes the close relationship between humans and ape species—chimpanzees, bonobos, and gorillas. Genetic analyses indicate that the distinctively human line split from the apes sometime between 5 and 8 million years ago.

Primatology

Studying the anatomy and behavior of the other primates helps us understand what we share with our closest living relatives and what makes humans unique. Therefore, **primatology**, or the study of living and fossil primates, is a vital part of physical anthropology. Primates include the

Penelope Breese/Liaison/Getty Images

Figure 1.7 **Primatologist Jane Goodall** Nearly forty-five years ago Jane Goodall began studying chimpanzees to shed light on the behavior of our distant ancestors. The knowledge she has amassed reveals striking similarities with our species. Goodall has devoted much of her career to championing the rights of our closest living relatives.

Asian and African apes, as well as monkeys, lemurs, lorises, and tarsiers.

Biologically, humans are members of the ape family—large-bodied, broad-shouldered primates with no tail. Detailed studies of ape behavior in the wild indicate that the sharing of learned behavior is a significant part of their social life. Increasingly, primatologists designate the shared, learned behavior of nonhuman apes as *culture.* For example, tool use and communication systems indicate the elementary basis of language in some ape societies.

Primate studies offer scientifically grounded perspectives on the behavior of our ancestors, as well as greater appreciation and respect for the abilities of our closest living relatives. As human activity encroaches on all parts of the world, many primate species are endangered. Primatologists, such as Jane Goodall (**Figure 1.7**), strongly advocate for the preservation of primate habitats so that these remarkable animals will be able to continue to inhabit the earth with us.

Human Growth, Adaptation, and Variation

Some physical anthropologists specialize in the study of human growth and development. They examine biological mechanisms of growth as well as the impact of the environment on the growth process. For example, Franz Boas, a pioneer of American anthropology of the early 20th century (see the Anthropologists of Note feature on the next page) compared the heights of immigrants who spent their

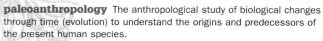

paleoanthropology The anthropological study of biological changes through time (evolution) to understand the origins and predecessors of the present human species.

biocultural An approach that focuses on the interaction of biology and culture.

primatology The study of living and fossil primates.

ANTHROPOLOGISTS OF NOTE

Franz Boas (1858–1942) • Matilda Coxe Stevenson (1849–1915)

Franz Boas on a sailing ship, about 1925.

Franz Boas was not the first to teach anthropology in the United States, but it was Boas and his students, with their insistence on scientific rigor, who made anthropology courses common in college and university curricula. Born and raised in Germany where he studied physics, mathematics, and geography, Boas did his first ethnographic research among the Inuit (Eskimos) in Arctic Canada in 1883 and 1884. After a brief academic career in Berlin, he came to the United States where he worked in museums interspersed with ethnographic research among the Kwakiutl (Kwakwaka'wakw) Indians in the Canadian Pacific. In 1896, he became a professor at Columbia University in New York City. He authored an incredible number of publications, founded professional organizations and journals, and taught two generations of great anthropologists, including numerous women and ethnic minorities.

As a Jewish immigrant, Boas recognized the dangers of ethnocentrism and especially racism. Through ethnographic fieldwork and comparative analysis, he demonstrated that white supremacy theories and other schemes ranking non-European peoples and cultures as inferior were biased, ill informed, and unscientific. Throughout his long and illustrious academic career, he promoted anthropology not only as a human science but also as an instrument to combat racism and prejudice in the world.

Among the founders of North American anthropology were a number of women, including **Matilda Coxe Stevenson**, who did fieldwork among the Zuni Indians of Arizona. In 1885, she founded the Women's Anthropological Society in Washington, DC, the first professional association for women scientists. Three years later, hired by the Smithsonian's Bureau of American Ethnology, she became one of the first women in the world to receive a full-time official position in science. Along with several other pioneering female anthropologists in North America, she was highly influential among women's rights advocates in the late 1800s. The tradition of women building careers in anthropology continues. In fact, since World War II more than half the presidents of the now 12,000-member American Anthropological Association have been women.

Matilda Coxe Stevenson in New Mexico, about 1900.

Recording observations on film as well as in notebooks, Stevenson and Boas were also pioneers in visual anthropology. Stevenson used an early box camera to document Pueblo Indian religious ceremonies and material culture, while Boas photographed Inuit and Kwakiutl Indians from the early 1890s for cultural as well as physical anthropological documentation. Today, their early photographs are greatly valued not only by anthropologists and historians, but also by indigenous peoples themselves.

childhood in the "old country" (Europe) to the increased heights reached by their children who grew up in the United States. Today, physical anthropologists study the impact of poverty, pollution, and disease on growth. Comparisons between human and nonhuman primate growth patterns can provide clues to the evolutionary history of humans. Detailed anthropological studies of the hormonal, genetic, and physiological bases of healthy growth in living humans also contribute significantly to the health of children today.

Studies of human adaptation focus on the capacity of humans to adapt or adjust to their material environment—biologically and culturally. This branch of physical anthropology takes a comparative approach to humans living today in a variety of environments. Human beings are the only primates to inhabit the entire earth. Although biological adaptations make it possible for people to live in environmentally extreme regions, cultural adaptations also contribute to our survival in places that are dangerously cold, hot, or of high altitude.

Some of these biological adaptations are built into the genetic makeup of populations. The long period of human growth and development provides ample opportunity for the environment to shape the human body. *Developmental adaptations* are responsible for some features of human variation, such as the enlargement of the right ventricle of the heart to help push blood to the lungs among the Aymara Indians of the Bolivian altiplano—an extensive area of high plateau at the widest part of the Andes. *Physiological adaptations* are short-term changes in response to a particular environmental stimulus. For example, if a woman who normally lives at sea level flies to La Paz, a large Bolivian city in the altiplano at an altitude of 3,660 meters (nearly 12,000 feet), her body will undergo a series of physiological responses, such as increased production of the red blood cells that carry oxygen. These kinds of biological adaptation contribute to present-day human variation.

Genetically based human differences include visible traits such as height, body build, and skin color, as well as biochemical factors such as blood type and susceptibility to certain diseases. Still, we remain members of a single

ANTHROPOLOGY APPLIED

Forensic Anthropology: Voices for the Dead

The work of Clyde C. Snow, Michael Blakey, and Amy Zelson Mundorff

Forensic anthropology is the analysis of skeletal remains for legal purposes. Law enforcement authorities call upon forensic anthropologists to use skeletal remains to identify murder victims, missing persons, or people who have died in disasters, such as plane crashes. Forensic anthropologists have also contributed substantially to the investigation of human rights abuses in all parts of the world by identifying victims and documenting the cause of their death.

Among the best-known forensic anthropologists is Clyde C. Snow. He has been practicing in this field for over forty years, first for the Federal Aviation Administration and more recently as a freelance consultant. In addition to the usual police work, Snow has studied the remains of General George Armstrong Custer and his men from the 1876 battle at Little Big Horn, and in 1985 he went to Brazil, where he identified the remains of the notorious Nazi war criminal Josef Mengele.

Snow was also instrumental in establishing the first forensic team devoted to documenting cases of human rights abuses around the world. This began in 1984 when he went to Argentina at the request of a newly elected civilian government to help with the identification of remains of the *desaparecidos,* or "disappeared ones," the 9,000 or more people who were eliminated by death squads during seven years of military rule. A year later, he returned to give expert testimony at the trial of nine junta members and to teach Argentineans how to recover, clean, repair, preserve, photograph, x-ray, and analyze bones. Besides providing factual accounts of the fate of victims to their surviving kin and refuting the assertions of revisionists that the massacres never happened, the work of Snow and his Argentinean associates was crucial in convicting several military officers of kidnapping, torture, and murder.

Since Snow's pioneering work, forensic anthropologists have become increasingly involved in the investigation of human rights abuses in all parts of the world, from Chile to Guatemala, Haiti, the Philippines, Rwanda, Iraq, Bosnia, and Kosovo. Meanwhile, they continue to do important work for more typical clients. In the United States these clients include the Federal Bureau of Investigation and city, state, and county medical examiners' offices.

Forensic anthropologists specializing in skeletal remains commonly work closely with forensic archaeologists. The relation between them is rather like that between a forensic pathologist, who examines a corpse to establish time and manner of death, and a crime scene investigator, who searches the site for clues. While the forensic anthropologist deals with the human remains—often only bones and teeth—the forensic archaeologist controls the site, recording the position of relevant finds and recovering any clues associated with the remains.

In Rwanda, for example, a team assembled in 1995 to investigate mass murder (genocide) for the United Nations, which included archaeologists from the U.S. National Park Service's Midwest Archaeological Center. They performed the standard archaeological procedures of mapping the site, determining its boundaries, photographing and recording all surface finds, and excavating, photographing, and recording buried skeletons and associated materials in mass graves.[a]

In 1991, in another part of the world, construction workers in New York City discovered an African burial ground from the 17th and 18th centuries.

species. Physical anthropology applies all the techniques of modern biology to achieve fuller understanding of human variation and its relationship to the different environments in which people have lived. Physical anthropologists' research on human variation has debunked false notions of biologically defined races, a belief based on widespread misinterpretation of human variation.

Forensic Anthropology

One of the many practical applications of physical anthropology is **forensic anthropology**—the identification of human skeletal remains for legal purposes. In addition to helping law enforcement authorities identify murder victims, forensic anthropologists investigate human rights abuses such as systematic genocide, terrorism, and war crimes. These specialists use details of skeletal anatomy to establish the age, sex, population affiliation, and stature of the deceased. Forensic anthropologists can also determine whether the person was right- or left-handed, exhibited any physical abnormalities, or had experienced trauma.

While forensics relies upon differing frequencies of certain skeletal characteristics to establish population affiliation, it is nevertheless false to say that all people from a given population have a particular type of skeleton. (See the Anthropology Applied feature to read about the work of several forensic anthropologists and forensic archaeologists.)

forensic anthropology The identification of human skeletal remains for legal purposes.

The excavation of mass graves by the Guatemalan Foundation for Forensic Anthropology (Fernando Moscoso Moller, director) documents the human rights abuses committed during Guatemala's bloody civil war, a conflict that left 200,000 people dead and another 40,000 missing. In 2009, in a mass grave in the Quiche region, Diego Lux Tzunux uses his cell phone to photograph the skeletal remains believed to belong to his brother Manuel who disappeared in 1980. Genetic analyses allow forensic anthropologists to confirm the identity of individuals so that family members can know the fate of their loved ones. The analysis of skeletal remains provides evidence of the torture and massacre sustained by these individuals.

Ground Project provided incontrovertible evidence of the horror of slavery in North America, in the busy northern port of New York City. The more than 400 individuals, many of them children, were worked so far beyond their ability to endure that their spines were fractured.

A decade after construction workers happened upon the African Burial Ground, terrorists attacked the World Trade Center in lower Manhattan. Amy Zelson Mundorff, a forensic anthropologist for New York City's Office of the Chief Medical Examiner, was injured in the September 11 attack. But two days later she returned to work where she supervised and coordinated the management, treatment, and cataloguing of people who lost their lives in the tragedy.

Thus, several kinds of anthropologists analyze human remains for a variety of purposes. Their work contributes to the documentation and correction of violence committed by humans of the past and present.

Researchers used a bioarchaeological rather than a strictly forensic approach to examine the complete cultural and historical context and lifeways of the entire population buried there. Directed by Michael Blakey, the African Burial

[a]Haglund, W. D., Conner, M., & Scott, D. D. (2001). The archaeology of contemporary mass graves. *Historical Archaeology 35* (1), 57–69.

Anthropology, Science, and the Humanities

Anthropology has sometimes been called the most humane of the sciences and the most scientific of the humanities—a designation that most anthropologists accept with pride. Given their intense involvement with people of all times and places, anthropologists have amassed considerable information about human failure and success, weakness and greatness—the real stuff of the humanities.

Anthropologists remain committed to the proposition that one cannot fully understand another culture by simply observing it; as the term *participant observation* implies, one must *experience* it as well. This same commitment to fieldwork and to the systematic collection of data, whether qualitative or quantitative, is also evidence of the scientific side of anthropology. Anthropology is an **empirical** social science based on observations or information taken in through the senses and verified by others rather than on intuition or faith. But anthropology is distinguished from other sciences by the diverse ways in which scientific research is conducted within the discipline.

Science, a carefully honed way of producing knowledge, aims to reveal and explain the underlying logic, the structural processes that make the world tick. The creative scientific endeavor seeks testable explanations for observed phenomena, ideally in terms of the workings of hidden but unchanging principles or laws. Two basic ingredients are essential for this: imagination and skepticism. Imagination, though having the potential to lead us astray, helps us recognize unexpected ways phenomena might be ordered and to think of old things in new ways. Without it, there can be no science. Skepticism allows us to distinguish fact (an observation verified by others) from fancy, to test our speculations, and to prevent our imaginations from running away with us.

In their search for explanations, scientists do not assume that things are always as they appear on the surface. After all, what could be more obvious to the scientifically uninformed observer than the earth staying still while the sun travels around it every day?

Like other scientists, anthropologists often begin their research with a **hypothesis** (a tentative explanation or hunch) about the possible relationships between certain observed facts or events. By gathering various kinds of data that seem to ground such suggested explanations on evidence, anthropologists come up with a **theory**, a coherent statement that provides an explanatory framework for understanding; an explanation or interpretation supported by a reliable body of data. In their effort to demonstrate links between *known* facts or events, anthropologists may discover *unexpected* facts, events, or relationships. An important function of theory is that it guides us in our explorations and may result in new knowledge. Equally important, the newly discovered facts may provide evidence that certain explanations, however popular or firmly believed, are unfounded. When the evidence is lacking or fails to support the suggested explanations, promising hypotheses or attractive hunches must be dropped. In other words, anthropology relies on empirical evidence. Moreover, no scientific theory—no matter how widely accepted by the international community of scholars—is beyond challenge. That includes the findings of some of anthropology's earliest and most respected scholars.

It is important to distinguish between scientific theories—which are always open to challenges born of new evidence or insights—and doctrine. A **doctrine**, or dogma, is an assertion of opinion or belief formally handed down by an authority as true and indisputable. For instance, those who accept a creationist doctrine on the origin of the human species as recounted in sacred texts or myths do so on the basis of religious authority, conceding that such views may be contrary to genetic, geological, biological, or other explanations. Such doctrines cannot be tested or proved one way or another: They are accepted as matters of faith.

Straightforward as the scientific approach may seem, its application is not always easy. For instance, once a hypothesis has been proposed, the person who suggested it is strongly motivated to verify it, and this can cause one to unwittingly overlook negative evidence and unanticipated findings. This is a familiar problem in all science as noted by paleontologist Stephen Jay Gould: "The greatest impediment to scientific innovation is usually a conceptual lock, not a factual lock" (Gould, 1989, p. 226). Because culture provides humans with concepts and shapes our very thoughts, it can be challenging to frame hypotheses or to develop interpretations that are not culture-bound. However, by encompassing both humanism and science, the discipline of anthropology can draw on its internal diversity to overcome conceptual locks.

empirical An approach based on observations of the world rather than on intuition or faith.

hypothesis A tentative explanation of the relationships among certain phenomena.

theory A coherent statement that provides an explanatory framework for understanding; an explanation or interpretation supported by a reliable body of data.

doctrine An assertion of opinion or belief formally handed down by an authority as true and indisputable.

culture shock In fieldwork, the anthropologist's personal disorientation and anxiety that may result in depression.

Fieldwork

Anthropologists are keenly aware that their personal identity and cultural background may shape their research questions, bear upon their factual observations, and even influence their interpretations and explanations. To avoid inadvertent bias or distortion, they immerse themselves in the data to the fullest extent possible through on-location research traditionally known as *fieldwork*.

Fieldwork, introduced earlier in this chapter in connection with cultural anthropology, is characteristic of *all* the anthropological subdisciplines. Archaeologists and paleoanthropologists excavate sites in the field, and, as already noted, cultural anthropologists observe human behavior while living and interacting with a group of people wherever the group may reside, work, or travel. Just as an ethnographer will study the culture of a human community by living in it, a primatologist might live among a group of chimpanzees or gorillas in the forest. Likewise, linguistic anthropologists interested in analyzing or comparing words and grammar from undocumented languages must first learn the languages, and they typically do so by living in communities where these are actually spoken. The same is true for colleagues studying how speech is actually "performed" in various social settings. Also, a physical anthropologist interested in the effects of globalization on nutrition and growth may reside in a particular community to research this issue.

Fieldwork requires researchers to step out of their cultural comfort zone into a world that is unfamiliar and sometimes unsettling. Anthropologists in the field are likely to face a host of challenges—physical, social, mental, political, and ethical. They often must deal with the physical challenges of unfamiliar food, climate, and hygiene conditions.

Typically, anthropologists in the field struggle with emotional challenges such as loneliness, feeling like a perpetual outsider, being socially awkward in their new cultural setting, and having to be alert around the clock because anything that is happening or being said may be significant to their research. Political challenges include the possibility of unwittingly letting oneself be used by factions within the community, or being regarded with suspicion by government authorities who may view the anthropologist as a spy. And there are ethical dilemmas: What does the anthropologist do if faced with a troubling cultural practice such as female circumcision? How does the anthropologist deal with demands for food supplies or medicine? Is it acceptable to use deception to gain vital information? Collectively, these multiple challenges may gradually amount to **culture shock**—personal disorientation and anxiety that may result in depression, forcing some anthropologists to abandon their fieldwork and return home for recovery.

More often, however, fieldwork leads to tangible and meaningful personal, professional, and social rewards, ranging from lasting friendships to significant knowledge and insights concerning the human condition. Something of the meaning of anthropological fieldwork—its usefulness and its impact on researcher and subject—is conveyed in the following Original Study by Suzanne Leclerc-Madlala, an anthropologist who left her familiar New England surroundings nearly thirty years ago to do AIDS research among Zulu-speaking people in South Africa. Her research interest has changed the course of her own life, not to mention the lives of many individuals who are dealing with AIDS/HIV.

Fighting HIV/AIDS in Africa: Traditional Healers on the Front Line BY SUZANNE LECLERC-MADLALA

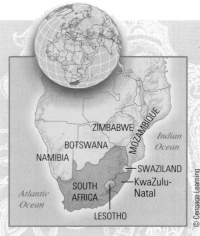

In the 1980s, as an anthropology graduate student at George Washington University, I met and married a Zulu-speaking student from South Africa. It was the height of apartheid (racial segregation), and upon moving to that country I was classified as "honorary black" and forced to live in a segregated township with my husband. The AIDS epidemic was in its infancy, but it was clear from the start that an anthropological understanding of how people perceive and engage with this disease would be crucial for developing interventions. I wanted to learn all that I could to make a difference, and this culminated in earning a doctorate from the University of Natal on the cultural construction of AIDS among the Zulu. The HIV/AIDS pandemic in Africa became my professional passion.

Faced with overwhelming global health-care needs, the World Health Organization passed a series of resolutions in the 1970s promoting collaboration between traditional and modern medicine. Such moves held a special relevance for Africa where traditional healers typically outnumber practitioners of modern medicine by a ratio of 100 to 1 or more. Given Africa's disproportionate burden of disease, supporting partnership efforts with traditional healers makes sense. But what sounds sensible today was once considered absurd, even heretical. For centuries Westerners generally viewed traditional healing as a whole lot of primitive mumbo jumbo practiced by witchdoctors with demonic powers who perpetuated superstition. Yet, its practice survived. Today, as the African continent grapples with an HIV/AIDS epidemic of crisis proportion, millions of sick people who are either too poor or too distant to access modern health care are proving that traditional healers are an invaluable resource in the fight against AIDS.

Of the world's estimated 35 million people currently infected by HIV, nearly 70 percent live in sub-Saharan Africa, and the vast majority of children left orphaned by AIDS are African. From the 1980s onward, as Africa became synonymous with the rapid spread of HIV/AIDS, a number of prevention programs involved traditional healers. My initial research in South Africa's KwaZulu-Natal province—where almost 40 percent of the population is HIV infected—revealed that traditional Zulu healers were regularly consulted for the treatment of sexually transmitted disease (STD). I found that such diseases, along with HIV/AIDS, were usually attributed to transgressions of taboos related to birth, pregnancy, marriage, and death. Moreover, these diseases were often understood within a framework of pollution and contagion, and like most serious illnesses, ultimately believed to have their causal roots in witchcraft.

I investigated a pioneer program in STD and HIV education for traditional healers in the province. It aimed to provide basic biomedical knowledge about the various modes of disease transmission, the means available for prevention, the diagnosing of symptoms, the keeping of records, and the making of patient referrals to local clinics and hospitals.

Interviews with the healers showed that many were deeply suspicious of modern medicine. They perceived AIDS education as a one-way street intended to press them into formal health structures and convince them of the superiority of modern medicine. Yet, today, few of the 6,000-plus KwaZulu-Natal healers who have been trained in AIDS education say they would opt for less collaboration; most want to have more.

Treatments by Zulu healers for HIV/AIDS often take the form of infusions of bitter herbs to "cleanse" the body, strengthen the blood, and remove misfortune and "pollution." Some treatments provide effective relief from common ailments associated with AIDS such as itchy skin rashes, oral thrush, persistent diarrhea, and general debility. Indigenous plants such as *unwele (Sutherlandia frutescens)* and African potato *(Hypoxis hemerocallidea)* are well-known traditional medicines that have proven immuno-boosting properties. Both have recently become available in modern pharmacies packaged in tablet form. With modern anti-retroviral treatments still well beyond the reach of most South Africans, indigenous medicines that can delay or alleviate some of the suffering caused by AIDS are proving to be valuable and popular treatments.

Knowledge about potentially infectious bodily fluids has led healers to change some of their practices. Where porcupine quills were once used to give a type of indigenous injection, patients are now advised to bring their own sewing needles to consultations. Patients provide their own individual razor blades for making incisions on their skin, where previously healers reused the same razor on many clients. Some healers claim they have given up the practice of biting clients' skin to remove foreign objects from the body. Today, especially in urban centers like Durban, it is not uncommon for healers to proudly display AIDS training certificates in their inner-city "surgeries" where they don white jackets and wear protective latex gloves.

Medical anthropologist Suzanne Leclerc-Madlala visits with "Doctor" Koloko in KwaZulu-Natal, South Africa. This Zulu traditional healer proudly displays her official AIDS training certificate.

Politics and controversy have dogged South Africa's official response to HIV/AIDS. But back home in the waddle-and-daub, animal-skin-draped herbariums and diving huts of traditional healers, the politics of AIDS holds little relevance. Here the sick and dying are coming in droves to be treated by healers who have been part and parcel of community life (and death) since time immemorial. In many cases traditional healers have transformed their homes into hospices for AIDS patients. Because of the strong negative stigma that still plagues the disease, those with AIDS symptoms are often abandoned or sometimes chased away from their homes by family members. They seek refuge with healers who provide them with comfort in their final days. Healers' homes are also becoming orphanages as healers respond to what has been called the "third wave" of AIDS destruction: the growing legions of orphaned children.

Those who are suffering go to traditional healers not only in search of relief for physical symptoms. They go to learn about the ultimate cause of their disease—something other than the immediate cause of a sexually transmitted "germ" or "virus." They go to find answers to the "why me and not him" questions, the "why now" and "why this." As with most traditional healing systems worldwide, healing among the Zulu and most all African ethnic groups cannot be separated from the spiritual concerns of the individual and the cosmo-logical beliefs of the community at large. Traditional healers help to restore a sense of balance between the individual and the community, on one hand, and between the individual and the cosmos, or ancestors, on the other hand. They provide health care that is personalized, culturally appropriate, holistic, and tailored to meet the needs and expectations of the patient. In many ways it is a far more satisfactory form of healing than that offered by modern medicine.

Traditional healing in Africa is flourishing in the era of AIDS, and understanding why this is so requires a shift in the conceptual framework by which we understand, explain, and interpret health. Anthropological methods and its comparative and holistic perspective can facilitate, like no other discipline, the type of understanding that is urgently needed to address the AIDS crisis.

For more details, see Leclerc-Madlala, S. (2002). Bodies and politics: Healing rituals in the democratic South Africa. *In V. Faure (Ed.),* Les cahiers de 'l'IFAS, no. 2. Johannesburg: The French Institute. *Leclerc-Madlala now works for USAID.*

Questions of Ethics

Anthropologists deal with matters that are private and sensitive, including information that individuals would prefer not to have generally known about them. In the early years of the discipline, many anthropologists documented traditional cultures they assumed would disappear due to disease, warfare, or changes imposed by colonialism, growing state power, or international market expansion. Some worked as government administrators or consultants gathering data used to formulate policies concerning indigenous peoples. Others helped predict the behavior of enemies during wartime.

How does one write about important but delicate issues and at the same time protect the privacy of the individuals who have shared their stories? The kinds of research carried out by anthropologists, and the settings within which they work, raise important moral questions about the potential uses and abuses of our knowledge. Who will utilize our findings and for what purposes? Who decides what research questions are asked? Who, if anyone, will benefit from the research? For example, in the case of research on an ethnic or religious minority whose values may be at odds with the dominant society, will government bureaucracies or industrial corporations use anthropological data to suppress that group? And what of traditional communities around the world? Who is to decide what changes should, or should not, be introduced for community development? And who defines "development"—the community, a national government, or an international agency like the World Bank?

After the colonial era ended in the 1960s, and in reaction to controversial research practices by some anthropologists in or near violent conflict areas, anthropologists formulated a code of ethics to ensure that their research would not harm the groups being studied. Formalized in 1971 and revised in 1998 and again in 2009, the American Anthropological Association's (AAA) ethics code outlines a range of moral responsibilities and obligations. It includes this core principle: Anthropological researchers must do everything in their power to ensure that their research does not harm the safety, dignity, or privacy of the people with whom they work, conduct research, or perform other professional activities.

In recent years, some of the debates regarding this code have focused on the potential ethical breaches if anthropologists work for corporations or undertake classified contract work for the military. Although the AAA has no legal authority, it does issue policy statements on research ethics questions as they come up. For example, recently the AAA recommended that research notes from medical settings should be protected and not subject to subpoena in court. This honors the ethical imperative to protect the privacy of individuals who have shared with anthropologists their stories about personal health issues.

Emerging technologies have ethical implications that impact anthropological inquiry. For example, the ability to sequence and patent particular genes has led to debates about who has the right to hold a patent—the individuals from whom the particular genes were obtained or the researcher who studies the genes? Similarly, do ancient remains belong to the scientist, to the people living in the region under scientific investigation, or to whoever happens to have possession of them? Global market forces have converted these remains into expensive collectibles, resulting in a systematic looting of archaeological and fossil sites.

While seeking answers to these questions, anthropologists recognize that they have special obligations to three sets of people: those whom they study, those who fund the research, and those in the profession who rely on published findings to increase our collective knowledge. Because fieldwork requires a relationship of trust between researchers and the community in which they work, the anthropologist's first responsibility clearly is to the people who have shared their stories and their community. Everything possible must be done to protect their physical, social, and psychological welfare and to honor their dignity and privacy. This task is frequently complex. For example, telling the story of a people gives information both to relief agencies who might help them and to others who might take advantage of them.

Maintaining one's own culture is an internationally recognized basic human right, and any connection with

Globalscape

A Global Body Shop?

Lakshmamma, pictured here with her daughter in southern India's rural village of Holalu, near Mandya, has sold one of her kidneys for about 30,000 rupees ($650). This is far below the average going rate of $6,000 per kidney in the global organ transplant business. But the broker took his commission, and corrupt officials needed to be paid as well. Although India passed a law in 1994 prohibiting the buying and selling of human organs, the business is booming. In Europe and North America, kidney transplants can cost over $200,000, plus the waiting list for donor kidneys is long, and dialysis is expensive. Thus "transplant tourism," in India and several other countries, caters to affluent patients in search of "fresh" kidneys to be harvested from poor people like Lakshmamma.[a]

The well-publicized arrest of Brooklyn-based organ broker Levy Izhak Rosenbaum in July 2009—part of an FBI sting operation that also led to the arrest of forty-five other individuals, including several public officials in New Jersey—represents some progress in combatting illegal trafficking of body parts. Charged with brokering illegal kidney transplants—purchasing the organs for $10,000–$25,000 and selling them for as much as $160,000—the Israeli immigrant pleaded guilty to three trafficking counts and agreed to forfeit $420,000 in broker fees. In July 2012, he was sentenced to 2½ years in prison and possible deportation.[b]

Medical anthropologist and activist Nancy Scheper-Hughes has researched the criminal and medical aspects of global organ trafficking for some two decades. Cofounder of Organs Watch in Berkeley, California, an organization working to stop the illegal traffic in organs, she notified the FBI about Rosenbaum in 2002.[c] International crackdowns and changes in local laws are now curbing illegal global networks in human organ trafficking.

Global Twister

Considering that $650 is a fortune in a poor village like Holalu, does medical globalization benefit or exploit people like Lakshmamma, who are looked upon as human commodities? What accounts for the gap between the $650 she received for her kidney and the fees Rosenbaum received for the organ sales he brokered?

[a]Vidya, R. (2002). Karnataka's unabating kidney trade. *Frontline*. www.frontlineonnet.com/fl1907/19070610.htm (retrieved June 10, 2012)

[b]Henry, S., & Porter, D. (2011, October 27). Levy Izhak Rosenbaum pleads guilty to selling black market kidneys. *Huffingtonpost.com*. www.huffingtonpost.com/2011/10/27/levy-izhak-rosenbaum-plea_n_1035624.html (retrieved June 10, 2012)

[c]Glovin, D., & Voreacos, D. (2012, July 12). Kidney broker sentenced to prison. *Bloomberg News*. Retrieved from http://www.businessweek.com/news/2012-07-11/n-dot-y-dot-man-gets-30-month-term-in-first-u-dot-s-dot-organ-case

outsiders can expose and therefore endanger the cultural integrity of the community being studied. To overcome some of these ethical challenges, anthropologists frequently collaborate with and contribute to the communities in which they are working, inviting the people being studied to have some say about if and how their stories are told. In research involving ancient human remains, collaboration with local people not only preserves the remains from market forces but also honors the connections of indigenous people to the places and remains under study.

Anthropology and Globalization

A holistic perspective and a long-term commitment to understanding the human species in all its variety equip anthropologists to grapple with a challenge that has overriding importance for each of us today: **globalization**. This concept refers to worldwide interconnectedness, evidenced in rapid global movement of natural resources, trade goods, human labor, finance capital, information, and infectious diseases. Although worldwide travel, trade relations, and information flow have existed for several centuries, the pace and magnitude of these long-distance exchanges have picked up enormously in recent decades; the Internet, in particular, has greatly expanded information exchange capacities.

The powerful forces driving globalization are technological innovations, cost differences among countries, faster knowledge transfers, and increased trade and financial integration among countries. Touching almost everybody's life on the planet, globalization is about economics as much as politics, and it changes human relations and ideas as well as our natural environments. Even geographically remote communities are quickly becoming interdependent—and often vulnerable—through globalization (see the Globalscape on the opposite page for an example).

Researching in all corners of the world, anthropologists witness the impact of globalization on human communities wherever they are located. They describe and try to explain how individuals and organizations respond to the massive changes confronting them. Dramatically increasing every year, globalization can be a two-edged sword. It may generate economic growth and prosperity, but it also undermines long-established institutions. Generally, globalization has brought significant gains to more-educated groups in wealthier countries, while at the same time contributing to the erosion of traditional cultures. Upheavals due to globalization are key causes for rising levels of ethnic and religious conflict throughout the world.

Because all of us now live in a global village, we can no longer afford the luxury of ignoring our neighbors, no matter how distant they may seem. In this age of globalization, anthropology may not only provide humanity with useful

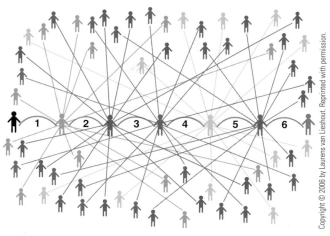

Figure 1.8 Six Degrees of Separation The phrase "six degrees of separation," diagrammed here, refers to the idea that everyone is on average approximately six steps away, by way of introduction, from any other person on earth. Thus, a chain of "a friend of a friend" statements can be made to connect any two people in six steps or fewer. Originally coined by Hungarian writer Frigyes Karinthy in his 1929 short story, "Chains," it was popularized by American playwright John Guare's 1993 film, *Six Degrees of Separation*. It became all the more popular after four college students invented the trivia game Six Degrees of Kevin Bacon, in which the goal is to link any actor to film star Kevin Bacon through no more than six performance connections.

insights concerning diversity, but it may also assist us in avoiding or overcoming significant problems born of that diversity. In countless social arenas, from schools to businesses to hospitals to emergency centers, anthropologists have done cross-cultural research that makes it possible for educators, businesspeople, doctors, and humanitarians to do their work more effectively.

As illustrated by many examples in this textbook, ignorance or ethnocentric (mis)information about other societies and their cultural beliefs and practices can cause or fuel serious problems throughout the world. This is especially true in an age when human interactions and interdependence have been transformed by global information exchange and transportation advances. As noted in the Challenge Issue at the start of this chapter, there are only six degrees of separation between each of us and any other person on earth (**Figure 1.8**). Anthropology offers a way of looking at and understanding the world's peoples—insights that are nothing less than basic skills for survival in this age of globalization.

globalization Worldwide interconnectedness, evidenced in rapid global movement of natural resources, trade goods, human labor, finance capital, information, and infectious diseases.

CHAPTER CHECKLIST

What is anthropology?

● Anthropology is the objective and systematic study of humankind in all times and places.

● Anthropology contains four major fields or subdisciplines: cultural anthropology, linguistic anthropology, archaeology, and physical or biological anthropology.

● In each of anthropology's fields some individuals practice applied anthropology, which uses anthropological knowledge to solve practical problems.

What do anthropologists do in each of its four fields?

● Cultural anthropologists study humans in terms of their cultures, the often-unconscious standards by which social groups operate.

● Linguistic anthropologists study human languages and may deal with the description of a language, with the history of languages, or with how languages are used in particular social settings.

● Archaeologists study human cultures through the recovery and analysis of material remains and environmental data.

● Physical anthropologists focus on humans as biological organisms; they particularly emphasize tracing the evolutionary development of the human animal and studying biological variation within the species today.

How is anthropology different from other disciplines?

● Unique among the sciences and humanities, anthropology has long emphasized the study of non-Western societies and a holistic approach, which aims to formulate theoretically valid explanations and interpretations of human diversity based on detailed studies of all aspects of human biology, behavior, and beliefs in all known societies, past and present.

● In anthropology, the humanities, social sciences, and natural sciences come together into a genuinely humanistic science. Anthropology's link with the humanities can be seen in its concern with people's beliefs, values, languages, arts, and literature—oral as well as written—but above all in its attempt to convey the experience of living in different cultures.

How do anthropologists conduct research?

● Fieldwork, characteristic of all the anthropological subdisciplines, includes complete immersion in research settings ranging from archaeological and paleoanthropological survey and excavation, to living with a group of primates in their natural habitat, to biological data gathered while living with a group. Ethnographic participant observation with a particular culture or subculture is the classic field method of cultural anthropology.

● After the fieldwork of archaeologists and physical anthropologists, researchers conduct laboratory analyses of excavated remains or biological samples collected in the field.

● The comparative method is key to all branches of anthropology. Anthropologists make broad comparisons among peoples and cultures—past and present. They also compare related species and fossil groups. Ethnology, the comparative branch of cultural anthropologists, uses a range of ethnographic accounts to construct theories about cultures from a comparative or historical point of view. Ethnologists often focus on a particular aspect of culture, such as religious or economic practices.

How do anthropologists face the ethical challenges that emerge through conducting anthropological research?

● Anthropologists must stay aware of the potential uses and abuses of anthropological knowledge and the ways that it is obtained.

● The anthropological code of ethics, first formalized in 1971 and continually revised, outlines the moral and ethical responsibilities of anthropologists to the people whom they study, to those who fund the research, and to the profession as a whole.

What can anthropology contribute to the understanding of globalization?

● A long tradition of studying the connections among diverse peoples over time gives anthropology a theoretical framework to study globalization in a world increasingly linked through recent technological advancements.

● Anthropology equips global citizens to challenge ethnocentrism and to understand human diversity.

● Anthropology has essential insights to offer the modern world, particularly today, when understanding our neighbors in the global village has become a matter of survival for all.

QUESTIONS FOR REFLECTION

1. As noted in this chapter's opening Challenge Issue, there are only six degrees of separation between you and the pictured coltan miner working in the heart of Africa. Many miners are poor or orphaned children forced into hard labor and living in squalor, with short life expectancies. When you buy a new electronic device that uses coltan, do you think you contribute to the miserable exploitation of fellow humans?

2. Anthropology embraces a holistic approach to explain all aspects of human beliefs, behavior, and biology. How might anthropology challenge your personal perspective on the question, who am I?

3. From the holistic anthropological perspective, humans have one leg in culture and the other in nature. Are there examples from your life that illustrate the interconnectedness of human biology and culture?

4. Globalization can be described as a two-edged sword. How does it foster growth and destruction simultaneously?

5. The Biocultural Connection in this chapter contrasts different cultural perspectives on brain death, while the Original Study features a discussion about traditional Zulu healers and their role in dealing with AIDS victims. What do these two accounts suggest about the role of applied anthropology in dealing with cross-cultural health issues around the world?

ONLINE STUDY RESOURCES

CourseMate

Access chapter-specific learning tools, including learning objectives, practice quizzes, videos, flash cards, glossaries, and more in your Anthropology CourseMate.

Log into **www.cengagebrain.com** to access the resources your instructor has assigned and to purchase materials.

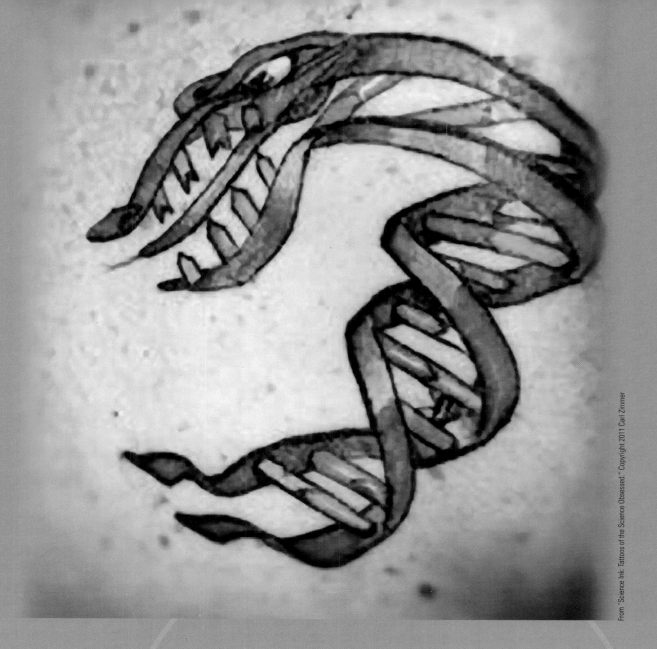

Challenge Issue

In the 21st century, a biomedical doctor in Brazil might urge his or her patient to undergo testing for a specific disease gene as part of predicting the patient's future health. A pregnant woman in Canada might choose to terminate her pregnancy if prenatal testing reveals the presence of genes for a specific disease in a developing fetus. A pregnant woman in India, a society that considers female children a liability, could opt for prenatal genetic testing to ensure she will have a boy. Genetic analyses have become routine in biomedicine. Genetics plays a role in law as well. Throughout the globe, police identify criminals through DNA fingerprinting. They also maintain DNA databases of convicts and suspects for solving crimes in the future. In the United States, individuals wrongfully imprisoned for many years have been freed after genetic testing. No wonder, then, that many individuals have come to see genes and DNA as integral to individual identity. This correspondence between self and genetics has even prompted some people to tattoo an image of the genetic code into their very skin. But is the human condition this simple? Are we merely our DNA? Do our genes determine our actions? And what will be the social consequences of depicting people as creatures programmed by their DNA, or by any other aspect of biology? Individuals and societies can answer these challenging questions using an anthropological perspective, which emphasizes the connections between human biology and culture.

Biology, Genetics, and Evolution

2

Evolution and Creation Stories

The mythology of most peoples includes a story explaining the appearance of humans on earth. The accounts of creation recorded in the Bible's Book of Genesis, for example, explain human origins. The Nez Perce, American Indians native to eastern Oregon and Idaho, provide us with a vastly different example that serves the same function. For the Nez Perce, human beings are the creation of Coyote, a trickster-transformer. Coyote chased the giant beaver monster Wishpoosh over the earth, leaving a trail to form the Columbia River. When Coyote caught Wishpoosh, he killed him, dragged his body to the riverbank, and cut it into pieces, each body part transforming into one of the various peoples of this region. The Nez Perce were made from Wishpoosh's head, thus conferring on them great intelligence and horsemanship (Clark, 1966).

Creation stories depict the relationship between humans and the rest of the natural world, sometimes reflecting a deep connection among people, other animals, and the earth. In the traditional Nez Perce creation story, groups of people derive from specific body parts—each possessing a special talent and relationship with a particular animal. By contrast, the story of creation in Genesis emphasizes human uniqueness and the concept of time. Creation takes place as a series of actions over the course of six days. God's final act of creation is to fashion the first human in his own image before the seventh day of rest.

This linear creation story from Genesis—shared by Jews, Christians, and Muslims—differs from the cyclical creation stories characteristic of Hinduism, which emphasize reincarnation and the cycle of life, including creation and destruction. For Hindus, the diversity of life on earth comes from three gods—Lord Brahma, the creator; Lord Vishnu, the preserver; and Lord Shiva, the destroyer and recreator—all of whom are part of the Supreme One. Lord Brahma destroys the world as he sleeps, then he recreates it again when he awakes. Similarly, intelligent design (ID)—championed by Seattle Washington's Discovery Institute to avoid the creation–evolution controversy and circumvent U.S. Supreme Court rulings—considers creation to be the result of an intelligent cause.

IN THIS CHAPTER YOU WILL LEARN TO

- Compare evolution to creation stories.

- Identify the place of humans in the classification of all living things.

- Explain the molecular basis of evolution and the four evolutionary processes: mutation, gene flow, genetic drift, and adaptation.

- Describe how evolutionary processes account for the diversity of life on earth.

- Contrast how evolutionary processes work at the individual and population level.

- Explain how humans have adapted to their environments.

- Identify how new species come into being.

Like creation stories, evolution, the major organizing principle of the biological sciences, accounts for the diversity of life on earth. Theories of evolution provide mechanisms for change and explanations for how the variety of organisms, both in the past and today, came into being. However, evolution differs from creation stories in that it explains the diversity of life in a consistent scientific language, using testable ideas (hypotheses). Contemporary scientists make comparisons among living organisms to test hypotheses drawn from evolutionary theory. Through their research, scientists have deciphered the molecular basis of evolution and the mechanisms through which evolutionary forces work on populations of organisms. At the same time, scientific thought does not come out of a vacuum. As you will see, historical and cultural processes contribute to scientific thought.

The Classification of Living Things

As European explorers exploited foreign lands, their approach to the natural world changed. The discovery of new life forms challenged the previously held notion of fixed, unchanging life on earth. As well, the invention of instruments, such as the microscope to study the previously invisible interior of cells, led to a new appreciation of life's diversity.

Before this time, Europeans organized living things and inanimate objects alike into a ladder or hierarchy known as the Great Chain of Being—an approach to nature first developed by the philosopher Aristotle in ancient Greece more than 2,000 years ago (**Figure 2.1**). The categories were based upon visible similarities, and one member of each category was considered its "primate" (from the Latin *primus*), meaning "the first" or "best" of the group. For example, the primate of rocks was the diamond, the primate of birds was the eagle, and so forth. Humans stood at the very top of the ladder, just below the angels.

This classificatory system was in place until Carolus Linnaeus (also known as Carl von Linné) developed the *Systema Naturae*, or system of nature, in the 18th century to classify the diversity of living things collected and brought

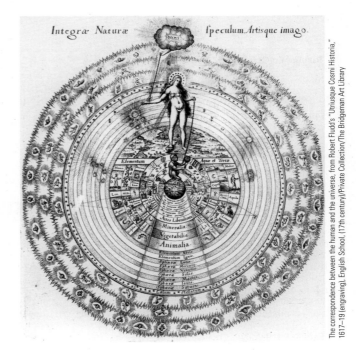

Figure 2.1 **The Great Chain of Being** This 17th-century drawing of the Great Chain of Being by Robert Flood shows that this system of classification was as much a spiritual system as a framework for organizing the natural world. Unlike Linnaeus's later classification scheme, the *Systema Naturae*, the Great Chain included minerals and astral bodies, which, though they can be studied scientifically, are not alive.

to Europe by ship from throughout the globe. Linnaeus's system reflected a new understanding of life on earth and of the place of humanity among the animals.

Linnaeus noted the similarity among humans, monkeys, and apes, classifying them together as **primates**. Not the first or the best of the animals on earth, primates are just one of several kinds of **mammal**, animals having body hair or fur who suckle or nurse their young. In other words, Linnaeus classified living things into a series of categories that are progressively more inclusive on the basis of internal and external visual similarities. **Species**, the smallest working units in biological classificatory systems, are reproductively isolated populations or groups of populations capable of interbreeding to produce fertile offspring. Species are subdivisions of larger, more inclusive groups, called **genera** (singular, **genus**). Humans, for example, are classified in the genus *Homo* and the species *sapiens*.

Linnaeus based his classificatory system on the following criteria:

1. *Body structure:* A Guernsey cow and a Holstein cow are the same species because they have identical body structure. A cow and a horse do not.
2. *Body function:* Cows and horses give birth to live young. Although they are different species, they are closer than either cows or horses are to chickens, which lay eggs and have no mammary glands.

---

primates The group of mammals that includes lemurs, lorises, tarsiers, monkeys, apes, and humans.

mammals The class of vertebrate animals distinguished by bodies covered with hair or fur, self-regulating temperature, and in females, milk-producing mammary glands.

species The smallest working units in biological classificatory systems; reproductively isolated populations or groups of populations capable of interbreeding to produce fertile offspring.

genus (genera) In the system of plant and animal classification, a group of like species.

TABLE 2.1

The Classification of Humans

Taxonomic Category	Category to Which Humans Belong	Biological Features Used to Define and Place Humans in This Category
Kingdom	Animalia	Humans are animals. We do not make our own food (as plants do) but depend upon intake of living food.
Phylum	Chordata	Humans are chordates. We have a **notochord** (a rodlike structure of cartilage) and nerve chord running along the back of the body as well as gill slits in the embryonic stage of our life cycle.
Subphylum*	Vertebrata	Humans are vertebrates, possessing an internal backbone with a segmented spinal column.
Class	Mammalia	Humans are mammals: warm-blooded animals covered with fur and possessing mammary glands for nourishing their young after birth.
Order	Primates	Humans are primates: a kind of mammal with a generalized anatomy, a relatively large brain, and grasping hands and feet.
Suborder	Anthropoidea	Humans are anthropoids: social, daylight-active primates.
Superfamily	Hominoid	Humans are hominoids with broad, flexible shoulders and no tail. Chimps, bonobos, gorillas, orangutans, gibbons, and siamangs are also hominoids.
Family Subfamily	Hominid Hominin	Humans are hominids. We are hominoids from Africa, genetically more closely related to chimps, bonobos, and gorillas than to hominoids from Asia. Some scientists use "hominid" to refer only to humans and their ancestors. Others include chimps and gorillas in this category, using the subfamily "hominin" to distinguish humans and their ancestors from chimps and gorillas and their ancestors. The two taxonomies differ according to emphasis on genetic versus morphological similarities. Those who use "hominin" do so to emphasize the genetic relationship among humans, chimps, and gorillas. Those who refer to humans and their ancestor as "hominids" give preference to the similarities in body shape among chimpanzees, gorillas, and orangutans.
Genus Species	*Homo sapiens*	Humans have large brains and rely on cultural adaptations to survive. Ancestral fossils are placed in this genus and species depending upon details of the skull shape and interpretations of their cultural capabilities. Genus and species names are always italicized.

© Cengage Learning

*Most categories can be expanded or narrowed by adding the prefix "sub" or "super." A family could thus be part of a superfamily and in turn contain two or more subfamilies.

3. *Sequence of bodily growth:* At the time of birth—or hatching out of the egg—young cows and chickens possess body plans basically like that of their parents. They are therefore more closely related to each other than either one is to the frog, whose tadpoles undergo a series of changes before attaining the basic adult form.

Modern **taxonomy**, or the science of classification (from the Greek for "naming divisions"), while retaining the structure of the Linnaean system, takes more than body structure, function, and growth into account. Today's scientists also compare protein structure and genetic material to construct the relationships among living things. Such molecular comparisons can even be aimed at parasites, bacteria, and viruses, allowing scientists to classify or trace the origins of particular diseases, such as swine flu or HIV (human immunodeficiency virus). An emphasis on genetics rather than morphology has led to a reworking of

taxonomic designation in the human family, among other families, as is described in **Table 2.1**. Alternative taxonomies based on genetics compared to body form in the primate order will be discussed in detail in the next chapter.

Cross-species comparisons identify anatomical features of similar function as **analogies**, while anatomical features that have evolved from a common ancestral feature are called **homologies**. For example, the arm and

---

notochord A rodlike structure of cartilage that, in vertebrates, is replaced by the vertebral column.

taxonomy The science of classification.

analogies In biology, structures possessed by different organisms that are superficially similar due to similar function but that do not share a common developmental pathway or structure.

homologies In biology, structures possessed by two different organisms that arise in similar fashion and pass through similar stages during embryonic development, although they may have different functions.

VISUAL COUNTERPOINT

Mark Carwardine/Getty Images/Peter Arnold

© Ellen B. Senisi/The Image Works

Figure 2.2   An Example of Homology The bat wing is homologous to the human hand. Look closely at the bones supporting the wing, and you can see that they are the same bones found in the human arm and hand. Homologous structures have the same embryonic origins but ultimately take on different functions. For humans, our grasping hands function in a variety of ways, including even language. Here two deaf children communicate through American Sign Language on their school playground.

hand of a human and the wing of a bat evolved from the front leg of a common ancestor, although they have acquired different functions: The human hand and bat wing are homologous structures (**Figure 2.2**). During their early embryonic development, homologous structures arise in a similar fashion and pass through similar stages before differentiating. The wings of birds and butterflies (**Figure 2.3**) look similar and have a similar function (flying): These are analogous, but not homologous, structures because they do not follow the same developmental sequence. When constructing evolutionary relationships, only homologies matter.

Through careful comparison and analysis of organisms, Linnaeus and his successors have grouped species into genera and into even larger groups such as families, orders, classes, phyla, and kingdoms. Characteristics shared by all the organisms in the group define each taxonomic level.

The Discovery of Evolution

Just as European seafaring and exploitation brought about an awareness of the diversity of life across the globe, industrialization in Europe brought about an awareness of change in life forms through time. As workers cut away the earth to lay railway tracks and excavated limestone for

Darrell Gulin/Getty Images/Photodisc

Figure 2.3   Analogous Wings Butterflies, like bats and birds, use their wings to fly. But any resemblance of the insect wing to the analogous structures in a bird or mammal derives solely from their similar function. The course of insect wing development, as well as its structure, differs from that of a bat or bird.

buildings, fossils—preserved remains of past life forms—were brought into the light.

At first, the fossilized remains of elephants and giant saber-toothed tigers in Europe were interpreted according to religious doctrine. For example, the early 19th-century theory of *catastrophism,* championed by French paleontologist and anatomist George Cuvier, invoked natural events like the Great Flood described in Genesis to account for the disappearance of these species on European lands.

Another French scientist, Jean-Baptiste Lamarck, was among the first to suggest a mechanism to account for diversity among living creatures that did not rely upon scriptures. His theory of the *inheritance of acquired characteristics* proposed that behavior brought about changes in organisms' forms. The famed example was that the first giraffe gained its long neck by stretching to reach the leaves on the highest treetop branches and in turn passed this acquired long neck onto its offspring. While Lamarck's theory has long since been disproved as a mechanism to account for biological change, he was the first to make the connection between organisms and the environments they inhabit. As well, the mechanism he proposed for change over time works for qualities inherited via culture.

At about the same time, British geologist Sir Charles Lyell proposed a nonreligious theory to account for variations in the earth's surface. His theory, *uniformitarianism,* maintained that just as changes in the earth's surface that are immediately observable are caused by erosion and other

natural processes, other changes are caused by gradual processes over extremely long periods of time. Lyell's theory was incompatible with religious accounts of creation because the length of time required for uniformitarianism far exceeded the biblical version that the earth is a mere 6,000 years old.

With industrialization, Europeans became more comfortable with the ideas of change and progress. In hindsight, it seems inevitable that someone would hit upon the idea of evolution. By the start of the 19th century, many naturalists had come to accept the idea that life had evolved, even though they were not clear about how it happened. It remained for Charles Darwin (1809–1882) to formulate a theory that has withstood the test of time.

Charles Darwin began the study of medicine at the University of Edinburgh in Scotland. Finding himself unfit for this profession, he went to Christ's College, Cambridge, to study theology. He then left Cambridge to take the position of companion to Captain Robert FitzRoy aboard the HMS *Beagle*, embarking on an expedition to various poorly mapped parts of the world. The voyage lasted almost five years, taking Darwin along the coasts of South America, to the Galapagos Islands, across the Pacific to Australia, and then across the Indian and Atlantic oceans to South America before returning to England in 1836 (**Figure 2.4**).

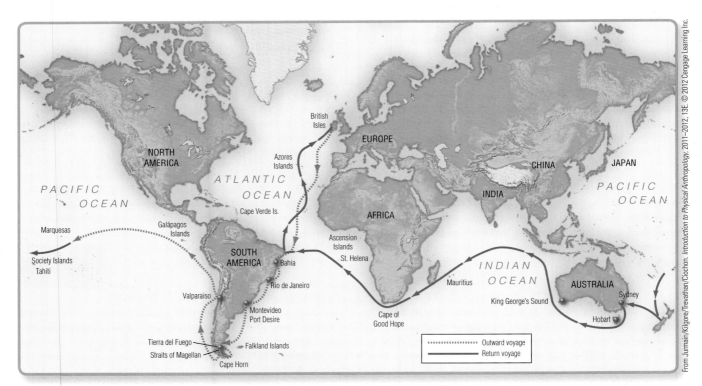

Figure 2.4 The Voyage of the HMS *Beagle* During his journey of almost five years, Darwin worked studiously on a manuscript about barnacles. At the same time, Darwin's exposure to the diversity of plant and animal life, as well as to the varied environments across the globe, planted the seeds of his evolutionary theory.

Observing the tremendous diversity of living creatures as well as the astounding fossils of extinct animals, Darwin began to note that species varied according to the environments they inhabited. The observations he made on this voyage, his readings of Lyell's *Principles of Geology* (1830), and the arguments he had with the orthodox and dogmatic FitzRoy all contributed to the ideas culminating in Darwin's most famous book, *On the Origin of Species*. This book, published in 1859, twenty years after he returned from his voyage, describes a theory of evolution accounting for change within species and for the emergence of new species in purely naturalistic terms.

Darwin added observations from English farm life and intellectual thought to the ideas he began to develop on the *Beagle*. He paid particular attention to domesticated animals and farmers' "artificial selection," a practice of breeding their stock to select for specific traits. Darwin's theoretical breakthrough derived from an essay by economist Thomas Malthus (1766–1834), which warned of the potential consequences of increased human population, particularly of the poor. Malthus observed that animal populations, unlike human populations, remained stable, due to an overproduction of young followed by a large proportion of animal offspring not surviving to maturity. Darwin wrote in his autobiography,

> It at once struck me that under these circumstances favourable variations would tend to be preserved, and unfavourable ones to be destroyed. The results of this would be the formation of a new species. Here, then I had at last got a theory by which to work. (Darwin, 1887)

Darwin combined his observations into the theory of **natural selection** as follows: All species display a range of variation, and all have the ability to expand beyond their means of subsistence. It follows that, in their "struggle for existence," organisms with variations that help them to survive in a particular environment will reproduce with greater success than those without such variations. Thus, as generation succeeds generation, nature selects the most advantageous variations and species evolve. In retrospect, the idea seemed so obvious that Thomas Henry Huxley, one of the era's most prominent scientists, remarked, "How extremely stupid of me not to have thought of that" (quoted in Durant, 2000, p. 11).

As often happens in the history of science, Darwin was not alone in authoring the theory of natural selection. A Welshman, Alfred Russel Wallace, independently came up with the same idea at the same time while on a voyage to the Malay archipelago in Southeast Asia to collect specimens for European zoos and museums.

According to his autobiography, a theory came to Wallace while he was in a feverish delirium from malaria. He shared excitedly his idea with other scientists in England, including Darwin, whose own theory was yet unpublished. The two scientists jointly presented their findings.

However straightforward the idea of evolution by natural selection may appear, the theory was (and has continued to be) a source of considerable controversy. Darwin avoided the most contentious question of human origins, limiting his commentary in the original work to a single sentence near the end: "much light will be thrown on the origin of man and his history." However, the feisty Thomas Henry Huxley, in his book *On Man's Place in Nature* (1863), took up the subject of human origins explicitly through comparative anatomy of apes and humans and an examination of the fossils.

Two problems plagued Darwin's theory throughout his career: First, how did variation arise in the first place? Second, what was the mechanism of heredity by which variable traits could be passed from one generation to the next?

Heredity

Ironically, some of the information Darwin needed was available by 1866. Gregor Mendel (1822–1884), a Roman Catholic monk, developed the basic laws of heredity while working in the monastery gardens in Brno, a city in today's Czech Republic. Mendel, who was raised on a farm, possessed two particular talents: a flair for mathematics and a passion for gardening. As with all farmers of his time, Mendel had an intuitive understanding of biological inheritance. He went a step farther, though, in that he recognized the need for theoretical explanations. At age 34, he began careful breeding experiments in the monastery garden, starting with pea plants.

Over eight years, Mendel planted more than 30,000 plants, controlling their pollination, observing the results, and figuring out the mathematics behind it all. This allowed him to unravel the basic laws of heredity. Though his findings were published in 1866 in a respected scientific journal, no one recognized the importance of Mendel's work during his lifetime. Interestingly, a copy of this journal was found in Darwin's own library with the pages still uncut (journals were printed on long continuous sheets of

---

natural selection The evolutionary process through which factors in the environment exert pressure, favoring some individuals over others to produce the next generation.

paper and then folded into pages to be cut by the reader), an indication that the journal had never been read.

In 1900, cell biology had advanced to the point where rediscovery of Mendel's laws was inevitable, and in that year three European botanists, working independently of one another, rediscovered not only the laws but also Mendel's original paper. With this rediscovery, the science of genetics began. Still, it would be another fifty-three years before the molecular mechanisms of heredity and the discrete units of inheritance would be discovered. Today, a comprehensive understanding of heredity, molecular genetics, and population genetics supports Darwinian evolutionary theory.

The Transmission of Genes

Today, we define **genes** as portions of the DNA molecule containing a sequence of base pairs that encodes a particular protein. When biologists coined the term from the Greek word for "birth" at the turn of the 20th century, however, the molecular basis of the gene was still fifty years away from discovery. Mendel had deduced the presence and activity of genes by experimenting with garden peas to determine how various traits are passed from one generation to the next. Specifically, he discovered that inheritance was *particulate*, rather than *blending*, as Darwin and many others thought. That is, the units controlling the expression of visible traits come in pairs, one from each parent, and retain their separate identities over the generations rather than blending into a combination of parental traits in offspring. This was the basis of Mendel's first **law of segregation**, which states that pairs of genes separate, keep their individuality, and are passed on to the next generation unaltered. Another finding—Mendel's **law of independent assortment**—states that different traits (under the control of distinct genes) are inherited independently of one another.

Mendel based his laws on statistical frequencies of observed characteristics, such as color and texture in generations of plants. When **chromosomes**, the cellular structures containing the genetic information, were discovered at the start of the 20th century, they provided a visible vehicle for transmission of traits proposed in Mendel's laws.

Then in 1953 James Watson and Francis Crick found that genes are actually portions of molecules of **DNA (deoxyribonucleic acid)**—long strands of which form chromosomes. (Rosalind Franklin, shown in **Figure 2.5**,

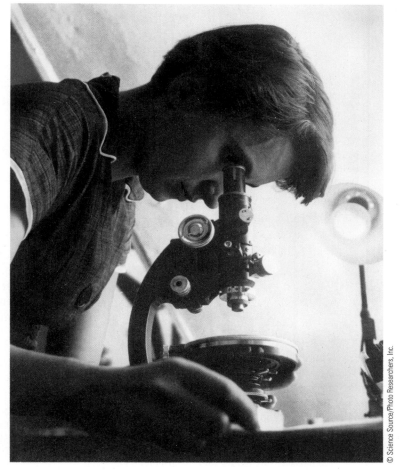

Figure 2.5 Rosalind Franklin and the Structure of DNA British scientist Rosalind Franklin's pioneering work in x-ray crystal photography played a vital role in unlocking the secret of the genetic code in 1953. Without her permission, Franklin's colleague Maurice Wilkins showed one of her images to James Watson. In his book *The Double Helix*, Watson wrote, "The instant I saw the picture my mouth fell open and my pulse began to race." While her research was published simultaneously in the prestigious journal *Nature* in 1953—alongside that of James Watson, Francis Crick, and Maurice Wilkins—her untimely death from cancer meant that only the gentlemen received the Nobel Prize for the double-helix model of DNA in 1962.

genes The portions of DNA molecules that direct the synthesis of specific proteins.

law of segregation The Mendelian principle that variants of genes for a particular trait retain their separate identities through the generations.

law of independent assortment The Mendelian principle that genes controlling different traits are inherited independently of one another.

chromosomes In the cell nucleus, the structures visible during cellular division containing long strands of DNA combined with a protein.

DNA (deoxyribonucleic acid) The genetic material consisting of a complex molecule whose base structure directs the synthesis of proteins.

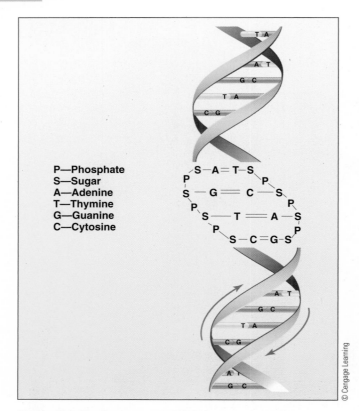

P—Phosphate
S—Sugar
A—Adenine
T—Thymine
G—Guanine
C—Cytosine

© Cengage Learning

Figure 2.6 The Structure of DNA This diagrammatic representation of a portion of DNA (deoxyribonucleic acid) illustrates its twisted ladderlike structure. Alternating sugar and phosphate groups form the structural sides of the ladder. The connecting "rungs" are formed by pairings between complementary bases—adenine with thymine and cytosine with guanine.

was a largely unknown contributor to this amazing breakthrough.) DNA is a complex molecule with an unusual shape, rather like two strands of a rope twisted around each other with ladderlike steps between the two strands (Figure 2.6). Alternating sugar and phosphate molecules form the backbone of these strands connected to each other by four base pairs: adenine, thymine, guanine, and cytosine (usually written as A, T, G, and C). Connections between the strands occur between so-called complementary pairs of bases (A to T, G to C).

chromatid One half of the X shape of chromosomes visible once replication is complete. Sister chromatids are exact copies of each other.

alleles Alternate forms of a single gene.

enzymes Proteins that initiate and direct chemical reactions.

karyotype The array of chromosomes found inside a single cell.

genome The complete structure sequence of DNA for a species.

codon Three-base sequence of a gene that specifies a particular amino acid for inclusion in a protein.

Sequences of three complementary bases specify the sequence of amino acids in protein synthesis. This arrangement also confers upon genes the unique property of replication—being able to make exact copies of themselves. The term **chromatid** refers to one half of the X shape of chromosomes visible once replication is complete. Sister chromatids are exact copies of each other.

Genes and Alleles

A sequence of chemical bases on a molecule of DNA (a gene) constitutes a recipe for making proteins. As science writer Matt Ridley puts it, "Proteins . . . do almost every chemical, structural, and regulatory thing that is done in the body: they generate energy, fight infection, digest food, form hair, carry oxygen, and so on and on" (Ridley, 1999, p. 40). Almost everything in the body is made of or by proteins.

There are alternate forms of genes, known as **alleles**. For example, the gene for a human blood type in the A-B-O system refers to a specific portion of a DNA molecule on chromosome 9 that in this case is 1,062 letters long (a medium-sized gene). This gene specifies the production of an **enzyme**, a kind of protein that initiates and directs a chemical reaction. This particular enzyme causes molecules involved in immune responses to attach to the surface of red blood cells. Alleles correspond to the specific blood type (the A allele and B allele). Genes, then, are not really separate structures, as had once been imagined, but locations, like dots on a map. (Figure 2.7 displays a **karyotype**, the array of chromosomes found inside a single cell.) These genes provide the recipe for the many proteins that keep us alive and healthy.

The human **genome**—the complete sequence of human DNA—contains 3 billion chemical bases, with 20,000 to 25,000 genes, a number similar to that found in most mammals. Of the 3 billion bases, humans and mice are about 90 percent identical. Both species have three times as many genes as does the fruit fly, but surprisingly humans and mice have half the number of genes found in the rice plant! In other words, the number of genes or base pairs does not explain every difference among organisms. At the same time, those 20,000 to 25,000 human genes account for only 1 to 1.5 percent of the entire genome, indicating that scientists still have far more to learn about how genes work. Frequently, genes themselves are split by long stretches of DNA that are not part of the known protein code; for example, the 1,062 bases of the A-B-O blood-group gene are interrupted by five such stretches. In the course of protein production, these stretches of DNA are metaphorically snipped out and left on the cutting room floor.

How is the DNA recipe converted into a protein? Through a series of intervening steps, each three-base sequence of a gene, called a **codon**, specifies production of a particular

Karyotype with a Few Genetic Loci

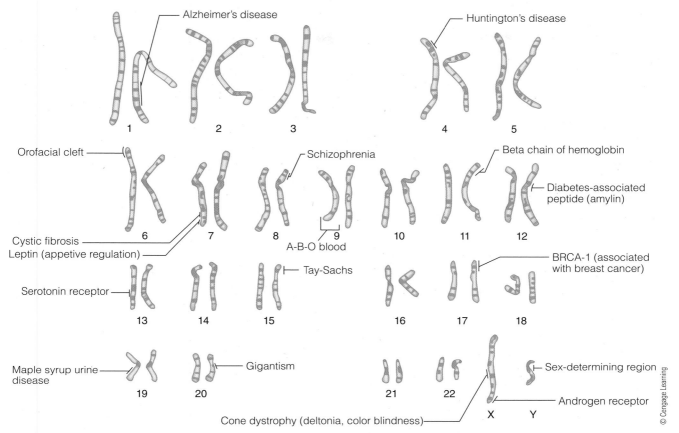

Figure 2.7 A Human Karyotype An array of chromosomes from inside the nucleus of one cell of one individual is called a karyotype. The twenty-three pairs of chromosomes humans possess include twenty-two pairs of somatic or body chromosomes, plus one pair of sex chromosomes, for a total of forty-six chromosomes. Here you can see the characteristic shape and relative size of each of the chromosomes. The locations of certain genes associated with various diseases and conditions identified by the Human Genome Project are labeled. Although we would need to sequence the DNA to see what alleles this individual had for various genes, a glance at the overall karyotype indicates a normal number of chromosomes and that this individual is genetically male. The female phenotype is determined by the presence of two X chromosomes. Offspring inherit an X chromosome from their mothers but either an X or a Y from their fathers, resulting in approximately equal numbers of male and female offspring in subsequent generations. Although the Y chromosome is critical for differentiation into a male phenotype, compared to other chromosomes the Y is tiny and carries little genetic information.

amino acid, strings of which build proteins. Because DNA cannot leave the cell's nucleus (**Figure 2.8**), the directions for a specific protein are first converted into **RNA (ribonucleic acid)** in a process called **transcription**. RNA differs from DNA in the structure of its sugar phosphate backbone and in the presence of the base uracil rather than thymine. Next, the RNA (called *messenger RNA* or *mRNA*) travels to the **ribosomes**, the cellular structure (**Figure 2.9**) where **translation** of the directions found in the codons occurs, producing proteins. Anticodons of *transfer RNA (tRNA)* transport the individual amino acids to the corresponding mRNA codons, and the amino acids are joined together by peptide bonds to form polypeptide chains. For example, the sequence of AUG specifies the amino acid methionine, CCC proline, GAU aspartic acid, and so on.

RNA (ribonucleic acid) Similar to DNA but with uracil substituted for the base thymine. Transcribes and carries instructions from DNA from the nucleus to the ribosomes, where it directs protein synthesis. Some simple life forms contain RNA only.

transcription The process of conversion of instructions from DNA into RNA.

ribosomes Structures in the cell where translation occurs.

translation The process of conversion of RNA instructions into proteins.

Figure 2.8 A Eukaryotic Cell The figure shows the three-dimensional structure of a generalized eukaryotic, or nucleated, cell. DNA is located in the nucleus. Because DNA cannot leave the nucleus, genes must first be transcribed into RNA, which carries genetic information to the ribosomes, where protein synthesis occurs. Note also the mitochondria, which contain their own circular chromosomes and mitochondrial DNA.

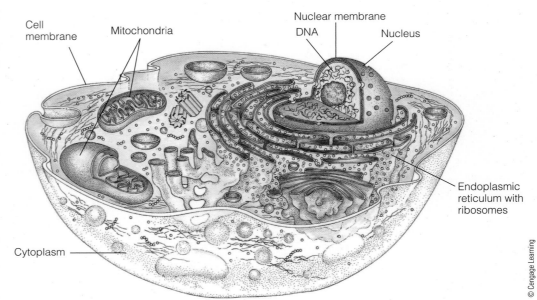

© Cengage Learning

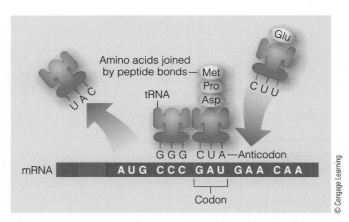

© Cengage Learning

Figure 2.9 Transcription and Translation of DNA into Proteins Codons of DNA (a sequence of three bases) are transcribed into the complementary codons of a kind of RNA called messenger RNA (mRNA) in order to leave the nucleus. In the ribosomes, these codons are translated into proteins by transfer RNA (tRNA), which strings the amino acids together into particular chains. Can you think of the bases that would have been found in the DNA that correspond to the section of mRNA pictured here?

There are twenty amino acids, which are strung together in different amounts and sequences to produce an almost infinite number of different proteins. This is the so-called **genetic code**, and it is the same for every living thing, whether a worm or a human being. In addition to the genetic information stored in the chromosomes of the nucleus, complex organisms also possess cellular structures

called *mitochondria,* each of which has a single circular chromosome. The genetic material known as *mitochondrial DNA* or *mtDNA* has figured prominently in human evolutionary studies. On the other end of the spectrum, simple living things without nucleated cells, such as the retrovirus that causes AIDS, contain their genetic information only as RNA.

Much of this seemingly useless, noncoding DNA (often called *junk DNA*) has been inserted by retroviruses. *Retroviruses* are some of the most diverse and widespread infectious entities of vertebrates—responsible for AIDS, hepatitis, anemias, and some neurological disorders (Amábile-Cuevas & Chicurel, 1993). Other junk DNA consists of decaying hulks of once useful but now functionless genes: damaged genes that have been "turned off." As cells divide and reproduce, junk DNA, like known genes, also replicates. Mistakes can occur in the replication process, adding or subtracting repeats of the four bases: A, C, G, and T. This happens with some frequency and differently in every individual. As these "mistakes" accumulate over time, each person develops his or her unique DNA fingerprint.

Cell Division

In order to grow and maintain good health, the body cells of an organism must divide and produce new cells. Cell division begins when the chromosomes replicate, forming a second pair that duplicates the original pair of chromosomes in the nucleus. To do this, the DNA "unzips" between the base pairs—adenine from thymine and guanine from cytosine—and then each base on each now-single strand attracts its complementary base, reconstituting the second half of the double helix. After they separate, a new cell membrane surrounds each new chromosome pair and becomes the

genetic code The sequence of three bases (a codon) that specifies the sequence of amino acids in protein synthesis.

Among wealthier parents-to-be, prenatal genetic testing has become increasingly common. As mentioned in this chapter's opening Challenge Issue, such testing aims to eliminate conditions not favored within a society. Generally, during the first two trimesters, women in the United States have a constitutionally protected right to decide whether to terminate or continue a pregnancy for any reason at all, including the diagnosis of a genetic anomaly. Following this window of time, federal law protects the rights of disabled individuals with these same anomalies. In other societies, the undesirable trait discovered through prenatal genetic testing can be as basic as the biological sex of the child (**Figure 2.10**). In India, where female children are undervalued, prenatal genetic testing has led to selective abortion of female fetuses (Arnold, Kishor, & Roy, 2002).

No aspect of human reproduction or genetics is simply biological. Social and political processes impact the interpretation and use of genetic technology. The technology, in turn, shapes social definitions of family, identity, and the types of citizens preferred by a given society. See this chapter's Biocultural Connection to read how DNA testing has made its way into the lives of African refugees seeking reunification with their families in the United States.

Sexual reproduction increases genetic diversity, which in turn has contributed to a multitude of adaptations among sexually reproducing species such as humans. Sexual reproduction involves the merging of two cells, one from each parent, to make a new individual. If two regular body cells, each containing twenty-three pairs of chromosomes, were to merge, the lethal result would be a new individual with forty-six pairs of chromosomes. Instead, sexual reproduction involves joining specialized sex cells (eggs and sperm) produced by a different kind of cell division, called **meiosis**.

Although meiosis begins like mitosis, with the replication and doubling of the original genes in chromosomes through the formation of sister chromatids, it proceeds to divide that number into four new cells rather than two

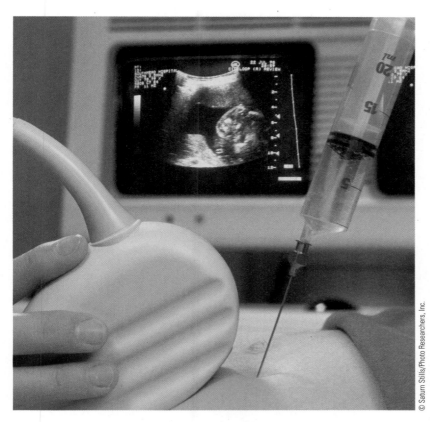

© Saturn Stills/Photo Researchers, Inc.

Figure 2.10 Prenatal Genetic Testing by Amniocentesis Prenatal genetic testing is conducted most frequently by amniocentesis, a technique that began in the 1960s through which a medical practitioner draws fluid, containing cells from the developing embryo, from the womb of a pregnant woman. Lab technicians then analyze the chromosomes and specific genes for abnormalities. Cultural anthropologists have shown that a biological fact (such as an extra 21st chromosome or Down syndrome) is open to diverse interpretations and reproductive choices by "potential parents" (Rapp, 1999). New reproductive technologies have far-reaching social consequences. Genetic testing may lead to the labeling of certain people as undesirable, pitting women's reproductive rights against the rights of the disabled.

nucleus that directs the activities of a new cell. This kind of cell division is called **mitosis**. Barring errors in this replication process, cells divide mitotically to form daughter cells that are exact genetic copies of the parent cell.

Like most animals, humans reproduce sexually. The "popularity" of sex from an evolutionary perspective derives from the genetic variation that it provides. All animals contain two copies of each chromosome, having inherited one from each parent. In humans this involves twenty-three pairs of chromosomes. Sexual reproduction can bring favorable alleles together, purge the genome of harmful ones, and allow beneficial alleles to spread without being held back by the baggage of disadvantageous variants of other genes.

While human societies have always regulated sexual reproduction in some ways, the science of genetics has had a tremendous impact on social aspects of reproduction.

mitosis A kind of cell division that produces new cells having exactly the same number of chromosome pairs, and hence copies of genes, as the parent cell.

meiosis A kind of cell division that produces the sex cells, each of which has half the number of chromosomes found in other cells of the organism.

BIOCULTURAL CONNECTION

Bonds Beyond Blood: DNA Testing and Refugee Family Unification

By Jason Silverstein

In February of 2008, the U.S. government began to assess the use of DNA testing as documentary proof of familial relationship among asylum seekers from Africa attempting reunification with family members already in the United States. The pilot study began with 500 residents of the Dadaab refugee camp in Nairobi, Kenya, where an estimated 465,000 refugees currently live in a space designed for 90,000. DNA testing was later expanded to include 3,000 refugees in Ethiopia, Uganda, Ghana, Guinea, and Côte d'Ivoire.

The pilot program operated on the assumption of "guilty until proven family." Anything other than DNA proof of relationship was recorded as fraud. Refusal to test was recorded as fraud. On a petition with multiple family members, if one person refused, did not

Reuters/Jonathan Ernst/Landov

Covering 50 square kilometers in northeastern Kenya, the Dadaab Refugee Camp is the largest such camp in the world. Originally designed in 1991 for 90,00, today over 400,000 people crowd into the camp. Each day, over 1,300 new refugees arrive seeking sanctuary from political persecution and starvation brought about by civil war and drought. Here Somali refugees pray during Eid al-Fitr, marking the end of the Muslim holy month of Ramadan.

(Figure 2.11). Thus, each new cell has only half the number of chromosomes compared to the parent cell. Human eggs and sperm have only twenty-three single chromosomes (half of a pair), whereas body cells have twenty-three pairs, or forty-six chromosomes.

The process of meiotic division has important implications for genetics. Because paired chromosomes are separated,

the daughter cells will not be identical. Two of the four new cells will have half of each pair of chromosomes, and the other two will have the second half of the original chromosome pair. In addition, corresponding portions of one chromosome may "cross over" to the other one, somewhat scrambling the genetic material compared to the original chromosomes.

Sometimes, the original pair is **homozygous**, possessing identical alleles for a specific gene. For example, if in both chromosomes of the original pair the gene for A-B-O blood type is represented by the allele for type A blood,

homozygous Refers to a chromosome pair that bears identical alleles for a single gene.

show up for, or failed the test, then the entire petition was recorded as fraud. Shockingly, the "anchor" (the person with whom the applicants desired to reunite) was never tested. Only the relationships between individuals on the application were tested. By the time the pilot phase ended, these policies resulted in the classification of 80 percent of family reunification claims as fraudulent, and the U.S. government suspended the reunification program. As DNA testing increasingly becomes the standard by which border security officials investigate kinship claims, what makes a family legitimate will be determined by the social prescriptions of the receiving community.

The definition of *family* is not necessarily portable across borders. Refugees are forced to conform their qualifications of family and, thus, their very life stories to the social norms of the receiving community. We should not confuse the neutrality of DNA as a hereditary material with the neutrality of those who collect, process, and interpret it. Far from value-neutral technology, DNA testing for family reunification reveals an allegiance to a particular social universe and often conceals the reality of the refugees' lived experience.

One especially lucid example of this claim is provided by a refugee case manager who remarked that polygamous families (those with more than one spouse) are never resettled (in other words, would never pass the family-relatedness test). Given the testing protocol of the pilot project (testing the genetic relationship between applicants and not between the applicant and the anchor), one readily can imagine that a mother as a primary applicant may not share DNA with her child. In such a case the entire application, and their relationship, would be officially recorded as fraudulent.

Family is not simply genetic or socially prescribed; it is also existentially evolved, especially for refugees, who have spent years if not decades in camps. An interviewer with the United Nations High Commissioner on Refugees related stories about parents who did not want to distinguish between their biological and adopted, often war-orphaned, children. Given that the verification interview takes place in front of the children, avoiding this distinction may have little to do with what security officials cruelly call fraud or abuse. As one case manager starkly put it, the DNA testing methodology overlooks that those who survive often do not survive unscathed.

For security officials, the DNA test is an attractive method of quantifying and eliminating fraud and abuse (and obeying the proposed refugee quota for the fiscal year). For caseworkers and interviewers, the DNA test alleviates officials' feelings of overwhelming responsibility and guilt stemming from their inability to resettle each of the worthy. But for the refugees themselves, the effect is a further widening of the divide between the world in which they are forced to live and a world of their own making. Indeed, if the refugee signifies that he or she is a person threatened by persecution, as defined by the 1951 United Nations Convention Relating to the Status of Refugees, then we must ask ourselves if our resettlement efforts return power to refugees or subject them to new narratives of domination and disregard.

BIOCULTURAL QUESTION

When DNA testing is used by the state for identification purposes, what rifts open between the truth of one's life and what can be extracted from one's blood? What should we be searching for when we want to know who a person truly is?

Adapted from Silverstein, J. (2012). Bonds beyond blood: DNA testing and refugee family resettlement. Anthropology News *53 (4), 11. Reprinted by permission of the American Anthropological Association.*

then all new cells will have the A allele. But if the original pair is **heterozygous**, with the A allele on one chromosome and the allele for type B blood on the other, then half of the new cells will contain only the B allele; the offspring have a 50–50 chance of getting either one. It is impossible to predict any single individual's **genotype**, or genetic composition, but, as Mendel originally discovered, statistical probabilities can be established.

What happens when a child inherits the allele for type O blood from one parent and that for type A from the other? Will the child have blood of type A, O, or some mixture of the two? **Figure 2.12** illustrates some of the possible outcomes. Many of these questions were answered by Mendel's original experiments.

Mendel discovered that certain alleles are able to mask the presence of others; one allele is **dominant**, whereas the

heterozygous Refers to a chromosome pair that bears different alleles for a single gene.
genotype The alleles possessed for a particular trait.
dominant In genetics, a term to describe the ability of an allele for a trait to mask the presence of another allele.

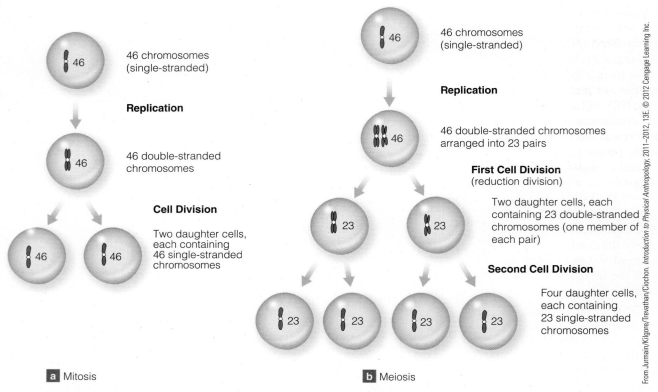

Figure 2.11 Cell Division: Mitosis and Meiosis in Humans Each chromosome consists of two sister chromatids, which are exact copies of each other. During mitosis, these sister chromatids separate into two identical daughter cells. In meiosis, the cell division responsible for the formation of gametes, the first division halves the chromosome number. The second meiotic division is essentially like mitosis and involves the separation of sister chromatids. Chromosomes in red came from one parent; those in blue came from the other. Meiosis results in four daughter cells that are not identical.

From Jurmain/Kilgore/Trevathan/Ciochon. *Introduction to Physical Anthropology*, 2011–2012, 13E. © 2012 Cengage Learning Inc.

Figure 2.12 Punnett Squares, Phenotype, and Genotype These four Punnett squares (named for British geneticist Reginald Punnett) illustrate some of the possible phenotypes and genotypes of offspring within the A-B-O system. Each individual possesses two alleles within this system, and together these two alleles constitute the individual's genotype. Phenotype refers to an individual's observed physical characteristics or traits. The alleles of one parent are listed on the left-hand side of the square, while the other parent's alleles are listed across the top. The potential genotypes of offspring are listed in the colored squares by letter. Offspring phenotypes are indicated by color: blue indicates the type A phenotype; orange indicates the B phenotype. Individuals with one A and one B allele have the AB phenotype and make both blood antigens. Individuals with the O phenotype (red) have two O alleles.

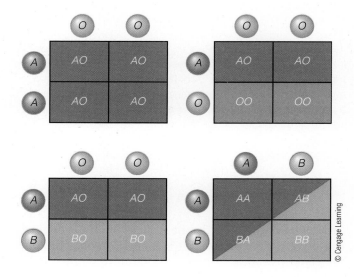

© Cengage Learning

---

recessive In genetics, a term to describe an allele for a trait whose expression is masked by the presence of a dominant allele.

phenotype The observable characteristic of an organism that may or may not reflect a particular genotype due to the variable expression of dominant and recessive alleles.

hemoglobin The protein that carries oxygen in red blood cells.

polygenetic inheritance Two or more genes contributing to the phenotypic expression of a single characteristic.

other is **recessive.** Actually, it is the traits that are dominant or recessive rather than the alleles themselves; geneticists merely refer to dominant and recessive alleles for the sake of convenience. Thus, one might speak of the allele for type A blood as being dominant to the one for type O. An individual whose blood type genes are heterozygous, with one A and one O allele, will have type A blood. In other words, the heterozygous condition (AO) will show exactly the same observed physical characteristic, or **phenotype**, as the homozygous (AA), even though the two have a somewhat different genetic composition, or genotype. Only the homozygous recessive genotype (OO) will show the phenotype of type O blood.

The dominance of one allele does not mean that the recessive one is lost or in some way blended. A type A heterozygous parent (AO) will produce sex cells containing both A and O alleles. (This is an example of Mendel's law of segregation, that alleles retain their separate identities.) Recessive alleles can be handed down for generations before they are matched with another recessive allele in the process of sexual reproduction and show up in the phenotype. The presence of the dominant allele simply masks the expression of the recessive allele.

All of the traits Mendel studied in garden peas showed this dominant–recessive relationship, and so for some years it was believed that this was the only relationship possible. Later studies, however, have indicated that patterns of inheritance are not always so simple. In some cases neither allele is dominant; they are both *co-dominant*. An example of co-dominance in human heredity can be seen also in the inheritance of blood types. Type A is produced by one allele; type B by another. A heterozygous individual will have a phenotype of AB because neither allele can dominate the other.

The inheritance of blood types points out another complexity of heredity. Although we each have at most two alleles for any given gene, the number of possible alleles for that gene found in a population is by no means limited to two. Certain traits have three or more allelic forms. For example, over 100 alleles exist for **hemoglobin**, the blood protein that carries oxygen. Only one allele can appear on each of the two homologous chromosomes, so each individual is limited to two genetic alleles.

Polygenetic Inheritance

So far, we have described the traits of organisms as if they are determined by just one gene. However, multiple genes control most physical traits, such as body build, skin color, or susceptibility to disease. In such cases, we speak of **polygenetic inheritance**, in which the respective alleles of two or more genes influence phenotype. For example, several individuals may have the exact same height, but because there is no single height gene that determines an individual's size, it is impossible to neatly unravel the genetic underpinnings of 5 foot 3 inches or 160 centimeters. Characteristics subject to polygenetic inheritance exhibit a continuous range of variation in their phenotypic expression that does not correspond to simple Mendelian rules. As biological anthropologist Jonathan Marks demonstrates in the following Original Study, the relationship between genetics and continuous traits remains a mystery.

ORIGINAL STUDY

Ninety-Eight Percent Alike: What Our Similarity to Apes Tells Us about Our Understanding of Genetics *BY JONATHAN MARKS*

It's not too hard to tell Jane Goodall from a chimpanzee. Goodall is the one with long legs and short arms, a prominent forehead, and whites in her eyes. She's the one with a significant amount of hair only on her head, not all over her body. She's the one who walks, talks, and wears clothing.

A few decades ago, however, the nascent field of molecular genetics recognized an apparent paradox: However easy it may be to tell Jane Goodall from a chimpanzee on the basis of physical characteristics, it is considerably harder to tell them apart according to their genes.

More recently, geneticists have been able to determine with

A true four-fielder, biological anthropologist Jonathan Marks is at the grave of Emile Durkheim, the French sociologist who profoundly influenced the founding of cultural anthropology.

By Jonathan Marks (2000) "98% Alike: What Our Similarity to Apes Tells Us about Our Understanding Genetics." The Chronicle of Higher Education May 12. 1987

precision that humans and chimpanzees are over 98 percent identical genetically, and that figure has become one of the most well-known factoids in the popular scientific literature. It has been invoked to argue that we are simply a third kind of chimpanzee, together with the common chimp and the rarer bonobo; to claim human rights for nonhuman apes; and to explain the roots of male aggression.

Using the figure in those ways, however, ignores the context necessary to make sense of it. Actually, our amazing genetic similarity to chimpanzees is a scientific fact constructed from two rather more mundane facts: our familiarity with the apes and our unfamiliarity with genetic comparisons.

To begin with, it is unfair to juxtapose the differences between the bodies of people and apes with the similarities in their genes. After all, we have been comparing the bodies of humans and chimpanzees for 300 years, and we have been comparing DNA sequences for less than 20 years.

Now that we are familiar with chimpanzees, we quickly see how different they look from us. But when the chimpanzee was a novelty, in the 18th century, scholars were struck by the overwhelming similarity of human and ape bodies. And why not? Bone for bone, muscle for muscle, organ for organ, the bodies of humans and apes differ only in subtle ways. And yet, it is impossible to say just how physically similar they are. Forty percent? Sixty percent? Ninety-eight percent? Three-dimensional beings that develop over their lifetimes don't lend themselves to a simple scale of similarity.

Genetics brings something different to the comparison. A DNA sequence is a one-dimensional entity, a long series of A, G, C, and T subunits. Align two sequences from different species and you can simply tabulate their similarities; if they match 98 out of 100 times, then the species are 98 percent genetically identical.

But is that more or less than their bodies match? We have no easy way to tell, for making sense of the question "How similar are a human and a chimp?" requires a frame of reference. In other words, we should be asking: "How similar are a human and a chimp, compared to what?" Let's try and answer the question. How similar are a human and a chimp, compared to, say, a sea urchin? The human and chimpanzee have limbs, skeletons, bilateral symmetry, a central nervous system; each bone, muscle, and organ matches. For all intents and purposes, the human and chimpanzee aren't 98 percent identical, they're 100 percent identical.

On the other hand, when we compare the DNA of humans and chimps, what does the percentage of similarity mean? We conceptualize it on a linear scale, on which 100 percent is perfectly identical, and 0 percent is totally different. But the structure of DNA gives the scale a statistical idiosyncrasy.

Because DNA is a linear array of those four bases—A, G, C, and T—only four possibilities exist at any specific point in a DNA sequence. The laws of chance tell us that two random sequences from species that have no ancestry in common will match at about one in every four sites.

Thus, even two unrelated DNA sequences will be 25 percent identical, not 0 percent identical. (You can, of course, generate sequences more different than that, but greater differences would not occur randomly.) The most different two DNA sequences can be, then, is 75 percent different.

Now consider that all multicellular life on earth is related. A human, a chimpanzee, and the banana the chimpanzee is eating share a remote common ancestry, but a common ancestry nevertheless. Therefore, if we compare any particular DNA sequence in a human and a banana, the sequence would have to be more than 25 percent identical. For the sake of argument, let's say 35 percent. In other words, your DNA is over one-third the same as a banana's. Yet, of course, there are few ways other than genetically in which a human could be shown to be one-third identical to a banana.

That context may help us to assess the 98 percent DNA similarity of humans and chimpanzees. The fact that our DNA is 98 percent identical to that of a chimp is not a transcendent statement about our natures, but merely a decontextualized and culturally interpreted datum.

Moreover, the genetic comparison is misleading because it ignores qualitative differences among genomes. Genetic evolution involves much more than simply replacing one base with another. Thus, even among such close relatives as human and chimpanzee, we find that the chimp's genome is estimated to be about 10 percent larger than the human's; that one human chromosome contains a fusion of two small chimpanzee chromosomes; and that the tips of each chimpanzee chromosome contain a DNA sequence that is not present in humans.

In other words, the pattern we encounter genetically is actually quite close to the pattern we encounter anatomically. In spite of the shock the figure of 98 percent may give us, humans are obviously identifiably different from, as well as very similar to, chimpanzees. The apparent paradox is simply a result of how mundane the apes have become and how exotic DNA still is.

Adapted from Marks, J. (2000, May 12). 98% alike (What our similarity to apes tells us about our understanding of genetics). The Chronicle of Higher Education, B7. Copyright © 2000 by Chronicle of Higher Education. Reprinted with permission of the author.

Evolution, Individuals, and Populations

At the level of the individual, the study of genetics shows how traits are transmitted from parent to offspring, enabling a prediction about the chances that any given individual will display some phenotypic characteristic. At the level of the group, the study of genetics takes on additional significance, revealing how evolutionary processes account for the diversity of life on earth.

A key concept in genetics is that of the **population**, or a group of individuals within which breeding takes place. **Gene pool** refers to all the genetic variants possessed by members of a population. Natural selection takes place within populations as some members contribute a disproportionate share of the next generation. Over generations, the relative proportions of alleles in a population change (biological evolution) according to the varying reproductive success of individuals within that population. In other words, at the level of population genetics, **evolution** can be defined as changes in allele frequencies in populations. This is also known as *microevolution*. Evolution could not occur without variation. Four evolutionary forces—mutation, genetic drift, gene flow, and natural selection—create and pattern biological diversity.

In theory, the characteristics of any given population should remain stable. For example, generation after generation, the bullfrogs in a farm pond look much alike, have the same calls, and exhibit the same behavior when breeding. The gene pool of the population—the genetic variation available to that population—appears to remain stable over time.

Although some alleles may be dominant over others, recessive alleles are not just lost or destroyed. Statistically, an individual who is heterozygous for a particular gene with one dominant (A) and one recessive (a) allele has a 50 percent chance of passing on the dominant allele and a 50 percent chance of passing on the recessive allele. Even if another dominant allele masks the presence of the recessive allele in the next generation, the recessive allele nonetheless will continue to be a part of the gene pool.

Because alleles are not lost in the process of reproduction, the frequency of the different alleles within a population should remain exactly the same from one generation to the next in the absence of evolution. In 1908, the English mathematician Godfrey H. Hardy (1877–1947) and the German obstetrician Wilhelm Weinberg (1862–1937) worked this idea into a mathematical formula called the **Hardy-Weinberg principle**. The principle algebraically demonstrates that the percentages of individuals homozygous for the dominant allele, homozygous for the recessive allele, and heterozygous will remain the same from one generation to the next provided that the following conditions are met: mating is entirely random; the population is sufficiently large for a statistical average to express itself; no new variants will be introduced into the population's gene pool; and all individuals are equally successful at surviving and reproducing. As you will see in the following sections of this chapter, each of these conditions relates to one of the four forces responsible for microevolution or changes in allele frequency.

Evolutionary Forces

Mutation

Mutation, the ultimate source of evolutionary change, constantly introduces new genetic variation. Mutation occurs randomly. Although some mutations may be harmful or beneficial to individuals, most mutations are neutral. But in an evolutionary sense, random mutation is inherently

positive: It provides the variation upon which the other evolutionary forces work. New body plans—such as walking on two legs compared to knuckle-walking like our closest relatives, chimpanzees and gorillas—ultimately depended on a series of genetic mutations. A random mutation might create a new allele that modifies protein, making possible a novel biological task. Without the variation brought in through random mutations, populations could not change over time in response to changing environments.

Mutations may arise whenever copying mistakes are made during cell division. This may involve a change in a single base of a DNA sequence or, at the other extreme, relocation of large segments of DNA, including entire chromosomes. As you read this page, the DNA in each cell of your body is being damaged (Culotta & Koshland, 1994). Fortunately, DNA repair enzymes constantly scan DNA for mistakes, slicing out damaged segments and patching up gaps. Moreover, for sexually reproducing species like humans, the only mutations of any evolutionary consequence are those occurring in sex cells because these cells form future generations.

New mutations arise continuously because no species has perfect DNA repair; thus all species continue to evolve. Geneticists have calculated the rate at which various types of mutant genes appear. In human populations, they run from a low of about five mutations per million sex cells formed, in the case of a gene abnormality that leads to the absence of an iris in the eye, to a high of about a hundred per million, in the case of a gene involved in a form of muscular dystrophy. The average is about thirty mutants per million. Environmental factors may increase the rate at which mutations occur. These factors include certain dyes, antibiotics, and chemicals used in the preservation of food. Radiation, whether of industrial or solar origin, represents another important cause of mutations (**Figure 2.13**). Even stress can increase mutation rates, augmenting the diversity necessary for selection if successful adaptation is to occur (Chicurel, 2001).

In humans, as in all multicellular animals, the very nature of genetic material ensures that mutations will occur. For instance, the fact that a gene can be split by stretches of DNA that are not part of that gene increases the chances that a mistake in the process of copying DNA will cause mutations. To cite one example, no fewer than fifty such segments of DNA fragment the gene for collagen—the main

population In biology, a group of similar individuals that can and do interbreed.

gene pool All the genetic variants possessed by members of a population.

evolution The changes in allele frequencies in populations; also known as *microevolution*.

Hardy-Weinberg principle The concept that demonstrates algebraically that the percentages of individuals that are homozygous for the dominant allele, homozygous for the recessive allele, and heterozygous should remain constant from one generation to the next, provided that certain specified conditions are met.

mutation The chance alteration of genetic material that produces new variation.

© Gerg Ludwig/INSTITUTE

Figure 2.13 From Toxic Dumps to Missing Hands These eight children, each missing a hand, were among 90 children born with missing terminal limbs over a twenty-year period in Moscow, Russia. Their family homes were all clustered in polluted industrialized sections of the city, and the missing limbs are the result of prenatal exposure to toxins. These children and their families certainly face many obstacles as a result of this birth defect. Yet from an evolutionary perspective, the mutations leading to limb loss will have no consequences unless they appear in the reproductive cells and are transmitted to future generations.

structural protein of the skin, bones, and cartilage. One possible benefit of this seemingly inefficient situation is that it allows the gene segments themselves to be shuffled like a deck of cards, sometimes creating new proteins with new functions. So although individuals may suffer as a result, mutations also confer versatility at the population level, making it possible for an evolving species to adapt more quickly to environmental changes. Remember, however, that mutations occur randomly and thus do not arise out of need for some new adaptation.

Genetic Drift

Genetic drift refers to chance fluctuations of allele frequencies in the gene pool of a population. This evolutionary force produces changes at the population level caused by random events at the individual level. Over the course of a lifetime, a number of random events affect each individual's survival. For example, an individual squirrel in good health and possessed of a number of advanta-

geous traits may be killed in a chance forest fire; a genetically well-adapted baby cougar may not live longer than a day if its mother gets caught in an avalanche, whereas the weaker offspring of another cougar mother may survive.

In a large population, such accidents of nature are unimportant; the accidents that preserve individuals with certain alleles will be balanced out by the accidents that destroy them. However, in small populations such averaging out may not be possible. Because today human populations are large, we might suppose that human beings are unaffected by genetic drift. But a chance event, like a rockslide that kills five people from a small town, say a population of 1,000, could significantly alter the frequencies of alleles in the local gene pool.

A specific kind of genetic drift known as **founder effects** may occur when an existing population splits up into two or more new ones, especially if a particularly small number of individuals founds one of the new populations. In such cases, the gene frequencies of the smaller population tend not to contain the full range of variation present in the larger one.

Isolated island populations may have limited variability due to founder effects. An interesting example can be seen on the Pacific Ocean island of Pingelap in Micronesia, where 5 percent of the population is completely colorblind, a condition known as *achromatopsia*. This is not the "normal"

---

genetic drift The chance fluctuations of allele frequencies in the gene pool of a population.

founder effects A particular form of genetic drift deriving from a small founding population not possessing all the alleles present in the original population.

red–green colorblindness that affects 8 to 20 percent of males in most populations but rather a complete inability to see color. The high frequency of achromatopsia occurred sometime around 1775 after a typhoon swept through the island, reducing its total population to only twenty individuals. Among the survivors was a single individual who was heterozygous for this condition. After a few genera-

tions, this gene became fully embedded in the expanding population. Today a full 30 percent of the island's inhabitants are carriers of the colorblind gene, compared to a mere .003 percent seen in the United States (Sacks, 1998).

Genetic drift is likely to have been an important factor in human evolution because until 10,000 years ago all humans were food foragers generally living in relatively small communities. Whenever biological variation is observed, whether it is the distant past or the present, it is always possible that chance events of genetic drift are responsible for it.

Gene Flow

Gene flow, or the introduction of new alleles from nearby populations, brings new genetic variation into a population: Interbreeding allows "road-tested" genes to flow into and out of populations. Migration of individuals or groups into the territory occupied by others may lead to gene flow. Geographic factors also affect gene flow. For example, if a river separates two populations of small mammals, preventing interbreeding, these populations will begin to accrue random genetic differences due to their isolation (genetic drift). If the river changes course and the two populations can again interbreed freely, new alleles that may have been present in only one population will now be present in both populations due to gene flow.

Among humans, social factors—such as mating rules, intergroup conflict, and our ability to travel great distances—affect gene flow. For example, the last 500 years have seen the introduction of alleles into Central and South American populations from both the Spanish colonists and the Africans whom Europeans imported as slaves. More recent migrations of people from East Asia have added to this mix. Throughout the history of human life on earth, gene flow has prevented populations from developing into separate species.

Natural Selection

Although gene flow and genetic drift may produce changes in the allele frequency of a population, that change would not necessarily make the population better adapted to its biological and social environment. Natural selection, the evolutionary force described by Darwin, accounts for adaptive change. **Adaptation**—a series of beneficial adjustments to a particular environment—is the outcome of natural selection. As we will explore throughout this text, humans can adapt to their environment through culture as well as biology. When biological adaptation occurs at a genetic level, natural selection is at work.

Natural selection shapes genetic variation at the population level to fit local environmental conditions. In other words, instead of random individuals passing their traits on to the next generation, selection by the forces of nature favors some individuals over others. In the process, the frequency of genetic variants for harmful or nonadaptive traits within the population reduces while the frequency of genetic variants for adaptive traits increases. Over time, changes in the genetic structure of the population can result in the formation of new species.

Popular writing often reduces natural selection to the notion of the "survival of the fittest," a phrase coined by British philosopher Herbert Spencer (1820–1903). The phrase implies that disease, predation, and starvation eliminate the physically weak from the population. Obviously, the survival of the fittest has some bearing on natural selection. But at times "less fit" individuals survive, and even do quite well, but do not reproduce. They may be incapable of attracting mates, or they may be sterile, or they may produce offspring that do not survive after birth. For example, among the Uganda kob, a kind of antelope native to East Africa, males that are unable to attract females form bachelor herds in which they live out their lives. As members of a herd, they are reasonably well protected against predators, and so they may survive to relatively old ages. They do not, however, pass on their genes to succeeding generations.

Ultimately, all natural selection is measured in terms of **reproductive success**—mating and production of viable offspring who will in turn carry on one's genes. In some human societies, a woman's social worth is assessed in terms of reproductive success or her ability to bear children. In these contexts infertility becomes a human rights issue (Figure 2.13)

In human populations, changes in allele frequencies take place slowly. For example, if an environment changed such that a recessive allele that had been present in humans

---

gene flow The introduction of alleles from the gene pool of one population into that of another.

adaptation A series of beneficial adjustments to a particular environment.

reproductive success The relative production of fertile offspring by a genotype. In practical terms, the number of offspring produced by individual members of a population is tallied and compared to that of others.

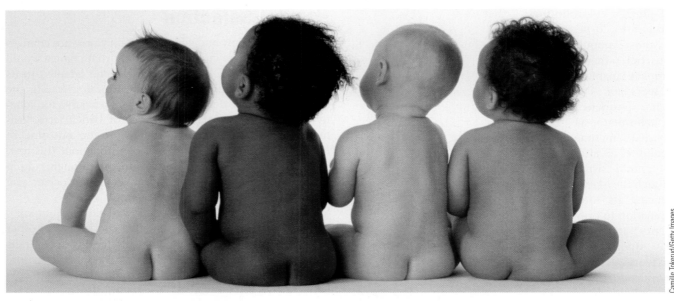

Camille Tokerud/Getty Images

Figure 2.14 **Birth Weight and Stabilizing Selection** Across the globe, newborn babies weigh on average between 5 and 8 pounds. Stabilizing selection seems to be operating here to keep infant size well matched to the size of the human birth canal for successful childbirth. Natural selection can promote stability as well as change.

at a modest frequency suddenly became lethal, this allele's frequency would still decrease only gradually. Even with complete selection against those homozygous for this allele, the allele would persist in the offspring of heterozygotes. In the first several generations, the frequency of the allele would decrease at a relatively rapid rate. However, with time, as the frequency of the recessive allele drops, the probability of forming a recessive homozygote also drops, so that it would take many generations to realize even a small decrease in allele frequency. Moreover, the twenty-five-year duration of a human generation (forty generations would span over a thousand years) contributes to the slow pace of evolutionary change. Nevertheless, even such small and slow changes can have a significant cumulative impact on both the genotypes and phenotypes of any population.

Through the process of natural selection, populations generally become well adapted to their environments. For example, consider the plants and animals that survive in the deserts of the western United States. Members of the cactus family have extensive root networks close to the surface of the soil, enabling them to soak up the slightest bit of moisture; they are able to store large quantities of water whenever it is available; they are shaped so as to expose the smallest possible surface to the dry air and are generally leafless as mature plants, thereby preventing water loss through evaporation; and a covering of spines discourages animals from chewing into the juicy flesh of the plant. Desert animals are also adapted to their environment. The kangaroo rat can survive without drinking water; many reptiles live in burrows where the temperature is lower; most animals are nocturnal or active only in the cool of the night. By extrapolation, biologists assume that the same adaptive mechanisms also work on behavioral traits.

Natural selection often promotes stability instead of change. **Stabilizing selection** occurs in populations that are already well adapted or where change would be disadvantageous (**Figure 2.14**). In cases where change is disadvantageous, natural selection will favor the retention of allele frequencies more or less as they are. Evolution tends not to proceed as a steady, stately progression over vast periods of time. Instead, the life history of most species consists of relative stability or gradual change punctuated by shorter periods of more rapid change (or extinction) when altered conditions require new adaptations or when a new mutation produces an opportunity to adapt to some other available environment. According to the fossil record, most species survive between 3 and 5 million years (Thomson, 1997).

Despite the importance of adaptation and natural selection in shaping living organisms, many traits have no adaptive function. All male mammals, for example, possess nipples, even though they serve no useful purpose. For female mammals, however, nipples are essential to reproductive success, which is why males have them. The two sexes are not separate entities, shaped independently by natural selection, but are variants upon a single body plan, elaborated in later embryology. All mammalian fetuses possess precursors of mammary glands, enlarging later in the development of females but remaining small and without function in males.

Further, traits that seem nonadaptive in the present may be coopted for later use, and traits that appear adaptive might have come about due to unrelated changes in the pattern of growth and development. For instance, the

stabilizing selection Natural selection acting to promote stability rather than change in a population's gene pool.

Figure 2.15 **Disproportionate Eggs** This x-ray showing the unusually large size of a kiwi egg illustrates that evolution does not continue by preplanned design but rather by a process of tinkering with preexisting body forms.

unusually large size of a kiwi's egg enhances the survivability of kiwi chicks, in that they are particularly large and capable when hatched (Figure 2.15). Nevertheless, large kiwi egg size probably did not evolve because the size is adaptive. Instead, kiwis evolved from an ancestor that was the size of an ostrich, and in birds, egg size reduces at a slower rate than does body size. Therefore, the outsized eggs of kiwi birds seem to be no more than a developmental byproduct of a reduction in body size (Gould, 1991a).

Similarly, an existing adaptation may come under strong selective pressure for some new purpose. For instance, insect wings arose as structures that were used to "row," and later skim, across the surface of the water (Kaiser, 1994). Later, the larger ones by chance proved useful for purposes of flight. In both the kiwi eggs and the insect wings, what we see is natural selection operating as "a creative scavenger, taking what is available and putting it to new use" (Dorit, 1997, p. 475).

Natural selection differs from the concept of design as it works only with the existing store of genetic variation; it cannot create something entirely new. Variation protects populations from dying out or species from going extinct in changing environments. Evolution is a process of tinkering. Often tinkering involves balancing beneficial and harmful effects of a specific allele in a specific environment, as the following case study of sickle-cell anemia illustrates.

The Case of Sickle-Cell Anemia

Among human beings, **sickle-cell anemia** is a particularly well-studied case of adaptation. This painful disease, in which the oxygen-carrying red blood cells change shape (sickle) and clog the finest parts of the

circulatory system, first came to the attention of geneticists in Chicago who observed that the disease disproportionately impacted African Americans. Further investigation found that populations that live in a clearly defined belt across Central Africa had the sickle-cell allele at surprisingly high frequencies. Geneticists were curious to know why such a harmful hereditary disability persisted in these populations. Figure 2.16 demonstrates the sickling shape of these abnormal red blood cells.

According to the theory of natural selection, any alleles that are harmful will tend to disappear from the group because the individuals who are homozygous for the abnormality generally die—are "selected out"—before they reproduce. Why, then, has this seemingly harmful condition persisted in populations from Central Africa?

The answer to this mystery began to emerge when researchers noticed that a particularly deadly form of malaria (falciparum malaria) was prevalent in the same areas that had high rates of sickle-cell anemia (Figure 2.17). This severe form of malaria causes many deaths or, in those who survive, high fever that significantly interferes with individuals' reproductive abilities. Moreover, researchers discovered hemoglobin abnormalities among people living in parts of the Arabian peninsula, Greece, Algeria, Syria, and India, all regions where malaria is (or was) common. Thus, selection favored heterozygous individuals with normal and sickling hemoglobin. The loss of alleles for abnormal hemoglobin caused by the death of those homozygous for it (from sickle-cell anemia) was balanced out by the loss of alleles for normal hemoglobin, as those homozygous for normal hemoglobin were more likely to die from malaria.

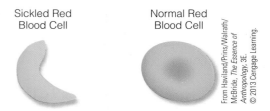

Figure 2.16 **Sickle and Normal Red Blood Cells** Sickle-cell anemia is caused by a genetic mutation in a single base of the hemoglobin gene, resulting in abnormal hemoglobin, called hemoglobin S or Hb^S. (The normal hemoglobin allele is called Hb^A not to be confused with blood type A.) Those afflicted by the disease are homozygous for the Hb^S allele, and all their red blood cells "sickle." Co-dominance is observable with the sickle and normal alleles. Heterozygotes (genotype $Hb^A Hb^S$) make 50 percent normal hemoglobin and 50 percent sickle hemoglobin. Shown here is a sickled red blood cell compared to a normal red blood cell.

sickle-cell anemia An inherited form of anemia produced by a mutation in the hemoglobin protein that causes the red blood cells to assume a sickle shape.

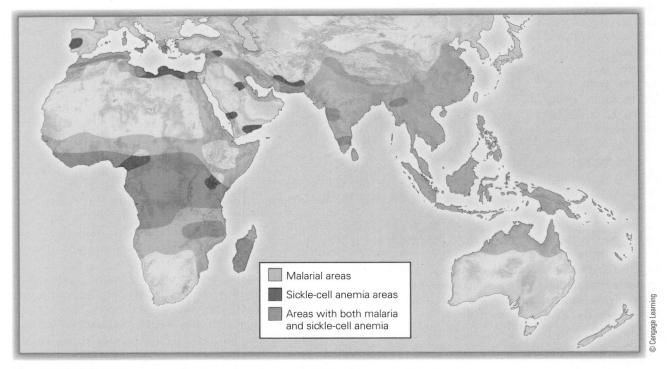

Figure 2.17 The Distribution of Malaria and the Sickle-Cell Allele In regions with a high incidence of falciparum malaria, people native to these areas have a higher than normal rate of the
allele that causes sickle-cell anemia. Researchers have surmised that natural selection preserved
the allele for the sickle-cell trait to protect individuals from the devastating effects of malaria.

The mutation that causes hemoglobin to sickle consists
of a change in a single base of DNA, so it can arise readily
by chance (**Figure 2.18**). The resulting mutant allele codes
for an amino acid substitution in the beta chain of the
hemoglobin protein that leads red blood cells to take on a
characteristic sickle shape. In homozygous individuals with
two sickle-hemoglobin alleles, collapse and clumping of the
abnormal red blood cells block the capillaries and create
tissue damage—causing the symptoms of sickle-cell disease.

Afflicted individuals commonly die before reaching adulthood. Except under low oxygen or other stressful conditions,
heterozygous individuals suffer no ill effects. In regions with
malaria, the heterozygous condition actually improves individuals' resilience to malaria and their reproductive success
relative to the "normal" homozygous condition.

This example also points out how adaptations tend to
be specific; the abnormal hemoglobin was adaptive only
in environments in which the malarial parasite flourished.

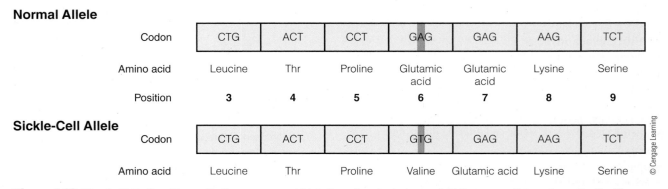

Figure 2.18 Simple Mutation, Dramatic Consequences Mutation of a single base of DNA can result in a dramatically different protein. Pictured here are codons 3 through 9 for the beta chain of hemoglobin, the protein that carries oxygen in red
blood cells and the amino acids these codons specify. The top row depicts the normal allele, and the bottom row shows the
single substitution that makes the red blood cells bend into a sickle shape (clogging the capillary beds and causing great
pain, which is what occurs with sickle-cell anemia). Sickling occurs because the amino acid valine, compared to glutamic acid
in the normal allele, gives the hemoglobin molecule different properties. The beta chain is 146 amino acids long. A simple
mutation (the substitution of thymine for adenine in position 6 as indicated in red) has dramatic and tragic consequences.

When individuals adapted to malarial regions came to regions relatively free of malaria, the abnormal hemoglobin became comparatively disadvantageous. Although the rates of sickle-cell trait remain relatively high among African Americans—about 9 percent have the sickling trait—this has significantly declined from the 22 percent estimated among the first African captives who were shipped across the Atlantic and sold as slaves. A similar decline in the sickle-cell allele would occur over the course of several generations in malarial zones if this deadly disease were brought under control.

This example also illustrates the important role culture plays in biological adaptation. In Africa, the severe form of malaria was not a significant problem until humans abandoned food foraging for farming a few thousand years ago. In order to farm, people had to clear areas of the natural forest cover. In the forest, decaying vegetation on the forest floor gave the ground an absorbent quality so that the heavy rainfall rapidly soaked into the soil. But once stripped of its natural vegetation, the soil lost this quality. In addition, without the forest canopy to break the force of the rainfall, the heavy rains compacted the soil further. The stagnant puddles that formed after rains provided the perfect breeding environment for the type of mosquito that hosts the malarial parasite. These mosquitoes then began to flourish and transmit the malarial parasite to humans.

Thus, humans unwittingly created the kind of environment that made a disadvantageous trait, the abnormal hemoglobin associated with sickle-cell anemia, advantageous. While the biological process of evolution accounts for the frequency of the sickle-cell allele, cultural processes shape the environment to which humans adapt.

Adaptation and Physical Variation

Anthropologists study biological diversity in terms of **clines**, or the continuous gradation over space in the form or frequency of a trait. The spatial distribution or cline for the sickle-cell allele allowed anthropologists to identify the adaptive function of this gene in a malarial environment. Clinal analysis of a continuous trait such as body shape, which is controlled by a series of genes, allows anthropologists to interpret human global variation in body build as an adaptation to climate.

Generally, people long native to regions with cold climates tend to have greater body bulk (not to be equated with fat) relative to their extremities (arms and legs) than do people native to regions with hot climates, who tend to be relatively tall and slender. Interestingly, tall, slender bodies show up in human evolution perhaps as early as 1.5 million years ago. A person with larger body bulk and relatively short extremities may suffer more from summer heat than someone with a slender body and relatively long extremities. But this person will conserve needed body heat under cold conditions because a bulky body has less surface area relative to volume. In hot, open country, by contrast, people benefit from a long, slender body that can get rid of excess heat quickly. A small slender body can also promote heat loss due to a high surface area to volume ratio.

In addition to these sorts of very long-term effects that climate may have imposed on human variation, climate can also contribute to human variation through its impact on the process of growth and development (developmental adaptation). For example, some of the biological mechanisms for withstanding cold or dissipating heat have been shown to vary depending upon the climate an individual experiences as a child. People spending their youth in very cold climates develop circulatory system modifications that allow them to remain comfortable at temperatures that those from warmer climates cannot tolerate. Similarly, hot climate promotes the development of a higher density of sweat glands, creating a more efficient system for sweating to keep the body cool.

Cultural processes complicate studies of biological adaptation to climate. For example, a poor diet during childhood affects the growth process and ultimately impacts adult body shape and size. Clothing also complicates these studies. In fact, culture rather than biology accounts for much of the way people adapt to cold. For instance, to cope with bitter Arctic climates, the Iñuit peoples of northern Canada long ago developed efficient clothing to keep the body warm. The Iñuit (and other Eskimos) created artificial tropical environments for themselves inside their clothing. Such cultural adaptations allow humans to inhabit the entire globe.

Some anthropologists have suggested that variation in features such as face and eye shape relate to climate. For example, biological anthropologists once proposed that the flat facial profile and round head—common in populations native to East and Central Asia, as well as Arctic North America—derive from adaptation to very cold environments. Though these features are common in Asian and Native American populations, considerable physical variation exists within each population. Some individuals who spread to North America from Asia have a head shape that is more common among Europeans. Furthermore, genetic drift could also account for regional variation of traits. Because specific examples of adaptation, particularly of continuous traits, can be difficult to prove, scientists sometimes suggest that their colleagues' scenarios about adaptation are "Just So" stories.

Macroevolution and the Process of Speciation

While *microevolution* refers to changes in the allele frequencies of populations, **macroevolution** focuses on **speciation**—the formation of new species—and on

---

clines The gradual changes in the frequency of an allele or trait over space.
macroevolution Evolution above the species level or leading to the formation of new species.
speciation The process of forming new species.

the evolutionary relationships among groups of species. The microevolutionary forces of mutation, genetic drift, gene flow, and natural selection can lead to macroevolutionary change as species diverge.

As defined earlier in the chapter, *species*—a population or group of populations capable of interbreeding and producing viable, fertile offspring—are reproductively isolated. The bullfrogs in one farmer's pond are the same species as those in a neighboring pond, even though the two populations may never actually interbreed; in theory, they could interbreed if brought together. But isolated populations may be in the process of evolving into different species, and it is hard to tell exactly when they become biologically distinct.

Certain factors, known as *isolating mechanisms*, can separate breeding populations and lead to the appearance of new species. Because isolation prevents gene flow, changes that affect the gene pool of one population cannot be introduced into the gene pool of the other. Random mutation may introduce new alleles in one of the isolated populations but not in the other. Genetic drift and natural selection may affect the two populations in different ways. Over time, as the two populations continue to differ from each other, speciation occurs in a branching fashion known as **clado-genesis**. Speciation can also happen without branching, as a single population accumulates sufficient new mutations over time to be considered a separate species. This process is known as **anagenesis** (Figure 2.19). Speciation is inferred in the fossil record when a group of organisms takes on a different appearance over time.

Because speciation is a process, it can occur at various rates. Scholars generally consider speciation through the process of natural selection as proposed by Darwin to occur at a slow rate. In this model, speciation happens as organisms become better adapted to their environments. Sometimes, however, speciation can occur quite rapidly. For example, a genetic mutation such as one involving a key *regulatory gene,* a gene that turns other genes off and on, can lead to the formation of a new body plan. Such genetic accidents may involve material that is broken off, transposed, or transferred from one chromosome to another.

Genes that regulate the growth and development of an organism may have a major effect on its adult form. Scientists have discovered certain key genes called *homeobox genes* that are responsible for large-scale effects on the growth and development of the organism (Figure 2.20). If a new body plan happens to be adaptive, natural selection will maintain this new form during long periods of time rather than promoting change.

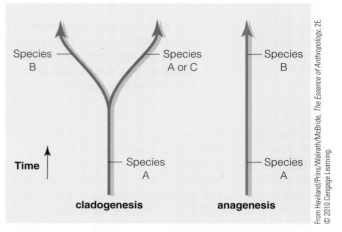

Figure 2.19 **Mechanisms of Speciation** Cladogenesis occurs as different populations of an ancestral species become reproductively isolated. Through genetic drift and differential selection, the number of descendant species increases. By contrast, anagenesis can occur through a process of variational change that takes place as small differences in traits that (by chance) are advantageous in a particular environment accumulate in a species' gene pool. Over time, this may produce sufficient change to transform an old species into a new one. Genetic drift may also account for anagenesis.

Figure 2.20 **Homeobox Genes and New Body Plans** Sometimes mutation in a single gene can cause reorganization of an organism's body plan. Here the "bithorax" homeobox gene has caused this fruit fly to have two thoraxes and two sets of wings. Another homeobox gene, "antennepedia," causes legs to develop in the place of antennae on the heads of fruit flies.

---

cladogenesis Speciation through a branching mechanism whereby an ancestral population gives rise to two or more descendant populations.

anagenesis A sustained directional shift in a population's average characteristics.

punctuated equilibria A model of macroevolutionary change that suggests evolution occurs via long periods of stability or stasis punctuated by periods of rapid change.

(a) Ground finch
  Main food: seeds
  Beak: heavy

(b) Tree finch
  Main food: leaves, buds,
  blossoms, fruits
  Beak: thick, short

(c) Tree finch (called
  woodpecker finch)
  Main food: insects
  Beak: stout, straight

(d) Ground finch (known
  as warbler finch)
  Main food: insects
  Beak: slender

Figure 2.21 Adaptation and Darwin's Finches Scientists have begun to unravel the genetic mechanisms controlling the shape and size of beaks of the finches studied by Darwin on the Galapagos Islands. Darwin noted how beak shape and size were related to each species' diet and used the birds to illustrate adaptation to a particular ecological niche. Finches with blunt crushing beaks are seedeaters while others with long probing beaks pick between cactus thorns for food or use the beaks to reach insects.

From Jurmain/Kilgore/Trevathan/Ciochon. *Introduction to Physical Anthropology,* 2009–2010, 12E. © 2010 Cengage Learning Inc.

Paleontologists Stephen Jay Gould and Niles Eldredge have proposed that speciation occurs in a pattern of **punctuated equilibria**, or the alternation between periods of rapid speciation and times of stability. Often this model of evolutionary change is contrasted with speciation through adaptation, sometimes referred to as *Darwinian gradualism.* A close look at the genetics and the fossil record indicates that evolutionary change occurs via both mechanisms.

Genetic mechanisms underlie both rapid and gradual changes because mutations can have small or large effects. It is particularly interesting to see how molecular genetics supports Darwinian evolutionary change. For example, the tailoring of beak shape and size to diet among finches on the Galapagos Islands, in the Pacific Ocean west of Ecuador, constituted Darwin's classic example of natural selection

(**Figure 2.21**). Recently, scientists identified two proteins along with the underlying genes that control beak shape and size in birds. It is all the more impressive that Darwin was able to make his inferences about natural selection without the benefit of molecular genetics.

In biological terms, evolution accounts for all that humans share as well as the broad array of human diversity. Evolution is also responsible for the creation of new species over time. Primatologist Frans de Waal has said, "Evolution is a magnificent idea that has won over essentially everyone in the world willing to listen to scientific arguments" (de Waal, 2001, p. 77). We will return to the topic of human evolution in chapters that follow, but first we will look at the other living primates in order to understand the kinds of animals they are, what they have in common with humans, and what distinguishes the various forms.

CHAPTER CHECKLIST

How does evolutionary theory differ from creation stories?

● Scientific theories are based on testable hypotheses.

● Unlike existential or faith-based explanations, scientific theories of evolution propose mechanisms to account for the diversity of life on earth.

How are living things classified, and how did this system come about?

● The science of taxonomy classifies living organisms into a series of progressively more inclusive categories on the basis of internal and external visual similarities.

● In the 18th century, Carolus Linnaeus devised his *System Naturae,* the first system to classify living things then known on the basis of similarities in body structure, body function, and sequence of bodily growth.

● Modern taxonomy still uses the basic Linnaean system but now looks at such characteristics as chemical reactions of blood, protein structure, and the makeup of the genetic material itself. These new kinds of data have led to the revision of some existing taxonomies.

● Species, the smallest working units in biological classificatory systems, are reproductively isolated populations or groups of populations capable of interbreeding to produce fertile offspring.

What is evolution, and when was this central biological theory formulated?

● Charles Darwin formulated a theory of evolution in 1859. His conception of evolution was based on differential reproductive success among members of a population (a group of interbreeding individuals) that becomes adapted to its environment through natural selection.

● Today, evolution is understood in terms of the four evolutionary forces—mutation, genetic drift, gene flow, and natural selection—that affect the genetic structures of populations. Evolution at the level of population genetics is change in allele frequencies, which is also known as microevolution.

● Different versions or alternate forms of a gene for a given trait are called alleles. The total number of different alleles of genes available to a population is called its gene pool.

● Macroevolution focuses on the formation of new species (speciation) and on the evolutionary relationships among groups of species.

What is the molecular basis of evolution?

● Genes, the units of heredity, are segments of molecules of DNA (deoxyribonucleic acid), and the entire sequence of DNA is known as the genome.

● DNA is a complex molecule resembling two strands of rope twisted around each other with ladderlike rungs connecting the two strands.

● The sequence of bases along the DNA molecule directs the production of proteins. Proteins, in turn, constitute specific identifiable traits such as blood type. Just about everything in the human body is made of or by proteins, and human DNA provides the instructions for the thousands of proteins that keep us alive and healthy.

How do cells and organisms reproduce?

● DNA molecules have the unique property of being able to produce exact copies of themselves. As long as no errors are made in the process of replication, new daughter cells will be exact genetic copies of the parent cell.

● DNA molecules are located on chromosomes, structures found in the nucleus of each cell. Chromosomes consist of two sister chromatids, which are exact copies of each other.

● Each kind of organism has a characteristic number of chromosomes, which are usually found in pairs in sexually reproducing organisms. Humans have twenty-three pairs of chromosomes.

● Mitosis, one kind of cell division that results in new cells, begins when the chromosomes (hence, the genes) replicate, forming a duplicate of the original pair of chromosomes in the nucleus. Sister chromatids separate during mitosis and form identical daughter cells.

● Meiosis is related to sexual reproduction; it begins with the replication of original chromosomes, but these are divided into four cells, in humans each containing twenty-three single chromosomes. Fertilization, the union of an egg and a sperm cell, reestablishes the normal human number of twenty-three pairs of chromosomes.

How do different traits get inherited across generations?

● In the late 19th century Gregor Mendel discovered the particulate nature of heredity: Individuals inherit traits independently from each parent.

● Dominant alleles are able to mask the presence of recessive alleles. The allele for type A blood in humans, for example, is dominant to the allele for type O blood. Alleles that are both expressed when present are termed *co-dominant*. For example, an individual with the alleles for type A and type B blood has the AB blood type.

● *Phenotype* refers to the physical characteristics of an organism, whereas *genotype* refers to its genetic composition. Two organisms may have different genotypes but the same phenotype. An individual with the type A blood phenotype may possess either the AO or the AA genotype, having inherited one allele from each parent.

How do the four evolutionary forces contribute to the diversity of life on earth?

● Mutation provides the ultimate source of genetic variation. These changes in DNA may be helpful or harmful to the individual organism, though most mutations are simply neutral. Although mutations are inevitable given the nature of cellular chemistry, environmental factors—such as heat, chemicals, or radiation—can increase the mutation rate.

● *Genetic drift* refers to the effects of random events on the gene pool of a small population. Genetic drift may have been an important factor in human evolution because until 10,000 years ago humans lived in small isolated populations.

● Gene flow, the introduction of new variants of genes from nearby populations, distributes new variation to all populations and serves to prevent speciation.

● Natural selection, the evolutionary force involved in adaptive change, reduces the frequency of alleles for harmful or maladaptive traits within a population and increases the frequency of alleles for adaptive traits.

What are some examples of human adaptation through natural selection?

● A well-studied example of adaptation through natural selection in humans is inheritance of the trait for sickling red blood cells. The sickle-cell trait, caused by the inheritance of an abnormal form of hemoglobin, is an adaptation to life in regions in which malaria is common.

● Physical anthropologists have determined that some human physical variation appears related to climatic adaptation. People native to cold climates tend to have greater body bulk relative to their extremities than individuals from hot climates; the latter tend to be relatively tall and slender.

● Studies involving body build and climate are complicated by other factors such as the effects on physique of diet and clothing.

How are new species formed?

● Speciation can occur in a branching fashion (cladogenesis) or without branching (anagenesis) as a single population accumulates sufficient new mutations over time to be considered a separate species.

● Microevolutionary forces of mutation, genetic drift, gene flow, and natural selection can lead to macroevolutionary change, but the tempo of evolutionary change varies.

● A mutation in a regulatory gene can bring about rapid change. The punctuated equilibrium model proposes that macroevolution is characterized by long spans of relative stability interspersed with periods of rapid change.

QUESTIONS FOR REFLECTION

1. Have genetics and DNA become a part of your everyday experience? If so, how? How has the popularization of the human genetic code challenged your conception of what it means to be human? How much of your life, or of the lives of the people around you, is dictated by the structure of DNA?

2. Scientific fact and theory can challenge other belief systems. Is it possible for scientific models of human evolution and religious stories of creation to coexist? How do you personally reconcile science and religion?

3. The four evolutionary forces—mutation, genetic drift, gene flow, and natural selection—all affect biological variation. Some are at work in individuals while others function at the population level. Compare and contrast these evolutionary forces, outlining their contributions to biological variation.

4. The frequency of the sickle-cell allele in populations provides a classic example of adaptation on a genetic level. Describe the benefits of this deadly allele. Are mutations good or bad?

5. Are you likely to witness the appearance of a new species in your lifetime? If so, how might this come about? How would you recognize that this is truly a new species?

ONLINE STUDY RESOURCES

CourseMate

Access chapter-specific learning tools, including learning objectives, practice quizzes, videos, flash cards, glossaries, and more in your Anthropology CourseMate.

Log into **www.cengagebrain.com** to access the resources your instructor has assigned and to purchase materials.

Challenge Issue

One quick glance at this female gorilla and two children at play attests to all that we share with our closest living relatives. We are equipped to read their body language, their facial expressions. Our bodies possess the same basic form. In them we can discern the joy of play and the ease across generations, perhaps recalling our own experiences just from looking at them. It is no small wonder, then, that the other primates have long fascinated humans. But despite our biological and emotional closeness, humans threaten the survival of our primate cousins. Today, largely due to human action, all of the other great ape species—chimps, bonobos, gorillas, and orangutans—are endangered. The same holds true for many other primate species. We humans have brought war, a hunger for natural resources, and infectious disease into their habitats, with devastating results. If the difference between our primate relatives and us is our greater intelligence and complex language, it is time to use both these gifts to protect them. We humans face the challenge of speaking out and engaging in actions that ensure that other primates do not become extinct.

Living Primates

3

In October 1960, the young Jane Goodall sent word back to her mentor, paleoanthropologist Louis Leakey, that she had observed two chimps turning sticks into tools for fishing termites out of their nesting mounds. Leakey replied, "Now we must redefine 'tool,' redefine 'man,' or accept chimpanzees as humans" (Jane Goodall Institute, 2012).

Field studies of primates by Western scientists have always contained a degree of anthropocentrism and a focus on what nonhuman primates can tell us about ourselves. Indeed, that is the purpose of this chapter. By looking at the biology and behavior of the primates, we gain a firmer understanding of those characteristics we share with other primates, as well as those that distinguish us from them and make us distinctively human. Studying communication and tool use among our primate cousins today, for example, can help anthropologists reconstruct how and why humans developed as they did. Studies of primate behavior might unravel an old nature–nurture question: How much of human behavior is biologically determined and how much of it derives from culture?

Today, we are the only primate to inhabit the entire globe. As human population size rises to unsustainable levels, many primate groups are hovering on the brink of extinction. **Figure 3.1** shows the natural global distribution of living and fossil primates. It also indicates where the twenty-five most endangered species are struggling to survive. In this light, the purpose of this chapter is not just to learn more about ourselves, but to learn how to protect our primate cousins and the planet we share.

IN THIS CHAPTER YOU WILL LEARN TO

- Identify the key methods of primatologists and the ethics they uphold.

- Situate primates in the animal kingdom and compare them to other mammals and reptiles.

- Construct evolutionary relationships among the primates.

- Recognize the basic features of primate anatomy and behavior.

- Distinguish the characteristics of the five natural groups of primates.

- Identify critical issues and methods in primate conservation.

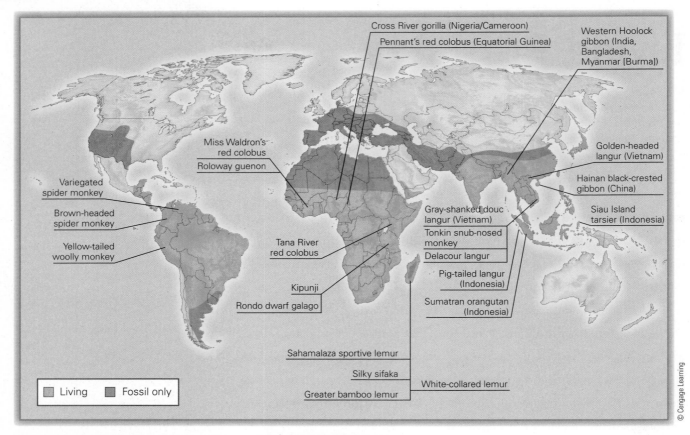

Figure 3.1 The Global Distribution of Living and Fossil Nonhuman Primates In the past, when more of the world was covered by tropical forests, the range of primates was far greater than it is now. Today, human activity threatens our primate cousins throughout the globe. The figure also shows the location of the twenty-five most endangered primate species today.

Methods and Ethics in Primatology

Just as anthropologists employ diverse methods to study humans, primatologists use a variety of methods to study the biology, behavior, and evolutionary history of our closest living relatives. Some primatologists concentrate on the comparative anatomy of ancient skeletons, whereas others trace evolutionary relationships by studying the comparative physiology and genetics of living species. Primatologists study the biology and behavior of living primates both in their natural habitats and in captivity in zoos, primate research colonies, and learning laboratories.

The primatologist most people recognize is Jane Goodall, a world-renowned British researcher who has devoted her career to in-depth observation of chimpanzees in their natural habitat. While documenting the range and nuance of chimpanzee behavior, she has also championed conservation of primate habitats and humane treatment of primates in captivity. The philosophy of conservation and

preservation has led to further innovations in research methods. For example, primatologists have developed a number of noninvasive methods that allow them to study primate biology and behavior in the field while minimizing physical disruption. Primatologists gather hair, feces, and other body secretions left by the primates in the environment for later analysis in the laboratory. These analyses provide invaluable information about characteristics such as dietary habits or genetic relatedness among a group of individuals.

Work with captive animals provides more than knowledge about the basic biology of primates. It has also allowed primatologists to document the humanity of our primate cousins. Many of the amazing linguistic and conceptual abilities of primates became known through studies of captive animals. Individual primatologists have devoted their careers to working with primates in captivity, teaching them to communicate through pictures on a computer screen or American Sign Language. Of course, even compassionate captivity imposes stress on primates. Still, the knowledge gained through these studies ultimately will contribute to primate conservation and survival.

At first glance it might seem inherently more humane to work with animals in the field compared to captivity. But even field studies raise important ethical issues for primatologists to consider. Primatologists must maintain an awareness of how their presence affects the behavior of the group. For example, does becoming tolerant of human observers make the primates more vulnerable? Primates habituated to humans commonly range beyond established wilderness preserves and come in close contact with other humans who may be more interested in hunting than observing. Contact between primates and humans can also expose endangered primates to infectious diseases carried by humans.

Whether working with primates in captivity or in the field, primatologists seriously consider the well-being of the primates they study. Primatologist Michele Goldsmith explores these issues in depth in this chapter's Original Study.

Gorilla Ecotourism: Ethical Considerations for Conservation BY MICHELE GOLDSMITH

For the past 13 years, I have been studying and writing about the impact of ecotourism on mountain gorillas living in Bwindi Impenetrable National Park, Uganda. As a biological anthropologist and conservationist, my main focus has been on habituation, which is a necessary prerequisite for tourism, and how it influences gorilla behavior and well-being. *Habituation* refers to the acceptance by wild animals of a human observer as a neutral element in their environment. Although information from habituated primates has been instrumental in providing a wealth of information for research and conservation, little attention has been given to the costs these animals bear when their fear of humans is removed.

Primatologist Michele Goldsmith making observations of gorillas in the field.

The first impacts of habituation occur during the process of acclimation. Habituators follow the animals from a distance and, over time, slowly get closer and closer. Many factors contribute to the speed and success of the process, such as the terrain (open areas versus thick forest), prior exposure to humans, hunting pressure, and so on. The process can be stressful for the gorillas and even dangerous for the habituators. During the habituation process, a group of western lowland gorillas exhibited fear in their vocalizations, increased their aggressive behavior, and changed their daily ranging pattern.[a] Such fear and stress can lead to loss of reproductive function and to a weakened immune system. Aggressive behavior has resulted in habituators being charged by silverback males with some humans being hit and bitten.

Once fully habituated, gorillas may then experience unforeseen consequences. For example, gorillas that have lost their fear of humans are especially vulnerable to hunting. Five Bwindi gorillas habituated for research were found dead, having been killed by poachers so they could capture a young infant gorilla. In addition, humans have also brought great instability and warfare to areas where gorilla populations live. Sudden evacuation of research and tourist sites leaves behind habituated gorillas that become easy targets for the poacher's gun.

With regard to long-term changes in ecology and behavior, my research has shown that the diet, nesting, and ranging patterns of habituated gorilla groups are different from other "wild" gorillas in the same study area. The Nkuringo group, habituated in 1998 for tourism that started in 2004, lives near the edge of the protected Bwindi Impenetrable National Park. These gorillas spend close to 90 percent of their time outside the park, in and around human-inhabited areas and farms. These behavioral changes have many costs to the gorillas, such as increased contact with humans and human waste,

Michele L. Goldsmith/Photograph © Nate Boesch

Posho, a blackback gorilla from the Nkuringo tourist-habituated group, looks out over an area outside Bwindi Impenetrable National Park.

conflict with farmers that could result in injury, increased exposure to hunting given that these areas are mostly open fields, and increased risk of disease transmission.[b]

Another effect on behavior may be an artificial increase in group size. For example, a group of some forty-four animals now exists in the Virungas, where the average group size is usually ten individuals. Furthermore, it is thought that, due to their fear of humans, "wild" adult male gorillas that would normally challenge other dominant males are either deterred from presenting a challenge or are less successful in their challenge against habituated groups.

Perhaps the biggest threat to habituated great apes is disease.[c] There are over nineteen viruses and eighteen parasites that are known to infect both great apes and humans. These diseases have been responsible for between sixty-three and eighty-seven ape deaths in habituated groups (both research and tourist groups) in the Virungas, Bwindi, Mahale, Tai, and Gombe. As for the gorillas in Bwindi, it has been shown that parasites such as *Cryptosporidium* and *Giardia* are most prevalent in habituated groups living near humans along the border of the park.

Is gorilla tourism sustainable? Early gorilla tourism in the 1980s did appear to be a salvation because it helped to halt poaching and provide value to the living animal that was lacking. However, now the balance seems to have tipped. As of 2011, *61 percent* of the entire mountain gorilla population *is now habituated* for either research (17%) or tourism (44%). We know habituated gorillas are more susceptible to stress, experience changes in their behavior, and are more vulnerable to human disease. The fear remains that one deadly, highly infectious disease could travel quickly through the small isolated populations and leave few survivors. *What is most important is not habituating more groups but better managing of the already habituated groups.* Ethical considerations are crucial as we continue to put gorilla populations at risk.[d] Habituation, especially for tourism, may not be an ape's salvation.

Michele L. Goldsmith is a primatologist who has been studying the behavioral ecology of gorillas in Uganda and the Congo since 1991.

---

[a]Blom, A., et al. (2004). Behavioral responses of gorillas to habituation in the Dzanga-Ndoki National Park, Central African Republic. *International Journal of Primatology 25*, 179–196.

[b]Goldsmith, M. L., Glick, J., & Ngabirano, E. (2006). Gorillas living on the edge: Literally and figuratively. In N. E. Newton-Fisher, et al. (Eds.), *Primates of Western Uganda* (pp. 405–422). New York: Springer.

[c]Woodford, M. H., Butynski, T. M., & Karesh W. (2002). Habituating the great apes: The disease risks. *Oryx 36*, 153–160.

[d]Goldsmith, M. L. (2005). Habituating primates for field study: Ethical considerations for great apes. In T. Turner (Ed.), *Biological anthropology and ethics: From repatriation to genetic identity* (pp. 49–64). New York: SUNY Press.

Primates as Mammals

Biologists classify humans within the primate order, a subgroup of the class Mammalia. The other primates include lemurs, lorises, tarsiers, monkeys, and apes. Humans—together with chimpanzees, bonobos, gorillas, orangutans, gibbons, and siamangs—form the hominoids, colloquially known as apes, a superfamily within the primate order. Biologically speaking, as hominoids, humans are apes.

The primates are only one of several different kinds of mammals, such as rodents, carnivores, and ungulates (hoofed mammals). Primates, like other mammals, are intelligent animals, having more in the way of brains than reptiles or other kinds of vertebrates. Increased brainpower and the mammalian growth and development form the biological basis of the flexible behavior patterns typical of mammals. In most species, the young are born live, the egg being retained within the womb of the female until the embryo achieves an advanced state of growth.

Once born, the young receive milk from their mothers' mammary glands, the physical feature from which the class Mammalia gets its name (**Figure 3.2**). During this period of infant dependency, young mammals learn many of the things they will need for survival as adults. Primates in general, and apes in particular, have a long period of infant and childhood dependency in which the young learn the ways of their social group. Thus, primate behavioral patterns derive from mammalian primate biology.

In this regard, a comparison of mammals to reptiles clarifies much about the primate adaptation. The mammalian diversity with which we are familiar today is the product of an **adaptive radiation**: the rapid diversification of an evolving population following a change in the environment. Evidence from ancient skeletons indicates the first mammals appeared over 200 million years ago as small, often **nocturnal** (active at night) creatures. With the mass extinction of many reptiles including the dinosaurs some 65 million years ago, a number of existing **ecological niches**, or functional positions in their habitats, became available to mammals. A species' niche incorporates factors such as diet, activity, terrain, vegetation, predators, prey, and climate. New niches opened as the earth cooled during this time period, permitting mammals to fill them.

By chance, mammals were **preadapted**—possessing the biological equipment to take advantage of the new opportunities available to them through the mass extinction of the dinosaurs and other reptiles. As **homeotherms**, mammals have the ability to maintain a constant body temperature. Mammals can be active at a wide range of environmental temperatures, whereas reptiles, as **isotherms** that take their body temperature from the surrounding environment, become progressively sluggish as the surrounding temperature drops.

However, mammals require a diet high in calories in order to maintain a constant body temperature. To meet this need, mammals developed superior senses of smell and

Martin Harvey/Getty Images/Peter Arnold

Figure 3.2 Nursing Chimp Nursing their young is an important part of the general mammalian tendency to invest high amounts of energy into rearing relatively few young at a time. The reptilian pattern is to lay many eggs, with the young fending for themselves. Ape mothers tend to nurse their young for four or five years. The practice of bottle-feeding infants in North America and Europe is a massive departure from the ape pattern. Although the health benefits for mothers (such as lowered breast cancer rates) and children (strengthened immune systems) are clearly documented, cultural norms sometimes present obstacles to breastfeeding. In the United States, for example, only 44 percent of mothers were breastfeeding their 6-month-old infants. By contrast, across the globe women nurse their children on average for about three years.

---

adaptive radiation The rapid diversification of an evolving population as it adapts to a variety of available niches.

nocturnal Active at night and at rest during the day.

ecological niche A species' way of life considered in the full context of its environment including factors such as diet, activity, terrain, vegetation, predators, prey, and climate.

preadapted Possessing characteristics that, by chance, are advantageous in future environmental conditions.

homeotherm An animal that maintains a relatively constant body temperature despite environmental fluctuations.

isotherm An animal whose body temperature rises or falls according to the temperature of the surrounding environment.

hearing relative to reptiles. The mammalian pattern also differs from reptiles in terms of how they care for their young. Compared to reptiles, mammalian species are **k-selected**. This means that they produce relatively few offspring at a time, providing them with considerable parental care. Reptiles are **r-selected**, which means that they produce many young at a time and invest little effort caring for their young after they are born. Although among mammals some species are relatively more k- or r-selected, the higher energy requirements of mammals, entailed by parental investment and the maintenance of a constant body temperature, demand more nutrition than that required by reptiles.

Mammals tend to be more active than other members of the animal kingdom. Their high activity levels depend upon a relatively constant body temperature, an efficient respiratory system featuring a separation between the nasal (nose) and mouth cavities (allowing them to breathe while they eat), a diaphragm to assist in drawing in and letting out breath, and an efficient four-chambered heart that prevents mixing of oxygenated and deoxygenated blood.

Mammals possess a skeleton in which the limbs are positioned beneath the body, rather than out to the sides. This arrangement allows for direct support and easy, flexible movement. The bones of the limbs have joints constructed to permit growth in the young while simultaneously providing strong, hard joint surfaces that will stand up to the stresses of sustained activity. Mammals stop growing when they reach adulthood, whereas reptiles continue to grow throughout their lifespan.

Mammals and reptiles also differ in terms of their teeth. Reptilian teeth are pointed, peglike, and nearly identical in shape; mammalian teeth are specialized for particular purposes: incisors for nipping, gnawing, and cutting; canines for ripping, tearing, killing, and fighting; premolars for either slicing and tearing or crushing and grinding (depending on the kind of animal); and molars for crushing and grinding (**Figure 3.3**). This enables mammals to eat a wide variety of foods—an advantage given that they require more food than reptiles to sustain their high activity level.

But mammals pay a price for their dental specialization: Reptiles can repeatedly replace teeth throughout their lifespan, whereas mammals are limited to two sets. The first set serves the immature animal and is replaced by the "permanent" or adult teeth. The specializations of mammalian teeth allow species and evolutionary relationships to be identified through dental comparisons.

The earliest primatelike creatures emerged when a milder climate returned favoring the spread of dense tropical and

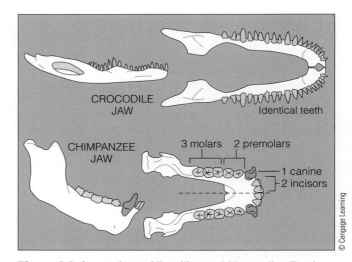

Figure 3.3 Comparison of Reptilian and Mammalian Teeth
The crocodile jaw, like the jaw of all reptiles, contains a series of nearly identical teeth. If a tooth breaks or falls out, a new tooth will emerge in its place. Mammals, by contrast, possess precise numbers of specialized teeth, each with a particular shape characteristic of the group, as indicated on the chimpanzee jaw: Incisors in front are shown in blue, canines behind in red, followed by two premolars and three molars in yellow (the last being the wisdom teeth in humans).

subtropical forests over much of the earth. The change in climate and habitat, combined with the earlier sudden extinction of dinosaurs, favored mammal diversification, including the evolutionary development of **arboreal** (tree-living) mammals from which primates evolved.

The ancestral primates possessed biological characteristics that allowed them to adapt to life in the forests. Their relatively small size enabled them to use tree branches not accessible to larger competitors and predators. Arboreal life opened up an abundant new food supply. The primates could gather leaves, flowers, fruits, insects, birds' eggs, and even nesting birds, rather than having to wait for them to fall to the ground. Natural selection favored those who judged depth correctly and gripped the branches tightly. Those individuals who survived life in the trees passed on their genes to succeeding generations.

Although the earliest primates were nocturnal, today most primate species are **diurnal**—active in the day. The transition to diurnal life in the trees involved important biological adjustments that helped shape the biology and behavior of humans today.

---

k-selected Reproduction involving the production of relatively few offspring with high parental investment in each.
r-selected Reproduction involving the production of large numbers of offspring with relatively low parental investment in each.
arboreal Living in the trees.
diurnal Active during the day and at rest at night.

Primate Taxonomy

Taxonomies reflect scientists' understanding of the natural world. Because scientific knowledge of evolutionary relationships among living things shifts over time, these classificatory systems are continually under construction. With new scientific discoveries, taxonomic categories have to be redrawn, and scientists often disagree about these categorical distinctions.

Taxonomies become contentious because classificatory systems make statements about evolutionary relationships. When creating a taxonomic grouping, scientists pay particular attention to features appearing more recently in evolutionary history that are unique to a group, calling these features **derived**. By contrast, **ancestral** characteristics occur not only in the present-day species but also in ancient forms. For example, bilateral symmetry, a body plan in which the right and left sides of the body are mirror images of each other, is an ancestral trait in humans. Because bilateral symmetry characterizes all vertebrates including fish, reptiles, birds, and mammals, it does not contribute to the reconstruction of evolutionary relationships among primates. Instead, scientists pay particular attention to recently evolved derived features in order to construct evolutionary relationships.

Convergent evolution—in which two more distant forms develop similarities to one another due to similar function rather than to shared ancestry—complicates taxonomic analyses. The classic examples of convergence involve analogies discussed in Chapter 2, such as the wings of birds and butterflies, which resemble each other because these structures serve similar functions. Convergent evolution occurs when an environment exerts similar pressures on distantly related organisms causing these species to resemble each other. Distinguishing the physical similarities produced by convergent evolution from those resulting from shared ancestry may be difficult.

Among more closely related groups, convergence of homologous structures can occur, such as when an identical structure present within several distinct species takes on a similar form in distantly related groups. Among the primates, an example is hind-leg dominance in both lemurs—a primate group found on Madagascar, an isolated but large island off the coast of Africa—and humans. Most primates possess hind limbs that are either shorter or of the same length as the forelimbs. Though their relationship is quite distant among the primates, lemurs and humans both have longer hind limbs because of their patterns of locomotion (**Figure 3.4**). Humans walk on two legs, while lemurs use their long legs to push off and propel them from tree to tree. Hind-leg dominance appeared separately in these two groups and is not indicative of a close evolutionary relationship. Only shared derived features can be used to establish relationships among groups of species.

Scientists have proposed alternate taxonomies to account for two hot spots in the classification of primates: one at the level of dividing the primate order into two suborders and the other at the level of the human family and subfamily. In both cases, the older classificatory systems, dating back to the time of Linnaeus, derive from shared visible physical characteristics. By contrast, the

Anup Shah/Getty Images/The Image Bank

Figure 3.4 Long-Legged Lemurs Lemurs, like humans, have longer hind limbs (legs) compared to their forelimbs (arms). Convergent evolution, rather than an especially close evolutionary relationship, accounts for this visible similarity. Long-legged lemurs move through the trees through vertical clinging and leaping, a mode of locomotion by which they cling to a tree trunk, push off with their powerful legs, do a "180," and grab another trunk. Human locomotion likewise benefits from long legs, but this characteristic evolved independently in these two primate groups.

newer taxonomic systems depend upon genetic analyses. Although molecular evidence has confirmed the close relationship between humans and other primates, these genetic comparisons have also challenged evolutionary relationships that had been inferred from physical characteristics. Laboratory methods involving genetic comparisons range from scanning species' entire genomes to comparing the precise sequences of base pairs in DNA, RNA, or amino acids in proteins.

Both genetic and morphological (body form and structure) data are useful. Biologists refer to the overall similarity

derived Characteristics that define a group of organisms and that did not exist in ancestral populations.

ancestral Characteristics that define a group of organisms that are due to shared ancestry.

convergent evolution In biological evolution, a process by which unrelated populations develop similarities to one another due to similar function rather than shared ancestry.

TABLE 3.1

Two Alternative Taxonomies for the Primate Order: Differing Placement of Tarsiers

Suborder	Infraorder	Superfamily (Family)	Location
I.			
Prosimii	Lemuriformes	Lemuroidea (lemurs, indriids, and aye-ayes)	Madagascar
(lower primates)	Lorisiformes	Lorisoidea (lorises)	Asia and Africa
		Tarsioidea (tarsiers)	Asia
Anthropoidea	Platyrrhini (New World monkeys)	Ceboidea	Tropical Americas
(higher primates)	Catarrhini	Cercopithecoidea (Old World monkeys)	Africa and Asia
		Hominoidea (apes and humans)	Africa and Asia (humans worldwide)
II.			
Strepsirhini	Lemuriformes	Lemuroidea (lemurs, indriids, and aye-ayes)	Madagascar
	Lorisiformes	Lorisoidea (lorises)	Asia and Africa
Haplorhini	Tarsiiformes	Tarsioidea (tarsiers)	Asia
	Platyrrhini (New World monkeys)	Ceboidea	Tropical Americas
	Catarrhini	Cercopithecoidea (Old World monkeys)	Africa and Asia
		Hominoidea (apes and humans)	Africa and Asia (humans worldwide)

© Cengage Learning

of body plans within taxonomic groupings as a **grade**. The examination of shared sequences of DNA and RNA allows researchers to establish a **clade**, a taxonomic grouping that contains a single common ancestor and all of its descendants. Genetic analyses allow for precise quantification, but it is not always clear what the numbers mean (recall the Original Study from Chapter 2).

© Cengage Learning

The Linnaean system divides primates into two suborders: the **prosimians** (Prosimii, from the Latin for "before monkeys"), which includes lemurs, lorises, and tarsiers, and the **anthropoids** (Anthropoidea, from the Greek for "humanlike"), which includes monkeys, apes, and humans. Some call prosimians the "lower primates" because they resemble the earliest fossil primates. On the whole, most prosimians are cat-sized or smaller, although some larger forms existed in the past. The prosimians also retain certain ancestral features common among nonprimate mammals that the anthropoids have lost over time, such as claws and moist, naked skin on their noses.

In Asia and Africa, all prosimians are nocturnal and arboreal creatures—again, like the fossil primates. However, a variety of diurnal ground-dwelling prosimians inhabit the island of Madagascar. In the rest of the world, the diurnal primates are all anthropoids. This group is sometimes called the "higher primates" because they appeared later in evolutionary history and because of a lingering belief that the group including humans was more "evolved." From a contemporary biological perspective, no species is more evolved than any other.

Molecular evidence led to the proposal of a new primate taxonomy (**Table 3.1**). A close genetic relationship was discovered between the tarsiers—nocturnal tree-dwellers who resemble lemurs and lorises—and monkeys and apes (Goodman et al., 1994). The taxonomic scheme reflecting this genetic relationship places lemurs and lorises in the subdivision **strepsirhine** (Strepsirhini, from the Greek for "turned nose"). In turn, the subdivision **haplorhine** (Haplorhini, Greek for "simple nose") contains the tarsiers, monkeys, and apes. Tarsiers are separated from monkeys and apes at the infraorder level in this taxonomic scheme. Although this classificatory scheme accurately reflects genetic relationships, comparisons among grades, or general levels of organization, in the older prosimian and anthropoid classification make more sense when examining morphology and lifeways.

grade A general level of biological organization seen among a group of species; useful for constructing evolutionary relationships.

clade A taxonomic grouping that contains a single common ancestor and all of its descendants.

prosimians The suborder of primates that includes lemurs, lorises, and tarsiers.

anthropoids The suborder of primates that includes New World monkeys, Old World monkeys, and apes (including humans).

strepsirhines The subdivision within the primate order based on shared genetic characteristics; includes lemurs and lorises.

haplorhines The subdivision within the primate order based on shared genetic characteristics; includes tarsiers, New World monkeys, Old World monkeys, and apes (including humans).

The older taxonomic scheme divides the anthropoid suborder into two infraorders: the **platyrrhines** (*Platyrrhini,* Greek for "flat-nosed"), or New World monkeys, and the **catarrhines** (*Catarrhini,* Greek for "drooping nose"), consisting of the superfamilies Cercopithecoidea (Old World monkeys) and Hominoidea (apes). Although the terms *New World* and *Old World* reflect a Eurocentric vision of history (whereby the Americas were considered new only to European explorers and not to the indigenous people already living there), these terms have evolutionary and geologic relevance with respect to primates, as we will see in Chapters 5 and 6. Old World monkeys and apes, including humans, have a 40-million-year shared evolutionary history in Africa distinct from the course taken by anthropoid primates in the tropical Americas. "Old World" in this context represents the evolutionary origins of anthropoid primates rather than a political or historical focus on Europe.

In terms of human evolution, most of the taxonomic controversy derives from relationships established by the molecular evidence among the hominoids. Humans are placed in the **hominoid** or ape superfamily—with gibbons, siamangs, orangutans, gorillas, chimpanzees, and bonobos—due to physical similarities such as broad shoulders, absent tail, and long arms. Human characteristics such as bipedalism (walking on two legs) and culture led scientists to think that all the other apes were more closely related to one another than any of them were to humans. Thus, humans and their ancestors were classified in the **hominid** family to distinguish them from the other apes.

Advances in molecular analysis of blood proteins and DNA later demonstrated that humans are more closely related to African apes (chimps, bonobos, and gorillas) than we are to orangutans and the smaller apes (siamangs and gibbons). Some scientists then proposed that African apes should be included in the hominid family, with humans and their ancestors distinguished from the other African hominoids at the taxonomic level of subfamily, as **hominins** (Figure 3.5).

Although all scientists today agree about the close relationship among humans, chimpanzees, bonobos, and gorillas, they differ as to whether they use the term *hominid* or *hominin* to describe the taxonomic grouping of humans and their ancestors. Museum displays and much of the popular press tend to retain the old term *hominid,* emphasizing the visible differences between humans and the other African apes. Scientists and publications using *hominin* (such as *National Geographic*) emphasize the importance of genetics in establishing relationships among species. More than name games, these word choices reflect theoretical relationships among closely related species.

Though the DNA sequences of humans and African apes are 98 percent identical, the organization of DNA into chromosomes differs between humans and the other

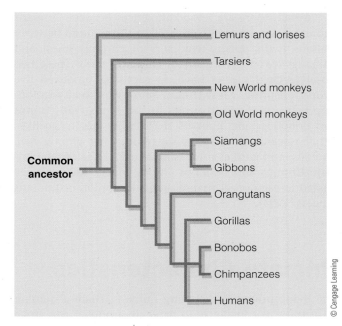

Figure 3.5 **Relationships among the Primates** Molecular evidence establishes these relationships among various primate groups. This evidence shows that tarsiers are more closely related to monkeys and apes than to the lemurs and lorises that they resemble physically. Present thinking is that the split between the human and African ape lines took place between 5 and 8 million years ago.

great apes. Bonobos and chimps, like gorillas and orangutans, possess an extra pair of chromosomes compared to humans, in which two medium-sized chromosomes have fused together to form chromosome 2. Chromosomes are numbered according to their size as they are viewed microscopically, so that chromosome 2 is the second largest of the human chromosomes (recall Figure 2.7). Of the other pairs, eighteen are virtually identical between humans and the African apes, whereas the remaining ones have been reshuffled.

platyrrhines The primate infraorder that includes New World monkeys.

catarrhines The primate infraorder that includes Old World monkeys, apes, and humans.

hominoid The taxonomic division superfamily within the Old World primates that includes gibbons, siamangs, orangutans, gorillas, chimpanzees, bonobos, and humans.

hominid African hominoid family that includes humans and their ancestors. Some scientists, recognizing the close relationship of humans, chimps, bonobos, and gorillas, use the term *hominid* to refer to all African hominoids. They then divide the hominid family into two subfamilies: the Paninae (chimps, bonobos, and gorillas) and the Homininae (humans and their ancestors).

hominin The taxonomic subfamily or tribe within the primates that includes humans and our ancestors.

Overall, there are fewer differences between humans and other African apes compared to those found between gibbons (with twenty-two pairs of chromosomes) and siamangs (twenty-five pairs of chromosomes). These two closely related species have, in captivity, produced live hybrid offspring. Most studies suggest a closer relationship between the two species in the genus *Pan* (chimps and bonobos) and humans than either has to gorillas. Other researchers disagree, suggesting that among *Pan*, humans, and gorillas there is an equal degree of relationship. Chimps and bonobos are, of course, more closely related to each other than either is to gorillas or humans (Rogers, 1994).

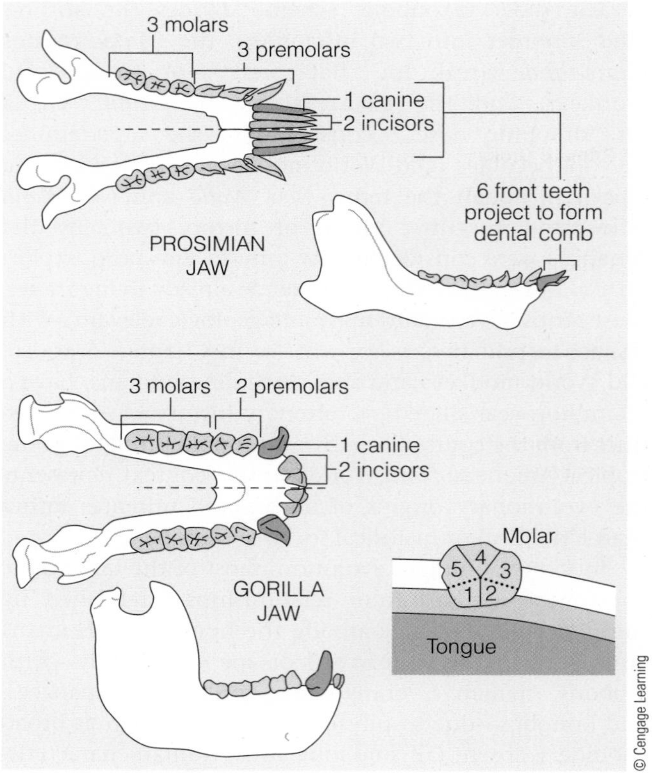

Primate Characteristics

The living primates, including humans, share a number of features. For instance, in baseball, a pitcher can strike out a batter due to the primate characteristics of grasping, throwing, and seeing in three dimensions. Compared to other mammals, primates possess a relatively unspecialized anatomy combined with diverse and flexible behavioral patterns.

Many primate characteristics developed from their arboreal niche. For animals preying upon the many insects living on the fruit and flowers of trees and shrubs, dexterous hands and keen vision would have been enormously adaptive. Life in the trees, along with the visual predation of insects, played a role in the evolution of primate biology.

Primate Teeth

The varied diet available to arboreal primates—shoots, leaves, insects, and fruits—did not require the specialization of teeth seen in other mammals. In most primates (humans included), on each side of each jaw, in front, are two straight-edged, chisel-like broad teeth called incisors (**Figure 3.6**). A large flaring and often fanglike canine tooth lies behind each incisor. The canines are used for defense as well as for tearing and shredding food.

Humans possess relatively small canine teeth with oversized roots, suggestive of larger canines some time back in our ancestry. Behind the canines, the premolars and molars (the "cheek teeth") grind and chew food. Molars erupt through the gums over the course of a young primate's growth and development (6-year molars,

Figure 3.6 Primate Dentition Because the exact number and shape of the teeth differ among primate groups, teeth are frequently used to identify evolutionary relationships and group membership. Prosimians (*top*), with a dental formula of 2-1-3-3, possess two incisors, one canine, three premolars, and three molars on each side of their upper and lower jaws. Also, lower canines and incisors project forward, forming a "dental comb," which is used for grooming. A dental formula of 2-1-2-3, typical of Old World monkeys and apes, can be seen in the gorilla jaw (*bottom*). Note the large projecting canines. On one of the molars, the cusps are numbered to illustrate the Y5 pattern found in hominoids.

12-year molars, and wisdom teeth in humans). Thus, the functions of grasping, cutting, and grinding were served by different kinds of teeth. The exact number of premolars and molars and the shape of individual teeth differ among primate groups (**Table 3.2**).

The course of primate evolution includes a trend toward a reduction in the number and size of the teeth. The ancestral **dental formula**, or pattern of tooth type and number in mammals, consists of three incisors, one canine, five premolars, and three molars (expressed as 3-1-5-3) on each side of the jaw, top and bottom, for a total of forty-eight teeth. In the early stages of primate evolution, one incisor and one premolar were lost on each side of each jaw, resulting in a dental pattern of 2-1-4-3 in the early fossil primates. This change differentiated primates from other mammals.

---

dental formula The number of each tooth type (incisors, canines, premolars, and molars) on one half of each jaw. Unlike other mammals, primates possess equal numbers on their upper and lower jaws so the dental formula for the species is a single series of numbers.

TABLE 3.2

Primate Anatomical Variation and Specialization

Primate Group	Skull and Face	Dental Formula and Specializations	Locomotor Pattern and Morphology	Tail and Other Skeletal Specializations
Earliest fossil primates	Eye not fully surrounded by bone	2-1-4-3		
Prosimians	Complete ring of bone surrounding eye Upper lip bound down to the gum Long snout	2-1-3-3 Dental comb for grooming	Hind-leg dominance for vertical clinging and leaping	Tail present
Anthropoids	Forward-facing eyes fully enclosed in bone Free upper lip Shorter snout			
New World monkeys		2-1-3-3	Quadrupedal	Prehensile (grasping) tail in some
Old World monkeys		2-1-2-3 Four-cusped molars	Quadrupedal	Tail present
Apes		2-1-2-3 Y5 molars on lower jaw	Suspensory hanging apparatus	No tail

© Cengage Learning

Over the millennia, as the first and second premolars became smaller and eventually disappeared altogether, the third and fourth premolars grew larger and added a second pointed projection, or cusp, thus becoming "bicuspid." In humans, all eight premolars are bicuspid, but in other Old World anthropoids, the lower first premolar is not bicuspid. Instead, it is a specialized, single-cusped tooth with a sharp edge to act with the upper canine as a shearing mechanism. The molars, meanwhile, evolved from a three-cusp pattern to one with four and even five cusps. The five-cusp pattern is characteristic of the lower molars of living and extinct hominoids (for instance, the mandrill in **Figure 3.7**). Because the grooves separating the five cusps of a hominoid lower molar looks like the letter Y, hominoid lower molars are said to have a Y5 pattern. Humans have departed somewhat from the Y5 pattern as tooth and jaw size reduced such that the second and third molars generally have only four cusps. Four- and five-cusp molars economically combined the functions of grasping, cutting, and grinding in one tooth.

The evolutionary trend for human dentition has generally been toward economy, with fewer, smaller, more efficient teeth doing more work. With thirty-two teeth (a 2-1-2-3 dental formula shared with the Old World monkeys and apes), we possess fewer teeth than some primates. However, this trend does not indicate that species with more teeth are less evolved; it only shows that their evolution followed a different path.

The canines of most primates develop into long daggerlike teeth that enable them to rip open tough husks of fruit and other foods (Figure 3.7). In many species, males possess larger canine teeth compared to females. This

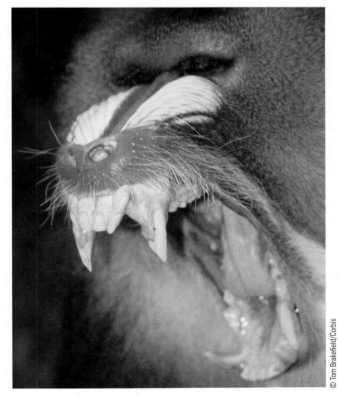

© Tom Brakefield/Corbis

Figure 3.7 Powerful Canines Though the massive canine teeth of some male primates are serious weapons, they are more often used to communicate rather than to draw blood. Raising his lip to flash his canines, this mandrill will get the young members of his group in line right away. Over the course of human evolution, overall canine size decreased as did differences in canine size between males and females.

sex difference is an example of **sexual dimorphism**—differences between the sexes in the shape or size of a feature. Adult males frequently use these large canines for social communication. If an adult male gorilla, baboon, or mandrill raises his upper lip to display his large, sharp canines, a youngster becomes submissive.

Primate Sensory Organs

The primates' adaptation to arboreal life involved changes in the form and function of their sensory organs. The sense of smell was vital for the earliest ground-dwelling, night-active mammals. It enabled them to operate in the dark, to sniff out their food, and to detect hidden predators. However, for active tree life during daylight, good vision is a better guide than smell in judging the location of the next branch or tasty morsel. Accordingly, the sense of smell declined in primates, while vision became highly developed.

Travel through the trees demands judgments concerning depth, direction, distance, and the relationships of objects hanging in space, such as vines or branches. Monkeys, apes, and humans achieved this through binocular stereoscopic color vision (**Figure 3.8**), the ability to see the world in the three dimensions of height, width, and depth. **Binocular vision** (in which two eyes sit next to each other on the same plane so that their visual fields overlap) and nerve connections that run from each eye to both sides of the brain confer complete depth perception characteristic of three-dimensional or **stereoscopic vision**. This arrangement allows nerve cells to integrate the images derived from each eye. Increased brain size in the visual area in primates, and a greater complexity at nerve connections, also contribute to stereoscopic color vision.

Visual acuity, however, varies throughout the primate order in terms of both color and spatial perception. Prosimians, most of whom are nocturnal, lack color vision. The eyes of lemurs and lorises (but not tarsiers) are capable of reflecting light off the retina, the surface where nerve fibers gather images in the back of the eye to intensify the limited light available in the forest at night. In

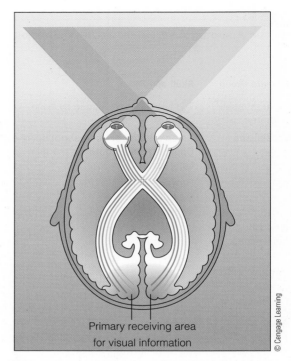

Primary receiving area
for visual information

© Cengage Learning

Figure 3.8 Primate Vision Monkeys, apes, and humans possess binocular stereoscopic vision. Binocular vision refers to overlapping visual fields due to forward-facing eyes. Three-dimensional or stereoscopic vision comes from binocular vision and the transmission of information from each eye to both sides of the brain.

addition, prosimian vision is binocular without the benefits of stereoscopy. Their eyes look out from either side of their muzzle or snout. Though there is some overlap of visual fields, their nerve fibers do not cross from each eye to both halves of the brain.

By contrast, monkeys, apes, and humans possess both color and stereoscopic vision. Color vision markedly improves the diet of these primates compared to most other mammals. The ability to distinguish colors allows anthropoid primates to choose ripe fruits or tender, immature leaves due to their red rather than green coloration. See this chapter's Biocultural Connection to see how our primate ancestry affects our response to color.

In addition to color vision, anthropoid primates possess a unique structure called the **fovea centralis**, or central pit, in the retina of each eye. Like a camera lens, this feature enables the animal to focus on a particular object for acutely clear perception without sacrificing visual contact with the object's surroundings.

The primates' emphasis on visual acuity came at the expense of their sense of smell. Smells are processed in the forebrain, and in animals that depend greatly on the sense of smell, the forebrain projects into the snout. A large protruding snout, however, interferes with stereoscopic vision. But as primates became diurnal tree-dwelling

---

sexual dimorphism Within a single species, differences between males and females in the shape or size of a feature not directly related to reproduction, such as body size or canine tooth shape and size.

binocular vision Vision with increased depth perception from two eyes set next to each other, allowing their visual fields to overlap.

stereoscopic vision Complete three-dimensional vision, or depth perception, from binocular vision and nerve connections that run from each eye to both sides of the brain, allowing nerve cells to integrate the images derived from each eye.

fovea centralis A shallow pit in the retina of the eye that enables an animal to focus on an object while maintaining visual contact with its surroundings.

BIOCULTURAL CONNECTION

Why Red Is Such a Potent Color

By Meredith F. Small

The Olympic athletes have been parading around like fashionistas in an array of colorful outfits, and we, their adoring public, can't resist commenting on the style and color of their high-end athletic wear. My favorite was the faux silk, faux embroidered, slinky red leotards of the Chinese women's gymnasts.

Apparently, as researchers have recently discovered, the choice of red for those leotards might also have given the Chinese gymnasts an advantage. But why is the color red so impressive?

The answer lies in our tree-living past.

The human response to the color red may well be rooted in our anthropoid heritage. Could this have given an edge to the Chinese gymnastic team? It is certain that our ape ancestry contributes to the human range of motion. Although we are all not able to move in the same ways that these talented gymnasts can, the human ability to grasp, swing, stretch, and throw things derives from characteristics of the hands and shoulders inherited from our ape ancestors.

In the back of the vertebrate eyeball are two kinds of cells called rods and cones that respond to light. Cones take in a wide range of light, which means they recognize colors, and they are stimulated best during daylight. Rods respond to a narrower range of light (meaning only white light) but notice that light from far away and at night.

Isaac Newton was the first person to hold up a prism and refract white light into a rainbow of colors and realize that there might be variation in what the eye can see. Color comes at us in electromagnetic waves. When the wavelength of light is short we perceive purple or blue. Medium wavelengths of lights tickle the cones in another way and we think green. Short light wavelengths make those cones stand up and dance as bright spots of yellow, orange, and red.

Various animals distinguish only parts of that rainbow because their cones respond in different ways. Butterflies, for example, see into the ultraviolet end of the rainbow, which allows them to see their own complex markings better than we can. Foxes and owls are basically colorblind, and it doesn't matter because they are awake at night when the light spectrum is limited anyway.

Humans are lucky enough to be primates, animals with decent color vision, and we can thank monkeys for this special ability.

Long ago, primitive primates that resemble today's lemurs and lorises saw only green and blue, the longer wavelengths of color. But when monkeys evolved, around 34 million years ago, their cones became sensitive to even shorter wavelengths of color and they saw red.

And what a difference. With red, the forest comes alive. Instead of a blanket of bluish-green leaves, the world is suddenly accented with ripe red, yellow, and orange fruits, and even the leaves look different.

For a monkey leaping through the forest canopy, color vision would be an essential advantage. Unripe fruit doesn't have enough carbs to sustain a hungry primate, and they taste really sour. Unripe leaves not only taste bad, they are toxic and indigestible.

For the first humans foraging about the forest and savannah around 5 million years ago, it would have been much more efficient to spot a ripe fruit or tuber than bite into a zillion just to get the right one. And so humans ended up with color vision even though we no longer live in trees.

But color is more than wavelengths, more than an indicator of ripeness, to us.

Color has become symbolic, meaning it has meaning, and that meaning is highly cultural.

Chinese athletes and Chinese brides wear red because red is considered lucky. The U.S. athletes also wear red because that bright color is in the U.S. flag, and because designers of athletic wear, as well as scientists, know that red gets you noticed.

BIOCULTURAL QUESTION

While the vast majority of humans see color as described here, 8 to 20 percent of human males have red-green color blindness. Do you know someone who is colorblind? What could a conversation with a colorblind person reveal about the anthropological perspective? What colors besides red have particular meanings? Do these meanings derive from biology or culture?

Adapted from Small, M. F. (2008, August 15). Why red is such a potent color. LiveScience. www.livescience.com/ 5043-red-potent-color.html (retrieved June 20, 2012). Reprinted by permission.

© Cheng Min/Xinhua/Landov

animals in search of insects, they no longer needed to live a "nose to the ground" existence, sniffing the earth in search of food. The anthropoids especially have the least-developed sense of smell of all land animals. Though our sense of smell allows humans to distinguish perfumes, and even to distinguish family members from strangers, our brains have come to emphasize vision rather than smell. Prosimians, by contrast, still rely more on smell than on vision, and they possess numerous scent glands for marking objects in their territories.

Arboreal primates also have an acute sense of touch. An effective feeling and grasping mechanism helps prevent them from falling and tumbling while speeding through the trees. The early mammals from which primates evolved possessed tiny touch-sensitive hairs at the tips of their hands and feet. In primates, sensitive pads backed up by nails on the tips of the animals' fingers and toes replaced these hairs.

The Primate Brain

These changes in sensory organs have corresponding changes in the primate brain. In addition, an increase in brain size, particularly in the cerebral hemispheres—the areas supporting conscious thought—occurred in the course of primate evolution. In monkeys, apes, and humans, the cerebral hemispheres completely cover the cerebellum, the part of the brain that coordinates the muscles and maintains body balance.

In turn, this development led to the flexibility seen in primate behavior. Rather than relying on reflexes controlled by the cerebellum, primates constantly react to a variety of features in the environment. Messages from the hands and feet, eyes and ears, and from the sensors of balance, movement, heat, touch, and pain are simultaneously relayed to the cerebral cortex. The cortex had to evolve considerably in order to receive, analyze, and coordinate these impressions and transmit the appropriate response back down to the motor nerves. This enlarged, responsive cerebral cortex provides the biological basis for flexible behavior patterns found in all primates, including humans.

The increased learning capacity of the primate brain likely started as the earliest primates, along with many other mammals, began to carry out their activities in the daylight hours. Prior to 65 million years ago, mammals seem to have been nocturnal in their habits. The extinction of the dinosaurs and climate change at that time opened new ecological niches. With the change to a diurnal

life, the sense of vision took on greater importance, and so visual acuity was favored by natural selection. Unlike reptiles, who process visual information with neurons in the retina, mammals process visual information in the brain, permitting integration with information received through other senses such as sound, touch, taste, and smell.

If the evolution of visual acuity led to larger brains, it is likely that the primates' insect predation in an arboreal setting also played a role in enlargement of the brain. This would have required great agility and muscular coordination, favoring development of the brain centers. Interestingly, many higher mental faculties developed in an area alongside the motor centers of the brain (Romer, 1945).

Another hypothesis that may account for primate brain enlargement involves the use of hands as tactile instruments to replace the teeth and jaws or snout. The hands assumed some of the grasping, tearing, and dividing functions of the jaws, again requiring development of the brain centers for more complete coordination.

The Primate Skeleton

The skeleton gives animals with internal backbones, or **vertebrates**, their basic shape or silhouette, supports the soft tissues, and helps protect vital internal organs (**Figure 3.9**). In primates, for example, the skull protects the brain and the eyes. A number of factors are responsible for the shape of the primate skull as compared with those of most other mammals: changes in dentition, changes in the sensory organs of sight and smell, and increased brain size.

The primate braincase, or **cranium**, tends to be high and vaulted. Anthropoid primates have a solid partition between the eye and the temple, affording maximum protection to the eyes from the contraction of the chewing muscles, which are positioned directly next to the eyes.

The **foramen magnum** (the large opening at the base of the skull through which the spinal cord passes and connects to the brain) provides important clues about evolutionary relationships. In most mammals, as in dogs and horses, this opening faces directly backward, with the skull projecting forward from the vertebral column. In humans, by contrast, the vertebral column joins the skull toward the center of its base, thereby placing the skull in a balanced position as required for habitual upright posture. Other primates, though they frequently cling, sit, or hang with their body upright, are not as fully committed to upright posture as humans, and so their foramen magnum is not as far forward.

In anthropoid primates, the snout or muzzle portion of the skull reduced as the acuity of the sense of smell declined. The smaller snout offers less interference with stereoscopic vision; it also enables the eyes to take a frontal position. As a result, primates have flatter faces than some other mammals.

vertebrates Animals with a backbone, including fish, amphibians, reptiles, birds, and mammals.

cranium The braincase of the skull.

foramen magnum A large opening in the skull through which the spinal cord passes and connects to the brain.

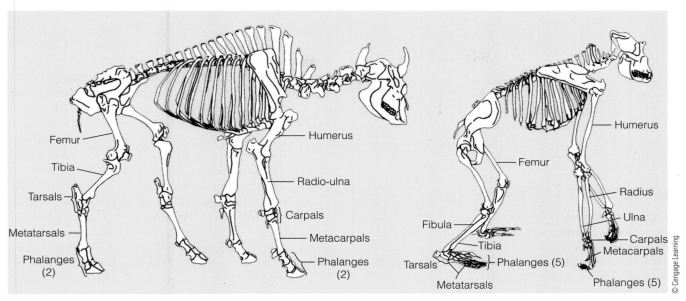

Figure 3.9 Skeletal Comparisons of Gorilla and Bison All primates possess the same ancestral vertebrate limb pattern seen in reptiles and amphibians, consisting of a single upper long bone, two lower long bones, and five radiating digits (fingers and toes), as seen in this gorilla skeleton (*right*). Other mammals such as bison (*left*) have a modified version of this pattern. In the course of evolution, bison have lost all but two of their digits, which form their hooves. The second long bone in the lower part of the limb is reduced. Note also the joining of the skull and vertebral column in these skeletons. In bison (as in most mammals) the skull projects forward from the vertebral column, but in semi-erect gorillas, the vertebral column is further beneath the skull.

Below the primate skull and the neck is the **clavicle**, or collarbone, a bone found in ancestral mammals though lost in some mammals such as cats. The size of the clavicle varies across the primate order according to pattern of locomotion. Quadrupedal primates like monkeys with a narrow, sturdy body plan possess smaller clavicles. Apes, by contrast, have broad clavicles that orient the arms at the side rather than at the front of the body and form part of the **suspensory hanging apparatus** of this group (see Table 3.2). The clavicle also supports the **scapula** (shoulder blade) and muscles required for flexible yet powerful arm movement—permitting large-bodied apes to hang suspended below tree branches and to move through **brachiation**, or swinging from tree to tree.

The limbs of the primate skeleton follow the same basic ancestral plan seen in the earliest vertebrates. Other animals possess limbs specialized to optimize a particular behavior, such as speed. In each primate arm or leg, the upper portion of the limb has a single long bone, the lower portion two long bones, and then hands or feet with five radiating digits (phalanges). Their grasping feet and hands have sensitive pads at the tips of their digits, backed up (except in some prosimians) by flattened nails. This unique combination of pad and nail provides the animal with an excellent **prehensile** (grasping) device for use when moving from branch to branch. The structural characteristics of the primate foot and hand make grasping possible; the digits are extremely flexible, the big toe is fully **opposable** to the other digits in all but humans and

their immediate ancestors, and the thumb is opposable to the other digits to varying degrees.

The retention of the flexible vertebrate limb pattern in primates was a valuable asset to evolving humans. It was, in part, having hands capable of grasping that enabled our own ancestors to manufacture and use tools and to embark on the pathway that led to the revolutionary ability to adapt through culture.

To sum up, a comparison of humans to other primates reveals how many of the characteristics we consider distinctly human are not in fact unique to us; rather, they are variants of typical primate traits. We humans look the way we do because we are primates, and the differences between us and our primate cousins—especially the apes—are more differences of degree than differences of kind.

clavicle The collarbone connecting the sternum (breastbone) with the scapula (shoulder blade).

suspensory hanging apparatus The broad powerful shoulder joints and muscles found in all the hominoids, allowing these large-bodied primates to hang suspended below the tree branches.

scapula The shoulder blade.

brachiation Moving from branch to branch using the arms, with the body hanging suspended below.

prehensile Having the ability to grasp.

opposable Having the ability to bring the thumb or big toe in contact with the tips of the other digits on the same hand or foot in order to grasp objects.

Living Primates

Except for a few species of Old World monkeys who live in temperate climates and humans who inhabit the entire globe, living primates inhabit warm areas of the world. We will briefly explore the diversity of the five natural groupings of living primates: lemurs and lorises, tarsiers, New World monkeys, Old World monkeys, and apes. We will examine each group's distinctive habitat, biological features, and behavior.

Lemurs and Lorises

Although the natural habitat of lemurs is restricted to the large island of Madagascar (off the east coast of Africa), lorises range from Africa to southern and eastern Asia. Only on Madagascar, where there was no competition from anthropoid primates until humans arrived, are lemurs diurnal, or active during the day; lorises, by contrast, are all nocturnal and arboreal (**Figure 3.10**).

All these animals are small, with none larger than a good-sized dog. In general body outline, they resemble rodents and insectivores, with short pointed snouts, large pointed ears, and big eyes. In the anatomy of the upper lip and snout, lemurs and lorises resemble nonprimate mammals in that the upper lip is bound down to the gums, thus limiting their range of facial expression. The split, moist naked skin on the nose around the nostrils facilitates a keen sense of smell. Most also have long tails, with that of a ring-tailed lemur somewhat like that of a raccoon.

Lemurs and lorises have typical primate "hands," although they use them in pairs, rather than one at a time. Their fingers and toes are particularly strong with sensitive pads and flattened nails located at their tips. However, they retain a claw on their second toe, sometimes called a grooming claw, which they use for scratching and cleaning. Lemurs and lorises possess another unique structure for grooming: a dental comb made up of the lower incisors and canines, which projects forward from the jaw and can be run through the fur. Behind the incisors and canines, lemurs and lorises have three premolars and molars, resulting in a dental formula of 2-1-3-3.

Lemurs and lorises have scent glands at their wrists, under their arms, and sometimes in their anal region that they use for communication. Individuals leave smelly messages for one another by rubbing their scent glands on tree branches or some other fixture of the environment. Through such olfactory clues, lemurs and lorises can recognize distinct individuals within their own group as well as pinpoint their location and physical state. They also use scent to mark their territory, thus communicating to members of other groups.

With hind legs longer than their front legs, lemurs and lorises keep their forelimbs in a palms-down position when they move on all fours. As mentioned previously, some species can also move from tree to tree by vertical clinging and leaping. With their distinctive mix of characteristics, lemurs and lorises appear to occupy a place between the anthropoid primates and insectivores, the mammalian order that includes moles and shrews.

VISUAL COUNTERPOINT

Figure 3.10 **Lemurs and Lorises** Wherever there is competition from the anthropoid primates, prosimian species, such as this loris on the right, retain the arboreal nocturnal patterns of the earliest fossil primates. Notice its large eyes, long snout, and moist split nose—all useful in its relatively solitary search for food in the trees at night. In contrast, only on the large island of Madagascar off the eastern coast of Africa, where no anthropoids existed until humans arrived, have prosimians come to occupy the diurnal ground-dwelling niche as do these ring-tailed lemurs. While all prosimians still rely on scent, marking their territory and communicating through smelly messages, daytime activity allowed the prosimians on Madagascar to become far less solitary. Also notice the difference in the size of the eyes in these two groups. Just as it would be incorrect to think of prosimians as "less evolved" than anthropoid primates because they bear a closer resemblance to the ancestral primate condition, it is also incorrect to think of lorises as less evolved compared to lemurs.

Tarsiers

Outwardly, tarsiers resemble lemurs and lorises (**Figure 3.11**). Molecular evidence, however, indicates a closer relationship to monkeys, apes, and humans. The head, eyes, and ears of these kitten-sized arboreal creatures are huge in proportion to the body. They have the remarkable ability to turn their heads 180 degrees, so they can see where they have been as well as where they are going. Their digits end in platelike adhesive discs.

Tarsiers are named for the elongated tarsal, or foot bone, that provides leverage for jumps of 6 feet or more. Tarsiers are mainly nocturnal insect-eaters and so occupy a niche that is similar to that of the earliest ancestral primates. In the structure of the nose and lips and in the part of the brain governing vision, tarsiers resemble monkeys.

Figure 3.11 Tarsiers With their large eyes, tarsiers are well adapted for nocturnal life. If humans possessed eyes proportionally the same size as tarsiers relative to the size of our faces, our eyes would be approximately as big as oranges. In their nocturnal habit and outward appearance, tarsiers resemble lemurs and lorises. Genetically, however, they are more closed related to monkeys and apes, causing scientists to rework the suborder divisions in primate taxonomy to reflect this evolutionary relationship.

New World Monkeys

New World monkeys live in tropical forests of South and Central America. In outward body plan they closely resemble Old World monkeys, except that New World monkeys possess flat noses with widely separated, outward-flaring nostrils. Their infraorder name platyrrhine (from the Greek for "flat-nosed") comes from this characteristic. There are five different families of New World monkeys, and they range in size from less than a pound to over 30 pounds.

New World monkeys have not been studied as extensively as other primates for two reasons. First, because of primatology's emphasis on human origins, researchers have tended to favor Old World species. The second reason is that the arboreal habitat of New World species makes it more difficult for researchers to observe them. In recent decades, however, primatologists have conducted numerous long-range field studies on a variety of species.

For example, anthropologist Karen Strier has studied the woolly spider monkey, or muriqui, in the state of Minas Gerais, Brazil, for close to three decades. Her field studies progressed from examining muriqui diet, social structure, and **demographics** (population characteristics such as the number of individuals of each age and sex) to tracking the reproductive cycles and health of these large, peaceful forest-dwellers. She pioneered a noninvasive method to measure reproductive hormone levels and the presence of parasites through analysis of the feces of individual animals—catching feces (in a gloved hand) the moment it dropped from the trees or quickly retrieving it from the ground. Through analysis of these samples, Strier was able to document correlations between diet and fertility.

Strier also documented a reduced parasite load in muriquis that consumed certain plants—apparently for their medicinal or therapeutic value. Amazonian peoples have been known to use some of these plants for the same reason. As these human populations have become increasingly removed from their traditional lifeways due to globalization and modernization, the muriqui remain a valuable source to reclaim knowledge of the forest.

demographics Population characteristics such as the number of individuals of each age and sex.

According to Strier, "While traditional peoples of the Amazon have survived long enough to impart some of their knowledge of forest plants, the indigenous human societies of the Atlantic forest are long gone. The muriqui and other monkeys may provide humans with their best guides to the forest's medicinal values" (Strier, 1993, p. 42). Field studies like Strier's not only have contributed to our understanding of the behavior and biology of New World monkeys but have also played a major role in bringing back a number of species from the brink of extinction.

New World monkeys—unlike Old World monkeys, apes, and humans—possess a 2-1-3-3 dental formula (three, rather than two, premolars on each side of each jaw). This is not as much a functional distinction as it is a difference in evolutionary path. The common ancestor of Old World anthropoids and New World anthropoids possessed this 2-1-3-3 dental pattern. In the New World this pattern remained, while in Old World species a molar was lost.

Like Old World monkeys, New World monkeys have long tails. All members of one group, the family Atelidae, possess prehensile or grasping tails that they use as a fifth limb (**Figure 3.12**). The naked skin on the underside of their tail resembles the sensitive skin found at the tips of our fingers and is even covered with whorls like fingerprints.

Platyrrhines walk on all fours with their palms down and scamper along tree branches in search of fruit, which they eat sitting upright. Although New World monkeys spend much of their time in the trees, they rarely hang suspended below the branches or swing from limb to limb by their arms and have not developed the extremely long forelimbs and broad shoulders characteristic of the apes.

Old World Monkeys

Divided from the apes at the superfamily taxonomic level, Old World or catarrhine (from the Greek for "sharp-nosed") primates resemble New World monkeys in their basic body plan, but their noses are distinctive, with closely spaced, downward-pointing nostrils. Two subfamilies, the Cercopithecinae and the Colobinae, contain eleven and

Ingo Arndt/Getty Images/Minden Pictures

Figure 3.12 New World Spider Monkey Grasping hands and three-dimensional vision enable primates like this South American spider monkey to lead an active life in the trees. In some New World monkey species, a grasping or prehensile tail makes tree life even easier. The naked skin on the underside of the tail resembles the sensitive skin found at the tips of our fingers and is even covered with whorls like fingerprints. This sensory skin allows New World monkeys to use their tails as a fifth limb.

ten genera, respectively. Old World monkeys occupy a broader range of habitats compared to New World monkey species, which occupy only tropical forests.

Some Old World monkeys such as mandrills (pictured in Figure 3.7) have brightly colored faces and genitals. Others, like proboscis monkeys (**Figure 3.13**), have long droopy noses. They all possess a 2-1-2-3 dental formula (two, rather than three, premolars on each side of each jaw) and tails that are never prehensile. They may be either arboreal or terrestrial, using a quadrupedal pattern of locomotion on the ground or in the trees in a palms-down position. Their body plan is narrow with hind limbs and forelimbs of equal length, a reduced clavicle (collarbone), and relatively fixed and sturdy shoulder, elbow, and wrist joints.

Arboreal species of Old World monkeys include the mantled guereza (*Colobus guereza*) monkey, a species known to have been hunted by chimpanzees. Other Old World monkeys are equally at home on the ground and in the trees. These include the macaques—some nineteen

Figure 3.13 **The Proboscis Monkey** Although all Old World monkeys share certain features like a narrow body plan, a non-prehensile tail, and a 2-1-2-3 dental formula, some unusual specializations are also seen. The proboscis monkey, found in the mangrove swamps of Borneo, is known for its unusual protruding nose, which provides a chamber for extra resonance for its vocalizations. When a monkey is alarmed, the nose fills with blood so that the resonating chamber becomes even more enlarged.

Other Old World species also have much to tell us. For example, over the past several decades primatologists have documented primate social learning and innovation in colonies of macaques in Japan. Similarly, field studies of vervet monkeys in eastern and southern Africa have revealed that these Old World monkeys possess sophisticated communication abilities. In short, wherever primatologists study primates they make fascinating discoveries. These discoveries contribute not only to the disciplines of primatology, evolutionary biology, and ecology but also to our deepening understanding of who we are as primates. Chapter 4 includes more on the behavior of baboons and a variety of other Old World species, particularly the apes.

Small and Great Apes

Like us, the apes, our closest cousins in the animal world, are large, wide-bodied primates with no tails. As members of the hominoid superfamily, apes and humans possess a shoulder anatomy specialized for hanging suspended below tree branches. All apes have this suspensory hanging apparatus, although among apes only small, lithe gibbons and talented gymnasts swing from branch to branch in the pattern known as *brachiation*. At the opposite extreme are gorillas, which generally climb trees, using their prehensile hands and feet to grip the trunk and branches. Although small gorillas may swing between branches,

species that range from tropical Africa and Asia to Gibraltar on the southern coast of Spain to Japan. At the northernmost portions of their range, these primates inhabit temperate rather than strictly tropical environments.

Baboons, a kind of Old World monkey, have been of particular interest to paleoanthropologists because they live in environments similar to those in which humans may have originated. Largely terrestrial, baboons have abandoned trees (except for sleeping and refuge) and live in the savannahs, deserts, and highlands of Africa. Somewhat dog-faced, they have long muzzles and a fierce look. They eat a diet of leaves, seeds, insects, lizards, and small mammals. Baboons live in large, well-organized troops composed of related females and adult males that have transferred out of other troops.

larger individuals limit their swinging to leaning outward while reaching for fruit and clasping a limb for support. Still, gorillas spend most of their time on the ground. All apes except humans and their immediate ancestors possess arms that are longer than their legs.

In moving on the ground, African apes "knuckle-walk" on the backs of their hands, resting their weight on the middle joints of the fingers. They stand erect when reaching for fruit, looking over tall grass, or doing any activity where they find an erect position advantageous. The semi-erect posture is natural in apes when on the ground because the curvature of their vertebral column places their center of gravity, which is high in their body, in front of their hip joint. Thus, they are both top heavy and front heavy. Though apes can walk on two legs, or bipedally, for short distances, the structure of the ape pelvis is not well suited to support the weight of the torso and limbs for more than several minutes.

Gibbons and siamangs, the small apes that are native to Southeast Asia and Malaysia, have compact, slim bodies and stand about 3 feet high. They have extraordinarily long arms compared to their short legs. In addition to moving through treetops by brachiation (**Figure 3.14**), they can run erect, holding their arms out for balance.

Figure 3.14 Gibbons Swinging from Branch to Branch All apes or hominoids possess a suspensory hanging apparatus that allows them to hang from the branches of the forest canopy. But only the gibbon is a master of brachiation—swinging from branch to branch. These hominoids can also walk bipedally for brief periods of time when they need their arms free for carrying, but they cannot sustain bipedal locomotion for more than 50 to 100 yards. Hominoid anatomy, the human line excepted, is better adapted to knuckle-walking and hanging in the trees.

Gibbon and siamang males and females are similar in size, living in family groups of two parents and offspring.

Orangutans, found in Borneo and Sumatra, are divided into two distinct species. Considerably taller and much heavier than gibbons and siamangs, orangutans possess the bulk characteristic of the great apes. With close-set eyes and facial prominence, orangutans appear to be quite human. The people of Sumatra gave orangutans their name "person of the forest," using the Malay term *oran*, which means "person." On the ground, orangutans walk with their forelimbs in a fists-sideways or a palms-down position. They are, however, more arboreal than the African apes (**Figure 3.15**).

Although sociable by nature, the orangutans of Borneo spend most of their time alone (except in the case of females with young) because they have to forage over a wide area to obtain sufficient food. By contrast, in the swamps of Sumatra an abundance of fruits and insects sustains groups of adults and permits coordinated group travel. Thus, gregariousness is a function of habitat productivity (Normile, 1998).

Gorillas, found in equatorial Africa, are the largest of the apes; an adult male can weigh over 450 pounds, with females about half that size (**Figure 3.16**). Scientists distinguish between two gorilla species: the lowland and mountain varieties. A thick coat of glossy black hair covers gorilla bodies, and mature males have a silvery gray upper back. With a strikingly human look about the face, gorillas, like humans, focus on things in their field of vision by directing the eyes rather than moving the head.

Gorillas are mostly ground-dwellers, but the lighter females and young may sleep in trees in carefully constructed nests. Because of their weight, adult males spend less time in the trees but raise and lower themselves among the tree branches when searching for fruit. Gorillas knuckle-walk, using all four limbs with the fingers of the hand flexed, placing the knuckles instead of the palm of the hand on the ground. They stand erect to reach for fruit, to see something more easily, or to threaten perceived sources of danger with their famous chest-beating displays. Although known for these displays (which protect the members of their troop), adult male silverback gorillas are the gentle giants of the forest. As vegetarians, gorillas devote a major portion of each day to eating volumes of plant matter to sustain their massive size.

© Terry Whittaker/Alamy

Figure 3.15 Go Fish This male orangutan was photographed off Kaja Island in the middle of the Gohong River in Borneo. A resident of a preserve where captive animals are rehabituated into the wild, the young male copied this hunting behavior by watching humans spear fishing along the same river. Although so far the orangutan has been unable to nab a fish with his spear tip, his intent is clear. This rare photograph, along with the first photograph of a swimming orangutan, appears in the beautiful book titled *Thinkers of the Jungle*, by Gerd Schuster, Willie Smits, and photographer Jay Ullal.

Figure 3.16 Gorillas and Sexual Dimorphism Compare this female gorilla to the adult male gorilla in this chapter's Globalscape. Not only are male gorillas nearly twice the size of females, but their faces also have a different shape. From the earliest embryological stage to adolescence, male and female sex hormones control the process of growth and development so that the male and female adult phenotypes differ in a variety of ways. Scientists have proposed that high levels of sexual dimorphism characterize primate groups in which male–male competition is high.

Although gorillas are gentle and tolerant, their behavioral repertoire includes bluffing aggression.

In the past, chimpanzees and bonobos (**Figure 3.17**), two closely related species of the genus (*Pan*), were thought to be the same species. Bonobos are restricted in their distribution to the rainforests of the Democratic Republic of Congo. The common chimpanzee, by contrast, widely inhabits the forested portions of sub-Saharan Africa. Probably the best known of the apes, chimpanzees and bonobos have long been favorites in zoos and circuses. When bonobos were recognized as a distinct species in 1929, they were commonly called "pygmy chimpanzees." *Bonobo* replaced this term because not only does their size range overlap with that of chimpanzees, but as we will explore in the next chapter, behavior rather than size constitutes the most striking difference between the two groups.

Although thought of as particularly quick and clever, all four great apes are of equal intelligence, despite some

© Steve Bloom Images/Alamy

Figure 3.17 A Bonobo Over a decade of civil war in the Democratic Republic of Congo, the natural habitat of bonobos, and the aftermath of the genocide in neighboring Rwanda have drastically threatened the survival of bonobos, a species known for harmonious social life. These violent times have prompted the hunting of bonobos to feed starving people and the illegal capture of baby bonobos as pets. Primatologists and local conservationists have turned from observational fieldwork to economic development projects aimed at restoring the stability in the region required for the continued survival of bonobos and mountain gorillas.

Threats to Primates

In Asia, the statistics are alarming, with more than 70 percent of species threatened and at least 80 percent at risk in Indonesia and Vietnam. Included among them are all of the great apes, as well as such formerly widespread and adaptable species as rhesus macaques. In the wild these animals are endangered by habitat destruction caused by economic development (farming, lumbering, cattle ranching, rubber tapping), as well as by hunters and trappers who pursue them for food, trophies, research, or as exotic pets. Primatologists have long known the devastating effects of habitat destruction through the traditional practice of slash-and-burn agriculture.

However, primate habitats are at far greater risk from contemporary hazards. War impacts primate habitats significantly, and the effects linger long after the battles. Hunters may use the automatic weapons left over from human conflicts in their pursuit of bushmeat. Also, because monkeys and apes are so closely related to humans, some scientists regard them as essential for biomedical research. Although captive breeding provides most of the primates used in laboratories, an active trade in live primates still threatens their native extinction. Globalization also exerts a profound impact on local conditions. This chapter's Globalscape illustrates how cell phones are impacting gorilla habitats and the survival of this species.

Primate Conservation

The aforementioned survey of living primates illustrates the diversity of our closest living relatives. To ensure that they will continue to share the planet with us, primate conservation has become an issue of vital importance. Nearly 50 percent of the known primate species and subspecies face extinction in the next decade (Kaplan, 2008).

differences in cognitive styles. More arboreal than gorillas but less so than orangutans, chimpanzees and bonobos forage on the ground much of the day, knuckle-walking like gorillas. At sunset, they return to the trees where they build their nests.

Conservation Strategies

Because of their vulnerability, the conservation of primates is an urgent matter. Traditional conservation efforts have emphasized habitat preservation above all else, but primatologists have expanded their efforts to include educating local communities and discouraging the hunting of primates for food and medical purposes. Some primatologists even help implement alternative economic strategies for local peoples so that human and primate populations can return to the successful coexistence that prevailed before colonialism and globalization contributed to the destabilization of tradition homelands. This chapter's Anthropology Applied looks at these economic development efforts in the Democratic Republic of Congo.

In direct conservation efforts, primatologists work to maintain some populations in the wild, either by

Globalscape

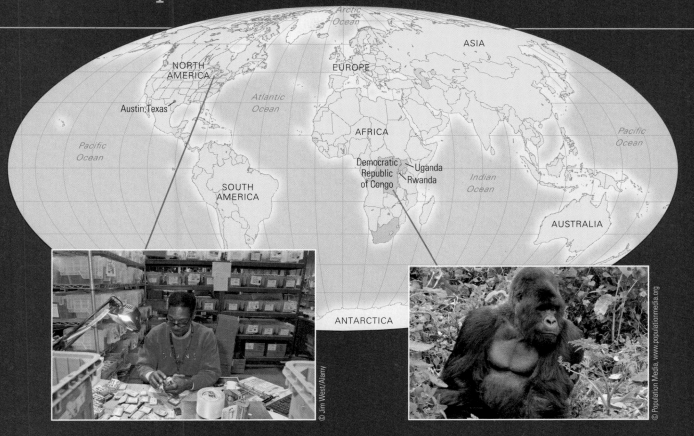

Gorilla Hand Ashtrays?

Tricia, a 20-year-old from Austin, Texas, once blogged: "At that party did you meet the guy from South Africa that looked like an exact replica of Dave Matthews (only skinnier) who was talking about gorilla hand ashtrays?"[a] The unnamed guy was talking about one of the many real threats to gorillas in the wild. With no natural enemies, human actions alone are responsible for the shrinking population of gorillas in their natural habitats in Rwanda, Uganda, and the Democratic Republic of Congo. Despite conservation work begun by the late primatologist Dian Fossey, who pioneered field studies of the gorillas in the 1970s, ashtrays made from gorilla hands and gorilla heads remain coveted souvenirs for unsavory tourists. A poacher can sell these body parts and the remaining bushmeat for a handsome profit.

Today, not only do logging and mining in gorilla habitats destroy these forests, but new roads make it easier for poach-ers to access the gorillas. Local governments of Rwanda and Uganda, in partnership with the Fossey Fund and the Bush Meat Project, have organized poaching patrols and community partnerships to protect the endangered gorillas. Thousands of miles away, Tricia and her friends can also help by recycling their cell phones. The mineral coltan (shown in Chapter 1's opening Challenge Issue) that is found in cell phones is mined primarily from gorilla habitats in the Democratic Republic of Congo. Recycling, as pictured here in a Michigan cell phone recycling plant, will reduce the amount of new coltan needed.

Global Twister

Encouraging recycling of cell phones and discouraging poaching both will impact gorilla survival. How would you go about convincing average cell phone users or poachers to change their habits or livelihood to protect endangered gorillas?

[a]http://profile.myspace.com/index.cfm?fuseaction=user.
viewprofile&friendid=40312227 (accessed July 3, 2006)

ANTHROPOLOGY APPLIED

The Congo Heartland Project

Under the leadership of Belgian primatologist Jef Dupain, the African Wildlife Foundation has embarked on a number of projects to support the continued survival of bonobos and mountain gorillas in the Democratic Republic of Congo (DRC). Called the Congo Heartland Project, this work is designed to support the local human populations devastated by a decade of civil war in the Congo itself as well as the impact of the massive influx of refugees from war and genocide in neighboring Rwanda.

The rich rainforests along the tributaries of the mighty Congo River in the

As part of the African Wildlife Foundation's Congo Heartland Project, primatologist Jef Dupain (*second from left*) trains workers in the forest near the Lomako Conservation Science Center. In addition to classic research activities, the Congo Heartland Project provides jobs for local families and serves as an anchor for research, conservation, and microenterprise activities in the largely undisturbed Lomako Forest, which is the habitat of the bonobo, a rare great ape.

DRC are the only natural habitats for bonobos in the world. Mountain gorillas can be found in the DRC and in neighboring Uganda and Rwanda. Primatological fieldwork thrived in sites established during the 1970s until the mid-1990s when war and genocide led to the forced removal of primatologists. Although many left the region, Dupain stayed and monitored the kinds of bushmeat brought into the markets in Kinshasa. With the human population

establishing preserves in areas the animals already occupy or by moving populations to suitable habitats. These approaches require constant monitoring and management to ensure that sufficient space and resources remain available. As humans encroach on primate habitats, translocation of primates to protected areas is a viable strategy for primate conservation, and primatologists provide invaluable field studies to guide these relocations.

For example, when the troop of free-ranging baboons that primatologist Shirley Strum had been studying for

fifteen years in Kenya began raiding crops and garbage on newly established farms, she was instrumental in successfully moving this troop and two other local troops—130 animals in all—to more sparsely inhabited country 150 miles away. Knowing their habits, Strum was able to trap, tranquilize, and transport the animals to their new home while preserving the baboons' vital social relationships. Strum's careful work allowed for a smooth transition. With social relations intact, the baboons did not abandon their new homes nor did they block the transfer of desperate and starving and the poachers armed with automatic weapons, the park rangers charged with protecting the great apes were outnumbered, and many primates perished. Since a fragile peace was achieved in the region in 2003, initiatives of the Congo Heartland Project have been reestablished, including involving local communities in agricultural practices to protect the Congo River and its tributaries and to preserve their precious animal populations.

Congo Heartland Project initiatives typically empower local communities in development efforts using a participative, interactive, and transparent approach. For example, a range of different ethnic groups, including marginalized people such as Pygmies and women, met with local authorities to reestablish the management policies of Dupain's field site (the Lomako-Yokokala Faunal Reserve) as it reopened for researchers and ecotourists. Forty percent of the income generated in park revenues is to return to the local communities. According to Dupain, success for these projects is defined as follows:

Local communities take part in decision making on how the protected area will be managed, on how revenue will be shared, and as a result, local communities take up the defense of their protected area. In time, densities of bonobo, bongo, forest elephant, Congo peacock, leopard, Allen's swamp monkey, black and white colobus, and many others will increase, more tourists and researchers will come and will be willing to pay for this environmental service, local communities will have increased access to education, medical treatment, electricity, clean water . . . the list goes on. Mange Bofaso put it best: "In Katanga they have diamonds. Here in Lomako, we have bonobos."[a]

The Congo Heartland Project also includes encouraging a variety of alternative economic practices in communities bordering existing wildlife preserves. For example, around the Virunga National Park, home to the endangered mountain gorilla, Congolese Enterprise Officer Wellard Makambo encourages and monitors beekeeping and a mushroom farm collective, run by Congolese women. He also advises members of a conflict resolution team dealing with gorillas that have left the wildlife preserve to raid human crops. Local communities require reassurance and restitution, while gorillas need to be returned safely to the park. When Makambo made his first trip back to the Bukima Ranger Station after the war, he wrote,

While I was standing on the hill surveying the amazing Bukima view I felt like a mighty silverback gorilla looking at his bountiful bamboo kingdom—one whose life would be hopeless if this kingdom is destroyed. I tried to measure the effects of the war on people and on our activities and projects. It was tough getting my head around it: how to re-start things when you realise effort alone is not sufficient. You need stability as well, which is slowly coming back to this area.[b]

These economic development projects are playing a crucial role in restoring the stability in the region required for the continued survival of bonobos and mountain gorillas.

---

[a]African Wildlife Foundation, Facebook blog. www.facebook.com/AfricanWildlife Foundation
[b]Ibid.

new males, with their all-important knowledge of local resources, into the troop. The success of her effort, which had never been tried with baboons, proves that translocation is a realistic technique for saving endangered primate species. However, this conservation effort depends first on available land, where preserves can be established to provide habitats for endangered primates.

A second strategy has been developed to help primates that have been illegally trapped—either for market as pets or for biomedical research. This approach involves returning these recovered animals to their natural habitats. Researchers have established orphanages in which specially trained human substitute mothers support the young primates so that they can gain enough social skills to return to living with their own species.

A third strategy to preventing primate extinction is to maintain breeding colonies in captivity. These colonies encourage psychological and physical well-being, as well as reproductive success. Primates in zoos and laboratories do not successfully reproduce when deprived of amenities such as opportunities for climbing, materials for nest building, others with whom to socialize, and places for privacy. Although such features contribute to the success of breeding colonies in captivity, ensuring the survival of our primate cousins in suitable natural habitats is a far greater challenge that humans must meet in the years to come.

Intense primate conservation efforts are beginning to pay off. For example, in recent years, the population size of the mountain gorilla (*Gorilla beringei beringei*) has increased despite the political chaos of the Democratic Republic of Congo. Western lowland gorilla populations (*Gorilla gorilla*) are also on the rise. Similarly, tamarin monkey populations in Brazil (**Figure 3.18**) have stabilized despite being on the brink of extinction thirty-five years ago, demonstrating the effectiveness of the conservation initiatives put into place. According to primatologist Sylvia Atsalis, "The presence alone of scientists has been shown to protect primates, acting as a deterrent to habitat destruction and hunting. . . . The more people we can send, the more we can help to protect endangered primates" (quoted in Kaplan, 2008).

© Martin Bennett/Alamy

Figure 3.18 The Golden Lion Tamarin Because of their exceptional beauty, golden lion tamarin monkeys (or golden marmosets) have been kept as pets since colonial times. More recently, they have also been threatened by development given that they reside in the tropical forest habitats around the popular tourist destination of Rio de Janeiro, Brazil. A major conservation effort, initiated in the 1980s to save these monkeys, included planting wildlife corridors to connect the remaining forest patches and releasing animals bred in captivity into these newly created environments. Today, live wild births have increased steadily, and the golden lion tamarin population is recovering from the threat of extinction.

CHAPTER CHECKLIST

How do primatologists conduct field research?

● Researchers rely on observation and collection of feces and hair samples left behind in order to minimize contact that could endanger primate populations.

● Conservation efforts are combined with research to ensure the future study of wild populations.

● Animals in captivity have provided opportunities to interact with and discover the communicative capabilities of many primates.

How does mammalian biology compare to reptilian biology?

● As homeotherms, mammals can survive in a wider variety of climates than isothermic reptiles, but mammals require more calories to survive.

● Mammals are k-selected, rather than r-selected, meaning that parents spend much time rearing few offspring.

● Mammals possess various types of specialized teeth that are replaced only once over a lifetime. Reptile teeth are all nearly identical with unlimited replacement.

How does taxonomy apply to primates, and what issues does it pose?

● Taxonomists use shared derived characteristics to establish evolutionary relationships.

● The Linnaean system focuses on the measure of anatomical similarity known as a grade. By this system, primates consist of two subfamilies called *Prosimii* and *Anthropoidea*. Anthropoids are divided into the infraorders Platyrrhini and Catarrhini.

● A new taxonomic scheme based on quantifying genetic similarities proposes a regrouping of primates into two suborders: Strepsirhini and Haplorhini. It also distinguishes the hominin subfamily of hominids (humans and their ancestors) from the other African apes.

What features distinguish primates from other mammals?

● Primates have a long period of childhood dependency and are large-brained, which enables both learned and adaptive behavior.

● Primates developed binocular stereoscopic color vision as they became both diurnal and arboreal. Primate teeth reflect the diversity of food sources available among the trees.

● The fovea centralis is unique to primates and allows focusing the eye without sacrificing peripheral vision. Enhanced visual acuity has come at the expense of sense of smell.

● The primate foramen magnum is closer to the base of the skull, allowing an upright posture.

● Primate digits have sensitive pads, usually accompanied by flattened nails. Most species have opposable thumbs and big toes.

What features characterize the five natural groups of primates?

● Lemurs and lorises have large ears, big eyes, pointed snouts that limit facial expression, a claw on their second toe used for grooming, and several scent glands for communication. As a group, they retain more ancestral primate characteristics.

● Tarsiers are tiny arboreal creatures with oversized eyes and heads and elongated foot bones that allow for far jumps. They are genetically closer to monkeys and apes, though as nocturnal insect-eaters, they resemble early ancestral primates.

● New World monkeys are flat-nosed tree-dwellers that walk on all fours and rarely hang from trees by their arms. One subgroup possesses long prehensile tails that are used as an extra limb.

● Old World monkeys are alternately terrestrial and arboreal and have downward-pointing nostrils and non-prehensile tails. They walk on all fours with palms down, and many species exhibit sophisticated social organization, communication, and learning abilities.

● Having no tails, apes are all adapted to hanging by their arms and in some species to brachiate. Their clavicles position their arms at the sides of the body. They are able to stand erect due to the curvature of their vertebrae. African apes knuckle-walk when on the ground, and all apes but humans have forelimbs that are longer than their legs.

What pressures do primate populations currently face?

● Habitat destruction caused by economic development and globalization has led to the endangered status of many primate species, especially the great apes.

● Primates in war-torn regions are particularly threatened by the presence of automatic weapons and disruption to conservation efforts.

● Relocation, reintroduction, and captive colony strategies have met with success in recent years, and some populations are rebounding due to such conservation efforts.

QUESTIONS FOR REFLECTION

1. Has learning more about the numerous similarities between our primate cousins and us motivated you personally to meet the challenge of preventing their extinction? What human factors are causing endangerment of primates, and how can we prevent their extinction?

2. What are the main differences between mammals and reptiles? Do we share any ancestral features with reptiles? What are some of the derived features characteristic of mammals including humans?

3. Considering some of the trends seen among the primates, such as increased brain size or fewer teeth, why is it incorrect to say that some primates are more evolved than others? What is wrong with the statement that humans are more evolved than chimpanzees?

4. Two systems exist for dividing the primate order into suborders because of difficulties with classifying tarsiers. Should classification systems be based on genetic relationships or based on the biological concept of grade? Is the continued use of the older terminology an instance of unwillingness to change or a difference in philosophy? How do the issues brought up by the tarsier problem translate to the hominoids?

5. What aspects of mammalian primate biology do you see reflected in yourself or in people you know?

ONLINE STUDY RESOURCES

CourseMate

Access chapter-specific learning tools, including learning objectives, practice quizzes, videos, flash cards, glossaries, and more in your Anthropology CourseMate.

Log into **www.cengagebrain.com** to access the resources your instructor has assigned and to purchase materials.

© Frans Lanting/Frans Lanting Stock

Challenge Issue

Each new observation of primate behavior challenges us to rethink the old nature–nurture question: How much of human behavior is biologically determined and how much of it derives from culture? Early on, primate behavior was considered wholly natural or "acultural": Any behavior that humans shared with other primates was considered to have a biological basis. But repeated demonstration of the range of behaviors among our primate cousins has complicated such theories of human biological determinism. Consider, for example, the diverse sexual behaviors of bonobos, the species of the genus *Pan* that inhabits the war-torn rainforests of the Congo. The genital-genital or G-G rubbing between two females pictured here is one among the many sexual practices bonobos use to reduce tension and resolve social conflicts. Among bonobos, primatologists have observed every possible combination of ages and sexes engaging in a remarkable array of sexual activities that goes far beyond male–female mating for purposes of biological reproduction. Interestingly, female bonobos, like female humans, have no visible biological display of ovulation, or the moment when a fertile egg is released from the womb. Does this biological factor alone determine bonobos' diverse sexuality? And by extension, does concealed ovulation in human females indicate that our sexuality as a species is also untethered from the biological task of reproduction? What does it mean when individuals argue for a biological basis for human homosexuality or its opposite, that among humans, only heterosexuality is natural? Biology and culture clearly interact not only in generating behavioral variation, but also with the theories we humans generate about our behaviors.

Primate Behavior

4

Research into primate behavior has shown again and again the behavioral sophistication of our closest living relatives. Primates use tools, learn, and can be dishonest, just as humans can. Although the young Jane Goodall was criticized for naming the chimpanzees she studied, social interactions, particularly among the apes, demonstrate that they recognize one another as individuals and adjust their behavior accordingly. (Many other long-lived social mammals, such as elephants and dolphins, do the same.) Certainly, biology plays a role in such primate behaviors, but often, as with humans, the social traditions of the group also determine behavior. Nevertheless, some broad biological factors underlie the social traditions of the primates.

Compared to many other mammals, primates require more time to reach adulthood. During their lengthy growth and development, young primates learn the behaviors of their social group. Observations of primates in their natural habitats over the past decades have shown that social interaction, organization, learning, reproduction, care of the young, and communication among our primate relatives resemble human behavior. As we study primate behavior to learn about ourselves, who we are as a species today, and how we got here, it becomes clear that many of our differences reflect only the degree of expression of shared characteristics.

Primates as Models for Human Evolution

As we will explore in the human evolution chapters to come, the human line split from a common ancestor that we share with the African apes. Although this split occurred millions of years ago, paleoanthropologists in the mid-20th century were hopeful that observations made among the living apes might shed light on the lifeways of the fossil species they were discovering. Indeed, paleontologist Louis Leakey encouraged Jane Goodall to begin her research with chimpanzees in Gombe Stream Chimpanzee Reserve (now a national park) on the eastern shores

IN THIS CHAPTER YOU WILL LEARN TO

- Identify the range of variation of primate behavior and the theories that account for it.

- Distinguish different forms of primate social organization.

- Examine the biological basis of primate behavior, with particular emphasis on the primate life cycle, social learning, and the environment.

- Explore the cultural influences on theories of primate behavior.

- Distinguish the diverse behavioral patterns of our closest relatives—orangutans, gorillas, chimpanzees, and bonobos—with particular emphasis on sexual behavior, cooperation, hunting, and tool use.

- Describe the linguistic capacities of the great apes.

- Define *primate culture* in the context of human evolution.

- Explore the moral questions surrounding the use of chimpanzees in biomedical research.

of Lake Tanganyika in Tanzania for this reason. He also supported the fieldwork of two other primatologists: Dian Fossey, working with mountain gorillas in Rwanda, and Biruté Galdikas, working with orangutans in Borneo.

But as forest-dwellers, each of these ape species inhabited an environment that differed considerably from the grassy savannahs inhabited by the earliest human ancestors known at that time. Instead, paleoanthropologists turned to baboons: an Old World monkey native to the savannah environments of eastern Africa where the richest fossil evidence of our ancestors had also been found.

Although baboons differ considerably from our two-legged ancestors, their survival strategies provide some clues as to how early humans adapted to the savannah environment. Members of the genus *Papio*, baboons are among the largest of the Old World monkeys. Fully terrestrial, troops of baboons can be seen sitting together on the dry savannah earth to forage for corms (thick, nutritious underground reproductive parts of plants). They keep a watchful eye out for predators while feeding. At the first sight or sound of danger, alarm calls by members of the troop will signal for all the individuals to retreat to safety.

Baboons live in groups that vary dramatically in size, from less than ten individuals to hundreds. In some species the groups are multi-male multi-female while others are made up of a series of polygynous groups—one male with several females that he dominates (Figure 4.1). Sexual dimorphism—anatomical differences between males and females—is high in baboons, and therefore males can use their physical advantages to overpower females easily. But the degree to which males choose to do so varies from group to group.

Extrapolating from baboons to theories about our ancestors poses problems. To use the words of primatologists Shirley Strum and William Mitchell, these baboon "models" often became baboon "muddles" (Strum & Mitchell, 1987).

Figure 4.1 Baboon Social Learning The behavior of baboons, a type of Old World monkey, has been particularly well studied. There are several distinct species of baboon, each with its own social rules. Troops of hamadryas baboons, the sacred baboons of ancient Egypt pictured here, consist of a series of smaller groups made up of a single male and several females over which he dominates. Female hamadryas baboons, if transferred to a troop of olive baboons, where females are not as submissive, maintain the passive behaviors learned in their original troop. But a female olive baboon placed in the hamadryas troop quickly learns submissive behaviors in order to survive.

Paleoanthropologists did not expect our ancestors to possess tails or **ischial callosities**—the hardened, nerveless buttock pads that allow baboons to sit for long periods of time. Tails are strictly a monkey characteristic, not an ape one, and among the hominoids only gibbons and siamangs possess ischial callosities. Instead, paleoanthropologists were looking for examples of *convergence*—of behaviors that might appear in large-bodied, dimorphic primates living in large multi-male multi-female groups in a savannah environment.

Paleoanthropology's "baboon hypothesis" led to many excellent long-term field studies of baboons that have yielded fascinating data on their social organization, omnivorous diet, mating patterns and other reproductive strategies, communication, and so forth. As with most primate field studies, the evolutionary questions remain in the background while the rich repertoire of primate behavior takes center stage.

While the savannah environment has certainly been important in human evolution, recent fossil discoveries and analyses have led paleoanthropologists back into the forest, where the earliest two-legged ancestors lived. Researchers now also focus on human origins and the transition from a forested environment to the savannah. Recent field studies of chimpanzees in more savannah-like environments, explored in this chapter, have yielded fascinating results.

Primate Social Organization

Primates are social animals, living and traveling in groups that vary in size and composition from species to species. Different environmental and biological factors have been linked to the group's size, and various primate species exhibit all the possible organizational forms (**Figure 4.2**).

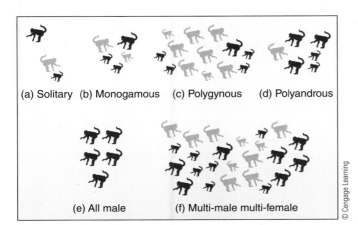

(a) Solitary (b) Monogamous (c) Polygynous (d) Polyandrous

(e) All male   (f) Multi-male multi-female

© Cengage Learning

Figure 4.2 Primate Social Organization Primate social organization ranges from (a) solitary to (b) monogamous to (c) polygynous (single male with many females and their young) to the rare (d) polyandrous (single female with multiple males and her young to (e) all male to (f) multi-male multi-female groups of various sizes and ages. In this figure, females are rust-colored, and males are dark brown.

For example, gibbons live in small nuclear family units consisting of a pair of bonded (*monogamous*) adults and their offspring, whereas orangutans tend to lead solitary existences, with males and females coming together only to mate. Young orangutans stay with their mothers until they reach adult status.

Some baboon species live in *polygynous* groups with one male and many females and their young. Only a very few New World species are *polyandrous* with a single female and more than one male and her young. Twins are common in these species, and the males all help with parenting.

Chimps and bonobos live in large multi-male multi-female groups. Among chimps and bonobos, the largest social organizational unit is the **community**, usually composed of fifty or more individuals who collectively inhabit a large geographic area. Rarely, however, do all of these animals congregate. Instead, they range singly or in small subgroups consisting of adult males, or females with their young, or males and females together with their young. In the course of their travels, subgroups may join forces and forage together, but sooner or later these will break up into smaller units. Typically, when some individuals split off, others join, so the composition of subunits shifts frequently.

The gorilla group is a "family" of five to thirty individuals led by a mature silver-backed male and including younger (black-backed) males, females, the young, and occasionally other silverbacks. The dominant male, however, usually prevents subordinate males from mating with the group's females. Thus, young, sexually mature males, who take on the characteristic silver color at the end of the sexual maturation process (about 11 to 13 years of age), are forced by the dominant silverback to leave their **natal group**—the community they have known since birth. After some time as a solitary male in the forest, a young silverback may find the opportunity to start his own social group by winning outside females. Occasionally, these solitary males will form an all-male group. In the natal group, if the dominant male is weakening with age, one of his sons may remain with the group to succeed to his father's position. Alternatively, an outside male may take over the group. With the dominant male controlling the group, gorillas rarely fight over food, territory, or sex, but they will fight fiercely to defend the group.

In many primate species, including humans, adolescence marks the time when individuals change the relationships they have had with the group they have known since birth. Among primates this change often takes the form of migration to new social groups. In many species, females constitute the core of the social system.

ischial callosities Hardened, nerveless pads on the buttocks that allow baboons and other primates to sit for long periods of time.

community In primatology, a unit of primate social organization composed of fifty or more individuals who collectively inhabit a large geographic area.

natal group The group or the community an animal has inhabited since birth.

For example, offspring tend to remain with the group to which their mother, rather than their father, belongs. Among gorillas, male adolescents leave their natal groups more frequently than females. However, adolescent female chimpanzees and bonobos are often the ones to migrate.

Among Tanzanian chimpanzee communities studied, about half the females leave the community they have known since birth to join another group (Moore, 1998). Other females may also temporarily leave their group to mate with males of another group. Among bonobos, adolescent females appear to always transfer to another group, where they promptly establish bonds with females of their new community. Although biological factors such as the hormonal influences on sexual maturity play a role in adolescent migration, the variation across species and within the chimpanzees in dispersal patterns indicates that differences may also derive from the learned social traditions of the group.

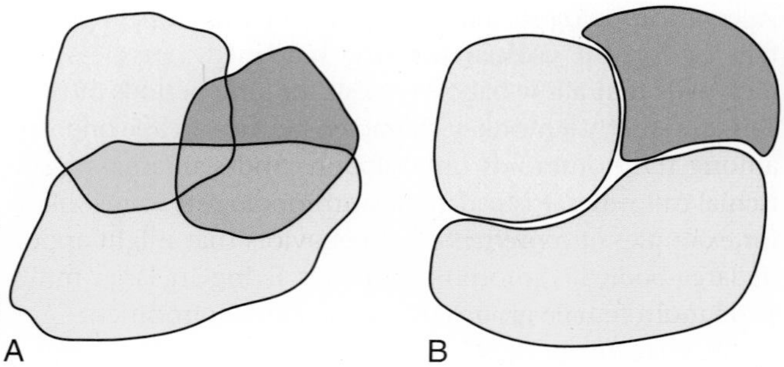

Home Range

Primates usually move about within a circumscribed area, or **home range**, which varies in size depending on the group and on ecological factors such as availability of food. Ranges often change seasonally, and the number of miles traveled daily by a group varies. Some areas, known as *core areas,* are used more often than others. Core areas typically contain water, food sources, resting places, and sleeping trees. The ranges of different groups may overlap, as among bonobos, where 65 percent of one community's range may overlap with that of another (Parish, 1998). By contrast, chimpanzee territories, at least in some regions, are exclusively occupied and will be defended from intrusion (**Figure 4.3**).

Gorillas do not defend their home range against incursions of others of their kind, although they will defend their group if it is in any way threatened. In the lowlands of Central Africa, it is not uncommon to find several families feeding in close proximity to one another (Parnell, 1999). In encounters with other communities, bonobos will defend their immediate space through vocalizations and displays but rarely through fighting. Usually, they settle down and feed side by side, not infrequently grooming, playing, and engaging in sexual activity between groups as well.

Chimpanzees, by contrast, have been observed patrolling their territories to ward off potential trespassers. Moreover, Jane Goodall (see Anthropologists of Note) has recorded the destruction of one chimpanzee community by another invading group. This sort of deadly intercommunity interaction has never been observed

home range The geographic area within which a group of primates usually moves.

dominance hierarchies An observed ranking system in primate societies, ordering individuals from high (alpha) to low standing corresponding to predictable behavioral interactions including domination.

© Cengage Learning

Figure 4.3 Home Range and Territory As illustrated in A, home ranges can overlap. When members of the same species meet one another in the shared parts of the range, there might be some tension, deference, or peaceful mingling. Some groups maintain clear territories (B) that are strictly defended from any intrusion by members of the same species.

among bonobos. Some have interpreted the apparent territorial behavior as an expression of the supposedly violent nature of chimpanzees. However, others have suggested that the violence Goodall witnessed was a response to overcrowding that resulted from human activity (Power, 1995).

Social Hierarchy

In the past, primatologists believed that male **dominance hierarchies**, in which some animals outrank and dominate others, formed the basis of primate social structures. They noted that physical strength and size play a role in determining an animal's rank. By this measure, males generally outrank females. However, the male-biased cultures of many early primatologists may have contributed to this theoretical perspective, with their emphasis on domination through superior size and strength. Male dominance hierarchies seemed "natural" to these initial researchers.

With the benefit of detailed field studies over the last fifty years, including cutting-edge research by female primatologists such as Goodall, the nuances of primate social behavior, the relative harmony of primate social life, and the importance of female primates are now documented. High-ranking female chimpanzees may dominate low-ranking males. And among bonobos, female rank determines the social order of the group far more than male rank. While greater strength and size do contribute to an animal's higher rank, several other factors also come into play in determining its social position. These include the rank of its mother, a factor largely determined through her cooperative social behavior and how effectively each individual animal creates alliances with others.

For males, drive or motivation to achieve high status also influences rank. For example, in the community studied by Goodall, one male chimp hit upon the idea of incorporating noisy kerosene cans into his charging displays, thereby intimidating all the other males (Goodall,

ANTHROPOLOGISTS OF NOTE

Jane Goodall (b. 1934) • Kinji Imanishi (1902–1992)

In July 1960, **Jane Goodall** arrived with her mother at the Gombe Chimpanzee Reserve on the shores of Lake Tanganyika in Tanzania. Goodall was the first of three women Kenyan anthropologist Louis Leakey sent to study great apes in the wild (the others were Dian Fossey and Biruté Galdikas, who studied gorillas and orangutans, respectively); her task was to begin a long-term study of chimpanzees. Little did she realize that, more than fifty years later, she would still be at it.

Jane Goodall in the field with chimpanzees at Gombe.

Born in London, Goodall grew up and was schooled in Bournemouth, England. As a child, she dreamed of going to live in Africa, so when an invitation arrived to visit a friend in Kenya, she jumped at the opportunity. While in Kenya, she met Leakey, who gave her a job as an assistant secretary. Before long, she was on her way to Gombe. Within a year, the outside world began to hear extraordinary things about this pioneering woman and her research: tales of tool-making apes, cooperative hunts by chimpanzees, and what seemed like exotic chimpanzee rain dances. By the mid-1960s, her work had earned her a doctorate from Cambridge University, and Gombe was on its way to becoming one of the most dynamic field stations for the study of animal behavior anywhere in the world.

Although Goodall is still very much involved with chimpanzees, she now spends a good deal of time lecturing, writing, and overseeing the work of other researchers. She is passionately committed to primate conservation and is dedicated to halting illegal trafficking in chimps as well as fighting for the humane treatment of captive chimps.

Long before Louis Leakey sent the first Western primatologists into the field, **Kinji Imanishi**—naturalist, explorer, and mountain climber—profoundly influenced primatology in Japan and throughout the world. Although fully aware of Western methods and theories, he developed a radically different approach to the scientific study of the natural world. Imanishi dates his transformation to a youthful encounter with a grasshopper:

> I was walking along a path in a valley, and there was a grasshopper on a leaf in a shrubbery. Until that moment I had happily caught insects, killed them with chloroform, impaled them on pins, and looked up their names, but I realized I knew nothing at all about how this grasshopper lived in the wild.[a]

Kinji Imanishi initiated the earliest field studies of bonobos in the 1940s.

In his most important work, *The World of Living Things*, first published in 1941, Imanishi developed a comprehensive theory about the natural world rooted in Japanese cultural beliefs and practices.

Imanishi's work challenged Western evolutionary theory in several ways. First, Imanishi's theory, like Japanese culture, does not emphasize differences between humans and other animals. Second, rather than focusing on the biology of individual organisms, Imanishi suggested that naturalists examine "specia" (a species society) to which individuals belong as the unit of analysis. Rather than focusing on time, Imanishi emphasized space in his approach to the natural world. He highlighted the harmony of all living things rather than conflict and competition among individual organisms.

Imanishi's research techniques, now standard worldwide, developed directly from his theories: long-term field study of primates in their natural societies using methods from ethnography. With his students, Imanishi conducted pioneering field studies of African apes and Japanese and Tibetan macaques. Japanese primatologists were the first to document the importance of kinship, the complexity of primate societies, patterns of social learning, and the unique character of each primate social group. Because of the work by Imanishi and his students, we now think about the distinct cultures of primate societies.

[a]Heita, K. (1999). Imanishi's world view. *Journal of Japanese Trade and Industry* 18 (2), 15.

1986). As a result, he rose from relatively low status to the number one (alpha) position.

On the whole, bonobo females form stronger bonds with one another than do chimpanzee females. Moreover, the strength of the bond between mother and son interferes with bonds among males. Bonobo males defer to females in feeding, and alpha (high-ranking) females have been observed chasing alpha males; such males may even yield to low-ranking females, particularly when groups of females form alliances. Further, allied females will band together to force an aggressive male out of the community. These bonobo females cooperate even though they are not genetically related to one another.

Alpha males even yield to low-ranking females, and groups of females form alliances in which they may cooperatively attack males, to the point of inflicting blood-drawing injuries (de Waal, Kano, & Parish, 1998). Thus, instead of the male dominance characteristic of chimps, female dominance prevails among bonobos.

Western primatologists' focus on social rank and attack behavior may be a legacy of the individualistic, competitive nature of the societies in which evolutionary theory originated. To a certain degree, natural selection relies upon struggle and competition among living creatures rather than peaceful coexistence within a fixed social order. By contrast, noted Japanese primatologist Kinji Imanishi (see Anthropologists of Note) developed a harmonious theory of evolution and initiated field studies of bonobos that have demonstrated the importance of social cooperation rather than competition. According to Dutch primatologist Frans de Waal, in social species that cooperate and depend upon one another, **reconciliation**—a friendly reunion between former opponents not long after a conflict—has more evolutionary import than the fight that preceded it (Aureli & de Waal, 2000; de Waal, 2000).

As pictured in the chapter opener, female bonobos reconcile by rubbing their clitorises and swollen genitals. Chimpanzees reconcile with a hug and mouth-to-mouth kiss. The reconciliation techniques of a wide range of other primates and other mammalian species including dolphins and hyenas have been observed in the wild. Although some attribute reconciliation behavior to simple biology, de Waal carried out a series of experiments that demonstrate that primates *learn* these social skills. He took two species of Old World monkey, the aggressive rhesus macaque and the mellower stump-tailed macaque, and housed some of them together for five months. At the end of this period, rhesus macaques that had learned reconciliation from the stump-tailed macaques continued to practice these behaviors when living strictly with rhesus macaques.

Chimps, as de Waal observed, take reconciliation a step further: Some individuals, generally an older female, take on the role of mediator. Recognizing a dispute between two other individuals in the group who sit near one another but avoid eye contact, this mediator will groom one of the combatants for a bit (**Figure 4.4**). When she gets up to groom the other combatant, the first fighter follows and grooms her. She eventually leaves the two fighters grooming each other.

Figure 4.4 Primate Grooming Grooming is an important activity among all catarrhine primates, as shown here in a group of chimps grooming one another in a pattern known as the *domino effect*. Such activity is important for strengthening bonds among individual members of the group.

Gunter Ziesler/Getty Images/Peter Arnold

Individual Interaction and Bonding

As shown in Figure 4.4, **grooming**, the ritual cleaning of another animal to remove parasites and other matter from its skin or coat, has social as well as practical consequences. The grooming animal deftly parts the hair of the one being groomed and removes any foreign object, often eating it. Besides serving hygienic purposes, grooming can signify friendliness, closeness, appeasement, reconciliation, or even submission. Bonobos and chimpanzees have favorite grooming partners. Embracing, touching, and the joyous welcoming of other members of the ape community also demonstrate group sociability. These important behavioral traits undoubtedly existed among human ancestors.

Interestingly, different chimp communities have different styles of grooming. In one East African group, for example, the two chimps groom each other face-to-face, with one hand, while clasping their partner's free hand. In another group 90 miles distant, the handclasp does not occur. In East Africa, all communities incorporate leaves in their grooming, but in West Africa they do not.

Gorillas, though gentle and tolerant, tend toward aloofness and independence. Restraint characterizes individual interaction among adults, whereas friendship and closeness appear to typify only the relationships between adults and infants. Among bonobos, chimpanzees, gorillas, and orangutans, as among most other primates, the mother–infant bond is the strongest and longest lasting. It may endure for many years—commonly for the lifetime of the mother. Gorilla infants share their mothers' nests but have also been seen sharing nests with mature childless females. Bonobo, chimpanzee, and gorilla males pay attention to juveniles, thus contributing to their socialization. Bonobo males even carry infants on occasion. Their interest in a youngster does not elicit the nervous reaction from the mother that it does among chimps; chimp mothers may be reacting to the occasional infanticide on the part of chimpanzee males, a behavior never observed among bonobos.

Sexual Behavior

Most mammals mate only during specified breeding seasons occurring once or twice a year. While some primates have a fixed breeding season tied to a simultaneous increase in body fat, or to the consumption of specific plant foods, many primate species can breed throughout the course of the year. Among the African apes, as with humans, there is no fixed breeding season. In chimps, frequent sexual activity—initiated by either the male or the female—occurs during **estrus**, the period when the female is receptive to impregnation. Physically visible as a signal to potential mates (**Figure 4.5**), in chimpanzees the skin around the genitals swells during estrus. Bonobo females, by contrast, appear as if they are fertile at all

© Michel Gunther/Photo Researchers, Inc.

Figure 4.5 Gelada Estrus Because geladas, a kind of Old World monkey, spend far more time sitting than upright, signaling ovulation through genital swelling is not as practical as is signaling it through the reddening of a patch of furless skin on their chests. This way it is easy for other members of the group to see that they are fertile even while they are foraging.

times due to their constantly swollen genitals and interest in sex. Gorillas appear to show less interest in sex compared to either chimps or bonobos.

When in estrus, a chimpanzee female engages in lots of sexual activity, sometimes with as many as fifty copulations in one day with a dozen different partners. For the most part, females mate with males of their own group. Dominant males often try to monopolize females in full estrus, although this will not succeed without cooperation from the female. In addition, an individual female and a lower-ranking male sometimes form a temporary bond, leaving the group together for a few "private" days during the female's fertile period. Interestingly, the relationship between reproductive success and social rank differs for males and females. In the chimpanzee community

reconciliation In primatology, a friendly reunion between former opponents not long after a conflict.

grooming The ritual cleaning of another animal's coat to remove parasites and other matter.

estrus In some primate females, the time of sexual receptivity during which ovulation is visibly displayed.

studied by Goodall, low- or midlevel males sired about half the infants. Although for females high rank is linked with successful reproduction, social success for males—achieving alpha status—does not translate neatly into the evolutionary currency of reproductive success (Figure 4.6).

In contrast to chimpanzees, bonobos (like humans) do not limit their sexual behavior to times of female fertility. The constant genital swelling of bonobos, in effect, conceals the females' **ovulation**, or moment when an egg released into the womb is receptive for fertilization. Ovulation is also concealed in humans, by the absence of genital swelling at all times. Concealed ovulation in humans and bonobos may play a role in separating sexual activity for social and pleasurable reasons from the purely biological task of reproduction. In fact, among bonobos (as among humans) sexuality goes far beyond male–female mating for purposes of biological reproduction.

Primatologists have observed virtually every possible combination of ages and sexes engaging in a remarkable array of sexual activities, including oral sex, tongue-kissing, and massaging each other's genitals (de Waal, 2001). Male bonobos may mount each other, or one may rub his scrotum against that of the other. Researchers have also observed bonobos "penis fencing"—hanging face-to-face from a branch and rubbing their erect penises together as if crossing swords. Among females, genital rubbing is particularly common.

Most of this sex, both hetero- and homosexual, functions to reduce tensions and resolve social conflicts. Bonobo sexual activity is very frequent but also very brief, lasting only 8 to 10 seconds. Since the documentation of sexual activities among bonobos, field studies by primatologists have documented a variety of sexual behaviors

ovulation The moment when an egg released from an ovary into the womb is receptive for fertilization.

© Martin Harvey/Alamy

Figure 4.6 Male Dominance Display and Reproductive Success Although early primates studies focused on male dominance hierarchies, later research has shown that social dominance or alpha status does not automatically confer greater reproductive success for males as it does for females. As primates themselves, were the early primatologists impressed by male displays of power and bluster, such as seen here? Or did this emphasis on dominance hierarchies stem from the fact that Darwinian theory—itself in sync with its own cultural milieu—emphasized competition and a struggle for existence? With time, careful scientific study has confirmed that for primate survival, cooperation outranks aggression.

among other species as well. This chapter's Original Study by primatologists Anna Maggioncalda, and Robert Sapolsky offers a disturbing example of the diversity of sexual behavior of primates.

Disturbing Behaviors of the Orangutan
BY ANNE NACEY MAGGIONCALDA AND ROBERT M. SAPOLSKY

An adult male orangutan is an impressive sight. The animal has a pair of wide cheek pads, called flanges, and a well-developed throat sac used for emitting loud cries known as long calls. The mature male also has long, brightly colored hair on its body and face. These are secondary sexual characteristics, the flamboyant signals that male orangutans flaunt to proclaim their fertility and fitness to the opposite sex. The features emerge during orangutan adolescence: Males reach puberty at around 7 to 9 years of age, then spend a few years in a far-from-impressive "subadult" stage, during which they are

about the same size as mature females. The males reach their adult size and develop secondary sexual traits by ages 12 to 14. Or at least that's what primate researchers used to think.

As stable social groups of orangutans were established in zoos, however, it became clear that an adolescent male could remain a subadult, in a state of arrested development, until his late teens. In the 1970s, studies of orangutans in the rainforests of Southeast Asia by Biruté M. F. Galdikas . . . and others produced the same finding: Sometimes males were arrested adolescents for a decade or more, about half their potential reproductive lives. Variability of this magnitude is fascinating—it is like finding a species in which pregnancy could last anywhere from six months to five years.

Biologists are keenly interested in studying cases of arrested development because they often shed light on the processes of growth and maturation. . . . Environmental factors can . . . slow or halt an organism's development. For instance, food shortages delay maturation in humans and many other animals. This response is logical from an evolutionary standpoint—if it is unclear whether you will survive another week, it makes no sense to waste calories by adding bone mass or developing secondary sexual characteristics. Gymnasts and ballet dancers who exercise to extremes and anorexics who starve themselves sometimes experience delayed onset of puberty.

Among male orangutans, though, the cause of arrested development seems to lie in the animals' social environment. The presence of dominant adult males appears to delay the maturation of adolescent males in the same vicinity. Until recently, researchers believed that they were observing a stress-induced pathology—that is, the adolescent orangutans stopped developing because the adult males bullied and frightened them. Over the past few years, however, we have conducted studies (by measuring stress, growth, and reproductive hormone levels in urine) suggesting that arrested development among orangutans is not a pathology but an adaptive evolutionary strategy. The arrested adolescent males are capable of impregnating females, and by staying small and immature (in terms of secondary sexual features) they minimize the amount of food they need and lower the risk of serious conflict with adult males. But the strategy of these arrested adolescents has a disquieting aspect: They copulate forcibly with females. In other words, they rape.

These findings overturned some long-held assumptions about orangutans. Apparently, arrested adolescents are neither stressed nor reproductively suppressed. What is going on? It turns out that there is more than one way for a male orangutan to improve his chances of reproducing.

A cornerstone of modern evolutionary theory is that animal behavior has evolved not for the good of the species or the social group but to maximize the number of gene copies passed on by an individual and its close relatives. For a long time, the study of primates was dominated by simplistic models of how animals achieve this goal. According to these models, male behavior consists of virtually nothing but aggression and competition to gain access to females. If only one female is sexually receptive in a group with many males, this competition would result in the highest-ranking male mating with her; if two females are receptive, the males ranking first and second in the hierarchy would mate with them, and so on.

But this kind of behavior is rarely seen among social primates. Instead male primates can choose alternative strategies to maximize their reproductive success. Why should there be alternatives? Because the seemingly logical strategy—developing powerful muscles and dramatic secondary sexual characteristics to excel at male–male competition—has some serious drawbacks. In many species, maintaining those secondary characteristics requires elevated testosterone levels, which have a variety of adverse effects on health. The aggression that comes with such a strategy is not great for health either.

Furthermore, increased body mass means greater metabolic demands and more pressure for successful food acquisition. During famines, the bigger primates are less likely to survive. For an arboreal species such as the orangutan, the heavier body of the mature male also limits which trees and branches can be accessed for food. And the development of secondary sexual characteristics makes a male more conspicuous, both to predators and to other males that view those characteristics as a challenge.

In contrast, the key impression that a developmentally arrested male communicates to an adult male is a lack of threat or challenge because the immature male looks like a kid. Arrested male orangutans are apparently inconspicuous enough to be spared a certain amount of social stress. What is more, the "low profile" of these animals may actually give them a competitive advantage when it comes to reproduction. In many primate species, the low-ranking males are actually doing a fair share of the mating. Genetic paternity testing of these primates has shown that the subordinate males are quite successful in passing on their genes. . . .

The great majority of adult female orangutans are sexually receptive only to mature males. So how do the arrested males mate? Observations of orangutans both in the wild and in captive populations have indicated that the arrested males forcibly copulate with females. *Rape* is an apt term for these copulations: The adult females usually resist the arrested adolescents fiercely, biting the males whenever they can and emitting loud, guttural sounds (called rape grunts) that are heard only under these circumstances. Adult males sometimes rape, too, but not nearly as often as the arrested males.

Thus, two reproductive strategies appear to have evolved for adolescent male orangutans. If no fully mature males are nearby, the adolescent will most likely develop quickly in the hopes of attracting female attention. When adult males are present, however, a strategy of arrested development has its advantages. If the social environment changes—say, if the nearby adult males die off or migrate—the arrested males will rapidly develop secondary sexual features and change their behavior patterns. Researchers are now trying to determine exactly how the presence or absence of adult males triggers hormonal changes in the adolescents.

What are the lessons we can learn from the male orangutan? First, a situation that seems stressful from a

VISUAL COUNTERPOINT

Kevin Shafter/Getty Images/The Image Bank

© Danita Delimont/Alamy

The male orangutan on the right has retained his adolescent physique even though his primary sex characteristics are fully mature, allowing him to father offspring. The male on the left has developed the secondary sexual characteristics typical of the adult male orangutan. Though strikingly different in appearance, these two individuals might be very close to the same age.

human's perspective may not necessarily be so. Second, the existence of alternative reproductive strategies shows that the optimal approach can vary dramatically in different social and ecological settings. There is no single blueprint for understanding the evolution of behavior. Third, although the recognition of alternative strategies built around female choice has generally met with a receptive audience among scientists, the rape-oriented strategy of arrested male orangutans is not so pleasing. But the study of primates has demonstrated time and again that the behavior of these animals is far from Disney-esque.

One must be cautious, however, in trying to gain insights into human behavior by extrapolating from animal studies. There is a temptation to leap to a wrongheaded conclusion: Because forcible copulation occurs in orangutans and something similar occurs in humans, rape has a natural basis and is therefore unstoppable. This argument ignores the fact that the orangutan is the only nonhuman primate to engage in forcible copulation as a routine means of siring offspring. Furthermore, close observations of orangutan rape show that it is very different from human rape: For example, researchers have never seen a male orangutan injure a female during copulation in an apparently intentional manner. Most important, the orangutan's physiology, life history, and social structure are completely unlike those of any other primate. Orangutans have evolved a unique set of adaptations to survive in their environment, and hence it would be the height of absurdity to draw simpleminded parallels between their behaviors and those of humans.

Adapted from Maggioncalda, A. N., & Sapolsky, R. M. (2002, May 13). Disturbing behaviors of the orangutan. Scientific American 286 (6), 60–65. Copyright © Scientific American, a division of Nature America, Inc. All rights reserved. Reprinted by permission.

The behavior of the orangutans disturbs us in part because we see ourselves in their actions. Maggioncalda and Sapolsky call the forced copulations by arrested male orangutans "rape," but they also take pains to show how this differs from rape in humans. Likewise, individuals uncomfortable with human sexual diversity might see the sexual behavior of bonobos as deviant. As we study the sexual behavior of primates we must stay particularly aware of how we might impose our own cultural notions onto the behaviors of our closest living relatives.

Consider, for example, how previous editions of this text explained gorilla sexuality in terms of male control as follows: The dominant silverback was said to have exclusive breeding rights with the females; sometimes the silverback would tolerate the presence of a young adult male and allow him occasional access to a low-ranking female. Young males then enticed partners away from other established groups, in order to have reproductive success. Today we can look at this situation from the female gorilla's perspective and find an explanation for why males leave the home group by the time they become silverbacks. Could it be that females recognize the future potential in an incipient silverback and the possibility of forming a new group and thus will mate with these young adult males? Today's scientists studying animal behavior recognize the importance of female choice in reproduction.

Field studies have revealed variation in the typical gorilla pattern of a single dominant male. Gorilla groups in Uganda and Rwanda contain multiple silverback males. Still, in one of these multi-male groups studied in Rwanda, a single dominant male fathered all but one of ten juveniles (Gibbons, 2001a).

Although the vast majority of primate species are not **monogamous**—bonded exclusively to a single sexual partner—in their mating habits, many smaller species of New World monkeys, a few island-dwelling populations of leaf-eating Old World monkeys, and all of the smaller apes (gibbons and siamangs) appear to mate for life with a single individual of the opposite sex. These monogamous species have a lower degree of sexual dimorphism—anatomical differences between males and females—compared to our closest primate relatives (the great apes) or that was characteristic of our own ancient ancestors.

Evolutionary biologists, dating back to Charles Darwin himself, have proposed that sexual dimorphism (for example, larger male size in apes, beautiful feathers in peacocks) relates to competition among males for access to females. Females only evolved by what Canadian primatologist Linda Fedigan has called the "coat-tails theory" of evolution (Fedigan, 1992). She points out that evolutionary theories about sexual dimorphism and reproductive behaviors are particularly susceptible to becoming "gendered." That is, the gender norms of the scientists can easily creep their way (subconsciously, of course) into the theories they are creating. Darwin's era, despite the reign of Queen Victoria, was firmly patriarchal, and male–male competition prevailed in British society. Women of Darwin's time and

class were denied basic rights, such as the right to vote. Inheritance laws favored first-born male heirs. Feminist analyses such as Fedigan's have contributed substantially to the developing discipline of primatology.

Primate field studies have revealed that male–male competition is just one of many factors playing a role in primate reproduction. Male–male competition can be reduced as it is in orangutans through arrested development. Further, a broad range of social processes contributes to reproductive success, with as much variation as the numerous biological factors that contribute to body size. For example, in baboons, a very sexually dimorphic species, the female chooses who her mate is just as often as the choice is determined through male–male competition. Females frequently choose to mate with lower-ranking males that show strong male–female **affiliative** actions (tending to promote social cohesion) and good parental behavior (Sapolsky, 2002).

Among baboons, paternal involvement has been shown to have distinct advantages for offspring, including more rapid growth in baboon infants if they receive attention from their fathers. In addition, adult males will also intercede on their offspring's behalf when the young ones are involved in fights. In short, choosing a good mate based on affiliative qualities can optimize the reproductive success of female baboons.

Reproduction and Care of Young

The average adult female monkey or ape spends most of her adult life either pregnant or nursing her young, times at which she is not sexually receptive. Apes generally nurse each of their young for about four to five years. After weaning her infant, she will come into estrus periodically, until she becomes pregnant again.

Among primates, as among some other mammals, females generally give birth to one infant at a time. Natural selection may have favored single births among primate tree-dwellers because the primate infant, having a highly developed grasping ability (human infants have this same grasping reflex), must be transported about by its mother. More than one clinging infant would interfere with movement in the trees. Only the smaller nocturnal prosimians, the primates closest to the ancestral condition, typically bear more than one infant at a time. Among the anthropoids, only the true marmoset, a kind of New World monkey, has a pattern of habitual twinning. Other species like humans will twin occasionally. In marmosets, both parents share infant care, with fathers doing most of the carrying. Polyandry also occurs

---

monogamous In primatology, mating for life with a single individual of the opposite sex.

affiliative Behaving in a manner that tends to promote social cohesion.

among marmosets, presumably as an adaptation to carrying multiple young.

Primates follow a pattern of bearing few young but devoting more time and effort to the care of each individual offspring. Compared to other mammals such as mice, which pass from birth to adulthood in a matter of weeks, primates spend a great deal of time growing up. As a general rule, the more closely related to humans the species is, the longer the period of infant and childhood dependency (**Figure 4.7**). For example, a lemur depends upon its mother for only a few months after birth, whereas an ape is dependent for four or five years. A chimpanzee infant cannot survive if its mother dies before it reaches the age of 4 at the very least. During the juvenile period, the larger social group, rather than just the mothers, sustain young primates. The young use this period to learn and refine a variety of behaviors. If the mother of a juvenile primate dies, an older male or female member of the social group may adopt the youngster. Among bonobos, a juvenile who has lost his or her mother has very little social standing in the group.

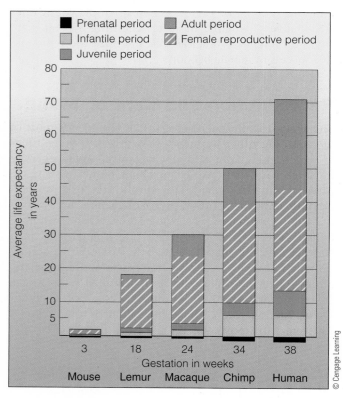

Figure 4.7 The Primate Life Cycle A long life cycle, including a long period of childhood dependency, is characteristic of the primates. In biological terms, infancy ends when young mammals are weaned, and adulthood is defined as *sexual maturation*. In many species, such as mice, animals become sexually mature as soon as they are weaned. Among primates, a juvenile period for social learning occurs between infancy and adulthood. For humans, the biological definitions of *infancy* and *adulthood* are modified according to cultural norms.

The long interval between births, particularly among the apes, results in small population size. A female chimpanzee, for example, does not reach sexual maturity until about the age of 10, and once she produces her first live offspring, five or six years passes before she will bear another. So, assuming that none of her offspring dies before adulthood, a female chimpanzee must survive for at least twenty or twenty-one years just to maintain the status quo in chimpanzee population. In fact, chimpanzee infants and juveniles do die from time to time, and not all females live full reproductive lives. This accounts for the lower population size of apes compared to monkeys. Likewise, the short intervals between births account for ever-increasing human population growth.

A long slow period of growth and development, particularly among the hominoids, also provides opportunities. Born without built-in responses dictating specific behavior in complex situations, the young monkey or ape, like the young human, learns how to strategically interact with others and even to manipulate them for his or her own benefit—by trial and error, observation, imitation, and practice. Young primates make mistakes along the way, learning to modify their behavior based on the reactions of other members of the group. Each member of the community has a unique physical appearance and personality. Youngsters learn to match their interactive behaviors according to each individual's social position and temperament. Anatomical features common to all monkeys and apes, such as a free upper lip (unlike lemurs and cats, for example), allow for varied facial expression, contributing to communication between individuals. Much of this learning takes place through play.

For primate infants and juveniles, play does more than pass the hours. Young primates play to learn about their environment, to learn social skills, and to test a variety of behaviors. Chimpanzee infants mimic the food-getting activities of adults, "attack" dozing adults, and "harass" adolescents. Observers have watched young gorillas do somersaults, wrestle, and play various organized games, such as jostling for position on the top of a hillside or following and mimicking a single youngster. One juvenile, becoming annoyed at repeated harassment by an infant, picked it up, climbed a tree, and deposited it on a branch from which it was unable to get down on its own; eventually, its mother came to retrieve it.

Communication and Learning

Primates, like many animals, vocalize. They have a great range of calls that are often used together with movements of the face or body to convey a message. Observers have not yet established the meaning of all the sounds, but a good number have been distinguished, such as warning calls, threat calls, defense calls, and gathering calls. Primatologists have studied the behavioral reactions of other animals hearing the call. Among bonobos, chimpanzees, and gorillas, most vocalizations communicate an emotional state rather than information. Much of the communication of these species takes place by using specific gestures and postures (**Figure 4.8**). Indeed, apes and humans share a number of these, such as kissing and embracing.

Primatologists have classified numerous chimpanzee vocalizations and visual communication signals. Facial expressions convey emotional states such as distress, fear, or excitement. Distinct vocalizations or calls have been associated with a variety of sensations. For example, chimps will smack their lips or clack their teeth to express pleasure with sociable body contact. Calls called "pant-hoots," which are used to announce the arrival of individuals or to inquire, can be differentiated into specific types. Together, these facilitate group protection, coordination of group efforts, and social interaction in general.

To what degree are various forms of communication universal and to what degree are they specific to a given group? On the group-specificity side, primatologists have recently documented within-species dialects of calls that emerge as groups are isolated in their habitats. Social factors, genetic drift, and habitat acoustics could all contribute to the appearance of these distinct dialects (de la Torre & Snowden, 2009).

Smiles and embraces have long been understood to be universal among humans and our closest relatives. But recently some additional universals have been documented. Athletes who are blind use the same gestures to express submission or victory that sighted athletes use at the end of a match, although they have never seen such gestures themselves (**Figure 4.9**) (Tracy & Matsumoto, 2008).

Figure 4.8 Universal Hominoid Expressions Many ape non-verbal communications are easily recognized by humans, as we share the same gestures. This capacity allows us to communicate across cultures and across species. Among humans, this capacity also makes miscommunication more likely when visual cues are missing or do not match the accompanying words.

This raises interesting questions about whether primate communications are biologically hardwired or learned.

Visual communication can also take place through objects. Bonobos do so with trail markers. When foraging, the community breaks up into smaller groups, rejoining

Figure 4.9 Gestures of the Blind Athletes who have been blind since birth use the same body gestures to express victory and defeat as sighted athletes. Because they do this without ever having seen an "end zone" celebration, this indicates that these body gestures are hardwired into humans and presumably derive from our primate heritage.

in the evening to nest together. To keep track of each party's whereabouts, those in the lead, at the intersections of trails or where downed trees obscure the path, will indicate their direction by deliberately stomping down the vegetation or by ripping off large leaves and placing them carefully. Thus, they all know where to come together at the end of the day (Recer, 1998).

Primatologists have also found that primates can communicate specific threats through their calls. Researchers have documented that the alarm calls of vervet monkeys communicate on several levels of meaning to elicit specific responses from others in the group (Seyfarth, Cheney, & Marler, 1980). The calls designated types of predators (birds of prey, big cats, snakes) and where the threat might arise. Further, they have documented how young vervets go about learning the appropriate use of the calls. If the young individual has uttered the correct call, adults will repeat the call, and the appropriate escape behavior will follow (heading into the trees to get away from a cat or into brush to be safe from an eagle). But if an infant utters the cry for an eagle in response to a leaf falling from the sky or for a nonthreatening bird, no adult calls will ensue.

From an evolutionary perspective, scientists have been puzzled about behaviors such as these vervet alarm calls. Biologists assume that the forces of natural selection work on behavioral traits just as they do on genetic traits. It seems reasonable that individuals in a group of vervet monkeys capable of warning one another of the presence of predators would have a significant survival advantage over those without this capability. However, these warning situations are enigmatic to evolutionary biologists because they would expect the animals to act in their own self-interest, with survival of self being paramount. By giving an alarm call, an individual calls attention to itself, thereby becoming an obvious target for the predator. How, then, could **altruism**, or concern for the welfare of others, evolve so that individuals place themselves at risk for the good of the group? One biologist's solution substitutes money for reproductive fitness to illustrate how such cooperative behavior may have come about:

> You are given a choice. Either you can receive $10 and keep it all or you can receive

Figure 4.10 **Bonobos and Pictorial Language** Kanzi, the 23-year-old bonobo at the Great Ape Trust of Iowa, communicates with primatologist Sue Savage-Rumbaugh by pointing to visual images called lexigrams. With hundreds of lexigrams, Kanzi can express his thoughts and feelings. He also understands spoken language and can reply in a conversation with the lexigrams. Kanzi began to learn this form of communication when he was a youngster, tagging along while his mother had language lessons. Though he showed no interest in the lessons, later he spontaneously began to use lexigrams himself.

> $10 million if you give $6 million to your next-door neighbor. Which would you do? Guessing that most selfish people would be happy with a net gain of $4 million, I consider the second option to be a form of selfish behavior in which a neighbor gains an incidental benefit. I have termed such selfish behavior benevolent. (Nunney, 1998, p. 1619)

Natural selection of beneficial social traits was probably an important influence on human evolution because in the primates some degree of cooperative social behavior became important for food-getting, defense, and mate attraction. Indeed, anthropologist Christopher Boehm argues, "If human nature were merely selfish, vigilant punishment of deviants would be expected, whereas the elaborate prosocial prescriptions that favor altruism would come as a surprise" (Boehm, 2000, p. 7).

With primate survival dependent on social cooperation, evolutionary forces have favored the development of strong communication skills. Experiments with captive apes, carried out over several decades, reveal remarkable communicative abilities. In some of these experiments, bonobos and chimpanzees have been taught to communicate using symbols, as in the case of Kanzi, a bonobo who uses a visual keyboard (**Figure 4.10**). Other chimpanzees, gorillas, and orangutans have been taught American Sign Language.

---

altruism Concern for the welfare of others expressed as increased risk undertaken by individuals for the good of the group.

Controversy surrounds this research in part because it challenges notions of human uniqueness. Nevertheless, it has become evident that apes are capable of understanding language quite well, even using rudimentary grammar. They generate original utterances, ask questions, distinguish naming something from asking for it, develop original ways to tell lies, coordinate their actions, and spontaneously teach language to others. Even though they cannot literally "speak," it is now clear that all of the great ape species can develop language skills to the level of a 2- to 3-year-old human child (Lestel, 1998; Miles, 1993). Interestingly, a Japanese research team recently demonstrated that chimps can outperform college students at a computer-based memory game (Inoue & Matsuzawa, 2007). The researchers propose that human brains have lost some of the spatial skill required to master this game to allow for more sophisticated human language.

Observations of monkeys and apes have shown learning abilities remarkably similar to those of humans. Numerous examples of inventive behavior have been observed among monkeys, as well as among apes. The snow monkeys or macaques of the research colony on Koshima Island, Japan, are particularly famous for demonstrating that individuals can invent new behaviors that then get passed on to the group through imitation.

In the 1950s and early 1960s, one particularly bright young female macaque named Imo (Japanese primatologists always considered it appropriate to name individual animals) started several innovative behaviors in her troop. She figured out that grain could be separated from sand if it was placed in water. The sand sank and the grain floated clean, making it much easier to eat. She also began the practice of washing the sweet potatoes that primatologists provided—first in fresh water but later in the ocean, presumably because of the pleasant taste the saltwater added. In each case, only the young animals imitated the innovations; Imo's mother was the lone older macaque to embrace them right away. Similarly, a female macaque named Mukbili at a field site in the Nagono Mountains initiated the

Figure 4.11 **Macaque Social Learning** In the same way that young Imo got her troop to begin washing sweet potatoes in saltwater, at Kyoto University's Koshima Island Primatology Research Preserve, another young female macaque recently taught other macaques to bathe in hot springs. In the Nagano Mountains of Japan, this macaque, named Mukbili, began bathing in the springs. Others followed her, and now this is an activity practiced by all members of the group.

practice of bathing in hot springs, a behavior that other members of the group adopted happily (Figure 4.11).

Another example of innovation in food manipulation was discovered among captive chimpanzees in the zoo of Madrid, Spain. It began when a 5-year-old female rubbed apples against a sharp corner of a concrete wall in order to lick the mashed pieces and juice left on the wall. From this youngster, the practice of "smearing" spread to her peers, and within five years most group members were performing the operation frequently and consistently. The innovation has become standardized and durable, having transcended two generations in the group (Fernandez-Carriba & Loeches, 2001).

Freely living chimpanzees in West Africa provide another dramatic example of learning in their method of cracking open hard-shelled oil-palm nuts. For this they use tools: an anvil stone with a level surface on which to place the nut and a good-sized hammer stone to crack it. Not just any stone will do; it must be of the right shape and weight, and the anvil may require leveling by placing smaller stones beneath one or more edges. Nor does random banging away do the job. The nut has to be hit at the right speed and the right trajectory, or else the nut simply flies off into the forest. Last but not least, the apes must avoid mashing their fingers, rather than the nut. According to fieldworkers, the expertise of the chimps far exceeds that of any human who tries cracking these hardest nuts in the world.

Youngsters learn this process by staying near to adults who are cracking nuts, where their mothers share some of the food. This teaches them about the edibility of the nuts but not how to get at what is edible. This they learn by observing and by "aping" (copying) the adults. At first they play with a nut or stone alone; later they begin to randomly combine objects. They soon learn, however, that placing nuts on anvils and hitting them with a hand or foot gets them nowhere.

Only after three years of futile effort do they begin to coordinate all of the multiple actions and objects, but even then only after a great deal of practice, by the age of 6 or 7 years, do they become proficient in this task. They practice this skill for over a thousand days. Evidently, social motivation accounts for their perseverance after at least three years of failure, with no reward to reinforce their effort. At first, a desire to act like the mother motivates them; only later does the desire to feed on the tasty nutmeat take over (de Waal, 2001).

Martin Harvey/Getty Images/Peter Arnold

Figure 4.12 Fishing for Termites Chimps use a variety of tools in the wild. Here a chimp uses a long stick stripped of its side branches to fish for termites—the first chimp tool use described by Jane Goodall in the 1960s. Chimps will select a stick when still quite far from the termite mound and modify its shape on the way to the snacking spot.

Use of Objects as Tools

A **tool** may be defined as an object used to facilitate some task or activity. The nut cracking just discussed is the most complex tool-use task observed by researchers in the wild, involving both hands, two tools, and exact coordination. Other examples of tool use among apes in the wild abound. Chimpanzees, bonobos, and orangutans all make and use tools.

Tool use and tool-making capacities remain distinct. Tool use, as in pounding something with a convenient stone, requires far less acumen compared to tool making, which involves deliberate modification of some material for its intended use. Thus, otters that use unmodified stones to crack open clams may be tool users, but they are not toolmakers. Not only do chimpanzees modify objects to make them suitable for particular purposes, but chimps also modify these objects into regular and set patterns. They pick up and even prepare objects for future use at some other location, and they can use objects as tools to solve new problems.

Chimps have been observed using stalks of grass, twigs that they have stripped of leaves, and even sticks up to 3 feet long that they have smoothed down to "fish" for termites (**Figure 4.12**). They insert the modified stick into a termite nest, wait a few minutes, pull the stick out, and eat the insects clinging to it, all of which requires considerable dexterity. Chimpanzees are equally deliberate in their own nest

---

tool An object used to facilitate some task or activity. Although tool making involves intentional modification of the material of which it is made, tool use may involve objects either modified for some particular purpose or completely unmodified.

building. They test the vines and branches to make sure they are usable. If they are not, the animal moves to another site.

Other examples of chimpanzee use of tools involve leaves, used as wipes or as sponges, to get water out of a hollow to drink. Large sticks may serve as clubs or as missiles (as may stones) in aggressive or defensive displays. Chimps use twigs as toothpicks to clean teeth as well as to extract loose baby teeth. They use these dental tools not just on themselves but on other individuals as well (McGrew, 2000).

In the wild, bonobos have not been observed making and using tools to the extent seen in chimpanzees. However, their use of large leaves as trail markers may be considered a form of tool use. Further, a captive bonobo who has figured out how to make tools of stone that are remarkably like the earliest such tools made by our own ancestors provides further evidence of their tool-making capacities (Toth et al., 1993).

Chimpanzees also use plants for medicinal purposes, illustrating their selectivity with raw materials, a quality related to tool manufacture. Chimps that appear to observers to be ill have been seen seeking out specific plants of the genus *Aspilia*. They will eat the leaves singly without chewing them, letting the leaves soften in their mouths for a long time before swallowing. Primatologists have discovered that the leaves pass through the chimp's digestive system whole and relatively intact, having scraped parasites off the intestinal walls in the process.

Although gorillas (like bonobos and chimps) build nests, they have not been observed to make and use other tools in the wild. The lack of tools among gorillas likely stems from the fact that their easy diet of leaves and nettles makes tools of no particular use.

Hunting

Prior to the 1980s, most primates were thought to be vegetarian while humans alone were considered meat-eating hunters. Among the vegetarians, *folivores* were thought to eat only leaves while *frugivores* feasted on fruits. Though some primates do have specialized adaptations—such as a complex stomach and shearing teeth to aid in the digestion of leaves or an extra-long small intestine to slow the passage of juicy fruits so they can be readily absorbed—primate field studies have revealed that the diets of monkeys and apes are extremely varied.

Many primates are *omnivores* who eat a broad range of foods. Goodall's fieldwork among chimpanzees in their natural habitat at Gombe Stream demonstrates that these apes supplement their primary diet of fruits and other plant foods with insects and meat. Even more surprising, she found that in addition to killing small invertebrate animals for food, they also hunt and eat monkeys. Goodall observed chimpanzees grabbing adult red colobus monkeys and flailing them to death. Since her pioneering work, other primatologists have documented hunting behavior in baboons and capuchin monkeys, among others.

Chimpanzee females sometimes hunt, but males do so far more frequently. When on the hunt, they may spend hours watching, following, and chasing intended prey. Moreover, in contrast to the usual primate practice of each animal finding its own food, hunting frequently involves teamwork to trap and kill prey, particularly when hunting for baboons. Once a potential victim has been isolated from its troop, three or more adult chimps will carefully position themselves so as to block off escape routes while another pursues the prey. Following the kill, most who participated get a share of the meat, either by grabbing a piece as chance affords or by begging for it.

In addition to the nutritional value of meat, hunting appears to have social and reproductive value as well. Anthropologist Craig Stanford, who has been doing fieldwork among the chimpanzees of Gombe since the early 1990s, found that these sizable apes (100-pound males are common) frequently kill animals weighing up to 25 pounds and eat much more meat than previously believed. Their preferred prey is the red colobus monkey that shares their forested habitat. Annually, chimpanzee hunting parties at Gombe kill about 20 percent of these monkeys, many of them babies, often shaking them out of the tops of 30-foot trees. They may capture and kill as many as seven victims in a raid. These hunts usually take place during the dry season when plant foods are less available and when females display genital swelling, which signals that they are ready to mate. On average, each chimp at Gombe eats about a quarter-pound of meat per day during the dry season. For female chimps, a supply of protein-rich food helps support the increased nutritional requirements of pregnancy and lactation.

Somewhat different chimpanzee hunting practices have been observed in West Africa. At Tai National Park in Côte d'Ivoire, for instance, chimpanzees engage in highly coordinated team efforts to chase monkeys hiding in very tall trees in the dense tropical forest. Individuals who have especially distinguished themselves in a successful hunt see their contributions rewarded with more meat.

Recent research shows that bonobos in the Democratic Republic of Congo's rainforest also supplement their diet with meat obtained by means of hunting. Although their behavior resembles that of chimpanzees, crucial differences exist. Among bonobos, females predominantly hunt. Also, female hunters regularly share carcasses with

BIOCULTURAL CONNECTION

Chimpanzees in Biomedical Research: Time to End the Practice

Biological similarities among humans, apes, and Old World monkeys have led to the extensive use of nonhuman primate species in biomedical research aimed at preventing or curing disease in humans. Some biomedical research disturbs animals minimally. For example, DNA can be extracted from the hair naturally shed by living primates, allowing for cross-species comparisons of disease genes. To facilitate this process, cell repositories have been established for researchers to obtain samples of primate DNA. Other biomedical research is far more invasive to the individual primate. For example, to document the infectious nature of kuru, a disease closely related to mad cow disease, extract from the brains of sick humans was injected into the brains of living chimpanzees. A year and a half later, the chimpanzees began to sicken. They

had the same classic features of kuru—uncontrollable spasticity, seizures, dementia, and ultimately death.

These research animals are subjected to procedures that would be considered morally questionable if done on humans. Mickey, pictured here, for example, was one of the hundreds of chimps who spent decades of her life alone in a concrete-and-steel windowless cage in a private research facility in New Mexico run by Frederick Coulston. After years of testing the effects of various infectious diseases, cosmetics, drugs, and pesticides on chimps like Mickey, the Coulston laboratory finally closed in 2002 when government research funding was withdrawn due to repeated violations of the Animal Welfare Act. But after years of abuse and neglect, research chimpanzees lack the skills to participate in chimpanzee social life. Furthermore,

research animals have often been infected with deadly diseases such as HIV or hepatitis and cannot be released into the wild. Fortunately, Mickey and the other research chimps were given sanctuary through Save the Chimps, one of several organizations that rescue research animals.

The biological similarities of humans and other primates leading to such research practices derive from a long, shared evolutionary history. By comparison, the cultural rules that allow our closest relatives to be the subjects of biomedical research are relatively recent. Jane Goodall makes a convincing case for ending this practice:

> Surely it should be a matter of moral responsibility that we humans, differing from other animals mainly by virtue of our more highly developed intellect and, with it, our greater capacity for understanding and compassion, ensure that the medical progress slowly detaches its roots from the manure of nonhuman animal suffering and despair. Particularly when this involves the servitude of our closest relatives.[a]

BIOCULTURAL QUESTION

Those who fully support the use of nonhuman primates in biomedical research argue that using a limited number of chimpanzees or rhesus macaques to lessen human suffering and spare human lives is justified. Do you agree or disagree? What kinds of alternatives might be developed to replace nonhuman primates in biomedical research?

The toll of a life spent in the Coulston research facility is evident in Mickey who has since been rescued by Save the Chimp

Courtesy of Save the Chimps, the world's largest sanctuary for rescued chimpanzees; www.savethechimps.org

[a]Goodall, J. (1990). *Through a window: My thirty years with the chimpanzees of Gombe.* Boston: Houghton Mifflin.

other females but less often with males. Even when the most dominant male throws a tantrum nearby, he may still be denied a share of meat (Ingmanson, 1998). Female bonobos behave in much the same way when it comes to sharing other foods such as fruits.

While it had long been assumed that male chimpanzees were the primary hunters, primatologist Jill Pruetz and her colleagues researching in Fongoli, Senegal, documented habitual hunting by groups of young female and male chimpanzees using spears (Pruetz & Bertolani, 2007). The chimps took spears they had previously prepared and sharpened to a point and jabbed them repeatedly into the hollow parts of trees where small animals, including primates, might be hiding. The primatologists even observed the chimps extract bush babies from tree hollows with the spears.

The observation that young chimpanzees, one adolescent female in particular, are the most frequent spear hunters indicates that this innovation appeared in the group quite recently. Just as the young female Japanese macaques mentioned previously were the innovators in those groups, this young female chimp seems to be leading this behavior in Senegal. Further, the savannah conditions of the Fongoli Reserve make these observations particularly interesting in terms of human evolutionary studies: Paleoanthropologists have suggested that among our ancestors out on the savannah, males hunted while females gathered, a theory that seems to be undermined by the Fongoli observations.

The Question of Culture

The more we learn of the behavior of our nearest primate relatives, the more we become aware of the importance of learned, socially shared practices and knowledge in these creatures. Do chimpanzees, bonobos, and the other apes have culture? The answer appears to be yes. The detailed study of ape behavior has revealed varied use of tools and patterns of social engagement that seem to derive from the traditions of the specific group rather than from a biologically determined script. Humans share with the other apes an ability to learn the complex but flexible patterns of behavior particular to a social group during a long period of childhood dependency.

If we agree that these other primates possess culture, does this demand a reorientation in how humans behave toward

them, such as stopping the use of monkeys and apes in biomedical research? Jane Goodall argues vehemently for this change. She emphasizes that cultural processes determine the place of animals within biomedical research, and she advocates eliminating the cultural distinction between humans and our closest relatives for research purposes. Governments have begun responding to her calls as seen by the 2008 approval by the Spanish Parliament of the "Declaration on Great Apes," which extends some human rights to gorillas, chimpanzees, bonobos, and orangutans (O'Carroll, 2008).

In December 2010 the U.S. National Institutes of Health (NIH) commissioned the Institute of Medicine to study whether there was a need for chimps in biomedical and behavioral research. The answer was such an unequivocal no that the NIH will no longer fund any new projects involving research chimpanzees. The NIH also committed to reviewing all existing studies and dismantling any that do not meet the stringent criteria outlined in the Institute of Medicine's report. See this chapter's Biocultural Connection for more on the use of chimpanzees in medical research and the efforts to stop this practice.

Despite this progress, powerful social barriers still work against the well-being of our animal relatives. In Western societies there has been an unfortunate tendency to erect what paleontologist Stephen Jay Gould refers to as "golden barriers" that set us apart from the rest of the animal kingdom (quoted in de Waal, 2001). Sadly, this mindset blinds us to the fact that a continuum exists between us (humans) and them (animals). We have already seen that the physical differences between humans and apes are largely differences of degree, rather than kind. It now appears that the same is true with respect to behavior. As primatologist Richard Wrangham put it,

> Like humans, [chimpanzees] laugh, make up after a quarrel, support each other in times of trouble, medicate themselves with chemical and physical remedies, stop each other from eating poisonous foods, collaborate in the hunt, help each other over physical obstacles, raid neighboring groups, lose their tempers, get excited by dramatic weather, invent ways to show off, have family traditions and group traditions, make tools, devise plans, deceive, play tricks, grieve, are cruel and are kind. (quoted in Mydens, 2001, p. 5)

This is not to say that we are "just" another ape; obviously, degree does make a difference. Nevertheless, the continuities between our primate kin and us reflect a common evolutionary heritage, giving us the responsibility to help our cousins today. Because of our shared evolutionary heritage, the biology and behavior of the other living primates, like the contemporary study of genetics, provide valuable insight into our understanding of human origins. The methods scientists use to recover data directly from fossilized bones and preserved cultural remains in order to study the human past are the subject of the next chapter.

CHAPTER CHECKLIST

How does primate social organization differ among species?

● Chimps and bonobos compose communities of up to fifty members split among subgroups that change as individuals join and leave.

● Gorillas group into "families" led by a silver-backed male who tends to have exclusive mating rights. Upon maturity, younger males are forced to leave their natal group and may go on to form their own family or join an all-male group.

● Baboons live in troops of varying size that may comprise several smaller single male multi-female (polygynous) groups.

● Gibbons and a few other species are monogamous and live with only their nuclear families.

How does primate biology reflect behavior and environmental factors?

● Natural selection has favored single births among tree-dwelling primates whose young must cling to their mothers for transport. The long period until maturity provides opportunity for learning social behaviors, communication, and practical skills.

● Bonobo genitals maintain a constant state of swelling, which conceals ovulation and reflects their frequent and regular sexual activity. Sexual interactions are an important component of bonobo social organization and often mark reconciliation.

● A free upper lip allows apes a greater range of facial expression than that present in other primates, which contributes to their advanced communicative abilities.

● Baboons and some other species possess ischial callosities, permitting them to sit for long durations—an important feature for ground-dwellers. Primatologists have proposed that sexual dimorphism varies among primate species according to the degree of male–male competition.

● Rebalance columns as needed.

What are some possible cultural influences on primate behavior theories?

● Primatologists from male-biased cultures supposed that male-dominated hierarchies were the natural order of other primate social structures. However, female dominance is prevalent among some species, such as bonobos.

● A host of characteristics—including size, the rank of one's mother, motivation, and alliances—contribute to an individual's rank within primate groups.

● Western social norms may skew perceptions of the importance of social hierarchy and male–male competition in primatology. Cooperation and reconciliation are vitally important aspects of primate behavior.

● Female's choices in selection of mates based on affiliative and paternal behavioral qualities are important evolutionary forces among many primates.

How do the behavioral patterns and linguistic capabilities of the great apes compare?

● Apes combine vocalizations, gesturing, and facial expressions to communicate a variety of messages directly. Survival for many species depends on strong communication skills and effective social cooperation.

● Individuals in captivity have been taught to communicate using visual symbols and have learned American Sign Language. Innovation and adoption of new skills by whole groups is widespread.

● Chimps and bonobos are known for making tools whereas gorillas do not. Furthermore, chimps know to use certain plants for medicinal purposes and regularly hunt monkeys and other smaller animals, even using prepared spears.

What ethical concerns arise from the use of primates in biomedical research?

● The use of primates in medical research traditionally derived from a firm distinction between us and the other primates.

● The existence of primate culture runs counter to suppositions of human uniqueness. As our closest relatives, apes deserve the same rights we extend to fellow humans.

● Recent laws in several countries have begun to ban the use of apes in biomedical research.

QUESTIONS FOR REFLECTION

1. The range of sexual behavior among primates and the biological similarities that we share particularly with bonobos, our closest primate cousins, challenge us to apply the nature–nurture question to human sexuality. What does it mean when individuals argue for or against a biological basis for human homosexuality? Is there any evidence that homosexuality or heterosexuality is "natural"? Is it possible to consider human sexuality without taking culture into account?

2. What kinds of communication systems have been observed in primates? How do these differ from human language? How are they the same?

3. This chapter describes several instances of scientists revising their paradigms when it appeared that their work was overly influenced by their own cultural norms, such as prevailing gender roles. Can you think of ways that this might still be occurring? How do researchers prevent this from happening?

4. Given the variation seen in the specific behaviors of chimp, bonobo, and gorilla groups, is it fair to say that these primates possess culture?

5. Many primate species are endangered today due to human action. What features of ape biology also contribute to apes' limited population size? Do these biological limitations pertain to humans? Why or why not?

ONLINE STUDY RESOURCES

CourseMate

Access chapter-specific learning tools, including learning objectives, practice quizzes, videos, flash cards, glossaries, and more in your Anthropology CourseMate.

Log into **www.cengagebrain.com** to access the resources your instructor has assigned and to purchase materials.

Challenge Issue

The radical changes taking place in the world today make a scientific understanding of the past ever more important. Investigating and preserving ancient remains challenges us to collectively solve the complex questions of who owns the past and how can we protect its precious remains. These questions came into sharp focus in the spring of 2012 as ethnically Tuareg freedom fighters/separatist rebels (depending on one's perspective) occupied the ancient city of Timbuktu and declared it the capital of the new independent state Azawad. In the landlocked country of Mali on the southern edge of the Sahara Desert, Timbuktu, originally founded in the 4th century, has long been a crossroads, a trade center, a melting pot, and a hub of Islamic learning. In addition to unique ancient earthen mosques, Timbuktu also houses nearly 100,000 ancient manuscripts dating from its golden age, between the 12th and 15th centuries. Within days of the political shift, the world began hearing reports of looting and pillaging of the ancient libraries. Fearing that Islamic Sharia law was behind the destruction of early manuscripts relating to mathematics, medicine, astronomy, and music, people locally and across the world are struggling to preserve the unique treasure of Timbuktu. To whom do such remains belong—to the local government, to the global community, to researchers or scientific institutions, to people living in the region, to a rebel faction that has possession of them at that moment? The archaeological perspective holds that for the collective benefit of local peoples and the global community alike, these questions must be answered with an eye to long-term preservation, cooperation, and peace.

Field Methods in Archaeology and Paleoanthropology

5

Paleoanthropologists and archaeologists, anthropological specialists, reconstruct the biology and behavior of humans and their ancestors using a remarkable array of techniques. They share a focus on **prehistory**, a conventional term used to refer to the period of time before written records. For some people, the term *prehistoric* might conjure up images of "primitive" cavemen and cavewomen, but it does not imply a lack of history or any inferiority—merely a lack of *written* history. Archaeologists also focus on the cultural remains of peoples living since the invention of writing, such as the authors of the Timbuktu manuscripts as described in the chapter opener. The next several chapters of this book focus on the past; this chapter examines the methods archaeologists and paleoanthropologists use to study that past.

Most of us are familiar with some kind of archaeological material: a coin dug out of the earth, a fragment of an ancient pot, a spear point used by some ancient hunter. Archaeology consists of far more than finding and cataloguing such cultural treasures. Instead, archaeologists use material and ecological remains to reconstruct the culture and worldview of past human societies. Archaeologists examine every recoverable detail from past societies, including all kinds of structures (not just palaces and temples), hearths, garbage dumps, bones, and plant remains. Although it may appear that archaeologists are digging up *things*, they are really digging up human biology, behavior, and beliefs.

Similarly, paleoanthropologists who study the physical remains of our ancestors and other ancient primates do more than find and catalogue old bones. Paleoanthropologists recover, describe, and organize these remains to see what they can tell us about human biological evolution. True, paleoanthropologists find ancient bones, but more than that, they find out what these bones mean.

prehistory A conventional term used to refer to the period of time before the appearance of written records; does not deny the existence of history, merely of *written* history.

Recovering Cultural and Biological Remains

Archaeologists and paleoanthropologists face a dilemma. Their main investigative technique—excavation of sites containing biological and cultural remains—involves destruction of that site. Thus, competent and conscientious researchers precisely record the location and context of everything recovered, no matter how small, as they excavate. These records help scientists make sense of the data and enhance our knowledge of the past. Knowledge that can be derived from physical and cultural remains diminishes dramatically without such accurate and detailed records of the excavation. As anthropologist Brian Fagan has put it, "The fundamental premise of excavation is that all digging is destructive, even that done by experts. The archaeologist's primary responsibility, therefore, is to record a site for posterity as it is dug because there are no second chances" (Fagan, 1995, p. 19).

Archaeologists work with **artifacts**, any object fashioned or altered by humans—a flint scraper, a basket, an axe, the ruins of a house or its walls. An artifact expresses a facet of human culture. Artifacts, as products or representations of human behavior and beliefs, help archaeologists define durable aspects of culture such as tools, structures, and art as **material culture**.

Archaeologists do not consider artifacts in isolation; rather, they integrate them with biological and ecological remains. Such **ecofacts**, the natural remains of plants and animals found in the archaeological record, convey much about associated artifacts. Archaeologists also focus on **features**—nonportable elements such as hearths and architectural elements such as walls—that are preserved in the archaeological record. Archaeologists take into account how the artifacts and physical remains make their way into the ground. What people do with the things they have made, how they dispose of them, and how they lose them reflect important aspects of human culture. In other words, context allows archaeologists to understand the cultures of the past.

Similarly, context provides important information about biological remains, telling researchers which fossils are earlier or later in time compared to other fossils. Also, by noting the association of ancient human fossils with the remains of other species, the paleoanthropologist may make significant progress in reconstructing environmental settings of the past.

Cultural and physical remains represent distinct kinds of data, but the most comprehensive interpretation of the human past requires the integration of ancient human biology and culture. Often paleoanthropologists and archaeologists work together to systematically excavate and analyze fragmentary remains, placing scraps of bone, shattered pottery, and scattered campsites into broad interpretive contexts.

The Nature of Fossils

Broadly defined, a **fossil** is any mineralized trace or impression of an organism that has been preserved in the earth's crust from a past geologic time. Fossilization typically involves the hard parts of an organism. Bones, teeth, shells, horns, and the woody tissues of plants are the most successfully fossilized materials. Although the soft parts of an organism are rarely fossilized, casts or impressions of footprints, brains, and even whole bodies are sometimes found. Because dead animals quickly attract meat-eating scavengers and bacteria that cause decomposition, they rarely survive long enough to become fossilized. For an organism to become a fossil, it must be covered by some protective substance soon after death.

Preservation of an organism or part of an organism can take place in a number of ways that do not necessarily lead to fossilization. The whole animal may be frozen in ice (**Figure 5.1**), like the famous mammoths found in Siberia, safe from the forces of predators, weathering, and bacteria. Natural resins exuding from evergreen trees may enclose an organism allowing it to later become hardened and fossilized as amber. Specimens of spiders and insects dating back millions of years have been preserved in the Baltic Sea area in northeastern Europe, which is rich in resin-producing evergreens such as pine, spruce, and fir trees.

Lake bottoms and sea basins provide optimal conditions for preservation because sediment can quickly cover the organism. An entire organism may also be mummified or preserved in tar pits, peat, oil, or asphalt bogs, in which the chemical environment prevents the growth of decay-producing bacteria.

Entire organisms rarely fossilize, let alone an entire human. Fossils generally consist of scattered teeth and fragments of bones found embedded in rock deposits. Most have been altered in some way in the process of becoming fossilized. **Taphonomy** (from the Greek for "tomb"), the study of the biologic and geologic processes by which dead organisms become fossils, provides

---

artifact Any object fashioned or altered by humans.

material culture The durable aspects of culture, such as tools, structures, and art.

ecofact The natural remains of plants and animals found in the archaeological record.

feature A nonportable element such as a hearth or an architectural element such as a wall that is preserved in the archaeological record.

fossil The mineralized remains of past life forms.

taphonomy The study of how bones and other materials come to be preserved in the earth as fossils.

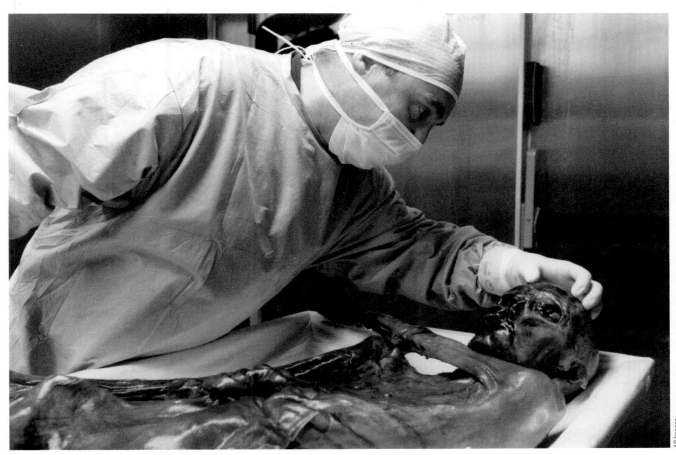

Figure 5.1 The Ice Man Ötzi In rare circumstances, human bodies are so well preserved that they could be mistaken for recent corpses. Such is the case of Ötzi, the 5,200-year-old Ice Man, exposed by the melting of an alpine glacier in the Tyrolean Alps in 1991. Both the Italian and the Austrian governments felt they had legitimate claims on this rare find, and they mounted legal, geographic, and taphonomic arguments for housing the body. These arguments continued as the specimen, just released from the ice, began to thaw.

systematic understanding of the fossilization process vital for the scientific interpretations of the fossils themselves.

Fossilization occurs most frequently among marine animals and other creatures living near water. Concentrations of shells and other parts of organisms are covered and completely enclosed by the soft waterborne sediments that eventually harden into shale and limestone in the following fashion: As the remains of organisms accumulate on the floor of shallow seas, rivers, or lakes, they become covered by sediment and silt, or sand. These materials gradually harden, forming a protective shell around the skeleton of the organism. The internal cavities of bones or teeth and other parts of the skeleton fill in with mineral deposits from the sediment immediately surrounding the specimen. Then the external walls of the bone decay and are replaced by calcium carbonate or silica.

Unless protected in some way, the bones of a land-dweller are generally scattered and exposed to the deteriorating influence of the elements, predators, and scavengers. Occasionally, terrestrial animals living near lakes or rivers become fossilized if they die next to or in the water. A land-dweller may also become fossilized if it happens to die in a cave (**Figure 5.2**), or if some other meat-eating animal drags its remains to a site protected from erosion and decay. In caves, conditions are often excellent for fossilization, as minerals contained in water dripping from the ceiling may harden over bones left on the cave floor. In northern China, for example, many fossils of *Homo erectus* (discussed in Chapter 7) and other animals were found in a cave near a village called Zhoukoudian, in deposits of consolidated clay and rock that had fallen from the cave's limestone ceiling. The cave had been frequented by both humans and predatory animals, which left the remains of many meals there.

Figure 5.2 **Sima de los Huesos** To excavate the ancient Stone Age site Sima de los Huesos or "Pit of Bones," Spanish paleoanthropologist Juan Luis Arsuaga and his team spend nearly an hour each day traveling underground through a narrow passage to a small enclosed space, rich with human remains. Here, the fossils are excavated with great care and transported back to the laboratory, where the long process of interpretation and analysis begins. Arsuaga's team has proposed that the high number of individuals recovered from this single cave site indicates some ritual surrounding death, a placement of the dead as in an ossuary rather than a burial. If true, this site, dated to sometime between 350,000 and 600,000 years ago, would provide the earliest evidence of ritualistic treatment of the dead.

Burial of the Dead

The cultural practice of burial that began (consistently) about 100,000 years ago has increased the preservation of complete fossil skeletons. The human fossil record from before this time consists primarily of fragmentary remains with an occasional complete skeleton. The fossil record for many other primates is even poorer because organic materials decay rapidly in the tropical forests where they lived. The records are more complete for primates (such as evolving humans) that lived on the grassy plains or in savannah environments, where conditions were more favorable to the formation of fossils. Places where ash deposited from volcanic eruptions or waterborne sediment along lakes and streams could quickly cover organisms

that died, favoring fossilization. Several localities in Ethiopia, Kenya, and Tanzania in East Africa, found near ancient lakes and streams and often sandwiched between layers of volcanic ash, yield numerous fossils important for our understanding of human evolution.

In more recent times, such complete remains are often quite spectacular and particularly informative. As an example, consider the recovery in 1994 of the remains of an Inupiat Eskimo girl in Barrow, Alaska, described in the Original Study. As seen in this case study, successful exploration of the past depends upon cooperation and respect between anthropologists and the living people with ancestral connections to the physical and cultural remains being studied.

Whispers from the Ice

BY SHERRY SIMPSON

People grew excited when a summer rainstorm softened the bluff known as Ukkuqsi, sloughing off huge chunks of earth containing remains of historic and prehistoric houses, part of the old village that predates the modern community of Barrow. Left protruding from the slope was a human head. Archaeologist Anne Jensen happened to be in Barrow buying strapping tape when the body appeared. Her firm, SJS Archaeological Services, Inc., was closing a field season at nearby Point Franklin, and Jensen offered the team's help in a kind of archaeological triage to remove the body before it eroded completely from the earth.

The North Slope Borough hired her and Glenn Sheehan, both associated with Pennsylvania's Bryn Mawr College, to conduct the work. The National Science Foundation, which supported the three-year Point Franklin Project, agreed to fund the autopsy and subsequent analysis of the body and artifacts. The Ukkuqsi excavation quickly became a community event. In remarkably sunny and calm weather, volunteers troweled and picked through the thawing soil, finding trade beads, animal bones, and other items. Teenage boys worked alongside grandmothers. The smell of sea mammal oil, sweet at first then corrupt, mingled with ancient organic odors of decomposed vegetation. One man searched the beach for artifacts that had eroded from the bluff, discovering such treasures as two feather parkas. Elder Silas Negovanna, originally of Wainwright, visited several times, "more or less out of curiosity to see what they have in mind," he said. George Leavitt, who lives in a house on the bluff, stopped by one day while carrying home groceries and suggested a way to spray water to thaw the soil without washing away valuable artifacts. Tour groups added the excavation to their rounds.

"This community has a great interest in archaeology up here just because it's so recent to their experience," says oral historian Karen Brewster, a tall young woman who interviews elders as part of her work with the North Slope Borough's division of Inupiat History, Language, and Culture. "The site's right in town, and everybody was really fascinated by it."

Slowly, as the workers scraped and shoveled, the earth surrendered its historical hoard: carved wooden bowls, ladles, and such clothing as a mitten made from polar bear hide, bird-skin parkas, and mukluks. The items spanned prehistoric times, dated in Barrow to before explorers first arrived in 1826.

The work prompted visiting elders to recall when they or their parents lived in traditional sod houses and relied wholly on the land and sea for sustenance. Some remembered sliding down the hill as children, before the sea gnawed away the slope. Others described the site's use as a lookout for whales or ships. For the archaeologists, having elders stand beside them and identify items and historical context is like hearing the past whispering in their ears. Elders often know from experience, or from stories, the answers to the scientists' questions about how items were used or made. "In this instance, usually the only puzzled people are the archaeologists," jokes archaeologist Sheehan.

A modern town of 4,000, Barrow exists in a cultural continuum, where history is not detached or remote but still pulses through contemporary life. People live, hunt, and fish where their ancestors did, but they can also buy fresh vegetables at the store and jet to other places. Elementary school classes include computer and Inupiaq language studies. Caribou skins, still ruddy with blood, and black brant carcasses hang near late-model cars outside homes equipped with television antennas. A man uses power tools to work on his whaling boat. And those who appear from the earth are not just bodies, but relatives. "We're not a people frozen in time," says Jana Harcharek, an Inupiat Eskimo who teaches Iñupiaq and nurtures her culture among young people. "There will always be that connection between us [and our ancestors]. They're not a separate entity."

The past drew still closer as the archaeologists neared the body. After several days of digging through thawed soil, they used water supplied by the local fire station's tanker truck to melt through permafrost until they reached the remains, about 3 feet below the surface. A shell of clear ice encased the body, which rested in what appeared to be a former meat cellar. With the low-pressure play of water from the tanker, the archaeologists teased the icy casket from the frozen earth, exposing a tiny foot. Only then did they realize they had uncovered a child. "That was kind of sad, because she was about my daughter's size," says archaeologist Jensen.

The girl was curled up beneath a baleen toboggan and part of a covering that Inupiat elder Bertha Leavitt identified as a kayak skin by its stitching. The child, who appeared to be 5 or 6, remained remarkably intact after her dark passage through time. Her face was cloaked by a covering that puzzled some onlookers. It didn't look like human hair, or even fur, but something with a feathery

In the long cool days of the Alaska summer, archaeologist Anne Jensen and her team excavate artifacts that will be exhibited at the Inupiat Heritage Center in Barrow, Alaska. In addition to traditional museum displays honoring the past, the center actively promotes the continuation of Inupiat Eskimo cultural traditions through innovations such as the elder-in-residence program.

residue. Finally, they concluded it was a hood from a feather parka made of bird skins. The rest of her body was delineated muscle that had freeze-dried into a dark brick-red color. Her hands rested on her knees, which were drawn up to her chin. Frost particles coated the bends of her arms and legs.

"We decided we needed to go talk to the elders and see what they wanted, to get some kind of feeling as to whether they wanted to bury her right away, or whether they were willing to allow some studies in a respectful manner—studies that would be of some use to residents of the North Slope," Jensen says. Working with community elders is not a radical idea to Jensen or Sheehan, whose previous work in the Arctic has earned them high regard from local officials who appreciate their sensitivity. The researchers feel obligated not only to follow community wishes, but to invite villagers to sites and to share all information through public presentations. In fact, Jensen is reluctant to discuss findings with the press before the townspeople themselves hear it.

"It seems like it's a matter of simple common courtesy," she says. Such consideration can only help researchers, she points out. "If people don't get along with you, they're not going to talk to you, and they're liable to throw you out on your ear." In the past, scientists were not terribly sensitive about such matters, generally regarding

human remains—and sometimes living natives—as artifacts themselves. Once, the girl's body would have been hauled off to the catacombs of some university or museum, and relics would have disappeared into exhibit drawers in what Sheehan describes as "hit-and-run archaeology."

"Grave robbers" is how Inupiat Jana Harcharek refers to early Arctic researchers. "They took human remains and their burial goods. It's pretty gruesome. But, of course, at the time they thought they were doing science a big favor. Thank goodness attitudes have changed."

Today, not only scientists but municipal officials confer with the Barrow Elders Council when local people find skeletons from traditional platform burials out on the tundra, or when bodies appear in the house mounds. The elders appreciate such consultations, says Samuel Simmonds, a tall, dignified man known for his carving. A retired Presbyterian minister, he presided at burial ceremonies of the famous "frozen family," ancient Inupiats discovered in Barrow [about thirty years ago]. "They were part of us, we know that," he says simply, as if the connection between old bones and bodies and living relatives is self-evident. In the case of the newly discovered body, he says, "We were concerned that it was reburied in a respectful manner. They were nice enough to come over and ask us."

The elders also wanted to restrict media attention and prevent photographs of the body except for a few showing her position at the site. They approved a limited autopsy to help answer questions about the body's sex, age, and state of health. She was placed in an orange plastic body bag in a stainless steel morgue with the temperature turned down to below freezing.

With the help of staff at the Indian Health Service Hospital, Jensen sent the girl's still-frozen body to Anchorage's Providence Hospital. There she assisted with an autopsy performed by Dr. Michael Zimmerman of New York City's Mount Sinai Hospital. Zimmerman, an expert on prehistoric frozen bodies, had autopsied Barrow's frozen family in 1982 and was on his way to work on the prehistoric man recently discovered in the Alps.

The findings suggest the girl's life was very hard. She ultimately died of starvation, but also had emphysema caused by a rare congenital disease—the lack of an enzyme that protects the lungs. She probably was sickly and needed extra care all her brief life. The autopsy also found soot in her lungs from the family's sea mammal oil lamps, and she had osteoporosis, which was caused by a diet exclusively of meat from marine mammals. The girl's stomach was empty, but her intestinal tract contained dirt and animal fur. That remains a mystery and raises questions about the condition of the rest of the family. "It's not likely that she would be hungry and everyone else well fed," Jensen says.

That the girl appears to have been placed deliberately in the cellar provokes further questions about precontact burial practices, which the researchers hope Barrow elders can help answer. Historic accounts indicate the dead often were wrapped in skins and laid out on the tundra on wooden platforms, rather than buried in the frozen earth. But perhaps the entire family was starving and too weak to remove the dead girl from the house, Jensen speculates. "We probably won't ever be able to say, 'This is the way it was,'" she adds. "For that you need a time machine."

The scientific team reported to the elders that radiocarbon dating places the girl's death in about AD 1200. If correct—for dating is technically tricky in the Arctic—the date would set the girl's life about 100 years before her people formed settled whaling villages, Sheehan says.

Following the autopsy and the body's return to Barrow . . . , one last request by the elders was honored. The little girl, wrapped in her feather parka, was placed in a casket and buried in a small Christian ceremony next to the grave of the other prehistoric bodies. Hundreds of years after her death, an Inupiat daughter was welcomed back into the midst of her community.

The "rescue" of the little girl's body from the raw forces of time and nature means researchers and the Inupiat people will continue to learn still more about the region's culture. Sheehan and Jensen returned to Barrow in winter 1994 to explain their findings to townspeople. "We expect to learn just as much from them," Sheehan said before the trip. A North Slope Cultural Center . . . will store and display artifacts from the dig sites.

Laboratory tests and analyses also will contribute information. The archaeologists hope measurements of heavy metals in the girl's body will allow comparisons with modern-day pollution contaminating the sea mammals that Inupiats eat today. The soot damage in her lungs might offer health implications for Third World people who rely on oil lamps, dung fires, and charcoal for heat and light. Genetic tests could illuminate early population movements of Inupiats.

The project also serves as a model for good relations between archaeologists and Native people. "The larger overall message from this work is that scientists and communities don't have to be at odds," Sheehan says. "In fact, there are mutual interests that we all have. Scientists have obligations to communities. And when more scientists realize that, and when more communities hold scientists to those standards, then everybody will be happier."

Adapted from Simpson, S. (1995, April). Whispers from the ice. Alaska, 23–28.

Searching for Artifacts and Fossils

Where are artifacts and fossils found? Places containing archaeological remains of previous human activity are known as *sites*. Many kinds of sites exist, and sometimes it is difficult to define their boundaries, for remains may be strewn over large areas. Sites are even found under water. Some examples of sites identified by archaeologists and paleoanthropologists are hunting campsites, from which hunters went out to hunt game; kill sites, in which game was killed and butchered; village sites, in which domestic activities took place; and cemeteries, in which the dead, and sometimes their belongings, were buried.

Although skeletons of recent peoples are frequently associated with their cultural remains, archaeological sites may or may not contain any physical remains. As we go back in time, the association of physical and cultural remains becomes less likely. Physical remains dating from before 2.5 to 2.6 million years ago are found in isolation. This does not prove the absence of material culture; it simply indicates that the earliest forms of material culture were not preserved in the archaeological record. The earliest tools used by our ancestors were likely made of organic materials (such as the termite-fishing sticks used by chimpanzees) that were much less likely to be preserved. Although only geologic contexts with conditions favorable for fossilization yield physical remains, archaeological sites may be found just about anywhere. The more recent time depth of archaeological remains helps their preservation as well.

Site Identification

Archaeologists must first identify sites to investigate. Archaeological sites, particularly very old ones, frequently are buried underground, covered by layers of sediment deposited since the site was in use. The presence of artifacts indicates a potential site. Chance may play a crucial role in the site's discovery, as in the case discussed in Barrow, Alaska. Usually, however, the archaeologist will conduct surveys of a region in order to plot the sites available for excavation.

A survey can be made from the ground, but more territory can be covered from the air. Aerial photographs have been used by archaeologists since the 1920s and are widely used today. Among other purposes, such photographs were used for the discovery and interpretation of the huge geometric and zoomorphic (from Latin for "animal-shaped") markings on the coastal desert of Peru (**Figure 5.3**). More recently a variety of innovations in the geographic and geologic sciences have been incorporated into archaeological surveys and other aspects of research. Innovations such as geographic information systems (GIS), remote sensing, and ground-penetrating radar (GPR) complement traditional archaeological exploration methods.

High-resolution aerial photographs, including satellite imagery, resulted in the astonishing discovery of over 500 miles of prehistoric roadways connecting sites in the Four Corners region of the United States (where Arizona, New Mexico, Colorado, and Utah meet) with other sites in ways that archaeologists had never suspected. This discovery led to a new understanding of prehistoric Pueblo Indian economic, social, and political organization. Evidently, large centers in this region governed a number of smaller satellite communities, mobilized labor for large public works, and allowed for the distribution of goods over substantial distances.

In open country, archaeologists can easily identify more obvious sites, such as the human-made mounds or *tells* of the Middle East, that rise as swells from the ground. But a heavy forest cover poses extra challenges for site identification even when ruins rise above ground. Thus, local geography and climate impact the discovery of archaeological sites.

In the forests, a change in vegetation might indicate a potential site. For example, topsoil that is richer in organic matter than that of the surrounding areas often covers ancient storage and refuse pits and grows distinctive vegetation. At Tikal, an ancient Maya site in Guatemala, breadnut trees usually grow near the remains of ancient houses, so archaeologists can use these trees as guideposts.

Figure 5.3 **Zoomorphs** Some archaeological features are best seen from the air, such as this massive figure of a monkey made in prehistoric times on the Nazca Desert of Peru. Ancient people selectively removed the top layer of reddish stones thus exposing the light-colored earth below.

On the ground, **soil marks** or stains, showing up on the surface of recently plowed fields, can indicate a potential site. Soil marks led archaeologists to many of the Bronze Age burial mounds in Hertfordshire and Cambridgeshire, England. The mounds hardly rose out of the ground, yet each was circled at its core by chalky soil marks. Sometimes the very presence of a particular chalky rock is significant.

Archaeologists also use documents, maps, and folklore in the search for sites. For example, Homer's *Iliad* led Heinrich Schliemann, the famous and controversial 19th-century German archaeologist, to the discovery of Troy. (As was typical of that time, Schliemann's excavation methods destroyed much of the actual remains.) He assumed that the city described by Homer as Ilium was really Troy. Place names and local lore often indicate the presence of an archaeological site in an area. Archaeological surveys therefore often depend upon amateur collectors and local people who are usually familiar with the history of the land.

Sometimes natural processes, such as soil erosion or droughts, expose sites or fossils. For example, in eastern North America erosion along the coastlines and riverbanks has exposed prehistoric refuse mounds known as **middens** (the general term for a trash deposit), which in these regions are filled with the remains of mussels and/or oysters, indicating that shellfish consumption was common. Similarly, the gradual action of wind blowing away sand exposed a whole village of stone huts dug into the ground at Skara Brae in Scotland's Orkney Islands.

Sometimes natural forces expose fossils and sites, and sometimes human actions unrelated to anthropological

---

soil marks Stains that show up on the surface of recently plowed fields that reveal an archaeological site.

middens A refuse or garbage disposal area in an archaeological site.

investigations reveal physical and cultural remains. In Chapter 2 we noted how construction and quarrying work in Europe led to the discovery of fossils of extinct animals, which then played a role in the development of evolutionary theory. Similarly, limestone quarrying at a variety of sites in South Africa early in the 20th century led to the discovery of the earliest humanlike fossils from millions of years ago (see Chapter 6). Disturbances of the earth on a smaller scale, such as plowing, sometimes turn up bones, fragments of pots, and other archaeological objects.

Cultural Resource Management

Because construction projects frequently uncover archaeological remains, in many countries, including the United States, such projects require government approval in order to ensure the identification and protection of those finds. *Cultural resource management*, introduced in Chapter 1, is routinely included in the environmental review process for federally funded or licensed construction projects in the United States, as it is in Europe. For example, in the United States, if the transportation department of a state government plans to replace a highway bridge, the state must first contract with archaeologists to identify and protect any significant resources that might be affected by this new construction.

Since passage of the Historic Preservation Act of 1966, the National Environmental Policy Act of 1969, the Archaeological and Historical Preservation Act of 1974, and the Archaeological Resources Protection Act of 1979, cultural resource management has been required for any construction project that is partially funded or licensed by the U.S. government. As a result, the field of cultural resource management has flourished. Many archaeologists are employed by U.S. government agencies such as the Army Corps of Engineers, the National Park Service, the Forest Service, and the Natural Resource Conservation Service, assisting in the preservation, restoration, and salvage of archaeological resources. Canada and the United Kingdom have programs very similar to those of the United States. From Chile to China, various governments use archaeological expertise to manage their cultural heritage.

When cultural resource management work or other archaeological investigation unearths Native American cultural items or human remains, federal laws come into the picture again. The Native American Graves Protection and Repatriation Act (NAGPRA), passed in 1990, outlines a process for the return of these remains to lineal descendants, culturally affiliated Indian tribes, and Native Hawaiian organizations. NAGPRA has become central to the work of anthropologists who study Paleo-Indian and more recent Indian cultures in the United States. The Kennewick Man

controversy featured later in this chapter highlights some of the ethics debates surrounding NAGPRA.

In addition to working in all the capacities mentioned, archaeologists also consult for engineering firms to help them prepare environmental impact statements. Some of these archaeologists operate out of universities and colleges, whereas others are on the staff of independent consulting firms. When state legislation sponsors any kind of archaeological work, it is referred to as *contract archaeology*.

Excavation

Once a researcher identifies an appropriate site, the next step is to plan and carry out excavation. If not already a part of cultural resource management, the next step of excavation planning involves obtaining permission to excavate from a variety of local and national authorities. The excavation team begins by clearing the land and plotting the site as a **grid system** (Figure 5.4). The excavators divide the surface of the site into squares of equal size and number and mark each square with stakes. Each object found then may be located precisely in the square from which it came. (Remember, context is everything!) The starting point of a grid system, which is located precisely in three dimensions, may be a large rock, the edge of a stone wall, or an iron rod sunk into the ground. This point is also known as the reference or **datum point**.

At a large site covering several square miles, archaeologists may plot individual structures, numbered according to their location in a particular square of a giant grid. Archaeologists dig each square of the grid separately with great care. (In Figure 5.5, notice how archaeologists use the grid system even when under water.) They use trowels to scrape the soil and screens to sift all the loose soil so that they recover even the smallest artifacts, such as flint chips or beads.

Flotation, a technique employed when looking for very fine objects, such as fish scales or very small bones, consists of immersing soil in water, causing the particles to separate. Some will float, others will sink to the bottom, allowing for easy retrieval of the remains.

If the site is **stratified**—that is, if the remains lie in layers one upon the other—archaeologists will dig

---

grid system A system for recording data in three dimensions for an archaeological excavation.

datum point The starting point or reference for a grid system.

flotation An archaeological technique employed to recover very tiny objects by immersion of soil samples in water to separate heavy from light particles.

stratified Layered; term used to describe archaeological sites where the remains lie in layers, one upon another.

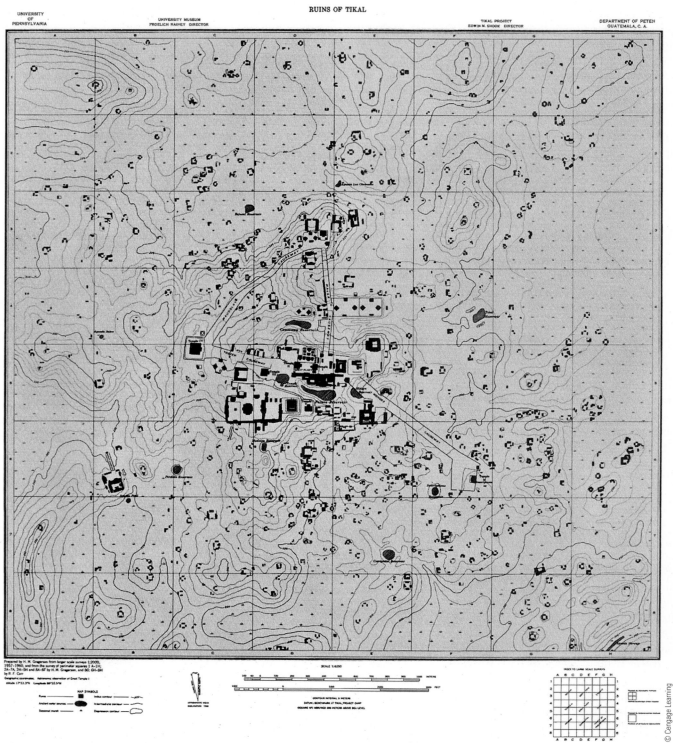

Figure 5.4 The Grid System At large sites covering several square miles, archaeologists construct a giant grid, as shown in this map of the center of the ancient Maya city of Tikal. Each square of the grid is one-quarter of a square kilometer; excavators number individual structures according to the square in which they are found.

each layer, or stratum, separately. Each layer represents a particular span of time and period of settlement. Thus, it will contain artifacts deposited at the same time and belonging to the same culture (**Figure 5.6**). Cultural change can be traced through the order in which artifacts were deposited—deeper layers reveal older artifacts.

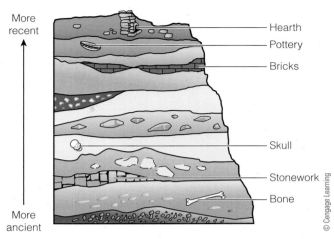

Figure 5.6 An Archaeological Profile Archaeologists create profiles or vertical representations of the sites they excavate. In stratified sites where archaeological remains lie in stacked layers, with older layers deeper or lower down and more recent layers above them, profiles are especially informative. Geologic processes will result in strata of different depths in different places. Interpretation of the site depends upon careful mapping of each stratum using the grid system.

Figure 5.5 Underwater Archaeology Here a diver recovers antique amphorae (the traditional containers for transporting wine, olives, olive oil, grain, and other commodities) from the site of a shipwreck in the Mediterranean Sea near the village of Kas, Turkey. The shipwreck dates back to the time of the Trojan War (over 3,000 years ago). Underwater archaeologists—led in this expedition by George Bass from the Institute of Nautical Archaeology of Texas A&M University collaborating with the Bodrum Museum of Underwater Archaeology in Istanbul, Turkey—reconstructs facets of the past, ranging from ancient trade routes and shipbuilding techniques, through the analysis of such remains.

However, archaeologists Frank Hole and Robert F. Heizer suggest care when analyzing stratified sites:

> because of difficulties in analyzing stratigraphy, archaeologists must use the greatest caution in drawing conclusions. Almost all interpretations of time, space, and culture contexts depend on stratigraphy. The refinements of laboratory techniques for analysis are wasted if archaeologists cannot specify the stratigraphic position of their artifacts. (Hole & Heizer, 1969, p. 113)

If no stratification is present, then the archaeologist digs by arbitrary levels. Each square must be dug so that its edges and profiles are straight; walls between squares are often left standing to serve as visual correlates of the grid system.

Paleoanthropologists working on older sites, without the benefit of archaeological layers, must employ geological expertise because interpretation of a fossil depends utterly on its place in the sequence of rocks that contain it. The geological context provides the dates that place specimens in the human evolutionary sequence. More recent archaeological sites can be dated more reliably. Paleoanthropological expeditions today generally are made up of teams of specialists in various fields in addition to physical anthropology so that all the necessary expertise is available.

Excavation of Bones

Removing a fossil from its burial place without damage requires surgical skill and caution. Unusual tools and materials are found in the kit of the paleoanthropologist—pickaxes, dental instruments, enamel coating, burlap for bandages, and sculpting plaster.

To remove newly discovered bones, the paleoanthropologist and archaeologist begin uncovering the specimen, using pick and shovel for initial excavation, then small camel-hair brushes and dental picks to remove loose and easily detachable debris surrounding the bones. Once

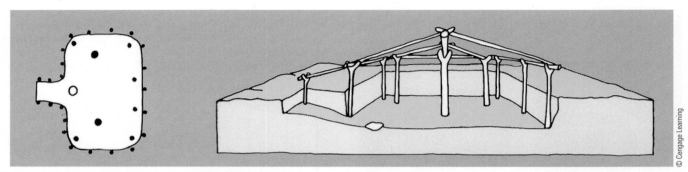

Figure 5.7 Reconstruction from Traces of Organic Remains Although the wooden posts of a house have long since decayed, their positions may still be marked by discoloration of the soil. The plan shown on the left—of an ancient post-hole pattern and depression at Snaketown, Arizona—permits the hypothetical house reconstruction on the right.

the researchers uncover the entire specimen (a process that may take days of back-breaking patient labor), they cover the bones with shellac and tissue paper to prevent cracking and damage during further excavation and handling.

The excavation team prepares both the fossil and the earth immediately surrounding it, or the *matrix*, for removal as a single block. They cut the bones and matrix out of the earth but do not remove them. Next they add more shellac to the entire block to harden it. They cover the bones with burlap bandages dipped in plaster. Then they enclose the block in more plaster and burlap bandages, perhaps splinted with tree branches, and allow it to dry overnight. After it has hardened, they carefully remove the entire block from the earth, now ready for packing and transport to a laboratory. Before leaving the discovery area, the investigator makes a thorough sketch map of the terrain and pinpoints the find on geological maps to aid future investigators.

State of Preservation of Archaeological and Fossil Evidence

The results of an excavation depend greatly on the condition of the remains. Inorganic materials such as stone and metal are more resistant to decay than organic ones such as wood and bone. Sometimes the anthropologist discovers an *assemblage*—a collection of artifacts—made of durable inorganic materials, such as stone tools, and traces of organic ones long since decomposed, such as woodwork (Figure 5.7), textiles, or food.

Climate, local geological conditions, and cultural practices also play a role in the state of preservation. For example, our knowledge of ancient Egyptian culture stems not only from their burial practices but from the effects of climate and soil on preservation. The ancient Egyptians believed that eternal life could be achieved only if the dead were buried with their worldly possessions. Hence, these tombs are usually filled with a wealth of artifacts, including the skeletons of other humans owned by dynastic rulers.

Under favorable climatic conditions, even the most perishable objects may survive over vast periods of time. The earliest Egyptian burials, consisting of shallow pits in the sand with bodies buried long before mummification was practiced, often yield well-preserved corpses. Their preservation is the result of rapid desiccation, or complete drying out, in the warm desert climate (Figure 5.8). The elaborate tombs of the rulers of dynastic Egypt often contain wooden furniture, textiles, flowers, and written scrolls on paper made from papyrus reeds, barely touched by time, seemingly as fresh as they were when deposited in the tombs as long as 5,000 years ago—a consequence of the region's arid climatic conditions. Of course, the ancient Egyptian burial practices selectively preserved more information about the elite members of society than the average individual.

The dryness of certain caves also promotes the preservation of **coprolites**, the scientific term for fossilized human or animal feces. Coprolites provide information on prehistoric diet and health. From the analysis of elements preserved in coprolites such as seeds, insect skeletons, and tiny bones from fish or amphibians, archaeologists and paleoanthropologists can directly determine diets from the past. This information, in turn, can shed light on overall health. Because many sources of food are available only in certain seasons, researchers can even determine the time of year in which the food was eaten.

Certain climates can obliterate all evidence of organic remains. Maya ruins found in the tropical rainforests

coprolites Preserved fecal material providing evidence of the diet and health of past organisms.

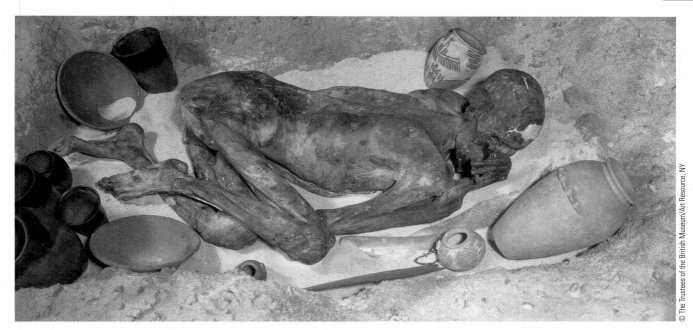

Figure 5.8 Preservation and Environment The preservation of archaeological remains is dependent upon the environment. Even before the invention of mummification technologies, buried bodies were very well preserved in Egypt because they dried so quickly in the extremely arid environment.

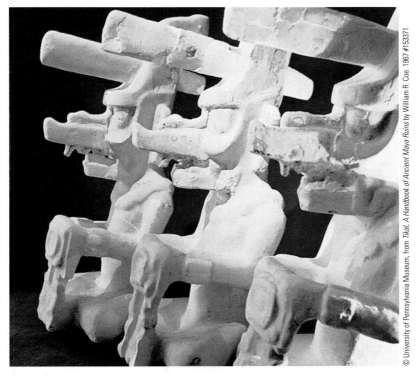

Figure 5.9 Reconstructing Decayed Wood Carvings At the Maya site of Tikal, these intricately carved figures, originally made of wood, were recovered from a king's tomb by pouring plaster into a cavity in the soil that was left when the original organic material decayed.

of Mesoamerica (the region encompassing central and southern Mexico and northern Central America) are often in a state of collapse—notwithstanding that many are massive structures of stone—as a result of the pressure exerted upon them by the heavy forest vegetation. The rain and humidity soon destroy almost all traces of woodwork, textiles, or basketry. Fortunately, impressions of these artifacts can sometimes be preserved in plaster (**Figure 5.9**). More easily preserved stone carvings and pottery figurines may depict some objects made of wood or plant fibers. Thus, even in the face of substantial decay of organic substances, archaeologists can still learn about these remains.

Sorting Out the Evidence

Excavation records include a scale map of all the features, the stratification of each excavated square, a description of the exact location and depth of every artifact or bone unearthed, and photographs and scale drawings of the objects. Such detailed records allow the researchers to piece together the archaeological and biological evidence so as to arrive at a plausible reconstruction of a culture. Although researchers conducting an excavation may focus only on certain kinds of remains, they must record every aspect of the site. Future researchers may need a piece of information to answer a question that no one thought of at the time of the initial investigation. In other words, archaeological sites are nonrenewable resources. Even the most meticulous excavation results in a permanent disturbance of the arrangement of artifacts.

Sometimes sites are illegally looted, which can result in loss not only of the artifacts themselves but of the site (**Figure 5.10**). Although looting has long been a threat to the archaeological record, today it is a high-tech endeavor. Avid collectors and fans of archaeological sites

unwittingly aid looting through sharing site and artifact location information on the Internet, which has also provided a market for artifacts.

Meticulous care does not end with excavation. Archaeologists and paleoanthropologists apply a variety of laboratory methods to studying the artifact or fossil, once freed from the surrounding matrix. Generally, archaeologists and paleoanthropologists plan on at least three hours of laboratory work for each hour of fieldwork (**Figure 5.11**).

In the lab, archaeologists first clean and catalogue—often a tedious and time-consuming job—all artifacts before beginning any analyses. From the shapes of the artifacts as well as from the traces of manufacture and wear, archaeologists can usually determine their function. For example, the Russian archaeologist S. A. Semenov devoted many years to the study of prehistoric technology. In the

Figure 5.10 Looting When looters harvest artifacts for sale on the black market, they simply pull them from the ground. These looters steal far more than the artifacts themselves: They also steal all the information that could have been gleaned from a proper excavation of the site. Even if police ultimately recover the artifacts from the looters, or from the collectors who purchase such artifacts illegally, lack of context and precise location of the artifacts in relation to every other detail of the site severely limits the opportunity to reconstruct lifeways of past peoples. Further, looters often completely destroy the sites they loot, erasing evidence of their crime along with any details archaeologists might have salvaged.

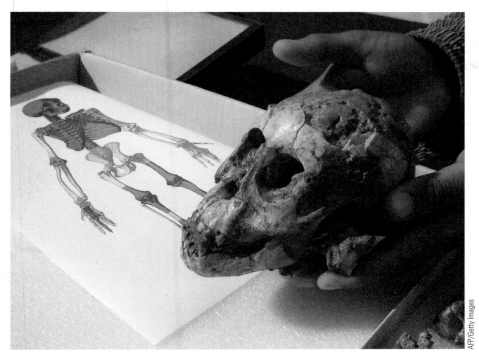

Figure 5.11 Lucy's Child In September 2006, researchers announced the discovery of a spectacular new fossil—the skeleton of a young child dated to 3.3 million years ago. The fossil was actually discovered in the Dikika area of northern Ethiopia in 2000. Since then, researchers worked on careful recovery and analysis of the fossilized remains so that when the announcement was made, much was already known about the specimen. Their analyses have determined that this child, a little girl about 3 years old who likely died in a flash flood, was a member of *Australopithecus afarensis*, the same species as the famous Lucy specimen (see Chapter 6). Due to the importance of this find, some scientists have referred to this specimen as "Lucy's Baby" or "Lucy's Child," although the individual lived about 150,000 years before Lucy.

case of a flint tool used as a scraper, he was able to determine, by examining the wear patterns of the tool under a microscope, that the prehistoric individuals who used it began to scrape from right to left and then scraped from left to right, and in so doing avoided straining the muscles of the hand (Semenov, 1964). From the work of Semenov and others, we now know that right-handed individuals made most stone tools preserved in the archaeological record, a fact that has implications for brain structure. The relationships among populations can also be traced through material remains (**Figure 5.12**).

Paleoanthropologists, bioarchaeologists, and forensic anthropologists use a variety of investigative techniques to examine bones and teeth. For example, the examination of dental specimens under the microscope might reveal markings on teeth that provide clues about diet. Paleoanthropologists often make imprints or **endocasts** of the insides of skulls to determine the size and shape of ancient brains.

Just as DNA fingerprinting might be used in forensic investigations, paleoanthropologists apply advances in genetic technology to ancient human remains. By extracting genetic material from skeletal remains, they can make DNA comparisons among the specimen, other fossils, and living people. Small fragments of DNA are amplified or copied repeatedly using **polymerase chain reaction (PCR)** technology to provide a sufficient amount of material to perform these analyses. However, unless DNA is preserved in a stable material such as amber, it will decay over time. Therefore, analyses of DNA extracted from specimens older than about 50,000 years become increasingly unreliable due to the decay of DNA.

The bioarchaeologist combines the biological anthropologist's expertise in skeletal biology with the archaeological reconstruction of human cultures. Examination of human skeletal material provides important insights into ancient peoples' diets, gender roles, social status,

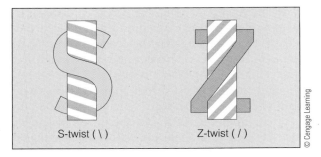

S-twist (\ )   Z-twist (/)

© Cengage Learning

Figure 5.12 Actions in Objects In northern New England, prehistoric pottery was often decorated by impressing the damp clay with a cord-wrapped stick. Examination of cord impressions reveals that coastal people made cordage by twisting fibers to the left (Z-twist), whereas those living inland did the opposite (S-twist). The nonfunctional differences reflect motor habits so deeply ingrained as to seem completely natural to the cordage makers. From this, we may infer two distinctively different populations.

endocast A cast of the inside of a skull; used to help determine the size and shape of the brain.

polymerase chain reaction (PCR) A technique for amplifying or creating multiple copies of fragments of DNA so that it can be studied in the laboratory.

and patterns of activity. For example, analysis of human skeletons shows that elite members of society had access to more nutritious foods, allowing them to reach their full growth potential.

Bioarchaeologists can assess the gender roles in a given society through skeletons as well. In fully preserved adult skeletons, the sex of the deceased individual can be determined with a high degree of accuracy, allowing for comparisons of male and female life expectancy, mortality, and health status (**Figure 5.13**). These analyses can help establish the social roles of men and women in past societies. Skeletal remains can also reveal aspects of an individual's social status (**Figure 5.14**).

Forensic anthropology, bioarchaeology's cousin discipline, also examines skeletal remains to determine characteristics of a deceased or injured individual. As does a bioarchaeologist, the forensic anthropologist integrates skeletal information with material remains. New biomedical technology also plays a role in the investigation of remains from both the past and the present. For example, CT (computed tomography) scans have added new information in forensic, bioarchaeological, and paleoanthropological investigations. Recent and ancient remains are now routinely scanned, yielding considerable information about the structural details of bones. Although a CT scan cannot substitute for an autopsy in forensic contexts, it facilitates identification in the context of mass disasters. In addition, it can provide evidence of past trauma that might otherwise remain hidden in an investigation aimed at determining the immediate cause of death (Leth, 2007).

In archaeological contexts, CT technology has been particularly useful for determining whether damage to remains took place during excavation or whether it preceded death. For example, after the remains of Egyptian King Tut were scanned, scientists uniformly agreed that the young king did not die of a head injury as previously thought; some suggested that a broken femur may have been the cause of his death (Handwerk, 2005). To minimize handling, scientists scan these rare specimens only once allowing future researchers to study the digital images instead of the remains.

Recently, it has become more complicated to carry out skeletal analyses, especially in the United States where the right of American Indian communities to request the return of archaeologically excavated skeletons for reburial is now supported by federal law. Anthropologists find themselves in a quandary over this requirement. As scientists, anthropologists know the importance of the information that can be gleaned from studies of human skeletons, but as scholars guided by ethical principles they are bound to respect the feelings of those for whom the skeletons possess cultural and spiritual significance.

New techniques, such as 3D digital images of Native American skeletons, help to resolve this conflict as they allow for both rapid repatriation and continued study

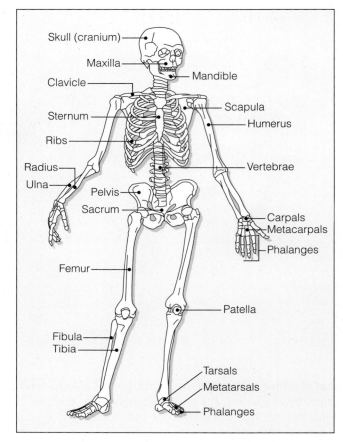

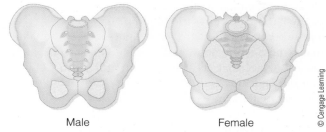

Male   Female

Figure 5.13 **The Human Skeleton** Learning the basic skeleton will be useful in the chapters ahead as we trace the history of human evolution. In addition, bear in mind that the complete male and female skeletons differ on average in some consistent ways that allow skeletal biologists to identify the sex of the deceased individual. Some of these differences relate to the fact that generally males outsize females. But the successful adaptation of the human female pelvis to childbirth makes it the most dimorphic bone of the body and the best way for researchers to determine the sex of skeletal remains. Notice the typically more open space on the interior of the female pelvis corresponding to the birth canal. In males, bones project into this space.

of skeletal remains. But globally, many aboriginal groups question the practice of digitizing remains of their people without permission. For example, the University of Vienna in Austria has been challenged by representatives of the

The National Park Service

Figure 5.14 African Burial Ground In 1991, federally mandated investigation of cultural remains, on the site of a proposed 34-story, $276-million federal office building in Lower Manhattan, led to the discovery of a massive African burial ground, covering nearly six acres. Though laws led to this discovery, ironically no laws automatically protected this site, one of the most important historical archaeological sites of colonial America. Activists, politicians, and anthropologists worked together to protect and ultimately excavate the site. The investigations documented the extreme physical hardships endured by these earliest American slaves, the vital contributions African men, women, and children made to economic and cultural development of colonial America, and the cultural continuity that these individuals maintained with their African homeland against great odds. After completing analyses of the skeletal remains of over 400 of the estimated 20,000 people buried there, the remains were respectfully reinterred in a commemorative ceremony, "Rites of Ancestral Return." Today, instead of an office building, a memorial and a historical exhibit mark the site.

Ju/'hoansi people of southern Africa because the remains that the Austrian ethnological museum holds were not donated; rather, they were taken early in the century by Rudolf Pöch, a Viennese anthropologist, as was common practice at that time. Roger Chennells, the South African legal advisor for the Ju/'hoansi, states their position as: "We have not been consulted, and we do not support any photographic archiving of our people's remains—we are opposed to it" (quoted in Scully, 2008, p. 1155).

By the standards of the 1990 Native American Graves Protection and Repatriation Act (NAGPRA), the Ju/'hoansi

would have legal decision-making authority over the fate of these remains; but the equivalent of NAGPRA has not yet been codified in international law. Even with NAGPRA in place, controversy still surrounds the handling of remains. Sometimes conflicting worldviews are at the heart of the controversy between scientists and American Indians, as seen with Kennewick Man, a 9,300-year-old skeleton that was dislodged by the Columbia River in Washington State in 1996. This chapter's Biocultural Connection focuses on how this controversy has been playing out in the federal courts.

BIOCULTURAL CONNECTION

Kennewick Man

The "Ancient One" and "Kennewick Man" both refer to the 9,300-year-old skeletal remains that were found in 1996 below the surface of Lake Wallula, part of the Columbia River, in Kennewick, Washington State. This discovery has been the center of continuing controversy since it was made. Who owns these human remains? Who can determine what shall be done with them? Do the biological characteristics preserved in these remains play a role in determining their fate?

This particular conflict involves three major parties. Because the skeleton was found on a location for which the U.S. Army Corps of Engineers is responsible, this federal agency first took possession of the remains. Appealing to NAGPRA, a nearby American Indian group—Confederated Tribes of the Umatilla Indian Reservation (representing the region's Umatilla, Cayuse, and Walla Walla nations)—claimed the remains. Because Kennewick Man was found within their ancestral homeland, they argue that they are "culturally affiliated" with the individual they refer to as the "Ancient One." Viewing these human bones as belonging to an ancestor, they wish to return them to the earth in a respectful ceremony.

This claim was challenged in federal court by a group of scientists, including archaeologists and biological anthropologists. They view these human remains, among the oldest ever discovered in the western hemisphere, as scientifically precious, with potential to shed light on the earliest population movements in the Americas. The scientists do not want to "own" the remains but want the opportunity to study them. By means of DNA analysis, for instance, these scientists expect to determine possible prehistoric linkages between this individual and ancient human remains found elsewhere, including Asia. Moreover, scientific analysis may determine whether there actually exists any biological connection between these remains and currently living Native peoples, including individuals residing on the Umatilla Indian Reservation.

Fearing the loss of a unique scientific specimen, the scientists filed a lawsuit in federal court to prevent reburial before the bones were researched and analyzed. Their legal challenge was based on the notion that "cultural affiliation" is a very difficult concept when it concerns such ancient human remains. The scientists focus on the fact that the region's Native peoples cannot prove they are

direct lineal descendants. Unless such ties have been objectively established, they argue, Kennewick Man should be released for scientific study.

In 2004 federal court rulings permitted initial scientific investigations. Just as these investigations were wrapping up in July 2005, the Senate Indian Affairs Committee heard testimony on a proposal by Arizona Senator John McCain to expand NAGPRA so that remains such as these would be once again prohibited from study. Congress adjourned without this bill becoming law, and the remains have been studied continually since then.

Doug Owsley, the forensic anthropologist from the Smithsonian Institution leading the research team, has said that scientific investigation is yielding even more information than expected. Because conflicting worldviews are at the center of this controversy, it is unlikely that it will be easily resolved.

BIOCULTURAL QUESTION

If the skeletons of your ancestors were the subject of scientific study, how would you react? Would you be comfortable donating your own body to biological research? What beliefs about life, death, and the body inform your responses to these questions?

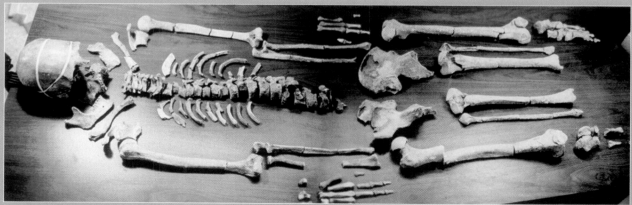

The names for this prehistoric skeleton, Ancient One and Kennewick Man, distill the debate between American Indians and scientists down to the level of two expressive words.

© Eurelios/Photo Researchers, Inc.

Dating the Past

With accurate and detailed records of their excavations in hand, archaeologists and paleoanthropologists can begin to investigate a crucial research issue: the question of age. As we have seen, analysis and interpretation of physical and cultural remains depends on accurate calculation of the age of the artifacts or specimens. How, then, do scientists reliably date the materials retrieved from excavations? Because archaeologists and paleoanthropologists often deal with peoples and events from long ago, the traditional calendar of historic times is of little use to them.

Scientists can date remains by noting their position in the earth, by measuring the amount of chemicals contained in fossil bones, or by association with other plant, animal, or cultural remains. These are known as **relative dating** techniques because they do not establish precise dates for specific remains but rather their relationship to a series of remains. Methods of **absolute dating** or **chronometric dating** (from the Latin for "measuring time") provide actual dates calculated in years "before the present" (BP). These methods rely on chemical and physical properties such as rates of decay of radioactive elements, which may be present in the remains themselves or in the surrounding soil. Absolute dating methods scientifically establish actual dates for the major events of geologic and evolutionary history. By comparing dates and remains across a variety of sites, anthropologists can reconstruct human origins, migrations, and technological developments.

Scientists use a wide range of relative and chronometric techniques. However, most of these methods work only for certain time spans and in certain environmental contexts. Bear in mind that each of the chronometric dating techniques also has a margin of error. Ideally, archaeologists and paleoanthropologists utilize as many methods as are appropriate, given the materials available and the funds at their disposal. By doing so, they significantly reduce the risk of error. Several of the most frequently employed dating techniques are presented in **Table 5.1**.

Relative Dating

Of the many relative dating techniques available, **stratigraphy** is probably the most reliable (recall Figure 5.6). Based on the simple principle that the oldest layer, or stratum, was deposited first (it is the deepest) whereas the newest layer was deposited last (in undisturbed situations, it lies at the top), stratigraphy establishes a reliable sequence of age at a given site. The archaeological evidence follows the same pattern with deposition in chronological order. The lowest stratum contains the oldest artifacts and possibly fossils whereas the uppermost stratum contains the most recent ones. Thus, even in the absence of precise dates, one knows the *relative* age of objects in one stratum compared with the ages of those in other strata. However, defining the stratigraphy of a given site can be complicated by geologic activities such as earthquakes that shift the position of stratigraphic layers.

Archaeologists also use the relative dating technique of **fluorine dating**, based on the fact that the amount of fluorine deposited in bones is proportional to the amount of time they have been in the earth. The oldest bones contain the greatest amount of fluorine and vice versa. The fluorine test can help date bones that cannot be ascribed with certainty to any particular stratum. The variation in the amount of naturally occurring fluorine from region to region limits the validity of this method for cross-site comparisons of fluorine values. Fluorine dating was vital for exposing the infamous Piltdown hoax in England, in which a human skull and orangutan jaw were placed together in the earth as false evidence for an early human ancestor (see Chapter 6).

Relative dating can also be done by **seriation**, a method of establishing sequences of plant, animal, or even cultural remains. With seriation, the order of appearance of a succession (or series) of plants, animals, or artifacts provides relative dates for a site based on a series established in another area. An example of seriation based on cultural artifacts is the Stone–Bronze–Iron Age series used by prehistorians. Within a given region, sites containing artifacts made of iron are generally more recent than sites containing only stone tools. In well-investigated cultural areas, archaeologists have developed series for particular styles of pottery.

Scientists make similar inferences with animal or faunal series. For example, very early North American Indian sites have yielded the remains of mastodons and mammoths—animals now extinct. These remains allow scientists to date these sites to a time before these animals died out, roughly 10,000 years ago. For dating some of the earliest African fossils in human evolution, paleoanthropologists have developed faunal series in regions where accurate chronometric dates can be established. They then

relative dating In archaeology and paleoanthropology, designating an event, object, or fossil as being older or younger than another by noting the position in the earth, by measuring the amount of chemicals contained in fossil bones and artifacts, or by identifying its association with other plant, animal, or cultural remains.

absolute or chronometric dating In archaeology and paleoanthropology, dating archaeological or fossil materials in units of absolute time using scientific properties such as rates of decay of radioactive elements; also known as *chronometric dating*.

stratigraphy In archaeology and paleoanthropology, the most reliable method of relative dating by means of strata.

fluorine dating In archaeology or paleoanthropology, a technique for relative dating based on the fact that the amount of fluorine in bones is proportional to their age.

seriation In archaeology and paleoanthropology, a technique for relative dating based on putting groups of objects into a sequence in relation to one another.

TABLE 5.1

Absolute and Relative Dating Methods Used by Archaeologists and Paleoanthropologists

Dating Method	Time Period	Process and Use	Drawbacks
Stratigraphy	Relative only	Based on the law of superposition, which states that lower layers or strata are older than higher strata; establishing the age of biological and cultural remains based on the layer in which they are found	Site specific; natural forces, such as earthquakes, and human activity, such as burials, disturb stratigraphic relationships
Fluorine analysis	Relative only	Comparing the amount of fluorine from surrounding soil absorbed by specimens after deposition; older remains will have absorbed more fluorine	Site specific
Faunal and floral series	Relative only	Sequencing remains into relative chronological order based on an evolutionary order established in another region with reliable absolute dates; called *palynology* when done with pollen grains	Dependent upon known relationships established elsewhere
Seriation	Relative only	Sequencing cultural remains into relative chronological order based on stylistic features	Dependent on known relationships established elsewhere
Dendrochronology	About 3,000 years before present (BP) maximum	Comparing tree growth rings preserved in a site with a tree of known age	Requires ancient trees of known age
Radiocarbon	Accurate < 50,000 BP	Comparing the ratio of radioactive carbon 14 (^{14}C), with a half-life of 5,730 years, to stable carbon (^{12}C) in organic material; after organisms die, only the ^{14}C decays (half of it every 5,730 years), so the ratio between ^{14}C and ^{12}C determines an actual date since death	Increasingly inaccurate when assessing remains from more than 50,000 years ago
Potassium argon (K-Ar)	> 200,000 BP	Using volcanic ash, comparing the amount of radioactive potassium (^{40}K), with a half-life of 1.25 billion years, to stable argon (^{40}Ar)	Requires volcanic ash; requires cross checking due to contamination from atmospheric argon
Amino acid racemization	40,000–180,000 BP	Comparing the ratio of right- and left-sided proteins in a three-dimensional structure; decay after death causes these proteins to change	Amino acids leached out from soil variably cause error
Thermoluminescence	Possibly up to 200,000 BP	Measuring the amount of light given off due to radioactivity when the specimen is heated to high temperatures	Technique developed for recent materials such as Greek pottery; not clear how accurate the dates are for older remains
Electron spin resonance	Possibly up to about 200,000 BP	Measuring the resonance of trapped electrons in a magnetic field	Works with tooth enamel, not yet developed for bone; problems with accuracy
Fission track	Wide range of times	Measuring the tracks left in crystals by uranium as it decays; good cross check for K-Ar technique	Useful for dating crystals only
Paleomagnetic reversals	Wide range of times	Measuring the orientation of magnetic particles in stones and linking them to whether the earth's magnetic field pulled toward the north or south during their formation	Large periods of normal or reversed magnetic orientation require dating by some other method; some smaller events are known to interrupt the sequence
Uranium series	40,000–180,000	Measuring the amount of uranium decaying in cave sites	Large error range

use these series to establish relative sequences in other regions. Similar series have been established for plants, particularly using grains of pollen. With this approach, known as **palynology**, the kind of pollen found in any geologic stratum depends on the kind of vegetation that existed at the time that stratum was deposited. Identifying the type of pollen associated with a site or locality can establish its relative dates. In addition, palynology also helps to reconstruct the environments in which prehistoric peoples lived.

Chronometric Dating

Some archaeological sites yield written records that provide archaeologists with a fascinating account of dates and times (**Figure 5.15**). But generally precise dates derive from a variety of absolute or chronometric dating methods. These techniques apply chemistry and physics to calculate the ages of physical and cultural remains. Several methods use naturally occurring radioactive elements that are present either in the remains themselves or in the surrounding soil.

One of the most widely used methods of absolute dating is **radiocarbon dating**. This method uses the fact that while they are alive, all organisms absorb radioactive carbon (known as carbon 14 or ^{14}C) as well as ordinary carbon 12 (^{12}C) in proportions identical to those found in the atmosphere. Absorption of ^{14}C ceases at the time of death, and the ratio between the two forms of carbon begins to change as the unstable radioactive element ^{14}C begins to "decay." Each radioactive element decays, or transforms into a stable nonradioactive form, at a specific rate. The amount of time it takes for one-half of the material originally present to decay is expressed as the "half-life." In the case of ^{14}C, it takes 5,730 years for half of the amount of ^{14}C present to decay to stable nitrogen 14. In another 5,730 years (11,460 years total), half of the remaining amount will also decay to nitrogen 14 so that only one-quarter of the original amount of ^{14}C will be present. Thus, the age of an organic substance such as charcoal, wood, shell, or bone can be measured through determining the changing proportion of ^{14}C relative to the amount of stable ^{12}C.

Though scientists can measure the amount of radioactive carbon left in even a few milligrams of a given organic substance of a recent specimen, the miniscule amount of carbon 14 present in remains from the distant past limits accurate detection. The radiocarbon method can adequately date organic materials up to about 50,000 years old, but dating older material is far less reliable.

Of course, one has to be sure that the organic remains were truly contemporaneous with the archaeological materials. For example, charcoal found on a site may have gotten there from a recent forest fire rather than a more ancient activity, or wood found at a site may have been retrieved by the people who lived there from some older context.

Because there is always a certain amount of error involved, radiocarbon dates (like all chronometric dating methods) are not as absolute as is sometimes thought. This is why any stated date always has a plus-or-minus ($\pm$) factor attached to it corresponding to one standard deviation above and below the mean value. For example, a date of 5,200 $\pm$ 120 years ago means that there is about a 2 out of 3 chance (or a 67 percent chance) that the true date

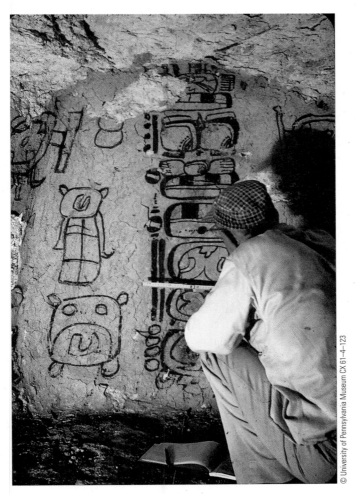

Figure 5.15 Maya Calendric Glyphs Some ancient societies devised precise ways of recording dates that archaeologists have been able to correlate with our own calendar. Here is the tomb of an important ruler, Siyaj Chan K'awil II, at the ancient Maya city of Tikal. The glyphs painted on the wall give the date of the burial in the Maya calendar, which is the same as March 18 of the year AD 457, in the Gregorian calendar.

palynology In archaeology and paleoanthropology, a technique of relative dating based on changes in fossil pollen over time.

radiocarbon dating In archaeology and paleoanthropology, a technique of chronometric dating based on measuring the amount of radioactive carbon (^{14}C) left in organic materials found in archaeological sites.

falls somewhere between 5,080 and 5,320 radiocarbon years ago. The qualification "radiocarbon years" is used because radiocarbon years are not precisely equivalent to calendar years.

That discovery—radiocarbon years are not precisely equivalent to calendar years—was made possible by another method of absolute dating: **dendrochronology** (derived from *dendron*, a Greek word meaning "tree"). Originally devised for dating Pueblo Indian sites in the North American Southwest, this method is based on the fact that in the right kind of climate, trees add one (and only one) new growth ring to their trunks every year. The rings vary in thickness, depending upon the amount of rainfall received in a year, so that tree ring growth registers climatic fluctuation. By taking a sample of wood, such as a beam from a Pueblo Indian house, and by comparing its pattern of rings with those in the trunk of a tree of known age, archaeologists can date the archaeological material.

Dendrochronology is applicable only to wooden objects. Furthermore, it works only in regions that contain trees of great age, such as giant sequoias and bristlecone pines. Radiocarbon dating of wood from bristlecone pines dated by dendrochronology allows scientists to correct the carbon 14 dates so as to bring them into agreement with calendar dates.

Potassium-argon dating, another commonly used method of absolute dating, is based on a technique similar to that of radiocarbon analysis. Following intense heating, as from a volcanic eruption, radioactive potassium decays at a known rate to form argon; any previously existing argon will have been released by the heating of the molten lava. The half-life of radioactive potassium is 1.3 billion years. Measuring the ratio of potassium to argon in a given rock accurately dates deposits dating back millions of years.

Potassium-argon analysis of volcanic debris at various fossil localities in East Africa indicates when the volcanic eruption occurred. Fossils or artifacts found sandwiched between layers of volcanic ash (as at Olduvai and other sites in East Africa) can be dated with some precision. As with radiocarbon dates, there are limits to that precision so potassium-argon dates are always stated with a plus-or-minus margin of error attached. Further, potassium-argon dating loses precision with materials younger than about 200,000 years.

Neither the radiocarbon nor the potassium-argon methods work well during the time period dating from about 50,000 years ago to about 200,000 years ago. Because this same time period happens to be very important in human evolutionary history, scientists have developed a number of other methods to obtain accurate dates for this critical period.

One such method, *amino acid racemization*, is based on the fact that amino acids trapped in organic materials gradually change, or racemize, after death, from left-handed forms to right-handed forms. Thus, the ratio of left- to right-handed forms should indicate the specimen's age. Unfortunately, in substances like bone, moisture and acids in the soil can leach out the amino acids, thereby introducing a serious source of error. However, ostrich eggshells have proved immune to this problem, the amino acids being so effectively locked up in a tight mineral matrix that they are preserved for thousands of years. Because ostrich eggs were widely used as food and the shells were used as containers in Africa and the Middle East, they provide a powerful means of dating sites of the later parts of the Old Stone Age (Paleolithic), between 40,000 and 180,000 years ago.

Electron spin resonance, which measures the number of trapped electrons in bone, and *thermoluminescence*, which measures the amount of light emitted from a specimen when heated to high temperatures, are two additional methods that have been developed to fill in prehistoric time gaps. Dates derived from these two methods changed the interpretation of key sites in present-day Israel vital for reconstructing human origins (see Chapters 7 and 8).

A few other chronometric techniques rely on the element uranium. *Fission track dating*, for example, counts radiation damage tracks on mineral crystals. Like amino acid racemization, all these methods have problems: They are complicated and tend to be expensive, many can be carried out only on specific kinds of materials, and some are so new that their reliability is not yet unequivocally established. It is for these reasons that they have not been as widely used as radiocarbon and potassium-argon dating techniques.

Paleomagnetic reversals contribute another interesting dimension to absolute dating methodologies by providing a method to crosscheck dates (**Figure 5.16**). This method is based on the shifting magnetic pole of the earth—the same force that controls the orientation of a compass needle. Today, a compass points to the north because we are in a period defined as the geomagnetic "normal." Over the past several million years, there have been extended periods of time during which the magnetic field of the earth pulled toward the south pole. Geologists call these periods *geomagnetic reversals*. Iron particles in stones will be oriented into positions determined by the dominant magnetic pole at the time of their formation, allowing scientists to derive broad ranges of dates for them. Human evolutionary history contains a geomagnetic reversal starting 5.2 million years ago that ended 3.4 million years ago, followed by a normal period until 2.6 million years ago; then a second reversal began, lasting until about 700,000 years ago when the present normal period began. This paleomagnetic sequence can be used to date sites to either normal or reversed periods and can be correlated with a variety of other dating methods to crosscheck their accuracy.

---

dendrochronology In archaeology and paleoanthropology, a technique of chronometric dating based on the number of rings of growth found in tree trunks.

potassium-argon dating In archaeology and paleoanthropology, a technique of chronometric dating that measures the ratio of radioactive potassium to argon in volcanic debris associated with human remains.

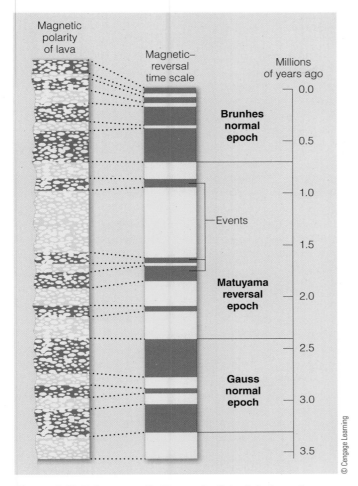

Figure 5.16 Paleomagnetic Reversals Scientists have documented a geomagnetic polarity time scale in which the changes in the earth's magnetic force—to north or south—have been calibrated. This geomagnetic time scale provides scientists with opportunities to cross check other dating methods.

Concepts and Methods for the Most Distant Past

As described previously, context and dating are vital for the interpretation of fossils and cultural remains. Because mammalian primate evolution extends so far back in time, paleoanthropologists reconstruct our evolutionary history in conjunction with information about the geologic history of the earth, which is 4.6 billion years old.

Continental Drift and Geologic Time

The geologic time scale is unfamiliar because few people deal with hundreds of millions of anything, let alone years, on a regular basis. To understand this type of scale, astronomer Carl Sagan correlated the geologic time scale for the history of the earth to a single calendar year. In this "cosmic calendar," the earth itself originates on January 1,

the first organisms appear approximately 9 months later around September 25, followed by the earliest vertebrates around December 20, mammals on December 25, primates on December 29, hominoids at 10:15 AM on New Year's Eve, bipeds at 9:30 PM, with our species appearing in the last minutes before midnight. Human evolutionary history begins with the December 25 appearance of the mammals in the Mesozoic era, roughly 245 million years ago (mya). **Figure 5.17** plots out the more recent events in

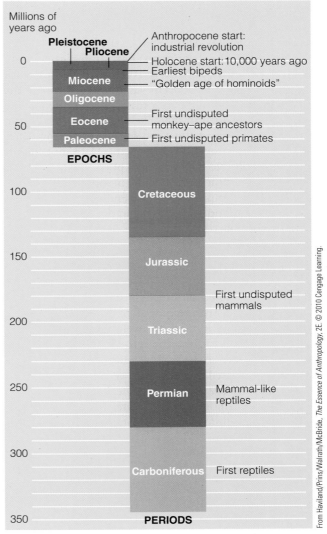

Figure 5.17 Milestones of Mammalian Primate Evolution This timeline highlights some major milestones in the course of mammalian primate evolution that ultimately led to humans and their ancestors. The Paleocene, Eocene, Oligocene, and Miocene epochs are subsets of the Tertiary period. The Quaternary period begins with the Pleistocene and continues today. It includes the Holocene epoch that began at the end of the last Ice Age around 12,000 years ago. In 2000, the Nobel Prize–winning chemist Paul Crutzen coined the term *Anthropocene* to describe the world since the industrial revolution because of the profound geologic changes human activity imposes on the earth. Geologic societies around the globe are currently debating the inclusion of Anthropocene as a formal geologic unit.

mammalian primate evolution that take place during the final week of Sagan's cosmic calendar.

By 190 million years ago—the end of what geologists call the Triassic period—true mammals were on the scene. Mammals from the Triassic, Jurassic (135–190 mya), and Cretaceous (65–135 mya) periods are largely known from hundreds of fossils, especially teeth and jaw parts. Because teeth are the hardest, most durable structures, they often outlast other parts of an animal's skeleton. Fortunately, investigators often are able to infer a good deal about the total animal on the basis of only a few teeth found in the earth.

Over such vast amounts of time, the earth itself has changed considerably. During the past 200 million years, the position of the continents has shifted through a process called **continental drift**, which accounts for the rearrangement of adjacent landmasses through the theory of plate tectonics. According to this theory, the continents, embedded in platelike segments of the earth, move their positions as the edges of the underlying plates are created or destroyed (**Figure 5.18**). Plate movements are also responsible for geologic phenomena such as earthquakes, volcanic activity, and mountain formation. Continental drift impacted the distribution fossil primates (recall Figure 3.1) and played a role in the earliest stages of human evolutionary history.

The Molecular Clock

In the 1960s, a molecular biochemist Allan Wilson from New Zealand (see Anthropologist of Note) and his U.S. graduate student Vince Sarich developed the revolutionary concept of a **molecular clock**. Although not a dating method per se, such clocks help detect when the branching of related species from a common ancestor took place in the distant past. They can establish a series of relationships among closely related species that then can reinforce absolute or relative dates established at specific fossil localities.

For the first molecular clock, Sarich and Wilson used a technique that had been around since the beginning of the 20th century: comparison of the blood proteins of living groups. Today, this technique has been expanded to include comparisons in bases of DNA. Sarich worked on serum albumin, a protein from the fluid portion of the blood (like the albumin that forms egg whites) that can be precipitated out of solution. *Precipitation* refers to

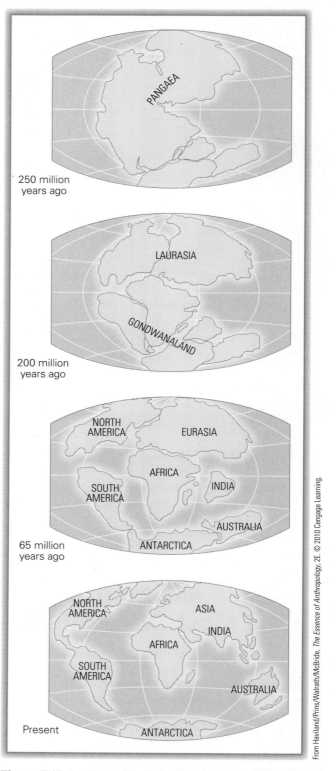

250 million years ago

200 million years ago

65 million years ago

Present

From Haviland/Prins/Walrath/McBride, *The Essence of Anthropology, 2E.* © 2010 Cengage Learning.

Figure 5.18 Continental Drift Continental drift is illustrated here during several geologic periods. At the time of the extinction of the dinosaurs 65 million years ago, the seas opened up by continental drift, creating isolating barriers between major landmasses. About 23 million years ago, at the start of the time period known as the Miocene epoch, African and Eurasian landmasses reconnected and the Indian subcontinent joined Asia.

---

continental drift According to the theory of plate tectonics, the movement of continents embedded in underlying plates on the earth's surface in relation to one another over the history of life on earth.

molecular clock The hypothesis that dates of divergences among related species can be calculated through an examination of the genetic mutations that have accrued since the divergence.

ANTHROPOLOGIST OF NOTE

Allan Wilson (1934–1991)

Though a biochemist by training, New Zealander **Allan Wilson** has made key contributions to anthropology through his pioneering work in applying the principles of biochemistry to human evolutionary questions. Wilson forged a new "hybrid science," combining fossil and molecular evidence with groundbreaking results. Because the molecular evidence required rethinking long-held theories about the relationships among fossil groups, Wilson's work has been

Allan Wilson (*right*) observes as Vince Sarich (*left*) injects a laboratory rabbit.

© Roger Ressmeyer/Corbis

surrounded by controversy. According to those close to Wilson, he enjoyed his role as an outsider—being on the edges of anthropology and shaking things up.

Wilson was born in Ngaruwahia, New Zealand, and grew up on a farm in Pukekohe. After attending school in New Zealand and Australia, he was invited to study biochemistry at the University of California, Berkeley, in 1955. His father was reluctant to have his son travel so far from home, but his mother saw this as an exciting opportunity and encouraged him to head to California.

Wilson stayed at Berkeley for the next thirty-five years, running one of the world's most creative biochemistry labs. In the 1960s, Berkeley was a center of academic liberalism and social protest. Wilson's highly original work was conducted with a similar revolutionary spirit, garnering him a MacArthur "Genius" grant, two Guggenheim fellowships, and a place on the short list for the Nobel Prize.

He developed the notion of a molecular clock with his graduate student Vince Sarich and published the groundbreaking paper "Immunological Time-Scale for Human Evolution" in the journal *Science* in 1967. The molecular clock proposes that evolutionary events such as the split between humans and apes can be dated through an examination of the number of genetic mutations that accumulated since two species diverged from a common ancestor. In the 1980s, his laboratory (including Rebecca Cann and Mark Stoneking) was also responsible for seminal work with the mitochondrial Eve hypothesis that continues to be widely debated today (see Chapters 8).

Wilson died from leukemia at the age of 56. Joseph Felsenstein, one of his biographers, stated in his obituary in the journal *Nature*, "While others concentrated on what evolution could tell them about molecules, Wilson always looked for ways that molecules could say something about evolution."

the chemical transformation of a substance dissolved in a liquid back into its solid form. One of the forces that will cause such precipitation is contact of this protein with antibodies directed against it. Antibodies are proteins produced by organisms as part of an immune response to an infection. The technique relies on the notion that the stronger the biochemical reaction between the protein and the antibody (the more precipitate), the closer the evolutionary relationship. The antibodies and proteins of closely related species resemble one another more than the antibodies and proteins of distant species.

Sarich made immunological comparisons between a variety of species and suggested that he could establish dates for evolutionary events by calculating a molecular rate of change over time. By assuming a constant rate of change in the protein structure of each species, Sarich used these results to predict times of divergence between related groups. Each molecular clock needs to be set, or calibrated, by the dates associated with a known event, such as the divergence between prosimian and anthropoid primates or a major change in the continental plates, as established by absolute dating methods.

Using this technique, Sarich proposed a sequence of divergence for the living hominoids showing that human, chimp, and gorilla lines split roughly 5 million years ago (mya). He boldly stated that it was impossible to have a separate human line before 7 million years ago "no matter what it looked like." Before this work, anthropologists had thought that the great apes—chimpanzees and bonobos, gorillas, and orangutans—were more closely related to one another than any of them were to humans. This work was the first proof that human origins are firmly in Africa and that humans, chimps and bonobos, and gorillas are more closely related to one another than any of them are to the orangutans. A discovery in the laboratory, like the molecular clock, can drastically change the interpretation of the fossil evidence.

Sciences of Discovery

The previous discussion demonstrates that anthropologists participate in an unusual kind of science. Paleoanthropology and archaeology are sciences of discovery. As new fossil discoveries and artifacts come to light, interpretations inevitably change, making for better understanding of human evolutionary and cultural history. Today, discoveries can occur in the laboratory as easily as on the site of an excavation. Molecular studies since the 1970s provide a new line of evidence in much the same way that a fossil or pottery figurine or the remains of a preserved plant provides new data as it is unearthed. Just like detectives at an investigation, scientists use each new discovery to refine our collective understanding of the past.

The archaeological and fossil records are imperfect. Chance circumstances of preservation have determined what has and what has not survived the consequences of time. Thus, scientists reconstruct the biology and culture of our ancestors on the basis of fragmentary and at times unrepresentative samples of physical and cultural remains. Chance also impacts the discovery of prehistoric remains. Vestiges may come to light due to factors ranging from changing sea level, vegetation, or even a local government's decision to build a highway.

Ancient cultural processes have also shaped the archaeological and fossil record. We know more about the past due to the cultural practice of deliberate burial. We also know more about the elite segments of past societies because they have left more material culture behind. However, as archaeologists have shifted their focus from gathering treasures to the reconstruction of human behavior, they have gained a more complete picture of ancient societies. Similarly, paleoanthropologists no longer simply catalogue fossils; they interpret data about our ancestors in order to reconstruct the biological processes responsible for who we are today. The challenge of reconstructing our past will be met by a continual process of reexamination and modification as anthropologists discover evidence in the earth, among living people, and in the laboratory leading to new understandings of human origins.

CHAPTER CHECKLIST

How do archaeologists and paleoanthropologists identify sites for excavation?

● Aerial photographs and other surveying tools reveal environmental clues such as soil markings. Survey may be combined with documents, folklore, and found artifacts in order to locate important sites.

● Many excavations take place where natural forces such as erosion or drought leave sites exposed.

● Chance discoveries, like those from mining or construction, have led to the recovery of significant historical remains.

What excavation practices are preferred?

● Excavators map the land into a grid system in order to precisely record the location of found objects, and they choose a fixed landmark to use as the reference (datum point) of the grid. Photographs and scale drawings supplement the written excavation data.

● The destructive nature of excavation demands that researchers record information on all found objects including those irrelevant to their original purpose.

● Where stratification is present, layers corresponding to distinct time periods are dug carefully, one at a time. If searching for smaller objects, the excavation team may utilize the flotation technique to separate particles of varying density.

● For bone excavation, the earth matrix containing the specimen is cut out and hardened using shellac and plaster bandages. Then, the entire block is removed and shipped to a laboratory for the final stages of extraction.

How do scientists continue excavation analysis in the lab?

● Close examination of wear patterns on artifacts can lead to understanding of early human behaviors. Similarly, markings on teeth suggest dietary habits, and endocasts reveal brain size and shape.

● Bioarchaeologists use anatomical data to reconstruct cultures of the past.

● Technology such as CT scanning minimizes handling and potential damage to specimens; 3D digital images permit the continued scientific study of remains that must be repatriated.

● DNA samples can be extracted from more recent skeletal remains.

What are the important dating methods, and how do they differ?

● Relative dating techniques establish the age of remains by association with the surrounding earth or other nearby remains. Researchers may combine several techniques to create accurate timelines of the past. Relative dating methods include stratigraphy, the fluorine method, and seriation.

● Most absolute dating techniques rely on rates of decay of radioactive elements present in remains in order to estimate a numerical age. Absolute methods include techniques such as radiocarbon dating, potassium-argon dating, amino acid racemization, and, in the case of wooden remains, dendrochronology.

How do geologic phenomena contribute to our understanding of human history?

● Knowledge of geomagnetic reversals can be used to date ancient remains by examining the position of iron particles in stone artifacts.

● Continental drift has impacted the course of human evolution by separating populations that then diverged to become distinct species.

What is the molecular clock, and what does it reveal about human evolution?

● The evolutionary proximities of living species can be estimated by comparing their blood proteins. Assuming these proteins have changed at a constant rate over time, scientists estimate when two species' last common ancestor lived.

● Molecular clocks were used to determine that humans, chimps, bonobos, and gorillas split into different evolutionary branches between 5 and 7 million years ago in Africa. All African hominoids are more closely related to one another than any is to the orangutan.

QUESTIONS FOR REFLECTION

1. How would you decide who owns the past? Have there been any examples of contested ownership in your community?

2. The cultural practice of burial of the dead altered the fossil record and provided valuable insight into the beliefs and practices of past cultures. The same is true today. What beliefs are reflected in the traditions for treatment of the dead in your culture?

3. Controversy has surrounded Kennewick Man since this skeleton was discovered on the banks of the Columbia River in Washington in 1996. Scientists and American Indians both feel they have a right to these remains.

What kinds of evidence support these differing perspectives? How should this controversy be resolved?

4. Why is dating so important for paleoanthropologists and archaeologists? Would an interpretation of physical or cultural remains change depending upon the date assigned to the remains? Why are metaphors used in the context of geologic time?

5. The interpretation of fossil material changes with the discovery of new specimens and with findings in the laboratory. How has that happened? Why do we know more about some places and peoples than others?

ONLINE STUDY RESOURCES

CourseMate

Access chapter-specific learning tools, including learning objectives, practice quizzes, videos, flash cards, glossaries, and more in your Anthropology CourseMate.

Log into **www.cengagebrain.com** to access the resources your instructor has assigned and to purchase materials.

© Frans Lanting/Frans Lanting Stock

Challenge Issue

Who are we? How did we get here? Where and when did the unique human line first appear? What distinguishes us from the other animals in general, the other primates in particular? Paleoanthropologists seek answers to all these questions through scientific study of the fossil record, of our closest relatives, of molecules, and of geology, and they use this disparate fragmentary evidence to reconstruct a coherent trajectory of our evolutionary history. Each aspect of this narrative of human origins challenges us to think about what it means to be human. Although we might be tempted to say that our intellects distinguish us from the other primates, the hallmark of the hominin or human line is *bipedalism*—our ability to walk on two legs. Bone structure indicating that a fossil was fully bipedal makes it, by definition, a hominin. But as Nellie, a graceful tightrope-walking chimp from Fongoli, Senegal, demonstrates, our closest relatives can do this extremely well, if only for a few minutes at a time. The opposable big toe makes it far easier for a chimp than a human to grip a branch thirty feet above the forest floor, but the chimp has difficulty maintaining this posture for long periods of time, due to the position of the bones and muscles of the trunk and legs. Still, the discovery of rich fossil evidence for bipedal forest-dwelling primates who lived from 4.4 to 5.8 million years ago has made some scientists wonder if, like Nellie, our ancestors took their first bipedal steps in the trees instead of on the ground.

From First Primates to First Bipeds

In geologic terms, humans appeared in the world recently, though not as recently as some new strains of bacteria. Our form—like that of any organism—came about only as a consequence of a whole string of accidental happenings in the past. The history of any species is an outcome of many such occurrences. This chapter begins our focus on human origins, starting with our earliest primate ancestors. Much of who we are, as culture-bearing biological organisms, derives from our mammalian primate heritage.

The successful adaptation of the primates largely reflects their intelligence, a characteristic that provides for behavioral flexibility. Other physical traits, such as stereoscopic vision and a grasping hand, have also been instrumental in the success of the primates. In addition, the continued survival of our species and of our world now depends on understanding evolutionary processes and the way all organisms interact with their environment.

Primate Origins

Early primates began to emerge during a time of great global change at the start of the Paleocene epoch 65 million years ago (mya). Evidence suggests that a meteor or some other sort of extraterrestrial body slammed into the earth where the Yucatan Peninsula of Mexico now exists, cooling global temperatures to such an extent as to cause the extinction of the dinosaurs (and numerous other species as well). For 100 million years, dinosaurs had dominated most terrestrial environments suitable for vertebrate animals and would probably have continued to do so had the climate not changed. Although mammals appeared at about the same time as reptiles, they existed as small, inconspicuous creatures. But with the demise of the dinosaurs, new opportunities became available, allowing mammals to begin their great adaptive radiation into a variety of species, including our own ancestors, the earliest primates (**Figure 6.1**).

IN THIS CHAPTER YOU WILL LEARN TO

- Identify the course of primate evolution and its major geologic events.

- Recognize the anatomy of bipedalism and how paleoanthropologists identify the hominin line and distinct species in the fossil record.

- Discuss how cultural biases interfered with scientific recognition of the African origins of humans.

- Describe paleoanthropology in action: how paleoanthropologists construct the trajectory of human origins from fragmentary remains.

- Compare the earliest bipeds to one another and to chimps and humans.

- Identify two grades of australopithecines: the gracile and the robust.

- Describe the earliest appearance of the genus *Homo* in the fossil record.

Figure 6.1 **Extinction of the Dinosaurs** Though popular media depict the coexistence of humans and dinosaurs, in reality the extinction of the dinosaurs occurred 65 million years ago (mya), while the first bipeds ancestral to humans appeared between 5 and 8 million years ago. The climatic changes beginning 65 million years ago allowed for the adaptive radiation of the mammals and a diversification of plant life. The appearance of the true seed plants (the angiosperms) provided not only highly nutritious fruit seeds and flowers but also a host of habitats for numerous edible insects and worms—just the sorts of food required by mammals with their higher metabolism. For species like mammals to continue to survive, a wide diversity of plants, insects, and even single-celled organisms needs to be maintained. In ecosystems these organisms are dependent upon one another.

Newly evolved grasses, shrubs, and other flowering plants proliferated enormously during this same time period. This diversification, along with a milder climate, favored the spread of dense, lush tropical and subtropical forests over the earth. The spread of these huge belts of forest set the stage for the movement of some mammals into the trees. Forests provided our early ancestors with the ecological niches in which they would flourish. Fossil evidence of primatelike mammals from the Paleocene forests has been found in North America and Eurasia. See Figure 6.2 for a full timeline of primate evolution.

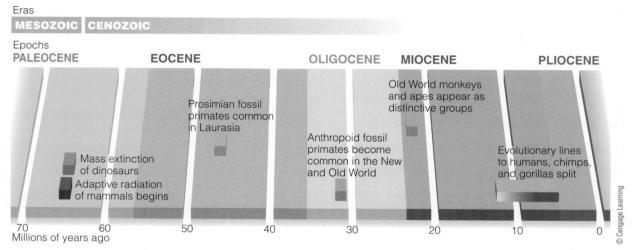

Figure 6.2 **Timeline of Primate Evolution** This timeline depicts some of the major events of primate evolution.

One theory for primate evolution, the **arboreal hypothesis**, proposes that life in the trees was responsible for enhanced visual acuity and manual dexterity in primates. Misjudgments and errors of coordination led to falls that injured or killed the individuals poorly adapted to arboreal life. Natural selection would favor those that judged depth correctly and gripped the branches strongly. Early primates that took to the trees were probably in some measure preadapted by virtue of behavioral flexibility, better vision, and more dexterous fingers than their contemporaries.

Primatologist Matt Cartmill's **visual predation hypothesis** suggests that primate visual and grasping abilities were also promoted through the activity of hunting for insects by sight. The relatively small size of the early primates allowed them to make use of the smaller branches of trees; larger, heavier competitors and most predators could not follow. The move to the smaller branches also gave them access to an abundant food supply; the primates were able to gather insects, leaves, flowers, and fruits directly rather than waiting for them to fall to the ground.

The strong selection in a new environment led to an acceleration in the rate of change of primate characteristics. Paradoxically, these changes eventually facilitated a return to the ground by some primates, including the ancestors of the genus *Homo*.

The first well-preserved "true" primates appeared by about 55 million years ago at the start of the Eocene epoch. During this time period, an abrupt warming trend caused the extinction of many older mammalian forms, which were replaced by recognizable forerunners of some of today's mammals, including the prosimians. Over fifty prosimian fossil genera have been found in Africa, North America, Europe, and Asia, where the warm, wet conditions of the Eocene sustained extensive rainforests. Relative to ancestral primatelike mammals, these early primate families had enlarged braincases, slightly reduced snouts, and a somewhat forward position of the eye orbits, which, though not completely walled in, were surrounded by a complete bony ring called a *postorbital bar* (**Figure 6.3**).

The fossil record indicates that Eocene primates, ancestors of today's prosimians and anthropoids, were abundant, diverse, and widespread. Among these, a spectacularly well-preserved 47-million-year-old specimen nicknamed "Ida" received a lot of media attention in 2009 when two sections of her remains were reunited (Dalton, 2009; Franzen et al., 2009; Gebo, Dagosto, Beard, & Tao, 2001; "Media frenzy," 2009; Seiffert et al., 2009; Simons et al., 2009). The remains of this potential anthropoid, originally discovered thirty years earlier during mining and drilling operations in Germany, were sold to two separate collections. Since being reunited, scientists are determining whether Ida is a true anthropoid, a distinction that places her on the line leading to humans.

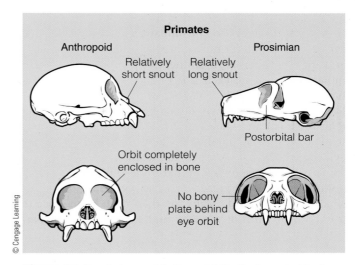

Figure 6.3 Prosimian and Anthropoid Skulls Ancestral features seen in Eocene and Oligocene primates are still seen in prosimians today. Like modern lemurs, these fossil prosimians have a postorbital bar, a bony ring around the eye socket that is open in the back. Anthropoid primates have orbits completely enclosed in bone. Note also the difference in the relative size of the snout in these two groups. Paleoanthropologists make these kinds of comparisons as they reconstruct our evolutionary history.

With the end of the Eocene, climates became somewhat cooler and drier, but then temperatures took a sudden dive, triggering the formation of an icecap over previously forested Antarctica. The result was a marked reduction in the range of suitable environments for primates. At the same time, cold climate led to lower sea levels through the formation of icecaps, perhaps changing opportunities for migration of primates. In North America, now well isolated from Eurasia, primates became extinct, and elsewhere their range seems to have been reduced considerably.

Oligocene Anthropoids

During the Oligocene epoch, from about 23 to 34 million years ago (mya), the anthropoid primates diversified and expanded their range, and prosimian fossil forms became far less prominent. Fossil evidence from Egypt's Fayum region has yielded sufficient fossils (more than 1,000) to reveal that by 33 million years ago, Old World anthropoid primates existed in considerable diversity.

arboreal hypothesis A theory for primate evolution that proposes that life in the trees was responsible for enhanced visual acuity and manual dexterity in primates.

visual predation hypothesis A theory for primate evolution that proposes that hunting behavior in tree-dwelling primates was responsible for their enhanced visual acuity and manual dexterity.

Some have the ancestral dental formula (2-1-3-3) seen in New World monkeys and prosimians, whereas others have the derived dental formula shared by Old World monkeys and apes: two incisors, a canine, two premolars, and three molars (2-1-2-3) on each side of the jaw. The eye orbits have a complete wall, a feature of anthropoid primates. Fayum, along with newly discovered localities in Algeria (North Africa) and Oman (Arabian Peninsula), continues to yield anthropoid fossil discoveries. At present, we have evidence of at least sixty genera included in two families.

Fossil evidence indicates that these Old World anthropoids were diurnal quadrupeds, as evidenced by their smaller orbits (eyes). Many of these Oligocene species possess a mixture of monkey and ape features. Of particular interest is the genus *Aegyptopithecus* (pronounced "Egypt-o-pith-ee-kus"; Greek for "Egyptian ape"), an Oligocene anthropoid that has sometimes been called a monkey with an ape's teeth. Its lower molars have the five cusps of an ape, and the upper canine and lower first premolar exhibit the sort of shearing surfaces found in monkeys and apes. Its skull has forward-facing eye sockets completely protected by a bony wall. The endocast of its skull indicates that it had a larger visual cortex than that found in prosimians. Relative to its body size, the brain of *Aegyptopithecus* was smaller than that of more recent anthropoids. Still, this primate seems to have had a larger brain than any prosimian, past or present. Possessed of a monkeylike skull and body, and fingers and toes capable of powerful grasping, it evidently moved about in a quadrupedal, monkeylike manner.

Although no bigger than a modern house cat, *Aegyptopithecus* was, nonetheless, one of the larger Oligocene primates. Primatologists consider the larger *Aegyptopithecus* fossils to be males, noting that these specimens also possess more formidable canine teeth and deeper mandibles (lower jaws) compared to the smaller females. In modern anthropoids, such sexual dimorphism correlates with social systems with high competition among males.

New World Monkeys

The earliest evidence of primates in Central and South America dates from the Oligocene epoch. Eyes fully encased in bone and limb bones for quadrupedal locomotion confirm these fossil primates' anthropoid status. Scientists hypothesize that these primates came to South America from Africa because the Old World contains the earliest fossil evidence of anthropoids.

Scientists surmise that some of the African anthropoids arrived in South America, which at the time was not attached to any other landmass, by means of giant floating clumps of vegetation of the sort that originate even today in the great rivers of West and Central Africa. In the Oligocene, the distance between the two continents, though still formidable, was far less than it is today. Favorable winds and currents could have carried New World monkey ancestors on these floating islands of vegetation to South America quickly enough for them to survive.

Miocene Apes and Human Origins

True apes first appeared in the fossil record during the Miocene epoch, 5 to 23 million years ago. It was also during this time period that the African and Eurasian landmasses made direct contact. For most of the preceding 100 million years, the Tethys Sea—a continuous body of water that joined what are now the Mediterranean Sea and the Black Sea to the Indian Ocean—created a barrier to migration between Africa and Eurasia. Once joined through the region of what is now the Middle East and Gibraltar, Old World primates, such as the apes, could extend their range from Africa into Eurasia. Miocene ape fossil remains have been found everywhere from the caves of China, to the forests of France, to East Africa, where scientists have recovered the oldest fossil remains of bipeds. So varied and ubiquitous were the fossil apes of this period that the Miocene has been called the "golden age of the hominoids." The word *hominoid* comes from the Latin roots *homo* and *homin* (meaning "human being") and the suffix *oïdes* ("resembling").

In addition to the Old World anthropoid dental formula of 2-1-2-3, hominoids can be characterized by the derived characteristics of Y5 molars, lack of a tail, and broad flexible shoulder joints. One of the Miocene apes is the direct ancestor of the human line; exactly which one remains a question. An examination of the history of the contenders for direct human ancestor among the Miocene apes demonstrates how reconstruction of evolutionary relationships draws on much more than simply bones. Scientists interpret fossil finds by drawing on existing beliefs and knowledge. With new discoveries, interpretations change.

The first Miocene ape fossil remains were found in Africa in the 1930s and 1940s by the British archaeologist A. T. Hopwood and the renowned Kenyan paleoanthropologist Louis Leakey. These fossils turned up on one of the many islands in Lake Victoria, the 27,000-square-mile lake where Kenya, Tanzania, and Uganda meet. Impressed with the chimplike appearance of these fossil remains, Hopwood suggested that the new species be named *Proconsul*, combining the Latin root for "before" (*pro*) with the stage name of a chimpanzee who was performing in London at the time.

Dated to the early Miocene (17 to 21 mya), *Proconsul* had some of the classic hominoid features, lacking a tail and having the characteristic pattern of Y5 grooves in the lower molar teeth. However, the adaptations of the upper body seen in later apes (including humans), such as a skeletal structure adapted for hanging suspended below tree branches, were absent. In other words, *Proconsul* had some apelike features as well as some features of four-footed Old World monkeys (**Figure 6.4**). This mixture of ape and monkey features makes *Proconsul* a contender for a missing link between monkeys and apes.

At least seven fossil hominoid groups besides *Proconsul* have been found in East Africa from the early to middle Miocene. Between 5 and 14 million years ago, however, this fossil record thins out because the tropical forests inhabited by ancestral chimps and gorillas were not optimal for the preservation of bones. The scarcity of African fossil evidence from this time period fit well with notions about human origins that prevailed in the past. European scientists in the early 20th century concentrated on the various species of European ape—all members of the genus *Dryopithecus* (pronounced "dry-o-pith-ee-kus"). They believed that humans evolved where "civilization" developed and that these apes could be the missing link to humans.

Moreover, investigators initially did not consider that humans were any more closely related to the African apes than they were to the other intelligent great ape—the Asian orangutan. Chimps, bonobos, gorillas, and orangutans were thought to be more closely related to one another than any of them were to humans. The construction of evolutionary relationships still relied upon visual similarities among species, much as it did in the mid-1700s

when Linnaeus developed the taxonomic scheme that grouped humans with other primates. Chimps, bonobos, gorillas, and orangutans all possess the same basic body plan, adapted to hanging by their arms from branches or knuckle-walking on the ground. Humans and their ancestors had an altogether different form of locomotion: walking upright on two legs. On an anatomical basis, the first Miocene ape to become bipedal could have come from any part of the vast Old World range of the Miocene apes.

Today, scientists agree that genetic evidence firmly establishes that the human line diverged from those leading to chimpanzees and gorillas between 5 and 8 million years ago. Although any fossil discoveries in Africa from this critical time period have the potential to be the missing link between humans and the other African ape species, the evidence from this period has been, until recently, particularly scrappy. Controversy surrounds the interpretation of many of these fossil finds, although scientists agree on the basic evolutionary relationships among the Old World anthropoid primates (**Figure 6.5**).

For example, in 2007 scientists announced a new 10-million-year-old ape species discovered in Ethiopia as ancestral to gorillas. Named *Chororapithecus abyssinicus,* after Chorora, the local area where the fossil was found, and Abyssinia, the ancient name of Ethiopia, the scientists who found the nine fossil teeth claim that this specimen indicates that the gorilla lineage had become distinct from the human and chimp lines 2 to 4 million years earlier than that. Other scientists require more fossil evidence before pushing back the timing of the split.

Some fossils have begun to fill in the critical period of 5 to 8 million years ago. In Chad in the summer of 2002, a team of international researchers led by Michael Brunet of France unearthed a well-preserved skull dated to between 6 and 7 million years ago (**Figure 6.6**). Calling their find *Sahelanthropus tchadensis* ("Sahel human of Chad," referring to the Sahel, a belt of semi-arid land bordering the southern edge of the Sahara Desert), the researchers suggested that this specimen represented the earliest known ancestor of humans (Brunet et al., 2002). Inclusion of any fossil specimen in the human evolutionary line depends upon evidence for **bipedalism** (also called *bipedality*), the shared derived characteristic distinguishing humans and their ancestors from the other African apes.

Some paleoanthropologists argue that this specimen, nicknamed "Toumai," from the region's Goran-language meaning "hope for life," cannot be established as a hominin from skull bones alone, especially considering the degree

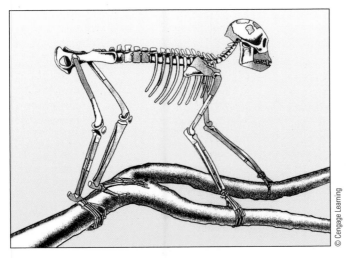

© Cengage Learning

Figure 6.4 A Reconstructed Skeleton of *Proconsul* Note the apelike absence of a tail but monkeylike limb and body proportions. *Proconsul*, however, was capable of greater rotation of forelimbs than monkeys.

bipedalism A special form of locomotion, distinguishing humans and their ancestors from the African great apes, in which the organism walks upright on two feet; also called *bipedality*.

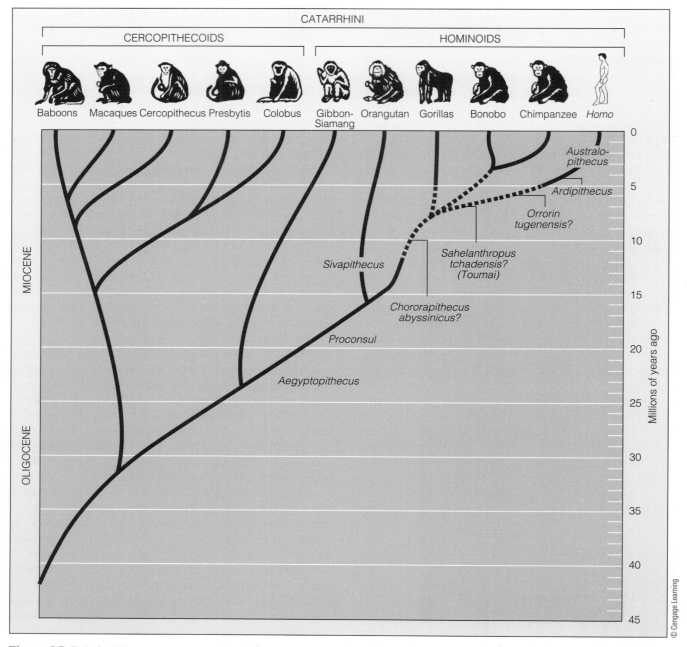

Figure 6.5 **Relationships among the Old World Anthropoids** Although debate continues over details, this chart represents a reasonable reconstruction of evolutionary relationships among the Old World anthropoid primates. (Extinct evolutionary lines are not shown.) The 2007 discovery of a fossil ancestor to gorillas has suggested a new interpretation of the timing and nature of the split between humans and the African apes.

of distortion present. The research team argues that derived features, such as a reduced canine tooth, indicate its status as a member of the human evolutionary line. Whether or not this specimen proves to be a direct human ancestor, as the only skull from this time period, it remains a very important find.

In 2001, 6-million-year-old fossils discovered in Kenya by French and British researchers Brigitte Senut and Martin Pickford were also reported as human ancestors (**Figure 6.7**). Officially given the species name *Orrorin tugenensis* (*Orrorin* meaning "original man" and *tugenensis* meaning "from the Tugen Hills") but nicknamed

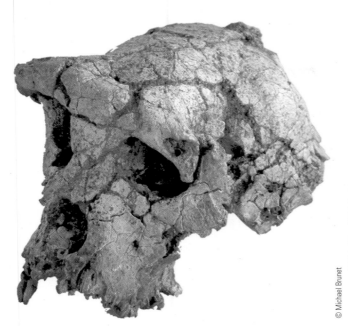

Figure 6.6 *Sahelanthropus tchadensis* The spectacular skull from Chad nicknamed "Toumai" ("hope for life") has been proposed as the earliest direct human ancestor. Although the 6- to 7-million-year-old specimen is beautifully preserved and has some derived features, some paleoanthropologists feel that alone, it does not establish bipedalism, the derived trait characteristic of the human line.

Figure 6.7 *Orrorin tugenensis* These 6-million-year-old fossils, discovered in Kenya in 2001, represent a new species, *Orrorin tugenensis*, which has also been proposed as the earliest human ancestor. Like Toumai, these bones are surrounded by controversy. The thighbones (femora) strongly suggest bipedalism, and the upper arm bone (humerus) may be more like that of humans than it is like some of the later bipeds. More discoveries and scientific comparisons will solve controversies surrounding both *Orrorin* and Toumai.

"Millennium Man," controversy also surrounds these specimens (Senut et al., 2001).

The evidence for *Orrorin* consists of bone fragments from the arm and thigh, a finger bone, some jaw fragments, and teeth of at least five individuals. The thighbones demonstrate possible but not definite bipedalism. Unfortunately, the distal, or far ends, of the thighbone that would prove this are not fully preserved. The humerus (upper arm) appears to be more like that of humans, but arm bones cannot confirm bipedalism. Surprisingly, many other unexpected fragments can provide strong evidence of bipedalism, as we will explore following.

The Anatomy of Bipedalism

Anatomical changes accompany bipedalism literally from head to toe. Even an isolated skull can indicate bipedalism (**Figure 6.8**) because balancing the head in an upright posture requires a skull position relatively centered above the spinal column. The spinal cord leaves the skull at its base through an opening called the *foramen magnum* (Latin for "big opening"). In a knuckle-walker like a chimp, the foramen magnum sits toward the back of the skull whereas in a biped it is toward the front.

Extending down from the skull of a biped, the spinal column makes a series of convex and concave curves that together maintain the body in an upright posture by positioning the body's center of gravity above the legs rather than forward. The curves correspond to the neck (cervical), chest (thoracic), lower back (lumbar), and pelvic (sacral) regions of the spine, respectively. In a chimp, the shape of the spine

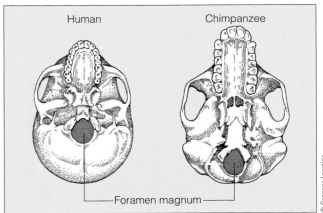

Figure 6.8 **The Foramen Magnum** Bipedalism can be inferred from the position of the foramen magnum, the large opening at the base of the skull. Note its relatively forward position on the human skull (*left*) compared to the chimpanzee skull.

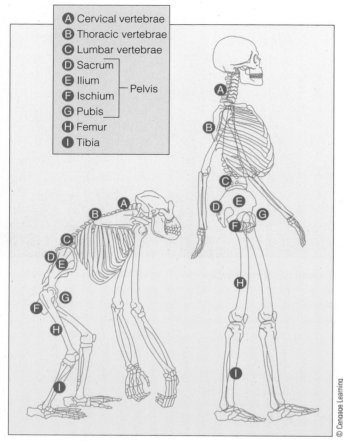

Figure 6.9 Chimp and Human Skeletons Differences between skeletons of chimps and humans reflect their habitual mode of locomotion. Notice the curves in the spinal column of the human as well as the basin-shaped pelvis.

Legend for Figure 6.9:

- Ⓐ Cervical vertebrae
- Ⓑ Thoracic vertebrae
- Ⓒ Lumbar vertebrae
- Ⓓ Sacrum ⎤
- Ⓔ Ilium   ⎥
- Ⓕ Ischium ⎬— Pelvis
- Ⓖ Pubis   ⎥
- Ⓗ Femur
- Ⓘ Tibia

© Cengage Learning

follows a single arching curve (**Figure 6.9**). Interestingly, at birth the spines of human babies have a single arching curve as seen in adult apes. As humans mature, the curves characteristic of bipedalism appear, the cervical curve at about 3 months on average and the lumbar curve at around 12 months—a time when many babies begin to walk.

The shape of the pelvis also differs considerably between bipeds and other apes. Instead of an elongated shape following the arch of the spine as seen in the chimp, the biped has a wider and foreshortened pelvis that provides structural support for the upright body. With a wide bipedal pelvis, the lower limbs would be oriented away from the body's center of gravity if the thighbones (femora) did not angle in toward each other from the hip to the knee, a phenomenon described as "kneeing-in." (Notice how your own knees and feet can touch when standing whereas

your hip joints remain widely spaced.) This angling does not continue past the knee to the shinbones (tibia), which are oriented vertically. The resulting knee joint is not symmetrical, allowing the thighbones and shinbones to meet despite their different orientations (**Figure 6.10**).

Other characteristics of bipeds are their stable arched feet and the absent opposable big toe. The position of the ape big toe is **abducted** (sticking out away from the midline) while the human big toe is **adducted** (pulled in

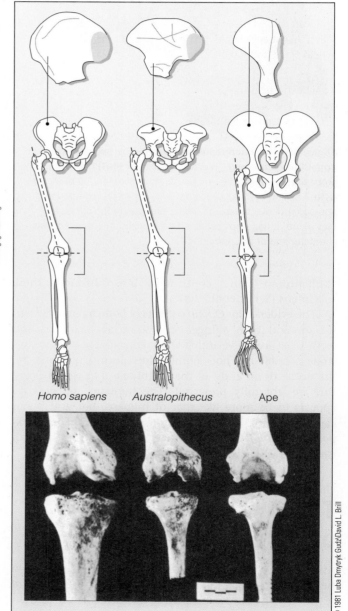

Homo sapiens   *Australopithecus*   Ape

© 1981 Luba Dmytryk Gudz/David L. Brill

Figure 6.10 Lower Limb Comparisons The upper hip bones and lower limbs of (*from left*) *Homo sapiens*, *Australopithecus* (an ancestral hominin species) and an ape can be used to determine means of locomotion. The striking similarities between the human and australopithecine bones are indicative of bipedal locomotion.

abduction Movement away from the midline of the body or from the center of the hand or foot.

adduction Movement toward the midline of the body or to the center of the hand or foot.

© Cengage Learning

Figure 6.11 **Bipedal Gait** The bipedal gait in some regards is really "serial monopedalism" or movement by means of one foot at a time through a series of controlled falls. Note how the body's weight shifts from one foot to the other as an individual moves through the swing phase to heel strike and toe off.

toward the midline). In general, humans and their ancestors possess shorter toes than the other apes.

These anatomical features allow paleoanthropologists to diagnose bipedal locomotion even in fragmentary remains such as the top of the shinbone or the base of a skull. Bipedal locomotion can also be established through fossilized footprints, which preserve the characteristic stride used by humans and their ancestors. In fact, bipedal locomotion is a process of shifting the body's weight from one foot to the other as the nonsupporting foot swings forward. While the body is supported in a one-legged stance, a biped takes a stride by swinging the other leg forward. The heel of the foot is the first part of the swinging leg to hit the ground. Then as the biped continues to move forward, the individual rolls from the heel toward the toe, pushing or "toeing off" into the next swing phase of the stride (**Figure 6.11**). While one leg is moving from

heel strike to toe off of the stance phase, the other leg is moving forward through the swing phase of walking.

The most dramatic confirmation of our ancestors' walking ability comes from Laetoli, Tanzania, where, 3.6 million years ago, two (perhaps three) individuals walked across newly fallen volcanic ash (**Figure 6.12**). Because it was damp, the ash took the impressions of their feet, and these were sealed beneath subsequent ash falls until discovered by chemist Paul Abell in 1978. Abell was part of a team led by British paleoanthropologist Mary Leakey in search of human origins at Laetoli (see Anthropologists of Note). The shape of the footprints and the linear distance between the heel strikes and toe offs are quite human.

Once bipedalism establishes a fossil specimen as a hominin, paleoanthropologists turn to other features, such as the skull or teeth, to reconstruct relationships among the various fossil hominin groups.

Photo by Denis Finnin and Craig Chesek, © American Museum of Natural History

Figure 6.12 **Laetoli Footprints** Paleoartists can reconstruct the soft tissues of individual fossil specimens using the data paleoanthropologists amass from their study of bones. They also reconstruct the setting based on data gathered by investigators. In this particular case, because the footprints were preserved in volcanic ash, paleoanthropologists can date when these steps were taken at the Laetoli site in Tanzania. The actual trail of footprints is 24 meters (80 feet) long. Does your sense of these ancient hominins change from looking at them fully fleshed out? What details are scientific? What details are imagined?

ANTHROPOLOGISTS OF NOTE

Louis S. B. Leakey (1903–1972) • Mary Leakey (1913–1996)

Few figures in the history of paleoanthropology discovered so many key fossils, received so much public acclaim, or stirred up as much controversy as **Louis Leakey** and his second wife, **Mary Leakey**.

Born in Kenya of missionary parents, Louis received his early education from an English governess and subsequently was sent to England for a university education. He returned to Kenya in the 1920s to begin his career there. It was in 1931 that Louis and his research assistant from England, Mary Nicol (whom he married in 1936), began working in their spare time at Olduvai Gorge in Tanzania, searching patiently and persistently for remains of early human ancestors. It seemed a good place to look, for there were numerous animal fossils as well as crude stone tools lying scattered on the ground and eroding out of the walls of the gorge.

Their patience and persistence were not rewarded until 1959, when Mary found the first fossil. A year later, another

skull was found, and Olduvai was on its way to being recognized as one of the most important sources of fossils relevant to human evolution in all of Africa. While Louis reconstructed, described, and interpreted the fossil material, Mary made the definitive study of the Oldowan tools, a very early stone tool industry.

The Leakeys' important discoveries were not limited to those at Olduvai. In the early 1930s they found the first fossils of Miocene apes in Africa at Rusinga Island in Lake Victoria. Also in the 1930s, Louis found a number of skulls at Kanjera, Kenya, that show a mixture of derived and more ancestral features. In 1948, at Fort Ternan, Kenya, the Leakeys found the remains of a late Miocene ape with features that seemed appropriate for an ancestor of the bipeds. After Louis's death, Paul Abell, a member of an expedition led by Mary Leakey, found the first fossilized footprints of early bipeds at Laetoli, Tanzania.

In addition to their own work, Louis Leakey promoted a good deal of important work on the part of others. He made it possible for Jane Goodall to begin her landmark field studies of chimpanzees; later, he was instrumental in setting up similar studies among gorillas (by Dian Fossey) and orangutans (by Biruté Galdikas). He set into motion the fellowship program responsible for the training of numerous paleoanthropologists from Africa. The Leakey tradition has been continued by son Richard, his wife Meave, and their daughter Louise.

Louis Leakey had a flamboyant personality and a way of interpreting fossil materials that frequently did not stand up to careful scrutiny, but this did not stop him from publicly presenting his views as if they were the gospel truth. It was this aspect of the Leakeys' work that generated controversy. Nonetheless, the Leakeys produced a great deal of work that resulted in a much fuller understanding of human origins.

Mary and Louis Leakey at work at Olduvai Gorge. Not only did they contribute substantially to paleoanthropology through numerous fossil finds, but they also created a lineage of paleoanthropologists.

© Des Bartlett/Photo Researchers, Inc.

Ardipithecus

In the fall of 2009, a dramatic paleoanthropological find was announced: a remarkably complete skeleton of a putative human ancestor dated to 4.4 million years ago

(**Figure 6.13**). Only half a dozen partially complete fossil skeletons on the human line older than 1 million years have ever been discovered, and this one is the oldest. Nicknamed "Ardi" for the new genus *Ardipithecus*, these fossil remains, first discovered between 1992 and

© T. White

Figure 6.13 ***Ardipithecus ramidus*** Early analyses of the Ardi remains in the early 1990s also established that there were forest- rather than savannah-dwellers on the human line. For the following fifteen-plus years, an international team of forty-seven scientists conducted painstaking excavation, reconstruction, and analysis to create a complete picture of the lifeways of this new species; through this process Ardi has become personified. A series of research papers in the prestigious journal *Science*, along with a Discovery Channel documentary about how the scientists went about their work, reveal not only the importance of the find but how Ardi has captured our collective imagination. Sophisticated computer graphics allow scientists to simulate how regulatory genes might have shaped the development of Ardi's bones that caused her to move in a more humanlike fashion. Gymnasts were asked to mimic her gait for scientific analysis, and advances in physics and chemistry were incorporated in the reconstruction of the ancient forested environment she inhabited.

1995, have dramatically changed what we know about the earliest bipeds (White et al., 2009). The genus actually contains two species, *Ardipithecus ramidus* and the older *Ardipithecus kadabba* dated to between 5.2 and 5.8 million years ago. The *Ardipithecus* remains show that some of the earliest bipeds inhabited a forested environment much like that of contemporary chimpanzees, bonobos, and gorillas; these remains were found in fossil-rich deposits along Ethiopia's Awash River accompanied by fossils of forest animals. The name *Ardipithecus ramidus* is fitting for an ultimate human ancestor as *Ardi* means "floor" and *ramid* means "root" in the local Afar language.

Now that the spectacular Ardi specimen has been sufficiently analyzed by the team who discovered her, paleoanthropologists debate her exact place on the human line. Because the other African apes share a body plan similar to one another, many paleoanthropologists expected the earliest bipeds to resemble something halfway between chimps and humans. Instead, Ardi shows that these forest creatures moved in a combination of ways: They traveled across the tops of branches with the palms of their hands and feet facing downward, and they walked between the trees on the ground in an upright position. The other African apes, as we saw in previous chapters, knuckle-walk on the forest floor and hang suspended below the branches. In other words, Ardi resembles some of the early Miocene apes more than she does the living African apes.

This calls into question what the last common ancestor of humans and the other African apes looked like. Does Ardi represent the more ancestral form, with the other apes evolving independently after they split from the human line but still converging to the typical African ape body plan? Or does Ardi represent a new body plan, characteristic of the earliest bipeds that evolved away from the African ape plan shared by chimps and gorillas? And what of Ardi's relationship to the later bipeds? Until fall 2009, *Ardipithecus* was generally considered a side branch on the human evolutionary tree. Now, the international team has proposed that Ardi may be a direct ancestor to the later bipeds, including humans.

In terms of size, at 120 centimeters tall and a weight of about 50 kilograms, Ardi resembles a female chimpanzee. The size and shape of this partial skeleton's brain and the enamel thickness of the specimen's teeth are similar to chimpanzees as well. Although possessing a grasping big toe like a chimp, scientists reconstruct Ardi's locomotion as bipedal when on the ground.

The *Ardipithecus* finds, along with the *Orrorin* and Toumai specimens, provide evidence for the time period

Ardipithecus One of the earliest genera of bipeds that lived in eastern Africa. *Ardipithecus* is actually divided into two species: the older, *Ardipithecus kadabba*, which dates to between 5.2 and 5.8 million years ago, and the younger, *Ardipithecus ramidus*, which dates to around 4.4 million years ago.

before the appearance of the ancient bipeds belonging to the genus *Australopithecus*. Paleoanthropologists discovered the first representatives of this group in the early 20th century, long before the majority of scientists were comfortable with the now-accepted notion that humans originated on the African continent.

Australopithecus

Most of the early bipeds from the Pliocene are members of the genus *Australopithecus*, a genus that includes species from southern and eastern Africa (**Figure 6.14**). The name for this group of fossils was coined back in 1924 when the first important fossil from Africa proposed to be a human ancestor came to light. This unusual fossil, consisting of a partial skull and natural brain cast of a young individual, was brought to the attention of anatomist Raymond Dart

of the University of Witwatersrand in Johannesburg, South Africa. The "Taung Child," named for the limestone quarry in the South African town of Taung (Tswana for "place of the lion") in which it was found, was unlike any creature Dart had seen before. Recognizing an intriguing mixture of ape and human characteristics in this unusual fossil, Dart proposed a new taxonomic category for his discovery—*Australopithecus africanus* or "southern ape of Africa"—suggesting that this specimen represented an extinct form that was ancestral to humans (**Figure 6.15**).

Although the anatomy of the base of the skull indicated that the Taung Child was probably a biped, the scientific community was not ready to accept the notion of a small-brained African ancestor to humans. Dart's original paper describing the Taung Child was published in the February 1925 edition of the prestigious journal *Nature*. The next month's issue was filled with venomous critiques rejecting Dart's proposal that this specimen represented a human ancestor. Criticisms of Dart ranged from biased to fussy to sound. Some scholars chastised Dart for incorrectly combining Latin and Greek in the genus and species name he coined. Other critics more justifiably questioned the wisdom of making inferences about the appearance of an adult of the species based only on the fossilized remains of a young individual. However, ethnocentric bias was the biggest obstacle to Dart's proposed human ancestor. Paleoanthropologists of the early 20th century expected that the ancestor to humans already had a large brain. Moreover, most European scientists expected to

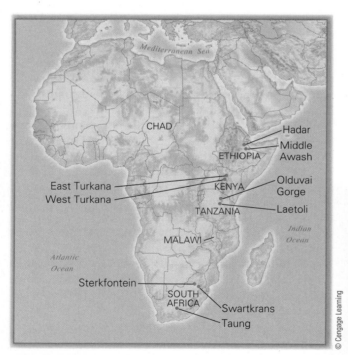

© Cengage Learning

Figure 6.14 **Map of *Australopithecus* Sites** Australopithecine fossils have been found in South Africa, Malawi, Tanzania, Kenya, Ethiopia, and Chad. In the Miocene, the Eurasian and African continents made contact at the eastern and western ends of what now is the Mediterranean Sea. As these landmasses met, rifting also occurred, gradually raising the elevation of the eastern third of Africa. The drier climates that resulted may have played a role in human evolution in the distant past. This rifting also gives us excellent geologic conditions for finding fossils today.

Australopithecus The genus including several species of early bipeds from southern and eastern Africa living between about 1.1 and 4.3 million years ago, one of whom was directly ancestral to humans.

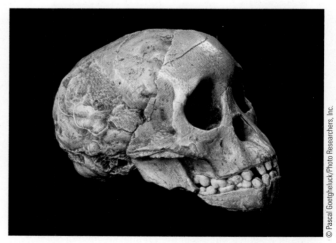

© Pascal Goetgheluck/Photo Researchers, Inc.

Figure 6.15 **The Taung Child** Discovered in South Africa in 1924, the Taung Child was the first fossil specimen placed in the genus *Australopithecus*. Though Raymond Dart correctly diagnosed the Taung Child's bipedal mode of locomotion as well as its importance in human evolution, other scientists rejected Dart's claims that this small-brained biped with a humanlike face was a direct ancestor to humans. In the early 20th century, scientists expected ancestors to humans to possess a large brain and an apelike face and to originate from Europe or Asia rather than Africa.

find evidence of this large-brained ancestor in Europe or, barring that, in Asia. No one at the time expected to find the ancestor to humans in Africa.

In fact, many scientists of the 1920s even believed that the ancestor to humans had already been found in the Piltdown gravels of Sussex, England, in 1910. The Piltdown specimens consisted of a humanlike skull and an apelike jaw that seemed to fit together, though the crucial joints connecting the two were missing (**Figure 6.16**). They were discovered along with the bones of some other animal species known to be extinct. Charles Dawson— the British amateur archaeologist, paleontologist, and practicing lawyer who found these remains—immodestly named them *Eoanthropus dawsoni* or "Dawson's Dawn Man." Until the 1950s the Piltdown remains were widely accepted as representing the missing link between apes and humans; today, they are known as one of the biggest hoaxes in the history of science.

There were several reasons for widespread acceptance of Dawson's Dawn Man. As Darwin's theory of evolution by natural selection began to gain acceptance in the early 20th century, intense interest developed in finding traces of prehistoric human ancestors. Accordingly, predictions were made as to what those ancestors looked like. Darwin himself, on the basis of his knowledge of embryology and the comparative anatomy of living apes and humans, suggested in his 1871 book *The Descent of Man* that early humans had, among other things, a large brain and an apelike face and jaw.

Although the tools made by prehistoric peoples were commonly found in Europe, their bones were not. A few fossilized skeletons had come to light in France and Germany, but they did not resemble the predicted missing link, nor had any human fossils been discovered in England ever before. Given this state of affairs, the Piltdown finds could not have come at a better time. Here at last was the long-awaited missing link, and it was almost exactly as predicted. Even better, so far as English-speaking scientists were concerned, it was found on English soil.

In the context of the evidence available in the early 1900s, the idea of an ancient human with a large brain

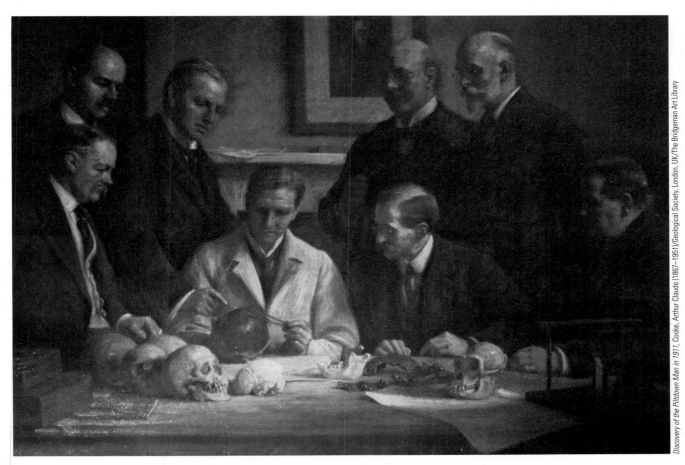

Discovery of the Piltdown Man in 1911, Cooke, Arthur Claude (1867–1951)/Geological Society, London, UK/The Bridgeman Art Library

Figure 6.16 The Piltdown Gang The Piltdown forgery was widely accepted as ancestral to humans, in large part because it fit with conventional expectations that the missing link would have a large brain and an apelike face. No one knows with certainty how many of the "Piltdown gang"—scientists supporting this specimen as the missing link—were actually involved in the forgery. It is likely that Charles Dawson had help from at least one scientist. Sir Arthur Conan Doyle, the author of the Sherlock Holmes detective stories, has also been implicated.

and an apelike face met expectations. Fortunately, the self-correcting nature of science has prevailed, exposing the Piltdown specimens as a forgery. First, discoveries—primarily in South Africa, China, and Java—of fossils of smaller-brained bipeds from the distant past caused scientists to question Piltdown's authenticity. Ultimately, the application of the newly developed fluorine dating method (described in Chapter 5) by British physical anthropologist Kenneth Oakley and colleagues in 1953 proved conclusively that Piltdown was a hoax. The forgery consisted of a human approximately 600 years old and a recent jaw from an orangutan. These findings fully vindicated Dart and the Taung Child.

The Pliocene Environment and Hominin Diversity

As mentioned previously, the Miocene epoch was a time of tremendous geologic change, and the effects of these changes continued into the Pliocene. The steady movement of geologic plates supporting the African and Eurasian continents resulted in a collision of the two landmasses at either end of what now is the Mediterranean Sea. This contact allowed for the spread of species between the continents.

A suite of geologic changes accompanied this collision. Among the changes was the creation of the Great Rift Valley system, a separation between geologic plates extending from the Middle East through the Red Sea and

eastern Africa into southern Africa. **Rifting** created the steady increase in the elevation of the eastern third of the African continent, which experienced a cooler and drier climate and a transformation of vegetation from forest to dry grassy **savannah**. The system also contributed to the volcanic activity in the region, which provides opportunities for accurate dating of fossil specimens.

Also in the Miocene, the Indian subcontinent, which had been a solitary landmass for many millions of years, came into its present position through a collision with Eurasia, contributing further to cooler, drier conditions globally. In addition to causing global climate change, these geologic events also provided excellent opportunities for the discovery of fossil specimens as layers of the earth became exposed through the rifting process.

Diverse Australopithecine Species

Since Dart's original find, hundreds of other fossil bipeds have been discovered, first in South Africa and later in Tanzania, Malawi, Kenya, Ethiopia, and Chad. As they were discovered, scientists defined a variety of different genera and species, but over time the single genus *Australopithecus* has come to include most of these species. Anthropologists recognize up to nine species of the genus (**Table 6.1**). In addition, some other groups of fossil bipeds from the Pliocene epoch (1.6 to around 5 mya) have been discovered, including the earliest representatives of the

---

TABLE 6.1

Species of *Australopithecus* and Other Pliocene Fossil Hominins*

Species	Location	Dates	Notable Features/Fossil Specimens
Ardipithecus ramidus	Ethiopia	4.4 mya[†]	Fossil remains of over thirty-five individuals including Ardi (another species, *Ardipithecus kadabba*, dates to 5.4–5.8 mya)
A. anamensis	Kenya	3.9–4.2 mya	Oldest australopithecine
Kenyanthropus platyops	Kenya	3.2–3.5 mya	Contemporary with australopithecines, believed by some to be a member of that genus
A. afarensis	East Africa	2.9–3.9 mya	Lucy, Lucy's Child, the Laetoli footprints
A. bahrelghazali	Chad	3–3.5 mya	Only australopithecine from Central Africa
A. africanus	South Africa	2.3–3 mya	First discovered, gracile, well represented in fossil record (Taung)
A. aethiopicus	Kenya	2.5 mya	Oldest robust australopithecine (Black Skull)
A. garhi	Ethiopia	2.5 mya	Later East African australopithecine with humanlike dentition
A. boisei	Kenya	1.2–2.3 mya	Later robust form coexisted with early *Homo* (Zinj)
A. robustus	South Africa	1–2 mya	Coexisted with early *Homo*
A. sediba	South Africa	1.97–1.98 mya	May be ancestral to early *Homo* and a descendant of *A. africanus*

*Paleoanthropologists differ in the number of species they recognize, some suggesting separate genera.
[†]Million years ago.

© Cengage Learning

genus *Homo*. Because the East African sites can be reliably dated we will look at these fossils first, followed by the South African australopithecines, and then we close the chapter with a late-appearing grade of australopithecine that coexisted with the genus *Homo*.

East Africa

The oldest australopithecine species known so far consists of some jaw and limb bones from Kenya that date to between 3.9 and 4.2 million years ago (see *Australopithecus anamensis* in Table 6.1). Meave and Louise Leakey, daughter-in-law and granddaughter of Louis and Mary Leakey, discovered these fossils in 1995 and decided to place them in a separate species from other known australopithecines. The name means "ape-man of the lake," and the jaw shows particularities in the teeth such as a true *sectorial*: a lower premolar tooth shaped to hone the upper canine as seen in apes. In humans and more recent ancestors, the premolar has a characteristic bicuspid shape and does not sharpen the canine each time the jaws come together. As in other australopithecines and humans, thick enamel coats the molar teeth. The limb bone fragments indicate bipedalism.

Moving closer to the present, the next species defined in the fossil record is *Australopithecus afarensis*. No longer considered the earliest australopithecine species, it still remains one of the best known due to the Laetoli footprints from Tanzania, the famous Lucy specimen (**Figure 6.17**), and the recent discovery of the 3.3-million-year-old remains of a young child called "Lucy's Baby," both from Ethiopia (recall Figure 5.11). Lucy consists of bones from almost all parts of a single 3.2-million-year-old skeleton discovered in 1974 in the Afar Triangle of Ethiopia (hence the name *afarensis*). Standing only 3½ feet tall, this adult female was named after the Beatles song "Lucy in the Sky with Diamonds," which the paleoanthropologists listened to as they celebrated her discovery. The Afar region also is the site of the "First Family"—a collection of bones from at least thirteen individuals, ranging in age from infancy to adulthood, who died together as a result of some single calamity.

Fossil localities in Ethiopia and Tanzania have yielded at least sixty individuals from *A. afarensis* (once the name of a genus has been established, it can be abbreviated with the first letter followed by the complete species name).

Figure 6.17 Lucy Here, Lucy, the 3.2-million-year-old fossil specimen, is on display in an exhibition space in New York City's Times Square as part of a traveling exhibit organized and curated by the Ethiopian government and the Houston Museum of Natural History. Though Lucy has done much to popularize paleoanthropology and evolutionary studies since her discovery in 1974, some paleoanthropologists have said that placing her fragile ancient skeleton on public display is far too risky. The Smithsonian Institution and the Cleveland Museum of Natural History declined to host the show for this reason. Others—like her discoverer Donald Johanson, pictured here with Lucy—feel that the benefits outweigh the risks. Benefits include the study of Lucy's remains via CT scans so that future generations of scientists can study them without actually handling the fragile bones. In addition, the revenues from the tour will be used to help modernize Ethiopia's museums. Finally, the exhibit will increase public awareness of human origins and the vital role of Africa and, in particular, Ethiopia in our evolutionary history. What's your opinion?

Potassium-argon techniques securely date the specimens from Ethiopia's Afar region to between 2.9 and 3.9 million years ago, and material from Laetoli, in Tanzania, to 3.6 million years ago. Altogether, *A. afarensis* appears to be a sexually

rifting In geology, the process by which a rift, or a long narrow zone of faulting, results when two geological plates come together.

savannah Semi-arid plains environment as in eastern Africa.

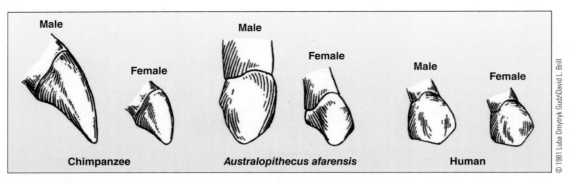

Figure 6.18 Sexual Dimorphism in Canine Teeth In addition to the difference in sexual dimorphism of canines seen in chimps, australopithecines, and humans, respectively, also note the more daggerlike shape of the chimp canines compared to the hominins.

dimorphic bipedal species with estimates of body size and weight ranging between 1.1 and 1.6 meters (3½–5 feet) and 29 and 45 kilograms (64–100 pounds), respectively.

Assuming that larger fossil specimens were males and smaller specimens females, males were about 1½ times the size of females. This resembles the sexual dimorphism of Miocene African apes but falls between the lesser degree of dimorphism present in a modern chimpanzee and the greater amount seen in gorillas and orangutans. Males possess canine teeth, significantly larger than those of females, though canine size is reduced compared to that of chimps (**Figure 6.18**).

Nearly 40 percent complete, the Lucy specimen has provided invaluable information about the shape of the pelvis and torso of early human ancestors. From the waist up, *A. afarensis* resembles an ape and from the waist down, a human (**Figure 6.19**). In addition, because her forearm bones are relatively shorter than those of apes, it is believed that Lucy's upper limbs were lighter and her center of gravity lower in the body than in apes. Still, Lucy and other early australopithecines possessed arms long in proportion to their legs when compared to the proportions seen in humans.

Though she lived about 150,000 years before her namesake, Lucy's Baby will add considerably to our knowledge about the biology and behavior of *A. afarensis* (Zeresenay et al., 2006). These well-preserved remains of a child, thought to have died in a flash flood, include a hyoid bone (located in the throat region) that will allow scientists to reconstruct australopithecine patterns of vocalization. Although the lower limbs clearly indicate bipedalism, the specimen's scapula and long curved finger bones are more apelike.

The curvature of the fingers and toes and the somewhat elevated position of the shoulder joint seen in adult specimens indicate that *A. afarensis* was better adapted to tree climbing compared to more recent human ancestors. In the following Original Study, paleoanthropologist John Hawks discusses the kinds of evidence used to reconstruct a behavior such as tree climbing in our ancestors.

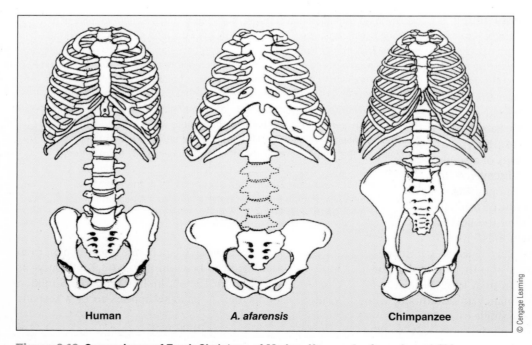

Figure 6.19 Comparisons of Trunk Skeletons of Modern Human, *A. afarensis,* and Chimp In its pelvis, the australopithecine resembles the modern human, but its rib cage shows the pyramidal configuration of the ape.

Ankles of the Australopithecines

BY JOHN HAWKS

Recent University of Michigan PhD Jeremy DeSilva gets some nice press about his work demonstrating that fossil hominins didn't climb like chimpanzees.

> "Frankly, I thought I was going to find that early humans would be quite capable, but their ankle morphology was decidedly maladaptive for the kind of climbing I was seeing in chimps," DeSilva told LiveScience. "It kind of reinvented in my mind what they were doing and how they could have survived in an African savannah without the ability to go up in the trees."[a]

This is a good example of the comparative method in paleoanthropology. We can't observe the behavior of extinct species; we can only observe the behavior of their living relatives. We can observe the anatomy of fossil specimens, but testing hypotheses about their behavior requires us to understand the relationship between anatomy and behavior in living species. We've known about the anatomy of fossil hominin ankles for a long time, but it's not so obvious how the anatomical differences between them and chimpanzee ankles relates to behavior.

DeSilva studied the tibiae and anklebones of early hominins and concludes "that if hominins included tree climbing as part of their locomotor repertoire, then they were performing this activity in a manner decidedly unlike modern chimpanzees."

DeSilva's conclusion is straightforward and easy to illustrate. Chimpanzees climb vertical tree trunks pretty much like a logger does. A logger slings a strap around the trunk and leans back on it. Friction from the strap holds him up as he moves his feet upward; spikes on his boots hold him while he moves the strap.

Of course, chimpanzees don't have spikes on their feet, and they don't use a strap. Instead, their arms are long enough to wrap around the trunk, and they can wedge a foot against the trunk by flexing their ankle upward—dorsiflexing it—or grip the trunk by bending the ankle sideways—inverting the foot—around it. . . .

You might wonder, yeah so what? Isn't it obvious that chimpanzees climb this way?

Well, it wasn't so obvious which features of the ankle might adapt chimpanzees to this style of climbing. By

The amount of dorsiflexion in a chimpanzee's foot allows it to climb trees with the feet in a position that is impossible for humans. Comparisons like this between living species allow paleoanthropologists to reconstruct the pattern of locomotion in fossil groups.

watching the chimpanzees (and other apes), DeSilva was able to determine the average amount (and range) of dorsiflexion and inversion of the feet while climbing, and could also assess the extent to which dorsiflexion is accomplished at the ankle joint (as opposed to the midfoot). In this case, the observations were pretty obvious—chimpanzees were habitually flexing their ankles in ways that would damage a human ankle. Then, by examining the bony limits on human ankle flexibility, DeSilva showed that fossil hominins shared the same constraints on ankle movement as recent people. They couldn't have climbed like chimpanzees.

Human Climbing

I would say that the ankle-joint observations match the rest of the skeleton. It seems pretty obvious that *Australopithecus afarensis* and later hominins couldn't possibly have climbed in the chimpanzee-like manner described in DeSilva's paper because the hominins' arms were too short. If a logger tried to climb with his arms instead of a strap, even spikes on his feet would be relatively ineffective holding him up. Dorsiflexion would be hopeless—the normal component of force against the tree trunk would be insufficient to prevent slipping.

Humans who *aren't* loggers use a different strategy to climb vertical tree trunks—they put a large fraction of the surface area of their legs directly in contact with the trunk. Wrapping legs around and pressing them together gives the necessary friction to hold the body up.

If you're like me, you'll remember this climbing strategy ruefully from gym class, where "rope climbing" is the lowest common denominator of fitness tests. The sad fact is that many otherwise-normal humans fall on the wrong side of the line between mass and muscle power. Straining my groin muscles to the max, I still could never pull my way up a rope.

There's nothing magical about getting a human to climb. Ladders, after all, are relatively easy for the large fraction of the population who can't climb a rope or tree trunk. The trick with a ladder is that friction is organized in a more effective way for our ankle mechanics and arm length. But you don't need to schlep a ladder, if you can manage a little extra arm strength and a low enough body mass.

Early Hominin Climbing

Australopithecines were light in mass, and from what we can tell, they had strong arms. So they had what it takes for humans today to climb trees effectively—not like chimpanzees, but like humans. Up to *A. afarensis*, every early hominin we know about lived in an environment that was at least partially wooded.

. . . DeSilva hypothesizes a trade-off between climbing ability and effective bipedality, so that early hominins could not have effectively adapted to both. I don't think a chimpanzee-like ankle would have been any use with arms as short as australopithecines'. So I don't see the necessity of a trade-off in ankle morphology. *A. afarensis*—long before any evidence of stone tool manufacture—had very non-apelike arms, hands and thumbs.

But there's one significant question that DeSilva omits discussing—the foot bones of a South African australopithecine: StW 573 (see Figure 6.22). Clarke and Tobias[b] describe the foot of StW 573 as having a big toe that is abducted (sticks out) from the foot, intermediate between the chimpanzee and human condition. They conclude:

> [W]e now have the best available evidence that the earliest South African australopithecine, while bipedal, was equipped to include arboreal, climbing activities in its locomotor repertoire. Its foot has departed to only a small degree from that of the chimpanzee. It is becoming clear that *Australopithecus* was not an obligate terrestrial biped, but rather a facultative biped and climber. (p. 524)

DeSilva studied the talus (an ankle bone), not the toe. StW 573 has a talus, and although it is not in DeSilva's sample, it probably would place very close to the other hominins in his comparison. Even Clarke and Tobias described its talus as humanlike—their argument for an intermediate form was based mostly on the toe.

But still, it's hard to believe that australopithecines would retain a chimpanzee-like big toe, if they couldn't use that big toe by inverting or dorsiflexing their foot in any significant way. By all other accounts, an abducted hallux (big toe) would only impede effective bipedality. It is of no use at all for a humanlike pattern of climbing. The only remaining utility would be for small-branch grasping, but small branches would seem unlikely as a support for hominin arboreality.

One possibility is that Clarke and Tobias were simply mistaken. That appears to be the explanation favored by Harcourt-Smith and Aiello[c] and McHenry and Jones,[d] who concluded that all known hominin feet appear to lack any "ape-like ability to oppose the big toe." They also point to the Laetoli footprint trails, most observers of which agree that the big toe was adducted, not abducted.

I tend to favor that explanation—australopithecines simply didn't have a grasping foot. But they may not have shared the medial longitudinal arch, at least not in the human configuration, and without it one might doubt that their gait featured as strong a toe-off as that of later humans. Who knows?

Adapted from Hawks, J. (2009, April 14). Ankles of the Australopithecines. John Hawks Weblog. http://johnhawks. net/weblog/reviews/early_hominids/anatomy/desilva-2009-chimpanzee-climbing-talus.html (retrieved July 5, 2012). Copyright © 2009 John Hawks, all rights reserved. Reprinted by permission of the author.

[a]DeSilva, J. M. (2009). Functional morphology of the ankle and the likelihood of climbing in early hominins. *Proceeding of the National Academy of Sciences, USA 106*, 6567–6572.

[b]Clarke, R. J., & Tobias, P. V. (1995). Sterkfontein Member 2 foot bones of the oldest South African hominid. *Science 269*, 521–524.

[c]Harcourt-Smith, W. E. H., & Aiello, L. C. (2004). Fossils, feet and the evolution of human bipedal locomotion. *Journal of Anatomy 204*, 412.

[d]McHenry, H. M., & Jones, A. L. (2006). Hallucial convergence in early hominids. *Journal of Human Evolution 50*, 534–539.

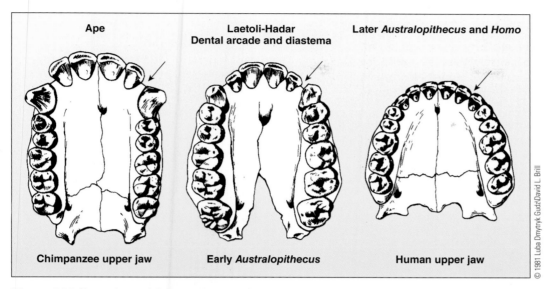

Ape

Laetoli-Hadar
Dental arcade and diastema

Later *Australopithecus* and *Homo*

Chimpanzee upper jaw

Early *Australopithecus*

Human upper jaw

© 1981 Luba Dmytryk Gudz/David L. Brill

Figure 6.20 **Upper Jaws of Chimps, Australopithecines, and Humans** The upper jaws and teeth of these three groups differ in several ways. Note the difference in the shape of the dental arch and the spacing between the canines and the adjoining teeth. Only the earliest australopithecines possess a diastema (a large gap between the upper canine and incisor), which is found in chimpanzees.

At the other end of the body, skull bones are vital for the reconstruction of evolutionary relationships. They allow paleoanthropologists to learn about the cognitive capacities of ancestral species. For example, the brow of an *A. afarensis* skull slopes backward to a relatively low height and has the ridge that helps give apes such massive-looking foreheads. Other ape features include large jaws relative to the size of the skull, no chin, and a small brain. Even the semicircular canal, a part of the ear crucial to maintenance of balance, is apelike. Cranial capacity, commonly used as an index of brain size for *A. afarensis*, averages about 420 cubic centimeters (cc), roughly equivalent to the size of a chimpanzee and about one-third the size of living humans. In addition to absolute brain size, the ratio of brain to body size contributes to intelligence. Unfortunately, with such a wide range of adult weights, this ratio cannot be determined for australopithecines.

Australopithecine teeth constitute one of the primary means for distinguishing among closely related groups. In *A. afarensis*, unlike humans, the teeth are all quite large, particularly the molars. The premolar is no longer fully sectorial as in *A. anamensis*, but most other features of the teeth represent a more ancestral rather than derived condition. For example, instead of the dental arch seen in humans, australopithecines possess more parallel tooth rows (the ancestral ape condition). The canines project slightly, and a slight space or gap known as a **diastema** remains between the upper incisors and canines as found in the apes (**Figure 6.20**).

To further complicate the diversity seen in *A. afarensis*, in 2001 Meave and Louise Leakey announced the discovery of an almost complete cranium, parts of two upper

jaws, and assorted teeth from a site in northern Kenya, dated to between 3.2 and 3.5 million years ago (Leakey et al., 2001). Contemporary with early East African *Australopithecus*, the Leakeys see this as a different genus and named it ***Kenyanthropus platyops*** ("flat-faced man of Kenya"). Unlike early australopithecines, *Kenyanthropus* has a small braincase and small molars set in a large, humanlike, flat face. The Leakeys regard the fossils as ancestral to the genus *Homo*. Other paleoanthropologists disagree suggesting that the Leakeys' interpretation rests on a questionable reconstruction of badly broken fossil specimens (White, 2003).

Central Africa

The first Central African australopithecine species, dated to the same time period as *Kenyanthropus platyops*, was discovered in Chad. Named *Australopithecus bahrelghazali* for a nearby riverbed, the specimen consists of a jaw and several teeth dated to between 3 and 3.5 million years ago. With time, perhaps more discoveries from this region (also home to the Toumai specimen discussed previously) will give a fuller understanding of the role of *A. bahrelghazali* in human evolution and its relationship to the possible bipeds from the Miocene.

---

diastema A space between the canines and other teeth allowing the large projecting canines to fit within the jaw.

Kenyanthropus platyops A proposed genus and species of biped contemporary with early australopithecines; may not be a separate genus.

South Africa

Throughout the 20th century and into the present, a variety of sites in South Africa have yielded australopithecine fossils. These include numerous fossils found beginning in the 1930s at Sterkfontein and Makapansgat, in addition to Dart's original find from Taung.

Absence of the clear stratigraphy and volcanic ash of East African sites makes these discoveries far more difficult to date and interpret (**Figure 6.21**). Paleomagnetism dates one unusually complete skull and skeleton and one partial foot skeleton (**Figure 6.22**) to about 3.3 million years ago. Until recently, dates for the other fossils remained hard to pin down. A faunal series established in East Africa places these specimens between 2.3 and 3 million years ago. Like the Taung Child, paleoanthropologists classify all these specimens as *A. africanus*, also known as **gracile australopithecines**.

Researchers debate the presence of human qualities in gracile australopithecines. Some see evidence for some

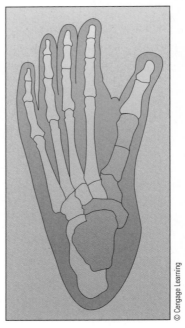

Figure 6.22 **Gracile Australopithecine Foot** Drawing of the foot bones of a 3- to 3.3-million-year-old *Australopithecus* from Sterkfontein, South Africa, as they would have been in the complete foot. Note the length and flexibility of the first toe (*at right*). This is a drawing of the StW 573 specimen referred to in this chapter's Original Study.

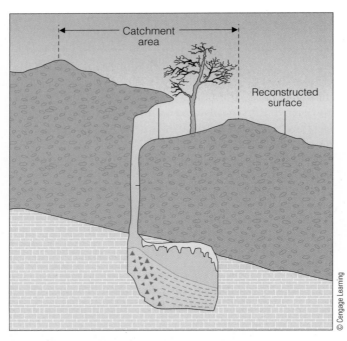

Figure 6.21 **South African Limestone Cave Sites** Many of the fossil sites in South Africa were limestone caverns connected to the surface by a shaft. Over time, dirt, bones, and other matter that fell down the shaft accumulated inside the cavern, becoming fossilized. In the Pliocene, trees that grew from earth next to the shaft's opening provided a sheltered location that may have been used by predators for eating without being bothered by scavengers.

gracile australopithecines Members of the genus *Australopithecus* possessing a more lightly built chewing apparatus; likely had a diet that included more meat than that of the robust *australopithecines*; best represented by the South African species *A. africanus*.

expansion of the brain in *A. africanus*, whereas others vigorously disagree. The same is true for analyses of the outer surface of the brain, as revealed by casts of the insides of skulls. At the moment, the weight of the evidence favors mental capabilities for all gracile australopithecines as being comparable to those of modern great apes (chimps, bonobos, gorillas, orangutans).

Using patterns of tooth eruption in young australopithecines such as Taung, some paleoanthropologists suggest that the developmental pattern of australopithecines was more humanlike than apelike, though other paleoanthropologists do not agree. Evidence from the recent discovery of the young *A. afarensis* specimen (Lucy's Baby) will help scientists to resolve this debate. Our current understanding of genetics and the macroevolutionary process indicates that a developmental shift likely underlies a change in body plan such as the emergence of bipedalism among the African hominoids.

Other South African sites have yielded fossils whose skulls and teeth looked quite different from the gracile australopithecines described previously. Relative to the size of their braincases, these South African fossils, known as *Australopithecus robustus*, possess massive (robust) teeth, jaws, and chewing muscles. The slightly smaller gracile forms lack such robust chewing structures. Over the course of evolution, several distinct groups of

robust australopithecines have appeared not only in South Africa but throughout East Africa as well.

Robust Australopithecines

The remains of robust australopithecines were first found at Kromdraai and Swartkrans in the 1930s in deposits that, unfortunately, cannot be securely dated. Current thinking puts them between 1 and 2 million years ago. Usually referred to as *A. robustus* (see Table 6.1), this species possessed a characteristic robust chewing apparatus including a **sagittal crest** running from front to back along the top of the skull (Figure 6.23). This feature provides sufficient area on a relatively small braincase for attachment of the huge temporal muscles required to operate powerful jaws. Present in robust australopithecines and gorillas today, the sagittal crest provides an example of convergent evolution.

The first East African robust australopithecine was discovered by Mary Leakey in the summer of 1959, the centennial year of the publication of Darwin's *On the Origin of Species*. She found it in Olduvai Gorge, a massive fossil-rich gash in the earth, near Ngorongoro Crater, on the Serengeti Plain of Tanzania. About 40 kilometers (25 miles) long and 91 meters (300 feet) deep, Olduvai Gorge cuts through Plio-Pleistocene and recent geologic strata revealing close to 2 million years of the earth's history.

Figure 6.24 Robust Australopithecines and the Genus *Homo* The robust australopithecines and the earliest members of genus *Homo* inhabited the earth at the same time. These particular skulls and leg bones were all found along the eastern shores of Lake Turkana in Kenya and are dated to between 1.7 and 1.9 million years ago. Many paleoanthropologists classify two specimens with the rounded skulls as members of the species *Homo habilis*. The robust australopithecine at the top of the photograph has the bony ridge (sagittal crest) along the top of its skull. Note that the dates for each of these species expands beyond the dates found at one particular site.

Louis Leakey reconstructed his wife Mary's discovery and gave it the name *Zinjanthropus boisei* (Zinj, an old Arabic name for East Africa that means literally "Land of the Blacks," *boisei* after the benefactor who funded their expedition). At first, the stone tools found in association with this specimen led Louis Leakey to suggest that this ancient fossil seemed more humanlike than *Australopithecus* and extremely close to modern humans in evolutionary development. Further study, however, revealed that *Zinjanthropus*, the remains of which consisted of a skull and a few limb bones, was an East African species of robust australopithecine, *Australopithecus boisei* (see Table 6.1). Potassium-argon dating places these fossils at about 1.75 million years old.

Since the time of Mary Leakey's original *A. boisei* find, numerous other fossils of this robust species have been found at Olduvai, as well as north and east of Lake Turkana in Kenya (Figure 6.24). These robust fossils date

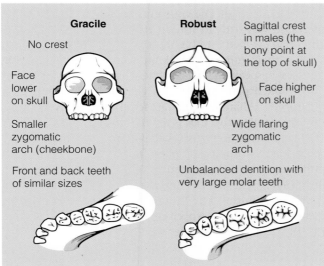

Gracile	Robust	
No crest		Sagittal crest in males (the bony point at the top of skull)
Face lower on skull		Face higher on skull
Smaller zygomatic arch (cheekbone)		Wide flaring zygomatic arch
Front and back teeth of similar sizes		Unbalanced dentition with very large molar teeth

Figure 6.23 Gracile and Robust Australopithecines The differences between gracile and robust australopithecines relate primarily to their chewing apparatus. Robust species have extremely large cheek teeth, large chewing muscles, and a bony ridge on the top of their skulls for the attachment of large temporal muscles for chewing. The front and back teeth of gracile species are balanced in size, and their chewing muscles (reflected in a less massive skull) are more like those seen in the later genus *Homo*. If you place your hands on the sides of your skull above your ears while opening and closing your jaw, you can feel where your temporal muscles attach to your skull. Glide your hands toward the top of your skull while still moving your jaw to feel where these muscles end in humans.

robust australopithecines Several species within the genus *Australopithecus*, who lived from 1 to 2.5 million years ago in eastern and southern Africa; known for the rugged nature of their chewing apparatus (large back teeth, large chewing muscles, and a bony ridge on their skull tops to allow for these large muscles).

sagittal crest A crest running from front to back on the top of the skull along the midline to provide a surface of bone for the attachment of the large temporal muscles for chewing.

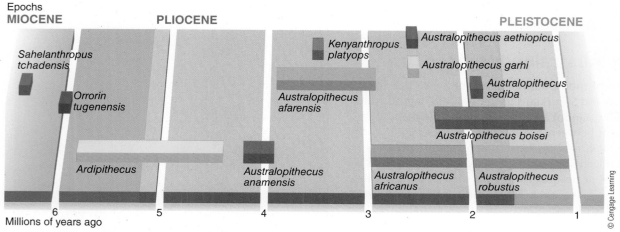

Figure 6.25 Timeline of Plio-Pleistocene Hominins This timeline shows the fossil bipeds who were not members of the genus *Homo* and the scientific names by which they have been known, arranged according to when they lived. The genus *Homo* first appears in the fossil record 2.5 million years ago and coexists with the gracile species *A. garhi* and *A. sediba*. There is also overlap between *Homo* and the robust australopithecines species *A. aethiopicus, A. boisei,* and *A. robustus.* Whether the different species names are warranted is a matter of debate.

from between 2.5 million years old and 1 mya. Like robust australopithecines from South Africa, East African robust forms possessed enormous molars and premolars. Despite a large mandible and palate, the anterior teeth (canines and incisors) were often crowded, owing to the room needed for the massive molars. The heavy skull, more massive even than seen in the robust forms from South Africa, has a sagittal crest and prominent brow ridges. Cranial capacity ranges from about 500 to 530 cubic centimeters. Body size, too, is somewhat larger; estimates for the weight of the South African robust forms range between 32 and 40 kilograms, while the East African robusts probably weighed from 34 to 49 kilograms.

Because the earliest robust skull from East Africa, the Black Skull from Kenya dated to 2.5 million years ago (see *A. aethiopicus* in Table 6.1), retains a number of ancestral features shared with earlier East African australopithecines, some suggest that it evolved from *A. afarensis*, giving rise to the later robust East African forms. Paleoanthropologists debate whether the South African robust australopithecines represent a southern offshoot of the East African line or convergent evolution from a South African ancestor. In either case, the later robust australopithecines developed molars and premolars that are both absolutely and relatively larger than those of earlier australopithecines, who possessed front and back teeth more in proportion to those seen in the genus *Homo*.

Larger teeth require more bone to support them, hence the prominent jaws of the robust australopithecines. Larger jaws and heavy chewing activity require more jaw musculature that attaches to the skull. The marked crests seen on skulls of the late australopithecines provide for the attachment of chewing muscles on a skull that has increased very little in size. In effect, robust australopithecines had evolved into highly efficient chewing machines. Clearly, their immense cheek teeth and powerful chewing muscles bespeak the heavy chewing required for a diet of uncooked plant foods. This general level of biological organization shared by separate fossil groups as seen in the robust australopithecines is referred to as a *grade*.

Many anthropologists believe that, by becoming a specialized consumer of plant foods, the late australopithecines avoided competing for the same niche with early *Homo*, with which they were contemporaries. In the course of evolution, the **law of competitive exclusion** dictates that when two closely related species compete for the same niche, one will outcompete the other, bringing about the loser's extinction. Their coexistence for 1.5 million years from about 1 to 2.5 million years ago suggests that early *Homo* and late *Australopithecus* did not compete for the same niche (**Figure 6.25**).

Australopithecines and the Genus *Homo*

A variety of bipeds inhabited Africa about 2.5 million years ago, around the time the first evidence for the genus *Homo* begins to appear. In 1999, discoveries in East Africa added another australopithecine to the mix. Found

law of competitive exclusion When two closely related species compete for the same niche, one will outcompete the other, bringing about the latter's extinction.

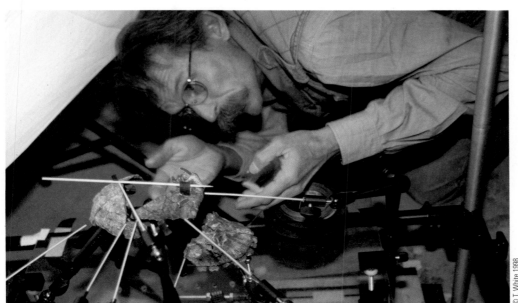

Figure 6.26
Reconstruction of Fossil Specimens Photographer David Brill, a specialist in images of fossils and paleoanthropologists, positions the upper jaw and the other skull fragments of *Australopithecus garhi* so that the fragments are aligned as they would be in a complete skull.

© T. White 1998

in the Afar region of Ethiopia, these fossils were named *Australopithecus garhi* from the word for "surprise" in the local Afar language (**Figure 6.26**). Though the teeth were large, this australopithecine possessed an arched dental arcade and a ratio between front and back teeth more like humans and South African gracile australopithecines than like robust groups. For this reason, some have proposed that *A. garhi* is ancestral to the genus *Homo*, though the question of which australopithecine was ancestral to humans remains particularly controversial.

The new discoveries continue. In 2010, a paleoanthropological team led by Lee Berger published a series of papers on a newly discovered South African gracile australopithecine they named ***Australopithecus sediba***. First discovered in 2008 by Berger's then 9-year-old son Matthew, who was exploring while his father excavated a formal site nearby, this new species consists of at least four partial skeletons, one of which is a well-preserved adolescent male. Best of all, *A. sediba* can be precisely dated to between 1.97 and 1.98 million years ago by paleomagnetism and uranium dating (Pickering et al., 2011). A variety of derived traits in the hand, forearm, and pelvis have led Berger's team to suggest that *A. sediba* is transitional between *A. africanus* and early *Homo* (**Figure 6.27**). Others argue that these specimens are part of the wide variation present in *A. africanus*. They also protest that *A. sediba* could not be ancestral to early *Homo* because the two groups seem to have coexisted.

A variety of scenarios have been proposed, each one giving a different australopithecine group the starring

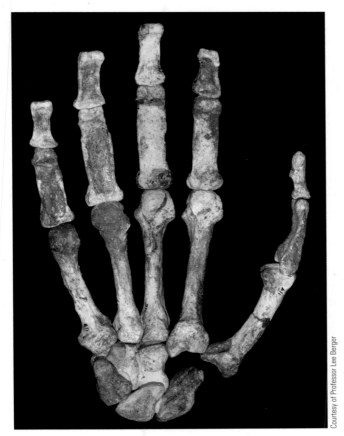

Courtesy of Professor Lee Berger

Figure 6.27 Exquisite Hands Derived features of the hand and forearm, which *Australopithecus sediba* shares with humans, have led some scientists to suggest that this is the ancestral hominin that gave rise to the human line. From the analysis of the well-preserved bones, it appears that these ancient hominins were anatomically capable of a "precision grip," a feature characteristic of humans. The *A. sediba* pelvis also has evidence of derived morphology that would contribute to a more efficient stride.

Australopithecus sediba A newly identified species of South African gracile australopithecine dated precisely to between 1.97 and 1.98 million years ago, with derived *Homo*-like characteristics in the hands and pelvis.

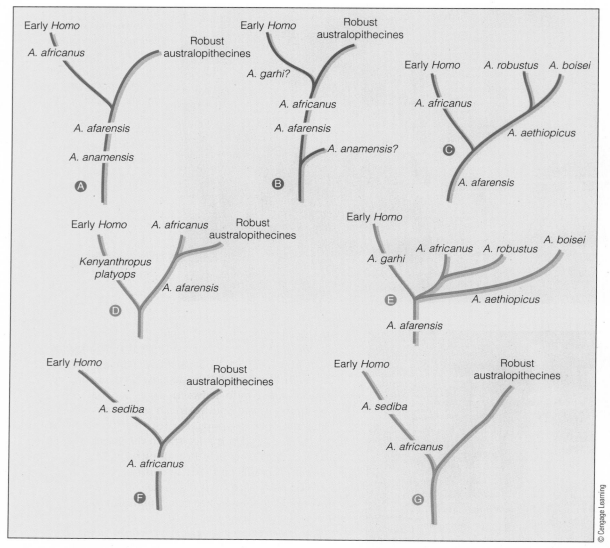

Figure 6.28 Scenarios for Human Origins Paleoanthropologists debate the relationship among the various australopithecine (and other) Pliocene groups and the question of which group is ancestral to the genus *Homo*. These diagrams present several alternative hypotheses. Most agree, however, that the robust australopithecines represent an evolutionary side branch and that *Ardipithecus ramidus* is ancestral to the australopithecines. The most recent point of contention is whether the newly discovered species, *Australopithecus sediba*, might be directly ancestral to the genus *Homo*.

role as the immediate human ancestor (Figure 6.28). Paleoanthropologists use the dates of the specimens as well as derived features to link the contending australopithecines to *Homo*. Pelvic shape and forearm anatomy make the case for *A. sediba*. An arched dental arcade is the evidence promoted for *A. garhi*. The flat face and perhaps larger cranial capacity of *Kenyanthropus platyops* is proposed as the link to *Homo*, but when cranial capacity becomes sufficiently large, the specimens are already classified as the genus *Homo*. Paleoanthropologists do agree, however, that the robust australopithecines, though successful in their time, ultimately represent an evolutionary side branch.

Environment, Diet, and Origins of the Human Line

How did evolutionary processes transform an early ape into a hominin? Hypotheses about hominin adaptation begin with the fossil evidence. For example, the fossil record indicates that once bipedalism appeared, over the next several million years the shape of the face and teeth shifted from an apelike to a humanlike condition. To refine their hypotheses, paleoanthropologists add scientific reconstructions of environmental conditions and

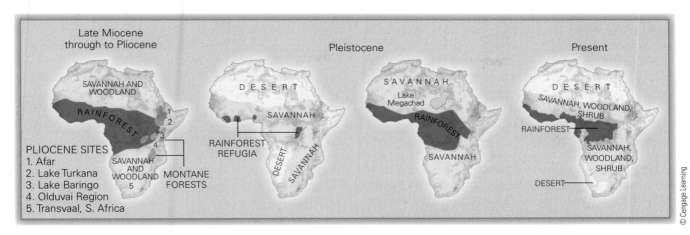

Figure 6.29 Climate Change and Vegetation Zones Since the late Miocene, the vegetation zones of Africa have changed considerably. Cooler, drier periods during the Pliocene reduced forested areas to far less than what exist today. The loss of forest likely created selective pressures that favored bipedalism.

inferences made from data gathered on living nonhuman primates and humans to the fossil evidence.

For many years, the emergence of the savannah environment in eastern Africa has dominated the human evolutionary narrative. Although the evidence from *Ardipithecus* shows that the earliest members of the human line were forest-dwellers, over time the size of tropical forests decreased or, more commonly, broke up into mosaics where patches of forest were interspersed with savannah or other types of open country. The forebears of the human line likely lived in places with access to both trees and open savannah.

With the breaking up of forests, these early ancestors found themselves spending more and more time on the ground and had to adapt to this new, more exposed environment. As the forest thinned or shrank, the traditional ape-type foods found in trees became less available, especially in seasons of reduced rainfall (Figure 6.29). Therefore, it became more and more necessary to forage on the ground for foods such as seeds, grasses, and roots. With reduced canine teeth, early bipeds were relatively defenseless when down on the ground and were easy targets for numerous carnivorous predators. The South African fossil evidence supports the notion that predators were a problem for early hominins. Most of the fossil specimens were dropped into rock fissures by predators such as leopards or, in the case of Dart's original find, by an eagle.

Many investigators have argued that the hands of early bipeds took over the weapon functions of reduced canine teeth. Hands enabled them to threaten predators by using wooden objects as clubs and throwing stones. Many of the other hominoids use their hands in this fashion. Recall the male chimpanzee (Chapter 4) clanging kerosene cans as part of his display to obtain alpha status. In australopithecines the use of clubs and throwing stones may have set the stage for the much later manufacture of more efficient weapons from bone, wood, and stone.

Although the hands of the later australopithecines were suitable for tool making, no evidence exists that any of them actually *made* stone tools. Still, using brain size as a measure, *Australopithecus* certainly had no less intelligence and dexterity than do modern great apes, all of whom make use of tools as described in Chapter 4. Most likely, the ability to make and use simple tools dates back to the last common ancestor of the Asian and African apes, before the appearance of the first bipeds.

Australopithecine tool use was likely similar to that of the other great apes. Unfortunately, these simple tools would not preserve well in the fossil record for a million and more years. Although we cannot be certain about this, in addition to clubs and objects thrown for defense, sturdy sticks may have been used to dig edible roots, and convenient stones may have been used (as some chimpanzees do) to crack open nuts. In fact, some animal bones from australopithecine sites in South Africa show microscopic wear patterns suggesting their use to dig edible roots from the ground. We may also allow the possibility that, like chimpanzees, females used tools more often to get and process food, while males more typically used tools as weapons. The female chimpanzees hunting with spears in Fongoli as described in Chapter 4 call into question these distinct roles for the sexes.

Humans Stand on Their Own Two Feet

From the broad-shouldered, long-armed, tailless ape body plan, the human line became fully bipedal. Our late Miocene forebears seem to have been primates that combined quadrupedal tree climbing with perhaps some swinging below the branches. On the ground, they were capable of assuming an upright stance, at least on occasion (optional, versus obligatory, bipedalism).

Paleoanthropologists generally take the negative aspects of bipedal locomotion into account when considering this pattern of locomotion. For example, paleoanthropologists have suggested that bipedalism makes an animal more visible to predators, exposes its soft underbelly or gut, and interferes with the ability to instantly change direction while running. They also emphasize that bipedalism does not result in particularly fast running; quadrupedal chimpanzees and baboons, for example, run 30 to 34 percent faster than we bipeds. For 100-meter distances, our best athletes today may attain speeds of 34 to 37 kilometers per hour, while the larger African carnivores from which bipeds might need to run can attain speeds up to 60 to 70 kilometers per hour. The consequences of a leg or foot injury are more serious for a biped whereas a quadruped can do amazingly well on three legs. Because each of these drawbacks would have placed our early ancestors at risk from predators, paleoanthropologists ask what made bipedal locomotion worth paying such a high price. What selective pressures favored bipedalism despite these disadvantages?

One older theory proposed that bipedal locomotion allowed males to obtain food on the savannah and transport it back to females, who were restricted from doing so by the dependence of their offspring. The fact that female apes, not to mention women among food-foraging peoples, routinely combine infant care with foraging for food negates this theory. Indeed, among most food foragers, it is the women who commonly supply the bulk of the food eaten by both sexes.

Moreover, this model presumed pair bonding (one male attached to one female), a form of social organization atypical of terrestrial primates displaying the degree of sexual dimorphism that was characteristic of *Australopithecus*. Nor is pair bonding really characteristic of *Homo sapiens*. In a substantial majority of recent human societies, including those in which people forage for their food, some form of polygamy—marriage to two or more individuals at the same time—is not only permitted but preferred. And even in the supposedly monogamous United States, many individuals marry (and hence mate with) two or more others (the only requirement is that the person not be married to more than one mate at the same time).

In the end, the idea of males provisioning stay-at-home moms appears to be more culture-bound than based on the fossil evidence. Paleoanthropologists, like all anthropologists, must exercise caution to avoid infusing theories about the fossil record with their own cultural beliefs. See the Biocultural Connection for another example of the influence of contemporary gender roles on paleoanthropological theories.

A fully erect biped on the ground—whether male or female—has the ability to gather food for transport back to a tree or other place of safety for consumption. The biped does not have to remain out in the open, exposed and vulnerable, to do all of its eating. Besides making it possible to carry food, bipedalism could have facilitated the food quest in other ways. With their hands free and body upright, the animals could reach otherwise unobtainable food on thorny trees too flimsy and too spiny to climb (Kaplan, 2007; Thorpe, Holder, & Crompton, 2007). Furthermore, with both hands free, they could gather other small foods more quickly using both hands. And in times of scarcity, being able to see farther, with the head in an upright position, would have helped them locate food and water sources.

Food may not have been the only thing transported by early bipeds. As we saw in Chapters 3 and 4, from birth primate infants must cling to their mothers, who use all their limbs in locomotion. Chimpanzee infants, for example, cling by themselves to their mother, and even up to 4 years of age they make long journeys on their mother's back. Injuries caused by falling from the mother account for a significant proportion of infant mortality among apes. Thus, the ability to carry infants would have made a significant contribution to the survival of offspring, and the ancestors of *Australopithecus* would have been capable of doing just this.

Although bipedalism appeared before our ancestors lived in the savannah, bipedalism likely served as a means to cope with heat stress out in the open as the forested environments disappeared. In addition to bipedalism, our relative nakedness constitutes one of the most obvious differences between humans and other living hominoids. Humans have only a fine sparse layer of body hair over most of the body with a very dense cover of hair limited primarily to the head. Peter Wheeler, a British physiologist, has suggested that bipedalism and the human pattern of body hair growth are both adaptations to the heat stress of the savannah environment. Building upon the earlier "radiator" theory of paleoanthropologist Dean Falk, Wheeler developed this hypothesis through comparative anatomy, experimental studies, and the observation that humans are the only apes to inhabit the savannah environment today.

Many other animals, however, inhabit the savannah, and each of them possesses some mechanism for coping with heat stress. Some animals, like many of the carnivores, limit their heavy activity to near dawn or dusk when the sun is low in the sky or to the cooler nights. Some, like antelope, have evolved to tolerate high body temperatures that would kill humans due to overheating of the brain tissue. They accomplish this through cooling their blood in their muzzles through evaporation before it enters the vessels leading to the delicate tissues of the brain.

BIOCULTURAL CONNECTION

Evolution and Human Birth

Because biology and culture have always shaped human experience, it can be a challenge to separate the influences of each of these factors on human practices. For example, in the 1950s, paleoanthropologists developed the theory that human childbirth is particularly difficult compared to birth in other mammals. This theory was based in part on the observation of a "tight fit" between the human mother's birth canal and the baby's head, though several other primates also possess similarly tight fits between the newborn's head or shoulders and the birth canal. Nevertheless, changes in the birth canal associated with bipedalism coupled with the evolution of large brains were held responsible for difficult birth in humans.

At the same historical moment, childbirth practices in the United States were changing. In one generation from the 1920s to the 1950s, birth shifted from the home to the hospital. In the process childbirth transformed from something a woman normally accomplished at home, perhaps with the help of a midwife or relatives, into the high-tech delivery of a neonate (the medical term for a newborn) with the assistance of medically trained personnel. Women in the 1950s were generally fully anesthetized during the birth process. Paleoanthropological theories mirrored the cultural norms, providing a scientific explanation for the change in U.S. childbirth practices.

As a scientific theory, the idea of difficult human birth stands on shaky ground. No fossil neonates have ever been recovered, and only a handful of complete pelves (the bones forming the birth canal) exist. Instead, scientists must examine the birth process in living humans and nonhuman primates to reconstruct the evolution of the human birth pattern.

Cultural beliefs and practices, however, shape every aspect of birth.

Tlazolteotl, the earth mother goddess of the Aztecs, is depicted here giving birth in a squatting position, which is favored by women throughout the world. For hospital births, women generally have to work against gravity to bring a child into the world because they tend to be placed on their backs with their legs in stirrups for the benefit of attending physicians.

© 2012 Man Ray Trust/Artists Rights Society (ARS), NY/ADAGP, Paris. Statuette of Ixcuina, Mexican Goddess of Maternity, 1890–1941. Gelatin silver print, 9-1/16 x 6-7/8". Gift of James Thrall Soby (204.1991). Digital Image © The Museum of Modern Art/Licensed by SCALA/Art Resource, NY.

Cultural factors determine where a birth occurs, the actions of the individuals present, and beliefs about the nature of the experience. When paleoanthropologists of the 1950s and 1960s asserted that human childbirth is more difficult than birth in other mammals, they were drawing upon their own cultural beliefs that childbirth is dangerous and belongs in a hospital.

A quick look at global neonatal mortality statistics indicates that in countries such as the Netherlands and Sweden, healthy well-nourished women give birth successfully outside of hospitals, as they did throughout human evolutionary history. In other countries, deaths related to childbirth reflect malnutrition, infectious disease, and the low social status of women, rather than an inherently faulty biology.

BIOCULTURAL QUESTION

Though well-nourished healthy women successfully birth their babies outside of hospital settings, caesarean section (C-section) rates have been rising in industrialized societies. In the United States one in three deliveries is by C-section, and in many Latin American countries more than half of all deliveries are by caesarean. What cultural factors have led to this practice? Would your personal approach to birth change with the knowledge that humans have successfully adapted to childbirth?

According to Wheeler, the interesting thing about humans and other primates is that

> We can't uncouple brain temperature from the rest of the body, the way an antelope does, so we've got to prevent any damaging elevations in body temperature. And of course the problem is even more acute for an ape, because in general, the larger and more complex the brain, the more easily it is damaged. So, there were incredible selective pressures on early hominids favoring adaptations that would reduce thermal stress-pressures that may have favored bipedalism. (quoted in *The Naked and the Bipedal* by Tim Folger, 1993, pp. 34–35)

Wheeler has studied this notion by taking measurements on the exposure of an early biped, like Lucy, to solar radiation in upright and quadrupedal stances. He found that the bipedal stance reduced exposure to solar radiation by 60 percent, indicating that a biped would require less water to stay cool in a savannah environment compared to a quadruped.

Wheeler further suggests that bipedalism made the human body hair pattern possible. Fur can keep out solar radiation as well as retain heat. A biped, with reduced exposure to the sun everywhere except the head, would benefit from hair loss on the body surface to increase the efficiency of sweating to cool down. On the head, hair serves as a shield, blocking solar radiation.

Some object to this scenario, citing that when bipedalism developed, savannah was not as extensive in Africa as it is today. In both East and South Africa, environments included closed and open bush and woodlands. Moreover, fossil flora and fauna found with *Ardipithecus* and the possible human ancestors from the Miocene are typical of a moist, closed, wooded habitat.

However, the presence of bipedalism in the fossil record without a savannah environment does not indicate that bipedalism was not adaptive to these conditions. It merely indicates that bipedalism appeared without any particular adaptive benefits at first, likely through a random macromutation. Bipedalism provided a body plan preadapted to the heat stress of the savannah environment.

Recall how in the early 20th century, larger brains were thought to have permitted the evolution of bipedalism. We now know not only that bipedalism preceded the evolution of larger brains by several million years, but we can also consider the possibility that bipedalism may have preadapted human ancestors for brain expansion. According to Wheeler,

> The brain is one of the most metabolically active tissues in the body. . . . In the case of humans it accounts for something like 20 percent of total energy consumption. So you've got an

organ producing a lot of heat that you've got to dump. Once we'd become bipedal and naked and achieved this ability to dump heat, that may have allowed the expansion of the brain that took place later in human evolution. It didn't cause it, but you can't have a large brain unless you can cool it. (quoted in *The Naked and the Bipedal* by Tim Folger, 1993, pp. 34–35)

Consistent with Wheeler's hypothesis is the fact that the system for drainage of the blood from the cranium of the earlier australopithecines is significantly different from that of the genus *Homo* (**Figure 6.30**).

Though paleoanthropologists cannot resolve every detail of the course of human evolution from the available data, over time the narrative they have constructed has improved. Human evolution evidently took place in fits and starts, rather than at a steady pace. Today, we know that bipedalism preceded brain expansion by several million years. Bipedalism likely occurred as a sudden shift in body plan and after a viable bipedal adaptation was achieved; then stabilizing selection took over, and little change took place for at least a few million years.

Change again occurred about 2.5 million years ago, resulting in the branching out of new forms, including several robust species as well as the first appearance of the

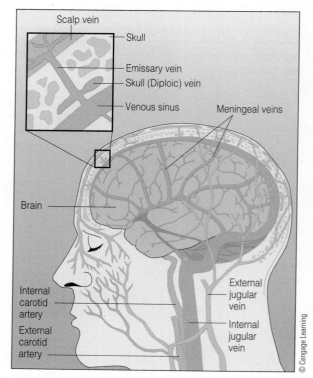

Figure 6.30 Cooling Hot-Headed Hominins In humans, blood from the face and scalp, instead of returning directly to the heart, may be directed instead into the braincase and then to the heart. Already cooled at the surface of the skin, blood is able to carry heat away from the brain.

genus *Homo*. From about 2.3 million years ago until robust australopithecines became extinct around 1 million years ago, however, the robust forms underwent relatively little alteration. By contrast, after its appearance 2.5 million years ago, *Homo* began a steady course of brain expansion that continued over the next 2.3 million years until brain size reached its current state. With the appearance of this new larger-brained hominin, the first stone tools appear in the archaeological record.

Early Representatives of the Genus *Homo*

Just as the Leakeys thought, Olduvai Gorge with its stone tool assemblages was a good place to search for human ancestors. Part of today's Olduvai Gorge was once a lake. Almost 2 million years ago, numerous wild animals including a variety of bipeds inhabited its shores. In 1959—when the Leakeys found the bones of the first specimen of robust *Australopithecus boisei* in association with some of these tools and the bones of birds, reptiles, antelopes, and pigs—they thought they had found the remains of one of the toolmakers. Fossils unearthed a few months later and a few feet below this first discovery led them to change their mind. These fossil remains consisted of more than one individual, including a few cranial bones, a lower jaw, a clavicle, some finger bones (**Figure 6.31**), and the nearly complete left foot of an adult (**Figure 6.32**). Skull and jaw fragments indicated that these specimens represented a larger-brained biped without the specialized chewing apparatus of the robust australopithecines.

The Leakeys and colleagues named that contemporary *Homo habilis* (Latin for "handy human") and suggested that tool-wielding *H. habilis* may have eaten the animals and possibly the *Australopithecus boisei*. Of course, we do not really know whether *A. boisei* from Olduvai Gorge met its end in this way, but we do know that cut marks from a stone tool are present on a jawbone from a 2.4-million-year-old australopithecine from South Africa (White & Toth, 2000). This was done, presumably, to remove the mandible, but for what purpose we do not know. In any event, it does lend credibility to the idea of *A. boisei* on occasion being dismembered by *H. habilis*.

Subsequent work at Olduvai has unearthed not only more skull fragments but other parts of the skeleton of *H. habilis* as well. Since the late 1960s, sites in South Africa, Ethiopia, and Kenya have yielded fossils of the genus *Homo* contemporaneous with those from Olduvai.

The eastern shores of Lake Turkana, on the border between Kenya and Ethiopia, have been particularly rich with fossils from earliest *Homo*. The Leakeys' son Richard discovered one well-known fossil, known as KNM ER 1470, at Koobi Fora. (The letters KNM stand for Kenya National

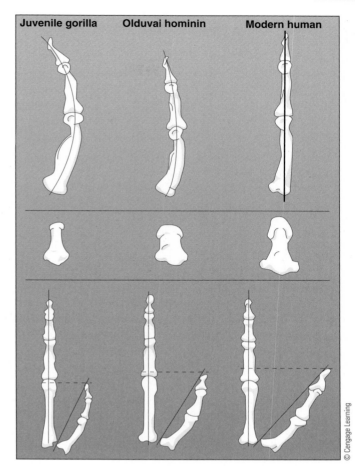

Figure 6.31 Comparative Anatomy of *Homo habilis* Hand Bones A comparison of hand bones of a juvenile gorilla, *Homo habilis* from Olduvai, and a modern human highlights important differences in the structure of fingers and thumbs. In the top row are fingers, and in the second row are terminal (end) thumb bones. Although terminal finger bones are more human, lower finger bones are more curved and powerful. The bottom row compares thumb length and angle relative to the index finger.

Museum; the ER, for East Rudolf, the name for Lake Turkana during the colonial era in Kenya.) The deposits in which it was found are about 1.9 million years old; these deposits, like those at Olduvai, also contain crude stone tools. The KNM ER 1470 skull is more modern in appearance than any *Australopithecus* skull and has a cranial capacity of 752 cubic centimeters (cc). However, the large

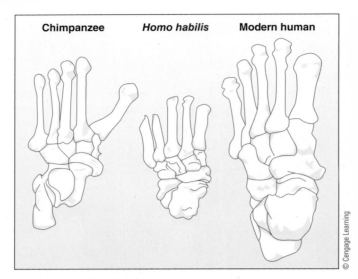

Figure 6.32 Comparative Anatomy of *Homo habilis* Foot
A partial foot skeleton of *Homo habilis* (*center*) is compared
with the same bones of a chimpanzee (*left*) and modern human
(*right*). Note how *H. habilis'* bone at the base of the great toe is
in line with the others, as it is in modern humans, making for
effective walking but poor grasping.

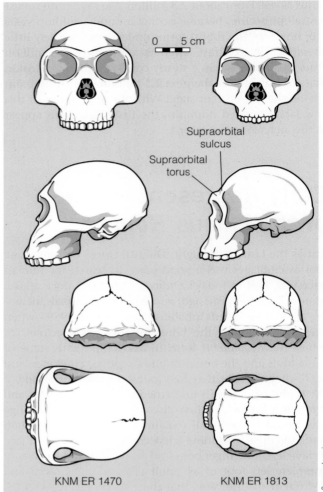

Figure 6.33 One Diverse Species? The KNM ER 1470 skull—
one of the most complete skulls of *Homo habilis*—is close to
2 million years old and is probably a male; it contrasts with the
considerably smaller KNM ER 1813 skull, probably a female.
Some paleoanthropologists feel this variation is too great to
place these specimens in the same species.

teeth and face of this specimen resemble the earlier australopithecines.

From this same site another well-preserved skull from
the same time period (KNM ER 1813) possesses a cranial
capacity of less than 600 cc but has the derived characteristics of a smaller, less projecting face and teeth (both
of these specimens are shown in Figure 6.24). Though
specimens attributed to *H. habilis* generally have cranial
capacities greater than 600 cc, the cranial capacity of any
individual is also in proportion to its body size. Therefore,
many paleoanthropologists interpret KNM ER 1813 and
ER 1470 as a female and male of a very sexually dimorphic
species, with the smaller cranial capacity of KNM ER 1813
a reflection of her smaller body size (**Figure 6.33**).

Lumpers or Splitters?

Other paleoanthropologists do not agree with placing
specimens as diverse as KNM ER 1813 and KNM ER 1470
in the single taxonomic group of *H. habilis*. Instead they
feel that the diversity represented in these specimens warrants separating the fossils like the larger-brained KNM
ER 1470 into a distinct coexisting group called *Homo
rudolphensis*. Whether one chooses to call these or any
other contemporary fossils *Homo rudolphensis* or *Homo
habilis* is more than a name game. Fossil names indicate
researchers' perspectives about evolutionary relationships among groups. Giving specimens separate species
names signifies that they form part of a reproductively
isolated group.

Some paleoanthropologists approach the fossil record
with the perspective that making such detailed biological determinations is arbitrary and that variability exists
within any group. Arguing that it is impossible to prove
whether a collection of ancient bones and teeth represents a distinct species, these paleoanthropologists tend
to be "lumpers," placing similar-looking fossil specimens
together in more inclusive groups. For example, gorillas
show a degree of sexual dimorphism that lumpers attribute to *H. habilis*.

"Splitters," by contrast, focus on the variation in the
fossil record, interpreting minor differences in the shape
of skeletons or skulls as evidence of distinct biological species with corresponding cultural capacities. The late great
South African paleoanthropologist Philip Tobias (to whose

Origins of the Genus *Homo*

7

In the quest for the origin of modern humans, paleoanthropologists confront mysteries by drawing from evidence that can be scant, misleading, and contradictory. Some of the mystery stems from the kind of evolutionary change that was set in motion with the appearance of the genus ***Homo***. Beginning 2.5 million years ago (mya), several million years after the appearance of bipedalism separated the human evolutionary line from those of the other African apes, the brain size of our ancestors began to increase. Simultaneously, these early ancestors increased their cultural manipulation of the physical world through their use of stone tools. These new bipeds were the first members of the genus *Homo*. Over time, they increasingly relied on cultural adaptation as a rapid and effective way to adjust to the environment.

Although the evolution of culture became critical for human survival, it was intricately tied to underlying biological capacities, specifically the evolution of the human brain. Over the course of the next 2.2 million years, increasing brain size and specialization of function (evidence preserved in fossilized skulls) permitted the development of language, planning, new technologies, and artistic expression. With the evolution of a brain that made versatile behavior possible, members of the genus *Homo* became biocultural beings.

U.S. biological anthropologist Misia Landau has noted that the narrative of human evolutionary history takes the form of the heroic epic (Landau, 1991). The hero, or evolving human, faces a series of natural challenges that cannot be overcome from a strictly biological standpoint. Endowed with the gift of intelligence, the hero meets these challenges to become fully human. In this narrative, cultural capabilities increasingly separate humans from other evolving animals. As we saw in earlier chapters, recent advances in primatology keep undercutting this notion of human uniqueness.

Biological change and cultural change are very different phenomena. Cultural equipment and techniques can develop rapidly with innovations

IN THIS CHAPTER YOU WILL LEARN TO

- Describe the cultural capacity of various members of the genus *Homo* and how these capacities relate to anatomy preserved in fossils.

- Situate humans' place in the animal kingdom and recognize the cultural biases that have influenced the development of scientific theories about human evolution.

- Describe the debates surrounding relationships among fossil groups of the genus *Homo*.

- Identify the features that characterize the distinct eras of toolmaking.

- Discuss the controversy surrounding Neandertals' place in human evolution.

Homo The genus of bipeds that appeared 2.5 million years ago, characterized by increased brain size compared to earlier bipeds. The genus is divided into various species based on features such as brain size, skull shape, and cultural capabilities.

occurring during the lifetime of individuals. By contrast, because it depends upon heritable traits, biological change requires many generations. Paleoanthropologists consider whether an evident cultural change, such as a new type of stone tool, corresponds to a major biological change, such as the appearance of a new species. Reconciling the relation between biological and cultural change is often a source of debate within paleoanthropology.

The Discovery of the First Stone Toolmaker

Paleoanthropologists Louis and Mary Leakey began their search for human origins at Olduvai Gorge, Tanzania, because of the presence of crude stone tools unearthed there. These tools found in deposits dating back to very early in the Pleistocene epoch (which began almost 2 mya), defined the **Oldowan tool tradition**.

These earliest identifiable tools consist of implements made using a system of manufacture called the **percussion method** (Figure 7.1). Sharp-edged flakes were obtained from a stone (often a large, water-worn cobble) either by using another stone as a hammer (a hammerstone) or by striking the cobble against a large rock (anvil) to remove the flakes. The finished flakes had sharp edges, effective for cutting and scraping. Microscopic wear patterns show that these flakes were used for cutting meat, reeds, sedges, and grasses and for cutting and scraping wood. Small indentations on their surfaces suggest that the leftover cores were transformed into choppers for breaking open bones, and they may also have been employed to defend the user. The appearance of these tools marks the beginning of the **Lower Paleolithic**, the first part of the Old Stone Age.

The tools from Olduvai Gorge are not the oldest stone tools known. Paleoanthropologists have dated the start of the Lower Paleolithic to between 2.5 and 2.6 million years ago from similar assemblages recently discovered in Gona, Ethiopia. (Figure 7.2 shows the captive bonobo Kanzi who has made tools and used tools similar to those found in

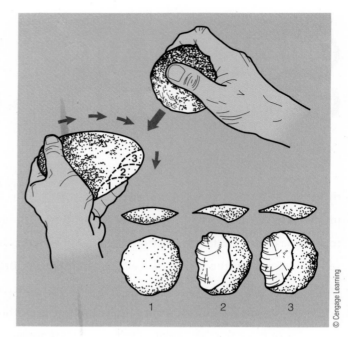

Figure 7.1 The Percussion Method By 2.5 million years ago, early *Homo* in Africa had invented the percussion method of stone tool manufacture. This technological breakthrough, which is associated with a significant increase in brain size, made the butchering of meat from scavenged carcasses possible.

Gona.) Lower Paleolithic tools have also been found in the vicinity of Lake Turkana in northwestern Kenya, in southern Ethiopia, as well as in other sites near Gona in the Afar Triangle of Ethiopia. With these earliest stone tools, we have the beginning of the hominin archaeological record. Before this time, tool use among early bipeds probably consisted of heavy sticks to dig up roots or ward off animals, unshaped stones to throw for defense or to crack open nuts, and perhaps simple carrying devices made of knotted plant fibers. Perishable tools are not preserved in the archaeological record.

Paleoanthropologists have applied the methodology of **experimental archaeology**, the systematic recreation of ancient lifeways in order to test hypotheses, interpretations, and assumptions about the past. To understand the process of toolmaking, researchers work with raw materials to make stone tools themselves (Figure 7.2). The process of becoming skilled at fashioning

Oldowan tool tradition The first stone tool industry, beginning between 2.5 and 2.6 million years ago.

percussion method A technique of stone tool manufacture performed by striking the raw material with a hammerstone or by striking raw material against a stone anvil to remove flakes.

Lower Paleolithic The first part of the Old Stone Age beginning with the earliest Oldowan tools spanning from about 200,000 or 250,000 to 2.6 million years ago.

experimental archaeology The recreation of ancient lifeways by modern paleoanthropologists in order to test hypotheses, interpretations, and assumptions about the past.

Sex, Gender, and the Behavior of Early *Homo*

Figure 7.2 Oldowan Toolmaking While we have no evidence of stone toolmaking by any hominoids in the wild, Kanzi, the captive bonobo, spontaneously began making stone tools thus providing us with some insight into the cognitive capacities that underlie this ancient task. The experimental archaeologist takes this many steps further. Through becoming skilled at ancient toolmaking techniques, an experimental archaeologist analyzes the exact processes involved. In essence, a form of participant observation across time, the experimental archaeologist takes on the lifeways of ancient hominins. He or she performs the same behaviors and creates the same artifacts, to discover which skills these lifeways required, knowledge that is indispensible for the interpretation of the material remains. Experimental archaeologists often master the entire range of ancient stone tool techniques described in this chapter in order to make comparisons among the various industries.

When paleoanthropologists from the 1960s and 1970s depicted the lifeways of early *Homo*, they concentrated on "man the hunter," a tough guy with a killer instinct wielding tools on a savannah teeming with meat, while the female members of the species stayed at home tending their young. Similarly, until the 1960s, most cultural anthropologists doing fieldwork among foragers stressed the role of male hunters and underreported the significance of female gatherers in providing food for the community. Western notions of **gender**, the cultural elaborations and meanings assigned to the biological differentiation between the sexes, played a substantial role in creating these biases.

tools allows researchers to analyze what skills toolmaking requires. Through this work it is clear that the makers of these early tools were highly skilled, consistently and efficiently producing many well-formed sharp-edged flakes from raw materials with the least effort (Ambrose, 2001). To do this, the toolmaker had to have in mind an abstract idea of the tool to be made, as well as a specific set of steps to transform the raw material into the finished product. Furthermore, the toolmaker would have to know which kinds of stone have the flaking properties that would allow the transformation to take place, as well as where such stone could be found.

Sometimes tool fabrication required the transport of raw materials over great distances. Such planning for the future undoubtedly was associated with natural selection favoring changes in brain structure. These changes mark the beginning of the genus *Homo*. As described in the previous chapter, ***Homo habilis*** was the name given to the oldest members of the genus when first discovered in 1959. With larger brains and the stone tools preserved in the archaeological record, paleoanthropologists began to piece together a picture of the life of early *Homo*.

As anthropologists became aware of their own biases, they began to set the record straight, documenting the vital role of "woman the gatherer" in provisioning the social group in foraging cultures, past and present. (See this chapter's Biocultural Connection for the specific contributions of female paleoanthropologists.) The division of labor among contemporary food foragers, like all gender relations, does not conform to fixed boundaries defined through biologically based sex differences. Instead, it is influenced by cultural and environmental factors. It appears likely that the same principle applied to our human ancestors. Uncovering such biases is as important as any new discovery for interpreting the fossil record (**Figure 7.3**).

Studies of extant primates can allow paleoanthropologists to see when gender might appropriately be incorporated into their theories. For example, by finding sex

Homo habilis "Handy human." The first fossil members of the genus *Homo* appearing 2.5 million years ago, with larger brains and smaller faces than australopithecines.

gender The cultural elaborations and meanings assigned to the biological differentiation between the sexes.

BIOCULTURAL CONNECTION

Sex, Gender, and Female Paleoanthropologists

Until the 1970s, the study of human evolution was permeated by a deep-seated bias reflecting the privileged status enjoyed by men in Western society. Beyond the obvious labeling of fossils as particular types of "men," irrespective of the sex of the individual represented, males were portrayed as the active players in human evolution. Thus, males were seen as providers and innovators, using their wits to become ever-more effective suppliers of food and protection for passive females. Females were depicted as spending their time preparing food and caring for offspring, while the males were getting ahead by becoming ever smarter. Central to such thinking was the idea of "man the hunter," constantly honing his wits through the pursuit and killing of animals. Hunting by men was seen as the pivotal humanizing activity in evolution.

We now acknowledge that such ideas are culture-bound, reflecting the hopes and expectations of Western culture in the late 19th and early 20th centuries. This recognition came in the 1970s and was a direct consequence of the entry of a number of highly capable women into the profession of paleoanthropology.

Up until the 1960s, there were few women in any field of physical anthropology, but with the expansion of graduate programs and changing attitudes toward the role of women in society, increasing numbers of women went on to earn doctorates. One of these was Adrienne Zihlman, who earned her doctorate at the University of California at Berkeley in 1967. Subsequently, she authored a number of important papers critical of "man the hunter" scenarios. She was not the first to do so; as early as 1971, Sally Linton had published a preliminary paper on "woman the gatherer." But it was Zihlman who, from 1976 on, especially elaborated on the importance of female activities for human evolution. Others have joined in the effort, including Zihlman's graduate school companion and professional colleague Nancy Tanner, who has produced important works of her own.

The work of Zihlman and her coworkers was crucial in forcing a reexamination of existing "man the hunter" scenarios; this produced recognition of the importance of scavenging in early human evolution as well as the value of female gathering and other activities.

Although there is still plenty to learn about human evolution, thanks to these women we now know that it was not a case of females being "uplifted" as a consequence of their association with progressively evolving males. Rather, the two sexes evolved together, with each making its own important contribution to the process.

BIOCULTURAL QUESTION

Can you think of any examples of how gender norms are influencing theories about the biological basis of male and female behavior today?

---

differences in the levels of the mineral strontium in the teeth of 2-million-year-old fossil hominins, paleoanthropologists have deduced that these ancestors followed the same pattern of female dispersal at adolescence seen in chimps and bonobos (Copeland et al., 2011). However, female dispersal patterns cannot be extended to explain theories regarding the evolution of pair bonding or biologically encoded male aggression without introducing gender bias.

Similarly, evidence from chimpanzees and bonobos casts further doubt on the notion of a strict sex-based division of labor in human evolutionary history. As described in Chapter 4, female chimpanzees have been observed participating in hunting expeditions, even leading the hunt behavior with spears. Meat gained from the successful hunt of a smaller mammal is shared within the group whether provided by a male or a female chimpanzee. Among bonobos, females hunt regularly and share meat as well as plant foods with one another. In other words, patterns of food sharing and hunting behaviors in these apes are variable, supporting the notion that culture plays a role in establishing these behaviors. Similarly, in our evolutionary history it is likely that culture—the shared learned behaviors of each early *Homo* group—played a role in food-sharing behaviors rather than strict biological differences between the sexes.

No evidence exists to establish definitively how procured foods may have been shared among our ancestors. When the evidence is fragmentary, as it is in all paleoanthropological reconstructions of behavior, gaps are too easily filled in with behaviors that seem "natural" and familiar, such as the contemporary gender roles of the paleoanthropologist.

Hunters or Scavengers?

As biases in paleoanthropological interpretations were addressed, it became clear that early members of the genus *Homo* were not hunters of large game. Assemblages of Oldowan tools and broken animal bones tell us that both *H. habilis* and large carnivorous animals were active at these locations. In addition to marks on the bones made by slicing, scraping, and chopping with stone tools, there

Figure 7.3 Gender Bias In this artist's reconstruction, separate roles are portrayed for males and females. Do the roles depicted here derive from biological differences between the sexes or culturally established gender differences?

are marks made by gnawing teeth. Some of the gnawing marks overlie the butcher marks, indicating that enough flesh remained on the bones after *Homo* was done with them to attract other carnivores. In other cases, though, the butcher marks overlie the tooth marks of carnivores, indicating that the animals got there first. This is what we would expect if *H. habilis* was scavenging the kills of other animals, rather than doing its own killing.

Further, areas that appear to be ancient butchering sites lack whole carcasses; apparently, only parts were transported away from the original location where they were obtained—again, the pattern that we would expect if they were stolen from the kill of some other animal. The stone tools, too, were made of raw material procured at distances of up to 60 kilometers from where they were used to process pieces of carcasses. Finally, the incredible density of bones at some of the sites and patterns of weathering indicate that the sites were used repeatedly for perhaps five to fifteen years.

By contrast, historically known and contemporary hunters typically bring whole carcasses back to camp or form camp around a large animal in order to fully process it. After processing, nothing edible remains—neither meat nor **marrow** (the fatty nutritious tissue inside long bones where blood cells are produced). The bones themselves are broken up not just to get at the marrow (as at Oldowan sites) but to fabricate tools and other objects of bone (unlike at Oldowan sites).

It appears that our Oldowan forebears were scavengers, getting their meat from the Lower Paleolithic equivalent of modern-day roadkill, taking the spoils of their scavenging to particular places where tools, and the raw materials for making them (often procured from faraway sources), had been stockpiled in advance for the purpose of butchering. At the least, this may have required fabrication of carrying devices such as net bags and trail signs of the sort (described in Chapter 4) used by modern bonobos. Quite likely, *H. habilis* continued to sleep in trees or rocky cliffs, as do modern small-bodied terrestrial or semiterrestrial primates, in order to be safe from predators.

Microscopic analysis of cut marks on bones has revealed that the earliest members of the genus *Homo* were actually **tertiary scavengers**—that is, third in line to get something from a carcass after a lion or leopard managed to kill the prey. After the initial kill, ferocious scavengers, such as hyenas and vultures, would swarm the rotting carcass. Next, our tool-wielding ancestors would scavenge for food, breaking open the shafts of long bones to get at the rich marrow inside. A small amount of marrow is a concentrated source of both protein and fat. Muscle alone, particularly from lean game animals, contains very little fat. Furthermore, as the following Original Study shows, perhaps evolving humans were prey themselves, and this selective pressure imposed by predators played a role in brain expansion (Hart & Sussman, 2005).

---

marrow The fatty nutritious tissue inside of long bones where blood cells are produced.

tertiary scavenger In a food chain, the third animal group (second to scavenge) to obtain meat from a kill made by a predator.

Humans as Prey BY DONNA HART

There's little doubt that humans, particularly those in Western cultures, think of themselves as the dominant form of life on earth. And we seldom question whether that view holds true for our species' distant past. . . . We swagger like the toughest kids on the block as we spread our technology over the landscape and irrevocably change it for other species.

. . . The vision of our utter superiority may even hold true for the last 500 years, but that's just the proverbial blink of an eye when compared to the 7 million years that our hominid ancestors wandered the planet.

"Where did we come from?" and "What were the first humans like?" are questions that have been asked since Darwin first proposed his theory of evolution. One commonly accepted answer is that our early ancestors were killers of other species and of their own kind, prone to violence and even cannibalism. In fact, a club-swinging "Man the Hunter" is the stereotype of early humans that permeates literature, film, and even much scientific writing. . . .

Even the great paleontologist Louis S. B. Leakey endorsed it when he emphatically declared that we were not "cat food." Another legendary figure in the annals of paleontology, Raymond A. Dart, launched the killer-ape-man scenario in the mid-20th century. . . .

Dart had interpreted the finds in South African caves of fossilized bones from savannah herbivores together with damaged hominid skulls as evidence that our ancestors had been hunters. The fact that the skulls were battered in a peculiar fashion led to Dart's firm conviction that violence and cannibalism on the part of killer ape-men formed the stem from which our own species eventually flowered. In his 1953 article "The Predatory Transition from Ape to Man," Dart wrote that early hominids were "carnivorous creatures, that seized living quarries by violence, battered them to death, tore apart their broken bodies, [and] dismembered them limb from limb, . . . greedily devouring livid writhing flesh."

But what is the evidence for Man the Hunter? Could smallish, upright creatures with relatively tiny canine teeth and flat nails instead of claws, and with no tools or weapons in the earliest millennia, really have been deadly predators? Is it possible that our ancestors lacked the spirit of cooperation and desire for social harmony? We have only two reliable sources to consult for clues: the fossilized remains of the human family tree and the behaviors and ecological relationships of our living primate relatives.

When we investigate those two sources, a different view of humankind emerges. First, consider the hominid fossils that have been discovered. Dart's first and most famous find, the cranium of an *Australopithecus* child who died over 2 million years ago (called the "Taung

Child" after the quarry in which the fossil was unearthed), has been reassessed by Lee Berger and Ron Clarke of the University of the Witwatersrand, in light of recent research on eagle predation. The same marks that occur on the Taung cranium are found on the remains of similarly sized African monkeys eaten today by crowned hawk eagles, known to clutch the monkeys' heads with their sharp talons.

C. K. Brain, a South African paleontologist like Dart, started the process of relabeling Man the Hunter as Man the Hunted when he slid the lower fangs of a fossil leopard into perfectly matched punctures in the skull of another australopithecine who lived between 1 million and 2 million years ago. The paradigm change initiated by Brain continues to stimulate reassessment of hominid fossils.

The idea that our direct ancestor *Homo erectus* practiced cannibalism was based on the gruesome disfigurement of faces and brain-stem areas in a cache of skulls a half-million years old, found in the Zhoukoudian cave, in China. How else to explain these strange manipulations except as relics of Man the Hunter? But studies over the past few years by Noel T. Boaz and Russell L. Ciochon—of the Ross University School of Medicine and the University of Iowa, respectively—show that extinct giant hyenas could have left the marks as they crunched their way into the brains of their hominid prey.

The list of our ancestors' fossils showing evidence of predation continues to grow. A 1.75-million-year-old hominid skull unearthed in the Republic of Georgia shows punctures from the fangs of a saber-toothed cat. Another skull, about 900,000 years old, found in Kenya, exhibits carnivore bite marks on the brow ridge. . . . Those and other fossils provide rock-hard proof that a host of large, fierce animals preyed on human ancestors.

It is equally clear that, outside the West, no small amount of predation occurs today on modern humans. Although we are not likely to see these facts in American newspaper headlines, each year 3,000 people in sub-Saharan Africa are eaten by crocodiles, and 1,500 Tibetans are killed by bears about the size of grizzlies. In one Indian state between 1988 and 1998, over 200 people were attacked by leopards; 612 people were killed by tigers in the Sundarbans delta of India and Bangladesh between 1975 and 1985. The carnivore zoologist Hans Kruuk, of the University of Aberdeen, studied death records in eastern Europe and concluded that wolf predation on humans is still a fact of life in the region, as it was until the 19th century in western European countries like France and Holland.

The fact that humans and their ancestors are and were tasty meals for a wide range of predators is further supported by research on nonhuman primate species still in

Whether hunters or hunted, early *Homo* was in competition with formidable adversaries like hyenas. Communication and cooperation helped early *Homo* avoid carnivores that saw them as prey.

existence. My study of predation found that 178 species of predatory animals included primates in their diets. The predators ranged from tiny but fierce birds to 500-pound crocodiles, with a little of almost everything in between: tigers, lions, leopards, jaguars, jackals, hyenas, genets, civets, mongooses, Komodo dragons, pythons, eagles, hawks, owls, and even toucans.

Our closest genetic relatives, chimpanzees and gorillas, are prey to humans and other species. Who would have thought that gorillas, weighing as much as 400 pounds, would end up as cat food? Yet Michael Fay, a researcher with the Wildlife Conservation Society and the National Geographic Society, has found the remnants of a gorilla in leopard feces in the Central African Republic. Despite their obvious intelligence and strength, chimpanzees often fall victim to leopards and lions. In the Tai Forest in the Ivory Coast, Christophe Boesch, of the Max Planck Institute, found that over 5 percent of the chimp population in his study was consumed by leopards annually. Takahiro Tsukahara reported, in a 1993 article, that 6 percent of the chimpanzees in the Mahale Mountains National Park of Tanzania may fall victim to lions.

The theory of Man the Hunter as our archetypal ancestor isn't supported by archaeological evidence, either. Lewis R. Binford, one of the most influential figures in archaeology during the last half of the 20th century, dissented from the hunting theory on the ground that reconstructions of early humans as hunters were based on a priori positions and not on the archaeological record. Artifacts that would verify controlled fire and weapons, in particular, are lacking until relatively recent dates.

And, of course, there's also the problem of how a small hominid could subdue a large herbivore. . . . Large-scale, systematic hunting of big herbivores for meat may not have occurred any earlier than 60,000 years ago—over 6 million years after the first hominids evolved.

What I am suggesting, then, is a less powerful, more ignominious beginning for our species. Consider this alternate image: smallish beings (adult females maybe weighing 60 pounds, with males a bit heavier), not overly analytical because their brain-to-body ratio was rather small, possessing the ability to stand and move upright, who basically spent millions of years as meat walking around on two legs. Rather than Man the Hunter, we may need to visualize ourselves as more like Giant Hyena Chow, or Protein on the Go.

Our species began as just one of many that had to be careful, to depend on other group members, and to communicate danger. We were quite simply small beasts within a large and complex ecosystem.

Is Man the Hunter a cultural construction of the West? Belief in a sinful, violent ancestor does fit nicely with Christian views of original sin and the necessity to be saved from our own awful, yet natural, desires. Other religions don't necessarily emphasize the ancient savage in the human past; indeed, modern-day hunter-gatherers, who have to live as part of nature, hold animistic beliefs in which humans are a part of the web of life, not superior creatures who dominate or ravage nature and one another.

Think of Man the Hunted, and you put a different face on our past. . . . We needed to live in groups (like most other primates) and work together to avoid predators. Thus an urge to cooperate can clearly be seen as a functional tool rather than a Pollyannaish nicety, and deadly competition among individuals or nations may be highly aberrant behavior, not hardwired survival techniques. The same is true of our destructive domination of the earth by technological toys gone mad.

Raymond Dart declared that "the loathsome cruelty of mankind to man . . . is explicable only in terms of his carnivorous, and cannibalistic origin." But if our origin was not carnivorous and cannibalistic, we have no excuse for loathsome behavior. Our earliest evolutionary history is not pushing us to be awful bullies. Instead, our millions of years as prey suggest that we should be able to take our heritage of cooperation and interdependency to make a brighter future for ourselves and our planet.

Adapted from Hart, D. (2006, April 21). Humans as prey. Chronicle of Higher Education Review, April 21, 2006. Reprinted by permission of Donna Hart.

Whether as hunters or as the hunted, brain expansion and tool use played a significant role in the evolution of the genus *Homo*. The advanced preparation for meat processing implied by the storing of stone tools, and the raw materials for making them, attest to considerable foresight, an ability to plan ahead, and cooperation among our ancestors.

Brain Size and Diet

From its appearance 2.5 million years ago, the genus *Homo* began a course of brain expansion that continued until about 200,000 years ago. By this point, brain size had approximately tripled, reaching the proportion of contemporary people. The cranial capacity of the largely plant-eating robust australopithecines ranged from 310 to 530 cubic centimeters (cc). Likewise the cranial capacity of the contemporaneous *Australopithecus sediba* was also small though they possessed some more *Homo*-like skeletal features. The cranial capacity of the earliest known meat-eater, *Homo habilis* from East Africa, ranged from 580 to 752 cc; whereas *Homo erectus*, who eventually hunted as well as scavenged for meat, possessed a cranial capacity of 775 to 1,225 cc.

Larger brains, in turn, required parallel improvements in diet. The energy demands of nerve tissue, of which the brain is made, are high—higher, in fact, than the demands of other types of tissue in the human body. Although a mere 2 percent of body weight, the brain accounts for about 20 to 25 percent of energy consumed at resting metabolic rate in modern human adults. One can meet the brain's energy demands on a vegetarian diet, but generally a given amount of plant food contains less energy compared to the same amount of meat. Large animals that live on plant foods, such as gorillas, spend all day munching on plants to maintain their large bodies. Meat-eaters, by contrast, have no need to eat so much, or so often. Consequently, meat-eating bipeds of both sexes may have had more leisure time to explore and manipulate their environment.

The archaeological record provides us with a tangible account of our ancestors' cultural abilities that corresponds with the simultaneous biological expansion of the brain. Toolmaking itself puts a premium on manual dexterity, precision, and fine manipulation (**Figure 7.4**). Stone tools provide evidence of handedness that bespeaks specialization and lateralization of the brain associated with language.

Beginning with the appearance of the genus *Homo* in Africa 2.5 million years ago, increasing brain size and cultural development each presumably acted to promote the other. The behaviors made possible by larger brains conferred advantages to large-brained individuals, increasing their reproductive success. Over time, large-brained individuals contributed more to successive generations, so that the population evolved to a larger-brained form. Natural selection for increases in learning ability thus led to the evolution of larger and more complex brains over about 2 million years.

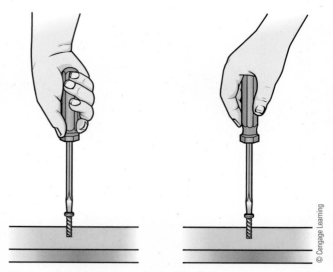

© Cengage Learning

Figure 7.4 **Power Versus Precision Grip** A power grip (*left*) utilizes more of the hand whereas the precision grip (*right*) relies on the fingers for control, requiring corresponding organizational changes in the brain. Though *A. sediba* possessed a small brain, their hand anatomy indicates they could execute a precision grip.

Though it preceded increases in brain size by several million years, bipedalism set the stage for the evolution of large brains and human culture. It freed the hands for activities such as toolmaking and carrying of resources or infants. Thus, the bipedal body plan opened new opportunities for change.

Homo erectus

In 1887, long before the discovery of *Australopithecus* and early *Homo* in Africa, the Dutch physician Eugène Dubois set out to find the missing link between humans and apes. The presence of the humanlike orangutan in the Dutch East Indies (now Indonesia) led him to start his search there. He joined the colonial service as an army surgeon and set sail.

When Dubois found fossilized remains consisting of a skullcap, a few teeth, and a thighbone at Trinil on the island of Java, the features seemed to him part ape, part human. The flat skull with its low forehead and enormous brow ridges resembled that of an ape; but at about 775 cubic centimeters it possessed a much larger cranial capacity, even though small by modern human standards. The femur, or thighbone, was clearly human in shape, and its proportions indicated the creature was a biped. Believing that his specimens represented the missing link and that the thighbone indicated this creature was bipedal, Dubois named his find *Pithecanthropus erectus* (from the Greek *pithekos* meaning "ape," *anthropus* meaning "man") or "erect ape-man." Dubois used the genus name proposed

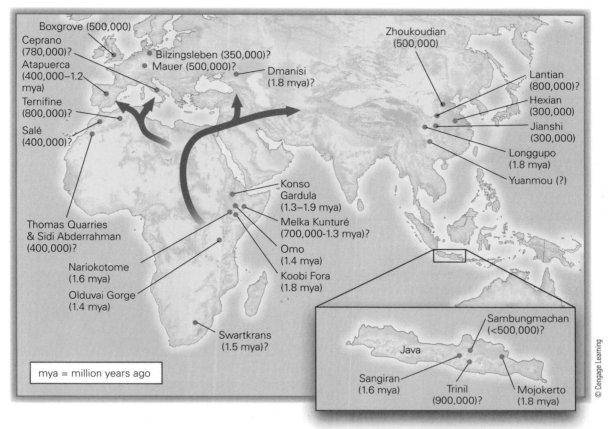

Figure 7.5 Map of *Homo erectus* Sites *Homo erectus* sites are shown here with their dates. The arrows indicated the proposed routes by which *Homo* spread from Africa to Eurasia. The question marks indicate the uncertain dating for particular sites. Splitters give some of these fossils different names.

in a paper by the German zoologist Ernst Haeckel, a strong supporter of Darwin's theory of evolution.

As with the Taung Child, the first australopithecine discovered in the 1920s, many in the scientific community ridiculed and criticized Dubois's claim, suggesting instead that the apelike skull and humanlike femur came from different individuals. Controversy surrounded these specimens throughout Dubois's lifetime. He eventually retreated from the controversy, keeping the fossil specimens stored safely under the floorboards of his dining room. Ultimately, the discovery of more fossils provided enough evidence to fully support his claim. In the 1950s, the Trinil skullcap and similar specimens from Indonesia and China were assigned to the species ***Homo erectus*** because they were more human than apelike.

Fossils of *Homo erectus*

Until about 1.8 million years ago, the bipedal primates inhabited only Africa. Both the first bipeds and the genus *Homo* originated there, and the first stone tools were also invented in Africa. But by the time of *H. erectus*, members

of the genus *Homo* had begun to spread far beyond their original homeland. Fossils of this species are now known from a number of localities not just in Africa, but in China, western Europe, Georgia (in the Caucasus Mountains), and India, as well as Java (**Figure 7.5**).

Although remains of *H. erectus* have been found in many different places in three continents, "lumpers," as discussed in the last chapter, emphasize that several shared characteristics unify them. However, because the fossil evidence also suggests some differences within and among populations of *H. erectus* inhabiting discrete regions of Africa, Asia, and Europe, "splitters" prefer to divide *H. erectus* into multiple distinct groups, limiting the species *H. erectus* only to the specimens from Asia. In this taxonomic scheme, *Homo ergaster* is used for African specimens from the early Pleistocene period that others describe as early *Homo erectus* (**Table 7.1**).

Homo erectus "Upright human." A species within the genus *Homo* first appearing just after 2 million years ago in Africa and ultimately spreading throughout the Old World.

TABLE 7.1

Alternate Species Designations for *Homo erectus* Fossils from Eurasia and Africa

Name	Explanation
Homo ergaster	Some paleoanthropologists feel that the large-brained successors to *H. habilis* from Africa and Asia are too different to be placed in the same species. Therefore, they use *H. ergaster* for the African specimens, saving *H. erectus* for the Asian fossils. Some paleoanthropologists place the recent discoveries from Dmanisi into this taxon.
Homo antecessor	This name was coined by "splitters" for the earliest *Homo* fossils from western Europe discovered in Spain; *antecessor* is Latin for "explorer" or "pioneer."
Homo heidelbergensis	Originally coined for the Mauer jaw (Mauer is not far from Heidelberg, Germany), this name is now used by some as a designation for all European fossils from about 500,000 years ago until the appearance of the Neandertals.

© Cengage Learning

Regardless of species designation, the fossil evidence indicates that beginning 1.8 million years ago these larger-brained members of the genus *Homo* lived not only in Africa but had also spread to Eurasia. Fossils dating to 1.8 million years old have been recovered from Dmanisi, Georgia, as well as from Mojokerto, Indonesia. A recently discovered and securely dated jaw from the Atapuerca site places the genus *Homo* in western Europe 1.2 million years ago (Carbonell et al., 2008). Many additional specimens have been found at a variety of sites in Europe and Asia.

Physical Characteristics of *Homo erectus*

Features of the skull best identify *H. erectus*. Cranial capacity ranges from 775 to 1,225 cc (average about 1,000 cc). Cranial capacity overlaps with both the nearly 2-million-year-old KNM ER 1470 skull from East Africa (752 cc) and the 1,000 to 2,000 cc range (average 1,300 cc) for modern human skulls (**Figure 7.6**).

The cranium itself has a low vault (height of the dome of the skull top), and the head is long and narrow. When viewed from behind, its width is greater than its height, with its greatest width at the base. The skulls of modern humans when similarly viewed are higher than they are wide, with the widest dimension in the region above the ears. The shape of the inside of *H. erectus'* braincase shows near-modern development of the brain, especially in the speech area. Although some anthropologists argue that the vocal apparatus was not adequate for speech, others claim that asymmetries of the brain suggest the same pattern of right-handedness with left cerebral dominance that, in modern peoples, is correlated with the capacity for language.

H. erectus possessed a massive brow ridge (**Figure 7.7**). When viewed from above, a marked constriction or "pinching in" of the skull can be seen just behind the brow ridge. *H. erectus* also possessed a sloping forehead and a receding chin. Powerful jaws with large teeth, a protruding mouth, and huge neck muscles added to *H. erectus'* generally rugged appearance. Nevertheless, the face, teeth, and jaws of this species are smaller than those of *H. habilis*.

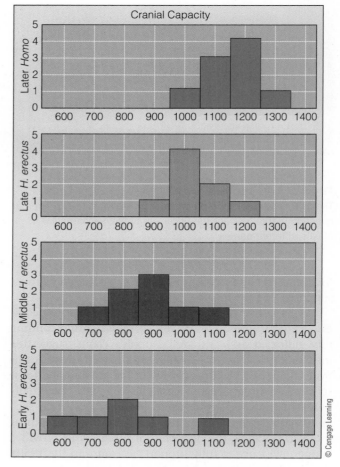

Figure 7.6 Ranges of Cranial Capacity Cranial capacity in *Homo erectus* increased over time, as illustrated by these bar graphs, shown in cubic centimeters. The cranial capacity of late *Homo erectus* overlaps with the range seen in contemporary humans.

© Cengage Learning

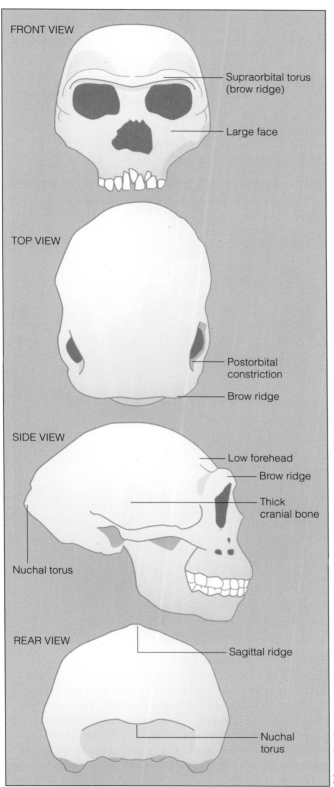

FRONT VIEW

Supraorbital torus (brow ridge)

Large face

TOP VIEW

Postorbital constriction

Brow ridge

SIDE VIEW

Low forehead

Brow ridge

Thick cranial bone

Nuchal torus

REAR VIEW

Sagittal ridge

Nuchal torus

© Cengage Learning

Figure 7.7 The Skull of *Homo erectus* Note the enormous brow ridge of the *Homo erectus* skull, along with the sloping forehead and receding chin.

Apart from its skull, the skeleton of *H. erectus* differs only subtly from that of modern humans. Its bodily proportions resemble ours but with more robust muscles. Stature seems to have increased from the smaller size typical of the australopithecines and the earliest members of the genus *Homo*. The best evidence for this comes from a remarkably well-preserved skeleton of an adolescent male from Lake Turkana in Kenya. Sexual dimorphism in body size also appears to have decreased in *H. erectus* compared to earlier bipeds. A reduction in sexual dimorphism may be due to the increase in female size as an adaptation to childbirth. The recent discovery of a capacious female *Homo erectus* pelvis in Gona, Ethiopia, supports this notion (Simpson et al., 2008), although the large pelvis of *Australopithecus sediba* indicates that this trait might predate brain enlargement (Kibii et al., 2011).

Relationship among *Homo erectus*, *Homo habilis*, and Other Proposed Fossil Groups

The smaller teeth and larger brains of *Homo erectus* seem to mark the continuation of a trend first seen in *Homo habilis*. Newly derived characteristics for *H. erectus* include increased body size, reduced sexual dimorphism, and a more "human" body form. Nonetheless, some skeletal resemblance to *H. habilis* exists, for example, in the shape of the thighbone, the long low vault and marked constriction of the skull behind the eyes, and the smaller brain size in the earliest *H. erectus* fossils.

Presumably *H. erectus* evolved from *H. habilis* fairly abruptly, around 1.8 to 1.9 million years ago. Although Asian *H. erectus* possesses thicker bones and more pronounced brow ridges compared to *H. erectus* from Africa, detailed anatomical comparisons indicate levels of variation approximating those seen in *H. sapiens* (Rightmire, 1998). That the 1.8-million-year-old specimens from Dmanisi, in the Caucasus—a region that lies along the overland route between Africa and Eurasia—show a mix of characteristics seen in African and Asian *H. erectus* populations supports the notion of a single species. The recent discovery of the small-brained 1.9-million-year-old "gracile" *Australopithecus sediba*, coexisting with these early members of the genus *Homo*, complicates this picture. Its discoverers proposed that derived aspects of its skeleton, such as a precision grip and a large pelvis, place it too as a contender for our direct ancestor.

Despite this complexity, paleoanthropologists state that throughout the globe, the most recent fossils possess a more derived appearance, and the oldest fossils (up to 1.8 million years old) display features reminiscent of earlier *H. habilis*. Indeed, distinguishing early *H. erectus* from late *H. habilis* is problematic—precisely what one would expect if one evolved from the other. We will next explore the *H. erectus* finds by region.

Homo erectus from Africa

Although our samples of *H. erectus* fossils from Asia remain among the best, Africa has yielded several important specimens. Fossils now assigned to this species were discovered there as long ago as 1933, but the better-known finds have been made since 1960, at Olduvai Gorge and at Lake Turkana, Kenya. These include the most complete *H. erectus* skeleton ever found, the Nariokotome Boy, an adolescent who died 1.6 million years ago (**Figure 7.8**). Paleoanthropologists infer the age of this specimen from his teeth (the 12-year molars are fully erupted) and the stage of maturity of the bones. With a height of about 5 feet 3 inches at adolescence, the Nariokotome Boy was expected to attain a stature of about 6 feet by adulthood.

Recently, paleoanthropologists discovered a trail of *H. erectus* footprints, like those from Laetoli, along Lake Turkana. These footprints support the estimates of *H. erectus* body mass (weight) and stature made from more fragmentary remains.

Homo erectus Entering Eurasia

The site of Dmanisi in the Caucasus Mountains of Georgia preserves evidence of the spread of *H. erectus* from Africa into Eurasia. Dmanisi was first excavated as an archaeological site because of its importance as a crossroads for the caravan routes of ancient Armenia, Persia, and Byzantium. When Oldowan stone tools were found at this site in 1984, the hunt for fossil specimens began there as well.

Since then, paleoanthropologists have recovered some remarkable remains that can be accurately dated to 1.8 million years ago through past volcanic activity in the region. In 1999, two well-preserved skulls, one with a partial face, were discovered. Thus, the early habitation of this region by members of the genus *Homo* is supported at Dmanisi with archaeological, anatomical, and geological evidence.

Because rising sea levels since the Pleistocene make it impossible for paleoanthropologists to document coastal routes for the spread of *Homo* from Africa to Eurasia, the evidence from Georgia constitutes the only direct evidence of the spread of evolving humans from Africa to Europe and to Asia.

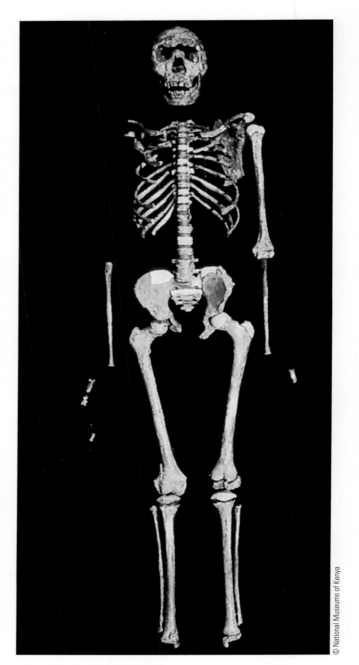

Figure 7.8 Nariokotome Boy One of the oldest and certainly one of the most complete *Homo erectus* fossils is the Nariokotome Boy from Lake Turkana, Kenya. How can scientists determine the age and sex of this specimen? Age comes from an examination of the degree to which bones have finished their growth and the emergence of the molar teeth; sex is determined from the shape of the pelvis, due to adaptations in the female pelvis that accommodate childbirth. Even though these remains come from a tall adolescent boy, this pelvis has been used to reconstruct theories about the evolution of human birth.

Homo erectus from Indonesia

Although it took many years for the skullcap and thighbone discovered by Dubois to be accepted as part of the human line, these specimens are now considered typical

Asian *H. erectus*. In the 1930s, a number of additional *H. erectus* fossils were discovered by German-Dutch paleoanthropologist G. H. R. von Königswald at Sangiran, Java (see Figure 7.5). Von Königswald found a small skull that fluorine analysis and (later) potassium-argon dating assigned to the early Pleistocene. This indicated that these fossils were older than the Trinil skullcap found by Dubois, dating to approximately 500,000 to 700,000 years ago.

Since 1960, additional fossils have been found in Java, and we now have remains of around forty individuals. A long continuity of *H. erectus* populations in Southeast Asia is indicated, from 500,000 to 1.8 million years ago. Interestingly, the teeth and jaws of some of the earliest Javanese fossils are in many ways quite similar to those of *H. habilis*. When considering the spread of *H. erectus* to Java, it is important to note that in the past, lower sea levels resulted in a continuous landmass between most of Indonesia and the Asian continent.

Homo erectus from China

In the mid-1920s a combination of serendipity and good anatomical knowledge led to the discovery of a site in China rich with fossils, now known as *H. erectus*. Davidson Black, a Canadian anatomist teaching at Peking Union Medical College, traveled to this site after purchasing a few ancient humanlike teeth offered for their medicinal properties from a Beijing drugstore. He set out for the nearby countryside to discover the "owner" of the teeth and perhaps a species of early human ancestor. At a place called Dragon Bone Hill in Zhoukoudian, 48 kilometers (30 miles) from Beijing (see Figure 7.5), on the day before closing camp at the end of his first year of excavation, he found one molar tooth. Subsequently, Chinese paleoanthropologist W. C. Pei, who worked closely with Black, found a skull encased in limestone.

Between 1929 and 1934, the year of his death from silicosis—a lung disease caused by exposure to silica particles in the cave—Black labored along with Pei and French Jesuit paleontologist Pierre Teilhard de Chardin in the fossil-rich deposits of Zhoukoudian, uncovering fragment after fragment of ancient remains. On the basis of the anatomy of that first molar tooth, Black

named these fossils *Sinanthropus pekinensis,* or "Chinese human of Peking" (Beijing), called "Peking Man" for short at the time. Today, paleoanthropologists consider these fossils an East Asian representative of *H. erectus*.

After Black's death, the Rockefeller Foundation sent Franz Weidenreich, a German anatomist and paleoanthropologist, to China to continue this work. As a Jew in Nazi Germany in the early 1930s, Weidenreich had sought refuge in the United States. By 1938, he and his colleagues recovered the remains of more than forty individuals, over half of them women and children, from the limestone deposits of Zhoukoudian. Fragmentary fossil remains included teeth, jawbones, and incomplete skulls. Weidenreich reconstructed a spectacular composite specimen from the most complete remains.

However, World War II (1939–1945) brought a halt to the digging, and the original Zhoukoudian specimens were lost during the Japanese occupation of China. The fossils had been carefully packed by Weidenreich and his team and placed with the U.S. Marines, but in the chaos of war, these precious fossils disappeared. Then, in 2012, an international team of paleoanthropologists followed the trail of the missing fossils, guided by information from a retired Marine, Richard Bowen Sr., who was stationed at the camp where the fossils were last seen. The potential location of the remains was pinpointed to a parking lot in the industrial city of Qinhuangdao (**Figure 7.9**).

Figure 7.9 Missing Peking Man Retired U.S. Marine Richard M. Bowen has led paleoanthropologists to think that the lost Peking Man fossils may be lying underneath this parking lot in Qinhuangdao, China. One of the last American soldiers to leave China at the end of World War II, Bowen vividly recalled finding a box of bones while digging a foxhole and reburying them when his small company was surrounded by the Communist 8th Route Army. After trying to pass this information on to Chinese authorities, Bowen's son Paul contacted paleoanthropologist Lee Berger, who has mobilized an investigation.

Courtesy of Professor Lee Berger

Paleoanthropologists are working with Chinese Cultural Heritage authorities to excavate the remains.

Fortunately, Weidenreich had made superb casts of most of the Zhoukoudian fossil specimens and sent them to the United States before leaving the site (**Figure 7.10**). After the war, other specimens of *H. erectus* were discovered in China, at Zhoukoudian and a number of other localities. The oldest skull is about 700,000 to 800,000 years old and comes from Lantian in central China. A fragment of a lower jaw from a cave in south-central China (Longgupo) is as old as the oldest Indonesian fossils. Like some of their Indonesian contemporaries, this Chinese fossil resembles African *H. habilis*. In contrast to these ancient remains, the original Zhoukoudian fossils appear to date between 300,000 and 600,000 years ago.

Although the two populations overlap in time, the majority of the Chinese fossils are, on the whole, slightly younger than those from Indonesia. Not surprisingly, Chinese *H. erectus* is less ancestral in appearance with an average cranial capacity of about 1,000 cc, compared to 900 cc for Indonesian *H. erectus*. The smaller teeth and short jaw of the Chinese fossil specimens provide further evidence of their more derived status.

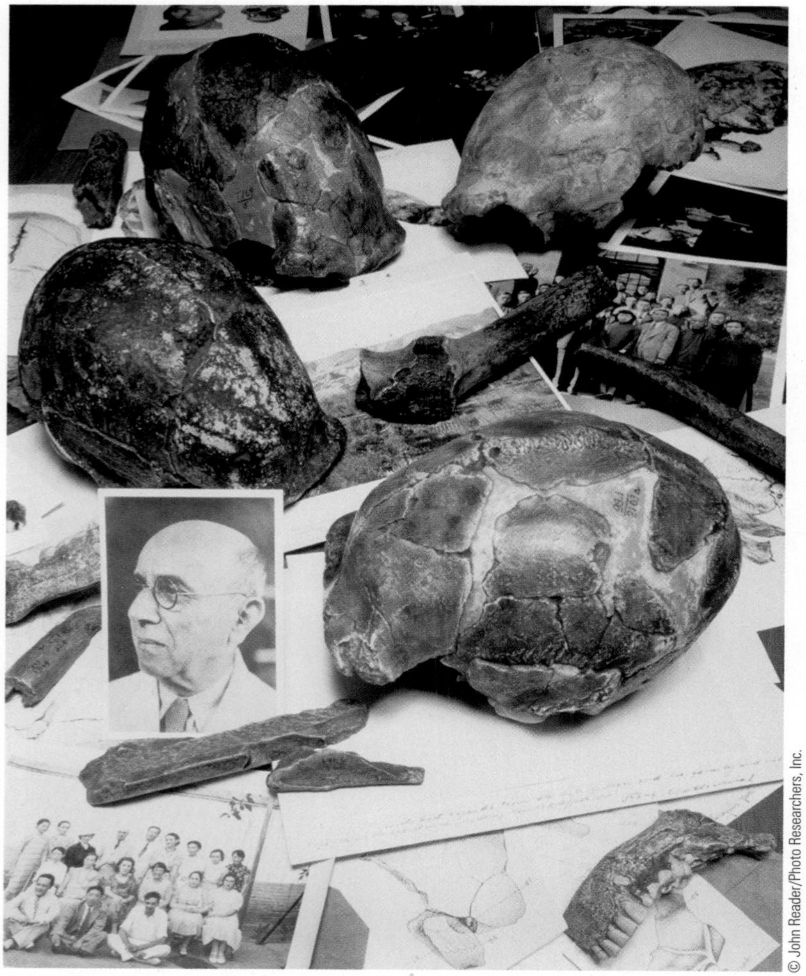

Homo erectus from Western Europe

Although the fossil evidence indicates the presence of the genus *Homo* on the Eurasian landmass 1.8 million years ago (at Dmanisi, Georgia), the fossil evidence from western Europe begins at about 1.2 million years ago with the new jawbone discovery at the Sima del Elefante ("Elephant's Pit") site in the Sierra de Atapuerca region of north-central Spain. The nearby Grand Dolina site has yielded fragments of four individuals dating to 1.2 million years ago. A skull from Ceprano in Italy is thought to be approximately the same age if not older. Again, whether one places these specimens into the inclusive but varied species *H. erectus* or into several separate species differs according to the approach taken by paleoanthropologists with regard to the fossil record (see Table 7.1).

Some other fossils attributable to *H. erectus*—such as a robust shinbone from Boxgrove, England, and a large lower jaw from Mauer, Germany—are close to half a million years old. The jaw came from a skull that was wide at the base, typical of *H. erectus*. These remains resemble *H. erectus* material from North Africa from the same time period. This observation and the fact that the earliest evidence of the genus *Homo* in western Europe comes from Spain and Italy suggest continued gene flow between this region and northern Africa (Balter, 2001). At the time, a mere 6 or 7 kilometers separated Gibraltar from Morocco (compared to 13 kilometers today), and islands dotted the straits from Tunisia to Sicily. The only direct land connection between Africa and Eurasia is through the Middle East and into Turkey and the Caucasus.

© John Reader/Photo Researchers, Inc.

Figure 7.10 Weidenreich and Zhoukoudian The original *Homo erectus* fossils from Zhoukoudian had been packed for shipment to the United States for safekeeping during World War II, but they mysteriously disappeared. Fortunately, Weidenreich had made excellent casts of the specimens and provided detailed anatomical descriptions before the fossils were lost during the war.

The Culture of Homo erectus

As one might expect given its larger brain, *Homo erectus* outstripped its predecessors in cultural ability. *H. erectus* refined the technology of stone toolmaking and at some point began to use fire for light, protection, warmth, and cooking, though precisely when is still a matter for debate. Indirect evidence indicates that the organizational and planning abilities of *H. erectus*, or at least the later ones, exceeded those of their predecessors.

Acheulean Tool Tradition

Implements of the **Acheulean tool tradition** accompany the remains of *H. erectus* in Africa, Europe, and southwestern Asia. Named for the stone tools first identified at St. Acheul, France, the signature piece of this tradition is the hand-axe: a teardrop-shaped tool pointed at one end with a sharp cutting edge all around (**Figure 7.11**).

The earliest hand-axes, from East Africa, date to about 1.6 million years ago. Those found in Europe are no older than about 500,000 years. At the same time that hand-axes appeared, archaeological sites in Europe became dramatically more common. This suggests an influx of individuals bringing Acheulean technology with them, implying continued gene flow into Europe. Because the spread of the genus *Homo* from Africa into Asia took place before the invention of the hand-axe, different forms of tools developed in East Asia.

Evidence from Olduvai Gorge indicates that the Acheulean grew out of the Oldowan tradition: In lower strata, chopper tools were found along with remains of *H. habilis*; above these, the first crude hand-axes intermingle with chopper tools; and higher strata contain more finished-looking Acheulean hand-axes along with *H. erectus* remains.

Early Acheulean tools represent a significant step beyond the generalized cutting, chopping, and scraping

tools of the Oldowan tradition. The original form, size, and mechanical properties of raw materials largely controlled the shapes of Oldowan tools. The shapes of hand-axes and some other Acheulean tools, by contrast, were more standardized, apparently reflecting arbitrary preconceived designs imposed upon a diverse range of raw materials (Ambrose, 2001). Overall, Acheulean toolmakers could produce a sharper point and a more regular and larger cutting edge from the same amount of stone.

During this part of the Lower Paleolithic, toolkits began to diversify. Besides hand-axes, *H. erectus* used tools that functioned as cleavers (hand-axes with a straight, sharp edge where the point would otherwise be), picks and knives (variants of the hand-axe form), and flake tools (generally smaller tools made by hitting a flint core with a hammerstone, thus knocking off flakes with sharp edges). Many flake tools were byproducts of hand-axe and cleaver manufacture. Their sharp edges made them useful as is, but many were retouched (modified again by ancient flint-knappers) to make points, scrapers, borers, and other sorts of tools.

Toolkits diversified regionally during this period. In northern and eastern Europe, the archaeological record contains reduced numbers of hand-axes compared to Africa and southwestern Asia. People relied on simple flaked choppers, a wide variety of unstandardized flakes, and supplementary tools made of bone, antler, and wood. In eastern Asia, by contrast, people developed a variety of choppers, scrapers, points, and burins (chisel-like tools) different from those in southwestern Asia, Europe, and Africa.

Besides direct percussion, anvil (striking the raw material against a stationary stone) and bipolar percussion (holding the raw material against an anvil, but striking it at the same time with a hammerstone) other methods were used in tool manufacture. Although tens of thousands of stone tools have been found with *H. erectus* remains at Zhoukoudian, stone implements are not at all common in Southeast Asia. Here, favored materials likely were ones that do not preserve well, such as bamboo (**Figure 7.12**) and other local woods, from which excellent knives, scrapers, and so on can be made.

Use of Fire

With *H. erectus* came the first evidence of ancestral populations living outside the Old World tropics. Controlled use of fire allowed early humans to move successfully into regions where winter temperatures regularly dropped to temperate climate levels—as they must have in northern China, the mountain highlands of Central Asia, and most of Europe. Members of the genus *Homo* spread to these colder regions some 780,000 years ago.

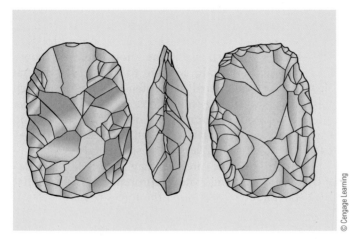

© Cengage Learning

Figure 7.11 Acheulean Hand-Axe To fabricate this Acheulean hand-axe from flint, the toolmaker imposed a standardized arbitrary form on the naturally occurring raw material. The crafter made many separate strikes to create the sharp edge visible in profile.

Acheulean tool tradition The prevalent style of stone tools associated with *Homo erectus* remains and represented by the hand-axe.

rocks, more readily available in the shelter, cannot be used for hearths because, when burned, limestone produces quicklime, a caustic substance that causes itching and burning skin rashes. The hearth is associated with bones, showing clear evidence of cut marks from butchering as well as burning.

Evidence from Swartkrans in South Africa indicates that *H. erectus* may have been using fire even earlier. Here, deposits dated to between 1 and 1.3 million years ago contain bones that had been heated to temperatures far in excess of what one would expect as the result of natural fires. Furthermore, the burned bones at Swartkrans do not occur in older, deeper deposits. If these fires were natural, all archaeological layers would contain burned bones. Because the bones indicate heating to such high temperatures that any meat on them would have been inedible, paleoanthropologists suggest that the Swartkrans fires functioned as protection from predators.

H. erectus may have used fire not just for protection from animals out in the open but also to frighten away cave-dwelling predators allowing the fire users to live in the caves themselves. In addition, fire provided warmth and light in these otherwise cold and dark habitations. Although earlier bipeds likely used caves as part of their temperature regulation strategy as has been observed in nonhuman primates (Barrett et al., 2004), controlled use of fire expands the ability to regulate temperature considerably.

Fire may have assisted in the quest for food as well. In the long, cold winters of places like central Europe and China, food would have been hard to come by. Edible plants were unavailable, and the large herds of animals dispersed and migrated. Our ancestors may have searched out the frozen carcasses of animals that had died naturally in the late fall and winter, using long wooden probes to locate them beneath the snow, wooden scoops to dig them out, and fire to thaw them so that they could be butchered and eaten. Furthermore, such fire-assisted scavenging would have made available meat and hides of woolly mammoths, woolly rhinoceroses, and bison, which were probably beyond the ability of *H. erectus* to kill, at least until late in the species' career.

Using fire to thaw carcasses may have led to the idea of cooking food. Some paleoanthropologists suggest that this behavioral change altered the forces of natural selection, which previously favored individuals with heavy jaws and large, sharp teeth (tough raw foods require more chewing), favoring instead further reduction in tooth size along with supportive facial structure.

Alternatively, the reduction of tooth size and supporting structure may have occurred outside the context of adaptation. For example, the genetic changes responsible

© Gunter Marx/Alamy

Figure 7.12 Bamboo Construction In regions where bamboo is readily available for the fabrication of effective tools, the same stone tool industries might not have developed. Here, contemporary Chinese construction workers erecting a bamboo scaffolding demonstrate this material's strength and versatility.

The 700,000-year-old Kao Poh Nam rock shelter in Thailand provides compelling evidence for deliberate, controlled use of fire. Here, a roughly circular arrangement of fire-cracked basalt cobbles was discovered in association with artifacts and animal bones. Because basalt rocks are not native to the rock shelter and are quite heavy, they were likely carried in by *H. erectus*. Limestone

© Cengage Learning

for increasing brain size may also have caused a reduction in tooth size as a secondary effect. The discovery of a genetic mutation, shared by all humans but absent in apes, that acts to prevent growth of powerful jaw muscles supports this hypothesis. Without heavy jaw muscles attached to the outside of the braincase, a significant constraint to brain growth was removed. In other words, humans may have developed large brains as an accidental byproduct of jaw-size reduction (Stedman et al., 2004).

Soft foods may have relaxed selection for massive jaws. But cooking does more than soften food. It detoxifies a number of otherwise poisonous plants; alters digestion-inhibiting substances so that important vitamins, minerals, and proteins can be absorbed while in the gut, rather than just passing through it unused; and makes high-energy complex carbohydrates like starch digestible. Cooking increased the nutritional resources available to humans and made them more secure.

The partial predigestion of food by cooking also may have allowed a reduction in the size of the digestive tract. Because paleoanthropologists do not have the benefit of fossilized digestive tracts to establish this biological change, they turn to comparative anatomy of the living hominoids. Despite its overall similarity of form to those of apes, contemporary humans possess substantially smaller digestive tracts. This reduced gut takes less energy to operate, thereby easing the competing energy demands of a larger brain.

Like tools, then, fire gave people more control over their environment. Fire modified the natural succession of day and night, perhaps encouraging *H. erectus* to stay up after dark to review the day's events and plan the next day's activities. Though we cannot know whether *H. erectus* enjoyed socializing and planning around campfires at night, we do have evidence at least of some planning behavior. The existence of populations in temperate climates implies planning because survival depended upon the ability to anticipate the needs of the winter season by advance preparation for the cold.

Although considerable variation exists, studies of modern humans indicate that most people can remain reasonably comfortable down to 50 degrees Fahrenheit (10 degrees Celsius) with minimal clothing as long as they keep active. Below that temperature, hands and feet cool to the point of pain. Clothing, like many other aspects of material culture, does not fossilize, so we have no direct evidence of the kind of clothing worn by *H. erectus*. We know only that colder climates required more sophisticated clothing. In short, when our human ancestors learned to use fire to warm and protect themselves and to cook their food, they dramatically increased their geographic range and nutritional options.

Hunting

Sites such as 400,000-year-old Ambrona and Torralba in Spain provide evidence that *Homo erectus* developed the ability to organize in order to hunt large animals.

The ancient swamp at Torralba contains dismembered scattered remains of several elephants, horses, red deer, wild oxen, and rhinoceroses. That no natural geologic process can account for this find indicates that these animals did not accidentally get mired in a swamp where they simply died and decayed. In fact, the bones are closely associated with a variety of stone tools—a few thousand of them. Furthermore, the site contains very little evidence of carnivorous animal activity and none at all for the really big carnivores. Clearly, the genus *Homo* was involved—not just in butchering the animals but evidently in killing them as well.

It appears that the animals were actually driven into the swamp so that they could be easily killed. The remains of charcoal and carbon, widely but thinly scattered in the vicinity, raise the possibility that grassfires were used to drive the animals into the swamp. This evidence indicates more than opportunistic scavenging. Not only was *H. erectus* able to hunt, but the evidence implies considerable organizational and communicative skills as well.

Other Evidence of Complex Thought

Other evidence of *H. erectus'* capabilities comes from the small island of Flores in Indonesia. Flores lies east of a deepwater strait that throughout the Pleistocene acted as a barrier to animals to and from Southeast Asia. Even at times of lowered sea levels, getting to Flores required crossing open water: at minimum 25 kilometers from Bali to Sumbawa, with an additional 19 kilometers to Flores. The presence of 800,000-year-old stone tools on Flores indicates that somehow our ancestors navigated across the deep, fast-moving water.

Flores is also the site where the "hobbit" species, *Homo floresensis* was discovered in 2003. Tiny in stature and possessing many ancestral characteristics, the Flores fossils date from 13,000 years ago to 73,000 years ago. Some paleoanthropologists have proposed that this dwarf species evolved directly from *H. erectus*, who arrived on the island with the aforementioned stone tools. In this model, the hominins then reduced in size, over generations, a phenomenon that can occur in isolated island populations.

Increased standardization and refinement of Acheulean hand-axes over time also provides evidence for a developing symbolic life. Moreover, deliberately marked objects of stone, bone, and ivory appear in Acheulean contexts at several sites in Europe. These include several objects from Bilzingsleben, Germany—among them a mastodon bone with a series of regular lines that appear to have been deliberately engraved. Similarly, the world's oldest known rock carvings are associated with Acheulean tools in a cave in India. Though a far cry from the later Upper Paleolithic cave art of France and Spain, these Paleolithic artifacts have no obvious utility or model in the natural world. Archaeologists have argued that the use of such symbolic images requires some sort of spoken language, not only to assign meaning to the images but to maintain the tradition they seem to represent.

The Question of Language

Though we have no definitive evidence of *Homo erectus'* linguistic abilities, indications of a developing symbolic life, as well as the need to plan for seasonal changes and to coordinate hunting activities (and cross stretches of open water), imply improving linguistic competence. In addition, the observation that right-handed individuals made the majority of stone tools supports the theory of the increased specialization and lateralization of the evolving brain. In other primates and most mammals, the right and left sides of the brain duplicate each other's function; these animals use the right and left sides of their bodies equally and interchangeably. In humans, the emergence of handedness seems closely linked both developmentally (at about the age of 1 year) and evolutionarily with the appearance of language. Thus, evidence of handedness in Lower Paleolithic tools indicates that the kind of brain specialization required for language was well under way (**Figure 7.13**).

The fossil record provides evidence for evolving humans' linguistic capability. The vocal tract and brain of *H. erectus* are intermediate between those of *H. sapiens* and earlier *Australopithecus*. The **hypoglossal canal**—the passageway through the skull that accommodates the nerve that controls tongue movement, which is so important for spoken language—has taken on the characteristic large size seen in contemporary humans in fossil skulls dated to 500,000 years ago (**Figure 7.14**).

Possibly, a changeover from reliance on gestural to spoken language was a driving force in these evolutionary changes. The reduction of tooth and jaw size, facilitating the ability to articulate speech sounds, may have also played a role. From an evolutionary standpoint, spoken language may provide some advantages over a gestural

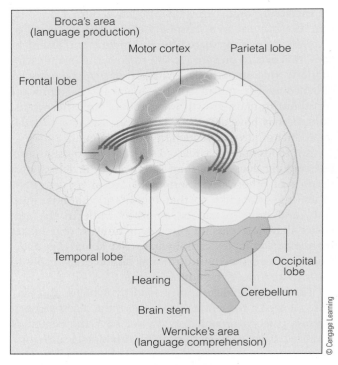

Figure 7.13 Language Areas of the Brain Language areas in the left side of the brain. The right side of the human brain has different specialized functions.

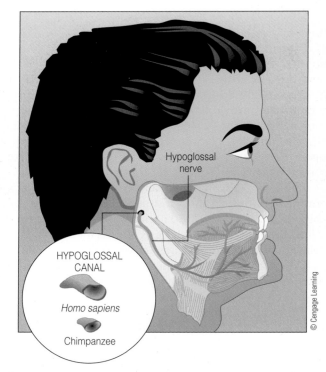

Figure 7.14 The Hypoglossal Canal The size of the hypoglossal canal is much larger in humans than in chimpanzees. The nerve that passes through this canal controls tongue movement, and complex tongue movements are involved in spoken language. All members of the genus *Homo* after about 500,000 years ago have an enlarged hypoglossal canal.

---

hypoglossal canal The opening in the skull that accommodates the tongue-controlling hypoglossal nerve.

one. Individuals do not have to stop whatever they are doing with their hands to "talk" (useful to a species increasingly dependent on tool use), and it is possible to communicate in the dark, past opaque objects, or among people whose gaze is concentrated on something else (potential prey, for example).

With *H. erectus*, then, we find a clearer manifestation of the interplay among cultural, physical, and environmental factors than ever before. However slowly, social organization, technology, and communication developed in tandem with an increase in brain size and complexity. In fact, the cranial capacity of late *H. erectus* is 31 percent greater than the mean for early *H. erectus*, a rate of increase more rapid than the average fossil vertebrate rate.

Archaic *Homo sapiens* and the Appearance of Modern-Sized Brains

Fossils from a number of sites in Africa, Asia, and Europe, dated to between 200,000 and 400,000 years ago, indicate that by this time cranial capacity reached modern proportions. Most fossil finds consist of parts of one or a very few individuals. The fossils from Sierra de Atapuerca in northern Spain provide the only evidence of a Paleolithic population (Figure 7.15). Dated to about 400,000 years ago (Parés et al., 2000), the remains of at least twenty-eight individuals of both sexes and of various ages were deliberately dumped (after defleshing their skulls) by their contemporaries into a deep cave shaft known today as Sima de los Huesos ("Pit of the Bones"). The presence of animal bones in the same pit with humans raises the possibility that early humans simply used the site as a dump. Alternatively, the treatment of the dead at Atapuerca may have involved ritual activity that presaged burial of the dead, a practice that became common after 100,000 years ago.

As with any population, this one displays a significant degree of variation. Cranial capacity, for example,

ranges from 1,125 to 1,390 cc, overlapping the upper end of the range for *H. erectus* and the average size of *H. sapiens* (1,300 cc). Overall, the bones display a mix of features, some typical of *H. erectus*, others of *H. sapiens*, including some incipient Neandertal characteristics. Despite this variation, the sample appears to show no more sexual dimorphism than displayed by modern humans.

Other remains from Africa and Europe dating from 200,000 to 400,000 years ago have shown a combination of *H. erectus* and *H. sapiens* features. Some—such as skulls from Ndutu in Tanzania, Swanscombe (England),

© Javier Trueba/Madrid Scientific Films

Figure 7.15 Sima de los Huesos These fossils from Sima de los Huesos ("Pit of the Bones"), Sierra de Atapuerca, Spain, are the best collection of *Homo* fossils from a single site. Although the remains possess cranial capacities overlapping with the average size of contemporary humans, the scientists who discovered them place them in the species *Homo antecessor*. These fossils fit into the complex period of our evolutionary history when brain size and cultural capability began to separate.

and Steinheim (Germany)—have been classified as *H. sapiens*, while others—from Arago (France), Bilzingsleben (Germany), Petralona (Greece), and several African sites—have been classified as *H. erectus*. Yet all have cranial capacities that fit within the range exhibited by the Sima de los Huesos skulls, which are classified as *H. antecessor* (see Table 7.1).

Comparisons of these skulls to those of living people or to *H. erectus* reflect their transitional nature. The Swanscombe and Steinheim skulls are large and robust, with their maximum breadth lower on the skull, more prominent brow ridges, larger faces, and bigger teeth. Similarly, the face of the Petralona skull from Greece resembles the later European Neandertals, whereas the back of the skull looks like *H. erectus*. Conversely, a skull from Salé in Morocco, which had a rather small brain for *H. sapiens* (930–960 cc), looks surprisingly modern from the back. Finally, various jaws from France and Morocco (in northern Africa) seem to combine features of *H. erectus* with those of the Neandertals. A similar situation exists in East Asia, where skulls from several sites in China exhibit the same mix of *H. erectus* and *H. sapiens* characteristics.

"Lumpers" suggest that calling some of these early humans "late *H. erectus*" or "early *H. sapiens*" (or any of the other proposed species names within the genus *Homo*) serves no useful purpose and merely obscures their transitional status. They tend to place these fossils in the **archaic *Homo sapiens*** category, a group that reflects both their large brain size and the ancestral features on the skull. "Splitters" use a series of discrete names for specimens from this period that take into account some of the geographic and morphologic variation exhibited by these fossils. Both approaches reflect their respective statements about evolutionary relationships among fossil groups.

Levalloisian Technique

With the appearance of large-brained members of the genus *Homo*, the pace of cultural change accelerated. These ancestors invented a new method of flake manufacture: the **Levalloisian technique**, so named for the French site where such tools were first excavated. Sites in Africa, Europe, southwestern Asia, and even China have yielded flake tools produced by this technique along with Acheulean tools. In China, the technique could represent a case of independent invention, or it could indicate the spread of ideas from one part of the inhabited world to another.

archaic *Homo sapiens* A loosely defined group within the genus *Homo* that "lumpers" use for fossils with the combination of large brain size and ancestral features on the skull.

Levalloisian technique Toolmaking technique by which three or four long triangular flakes are detached from a specially prepared core; developed by members of the genus *Homo* transitional from *H. erectus* to *H. sapiens*.

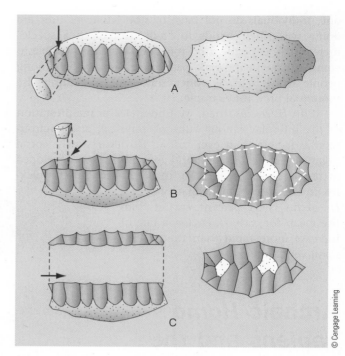

© Cengage Learning

Figure 7.16 The Levalloisian Technique These drawings show side (*left*) and top (*right*) views of the steps in the Levalloisian technique. Arrows indicate where the toolmaker strikes the core with another stone in order to shape it. Drawing A shows the preparatory flaking of the stone core; B, the same on the top surface of that core (the dotted line indicates what will ultimately become a tool; and C, the final step of detaching a flake tool of a size and shape predetermined by the preceding steps.

The Levalloisian technique initially involves preparing a core by removing small flakes over the stone's surface. Following this, the toolmaker sets up a platform by striking a crosswise blow at one end of the core of stone (**Figure 7.16**). Striking the platform removes three or four long flakes, whose size and shape have been predetermined by the preceding preparation, leaving behind a core nodule that looks like a tortoise shell and from which large preshaped flake tools can be removed. This method produces a longer edge for the same amount of flint than the previous ones used by evolving humans. It also produces sharper edges in less time.

Other Cultural Innovations

At about the same time the Levalloisian technique developed, our ancestors invented hafting—the fastening of small stone bifaces and flakes to handles of wood (**Figure 7.17**). Hafting led to the development of knives and more complex spears. Unlike the older handheld tools made simply by reduction (flaking of stone or working of wood), these new composite tools involved three components: a handle or shaft, a stone insert, and the materials to bind them. Manufacture involved planned sequences of actions that could be performed at different times and places.

© PhotoDisc/Getty Images

Figure 7.17 Hafting The practice of hafting, the fastening of small stone bifaces and flakes to handles of wood, was a major technological advance appearing in the archaeological record at about the same time as the invention of the Levalloisian technique.

With this new technology, regional stylistic and technological variants become more marked in the archaeological record, suggesting the emergence of distinct cultural traditions and culture areas. At the same time, the proportions of raw materials procured from faraway sources increased; whereas sources of stone for Acheulean tools were rarely more than 20 kilometers (12 miles) away, Levalloisian tools are found up to 320 kilometers (200 miles) from the sources of their stone (Ambrose, 2001).

The use of yellow and red pigments of iron oxide, called ochre, a development first identified in Africa, became especially common by 130,000 years ago. The use of ochre may signal a rise in ritual activity, similar to the deliberate placement of the human remains in the Sima de los Huesos, Atapuerca, already noted. The use of red ochre in ancient burials may relate to its similarity to the color of blood as a powerful symbol of life.

The Neandertals

To many outside the field of anthropology, **Neandertals** are the quintessential cavemen, portrayed by imaginative cartoonists as a slant-headed, stooped, dimwitted individuals clad in animal skins and carrying a big club as they plod across the prehistoric landscape, perhaps dragging an unwilling female or a dead saber-toothed tiger. The stereotype has been perpetuated in novels and film. The popular image of Neandertals as brutish and incapable of spoken language, much less abstract or innovative thinking, may, in turn, have influenced the interpretation of the fossil and archaeological evidence. One of the most contentious issues in paleoanthropology is the theory that the Neandertals represent an inferior side branch of human evolution that went extinct following the appearance of modern humans. The alternative view is that descendants of the Neandertals walk the earth today, and you may be one of them.

Neandertals were an extremely muscular people living from approximately 30,000 to 125,000 years ago in Europe, and southwestern and central Asia. Although having brains larger than the modern average size, Neandertals possessed faces distinctively different from those of modern humans. Their large noses and teeth projected forward. They had prominent bony brow ridges over their eyes. On the back of their skull, there was a bunlike bony mass for attachment of powerful neck muscles. These features, not in line with classic forms of Western beauty, may have contributed to the depiction of Neandertals as brutes. Their rude reputation may also derive from the timing of their discovery.

One of the first Neandertals was found in a cave in the Neander Valley (*tal* means "valley" in German, *thal* was the old German spelling) near Düsseldorf, Germany, in 1856. This was well before scientific theories to account for human evolution had gained acceptance. (Darwin published *On the Origins of Species* three years later in 1859.)

Initially, experts were at a loss as to what to make of this discovery. Examination of the fossil skull, a few ribs, and some limb bones revealed that the individual was a human being, but it did not look "normal." Some people believed the bones were those of a sickly and deformed contemporary. Others thought the skeleton belonged to a soldier who had succumbed to "water on the brain" during the Napoleonic Wars earlier that century. One prominent anatomist thought the remains were those of an idiot suffering from malnutrition, whose violent temper

Neandertals A distinct group within the genus *Homo* inhabiting Europe and southwestern Asia from approximately 30,000 to 125,000 years ago.

VISUAL COUNTERPOINT

Figure 7.18 **Neandertal Depiction** When Neandertals are portrayed as brutes as they were in this sketch from the early 20th century (*left*), based on the La Chapelle-aux-Saints skeleton, it is difficult to welcome them into our human ancestry. But when reconstructions portray them in a positive light, Neandertal ancestry seems more palatable. The image on the right depicts the reconstruction of Neandertal remains from the Shanidar site located in the Kurdistan region of today's Iraq. Excavated between 1957 and 1961, evidence from this site includes the deliberate burial of nine individuals. Ochre and pollen associated with the skeletons led to the nickname the "original flower people" for the Shanidar remains, as depicted here. Although some have claimed that the pollen is a modern contaminant, analysis of the bones reveals a rich cultural system. One of the buried individuals, an older male, had survived for many years after severe injuries that required amputating the lower half of one arm as well as a wound to his eye socket that would have left him partially blind. (The humerus or upper arm bone had withered—a gradual response to amputation of the lower arm.) Such survival demonstrates the caregiving capacities of his community to nurse him through these injuries.

had gotten him into many fights, flattening his forehead and making his brow ridges bumpy. Similarly, an analysis of a skeleton found in 1908 near La Chapelle-aux-Saints in France mistakenly concluded that the specimen's brain was apelike and that he walked like an ape (**Figure 7.18**).

The evidence indicates that Neandertals were nowhere near as brutish and apelike as originally portrayed, and some scholars now see them as the archaic *H. sapiens* of Europe and southwest and central Asia, ancestral to the more derived, anatomically modern populations of these regions of the last 30,000 years. For example, paleoanthropologist C. Loring Brace observed that "classic" Neandertal features (**Figure 7.19**) are commonly present in 10,000-year-old skulls from Denmark and Norway (Ferrie, 1997).

Nevertheless, Neandertals are somewhat distinctive when compared to more recent populations. Although they held modern-sized brains (average cranial capacity 1,400 cc versus 1,300 cc for modern *H. sapiens*), Neandertal skulls are notable for the protruding appearance of the midfacial region. The wear patterns on their large front teeth indicate that they may have been heavily used for tasks other than chewing. In many specimens,

front teeth were worn down to the root stub by 35 to 40 years of age. The large noses of Neandertals probably were necessary to warm, moisten, and clean the dry, dusty frigid air of the glacial climate, preventing damage to the lungs and brain as seen in cold-adapted people of recent times. At the back of the skull, the occipital bony bun allowed for attachment of the powerful neck muscles and counteracted the weight of a heavy face.

All Neandertal fossils indicate that both sexes were muscular, with extremely robust and dense limb bones. Relative to body mass, the limbs were short (as they are in modern humans native to especially cold climates). Their shoulder blades indicate the importance of over-arm and downward thrusting movements. Their arms were exceptionally powerful, and pronounced attachments on their hand bones attest to a remarkably strong grip. Science writer James Shreeve has suggested that a healthy Neandertal could lift an average North American football player over his head and throw him through the goalposts (Shreeve, 1995). Their massive, dense foot and leg bones suggest high levels of strength and endurance, comparable to robust individuals who live today (**Figure 7.20**).

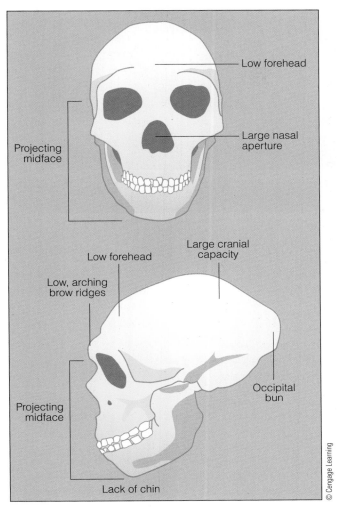

Figure 7.19 Neandertal Skulls Features of the skull seen in "classic" Neandertals.

Because brain size is related to overall body mass, heavy robust Neandertal bodies account for the large average size of the Neandertal brain. With *H. habilis* and *H. erectus*, increasing brain size has been linked to increasing cultural capabilities. Because Neandertal brain size falls at the high end of the human size range, paleoanthropologists have shifted to debating whether changes in the *shape*, rather than just the size, of the brain and skull is associated with changes in cultural capabilities.

Though the interpretation of Neandertal fossils has changed dramatically compared to when first discovered, they are still surrounded by controversy. Those who propose that the Neandertal line went extinct emphasize a notion of Neandertal biological difference and cultural inferiority. Those who include Neandertals in our direct ancestry emphasize the sophistication of Neandertal culture, attributing differences in skull shape and body form to regional adaptation to an extremely cold climate and the retention of ancestral traits in a somewhat isolated population.

Javanese, African, and Chinese Archaic *Homo sapiens*

While the large-brained Neandertals inhabited Europe and Southwest Asia, variants of archaic *H. sapiens* inhabited other parts of the world; these lacked the extreme midfacial projection and massive muscle attachments on the back of the skull characteristic of the Neandertals

Figure 7.20

Wolpoff Versus Neandertal As this face-off between paleoanthropologist Milford Wolpoff and his reconstruction of a Neandertal shows, the latter did not differ all that much from modern humans of European descent.

© The Natural History Museum, London

Figure 7.21 Comparing Crania The African archaic *Homo sapiens* from Kabwe, Zambia (*fourth from the left*) is pictured here with a variety of earlier hominins as well as Kabwe's contemporaries and later members of the genus *Homo*. The Kabwe specimen is likely to have died from a dental infection that spread to the brain of this individual. To the right of the Kabwe specimen is his contemporary, the original Neandertal cranium discovered in the Neander Valley, Germany, in 1856 (the only one without a face), followed by a cranium from a recent *Homo sapiens*. The other fossils, from the left, are a gracile australopithecine; *Homo habilis* (KNM ER 1470) discovered at Koobi Fora, Kenya; *Homo erectus* also from Koobi Fora. Increasing cranial capacity over time is evident from this series, as is the fact that Neandertal brains and that of Kabwe are in the modern human range. Even without the Neandertal face, some of the differences in the shape of the skull compared to *H. sapiens* are evident. The African archaic *H. sapiens* is also quite different from the contemporary skeleton.

(**Figure 7.21**). Skulls found in Java, Africa, and China date from roughly the same time period.

Eleven skulls found near the Solo River in Ngandong, Java, are a prime example. These skulls indicated modern-sized brains ranging from 1,013 to 1,252 cc, while retaining features of earlier Javanese *H. erectus*. When their dating was recently revised (to between 27,000 and 53,000 years ago), some researchers concluded that this proved a late survival of *H. erectus* in Asia, contemporary with *H. sapiens* elsewhere. But the Ngandong skulls remain what they always were: representatives of archaic *H. sapiens,* with modern-sized brains in otherwise ancient-looking skulls.

Fossils from various parts of Africa show a similar combination of ancient and modern traits. Equivalent remains have been found at several localities in China. Thus, the Neandertals could be said to represent an extreme form of archaic *H. sapiens*. Elsewhere, the archaics look like robust versions of the early modern populations that lived in the same regions or like somewhat more derived versions of the *H. erectus* populations that preceded them. All appear to have contained modern-sized brains, with their skulls retaining some ancestral features.

Exciting recent discoveries in southern Siberia bring a new group of archaic *Homo sapiens*, the **Denisovans**, into this mix. Dated to between 30,000 and 50,000 years ago and named for the cave in which they were discovered, the fossil evidence for Denisovans consists of a finger bone, a toe bone, and two molar teeth. Though scanty, these relatively recent remains were well enough preserved to allow for genetic analyses (Reich et al., 2010, 2012). They were also associated with blade tools and burins, more sophisticated stone tools characteristic of later peoples, as well as pendants made from the teeth of a variety of animals. Genetic analyses indicate that the Denisovans were local descendants of *Homo erectus*, who may have interbred with Neandertals, who also inhabited this region for a period of time, and with later waves of *Homo sapiens*. Features of both the Neandertal genome and the Denisovan genome live on in contemporary people today.

Middle Paleolithic Culture

Adaptations to the environment by *Homo* from the **Middle Paleolithic**, or middle part of the Old Stone Age, were both biological and cultural, but the capacity for cultural adaptation was predictably superior to what it had been in earlier members of the genus *Homo*. Possessing

Denisovans A newly discovered group of archaic *Homo sapiens* from southern Siberia dated to between 30,000 and 50,000 years ago.

Middle Paleolithic The middle part of the Old Stone Age characterized by the development of the Mousterian tool tradition and the earlier Levalloisian traditions.

brains of modern size, these members of the genus *Homo* had, as we would expect, greater cultural capabilities than their ancestors. Such a brain played a role in technological innovations, conceptual thought of considerable sophistication, and, almost surely, communication through spoken language. In addition to the Levalloisian technique already described, the Middle Paleolithic also included the development of the Mousterian tool tradition.

The Mousterian Tool Tradition

The **Mousterian tool tradition** and similar techniques of Europe, southwestern Asia, and northern Africa, dating between about 40,000 and 125,000 years ago, are the best known of these industries (Figure 7.22). Comparable traditions are found in China and Japan, where they likely arose independently from local toolmaking traditions.

All these traditions represent a technological advance over preceding industries. For example, the 40 centimeters (16 inches) of working edge that an Acheulean flint worker could get from a kilogram (2.2 pound) core compares with the nearly 200 centimeters (6 feet) of working edge the Mousterian could obtain from the same core. All people—Neandertals as well as other members of the genus *Homo* of this same time period who were said to possess more anatomically modern skulls, in Europe, northern Africa,

and southwestern Asia—used Mousterian tools. At around 35,000 years ago, the Mousterian traditions were replaced by the Upper Paleolithic traditions, which are the subject of Chapter 8. The following Anthropology Applied feature shows that stone tools continue to be important for humans today.

The Mousterian tradition is named after the Neandertal cave site of Le Moustier in southern France. The presence of Acheulean hand-axes at Mousterian sites is one indication that this culture was ultimately rooted in the older Acheulean tradition. Mousterian tools are generally lighter and smaller than those of earlier industries. Whereas previously only two or three flakes could be obtained from the entire core, Mousterian toolmakers obtained many smaller flakes, which they skillfully retouched and sharpened. Their toolkits also contained a greater variety of tool types: hand-axes, flakes, scrapers, borers, notched flakes for shaving wood, and many kinds of points that could be attached to wooden shafts to make spears. This variety of tools facilitated more effective use of food resources and enhanced the quality of clothing and shelter.

With the Mousterian cultural traditions, members of the genus *Homo* could cope with the frigid conditions that supervened in Eurasia as the glaciers expanded about 70,000 years ago. People likely came to live in cold climates as a result of a slow but steady population increase during the Pleistocene. Once there, they had little choice but to adapt as climates turned even colder.

Population expansion into previously uninhabited colder regions was made possible through a series of cultural adaptations. Under such cold conditions, vegetable foods are only rarely or seasonally available, and meat becomes a critical staple. In particular, animal fats, rather than carbohydrates, become the chief source of energy. Energy-rich animal fat in the diets of cold-climate meat-eaters provides them with the extra energy needed for hunting, as well as for keeping the body warm.

An abundance of associated animal bones, often clearly showing cut marks, indicates the importance of meat to Mousterian toolmakers. Frequently, the remains consist almost entirely of very large game—wild cattle (including the European bison known as the aurochs), wild horses, and even mammoths and woolly rhinoceroses. At several sites evidence indicates that particular species were singled out for the hunt. For example, at one site in the French Pyrenees, well over 90 percent of the faunal assemblage (representing at least 108 animals) consists of large members of the wild cattle family. These bones accumulated at the foot of a steep riverside escarpment, over which the animals were evidently stampeded. Evidence of similar cliff-fall hunting strategy is also found

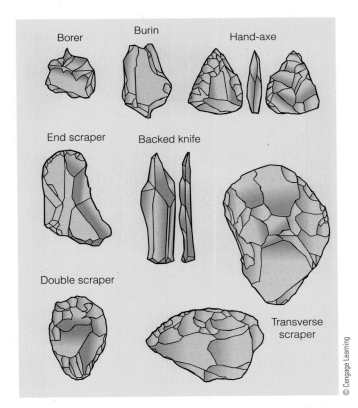

Borer

Burin

Hand-axe

End scraper

Backed knife

Double scraper

Transverse scraper

© Cengage Learning

Figure 7.22 The Mousterian Toolkit The Mousterian tool tradition includes a wide range of tool types with specific functions, which resulted in finer workmanship.

Mousterian tool tradition The tool industry of the Neandertals and their contemporaries of Europe, Southwest Asia, and North Africa from 40,000 to 125,000 years ago.

ANTHROPOLOGY APPLIED

Stone Tools for Modern Surgeons

When anthropologist Irven DeVore of Harvard University was to have some minor melanomas removed from his face, he did not leave it up to the surgeon to supply his own scalpels. Instead, he had graduate student John Shea create a scalpel. Making a blade of obsidian (a naturally occurring volcanic "glass") by the same techniques used by Upper Paleolithic people to create blades, he hafted this in a wooden handle, using melted pine resin as glue and then lashing it with sinew. After the procedure, the surgeon reported that the obsidian scalpel was superior to metal ones.[a]

DeVore was not the first to undergo surgery in which stone scalpels were used. In 1975, Don Crabtree, then at Idaho State University, prepared the scalpels that his surgeon would use in Crabtree's heart surgery. In 1980, Payson Sheets at the University of Colorado created obsidian scalpels that were used successfully in eye surgery. And in 1986, David Pokotylo of the Museum of Anthropology at the University of British Columbia underwent reconstructive surgery on his hand with blades he himself had made (the hafting was done by his museum colleague, Len McFarlane).

The reason for the use of scalpels modeled on ancient stone tools is that the anthropologists realized that obsidian is superior in almost every way to materials normally used to make scalpels: It is 210 to 1,050 times sharper than surgical steel, 100 to 500 times sharper than a razor blade, and three times sharper than a diamond blade (which not only costs much more but cannot be made with more than 3 millimeters of cutting edge).

Obsidian blades are easier to cut with and do less damage in the process (under a microscope, incisions made with the sharpest steel blades show torn, ragged edges and are littered with bits of displaced flesh).[b] As a consequence, the surgeon has better control over what she or he is doing, and the incisions heal faster with less scarring and pain. Because of the superiority of obsidian scalpels, Sheets went so far as to form a corporation in partnership with eye surgeon Dr. Firmon Hardenbergh. Together, they developed a means of producing cores of uniform size from molten glass, as well as a machine to detach blades from the cores.

---

[a]Shreeve, J. (1995). *The Neandertal enigma: Solving the mystery of modern human origins* (p. 134). New York: William Morrow.

[b]Sheets, P. D. (1993). Dawn of a New Stone Age in eye surgery. In R. J. Sharer & W. Ashmore (Eds.), *Archaeology: Discovering our past*. Palo Alto, CA: Mayfield.

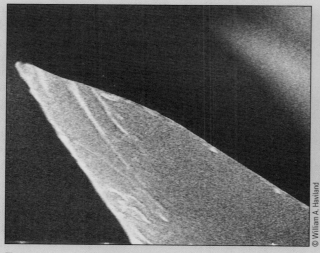 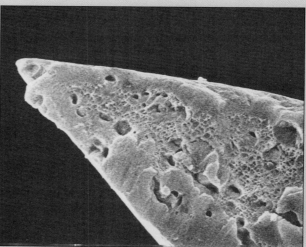

These electron micrographs of the tips of an obsidian blade (*left*) and a modern steel scalpel (*right*) illustrate the superiority of the obsidian.

at La Quina in southwestern France and at a site in the Channel Islands just off the northwest coast of France.

Clearly, the Neandertals were not merely casual or opportunistic hunters but engaged in carefully planned and organized hunting of very large and potentially dangerous game. The standardization of Mousterian hunting implements compared to household tools also reflects the importance of hunting for these ancient peoples. At the same time, the complexity of the toolkit needed for survival in a cold climate may have decreased the users' mobility. Decreased mobility is suggested by the greater depth of deposits and thus longer habitation at Mousterian sites compared with those from the earlier Lower Paleolithic. Such sites contain evidence of long production sequences, resharpening and discarding of tools, and large-scale butchering and cooking of game. Pebble paving, construction of simple walls, and the digging of post holes and artificial pits show how the inhabitants worked to improve living conditions in some caves and rock shelters. This evidence suggests that Mousterian sites were not simply stopovers in a people's constant quest for food.

In addition, evidence suggests that Neandertal social organization had developed to the point of providing care for physically disabled members of the group. For the first time, the remains of old people are well represented in the fossil record. Furthermore, many elderly Neandertal skeletons show evidence of treatment for trauma, with extensive healing of wounds and little or no infection. The partially blind man with a withered upper arm from Shanidar in Iraq, described in Figure 7.18, provides one particularly dramatic example. Remains of another individual found at Krapina in Croatia suggest the possibility of surgical amputation of a hand. In La Chapelle, France, fossil remains indicate prolonged survival of a man badly crippled by arthritis. The earliest example comes from a 200,000-year-old site in France, where a toothless man was able to survive, probably because others in his group processed or prechewed his food so he could swallow it. Whether this evidence indicates true compassion on the part of these early people is not clear, but it is certain that cultural factors helped ensure survival, allowing individuals to provide care for others.

The Symbolic Life of Neandertals

There are indications of a rich symbolic life among the Neandertals. For example, several sites contain clear evidence for deliberate burial of the dead. This is one reason for the relative abundance of reasonably complete Neandertal skeletons. The difficulty of digging an adult-sized grave without access to metal shovels suggests how important a social activity this was. Moreover, intentional positioning of dead bodies, whatever the specific reason may have been, constitutes evidence of symbolism.

To date, at least seventeen sites in Europe, South Africa, and Southwest Asia include Middle Paleolithic burials. For example, at Kebara Cave in Israel, around 60,000 years ago, a Neandertal male between 25 and 35 years of age was placed in a pit on his back, with his arms folded over his chest and abdomen (**Figure 7.23**). Some time later, after complete decay of attaching ligaments, the grave was reopened and the skull removed (a practice that, interestingly, is sometimes seen in burials in the same region roughly 50,000 years later).

The rich Neandertal site of Krapina in Croatia contains the remains of at least 70 individuals. At first, cut marks on the bones were interpreted as evidence of cannibalism. Now scientists have come to recognize that these marks indicate deliberate defleshing of the skeletons of the dead that are consistent with later ceremonial practices.

Shanidar Cave provides evidence of a burial accompanied by what may have been a funeral ceremony. In the back of the cave a Neandertal was buried in a pit. Pollen analysis of the soil around the skeleton indicates that flowers had been placed below the body and in a wreath about the head. Because the key pollen types came from insect-pollinated flowers, few if any of the pollen grains could have found their way into the pit via air currents. The flowers in question consist solely of varieties valued in historic times for their medicinal properties.

Other evidence for symbolic behavior in Mousterian culture comes from the naturally occurring pigments: manganese dioxide and the red and yellow forms of ochre. Recovered chunks of these pigments reveal clear evidence of scraping to produce powder, as well as facets, like those that appear on a crayon, from use. A Mousterian artist also applied color to the carved and shaped section of a mammoth tooth about 50,000 years ago. This mammoth tooth may have been made for cultural symbolic purposes. Noteworthy is its similarity to ceremonial objects made

© Cengage Learning

Figure 7.23 Kebara Burial The position of the body remains and the careful removal of the skull, without the lower jaw, indicate that the individual from Kebara Cave in Israel was deliberately buried there about 60,000 years ago.

of bone and ivory dated to the later Upper Paleolithic and to the *churingas* made of wood by Australian Aborigines.

The mammoth tooth, which was once smeared with red ochre, has a highly polished face suggesting it was handled a lot. Microscopic examination reveals that it was never provided with a working edge for any utilitarian purpose. Such objects imply, as archaeologist Alexander Marshack has observed, "that the Neandertals did in fact have conceptual models and maps as well as problem-solving capacities comparable to, if not equal to, those found among anatomically modern humans" (Marshack, 1989, p. 22).

Recent discovery of a painting "toolkit" in a South African cave push this behavior back to 100,000 years ago and also to a region outside of the Neandertal range. Here we have evidence that the ancient artists made paint by mixing ground-stone pigments with bone marrow and charcoal (as binders) and a liquid, most likely water (Henshilwood et al., 2011). Whether a new kind of species is responsible for this or whether this paint manufacture was just a part of Mousterian culture will be taken up in detail in the next chapter.

Evidence for symbolic activity on the part of Neandertals raises the possibility of the presence and use of musical instruments, such as a proposed bone flute from a Mousterian site in Slovenia in southern Europe (**Figure 7.24**). This object, consisting of a hollow bone with perforations, has sparked controversy. Some see it as nothing more than a bone from a cave bear that was chewed on by carnivores—hence the perforations. Its discoverer, French archaeologist Marcel Otte, on the other hand, sees it as a flute.

Unfortunately, the object is fragmentary; surviving are five holes, four on one side and one on the opposite side. The regular spacing of the four holes, fitting perfectly to the fingers of a human hand, and the location of the fifth hole at the base of the opposite side, at the natural location of the thumb, all lend credence to the flute hypothesis. Although signs of gnawing by animals are present on this bone, they are superimposed on traces of human activity (Otte, 2000). Were it found in an Upper Paleolithic context as was the flute discovered in Hohle Fels Cave in southwestern Germany, it would probably be accepted as a flute without argument. However, because its early date indicates a Neandertal made it, the interpretation of this object is tied to the larger controversy about Neandertals' cultural abilities and their place in human evolutionary history.

Speech and Language in the Middle Paleolithic

Among modern humans, the sharing of thoughts and ideas, as well as the transmission of culture from one generation to the next, is dependent upon language. Because the Neandertals and other Middle Paleolithic *Homo* had modern-sized brains and a sophisticated Mousterian toolkit, or one that was even more sophisticated such as the Denisovan toolkit, it might be supposed that they had some form of language.

As pointed out by paleoanthropologist Stanley Ambrose, the Mousterian toolkit included composite tools involving the assembly of parts in different configurations to produce functionally different tools. He likens this ordered assembly of parts into tools to grammatical language "because hierarchical assemblies of sounds produce meaningful phrases and sentences, and changing word order changes meaning" . . . "a composite tool may be analogous to a sentence, but explaining how to make one is the equivalent of a recipe or a short story" (Ambrose, 2001, p. 1751). In addition, the evidence

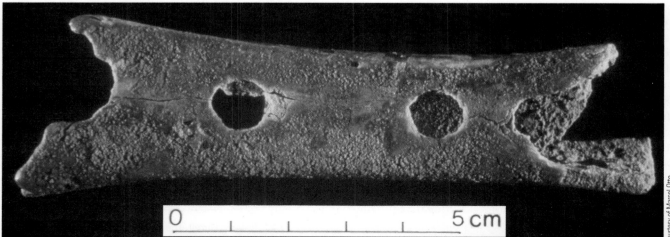

Figure 7.24 The First Musical Instrument? There is a strong possibility that this object, found in trash left by Neandertals, is the remains of a flute made of bone.

Courtesy of Marcel Otte

for the manufacture of objects of symbolic significance supports the presence of language in Middle Paleolithic *Homo*. Objects such as the colored section of mammoth tooth already described would seem to have required some form of explanation through language.

Although the archaeological evidence supports the symbolic thinking characteristic of language, specific anatomical features can be examined to determine whether this language was spoken or gestural. Some have argued that the Neandertals lacked the physical features necessary for speech. For example, an early 20th-century reconstruction of the angle at the base of the Neandertal skull was said to indicate that the larynx was higher in the throat than it is in modern humans, precluding humanlike speech. This reconstruction is now known to be faulty. Further, the hyoid bone associated with the muscles of speech in the larynx is preserved from the skeleton from the Kebara Cave burial in Israel. Its shape is identical to that of contemporary humans, indicating that the vocal tract was adequate for speech.

With respect to the brain, paleoneurologists, working from endocranial casts, agree that Neandertals had the neural development necessary for spoken language. Indeed, they argue that the changes associated with language began even before the appearance of archaic *Homo sapiens*, as described previously. Consistent, too, is an expanded thoracic vertebral canal (the thorax is the upper part of the body), a feature Neandertals share with modern humans but not with early *Homo erectus* (or any other primate). This feature suggests the increased breath control required for speech. This control enables production of long phrases or single expirations of breath, punctuated with quick inhalations at meaningful linguistic breaks.

Another argument—that a relatively flat base in Neandertal skulls would have prevented speech—has no merit, as some modern adults show as much flattening, yet have no trouble talking. Clearly, when the anatomical evidence is considered in its totality, there seems no compelling reason to deny Neandertals the ability to speak.

The discovery of a "language gene" by Swedish paleogeneticist Svante Pääbo and colleagues at the Max Planck Institute for Evolutionary Anthropology in Leipzig, Germany, adds an interesting new dimension to the study of the evolution of language (Lai et al., 2001). The gene, called FOXP2 found on chromosome 7, was identified through the analysis of a family in which members spanning several generations have severe language problems. Changes in the gene are hypothesized to control the ability to make fine movements of the mouth and larynx necessary for spoken language. The identification of this gene in humans allowed scientists to compare its structure to that found in other mammalian species.

The human FOXP2 gene differs from versions of the gene found in the chimpanzee, gorilla, orangutan, rhesus macaque, and mouse. Although these differences among living species can be known, applying this knowledge to the earlier members of the genus *Homo* is far more difficult. We do not know precisely when in human evolution the human form of the FOXP2 gene appeared or whether this gene was associated with the formation of a new species of *Homo*.

In light of these genetic discoveries it is also interesting to consider the work done on language capacity in the great apes. For example, in her work with the bonobo named Kanzi, Sue Savage-Rumbaugh documented his ability to understand hundreds of spoken words and associate them with lexigrams (pictures of words) on a computer display while unable to create the sounds himself (Savage-Rumbaugh & Lewin, 1994). Speech and language are not identical.

Culture, Skulls, and Modern Human Origins

For Middle Paleolithic *Homo*, cultural adaptive abilities relate to the fact that brain size was comparable to that of people living today. Archaeological evidence indicates sophisticated technology, as well as conceptual thought of considerable complexity, matching the increased cranial capacity. During this same time period, large-brained individuals with skulls with an anatomically modern shape began to appear. The earliest specimens with this skull shape—a more vertical forehead, diminished brow ridge, and a chin—appear first in Africa and later in Asia and Europe. Whether the derived features in the skull indicate the appearance of a new species with improved cultural capabilities is hotly debated.

The transition from the Middle Paleolithic to the tools of the Upper Paleolithic occurred around 40,000 years ago, some 100,000 years or so after the appearance of the first anatomically modern specimens in Africa. The Upper Paleolithic is known not only for a veritable explosion of tool industries, but also for clear artistic expression preserved in representative sculptures, paintings, and engravings (see Chapter 8). But the earliest anatomically modern humans, like the Neandertals and other archaic forms, used tools of the Middle Paleolithic traditions.

The relationship between cultural developments of the Upper Paleolithic and underlying biological differences between anatomically modern humans and archaic forms remains one of the most contentious debates in paleoanthropology. Discussions concerning the fate of the Neandertals and their cultural abilities are integral to this debate. Whether or not a new kind of human—anatomically modern with correspondingly superior intellectual and creative abilities—is responsible for the cultural explosion of the Upper Paleolithic is considered in Chapter 8.

CHAPTER CHECKLIST

What are the characteristics of the genus *Homo*?

● The genus *Homo* first appeared in East Africa and is marked by increasing cranial capacity and the earliest stone tools.

● Lumpers identify the first species as *Homo habilis* whereas splitters consider these fossils to be too varied to constitute a single species.

● *Homo erectus* appeared first in Africa around 1.9 million years ago and began spreading throughout the Old World.

● Cranial capacity in the genus *Homo* increased steadily from 2.5 million years ago until about 200,000 years ago when it reached modern proportions. Other trends include reduced jaws and teeth reduced sexual dimorphism, and an increase in overall body size.

How and when did stone tool industries develop for the genus *Homo*?

● The first evidence of stone tools is dated to about 2.6 million years ago from Gona, Ethiopia. Ancient toolmakers, presumably *Homo habilis*, used the percussion method of manufacture for these tools. The Lower Paleolithic or Lower Stone Age began with these early tools of the Oldowan tradition.

● *H. erectus* originated the hand-axe of the Acheulean tradition and exercised superior, more standardized craftsmanship compared to the preceding Oldowan tradition.

● Cranial capacity reached modern proportions between 200,000 and 400,000 years ago, roughly coincident with the Levalloisian tradition of stone tool manufacture and the practice of hafting.

● The Neandertal timespan coincides with the Mousterian tool era, although all the members of the genus *Homo* living at that time employed these methods. Together the Levalloisian and the Mousterian traditions constitute the Middle Paleolithic. It surpassed the Lower Paleolithic in variety and refinement, signifying our ancestors' developing reliance on cultural adaptation for survival.

What is the relationship between biological and cultural change among early *Homo*?

● Brain size increased over the course of 2.2 million years after the appearance of *H. habilis*, becoming the biological foundation for the cultural adaptation on which humans would rely for survival.

● As brain size reached modern proportions, the one-to-one correspondence between cultural innovation and larger brains no longer held.

● Meat eating satisfied the high-energy demands of larger brains and perhaps afforded leisure time for the development of culture and planning.

● Soft, cooked foods may have relaxed selection for large teeth and powerful jaws, permitting the cranium of *Homo erectus* to expand significantly.

● Increased overall size and decreased sexual dimorphism may have contributed to successful adaptation to bearing large-brained young.

● Fossil evidence indicates that early *Homo* was a scavenger rather than a hunter of big game, as the biases of Western tradition had suggested. Early tools were used to butcher scavenged carcasses in order to extract as much nutrition as possible.

How do we describe the history and lifeways of *Homo erectus*?

● *Homo erectus* appeared 1.8 million years ago, dispersing from Africa into Eurasia and Indonesia. A large cranial capacity, brow ridges, and a protruding mouth are some of the features that distinguish the *H. erectus* skull.

● Regional variation in fossils that are otherwise considered *Homo erectus* has led some scientists to create alternate species designations.

● Evidence of controlled use of fire dates to 1.3 million years ago. This skill presumably enabled *H. erectus* to expand into colder regions of Eurasia as well as to scavenge for frozen meat. Fire also provided the enormous nutritional benefits of cooked food.

● Evidence of handedness in tool manufacture and an enlarged hypoglossal canal support claims of late *H. erectus*' ability for language.

How do Neandertals compare to other members of *Homo*?

● Neandertal brains were larger than the modern average size, though their bulging facial features and muscular statures made them susceptible to derision by early Western scientists, especially before the theory of evolution was introduced.

● Aided by their implements and cognitive abilities, Neandertals could hunt large game effectively and relied upon it during the winter when vegetation was scarce.

● Neandertals practiced ritual burial and cared for ill and disabled members of their groups.

● Genetic, paleoneurological, anatomical, and artifact evidence all suggest Neandertals were capable of and used language, just as with other members of the genus *Homo* (generally classified as archaic *Homo sapiens*) who were living at that time.

QUESTIONS FOR REFLECTION

1. Members of the genus *Homo* draw upon integrated biological and cultural capabilities to face the challenges of existence. How do these factors play into the designation of species in the fossil record? How do paleoartists avoid introducing biases when they flesh out fossil species?

2. Paleoanthropologists can be characterized as lumpers or splitters depending upon their approach to the identification of species in the fossil record. Which of these approaches do you prefer and why?

3. In his 1871 book *Descent of Man, and Selection in Relation to Sex*, Charles Darwin stated, "Thus man has ultimately become superior to woman. It is indeed fortunate that the law of equal transmission of characters prevails with mammals. Otherwise it is probable that man would have become as superior in mental endowment to woman as the peacock is in ornamental plumage to the peahen." How were the cultural norms of Darwin's time reflected in his statement? Can 21st-century paleoanthropologists speak about differences between the sexes in an evolutionary context without introducing their own cultural biases?

4. Life forms ranging from rabbits to plants have come to occupy new niches without the benefits of culture. Was the spread of *Homo* out of the African continent possible without the benefit of culture?

5. Though language itself does not "fossilize," the archaeological and fossil records provide some evidence of the linguistic capabilities of our ancestors. Using the evidence available, what sort of linguistic abilities do you think early *Homo* possessed?

ONLINE STUDY RESOURCES

CourseMate

Access chapter-specific learning tools, including learning objectives, practice quizzes, videos, flash cards, glossaries, and more in your Anthropology CourseMate.

Log into **www.cengagebrain.com** to access the resources your instructor has assigned and to purchase materials.

Challenge Issue

We all recognize this stencil of a hand, made by spraying paint on a cave wall, as human. Or is it? Scientists recently dated this ancient rock art from Spain's El Castillo Cave to 40,800 years ago, indicating that the outline may be of a Neandertal hand. Uranium-series techniques yielded these new dates in June 2012, making the cave art a good 10,000 years older than previously thought. What prompted this ancient being to venture deep into a pitch-black cave, guided perhaps by a burning flame for light, to leave a record of him- or herself or of another member of the group? Do these marks represent the urge of these ancient beings to connect people to one another across time and space? It these were made by Neandertals, are they speaking to us, directly asserting their humanity through the handprints they left behind? For many years, some paleoanthropologists have argued that a biological shift accounted for the creative urges, symbolic thought, and cultural sophistication necessary to execute such a stencil. They attribute the explosion of art and complex tool industries that begin to appear in the archaeological record from this point on to an intrinsic biological change, perhaps even a speciation event responsible for the appearance in the fossil record of anatomically modern humans. These ancient handprints challenge us to consider whether a biological change was at the root of this creative expression and whether biology separates us from these ancestors or other archaic forms that preceded them. These marks also suggest that humans, as a thoughtful and self-reflecting species, have always faced the challenge of understanding where and how we fit in the larger natural system of all life forms, past and present.

The Global Expansion of *Homo sapiens* and Their Technology

8

In 1868, at the back of a rock shelter near the banks of the bucolic Vézère River, in a region of France now known for its delicious truffle mushrooms, the remains of eight ancient people were first discovered. These people, commonly referred to as **Cro-Magnons** after the rock shelter in which they were found (**Figure 8.1**), resembled contemporary Europeans more than Neandertals and were associated with tools of the **Upper Paleolithic**, the last part of the Old Stone Age. The Cro-Magnon name was extended to thirteen other specimens recovered between 1872 and 1902 in the caves of southwestern France and, since then, to Upper Paleolithic skeletons discovered in other parts of Europe.

Because Cro-Magnons were found with Upper Paleolithic tools and seemed to be responsible for the production of impressive works of art that abound in the caves of this region, scientists and laypeople alike considered them particularly clever when compared with the Neandertals. The idea of dimwitted Neandertals comfortably supported prevailing stereotypes based on their supposedly brutish appearance. Mousterian tools provided evidence of Neandertal cultural inferiority. Cro-Magnons, an anatomically modern people with a superior culture, swept into Europe and replaced a primitive local population. This idea mirrored the European conquest of other parts of the world during the colonial expansion that was concurrent with the discovery of these fossils.

With the invention of reliable dating techniques in the 20th century, we now know that many Neandertal specimens of Europe and the later Cro-Magnon specimens date from different time periods. The Middle Paleolithic Mousterian technology is associated with earlier fossil specimens, whereas the Upper Paleolithic technology and art belongs with later fossil specimens.

However, probably the most ethnocentric aspect of these beliefs is that the discussion focused on the

Cro-Magnons Europeans of the Upper Paleolithic after about 36,000 years ago.
Upper Paleolithic The last part (10,000 to 40,000 years ago) of the Old Stone Age, featuring tool industries characterized by long slim blades and an explosion of creative symbolic forms.

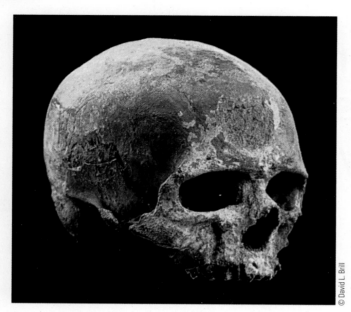

Figure 8.1 Cro-Magnon With a high forehead, the Cro-Magnon skull is more like contemporary Europeans compared to the prominent brow ridge and sloping forehead seen in the Neandertal skull. Whether these differences in skull shape account for their cultural differences rather than their relative age is hotly debated. The more recent Cro-Magnon skull even preserves evidence of continuity in diet with local contemporary French people because it exhibits signs of a fungal infection, perhaps caused by eating tainted mushrooms. Mushrooms are a delicacy in this region of France to this day.

European fossil evidence instead of incorporating evidence from throughout the globe. Recent fossil evidence for early anatomical modernity in Africa, evidence of regional continuity from Asia, new discoveries of earlier art such as that from the cave at El Castillo in Spain (Pike et al., 2012), and associated genetic studies (including the recent studies of the Denisovans) allow paleoanthropologists to develop more comprehensive theories for the origins of modern humans.

Upper Paleolithic Peoples: The First Modern Humans

What do we mean by *modernity*? Paleoanthropologists look at both skull shape and cultural practices, but still this is a difficult designation to make. Although Cro-Magnons resemble later populations of modern Europeans—in braincase shape, high broad forehead, narrow nasal openings, and common presence of chins—their faces were on average shorter and broader than those of modern Europeans, their brow ridges were a bit more prominent, and their teeth and jaws were as large as those of Neandertals. Some (a skull from the original Cro-Magnon site, for instance) even display the distinctive occipital bun of the Neandertals on the back of the skull. Nor were they particularly tall, as their average height of 5 feet 7 or 8 inches (170–175 centimeters) does not fall outside the Neandertal range. Similarly, early Upper Paleolithic skulls from Brno, Mladec, and Predmosti in the Czech Republic retain heavy brow ridges and Neandertal-like muscle attachments on the back of the skull.

Although paleoanthropologists routinely refer to the Cro-Magnons and Upper Paleolithic peoples from Africa and Asia as "anatomically modern," this definition lacks precision. We think of people with brains the size of modern people, but this had already been achieved by archaic *Homo sapiens*. Average brain size actually peaked in Neandertals at 10 percent larger than the contemporary human average. The reduction to today's average size correlates with a reduction in brawn, as bodies have become less massive overall. Living humans, in general, have faces and jaws smaller than those of Neandertals, but there are exceptions. For example, paleoanthropologists Milford Wolpoff and Rachel Caspari have pointed out that any definition of *modernity* that excludes Neandertals also excludes substantial numbers of recent and living Aborigines in Australia, although they are, quite obviously, a contemporary people (**Figure 8.2**). The fact is, no multidimensional diagnosis of anatomical modernity includes all living humans while excluding archaic populations (Wolpoff & Caspari, 1997).

Defining *modernity* in terms of culture also raises questions. The appearance of modern-sized brains in archaic *Homo* was related to increased reliance on cultural adaptation, but the Upper Paleolithic was a time of great technological innovation and a creative explosion. Upper Paleolithic toolkits contain a preponderance of blade tools, with flint flakes at least twice as long as they are wide. The earliest blade tools come from sites in Africa, but these tools do not make up the majority of the tool types until well into the Upper Paleolithic. The Upper Paleolithic archaeological record also contains a proliferation of expressive arts.

Technological improvements may have reduced the intensity of selective pressures that had previously favored especially massive robust bodies, jaws, and teeth. A marked reduction in overall muscularity accompanied the new emphasis on elongated tools with greater mechanical advantages, more effective techniques of hafting, a switch from thrusting to throwing spears, and the development of net hunting. A climate shift from the extreme cold that prevailed in Eurasia during the last Ice Age to milder conditions may have diminished selective pressure for short stature as an adaptation to conserve body heat.

Michael Conye/Getty Images

Figure 8.2 **A Problematic Definition** Living people today such as Aborigines in Australia do not meet the definition of anatomical modernity proposed in the recent African origins model. Some paleoanthropologists suggest that this proves the definition itself is problematic. All living people are clearly full-fledged members of the species *Homo sapiens*.

The Human Origins Debate

On a biological level, the great human origins debate distills down to the question of whether one, some, or all populations of the archaic groups played a role in the evolution of modern *Homo sapiens*. Those supporting the multiregional hypothesis argue for a simultaneous local transition from *Homo erectus* to modern *Homo sapiens* throughout the parts of the world inhabited by members of the genus *Homo*. By contrast, those supporting a theory of recent African origins argue that all contemporary peoples derive from one single population of archaic *Homo sapiens* from Africa. This model proposes that the improved cultural capabilities of anatomically modern humans allowed this group to replace other archaic forms as they began to migrate out of Africa sometime after 100,000 years ago. Both theories are explored in detail following.

The Multiregional Hypothesis

Shared regional characteristics among African, Chinese, and southeastern Asian fossils of archaic *Homo sapiens* imply continuity within these respective populations,

from *H. erectus* through to modern *H. sapiens*. This observation in the fossil evidence strongly supported the interpretation that there was genetic continuity in these regions. For example, in China, Pleistocene fossils from the genus *Homo* consistently have small forward-facing cheeks and flatter faces than their contemporaries elsewhere, as is still true today. In Southeast Asia and Australia, by contrast, skulls are consistently robust, with huge cheeks and forward projection of the jaws. As new molecular research techniques have developed over the past two decades, scientists have amassed genetic data to support the physical evidence.

In this model, gene flow among populations keeps the human species unified throughout the Pleistocene. No speciation events remove ancestral populations such as Asian *H. erectus*, Denisovans, or Neandertals from the line leading to *H. sapiens*. Although proponents of the **multiregional hypothesis** accept the idea of continuity

---

multiregional hypothesis The hypothesis that modern humans originated through a process of simultaneous local transition from *Homo erectus* to *Homo sapiens* throughout the inhabited world.

from the earliest European fossils through the Neandertals to living people, many other paleoanthropologists reject the idea that Neandertals were involved in the ancestry of modern Europeans.

The Recent African Origins Hypothesis

The **recent African origins hypothesis** (also called the *Eve hypothesis* and the *out of Africa hypothesis*) states that anatomically modern humans descended from one specific population of *Homo sapiens*, replacing not just the Neandertals but other populations of archaic *H. sapiens* as our ancestors spread out from their original homeland. This idea did not originate from fossils but from a relatively new technique pioneered in the 1980s that uses mitochondrial DNA (mtDNA) to reconstruct family trees (**Figure 8.3**).

Unlike nuclear DNA (in the cell nucleus), mtDNA is located in the mitochondria, the cellular structures that produce the energy needed to keep cells alive. Because sperm contribute virtually no mtDNA to the fertilized egg, mtDNA is inherited essentially from one's mother and is not subject to recombination through meiosis and fertilization with each succeeding generation as is nuclear DNA. Therefore, changes in mtDNA over time occur only through mutation.

By comparing the mtDNA of living individuals from diverse geographic populations, anthropologists and molecular biologists seek to determine when and where modern *Homo sapiens* originated. As widely reported in the popular press (including cover stories in *Newsweek* and *Time*), preliminary results suggested that the mitochondrial DNA of all living humans could be traced back to a "mitochondrial Eve" who lived in Africa some 200,000 years ago. If so, all other populations of archaic *H. sapiens*, as well as non-African *H. erectus*, would have to be ruled out of the ancestry of modern humans.

For many years, the recent African origins theory has been weakened by the lack of good fossil evidence from Africa. In 2003, however, skulls of two adults and one child, discovered in Ethiopia in East Africa in 1997 (see Anthropologist of Note), were described as anatomically modern (**Figure 8.4**) and were reconstructed and dated to 160,000 years ago (White et al., 2003). The discoverers of these fossils called them *Homo sapiens idaltu* (meaning "elder" in the local Afar language). Although conceding that the skulls are robust, they believe that these skulls have conclusively proved the recent African origins hypothesis, relegating Neandertals to a side branch of human evolution.

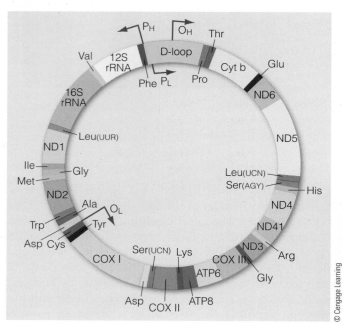

Figure 8.3 Mitochondrial DNA The 16,569 bases in mitochondrial DNA (mtDNA) are organized into circular chromosomes present in large numbers in every cell. The human mtDNA sequence has been entirely sequenced, with functional genes identified. Because mtDNA is maternally inherited and not subject to recombination, it can be used to establish evolutionary relationships. However, population size impacts the preservation of variation in the mtDNA genome and complicates using contemporary mtDNA variation to calibrate a molecular clock.

recent African origins hypothesis The theory that modern humans are all derived from one single population of archaic *Homo sapiens* who migrated out of Africa after 100,000 years ago, replacing all other archaic forms due to their superior cultural capabilities; also called the *Eve hypothesis* and the *out of Africa hypothesis*.

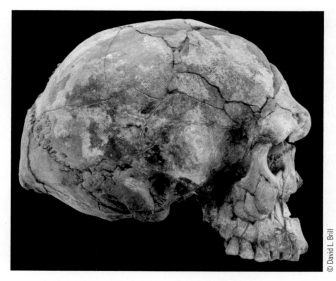

Figure 8.4 African Evidence for Anatomical Modernity The recently discovered well-preserved specimens from Herto, Ethiopia, provide the best fossil evidence in support of the recent African origins hypothesis. Though these fossils unquestionably possess an anatomically modern appearance, they are still relatively robust. In addition, it is not clear whether the higher skull and forehead indicate superior cultural abilities.

ANTHROPOLOGISTS OF NOTE

Berhane Asfaw (b. 1953) • Xinzhi Wu (b. 1928)

Born in Addis Ababa, Ethiopia, in 1953, **Berhane Asfaw** is a world-renowned paleoanthropologist leading major expeditions in Ethiopia. He is coleader of the international Middle Awash Research Project, the research team responsible for the discovery of spectacular ancestral fossils dating from the entire 6-million-year course of human evolutionary history, including *Ardipithecus ramidus, Australopithecus afarensis, Australopithecus garhi, Homo erectus,* and, most recently, the *Homo sapiens idaltu* fossils from Herto, Ethiopia.

Xinzhi Wu pictured here at Zhoukoudian is one of the original formulators of the multiregional continuity hypothesis.

Berhane Asfaw has been involved with most of the major recent finds in Ethiopia and has trained a generation of African paleoanthropologists.

At the June 2003 press conference, organized by Teshome Toga, Ethiopia's minister of culture, Asfaw described the Herto specimens as the oldest anatomically modern humans, likening Ethiopia to the Garden of Eden. This conference marked a shift in the Ethiopian government's stance toward the paleoanthropological research spanning Asfaw's career. Previous discoveries in the Middle Awash were also very important, but the government did not participate in or support this research.

Asfaw entered the discipline of paleoanthropology through a program administered by the Leakey Foundation providing fellowships for Africans to pursue graduate studies in Europe and the United States. Since this program's inception in the late 1970s, the Leakey Foundation has awarded sixty-eight fellowships totaling $1.2 million to Kenyans, Ethiopians, and Tanzanians to pursue graduate education in paleoanthropology.

Asfaw, mentored by U.S. paleoanthropologist Desmond Clark at the University of California, Berkeley, was among the earliest fellows in this program. They first met in 1979 when Asfaw was a senior studying geology in Addis Ababa. Asfaw obtained his doctorate in 1988 and returned to Ethiopia, where he had few Ethiopian anthropological colleagues, and the government had halted fossil exploration. Since that time, Asfaw has recruited and mentored many Ethiopian scholars and now has about a dozen on his team. Local scientists can protect the antiquities, keep fossils from disappearing, and mobilize government support. Asfaw's leadership in paleoanthropology has played a key role in helping the government recognize how important prehistory is for Ethiopia.

Xinzhi Wu is one of China's foremost paleoanthropological scholars, contributing to the development of the discipline for over a half-century. As with many other paleoanthropologists,

the study of human anatomy has been of vital importance to him.

He began his academic career with a degree from Shanghai Medical College followed by teaching in the Department of Human Anatomy at the Medical College in Dalian before beginning graduate studies in paleoanthropology. He is presently a professor at the Chinese Academy of Sciences Institute of Vertebrate Paleontology and Paleoanthropology in Beijing and the honorary president of the Chinese Society of Anatomical Sciences.

In addition to managing excavations in China and other parts of Asia, Wu has played a major role in the development of theories about modern human origins in cooperation with scholars internationally. He collaborated with Milford Wolpoff of the United States and Alan Thorne of Australia in the development of the theory of multiregional continuity for modern human origins. This theory fits well with the Asian fossil evidence proposing an important place for *Homo erectus* in modern human origins. Interestingly, it builds upon the model for human origins developed by Franz Weidenreich (see Chapter 7).

According to Wu, early humans from China are as old if not older than humans anyplace else. He suggests that the reason more fossils have been found in Africa recently is that Africa has been the site for more excavations.

Zhoukoudian remains a site of particular importance for Wu, as it documents continuous habitation of early humans and one of the earliest sites with evidence of controlled use of fire. Wu has predicted that more important discoveries will still be made at Zhoukoudian because a third of this site has still not been fully excavated. The Chinese government has responded to Wu's suggestions and is presently constructing a 2.4-square-kilometer Peking Man exhibition and paleoanthropology research area at Zhoukoudian.

Wu has welcomed many international scholars to China to study the Asian evidence. He also has led efforts to make descriptions of fossil material available in English. Collaborating with anthropologist Frank Poirier, he published the comprehensive volume *Human Evolution in China,* describing the fossil evidence and archaeological sites with great accuracy and detail.

Reconciling the Evidence

For many years, the recent African origins hypothesis has been the majority position among Western paleo-anthropologists, but it does not prevail throughout the international scientific community. Chinese paleoanthropologists, for example, favor the multiregional hypothesis because it fits well with the fossil discoveries from Asia and Australia. By contrast, the recent African origins hypothesis depends more upon the interpretation of fossils and cultural remains from Europe, Africa, and Southwest Asia.

Recent sequencing of the entire human genome for a variety of contemporary populations—as well as for fossil hominins including Cro-Magnons, Neandertals, and Denisovans—has added substantially to the evidence. Genetic studies show that features unique to the Neandertal genome remain in contemporary humans, particularly those of regions inhabited by Neandertals in the past. Further, some contemporary Melanesians share 4 to 6 percent of their DNA with Denisovans, as will be discussed following.

As we have seen, paleoanthropologists on both sides of the modern human origins debate marshal genetic, anatomical, and cultural evidence to both support and critique each hypothesis.

The Genetic Evidence

Though genetic evidence had been the cornerstone of the recent African origins hypothesis, molecular evidence also provided the grounds to challenge it. For example, reanalysis of the original mtDNA data set showed that Africa was not the sole source of mtDNA in modern humans. In addition, because both theories propose African origins for the human line, the genetic evidence could also support the African origins of the genus *Homo* instead of the more recent species *Homo sapiens*. Each model assumes a distinct rate of molecular change. Both models place ultimate human origins firmly in Africa.

DNA analyses contain other problematic assumptions. For example, these models assume steady rates of mutation, when in fact they can be notoriously uneven. They also rely upon the assumption that selective pressures do not impact mtDNA, when in fact variants have been implicated in epilepsy and in a disease of the eye.

Another issue is that DNA is seen as traveling exclusively *from* Africa, when it is known that, over the past 10,000 years, there has been plenty of movement of humans *into* Africa as well. In fact, one study of DNA carried on the Y chromosome (the sex chromosome inherited exclusively in the male line) suggests that DNA on the Y chromosome of some Africans was introduced from Asia, where it originated some 200,000 years ago (Gibbons, 1997). Nevertheless, recent work on the Y chromosome by anthropologist and geneticist Spencer Wells traces the human lineage to a single population living in Africa about 60,000 years ago (Wells, 2002).

Despite the seeming conflict, these data all confirm the importance of gene flow in human evolutionary history. Where the hypotheses differ is in terms of whether this gene flow occurred over the course of 200,000 years or 2 million years.

Starting in 1997, molecular paleoanthropologists under the direction of Svante Pääbo of the Max Planck Institute, began to study the mitochondrial DNA of fossil specimens, starting with the extraction of mtDNA from the original German Neandertal remains, followed by two other Neandertals. Today, this work has expanded to nuclear DNA including the entire Neandertal genome in 2010 (Green et al., 2010), as well as that of the ancient Denisovans (Max Planck Institute for Evolutionary Anthropology, 2012), and Cro-Magnons. Now scientists can quantify how much of a genome the ancient peoples share with contemporary peoples. Neandertals seem to share about 1 percent with living Eurasian peoples, but not with Africans, whereas contemporary Melanesians share 4 to 6 percent genetic identity with ancient Denisovans. Both these observations support regional continuity, though the case might seem to be less strong in Neandertals.

Lower amounts of genetic identity, however, do not necessarily exclude hominin species from human ancestry. The amount of isolation and the inflow of new genes have an impact on the precise percentages of ancient molecular features retained. The Denisovan features may be better preserved in more isolated island populations compared to the Eurasian mainland, which was inhabited by Neandertals and where gene flow occurred more readily.

Further evidence from Australia illustrates that specific gene sequences can "go extinct" though the species itself does not. In this case, an mtDNA sequence present in a skeleton from Australia that is 40,000 to 62,000 years old (and that everyone agrees is anatomically modern) does not appear in recent native Australians (Gibbons, 2001). In short, the genetic evidence that was once the mainstay of the recent African origins hypothesis has now come to favor the multiregional continuity hypothesis.

The Anatomical Evidence

Though the recent fossil discoveries certainly provide evidence of the earliest anatomically modern specimens in Africa, they do not resolve the relationship between biological change in the shape of the skull and cultural change as preserved in the archaeological record (Figure 8.5). The changes in the archaeological record and the appearance of anatomically modern skulls are separated by some 100,000 years. The evidence from Southwest Asia is particularly interesting in this regard. Here, at a variety of sites dated to between 50,000 and 100,000 years ago, there are fossils described as both anatomically modern and Neandertal, and they are associated with Mousterian technology.

VISUAL COUNTERPOINT

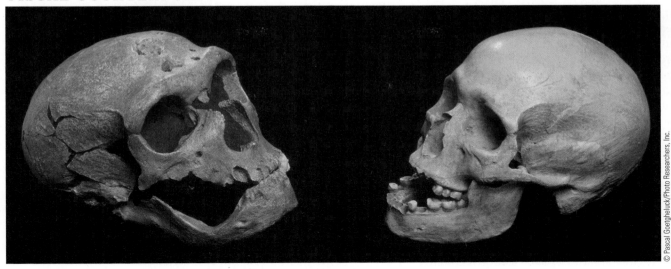

Figure 8.5 **Neandertals Compared to Recent *Homo sapiens*** A comparison of the Neandertal (*left*) and the contemporary *Homo sapiens* (*right*) shows that although both possess large brains, there are distinctive differences in the shape of the skull. The Neandertal has a large face, pronounced brow ridges, and a low, sloping forehead whereas the contemporary *H. sapiens* has a high forehead and a chin. The back of the Neandertal, though not visible from this angle, is robust (as seen in the Herto skull pictured in Figure 8.4). In what other ways is Herto like these two specimens? How do these three skulls compare to the Cro-Magnon skull pictured in Figure 8.1?

Nevertheless, recent African origins proponents argue that anatomically modern peoples coexisted for a time with other archaic populations until the superior cultural capacities of the "moderns" resulted in extinction of the archaic peoples. Especially clear evidence of this is said to exist in Europe, where Neandertals and moderns are said to have coexisted in close proximity between 30,000 and 40,000 years ago. However, defining fossils as either Neandertals or moderns illustrates the difficulty with defining a distinct biological species, given the presence of variation found in humans.

If we think in terms of varied populations, as seen in living humans today, we find that features reminiscent of modern humans can be discerned in some of the later Neandertals. A specimen from Saint Césaire in France, for example, has a higher forehead and a notable chin. A number of other Neandertals, too, show incipient chin development as well as reduced facial protrusion and smaller brow ridges. Conversely, the earliest anatomically modern human skulls from Europe often exhibit features reminiscent of Neandertals (see Chapter 7). In addition, some typical Neandertal features such as the occipital bun are found in diverse living populations today such as Bushmen from southern Africa, Finns and Saami from Scandinavia, and Australian Aborigines. Accordingly, we might view the population of this region between 30,000 and 40,000 years ago as a varied one, with some individuals retaining a stronger Neandertal heritage than others, in whom modern characteristics are more prominent (**Figure 8.6**). If all these groups were members of the same species, gene flow would be expected, and individuals would express a mosaic of traits. The genetic evidence supports such blending.

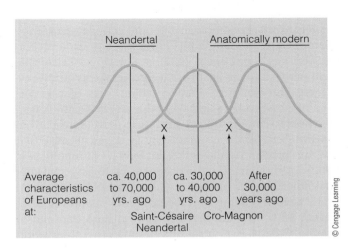

Figure 8.6 **Population Variation** This graph portrays a shift in average characteristics of an otherwise varied population over time from Neandertal to more modern features. Between 30,000 and 40,000 years ago, we would expect to find individuals with characteristics such as those of the Saint-Césaire Neandertal and the almost (but not quite) modern Cro-Magnon. Before and after this period of transition, both Neandertals and moderns had more classic features.

A mix of modern and Neandertal features is so strong in a child's skeleton found in Portugal as to lead several specialists to regard it as clear evidence of hybridization, or successful reproduction between the two groups. This would mean that the two forms are of a single species, rather than separate ones. Others, of course, argue that features interpreted as Neandertal-like might instead be related to this child's "chunky" build.

Scientists supporting the hypothesis that Neandertals are members of the species *Homo sapiens* suggest that the simplest explanation that accounts for all the evidence is that all of these fossils belong to a single varied population, with some individuals showing more typical Neandertal features than others. This accords with archaeological evidence that the intellectual abilities of late Neandertals were no different from those of early moderns.

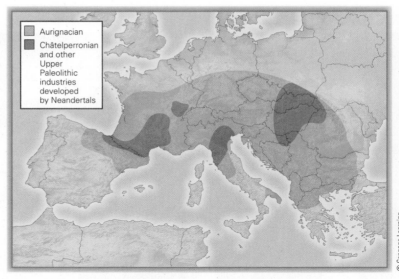

Legend:
- Aurignacian
- Châtelperronian and other Upper Paleolithic industries developed by Neandertals

© Cengage Learning

Figure 8.7 **Aurignacian and Châtelperronian Traditions** Between 30,000 and 36,500 years ago, Upper Paleolithic industries developed from the Mousterian tradition by European Neandertals coexisted with the Aurignacian industry, usually associated with anatomically modern humans.

The Cultural Evidence

In addition to the difficulties inherent with finding definitive fossil evidence that the physical or mental makeup of Neandertals would have prevented them from leading a typical Upper Paleolithic way of life, problems also exist with using technology to distinguish Neandertals from their contemporaries. Neandertals and anatomically modern humans alike used Mousterian toolkits during the Middle Paleolithic. At the time of the Upper Paleolithic transition, the latest Neandertals of Europe developed their own Upper Paleolithic technology (the Châtelperronian) comparable to the industries used by anatomically modern *Homo sapiens*. No earlier than 36,500 years ago (Zilhão, 2000), a new Upper Paleolithic technology known as the **Aurignacian tradition**—named after Aurignac, France, where tools of this sort were first discovered—appeared in Europe (**Figure 8.7**).

Though commonly considered to have spread from southwestern Asia, a recent reanalysis suggests instead that the Aurignacian developed exclusively in Europe (Clark, 2002). Although some paleoanthropologists consider anatomically modern humans the makers of Aurignacian tools, skeletal remains and tools are rarely found in association with one another. The central European site of Vindija, Croatia, is a notable exception to this observation because Neandertal remains were found there with an Aurignacian split-bone point (Karavanič & Smith, 2000).

Some have argued that the Upper Paleolithic technology of the Neandertals was a crude imitation of the true technological advancements practiced by anatomically modern humans. In some respects, however, Neandertals outdid their anatomically modern contemporaries, as in the use of red ochre, a substance less frequently used by Aurignacian peoples than by their late Neandertal neighbors. This cannot be a case of borrowing ideas and techniques from Aurignacians because these developments clearly predate the Aurignacian (Zilhão, 2000).

Coexistence and Cultural Continuity

Neandertals and anatomically modern humans also coexisted in Southwest Asia long before the cultural innovations of the Upper Paleolithic (**Figure 8.8**). Here neither the skeletal nor the archaeological evidence supports cultural difference between the fossil groups or absolute biological difference. Although Neandertal skeletons are clearly present at sites such as the caves of Kebara and Shanidar in Israel and Iraq, respectively, skeletons from some older sites have been described as anatomically modern.

At the cave site of Qafzeh near Nazareth in Israel, for example, 90,000-year-old skeletons show none of the Neandertal hallmarks; although their faces and bodies are large and heavily built by today's standards, they are nonetheless claimed to be within the range of living peoples. Yet, a statistical study comparing a number of measurements from among Qafzeh, Upper Paleolithic, and Neandertal skulls found those from Qafzeh to fall in between the anatomically modern and Neandertal norms, though slightly closer to the Neandertal. Nor is the

---

Aurignacian tradition Toolmaking tradition in Europe and western Asia at the beginning of the Upper Paleolithic.

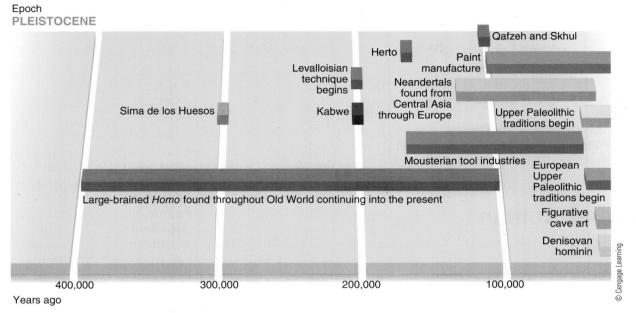

Epoch
PLEISTOCENE

Qafzeh and Skhul

Herto

Paint manufacture

Levalloisian technique begins

Neandertals found from Central Asia through Europe

Sima de los Huesos

Kabwe

Upper Paleolithic traditions begin

Mousterian tool industries

European Upper Paleolithic traditions begin

Large-brained *Homo* found throughout Old World continuing into the present

Figurative cave art

Denisovan hominin

400,000   300,000   200,000   100,000

Years ago

© Cengage Learning

Figure 8.8 **The Cultural Milestones in Human Evolution** Around 400,000 years ago, large-brained members of the genus *Homo* began to be found throughout Africa and Eurasia; corresponding cultural changes are evident as well. Analyses of DNA recovered from the Asian Denisova hominins and late Neandertals indicate a deeper time depth for these "sibling" fossil groups whose lines diverged around 640,000 ago. Large-brained members of the genus *Homo* continue into the present, of course, all members of the unified species *Homo sapiens*.

dentition functionally distinguishable when Qafzeh and Neandertal are compared (Brace, 2000).

Although skeletons from Skhul, a site on Mount Carmel of the same period, resemble those from Qafzeh, they were also part of a population whose continuous range of variation included individuals with markedly Neandertal characteristics. Furthermore, the idea of two distinctly different but coexisting populations receives no support from the archaeological evidence. Individuals living at Skhul and Qafzeh were making and using the same Mousterian tools as those at Kebara and Shanidar, a fact that undercuts the notion of biologically distinct groups with different cultural abilities. Indeed, recent genetic studies also support the notion that these were not biologically distinct groups.

The examination of sites continuously inhabited throughout the Upper Pleistocene provides no significant evidence for behavioral differences between the Middle Paleolithic and early Upper Paleolithic at these sites. For example, the Upper Paleolithic peoples who used Kebara Cave continued to live in exactly the same way as their Neandertal predecessors: They procured the same foods, processed them similarly, used comparable hearths, and disposed of their trash in the same way. The only evident difference is that the Neandertals did not use small stones or cobbles to bank their fires for warmth as did their Upper Paleolithic successors.

Nevertheless, by 28,000 years ago, many of the extreme anatomical features seen in archaic groups like

Neandertals seem to disappear from the European and Southwest and Central Asian fossil record. Instead, people with higher foreheads, smoother brow ridges, and distinct chins seemed to have Eurasia more or less to themselves. However, an examination of the full range of individual human variation across the globe and into the present reveals contemporary humans with skulls not meeting the anatomical definition of *modernity* proposed in the standard evolutionary arguments (recall Figure 8.2). Similarly, living people today possess many Neandertal features such as the occipital buns mentioned earlier. Human populations both now and during the Upper Paleolithic contain considerable physical variability.

Just how much gene flow took place among ancient human populations cannot be known precisely, but the sudden appearance of novel traits in one region later than their appearance elsewhere provides evidence of its occurrence. For example, some Upper Paleolithic remains from North Africa exhibit the kind of midfacial flatness previously seen only in East Asian fossils; similarly, various Cro-Magnon fossils from Europe show the short upper jaws, horizontally oriented cheekbones, and rectangular eye orbits previously seen in East Asians. Conversely, the round orbits, large frontal sinuses, and thin cranial bones seen in some archaic *H. sapiens* skulls from China represent the first appearance there of traits that have greater antiquity in Europe. The movement of these physical traits has a complex genetic basis that depends upon gene flow among populations.

Humans have a remarkable tendency to swap genes between populations, even in the face of cultural barriers. So do our primate cousins who tend to produce hybrids when two subspecies (and sometimes even species) come into contact either naturally or when bred in captivity. Moreover, without such gene flow, evolution inevitably would have resulted in the appearance of multiple species of modern humans, something that clearly has not happened. In fact, the low level of genetic differentiation among modern human populations can be explained easily as a consequence of high levels of gene flow.

Race and Human Evolution

The Neandertal question involves far more than simple interpretation of the fossil evidence. It raises fundamental issues about the relationship between biological and cultural variation. Can a series of biological features indicate particular cultural abilities?

As we examined the fossil record throughout this chapter and others, we made inferences about the cultural capabilities of our ancestors based on biological features in combination with archaeological features. The increased brain size of *Homo habilis* around 2.5 million years ago supported the notion that these ancestors were capable of more complex cultural activities than australopithecines, including the manufacture of stone tools. When we get closer to the present, can we make the same kinds of assumptions? Can we say that only the anatomically modern humans, with high foreheads and reduced brow ridges, and not archaic *Homo sapiens*, even with their modern-sized brains, were capable of making sophisticated tools and representational art?

Supporters of the multiregional hypothesis argue that we cannot. They suggest that using a series of biological features to represent a type of human being (Neandertals) with certain cultural capacities (inferior) is like making assumptions about cultural capabilities of living humans based on their appearance. In living peoples, such an assumption involves stereotyping or even racism. Supporters of the recent African origins hypothesis counter that because their theory embraces African human origins, it could hardly be considered prejudicial.

Although paleoanthropologists all acknowledge African origins for the first bipeds and the genus *Homo*, considerable disagreement exists with regard to the interpretation of the relationship between biological change and cultural change as we approach the present. The fossil and archaeological evidence from the Middle Paleolithic does not indicate a simple one-to-one correspondence between cultural innovations and a biological change preserved in the shape of the skull.

Upper Paleolithic Technology

In the Upper Paleolithic new techniques of core preparation allowed for more intensive production of highly standardized blades and permitted the proliferation of this tool type. The toolmaker formed a cylindrical core, struck the blade off near the edge of the core, and repeated this procedure, going around the core in one direction until finishing near its center (Figure 8.9). The procedure is analogous to peeling long leaves off an artichoke. With this **blade technique**, an Upper Paleolithic flint-knapper could get 75 feet of working edge from a 2-pound core; a Mousterian knapper could get only 6 feet from the same-sized core.

Other efficient techniques of tool manufacture also came into common use at this time. One such method

Upper Paleolithic Tools

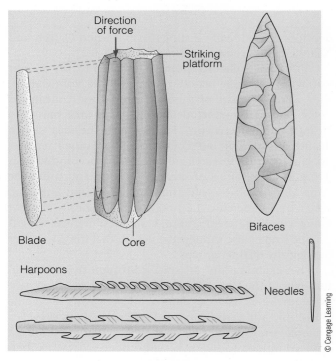

Figure 8.9 Upper Paleolithic Industries The techniques of the Upper Paleolithic allowed for the manufacture of a wide variety of tools including the efficient production of blade tools from carefully prepared cores. In addition, pressure-flaking techniques let toolmakers work with bone and antler, as well as stone, to produce finely shaped harpoons and eyed needles, and finely wrought leaf-shaped bifaces characteristic of the Solutrean industry of Europe.

---

blade technique A method of stone tool manufacture in which long, parallel-sided flakes are struck off the edges of a specially prepared core.

Figure 8.10 Pressure Flaking Flintknapper Willy Kemps, like others engaged in experimental archaeology, has mastered ancient toolmaking techniques such as pressure flaking, as well as an understanding of raw materials used at various sites. Here, he uses a moose-antler billet to press rather than strike small flakes off the edges of a core. This technique allows flint-knappers past and present to create tools far more intricate than those of the Mousterian, as you can see from his finished products.

Courtesy of Willy Kemps

is **pressure flaking**, in which a bone, antler, or wooden tool is used to press rather than strike off small flakes as the final step in stone tool manufacture (**Figure 8.10**). The advantage of this technique is that the toolmaker has greater control over the final shape of the tool than is possible with percussion flaking alone. The so-called Solutrean laurel leaf bifaces found in Spain and France are examples of this technique. The longest of these tools is 33 centimeters (13 inches) in length but less than a centimeter (about a quarter of an inch) thick. Through pressure flaking, tools could be worked with great precision into a variety of final forms, and worn tools could be effectively resharpened over and over until they were too small for further use.

Although invented in the Middle Paleolithic, the **burin**, a tool with a chisel-like edge, became more common in the Upper Paleolithic. Burins facilitated the working of bone, horn, antler, and ivory into such useful things as fishhooks, harpoons, and eyed needles. These implements made life easier for *Homo sapiens*, especially in colder northern regions where the ability to stitch together animal hides was particularly important for warmth.

The spear-thrower, also known by its Aztec (Nahuatl) name *atlatl*, appeared at this time as well. Atlatls are devices made of wood horn or bone, one end of which is gripped in the hunter's hand, while the other end has a hole or hook, in or against which the end of the spear is placed. It is held so as to effectively extend the length of the hunter's arm, thereby increasing the velocity of the spear when thrown. The greater thrust made possible through the use of a spear-thrower greatly added to the efficiency of the spear as a hunting tool (**Figure 8.11**). Ancient toolmakers often carved elaborate animal totems into the handles for their spear-throwers (**Figure 8.12**).

pressure flaking A technique of stone tool manufacture in which a bone, antler, or wooden tool is used to press, rather than strike off, small flakes from a piece of flint or similar stone.

burin A stone tool with chisel-like edges used for working bone, horn, antler, and ivory.

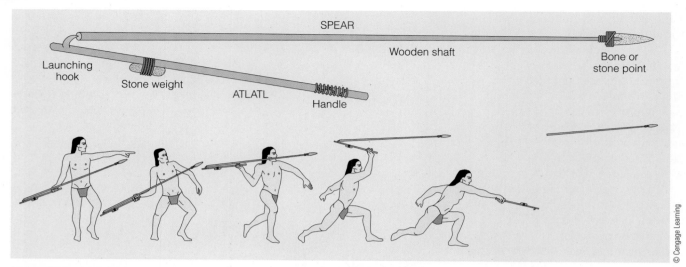

Figure 8.11 Spear-Throwers Spear-throwers (atlatls) allowed Upper Paleolithic individuals to throw spears at animals from a safe distance while still maintaining reasonable speed and accuracy. Upper Paleolithic artists frequently combined artistic expression with practical function, ornamenting their spear-throwers with animal figures.

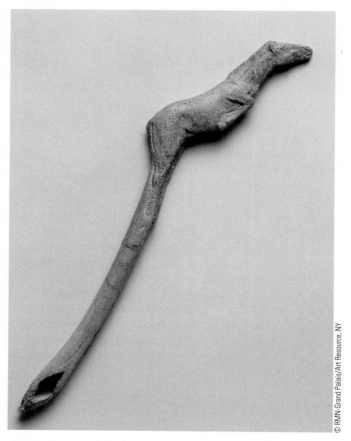

Figure 8.12 Early Production Art Some of the atlatl handles appear to have been relatively mass produced with the identical animal figure such as this 15,000-year-old horse appearing in the archaeological record multiple times. This could be the sign of an individual toolmaker or of a cultural group, or, in some cases, perhaps related to hunting a particular species of animal.

With handheld spears, hunters had to get close to their prey to make the kill. Because many of the animals they hunted were large and fierce, this was a dangerous business. The need to get within close striking range and the improbability of an instant kill exposed the hunter to considerable risk. But with the spear-thrower, the effective killing distance was increased; experiments demonstrate that the effective killing distance of a spear when used with a spear-thrower is between 18 and 27 meters as opposed to significantly less without.

Hunters can safely shorten the killing distance when their kill is assured. The use of poison on spear tips, as employed by contemporary hunters such as the Hadza of Tanzania, will decrease the risk to a hunter at shorter range. The archaeological record provides evidence of this innovation with the invention of tiny sharp stone blades that could possibly serve as dart tips and provide a vehicle for poison delivery. The earliest examples of these "microliths" began during the Upper Paleolithic in Africa but did not become widespread until the Mesolithic or Middle Stone Age, as will be described in detail in Chapter 9.

Another important innovation, net hunting, appeared sometime between 22,000 and 29,000 years ago. Knotted nets, made from the fibers of wild plants such as hemp or nettle, left their impression on the clay floors of huts when people walked on them. When the huts later burned, these impressions, baked into the earth, provide evidence that nets existed. Their use accounts for the high number of hare, fox, and other small mammal and bird bones at archaeological sites. Like historically known and contemporary net hunters, such as the Mbuti of the Congo, everyone—men, women, and children—probably participated, frightening animals with loud noises to drive them to where hunters were stationed with their nets.

This method lets hunters amass large amounts of meat without the requirement of great speed or strength.

The invention of the bow and arrow, which appeared first in Africa and arrived in Europe at the end of the Upper Paleolithic, marked another innovation in hunting techniques invented or adopted by some ancient peoples. The bow improves safety by increasing the distance between hunter and prey. Beyond 24 meters (79 feet), the accuracy and penetration of a spear thrown with a spear-thrower diminishes considerably whereas even a poor bow will shoot an arrow farther, with greater accuracy and penetrating power. With a good bow, effective even at nearly 91 meters (300 feet), hunters were able to maintain more distance between themselves and dangerous prey. This dramatically decreased both the risk to the hunter of being seriously injured by an animal fighting for survival and the chance of startling an animal and triggering its flight.

Upper Paleolithic peoples not only had better tools but also a greater diversity of tool types. The highly developed Upper Paleolithic toolkit included implements that varied seasonally as well as geographically. Thus, it is really impossible to speak of a single Upper Paleolithic culture even in Europe, a relatively small and isolated region compared to Asia and Africa. Geologic features such as mountain ranges, oceans, and glaciers isolated groups of people from one another.

Upper Paleolithic industries allowed past peoples to adapt specifically to the various environments in which they were living. Bone yards containing thousands of animal skeletons indicate just how proficient people had become at securing food. For example, at Solutré in France, over a period of many years, Upper Paleolithic hunters killed 10,000 horses; at Predmostí in the Czech Republic, they were responsible for the deaths of 1,000 mammoths. The favored big game of European hunters, however, was reindeer, which they killed in even greater numbers.

to manipulate symbols and make images. However, the modern-sized brains of archaic *Homo sapiens* and increasingly compelling evidence of the presence of language or behaviors involving symbolism—such as burials—undercut this notion. Like agriculture, which came later (see Chapter 9), the artistic explosion may have been no more than a consequence of innovations made by a people who already had possessed that capacity for tens of thousands of years.

In fact, just as many of the distinctive tools that were commonly used in Upper Paleolithic times first appear in the Middle Paleolithic, so too do objects of art. In Southwest Asia, a crude figurine of volcanic tuff is some 250,000 years old. Although some scholars contest whether this was carved, others believe that it indicates that people had the ability to carve all sorts of things from wood, a substance easier to fashion than volcanic tuff but rarely preserved for long periods of time. But with the Upper Paleolithic transition, the archaeological record becomes quite rich with figurative art that has no apparent utilitarian function. Most notable among these are the various Venus figurines found throughout Eurasia that will be discussed below (**Figure 8.13**).

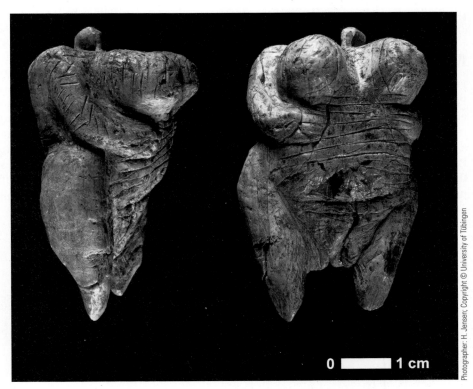

Figure 8.13 The Hohle Fels Cave Venus This tiny 35,000-year-old Venus figurine (about the size and weight of a small cluster of grapes) was recently discovered in the archaeologically rich Hohle Fels Cave in southwestern Germany. Because it was associated with the assumed earliest presence of undisputed *Homo sapiens* in Europe, the piece changed paleoanthropological interpretations of the origins of figurative art. Prior to this discovery, the earliest figurative art had included only representations of animals; female figurines did not appear until about 30,000 years ago. The exaggerated breasts and vulva and stylized markings on this carving, as on similar prehistoric statuettes known as Venus figurines, indicate the importance of female fertility to our ancestors. Some suggest that these figurines demonstrate that our ancestors may have worshiped the power of females to give birth. Could this worship have predated the appearance of stone carved figurines?

Upper Paleolithic Art

Although tools and weapons demonstrate the ingenuity of Upper Paleolithic peoples, artistic expression provides the best evidence of their creativity. Some have argued that this artistry was made possible by a newly evolved biological ability

Middle Paleolithic archaeological contexts in various parts of the world also included ochre "crayons" used by ancient peoples to decorate or mark. In southern Africa, for example, regular use of yellow and red ochre goes back 130,000 years, with some evidence as old as 200,000 years. Systematic production of paint took place by 100,000 years ago, as seen in the South African paint factory mentioned in Chapter 7 (Henshilwood et al., 2011). In that site, the Blombos Cave, archaeologists discovered large abalone shells and specialized stones used for grinding ochre pigment. They also found the shoulder bone of a seal from which marrow, a key ingredient in paint, had been removed. Ancient artists had apparently blended the pigment with the marrow, charcoal, and water to make paint. Associated artifacts at this site include large crosshatched chunks of ochre as well as beads smeared with ochre dating to 77,000 years ago.

Ancient people may well have used these pigmented paints on their bodies, as well as objects such as beads and the 50,000-year-old mammoth-tooth *churinga* described in Chapter 7. Recall as well, the use of ochre in burials in Mousterian contexts. The timeline in Figure 8.14 shows some of the cultural events of the Upper Paleolithic and the years leading into it.

Music

Evidence that music played a role in the lives of Upper Paleolithic peoples is documented through the presence of bone flutes and whistles in various sites, the most recently discovered dated to 35,000 years old. But again, such instruments may have their origin in Middle Paleolithic prototypes, such as the probable Neandertal flute discussed in Chapter 7. Although we cannot know just where and when it happened, some genius discovered that bows could do more than kill prey. They could make music as well. Because the bow and arrow first appeared during the Upper Paleolithic, the musical bow likely got its start then as well. The oldest of the stringed instruments, the musical bow ultimately made possible the rich array of such instruments in use today.

Cave or Rock Art

The earliest evidence of cave art comes from Australia and dates back at least 45,000 years. This consists entirely of geometric patterns and repetitive motifs. Figurative pictures go back 40,000 years in Europe as seen at the cave at El Castillo pictured in the Challenge Issue at the opening of the chapter. Equally old evidence of both engravings and paintings come from rock shelters and outcrops in southern Africa. The 100,000-year-old paint factory in South Africa provides evidence that pictorial art may have appeared there even earlier. Bushmen peoples have continued to make various forms of rock art into the present. Scenes feature both humans and animals, depicted with extraordinary skill, often in association with geometric and other abstract motifs. Some sites reveal that ancient peoples had the seemingly irresistible urge to add to existing rock paintings, whereas others used new sites for creating what we today call graffiti.

The continuation of this rock art tradition, unbroken into the present, has allowed scientists to discover what this art means. Living peoples maintain a close connection between art and shamanism, with many scenes depicting visions seen in states of trance. Distortions in the art, usually of human figures, represent sensations felt by individuals in a state of trance, whereas the geometric designs depict illusions that originate in the central nervous system in altered states of consciousness. These

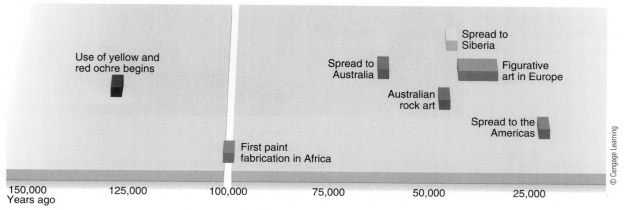

Epoch
PLEISTOCENE

Use of yellow and red ochre begins

Spread to Australia

Australian rock art

Spread to Siberia

Figurative art in Europe

Spread to the Americas

First paint fabrication in Africa

150,000 Years ago   125,000   100,000   75,000   50,000   25,000

© Cengage Learning

Figure 8.14 Cultural Innovation of the Upper Paleolithic This timeline indicates the dates for some for the cultural innovations associated with the Upper Paleolithic. Evidence exists to support the presence of other innovations such as deliberate burial and music during this time period.

© William D. Bachman/Photo Researchers, Inc.

Figure 8.15 Entoptic Phenomena in Cave Art These rock art paintings from the Kimberley Region of western Australia, depict things seen by dancers communicating with Wandjina (creation spirits) while in states of trance. Simple geometric designs such as zigzags, notches, dots, and spirals (as on the cave ceiling) as well as human and animal figures are common in these paintings.

entoptic phenomena are luminous grids, dots, zigzags, and other designs that seem to shimmer, pulsate, rotate, and expand and are seen as one enters a state of trance (Figure 8.15). Sufferers of migraines experience similar hallucinations. Entopic phenomena are typical of the Australian cave art mentioned previously.

In many recent cultures, geometric designs are used as symbolic expressions of genealogical patterns, records of origins, and the afterlife. The animals depicted in this art, often with startling realism, are not the ones most often eaten. Rather, they are powerful beasts like the eland (a large African antelope); this power is important to shamans—individuals skilled at manipulating supernatural forces and spirits for human benefit—who try to harness it for their rain-making, healing, and other rituals.

The most famous Upper Paleolithic art is that of Europe, largely because most researchers of prehistoric art are themselves of European background. Though the earliest of this art took the form of sculpture and engravings—often portraying such animals as reindeer, horses, bears, and ibexes—figurative art abounds in the spectacular paintings on the walls of 200 or so caves in southern France and northern Spain. Until El Castillo was recently dated, the oldest of these are from about 32,000 years ago (Figure 8.16). Visually accurate portrayals of Ice Age

mammals—including bison, aurochs, horses, mammoths, and stags—were often painted one on top of another.

Although well represented in other media, humans are not commonly portrayed in cave paintings; neither are scenes of events typical. Instead, the animals are often abstracted from nature and rendered two-dimensionally—no small achievement for these early artists. Sometimes the artists made use of bulges and other features of the rock to impart a more three-dimensional feeling. Frequently, the paintings are in hard-to-get-at places although suitable surfaces in more accessible locations remain untouched. In some caves, the lamps by which the artists worked have been found; these are spoon-shaped objects of sandstone in which animal fat was burned. Experimentation has shown that such lamps would have provided adequate illumination over several hours.

The techniques used by Upper Paleolithic peoples to create their cave paintings were unraveled a decade ago through the experimental work of Michel Lorblanchet. Interestingly, they turn out to be the same ones used by Aboriginal rock painters in Australia and in El Castillo. Lorblanchet's experiments are described in the following Original Study by science writer Roger Lewin.

entoptic phenomena Bright pulsating forms that are generated by the central nervous system and seen in states of trance.

Figure 8.16 Grotte de Chauvet
Ancestral humans painted these images of bison, panthers, and rhinoceroses some 32,000 years ago in the Chauvet Cave in France. These ancient paintings reflect a fundamental need to communicate, to record, and to share observations. Yet the ability to make these ancient paintings, like contemporary human culture, is rooted in the biology of the human hand, eye, and brain. Because these forms of expression appear in the Upper Paleolithic, does that provide evidence of a new species with such capabilities? Or does it simply demonstrate a cultural progression seen throughout the course of human evolutionary history? Do you think that our earlier ancestors made art that did not survive in the archaeological record?

AP Images/Jean Clottes

ORIGINAL STUDY

Paleolithic Paint Job *BY ROGER LEWIN*

© Cengage Learning

Lorblanchet's recent bid to recreate one of the most important Ice Age images in Europe was an affair of the heart as much as the head. "I tried to abandon my skin of a modern citizen, tried to experience the feeling of the artist, to enter the dialogue between the rock and the man," he explains. Every day for a week in the fall of 1990 he drove the 20 miles from his home in the medieval village of Cajarc into the hills above the river Lot. There, in a small, practically inaccessible cave, he transformed himself into an Upper Paleolithic painter.

And not just any Upper Paleolithic painter, but the one who 18,400 years ago crafted the dotted horses inside the famous cave of Pech Merle.

You can still see the original horses in Pech Merle's vast underground geologic splendor. You enter through a narrow passageway and soon find yourself gazing across a grand cavern to where the painting seems to hang in the gloom. "Outside, the landscape is very different from the one the Upper Paleolithic people saw," says Lorblanchet. "But in here, the landscape is the same as it was more than 18,000 years ago. You see what the Upper Paleolithic people experienced." No matter where you look in this cavern, the eye is drawn back to the panel of horses.

The two horses face away from each other, rumps slightly overlapping, their outlines sketched in black. The animal on the right seems to come alive as it merges with a crook in the edge of the panel, the perfect natural shape for a horse's head. But the impression of naturalism quickly fades as the eye falls on the painting's dark dots. There are more than 200 of them, deliberately distributed within and below the bodies and arcing around the right-hand horse's head and mane. More cryptic still are a smattering of red dots and half-circles and the floating outline of a fish. The surrealism is completed by six disembodied human hands stenciled above and below the animals.

Lorblanchet began thinking about recreating the horses after a research trip to Australia over a decade ago. Not only is Australia a treasure trove of rock art, but its aboriginal people are still creating it. "In Queensland I learned how people painted by spitting pigment onto the rock," he recalls. "They spat paint and used their hand, a piece of cloth, or a feather as a screen to create different lines and other effects. Elsewhere in Australia people used chewed twigs as paintbrushes, but in Queensland the spitting technique worked best." The rock surfaces there were too uneven for extensive brushwork, he adds—just as they are in Quercy.

An upper Paleolithic artist painted this spotted horse in the French cave of Pech Merle. Note the same hand motif as is seen at El Castillo.

When Lorblanchet returned home he looked at the Quercy paintings with a new eye. Sure enough, he began seeing the telltale signs of spit-painting—lines with edges that were sharply demarcated on one side and fuzzy on the other, as if they had been airbrushed—instead of the brushstrokes he and others had assumed were there. Could you produce lines that were crisp on both edges with the same technique, he wondered, and perhaps dots too? Archeologists had long recognized that hand stencils, which are common in prehistoric art, were produced by spitting paint around a hand held to the wall. But no one had thought that entire animal images could be created this way. Before he could test his ideas, however, Lorblanchet had to find a suitable rock face—the original horses were painted on a roughly vertical panel 13 feet across and 6 feet high. With the help of a speleologist, he eventually found a rock face in a remote cave high in the hills and set to work.

Following the aboriginal practices he had witnessed, Lorblanchet first made a light outline sketch of the horses with a charred stick. Then he prepared black pigment for the painting. "My intention had been to use manganese dioxide, as the Pech Merle painter did," says Lorblanchet, referring to one of the minerals ground up for paint by the early artists. "But I was advised that manganese is somewhat toxic, so I used wood charcoal instead." (Charcoal was used as pigment by Paleolithic painters in other caves, so Lorblanchet felt he could justify his concession to safety.) To turn the charcoal into paint, Lorblanchet ground it with a limestone block, put the powder in his mouth, and diluted it to the right consistency with saliva and water. For red pigment he used ochre from the local iron-rich clay.

He started with the dark mane of the right-hand horse. "I spat a series of dots and fused them together to represent tufts of hair," he says, unselfconsciously reproducing the spitting action as he talks. "Then I painted the horse's back by blowing the pigment below my hand held so"—he holds his hand flat against the rock with his thumb tucked in to form a straight line—"and used it like a stencil to produce a sharp upper edge and a diffused lower edge. You get an illusion of the animal's rounded flank this way."

He experimented as he went. "You see the angular rump?" he says, pointing to the original painting. "I reproduced that by holding my hand perpendicular to the rock, with my palm slightly bent, and I spat along the edge formed by my hand and the rock." He found he could produce sharp lines, such as those in the tail and in the upper hind leg, by spitting into the gap between parallel hands.

The belly demanded more ingenuity; he spat paint into a V-shape formed by his two splayed hands, rubbed it into a curved swath to shape the belly's outline, then finger-painted short protruding lines to suggest the animals' shaggy hair. Neatly outlined dots, he found, could not be made by blowing a thin jet of charcoal onto the wall. He had to spit pigment through a hole made in an animal skin. "I spent seven hours a day for a week," he says. "Puff . . . puff . . . puff. . . . It was exhausting, particularly because there was carbon monoxide in the cave. But you experience something special, painting like that. You feel you are breathing the image onto the rock—projecting your spirit from the deepest part of your body onto the rock surface."

Was that what the Paleolithic painter felt when creating this image? "Yes, I know it doesn't sound very scientific," Lorblanchet says of his highly personal style of investigation, "but the intellectual games of the structuralists haven't got us very far, have they? Studying rock art shouldn't be an intellectual game. It is about understanding humanity. That's why I believe the experimental approach is valid in this case."

Excerpted from Lewin, R. (1993). Paleolithic paint job. Discover 14 (7), 67–69. Copyright ©1993 The Walt Disney Co. Reprinted with permission of Discover Magazine.

© Bildarchiv/Preussischer Kulturbesitz/Art Resource, NY

Theories to account for the early European cave art often depend on conjectural and subjective interpretations. Some have argued that it is art for art's sake, but if that is so, why were animals often painted over one another, and why were they placed in inaccessible places? The latter might suggest that they served ceremonial purposes and that the caves were religious sanctuaries.

One suggestion is that the animals were drawn to ensure success in the hunt, another that their depiction was seen as a way to promote fertility and increase the size of the herds on which humans depended. In Altamira Cave in northern Spain, for example, the art shows a pervasive concern for the sexual reproduction of the bison. In cave art generally, though, the animals painted show little relationship to those most frequently hunted. Furthermore, cave art rarely includes depictions of animals being hunted, killed, copulating, birthing, or with exaggerated sexual parts, as is shown in the Venus figurines (Conard, 2009).

Another suggestion is that initiation rites, such as those marking the transition to adulthood, took place in the painted galleries. In support of this idea, footprints, most of which are small, have been found in the clay floors of several caves, and in one they even circle a modeled clay bison. As well, it appears that the small hands of ancient children created some of the finger "flutings," unpigmented grooves made into the soft surface of the cave walls (Sharpe & Van Gelder, 2006). The presence of children in the caves suggests that elders were transmitting knowledge to the new generation through painted animals and the countless "signs" and abstract designs that accompany much Upper Paleolithic art. Some have interpreted these markings as tallies of animals killed or as a reckoning of time according to a lunar calendar.

The abstract designs, including those such as the spots on the Pech Merle horses, suggest yet another possibility. For the most part, these are just like the entoptic designs seen by subjects in experiments dealing with altered states of consciousness and that are so consistently present in the rock art of southern Africa. Furthermore, the rock art of southern Africa shows the same painting of new images over older ones, as well as the same sort of fixation on large, powerful animals instead of the ones most often eaten. Thus, the cave art of Europe may well represent the same depictions of trance experiences, painted after the fact. Consistent with this interpretation, the isolation of the caves and the shimmering light on the cave walls themselves are conducive to the sort of sensory distortion that can induce trance.

Ornamental Art

Artistic expression, whatever its purpose may have been, was not confined to rock surfaces and portable objects. Upper Paleolithic peoples also ornamented their bodies with necklaces, rings, bracelets, and anklets made of perforated animal teeth, shells, and beads of bone, stone, and ivory. Clothing, too, was adorned with beads. Quite a lot of art was probably also executed in more delicate materials such as wood carving, painting on bark, and animal skins, which have not been preserved. Thus, the rarity of Upper Paleolithic art in some parts of the inhabited world may be due to the fact that some materials did not survive in the archaeological record, not that they never existed.

Gender and Art

As shown in Figure 8.13, the Upper Paleolithic also includes numerous portrayals of voluptuous women with body parts often described as exaggerated. Many appear to be pregnant, and some are shown in birthing postures. These so-called Venus figures have been found at sites from southwestern France to as far as Siberia. Made of stone, ivory, antler, or baked clay, they differ little in style from place to place, testifying to the sharing of ideas over vast distances. Although some have interpreted the Venuses as objects associated with a fertility cult, others suggest that they may have been exchanged to cement alliances between groups.

Art historian LeRoy McDermott has suggested that the Venus figurines are "ordinary women's views of their own bodies" and the earliest examples of self-representation (McDermott, 1996). He suggests that the distortions and exaggerations of the female form visible in the Venus figurines derive from the ancient artist looking down over her own pregnant body. Paleolithic archaeologist Margaret Conkey opened the door to such interpretations through her work combining gender theory and feminist theory with the science of archaeology.

With a particular interest in the Upper Paleolithic art of Europe, Conkey has spent decades challenging the traditional notion that Paleolithic art was made by male artists as an expression of spiritual beliefs related to hunting activities. She emphasizes that many reconstructions of behavior in the past rely upon contemporary gender norms to fill in blanks left in the archaeological record. Conkey, believing that today's stereotypes may be distorting our view of the past, seeks clues about the role of gender in the archaeological research she conducts (Gero & Conkey, 1991).

In this regard, note that current scientists tend to describe Venus figurines largely in sexual terms rather than in terms of fertility and birth. For example, in a commentary in the prestigious journal *Nature* that accompanied the description of the Hohle Fels Cave Venus, British archaeologist Paul Mellars states: "The figure is explicitly—and blatantly—that of a woman, with an exaggeration of sexual characteristics (large, projecting breasts, a greatly enlarged and explicit vulva, and bloated belly and thighs) that by twenty-first-century standards could be seen as bordering on the pornographic" (Mellars, 2009, p. 176).

Mellars's reaction to the Venus figurine reflects present-day attitudes toward the nude female form rather than the intent of an ancient artist. Perhaps the artist was a female, looking at her own pregnant form or remembering the experience of giving birth. Although the gender and the intention of the artist behind the Venus figurine cannot be known for sure, it is easy to imagine that pregnancy and the birth process were at least as awe-inspiring to Paleolithic peoples as were hunting experiences.

Human biology also provides us with some clues. Breasts and belly enlarge during pregnancy; the tissues around the vulva enlarge and stretch dramatically during the birth process. Breasts swell further with milk after a birth. Mellars's interpretation of the artistic depiction of these biological changes as "pornographic" derives from the gender norms of his particular culture. Many contemporary peoples with different worldviews would not react to the figurine in these terms.

Figure 8.17 Upper Paleolithic Mammoth Bone Dwelling Pictured is a reconstructed dwelling made from interlocked and lashed mammoth bones. These dwellings are typically round in form with a central hearth or several scattered hearths. Pits with bones and butchering areas and flint-knapping areas often surround the dwellings. They tend to be strategically built along old river terraces near migration pathways that grazing animals would take between steppes and rivers. Although most of these dwellings date to between 14,000 and 20,000 years ago, one from the site of Moldova dates back to 44,000 years ago and is associated with typical Neandertal tools. Others argue that the Moldova site represents the remains of a hunting blind.

Other Aspects of Upper Paleolithic Culture

Upper Paleolithic peoples lived not only in caves and rock shelters but also in structures built out in the open. In Ukraine, for example, remains of sizable settlements have been found in which huts were built on frameworks of intricately stacked mammoth bones (**Figure 8.17**). Where the ground was frozen, cobblestones were heated and placed in the earth to sink in, thereby providing sturdy, dry floors. Instead of shallow depressions or flat surfaces that radiated little heat, their hearths were stone-lined pits that conserved heat for extended periods and made for more efficient cooking.

For the outdoors, Upper Paleolithic peoples had the same sort of tailored clothing worn in historic times by Arctic and sub-Arctic peoples. Further, they engaged in long-distance trade, as indicated, for example, by the presence of seashells and amber from the Baltic Sea in northern Europe at sites several hundred kilometers from the sources of these materials. Although Middle Paleolithic peoples also made use of rare and distant materials, these practices became far more regular in the Upper Paleolithic.

The Spread of Upper Paleolithic Peoples

Upper Paleolithic peoples expanded into regions previously uninhabited by their archaic forebears. Colonization of southern Siberia by the Denisovans dates back about 280,000 years, and it appears that the Denisovans were interbreeding with *Homo sapiens* there between 40,000 and 50,000 years ago. Upper Paleolithic peoples reached the northeastern part of that region about 10,000 years later. Although reaching this region did not involve crossing large bodies of water, inhabiting Greater Australia and the Americas did require such voyages.

The Sahul

Much earlier, possibly by at least 60,000 years ago, people managed to get to Australia, Tasmania, and New Guinea, then connected to one another in a single landmass called the **Sahul** (Rice, 2000). To do this, they had to use some kind of watercraft because the Sahul was separated from the islands (which are geologically a part of the Asian landmass) of Java, Sumatra, Borneo, and Bali. At times of maximum glaciation and low sea levels, these islands were joined to one another in a single landmass called **Sunda**, but a deep ocean trench (called the Wallace Trench, after Alfred Russel Wallace, who, as described in Chapter 2, discovered natural selection at the same time as Charles Darwin) always separated Sunda and Sahul (**Figure 8.18**).

Anthropologist Joseph Birdsell suggested several routes of island hopping and seafaring to make the crossing between these landmasses (Birdsell, 1977). Each of these routes involves crossing open water without land visible on the horizon. The earliest known site in New Guinea dates to 40,000 years ago. Sites in Australia are dated to even earlier, but these dates are especially contentious because they involve the critical question of the relationship between anatomical modernity and the presence of humanlike culture.

Early dates for habitation of the Sahul indicate that archaic *Homo* rather than anatomically modern forms possessed the cultural capacity for oceanic navigation. Evidence from a recent genetic analysis of a hair sample taken from an Australian Aborigine over a century ago indicates direct spread from Africa for some of these people (Rasmussen et al., 2011). Once in Australia, these people used ochre to create some of the world's earliest sophisticated rock art, perhaps even earlier than the more famous European cave paintings. One painting in the Arnhem Land plateau depicts a species of giant bird thought to have gone extinct around 40,000 years ago.

Interestingly, considerable physical variation is seen in Australian fossil specimens from this period. Some specimens have the high forehead characteristic of anatomical modernity whereas others possess traits providing excellent evidence of continuity between living Aborigines and the earlier *Homo erectus* and archaic *Homo sapiens* fossils from Indonesia. Willandra Lakes—the fossil lake region of southeastern Australia, far from where the earliest archaeological evidence of human habitation of the continent was found—is particularly rich with fossils. The variation present in these fossils illustrates the problems inherent with making a one-to-one correspondence between the skull of a certain shape and cultural capabilities.

Figure 8.18 **Sea Level and the Coastlines of Sunda and Sahul** Habitation of Australia and New Guinea (joined together with Tasmania as a single landmass called Sahul) was dependent upon travel across the open ocean even at times of maximum glaciation when sea levels were low. This figure shows the coastlines of Sahul and Sunda (Southeast Asia plus the islands of Java, Sumatra, Borneo, and Bali) now and in the past. As sea levels rose with melting glaciers, sites of early human habitation were submerged under water.

Other evidence for sophisticated ritual activity in early Australia is provided by the burial of a man at least 40,000 and possibly 60,000 years ago from the Willandra Lakes region. His body was positioned with his fingers intertwined around one another in the region of his penis, and red ochre had been scattered over the body. It may be that this pigment had more than symbolic value; for example, its iron salts have antiseptic and deodorizing properties, and there are recorded instances in which red ochre is associated with prolonging life and is used medicinally to treat particular conditions or infections. One historically known Aborigine society is reported to have used ochre to heal wounds, scars, and burns and to use it for those in pain, covering the body with the substance and placing it in the sun to promote sweating. See this chapter's Globalscape to learn about the importance of Willandra Lakes to global and local heritage today.

As in many parts of the world, paleoanthropologists conducting research on human evolution in Australia are essentially constructing a view of history that conflicts with the beliefs of Aborigines. The story of human evolution is utterly dependent on Western conceptions of time, relationships established through genetics, and

---

Sahul The greater Australian landmass including Australia, New Guinea, and Tasmania. At times of maximum glaciation and low sea levels, these areas were continuous.

Sunda The combined landmass of the contemporary islands of Java, Sumatra, Borneo, and Bali that was continuous with mainland Southeast Asia at times of low sea levels corresponding to maximum glaciation.

Globalscape

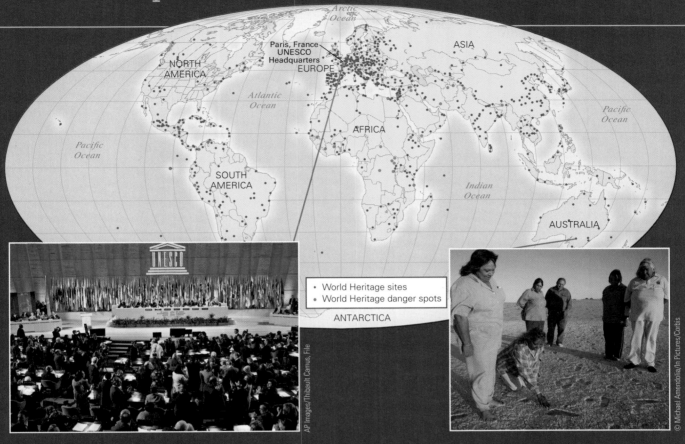

- World Heritage sites
- World Heritage danger spots

NORTH AMERICA · Paris, France UNESCO Headquarters · EUROPE · ASIA · Atlantic Ocean · Pacific Ocean · AFRICA · SOUTH AMERICA · Pacific Ocean · Indian Ocean · AUSTRALIA · ANTARCTICA · Arctic Ocean

AP Images/Thibault Camus, File

© Michael Amendolia/In Pictures/Corbis

Whose Lakes Are These?

Paleoanthropologists regularly travel to early fossil sites and to museums where original fossil specimens are housed. Increasingly, these same destinations are becoming popular with tourists. Making sites accessible to everyone while protecting the sites requires considerable skill and knowledge. But most importantly, long before the advent of paleoanthropology or paleotourism, these sites were and are the homelands of living people.

Aboriginal people have lived along the shores of the Willandra Lakes region of Australia for at least 50,000 years. They have passed down their stories and cultural traditions even as the lakes dried up and a spectacular crescent-shaped, wind-formed dune (called a *lunette*) remained. The Mungo lunette has particular cultural significance to three Aboriginal tribal groups. Several major fossil finds from the region include cremated remains as well as an ochred burial, both dated to at least 40,000 years ago. Nearly 460 fossilized footprints dated to between 19,000 and 23,000 years ago were made by people of all ages who lived in the region when the Willandra Lakes were still full of water. How can a place of local and global significance be appropriately preserved and honored?

Since 1972, UNESCO's World Heritage List has been an important part of maintaining places like Willandra Lakes, which was itself inscribed as a World Heritage Site in 1981. Individual states apply to UNESCO for site designation, and if approved they receive financial and political support for maintaining the site. When designated sites are threatened by natural disaster, war, pollution, or poorly managed tourism, they are placed on a danger list, indicated with a red dot on the map above, forcing the local governments to institute measures to protect the sites in order to continue receiving UNESCO support.

Each year approximately thirty new World Heritage sites are designated. In 2011 the list included 962 properties: 188 natural preserves, 745 cultural sites, and 29 mixed sites. Fossil and archaeological sites are well represented on the World Heritage List. The Willandra Lakes site is recognized for both natural and cultural value.

Although important to the world community, Willandra Lakes has particular meaning to the Aborigines. Aunty Beryl Carmichael, an elder of the Ngiyaampaa people, explains that this land is integrated with her culture:

Because when the old people would tell the stories, they'd just refer to them as "marrathal warkan," which means long, long time ago, when time first began for our people, as people on this land after creation. We have various sites around in our country, we call them the birthing places of all our stories. And of course, the stories are embedded with the lore that governs this whole land. The air, the land, the environment, the universe, the stars.[a]

Not only are Aunty Beryl's stories and the land around Willandra Lakes critical for the Ngiyaampaa and other Aboriginal groups, but their survival ultimately contributes to all of us.

The following lists the sites considered endangered at the June 2011 meeting of the World Heritage Committee. Committee members included representatives from countries throughout the globe including: Australia, Bahrain, Barbados, Brazil, Cambodia, China, Egypt, France, Iraq, Jordan, Mali, Mexico, Nigeria, Russia, South Africa, Sweden, Switzerland, Thailand, and the United Arab Emirates.

Afghanistan
Cultural Landscape and Archaeological Remains of the Bamiyan Valley (2003)
Minaret and Archaeological Remains of Jam (2002)

Belize
Belize Barrier Reef Reserve System (2009)

Central African Republic
Manovo-Gounda St. Floris National Park (1997)

Chile
Humberstone and Santa Laura Saltpeter Works (2005)

Colombia
Los Katíos National Park (2009)

Côte d'Ivoire
Comoé National Park (2003)
Mount Nimba Strict Nature Reserve (1992)

Democratic Republic of the Congo
Garamba National Park (1996)
Kahuzi-Biega National Park (1997)
Okapi Wildlife Reserve (1997)
Salonga National Park (1999)
Virunga National Park (1994)

Egypt
Abu Mena (2001)

Ethiopia
Simien National Park (1996)

Georgia
Bagrati Cathedral and Gelati Monastery (2010)
Historical Monuments of Mtskheta (2009)

Guinea
Mount Nimba Strict Nature Reserve (1992)

Honduras
Río Plátano Biosphere Reserve (2011)

Indonesia
Tropical Rainforest Heritage of Sumatra (2011)

Iran, Islamic Republic of
Bam and Its Cultural Landscape (2004)

Iraq
Ashur (Qal'at Sherqat) (2003)
Samarra Archaeological City (2007)

Jerusalem (site proposed by Jordan)
Old City of Jerusalem and Its Walls (1982)

Madagascar
Rainforests of the Atsinanana (2010)

Niger
Air and Ténéré Natural Reserves (1992)

Pakistan
Fort and Shalamar Gardens in Lahore (2000)

Peru
Chan Chan Archaeological Zone (1986)

Philippines
Rice Terraces of the Philippine Cordilleras (2001)

Senegal
Niokolo-Koba National Park (2007)

Serbia
Medieval Monuments in Kosovo (2006)

Tanzania, United Republic of
Ruins of Kilwa Kisiwani and Ruins of Songo Mnara (2004)

Uganda
Tombs of Buganda Kings at Kasubi (2010)

United States of America
Everglades National Park (2010)

Venezuela
Coro and Its Port (2005)

Yemen
Historic Town of Zabid (2000)

Global Twister

The listing of endangered sites brings global pressure on a state to find ways to protect the natural and cultural heritage contained within its boundaries. Do you think this method of global social pressure is effective?

---

[a]"Why the stories are told," Aunty Beryl Carmichael. *Aboriginal Culture: Dreamtime Stories.* www.rmwebed.com.au/HSIE/y10/abc/dreamtime/dreamtime.htm

a definition of what it means to be human. All of these theories are at odds with Aboriginal beliefs about human origins. Still, while conducting their research on human evolution, paleoanthropologists working in Australia have advocated and supported the Aboriginal culture.

The Americas

Although scientists concur that American Indian ancestry can be traced ultimately back to Asian origins, just when people arrived in the Americas has been a matter of lively debate. This debate draws upon geographical, cultural, and biological evidence.

The conventional wisdom has long been that the first people migrated into North America over dry land that connected Siberia to Alaska. This land bridge was a consequence of the buildup of great continental glaciers. As the ice masses grew, there was a worldwide lowering of sea levels, causing an emergence of land in places like the Bering Strait where seas today are shallow. Thus, Alaska became, in effect, an eastward extension of Siberia (**Figure 8.19**). Climatic patterns of the Ice Age kept this land bridge, known as Beringia or the Bering Land Bridge, relatively ice free and covered instead with lichens and mosses that could support herds of grazing animals. It is possible that Upper Paleolithic peoples could have come to the Americas simply by following herd animals. The latest genetic evidence indicates movement took place back and forth across Beringia.

According to geologists, conditions were right for ancient humans and herd animals to traverse Beringia between 11,000 and 25,000 years ago. Though this land bridge was also open between 40,000 and 75,000 years ago, there is no evidence that conclusively confirms human migration at these earlier dates. As with the Sahul, early dates open the possibility of spread to the Americas by archaic *Homo.*

Although ancient Siberians did indeed spread eastward, it is now clear that massive glaciers blocked their way until 13,000 years ago at the earliest (Marshall, 2001). By then, people were already living farther south in the Americas. Thus, the question of how people first came to this hemisphere has been reopened. One possibility is that, like the first Australians, the first Americans may have come by boat or rafts, perhaps traveling between islands or ice-free pockets of coastline, from as far away as the Japanese islands and down North America's northwestern coast. Hints of such voyages are provided by a handful of North American skeletons (such as Kennewick Man) that bear a closer resemblance to the aboriginal Ainu people of northern Japan and their forebears than they do to other Asians or contemporary Native Americans. Unfortunately, because sea levels were lower than they are today, coastal sites used by early voyagers would now be under water.

Figure 8.19 Land Bridge to the Americas The Arctic conditions and glaciers in northeastern Asia and northwestern North America provided both opportunities and challenges for ancient peoples spreading to the Americas. On the one hand, the Arctic climate provided a land bridge (Beringia) between the continents, but on the other hand, the harsh environment posed considerable difficulties to humans. Ancient peoples may have also come to the Americas by sea. Once in North America, glaciers spanning a good portion of the continent determined the areas open to habitation.

Securely dated objects from Monte Verde, a site in south-central Chile, place people in southern South America by 14,500 years ago, if not earlier. Assuming the first populations spread from Siberia to Alaska, linguist Johanna Nichols suggests that the first people to arrive in North America did so by 20,000 years ago. She bases this estimate on the time it took various other languages to spread from their homelands—including Eskimo languages in the Arctic and Athabaskan languages from interior western Canada to New Mexico and Arizona (Navajo). Nichols's conclusion is that it would have taken at least 7,000 years for people to reach south-central Chile (Nichols, 2008). Others suggest people arrived in the Americas closer to 30,000 years ago or even earlier.

A recent genetic study using mitochondrial and nuclear DNA indicates that the American Indian Upper Paleolithic peoples separated from Asian peoples prior to 40,000 years ago and occupied Beringia for about 20,000 years with little population growth (Kitchen, Miyamoto, & Mulligan, 2008). Population size then expanded again as these peoples crossed Beringia between 15,000 and 17,000 years ago but then took different paths. One group traveled down the Pacific Coast and the other down the center of the continent. Although the dates generated in this study are as early as others have suggested, these findings support the notion that distinct language groups made separate migrations.

Another study suggests back and forth exchanges between Siberia and North America (Tamm et al., 2007). Yet a third study suggests three waves of migration across Beringia (Reich et al., 2012). As is the case with all investigations of the distant past, the narrative of how the Americas were peopled is under construction. Genetic data must be crosschecked with morphological data, linguistic data, and with the archaeological evidence. Each new discovery in the field or in the lab contributes to this chronicle. Careful verifications among various kinds of data allow for the eventual refinement of the account.

The picture currently emerging, then, is of people, who may not have looked like modern Native Americans, arriving by boats or rafts and spreading southward and eastward over time. In fact, contact back and forth between North America and Siberia never stopped. In all probability, it became more common as the glaciers melted away. As a consequence, through gene flow as well as later arrivals of people from Asia, people living in the Americas came to have the broad faces, prominent cheekbones, and round cranial vaults that tend to characterize the skulls of many Native Americans today. Still, Native Americans, like all human populations, are physically variable. The Kennewick Man controversy described in Chapter 5 illustrates the complexities of establishing ethnic identity based on the shape of the skull. In order to trace the history of the peopling of the Americas, anthropologists must combine archaeological, linguistic, and cultural information with evidence of biological variation.

Although the earliest technologies in the Americas remain poorly known, they gave rise in North America, about 12,000 years ago, to the distinctive fluted spear points of **Paleoindian** hunters of big game, such as mammoths, mastodons, caribou, and now extinct forms of bison. Fluted points are finely made, with large channel flakes removed from one or both surfaces. This thinned section was inserted into the notched end of a spear shaft for a sturdy haft. Fluted points are found from the Atlantic seaboard to the Pacific Coast, and from Alaska down into Panama. The efficiency of the hunters who made and used these points may have hastened the extinction of the mammoth and other large Pleistocene mammals. By driving large numbers of animals over cliffs, they killed many more than they could possibly use, thus wasting huge amounts of meat.

This does not mean, however, that the first Americans were all big game hunters. Other Paleoindians, including those who inhabited Monte Verde in Chile, far distant from Beringia, provide evidence of a very different way of life. These people foraged for plants and seafood and consumed a variety of smaller mammals.

Upper Paleolithic peoples in Australia and the Americas, like their counterparts in Africa and Eurasia, possessed sophisticated technology that was efficient and appropriate for the environments they inhabited. As in other parts of the world, when a technological innovation such as the fluted points begins, this technology is rapidly disseminated among the people inhabiting the region.

Still, some innovations never became a part of a group's cultural repertoire. For example, Australian Aborigines retained the spear and spear-thrower, never adopting or inventing the bow and arrow. The bow and arrow was eventually widely used in the Americas, but it appeared there much later than it did in Africa and Eurasia. In each place, subsistence practices synchronized with the environment and other aspects of the local culture.

Major Paleolithic Trends

As we look at the larger picture, since the time the genus *Homo* appeared, evolving humans came to rely increasingly on cultural, as opposed to biological, adaptation. To handle environmental challenges, evolving humans developed appropriate tools, clothes, shelter, use of fire, and so forth rather than relying upon biological adaptation of the human organism. This was true whether human populations lived in regions that were hot or cold, wet or dry, forested or grassy. Though culture is ultimately based on what might loosely be called brainpower or, more formally, **cognitive capacity**, it is learned and not carried by genes. Therefore, cultural innovations may occur rapidly and can easily be transferred among individuals and groups.

Scientists have recently documented key differences in the proteins involved in brain metabolism in humans compared to other species that may account for some of this brainpower. Unfortunately, these metabolic changes are also associated with schizophrenia, indicating that there may have been some costs in the process. This study suggests that the cultural practice of cooking freed the body to devote more energy to brain metabolism. Although cooking was certainly an innovation of ancient *Homo*, the varied low-fat diet and high exercise of our ancestors were in general healthier than the dietary patterns prevailing in many parts of the world today. See this chapter's Biocultural Connection for a discussion of how a return to the diets and lifestyles of our forebears may improve human health.

Paleoindians The earliest inhabitants of North America.

cognitive capacity A broad concept including intelligence, educability, concept formation, self-awareness, self-evaluation, attention span, sensitivity in discrimination, and creativity.

BIOCULTURAL CONNECTION

Paleolithic Prescriptions for Diseases of Today

Throughout most of our evolutionary history, humans led more physically active lives and ate a more varied low-fat diet than we do now. Our ancestors did not drink alcohol or smoke. They spent their days scavenging or hunting for animal protein while gathering vegetable foods, with some insects thrown in for good measure. They stayed fit through traveling great distances each day over the savannah and beyond.

Though we hail increased life expectancy as one of modern civilization's greatest accomplishments, this phenomenon, brought about in part by the discovery and dissemination of antibiotics during the middle of the twentieth century, is quite recent. Anthropologists George Armelagos and Mark Nathan Cohen suggest that the downward trajectory for human health began when we left behind our Paleolithic lifeways and began farming instead of hunting and gathering and settled into permanent villages some 10,000 years ago.[a] The chronic diseases that linger—such as diabetes, heart disease, substance abuse, and high blood pressure—have their roots in this shift.

The prevalence of these "diseases of civilization" has increased rapidly over the past sixty-five years. Anthropologists Melvin Konner and Marjorie Shostak and physician Boyd Eaton have suggested that our Paleolithic ancestors left us with a prescription for a cure. They propose that as "stone-agers in a fast lane," people's health will improve by returning to the lifestyle to which their bodies are adapted.[b] Such Paleolithic prescriptions are an example of evolutionary medicine—a branch of medical anthropology that uses evolutionary principles to contribute to human health.

Evolutionary medicine bases its prescriptions on the idea that rate of cultural change exceeds the rate of biological change. Our food-forager physiology was shaped over millions of years, whereas the cultural changes leading to contemporary lifestyles have occurred rapidly. For example, tobacco was domesticated in the Americas only a few thousand years ago and was widely used as both a narcotic and an insecticide. Alcoholic beverages, which depend on the domestication of a variety of plant species such as hops, barley, and corn, also could not have arisen without village life, as the fermentation process requires time and watertight containers. However, the high-starch diets and sedentary lifestyle of village life contributes to diabetes and heart disease.

Our evolutionary history offers clues about the diet and lifestyle to which our bodies evolved. By returning to our ancient lifeways, we can make the diseases of civilization a thing of the past.

BIOCULTURAL QUESTION

Can you imagine what sort of Paleolithic prescriptions our evolutionary history would contribute for modern behaviors, such as childrearing practices, sleeping, and work patterns? Are there any ways that your culture or personal lifestyle is well aligned with past lifeways?

---

[a]Cohen, M. N., & Armelagos, G. J. (Eds.). (1984a). *Paleopathology at the origins of agriculture.* Orlando: Academic Press.

[b]Eaton, S. B., Konner, M., & Shostak, M. (1988). Stone-agers in the fast lane: Chronic degenerative diseases in evolutionary perspective. *American Journal of Medicine 84* (4), 739–749.

Certain trends stand out from the information anthropologists have gathered about the Old Stone Age in most parts of the world. One was toward increasingly more sophisticated, varied, and specialized toolkits. Tools became progressively lighter and smaller, resulting in the conservation of raw materials and a better ratio between length of cutting edge and weight of stone. Tools also became specialized according to region and function. Instead of crude all-purpose tools, more effective particularized devices were made to deal with the differing conditions of savannah, forest, and shore.

As humans came to rely increasingly on culture as a means to meet the challenges of existence, they were able to inhabit new environments. With more efficient tool technology, population size could increase, allowing humans to spill over into more diverse environments.

Improved cultural abilities may also have played a role in the reduction of heavy physical features, favoring instead decreased size and weight of face and teeth, the development of larger and more complex brains, and ultimately a reduction in body size and robustness. This dependence on intelligence rather than bulk provided the key for humans' increased reliance on cultural rather than physical adaptation. The development of conceptual thought can be seen in symbolic artifacts and signs of ritual activity throughout the world.

Through Paleolithic times, at least in the colder parts of the world, hunting became more important, and people became more proficient at it. Humans' intelligence enabled them to develop composite tools as well as the social organization and cooperation so important for survival and population growth. As discussed in the next chapter, this trend was reversed during the Mesolithic, when hunting lost its preeminence, and the gathering of wild plants and seafood became increasingly important.

As human populations grew and spread, cultural differences between regions also became more marked. Although some indications of cultural contact and intercommunication are evident in the development of long-distance trade networks, tool assemblages developed in response to the specific challenges and resources of specific environments.

As Paleolithic peoples eventually spread over all the continents of the world, including Australia and the Americas, changes in climate and environment called for new kinds of adaptations. In forest environments, people needed tools for working wood; on the open savannah and plains, humans began to use the bow and arrow to hunt the game they could not stalk closely; the people in settlements that grew up around lakes and along rivers and coasts developed harpoons and hooks; in the sub-Arctic regions, they needed tools to work the heavy skins of seals and caribou. Because culture is first and foremost a mechanism by which humans adapt, throughout the globe regional differentiations allowed Upper Paleolithic humans to face the challenges of their distinct environments.

CHAPTER CHECKLIST

What evidence supports the recent African origins hypothesis (or Eve hypothesis) for modern human origins? What are its assumptions?

● Evidence to support the recent African origins hypothesis originally came from the study of mitochondrial DNA of modern humans and extrapolating to the past based on an assumed rate of constant change.

● The earliest anatomically modern fossils have been found in Africa dating 160,000 old, relatively near in time to the estimation of when "Eve" should have existed.

● Issues with the recent African origins hypothesis include the movement of people into Africa, other geographical sources of mtDNA, and variable rates of molecular change.

● The recent African origins hypothesis supposes a strong connection between modern anatomy and cultural capacity that is inconsistent with findings on Neandertal culture.

What evidence supports the multiregional hypothesis for human origins? What are its assumptions?

● Modern humans retain certain anatomical characteristics of the *Homo erectus* fossils from the same region. This supports the idea that archaic humans all over the world simultaneously evolved into *Homo sapiens* and that gene flow kept humans connected as a single species.

● Distinguishing between various archaic and anatomically modern fossils poses a great challenge because many specimens and modern humans exhibit a mix of features.

● The anatomical variety of both archaic and modern humans and evidence of high levels of gene flow throughout human history support the multiregional hypothesis.

● Recent cultural innovations have no correspondence to changes in human appearance.

● Comparison of genomes of ancient peoples such as the Neandertals and the Denisovans with living human groups demonstrates genetic continuity.

What were the major technological developments of the Upper Paleolithic era?

● Throughout the globe blade tools became widespread along with an explosion of expressive arts. Spear throwing, the bow and arrow, and net hunting originated in this period. Hunting became a less dangerous and more effective manner of acquiring food.

● Pressure flaking gave toolmakers greater control over the shape of the tool whereas the blade technique yielded greater efficiency.

● In Europe Mousterian toolkits gave way to the earliest Upper Paleolithic industries—the Châtelperronian and Aurignacian traditions—shared by Neandertals and anatomically modern humans. Cultural distinction between the two groups in Europe does not clearly bear on either as superior.

How did the role of art in human societies evolve over this period?

● Starting 40,000 years ago, figurative art proliferated, including carved figurines, flutes, and cave art that most frequently depicted large mammals and abstract patterns seen perhaps in trance states.

● Evidence of paint manufacture goes back to 100,000 years ago when pigments were used as part of burial rituals and likely as body decoration. Figurative art that was not preserved in the archaeological record was also likely to have been created.

● Art began to be used in rituals and decorations, reflecting visions seen in altered states of consciousness known as entoptic phenomena.

● Interpretation of the artistic legacy of the Paleolithic remains subject to the biases of current social norms, as in the case of the Venus figurines.

How did humans spread throughout the globe during the Upper Paleolithic period?

● Spreading throughout the entire globe, Upper Paleolithic people built dwellings and tailored warm clothing that permitted habitation in harsh climates.

● Humans arrived in Australia at least 40,000 years ago by crossing wide bodies of open water. Original migration to North America may also have occurred by sea, with continued exchange happening while the Bering Land Bridge existed.

● Given their vast geographic distribution, disparate societies developed distinct art, technology, lifestyle, and anatomy.

QUESTIONS FOR REFLECTION

1. Upper Paleolithic art suggests that humans have always been challenged to understand where we fit in the larger system of life forms, past and present. What are your thoughts about how the impulse to create art relates to human efforts to make sense of our place in nature? What is your conception of the artist, a Neandertal perhaps, who had the impulse to create images of his or her hand shown in the chapter's Challenge Issue?

2. What does it mean to be "modern," biologically or culturally? How should we define *human*?

3. How do you feel personally about the possibility of having Neandertals as part of your ancestry? How might you relate the Neandertal debates to stereotyping or racism in contemporary society?

4. Why do you think that most of the studies of prehistoric art have tended to focus on Europe? Do you think this focus reflects ethnocentrism or bias about the definition of *art* in Western cultures?

5. Do you think that gender has played a role in anthropological interpretations of the behavior of our ancestors and the way that paleoanthropologists and archaeologists conduct their research? Do you believe that feminism has a role to play in the interpretation of the past?

ONLINE STUDY RESOURCES

CourseMate

Access chapter-specific learning tools, including learning objectives, practice quizzes, videos, flash cards, glossaries, and more in your Anthropology CourseMate.

Log into **www.cengagebrain.com** to access the resources your instructor has assigned and to purchase materials.

Challenge Issue

With the start of the Neolithic some 10,000 years ago—when some humans shifted to farming and to the domestication of animals as they settled into village life—competition for critical resources began to intensify. Today, the competition set into motion at the start of the Neolithic takes place on a global scale and places untenable pressures on the world's natural resources. Consider potato farming, water, and a way of life in the Ica region of Peru, in the foothills of the Andes. Ancient peoples in the region domesticated numerous plants and animals including some 3,000 varieties of potato, cultivating different types at various elevations. According to legend, the gods gave potatoes to Andean peoples to help them overthrow invaders, who were led instead to the inedible leaves hiding the rich underground treasure. Potatoes also play a role in aboriginal peoples' marriage ceremonies and religious rituals because raw potatoes' natural alkaloids help healers in their communications with spirits. Today, this complete way of life is threatened by the large-scale industrial farming of asparagus, a water-intensive crop native to Europe, western Asia, and northern Africa. Over the past decade, Peru has become the largest global exporter of asparagus, earning about $500 million per year on this crop. In Peru's sunny Ica region where 95 percent of the asparagus is grown, the industrial farms are draining the aquifers at alarming rates, and nearby potato farmers are losing their livelihood. In such a competition for resources, global corporations are greatly advantaged over local inhabitants, but ultimately, for all of us to win, we need to implement strategies to ensure a planet in balance.

The Neolithic Revolution: The Domestication of Plants and Animals

9

IN THIS CHAPTER YOU WILL LEARN TO

- Identify the Mesolithic roots of farming and pastoralism.

- Describe the mechanisms of and evidence for plant and animal domestication.

- Compare theories about the reasons for this shift in lifeways.

- Identify the various centers of domestication globally.

- Examine the effects of food production on population size.

- Describe how the means of subsistence affect other aspects of social organization.

- Summarize the health consequences of the Neolithic revolution.

- Compare the cultural changes of the Neolithic to hunter-gatherer lifeways and to hierarchical notions of progress.

Throughout the Paleolithic, people depended exclusively on wild sources of food for their survival. They hunted and trapped wild animals, fished and gathered shellfish, eggs, berries, nuts, roots, and other plant foods, relying on their wits and muscles to acquire what nature provided. Whenever favored sources of food became scarce, people adjusted by increasing the variety of foods eaten and incorporating less desirable foods into their diets.

Over time, the subsistence practices of some peoples began to change in ways that radically transformed their way of life as they became food producers rather than food foragers. For some human groups, a more sedentary existence accompanied food production. This in turn permitted a reorganization of the workload in society: Some individuals could be freed from the food quest to devote their energies to other tasks. Over the course of thousands of years, these changes brought about an unforeseen way of life. With good reason, the **Neolithic** era (literally, the New Stone Age), when this change took place, has been called revolutionary in human history.

The Mesolithic Roots of Farming and Pastoralism

As seen in the previous chapter, by the end of the Paleolithic humans had spread throughout the globe. During this period glaciers covered much of the northern hemisphere. By 12,000 years ago, warmer climates prevailed, and these glaciers receded, causing changes in human habitats globally. Sea levels rose throughout the world, and areas flooded that had been dry land during periods of glaciation, such as the Bering Strait, parts of the North Sea, and an extensive land area that had joined the eastern islands of Indonesia to mainland Asia (recall Figure 8.19).

Neolithic The New Stone Age; a prehistoric period beginning about 10,000 years ago in which peoples possessed stone-based technologies and depended on domesticated crops and/or animals for subsistence.

In some northern regions, warmer climates brought about particularly marked changes, allowing the replacement of barren tundra with forests. In the process, the herd animals—upon which northern Paleolithic peoples had depended for much of their food, clothing, and shelter—disappeared from many areas. Some, like the caribou and musk ox, moved to colder climates; others, like the mammoths, died out completely. In the new forests, animals were often more solitary in their habits. As a result, large cooperative hunts were less productive than previously. Diets shifted to abundant plant foods as well as fish and other foods in and around lakes, bays, and rivers. In Europe, Asia, and Africa, anthropologists call this transitional period between the Paleolithic and the Neolithic the **Mesolithic**, or Middle Stone Age. In the Americas, comparable cultures are referred to as **Archaic cultures**.

New technologies accompanied the changed postglacial environment. Toolmakers began to manufacture ground stone tools, shaped and sharpened by grinding the tool against sandstone, often using sand as an additional abrasive. Once shaped and sharpened, these stones were set into wooden or sometimes antler handles to make effective axes and *adzes* (cutting tools with a sharp blade set at right angles to a handle). Though such implements take longer to make, with heavy-duty usage, they break less often than those made of chipped stone. Thus, they were helpful in clearing forest areas and in the woodwork needed for the creation of dugout canoes and skin-covered boats. Evidence of seaworthy watercraft at Mesolithic sites indicates that human foraging for food took place on the open water—coastal areas, rivers, and lakes—as well as on the land.

The **microlith**—a small, hard, sharp blade—tradition flourished in the Mesolithic. Although microlithic ("small stone") tools existed in Central Africa by about 40,000 years ago, they did not become common elsewhere until the Mesolithic. Microliths could be mass-produced because they were small, easy to make, and could be fashioned from sections of blades. This tool could be attached to an arrow or another tool shaft by using melted resin (from pine trees) as a binder.

Microliths provided Mesolithic people with an important advantage over their Upper Paleolithic forebears: The small size of the microlith enabled them to devise a wider array of composite tools made out of stone and wood or bone. Thus, they could make sickles, harpoons, arrows, knives, and daggers by fitting microliths into slots in wood, bone, or antler handles. Later experimentation with these forms led to more sophisticated tools and weapons, such as bows to propel arrows.

Dwellings from the Mesolithic provide evidence of a somewhat more settled lifestyle during this period. People subsisting on a dietary mixture of wild game, seafood, and plants in the now milder forested environments of the north did not need to move regularly over large geographic areas in pursuit of migratory herds. In the warmer parts of the world, wild plant foods were more readily available, and so collection already had complemented hunting in the Upper Paleolithic. Thus, in areas like Southwest Asia, the Mesolithic represents less of a changed way of life than was true in Europe. Here, the important **Natufian culture** flourished.

The Natufians lived between 10,200 and 12,500 years ago at the eastern end of the Mediterranean Sea in caves, rock shelters, and small villages with stone- and mud-walled houses. They are named after Wadi en-Natuf, a ravine near Jerusalem, Israel, where the remains of this culture were first found. Natufians buried their dead in communal cemeteries, usually in shallow pits without any other objects or decorations. One of their villages, a 10,500-year-old settlement at Jericho in the Jordan River Valley, contained a small shrine. Basin-shaped depressions in the rocks found outside homes and plastered pits beneath the floors of the houses indicate that the Natufians stored plant foods. Natufians also used sickles—small stone blades set in straight handles of wood or bone. The sickles were originally used to harvest sedge for baskets but later came to be used to cut grain (**Figure 9.1**).

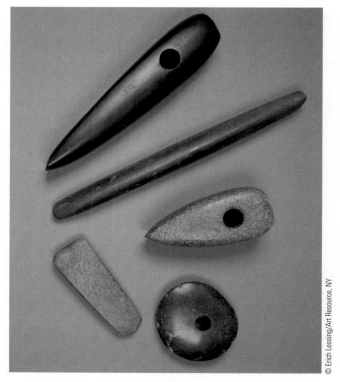

Figure 9.1 Tools of the Neolithic The Neolithic gets its name from the polished stone tools that appeared during this period. Archaeologists have also recovered hafted sickles, mortars, and pestles as well as grain storage pits at some of the earliest Natufian settlements. The polished stone axes and hammerheads pictured here would have been hafted to handles made of wood. The handle would pass through the hole created in the tool or fitted up to the side of the polished stone and then secured with sinew and various glues.

Mesolithic The Middle Stone Age of Europe, Asia, and Africa beginning about 12,000 years ago.

Archaic cultures The term used to refer to Mesolithic cultures in the Americas.

microlith A small blade of flint or similar stone, several of which were hafted together in wooden handles to make tools; widespread in the Mesolithic.

Natufian culture A Mesolithic culture from the lands that are now Israel, Lebanon, and western Syria, between about 10,200 and 12,500 years ago.

The new way of life and abundant food supplies of the various Mesolithic and Archaic cultures permitted peoples in some parts of the world to live in larger and more sedentary groups. Some of these settlements went on to expand into the first farming villages, towns, and ultimately cities.

The Neolithic Revolution

The Neolithic, or New Stone Age, named for the polished stone tools characteristic of this period, represents a major cultural change. The transition from a foraging economy based on hunting, gathering, and fishing to one based on food production outweighs the importance of the tool type for which this period gets its name. Food foragers and village-dwellers alike used these Neolithic tools.

The **Neolithic revolution** (also known as the *Neolithic transition*) was by no means smooth or instantaneous; in fact, the switch to food production spread over many centuries—even millennia—and grew directly from the preceding Mesolithic. Where to draw the line between the two periods is not always clear. Food production in the early Neolithic included both **horticulture**, the cultivation of crops in food gardens carried out with simple hand tools such as digging sticks and stone- or bone-bladed hoes, and **pastoralism**, breeding and managing migratory herds of domesticated grazing animals, such as goats, sheep, cattle, llamas, and camels.

The ultimate source of all cultural change is **innovation**: any new idea, method, or device that gains widespread acceptance in society. **Primary innovation** refers to the creation, invention, or discovery by chance of a completely new idea, method, or device. For example, take the discovery that clay permanently hardens when exposed to high temperatures. Presumably, accidental firing of clay took place around numerous ancient campfires. This chance occurrence became a primary innovation when someone perceived its potential use. This perception allowed our ancestors to begin to make figurines of fired clay some 35,000 years ago.

A **secondary innovation** involves a deliberate application or modification of an existing idea, method, or device. For example, ancient peoples applied the knowledge about fired clay to make pottery containers and cooking vessels. Recent evidence from Yuchanyan Cave, located in the southwest of China's Hunan Province, indicates the presence of the earliest pottery vessels; these are radiocarbon dated to between 15,430 and 18,300 years ago.

The shift to relatively complete reliance on domesticated plants and

animals took several thousand years. Although this transition has been particularly well studied in Southwest Asia, archaeological evidence for food production also exists from other parts of the world, such as China and Central America and the Andes at similar or somewhat younger dates. Human groups throughout the globe independently, but more or less simultaneously, invented food production.

What Is Domestication?

Domestication takes place as humans modify, intentionally or unintentionally, the genetic makeup of a population of wild plants or animals, sometimes to the extent that members of the population are unable to survive and/or reproduce without human assistance. Domestication resembles the interdependence between different species frequently seen in the natural world, where one species depends on another (that feeds upon it) for its protection and reproductive success. For example, certain ants native to the American tropics grow fungi in their nests, and these fungi provide the ants with most of their nutrition. Like human farmers, the ants add manure to stimulate fungal growth and eliminate competing weeds, both mechanically and through use of antibiotic herbicides. The fungi are protected and ensured reproductive success while providing the ants with a steady food supply.

In plant–human interactions, domestication ensures the plants' reproductive success while providing humans with food. Selective breeding eliminates thorns, toxins, and bad-tasting chemical compounds, which in the wild had served to ensure a plant species' survival, at the same time producing larger, tastier edible parts attractive to humans. Environmentalist Michael Pollan suggests that domesticated plant species successfully exploit human desires so that they are able to outcompete other plant species; he has even proposed that agriculture is something the grasses did to people as a way to conquer trees (Pollan, 2001).

Neolithic revolution The domestication of plants and animals by peoples with stone-based technologies, beginning about 10,000 years ago and leading to radical transformations in cultural systems; sometimes referred to as the *Neolithic transition*.

horticulture The cultivation of crops in food gardens, carried out with simple hand tools such as digging sticks and hoes.

pastoralism The breeding and managing of migratory herds of domesticated grazing animals, such as goats, sheep, cattle, llamas, and camels.

innovation Any new idea, method, or device that gains widespread acceptance in society.

primary innovation The creation, invention, or chance discovery of a completely new idea, method, or device.

secondary innovation The deliberate application or modification of an existing idea, method, or device.

domestication An evolutionary process whereby humans modify, intentionally or unintentionally, the genetic makeup of a population of wild plants or animals, sometimes to the extent that members of the population are unable to survive and/or reproduce without human assistance.

Evidence of Early Plant Domestication

Domesticated plants generally differ from their wild ancestors in ways favored by humans. These features include increased size, at least of edible parts; reduction or loss of natural means of seed dispersal; reduction or loss of protective devices such as husks or distasteful chemical compounds; loss of delayed seed germination (important to wild plants for survival in times of drought or other temporarily adverse conditions); and development of simultaneous ripening of the seed or fruit.

For example, wild cereals have a very fragile stem, whereas domesticated ones have a tough stem. Under natural conditions, plants with fragile stems scatter their seed for themselves, whereas those with tough stems do not. At harvest time, the grain stalks with soft stems would shatter at the touch of a sickle or flail, scattering the seeds to the wind. Inevitably, though unintentionally, most of the seeds that people were able to harvest would have come from the tough plants. Early domesticators probably also tended to select seed from plants having few husks or none at all—eventually breeding them out—because husking prior to pounding the grains into meal or flour required extra labor.

Many of the distinguishing characteristics of domesticated plants can be seen in remains from archaeological sites. One way that paleobotanists can often tell the fossil of a wild plant species from a domesticated one is by studying the shape and size of various plant structures (Figure 9.2).

Evidence of Early Animal Domestication

Domestication also produced changes in the skeletal structure of some animals. For example, the horns of wild goats and sheep differ from those of their domesticated counterparts. Some types of domesticated sheep have no horns at all. Similarly, the size of an animal or its parts can vary with domestication as seen in the smaller size of certain teeth of domesticated pigs compared to those of wild ones.

The age and sex ratios of butchered animals at an archaeological site can indicate the presence of animal domestication. For example, archaeologists found that the age and/or sex ratios at the 10,000-year-old site in

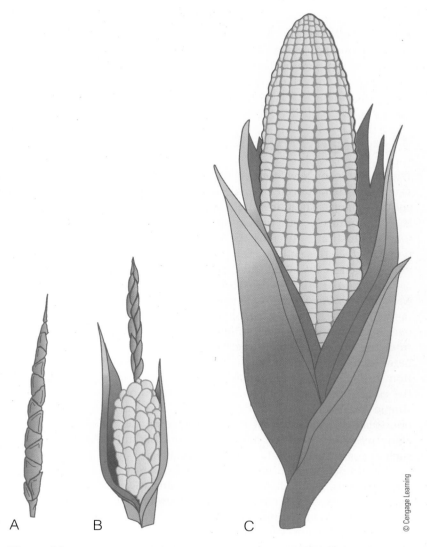

A   B   C

© Cengage Learning

Figure 9.2 Domestication of Maize Increased size of edible parts is a common feature of domestication. The large ear of corn or maize (C) that we know today is a far cry from the tiny ears (about an inch long) characteristic of 5,500-year-old maize (B). Maize may have arisen when a simple gene mutation transformed male tassel spikes of the wild grass called teosinte (A) into the small, earliest versions of the female maize ear. Teosinte, a wild grass from highland Mexico, is far less productive than maize and does not taste good. Like most plants that were domesticated, it was not a favored food for foraging peoples. Domestication transformed it into something highly desirable.

the Zagros Mountains of Iran differed from those of wild herds. A sharp rise in the number of young male goats killed indicates that people were slaughtering the young males for food and saving the females for breeding. Although such herd management does not prove that the goats were fully domesticated, it indicates a step in that direction (Zeder & Hesse, 2000). Similarly, the archaeological sites in the Andean highlands, dating to around 6,300 years ago, contain evidence that animals were penned up, indicating the beginning of domestication.

Why Humans Became Food Producers

Although it might seem that a sudden flash of insight about the human ability to control plants and animals underlies the rise of domestication, the evidence points us in different directions. Contemporary foragers, for example, choose to forgo food production, even though they know full well the role of seeds in plant growth and that plants grow better under certain conditions than others. In fact, Jared Diamond aptly describes contemporary food foragers as "walking encyclopedias of natural history with individual names for as many as a thousand or more plant and animal species, and with detailed knowledge of those species' biological characteristics, distribution, and potential uses" (Diamond, 1997, p. 143).

Food foragers clearly have the knowledge to undertake food production and frequently apply their expertise to actively manage the resources on which they depend. For example, indigenous peoples living in northern Australia deliberately alter the runoff channels of creeks to flood extensive tracts of land, converting them into fields of wild grain. Indigenous Australians choose to continue to forage while also managing the land.

Food foragers may avoid food production simply because of the hard work it involves. In fact, available ethnographic data indicate that farmers, by and large, work far longer hours compared to most food foragers. Also, food production is not necessarily a more secure means of subsistence than food foraging. Low species diversity makes highly productive seed crops—of the sort originally domesticated in Southwest Asia, Central America, and the Andean highlands—unstable from an ecological perspective. Without constant human attention, their productivity suffers.

For these reasons, contemporary food foragers do not necessarily regard farming and animal husbandry as superior to hunting, gathering, or fishing. Farming ushers in whole new systems of relationships that disturb an age-old balance between humans and nature. As long as existing practices work well, food foragers have no need to abandon them, especially if they provide an eminently satisfactory way of life. Noting that food foragers have more time for play and relaxation than food producers, anthropologist Marshall Sahlins has labeled hunter-gatherers the original "affluent society" (Sahlins, 1972). Nevertheless, as food-producing peoples (including postindustrial societies) have deprived them of more and more of the land base necessary for their way of life, foraging has become more difficult. The competition for resources ushered in during the Neolithic favors those cultures that develop concepts of land ownership.

Given this, we may well ask why any human group abandoned food foraging in favor of food production. Several theories account for this change in human subsistence practices. The desiccation or oasis theory, first championed by Australian archaeologist V. Gordon Childe in the mid-20th century, suggests environmental determinism. Glacial cover over Europe and Asia caused a shift in rain patterns from Europe to North Africa and Southwest Asia so that when the glaciers retreated northward, so did the rain. As a result, North Africa and Southwest Asia became drier, and people were forced to congregate at oases for water.

Relative food scarcity in such an environment drove people to collect the wild grasses and seeds growing around the oases, congregating in a part of Southwest Asia known as the Fertile Crescent (Figure 9.3). Eventually, they began to cultivate the grasses to provide enough food for the community. According to this theory, animal domestication began because the oases attracted hungry animals, such as wild goats, sheep, and cattle, which came to graze on the stubble of the grain fields and to drink. Finding that these animals were often too thin to kill for food, people began to fatten them up.

Although many other theories have been proposed to account for the shift to domestication, the oasis theory remains historically significant as the first scientifically testable explanation for the origins of food production. Childe's theory set the stage for the development of archaeology as a science. Later theories developed by archaeologists built on Childe's ideas.

The Fertile Crescent

Present evidence indicates that the earliest plant domestication took place gradually in the Fertile Crescent, the long arc-shaped sweep of river valleys and coastal plains extending from the Upper Nile (Sudan) to the Lower Tigris (Iraq). Archaeological data suggest the domestication of rye as early as 13,000 years ago by people living at a site (Abu Hureyra) east of Aleppo, Syria, although wild plants and animals continued to be their major food sources. Over the next several millennia they became full-fledged farmers, cultivating rye and wheat. By 10,300 years ago, crop cultivation spread to others in the region.

The domestication process was a consequence of a chance convergence of independent natural events and other cultural developments. The Natufians, whose culture we looked at earlier in this chapter, illustrate this process. These people lived at a time of dramatically changing climates in Southwest Asia. With the end of the last glaciation, temperatures not only became significantly warmer but markedly seasonal as well. Between 6,000 and 12,000 years ago, the region experienced the most extreme seasonality in its history, with dry summers significantly longer and hotter than today. As a consequence, many shallow lakes dried up, leaving just three in the Jordan River Valley.

At the same time, the region's plant cover changed dramatically. Among plants, the annuals, including wild cereal grains and legumes (such as peas, lentils, and chickpeas), adapt well to environmental instability and seasonal dryness. Because they complete their life cycle

Figure 9.3 The Fertile Crescent
This area of Southwest Asia and North Africa shows the Fertile Crescent, the site of the beginning of domestication.

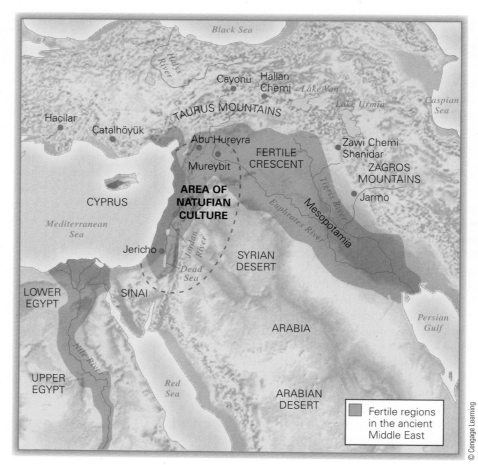

in a single year, annuals can evolve very quickly under unstable conditions. Moreover, they store their reproductive abilities for the next wet season in abundant seeds, which can remain dormant for prolonged periods.

The Natufians, who lived where these conditions were especially severe, adapted by modifying their subsistence practices in two ways: First, they probably burned the landscape regularly to promote browsing by red deer and grazing by gazelles, the main focus of their hunting activities. Second, they placed greater emphasis on the collection and storage of wild seeds from the annual plants that they used for food through the dry season. The importance of stored foods, coupled with the scarcity of reliable water sources, promoted more sedentary living patterns, reflected in the substantial villages of late Natufian times. Because they already possessed sickles (originally used to cut reeds and sedges for baskets) for harvesting grain and grinding stones to process a variety of wild foods, it was easier for the Natufians to shift to a reliance on seed.

The Natufians' use of sickles to harvest grain turned out to have important if unexpected consequences. In the course of harvesting, the easily dispersed seeds fell at the harvest site, whereas those that clung to the stems came back to the settlement where people processed and stored them. The periodic burning of vegetation carried

out to promote the deer and gazelle herds may have also affected the development of new genetic variation. Heat impacts mutation rates. Also, fire removes individuals from a population, which changes the genetic structure of a population drastically and quickly.

Inevitably, some seeds from nondispersing variants were carried back to settlements and germinated, growing on dump heaps and other disturbed sites (latrines, areas cleared of trees, or burned-over terrain). Certain variants known as *colonizers* do particularly well in disturbed habitats, making them ideal candidates for domestication. Sedentism itself disturbs habitats as resources closer to settlements become depleted over time. Thus, variants of plants particularly susceptible to human manipulation had more opportunities to flourish where people were living. Under such circumstances, humans began to actively promote the growth of these plants, even by deliberately sowing them. Ultimately, people realized that they could play a more active role in the process by deliberately trying to breed the strains they preferred. With this, domestication shifted from an unintentional to an intentional process.

The development of animal domestication in Southwest Asia seems to have proceeded along somewhat similar lines in the hilly country of southeastern Turkey, northern Iraq, and the Zagros Mountains of Iran. This region of rich environmental diversity contained large herds of wild sheep and goats. From the flood plains of the valley of the Tigris and Euphrates Rivers, for example, travel to the north or east takes one into high country through three other ecological zones: first steppe; then oak and pistachio woodlands; and finally high plateau country with grass, scrub, or desert vegetation. Valleys that run at right angles to the mountain ranges afford relatively easy access across these zones. Today, a number of peoples in the region still graze their herds of sheep and goats on the low steppe in the winter and move to high pastures on the plateaus in the summer.

Food foragers inhabited these regions prior to the domestication of plants and animals. Each ecological zone contained distinct plant species, and because of the variation in altitude, plant foods matured at different times in different zones. These ancient peoples hunted a variety of animal species for meat and hides. The bones of hoofed animals—deer, gazelles, wild goats, and wild sheep—dominate the human refuse piles from these periods. Most of these hoofed animals naturally move back and forth from low winter pastures to high summer pastures. People followed the animals in their seasonal migrations, eating and storing other wild foods as they passed through different zones: palm dates in the lowlands; acorns, almonds, and pistachios higher up; apples and pears higher still; wild grains maturing at different times in different areas; woodland animals in the forested region between summer and winter grazing lands. All in all, it was a rich, varied fare.

The archaeological record indicates that, at first, the people of the southwestern Asian highlands hunted animals of all ages and sexes. But, beginning about 11,000 years ago, the percentage of immature sheep consumed increased to about 50 percent of the total. At the same time, people ate fewer of the female animals. (Feasting on male lambs increases yields by sparing the females for breeding.) This marks the beginning of human management of sheep.

The human management of flocks shielded sheep from the effects of natural selection, affording the variants preferred by humans to have increased reproductive success. Variants attractive to humans did not arise out of need but randomly, as mutations do. But then humans selectively bred the varieties they favored. In such a way, those features characteristic of domestic sheep—such as greater fat and meat production, excess wool, and so on—began to develop (**Figure 9.4**). By 9,000 years ago, the shape and size of the bones of domestic sheep had become distinguishable from those of wild sheep. At about the same time and by similar means, ancient humans domesticated pigs in southeastern Turkey and the lower Jordan River Valley.

Some researchers link animal domestication to the development of fixed territories and settlements. They suggest that resource ownership promotes postponing the short-term gain of killing prey for the long-term gain of continued access to animals in the future (Alvard & Kuznar, 2001). Eventually, ancient peoples introduced animal species domesticated in one area to regions outside their natural habitat. However, not all scientists believe that domestication occurred in this way, with humans directing the process. Evolutionary anthropologist Brian Hare, featured in this chapter's Biocultural Connection, turns the theory around, arguing instead that animals (specifically, dogs) took advantage of new survival opportunities created by human settlements in the villages of the Neolithic.

The notion that dogs might have played a more active role in creating their own evolutionary relationship with humans underscores the fact that domestication took place as a series of interactions between species. Unaware of the long-term and revolutionary cultural consequences of their actions, the domesticators and domesticates alike sought only to maximize their available food sources. But as the domestication process continued, humans throughout the globe realized that the productivity of

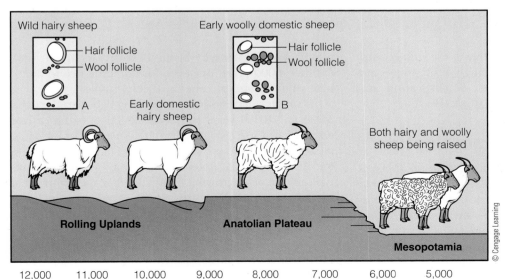

Figure 9.4 The Domestication of Sheep Domestication of sheep resulted in evolutionary changes that created more wool. Inset A shows a section of the skin of wild sheep, as seen through a microscope, with the arrangement of hair and wool follicles. Inset B shows how this arrangement changed with domestication so that the sheep produced more wool.

BIOCULTURAL CONNECTION

Dogs Get Right to the Point

Some dog breeds have a receptive vocabulary; that is, they can understand hundreds of words. How can they do this? In turn, do their soulful eyes, head tipped to the side, or wagging tail really speak of unconditional love? What if they could speak themselves? Would they say something different from what their bodies seem to tell us?

Poet Billy Collins reveals in the poem "The Revenant" what one cranky dog, just put to sleep by his owner, came back to tell him:

I never liked you—not one bit.

When I licked your face,
I thought of biting off your nose.[a]

Likewise, evolutionary anthropologist Brian Hare suggests that we view dog behavior, cognition, and communication through an anthropocentric lens.[b] He warns that these biases are in play when we speak of *Canis lupus familiaris*, a subspecies of wolf, as humankind's "best friend."

Hare came to this topic while researching chimpanzee cognition. Chimps, like the other great apes, can master human language at the level of a 2- to 3-year-old, and they can follow one another's gaze and figure out what might be in another chimp's

Dogs and humans are unique among mammals in their ability to interpret and act upon the meaning of pointing with a human hand.

line of sight. However, they struggle to comprehend the gesture of pointing.

Instead of relegating pointing to another area of human uniqueness, Hare thought of his own pet dogs, which, like all dogs, grasped this gesture immediately. Hare set about researching how and why dogs and humans, seemingly the lone species among mammals, understand the meaning of pointing. He conducted

pointing experiments using a "shell game" scenario, with dogs, chimps, wolves, and humans of all ages. Even puppies, like babies, understand pointing, which indicates that this ability is encoded in their genome and not a learned behavior. And like babies, they rely on social cues to interpret the meaning of a pointing finger.

The notion of a domesticated species, such as the dog, of course implies

the domestic species increased relative to the wild species. Thus, these species became increasingly more important to subsistence, resulting in further domestication and further increases in productivity (**Figure 9.5**).

Other Centers of Domestication

In addition to Southwest Asia, the domestication of plants and, in some cases, animals took place simultaneously in parts of the Americas (Central America, the Andean highlands, the tropical forests of South America, and eastern North America), northern China, and Africa (**Figure 9.6**). In China, domestication of rice was underway along the

middle Yangtze River by about 11,000 years ago. It took another 4,000 years, however, for domestic rice to dominate wild rice and become the dietary staple.

Similarly, decorations on pottery dated to between 5,000 and 8,800 years ago document rice as the earliest domesticated species of Southeast Asia. Other domesticates, particularly root crops such as yams and taro, dominate this region (**Figure 9.7**). Root crop farming, or **vegeculture**, typically involves growing many different species together in a single field. Because this approximates the complexity of the natural vegetation, vegeculture tends to be more stable than seed crop cultivation. Propagation or breeding of new plants usually occurs through vegetative means— the planting of cuttings—rather than the planting of seeds.

In the Americas, the domestication of plants began about as early as it did in these other regions. Evidence for one species of domestic squash appears as early as

vegeculture The cultivation of domesticated root crops, such as yams and taro.

that one species has effectively altered the genetic makeup of another. To avoid anthropocentrism, Hare has used a dog's eye view to think about domestication. Instead of seeing humans as the leaders in the process, he proposes that dogs domesticated themselves as humans began to live in discrete settlements during the Neolithic. Ancestral dogs, like wolves today, were probably partly scavengers and so came to orient to human habitations because of edible discarded material left by people. He suggests that those wolves that were least timid about humans had a selective advantage in the "human cohabitation" niche and eventually evolved into domesticated dogs.

Social acceptance of dogs by humans, and vice versa, has led to many interesting and humanlike behavioral adaptations in dogs. A dog "kissing" its owner's face may seem like love but really has its antecedents in the spitting up of prechewed food by wolves for their pack mates upon their return to the den. Although human owners do not spit up food for their dogs, they reward their dog's "love" through edible treats. Natural selection often produces such win–win scenarios among species—it's

just that when humans are involved, we call it domestication!

This reconstruction of the history of the canine–human partnership provides an interesting context to those who have had to clean up after their dog has upset the household trash bin. As the sequel to such an escapade, when the dog owner scolds his or her dog, the dog may show what we interpret as shame: head down, tail between the legs, body turned aside or walking away. Hare's experiments show that dogs will perform this behavior when scolded *even when they haven't broken any rule.* Their sensitivity to social judgment is so attuned that they can be in effect coerced into expressing what humans interpret as guilt when they are actually innocent. Evolutionary processes have favored dogs who could best manipulate humans.

Pointing has particular significance to a phenomenon in human psychology termed *joint attention*, which means that two individuals share an awareness that both are visually fixing on a common visual target. The connection of joint attention exists when a dog explores an area to which a human points or when one person "points out" a path to another. But most importantly,

joint attention lies at the heart of social awareness: Without it, we cannot function in groups. Interestingly, people with autism, who characteristically struggle with social cues and responses, also have a deficiency with pointing.

But not dogs. In the end they know just how to control us. The revenant dog from Billy Collins's poem gets the last laugh when he tells his owner about heaven:

> . . . that everyone here can read
> and write,
> the dogs in poetry, the cats and
> the others in prose.[c]

BIOCULTURAL QUESTION

Can you think of other examples of how we may impose human norms of behavior onto other species? How is this the same or different from imposing notions specific to one culture onto another?

---

[a]Collins, B. (2005). The revenant. In *The trouble with poetry.* New York: Random House. Reprinted by permission of the Chris Calhoun Literary Agency.

[b]Hare, B., et al. (2002). The domestication of social cognition in dogs. *Science 298* (5598). 1634–1636.

[c]Collins, 2005.

© Wolfgang Flamisch/Corbis

Figure 9.5 Manufacturing Food Today, deliberate attempts to create new varieties of plants take place in many greenhouses, experiment stations, and labs. But when first begun, the creation of domestic plants was not deliberate; rather, it was the unforeseen outcome of traditional food-foraging activities. Today, genetic engineering creates crops (GMOs, or genetically modified organisms) designed to survive massive applications of herbicides and pesticides. The crops are also engineered to *not* produce viable seeds so that corporations can solidify their control of the food industry. Here researchers study a strain of genetically modified corn.

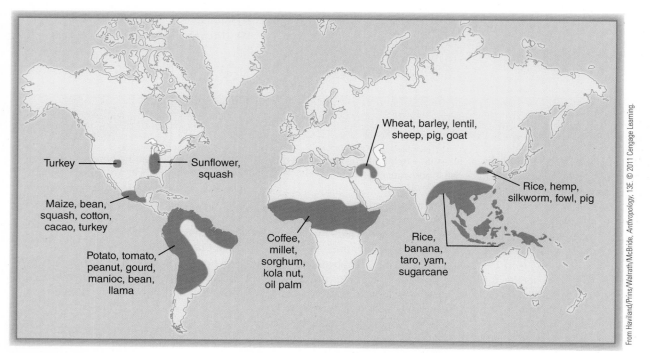

Figure 9.6 Early Plant and Animal Domestication Domestication of plants and animals took place in widely scattered areas more or less simultaneously. The figure indicates some of the domesticates typical to each area such as wheat and sheep in Southwest Asia; sorghum and millet in Central Africa, rice and pigs in China; taro and bananas in Southeast Asia; maize and dogs in Central America; potatoes and llamas in South America; and squash and sunflowers in North America. Although the domesticated plants and animals appeared independently in distinct regions, today humans use all of them throughout the globe.

Figure 9.7 Vegeculture The Dani people of Papua New Guinea, specialize in growing sweet potatoes through vegeculture, or root crop farming. Although vegeculture typically involves many species of root crop planted together in one area, the Dani fill vast irrigated fields exclusively with more than seventy varieties of sweet potato. The Dani have incorporated this important food into many of their rituals. Here, Dani women roast sweet potatoes on a fire as part of a ceremonial pig roast.

10,000 years ago in the coastal forests of Ecuador, the same time that another species independently appeared in an arid region of highland Mexico. The ecological diversity of the highland valleys of Mexico, like the hill country of Southwest Asia, provided an excellent environment for domestication (Figure 9.8). Movement of people through a variety of ecological zones as they changed altitude brought plant and animal species into new habitats, providing opportunities for "colonizing" species and humans alike.

Domestication in the Andean highlands of Peru, another environmentally diverse region, emphasized root crops, the best known being the thousands of varieties of potatoes discussed in the Challenge Issue at the opening of the chapter. They also domesticated plants for purposes other than eating, such as gourds (Figure 9.9) and cotton. South Americans also domesticated guinea pigs, llamas, alpacas, and ducks, whereas peoples in the Mexican highlands never did much with domestic livestock. They limited themselves to dogs, turkeys, and bees. American Indians living north of Mexico developed some of their own indigenous domesticates. These included local varieties of squash and sunflowers.

Ultimately, American Indians domesticated over 300 food crops, including two of the four most important ones in the

Figure 9.9 Domesticates for More than Food In coastal Peru, the earliest domesticates were the inedible bottle gourd (like the one shown here) and cotton. They were used to make nets and floats to catch fish, which was an important source of food.

CULTIGENS		PERCENTAGE			
		Hunting	Horticulture	Wild plant use	Years ago
Squash	Cotton	29%	31%		3,000
Chili	Maize				3,500
Amaranth	Beans				
Avocado	Gourd				4,000
	Sapote				
Squash	Maize				4,500
Chili	Beans	25%	50%		5,000
Amaranth	Gourd				
Avocado	Sapote				
Squash	Maize				5,500
Chili	Beans				6,000
Amaranth	Gourd	34%	52%		
Avocado	Sapote				6,500
					7,000
Squash					
Chili					7,500
Amaranth					
Avocado		54%	40%		8,000
					8,500

Figure 9.8 Patterns of Neolithic Domestication in Mesoamerica Subsistence trends in Mexico's Tehuacan Valley show that here, as elsewhere, dependence of horticulture came about gradually, over a prolonged period of time.

world today: potatoes and maize (the other two are wheat and rice). In fact, America's indigenous peoples first cultivated 60 percent of the crops grown in the world today; they not only developed the world's largest array of nutritious foods but also are the primary contributors to the world's varied cuisines. After all, where would Italian cuisine be without tomatoes? Thai cooking without peanuts? Northern European cooking without potatoes? Small wonder American Indians have been called the world's greatest farmers.

The domestication of plant species brought about the development of horticultural societies. Using neither irrigation nor plows, small communities of gardeners worked together with simple hand tools. Horticulturists typically cultivate a variety of crops in small gardens they have cleared by hand. Indians in the Amazon rainforest used sophisticated farming methods, as is evident in the research conducted by an international team of archaeologists and other scientists. These ancient methods, which left behind rich dark soils, may have important current applications. Reviving these ancient soil-enrichment techniques could contribute to better global management of rainforests and climate today.

Although plant domestication took place independently across the globe, at the same time people everywhere developed the same categories of foods: starchy grains (or root crops) accompanied by one or more legumes. For example, people in Southwest Asia combined wheat and barley with peas, chickpeas, and lentils, and people in Mexico combined maize with various kinds of beans. Together, the amino acids (building blocks of proteins) in these starch

Figure 9.10 **The Many Uses of Chilies** Mexicans, have used chili peppers for millennia. Chili peppers enhance the flavors of food and aid in digestion by helping with the breakdown of cellulose in diets heavy in plant foods. Chilies have other uses as well: This illustration from a 16th-century Aztec manuscript shows a mother threatening to punish her child with the smoke from chili peppers. Chili smoke was also used as a chemical weapon in warfare.

and legume combinations provide humans with sufficient protein. The starchy grains eaten at every meal in the form of bread, some sort of food wrapper (like a tortilla), or a gruel or thickening agent in a stew along with one or more legumes form the core of the diet. Each culture combines these rather bland sources of carbohydrates and proteins with flavor-giving substances that help the food go down.

In Mexico, for example, the chili pepper serves as the flavor enhancer par excellence (**Figure 9.10**); in other cuisines bits of meat or fat, dairy products, or mushrooms add the flavor. Anthropologist Sidney Mintz refers to this as the *core-fringe-legume pattern* (CFLP), noting its stability until the recent worldwide spread of processed sugars and high-fat foods.

Food Production and Population Size

Human population size has grown steadily since the Neolithic. The exact relationship between population growth and food production resembles the old chicken and egg question: Does population growth create the pressures that result in innovations, such as food production, or is population growth a consequence of food production? As already noted, domestication inevitably leads to higher yields, and higher yields make it possible to feed more people, albeit at the cost of more work.

Across human populations, increased dependence on farming and increased fertility seem to go hand in hand: Farming populations tend to have higher rates of fertility compared to hunter-gatherers. Hunter-gatherer mothers have their children about four to five years apart while some contemporary farming populations not practicing any form of birth control have another baby every year and a half (**Figure 9.11**). A complex interplay between human biology and culture lies at the heart of this difference. Some researchers suggest that the availability of soft foods for infants brought about by farming promoted population growth. In humans, frequent breastfeeding has a dampening effect on mothers' ovulation, inhibiting pregnancy in nursing mothers who breastfeed exclusively. Because breastfeeding frequency declines when soft foods are introduced, fertility tends to increase.

However, many other pathways can also lead to fertility changes. For example, farming cultures tend to view numerous children as assets to help out with the many

VISUAL COUNTERPOINT

Figure 9.11 **Diet and Fertility** The higher fertility of the Amish, a religious farming culture in North America, compared to that of the Ju/'hoansi hunter-gatherers from the Kalahari Desert, was originally attributed to nutritional stress among the hunter-gatherers. We now know that childrearing beliefs and practices account for these differences. The Ju/'hoansi fertility pattern derives from the belief that a crying baby should be breastfed, an action that biologically suppresses fertility. In farming populations families view children as assets to help work the farm, and infant feeding practices reinforce high fertility rates. Children are weaned at young ages and transitioned to soft foods, a practice that promotes the next pregnancy. All human activity includes a complex interplay between human biology and culture.

household chores. Further, higher fertility rates among farmers might derive from higher mortality rates due to infectious diseases brought about by the sedentary lifestyles and narrow diets characteristic of the Neolithic. High infant mortality, in turn, could raise the cultural value placed on fertility.

In the past, biases contributed to oversimplified anthropological explanations of fertility differences among peoples. Early anthropologists viewed the hunter-gatherer lifestyle as inferior and interpreted the differences in fertility to be the consequence of nutritional stress among the hunter-gatherers. This theory was based in part on the observation that humans and many other mammals require a certain percentage of body fat in order to reproduce successfully (see Chapter 12 for more on this biological phenomenon).

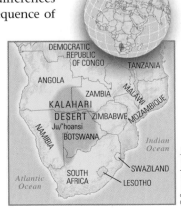

However, detailed studies among the !Kung or Ju/'hoansi (pronounced "zhutwasi") of the Kalahari Desert in southern Africa disproved this nutritional theory. The low fertility among the Ju/'hoansi ultimately derives from cultural beliefs about the right way to handle a baby: The Ju/'hoansi mother responds rapidly to her baby, breastfeeding whenever the infant shows any signs of fussing, day or night. On a biological level, the Ju/'hoansi pattern of breastfeeding in short, very frequent bouts suppresses ovulation, or the release of a new egg into the womb for fertilization. Biology and culture interact in all aspects of the human experience.

The Spread of Food Production

Paradoxically, although domestication increases productivity, it also increases instability. As humans increasingly focus on varieties with the highest yields, other varieties become less valued and ultimately ignored. As a result, farmers depend on a rather narrow choice of resources, compared to the wide range utilized by food foragers.

Today, modern agriculturists rely on a mere dozen species for about 80 percent of the world's annual tonnage of all crops.

This dependence on fewer varieties means that when a crop fails, for whatever reason, farmers have less to fall back on compared to food foragers. Furthermore, the common farming practice of planting crops together in one locality increases the likelihood of failure because proximity promotes the spread of disease among neighboring plants. Moreover, by relying on seeds from the most productive plants of a species to establish next year's crop, farmers favor genetic uniformity over diversity. In turn, some virus, bacterium, or fungus could wipe out vast fields of genetically identical organisms all at once as in the terrible Irish potato famine of 1845–1850. This disaster caused the deaths of about 1 million people due to hunger and disease and forced another 2 million to abandon their homes and emigrate. The population of Ireland dropped from 8 million to 5 million as a result of the famine.

This concentration of domesticates and the consequent vulnerability to disease intensify with contemporary agribusiness and factory farming. This chapter's Globalscape examines the role of pig farming in the swine flu pandemic that began to sweep the world early in 2009.

The Irish potato famine illustrates how the combination of increased productivity and vulnerability may contribute to the geographic spread of farming. Time and time again in the past, population growth, followed by crop failure, has triggered movements of peoples from one place to another, where they have reestablished their familiar subsistence practices.

Once farming came into existence, its instability more or less guaranteed that it would spread to neighboring regions through such migrations. From Southwest Asia, for instance, farming spread northeastward eventually to all of Europe, westward to North Africa, and eastward to India. Domesticated variants also spread from China and Southeast Asia westward. Those who brought crops to new locations brought other things as well, including languages, beliefs, and new alleles for human gene pools. The spread of certain ideas, customs, or practices from one culture to another is termed **diffusion**.

A similar diffusion occurred from West Africa to the southeast, creating the modern far-reaching distribution of speakers of Bantu languages. Crops including sorghum (so valuable today it is grown in hot, dry areas on all continents), pearl millet, watermelon, black-eyed peas, African yams, oil palms, and kola nuts (the source of modern cola drinks) were first domesticated in West Africa but began spreading eastward by 5,000 years ago. Between 2,000 and 3,000 years ago, Bantu speakers with their crops reached the continent's east coast and a few centuries later reached its southern tip.

The Culture of Neolithic Settlements

Excavations of Neolithic settlements have revealed much about the daily activities of their former inhabitants. Archaeologists can reconstruct the business of making a living from structures, artifacts, and even the food debris found at these sites. Jericho, an early farming community located on the Jordan River's West Bank in the Palestinian territories, provides an excellent case in point.

Jericho: An Early Farming Community

Excavations at the Neolithic settlement that later grew to become the biblical city of Jericho have revealed the remains of a sizable farming community inhabited as early as 10,350 years ago. Here, in the Jordan River Valley, crops could be grown almost continuously due to the presence of a bounteous spring and the rich soils of an Ice Age lake that had dried up some 3,000 years earlier. In addition, waterborne deposits originating in the Judean highlands to the west regularly renewed the fertility of the soil.

To protect their settlement against floods and associated mudflows, as well as invaders, the people of Jericho built massive walls of stone around the settlement. Within these walls (6½ feet wide and 12 feet high), as well as a large rock-cut ditch (27 feet wide and 9 feet deep), an estimated 400 to 900 people lived in houses of mud brick with plastered floors arranged around courtyards.

Jericho's inhabitants also built a stone tower inside one corner of the wall, near the spring (**Figure 9.12**). It would have taken 100 people 104 days to build this tower. A staircase inside it probably led to a building on top. Recently archaeologists have suggested that this tower provides one of the earliest examples of an archaeological structure connected to the astronomical movement of the planet and seasonal cycles. The tower is oriented so that at the sunset of the summer solstice, the shadow of nearby mountains hit it first and then spread throughout the village (Barkai & Liran, 2008). The village also included storage facilities as well as ceremonial structures, all made of mud brick. A village cemetery also reflects the sedentary life of these early people. Nomadic groups, with few exceptions, rarely buried their dead in a single central location.

Common features in art, ritual, use of prestige goods, and burial practices indicate close contact between the farmers of Jericho and other nearby villages. Discovered inside the walls of Jericho, obsidian and turquoise from Sinai and marine shells from the coast document trade among neighboring villages.

---

diffusion The spread of certain ideas, customs, or practices from one culture to another.

Globalscape

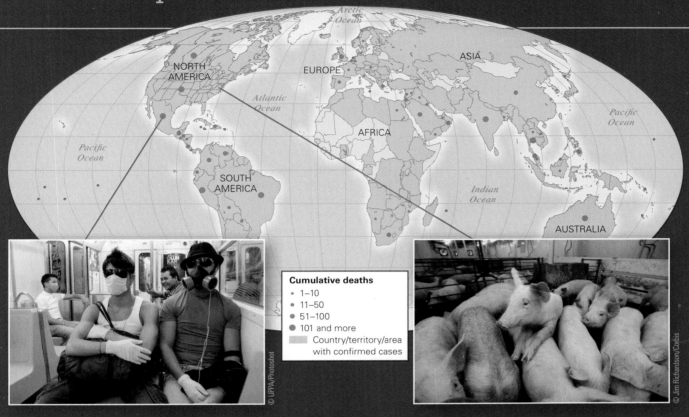

Cumulative deaths
- 1–10
- 11–50
- 51–100
- 101 and more
- Country/territory/area with confirmed cases

© UPPA/Photoshot

© Jim Richardson/Corbis

Factory Farming Fiasco?

In April 2009 protective masks and gloves were a common sight in Mexico City as the news of the first cases of swine flu pandemic appeared in the United States and Mexico. On June 11, 2009, the World Health Organization (WHO) made the pandemic official, and by July cases had been reported in three-quarters of the states and territories monitored by the WHO. Scientists across the world are examining the genetic makeup of the virus to determine its origins.

From the outset of the pandemic, many signs have pointed to a pig farming operation in Veracruz, Mexico, called Granjas Caroll, which is a subsidiary of Smithfield Foods, the world's largest pork producer. However, Ruben Donis, an expert virologist from the U.S. Centers for Disease Control and Prevention in Atlanta, Georgia, has come to a different conclusion based on genetic analysis. According to an article in the journal *Science*, Donis "suggests that the virus may have originated in a U.S. pig that traveled to Asia as part of the hog trade. The virus may have infected a human there, who then traveled back to North America, where the virus perfected human-to-human spread, maybe even moving from the United States to Mexico."[a] Another report has linked the current strain of swine flu to a strain that ran through factory farms in North Carolina in 1998 and to the avian flu that killed over 50 million people in 1918.[b]

While scientists examine the genetic evidence for swine flu, a look at factory farming shows how these practices facilitate the proliferation of disease. For example, the pig population of North Carolina numbers about 10 million, and most of these pigs are crowded onto farms of over 5,000 animals. These pigs travel across the country as part of farming operations. A pig may be born in North Carolina, then travel to the heartland of the United States to fatten up before a final trip to the slaughterhouses in California.

The crowded conditions in pig farms mean that if the virus enters a farm it quickly can infect many pigs, which are then shipped to other places spreading the virus further, with many opportunities for the virus to pass between species. Health risks of global food distribution have long been a concern, and the swine flu outbreak elevates these concerns to a new level.

Global Twister

Do you think the swine flu pandemic should lead to changes in meat production and distribution globally?

---

[a]Cohen, J. (2009). Out of Mexico? Scientists ponder swine flu's origin. *Science 324* (5928), 700–702.

[b]Trifonov, V., et al. (2009). The origin of the recent swine influenza A (H1N1) virus infecting humans. *Eurosurveillance 14* (17). www.eurosurveillance.org/ViewArticle.aspx?ArticleId=19193

© Nathan Benn/Ottochrome/Corbis

Figure 9.12 The Tower of Jericho The Natufian settlement of Jericho, located in the Palestinian West Bank of today's Israel, demonstrates that these ancient people had impressive social coordination, allowing them to build substantial structures. The defensive walls and the famous tower that stretched upward over 9 meters (28 feet) referenced in the Bible and gospel songs provide an example of cultural continuity in this region and beyond. The tower may have been part of a calendric ritual as the tower is built such that the shadows of mountains hit it first and then spread across the town at the sunset of the summer solstice.

Neolithic Material Culture

Life in Neolithic villages included various innovations in the realms of toolmaking, pottery, housing, and clothing. These aspects of material culture illustrate the dramatic social changes that took place during the Neolithic.

Toolmaking

Early harvesting tools consisted of razor-sharp flint blades inserted into handles of wood or bone. Later toolmakers added grinding and polishing the hardest stones to this toolmaking, technique. Scythes, forks, hoes, and simple plows replaced basic digging sticks. Later, when domesticated animals became available for use as draft animals, these early farmers redesigned their plows. Villagers used mortars and pestles to grind and crush grain. Along with the development of diverse technologies, individuals acquired specialized skills for creating a variety of craft specialties including leatherwork, weavings, and pottery.

Pottery

Hard work on the part of those producing the food supported other members of the society who could then apply their skills and energy to various craft specialties such as pottery. In the Neolithic, different forms of pottery developed for transporting and storing food, water, and various material possessions (Figure 9.13). Impervious to damage by insects, rodents, and dampness, pottery vessels could be used for storing small grains, seeds, and other materials. Moreover, villagers could boil their food in pottery vessels directly over the fire instead of dropping fire-heated stones directly into food to cook it. Neolithic peoples used pottery for pipes, ladles, lamps, and other objects; some cultures even used large pottery vessels for disposal of the dead. Significantly, pottery containers remain important for much of humanity today.

Widespread use of pottery made of clay and fired in very hot ovens likely indicates a sedentary community. Archaeologists have found pottery in abundance in all but a few of the earliest Neolithic settlements. Its fragility and weight make it less practical for use by nomads and hunters, who more typically use woven bags, baskets, and containers made of animal hide. Nevertheless, some modern nomads make and use pottery, just as there are farmers today who do not. In fact, food foragers in East Asia were making pottery vessels by about 15,000 years ago, long before pottery appeared in Southwest Asia.

The manufacture of pottery requires artful skill and some technological sophistication. To make a useful vessel requires knowledge of clay: how to remove impurities from it, how to shape it into desired forms, and how to dry it in a way that does not cause cracking. Proper firing requires knowledge and care so that the clay heats enough to harden and resists future disintegration from moisture without cracking or even exploding as it heats and later cools down.

Neolithic peoples decorated their pottery in various ways. Some engraved designs on the vessel before firing whereas others shaped special rims, legs, bases, and other details separately and fastened them to the finished pot. Painting, the most common form of pottery decoration, accounts for literally thousands of unique designs found among the pottery remains of ancient cultures.

Housing

Food production and the new sedentary lifestyle brought about another technological development—house building. Because most food foragers move around frequently, they care little for permanent housing. Cave shelters, pits dug in the earth, and simple lean-tos made of hides and wooden poles serve the purpose of keeping the weather

Figure 9.13 Domesticated Art Ancient pottery provides evidence of animal domestication as well as the craft specializations that developed as a consequence of the Neolithic revolution. This howling canine came from Remojadas, a culture that flourished between 1,000 and 2,100 years ago along the Gulf Coast of present-day Mexico. Dogs, one of the few domesticated animal species found in Mesoamerica, were frequently incorporated into vessels or freestanding pieces such as this hollow ceramic figure. Throughout the world, species valued as domesticates appear in the ancient pottery and other decorative arts of the region. Rice appears in the pottery of East Asia, and pigs in the pottery of southeastern Turkey.

out. In the Neolithic, however, dwellings became more complex in design and more diverse in type. Some were constructed of wood, whereas others included more elaborate shelters made of stone, sun-dried brick, or branches plastered together with mud or clay.

Although permanent housing frequently goes along with food production, some cultures created substantial housing without shifting to food production. For example, on the northwestern coast of North America, people lived in sturdy houses made of heavy planks hewn from cedar logs, yet their food consisted entirely of wild plants and animals, especially salmon and sea mammals.

Clothing

Neolithic peoples were the first in human history to wear clothing made of woven textiles. The raw materials and technology necessary for the production of such clothing came from several sources: flax and cotton from farming; wool from domesticated sheep, llamas, or goats; silk from silkworms. Human invention contributed the spindle for spinning and the loom for weaving.

Social Structure

The economic and technological developments listed thus far enabled archaeologists to draw certain inferences concerning the organization of Neolithic societies. Although archaeological sites contain indications of ceremonial and spiritual activity, village life seemed to lack central organization and hierarchy. Burials, for example, reveal a marked absence of social differentiation. Only rarely did early Neolithic peoples use stone slabs to construct or cover graves or include elaborate objects with the dead. Evidently, no person had attained the kind of exalted status that required an elaborate funeral. The smallness of most villages and the absence of extravagant buildings suggest that the inhabitants knew one another very well and were even related, so that most of their relationships were probably highly personal ones, with equal emotional significance. Still, Neolithic peoples sometimes organized themselves to carry out impressive communal works preserved in the archaeological record, such as the site of Stonehenge in England (**Figure 9.14**).

Figure 9.14 Druids of Stonehenge Sometimes Neolithic peoples organized themselves to carry out large projects, such as constructing Stonehenge, the famous ceremonial and astronomical center built in England some 4,500 years ago. Used as a burial ground long before the massive stone circle was erected, Stonehenge reflects the builders' understanding of the forces of nature and their impact upon food production. For instance, the opening of the stone circles aligns precisely with the sunset of the winter solstice. This careful alignment indicates that Neolithic peoples were paying close attention to the movement of the sun and to the seasonal growing cycle. Today people, such as the Wiltshire Druids pictured here, still gather at Stonehenge for rituals associated with the summer solstice.

In general, Neolithic social structure had minimal division of labor, but there is some evidence of new and more specialized social roles. In such **egalitarian societies** everyone has about the same rank and shares equally in the basic resources that support income, status, and power. Villages seem to have consisted of several households, each providing for most of its own needs. Kinship groups probably met the organizational needs of society beyond the household level.

Neolithic Cultures in the Americas

In the Americas the Neolithic revolution had a different shape and timing. For example, Neolithic farming villages were common in Southwest Asia between 8,000 and 9,000 years ago. But in **Mesoamerica**, the region from central Mexico to the northern regions of Central America, and in the Andean highlands, similar villages did not appear until about 4,500 years ago. Moreover, pottery, which developed in Southwest Asia shortly after plant and animal domestication, did not emerge in the Americas until about 4,500 years ago. Early Neolithic peoples in the Americas did not use the potter's wheel. Instead, they manufactured elaborate pottery by hand. Looms and the hand spindle appeared in the Americas about 3,000 years ago.

These absences do not indicate backwardness on the part of Native American peoples, many of whom, as we have already seen, were highly sophisticated farmers and plant breeders. Instead, we can surmise that Neolithic peoples in the Americas were satisfied with existing practices. Food production in Mesoamerica and the Andean highlands developed wholly independently from domestication in Eurasia and Africa, with different crops, animals, and technologies.

Outside Mesoamerica and the Andean highlands, hunting, fishing, and the gathering of wild plant foods remained important to the economy of Neolithic peoples in the Americas. Apparently, most American Indians continued to emphasize a food-foraging rather than a food-producing mode of life, even though maize and other domestic crops came to be cultivated just about everywhere that climate permitted. These groups, like hunter-gatherers in other parts of the world, opted not to take on the challenges of food production. These cultures remained stable until the arrival of European explorers, which instigated a pattern of disease and domination (Mann, 2005).

egalitarian societies Societies in which people have about the same rank, and share equally in the basic resources that support income, status, and power.

Mesoamerica The region extending from central Mexico to the northern regions of Central America.

The Neolithic and Human Biology

Although we tend to think of the invention of food production in terms of its cultural consequences, it had obvious biological impact as well. Physical anthropologists studying human skeletons from Neolithic burial grounds have found evidence for a somewhat lessened mechanical stress on peoples' bodies and teeth. Although exceptions exist, the teeth of Neolithic peoples generally show less wear, their bones are less robust, and compared to the skeletons of Paleolithic and Mesolithic peoples, they had less osteoarthritis (the result of stressed joint surfaces).

On the other hand, other skeletal features provide clear evidence for a marked deterioration in health and mortality. Skeletons from Neolithic villages show evidence of severe and chronic nutritional stress as well as pathologies related to infectious and deficiency diseases, as seen in this chapter's Original Study by Anna Roosevelt.

ORIGINAL STUDY

The History of Mortality and Physiological Stress

BY ANNA ROOSEVELT

Although there is a relative lack of evidence for the Paleolithic stage, enough skeletons have been studied that it seems clear that seasonal and periodic physiological stress regularly affected most prehistoric hunting-gathering populations, as evidenced by the presence of enamel hypoplasias [horizontal linear defects in tooth enamel] and Harris lines [horizontal lines near the ends of long bones].

What also seems clear is that severe and chronic stress, with high frequency of hypoplasias, infectious disease lesions, pathologies related to iron-deficiency anemia, and high mortality rates, is not characteristic of these early populations. There is no evidence of frequent, severe malnutrition, and so the diet must have been adequate in calories and other nutrients most of the time.

During the Mesolithic, the proportion of starch in the diet rose, to judge from the increased occurrence of certain dental diseases, but not enough to create an impoverished diet. At this time, diets seem to have been made up of a rather large number of foods, so that the failure of one food source would not be catastrophic. There is a possible slight tendency for Paleolithic people to be healthier and taller than Mesolithic people, but there is no apparent trend toward increasing physiological stress during the Mesolithic. Thus, it seems that both hunter-gatherers and incipient agriculturalists regularly underwent population pressure, but only to a moderate degree.

During the periods when effective agriculture first comes into use, there seems to be a temporary upturn in health and survival rates in a few regions: Europe, North America, and the eastern Mediterranean. At this stage, wild foods are still consumed periodically, and a variety of plants are cultivated, suggesting the availability of adequate amounts of different nutrients. Based on the increasing frequency of tooth disease related to high carbohydrate consumption, it seems that cultivated plants probably increased the storable calorie supply, removing for a time any seasonal or periodic problems in food supply. In most regions, however, the development of agriculture seems not to have had this effect, and there seems to have been a slight increase in physiological stress.

Stress, however, does not seem to have become common and widespread until after the development of high degrees of sedentism, population density, and reliance on intensive agriculture. At this stage in all regions the incidence of physiological stress increases greatly, and average mortality rates increase appreciably.

Most of these agricultural populations have high frequencies of porotic hyperostosis and cribra orbitalia [bone deformities indicative of chronic iron-deficiency anemia], and there is a substantial increase in the number and severity of enamel hypoplasias and pathologies associated with

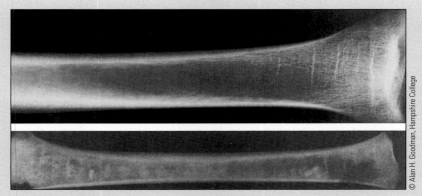

Harris lines near the ends of these youthful thighbones, found in a prehistoric farming community in Arizona, are indicative of recovery after growth arrest, caused by famine or disease.

© Alan H. Goodman, Hampshire College

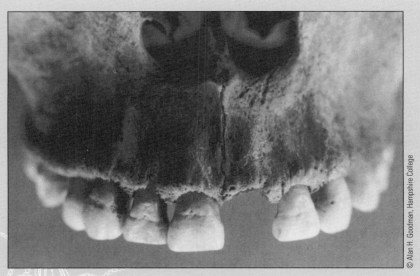

Enamel hypoplasias, such as those shown on these teeth, are indicative of arrested growth caused by famine or disease. These teeth are from an adult who lived in an ancient farming community in Arizona.

disease increases, apparently because subsistence by this time is characterized by a heavy emphasis on a few starchy food crops. Populations seem to have grown beyond the point at which wild food resources could be a meaningful dietary supplement, and even domestic animal resources were commonly reserved for farm labor and transport rather than for diet supplementation.

It seems that a large proportion of most sedentary prehistoric populations under intensive agriculture underwent chronic and life-threatening malnutrition and disease, especially during infancy and childhood. The causes of the nutritional stress are likely to have been the poverty of the staple crops in most nutrients except calories, periodic famines caused by the instability of the agricultural system, and chronic lack of food due to both population growth and economic expropriation by elites. The increases in infectious disease probably reflect both a poorer diet and increased interpersonal contact in crowded settlements, and it is, in turn, likely to have aggravated nutritional problems.

Adapted from Roosevelt, A. C. (1984). Population, health, and the evolution of subsistence: Conclusions from the conference. In M. N. Cohen & G. J. Armelagos (Eds.), Paleopathology at the origins of agriculture (pp. 572–574). Orlando: Academic Press.

infectious disease. Stature in many populations appears to have been considerably lower than would be expected if genetically determined height maxima had been reached, which suggests that the growth arrests associated with pathologies were causing stunting.

Accompanying these indicators of poor health and nourishment, there is a universal drop in the occurrence of Harris lines, suggesting a poor rate of full recovery from the stress. Incidence of carbohydrate-related tooth

In addition to this evidence of stress preserved in Neolithic skeletons, dental decay increased during this period due to the high-starch diet. Scientists have recently documented dental drilling of teeth in a 9,000-year-old Neolithic site in Pakistan (Coppa et al., 2006). This resembles the high frequency of dental decay seen in contemporary populations when they switch from a varied hunter-gatherer diet to a high-starch diet.

Domestication encourages a sedentary lifestyle with the great potential for overpopulation relative to the resource base. Under these conditions, even minor environmental fluctuations can lead to widespread hunger and malnutrition. Evidence of stress and disease increased proportionally with population density and the reliance on intensive agriculture. Further, the crowded conditions in settlements led to competition for resources with other villages, increasing the mortality rate due to warfare.

For the most part, Neolithic peoples depended on crops selected for their higher productivity and storability rather than for nutritional balance. Moreover, as already noted, the crops' nutritional shortcomings would have been exacerbated by their susceptibility to periodic failure, particularly as populations grew in size. Thus, it comes as no surprise that Neolithic peoples experienced worsened health and higher mortality compared to their Paleolithic forebears. Some have gone so far as to assert that the switch from food foraging to food production was the worst mistake that humans ever made!

Sedentary life in fixed villages likely increased the incidence of disease and mortality characteristic of the Neolithic. With a sedentary, settled lifestyle come problems such as the accumulation of garbage and human waste. Small groups of people, who move about from one campsite to another, leave their waste behind. Moreover, transmission of airborne diseases increases where people are gathered into villages. As we saw in Chapter 2, farming practices also created the ideal environment for the species of mosquito that spreads malaria.

TABLE 9.1

Diseases Acquired from Domesticated Animals

Disease	Animal with Most Closely Related Pathogen
Measles	Cattle (rinderpest)
Tuberculosis	Cattle
Smallpox	Cattle (cowpox) or other livestock with related pox viruses
Influenza	Pigs, ducks
Pertussis (whooping cough)	Pigs, dogs

Close contact with animals provides a situation in which variants of animal pathogens may establish themselves in humans. For example, humans have developed symptoms from infection with avian influenza (bird flu) following contact with domesticated birds.

© Cengage Learning

Source: Diamond, J. (1997). *Guns, germs, and steel* (p. 207). New York: Norton.

The close association between humans and their domestic animals facilitated the transmission of some animal diseases to people. A host of life-threatening diseases—including smallpox, chicken pox, and in fact all of the infectious diseases of childhood, overcome by medical science only in the latter half of the 20th century—came to humans through their close association with domestic animals (**Table 9.1**). Again we see that domestication and the changes of the Neolithic revolution had unforeseen biological consequences to the human population.

The Neolithic and the Idea of Progress

Although the overall health of Neolithic peoples suffered as a consequence of this cultural shift, many view the transition from food foraging to food production as a great step upward on a ladder of progress. In part this interpretation derives from one of the more widely held beliefs of Western culture—that humans and their lifeways have progressed steadily over time. To be sure, farming allowed people to increase the size of their populations, to live together in substantial sedentary communities, and to reorganize the workload in ways that permitted craft specialization. However, this is not progress in a universal sense but, rather, a set of cultural beliefs about the nature of progress. Each culture defines *progress* (if it does so at all) in its own terms.

Whatever the benefits of food production, Neolithic humans paid a substantial price for the development of **agriculture**—intensive crop cultivation, employing plows, fertilizers, and/or irrigation. As anthropologists Mark Cohen and George Armelagos put it, "Taken as a whole, indicators fairly clearly suggest an overall decline in the quality—and probably in the length—of human life associated with the adoption of agriculture" (Cohen & Armelagos, 1984b, p. 594).

Rather than imposing ethnocentric notions of progress on the archaeological record, anthropologists view the advent of food production as part of the diversification of cultures, something that began in the Paleolithic. Although some societies continued to practice various forms of hunting, gathering, and fishing, others became horticultural. But the resource competition that began in the Neolithic has pushed hunter-gatherers into increasingly marginalized territories over time.

Some horticultural societies developed agriculture. Technologically more complex than horticultural societies, agriculturalists practice intensive crop cultivation, employing plows, fertilizers, and possibly irrigation. They may use a wooden or metal plow pulled by one or more harnessed draft animals, such as horses, oxen, or water buffaloes, to produce food on larger plots of land. At times, the distinction between horticulturalist and intensive agriculturalist blurs. For example, the Hopi Indians of the North American Southwest traditionally employed irrigation in their farming while at the same time using basic hand tools.

Pastoralism arose in environments that were too dry, too grassy, too steep, too cold, or too hot for effective horticulture or intensive agriculture. Pastoralists breed and manage migratory herds of domesticated grazing animals, such as goats, sheep, cattle, llamas, or camels. For example, without plows early Neolithic peoples could not farm the heavy grass cover of the Russian steppe, but they could graze their animals there. Thus, a number of peoples living in the arid grasslands and deserts that stretch from northwestern Africa into Central Asia kept large herds of domestic animals, relying on their neighbors for plant foods. Finally, some societies went on to develop civilizations—the subject of the next chapter.

---

agriculture Intensive crop cultivation, employing plows, fertilizers, and/or irrigation.

CHAPTER CHECKLIST

What is the Mesolithic?

⬤ The period between the Paleolithic and Neolithic, this period of warming after the last glacial period included rising sea levels, changes in vegetation, and the disappearance of herd animals from many areas.

⬤ The Mesolithic included a shift from the hunting of big game to hunting of smaller game and gathering a broad spectrum of plants and aquatic resources.

⬤ Increased reliance on seafood and plants allowed some people to become more sedentary.

⬤ Many Mesolithic tools in the Old World were made with microliths—small, hard, sharp blades of flint or similar stone that could be mass-produced and hafted. Mesolithic peoples also hafted larger blades to produce implements like sickles.

⬤ In the Americas, Archaic cultures are comparable to the Old World Mesolithic.

What is the Neolithic Revolution, and how did it come about?

⬤ A shift to food production through the domestication of plants and animals constitutes most of the change of this period.

⬤ Settlement in permanent villages accompanied food production in many cases, though some Neolithic peoples who depended on domesticated animals did not become sedentary. Still others maintained a hunter-gatherer lifestyle. The use of polished stone tools by all peoples of this period gives the Neolithic its name.

⬤ During the Neolithic, stone that was too hard to be chipped was ground and polished for tools. People developed scythes, forks, hoes, and plows to replace simple digging sticks. Axes and adzes made of polished stone were far stronger and less likely to chip than those with blades made of chipped stone.

⬤ Village life allowed for a reorganization of the workload, letting some individuals pursue specialized tasks.

⬤ The change to food production took place independently and more or less simultaneously in various regions of the world: Southwest and Southeast Asia, highland Mexico and Peru, South America's Amazon forest, eastern North America, China, and Africa. In all cases, people developed food complexes based on starchy grains and/or roots that were consumed with protein-containing legumes plus flavor enhancers.

⬤ Southwest Asia contains the earliest known Neolithic sites consisting of small villages of mud huts with individual storage pits and clay ovens along with evidence of food production and trade.

⬤ At ancient Jericho, remains of tools, houses, and clothing indicate Neolithic people occupied the oasis as early as 10,350 years ago. At its height, Neolithic Jericho had a population of 400 to 900 people. Comparable villages developed independently in Mexico and Peru by about 4,500 years ago.

⬤ The most probable theory to account for the Neolithic revolution is that domestication came about as a consequence of a chance convergence of separate natural events and cultural developments.

What is domestication, and how can we recognize it?

⬤ A domesticated plant or animal is one that has become genetically modified as an intended or unintended consequence of human manipulation.

⬤ Analysis of plant and animal remains at a site usually indicates whether its occupants were food producers. Wild cereal grasses, for example, typically have fragile stems, whereas cultivated ones have tough stems. Domesticated plants can also be identified because their edible parts are generally larger than those of their wild counterparts.

⬤ Domestication produces skeletal changes in some animals. The horns of wild goats and sheep, for example, differ from those of domesticated ones. Age and sex imbalances in herd animals may also indicate manipulation by human domesticators.

⬤ Domesticated crops are more productive but also more vulnerable. Food production also requires more labor compared to hunting and gathering.

How did the Neolithic revolution impact social structure?

⬤ Human population sizes have increased steadily since the Neolithic. Some scholars argue that pressure from increasing population size led to innovations such as intensive agriculture. Others suggest that these innovations allowed population size to grow.

⬤ Periodic crop failures forced Neolithic peoples to move into new regions, spreading farming from one region to another, as into Europe from Southwest Asia. Sometimes, food foragers will adopt the cultivation of crops from neighboring peoples in response to a shortage of wild foods.

⬤ Trade specializations came about due to the increased yields of food production. This included the extensive manufacture and use of pottery, the building of permanent houses, and the weaving of textiles.

● Archaeological evidence indicates that social organization was probably relatively egalitarian, with minimal division of labor and little development of specialized social roles.

● Neolithic peoples sometimes organized themselves to create monumental structures related to their belief systems, such as the ring of massive boulders at Stonehenge whose opening lines up precisely with the sunset of the winter solstice.

What were the biological consequences of the Neolithic revolution?

● New diets, living arrangements, and farming practices led to increased incidence of disease and higher

mortality rates. Increased fertility, however, more than offset mortality, and globally human population has grown since the Neolithic.

● Many infectious diseases originated in the Neolithic because of close contact between humans and animal domesticates.

● Many of the health problems humans face today originated in the Neolithic.

● Increased competition for resources began in the Neolithic. Hunter-gatherers have become increasingly marginalized over time due to this competition.

QUESTIONS FOR REFLECTION

1. The changed lifeways of the Neolithic included the domestication of plants and animals as well as settlement into villages. This new way of life created a competition for resources. How is this competition manifest in the world today?

2. Why do you think some people of the past remained food foragers instead of becoming food producers? To what degree was the process of domestication conscious and deliberate? Were humans always directing this process?

3. Consider the reduction of diversity and the vulnerability to disease brought about by the domestication of wild species during the Neolithic. Are these same

factors relevant to today's genetically modified foods? Who benefits most directly from these genetically engineered products?

4. Why are the changes of the Neolithic sometimes mistakenly associated with progress? Why have the social forms that originated in the Neolithic come to dominate the earth?

5. Although the archaeological record indicates some differences in the timing of domestication of plants and animals in different parts of the world, why is it incorrect to say that one region was more advanced than another?

ONLINE STUDY RESOURCES

CourseMate

Access chapter-specific learning tools, including learning objectives, practice quizzes, videos, flash cards, glossaries, and more in your Anthropology CourseMate.

Log into **www.cengagebrain.com** to access the resources your instructor has assigned and to purchase materials.

Challenge Issue

With the emergence of cities and states, human societies began to develop organized central governments and concentrated power that made it possible to build monumental structures such as the magnificent 12th-century Angkor Wat temple complex in Cambodia. But cities and states also ushered in a series of problems, many of which we still face today, such as large-scale warfare. Like monumental civic works, warfare requires elaborate organization under a centralized authority, both to mount attacks and for defense. Within decades of the dedication of this 500-acre temple to the Hindu god Vishnu, a neighboring group sacked it. The original Khmer rulers then took the temple back, restored it, ultimately dedicating the temple to Buddhism. In more recent times, this temple again was the site of violence when the army of Khmer Rouge, a murderous regime responsible for the deaths of at least 1.5 million Cambodians, retreated to the sacred ruins as they were ousted from power in 1979. Although the Khmer Rouge professed a doctrine of "complete eradication of the past" to justify their genocidal policies, in an ironic twist international concern for preservation of these sacred ruins protected the Khmer army from massive bombings. Today, peace has returned to Cambodia, and collective global infrastructure protects the temple of Angkor Wat for all of us.

The Emergence of Cities and States

A walk down a busy street in a city like New York or Cairo brings us into contact with numerous activities essential to life in contemporary urban society. People going to and from offices and stores fill crowded sidewalks. Heavy traffic of cars, taxis, and trucks periodically comes to a standstill. A brief two-block stretch may contain a grocery store; shops selling clothing, appliances, or books; a restaurant; a newsstand; a gasoline station; and a movie theater. Other neighborhoods may feature a museum, a police station, a school, a hospital, or a church.

Each of these services or places of business depends on others from outside this two-block radius. A butcher shop, for instance, depends on slaughterhouses and beef ranches. A clothing store could not exist without designers, farmers who produce cotton and wool, and workers who manufacture synthetic fibers. Restaurants rely on refrigerated trucking and vegetable and dairy farmers. Hospitals need insurance companies, pharmaceutical companies, and medical equipment industries to function. All institutions, finally, depend on the public utilities—the telephone, gas, water, and electric companies, not to mention the Internet. Although not perceptible at first glance, interdependence defines modern cities.

The interdependence of goods and services in a big city makes a variety of products readily available. But interdependence also creates vulnerability. If labor strikes, bad weather, or acts of violence cause one service to stop functioning, other services can deteriorate. At the same time, cities are resilient. When one service breaks down, others take over its functions. A long newspaper strike in New York City in the 1960s, for example, opened opportunities for several new newsmagazines as well as expanded television coverage of news and events. This phenomenon also occurred with the explosion of reality television programs in the United States during the 2007–2008 Hollywood writers' strike.

In many parts of the world, wars have caused extensive damage to basic infrastructure, leading to the development of alternative systems to cope with everything from the most basic tasks such as procuring food and water to communication

IN THIS CHAPTER YOU WILL LEARN TO

- Define *civilization*, *cities*, and *states* and identify their global origins.

- Identify the elements of archaeological exploration of ancient civilizations through a case study of the Maya city of Tikal.

- Examine the four major cultural changes that mark the transition from the Neolithic to life in urban centers.

- Compare theories for the development of states.

- Identify the problems that accompany the development of cities and states.

Figure 10.1 **Urban Growth amid Destruction** Decades of violence have severely compromised the infrastructure of Afghanistan, yet the size of Kabul, the fifth fastest-growing city in the world, has swelled to over 4 million people. Streets consist of rubble, and building facades stand as empty shells. Here children go to a public spigot to get their family's daily supply.

within global political systems (**Figure 10.1**). People coping with the aftermath of a natural disaster such as Hurricane Katrina in 2005 or the massive earthquake and tsunami that hit Japan in 2011 must also find such alternatives.

With the interconnectedness of modern life due to the Internet and globalization, the interdependence of goods and services transcends far beyond city limits. Social media such as Facebook and Twitter allow for instantaneous communication about geopolitical events and can mobilize global support, as occurred with the Arab Spring of 2011.

On the surface, city life seems so orderly that we take it for granted; but a moment's reflection reminds us that the intricate metropolitan fabric of life did not always exist, and the concentrated availability of diverse goods developed only very recently in human history.

Defining Civilization

The word *civilization* comes from the Latin *civis*, meaning "an inhabitant of a city," and *civitas*, "the urban community in which one dwells." In everyday North American and European usage, the word *civilization* connotes refinement and progress and may imply ethnocentric judgments about cultures. In anthropology, by contrast, the term has a more

precise meaning that avoids culture-bound notions. As used by anthropologists, **civilization** refers to societies in which large numbers of people live in cities, are socially stratified, and are governed by a ruling elite working through centrally organized political systems called states. We shall elaborate on all of these points in the course of this chapter.

As Neolithic villages grew into towns, the world's first cities developed (**Figure 10.2**). This happened between 4,500 and 6,000 years ago, first in Mesopotamia (modern-day Iraq and Syria), then in Egypt's Nile Valley and the Indus Valley (today's India and Pakistan). In China, civilization was underway by 5,000 years ago. Independent of these developments in Eurasia and Africa, the first American Indian cities appeared in Peru around 4,000 years ago and in Mesoamerica about 2,000 years ago.

What characterized these first cities? Why are they called the birthplaces of civilization? The most obvious feature of cities—and of civilization—is their large size and population. But cities include more than overgrown towns.

Consider the case of Çatalhöyük, a compact 9,500-year-old settlement in south-central Turkey that, though well populated, was not a true city (Balter, 1998, 1999, 2001a; Kunzig, 1999). The tightly packed houses for its more than 5,000 inhabitants left no room for streets. People traversed the tops of neighboring houses and dropped through a hole in the roof to get into their own homes. Although house walls were covered with paintings and bas-reliefs, the houses were structurally similar to one another. People grew some crops and tended livestock but also collected significant amounts of food from wild plants and animals, never

civilization In anthropology, societies in which large numbers of people live in cities, are socially stratified, and are governed by a ruling elite working through centrally organized political systems called states.

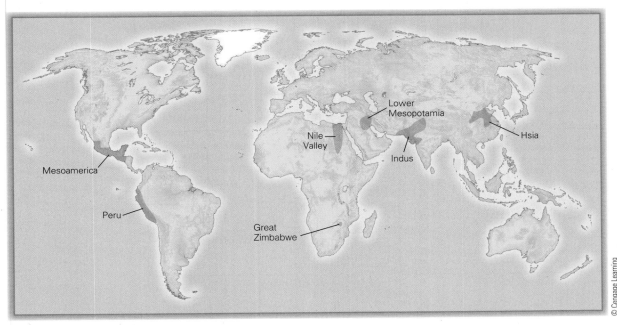

Figure 10.2 Early Civilizations The major early civilizations sprang from Neolithic villages in various parts of the world. Those of the Americas developed wholly independently of those in Africa and Eurasia. Chinese civilization seems to have developed independently of Southwest Asia, including the Nile and Indus civilizations. Although the Bantu city of Great Zimbabwe dates to later than some of these, it likewise was a major civilization that arose independently.

intensifying their agricultural practices. There is no evidence of public architecture and only minimal evidence of a division of labor or a centralized authority. It was as if several Neolithic villages were crammed together in one place at Çatalhöyük.

Archaeological evidence from early urban hubs, by contrast, demonstrates organized planning by a central authority, technological intensification, and social stratification. For example, flood control and protection were vital components of the great ancient cities of the Indus River Valley, located in today's India and Pakistan. Mohenjo-Daro, an urban center at its peak some 4,500 years ago with a population of at least 20,000, was built on an artificial mound, safe from floodwaters. The city streets were laid out in a grid pattern with sophisticated drainage systems for individual homes, indicating further centralized planning.

Ancient peoples incorporated their spiritual beliefs and social order into the cities they built. For example, the layout of the great Mesoamerican city Teotihuacan, founded 2,200 years ago, translated the solar calendar into a unified spatial pattern. Ancient city planners oriented the Street of the Dead—a grand north-south axis originating at the Pyramid of the Moon and bordered by the Pyramid of the Sun and the royal palace compound—to an astronomical marker, east of true north. They even channeled the San Juan River to conform to their pattern where it runs through the city (**Figure 10.3**). Thousands of apartment compounds surrounded this core, separated from one another by a grid of narrow streets, maintaining the east-of-north orientation throughout the city. Archaeologists estimate that over 100,000 people inhabited this great city until its sudden collapse possibly in the 7th century.

Archaeologists have recovered clear evidence of both social and economic diversity in Teotihuacan. Variation in size and quality of apartment rooms indicates at least six levels of society. Those at the top of the social scale lived on or near the Street of the Dead (**Figure 10.4**). The Pyramid of the Sun, built along this avenue above a cave, was seen as a portal to the underworld and as the home of deities associated with death. Teotihuacan artisans worked

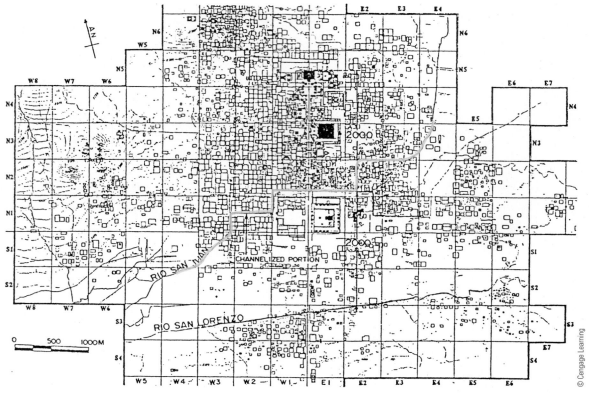

Figure 10.3 Aztec City Planning The founders of Teotihuacan imposed an audacious plan on several square kilometers of landscape in central Mexico. At the center is the Street of the Dead, originating at the Pyramid of the Moon (*near top*) and running past the Pyramid of the Sun, and, south of the San Juan River (Rio), the palace compound. Note the gridded layout of surrounding apartment compounds and the channeled San Juan River.

VISUAL COUNTERPOINT

Figure 10.4 The Grand Avenues of Cities The view looking south down Teotihuacan's principal avenue, the Street of the Dead (*left*), was unequaled in scale until the construction of such modern-day avenues as the Champs-Élysées in Paris (*right*). Archaeologists estimate that 100,000 people lived in this city in various neighborhoods according to their social position. This major avenue was home to the elite.

on exotic goods and raw materials imported from distant regions, and at least two neighborhoods housed people with foreign affiliations: one for those from Oaxaca, the other (the "merchant's quarter") for those from the Gulf and Maya lowlands. Farmers, whose labor in fields (some of them irrigated) supplied the food to fellow city-dwellers, also resided in the city.

Mohenjo-Daro and Teotihuacan, like other early cities throughout the globe, represent far more than expanded Neolithic villages. Some consider the array of changes accompanying the emergence of urban living as one of the great developments in human culture. The following case study provides a glimpse into another of the world's ancient cities and reveals how archaeologists went about studying this city—from the first exploratory surveys, to the excavations, to the theories proposed about its development.

Tikal: A Case Study

The ancient city of Tikal, one of the largest lowland Maya centers in existence, is situated in Central America about 300 kilometers north of Guatemala City. Here, on a broad limestone terrace in a rainforest, the Maya settled 3,000 years ago. Because archaeologists have correlated the Maya calendar precisely with our own, we know that their civilization flourished until 1,100 years ago.

At its height, Tikal covered about 120 square kilometers (km²). The Great Plaza, a large paved area surrounded by about 300 major structures and thousands of houses, stood at Tikal's center, or nucleus (**Figure 10.5**). Starting from a small, dispersed population, Tikal swelled to at least

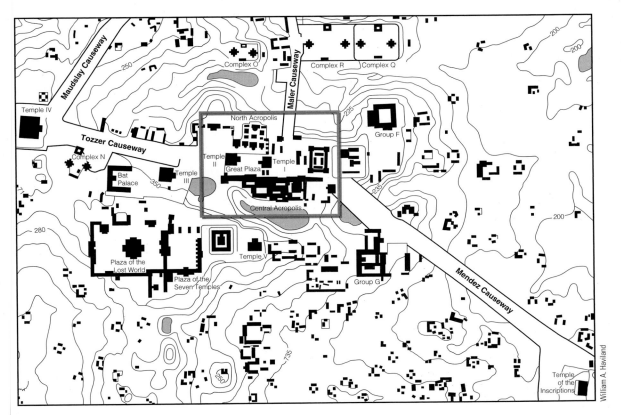

Figure 10.5 Layout of Tikal Tikal spreads far beyond the Great Plaza and the monumental buildings that have been excavated and are mapped here. Archaeologists used surveying techniques, test pits, and other strategies to define the city's boundaries and to understand the full spectrum of lifeways that took place there. The red outline in the center of the map delineates the royal court, royal burial ground, and central marketplace. In addition to what is pictured here, Tikal extends several kilometers outward in every direction. Those familiar with the original *Star Wars* movie will be interested to know that the aerial views of the rebel camp were filmed at Tikal, where monumental structures depicted in this map rise high above the forest canopy.

45,000 people. By 1,550 years ago, its population density had reached 600 to 700 persons per square kilometer, which was three times that of the surrounding region.

Archaeologists explored Tikal and the surrounding region under the joint auspices of the University of Pennsylvania Museum and the Guatemalan government from 1956 through the 1960s. At the time, it was the most ambitious archaeological project undertaken in the western hemisphere.

In the first few years of the Tikal Project, archaeologists investigated only the major temple and palace structures found in the vicinity of the Great Plaza, at the site's epicenter. But in 1959, aiming to gain a balanced view of Tikal's development and composition, they turned their attention to the hundreds of small mounds, thought to be the remains of dwellings that surrounded larger buildings. This represented a shift in the practice of archaeology toward studying the complexities of everyday life. Imagine trying to get a realistic view of life in a major city such as Chicago or Beijing by looking only at their monumental public buildings. Similarly, archaeologists realized that they needed to examine the full range of ruins at Tikal in order to accurately reconstruct past lifeways.

With data from the excavation of small structures, most of which were probably houses, archaeologists estimated Tikal's population size and density. In turn, this information allowed archaeologists to test the conventional assumption that the subsistence practices of the Maya inhabitants could not sustain large population concentrations.

Extensive excavation also provided a sound basis for a reconstruction of the everyday life and social organization of the Maya, a people who had been known almost entirely through the study of ceremonial remains. For example, differences in architecture, house construction, and associated artifacts and burials suggest differences in social class. Features of house distribution might reflect the existence of extended families or other types of kin groups. The excavation of both large and small structures revealed the social structure of the total population of Tikal (Haviland, 2002).

Surveying and Excavating the Site

Mapping crews extensively surveyed 6 square kilometers of forested land surrounding the Great Plaza, providing a preliminary map to guide the small-structure excavation process. The dense, tall rainforest canopy prevented the use of aerial photography for this mapping. Trees obscured all but the tallest temples. Many of the small ruins remain practically invisible even to observers on the ground. Four years of mapping revealed that ancient Tikal extended far beyond the original 6 km² surveyed. More time and money allowed continued surveying of the area in order to fully define the city's boundaries and calculate its overall size.

The initial excavation of six structures, two plazas, and a platform revealed new structures not visible before excavation, the architectural complexity of the structures, and an enormous quantity of artifacts. Some structures were partially excavated, and some remained uninvestigated. Following this initial work, the archaeological team excavated over a hundred additional small structures in different parts of the site in order to ensure investigation of a representative sample. The team also sank numerous test pits in various other small-structure groups to supplement the information gained from more extensive excavations. They also washed and catalogued every artifact recovered.

Evidence from the Excavation

Excavation at Tikal produced considerable evidence about the social organization, technology, and diversity in this ancient city, as well as the relationship between people in Tikal and other regions. For example, the site provides evidence of trade in nonperishable items. Granite, quartzite, hematite, pyrite, jade, slate, and obsidian all were imported, either as raw materials or finished products. Marine materials came from Caribbean and Pacific coastal areas. In turn, Tikal residents exported chert (a flintlike stone used to manufacture tools) both in its raw form and as finished objects. Tikal's location between two river systems may have facilitated an overland trade route. Evidence of trade in perishable goods—such as textiles, feathers, salt, and cacao—indicated the presence of full-time traders among the Tikal Maya.

In the realm of technology, archaeologists found specialized woodworking, pottery, obsidian, and shell workshops. The skillful carving displayed on stone monuments suggests that occupational specialists did this work. Similarly, the fine artwork glazed into ceramic vessels demonstrates that ancient artists could envision the transformation of their pale, relatively colorless ceramics into their finished fired form.

To control the large population, some form of bureaucratic organization must have existed in Tikal. From Maya written records (glyphs), we know that the government was headed by a hereditary ruling dynasty with sufficient power to organize massive construction and maintenance (**Figure 10.6**). This included a system of defensive ditches and embankments on the northern and southern edges of the city. The longest of these ran for a distance of perhaps 19 to 28 kilometers. We also know that astrological experts constructed detailed and accurate calendars for tracking the dynasties and their conquests (**Figure 10.7**). Although we do not have direct evidence, clues indicate the presence of textile workers, dental workers, makers of bark cloth "paper," scribes, masons, astronomers, and other occupational specialists.

Archaeologists suggest that the religion of the Tikal Maya developed initially as a means to cope with the uncertainties of agriculture. With thin soils and no streams, Tikal residents

Figure 10.6 Stone Documents Carved monuments like this were commissioned by Tikal's rulers to commemorate important events in their regions. Archaeologists have deciphered the glyphs or written language chiseled into the stone. This monument portrays the reign of a king who ruled about 1,220 years ago. Only a specialist could have accomplished such skilled stone carvings. The glyphs also provide indirect evidence of writing specialists or scribes who may have kept records on perishable materials such as bark cloth paper. (For a translation of the inscription on the monument's left side, see Figure 10.13.)

depended on rainwater collected in reservoirs. Rain is abundant in season, but its onset is unreliable. The ancient Maya may have perceived Tikal, with a high elevation relative to surrounding terrain, as a "power place," especially suited for making contact with supernatural forces and beings (**Figure 10.8**).

The Maya priests tried not only to win over and please the deities in times of drought but also to honor them in times of plenty. Priests—experts on the Maya calendar—determined the most favorable time to plant crops and were involved with other agricultural matters. This tended to keep people in or near the city so that they could receive guidance on their crops. The population in and around Tikal depended upon their priests to influence supernatural beings and forces on their behalf.

As the population increased, land for agriculture became scarce, forcing the Maya to find new methods of food production that could sustain Tikal's dense population. They added the planting and tending of fruit trees and other crops that could be grown around their houses in soils enriched by human waste. (Unlike houses at Teotihuacan, those at Tikal were not built close to one another.) Along with increased reliance on household gardening, the Maya constructed artificially raised fields in areas that flooded during the rainy season. Careful maintenance allowed for intensive cultivation of these raised fields, year after year. By converting low areas into reservoirs and constructing channels to carry runoff from plazas and other architecture into these reservoirs, the Maya at Tikal maximized the collection of water for the dry season.

As these agricultural changes took place, a class of artisans, craftspeople, and other occupational specialists emerged to serve the needs of an elite consisting of the priesthood and a ruling dynasty. The Maya built numerous

Figure 10.7 Maya Calendar Mesoamerican cultures like the Maya and the Olmec used a nonrepeating "long count" calendar system that tallied the number of days that had passed since a mythical creation date, corresponding to August 11, 3114 BCE. According to Mayan mythology, we live in the fourth world, the first three creations having been failed attempts by the gods. The end of the current long count on December 12, 2012, caused numerous doomsday predictions. Also, in 2012, a team of archaeologists lead by William Saturno of Boston Univeristy uncovered a remarkable series of glyphs at the Guatemalan site of Xultun that confirmed the astronomically accurate Maya calendars extend far into the future.

Figure 10.8 **Modern Maya at Tikal** Archaeologists have proposed that Tikal emerged as an important religious center due to its relative altitude in the region. Altitude may have created a perception of power and access to supernatural forces. Today, Tikal remains an important religious center for local Maya, who gather in front of the acropolis for a traditional ceremony.

temples, public buildings, and various kinds of houses appropriate to the distinct social classes of their society.

For several hundred years, Tikal sustained its ever-growing population. When the pressure for food and land reached a critical point, population growth stopped. At the same time, warfare with other cities had increasingly destructive effects on Tikal. Archaeologists diagnosed the damage caused by warfare from abandoned houses situated on prime lands in rural areas, from nutritional problems visible in skeletons recovered from burials, and from construction of the previously mentioned defensive ditches and embankments. The archaeological record shows that there was a period of readjustment directed by an already strong central authority. Activities then continued as before, but without further population growth for another 250 years or so.

As this case study shows, excavations at Tikal demonstrated the splendor, the social organization, the belief systems, and the agricultural practices of the ancient Maya civilization. This chapter's Original Study illustrates a very different Maya site just a day's walk from Tikal.

ORIGINAL STUDY

Action Archaeology and the Community at El Pilar BY ANABEL FORD

Resource management and conservation are palpable themes of the 21st century. Nowhere is this more keenly felt than in the tropics, seemingly our last terrestrial frontier. The Maya forest, one of the world's most biodiverse areas, is experiencing change at a rapid rate. Over the next two decades this area's population will double, threatening the integrity of the tropical ecosystems with contemporary development strategies that are at odds with the rich biodiversity of the region.

Curiously, in the past the Maya forest was home to a major civilization with at least three to nine times the current population of the region. The prosperity of the Classic Maya civilization has been touted for the remarkable quality of their unique hieroglyphic writing; the beauty of their art expressed in stone, ceramics, and plaster; and the precision of their mathematics and astronomy. What was the secret

of Maya conservation and prosperity? How can archaeology shed light on the conservation possibilities for the future? These are the questions I address in my research at El Pilar.

I began my work as an archaeologist in the Maya forest in 1972. Eschewing the monumental civic centers that draw tourist and scholar alike, I was interested in the everyday life of the Maya through the study of their cultural ecology—the multifaceted relationships of humans and their environment. Certainly, the glamorous archaeological centers intrigued me; they were testaments to the wealth of the

Maya civilization. Yet, it seemed to me that an understanding of the ancient Maya landscape would tell us more about the relationship of the Maya and their forest than yet another major temple. After all, the Maya were an agrarian civilization.

The ancient Maya agricultural system must be the key to their growth and accomplishments. With more than a century of exploration of the temple centers, we know that the civic centers were made for the ceremonial use of the ruling elite, that the temples would hold tombs of the royals and would include dedications of some of the most astounding artworks of the ancient world. Centers, too, would present stone stele erected in commemoration of regal accomplishments with hieroglyphic writing that is increasingly understood as codification of the Mayan language. These facts about the Maya point to successful development founded in their land use strategies that supported the increasing populations, underwrote the affluent elite glamor, and allowed for the construction of major civic centers over 2 millennia. The Maya farmers were at the bottom of this astounding expansion, and that is where I thought there could be a real discovery.

Because agriculture figures so importantly in preindustrial agrarian societies, such as the Maya, we would expect that the majority of the settlements would be farming ones. But how can we understand the farming techniques and strategies? Our appreciation of the traditional land use methods has been subverted with technology and a European ecological imperialism that inhibits a full understanding of other land use systems.

During the conquest of the Maya area, Spaniards felt there was nothing to eat in the forest; presented with a staggering cornucopia of fruits and vegetables that could fill pages, they asserted they were starving because there was no grain or cattle. Today, we use European terms to describe agricultural lands around the world that are in many ways inappropriate to describe traditional systems. The word *arable* specifically means "plowable" and is derived from the Egyptian word *Ard*, or "plow." *Arable* is equated with *cultivable* by the United Nations Food and Agriculture Organization, and by doing so eliminates realms of land use and management that have a subtler impact on the environment. *Fallow* is loosely used to indicate abandoned fields, but really *fallow* means "unseeded plowed field." For European eyes, plowing was equivalent to cultivating, but in the New World cultivating embraced a much broader meaning that included fields of crops, selective succession, diverse orchards, and managed forests. In fact, it meant the entire landscape mosaic.

It is important to remember that the Maya, like all Native Americans prior to the tumultuous conquest 500 years ago, lived in the Stone Age without metal tools and largely without domesticated animals. This was not a hindrance, as it would seem today, but a fact that focused land use and intensification in other realms. Farmers were called upon to use their local skill and knowledge to provide for daily needs. And, as with all Native Americans, this skill would involve the landscape and most particularly the plants.

Reports of yields of grain from the Mesoamerican maize fields, or *milpas*, suggest that they were more than two to three times as productive as the fertile fields of the Seine River near Paris of the 16th century, the time of the conquest. The Maya farmed in cooperation with the natural environment. Like the Japanese rice farmer Masanubu Fukuoka describes in his book *One Straw Revolution*, Maya farmers today use their knowledge of the insects to ensure pollination, their understanding of animals to promote propagation, their appreciation of water to determine planting, and their observations of change and nuance to increase their yields. This is not at all like the current agricultural development models that rely on increasingly complex techniques to raise production, disregarding nature in the process.

My focus on the patterns of the ancient Maya settlements has guided me along a path that I believe can provide important answers to questions of how the Maya achieved their success. The answers lie in finding where the everyday Maya lived, when they lived there, and what they did there. Although popular notions would have you think that the Maya were a seething sea of humanity displacing the forest for their cities, I have discovered patterns on the landscape indicating that at their height in the Late Classic from 600 to 900 CE, the Maya occupied less than two-thirds of the landscape. More than 80 percent of the settlements were concentrated into less than 40 percent of the area, whereas another 40 percent of the region was largely unoccupied.

This diversity of land use intensity created a patchwork of stages of what traditional farmers see as a cycle from forest to field and from field to orchard and back to forest again. The result in the Maya forest garden was an economic landscape that supported the ancient Maya, fueled wealth in the colonial and independence eras with lumber, and underwrote capitalism with the natural gum chicle. Today, more than 90 percent of the dominant trees of the forest are of economic value. The Maya constructed this valuable forest over the millennia.

Despite my interest in daily life in the forest, monumental buildings became a part of my work. While conducting a settlement survey in the forest, I uncovered and mapped El Pilar, a major ancient Maya urban center with enormous temples towering more than 22 meters high and plaza expanses greater than soccer fields. The whole center of civic buildings covers more than 50 hectares. El Pilar is the largest center in the Belize River area and is located only 50 kilometers from Tikal. This center was bound to become a tourist destination, presenting an opportunity to explore new ways to tell the Maya story. My observation that the ancient Maya evolved a sustainable economy in the tropics of Mesoamerica led my approach to developing El Pilar.

Astride the contemporary border separating Belize from Guatemala, El Pilar has been the focus of a bold conservation design for an international peace park on a long-troubled border. The vision for El Pilar is founded on the preservation of cultural heritage in the context of the natural environment. With a collaborative and interdisciplinary team of local villagers, government administrators, and scientists, we have established the El Pilar Archaeological Reserve for Maya Flora and Fauna. Since 1993, the innovations of the El Pilar program have forged new ground in testing novel strategies for community participation in the conservation development of the El Pilar Archaeological Reserve.

This program touches major administrative themes of global importance: tourism, natural resources, foreign affairs, agriculture, rural development, and education. Yet the program's impact goes further. Working with traditional forest gardeners affects agriculture, rural enterprise, and capacity building. There are few areas untouched by the program's inclusive sweep, and more arenas can contribute to its evolution.

At El Pilar, I practice what I call "action archaeology," a pioneering conservation model that draws on lessons learned from the recent and distant past to benefit contemporary populations. For example, the co-evolution of Maya society and the environment provide clues about sustainability in this region today. At El Pilar we have advanced programs that will simulate Maya forest gardens as an alternative to resource diminishing plow-and-pasture farming methods. Working with the traditional farmers, school models are being established. These models will help to transfer knowledge to the younger generation and carry on important conservation strategies. The forest survives and demonstrates resilience to impacts brought on by human expansion. The ancient Maya lived with this forest for millennia, and the El Pilar program argues there are lessons to be learned from that past.

The El Pilar program recognizes the privilege it has enjoyed in forging an innovative community participatory process, in creating a unique management planning design, and in developing a new tourism destination. The success of local outreach at El Pilar can best be seen in the growth of the community organizations such as the El Pilar Forest Garden Network and Amigos de El Pilar (Friends of El Pilar). With groups based in both Belize and Guatemala working together, the El Pilar program can help build an inclusive relationship between the community and the reserve that is mutually beneficial. The development of this dynamic relationship lies at the heart of the El Pilar philosophy—resilient and with the potential to educate communities, reform local-level resource management, and inform conservation designs for the Maya forest.

Written expressly for this text, 2005. Anabel Ford is the director of the Mesoamerican Research Center, University of California, Santa Barbara, and president of the nonprofit Exploring Solutions Past: The Maya Forest Alliance. www.marc.ucsb.edu/elpilar/. Reprinted by permission of Professor Anabel Ford.

Archaeologist Anabel Ford at work in El Pilar.

© Rolex Awards for Excellence, Susan Gray

Cities and Cultural Change

If a person who grew up in a rural North American village today moved to Philadelphia, Montreal, or Los Angeles, she or he would experience a very different way of life. The same would be true for a Neolithic village-dweller who moved into one of the world's first cities in Mesopotamia 5,500 years ago. Because cultures are dynamic and integrated systems of adaptation that respond to external and internal factors, a shift from food production to living in urban centers also includes changes in the social structure and ideology. Four basic changes mark the transition from Neolithic village life to life in the first urban centers: agricultural innovation, diversification of labor, central government, and social stratification.

Agricultural Innovation

Changes in farming methods distinguished early civilizations from Neolithic villages. The ancient Sumerians, for example, built an extensive system of dikes, canals, and reservoirs to irrigate their farmlands. With such a system, they could control water resources at will; water could be held and then run off into the fields as necessary. Such innovations also contributed to large-scale production and management of animals needed to sustain large populations. As described in this chapter's Anthropology Applied feature, an understanding of these ancient techniques can provide models for effective land use in the present.

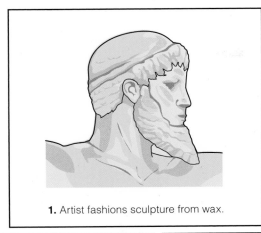

1. Artist fashions sculpture from wax.

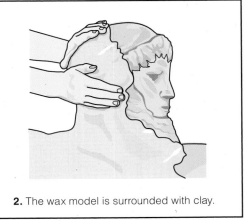

2. The wax model is surrounded with clay.

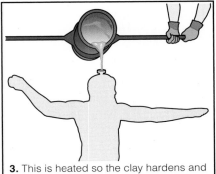

3. This is heated so the clay hardens and the wax melts.
4. The now hollow mold is inverted, and molten bronze metal is poured into it.

5. When the metal has cooled, the clay model is broken open to reveal a solid bronze sculpture.

© Cengage Learning

Figure 10.9 Lost Wax Casting Method The Bronze Age included manufacture of wholly practical metal items such as knives and plows, but it also contributed symbolically to maintaining the power of the ruling elite. Elaborate lifelike, large-scale sculptures of deities—such as the 3,000-year-old bronze Zeus, from the National Museum of Archaeology in Athens, Greece—or of the rulers themselves, demonstrated their power. This cultural tradition has continued into the present. Artists today employ the same methods of lost wax casting.

Irrigation improved crop yield: Not having to depend upon the seasonal rain cycles allowed farmers to harvest more crops in one year. Increased crop yields, resulting from agricultural innovations, contributed to the high population densities of ancient civilizations.

Diversification of Labor

Diversified labor activity also characterized early civilizations. In a Neolithic village without irrigation or plow farming, every family member participated in the raising of crops. In contrast, the high crop yields made possible by new farming methods and the increased population of civilizations permitted a sizable number of people to pursue nonagricultural activities on a full-time basis.

Ancient public records document a variety of specialized workers. For example, an early Mesopotamian document from the old Babylonian city of Lagash (modern-day Tell al-Hiba, Iraq) lists the artisans, craftspeople, and others paid from crop surpluses stored in the temple granaries. These lists included coppersmiths, silversmiths, sculptors, merchants, potters, tanners, engravers, butchers, carpenters, spinners, barbers, cabinetmakers, bakers, clerks, and brewers.

With specialization came the expertise that led to the invention of new ways of making and doing things. In Eurasia and Africa, civilization ushered in the **Bronze Age**, a period marked by the production of tools, ornaments, and monuments made of this metal alloy (**Figure 10.9**). Metals were in great demand for the manufacture of farmers' and artisans' tools, as well as for weapons. Copper and tin (the raw materials from which bronze is made) were smelted, or separated from their ores, then purified and cast to make plows, swords, axes, and shields.

Bronze Age In the Old World, the period marked by the production of tools and ornaments of bronze; began about 5,000 years ago in China, the Mediterranean, and South Asia and about 500 years earlier in Southwest Asia.

ANTHROPOLOGY APPLIED

Pre-Columbian Fish Farming in the Amazon

By Clark L. Erickson

Popular images associated with the Amazon today include the towering continuous green forest canopy, Day-Glo poison dart frogs, and natives' faces painted red. These potent images have been used to raise funds for conservation, educate the public in "green" politics, and promote ecotourism. Two themes have long dominated the popular and scientific literature on the Amazon: (1) the Myth of the Pristine Environment and (2) the Myth of the Noble Savage. The Myth of the Pristine Environment is the belief that the landscapes of the Americas were largely undisturbed Nature until the arrival of Europeans, who have destroyed the environment with their agriculture, mining, urbanism, and industry. The Myth of the Noble Savage posits that indigenous peoples of the past and present exist as a harmonious part of an undisturbed Nature. We now know that much of what has been traditionally recognized as Wilderness in the Amazon is the indirect result of massive depopulation after the arrival of Europeans. The introduction of Old World diseases, slavery, missionization, resettlement, and warfare removed most of the native peoples from the land within 100 years. Many areas of Amazonia were not repopulated until this century, and many still remain underpopulated.

My colleagues and I are documenting numerous cases of how native peoples of the Amazon (past and present) transformed, shaped, and in some cases, constructed what is often misidentified as pristine "wilderness." We find that high biodiversity is clearly related to past human activities such as gap formation, burning, and gardening. Our approach, called historical ecology or the archaeology of landscapes, assumes that all landscapes have long, complex histories. We find that high biodiversity is clearly related to past human activities such as opening up the forest, burning, and gardening. Since 1990, my research team has studied the vast networks of earthworks in the Bolivian Amazon built before the arrival of Europeans. These features include causeways of earth, artificial canals for canoe traffic, raised fields for growing crops in the savannahs, and settlement mounds of urban scale.

In 1995, we were invited by the local governor to begin archaeological investigations in Baures, a remote region of seasonally flooded savannahs, wetlands, and forest islands in northeast Bolivia. He loaned us his Cessna and pilot for an initial aerial survey of the region. As the plane circled the landscape, we saw an amazingly complex web of straight roads, canals, and moated earthwork enclosures below. During the dry season of 1996, I surveyed the area accompanied by a group of local hunters.

One artificial feature, referred to as a zigzag earthwork, particularly intrigued me. Low earthen walls zigzag across the savannahs between forest islands. Because of their changing orientations, they did not make sense as roads between settlements. As we mapped them with tape measure and compass, I noted that there were small funnel-like openings where the earthworks changed direction. I immediately realized that these matched the description of fish weirs that are reported in the ethnographic and historical literature on Amazonian peoples.

Later, such tools were made from smelted iron. In wars, stone knives, spears, and slings could not stand up against metal spears, arrowheads, swords, helmets, and armor.

The indigenous civilizations of the Americas also used metals. South American peoples used copper, silver, and gold for tools as well as for ceremonial and ornamental objects. The Aztecs and Maya used the same soft metals for ritual and decorative objects while continuing to rely on stone for their everyday tools. To those who assume the inherent superiority of metal, this seems puzzling. However, the ready availability of obsidian (a glass formed by volcanic activity), its extreme sharpness (many times sharper than the finest steel), and the ease with which toolmakers can work it made it perfectly suited to their needs. Moreover, unlike bronze—and especially iron—copper, silver, and gold are soft metals and have limited practical use. Obsidian tools provide some of the sharpest cutting edges ever made (recall Chapter 7's Anthropology Applied, "Stone Tools for Modern Surgeons").

Early civilizations developed extensive trade systems to procure the raw materials needed for their technologies. In many parts of the world, boats provided greater

Working with archaeologist Clark Erickson, artist Dan Brinkmeier of the Field Museum of Natural History has illustrated the fish weirs and ponds of ancient Baures, Bolivia.

© Dan Brinkmeier

season. I believe that in the past these were used to store live fish until needed. Our studies show that the weirs were used before the arrival of Europeans to the region.

The scale of the fish weir complex is larger than any previously reported. The native peoples of Baures shaped the environment into a productive landscape capable of providing sufficient protein to sustain large populations. The people responsible for this impressive land management are long gone or have forgotten the technology. Archaeology provides the only means of documenting this important lost knowledge. As politicians, conservationists, and aid agencies seek sustainable solutions to both develop and conserve the Amazon, archaeologists can play a key role by providing time-tested models of land use.

Fish weirs are fences made of wood, brush, basketry, or stones with small openings that extend across bodies of water. Baskets or nets are placed in the openings to trap migrating fish. Although most fish weirs are simple ephemeral structures crossing a river or shallow lake, those of Baures are permanent earthen features covering more than 500 square kilometers. In addition, small artificial ponds are associated with the fish weirs. Today, these ponds are filled with fish as the floodwaters recede in the dry

Adapted from Erickson, C. L. (2001). Pre-Columbian fish farming in the Amazon. Expedition 43 (3), 7–8. Copyright © 2001 Clark L. Erickson. Reprinted by permission of the author.

access to trade centers, transporting large loads of imports and exports between cities at lower costs than if they had been carried overland. A one-way trip from the ancient Egyptian cities along the Nile River to the Mediterranean port city of Byblos in Phoenicia (not far from today's Beirut, Lebanon) took far less time by rowboat compared to the overland route. With a sailboat, it was even faster.

Egyptian kings, or pharaohs, sent expeditions in various directions for prized resources: south to Nubia (northern Sudan) for gold; east to the Sinai Peninsula for copper; to Arabia for spices and perfumes; to Asia for lapis lazuli (a blue semiprecious stone) and other jewels; north to Lebanon for cedar, wine, and funerary oils; and southwest to Central Africa for ivory, ebony, ostrich feathers, leopard skins, cattle, and the captives they enslaved. Evidence of trading from Great Zimbabwe (**Figure 10.10**) in southern Africa indicates that by the 11th century these trading networks extended throughout the Old World. Increased contact with foreign peoples through trade brought new information to trading economies, furthering the spread of innovations and bodies of knowledge such as geometry and astronomy.

Figure 10.10 Great Zimbabwe The construction of elliptical granite walls held together without any mortar at Great Zimbabwe in southern Zimbabwe, Africa, attests to the skill of the people who built these structures. When European explorers, unwilling to accept the notion of civilization in sub-Saharan Africa, discovered these magnificent ruins, they wrongly attributed them to white non-Africans. This false notion persisted until archaeologists demonstrated that these structures were part of a city with 12,000 to 20,000 inhabitants that served as the center of a medieval Bantu state.

Central Government

A governing elite also emerged in early civilizations. The challenges new cities faced because of their size and complexity required a strong central authority. The governing elite saw to it that different interest groups, such as farmers or craft specialists, provided their respective services and did not infringe on one another.

Just as they do today, governments of the past ensured that cities were safe from their enemies by constructing fortifications and raising an army. They levied taxes and appointed tax collectors so that construction workers, the army, and other public expenses could be paid. They saw to it that merchants, carpenters, or farmers who made legal claims received justice according to their legal system's standards. They guaranteed safety for the lives and property of ordinary people and assured them that any harm done to one person by another would be justly handled. In addition, they arranged for storage of surplus food for times of scarcity and supervised public works such as extensive irrigation systems and fortifications.

Evidence of Centralized Authority

Evidence of centralized authority in ancient civilizations comes from sources such as law codes, temple records, monuments, and royal chronicles. Excavation of the city structures themselves provides additional evidence because these remains can show definitive signs of city planning. The precise astronomical layout of the Mesoamerican city of Teotihuacan, described earlier, attests to strong, centralized control.

Monumental buildings and temples, palaces, and large sculptures are usually found in ancient civilizations. For example, the Great Pyramid for the tomb of Khufu, the Egyptian pharaoh, is 755 feet long (236 meters) and 481 feet high (147 meters); it contains about 2.3 million stone blocks, each with an average weight of 2.5 tons. The Greek historian Herodotus reports that it took 100,000 men twenty years to build this tomb. Such gigantic structures could be built only because a powerful central authority was able to harness the considerable labor force, engineering skills, and raw materials necessary for their construction.

Writing or some form of recorded information provides another indicator of the existence of centralized authority. With writing, governors could disseminate information and store, systematize, and deploy written records for political, religious, and economic purposes. Of course, the development of writing went hand in hand with the development of specialized laborers: scribes responsible for physically creating the centralized authorities' records.

Scholars attribute the initial motive for the development of writing in Mesopotamia to recordkeeping of state affairs. Writing allowed early governments to track accounts of their food surplus, tribute records, and other business receipts. Some of the earliest documents appear to be just such records—lists of vegetables and animals bought and sold, tax lists, and storehouse inventories.

Before 5,500 years ago, records consisted initially of "tokens," ceramic pieces with different shapes indicative of different commercial objects. Thus, a cone shape could represent a measure of grain or a cylinder could be an animal. As the system became more sophisticated, tokens came to represent different animals, as well as processed foods (such as oil, trussed ducks, or bread) and manufactured or imported goods (such as textiles and metal) (Lawler, 2001). Ultimately, clay tablets with impressed marks representing objects replaced these tokens.

By 5,000 years ago, in the Mesopotamian city of Uruk in Iraq (which likely derives its modern country name

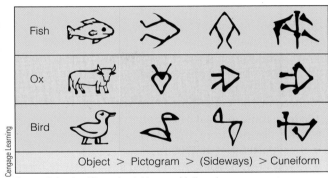

Object > Pictogram > (Sideways) > Cuneiform

Source: University of Pennsylvania Museum of Anthropology

Figure 10.11 Cuneiform Cuneiform writing developed from representational drawings of objects. Over time the drawings became simplified and more abstract, as well as being wedge-shaped so that they could be cut into a clay tablet with a stylus.

from this ancient place), a new writing technique emerged. Writers would use a reed stylus to make wedge-shaped markings on a tablet of damp clay. Originally, each marking stood for a word. Because most words in this language were monosyllabic, over time the markings came to stand for syllables, and cuneiform writing developed (Figure 10.11).

Controversy surrounds the question of the earliest evidence of writing (Figure 10.12). Traditionally, the earliest writing was linked to Mesopotamia. However, in 2003 archaeologists working in the Henan Province of central China discovered signs carved into 8,600-year-old tortoise shells; these markings resemble later-written characters and predate the Mesopotamian evidence by about 2,000 years (Li et al., 2003).

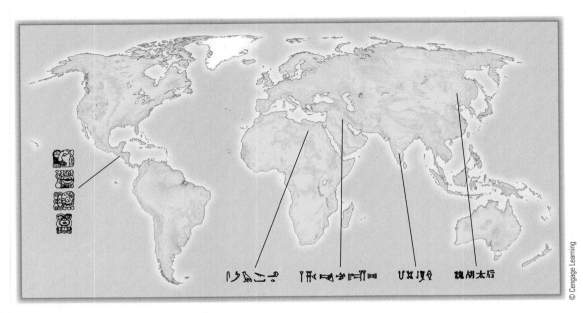

Figure 10.12 The Birthplaces of Writing The transience of spoken words contrasts with the relative permanence of written records. In all of human history, writing has been independently invented at least five times.

In the Americas, writing systems came into use among various Mesoamerican peoples, but the Maya had a particularly sophisticated one. The Maya system, like other aspects of that culture, first appeared to be rooted in the earlier writing system of the Olmec civilization (Pohl, Pope, & von Nagy, 2002). However, discoveries announced in 2006 of a stone tablet with a different writing system indicate that the Olmec had another form of writing distinct from the Maya glyphs (del Carmen Rodríguez Martínez et al., 2006).

The Maya hieroglyphic system had less to do with keeping track of state properties than with extravagant celebrations of the accomplishments of their rulers (**Figure 10.13**). Maya lords glorified themselves by recording their dynastic genealogies, important conquests, and royal marriages; by using grandiose titles to refer to themselves; and by associating their actions with important astronomical events. Different though this may be from the recordkeeping of ancient Mesopotamia, all writing systems share a concern with political power and its maintenance.

The Earliest Governments

A king and his advisors typically headed the earliest city governments although a few ancient queens also ruled. Of the many ancient kings known, one stands out as truly remarkable for the efficient government organization and highly developed legal system characterizing his reign: Hammurabi, the Babylonian king who lived in Mesopotamia (modern Iraq) between 3,700 and 3,950 years ago. From Babylon, the capital of his empire, he issued a set of laws now known as the Code of Hammurabi, notable for its thorough detail and standardization. In 1901, a French archaeological team first discovered this code, entirely inscribed in stone with cuneiform writing. It prescribed the correct form for legal procedures and determined penalties for perjury and false accusation. It contained laws applying to property rights, loans and debts, family rights, and even damages paid for malpractice by a physician. It defined fixed rates to be charged in various trades and branches of commerce, and it instituted mechanisms to protect vulnerable people—the poor, women, children, and slaves—from injustice.

Officials ordered that the code be publicly displayed on huge stone slabs so that no one could plead ignorance. Even the neediest citizens were supposed to know their rights and responsibilities. Distinct social classes were clearly

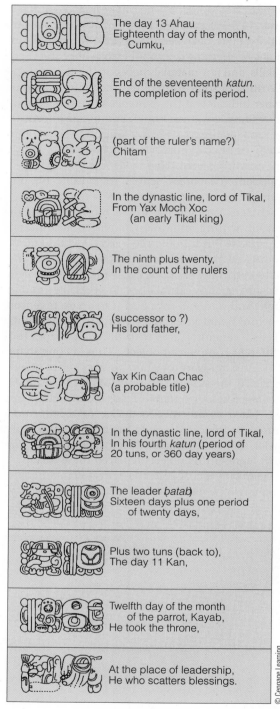

The day 13 Ahau Eighteenth day of the month, Cumku,

End of the seventeenth *katun*. The completion of its period.

(part of the ruler's name?) Chitam

In the dynastic line, lord of Tikal, From Yax Moch Xoc (an early Tikal king)

The ninth plus twenty, In the count of the rulers

(successor to ?) His lord father,

Yax Kin Caan Chac (a probable title)

In the dynastic line, lord of Tikal, In his fourth *katun* (period of 20 tuns, or 360 day years)

The leader *batab*, Sixteen days plus one period of twenty days,

Plus two tuns (back to), The day 11 Kan,

Twelfth day of the month of the parrot, Kayab, He took the throne,

At the place of leadership, He who scatters blessings.

Figure 10.13 Maya Writing The translation of the text on the monument in Figure 10.6 gives some indication of the importance of dynastic genealogy to Maya rulers. The "scattering" mentioned may refer to bloodletting as part of the ceremonies associated with the end of one twenty-year period, or *katun*, and the beginning of the next. Archaeologists cracked the meaning of these glyphs over the course of many decades of intense study. The base 20 numerical system of bars and dots was the first breakthrough followed by the realization that the symbols represented syllables instead of an alphabet.

reflected in the law ("rule of law" does not necessarily mean "equality before the law"). For example, if an aristocrat put out the eye of a fellow aristocrat, the law required that his own eye be put out in turn; hence the saying "an eye for an eye." However, if the aristocrat put out the eye of a commoner, he simply owed this person a payment of silver.

Although some civilizations flourished under a single ruler with extraordinary governing abilities, other civilizations prospered with a widespread governing bureaucracy that was very efficient at every level. The government of the Inca empire is one such example.

The Inca civilization of Peru (**Figure 10.14**) and its surrounding territories reached its peak 500 years ago, just before the arrival of the Spanish invaders. By 1525, it stretched 4,000 kilometers (2,500 miles) from north to south and 800 kilometers (500 miles) from east to west, making it one of the largest empires of its time. Its population, which numbered in the millions, was composed of people of many different ethnic groups. In the achievements of its governmental and political system, Inca

civilization surpassed every other civilization of the Americas and most of those of Eurasia. An emperor, regarded as the divine son of the Sun God, headed the government. Below him came the royal family, the aristocracy, imperial administrators, and lower nobility. Below them were the masses of artisans, craftspeople, and farmers.

The empire was divided into four administrative regions, further subdivided into provinces, and so on down to villages and families. Governmental agriculture and tax officials closely supervised farming activities such as planting, irrigation, and harvesting. Teams of professional relay runners could carry messages

Figure 10.14 Machu Picchu The Inca civilization spanned a vast territory and was responsible for monumental structures such as Machu Picchu, located high in the Andes Mountains at an altitude of almost 2,500 meters (nearly 8,000 feet). Scholars believe that the monument was built for the Inca ruler Pachacuti (1438–1472). The archaeological record indicates Machu Picchu may have been a sacred site as well. By the time of the Spanish conquistadores, the Inca people had abandoned the site, possibly because of a smallpox epidemic that had been brought to the Americas by Europeans.

Figure 10.15 **Terra Cotta Warriors** Grave goods frequently indicate the status of deceased individuals in stratified societies. For example, China's first emperor was buried with 7,000 life-sized terra cotta figures of warriors complete with chariots and horses. In fact, an entire necropolis or "dead city" was built for the emperor, which, according to some historians, required 700,000 workers to complete.

up to 400 kilometers (250 miles) in a single day over a network of roads and bridges that remains impressive even today.

Despite the complexity of the Inca civilization, they had no known form of conventional writing. Instead, they used an ingenious coding system of colored strings with knots known as *quipus* (the Quechua word for "knot") to keep public records and historical chronicles.

Social Stratification

The rise of large, economically diversified populations presided over by centralized governing authorities brought with it the fourth cultural change characteristic of civilization: social stratification, or the emergence of social classes. With social stratification, symbols of special status and privilege that ranked people according to the kind of work they did or the family into which they were born appeared in the ancient cities of Mesopotamia.

A social position at or near the head of government conferred high status. Although specialists—metalworkers, tanners, traders, or the like—generally outranked farmers, the people engaged in these kinds of economic activities were either members of the lower classes or outcasts.

grave goods Items such as utensils, figurines, and personal possessions, symbolically placed in the grave for the deceased person's use in the afterlife.

Merchants of the past could sometimes buy their way into a higher class. With time, the possession of wealth and the influence it could buy became their own prerequisite for high status, as seen in some contemporary cultures.

How do archaeologists know that different social classes existed in ancient civilizations? As described earlier, laws and other written documents, as well as archaeological features including dwelling size and location, can reflect social stratification. Burial customs also provide evidence of social stratification. Graves excavated at early Neolithic sites consist mostly of simple pits dug in the ground. They contained few, if any, **grave goods**—utensils, figurines, and personal possessions, symbolically placed in the grave for the deceased person's use in the afterlife (**Figure 10.15**).

The uniformity of early Neolithic gravesites indicates essentially classless societies. In contrast, graves excavated in civilizations vary widely in size, mode of burial, and the number and variety of grave goods. This reflects a stratified society, divided into social classes. The graves of important people contain not only various artifacts made from precious materials, but sometimes, as in some early Egyptian burials, the remains of servants evidently killed to serve their master in the afterlife.

Skeletons from the gravesites also provide evidence of stratification. Age at death, nutritional stress during childhood, as well as presence of certain diseases can be determined from skeletal remains. In stratified societies of the past, the dominant groups usually lived longer, ate better, and enjoyed an easier life than lower-ranking members of society, just as they do today.

The Making of States

From Africa to China to the South American Andes, ancient civilizations have created magnificent palaces built high above the ground, sculptures beautifully rendered using techniques that continue into the present, and vast, awe-inspiring engineering projects. These impressive accomplishments could indicate the superiority of civilization compared to other cultural forms, particularly when civilizations have come to dominate other social systems. But domination reflects aggression, size, and power—not cultural superiority. In other words, the emergence of centralized governments, characteristic of civilizations, has allowed some cultures to dominate others and for civilizations to flourish. Anthropologists have proposed several theories to account for the transition from small, egalitarian farming villages to large urban centers in which population density, social inequality, and diversity of labor required a centralized government.

Figure 10.16 **Policing Ancient Cities** To build a monument such as the Great Ziggurat of Ur, a temple in the ancient Mesopotamian city, a centralized authority needed to be able to mobilize the laborers to build the structures and to amass defensive armies. In the present, centralized authorities such as the U.S. military turn to archaeologists at times of war in order to protect cultural resources. The Archaeological Institute of America instituted an innovative program to educate troops before their deployment. For example, the mandatory class taken by both officers and enlisted men and women heading to Iraq included topics such as Mesopotamia's role in the development of writing, schools, libraries, law codes, calendars, and astronomy. Archaeologists taught troops basic archaeological techniques including effective strategies to protect sites against looters. Similar courses appropriate to each region will accompany future U.S. military deployments.

Ecological Theories

Ecological approaches emphasize the role of the environment in the development of states. Among these, the **hydraulic theory**, or *irrigation theory*, holds that civilizations developed when Neolithic peoples realized that the best farming occurred in the fertile soils of river valleys, provided that they could control the periodic flooding. The centralized effort to control the irrigation process blossomed into the first governing body, elite social class, and civilization.

Another theory suggests that in regions of ecological diversity, procuring scarce resources requires trade networks. In Mexico, for example, trade networks distributed chilies grown in the highlands, cotton and beans from intermediate elevations, and salt from the coasts to people throughout the region. Some form of centralized authority developed to organize the procurement and redistribution of these commodities.

A third theory developed by anthropologist Robert Carneiro (1970) suggests that states develop where populations are hemmed in by environmental barriers such as mountains, deserts, seas, or other human populations as an outcome of warfare and conflict in these circumscribed regions. As these populations grow, they have no space in which to expand, and so they begin to compete for increasingly scarce resources. Internally, this may result in the development of social stratification, in which an elite controls important resources to which lower classes have limited access. Externally, this leads to warfare and even conquest, which, to be successful, requires elaborate organization under a centralized authority (**Figure 10.16**). See this chapter's Globalscape for an example of warfare's current impact on archaeology.

Each of these ecological theories has limitations. Across the globe and through time, anthropologists find cultures

---

hydraulic theory The theory that explains civilization's emergence as the result of the construction of elaborate irrigation systems, the functioning of which required full-time managers whose control blossomed into the first governing body and elite social class; also known as *irrigation theory*.

Globalscape

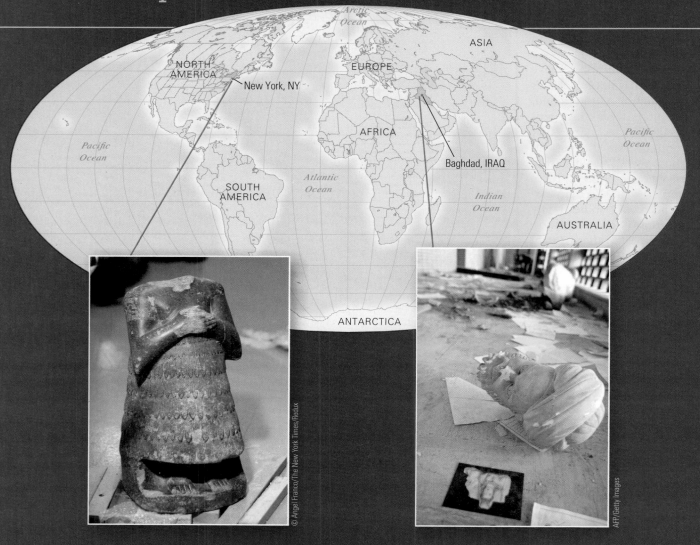

NORTH AMERICA

New York, NY

EUROPE

ASIA

AFRICA

Baghdad, IRAQ

SOUTH AMERICA

Pacific Ocean

Atlantic Ocean

Indian Ocean

Pacific Ocean

AUSTRALIA

ANTARCTICA

Arctic Ocean

© Angel Franco/The New York Times/Redux

AFP/Getty Images

Iraqi Artifacts in New York City?

A clandestine operation carried out by the U.S. government led to the recovery in New York City of a priceless (though headless) 4,400-year-old stone statue of the Sumerian King Entemena of Lagash. The statue was returned to its rightful place in the center of the Sumerian Hall of the Iraqi National Museum in Baghdad.

The modern-day state of Iraq, located in an area known as the cradle of civilization, is home to 10,000 archaeological sites preserving evidence of the earliest cities, laws, and civilizations. Though many Mesopotamian artifacts were brought to museums in Europe and the United States in the 19th and early 20th centuries, the Iraqi National Museum in Baghdad still housed an extraordinary collection of priceless artifacts.

That was the case until the weeks following the U.S. invasion in 2003, when several waves of looters removed tens of thousands of artifacts. According to Matthew Bogdanos, the Marine colonel who led the task force to track down and recover these artifacts, "The list of missing objects read like a 'who's who' of Near Eastern archaeology." Ironically, looting during the first Gulf War had led local archaeologists to move artifacts from regional museums to the National Museum of Baghdad for safekeeping.

This statue, like many other stolen artifacts, was first taken across the border into Syria and then made its way into the international black market in antiquities. Many artifacts have been returned to the museum through a no-questions-asked amnesty program. Others have required a combination of international cooperation and investigation, along with raids and seizures once artifacts have been tracked down.

Global Twister

If artifacts from ancient civilizations from throughout the world represent our shared global heritage, how can such treasures be kept safe from the chaos and desperation that result from war?

Figure 10.17 Mesa Verde Although the Ancient Pueblo cultures did not develop sprawling, crowded cities with vast monumental structures, their housing and farming methods demonstrate remarkable sophistication. They built a series of linked enclaves, with about 100 inhabitants each, into the dramatic cliff faces and farmed the top of the mesa they inhabited by using reservoirs and irrigation channels. They also built shrines within their villages of the sort still used by their descendants in the U.S. Southwest today. Other native North Americans built large cities such as Cahokia, a city with an estimated population of 40,000 people dating from 650 to 1400, located in southern Illinois. Until 1800, when Philadelphia surpassed it, Cahokia was the largest city in the land that is now the United States. The development of civilization does not make a people better—just better able to dominate.

that do not fit these models. For example, some of the earliest large-scale irrigation systems developed in highland New Guinea, where strong centralized governments never emerged. North American Indians (**Figure 10.17**) possessed trade networks that extended from Labrador in northeastern Canada to the Gulf of Mexico and the Yellowstone region of the Rocky Mountains and even to the Pacific—all without centralized control. And in many of the cultures that do not fit the theories of ecological determinism, neighboring cultures learned to coexist rather than pursuing warfare to the point of complete conquest.

Although few anthropologists would deny the importance of the human–environment relationship, many are dissatisfied with approaches that do not take into account beliefs and values (Adams, 2001). For example, as described in the case study of Tikal, even though their religion had some ties to natural cycles and the Maya astronomers created elaborate and accurate calendars, the beliefs and power relations that developed within Maya culture were not environmentally determined. Human societies past and present bring their beliefs and values into their interactions with the environment.

Action Theory

Scholars have criticized the aforementioned theories because they fail to recognize the capacity of ambitious, charismatic leaders to shape the course of human history. Accordingly, U.S. anthropologists Joyce Marcus and Kent Flannery (1996) have developed what they call **action theory**. This theory acknowledges the relationship of society to the environment in shaping social and cultural behavior, but it also recognizes that forceful leaders strive to advance their positions through self-serving actions. In so doing, they may create change.

In the case of Maya history, for example, local leaders, who once relied on personal charisma for the economic and political support needed to sustain them in their positions, may have seized upon religion to solidify their power. Through religion they developed an ideology that endowed them and their descendants with supernatural

---

action theory The theory that self-serving actions by forceful leaders play a role in civilization's emergence.

ancestry and gave them privileged access to the gods, on which their followers depended. In this case, certain individuals could monopolize power and emerge as divine kings, using their power to subjugate any rivals.

This example demonstrates the importance of the context in which a forceful leader operates. In the case of the Maya, the combination of existing cultural and ecological factors opened the way to the emergence of political dynasties. Thus, explanations of civilization's emergence tend to involve multiple causes, rather than just one. Furthermore, we may have the cultural equivalent of what biologists call *convergence*, where similar societies come about in different ways. Consequently, a theory that accounts for the rise of civilization in one place may not account for its rise in another.

Civilization and Its Discontents

Living in the context of civilization ourselves, we are inclined to view its development as a great step up on a so-called ladder of progress. Whatever benefits civilization has brought, these cultural changes have produced new problems. Among them is the challenge of waste disposal and its consequences. In fact, waste disposal probably began to be a difficulty in settled farming communities even before civilizations emerged. But as villages grew into towns and towns grew into cities, the situation became far more serious, as crowded conditions and the buildup of garbage and sewage created optimal environments for infectious diseases such as bubonic plague, typhoid, and cholera. As a result, early cities were disease-ridden places, with relatively high death rates.

Genetic adaptation to urban disease has influenced the course of history globally. Among northern Europeans, for example, the mutation of a gene on chromosome 7 makes carriers resistant to cholera, typhoid, and other bacterial diarrheas, all of which spread easily in urban environments. Because of the mortality caused by these diseases, selection favored spread of this allele among northern Europeans. But, as with sickle-cell anemia, protection comes at a price: cystic fibrosis, a usually fatal disease present in people who are homozygous for the altered gene.

Other acute infectious diseases accompanied the rise of towns and cities. In a small population, diseases such as chicken pox, influenza, measles, mumps, pertussis, polio, rubella, and smallpox will kill or immunize so high a proportion of the population that the virus cannot continue to propagate. Measles, for example, tends to die out in any human population with fewer than half a million people. The continued existence of such diseases depends upon the presence of a large population, as is found in cities. Survivors possessed immunity to these deadly diseases.

Other conditions unique to cities also promote disease. For example, the bacteria that cause tuberculosis (TB) cannot survive in the presence of sunlight and fresh air.

Before people began working and living in dark, crowded urban centers, if an infected individual coughed and released the TB bacteria into the air, sunlight would prevent the spread of infection. TB, like many other sicknesses, can be called a disease of civilization.

Social Stratification and Disease

Civilization affects disease in another powerful way. Social stratification impacts who gets sick as much as any bacterium, past and present. For example, Ashkenazi Jews of eastern Europe were forced into urban ghettos over several centuries, becoming especially vulnerable to the TB thriving in crowded, dark, confined neighborhoods. As with the genetic response to malaria (the sickle-cell allele) and bacterial diarrheas (the cystic fibrosis gene), TB triggered a genetic response in the form of the Tay-Sachs allele, which protects heterozygous individuals from TB.

Unfortunately, homozygotes for the Tay-Sachs allele develop a lethal, degenerative condition that remains common in Ashkenazi Jews. Without the selective pressure of TB, the frequency of the Tay-Sachs allele would never have increased. Similarly, without the strict social rules confining poor Jews to the ghettos (compounded by social and religious rules about marriage), the frequency of the Tay-Sachs allele would never have increased.

Today, not only are poor individuals more likely to become infected with TB, they are also less likely to be able to afford the medicines to treat this disease. For people in poor countries and for disadvantaged people in wealthier countries, tuberculosis, like AIDS, can be an incurable, fatal, infectious disease. As Holger Sawert from the World Health Organization has said, both TB and HIV thrive on poverty (Sawert, 2002). The poor of the world have borne a higher disease burden since the development of stratified societies characteristic of cities and states.

Colonialism and Disease

Infectious disease played a major role in European colonization of the Americas. When Europeans with immunity to so-called Old World diseases came to the Americas for the first time, they brought these devastating diseases with them. Millions of Native Americans—who had never been exposed to influenza, smallpox, typhus, and measles—died as a result. The microbes causing these diseases and the human populations upon which they depend developed in tandem over thousands of years of urban life in Eurasia, and before that in village life with a variety of domesticated animal species. Thus, anyone who survived had acquired immunity in the process. See this chapter's Biocultural Connection for more on the death and disease Europeans brought with them when they colonized the Americas.

Very few diseases traveled back to Europe from the Americas. Instead, these colonizers brought back the riches that they had pillaged and papers that gave them ownership of the lands they had claimed.

BIOCULTURAL CONNECTION

Perilous Pigs: The Introduction of Swine-Borne Disease to the Americas

By Charles C. Mann

On May 30, 1539, Hernando de Soto landed his private army near Tampa Bay, in Florida. . . . Half warrior, half venture capitalist, Soto had grown very rich very young by becoming a market leader in the nascent trade for Indian slaves. The profits had helped to fund Pizarro's seizure of the Incan empire, which had made Soto wealthier still. Looking quite literally for new worlds to conquer, he persuaded the Spanish Crown to let him loose in North America. . . . He came to Florida with 200 horses, 600 soldiers, and 300 pigs.

From today's perspective, it is difficult to imagine the ethical system that would justify Soto's actions. For four years his force, looking for gold, wandered through what is now Florida, Georgia, North and South Carolina, Tennessee, Alabama, Mississippi, Arkansas, and Texas, wrecking almost everything it touched. The inhabitants often fought back vigorously, but they had never before encountered an army with horses and guns. . . . Soto's men managed to rape, torture, enslave, and kill countless Indians. But the worst thing the Spaniards did, some researchers say, was entirely without malice— bring the pigs.

According to Charles Hudson, an anthropologist at the University of Georgia, . . . [t]he Spaniards approached a cluster of small cities, each protected by earthen walls, sizeable moats, and deadeye archers. In his usual fashion, Soto brazenly marched in, stole food, and marched out.

After Soto left, no Europeans visited this part of the Mississippi Valley for more than a century. Early in 1682 whites appeared again, this time Frenchmen in canoes. . . area[s] where Soto had found cities cheek by jowl . . . [were] deserted [without an] Indian village for 200 miles. About fifty settlements existed in this strip of the Mississippi when Soto showed up, according to Anne Ramenofsky, an anthropologist at the University of New Mexico. . . . Soto "had a privileged glimpse" of an Indian world,

Hudson says. "The window opened and slammed shut. When the French came in and the record opened up again, it was a transformed reality. A civilization crumbled. The question is, how did this happen?"

The question is even more complex than it may seem. Disaster of this magnitude suggests epidemic disease. In the view of Ramenofsky and Patricia Galloway, an anthropologist at the University of Texas, the source of the contagion was very likely not Soto's army but its ambulatory meat locker: his 300 pigs. Soto's force itself was too small to be an effective biological weapon. Sicknesses like measles and smallpox would have burned through his 600 soldiers long before they reached the Mississippi. But the same would not have held true for the pigs, which multiplied rapidly and were able to transmit their diseases to wildlife in the surrounding forest. When human beings and domesticated animals live close together, they trade microbes with abandon. Over time mutation spawns new diseases: Avian influenza becomes human influenza, bovine rinderpest becomes measles. Unlike Europeans, Indians did not live in close quarters with animals—they domesticated only the dog, the llama, the alpaca, the guinea pig, and, here and there, the turkey and the Muscovy duck. . . . [W]hat scientists call zoonotic disease was little known in the Americas. Swine alone can disseminate anthrax, brucellosis, leptospirosis, taeniasis, trichinosis, and tuberculosis. Pigs breed exuberantly and can transmit diseases to deer and turkeys. Only a few of Soto's pigs would have had to wander off to infect the forest.

Indeed, the calamity wrought by Soto apparently extended across the whole Southeast. The Coosa city-states, in western Georgia, and the Caddoan-speaking civilization, centered on the Texas-Arkansas border, disintegrated soon after Soto appeared. The Caddo had had a taste for monumental architecture: public plazas, ceremonial platforms, mausoleums. After Soto's army

left, notes Timothy K. Perttula, an archaeological consultant in Austin, Texas, the Caddo stopped building community centers and began digging community cemeteries. . . . [After] Soto's . . . visit, Perttula believes, the Caddoan population fell from about 200,000 to about 8,500—a drop of nearly 96 percent. . . . "That's one reason whites think of Indians as nomadic hunters," says Russell Thornton, an anthropologist at the University of California at Los Angeles. "Everything else—all the heavily populated urbanized societies—was wiped out."

How could a few pigs truly wreak this much destruction? . . . One reason is that Indians were fresh territory for many plagues, not just one. Smallpox, typhoid, bubonic plague, influenza, mumps, measles, whooping cough—all rained down on the Americas in the century after Columbus. . . .

To Elizabeth Fenn, the smallpox historian, the squabble over numbers obscures a central fact. Whether one million or 10 million or 100 million died, . . . the pall of sorrow that engulfed the hemisphere was immeasurable. Languages, prayers, hopes, habits, and dreams— entire ways of life hissed away like steam. . . . In the long run, Fenn says, the consequential finding is not that many people died but that many people once lived. The Americas were filled with a stunningly diverse assortment of peoples who had knocked about the continents for millennia. "You have to wonder," Fenn says. "What were all those people *up* to in all that time?"

BIOCULTURAL QUESTION

Does the history of the decimation of American Indians through infectious disease have any parallels in the contemporary globalized world? Do infectious diseases impact all peoples equally?

Adapted from Mann, C. C. (2005). 1491: New revelations of the Americas before Columbus. *New York: Knopf.*

Anthropology and Cities of the Future

Not until relatively recent times did public health measures reduce the risk of living in cities, and had it not been for a constant influx of rural peoples, areas of high population density might not have persisted. Europe's urban population, for example, did not become self-sustaining until early in the 20th century.

What led humans to live in such unhealthy places? Most likely, our ancestors were attracted by the same things that lure people to cities today. Cities are vibrant, exciting places that provide new opportunities and protection in times of warfare. Of course, people's experience in the cities did not always live up to expectations, particularly for the poor.

In addition to health problems, many early cities faced social problems strikingly similar to those found in contemporary cities all over the world. Dense population and the inequalities of class systems and oppressive centralized governments created internal stress. The poor saw that the wealthy had all the things that they themselves lacked. It was not just a question of luxury items; the poor did not have enough food or space in which to live with comfort, dignity, and health (Figure 10.18).

In addition to these challenges, abundant archaeological evidence also documents warfare in early civilizations. Cities were fortified. Ancient documents list battles, raids, and wars between groups. Cylinder seals, paintings, and sculptures depict battle scenes, victorious kings, and captured prisoners of war. Increasing population and the accompanying scarcity of fertile farmland often led to boundary disputes and quarrels between civilized states or between so-called tribal peoples and a state. When war broke out, people crowded into walled cities for protection and for access to irrigation systems.

It is discouraging to note that many of the problems associated with the first civilizations are still with us. Waste disposal, pollution-related health problems, crowding, social inequities, and warfare continue to challenge humanity. Through the study of past civilizations, and through comparison of contemporary societies, we now stand a chance of understanding these problems. Such understanding represents a central part of the anthropologist's mission and can contribute to the ability of our species to transcend human-made problems.

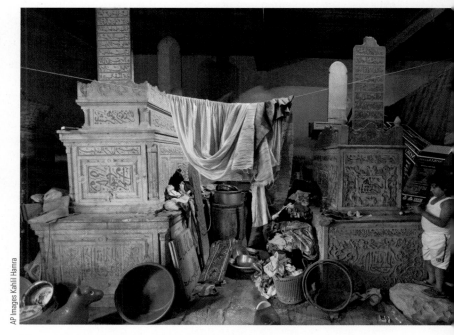

Figure 10.18 **"City of the Dead," Cairo, Egypt** One of Cairo's poorest neighborhoods, the "City of the Dead" is actually a cemetery. Thousands of poor families use centuries-old mausoleums, built for some of Cairo's wealthy inhabitants, as makeshift homes. For the poor, a gravestone might serve as a table or a bed. Children play among the graves. Because the land on which these families live is officially a cemetery, this neighborhood lacks basic services such as running water and a sewer system.

AP Images Kahlil Hamra

CHAPTER CHECKLIST

When did the first cities and states develop, and how did this occur?

The world's first cities grew out of Neolithic villages between 4,500 and 6,000 years ago—first in Mesopotamia, then in Egypt and the Indus Valley. In China, the process was underway by 5,000 years ago. Somewhat later, and completely independently, similar changes took place in Mesoamerica and the central Andes.

Four basic cultural changes mark the transition from Neolithic village life to life in civilized urban centers: agricultural innovation, diversification of labor, emergence of centralized government, and social stratification.

What characteristics distinguished the four cultural changes leading to the development of urban centers?

Agricultural innovation involved the development of new farming methods such as irrigation that increased crop yields. Agricultural innovations brought about other changes such as increased population size.

Diversification of labor occurred as a result of population growth in cities. Some people could provide sufficient food for everyone so that others could devote themselves to specialization as artisans and craftspeople. Specialization led to the development of new technologies and the beginnings of extensive trade systems.

The emergence of a central government provided an authority to deal with the complex problems associated with cities and permitted governors to mobilize workers to erect monumental structures. With the invention of writing, governments began keeping records and boasting of their own power and glory.

Symbols of status and privilege appeared with the emergence of social classes, as individuals were ranked according to the work they did or the position of their families. Graves, burial customs, grave goods, dwelling size, and records in documents and art provide evidence of social stratification.

Why did cities and states develop?

Ecological theories emphasize the interrelation of the actions of ancient peoples with their environment. According to these theories, civilizations developed as centralized governments began to control irrigation systems, trade networks, and scarce resources.

These theories omit the importance of the beliefs and values of the cultures of the past as well as the actions of forceful, dynamic leaders, whose efforts to promote their own interests may play a role in social change.

Several factors probably acted together to bring about the emergence of cities and states.

What problems beset early cities?

Poor sanitation in early cities, coupled with large numbers of people living in close proximity, created environments in which infectious diseases were rampant.

Early urban centers also faced social problems strikingly similar to those persisting in the world today. Dense population, class systems, and a strong centralized government created internal stress.

Warfare was common; cities were fortified, and armies served to protect the state.

European city-dwellers had already adapted to urban diseases that decimated both urban and rural Indian populations when the European colonial explorers arrived in the Americas.

QUESTIONS FOR REFLECTION

1. Since the origins of cities and states, humans have engaged in large-scale elaborate warfare. Is warfare an inevitable outcome to this form of social organization?

2. In large-scale societies of the past and present, elite classes have disproportionate access to and control of all resources. Is this social stratification an inevitable consequence of the emergence of cities and states? How can the study of social stratification in the past contribute to the resolution of contemporary issues of social justice?

3. What are some of the ways that differences in social stratification are expressed where you live? Does your community have any traditions surrounding death that serve to restate the social differentiation of individuals?

Are there local traditions that serve to redistribute the wealth so that it is shared more evenly?

4. With today's global communication and economic networks, will it be possible to shift away from social systems involving centralized governments, or is a global, centralized authority inevitable?

5. With many archaeological discoveries, there is a value placed on "firsts," such as the earliest writing, the first city, or the earliest government. Given the history of the independent emergence of cities and states throughout the world, do you think that scientists should place more value on these events just because they are older?

ONLINE STUDY RESOURCES

CourseMate

Access chapter-specific learning tools, including learning objectives, practice quizzes, videos, flash cards, glossaries, and more in your Anthropology CourseMate.

Log into **www.cengagebrain.com** to access the resources your instructor has assigned and to purchase materials.

Chris Trotman/Getty Images

Challenge Issue

The biological forces of evolution have resulted in a unified but pheno-typically diverse human species. Yet social factors impact how people think about this diversity. In some societies, the false belief that there are natural and separate divisions within our species fuels racism, a doctrine of superiority by which one group justifies the dehumanization of others based on their distinctive physical characteristics. Although there are obvious physical differences among humans, biological evidence demonstrates unequivocally that separate races do not exist. No human subspecies exists that would indicate distinct biological races, and far more genetic diversity exists within a single so-called racial category than between any two. However, racism and its vocabulary continually surface in different cultures, whether in security profiling, wage disparities, or media commentary. When basketball's Jeremy Lin moved from the bench to stardom in the NBA, sports reporters everywhere spoke about the new Asian American phenomenon in terms of breaking cultural barriers. Critics of "Linsanity" thought of Lin as a middle-range player who received undue attention only because of his Chinese ancestry. But when ESPN posted a photo of Lin alongside the headline "Chink in the Armor," uproar ensued: One reporter was fired and another suspended. The challenge for all of us is to under-stand that although distinct biological races do not exist, the social and political reality of race impacts, if not determines, the human experience in some societies including the United States.

Modern Human Diversity: Race and Racism

From male to female, short to tall, light to dark, we can categorize biological variation in a number of ways, but in the end we are all members of the same species. Minute variations of our DNA give each of us a unique genetic fingerprint, yet this variation remains within the bounds of being genetically human. Any visible differences among modern humans exist within the framework of biological features shared throughout the species, and as a species, humans vary. Although we use the terms *black*, *white*, and *race* in this chapter, they signify purely cultural concepts.

Human genetic variation generally is distributed across the globe in a continuous fashion. From a biological perspective, this variation sometimes follows a pattern imposed by interaction with the environment through the evolutionary process of natural selection. Random genetic drift accounts for the remainder. But the significance we give our biological variation is anything but random because cultures determine the way we perceive variation—in fact, whether we perceive it at all. For example, in many Polynesian cultures, where skin color bears no relationship to social status, people pay little attention to this physical characteristic. By contrast, people in countries such as the United States, Brazil, and South Africa notice skin color immediately because it remains a significant social and political category. The study of biological diversity, therefore, requires an awareness of the cultural dimensions that shape the questions asked about diversity as well as an understanding of how this knowledge has been used historically.

When European scholars first began their systematic study of human variation in the 18th and 19th centuries, they focused on documenting differences among human groups in order to divide them hierarchically into progressively "better types" of humans. Today, this hierarchical approach has been appropriately abandoned. Before exploring how we study contemporary biological variation today, let's examine the effects of social ideas about race and racial hierarchy on the interpretation of biological variation, past and present.

IN THIS CHAPTER YOU WILL LEARN TO

- Examine the history of human classification.

- Describe how the biological concept of race cannot be applied to humans.

- Recognize the conflation of biological race into cultural race in theories that attempt to link race to behavior and intelligence.

- Discuss physical anthropological approaches to the study of human biological variation.

- Describe the role of adaptation in human variation in skin color.

- Examine the interaction between biological and cultural components of the human adaptive complex.

The History of Human Classification

Early European scholars tried to systematically classify *Homo sapiens* into subspecies, or races, based on geographic location and phenotypic features such as skin color, body size, head shape, and hair texture. The 18th-century Swedish naturalist Carolus Linnaeus (recall him from Chapter 2) originally divided humans into subspecies based on geographic location and classified all Europeans as white, Africans as black, American Indians as red, and Asians as yellow.

The German physician Johann Blumenbach (1752–1840) introduced some significant and pernicious changes to this four-race scheme in the 1795 edition of his book *On the Natural Variety of Mankind*. Most notably, this book formally introduced a hierarchy of human types (**Figure 11.1**). Blumenbach considered the skull of a woman from the Caucasus Mountains (located between the Black and Caspian Seas of southeastern Europe and southwestern Asia) the most beautiful in his collection. More symmetrical than the others, he saw it as a reflection of nature's ideal form: the circle. Surely, Blumenbach reasoned, this "perfect" specimen resembled God's original creation. Moreover, he thought that the living inhabitants of the Caucasus region were the most beautiful in the world. Based on these criteria, he concluded that this high

mountain range, not far from the lands mentioned in the Bible, was the place of human origins.

Blumenbach concluded that all light-skinned peoples in Europe and adjacent parts of western Asia and northern Africa belonged to the same race. On this basis, he dropped the "European" race label and replaced it with "Caucasian." Although he continued to distinguish American Indians as a separate race, he regrouped dark-skinned Africans as "Ethiopian" and split those Asians not considered Caucasian into two separate races: "Mongolian" (referring to most inhabitants of Asia, including China and Japan) and "Malay" (indigenous Australians, Pacific Islanders, and others).

Convinced that Caucasians were closest to the original ideal humans supposedly created in God's image, Blumenbach ranked them as superior. The other races, he argued, were the result of "degeneration"; by moving away from their place of origin and adapting to different environments and climates, they had degenerated physically and morally into what many Europeans came to think of as inferior races (Gould, 1994).

We now clearly recognize the factual errors and ethnocentric prejudices embedded in Blumenbach's work, as well as others, with respect to the concept of race. Political leaders have used this notion of superior and inferior races to justify brutalities ranging from repression to slavery to mass murder to genocide. The tragic story of

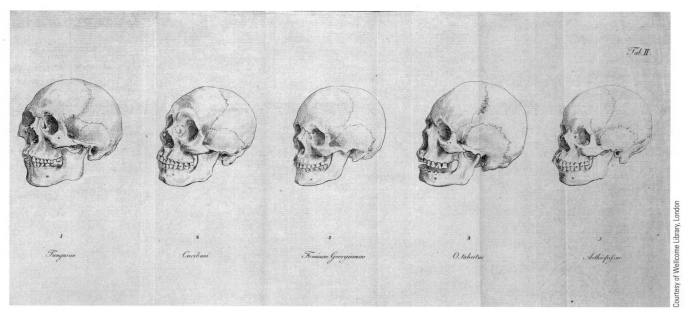

Courtesy of Wellcome Library, London

Figure 11.1 Blumenbach's Skulls Johann Blumenbach ordered humans into a hierarchical series with Caucasians (his own group) ranked the highest and created in God's image. He suggested that the variation seen in other races was a result of "degeneration" or movement away from this ideal type. (The five types he identified from left to right are: Mongolian, American Indian, Caucasian, Malay, and Ethiopian.) This view is both racist and an oversimplification of the expression of human variation in the skeleton. Although people from one part of the world might be more likely to possess a particular nuance of skull shape, within every population there is significant variation. Humans do not exist as discrete types.

Figure 11.2 **Ota Benga** The placement of Ota Benga on display in the Bronx Zoo illustrates the depths of racism in the early 20th century. Here's Ota Benga posing for the camera when he was part of the African Exhibit at the St. Louis World's Fair.

Missouri History Museum, St. Louis

Ota Benga, a Twa Pygmy man who in the early 1900s was caged in a New York zoo with an orangutan, painfully illustrates the disastrous impact of this dogma (**Figure 11.2**).

Captured in a raid in Congo, Ota Benga came into the possession of North American businessman Samuel Verner, who was looking for exotic "savages" for exhibition in the United States. In 1904, Ota and a group of fellow Twa were shipped across the Atlantic and exhibited at the World's Fair in St. Louis, Missouri. About 23 years old at the time, Ota was 4 feet 11 inches in height and weighed 103 pounds. Throngs of visitors came to see displays of dozens of indigenous peoples from around the globe, shown in their traditional dress and living in replica villages doing their customary activities. The fair was a success for the organizers, and all the Twa Pygmies survived to be shipped back to their homeland. Verner also returned to Congo and with Ota's help collected artifacts that he intended to sell to the American Museum of Natural History in New York City.

In the summer of 1906, Ota came back to the United States with Verner, who soon went bankrupt and lost his entire collection. Left stranded in the big city, Ota was placed in the care of the museum and then taken to the Bronx Zoo and exhibited in the monkey house, with an orangutan as company. Ota's sharpened teeth (a cultural practice among his people) were seen as evidence of his supposedly cannibal nature. After intensive protest, zoo officials released Ota

from his cage and during the day let him roam free in the park, where teasing visitors often harassed him. Ota (usually referred to as a "boy") was then turned over to an orphanage for African American children. In 1916, upon hearing that he would never return to his homeland, he took a revolver and shot himself through the heart (Bradford & Blume, 1992).

The racist display at the Bronx Zoo a century ago was by no means unique. Ota Benga's tragic life was the manifestation of a powerful ideology in which one small part of humanity sought to demonstrate and justify its claims of biological and cultural superiority. Indeed, such claims, based on false notions of race, have resulted in the oppression and genocide of millions of humans because of the color of their skin or the shape of their skull. This ideology had particular resonance in North America, where people of European descent colonized lands originally inhabited by Native Americans and then went on to exploit African slaves and (later) Asians imported as a source of cheap labor.

According to U.S. anthropologist Audrey Smedley, the earliest settlers who came over from England had already refined this ideology of dehumanization and the practice of slavery in their dealings with the Irish (Smedley, 2007). They even imported Irish slaves and indentured servants. Indeed, in Bacon's Rebellion of 1676, Irish and African slaves fought side by side. Only later did North American slavery become the exclusive burden of Africans.

Although the Emancipation Proclamation ended slavery in 1863, dismantling its pseudoscientific bases took much longer. In the early 20th century, some scholars began to challenge the concept of racial hierarchies. Among the strongest critics was Franz Boas (1858–1942), a Jewish scientist who immigrated to the United States because of rising anti-Semitism in his German homeland and who became a founder of North America's four-field anthropology. As president of the American Association for the Advancement of Science, Boas criticized false claims of racial superiority in an important speech titled "Race Problems in America," published in the prestigious journal *Science* in 1909. Boas's scholarship in both cultural and biological anthropology contributed to the depth of his critique.

Ashley Montagu (1905–1999), a student of Boas and one of the best-known anthropologists of his time, devoted much of his career to combating scientific racism. Born Israel Ehrenberg to a working-class Jewish family in England, he also felt the sting of anti-Semitism. After changing his name in the 1920s, he immigrated to the United States, where he went on to fight racism in his writing and in academic and public lectures. His book *Man's Most Dangerous Myth: The Fallacy of Race*, published in 1942, took the lead in debunking the concept of clearly bounded races as a "social myth." The book has since gone through six editions, the last in 1998. Montagu's once controversial ideas have now become mainstream, and his text remains one of the most comprehensive treatments of its subject. (For a contemporary approach to human biological variation, see this chapter's Anthropologist of Note.)

ANTHROPOLOGIST OF NOTE

Fatimah Jackson 1950

Although at first glance **Fatimah Jackson's** research areas seem quite diverse, they are unified by consistent representation of African American perspectives in biological anthropological research.

With a keen awareness of how culture determines the content of scientific questions, Jackson chooses hers carefully. One of her earliest areas of research concerned the use of

Fatimah Jackson, a leader in the investigations of human biological diversity, emphasizes the social and political reality of race in her work.

common African plants as foods and medicines. She has examined the coevolution of plants and humans and the ways plant compounds serve to modify human biology and behavior. Through laboratory and field research, she has documented that cassava, a New World root crop providing the major source of dietary energy for over 500 million people, also helps protect against malaria. This crop has become a major food throughout Africa in areas where malaria is common.

Jackson, who received her PhD from Cornell in 1981, is also the genetics group leader for the African Burial Ground Project (mentioned in Chapter 1). In a small area uncovered during a New York City construction project, scientists found the remains of thousands of Africans and people of African descent. Jackson is recovering DNA from skeletal remains and attempting to match the dead with specific regions of Africa through the analysis of genetic markers in living Africans.

Jackson, one of the early advocates for appropriate ethical treatment of minorities in the human genome project, is concerned with ensuring that the genetic work for the African Burial Ground Project is conducted with sensitivity to African people. She has worked to establish genetic repositories in Africa that capture both environmental and genetic data on local groups. For Jackson, these laboratories are symbolic of the fact of human commonality and that all humans today have roots in Africa.

Jackson has also developed models to better understand the biological and cultural substructure of peoples of African descent worldwide. Using these models, she has been able to link certain subgroups of African descended peoples to increased risk for certain diseases, including breast cancer and hypertension.

Race as a Biological Concept

To understand why the racial approach to human variation has been so unproductive and even damaging, we must first understand the race concept in strictly biological terms. Biologists define **race** as a subspecies,

or a population of a species differing geographically, morphologically, or genetically from other populations of the same species.

As simple and straightforward as such a definition may seem, there are three very important things to note about it. First, it is arbitrary; no scientific criteria exist on how many differences it takes to make a race. For example, if one researcher emphasizes skin color while another emphasizes fingerprint differences, they will not classify people in the same way (**Figure 11.3**).

Second, this biological definition of race does not mean that any one race has exclusive possession of any particular variant of any gene or genes. In human terms, the frequency of a trait like the type O blood

race In biology, the taxonomic category of subspecies that is not applicable to humans because the division of humans into discrete types does not represent the true nature of human biological variation. In some societies race is an important social category.

Figure 11.3 An Alternative Grouping Fingerprint patterns of loops, whorls, and arches are genetically determined. Grouping people on this basis would place most Europeans, sub-Saharan Africans, and East Asians together as "loops." Australian Aborigines and the people of Mongolia would be together as "whorls." The Bushmen of southern African would be grouped as "arches."

group, for example, may be high in one population and low in another, but it is present in both. In other words, populations are genetically "open," meaning that genes flow between them (**Figure 11.4**). The only reproductive barriers that exist for humans are the cultural rules some societies impose regarding appropriate mates.

As President Obama's family illustrates (Luo father from western Kenya and Anglo-American mother born in Kansas, who, incidentally, was an anthropologist), these social barriers change through time. As well, in July 2012, Ancestry.com, a genealogy business, released a report indicating that the president's mother, like so many white Americans, was descended from a slave ancestor ("President Obama descends from the first African enslaved for life in America," 2012). This news made a splash, particularly because the ancestor was a man named John Punch, one of the first African slaves to be documented in this country (Thompson, 2012). This chapter's Original Study by biological anthropologist Jonathan Marks explores the hype and folk appeal of such genealogical analyses and the ultimate biological truth: We are all related.

Figure 11.4 Jefferson's Family Many people have become accustomed to viewing racial groups as natural and separate divisions within our species based on visible physical differences. However, these groups differ from one another in only 7 percent of their genes. For many thousands of years, individuals belonging to different human social groups have been in sexual contact. Exchanging their genes, they maintained the human species in all its colorful variety and prevented the development of distinctive subspecies (biologically defined races). This continued genetic mixing is effectively illustrated by the above photo of distant relatives, all of whom are descendants of Sally Hemings, an African American slave, and Thomas Jefferson, the Anglo-American gentleman-farmer who had 150 slaves working for him at his Virginia plantation and served as third U.S. president (1801–1809).

Caveat Emptor: Genealogy for Sale BY JONATHAN MARKS

We are related, you and I.

Darwin says so. The Bible says so. Not much controversy about it.

The question is, How related? If we're too close, there will be restrictions on our sexual behavior toward one another. If we're too distant—that is to say, if you're a chimpanzee—there will be restrictions as well, of a different sort.

But the middle ground is very large—about seven billion people large—and we all form a network of biological kin (if not social kin). The structure of that network is the domain of human population genetics, a field newly reinvigorated by free-market genomics.

The power of molecular genetic data to address issues of identity and relatedness with scientific authority has been appreciated for decades, particularly in the domains of paternity, genealogy, and forensics. Only recently, however, has the field branched out, so to speak, into the field of family trees, and what is now often called "recreational ancestry," tapping into a universal human desire to situate ourselves within a complex social universe. The math is simple: genomic data + folk ideology = profits, and tests have been available for several years purporting to match your Y chromosome with Genghis Khan or Moses, or your mitochondrial DNA with any of seven imaginary European "clan mothers" who lived 15,000 years ago.

The commercial success of these tests lies in how successfully they can represent biological relatedness to be the equivalent of meaningful relatedness. In fact, the two never map on to one another particularly well, as anthropologists have long appreciated. Kinship (meaningful relatedness) is constructed by human societies from a locally particular calculus combining biological ties of heredity and legal ties of marriage and adoption. Your mother's sister's child and mother's brother's child are genetically equivalent, but the first is widely considered an incestuous relationship, while the second may be a preferred spouse across diverse cultures and eras. Charles Darwin, for example, married his mother's brother's daughter, yet his face nevertheless graces the English £10 note.

The mode of transmission of mitochondrial DNA makes it particularly vexing as a surrogate for biological ancestry. Most DNA, the nuclear human genome, is transmitted probabilistically; you have a 50% chance of having inherited any particular DNA segment from any particular parent. MtDNA, however, is inherited only through the maternal line: Thus, you are a mitochondrial clone of your mother and mitochondrially unrelated to your father.

Such a fundamental discrepancy between the heredity of mtDNA and our understandings of heredity ought to raise caution about glibly confounding the two. A generation further removed, the discrepancy becomes more glaring: You are equally descended from all four grandparents, but only mitochondrially descended from one of them (your mother's mother). And of your eight great-grandparents, only one is your mitochondrial ancestor.

In general terms, as you proceed upward in your genealogical tree, the number of ancestors you have in every generation increases exponentially (every ancestor had two parents), whereas the number of mitochondrial ancestors remains constant (one—your mother's mother's . . . mother). From a different angle, 75 percent of your grandparents are invisible to an mtDNA analysis—and every generation back, that percentage increases.

Or from yet another angle, a test for relatedness derived from mtDNA carries a risk of producing a false negative result that is incalculably high. A mitochondrial match is good evidence that the two bearers are genealogically linked, but a nonmatch means nothing at all. Moreover, there is a wide zone between a match and a nonmatch: Geneticists can cluster mtDNA sequences by their degrees of similarity to one another. Thus, the coalescence of the mtDNA sequences of a large population into a small number of basic groups can suggest a founder—a mother—for each of those groups.

Consider, though, what being a "member" of a 15,000-year-old mitochondrial "clan" actually implies. How many ancestors did you actually have 15,000 years ago? Conservatively assuming 25 years per generation yields 600 generations, and your 2-to, the-six-hundredth-power ancestors comprise a number with 180 zeroes, or about 173 orders of magnitude larger than the number of people alive at the time, and effectively beyond the power of language to express.

Let us call this a squijillion.

Not only do you have a squijillion ancestors 15,000 years ago, but so does everybody else. How could you have so many ancestors? Many of them are the same people—specific ancestors recur in your own tree, and many of your ancestors are other people's ancestors as well. That is to say, to some extent you are inbred, and to some extent you are related to everyone else. And of those squijillion ancestors distributed among the 10,000,000 or so people alive back then—the ones who all contributed nuclear DNA to your genome—how many are being detected by your mtDNA? One.

Here the tenuous connection between meaningful relatedness and biological relatedness becomes helpful. There is almost nothing biological there, but the cultural associations of DNA give these data the appearance of familial association, of science, of reality. The mtDNA similarity is symbolically powerful in spite of being biologically trivial in this context.

The intersection of that symbolic power with the free market has created a hybrid nature for the science of human population genetics: partly derived from Watson and Crick, that is to say, from molecular genetics; and partly derived from P. T. Barnum, that is to say, from the fellow who said epigrammatically, "There's a sucker born every minute."

Suppose there were a scientific test that allowed you to identify all of your family members and distinguish them from people to whom you were not related? You might find distant relatives you never knew you had; you might find that you are descended from someone noteworthy; you might find something exotic, romantic, interesting, or even admirable in your DNA. You might even be able to fill in gaps in your self-identity and find out who you "really" are and where you "really" come from. That is, after all, the source of a classic dramatic arc, from Oedipus to Skywalker.

But what would such a test entail? After all, heredity is probabilistic. You have, on the average, 25 percent of your DNA from each of your grandparents. Or more to the point, any bit of any grandparent's DNA has a 25 percent chance of showing up in your genome. Consequently, you may not necessarily match any specific bit of your grandfather's DNA—given you have three other grandparents and only two sets of DNA.

Moreover, because you are related to every other human being, there is no qualitative break between your family members and nonrelatives that a genetic test could detect. That is the "constructedness" of human kinship systems: Some people are defined as relatives and some people are not, regardless of their biological relationships. The only kind of test that can reliably sort people into your relatives and your nonrelatives would be a magic test.

In America, hardly any social fact can be understood outside the historical context of slavery. One modern legacy is the obliteration of the preslavery ancestry of African Americans. But what if your DNA matched that of an African tribe? Would that not provide a grounding in African soil and establish African kin? For a few hundred dollars, indeed that service is now provided.

One pioneering company's website "allows you to reconnect to your ancestral past—easily, accurately and profoundly" and will "connect your ancestry to a specific country in Africa and often to a specific African ethnic group." And there is no doubt that it does what it promises—it connects black Americans to black Africa. But of course, that is a sloppy term—"connects"—sounding as if it has profound biological meaning, when the profound connection it provides may be more emotional than genetic. After all, of the literally thousands of genetic ancestors you had 12 generations ago—say, about the year 1700—mtDNA is connecting you with only one. On the other hand, isn't that better than nothing?

Well, when you consider the fact that all of these mtDNA forms are polymorphic—that is to say, varying within any population, and that the sampling of Africans is very poor, you have to begin to wonder whether a mitochondrial DNA match to a Yoruba may actually be worse than nothing. Being biologically meaningless, yet mimicking a hereditary identity, the mtDNA match might well be giving you a false identity in the name of science.

As the classic 1973 film *The Sting* showed clearly, the best scams are the ones in which the victim does most of the work. You give them the dots, and they connect them—to your advantage. In this case, the clients are paying for science and are getting it. They are getting accurate DNA results and true matches. The companies certify the match, and allow their clients to make the meaningful "connection."

Testimonials vouch for the lives thereby changed, and why shouldn't they? The only problem might be if you confuse them for scientific evidence.

Ultimately, this essay is not intended as a public service or a whistle-blowing venture. Nothing illegal or even necessarily immoral is going on. Instead, this is an illustration of the way in which science has changed during our lifetimes. Science—and in particular, genetics—may never have been "pure," but until quite recently it never had to compete seriously with the profit motive for its public credibility.

In short, this isn't your grandfather's genetics.

Adapted from Marks, J. (2008). Caveat emptor: Genealogy for sale. Newsletter of the ESRC Genomics Network *7, 23. Reprinted by permission.*

In addition to the genetic openness of populations, and the arbitrary nature of criteria, a third problem with applying the biological definition of *race* to humans exists: The differences among individuals within a so-called racial population are greater than the differences among separate populations. Evolutionary biologist Richard Lewontin demonstrated this in the 1970s. He compared the amount of genetic variation within populations and among racial groups, finding a mere 7 percent of human variation existing among groups (Lewontin, 1972). Instead, the vast majority of genetic variation exists *within* groups. As the science writer James Shreeve puts it, "Most of what separates me genetically from a typical African or Eskimo also separates me from another average American of European ancestry" (Shreeve, 1994, p. 60). In other words, no one race has an exclusive claim to any particular form of a gene or trait.

The Conflation of the Biological into the Cultural Category of Race

Although the biological race concept does not pertain to human variation, race remains a significant cultural category. Human groups frequently insert a false notion of biological difference into the cultural category of race to make it appear more factual and objective. In various ways, cultures define religious, linguistic, and ethnic groups as races, thereby confusing linguistic and cultural traits with physical traits.

For example, people in many Latin American countries classify one another as Indian, Mestizo (mixed), or Ladino (of Spanish descent). But despite the biological connotations of these terms, the criteria used for assigning individuals to these categories are determined by whether they wear shoes, sandals, or go barefoot; speak Spanish or an Indian language; live in a thatched hut or a European-style house; and so forth. By speaking Spanish, wearing Western-style clothes, and living in a house in a non-Indian neighborhood, Indian people shed their indigenous identity and acquire a national identity as citizens of the country.

Similarly, the ever-changing racial categories used by the U.S. Census Bureau both reflect and reinforce the conflation of the biological and the cultural. The 2010 list includes large catchall political categories such as white and black as well as specific tribal affiliations of American Indians or Alaskan Natives, a designation that comes much closer to a population in the biological sense. The Census Bureau asks people to identify Hispanic ethnicity, independent of the category of race, but considers Arabs and Christians of Middle Eastern ancestry as white (Caucasian) despite the political relevance of their ancestry. The observation that the purported race of an individual can vary over the course of his or her lifetime speaks to the fact that cultural forces shape the designation of membership in a particular racial category (Hahn, 1992).

The Census Bureau gathers health statistics by racial categories for the purposes of correcting health disparities among social groups. Unfortunately, the false biological concept of race gets inferred in these analyses. As a result, the increased risk of dying from a heart attack for African Americans compared to whites is falsely attributed to biological differences rather than to health-care disparities or other social factors.

Similarly, medical genetics research is regularly oversimplified into comparisons of the racial types defined in the 18th and 19th centuries. Whether this genetic research will avoid the trap of recreating false genetic types that do not reflect the true nature of human variation remains to be seen. The recent claims made for race-specific drugs and vaccines based on limited scientific data indicate that the social category of race may again be interfering with our understanding of the true nature of human genetic diversity.

Against a backdrop of prejudice, the conflation of the social with the biological has historically provided a "scientific" justification for the exclusion of whole categories of people from certain roles or positions in society. For example, in colonial North America, a racial worldview assigned American Indians and Africans imported as slaves to perpetual low status. A supposed biological inferiority was used to justify this low status, whereas access to privilege, power, and wealth was reserved for favored groups of European descent (American Anthropological Association, 1998). Before the civil rights era brought equal legal rights to all U.S. citizens, the "one drop rule," also known as *hypodescent*, would assign individuals with mixed ethnicity or socioeconomic class to the subordinate group in the hierarchy. Similarly, the historical caste system in Mexico took into account intermarriage between various groups to position people within the hierarchical order (Figure 11.5).

Because of the colonial association of lighter skin with greater power and higher social status, people whose history includes domination by lighter-skinned Europeans have sometimes valued this phenotype. In Haiti, for example, the "color question" has been the dominant force in social and political life. Skin texture, facial features, hair color, and socioeconomic class collectively play a role in the ranking. According to Haitian anthropologist Michel-Rolph Trouillot, "a rich black becomes a mulatto, a poor mulatto becomes black" (Trouillot, 1996).

The Nazis in Germany elevated a racialized worldview to state policy, with particularly evil consequences. Hitler's agenda was inspired by the American eugenics movement of the early 20th century. He considered a 1916 book by Madison Grant, from the American Museum of Natural History, titled *The Passing of the Great Race*, his bible. The Nuremberg race laws of 1935 codified the superiority of the Aryan race and the inferiority of the Gypsy and Jewish races (Figure 11.6). The Nazi doctrine justified, on supposed biological grounds, political repression and extermination. In all, 11 million people (Jews, Gypsies, homosexuals, and other so-called inferior people, as well as political opponents of the Nazi regime) were deliberately put to death or died from starvation, disease, and exposure in labor camps.

Tragically, human history contains many atrocities on the scale of the Nazi Holocaust (from the Greek word for "wholly burnt" or "sacrificed by fire"). Such **genocides**, programs of extermination of one group by another, have a long history that predates World War II and continues today. From the massacre of 1.5 million Armenians during WWI, to the slaughter of 1.7 million Cambodians in the 1970s, to selective elimination of indigenous Guatemalans in the 1980s, to the massacre of nearly a million Tutsis by Hutus in Rwanda in the 1994, an estimated 83 million people died from genocides in the 20th century (White, 2001). A rhetoric of dehumanization and a depiction of the people being exterminated as a lesser type of human has accompanied each of these (Figure 11.7).

---

genocide The physical extermination of one people by another, either as a deliberate act or as the accidental outcome of activities carried out by one people with little regard for their impact on others.

Español con India.
Mestizo.

Mestizo con Española
Castizo.

Castizo con Española
Español.

Español con Mora.
Mulato.

5

6

7

Mulato con Española.
Morisco.

Morisco con Española
Chino.

Chino con India.
Salta atras.

Salta atras con Mulata.
Lobo.

9

10

11

12

Lobo con China
Gibaro.

Gibaro con Mulata
Albarazado.

Albarazado con Negra
Canbujo.

Canbujo con India.
Sanbaigo.

13

14

15

16

Sanbaigo con Loba
Calpamulato.

Calpamulato con Canbuja
Tente en el Aire.

Tente en el Aire con Mulata
Noteentiendo.

Noteentiendo con India
Tornaatras.

© Schalkwijik/Art Resource, NY

Figure 11.5 *Castas* In colonial Mexico, sixteen different *castas* ("castes") were designated, giving specific labels to individuals who were various combinations of Spanish, Indian, and African ancestry. These paintings of *castas* are traditionally arranged from light to dark as a series and reflect an effort to impose hierarchy despite the fluid social system in place. In the United States, despite the use of descriptors such as *quadroon, octoroon, sambo,* and *mulatto* that attempt to quantify the amount of mixture among races, the hierarchy was more rigid; the "one drop rule" would ascribe individuals to a subordinate position within the hierarchy if they had even one drop of blood from a "lower" ranking group.

Figure 11.6 The Aryan Race Members of the SS Tibet expedition team sit with local people at a banquet in Lhasa, Tibet, in 1939. Second from the left is anthropologist Bruno Beger, whose work for the German SS on this expedition included measuring skulls and cataloguing the physical traits of Tibetans as part of a search for the origins of the purportedly superior Aryan Race. After this expedition, Beger continued an even darker side of this racialized agenda at Auschwitz. There, through measurement of physical characteristics, he selected and prepared individuals for lethal experimentation, and for death in order to be included in the Jewish skeletal collection. Though a West German court found Beger guilty as an accessory to murder for his role at Auschwitz, he never served time.

© ullstein bild/The Image Works

© blickwinkel/Alamy

Figure 11.7 Victims of Genocide These skulls, from the genocide war memorial in Rwanda, record some of the horror that took place in this Central African country in 1994. Over the course of only about a hundred days, a militia of the ruling Hutu majority brutally murdered close to 1 million ethnic Tutsis. With clear genocidal intent, systematic organization, and intense speed, Hutu actions, resembling those of the Nazi regime, remind us that genocide is far from a thing of the past. The global effects of the Rwandan genocide have been massive. Millions of Rwandans, both refugees and killers, now live in neighboring regions, disrupting the stability of these states. Through the United Nations and individual governments, the international community has recognized that it failed to act to prevent this genocide and collectively has taken steps toward maintaining peace in the region. The parallels between Rwanda and current conflicts in Congo, Burundi, and Sudan are chilling.

The Social Significance of Race: Racism

Scientific facts, unfortunately, have been slow to change what people think about race. **Racism**, a doctrine of superiority by which one group justifies the dehumanization of others based on their distinctive physical characteristics, persists as a major political problem. Indeed, politicians have often exploited this concept as a means of mobilizing support, demonizing opponents, and eliminating rivals. Racial conflicts result from social stereotypes, not scientific facts.

Race and Behavior

The assumption that behavioral differences exist among human races remains an issue to which many people still cling tenaciously. Throughout history, certain characteristics have been attributed to groups of people under a variety of names—national character, spirit, temperament—all of them vague and standing for concepts unrelated to any biological phenomena. Common myths involve the coldness of Scandinavians or the rudeness of Americans or the fierceness of the Yanomami Indians. Such unjust characterizations rely upon a false notion of biological difference.

To date, no inborn behavioral characteristic can be attributed to any group of people (which the nonscientist might call a race) that cannot be explained in terms of cultural practices. If the Chinese happen to exhibit exceptional visual-spatial skills, it is probably because the business of learning to read Chinese characters requires a visual-spatial mastery that Western alphabets do not (Chan & Vernon, 1988). Similarly, the almost complete exclusion of non-whites from achievements in the sport of golf (until Tiger Woods) had everything to do with the social rules of country clubs and the sport's expense.[1] All such differences or characteristics can be explained in terms of culture.

In the same vein, high crime rates, alcoholism, and drug use among certain groups can be explained with reference to culture rather than biology. Individuals alienated and demoralized by poverty, injustice, and unequal opportunity tend to abandon the traditional paths to success of the dominant culture because these paths are blocked. In a racialized society, poverty and all its ill consequences affect some groups of people much more severely than others.

Slowly, some of this systemic racism, a form of **structural violence**—physical and/or psychological harm caused by impersonal, exploitative, and unjust social, political and economic systems—has been rectified. For example in 2010 the U.S. Congress passed the Fair Sentencing Act, legislation aimed at redressing many years of harsher penalties associated with crack cocaine use; crack is primarily associated with African Americans, as compared to the more expensive and equally potent powdered form of cocaine more often associated with white drug users. Before this legislation, the typical white user would have to possess 100 times the amount of powdered cocaine to receive the same sentence as his or her African American crack-using counterpart (King, 2010).

Race and Intelligence

Scholars and laypeople alike, unfamiliar with the fallacy of biological race in humans, have asked whether some races are inherently more intelligent than others. To address this issue requires, first, clarification of the term *intelligence*. Unfortunately, deciding what abilities or talents actually make up what we call intelligence remains contentious, even though some psychologists insist that it is a single quantifiable thing measured by IQ tests. Many more psychologists consider intelligence to be the product of the interaction of different sorts of cognitive abilities: verbal, mathematical-logical, spatial, linguistic, musical, bodily-kinesthetic, social, and personal (Jacoby & Glauberman, 1995). Each of these kinds of intelligence seems unrelated to the others in that individuals possess unique combinations of strengths in each of these areas. Just as humans inherit height, blood type, skin color, and so forth independently, it seems likely that to the degree that intelligence is heritable, each of these kinds of intelligence would be inherited independently.

Furthermore, scholars have shown the limits of IQ tests as a fully valid measure of inborn intelligence. An IQ test measures *performance* (something that one does) rather than *genetic disposition* (something that the individual is born with). Performance reflects past experiences and present motivational state, as well as innate ability.

Despite these limits, for at least a century some researchers have used IQ tests to try to prove the existence of significant differences in intelligence among human populations. In the United States, systematic comparisons of intelligence between whites and blacks began in the early 20th century and were frequently combined with data gathered by physical anthropologists about skull shape and size.

During World War I, for example, draftees were regularly given a series of IQ tests, known as Alpha and Beta. The results showed that on average white Americans attained higher scores compared to African Americans. Even though African Americans from the urban northern states scored higher than white Americans from the rural South, and some African Americans scored higher than most white Americans, many people took this as proof of the intellectual superiority of white people. But all the tests really showed was that, on

[1] Before Tiger Woods came Charles Sifford (b. 1922), the first African American to win honors in golf. Sifford did so at a time when desegregating the sport meant being subjected to threats and racial abuse. In 2004, the World Golf Hall of Fame inducted him as their first African American member.

racism A doctrine of superiority by which one group justifies the dehumanization of others based on their distinctive physical characteristics.
structural violence Physical and/or psychological harm caused by impersonal, exploitative, and unjust social, political, and economic systems.

the average, whites outperformed blacks in the social situation of IQ testing. The tests did not measure intelligence per se, but the ability, conditioned by culture, of certain individuals to respond appropriately to certain questions conceived by Americans of European descent for comparable middle-class whites. These tests frequently require knowledge of white middle-class values and linguistic behavior.

For such reasons, intelligence tests continue to be the subject of controversy. Many psychologists as well as anthropologists have shown that the tests have only limited application in particular cultural circumstances. In turn, holding cultural and environmental factors constant results in African and European Americans scoring equally well (Sanday, 1975).

Nevertheless, some researchers still insist that there are significant differences in intelligence among human populations. Richard Herrnstein, a psychologist, and Charles Murray, a political scientist and longtime fellow of a conservative think tank called the American Enterprise Institute, are among these researchers. In a lengthy and highly publicized book entitled *The Bell Curve*, they argue for immutable genetic origins for the difference in IQ scores between Americans of African, Asian, and European descent.

Scholars have criticized Herrnstein and Murray's book on many grounds, including violation of basic rules of statistics and their practice of utilizing studies, no matter how flawed, that appear to support their thesis while ignoring or barely mentioning those that contradict it. In addition, the basic laws of heredity also discredit their argument. As Mendel discovered with his pea plants back in the late 19th century, genes are inherited independently of one another. Whatever the alleles that may be associated with intelligence, they bear no relationship with the ones for skin pigmentation or with any other aspect of human variation such as blood type. Further, the expression of genes always occurs in an environment, and among humans culture shapes all aspects of the environment.

Separating genetic components of intelligence (or any other continuous trait) from environmental contributors poses enormous problems (Andrews & Nelkin, 1996). Most studies of intelligence rely on comparisons between identical twins, genetically identical individuals raised in the same or different environments. A host of problems plague twin studies: inadequate sample sizes, biased subjective judgments, failure to make sure that "separated" twins really were raised separately, unrepresentative samples of adoptees to serve as controls, untested assumptions about similarity of environments. In fact, children reared by the same mother resemble her in IQ to the same degree, whether or not they share her genes (Lewontin, Rose, & Kamin, 1984). Clearly, the degree to which intelligence is inherited through genes is far from understood.

Undoubtedly, the social environment contributes substantially to intelligence. This should not surprise us, as environmental factors influence other genetically determined traits. Height in humans, for example, has a genetic basis, but it also depends upon both nutrition and health status (severe illness in childhood arrests growth, and renewed growth never makes up for this loss).

Moreover, scientists have not yet teased apart the exact relative contributions of genetic and environmental factors on either the height or the intelligence of an individual (**Figure 11.8**). Although the burgeoning field of epigenetics has begun to unravel these interactions, the work is meaningful only in the context of individuals and discrete populations, not in the biologically false category of race (Marks, 2008b; Rose, 2009).

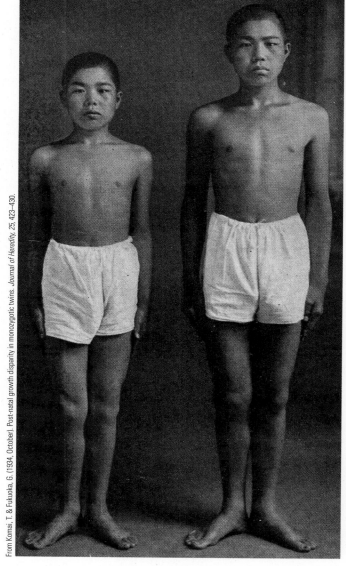

From Komai, T. & Fukuoka, G. (1934, October). Post-natal growth disparity in monozygotic twins. *Journal of Heredity*, 25, 423–430.

Figure 11.8 Duplicate Genes, Unique Experiences Differences in the growth process can lead to very different outcomes in terms of size as seen in these twins, who are genetically identical. Starting from inside their mother's womb, twins may experience environmental differences in terms of blood and nutrient supply. This can impact not only size but cognitive development.

Research on the importance of the environment in the expression of intelligence further exposes the problems with generalizations about IQ and race. For example, IQ scores of all groups in the United States, as in most industrial and postindustrial countries, have risen some 15 points since World War II. In addition, the gap between Americans of African and European descent has narrowed in recent decades. Other studies show impressive IQ scores for African American children from socially deprived and economically disadvantaged backgrounds who have been adopted into highly educated and prosperous homes. Studies have shown that underprivileged children adopted into such privileged families can boost their IQs by 20 points. Also, IQ scores rise in proportion to the test-takers' amount of schooling.

More such cases could be cited, but these suffice to make the point and lead to three conclusions. First, there is a bias in IQ testing based on social class. Second, the assertion that IQ is biologically fixed and immutable is clearly false. Third, ranking human beings with respect to their intelligence scores in terms of racial difference is doubly false.

Over the past 2.5 million years, all populations of the genus *Homo* have adapted primarily through culture—actively inventing solutions to the problems of existence rather than relying only on biological adaptation. Thus, we would expect a comparable degree of intelligence in all present-day human populations. The only way to be sure that individual human beings develop their innate abilities and skills to the fullest is to make sure they all have access to the necessary resources and the opportunity to do so (**Figure 11.9**).

Figure 11.9 **The Legacy of Slavery** Any discussion of race and behavior or intelligence in the United States must include the history of slavery and of legal segregation in the South, as well as other forms of structural violence that favored the white race at the expense of minorities. These social, political, and historical facts influence race relations in the United States today far more than minute genetic differences.

Studying Human Biological Diversity

Considering the problems, confusion, and horrendous consequences, anthropologists have abandoned the race concept as being of no utility in understanding human biological variation. Instead, they have found it more productive to study *clines*, the distribution and significance of single, specific, genetically based characteristics and continuous traits related to adaptation.

The physical characteristics of both populations and individuals derive from the interaction between genes and environments. For example, genes predispose people to a particular skin color, but the color of an individual's skin is also influenced by cultural and environmental factors. The skin of sailors, for example, darkens or burns after many hours of exposure to the sun, depending on not only genetic predisposition but cultural practices regarding exposure to the sun. In other cases, such as A-B-O blood type, phenotypic expression closely reflects genotype.

For characteristics controlled by a single gene, different versions of that gene, known as alleles (see Chapter 2), also mediate variation. Such traits are called **polymorphic** (meaning "many shapes"). Our blood types—determined by the alleles for types A, B, and O blood—are an example of polymorphism and may appear in any of four distinct phenotypic forms (A, B, O, and AB).

A species can also be considered polymorphic, meaning that there is wide variation among individuals (beyond differences between males and females). Here *polymorphic* refers to continuous phenotypic variation that may be genetically controlled by interactions among multiple different genes, in addition to the allelic variation described previously. When a polymorphic species faces changing

polymorphic Describing species with alternative forms (alleles) of particular genes.

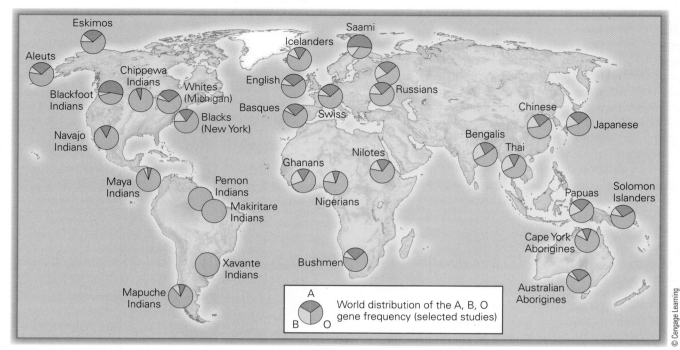

Figure 11.10 Blood Types Frequencies of the three alleles for the A, B, and O blood groups for selected samples around the world illustrate the polytypic nature of *Homo sapiens*. The frequency of the alleles differs among "populations." Which of the groups here best represent populations (a group of individuals within which breeding takes place) in the biological sense?

environmental conditions, the variation it has within its gene pool fosters survival of the species because some of those individuals may possess traits that prove adaptive in the altered environment. Individuals whose physical characteristics enable them to do well in the new environment will usually reproduce more successfully, so that their genes become more common in subsequent generations. Similarly, the polymorphism of the human species has allowed us to thrive in a wide variety of environments.

When polymorphisms are distributed into geographically dispersed populations, biologists describe this species as **polytypic** ("many types") for that feature; that is, uneven distribution of genetic variability among populations. For example, consider the polytypic distribution of the polymorphism for blood type (four distinct phenotypic groups: A, B, O, or AB). American Indian populations possess the highest frequency of the O allele, especially some populations native to South America; certain European populations have the highest frequencies of the allele for type A blood (although the highest frequency is found among the Blackfoot Indians of the northern Plains in North America); some Asian populations have the highest frequencies of the B allele (**Figure 11.10**). Even though single traits may be grouped within specific geographic regions, when a greater number of traits are considered,

specific human "types" cannot be identified. Instead, evolutionary forces work independently on each of these traits.

Scientists also use clinal analyses to examine continuous traits such as body shape. These studies have allowed anthropologists to interpret human global variation in body build as an adaptation to climate as we will explore in the next chapter. Relevant to the false notion of biological race, some anthropologists have also suggested that variation in features such as face and eye shape relate to climate. For example, some early biological anthropologists once proposed that the "Mongoloid" face, common in populations native to East and Central Asia, as well as Arctic North America, exhibits features adapted to life in very cold environments (Coon, 1962). The **epicanthic eye fold** (which minimizes the eye's exposure to the cold), a flat facial profile, and extensive fatty deposits may help to protect the face against frostbite.

Although experimental studies have failed to sustain the frostbite hypothesis, a flat facial profile generally goes with a round head. Because a significant percentage of body heat may be lost from the head, a round-shaped head, with less surface area relative to volume, loses less heat than a longer, more elliptical-shaped head. Predictably, populations with more elliptical-shaped heads are generally found in hotter climates; those with rounder-shaped heads are more common in cold climates. However, these same features also could be present in populations due to genetic drift. This chapter's Biocultural Connection on ethnic plastic surgery illustrates a very different approach to phenotypic variation in which individuals undergo elective surgery to attain the phenotype of the dominant culture.

polytypic Describing the expression of genetic variants in different frequencies in different populations of a species.

epicanthic eyefold A fold of skin at the inner corner of the eye that covers the true corner of the eye; common in Asian populations.

BIOCULTURAL CONNECTION

Beauty, Bigotry, and the Epicanthic Eyefold of the Beholder

One need look no farther than the magazines displayed at a store's checkout aisle to determine that appearance matters in the United States. It is not surprising that a society that once used skin color to determine social status should continue to emphasize the superiority of specific physical traits and to encourage people to acquire these desired traits through plastic surgery.

Plastic surgery began in the United States during World War I, as medical doctors developed procedures to reconstruct disfigured soldiers. Soon doctors began finding other applications for these new techniques. The physical traits associated with ethnic groups considered inferior provided new work for the fledgling medical specialty. Rhinoplasty, or the nose job, was originally a surgical procedure used to treat the "deformity" referred to in scientific literature as "Jewish nose," an angular prominence of the nose. Doctors considered this a medical condition that affected the entire well-being of the patient and demanded intervention. The modern plastic surgery literature still refers to various aspects of human variation as "deformities" that cause psychological and physical impairment to the patient.

For immigrant groups, including European Jews who endured significant psychological scarring as a result of discrimination and racism, cosmetic surgery provided one means of gaining acceptance into this new culture promising the American Dream. Cosmetic procedures offered a way to adapt to the stressor of discrimination. As a result, the United States, with its history of racism and discrimination, inherited a significant market for dealing in certain phenotypic traits. In this sense, plastic surgery continues the work of the eugenics movement by eliminating undesirable phenotypes.

Of course, plastic surgeons maintain that individual pursuit of beauty and a natural desire to look one's best motivate their practice and that it has nothing to do with race. Yet, roughly 30 percent of all cosmetic procedures occur in minority populations—a relatively high proportion. Many of these procedures, especially ones that alter features strongly identified with a particular ethnic group, have been criticized as a means of "occidentalizing" ethnic populations.

In response to the controversy, plastic surgeons published *Ethnic Considerations in Facial Aesthetic Surgery*, with the goal of outlining a "universal standard of beauty" while making considerations for each ethnic group. This difficult task quickly unraveled as the authors relied heavily on Western aesthetic principles derived from classical Greek concepts of beauty. The so-called universal standard was criticized as no more than a Western standard written in a politically correct style.

Double eyelid surgery, a procedure that removes the epicanthic eyefold common in people with East Asian ancestry, is at the center of the debate. The procedure gives the eyes a rounder look and occurs among East Asian almost exclusively. It is the third most common cosmetic procedure—after breast augmentation and nose reshaping.

Imagine a commercial in which a man with an epicanthic eyefold continually struggles to find employment. He comes home to his family after job searching, anxious and insecure. Then he gets double eyelid surgery, giving his eyes a rounder, more European look. His anxiety suddenly is transformed into confidence, and his wife embraces him as he proudly declares "I got the job, honey." A doctor writing in 1954 in the *American Journal of Ophthalmology* described a patient whose story almost exactly mirrors such a tale. The social pressures in a racialized society had already persuaded this patient to have the surgery. The patient, a Chinese American, recounted people consistently mocking the shape of his eyes, saying that he looked sleepy so his business must be sleepy too. After double eyelid surgery, he found both that he was treated more respectfully and that his business became more successful.[a] This account tells of no individual pursuit of beauty or natural desire to look one's best. Instead, it illustrates how years of persecution

REUTERS/Nir Elias/Landov

Here a plastic surgeon explains to a patient how double eyelid surgery could remove the epicanthic eyefold of her eye (*top*) and give her eyes a rounder and more Western look.

BIOCULTURAL CONNECTION (CONTINUED)

become internalized, only to morph into an expression of aesthetic preference.

Regardless of its cultural consequences, cosmetic surgery—whether chosen for its aesthetic properties or for the perceived social advantages of fitting in with a specific race—demonstrates the high value still attached to certain phenotypic traits. Yet the very ability to manipulate these traits illustrates both their superficiality and the fundamental flaws in the concept of discrete biological races. Ethnic plastic surgery, at best a harmless pursuit to look good and at worst a subversive continuation of racism's grip on society, shows us that the cost of beauty, or at least an idea of it, can be high indeed.

BIOCULTURAL QUESTION

Where would you draw the line for determining when plastic surgery was medically required and when it was a luxury item? Are there any aspects of your own appearance about which you have internalized a negative perception on account of the social value of this characteristic?

———

[a]Kaw, E. (1993). Medicalization of racial features: Asian American women and cosmetic surgery. *Medical Anthropology Quarterly* 7 (1), 74–89.

In contrast to facial features and shape, skin color—the trait so often used to separate people into groups—provides an excellent example of the role of natural selection in shaping human variation.

Skin Color: A Case Study in Adaptation

Several key factors impact variation in skin color: the transparency or thickness of the skin; a copper-colored pigment called carotene; reflected color from the blood vessels (responsible for the rosy color of lightly pigmented people); and, most significantly, the amount of **melanin** (from *melas*, a Greek word meaning "black")—a dark pigment in the skin's outer layer. People with dark skin have more melanin-producing cells than those with light skin, but everyone (except albinos) has a measure of melanin. Exposure to sunlight increases melanin production, causing skin color to deepen.

Melanin protects skin against damaging ultraviolet solar radiation conferring less susceptibility to skin cancers and sunburn on dark-skinned peoples compared to those with less melanin. Dark skin also helps to prevent the destruction of certain vitamins under intense exposure to sunlight. Because the highest concentrations of dark-skinned people tend to be found in the tropical regions of the world, it appears that natural selection has favored heavily pigmented skin as a protection against exposure where ultraviolet radiation is most constant.

The inheritance of skin color involves several genes (rather than variants of a single gene), each with several alleles, thus creating a continuous range of expression for this trait. In addition, the geographic distribution of skin color tends to be continuous (**Figure 11.11** and **Figure 11.12**). In northern latitudes, light skin has an adaptive advantage related to the skin's important biological function as the manufacturer of vitamin D through a chemical reaction dependent upon sunlight. Vitamin D maintains the balance of calcium in the body essential for healthy bones and balance in the nervous system. In northern climates with little sunshine, light skin allows enough sunlight to penetrate the skin and stimulate the formation of vitamin D. Dark pigmentation interferes with this process in environments with limited sunlight.

Cultural practices can contribute to avoiding the severe consequences of vitamin D deficiency (**Figure 11.13**). Only about 50 years ago, parents in northern Europe and northern North America fed their children a spoonful of cod liver oil, rich in vitamin D, during the dark winter months. Today, pasteurized milk is fortified with vitamin D.

Culture and Biological Diversity

Although cultural adaptation has reduced the importance of biological adaptation and physical variation, at the same time cultural forces impose their own selective pressures. For example, take the reproductive fitness of individuals with diabetes—a disease with a known genetic predisposition. Ready medication in North America and Europe makes people with diabetes as biologically fit as anyone else. However, without access

---

melanin A dark pigment produced in the outer layer of the skin that protects against damaging ultraviolet solar radiation.

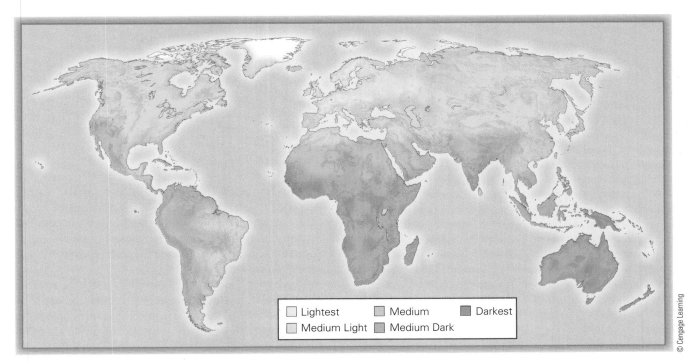

© Cengage Learning

Figure 11.11 **Global Distribution of Skin Pigmentation** This map illustrates the distribution of dark and light human skin pigmentation before 1492. The earliest members of the genus *Homo*, who inhabited the tropics, likely had dark skin, which is protective from UV radiation. In the tropics and at high altitudes, darker skin has selective advantages. As humans spread to regions with less UV exposure, some pigmentation was lost. Medium-light skin color in Southeast Asia reflects the spread into that region of people from southern China, whereas the medium darkness of people native to southern Australia is a consequence of their tropical Southeast Asian ancestry. Lack of dark skin pigmentation among tropical populations of Native Americans reflects their more recent ancestry in northeastern Asia a mere 20,000 or so years ago.

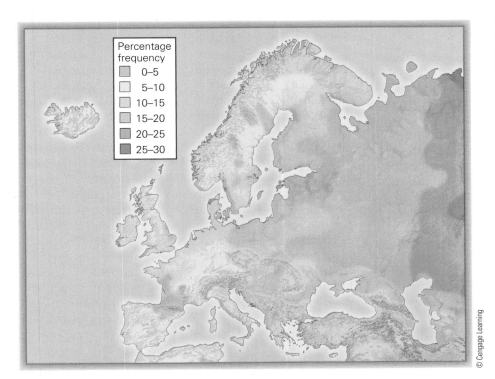

© Cengage Learning

Figure 11.12 **Distribution of Type B Blood in Europe** The east-west gradient in the frequency of type B blood in Europe contrasts with the north-south gradient in skin color shown in Figure 11.11. Just as the clines for skin color and blood type must be considered independently, so too must be whatever genes are involved in the complex of abilities known as intelligence.

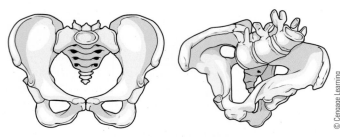

© Cengage Learning

Figure 11.13 When Skin Color Counts Bone diseases such as osteomalacia and rickets caused by vitamin D deficiency can deform the birth canal of the pelvis to the degree that it can interfere with successful childbirth. Because sunshine is vital to the body's production of vitamin D, this disease was very common in the past among the poor in northern industrial cities because they had limited exposure to sunlight. Dietary supplements have reduced the impact of bone diseases, such as rickets, although they continue to be a problem in cultures that require women and girls to dress so that they are completely veiled from the sun.

to the needed medication, a situation all too common globally, diabetes results in death. In fact, one's financial status affects one's access to medication, and so, however unintentional it may be, financial status determines biological fitness.

Culture can also contribute directly to the development of disease. For example, one type of diabetes very common among overweight individuals who get little exercise—a combination that describes 61 percent of people from the United States today—disproportionately affects the poor. Further, when people from traditional cultures adopt the Western high-sugar diet and low activity pattern, the incidence of diabetes and obesity skyrockets.

For years scientists attributed a tendency toward diabetes among American Indians to their **thrifty genotype**, a genotype thought to characterize all humans until about 6,000 years ago (Allen & Cheer, 1996). The thrifty genotype permitted efficient storage of fat to draw on in times of food shortage. In times of scarcity, individuals with the thrifty genotype conserve glucose (a simple sugar) for use in brain and red blood cells (as opposed to other tissues such as muscle), as well as nitrogen (vital for growth and health). Among Europeans, regular access to glucose particularly through the lactose in milk led to selection for

thrifty genotype Human genotype that permits efficient storage of fat to draw on in times of food shortage and conservation of glucose and nitrogen.

lactose A sugar that is the primary constituent of fresh milk.

lactase An enzyme in the small intestine that enables humans to assimilate lactose.

the nonthrifty genotype as protection against adult-onset diabetes, or at least its onset relatively late in life (at a nonreproductive age).

Recently, conservation biologist Gary Nabhan and his wife, anthropologist Laurie Monti, have enriched the discussion of diabetes among American Indians by focusing on diet and activity instead of a genetic difference. They show that native "slow release foods" such as the prickly pear lower the glucose levels of American Indians prone to diabetes (Nabhan, 2004). They chronicle the ability of these desert foods to sustain American Indians during long treks into the desert. These "treatments," unlike biomedical shots and pills, predate the appearance of the disease and also empower and preserve native cultures. Each culture developed as a complete adaptive system so it stands to reason that biological variation and cultural variation would be linked.

And what of the northern European adaptive system? In this context, cultural practices acted as an agent of biological selection for lactose tolerance: the ability to digest **lactose**, the primary constituent of fresh milk. This ability depends on the capacity to make a particular enzyme, **lactase**. Most mammals as well as most human populations—especially Asian, Native Australian, Native American, and many African populations—do not continue to produce lactase into adulthood. Adults with lactose intolerance suffer from gas pains and diarrhea when they consume milk or milk products. Only 10 to 30 percent of Americans of African descent and 0 to 30 percent of adult Asians are lactose tolerant. By contrast, lactase retention and lactose tolerance are normal for over 80 percent of adults of northern European descent. Eastern Europeans, central Asians, Arabs, and some East Africans resemble northern Europeans in lactase retention more than Asians and other Africans (**Figure 11.14**).

Generally speaking, populations with a long tradition of dairying tend to retain lactase into adulthood. With fresh milk contributing significantly to their diets, selection in the past favored those individuals with the allele that confers the ability to assimilate lactose, selecting out those without this allele.

At times, the usual synchronicity between genetic and cultural adaptations goes awry. Interactions between populations whose histories have produced distinct genetic adaptations illustrate such clashes. For example, because North American and European societies associate milk with health, powdered milk has long been a staple of economic aid to other countries. But populations who do not retain lactase into adulthood cannot utilize the many nutrients in milk. Frequently, they also suffer diarrhea, abdominal cramping, and even bone degeneration, with serious results. In fact, the shipping of powdered milk to earthquake victims in the 1960s caused many deaths among South Americans. Since this tragedy, relief workers have learned to take global variation of lactase retention into account.

form of cultural practices such as local cuisine. Biological and dietary adaptations to malaria converge with the interaction between one form of the glucose-6-phosphate-dehydrogenase (G-6-PD) enzyme and fava bean consumption.

The broad, flat fava bean (*Vicia faba*) is a dietary staple in malaria-endemic areas along the Mediterranean coast (**Figure 11.15**). G-6-PD is an enzyme that serves to reduce one sugar, glucose-6-phosphate, to another sugar—in the process releasing an energy-rich molecule. The malaria parasite lives in red blood cells off of energy produced via G-6-PD. Individuals with a mutation in the G-6-PD gene, so-called G-6-PD deficiency, produce energy by an alternate pathway not involving this enzyme that the parasite cannot use. Furthermore, G-6-PD-deficient red blood cells seem to turn over more quickly, thus allowing less time for the parasite to grow and multiply. Although a different form of G-6-PD deficiency is also found in some sub-Saharan African populations, the form found in Mediterranean populations is at odds with an adaptation embedded in the cuisine of the region.

Enzymes naturally occurring in fava beans also contain substances that interfere with the development of the malarial parasite. In cultures around the Mediterranean Sea where malaria is common, fava beans are incorporated into the diet through foods eaten at the height of the malaria season. However, if an individual with G-6-PD deficiency eats fava beans, the substances toxic to the parasite become toxic to humans. With G-6-PD deficiency, fava bean consumption leads to *hemolytic crisis* (Latin for "breaking of red blood cells") and a series of chemical reactions that release free radicals and hydrogen peroxide into the bloodstream. This condition is known as *favism*.

AP Images Jennifer Graylock

Figure 11.14 Got Milk? The "Got Milk?" campaign emphasizes the health benefits of milk for all people, yet globally, the vast majority of adults cannot digest milk. Instead it makes them quite sick. Mexican born Academy Award–nominated actress Salma Hayek, whose parents are of Lebanese and Spanish descent, can "get milk" because some of her ancestors had a tradition of dairying. Only populations with long traditions of dairying have high frequencies of the alleles for this biological capacity.

Beans, Enzymes, and Adaptation to Malaria

We have already explored some of the human biological adaptations to the deadly malarial parasite through the sickle-cell allele. Other adaptations to malaria take the

© Charles O. Cecil/Alamy

Figure 11.15 Fava Beans at Market Fava beans, a dietary staple in the countries around the Mediterranean Sea, also provide some protection against malaria. However, in individuals with G-6-PD deficiency, the protective aspects of fava beans turn deadly. This dual role has led to a rich folklore surrounding fava beans.

Unfortunately, apprehension about the fava bean has sometimes generalized to fear about many excellent sources of protein such as peanuts, lentils, chickpeas, soybeans, and nuts. Language accounts for this unnecessary deprivation. The Arabic name for fava beans is *foul* (pronounced "fool"), and the soybeans are called *foul-al-Soya*, and peanuts are *foul-al-Soudani*; in other words, the plants are linked linguistically even though they are unrelated biologically (Babiker et al., 1996).

An environmental stressor as potent as malaria has led to a number of human adaptations. In the case of fava beans and G-6-PD deficiency, these adaptations can work at cross-purposes. Just as understanding the history of lactose tolerance and intolerance has improved global health, cultural knowledge of the biochemistry of these interactions will allow humans to adapt, regardless of their genotype. The complexity of ongoing genetic and cultural adaptations highlights the flaws of a strictly biological definition of *race*.

Race and Human Evolution

Throughout this chapter we have explored the fallacy of the biological category of race when applied to the human species. Generalizations cannot be made about types of humans because no discrete types of humans exist. By contrast, the paleoanthropological analysis of the fossil record

The toxic effect of fava bean consumption in G-6-PD individuals has prompted a rich folklore around this simple food, including the ancient Greek belief that fava beans contain the souls of the dead. The link between favism and G-6-PD deficiency has led parents of children with this condition to limit their consumption of this favorite dietary staple.

explored in previous chapters includes defining specific types of ancestors based on biological and cultural capacities that go hand in hand.

The increased brain size of *Homo habilis* noted around 2.5 million years ago supports the notion that these ancestors were capable of more complex cultural activities than australopithecines, including the manufacture of stone tools. Closer to the present, the same assumptions do not hold. At some point in our evolutionary history we became a single, unified global species. Bearing this in mind, we can frame the modern human origins debate in the terms of the content of this chapter.

The modern human origins debate hinges on the question of whether cultural abilities and intelligence can be inferred from details of skull and skeletal shape and size. Supporters of the multiregional hypothesis argue that they cannot. They suggest that using a series of biological features to represent a type of human being (Neandertals) with certain cultural capacities (inferior) is like making assumptions about the cultural capabilities of living humans based on their appearance. In living people, such assumptions are considered stereotypes or racism. By arguing that ancient groups like Neandertals represent a distinct species, supporters of the recent African origins hypothesis bypass the potential prejudice inherent in these assumptions. Both theories embrace African human origins, and in doing so they confront the issue of skin color—the physical feature with extreme political significance today.

Given what we know about the adaptive significance of human skin color, and the fact that, until 800,000 years ago, members of the genus *Homo* were exclusively creatures of the tropics, lightly pigmented skins are likely a recent development in human history. Conversely, and consistent with humanity's African origins, darkly pigmented skins are likely quite ancient. Lightly pigmented peoples possess the enzyme tyrosinase, which converts the amino acid tyrosine into the compound that forms melanin, in sufficient quantity to make them very black. But they also possess genes that inactivate or inhibit it (Wills, 1994).

Human skin, more liberally endowed with sweat glands and lacking heavy body hair compared to other primates, effectively eliminates excess body heat in a hot climate. This would have been especially advantageous to our ancestors on the savannah, who could have avoided confrontations with large carnivorous animals by carrying out most of their activities in the heat of the day. For the most part, tropical predators rest during this period, hunting primarily from dusk until early morning. Without much hair to cover their bodies, selection would have favored dark skin in our human ancestors. In short, based on available scientific evidence, all humans appear to have a black ancestry, no matter how white some of them may appear to be today.

Light pigmentation developed later in populations living outside the tropics; exactly when this occurred remains an interesting question. Whether one subscribes to the multiregional continuity model or to the recent African origins hypothesis, the settling of Greater Australia helps answer this question, as we know that the first people to reach Australia did so sometime between 40,000 and 60,000 years ago. These people came there from tropical Southeast Asia, spreading throughout Australia eventually to what is now the island of Tasmania, with the latitude and levels of ultraviolet radiation similar to New York City, Rome, or Beijing. Multiregionalists see

these earliest Australians as direct ancestors of early *Homo* in Asia. The recent Denisova fossils and associated genetic studies support this notion.

As Aboriginal Australians originally came from the tropics, we would expect them to have had darkly pigmented skin. In Australia, those populations that spread south of the tropics (where, as in northern latitudes, ultraviolet radiation is less intense) underwent some reduction of pigmentation. But for all that, their skin color is still far darker than that of Europeans or East Asians (recall Figure 11.11). Most of today's Southeast Asian population spread there from southern China following the invention of farming. This expansion of lighter-skinned populations effectively "swamped" the original populations of this region, except in a few out-of-the-way places like the Andaman Islands, in the Bay of Bengal between India and Thailand (Diamond, 1996).

The obvious conclusion is that 40,000 to 60,000 years is not enough to produce significant depigmentation (Ferrie, 1997). These observations also suggest that Europeans and East Asians may have lived outside the tropics for far longer than the people of Tasmania or that settlement in latitudes even more distant from the equator were required for depigmentation to occur.

One should not conclude that because it is relatively new lightly pigmented skin is better or more highly evolved. Darker skin better suits the conditions of life in the tropics or at high altitudes, although with cultural adaptations like protective clothing, hats, and more recently invented sunscreen lotions lightly pigmented people can survive there. Conversely, the availability of supplementary sources of vitamin D allows more heavily pigmented people to do quite well far away from the tropics. In both cases, culture has rendered skin color differences largely irrelevant from a purely biological perspective. With time and effort, skin color may eventually lose its social significance as well.

CHAPTER CHECKLIST

Does the biological concept of race apply to human variation?

● Humans are a single, highly variable species inhabiting the entire globe. Though biological processes are responsible for human variation, the biological concept of race or subspecies cannot be applied to human diversity. No discrete racial types exist.

● Scientists of the past placed humans into discrete races and then ordered them hierarchically. This work was dismantled and discredited beginning in the early 20th century.

● Individual traits appear in continuous gradations (clines) from one population to another without sharp breaks. Traits are inherited independently, and populations are genetically open.

● The vast majority of human variation exists within single populations rather than across different populations.

How does the race concept function within cultures?

● In many countries such as the United States, Haiti, Brazil, and South Africa, the sociopolitical category of race significantly impacts social identity and opportunity.

● Racial conflicts result from social stereotypes and not scientific facts.

● Racists of the past and present frequently invoke the notion of biological difference to support unjust social practices.

● Behavioral characteristics attributed to race can be explained in terms of experience as well as a hierarchical social order affecting the opportunities and challenges faced by different groups of people, rather than biology.

What are the flaws with studies that attempt to link race and intelligence?

● These studies imply a biological basis and do not take into account that biological race does not exist.

● The inherited components of intelligence cannot be separated from those that are culturally acquired.

● There is still no consensus on what intelligence really is, but it is generally agreed that intelligence is made up of several different talents and abilities, each of which would be separately inherited.

● The cultural and environmental specificity of IQ testing makes it invalid for broad comparisons.

Why does human skin color vary across the globe?

● Subject to tremendous variation, skin color is a function of several factors: transparency or thickness of the skin, distribution of blood vessels, and amount of carotene and melanin in the skin.

● Exposure to sunlight increases the amount of melanin, darkening the skin.

● Natural selection has favored heavily pigmented skin as protection against the strong solar radiation of equatorial latitudes.

● In northern latitudes, natural selection has favored relatively depigmented skin, which can utilize relatively weak solar radiation in the production of vitamin D.

● Cultural factors such as social rules about mating and slavery play a part in contemporary skin color distribution globally.

How have human cultures shaped human biology?

● Cultural practices shape human environments, which in turn can act on gene pools.

● Peoples with a dairying tradition possess the ability to digest milk sugars (lactose) into adulthood.

● Foods and activity patterns are a complete adaptive package.

● Western-style lifeways, which are characterized by diets high in sugar and low levels of activity, produce a greater incidence of obesity and diabetes. These diseases skyrocket in populations with dietary traditions of "slow release" foods and high activity.

● The cline of global variation in skin color derives from a balance between selective pressures: synthesis of vitamin D through the skin and protection from solar ultraviolet radiation.

● Cultural and biological adaptations at times work at cross-purposes as seen with the example of G-6-PD deficiency and fava beans as adaptations to malaria.

What is the relationship between race and human evolution?

● The one-to-one correspondence between phenotype and cultural capacity that pertains to early human evolution is problematic when applied to modern human origins and contemporary human variation.

● Light pigment appeared relatively late in the course of human evolution.

● All humans have black ancestry no matter how white they might appear today.

QUESTIONS FOR REFLECTION

1. As a species humans are extremely diverse, and yet our biological diversity cannot be partitioned into discrete types, subspecies, or races. At the same time, race functions as a social and political category, imposing inequality in some societies. How did so-called biological race and very real sociopolitical race play out in the "Linsanity" of the spring of 2012? What are the beliefs about biological diversity and race in your community today?

2. Although we can see and scientifically explain population differences in skin color, why is it invalid to use the biological concept of subspecies or race when referring to humans? Can you imagine another species of animal, plant, or microorganism for which the subspecies concept makes sense?

3. Globally, health statistics are gathered by country. In addition, some countries such as the United States gather health statistics by so-called racial categories. How are these two endeavors different and similar? Should health statistics be gathered by group?

4. How do you define the concept of intelligence? Do you think scientists will ever be able to discover the genetic basis of intelligence?

5. Cultural practices affect microevolutionary changes in the human species and often have dramatic effects on human health. Do you see examples of structural violence in your community that make some individuals more vulnerable to disease than others? Do you see examples globally?

ONLINE STUDY RESOURCES

CourseMate

Access chapter-specific learning tools, including learning objectives, practice quizzes, videos, flash cards, glossaries, and more in your Anthropology CourseMate.

Log into **www.cengagebrain.com** to access the resources your instructor has assigned and to purchase materials.

Challenge Issue

In the early 21st century, the human species faces novel challenges due to the massive changes our societies have imposed on the world. An ever-expanding population size consumes the earth's natural resources leaving humans to compete for everything from water to fossil fuels to antiretroviral therapy for HIV and AIDS. But, just as we have done over the course of human evolutionary history, our entwined cultural and biological capabilities help us to adapt as a species. In South Africa, for example, a group from the Bambanani Women's Group—HIV-positive women who receive therapy through Doctors Without Borders—have turned to making body maps that convey their experiences and to show the privilege inherent in access to medical treatment. In her body map, a life-sized tracing made with the help of Cape Town artist Jane Solomon, each woman includes her name, a personal symbol of power, her hand- and footprints, and her own visualization of her biological and life history. Here, Nondomiso Hlwele stands outside of her mother's house in Khayelitsha township with the body map she made. These maps become objects of hope and inspiration for the makers and a means for these women to transfer their personal stories to their children. The maps in turn challenge us to directly engage with the individual suffering of others. Only through such engagement—through awareness of how social and biological processes shape one another and through recognition of our shared humanity—can we ensure the future of our species and our planet.

Human Adaptation to a Changing World

12

Throughout millions of years of human evolutionary history, biology and culture interacted to make humans the species we are today. The archaeological record and contemporary human variation reveal that biology and culture continue to shape all areas of human experience, including health and disease. Indeed, an inside joke among anthropologists is that if you do not know the answer to an exam question about biology and culture, the answer is either "both" or "malaria." Our current understanding of malaria, as explained in previous chapters, illustrates how answering "malaria" is just like answering "both." Farming practices (culture) of the past created the perfect environment for the malarial parasite. The genetic response (biology) to this environmental change was increased frequencies of the sickle-cell allele.

To add a few more biocultural layers closer to the present, think about how contemporary global inequalities contribute to the continuing devastation of malaria in poorer countries today. If malaria were a problem plaguing North America or Europe, would most citizens of these countries still be without adequate treatment or cure? Similarly, African Americans, who have experienced racism rooted in a false message of biological difference, have distrusted the public health initiatives for genetic counseling to reduce frequencies of sickle-cell anemia in the United States (Tapper, 1999; Washington, 2006). Would average Americans of European descent feel comfortable with genetic testing to eliminate a disease gene if they had experienced the wrongs underprivileged ethnic minorities have experienced in the name of science?

Consider, for example, the Tuskegee Syphilis Study, carried out by the U.S. Public Health Service in Macon County, Alabama, from 1932 to 1972. This study involved withholding syphilis medication from a group of poor African American men without their knowledge, so that the scientists could learn more about the biology of syphilis in the "Negro" (**Figure 12.1**). Today, this could not happen. Any kind of biological research on human subjects without informed consent is illegal in the United States and in many other countries.

IN THIS CHAPTER YOU WILL LEARN TO

- Recognize old and new pressures to human survival across the globe.

- Describe human biological adaptations to high altitude, cold, and heat.

- Identify patterns of human growth and how the process allows humans to adapt.

- Explain the challenges that we humans have created for ourselves and how their effects fall upon distinct yet interconnected communities.

- Describe modern humans' variety of coping methods and treatments for health issues.

- Define *disease* versus *illness*, and discuss cultural attitudes about both.

- Investigate the multiple causes of health problems from a medical anthropological perspective.

Figure 12.1 The Tuskegee Experiments The Tuskegee Syphilis Study denied appropriate medical treatment to African American men in order to study the supposed differences in the biology of the disease in the "Negro." This human experimentation was not only false from a biological perspective but represented a moral breach in research conduct. Public outcry about this experiment led to regulations that protect all human subjects in biomedical research. Today, laws in the United States and in many other countries require informed consent of study participants for all research on human subjects.

When examining a seemingly biological phenomenon such as disease, cultural factors must be considered at every level—from how that phenomenon is represented in social groups (reflected in this case in the false notion that the biology of syphilis would differ between people of different skin colors) to how biological research is conducted.

The integration of biology and culture is the hallmark of anthropology. Throughout this book we have emphasized biocultural connections in examples ranging from infant feeding and sleeping practices to the relationship between poverty and tuberculosis. In this chapter, we take a deeper look at this connection and examine some of the theoretical approaches biological and medical anthropologists use to examine the interaction of biology and culture.

Although humans possess a number of exquisite biological mechanisms through which they have adapted to the natural environment, these mechanisms can fall short in a globalizing world. But before turning to the challenges we face from the dramatic changes in the human-made environments of today, we will explore the biological mechanisms people have used over millennia to adapt to three naturally occurring environmental extremes: high altitude, cold, and heat.

Human Adaptation to Natural Environmental Stressors

Studies of human adaptation traditionally focus on the capacity of humans to adapt or adjust to their environment through biological and/or cultural mechanisms. Darwin's theory of natural selection accounts for **genetic adaptations**—discrete genetic changes built into the allele frequencies of populations, such as the various adaptations to malaria that we have examined. It also provides the mechanism for understanding that adaptations, evident in population variation of continuous phenotypic traits, depend upon multiple interacting genes.

---

genetic adaptations Discrete genetic changes built into the allele frequencies of populations or microevolutionary change brought about by natural selection.

Figure 12.2 Twins Diana Bozza and her identical twin, Deborah Faraday, share 100 percent genetic identity. Yet only Deborah suffers from early onset Alzheimer's disease. Here Diana comforts Deborah at an assisted living facility in Front Royal, Virginia. Diagnosed in 2004, Deborah is completely disabled while Diana has no symptoms of Alzheimer's. Though identical twins share 100 percent of their genetic material, their phenotypes can be distinct because of interactions between these genes and the environment over the course of each individual's distinct life.

Jodi Cobb/National Geographic Stock

Even without knowing the precise genetic bases to these adaptations (such as skin color or body build), scientists can study them through comparative measurement of the associated phenotypic variation. In both these cases, differential reproductive success accounts for differences in allele frequency.

Humans possess two additional biological mechanisms through which they can adapt. The first of these, **developmental adaptation**, also produces permanent phenotypic variation through environmental shaping of individual gene expression (**Figure 12.2**). The extended period of growth and development characteristic of humans allows for a prolonged time period during which the environment can exert its effects on the developing organism. Humans inherit this capacity to adapt through the process of growth and development, but the specific permanent phenotypic changes brought about through environmental interaction do not get directly passed onto future generations. Even after most physical growth ceases, our genomes interact with the environment, producing discrete biological changes.

The anthropological focus on growth and development has a long history dating back to the work of Franz Boas, the founder of American four-field anthropology. Boas is credited with discovering the features of the human growth curve (**Figure 12.3**). He demonstrated that the rate of human growth varies in typical patterns until adulthood, when physical growth ceases. Humans experience a period of very rapid growth after birth through infancy, followed by a gradually slower rate of growth during childhood. At adolescence, the rate of growth increases again during the adolescent growth spurt. Growth in height or stature results from the addition of

new cells throughout the body, but particularly in the bones where growth takes place at specific growth plates (**Figure 12.4**).

In addition to describing the long-term pattern of human growth, anthropologists have also demonstrated that within periods of growth, the actual process proceeds as a series of alternating bursts and relative quiet (Lampl, Velhuis, & Johnson, 1992). When challenged by malnutrition, physical growth slows to permit immediate survival at the expense of height in adulthood. This adaptive mechanism may have negative consequences for subsequent generations given individuals who were malnourished as children have been shown to experience reduced reproductive success as adults (Martorell, 1988).

Boas also demonstrated differences in the growth of immigrant children in the United States compared to their parents. This work was the earliest documentation of the variable effects of different environments on the growth process. Presumably, immigrant children resemble their parents genetically; therefore, size differences between immigrant children and their parents could be attributed to the environment alone. This kind of difference, known as a **secular trend**, allows anthropologists to make inferences about environmental effects on growth and development.

---

developmental adaptation A permanent phenotypic variation derived from interaction between genes and the environment during the period of growth and development.

secular trend A physical difference among related people from distinct generations that allows anthropologists to make inferences about environmental effects on growth and development.

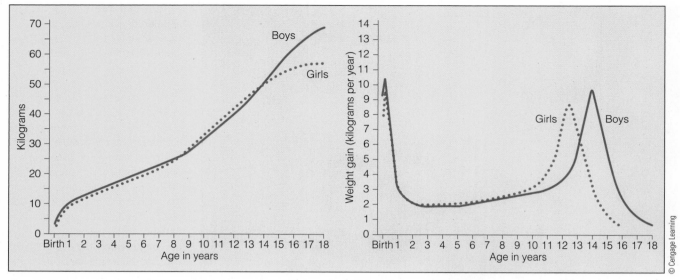

Figure 12.3 Human Growth Curves Franz Boas defined the features of the human growth curve. The graph on the left depicts distance, or the amount of growth attained over time, and the graph on the right shows the velocity, or rate of growth over time. These charts are widely used throughout the globe to determine the health status of children.

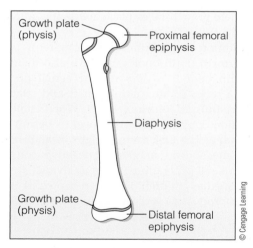

Figure 12.4 Long Bone Growth Each long bone has specific regions (in red) of cartilage where growth occurs; these are called growth plates. This allows the harder bony tissue of the diaphysis to support the body and for the epiphyses to function within the joint while an individual is developing. This thighbone, or femur, has four distinct areas of growth. In an x-ray of a child who is still growing, the cartilage does not appear white like bone. Each bone has a particular sequence of maturation that is regulated by hormones. Growth stops when the epiphyses fuse with the rest of the bone, a process regulated by estrogens in both males and females. In males, the clavicle or collarbone is one of the last bones to fuse. In females, the pubic bone of the pelvis is one of the last bones to fuse.

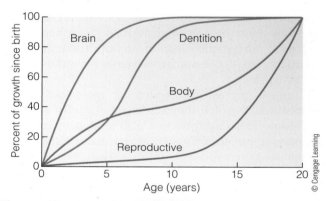

Figure 12.5 Development Trajectories The various systems of the human body each follow their own trajectory of growth. Brain growth is most rapid in the first five years of life but continues at a slower pace into young adulthood. Children's immune systems also undergo rapid development early in life. Human children acquire most of their permanent dentition by the time their reproductive systems start to mature at adolescence; their 12-year molars have emerged, and only the wisdom teeth have not yet erupted. The pace of growth for the reproductive system and the body both increase rapidly at adolescence.

The various systems of the human body have their own trajectory of growth and development (**Figure 12.5**). Over the past sixty years, a downward secular trend in the age at **menarche** (first menstruation) has become evident in North America. Whether this secular trend is attributable to healthy or problematic stimuli (such as childhood obesity or hormones in the environment) has yet to be determined. Likewise, age at menarche varies tremendously across the globe. Genetic differences from population to population

menarche First menstruation in the maturation of a human female.

© Friedrich Stark/Alamy

Figure 12.6 Nutrition and Fertility The theory that human females require a minimum percentage of body fat in order to attain menarche accounts for some of the global variation in the age at which this occurs. Around the world, many women stay incredibly lean through a combination of hard labor and limited food availability, a condition that limits their fertility. Further, sufficient body fat maintains menstrual cycles throughout adulthood. Thus, female bodies regulate their potential pregnancies in times of limited food because successful pregnancy and breastfeeding require extra nutrition. In postindustrial societies, loss of periods, or amenorrhea, is common among athletes and among women with anorexia nervosa, a disorder in which individuals starve themselves.

account for some of this variation, and environmental effects account for the remainder. The Bundi of New Guinea have the oldest average age (18) at menarche. By comparison, U.S. girls reach menarche on average at the age of 12.4 years.

An important theory accounting for the timing of sexual maturation ties age at menarche to the percentage of body fat possessed by growing individuals as a regulator of hormonal production (Frisch, 2002). Most female bodies seem to require a minimum ratio of 17 percent body fat to lean mass for menarche to occur (Figure 12.6). This body fat helps with the conversion of androgens (the male hormones) to the female hormonal counterpart, estrogens. Highly active lean women, whether from athletics or some kind of labor, may experience a delayed menarche or a secondary loss of menstruation. Starvation has the same effect. A massive excess of body fat also interferes with fertility.

Hormones impact fertility into adulthood, but teasing apart the role of biology and culture with respect to hormones has proven to be complex. Take, for example, the case of androgen hormone levels, waist-to-hip ratio, and fertility

levels of women in high-powered careers. These women tend to have a more cylindrical shape, which could be because their bodies produce relatively more androgen than hourglass-shaped women. A higher androgen level, however, may be the reason for lower fertility among these women. High androgen levels may also represent a biological response to a specific work environment that ultimately impedes the fertility of women in high-powered careers (Cashdan, 2008). Similarly, diminishing estrogens after **menopause** (the cessation of menstrual cycles) causes female body fat distribution patterns to shift to a more male pattern.

The bottom line is that human hormonal systems are highly sensitive to a variety of environmental stimuli. Biological anthropologist Peter Ellison works extensively on the connections between hormones and the environment—a subspecialty defined as reproductive ecology (see the Anthropologist of Note).

menopause The cessation of menstrual cycles.

ANTHROPOLOGIST OF NOTE

Peter Ellison

Reproductive biology and human health across cultures have been the focus of the work of biological anthropologist **Peter Ellison**. In the 1970s, Ellison first read Darwin's *Origin of Species* as a college student at St. John's College in Annapolis, Maryland. He found Darwin's text transformative and went to the University of Vermont to study biology; later he earned a doctorate in biological anthropology from Harvard, where he now runs a comprehensive program in reproductive ecology.

Ellison has pioneered techniques for hormonal analysis from saliva, and he uses this technique to monitor individuals' hormonal response to a variety of environmental stressors. This noninvasive technique has allowed Ellison to conduct hormonal studies throughout the world and to correlate hormonal levels with social events. People from long-term field sites in Congo, Poland, Japan, Nepal, and Paraguay have participated in this research, allowing Ellison to document the hormonal variation around biological events, such as egg implantation and breastfeeding, as well as cultural factors such as farm work or foraging.

Dr. Ellison is especially interested in how behavior and social stimuli affect reproductive physiology. In Western societies, he has explored hormonal levels of males and females in response to stimuli, such as winning a championship or taking a stressful exam. He has also studied the relationship between cancer development and exercise and stress. In his book *On Fertile Ground*, Ellison illustrates how evolutionary forces have shaped human reproductive physiology into a system capable of precise responses to environmental stimuli.

Peter Ellison (*left*) and Peter Gray discuss how male testosterone levels differ between married and single men and among men of different cultures.

© Kris Snibbe/Staff Photo Harvard News Office

Although genetic and developmental adaptations become permanent parts of an adult's phenotype, **physiological adaptations** come and go in response to a specific environmental stimulus. Along with cultural adaptations, these various biological mechanisms allow humans to be the only primate species to inhabit the entire globe. Over the course of our evolutionary history, most environmental stressors were climatic and geographic. Today, humans face a series of new environmental stressors of their own making.

Adaptation to High Altitude

High altitude differs from other natural environmental stressors because it is the least amenable to cultural adaptation. Humans can heat the cold and cool the heat, but the reduced availability of oxygen at high altitude poses more of a challenge. At a cellular level, this results in reduced oxygen availability, or **hypoxia** (from the Greek *hypo*, for "low" or "under" and the word *oxygen*). Before

physiological adaptation A short-term physiological change in response to a specific environmental stimulus. An immediate short-term response is not very efficient and is gradually replaced by a longer-term response; see *acclimatization*.

hypoxia The reduced availability of oxygen at a cellular level.

the invention of oxygen masks and pressurized cabins in airplanes, there was no way to modify this environmental stressor via culture.

When people speak of the air being "thinner" at high altitude, they are referring to the concentration (partial pressure) of oxygen available to the lungs, and so to the circulatory system. At high altitudes, the partial pressure of oxygen is sufficiently reduced so that most lowlanders experience severe oxygen deprivation (**Figure 12.7**).

Populations that have lived at high altitudes for generations, such as the Quechua Indians of the highlands of Peru and the Sherpa native to the Himalaya Mountains, possess a remarkable ability to tolerate oxygen deprivation, living and working at altitudes as high as 20,000 feet above sea level. Some of these abilities have been encoded in the genetic makeup of these populations. In addition, developmental and physiological adaptations to the lower partial pressure of oxygen in the environment have rendered their body tissues resistant to oxygen deprivation (**Figure 12.8**).

Typical lowlanders can make both short- and long-term physiological adjustments to high altitude. In general, short-term changes help an individual avoid an immediate crisis, but the poor efficiency of these changes makes them difficult to sustain. Instead, long-term responses take over as the individual's physiological

Kyodo/Landov

Figure 12.8 Born to Run Observing that East African runners, like Ethiopian Tiki Gelana crossing the women's marathon finish line at the 2012 Olympics, have won most of the major marathon competitions over the past several decades, coaches have emulated the East African approach. Adaptation to the hot, dry yet mountainous region leads to a long, lean build (a product of the heat adaptation) and increased oxygen-carrying capacity. Although runners worldwide tend to be long and lean, many athletes now train at high altitude so that when race day comes, their red blood cell count and hemoglobin levels allow them to carry more oxygen.

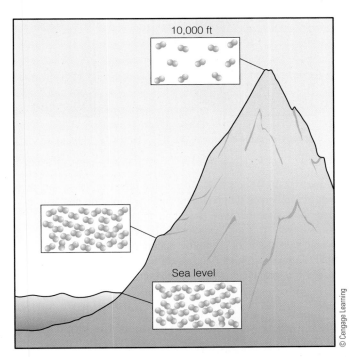

10,000 ft

Sea level

© Cengage Learning

Figure 12.7 Atmospheric Pressure The amount of atmosphere above us determines the amount of pressure being exerted on oxygen molecules in the air. At sea level, the pressure of the atmosphere packs oxygen molecules more tightly together compared to the density of oxygen molecules at higher altitudes. This in turn impacts the ease at which oxygen can enter the lungs when we breathe.

responses attain equilibrium with the environment. This process is known as **acclimatization**. Most lowlanders stepping off an airplane in Cuzco, Peru, for example will experience increased respiratory rate, cardiac output, and pulse rate. Their arteries will expand as blood pressure increases in order to get oxygen to the tissues. This kind of response cannot be maintained indefinitely. Instead, lowlanders acclimatize as their bodies begin to produce more red blood cells and hemoglobin in order to carry more oxygen. Because of differences in genetic makeup, individuals' physiological responses begin at varying altitudes.

Developmental adaptations are seen in individuals who spend their childhood years of growth and development at high altitude. Among the highland Quechua, for

acclimatization Long-term physiological adjustments made in order to attain equilibrium with a specific environmental stimulus.

example, both the chest cavity and the right ventricle of the heart (which pushes blood to the lungs) are enlarged compared to lowland Quechua. This may have genetic underpinnings in that all Quechua experience a long period of growth and development compared to the average person in the United States.

The process of growth and development begins with reproduction, and high altitude has a considerable impact on this process. For populations that have not adapted to high altitude, successful reproduction requires some cultural interventions. For example, take the case of fertility among Spanish colonialists in the city of Potosi high in the Andes. For the first fifty-four years of this city's existence, founded to mine the "mountain of silver" that towers above the community, no Spanish child was born who survived childhood. Indigenous populations did not have this problem. To ensure reproductive success, Spanish women began the cultural practice of retreating to lower altitude for their pregnancy and the first year of their child's life (Wiley, 2004).

At high altitudes cold stress is also a problem. A stocky body and short limbs help individuals conserve heat whereas the opposite facilitates heat loss. We dissipate heat through the surface of our bodies. A stocky build has a lower surface area to volume ratio compared to a long, linear build. Small body size also results in a higher surface area to volume ratio. These phenomena have been formalized into two rules named after the naturalists who made such observations in mammals. **Bergmann's rule** refers to the tendency for the bodies of mammals living in cold climates to be more massive than members of the same species living in warm climates (**Figure 12.9**). **Allen's rule** refers to the tendency of mammals living in cold climates to have shorter appendages (arms and legs) than members of the same species living in warm climates (**Figure 12.10**).

Adaptation to Cold

Cold stress can exist without high altitude, as it does in the Arctic. In addition to the previously mentioned patterns of body and limb shape and size, other cold responses are also evident in Arctic populations.

In extreme cold, the limbs need enough heat to prevent frostbite, but giving up heat to the periphery takes it away from the body core. Humans balance this through

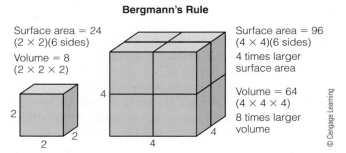

Bergmann's Rule

Surface area = 24 (2 × 2)(6 sides)
Volume = 8 (2 × 2 × 2)

Surface area = 96 (4 × 4)(6 sides)
4 times larger surface area

Volume = 64 (4 × 4 × 4)
8 times larger volume

© Cengage Learning

Figure 12.9 Bergmann's Rule Bergmann's rule refers to the observation that as overall body size increases, the amount of surface area increases less rapidly than the amount of volume. This accounts for the tendency for mammals living in cold climates to be more massive than members of the same species living in warmer climates. This allows for the conservation of heat in cold climates and its dissipation in warm climates.

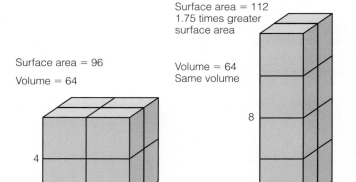

Allen's Rule

Surface area = 96
Volume = 64

Surface area = 112 1.75 times greater surface area

Volume = 64 Same volume

(4×4 of each side) × 6 sides = 96

[(2×4) × 2 sides] + [(2×8) × 2 sides] + [(4×8) × 2 sides] = 112

© Cengage Learning

Figure 12.10 Allen's Rule Allen's rule refers to the observation that in two bodies that have the same volume, the one that is long and lean rather than short and squat will have a greater surface area. This accounts for the tendency for mammals living in cold climates to have shorter appendages (arms and legs) than the same species living in warmer climates. Heat can be dissipated through long limbs or conserved through short ones.

Bergmann's rule The tendency for the bodies of mammals living in cold climates to be shorter and rounder than members of the same species living in warm climates.

Allen's rule The tendency for the bodies of mammals living in cold climates to have shorter appendages (arms and legs) than members of the same species living in warm climates.

hunting response A cyclic expansion and contraction of the blood vessels of the limbs that balances releasing enough heat to prevent frostbite with maintaining heat in the body core.

a cyclic expansion and contraction of the blood vessels of their limbs called the **hunting response**. Blood vessels oscillate between closing down to prevent heat loss and opening up to warm the hands and feet. When first exposed to cold as gloves are taken off, blood vessels immediately constrict. Initial alternations between open (warm) and shut (cold) and the corresponding temperature of the skin range dramatically. But the oscillations become smaller and more rapid, allowing a hunter to

Figure 12.11 **Whale Hunting** Arctic populations adapt to frigid conditions through a variety of biological and cultural adaptations. Often biology and culture interact. The high-energy readily available whale blubber diet, integral to Eskimo cultural systems, also stimulates the body to burn this energy at a high metabolic rate. A high metabolic rate, in turn, helps the body stay warm in very cold climates.

maintain the warmth-derived manual dexterity required for tying knots or positioning arrows.

Eskimos (including the Inuit) also deal with cold through a high **metabolic rate**: the rate at which their bodies burn energy. This may result from a diet high in protein and fat (whale blubber is the common food; see Figure 12.11). In addition, genetic factors likely also contribute to Eskimos' high metabolic rate.

Shivering provides a short-term physiological response to cold. Shivering quickly generates heat for the body but cannot be maintained for long periods of time. Instead, as an individual acclimatizes to the cold, adjustments to diet, activity pattern, metabolic rate, and the circulatory system must occur.

Adaptation to Heat

Sweating or perspiring provides the human body's primary physiological mechanism for coping with extreme heat. Through sweating, the body gives up heat as water released from sweat glands evaporates (Figure 12.12).

Without water, exposure to heat can be fatal. We must drink enough water to replace whatever we lose through sweating.

Each human has roughly 2 million sweat glands though this number varies among individuals and populations. Sweat glands spread out over a greater surface area on tall, thin bodies, facilitating water evaporation and heat loss. Thus, Bergmann's and Allen's rules also apply to heat adaptation. The more surface area a body has, the more surface for the sweat glands. In addition, because heat is produced by unit of volume, having a high surface area to volume ratio is beneficial for heat loss. Long, slender bodies dissipate heat best. In hot and humid environments such as rainforests, water evaporation poses a challenge. In this environment, human populations have adapted to minimize heat production through a reduction in overall size while keeping a slender, lean build.

metabolic rate The rate at which bodies burn energy (food) to function.

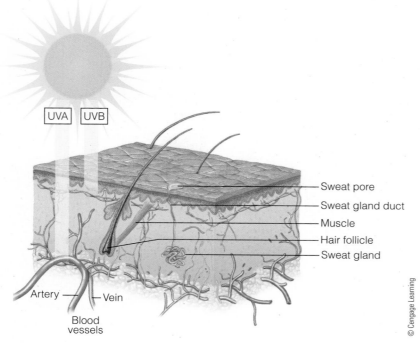

Figure 12.12 Cross-Section of Human Skin Skin—a sensitive, functional, and highly diffuse organ of the human body—responds exquisitely to the environment. As described in Chapter 11, vitamin D is synthesized here. In addition, skin regulates our adaptive response to heat through sweating. Blood vessels carry heat to the surface of the body. Water released through the sweat glands onto the surface of the skin through pores will evaporate and dissipate this body heat. Individuals who spend their growth and development in hotter climates possess more sweat glands as a developmental adaptation to heat. In addition, body build impacts heat dissipation. More skin or surface area allows an individual to dissipate heat more easily because of the increased number of sweat glands distributed on the skin.

Human-Made Stressors of a Changing World

Traditionally, culture has allowed humans to modify natural stressors such as heat and cold through means such as housing, diet, and clothing. But in today's globalizing world, the effects of culture are much more complex. Rather than simply alleviating physical stressors, cultural processes can *add* new stressors such as pollution, global warming, and exhaustion of the world's natural resources. Indeed, as you will recall from Chapter 5, geologists have added "Anthropocene" to the geological epochs to reflect the profound human modification of the earth since the industrial revolution.

Biological adaptation to these human-made stressors cannot keep pace with the rapid rate at which humans are changing the earth. Biological adaptation still occurs, but it takes many generations for beneficial alleles and phenotypes to be incorporated into a population's genome. Until human cultures cooperate to collectively address these global challenges, unnatural stressors will inevitably lead to sickness and suffering. An integrated, holistic anthropological perspective has much to contribute to alleviating if not eliminating these human-made stressors.

The Development of Medical Anthropology

Medical anthropology, a specialization that cuts across all four fields of anthropology, contributes significantly to the understanding of sickness and health in the 21st century. Some of the earliest medical anthropologists were individuals trained as physicians and ethnographers who investigated the health beliefs and practices of peoples in "exotic" places while also providing them with Western medicine. Medical anthropologists during this early period translated local experiences of sickness into

VISUAL COUNTERPOINT

© Topham/The Image Works

© Ronnie Kaufman/Corbis

Figure 12.13 Cultural Symbols of Authority Shamans and biomedical doctors both rely upon symbols to heal their patients. The physician's white coat is a powerful symbol of medical knowledge and authority that communicates to patients just as clearly as does the pattern on the skin of the shaman's drum. Interestingly, medical schools in the United States are increasingly incorporating a "white coat" ceremony into medical education, conferring the power of the white coat onto new doctors.

the scientific language of Western biomedicine. Following a reevaluation of this ethnocentric approach in the 1970s, medical anthropology emerged as a specialization that brings theoretical and applied approaches from cultural and biological anthropology to the study of human health and sickness.

Medical anthropologists study **medical systems**, or patterned sets of ideas and practices relating to illness. Medical systems are cultural systems, similar to any other social institution. Medical anthropologists examine healing traditions and practices cross-culturally and the qualities all medical systems have in common. For example, the terms used by French cultural anthropologist Claude Lévi-Strauss to describe the healing powers of *shamans* (the name for indigenous healers, originally from Siberia, and now applied to many traditional healers) also apply to medical practices in Europe and North America (Lévi-Strauss, 1963). In both situations, the healer has access to a world of restricted knowledge (spiritual or scientific) from which the average community member is excluded (Figure 12.13).

Medical anthropologists also use scientific models drawn from biological anthropology, such as evolutionary theory and ecology, to understand and improve human health. Moreover, they have turned their attention to the connections between human health and political and economic forces, both globally and locally. Because global flows of people, germs, cures, guns, and pollution underlie the distribution of sickness and health in the world today, a broad anthropological understanding of the origins of sickness is vital for alleviating human suffering.

The medical anthropological perspective recognizes poverty as one of the major determinants of sickness; anthropologists throughout the globe have demonstrated this connection and worked to improve health through social justice. This perspective has gained support from the World Bank, a global financial institution that provides loans to developing countries, with U.S. medical anthropologist and physician Jim Yong Kim as its new president. Kim, the cofounder (with physician-anthropologist Paul Farmer) of Partners in Health, has spent his career improving human health through the eradication of poverty.

medical system A patterned set of ideas and practices relating to illness.

Science, Illness, and Disease

During the course of medical anthropology's development as a distinct specialty within anthropology, there was a concurrent transformation in the relationship between biological and cultural knowledge. The earliest research on medical systems was carried out by physician-anthropologists—individuals trained as medical doctors and as anthropologists who participated in the international public health movement emerging early in the 20th century. While delivering the medical care developed in Europe and North America, these physician-anthropologists simultaneously studied the health beliefs and practices of the cultures they were sent to help. Local cultural categories about sickness were translated into Western biomedical terms.

Initially, these Western approaches were thought to be culture-free depictions of human biology and were therefore used as an interpretive framework for examining the medical beliefs and practices of other cultures. Implicit in this work was the notion that the Western approach, with its supposed objectivity, was superior. Fieldwork conducted by cultural anthropologists, however, has shown that medical categories, like other aspects of a people's unique worldview, reflect the value system of their particular culture. For example, the Subanun people of Mindinao, one of the large islands of the Philippines, give different names to fungal infections of the skin depending on whether the infection is openly visible or hidden under clothes. In contrast, the biomedical and scientific categorization of fungal infections refers only to genus and species of the fungus.

In the 1970s the place of biological and cultural knowledge in medical anthropology was dramatically reorganized. The admission of the People's Republic of China to the United Nations in 1971, and the subsequent improvement of diplomatic and other relationships between that communist country and Western powers, played a role in this theoretical shift. Cultural exchanges revealed a professional medical system in the East rivaling that of Western biomedicine in its scientific basis and technical feats. For example, the practice of open-heart surgery in China, using only acupuncture needles as an anesthetic, challenged the assumption of biomedical superiority within anthropological thought. Scholars began proposing that biomedicine is a cultural system, just like the medical systems in other cultures, and that it, too, is worthy of anthropological study.

To effectively compare medical systems and health cross-culturally, medical anthropologists have made a theoretical distinction between the terms *disease* and *illness*. **Disease** refers to a specific pathology: a physical or biological abnormality. **Illness** refers to the meanings and elaborations given to particular physical states. Disease and illness do not necessarily overlap. An individual may experience illness without having a disease, or a disease may occur in the absence of illness.

In cultures with scientific medical systems, a key component of the social process of illness involves delineating human suffering in terms of biology. At times this extends to labeling an illness as a disease even though the biology is poorly understood. Think about alcoholism in the United States, for example. A person who is thought of as a drunk, partier, barfly, or boozer tends not to get sympathy from the rest of society. By contrast, a person struggling with the disease of alcoholism receives cultural help from physicians, support from groups such as Alcoholics Anonymous, and financial aid from health insurance covering medical treatment. It matters little that the biology of this "disease" is still poorly understood and that alcoholism is treated through social support rather than expert manipulation of biology. By calling alcoholism a disease, it becomes a socially sanctioned and recognized illness within the dominant medical system of the United States. See this chapter's Globalscape for an innovative method of reducing the stigma and improving health through a focus on the social aspects of sickness.

Disease can also exist without illness. Schistosomiasis, infection with a kind of parasitic flatworm called a blood fluke, is an excellent example. Scientists have fully documented the life cycle of this parasite that alternates between water snail and human hosts. The adult worms live for many years inside human intestine or urinary tract. Human waste then spreads the mobile phase of the parasite to freshwater snails. Inside the snails, the parasite develops further to a second mobile phase of the flatworm life cycle, releasing thousands of tiny creatures into freshwater. If humans swim, wade, or do household chores such as laundry in this infested water, the parasite can bore its way through the skin, traveling to the intestine or bladder where the life cycle continues.

The idea of parasites boring through the skin and living permanently inside the bladder or intestine may well be revolting; ingesting poisons to rid the body of these parasites is an acceptable treatment for people at certain social and economic levels. But to people living where schistosomiasis is **endemic** (the public health term for a disease that is widespread in the population), this disease state is normal, and thus they seek no treatment. In other words, schistosomiasis is not an illness. Individuals may know about expensive effective biomedical treatments, but given the likelihood of reinfection and the inaccessibility of the drugs, they tend not to seek treatment with pharmaceutical agents.

Over time, the forces of evolution generally lead to a tolerance between parasite and host so that infected

---

disease A specific pathology; a physical or biological abnormality.

illness The meanings and elaborations given to a particular physical state.

endemic The public health term for a disease that is widespread in a population.

Globalscape

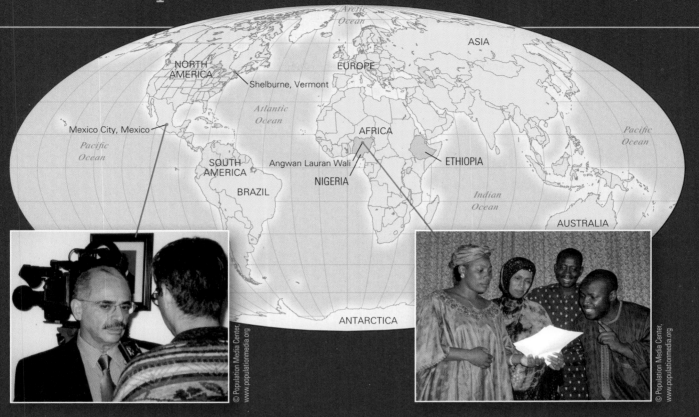

© Population Media Center, www.populationmedia.org

© Population Media Center, www.populationmedia.org

From Soap Opera to Clinic?

When Hajara Nasiru in Angwan Lauran Wali, Nigeria, listened to the radio soap opera *Gugar Goge* (*Tell It to Me Straight*), she learned something that changed her life. Created in Nigeria using a methodology developed originally in Mexico, the radio drama tells the story of 12-year-old Kande, who is forced to marry a man more than twice her age. She soon becomes pregnant. After a prolonged labor, her baby dies, and Kande develops an obstetric fistula (a hole between either the rectum and vagina or the bladder and vagina) leading to incontinence, infection, and nerve damage. Kande's husband abandons her, but a neighbor brings her to the hospital in the nearby city of Zaira. After the fistula is repaired, Kande is able to return to her father's home in full health.

Like Kande, Hajara married young (at 15), and by the age of 25 she had experienced eight labors, lost five children, and developed a fistula with her last labor. After living with the debilitating discomfort for nine weeks, she invited her husband to listen to the soap opera too. *Gugar Goge* gave Hajara and her husband the information they needed. From the show, they learned that the fistula could be repaired and that Hajara need not suffer.

This radio drama is one of many created by the local branches of the Population Media Center (PMC), a U.S.-based international nongovernmental organization, headquartered in Shelburne, Vermont, that uses "entertainment-education for social change." Mexican television producer Miguel Sabido, pictured above, developed PMC's methodology and created *telenovelas* that prompted dramatic social change across Mexico during the 1970s. For example, one program resulted in an eightfold increase in adult education, and another led to a 50 percent increase in contraceptive use.

Population Media Center is bringing the Sabido methodology to the world, through work with local radio and television broadcasters, appropriate government ministries, and nongovernmental organizations. Their goal is to design and implement a comprehensive media strategy for addressing family and reproductive health issues. This collaborative process takes place with local constituents, identifying and addressing various health issues. Transformed into a radio drama such as *Guga Goge* and performed by professional radio actors, the issues gain broad attention.

In addition to the individual success stories like Hajara's, success can be measured quantitatively at the countrywide level. For example, radio programs broadcast in Ethiopia in two different languages between 2002 and 2004 changed the reproductive health behavior in that region. The percentage of married women using contraception increased from 23 percent to 79 percent, and the birth rates for Ethiopia decreased. Reduction in fertility is a vital part of the transition each society must make to achieve better overall health. In exit interviews at family planning clinics, one-fourth of the 14,000 people surveyed cited the radio drama as their reason for coming.

Global Twister

Would the Sabido method work in your community? Is it already at work? What health issues would you like to see embedded in soap operas?

individuals can live normal lives. Some peoples are so accustomed to this parasitic infection that they regard the appearance of bloody urine in a teenage boy (due to a sufficient parasite load to cause this symptom) as a male version of menstruation. Cultural perspectives can thus be at odds with international public health goals that are based on a strictly Western biomedical understanding of disease.

Medical anthropologists working on global public health issues are careful to not impose their own interpretations and meanings as they work to improve the health of others. In the following Original Study, biological anthropologist Katherine Dettwyler explains how she was challenged to rethink Down syndrome as she worked on childhood growth and health in Mali.

Dancing Skeletons: Life and Death in West Africa BY KATHERINE DETTWYLER

I stood in the doorway, gasping for air, propping my arms against the door frame on either side to hold me up. I sucked in great breaths of cool, clean air and rested my gaze on the distant hills, trying to compose myself. Ominous black thunderclouds were massed on the horizon and moved rapidly toward the schoolhouse. . . .

The morning had begun pleasantly enough, with villagers waiting patiently under the huge mango tree in the center of the village. But before long, the approaching storm made it clear that we would have to move inside. The only building large enough to hold the crowd was the one-room schoolhouse, located on the outskirts of the village. . . .

Inside the schoolhouse, chaos reigned. It was 20 degrees hotter, ten times as noisy, and as dark as gloom. What little light there was from outside entered through the open doorway and two small windows. The entire population of the village crowded onto the rows of benches, or stood three deep around the periphery of the room. Babies cried until their mothers pulled them around front where they could nurse, children chattered, and adults seized the opportunity to converse with friends and neighbors. It was one big party, a day off from working in the fields, with a cooling rain thrown in for good measure. I had to shout the measurements out to Heather, to make myself heard over the cacophony of noise. . . .

A middle-aged man dressed in a threadbare pair of Levis shoved a crying child forward. I knelt down to encourage the little boy to step up onto the scales and saw that his leg was wrapped in dirty bandages. He hesitated before lifting his foot and whimpered as he put his weight onto it. . . .

"What's the matter with his leg?" I asked his father.

"He hurt it in a bicycle accident," he said.

I rolled my eyes at Heather. "Let me guess. He was riding on the back fender, without wearing long pants, or shoes, and he got his leg tangled in the spokes." Moussa translated this aside into Bambara, and the man acknowledged that was exactly what had happened. . . .

The festering wound encompassed the boy's ankle and part of his foot, deep enough to see bone at the bottom. His entire lower leg and foot were swollen and putrid; it was obvious that gangrene had a firm hold. . . .

"You have to take him to the hospital in Sikasso immediately," I explained.

"But we can't afford to," he balked.

"You can't afford not to," I cried in exasperation, turning to Moussa. "He doesn't understand," I said to Moussa. "Please explain to him that the boy is certain to die of gangrene poisoning if he doesn't get to a doctor right away. It may be too late already, but I don't think so. He may just lose his leg." Moussa's eyes widened with alarm. Even he hadn't realized how serious the boy's wounds were. As the father took in what Moussa was saying, his face crumpled. . . . Father and son were last seen leaving Merediela, the boy perched precariously on the back of a worn-out donkey hastily borrowed from a neighbor, while the father trotted alongside, shoulders drooping, urging the donkey to greater speed. . . .

Lunch back at the animatrice's compound provided another opportunity for learning about infant feeding beliefs in rural Mali, through criticism of my own child feeding practices. This time it was a chicken that had given its life for our culinary benefit. As we ate, without even thinking, I reached into the center pile of chicken meat and pulled pieces of meat off the bone. Then I placed them over in Miranda's section of the communal food bowl and encouraged her to eat.

"Why are you giving her chicken?" Bakary asked.

"I want to make sure she gets enough to eat," I replied. "She didn't eat very much porridge for breakfast because she doesn't like millet."

"But she's just a child. She doesn't need good food. You've been working hard all morning, and she's just been lying around. Besides, if she wanted to eat, she would," he argued.

"It's true that I've been working hard," I admitted, "but she's still growing. Growing children need much more food, proportionately, than adults. And if I didn't encourage her to eat, she might not eat until we get back to Bamako."

Bakary shook his head. "In Dogo," he explained, "people believe that good food is wasted on children. They don't appreciate its good taste or the way it makes you feel. Also, they haven't worked hard to produce the food. They have their whole lives to work for good food for themselves, when they get older. Old people deserve the best food because they're going to die soon." . . .

. . . In rural southern Mali, "good food" (which included all the high protein/high calorie foods) was reserved for elders and other adults. Children subsisted almost entirely on the carbohydrate staples, flavored with a little sauce. My actions in giving Miranda my share of the chicken were viewed as bizarre and misguided. I was wasting good food on a mere child, and depriving myself. . . .

In N'tenkoni the next morning, we were given use of the men's sacred meeting hut for our measuring session. A round hut about 20 feet in diameter, it had a huge center pole made from the trunk of a tree that held up the thatched roof. Because it had two large doorways, it was light and airy and would provide protection in the event of another thunderstorm. . . .

There was some initial confusion caused by the fact that people outside couldn't really see what we were doing, and everyone tried to crowd in at once. That was straightened out by the chief, however, and measuring proceeded apace, men, women, children, men, women, children. One family at a time filed into the hut through one door, had their measurements taken, and departed through the other door. It was cool and pleasant inside the hut, in contrast to the hot sun and glare outside. Miranda sat off to one side, reading a book, glancing up from time to time, but generally bored by the whole thing.

"Mommy, look!" she exclaimed in mid-morning. "Isn't that an *angel*?" she asked, using our family's code word for a child with Down syndrome. Down syndrome children are often (though not always!) sweet, happy, and affectionate kids, and many families of children with Down syndrome consider them to be special gifts from God and refer to them as angels. I turned and followed the direction of Miranda's gaze. A little girl had just entered the hut, part of a large family with many children. She had a small round head, and all the facial characteristics of a child with Down syndrome—Oriental-shaped eyes with epicanthic folds, a small flat nose, and small ears. There was no mistaking the diagnosis. Her name was Abi, and she was about 4 years old, the same age as Peter.

I knelt in front of the little girl. "Hi there, sweetie," I said in English. "Can I have a hug?" I held out my arms, and she willingly stepped forward and gave me a big hug.

I looked up at her mother. "Do you know that there's something 'different' about this child?" I asked, choosing my words carefully.

"Well, she doesn't talk," said her mother, hesitantly, looking at her husband for confirmation. "That's right," he said. "She's never said a word."

"But she's been healthy?" I asked.

"Yes," the father replied. "She's like the other kids, except she doesn't talk. She's always happy. She never cries. We know she can hear because she does what we tell her to. Why are you so interested in her?"

"Because I know what's the matter with her. I have a son like this." Excitedly, I pulled a picture of Peter out of my bag and showed it to them. They couldn't see any resemblance, though. The difference in skin color swamped the similarities in facial features. But then, Malians think all white people look alike. And it's not true that all kids with Down syndrome look the same. They're "different in the same way," but they look most like their parents and siblings.

"Have you ever met any other children like this?" I inquired, bursting with curiosity about how rural Malian culture dealt with a condition as infrequent as Down syndrome. Children with Down syndrome are rare to begin with, occurring about once in every 700 births. In a community where thirty or forty children are born each year at the most, a child with Down syndrome might be born only once in twenty years. And many of them would not survive long enough for anyone to be able to tell that they were different. Physical defects along the midline of the body (heart, trachea, intestines) are common among kids with Down syndrome; without immediate surgery and neonatal intensive care, many would not survive. Such surgery is routine in American children's hospitals, but nonexistent in rural Mali. For the child without any major physical defects, there are still the perils of rural Malian life to survive: malaria, measles, diarrhea, diphtheria, and polio. Some, like Peter, have poor immune systems, making them even more susceptible to childhood diseases. The odds against finding a child with Down syndrome, surviving and healthy in a rural Malian village, are overwhelming.

Not surprisingly, the parents knew of no other children like Abi. They asked if I knew of any medicine that could cure her. "No," I explained, "this condition can't be cured. But she will learn to talk, just give her time. Talk to her a lot. Try to get her to repeat things you say. And give her lots of love and attention. It may take her longer to learn some things, but keep trying. In my country, some people say these children are special gifts from God." There was no way I could explain cells and chromosomes and nondisjunction to them, even with Moussa's help. And how, I thought to myself, would that have helped them anyway? They just accepted her as she was.

We chatted for a few more minutes, and I measured the whole family, including Abi, who was, of course, short for her age. I gave her one last hug and a balloon and sent her out the door after her siblings. . . .

I walked out of the hut, . . . trying to get my emotions under control. Finally I gave in, hugged my knees close to my chest, and sobbed. I cried for Abi—what a courageous heart she must have; just think what she might have achieved given all the modern infant stimulation programs available in the West. I cried for Peter—another courageous heart; just think of what he might achieve given the chance to live in a culture that simply accepted him, rather than stereotyping and pigeonholing him, constraining him because people didn't think he was capable of more. I cried for myself—not very courageous at all; my heart felt as though it would burst with longing for Peter, my own sweet angel.

There was clearly some truth to the old adage that ignorance is bliss. Maybe pregnant women in Mali had to worry about evil spirits lurking in the latrine at night, but they didn't spend their pregnancies worrying about chromosomal abnormalities, the moral implications of amniocentesis, or the heart-wrenching exercise of trying to evaluate handicaps, deciding which ones made life not worth living. Women in the United States might have the freedom to choose not to give birth to children with handicaps, but women in Mali had freedom from worrying about it. Children in the United States had the freedom to attend special programs to help them overcome their handicaps, but children in Mali had freedom from the biggest handicap of all—other people's prejudice.

I had cried myself dry. I splashed my face with cool water from the bucket inside the kitchen and returned to the task at hand.

Although diseases are generally described in biological terms as understood through scientific investigation, the medical anthropological framework admits that these notions are not universal. Each culture's medical system provides individuals with a map of how to think about themselves in sickness and health, and each system defines specific terms and mechanisms for thinking about, preventing, and managing illness.

Evolutionary Medicine

Evolutionary medicine—an approach to human sickness and health combining principles of evolutionary theory and human evolutionary history—draws from both scientific medicine and anthropology. Although it may seem at first to concentrate on human biological mechanisms, evolutionary medicine emphasizes the biocultural integration characteristic of anthropology: Humans give cultural meaning to biological processes, and cultural practices impact human biology.

As with evolutionary theory in general, it is difficult to prove conclusively that specific ideas and theories from evolutionary medicine are indeed beneficial to human health. Instead, scientists work to amass a sufficient body of knowledge that supports their theories. Where appropriate, the theories can lead to hypotheses that can be tested experimentally. Frequently, treatments derived from evolutionary medicine lead to alterations in cultural practices and to a return to a more natural state in terms of human biology. As described in the Biocultural Connection on Paleolithic prescriptions, evolutionary medicine has contributed to current attitudes about the diseases of civilization.

The work of biological anthropologist James McKenna mentioned in our opening chapter provides an excellent example of evolutionary medicine. McKenna has suggested that the human infant, immature compared to some other mammals, has evolved to co-sleep with adults who provide breathing cues to the sleeping infant, protecting the child from sudden infant death syndrome (SIDS) (McKenna, Ball, & Gettler, 2007). He has used cross-cultural data of sleeping patterns and rates of SIDS to support his claim.

McKenna conducted a series of experiments documenting differences between the brainwave patterns of mother–infant pairs who co-sleep compared to mother–infant pairs who sleep in separate rooms. These data fit McKenna's theory, challenging the cultural practice of solitary sleeping that predominates in North America. Further, McKenna showed how the cultural pattern of sleeping directly impacts infant feeding practices, demonstrating that co-sleeping and breastfeeding are mutually reinforcing behaviors.

Evolutionary medicine suggests that cultural practices in industrial and postindustrial societies promote a variety of other biomedically defined diseases, ranging from psychological disorders to hepatitis (inflammation of the liver).

Symptoms as Defense Mechanisms

Scientists have documented that when faced with infection from a bacterium or virus, the human body mounts a series of physiological responses. For example, as a young individual learns the culture's medical system, the person

evolutionary medicine An approach to human sickness and health combining principles of evolutionary theory and human evolutionary history.

might learn to recognize an illness as a cold or flu by responses of the body, such as fever, aches, runny nose, sore throat, vomiting, or diarrhea.

Think of how you may have learned about sickness as a young child. A caregiver or parent might have touched your forehead or neck with the back of the hand or lips to gauge your temperature. Maybe you had a thermometer placed under your arm, in your mouth, or in your ear to see if you had an elevated temperature or fever. (In the past, young children's temperatures were usually taken rectally in North America.) If any of these methods revealed a temperature above the value defined as normal, a medicine might have been given to lower the fever.

Evolutionary medicine proposes that many of the symptoms that biomedicine treats are themselves nature's treatments developed over millennia. Some of these symptoms, such as fever, perhaps should be tolerated rather than suppressed, so the body can heal itself. An elevated temperature is part of the human body's response to infectious particles, whereas eliminating the fever provides favorable temperatures for bacteria or viruses. Further, within some physiological limits, vomiting, coughing, and diarrhea may be adaptive because they remove harmful substances and organisms from the body. In other words, the cultural prescription to lower a fever or suppress a cough might actually prolong the disease.

Similarly, the nausea and vomiting during early pregnancy may also represent an adaptive mechanism to avoid toxins during this most sensitive phase of fetal development. Many plants, particularly those in the broccoli and cabbage family, naturally contain toxins developed through the plants' evolutionary process to prevent them from being eaten by animals. Eating these plants during the first weeks of pregnancy, when the developing embryo is rapidly creating new cells through mitosis and differentiating into specific body parts, makes the embryo vulnerable to mutation. Therefore, a heightened sense of smell and lowered nausea threshold serve as natural defenses for the body. Pregnant women tend to avoid these foods, thus protecting the developing embryo.

Evolution and Infectious Disease

In a globalizing world where people, viruses, and bacteria cross national boundaries freely, evolutionary medicine provides key insights with regard to infectious disease.

First, if infectious disease is viewed as competition between microorganisms and humans—as it is in biomedicine where patients and doctors "fight" infectious disease—microorganisms possess one very clear advantage (**Figure 12.14**). Viruses, bacteria, fungi, and parasites all have very short life cycles compared to humans. Therefore, when competing on an evolutionary level, they will continue to pose new threats to health because any new genetic variants appearing through a random mutation will quickly become incorporated in the population's

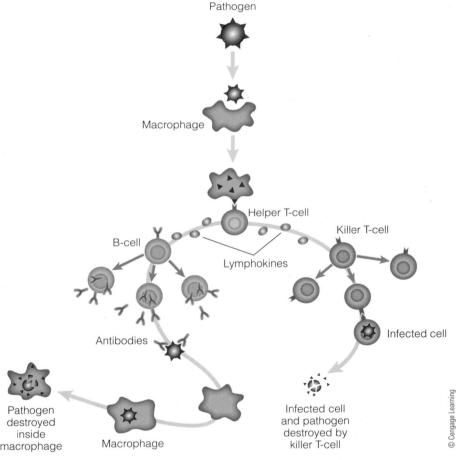

Figure 12.14 The Immune System Biomedical descriptions of the human immune system concentrate on "invading" pathogens, "triggering" the immune response, and "killer T-cells" that destroy the pathogens, as shown in this image introducing the fundamentals of the immune response. Medical anthropologist Emily Martin (1994, 1999) has shown that scientific depictions of infectious disease draw upon violent imagery common to the culture of the United States. Biomedical treatments involve taking antibiotics to kill "invading" organisms adding additional weapons to the "natural" human defenses. An evolutionary perspective suggests that the quick life cycle of microorganisms makes this "battle" a losing proposition for humans.

From *A Positron Named Priscilla: Scientific Discovery at the Frontier*, 1994. Reprinted with permission from National Academies Press, Washington, D.C.

© Cengage Learning

genome. This notion is of particular importance with regard to the use of antibiotics to fight infectious disease.

Although antibiotics do kill many bacteria, increasingly resistant strains are becoming more common. *Resistant strains* refers to genetic variants of a specific bacterium that are not killed by antibiotics. If a resistant strain appears in an infected individual who is being treated with antibiotics, the removal of all the nonresistant strains essentially opens up an entire ecological niche for that resistant strain inside the infected human. Here, without competition from the original form of the bacterium wiped out by the antibiotic, this mutant can proliferate easily and then spread to other individuals. The practice of taking antibiotics artificially alters the environment inside the human body.

In order to avoid the development of resistant strains, complex lengthy treatment regimes, often of multiple drugs, must be followed exactly. These treatments are prohibitively expensive in many parts of the world. The unfortunate result is not only increased human suffering but also the possibility of creating environments for the development of resistant strains as individuals receive partial treatments.

Another problem is that although individuals seek treatment within their own country's health-care system, infectious microbes do not observe national boundaries. To eradicate or control any infectious process, the world has to be considered in its entirety.

Evolutionary process provides a long-term natural mechanism for fighting infectious disease: Those individuals who survive the infection possess genes that provide them with immunity. At times these same genes also have potentially lethal consequences, as seen with the examples of sickle-cell anemia and malaria, cystic fibrosis and cholera, and Tay-Sachs disease and tuberculosis. An interesting recent example of population-based resistance to disease is that of a group of sex workers in Kenya who escape the HIV infection despite constant exposure (Fowke et al., 1996; Songok et al., 2012). This may represent a case of hosts and microbes adjusting to one another through the process of evolution. In order to survive, microbes cannot afford to eliminate all their hosts. Thus, over time a population and a microbe will become balanced, with the host population better able to resist and the microbe less virulent.

One positive note is that treatments can also be allowed to flow freely across the globe. For example, Brazil's HIV/AIDS program is internationally recognized as a model for prevention, education, and treatment for several reasons. Through a national policy of developing alternative generic antiretroviral agents and negotiating for reduced prices on patented agents, in 1996 Brazil became the first country to guarantee free antiretroviral access to all its citizens. At the same time, Brazilian public health officials developed counseling and prevention programs in collaboration with community groups and religious organizations. Their AIDS program's success derives, in part, from the candid public education on disease transmission targeted at heterosexual women and young people, who are now the fastest-growing groups affected by HIV.

In 2004, Brazil continued its innovations with the South to South Initiative providing assistance to the HIV and AIDS programs in the Portuguese-speaking African countries of Mozambique and Angola. These African countries directly replicate the Brazilian approach of providing free antiretroviral agents and collaborating with civil and religious groups to develop appropriate counseling, education, and prevention programs (D'Adesky, 2004).

Vaccines are another method for fighting infectious disease. Vaccines stimulate the body to mount its own immune response that will protect the individual from the real infectious agent if the individual is exposed at a later date. Vaccinations have been responsible for major global reduction of disease, as in the case of smallpox.

Historical records show that people in Asia, Africa, Europe, and the colonizers of North America practiced a form of vaccination for this deadly disease through what were known as "pox parties." Parents in recent years have revived this tradition, deliberately exposing their children to chicken pox rather than opt for the vaccine.

Despite numerous medical reports to the contrary, some parents believe that vaccinations may lead to other health problems. Although the vaccine to eradicate smallpox—a disease that killed 300 million people in the 20th century alone—is clearly beneficial, it is harder to convince parents of the need for vaccines for less fatal, although still serious, childhood diseases. But opting out has had grim consequences: The rates of pertussis (whooping cough) have reached epidemic proportions in some parts of the United States, and other regions are not far behind. The pertussis problem has become so severe that a booster for it is now routinely added to tetanus shots.

Vaccinations, like all medical procedures, change the social fabric. The vaccine for chicken pox in the United States provides an interesting case in point. Before this vaccination became standard care, most American children experienced chicken pox as a rite of childhood. Parents watched their children become covered with ugly poxes that then disappeared. This experience modeled for parents that intense sickness can be followed by full recovery, which, in and of itself, can provide some comfort. Only extremely rarely is chicken pox fatal.

Infectious disease and the human efforts to stop it always occur in the context of the human-made environment. Humans have been altering their external environments with increasing impact since the Neolithic revolution, resulting in an increase in a variety of infectious diseases. In this regard, evolutionary medicine shares much with political ecology—a discipline closely related to medical anthropology and described next.

The Political Ecology of Disease

An ecological perspective considers organisms in the context of their environment. Because human environments are shaped not only by local culture but by global political and economic systems, these features must all be included in a comprehensive examination of human disease. Simply describing disease in terms of biological processes leaves out the deeper, ultimate reasons that some individuals are likelier than others to become sick. A strictly biological approach also leaves out differences in the resources available to individuals, communities, and states to cope with disease and illness. Prion diseases provide excellent illustrations of the impact of local and global factors on the social distribution of disease.

Prion Diseases

In 1997 physician-scientist Stanley Prusiner won the Nobel Prize in medicine for his discovery of an entirely new disease agent called a **prion**—a protein lacking any genetic material that behaves as an infectious particle. Prions are a kind of protein that can cause the reorganization and destruction of other proteins, which may result in neurodegenerative disease as brain tissue and the nervous system are destroyed.

This discovery provided a mechanism for understanding mad cow disease, a serious problem in postindustrial societies. But knowing the biological mechanism alone is not enough to truly grasp how this disease spreads. The beef supply of several countries in Europe and North America became tainted by prions introduced through the cultural practice of grinding up sheep carcasses and adding them to the commercial feed of beef cattle. This practice began before prions were discovered, but postindustrial farmers were aware that these sheep had a condition known as *scrapie*; they just did not know that this condition was infectious. Through the wide distribution of tainted feed, prion disease spread from sheep to cows, and then to humans who consumed tainted beef. Today, countries without confirmed mad cow disease ban the importation of beef from neighboring countries with documented prion disease. Such bans have a tremendous negative impact on the local economies.

Mad cow disease is not new. This type of disease was a major concern for the Fore (pronounced "foray") people of Papua New Guinea during the middle of the 20th century. The Fore gave the name *kuru* to the prion disease that claimed the lives of great numbers of women and children in their communities. To deal with the devastation, the Fore welcomed assistance provided by an international team of health workers led by a physician from the United States, Carleton Gajdusek. As with mad cow disease, local

and global cultural processes affected both the transmission of kuru and the measures taken to prevent its spread long before prion biology was understood.

Kuru did not fit neatly into any known biomedical categories. Because the disease seemed to be limited to families of related individuals, cultural anthropologists Shirley Lindenbaum from Australia and Robert Glasse from the United States, who were doing fieldwork in the region, were recruited to contribute documentation of Fore kinship relationships. It was hoped this knowledge would reveal an underlying genetic mechanism for the disease.

When kinship records did not reveal a pattern of genetic transmission, the medical team turned instead to the notion of infectious disease, even though the slow progression of kuru seemed to weigh against an infectious cause. Material derived from infected individuals was injected into chimpanzees (recall Chapter 4's discussion of the ethics of this practice) to see whether they developed the disease. After 18 months, injected chimpanzees succumbed to the classic symptoms of kuru, and their autopsied brains indicated the same pathologies as seen in humans with kuru. At this point, the disease was defined as infectious (garnering Gajdusek a Nobel Prize). Because prions had not yet been discovered, scientists defined this infectious agent as an unidentified "slow virus."

Scientists knew that kuru is infectious, but they still did not understand why some individuals were infected but not others. The explanation requires a wider anthropological perspective, as Lindenbaum explains in her book *Kuru Sorcery*. Lindenbaum demonstrates that kuru is related to cultural practices regarding the bodies of individuals who have died from kuru and the way global factors impacted local practices.

Culturally, Fore women are responsible for preparing the bodies of their loved ones for the afterlife. This practice alone put women at a greater risk for exposure to kuru. Lindenbaum also discovered that women and children were at risk due to a combination of these local practices with global economic forces. In Fore society, men were responsible for raising pigs and slaughtering and distributing meat. The middle of the 20th century was a time of hardship and transition for the Fore people. Colonial rule by Australia had changed the fabric of

---

prion An infectious protein lacking any genetic material but capable of causing the reorganization and destruction of other proteins.

society, threatening traditional subsistence patterns and resulting in a shortage of protein in the form of pigs. Fore men preferentially distributed the limited amount of pig meat available to other men.

Fore women told Lindenbaum that, as a practical solution to their hunger, they consumed their own dead. Fore women preferred eating their loved ones who had died in a relatively "meaty" state from kuru compared to eating individuals wasted away from malnutrition. This temporary practice was abandoned as the Fore subsistence pattern recovered, and the Fore learned of the biological mechanisms of kuru transmission.

Medical Pluralism

The Fore medical system had its own explanations for the causes of kuru, primarily involving sorcery, that were compatible with biomedical explanations for the mechanisms of disease. Such blending of medical systems is common throughout the globe today.

Medical pluralism refers to the practice of multiple medical systems, each with its own techniques and beliefs, in a single society. As illustrated with the Fore, individuals generally can reconcile conflicting medical systems and incorporate diverse elements from a variety of systems to ease their suffering. Although Western biomedicine has contributed some spectacular treatments and cures for a variety of diseases, many of its practices and values are singularly associated with the European and North American societies in which they developed. The international public health movement attempts to bring many of the successes of biomedicine based on the scientific understanding of human biology to the rest of the world. But to do so successfully, local cultural practices and beliefs must be taken into account.

Both mad cow disease and kuru illustrate that no sickness in the 21st century can be considered in isolation; an understanding of these diseases must take into account political and economic influences as well as how these forces affect the ability to treat or cure.

Globalization, Health, and Structural Violence

One generalization that can be made with regard to most diseases is that wealth means health. In 1948, the World Health Organization defined *health* as "a complete state of physical, mental, and social well-being and not merely

the absence of disease or infirmity," a definition that has never been amended (World Health Organization, 1948). While the international public health community works to improve health throughout the globe, heavily armed states, megacorporations, and very wealthy elites are using their powers to rearrange the emerging world system to their own competitive advantage. When such power relationships undermine the well-being of others, we are witnessing the *structural violence* we discussed in Chapter 11.

Health disparities, or differences in the health status between the wealthy elite and the poor in stratified societies, are nothing new. Globalization has expanded and intensified structural violence, leading to enormous health disparities among individuals, communities, and even states. Medical anthropologists have examined how structural violence leads not only to unequal access to treatment but also to the likelihood of contracting disease through exposure to malnutrition, crowded conditions, and toxins.

Population Size and Health

At the time of the speciation events of early human evolutionary history, population size was extraordinarily small compared to what it is today. With human population size at over 7 billion and still climbing, we are reaching the carrying capacity of the earth (Figure 12.15). India and China alone have well over 1 billion inhabitants each. And population growth is still rapid in South Asia, which will become even more densely populated in the 21st century. Population growth threatens to increase the scale of hunger, poverty, and pollution—and the many problems associated with these issues.

Although human population growth must be curtailed, government-sponsored programs to do so have posed new problems. For example, China's much-publicized "one child" policy, introduced in 1979 to control its soaring population growth, led to sharp upward trends in sex-selective abortions, female infanticide, and female infant mortality due to abandonment and neglect. The resulting imbalance in China's male and female populations is referred to as the "missing girl gap." One study reported that China's male-to-female ratio has become so distorted that 111 million men would not be able to find a wife. Government regulations softened slightly in the 1990s, when it became legal for rural couples to have a second child if their first was a girl—and if they paid a fee. Millions of rural couples have circumvented regulations by not registering births—resulting in millions of young people who do not officially exist (Bongaarts, 1998).

But human cultures adapt and change. Some rural families in northeastern China have instead chosen to have only one daughter, reshaping the culture's gender norms (Shi, 2009).

---

medical pluralism The practice of multiple medical systems, each with its own techniques and beliefs, in a single society.

health disparity A difference in the health status between the wealthy elite and the poor in stratified societies.

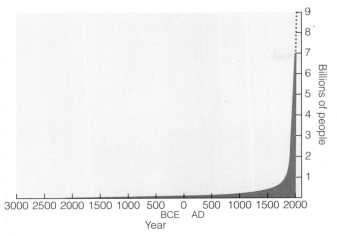

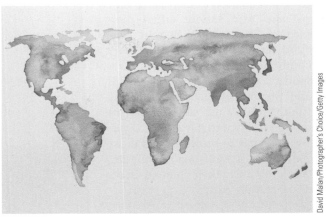

Figure 12.15 **World Population** Human population size grew at a relatively steady pace until the industrial revolution, when a geometric pattern of growth began. Since that time, human population size has been doubling at an alarming rate. The earth's natural resources will not be able to accommodate the ever-increasing human population if the rates of consumption seen in Western industrialized nations, particularly in the United States, persist. Notice, as well, that human populations are not distributed evenly across the globe; the highest concentrations are in urban centers and regions with fertile land. Climatic extremes and lack of natural resources like water characterize the sparsely populated areas, such as the Sahara Desert and Greenland.

Poverty and Health

With an ever-expanding population, a shocking number of people worldwide face hunger on a regular basis, leading to a variety of health problems including premature death. It is no accident that poor countries and poorer citizens of wealthier countries are disproportionately malnourished. All told, about 1 billion people in the world are undernourished. Some 7.6 million children age 5 and under die every year due to hunger, and those who survive often suffer from physical and mental impairment (World Health Organization, 2012).

In wealthy industrialized countries, obesity, a particular version of malnourishment, is becoming increasingly common (**Figure 12.16**). Obesity primarily affects poor working-class people who are no longer physically active

VISUAL COUNTERPOINT

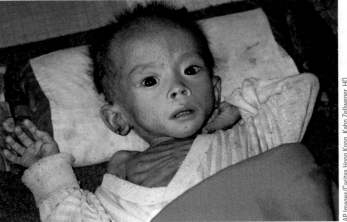

Figure 12.16 **Extremes of Malnutrition** The scientific definition of *malnutrition* includes undernutrition as well as excess consumption of foods, healthy or otherwise. Malnutrition leading to obesity is increasingly common among poor working-class people in industrialized countries. Obesity and Type 2 diabetes, previously degenerative diseases of adulthood only, now occur at alarming rates among children in the United States. Starvation is more common in poor countries or in those facing years of political turmoil, as is evident in this emaciated North Korean child.

at their work (because of increasing automation) and who cannot afford more expensive, healthy foods to stay fit. High sugar and fat content of mass-marketed foods and "super-sized" portions underlie this dramatic change. Obesity also greatly increases the risk of diabetes, heart disease, and stroke. High rates of obesity among American youth have led U.S. public health officials to project that the current generation of adults may be the first generation to outlive their children due to a cause other than war.

Environmental Impact and Health

Just as the disenfranchised experience a disproportionate share of famine and associated death, this same population also must contend with the lion's share of contaminants and pollution (Figure 12.17). The industries of wealthier communities and states create the majority of the pollutants that are changing the earth today. Yet those who do not have the resources to consume and thus pollute the earth at high rates often feel the impact of these pollutants most keenly.

For example, increasing emissions of greenhouse gases, as a consequence of deforestation and human industrial activity, have resulted in global warming. As the carbon emissions from the combustion of petroleum in wealthy nations warm the climate globally, the impact will be most severe for individuals in the tropics because these populations must contend with increases in deadly infectious diseases such as malaria.

Experts predict that global warming will lead to an expansion of the geographic ranges of tropical diseases and to an increase in the incidence of respiratory diseases due to additional smog caused by warmer temperatures. Similarly, the summer of 2012 included record heat waves, fires, and fatalities. To solve the problem of global warming, our species needs to evolve new cultural tools in order to anticipate environmental consequences that eventuate over decades. Regulating human population size globally and using the earth's resources more conservatively are necessary to ensure our survival.

© Ian Berry/Magnum Photos

Figure 12.17 **Ship-Breakers** For wages of about a dollar a day, workers at the ship-breaking yards of Bangladesh risk their health if not their lives as they toil in conditions of extreme heat, humidity, and exposure to a wide variety of toxins. Here, the large rusty tankers that have transported everything from crude oil to passengers throughout the globe are broken apart for recycling in an area that was pristine beach just decades ago. Workers dismember these ships by hand and are often barefoot; they have very little in the way of protective gear. Explosions and other accidents kill on average one worker a week. The long-term effects of toxins from the ships set other disease processes in motion. Some individuals might possess genotypes that can better process the toxins (comparable to the 90-year-old who has smoked two packs of cigarettes a day for over seventy years). And over time a population might become better able to tolerate these poisons through the process of biological adaptation. But in this case, a cultural solution—environmental regulation of the ship-breaking process—would protect these workers and our oceans and beaches and is a requirement for our collective human survival. As well, our global health requires addressing the social justice issues inherent in poor countries taking on the health burden of privileges enjoyed by the wealthy.

Global warming is merely one of a host of problems today that will ultimately have an impact on human gene pools. In view of the consequences for human biology of seemingly benign innovations such as dairying or farming (as discussed in Chapter 9), we may wonder about many recent practices—for example, the effects of increased exposure to radiation from use of x-rays, nuclear accidents, production of radioactive waste, ozone depletion (which increases human exposure to solar radiation), and the like.

Again the impact is often most severe for those who have not generated the pollutants in the first place. Take, for example, the flow of industrial and agricultural chemicals via air and water currents to Arctic regions. Icy temperatures allow these toxins to enter the food chain. As a result toxins generated in temperate climates end up in the bodies (and breast milk) of Arctic peoples who do not produce the toxins but who eat primarily foods that they hunt and fish.

In addition to exposure to radiation, humans also face increased exposure to other known mutagenic agents, including a wide variety of chemicals, such as pesticides. Despite repeated assurances about their safety, there have been tens of thousands of cases of poisonings in the United States alone and thousands of cases of cancer related to the manufacture and use of pesticides. The impact may be greater in so-called underdeveloped countries, where substances banned in the United States are routinely used.

Pesticides are responsible for millions of birds being killed each year (which would have been happily gobbling down bugs and other pests), serious fish kills, and decimation of honeybees (bees are needed for the efficient pollination of many crops). In all, pesticides alone (not including other agricultural chemicals) are responsible for billions of dollars of environmental and public health damage in the United States each year. Anthropologists document the effects on individuals, as described in the Biocultural Connection feature.

The shipping of pollutant waste between countries represents an example of structural violence. Individuals in the government or business sector of either nation may profit from these arrangements, creating another obstacle to addressing the problem. Similar issues may arise within countries, when authorities attempt to coerce ethnic minorities to accept disposal of toxic waste on their lands.

In particular, hormone-disrupting chemicals raise serious concerns because they interfere with the reproductive process. For example, in 1938 a synthetic estrogen known as DES (diethylstilbestrol) was developed and subsequently prescribed for a variety of ailments ranging from acne to prostate cancer. Moreover, DES was routinely added to animal feed. But, in 1971 researchers realized that DES causes vaginal cancer in young women. Subsequent studies have shown that DES causes problems with the male reproductive system and can produce deformities of the female reproductive tract of individuals exposed to DES in utero. DES mimics the natural hormone, binding with appropriate receptors in and on cells, and thereby turns on biological activity associated with the hormone (Colborn, Dumanoski, & Myers, 1996).

DES is not alone in its effects: Scientists have identified at least fifty-one chemicals—many of them in common use—that disrupt hormones, and even this could be the tip of the iceberg. Some of these chemicals mimic estrogens in the manner of DES, whereas others interfere with other parts of the endocrine system, such as thyroid and testosterone metabolism. The list includes such supposedly benign and inert substances as plastics widely used in laboratories and chemicals added to polystyrene and polyvinyl chloride (PVCs) to make them more stable and less breakable. These plastics are widely used in plumbing, food processing, and food packaging.

In addition, many detergents and personal care products, contraceptive creams, the giant jugs used to bottle drinking water, and plastic linings in cans contain hormone-disrupting chemicals. Plastics line about 85 percent of food cans in the United States. Similarly, after years of plastics use in microwave ovens, the deleterious health consequences of the release of compounds from plastic wrap and plastic containers during microwaving have come to light. Most concerning is bisphenol-A (BPA)—a chemical widely used in the manufacturing of water bottles and baby bottles (hard plastics). Researchers have documented an association between BPA and higher rates of chronic diseases such as heart disease and diabetes. It also disrupts a variety of other reproductive and metabolic processes. Infants and fetuses are at the greatest risk from exposure to BPA.

Consensus in the scientific community has led governments to start taking action (the Canadian government declared BPA a toxic compound). However, removing this compound from the food industry may be easier than ridding the environment of this contaminant. For decades billions of pounds of BPA have been produced each year, and in turn it has been dumped into landfills and into bodies of water. As with the Neolithic revolution and the development of civilization, each invention creates new challenges for humans.

The Future of *Homo sapiens*

One of the difficulties with managing environmental and toxic health risks is that serious consequences of new cultural practices often do not appear until years or even decades later. By then, of course, the cultural system has fully absorbed these practices, and huge financial interests function to keep them there. Today, cultural practices, probably as never before, impact human gene pools. The long-term effects on the human species as a whole remain to be seen, but as with disease today, poor people and people of color will bear a disproportionate burden for these practices.

BIOCULTURAL CONNECTION

Picturing Pesticides

The toxic effects of pesticides have long been known. After all, these compounds are designed to kill bugs. However, documenting the toxic effects of pesticides on humans has been more difficult, because they are subtle—sometimes taking years to become apparent.

Anthropologist Elizabeth Guillette, working in a Yaqui Indian community in Mexico, combined ethnographic observation, biological monitoring of pesticide levels in the blood, and neurobehavioral testing to document the impairment of child development by pesticides.[a] Working with colleagues from the Technological Institute of Sonora in Obregón, Mexico, Guillette compared children and families from two Yaqui communities: one living in a valley farm who was exposed to large doses of pesticides and one living in a ranching village in the foothills nearby.

Guillette documented the frequency of pesticide use among the farming Yaqui to be forty-five times per crop cycle with two crop cycles per year. In the farming valleys she also noted that families tended to use household bug sprays on a daily basis, thus increasing their exposure to toxic pesticides. In the foothill ranches, she found that the only pesticides that the Yaqui were exposed to consisted of DDT sprayed by the government to control malaria. In these communities, indoor bugs were swatted or tolerated.

Pesticide exposure was linked to child health and development through two sets of measures. First, levels of pesticides in the blood of valley children at birth and throughout their childhood were examined and found to be far higher than in the children from the foothills. Further, the presence of pesticides in breast milk of nursing mothers from the valley farms was also documented.

Second, children from the two communities were asked to perform a variety of normal childhood activities, such as jumping, memory games, playing catch, and drawing pictures. The children exposed to high doses of pesticides had significantly less stamina, eye–hand coordination, large motor coordination, and drawing ability compared to the Yaqui children from the foothills. These children exhibited no overt symptoms of pesticide poisoning—instead exhibiting delays and impairment in their neurobehavioral abilities that may be irreversible.

Though Guillette's study was thoroughly embedded in one ethnographic community, she emphasizes that the exposure to pesticides among the Yaqui farmers is typical of agricultural communities globally and has significance for changing human practices regarding the use of pesticides everywhere.

BIOCULTURAL QUESTION

Given the documented developmental damage these pesticides have inflicted on children, should their sale and use be regulated globally? Are there potentially damaging toxins in use in your community?

---

[a]Guillette, E. A., et al. (1998, June). An anthropological approach to the evaluation of preschool children exposed to pesticides in Mexico. *Environmental Health Perspectives* 106(6), 347–353. Courtesy of Dr. Elizabeth A. Guillette.

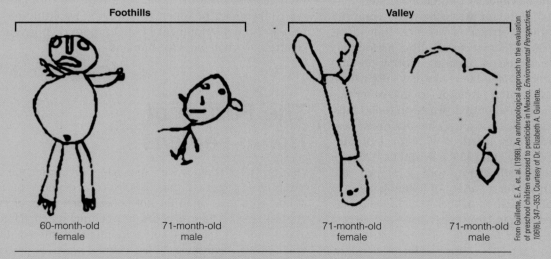

Foothills		Valley	
60-month-old female	71-month-old male	71-month-old female	71-month-old male

From Guillette, E. A. et. al. (1998). An anthropological approach to the evaluation of preschool children exposed to pesticides in Mexico. *Environmental Perspectives, 106(6), 347–353.* Courtesy of Dr. Elizabeth A. Guillette.

Compare the drawings typically done by Yaqui children heavily exposed to pesticides (*right, valley*) to those made by Yaqui children living in nearby areas who were relatively unexposed (*left, foothills*).

Further, with globalization, the values of wealthy consumers living in industrialized countries have spread to the inhabitants of poorer and developing countries, influencing their expectations and dreams. Of course, a luxurious standard of living requires a disproportionate share of the earth's limited resources. Instead of globalizing a standard of living that the world's natural resources cannot meet, it is time for all of humanity to use today's global connections to learn how to live within the carrying capacity of the earth (**Figure 12.18**).

We are a social species with origins on the African continent over 5 million years ago. Over the course of our evolutionary history, we came to inhabit the entire globe. From cities, to deserts, to mountaintops, to grassy plains, to rich tropical forests, human cultures in these varied places became distinct from one another. In each environment, human groups devised their own specific beliefs and practices to meet the challenges of survival. In the future, dramatic changes in cultural values will be required if our species is to thrive. "New, improved" values might, for example, include a worldview that sees humanity as *part of* the world, rather than as *master over* it, as it is in many of the world's cultures today. Included, too, might be a sense of social responsibility that recognizes and affirms respect among ethnic groups as well as our collective stewardship of the earth we inhabit.

Our continued survival will depend on our ability to cultivate positive social connections among all kinds of people and to recognize the ways we impact one another in a world interconnected by the forces of globalization. Together, we can use the adaptive faculty of culture, the hallmark of our species, to ensure our continued survival.

Lok Samiti (translation: People's Committee) of Mehdiganj, India. Photograph by Nandal Master

Figure 12.18 Water Troubles Women in Mehdiganj, India, hold water urns called *gharas* with the words "Water Is Life" written on them to protest the nearby Coca-Cola bottling plant. Because the plant uses up the local water, nearby farmers lose their livelihood and way of life. In a competition for resources such as this, global corporations like Coca-Cola have advantages over local inhabitants.

CHAPTER CHECKLIST

What biological mechanisms allow humans to adapt to a variety of environments?

● Genetic adaptations such as shorter limbs and stocky build for colder climates and long linear builds for hotter climates have developed in regions where continuous experience over generations has allowed for reproductive selection of such traits.

● Developmental adaption in response to an individual's environment occurs over the growth stages of life to shape gene expression in the way that best suits that individual to that specific environment.

● Developmental adaptations become permanent parts of an individual's phenotype, but they are not encoded directly into the genome and therefore do not get passed on directly to the next generation. Examples include growth stunting due to malnutrition, and the increased number of sweat glands in hot environments.

● Physiological adaptation allows the body to accustom itself to environmental stressors, such as low partial pressure of oxygen at high altitude or extremes of temperature.

● Individuals first experience short-term physiological responses that cannot be sustained indefinitely. *Acclimatization* refers to reversible long-term adaptations in the form of modulation of ongoing bodily processes such as metabolism rates or hemoglobin production.

● The human biological adaption cannot keep pace with the environmental changes impacting global environments today.

What are medical systems, and how do they vary across cultures?

● Medical systems are the idea patterns and practices relating to illness. Medical anthropologists study them cross-culturally, including western biomedicine.

● Medical systems globally are all alike in that they include a healer who possesses specialized, restricted knowledge from which others are excluded. Where multiple medical systems coexist (medical pluralism), individuals freely use what works from the various systems in order to alleviate their suffering.

● Medical systems define whether a given pathophysiological state (a disease) will be defined as an illness. For example, in regions where schistosomiasis is endemic, it may not be considered an illness. Without access to costly medicine or parasite free water, people tolerate a moderate parasite load.

What health hazards are attributable to the global political economy and population size?

● Privileged states, corporations, and individuals maintain systems that exercise structural violence upon the poor worldwide resulting in an unequal distribution of disease.

● Hunger and obesity both impact poor communities and cause chronic health problems and early mortality.

● Environmental contaminants such as carcinogenic pesticides and plastics or byproducts created by wealthier communities also affect the poor disproportionately.

● The effects of global warming, largely caused by pollution from industries to supply rich nations, will increase the incidence of tropical disease.

● With a global human population of over seven billion and rising, the carrying capacity of the earth may soon max out. Wealthy nations use a disproportionate portion of resources.

How have humans responded to the widening array of health threats?

● Evolutionary medicine emphasizes the importance of a body's natural responses to disease and recreation of lifestyle conditions that led to our current evolutionary state as methods of health care.

● Western scientific medicine has effectively introduced pharmaceutical and procedural innovation to fight pathogens, but it often ignores deeper reasons for the causes of sickness and the levels of resource availability in other communities.

● Analysis of the political and economic causes of sickness has led to successful treatment and prevention of diseases such as AIDS, kuru, and mad cow disease.

● Recognition of the political and economic causes of disease can lead to cooperation on global health issues with the effect of mitigating suffering worldwide.

QUESTIONS FOR REFLECTION

1. If you were to create a body map of yourself, what would you include to show aspects of your biology, health, and your place in the global political economy?

2. The anthropological distinction between illness and disease provides a way to separate biological states from cultural elaborations given to those biological states. Can you think of some examples of illness without disease and disease without illness?

3. What do you think of the notion of letting a fever run its course instead of taking a medicine to lower it? Do these prescriptions suggested by evolutionary medicine run counter to your own medical beliefs and practices?

4. Are there any examples in your experience of how the growth process or human reproductive physiology helped you adapt to environmental stressors? Does this ability help humans from an evolutionary perspective?

5. Do you see examples of structural violence in your community that make some individuals more vulnerable to disease than others?

ONLINE STUDY RESOURCES

CourseMate

Access chapter-specific learning tools, including learning objectives, practice quizzes, videos, flash cards, glossaries, and more in your Anthropology CourseMate.

Log into **www.cengagebrain.com** to access the resources your instructor has assigned and to purchase materials.

Challenge Issue

Born naked and speechless, humans are naturally incapable of surviving without culture—a socially learned adaptive system designed to help us meet our challenges of survival. Each culture is distinct, expressing its unique qualities in numerous ways, including the way we speak, what we eat, the clothes we wear, and with whom we live. Although culture goes far beyond what meets the eye, it is inscribed everywhere we look. Here we see a family of Kuchi ("migrant") herders in northeast Afghanistan. Because mobility is a key element in their successful adaptation to an arid environment, nearly everything they own is movable. Coming from different ethnic groups, Kuchi do not all share the same language. The particular fabrics, forms, and colors of their belongings and apparel mark their cultural identity. Many Kuchi have recently settled down, but about 1.5 million are still fully nomadic, with livelihoods dependent upon herds of goats and sheep. Using camels and donkeys to carry their belongings, this family follows age-old migration routes across mountains and valleys. They exchange their surplus animal products—meat, hides, wool, hair, *ghee* (butter), and *quroot* (dried yoghurt)—for wheat, sugar, salt, metal and plastic tools, and other trade goods. Ecological adaptation and symbolic expression of group identity are among the many interrelated functions of culture.

Characteristics of Culture

13

An introductory anthropology course presents what may seem like an endless variety of human societies, each with its own distinctive way of life, manners, beliefs, arts, and so on. Yet for all this diversity, these societies have one thing in common: Each is a group of human beings cooperating to ensure their collective survival and well-being.

Group living and cooperation are impossible unless individuals know how others are likely to behave in any given situation. Thus, some degree of predictable behavior is required of each person within the society. In humans, it is culture that sets the limits of behavior and guides it along predictable paths that are generally acceptable to those within the culture. The culturally specified ways in which we learn to act so that we conform to the social expectations in our community did not develop randomly. Among the major forces guiding how each culture has developed in its own distinctive way is a process known as adaptation.

Culture and Adaptation

From generation to generation, humans, like all animals, have continuously faced the challenge of adapting to their environment, its conditions and its resources, as well as to changes over time. The term **adaptation** refers to a gradual process by which organisms adjust to the conditions of the locality in which they live. Organisms have generally adapted biologically as the frequency of advantageous anatomical and physiological features increases in a population through the process of natural selection. For example, body hair protects mammals from extremes of temperature, specialized teeth help them to procure the kinds of food they need, and so on. Short-term physiological responses to the environment—along with responses that become incorporated into an organism through interaction with the environment during growth and development—are other kinds of biological adaptations.

adaptation A series of beneficial adjustments to a particular environment.

IN THIS CHAPTER YOU WILL LEARN TO

- Explain culture as a dynamic form of adaptation.

- Distinguish between culture, society, and ethnicity.

- Identify basic characteristics common to all cultures.

- Describe the connection among culture, society, and the individual.

- Define and critique *ethnocentrism*.

Marcus Fornell

Figure 13.1 **A Living Bridge** This bridge in Meghalaya, India, is made of the roots of living strangler fig trees (*Ficus elastica*). Meghalaya ("Abode of the Clouds") is the wettest place on earth with an average rainfall of some 40 feet a year. Nearly all of the rain is during the summer monsoon season, turning rivers and streams into raging torrents. The tangled roots of strangler figs help keep riverbanks from washing away, and the Khazi people living in this region train the roots into living bridges. Shaping a bridge is an epic project that cannot be accomplished in a single lifetime. From one generation to the next, individuals pass on the knowledge of how to guide and connect the hanging roots so they grow into a strong bridge. Dozens of these bridges form part of an essential and complex network of forest paths connecting the valleys of Meghalaya. Some of them are many centuries old.

Humans, however, have increasingly come to depend on **cultural adaptation**, a complex of ideas, technologies, and activities that enables them to survive and even thrive in their environment. Biology has not provided people with built-in fur coats to protect them in cold climates, but it has given us the ability to make our own coats, build fires, and construct shelters to shield ourselves against the cold. We may not be able to run as fast as a cheetah, but we are able to invent and build vehicles that can carry us faster and farther than any other creature.

Through culture and its many constructions, the human species has secured not just its survival but its expansion as well—at great cost to other species and, increasingly, to the planet at large. And by manipulating environments through cultural means, people have been able to move into a vast range of environments, from the icy Arctic to the searing Sahara Desert to the rainiest place on earth in northeast India (**Figure 13.1**).

This is not to say that everything human beings do is *because* it is adaptive to a particular environment. For one thing, people do not just react to an environment as given; rather, they react to it as they perceive it, and different groups may perceive the same environment in radically different ways. People also react to things other than the environment: their own biological traits, their beliefs and attitudes, and the short- and long-term consequences of their behavior for themselves and other people and life forms that share their habitats.

---

cultural adaptation A complex of ideas, technologies, and activities that enables people to survive and even thrive in their environment.

Figure 13.2 **Center-Pivot Irrigation** What is adaptive at one time may not be at another. In the Central Plains of North America, irrigation systems and chemical fertilizers have resulted in large but unsustainable crop yields in a principal region of grain cultivation. Here we see crop fields in western Kansas that are watered by a center-pivot irrigation system fed by the Ogallala aquifer. The aquifer, which underlies eight states from southern South Dakota to northwestern Texas, provides about 30 percent of the nation's groundwater used for irrigation, plus drinking water to 82 percent of the people who live within the aquifer boundary. However, over the past five decades, the aquifer's water table has dropped dramatically, and some experts estimate it will dry up in as little as two decades. Moreover, in semi-arid regions steady winds hasten evaporation of surface water. This leads to a buildup of salts in the soil, eventually resulting in toxic levels for plants. Chemical fertilizers also contribute to the pollution problem.

Although people maintain cultures to deal with problems, some cultural practices have proved to be inadequate or ill-fitting, sometimes creating new problems—such as toxic air and water resulting from certain industrial practices and a growing worldwide obesity epidemic spurred on by fast food, spectator sports, motorized transport, electronic media, and other technologies reducing people's physical activity.

A further complication is the relativity of any particular adaptation: What is adaptive in one setting may be seriously maladaptive in another. For example, the hygiene practices of food-foraging peoples—their habits of garbage and human waste disposal—are appropriate to contexts of low population densities, a degree of residential mobility, and organic materials. But these same practices become serious health hazards in large, fully sedentary populations such as urban slums without space to dump (in)disposable waste, including plastic and chemicals. In fact, with almost 4 billion people living in cities, waste management is turning into a huge challenge in many parts of the world.

Similarly, behavior that is adaptive in the short run may be maladaptive over a longer period of time. For instance, the development of irrigation in ancient

Mesopotamia (southern Iraq) made it possible for people to increase food production, but it also caused a gradual accumulation of salt in the soil, which contributed to the downfall of that civilization about 4,000 years ago. Similar situations exist in parts of the United States today (**Figure 13.2**).

Today, in many parts of the world the development of prime farmland for purposes other than food production increases dependency on food raised in less than optimal environments. Marginal farmlands can produce high yields with costly technology. However, over time these yields will not be sustainable due to loss of topsoil, increasing salinity of soil, and silting of irrigation works, not to mention the high cost of fresh water and fossil fuel.

All told, for any culture to be successful across generations, it must produce collective human behavior that does not destroy its natural environment. Successful adaptation has been, and continues to be, a major challenge facing every society in its long-term quest for survival. In response to this challenge, our species has developed a great variety of cultures, each with its own unique features befitting the particular needs of societies located in different corners of the globe. So, what do we mean by *culture*?

The Concept of Culture

Anthropologists conceived the modern concept of culture toward the end of the 19th century. The first comprehensive definition came from the British anthropologist Sir Edward Tylor. Writing in 1871, he defined *culture* as "that complex whole which includes knowledge, belief, art, law, morals, custom, and any other capabilities and habits acquired by man as a member of society" (Tylor, 1871, p. 1).

Recent definitions tend to distinguish more clearly between actual behavior and the abstract ideas, values, feelings, and perceptions of the world that inform that behavior. To put it another way, **culture** goes deeper than observable behavior; it is a society's shared and socially transmitted ideas, values, emotions, and perceptions that are used to make sense of experience, generate behavior, and are reflected in that behavior.

Characteristics of Culture

Through the comparative study of many human cultures, past and present, anthropologists have gained an understanding of the basic characteristics evident in all of them: Every culture is socially learned, shared, based on symbols, integrated, and dynamic. A careful study of these characteristics helps us to see the importance and the function of culture itself.

Culture Is Learned

All culture is socially learned rather than biologically inherited. One learns one's culture by growing up with it, and the process whereby culture is passed on from one generation to the next is called **enculturation** (Figure 13.3).

Most animals eat and drink whenever the urge arises. Humans, however, are enculturated to do most of their eating and drinking at certain culturally prescribed times and feel hungry as those times approach. These eating times vary from culture to culture, as does what is eaten, how it is prepared, how it is consumed, and where. To add complexity, food is used to do more than merely satisfy nutritional requirements. When used to celebrate rituals and religious activities, as it often is, food "establishes relationships of give and take, of cooperation, of sharing, of an emotional bond that is universal" (Caroulis, 1996, p. 16).

Through enculturation every person learns socially appropriate ways of satisfying the basic biologically determined needs of all humans: food, sleep, shelter, companionship, self-defense, and sexual gratification. It is important to distinguish between the needs themselves, which are not learned, and the learned ways in which they are satisfied—for each culture determines in its own way how these needs will be met. For instance, a French Canadian fisherman's idea of a great dinner and a comfortable way to sleep may vary greatly from that of a Kazakh nomad in Mongolia.

Most, if not all, mammals exhibit some degree of learned behavior. Several species may even be said to have elementary culture, in that local populations share patterns of behavior that, as among humans, each generation learns from the one before and that differ from one population to another. For example, research shows a distinctive pattern of behavior among lions of southern Africa's Kalahari Desert—behavior that fostered nonaggressive interaction with the region's indigenous hunters and gatherers and that each generation of lions passed on to the next. Moreover, Kalahari lion culture changed over a thirty-year period in response to new circumstances (Thomas, 1994). That said, it is important to note that not all learned behavior is cultural. For instance, a pigeon may learn tricks, but this behavior is reflexive, the result of conditioning by repeated training, not the product of enculturation.

Beyond our species, examples of socially learned behavior are particularly evident among other primates. An example of this is the way a chimpanzee will take a twig, strip it of all leaves, and smooth it down to fashion a tool for extracting termites from their nest. Such toolmaking, which juveniles learn from their elders, is unquestionably a form of cultural behavior once thought to be exclusively human. In Japan, macaque monkeys have learned the advantages of washing sweet potatoes before eating them and passed the practice on to the next generation.

Within any given primate species, one population's way of life often differs from that of others, just as it does among humans. We have discovered both in captivity and in the wild that primates in general and apes in particular "possess a near-human intelligence, generally including the use of sounds in representational ways, a rich awareness of the aims and objectives of others, the ability to engage in tactical deception, and the faculty to use symbols in communication with humans and each other" (Reynolds, 1994, p. 4).

Our increasing awareness of such traits in our primate relatives has spawned numerous movements to extend human rights to apes—rights such as freedom from living in fear, respect for dignity, and not being subjected to incarceration (caging), exploitation (medical experimentation), or other mistreatment. The movement reached a milestone with the Kinshasa Declaration on Great Apes. Signed by over seventy representatives from twenty-four countries and many nongovernmental organizations, convening in the capital of the Democratic Republic of the Congo in 2005, this document affirms a commitment to protect great apes, like chimps, gorillas, and orangutans, and extends some human rights to our closest animal relatives (O'Carroll, 2008).

---

culture A society's shared and socially transmitted ideas, values, emotions, and perceptions, which are used to make sense of experience and generate behavior and are reflected in that behavior.

enculturation The process by which a society's culture is passed on from one generation to the next and individuals become members of their society.

Trent Burkholder Photography

Figure 13.3 Stilt Fishing A father practices the traditional art of stilt fishing with his son in Ahangama, Sri Lanka. It's a tough job, wading through shallow waters before dawn and sitting atop the uncomfortable platform for hours to catch small fish that sell for about 2 cents apiece. The art of stilt fishing has been passed from father to son for generations, but fewer and fewer families are building their lives around this profession today due to low profits, harsh conditions, and tourists who are scaring the fish away.

Culture Is Shared

As a shared set of ideas, values, perceptions, and standards of behavior, culture is the common denominator that makes the actions of individuals intelligible to other members of their society. Culture enables individuals in a society to predict how fellow members are most likely to behave in a given circumstance, and it informs them how to react accordingly. **Society** may be defined as an organized group or groups of interdependent people who generally share a common territory, language, and culture and who act together for collective survival and well-being. The ways in which these people depend upon one another can be seen in such features as their economic, communication, and defense systems. They are also bound together by a general sense of common identity.

Because culture and society are such closely related concepts, anthropologists study both. Obviously, there can be no culture without a society. Conversely, there are no known human societies that do not exhibit culture. Without culture, human society quickly falls apart. This cannot be said for all other animal species. Ants and bees, for example, instinctively cooperate in a manner that clearly indicates a remarkable degree of social organization, yet this instinctual behavior is not a culture.

Although members of a society share a culture, it is important to realize that all is not uniform. For one thing, no two people share the exact same version of their culture. At the very least, there is some distinction between the roles of children and elders, men and women. This stems from the fact that there are obvious differences between infants, fully matured, and highly aged individuals, as well as between female and male reproductive anatomy and physiology. Every society gives cultural meaning to biological sex differences by explaining them in a particular way and specifying what their significance is in terms of social roles and expected patterns of behavior.

Because each culture does this in its own way, there can be tremendous variation from one society to another. Anthropologists use the term **gender** to refer to the cultural elaborations and meanings assigned to the biological differentiation between the sexes. So, although one's sex is biologically determined, one's gender is socially constructed within the context of one's particular culture (**Figure 13.4** on the next page).

Apart from sexual differences directly related to reproduction, biological underpinnings for contrasting gender roles have largely disappeared in modern industrialized and postindustrial societies. For example, men and women are equally capable of accomplishing tasks requiring muscular strength, such as moving heavy automobile engines, because assembly lines use hydraulic lifts for the job. Nevertheless, all cultures exhibit at least some role differentiation related to biology—some far more so than others.

In addition to cultural variation associated with gender, there is also variation related to age. In any society, children are not expected to behave as adults, and the

society An organized group or groups of interdependent people who generally share a common territory, language, and culture and who act together for collective survival and well-being.

gender The cultural elaborations and meanings assigned to the biological differentiation between the sexes.

Figure 13.4 Gender Identification
In U.S. hospital nurseries, newborn girls are typically wrapped in pink blankets and boys in blue blankets. This is in response to popular expectations in the United States and many other countries that newborn infants be assigned a gender identity of either male or female. Yet significant numbers of infants are born each year whose genitalia do not conform to cultural expectations. Because only two genders are recognized, the usual reaction is to make the young bodies conform to cultural requirements through gender assignment surgery that involves constructing male or female genitalia. This is in contrast to many Native American cultures (among others), which have traditionally recognized more than two genders (Blackless et al., 2000).

© Randy Duchaine/Alamy

reverse is equally true. But then, who is a child and who is an adult? Again, although age differences are natural, cultures give their own meaning and timetable to the human life cycle. In North America, for example, individuals are generally not regarded as adults until the age of 18; in many other cultures, adulthood begins earlier—often around age 12, an age closer to the biological changes of adolescence.

Subcultures: Groups Within a Larger Society

Besides age and gender differentiation, there may be cultural variation between subgroups in societies that share an overarching culture. These may be occupational groups in societies where there is a complex division of labor, or social classes in a stratified society, or ethnic groups in other societies. When such groups exist within a society—each functioning by its own distinctive set of ideas, values, and behavior patterns while still sharing some common standards—we call them **subcultures**.

Amish communities are one example of a subculture in North America. Specifically, they are an **ethnic group**—people who collectively and publicly identify

themselves as a distinct group based on various cultural features such as shared ancestry and common origin, language, customs, and traditional beliefs. The Amish originated in western Europe during the Protestant revolutions of the 16th century. Today, members of this group number about 100,000 and live mainly in the United States—in Pennsylvania, Ohio, Illinois, and Indiana—as well as in Ontario, Canada (**Figure 13.5**).

These rural pacifists base their lives on their traditional Anabaptist beliefs, which hold that only adult baptism is valid and that "true Christians" (as they define them) should not hold government office, bear arms, or use force. They prohibit marriage outside their faith, which calls for obedience to radical Christian teachings, including social separation from what they see as the wider evil world and rejection of material wealth as vainglorious.

Among themselves, Amish people usually speak a German dialect known as Pennsylvania Dutch (from *Deutsch*, meaning "German"). They use formal German for religious purposes, although children learn English in school. Valuing simplicity, hard work, and a high degree of neighborly cooperation, they dress in a distinctive plain garb and even today rely on the horse for transportation as well as agricultural work (Hostetler & Huntington, 1992). In sum, the Amish share the same **ethnicity**. This term, rooted in the Greek word *ethnikos* ("nation") and related to *ethnos* ("custom"), is the expression for the set of cultural ideas held by an ethnic group.

The goal of Amish education is to teach youngsters reading, writing, and arithmetic, as well as Amish values. Adults in the community reject what they regard

---

subculture A distinctive set of ideas, values, and behavior patterns by which a group within a larger society operates, while still sharing common standards with that larger society.

ethnic group People who collectively and publicly identify themselves as a distinct group based on shared cultural features such as common origin, language, customs, and traditional beliefs.

ethnicity This term, rooted in the Greek word *ethnikos* ("nation") and related to *ethnos* ("custom"), is the expression for the set of cultural ideas held by an ethnic group.

Figure 13.5 Amish Barn Raising The Amish people have held onto their traditional agrarian way of life in the midst of industrialized North American society. Their strong community spirit—reinforced by close social ties between family and neighbors, common language, traditional customs, and shared religious beliefs that set them apart from non-Amish people—is also expressed in a traditional barn raising, a large collective construction project.

as worldly knowledge and the idea of schools producing good citizens for the state. Resisting all attempts to force their children to attend regular public schools, they insist that education take place near home and that teachers be committed to Amish ideals.

Amish nonconformity to mainstream culture has frequently resulted in conflict with state authorities, as well as personal harassment from people outside their communities. Pressed to compromise, they have introduced vocational training beyond junior high to fulfill state requirements, but they have managed to retain control of their schools and to maintain their way of life.

Confronted with economic challenges that make it impossible for most to subsist solely on farming, some Amish work outside their communities. Many more have established cottage industries and actively market homemade goods to tourists and other outsiders. Yet, although their economic separation from mainstream society has declined somewhat, their cultural separation has not (Kraybill, 2001). They remain a reclusive community, more distrustful than ever of the dominant North American culture surrounding them and mingling as little as possible with non-Amish people.

The Amish are but one example of the way a subculture may develop and be dealt with by the larger culture within which it functions. Different as they are, the Amish actually put into practice many values that other North Americans often respect in the abstract: thrift, hard work, independence, a close family life. The degree of tolerance accorded to them, in contrast to some other ethnic groups, is also due in part to the fact that the Amish are white Europeans; they are defined as being of the same race as those who historically comprise dominant mainstream

society. Notably, as elaborated upon elsewhere in this text, the concept of race has no biological validity when applied to humans, yet it still persists as a powerful social classification. This can be seen in the spatial organization of many U.S. cities in which certain neighborhoods are predominantly Asian, black, white, or Hispanic. This organizational pattern conforms to the racial categories long imposed by U.S. government bureaucracies, which officially reinforce and culturally reproduce a historical race-based ideology in U.S. society.

Implicit in the discussion thus far is that subcultures may develop in different ways. On the one hand, Amish subculture in the United States developed gradually in response to how these members of a strict evangelical Protestant sect have adapted to survive within the wider North American society, while holding tightly to the traditional way of life of their European ancestors. In contrast, North American Indian subcultures are distinctive ways of life rooted in traditions of formerly independent societies. The Native Americans endured invasion of their own territories and colonization by European settlers and were brought under the control of federal governments in the United States, Canada, and Mexico.

Although all American Indian groups have experienced enormous changes due to colonization, many have retained traditions significantly different from those of the dominant Euramerican culture surrounding them. This makes it difficult to determine whether they endure as distinct cultures as opposed to subcultures. In this sense, *culture* and *subculture* represent opposite ends of a continuum, with no clear dividing line between them. The Anthropology Applied feature examines the intersection of culture and subculture with an example concerning Apache Indian housing.

ANTHROPOLOGY APPLIED

New Houses for Apache Indians

By George S. Esber

The United States, in common with other industrialized countries of the world, contains a number of more or less separate subcultures. Those who live by the standards of one particular subculture have their closest relationships with one another, receiving constant reassurance that their perceptions of the world are the only correct ones and coming to take it for granted that the whole culture is as they see it. As a consequence, members of one subculture frequently have trouble understanding the needs and aspirations of other such groups. For this reason anthropologists, with their special understanding of cultural differences, are frequently employed as go-betweens in situations requiring interaction between peoples of differing cultural traditions.

As an example, while I was still a graduate student in anthropology, one of my professors asked me to work with architects and the Tonto Apache Indians in Arizona to research housing needs for a new tribal community. Although the architects knew about cross-cultural differences in the use of space, they had no idea how to get relevant information from the Indian people. For their part, the Apaches had no explicit awareness of their needs, for these were based on unconscious patterns of behavior. For that matter, few people are consciously aware of the space needs for their own social patterns of behavior.

My task was to persuade the architects to hold back on their planning long enough for me to gather, through participant observation and a review of written records, the data from which Apache housing needs could be abstracted. At the same time, I had to overcome Apache anxieties over an outsider coming into their midst to learn about matters as personal as their daily lives as they are acted out, in and around their homes. With these hurdles overcome, I was able to identify and successfully communicate to the architects those features of Apache life having importance for home and community design. At the same time, discussions of my findings with the Apaches enhanced their own awareness of their unique needs.

As a result of my work, the Apaches moved into houses that had been designed with *their* participation, for *their* specific needs. Among my findings was the realization that the Apaches preferred to ease into social interactions rather than to shake hands and begin interacting immediately, as is more typical of the Anglo pattern. Apache etiquette requires that people be in full view of one another so each can assess the behavior of others from a distance prior to engaging in social interaction with them. This requires a large, open living space. At the same time, hosts feel compelled to offer food to guests as a prelude to further social interaction. Thus, cooking and dining areas cannot be separated from living space. Nor is standard middle-class Anglo kitchen equipment suitable because the need for handling large quantities among extended families requires large pots and pans, which in turn calls for extra-large sinks and cupboards. Built with such ideas in mind, the new houses accommodated long-standing native traditions.

On a return visit to the Tonto Apache reservation in 2010, I found that the original houses were fine, but many more units had been squeezed in to accommodate growing needs on a restricted land base. A recent acquisition of new lands, which more than doubled the size of the tiny reservation, offers new possibilities. The Tonto Apache opened a casino in 2007. Its success has resulted in significant changes—from impoverishment to being one of the biggest employers in the area.

Adapted from Esber, G. S. (1987). Designing Apache houses with Apaches. In R. M. Wulff & S. J. Fiske (Eds.), Anthropological praxis: Translating knowledge into action. Boulder, CO: Westview, 2007. Reprinted by permission of George S. Esber.

Pluralism

Our discussion raises the issue of the multi-ethnic or **pluralistic society** in which two or more ethnic groups or nationalities are politically organized into one territorial state but maintain their cultural differences. Pluralistic societies could not have existed before the first politically centralized states arose a mere 5,000 years ago. With the rise of the state, it became possible to bring about the political unification of two or more formerly independent societies, each with its own culture, thereby creating a more complex order that transcends the theoretical one culture–one society linkage.

Anthropology makes an important distinction between state and nation. *States* are politically organized territories that are internationally recognized, whereas

pluralistic society A society in which two or more ethnic groups or nationalities are politically organized into one territorial state but maintain their cultural differences.

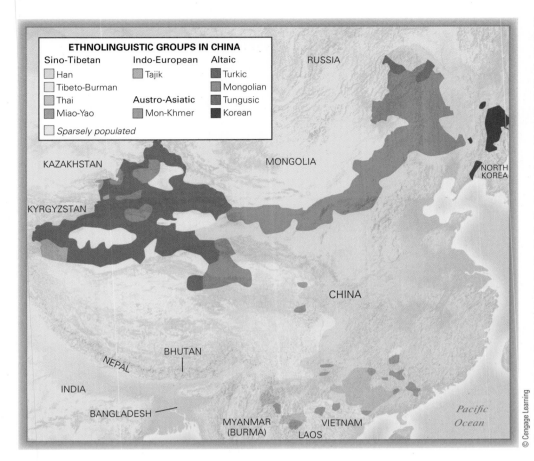

ETHNOLINGUISTIC GROUPS IN CHINA

Sino-Tibetan
- Han
- Tibeto-Burman
- Thai
- Miao-Yao

Indo-European
- Tajik

Austro-Asiatic
- Mon-Khmer

Altaic
- Turkic
- Mongolian
- Tungusic
- Korean

☐ *Sparsely populated*

RUSSIA

KAZAKHSTAN

MONGOLIA

NORTH KOREA

KYRGYZSTAN

CHINA

BHUTAN

NEPAL

INDIA

BANGLADESH

MYANMAR (BURMA)

LAOS

VIETNAM

Pacific Ocean

© Cengage Learning

Figure 13.6 Ethnolinguistic Groups in China China is the largest country in the world, with a population of 1.3 billion people. A pluralistic society, it has fifty-five officially recognized nationalities. By far the largest nationality, or ethnic group, is the Han, comprising about 90 percent of the population. However, there are many ethnic minorities speaking radically different languages and having different cultural traditions. For example, the Uyghur (pictured in Figure 13.7), numbering over 8 million, are a Turkic-speaking people in Xinjiang Province in northwestern China. Unlike most Han, who are Buddhists, most Uyghur are Sunni Muslims. Historically dominating the Chinese state, the Han typically see themselves as the "real" Chinese and ignore the ethnic minorities or view them with contempt. This ethnocentrism is also reflected in names historically used for these groups.

nations are socially organized bodies of people who share ethnicity—a common origin, language, and cultural heritage. For example, the Kurds constitute a nation, but their homeland is divided among several states: Iran, Iraq, Turkey, and Syria. The international boundaries among these states were drawn up after World War I (1914–1918), with little regard for the region's indigenous ethnic groups or nations. Similar state formation processes have taken place throughout the world, especially in Asia and Africa, often making political conditions in these countries inherently unstable.

Pluralistic societies, which are common in the world today, all face the same challenge: They are composed of groups that, by virtue of their high degree of cultural variation, are all essentially operating by different sets of rules. Because social living requires predictable behavior, it may be difficult for the members of any one subgroup to accurately interpret and follow the different standards by which the others operate.

Unfortunately, *ethnocentrism*—defined in Chapter 1 as a belief that the ways of one's own culture are the only proper ones—may open the door to cross-cultural misunderstanding and distrust among different subgroups within a pluralistic society. Under stressful circumstances, such as lack of resources due to drought, neighboring ethnic groups may become rivals and intolerance may escalate into violence. There are many examples of troubled pluralistic societies in the world today, including Afghanistan and Nigeria, where central governments face major challenges in maintaining peace and lawful order. In countries where one ethnic group is substantially larger than others, such as the Han in China, greater numbers may be used to political and economic advantage at the expense of minority groups (**Figure 13.6** and **Figure 13.7**). We will return to the topic of ethnocentrism a bit later in this chapter.

Culture Is Based on Symbols

Much of human behavior involves **symbols**—sounds, gestures, marks, and other signs that are linked to something else and represent them in a meaningful way. Because often there is no inherent or necessary relationship between a thing and its representation, symbols are arbitrary, acquiring specific meanings when people agree on usage in their communications.

symbol A sound, gesture, mark, or other sign that is arbitrarily linked to something else and represents it in a meaningful way.

© TAO Images Limited/Alamy

Figure 13.7 The Uyghur Minority in China The Uyghur, a Turkic-speaking Muslim ethnic minority in China, live in the country's northwestern province of Xinjiang. Politically dominated by China's Han ethnic majority, who comprise 90 percent of the population, Uyghurs are proud of their cultural identity and hold onto their distinctive traditional heritage—as evident in this photo of a Uyghur family group eating together on carpets woven with traditional Uyghur designs.

In fact, symbols—ranging from national flags to wedding rings to money—enter into every aspect of culture, from social life and religion to politics and economics. We are all familiar with the fervor and devotion that a religious symbol can elicit from a believer. An Islamic crescent, Christian cross, or a Jewish Star of David—as well as the sun among the Inca, a cow among the Hindu, a white buffalo calf among Plains Indians, or any other object of worship—may bring to mind years of struggle and persecution or may stand for a whole philosophy or religion.

The most important symbolic aspect of culture is language—using words to represent objects and ideas. Through language humans are able to transmit culture from one generation to another. In particular, language makes it possible to learn from cumulative, shared experience. Without it, one could not inform others about events, emotions, and other experiences. Language is so important that one of the four main subfields of anthropology is dedicated to its study.

Culture Is Integrated

The breadth and depth of every culture is remarkable. It includes what people do for a living, the tools they use, the ways they work together, how they transform their environments and construct their dwellings, what they eat and drink, how they worship, what they believe is right or wrong, what gifts they exchange and when, who they marry, how they raise their children, how they deal with misfortune, sickness, death, and so on. Because these and all other aspects of a culture must be reasonably well integrated in order to function properly, anthropologists seldom focus on one cultural feature in isolation. Instead, they view each in terms of its larger context and carefully examine its connections to related features.

For purposes of comparison and analysis, anthropologists customarily imagine a culture as a structured system made up of distinctive parts that function together as an organized whole. Although they may sharply identify each part as a clearly defined unit with its own characteristics

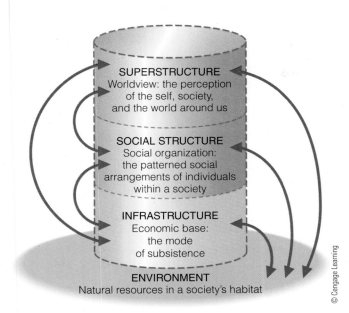

Figure 13.8 The Barrel Model of Culture Every culture is an integrated and dynamic system of adaptation that responds to a combination of internal factors (economic, social, ideological) and external factors (environmental, climatic). Within a cultural system, there are functional relationships among the economic base (infrastructure), the social organization (social structure), and the ideology (superstructure). A change in one leads to a change in the others.

and distinctive place within the larger system, anthropologists recognize that social reality is complex and subject to change and that divisions among cultural units are seldom clear-cut.

Broadly speaking, a society's cultural features fall within three categories: social structure, infrastructure, and superstructure, as depicted in our "barrel model" (**Figure 13.8**).

To ensure a community's biological continuity, a culture must provide a social structure for reproduction and mutual support. **Social structure** concerns rule-governed relationships—with all their rights and obligations—that hold members of a society together. Households, families, associations, and power relations, including politics, are all part of social structure. It establishes group cohesion and enables people to consistently satisfy their basic needs, including food and shelter for themselves and their dependents, by means of work.

There is a direct relationship between a group's social structure and its economic foundation, which includes subsistence practices and the tools and other material equipment used to make a living. Because subsistence practices involve tapping into available resources to satisfy a society's basic needs, this aspect of culture is known as **infrastructure**. It comprises strategies for the production and distribution of goods and services considered necessary for life.

Supported by this economic foundation, a society is held together by a shared sense of identity and worldview composed of a collection of ideas, beliefs, and values by which members of a society make sense of the world—its shape, challenges, and opportunities—and understand their place in it. Also known as ideology, this worldview is theoretically arranged in the model's **superstructure**. Including religion and political ideology, superstructure comprises a people's overarching ideas about themselves and the world around them—and it gives meaning and direction to their lives.

Influencing and reinforcing one another—continually adapting to changing demographic, technological, political-economic, and ideological factors—the interconnected features in these three interdependent structures together form part of a cultural system.

Kapauku Culture as an Integrated System

The integration of economic, social, and ideological aspects of a culture can be illustrated by the Kapauku Papuans, a mountain people of Western New Guinea, studied in 1955 by anthropologist Leopold Pospisil (1963). The Kapauku economy relies on plant cultivation, along with pig breeding, hunting, and fishing. Although plant cultivation provides most of the people's food, it is through pig breeding that men achieve political power and positions of legal authority.

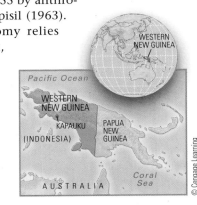

Among the Kapauku, living in an area now claimed by Indonesia, pig breeding is a complex business. Raising a lot of pigs requires a lot of food to feed them. The primary fodder is sweet potatoes, grown in garden plots. According to Kapauku culture, certain garden activities and the tending of pigs are tasks that fall exclusively in the domain of women's work. Thus, to raise many pigs a man needs numerous women in the household. As a result, in Kapauku society multiple wives are not only permitted, they are highly desired. For each

social structure The rule-governed relationships—with all their rights and obligations—that hold members of a society together. This includes households, families, associations, and power relations, including politics.

infrastructure The economic foundation of a society, including its subsistence practices and the tools and other material equipment used to make a living.

superstructure A society's shared sense of identity and worldview. The collective body of ideas, beliefs, and values by which members of a society make sense of the world—its shape, challenges, and opportunities—and understand their place in it. This includes religion and national ideology.

Figure 13.9 Kapauku Papuan Village, Western New Guinea Kapauku economy relies on plant cultivation, hunting, fishing, and especially on the breeding of pigs. Women are responsible for raising the pigs and their main fodder, sweet potatoes. Only men with numerous wives manage to acquire many pigs needed for wealth and prestige. As a result, in Kapauku society multiple wives are not only permitted, they are highly desired.

Courtesy © Jutka Rona

wife, however, a man must pay a bride-price, and this can be expensive. Furthermore, wives have to be compensated for their care of the pigs. Put simply, it takes pigs, by which wealth is measured, to get wives, without whom pigs cannot be raised in the first place. Needless to say, this requires considerable entrepreneurship. It is this ability that produces leaders in Kapauku society (**Figure. 13.9**).

The interrelatedness of these elements with various other features of Kapauku culture is even more complicated. For example, one condition that encourages men to marry several women is a surplus of adult females, sometimes caused by loss of males through warfare. Among the Kapauku, recurring warfare has long been viewed as a necessary evil. By the rules of war, men may be killed but women may not. This system works to promote the imbalanced sex ratio that fosters the practice of having more than one wife. Having multiple wives tends to work best if all of them come to live in their husband's village, and so it is among the Kapauku. With this arrangement, the men of a village are typically blood relatives of one another, which enhances their ability to cooperate in warfare.

Considering all these factors, it makes sense that Kapauku typically trace descent (ancestry) through men, which, coupled with near-constant warfare, tends to promote male dominance. So it is not surprising to find that only men hold positions of leadership in Kapauku, as they appropriate the products of women's labor in order to enhance their political stature. Such male dominance is by no means characteristic of all human societies. Rather, as with the Kapauku, it arises only under particular sets of circumstances that, if changed, will alter the way in which men and women relate to each other.

Culture Is Dynamic

Cultures are dynamic systems that respond to motions and actions within and around them. When one element within the system shifts or changes, the entire system strives to adjust, just as it does when an outside force applies pressure. To function adequately, a culture must be flexible enough to allow such adjustments in the face of unstable or changing circumstances.

All cultures are, of necessity, dynamic, but some are far less so than others. When a culture is too rigid or static and fails to provide its members with the means required for long-term survival under changing conditions, it is not likely to endure. On the other hand, some cultures are so fluid and open to change that they may lose their distinctive character. The Amish mentioned earlier in this chapter typically resist change as much as possible but are constantly making balanced decisions to adjust when absolutely necessary. North Americans in general, however, have created a culture in which change has become a positive ideal, reflecting the ongoing technological, demographic, and social transformations in their society.

Every culture is dynamically constructed and, not unlike a thermostat regulating room temperature, able to cope with recurrent strains and tensions, even dangerous disruptions and deadly conflicts. Sharing a culture, members of a society are capable of dealing with crises, solving their conflicts, and restoring order. Sometimes, however, the pressures are so great that the cultural features in the system are no longer adequate or acceptable, and the established order is changed.

ANTHROPOLOGIST OF NOTE

Bronislaw Malinowski (1884–1942)

Bronislaw Malinowski in the Trobriand Islands about 1916.

Courtesy Phoebe Apperson Hearst Museum of Anthropology

Bronislaw Malinowski, born in Poland, earned his doctorate in anthropology at the London School of Economics and later, as a professor there, played a vital role in making it an important center of anthropology. Renowned as a pioneer in participant observation, he stated that the ethnographer's goal is "to grasp the native's point of view . . . to realize *his* vision of *his* world."[a]

Writing about culture, Malinowski argued that people everywhere share certain biological and psychological needs and that the ultimate function of all cultural institutions is to fulfill those needs. Everyone, for example, needs to feel secure in relation to the physical universe. Therefore, when science and technology are inadequate to explain certain natural phenomena—such as eclipses or earthquakes—people develop religion and magic to account for those phenomena and to establish a feeling of security.

The quantity and quality of data called for by Malinowski's approach set new scientific standards for anthropological fieldwork. He argued that it was necessary to settle into the community being studied for an extended period of time in order to fully explain its culture. He demonstrated this approach with his research in the Trobriand Islands of the southern Pacific Ocean between 1915 and 1918. Never before had such intensive fieldwork been done nor had such theoretical insights been gained into the functioning of another culture.

[a]Malinowski, B. (1961). *Argonauts of the western Pacific* (p. 25). New York: Dutton.

Functions of Culture

Polish-born British anthropologist Bronislaw Malinowski argued that people everywhere share certain biological and psychological needs and that the ultimate function of all cultural institutions is to fulfill these needs (see Anthropologist of Note). Others have marked out different criteria, but the idea is basically the same: A culture cannot endure if it does not deal effectively with basic challenges. It has to equip members of a society with strategies for the production and distribution of goods and services considered necessary for life. To ensure the biological continuity of the group, it must also offer a social structure for reproduction and mutual support. Further, it has to provide ways and means to pass on knowledge and enculturate new members so they can contribute to their community as well-functioning adults. Moreover, it must facilitate social interaction and provide ways to

avoid or resolve conflicts within their group as well as with outsiders.

Because a culture must support all aspects of life, as indicated in our barrel model, it must also meet the psychological and emotional needs of its members. This last function is met, in part, simply by the measure of predictability that each culture, as a shared design for thought and action, brings to everyday life. Of course, it involves much more than that, including a worldview that helps individuals understand their place in the world and face major changes and challenges. For example, every culture provides its members with certain customary ideas and rituals that enable them to think creatively about the meaning of life and death. Many cultures even make it possible for people to imagine an afterlife. Invited to suspend disbelief and engage in such imaginings, people find the means to deal with the grief of losing a loved one and to face their own demise with certain expectations.

In Bali, for instance, Hindu worshipers stage spectacular cremation rituals at special places where they burn the physical remains of their dead. After a colorful procession with musicians, the corpse is carried to a great cremation tower, or *wadah*, representing the three-layered cosmos. It is then transferred into a beautifully decorated sarcophagus, made of wood and cloth artfully shaped in the form of an animal—a bull when the deceased belonged to the island's highest Hindu status group ("caste") of priests and lawgivers (Brahmanas), a winged lion for the second highest status of warriors and administrators (Satrias), and a half-fish/half-elephant for the next status of merchants and traders (Wesias).

After relatives and friends place their offerings atop or inside the sarcophagus, a Hindu priest sets the structure on fire. Soon, the body burns, and according to Balinese Hindu belief, the animal sarcophagus symbolically guides the soul of the deceased to Bali's "mother" mountain Gunung Angung. This is the sacred dwelling place of the island's gods and ancestors, the place to which many Balinese believe they return when they die. Freed from the flesh, the soul may later transmigrate and return in corporeal form. This belief in reincarnation of the soul allows the Balinese to cope with death as a celebration of life.

In sum, for a culture to function properly, its various parts must be consistent with one another. But consistency is not the same as harmony. In fact, there is friction and potential for conflict within every culture—among individuals, factions, and competing institutions. Even on the most basic level of a society, individuals rarely experience the enculturation process in exactly the same way, nor do they perceive their reality in precisely identical fashion. Moreover, conditions may change, brought on by inside or outside forces.

Culture, Society, and the Individual

Ultimately, a society is no more than a union of individuals, all of whom have their own special needs and interests. To survive, it must succeed in balancing the immediate self-interest of its individual members with the needs and demands of the collective well-being of society as a whole. To accomplish this, a society offers rewards for adherence to its culturally prescribed standards. In most cases, these rewards assume the form of social approval. For example, in contemporary North American society a person who holds a good job, takes care of family, pays taxes, and does volunteer work in the neighborhood may be spoken of as a "model citizen" in the community.

To ensure the survival of the group, each person must learn to postpone certain immediate personal satisfactions. Yet the needs of the individual cannot be overlooked entirely or emotional stress and growing resentment may erupt in the form of protest, disruption, and even violence.

Consider, for example, the matter of sexual expression, which, like anything that people do, is shaped by culture. Sexuality is important in every society for it helps to strengthen cooperative bonds among members, ensuring the perpetuation of the social group itself. Yet sex can be disruptive to social living. Without clear rules about who has sexual access to whom, competition for sexual privileges can destroy the cooperative bonds on which human survival depends. In addition, uncontrolled sexual activity can result in reproductive rates that cause a society's population to outstrip its resources. Hence, as it shapes sexual behavior, every culture must balance the needs of society against the individual's sexual needs and desires so that frustration does not build up to the point of being disruptive in itself.

Cultures vary widely in the way they go about this. On one end of the spectrum, societies such as the Amish in North America or the Muslim Brotherhood in Egypt have taken an extremely restrictive approach, specifying no sex outside of marriage. On the other end are societies such as the Norwegians who generally accept premarital sex and often choose to have children outside marriage, or even more extreme, the Canela Indians in Brazil, whose social codes guarantee that, sooner or later, everyone in a given village has had sex with just about everyone of the opposite sex. Yet, even as permissive as the latter situation may sound, there are nonetheless strict rules as to how the system operates (Crocker & Crocker, 2004).

In all life issues, cultures must strike a balance between the needs and desires of individuals and those of society as a whole. When those of society take precedence, people may experience excessive stress. Symptomatic of this are increased levels of social tension, disruptive behavior, emotional depression, even suicide.

Although some societies require a greater degree of cultural uniformity from its members than others, every organized social group imposes pressure on its members to conform to certain cultural models, or standards, of acceptable public behavior, speech, and so on. These standards are commonly accepted and adhered to, and each society has institutions in place with a repertoire of cultural mechanisms to promote or enforce conformity. In many traditional societies, religious institutions play a major role in doing this, whereas a political party may impose conformity in communist state societies. In capitalist societies, business corporations operating on the basis of economic market principles impose conformity in numerous ways, including standards of beauty (see the Biocultural Connection).

BIOCULTURAL CONNECTION

Modifying the Human Body

Each healthy human individual, like any other biological organism, is genetically programmed to develop to its full potential. This includes reaching a certain maximum height as a fully mature adult. What that height is, however, varies per population group. Dutch adult males, for example, average well over 1 foot taller than Mbuti men, who do not generally grow taller than 5 feet (150 cm). Whether we actually become as tall as our genes would allow, however, is influenced by multiple factors, including nutrition and disease.

In many cultures, being tall is viewed positively, especially for men. To make up for any perceived flaw in height, there is not much men can do to appear taller beyond wearing shoes with thick soles. But, in other areas, there are many alternatives to increase attraction and improve social status. Playing on this desire, and fueling it, the fashion industry creates and markets ever-changing styles of shoes, dresses, hairstyles, lipstick, perfumes, nail polish, hats, and whatever else to beautify the human body.

For thousands of years, people across the world have also engaged in modifying the human body itself—with tattoos, piercings, circumcision, footbinding, and even altering skull shape. In addition, modern medical technology has provided a whole new range of surgical procedures aimed at this goal.

With medicine as big business, many surgeons have joined forces with the beauty industry in what anthropologist Laura Nader calls "standardizing" bodies. Focusing on women's bodies, she notes "images of the body appear natural within their specific cultural milieus."[a] For example, breast implants are not seen as odd within the cultural milieu of the United States, and female circumcision and infibulation (also known as female genital mutilation or

PROCEDURE	NUMBER DONE IN 2011
Facial resurfacing and fillers (chemical peel, laser, collagen, etc.)	5,000,000
Brow lift	47,000
Eyelid surgery	196,000
Nose reshaping	244,000
Botox injection	5,700,000
Facelift	119,000
Upper arm lift	15,000
Breast augmentation	307,000
Tummy tuck	116,000
Liposuction	205,000

© Cengage Learning

This figure shows selected cosmetic surgical and nonsurgical procedures in the United States in 2011. In total, there were 1.6 million cosmetic surgeries and 12.2 million nonsurgical procedures (chemical peels, laser treatments, Botox injections, and so on) at a total cost of about $10.4 billion. Ninety-one percent of the total were done on women.

FGM) are not considered odd among people in several African countries.

Many feminist writers "differentiate [FGM] from breast implantation by arguing that American women *choose* to have breast implants whereas in Africa women are subject to indoctrination"[b] given they experience circumcision as young girls. But is a woman's decision to have breast implants, in fact, the result of indoctrination by the beauty-industrial complex?

This multibillion-dollar industry, notes Nader, "segments the female body and manufactures commodities of and for the body."[c] Among millions of women

getting "caught in the official beauty ideology" are those in the United States who have breast implantation. On average, they are 36 years old with two children. Designated as the beauty industry's "insecure consumers," these women are "recast as patients" with an illness defined as hypertrophy (small breasts). Psychological health can be restored by cosmetic surgery correcting this so-called deformity in the female body.

The doctors who perform these operations are often regarded as therapists and artists as well as surgeons. One pioneering breast implant surgeon "took as his ideal female figure that of ancient Greek statues, which he carefully measured, noticing the exact size and shape of the breasts, their vertical and horizontal locations."[d] In response to beauty marketing, the business of plastic surgery is now booming, and breast implantation is spreading across the globe.

BIOCULTURAL QUESTION

Have you or anyone close to you made body alterations? If so, were these changes prompted by an "official beauty ideology" or something else?

[a] Nader, L. (1997). Controlling processes: Tracing the dynamics of power. *Current Anthropology* 38, 715–717.
[b] Ibid.
[c] Ibid. See also Coco, L. E. (1994). Silicone breast implants in America: A choice of the official breast? In L. Nader (Ed.), *Essays on controlling processes* (pp. 103–132). *Kroeber Anthropological Society Papers* (no. 77). Berkeley: University of California Press; and Claeson, B. (1994). The privatization of justice: An ethnography of control. In L. Nader (Ed.), *Essays on controlling processes* (pp. 32–64). *Kroeber Anthropological Society Papers* (no. 77). Berkeley: University of California Press.
[d] Nader, 1997.

Culture and Change

Anthropologists today recognize that few peoples still exist in total or near-total isolation; in our current age of globalization, we are witnessing a much accelerated pace of widespread and radical change, discussed in detail in the last chapter of this book. Like our ancestors, all of us experience changes in our lives, but not all change is cultural change.

As living creatures, we humans typically experience multiple changes in the course of a lifetime. Such changes are part of the human life cycle. The average life expectancy for people today is about 64 years (3 years more for women than for men). But in many countries it is at least 20 years less, whereas in others it is a decade or more longer (Japanese may expect to live, on average, 80 years).

No matter how long we live or the changes we experience in our personal lives, few of us have any impact on how our culture is structured or how it operates. For that reason, cultures have been known to remain unchanged for many centuries, sometimes even longer. For anthropologists, an understanding of how cultures change and how people create or respond to change is crucially important—not only for the sake of knowledge itself but also because this knowledge can be applied in preventing or solving problems triggered by change.

Change in a culture may result from one or more factors, such as new technology, foreign invasion, new trade goods, population growth, ecological shifts, and so on. Cultural changes may be generated by forces within a society or may be imposed from the outside. Either way, they lead to a modification of cultural ideas, values, and practices.

Although cultures must have some flexibility to remain adaptive, cultural change can also bring unexpected and sometimes disastrous results. For example, consider the relationship between culture and the droughts that periodically afflict so many people living in African countries just south of the Sahara Desert. The lives of some 14 million nomadic herders native to this region are centered on cattle and other grazing animals. For thousands of years these nomads have migrated seasonally to provide their herds with pasture and water, utilizing vast areas of arid lands in ways that allowed them to survive severe droughts many times in the past.

Today, however, the nomadic way of life is frowned upon by the central governments of modern states in the region. Government officials actively discourage nomadism because it involves moving back and forth across relatively new international boundaries that are often impossible to guard, making it difficult to track the people and their animals for purposes of taxation and other government controls.

Viewing nomads as evading their authority, these governments have tried to stop the migratory herders from ranging through their traditional grazing territories and to convert them into sedentary villagers. Simultaneously, governments have aimed to press pastoralists into a market economy by giving them incentives to raise many more animals than required for their own needs so that the surplus could be sold to augment the tax base. Combined, these policies have led to overgrazing, erosion, and a lack of reserve pasture during recurring droughts. Thus, droughts today are far more disastrous than in the past because when they occur, they jeopardize the nomads' very existence (**Figure 13.10**).

The market economy that led nomads to increase their herds beyond sustainability is a factor in a huge range of cultural changes. Many nomads, including thousands of Kuchi herder families in Afghanistan pictured on the first page of this chapter, settle down as farmers or move to cities for cash-earning work opportunities. Across the globe, swift and often radical cultural change is driven by capitalism and its demand for market growth. Many welcome these changes, but others experience the loss of their traditional way of life as disturbing and feel powerless to stop, let alone reverse, the process.

Figure 13.10

Consequences of Cultural Change Climate and politics have conspired to create serious cultural change among migratory herders. So it is in the arid African grassland regions of Kenya pictured here, where severe drought combined with restrictions on grazing lands have resulted in the death of many animals and turned others into "bones on hoofs." Such catastrophes have forced many herders in Kenya and elsewhere to give up their old lifeways entirely.

Tony Karumba/AFP/Getty Images

VISUAL COUNTERPOINT

© David Kadlubowski/Corbis

AP Images/Sergey Ponomarev

Figure 13.11 Perpetrating Ethnocentrism Many people in the world consider their own nation superior to others, framing their nationalist pride by proclaiming to be a "master race," "divine nation," or "chosen people" and viewing their homeland as sacred. Such nationalist ideology is associated with militant ethnocentrism and dislike, fear, or even hatred of foreigners, immigrants, and ethnic minorities. For instance, most Russians now agree with the Nationalist slogan "Russia for the Russians," and almost half believe their nation has a natural right to dominate as an empire. Russian Nationalists (*right*) are right-wing extremists, 10,000 of whom recently marched to St. Petersburg to protest the immigration of Azeri Tajiks, Turks, and other foreigners into Russia. In their extremism, they are matched by the Minutemen Civil Defense Corps in the United States. Active nationwide, Minutemen view whites as the only "true" Americans and are strongly anti-immigrant. The left photo shows the Minutemen in Palominas, Arizona, erecting a U.S.–Mexico border fence on private ranchland.

Ethnocentrism and Cultural Relativism

There are numerous highly diverse cultural solutions to the challenges of human existence. Anthropologists have been intrigued to find that people in most cultures tend to be ethnocentric and see their own way of life as the best of all possible worlds. This is reflected in the way individual societies refer to themselves: Typically, a society's traditional name for itself translates roughly into "true human beings." In contrast, their names for outsiders commonly translate into various versions of "subhumans," including "monkeys," "dogs," "weird-looking people," "funny talkers," and so forth. When it comes to ethnocentrism, it is easy to find examples (**Figure 13.11**).

Anthropologists have been actively engaged in the fight against ethnocentrism ever since they started to study and actually live among traditional peoples with radically different cultures, thus learning by personal experience that these "others" were no less human than anyone else. Resisting the common urge to rank cultures, anthropologists have instead aimed to understand individual cultures and the general concept of culture. To do so, they have examined each culture on its own terms, discerning whether or not the culture satisfies the needs and expectations of the people themselves. If a people practiced human sacrifice or capital punishment, for example, anthropologists asked about the circumstances that made the taking of human life acceptable according to that particular group's values.

This brings us to the concept of **cultural relativism**—the idea that one must suspend judgment of other peoples'

practices in order to understand those practices in their own cultural terms. Only through such an approach can one gain a meaningful view of the values and beliefs that underlie the behaviors and institutions of other peoples and societies as well as clearer insights into the underlying beliefs and practices of one's own society.

Take, for example, the 16th-century Aztec practice of sacrificing humans for religious purposes. Few (if any) North Americans today would condone such practices, but by suspending judgment one can get beneath the surface and discern how it functioned to reassure the populace that the Aztec state was healthy and that the sun would remain in the heavens.

Moreover, an open-minded exploration of Aztec sacrifice rituals may offer a valuable comparative perspective on the death penalty today. Over two-thirds of the countries in the world—141—have now abolished it in law or practice. Among those countries where it continues, China, Iran, Saudi Arabia, the United States, and Yemen are the most frequent executioners (Amnesty International, 2012).

Numerous studies by social scientists have clearly shown that the U.S. death penalty does not deter violent crime, any more than Aztec sacrifice really provided sustenance for the sun. In fact, cross-cultural studies show that homicide rates mostly decline after its abolition (Radelet & Lacock, 2009). Similar to Aztec human sacrifice, capital punishment may be seen as an institutionalized magical

cultural relativism The idea that one must suspend judgment of other people's practices in order to understand them in their own cultural terms.

response to perceived disorder—an act that "reassures many that society is not out of control after all, that the majesty of the law reigns, and that God is indeed in his heaven" (Paredes & Purdum, 1990, p. 9).

Cultural relativism is essential as a research tool. However, employing it for research does not mean suspending judgment forever, nor does it require that anthropologists defend a people's right to engage in any cultural practice, no matter how destructive. All that is necessary is that we avoid *premature* judgments until we have a full understanding of the culture in which we are interested. Only then may anthropologists adopt a critical stance and in an informed way consider the advantages and disadvantages of particular beliefs and behaviors for a society and its members.

Evaluation of Cultures

A valid question to ask is how well does a given culture satisfy the biological, social and psychological needs of those whose behavior it guides (Bodley, 2008). Specific indicators to answer this question are found in the nutritional status and general physical and mental health of its population; the incidence of violence, crime, and delinquency; the demographic structure, stability, and tranquility of domestic life; and the group's relationship to its resource base. The culture of a people who experience high rates of malnutrition (including obesity), violent crime, emotional disorders and despair, and environmental degradation may be said to be operating less well than that of another people who exhibit few such problems (**Figure 13.12**).

In a well-working culture, people "can be proud, jealous, and pugnacious, and live a very satisfactory life without feeling '*angst*,' 'alienation,' 'anomie,' 'depression,' or any of the other pervasive ills of our own inhuman and civilized way of living" (Fox, 1968, p. 290). When traditional ways of coping no longer seem to work, and people feel helpless to shape their lives in their own societies, symptoms of cultural breakdown become prominent.

In short, a culture can be understood as a complex maintenance system designed to ensure the continued well-being of a group of people. Therefore, it may be

Figure 13.12 Signs of Cultural Dissatisfaction High rates of crime and delinquency are signs that a culture is not adequately satisfying a people's needs and expectations. This San Quentin Prison cellblock in California can be seen as such evidence. It is sobering to note that 25 percent of all imprisoned people in the world are incarcerated in the United States. In the past fifteen years the country's jail and prison population jumped from 1.6 million to 2.3 million. Ironically, people in the United States think of their country as "the land of the free," yet it has the highest incarceration rate in the world (about 750 per 100,000 inhabitants). The median among all countries is about 125 per 100,000 inhabitants.

deemed successful as long as it secures the survival of a society in a way that satisfies its members.

What complicates matters is that any society is made up of groups with different interests, raising the possibility that some people's interests may be better served than those of others. For this reason, anthropologists must always ask *whose* needs and *whose* survival are best served by the culture in question. Only by looking at the overall situation can a reasonably objective judgment be made as to how well a culture is working.

Our species today is challenged by rapid changes all across the globe, much of it triggered by powerful technology and dramatic population growth. In our current age of globalization, we must widen our scope and develop a truly worldwide perspective that enables us to appreciate cultures as increasingly open and interactive systems.

CHAPTER CHECKLIST

What is cultural adaptation?

● Cultural adaptation—a complex of ideas, activities, and technologies that enables people to survive and even thrive in their environment—has enabled humans to survive and expand into a wide variety of environments.

● Cultures have always changed over time, although rarely as rapidly or massively as many are doing today. Sometimes what is adaptive in one set of circumstances or over the short run is maladaptive over time.

What is culture, and what characteristics are common to all cultures?

● Culture is a society's shared and socially transmitted ideas, values, and perceptions that are used to make sense of experience and generate behavior and are reflected in that behavior.

● Although every culture involves a group's shared values, ideas, and behavior, this does not mean that everything within a culture is uniform. For instance, in all cultures people's roles vary according to age and gender, and in some cultures there are other subcultural variations.

● A subculture (for example, the Amish) shares certain overarching assumptions of the larger culture, while observing its own set of distinct rules. Pluralistic societies are those in which two or more ethnic groups or nationalities are politically organized into one territorial state but maintain their cultural differences.

● In addition to being shared, all cultures are learned, with individual members learning the accepted norms of social behavior through the process of enculturation. Also, every culture is based on symbols—transmitted through the communication of ideas, emotions, and desires—especially language. And culture is integrated, so that all aspects function as an integrated whole (albeit not without tension, friction, and even conflict). Finally, all cultures are dynamically designed to adjust to recurrent strains and tensions.

● As illustrated in the barrel model, all aspects of a culture fall into one of three broad, interrelated categories: infrastructure (the subsistence practices or economic system), social structure (the rule-governed relationships), and superstructure (the ideology or worldview).

● Cultural change takes place in response to events such as population growth, technological innovation, environmental crisis, intrusion of outsiders, or modification of values and behavior within the culture. Although cultures must change to adapt to new circumstances, sometimes the unforeseen consequences of change are disastrous for a society.

What is the connection between culture, society, and the individual?

● As a union of individuals, a society must strike a balance between the self-interest of individuals with the needs and demands of the collective well-being of the group. To accomplish this, a society rewards adherence to its culturally prescribed standards in the form of social approval.

● When individual needs and desires are eclipsed by those of society, the result may be stress and mental illness expressed in antisocial behavior such as alienation, substance abuse, or violence.

What are ethnocentrism and cultural relativism, and what is the measure of a society's success?

● Ethnocentrism is the belief that one's own culture is superior to all others. To avoid making ethnocentric judgments, anthropologists adopt the approach of cultural relativism, which requires suspending judgment in order to understand each culture in its own terms.

● One unbiased measure of a culture's success is based on answering this question: How well does a particular culture satisfy the physical and psychological needs of those whose behavior it guides? The following indicators provide answers: the nutritional status and general physical and mental health of the population, the incidence of violence, the stability of domestic life, and the group's relationship to its resource base.

QUESTIONS FOR REFLECTION

1. The barrel model offers a simple framework for imagining what a culture looks like from an analytical point of view. How would you apply that model to your own community and that of the Kuchi herders pictured at the beginning of this chapter?

2. Are you familiar with any subcultures or ethnic minorities in your own society? Could you make friends with or even marry someone from another subculture? What kind of problems would you be likely to encounter?

3. Peoples in all cultures across the world display ethnocentrism, but some more so than others. Considering today's globalization (as described in Chapter 1), do you think ethnocentrism poses more of a problem than in the past?

4. An often overlooked first step for developing an understanding of another culture is having knowledge and respect for one's own cultural traditions. Do you know the origins of the worldview commonly held by most people in your community? How do you think it developed over time, and what makes it so accepted or popular in your group today?

5. Currently, about 57 million humans die every year, and 135 million newborns join the more than 7 billion already crowding our planet. With finite natural resources and escalating piles of waste, do you think that technological inventions alone are sufficient to guarantee an additional 78 million more people annually a long and healthy life in pursuit of happiness?

ONLINE STUDY RESOURCES

CourseMate

 Access chapter-specific learning tools, including learning objectives, practice quizzes, videos, flash cards, glossaries, and more in your Anthropology CourseMate.

Log into **www.cengagebrain.com** to access the resources your instructor has assigned and to purchase materials.

Challenge Issue

Anthropologists take on the challenge of studying and describing cultures around the world and finding scientific explanations for their differences and similarities. Why do people think, feel, and act in certain ways—and find it wrong or impossible to do otherwise? Answers must come from fact-based knowledge about cultural diversity—knowledge that is not culture-bound and is widely recognized as significant. Over the years, anthropology has generated such knowledge through various theories and research methods. In particular, anthropologists obtain information through long-term, full-immersion fieldwork based on participant observation. Here we see anthropologist Lucas Bessire enjoying the taste of *ajidabia* (a variety of wild honey) with Ayoreo Indian companions alongside a newly found beehive in the dry forest of the Gran Chaco in Paraguay, South America—one involved moment among many in the all-engaging challenge of anthropological fieldwork.

Ethnographic Research: Its History, Methods, and Theories

14

As briefly discussed in Chapter 1, cultural anthropology has two main scholarly components: *ethnography* and *ethnology*. Ethnography is a detailed description of a particular culture primarily based on firsthand observation and interaction. Ethnology is the study and analysis of different cultures from a comparative or historical point of view, utilizing ethnographic accounts and developing anthropological theories that help explain why certain important differences or similarities occur among groups.

Historically, anthropology focused on non-Western traditional peoples whose languages were not written down—people whose communication was often direct and face-to-face, and whose knowledge about the past was based primarily on oral tradition. Even in societies where writing exists, not much of what is of interest to anthropologists is recorded in writing. Thus, anthropologists have made a point of going to these places in person to observe and experience peoples and their cultures firsthand. This is called *fieldwork*.

Today, anthropological fieldwork takes place not only in small-scale communities in distant corners of the world, but also in modern urban neighborhoods in industrial or postindustrial societies. Anthropologists can be found doing fieldwork in a wide range of places and within a host of diverse groups and institutions, including global corporations, nongovernmental organizations (NGOs), migrant labor communities, and peoples scattered and dispersed because of natural or human-made catastrophes.

In our rapidly changing and increasingly interconnected world, where long-standing cultural boundaries between societies are being erased, new social networks and cultural constructs are emerging, made possible by long-distance mass transportation and communication technologies. To better describe, explain, and understand these complex but fascinating dynamics in a globalizing world, anthropologists today are adjusting their theoretical frameworks and research methods and approaches.

IN THIS CHAPTER YOU WILL LEARN TO

- Explain why fieldwork is essential to ethnography.

- Situate historical changes in research questions and applications within their economic, social, and political contexts.

- Describe ethnographic research—its challenges and methods.

- Discuss the relationship between methods and theory.

- Contrast distinctive key theoretical perspectives in anthropology.

- Recognize the ethical responsibilities of anthropological research.

Our research questions are often influenced or even driven by the environmental, economic, political, military, or ideological concerns of a particular period. What we observe and consider significant is shaped or modified by a worldview, and our explanations or interpretations are framed in theories that gain and lose currency depending on ideological and political-economical forces beyond our individual control.

Taking all of this into consideration, this chapter presents a historical overview of anthropology, its research methods and theories—underscoring the idea that ethnographic research does not happen in a timeless vacuum.

History of Ethnographic Research and Its Uses

Anthropology emerged as a formal discipline during the heyday of colonialism (1870s–1930s) when many European anthropologists focused on the study of traditional peoples and their cultures in the colonies overseas. For instance, French anthropologists did most of their research in North and West Africa and Southeast Asia; British anthropologists in southern and East Africa; Dutch anthropologists in what has become Indonesia, Western New Guinea, and Suriname; and Belgian anthropologists in Congo of Africa. Meanwhile, anthropologists in North America focused primarily on their own countries' Native Indian and Eskimo communities—usually residing on tracts of land known as reservations or in remote Arctic villages.

At one time it was common practice to compare peoples still pursuing traditional lifeways—based on hunting, fishing, gathering, and/or small-scale farming or herding—with the ancient prehistoric ancestors of Europeans and to categorize the cultures of these traditional peoples as "primitive." Although anthropologists have long abandoned such ethnocentric terminology, many others still think and speak of these traditional cultures as underdeveloped or even undeveloped. This misconception helped state societies, commercial enterprises, and other powerful outside groups justify expanding their activities and invading the lands belonging to these peoples, often exerting overwhelming pressure on them to change their ancestral ways.

Salvage Ethnography or Urgent Anthropology

In this disturbing and often violent historical context, the survival of thousands of traditional communities worldwide has been at stake. In fact, many of these threatened peoples have become physically extinct. Others survived but were forced to surrender their territories and lifeways.

Although anthropologists have seldom been able to prevent such tragic events, they have tried to make a record of these cultural groups. This important early anthropological practice of documenting endangered cultures was initially called *salvage ethnography* and later became known as **urgent anthropology**, and it continues to this day (**Figure 14.1**).

By the late 1800s, many European and North American museums were sponsoring anthropological expeditions to collect cultural artifacts and other material remains (including skulls and bones), as well as vocabularies, myths, and other relevant cultural data. Early anthropologists also began taking ethnographic photographs, and by the 1890s some began shooting documentary films or recording the speech, songs, and music of these so-called vanishing peoples.

The first generation of anthropologists often began their careers working for museums, but those coming later were academically trained in the emerging discipline and became active in newly founded anthropology departments. In North America, most of the latter did their fieldwork on tribal reservations where indigenous communities were falling apart in the face of disease, poverty, and despair brought on by pressures of forced cultural change. These anthropologists interviewed American Indian elders still able to recall the ancestral way of life prior to the disruptions forced upon them. The researchers also collected oral histories, traditions, myths, legends, and other information, as well as old artifacts for research, preservation, and public display.

Beyond documenting social practices, beliefs, artifacts, and other disappearing cultural features, anthropologists also sought to reconstruct abandoned traditional lifeways remembered only by surviving elders. Although anthropological theories have come and gone during the past few hundred years or so, the plight of indigenous peoples struggling for cultural survival endures. Anthropologists can and still do contribute to that effort, assisting in cultural preservation efforts. In that work, utilizing a variety of new methods, they can tap into and continue to build on a professional legacy of salvage ethnography and urgent anthropology.

Acculturation Studies

In the 1930s, anthropologists began researching *culture contact*, studying how traditional cultures change when coming in contact with expanding capitalist societies. For several centuries, such contact primarily took place in the context of European *colonialism*—a system by which a society claims and controls a foreign territory for purposes of economic exploitation.

In contrast to Africa and Asia, where the natives vastly outnumbered the colonists, European settlers in the Americas, Australia, and New Zealand expanded their

urgent anthropology Ethnographic research that documents endangered cultures; also known as *salvage ethnography*.

Figure 14.1 Endangered Culture Until recently, Ayoreo Indian bands lived largely isolated in the Gran Chaco, a vast wilderness in South America's heartland. One by one, these migratory foragers have been forced to "come out" due to outside encroachment on their habitat. Today, most dispossessed Ayoreo Indians find themselves in different stages of acculturation. This photo shows Ayoreo women of Zapocó in Bolivia's forest. Dressed in Western hand-me-downs and surrounded by plastic from the modern society that is pressing in on them, they weave natural plant fibers into traditionally patterned bags to sell for cash, while men make money by cutting trees for logging companies.

territories, decimating and overwhelming the indigenous inhabitants. These settler societies became politically independent, turning colonies into new states. Several, such as Canada, Brazil, and the United States, recognized that the indigenous peoples had rights to lands on which they could remain, but not as independent nations. Surviving on reservations surrounded by a dominant mainstream society, these indigenous peoples, or tribal nations, are bureaucratically controlled as *internal colonies.*

Typically, as the dominant (often foreign) power establishes its superiority, local indigenous cultures are made to appear inferior, ridiculous, or otherwise unequal, and ethnic groups or smaller nations are often forced to adopt the ways of the more powerful society pressing in on them. Government-sponsored programs designed to compel tribal communities or ethnic minorities to abandon their ancestral languages and cultural traditions for those of the controlling society have ripped apart the unique cultural fabric of one group after another. These programs left many indigenous families impoverished, demoralized, and desperate.

In the United States, this asymmetrical culture contact became known as *acculturation.* This is the often-disruptive process of cultural change occurring in traditional societies as they come in contact with more powerful state societies—in particular, industrialized or capitalist societies.

One of the first anthropologists to study acculturation was Margaret Mead in her 1932 fieldwork among the Omaha Indians of Nebraska. In that research (one of many projects she undertook), she focused on community breakdown and cultural disintegration of this traditional American Indian tribe. In the course of the 20th century, numerous other anthropologists carried out acculturation studies in Asia, Africa, Australia, Oceania, the Americas, and even in parts of Europe, thereby greatly contributing to our knowledge of complex and often disturbing processes of cultural change.

Applied Anthropology

Anthropologists had a unique perspective on the impact of culture contact, but they were not the only ones interested in acculturation. In fact, business corporations, religious institutions, and government agencies responsible for the administration of colonies or tribal reservations actively promoted cultural change.

The British and Dutch governments, for example, had a vested interest in maintaining order over enormous colonies overseas, ruling foreign populations many times larger than their own. For practical purposes, these governments imposed a colonial system of *indirect rule* in which they depended on tribal chiefs, princes, kings, emirs, sultans, maharajas, or whatever their titles. These indigenous rulers, supported by the colonial regimes, managed the peoples under their authority by means of customary law. In the United States and Canada, a somewhat similar political system of indirect rule was established in which indigenous communities residing on tribal reservations were (and still are) governed by their own leaders largely according to their own rules, albeit under the surveillance of federal authorities.

Whatever the political condition of indigenous peoples—whether they reside on reservations, in colonies, or under some other form of authority exercised by a foreign controlling state—the practical value of anthropology became increasingly evident in the course of time. In identifying the disintegrating effects of asymmetrical culture contact, acculturation studies gave birth to *applied anthropology*—the use of anthropological knowledge and methods to solve practical problems in communities confronting new challenges.

In 1937 the British government set up an anthropological research institute in what is now Zambia to study the impact of international markets on Central Africa's traditional societies. In the next decade, anthropologists worked on a number of problem-oriented studies throughout Africa, including the disruptive effects of the mining industry and labor migration on domestic economies and cultures.

Facing similar issues in North America, the U.S. Bureau of Indian Affairs (BIA), which oversees federally recognized tribes on Indian reservations, established an applied anthropology branch in the mid-1930s. Beyond studying the problems of acculturation, the handful of applied anthropologists hired by the BIA were to identify culturally appropriate ways for the U.S. government to introduce social and economic development programs to reduce poverty, promote literacy, and solve a host of other problems on the reservations.

The international Society for Applied Anthropology, founded in 1941, aimed to promote scientific investigation of the principles controlling human relations and their practical application. Applied anthropology developed into an important part of the discipline and continued to grow even after colonized countries in Asia and Africa became self-governing states in the mid-1900s.

In Mexico—perhaps more than anywhere else in the world—anthropology has gained considerable prestige as a discipline, and its practitioners have been appointed to high political positions. The reasons for this are complex, but one factor stands out: Mexico, a former Spanish colony, is a large multi-ethnic democracy inhabited by millions of indigenous peoples who form the demographic majority in many regions. Converting acculturation theory into state-sponsored policies, influential government officials such as anthropologist Gonzalo Aguirre Beltrán sought to integrate myriad indigenous communities into a Mexican state that embraces ethnic diversity in a national culture (Aguirre Beltrán, 1974; Weaver, 2002) (**Figure 14.2**).

Figure 14.2 Postage stamp honoring Gonzalo Aguirre Beltrán First trained as a medical doctor, Dr. Gonzalo Aguirre Beltrán (1908–1996) became one of Mexico's most important anthropologists. He pioneered research on Afro-Mexicans and studied land tenure conflict among Mexican Indian communities in the 1930s. Theoretically influenced by the acculturation approach developed by Melville Herskovits of Northwestern University and Robert Redfield of the University of Chicago, he headed the Instituto Nacional Indigenista (National Indigenous Institute) in the 1950s and 1960s. As an influential government official, he converted acculturation theory into state-sponsored policies integrating and assimilating millions of indigenous Mexican Indians into a national culture embracing ethnic diversity in a democratic state society.

Voicing the need for an applied anthropology to address the negative effects of culture contact on indigenous peoples, Polish-born British anthropologist Bronislaw Malinowski commented, "The anthropologist who is unable to register the tragic errors committed at times with the best intentions remains an antiquarian covered with academic dust and in fool's paradise" (quoted in Mair, 1957, p. 4; see also Malinowski, 1945). Today, many academically trained anthropologists specialize in applied research, working for a variety of local, regional, national, and international institutions, in particular nongovernmental organizations (NGOs), and are active on numerous fronts in every corner of the world.

Studying Cultures at a Distance

During World War II (1939–1945) and the early years of the Cold War (over forty years of political hostility and conflict in diplomacy, economics, and ideology between blocks of capitalist countries led by the United States and rival blocks of communist countries led by Russia), some anthropologists shifted their attention from small-scale traditional communities to modern state societies.

Aiming to discover basic personality traits, or psychological profiles, shared by the majority of the people in modern state societies, several U.S. and British anthropologists became involved in a wartime government program of "national character" studies. Officials believed such studies would help them to better understand and deal with the newly declared enemy states of Japan and Germany (in World War II) and later Russia and others.

During wartime, on-location ethnographic fieldwork was impossible in enemy societies and challenging at best in most other foreign countries. So, Margaret Mead and her close friend Ruth Benedict (one of her former professors at Columbia University), along with several other anthropologists, developed innovative techniques for studying "culture at a distance." Their methods included the analysis of newspapers, literature, photographs, and popular films. They also collected information through structured interviews with immigrants and refugees from the enemy nations, as well as foreigners from other countries (Mead & Métraux, 1953).

The efforts of these anthropologists to portray the national character of peoples inhabiting distant countries included investigating topics such as childrearing beliefs, attitudes, and practices, in conjunction with examining print or film materials for recurrent cultural themes and values. This cultural knowledge was also used for propaganda and psychological warfare. After the war, some of the information and insight based on such long-distance anthropological studies were found useful in temporarily governing the occupied territories and dealing with newly liberated populations in other parts of the world.

Studying Contemporary State Societies

Although there were theoretical flaws in the national character studies and methodological problems in studying cultures at a distance, research on contemporary state societies was more than just a war-related endeavor. Even when anthropologists devoted themselves primarily to researching non-Western small-scale communities, they recognized that a generalized understanding of human relations, ideas, and behavior depends upon knowledge of *all* cultures and peoples, including those in complex, large-scale industrial societies organized in political states. Already during the years of the Great Depression (1930s) several anthropologists worked in their own countries in settings ranging from factories to farming communities and suburban neighborhoods.

One interesting example of an early anthropologist doing research on the home front is Hortense Powdermaker. Born in Philadelphia, Powdermaker went to London to study anthropology under Malinowski and did her first major ethnographic fieldwork among Melanesians in the southern Pacific. When she returned to the United States, she researched a racially segregated town in Mississippi in the 1930s (Powdermaker, 1939). During the next decade, she focused on combating U.S. dominant society's racism against African Americans and other ethnic minorities.

While in the South, Powdermaker became keenly aware of the importance of the mass media in shaping people's worldviews (Wolf & Trager, 1971). To further explore this ideological force in modern culture, she cast her critical eye on the domestic film industry and did a year of fieldwork in Hollywood (1946–1947).

As Powdermaker was wrapping up her Hollywood research, several other anthropologists were launching other kinds of studies in large-scale societies. Convinced that governments and colonial administrations, as well as new global institutions such as the United Nations (founded in 1945), could and should benefit from anthropological insights, Ruth Benedict and Margaret Mead initiated a team project in comparative research on contemporary cultures based at Columbia University in New York (1947–1952).

In 1950, Swiss anthropologist Alfred Métraux put together an international team of U.S., French, and Brazilian researchers to study contemporary race relations in Brazil. The project, sponsored by UNESCO (the United Nations Education, Science, and Culture Organization), was part of the UN's global campaign against racial prejudice and discrimination. Headquartered in Paris, Métraux selected this South American country as a research site primarily for comparative purposes. Like the United States, Brazil was a former European colony with a large multi-ethnic population and a long history of black slavery. It had abolished slavery twenty-five years later than the United States but had made much more progress in terms of its race relations.

In contrast to the racially segregated United States, Brazil was believed to be an ideal example of harmonious, tolerant, and overall positive cross-racial relations. The research findings yielded unexpected results, showing that dark-skinned Brazilians of African descent did face systemic social and economic discrimination—albeit not in the political and legal form of racial segregation that pervaded the United States at the time (Prins & Krebs, 2006).

In 1956 and 1957, anthropologist Julian Steward left the United States to supervise an anthropological research team in developing countries such as Kenya, Nigeria, Peru, Mexico, Japan, Myanmar (Burma), Malaya, and Indonesia. His goal was to study the comparative impact of industrialization and urbanization upon these different populations. Other anthropologists launched similar projects in other parts of the world.

Peasant Studies

In the 1950s, as anthropologists widened their scope to consider the impact of complex state societies on the traditional indigenous groups central to early anthropological study, some zeroed in on peasant communities. Peasants represent an important social category, standing midway between modern industrial society and traditional subsistence foragers, herders, farmers, and fishers (**Figure 14.3**). Part of larger, more complex societies, peasant communities exist worldwide, and peasants number in the many hundreds of millions.

Peasantry represents the largest social category of our species to date. Because peasant unrest over economic and social problems fuels political instability in many developing countries, anthropological studies of these rural populations in Latin America, Africa, Asia, and elsewhere are considered both significant and practical. In addition to improving policies aimed at social and economic development in rural communities, anthropological peasant studies may offer insights into how to deal with peasants resisting challenges to their traditional way of life. Such anthropological research may be useful in promoting social justice by helping to solve, manage, or avoid social conflicts and political violence, including rebellions and guerrilla warfare or insurgencies.

Advocacy Anthropology

By the 1960s, European colonial powers had relinquished almost all of their overseas domains. Many anthropologists turned their attention to the newly independent countries in Africa and Asia, whereas others focused on South and Central America. However, as anti-Western sentiment and political upheaval seriously complicated fieldwork in many parts of the world, significant numbers of anthropologists investigated important issues of cultural change and conflict inside Europe and North America.

Figure 14.3 **A Voice for Peasants** Peasant studies came to the fore during the 1950s as anthropologists began investigating rural peoples in state societies and the impact of capitalism on traditional small-scale communities. Here a Guarani-speaking peasant leader addresses a crowd in front of the presidential palace in Paraguay's capital city of Asunción at a massive protest rally against land dispossession.

Many of these issues, which remain focal points to this day, involve immigrants and refugees coming from places where anthropologists have conducted research.

Some anthropologists have gone beyond studying such groups to playing a role in helping them adjust to their new circumstances—an example of applied anthropology. Others have become advocates for peasant communities, ethnic or religious minorities, or indigenous groups struggling to hold onto their ancestral lands, natural resources, and customary ways of life. Both focus on identifying, preventing, or solving problems and challenges in groups that form part of complex societies and whose circumstances and affairs are conditioned or even determined by powerful outside institutions or corporations over which they generally have little or no control.

Although anthropologists have privately long championed the rights of indigenous peoples and other cultural groups under siege, one of the first anthropological research

Figure 14.4 Advocacy anthropologist Rodolfo Stavenhagen, UN Special Rapporteur on the Situation of Human Rights and Fundamental Freedom of Indigenous People. Here he appears with Victoria Tauli-Corpuz, chairperson of the UN Permanent Forum on Indigenous Issues, at a press conference near Manilla in the Phillipines in 2007.

AP Images/Pat Roque

projects explicitly and publicly addressing the quest for social justice and cultural survival took place among the Meskwaki, or Fox Indians, on their reservation in the state of Iowa (1948–1959). Based on long-term fieldwork with this North American Indian community, anthropologist Sol Tax challenged government-sponsored applied anthropological research projects and proposed instead that researchers work directly with "disadvantaged, exploited, and oppressed communities [to help *them*] identify and solve their [*own*] problems" (Field, 2004; see also Lurie, 1973).

Over the past few decades, anthropologists committed to social justice and human rights have become actively and increasingly involved in efforts to assist indigenous groups, peasant communities, and ethnic minorities. Today, most anthropologists committed to community-based and politically involved research refer to their work as **advocacy anthropology**.

Anthropologist Robert Hitchcock has practiced advocacy anthropology for over three decades. Specializing in development issues, he has focused primarily on land rights, as well as the social, economic, and cultural rights, of indigenous peoples in southern Africa—especially Bushmen (San, Basarwa) groups in Botswana. Hitchcock's work has involved helping Bushmen to ensure their rights to land—for foraging, pasturing, farming, and income-generation purposes—in the face of development projects aimed at setting aside land for the ranching, mining, or conservation interests of others. He helped draw up legislation on subsistence hunting in Botswana, making it the only country in Africa that allows broad-based hunting rights for indigenous peoples who forage for part of their livelihood (Hitchcock & Enghoff, 2004).

Today's most wide-ranging advocacy anthropologist is Rodolfo Stavenhagen, the UN's specialist on indigenous rights (**Figure 14.4**). A research professor at the Colegio de Mexico since 1965, he is founder and first president of the Mexican Academy of Human Rights. Stavenhagen leads investigations on the human rights and fundamental freedoms of indigenous peoples throughout the world.

Studying Up

Given anthropology's mission to understand the human condition in its full cross-cultural range and complexity—not just in distant places or at the margins of our own societies—some scholars have urged ethnographic research in the centers of political and economic power in the world's dominant societies. This wide scope is especially important for applied and advocacy anthropologists researching groups or communities embedded in larger and more complex processes of state-level politics and economics or even transnational levels of global institutions and multinational corporations. Of particular note in this effort is anthropologist Laura Nader. Coining the term *studying up*, she has called upon anthropologists to focus on Western elites, government bureaucracies, global corporations, philanthropic foundations, media empires, business clubs, and so on.

Studying up is easier said than done because it is a formidable challenge to do participant observation in such well-guarded circles. And when these elites are confronted

advocacy anthropology Research that is community based and politically involved.

with research projects or findings not to their liking, they have the capacity and political power to stop or seriously obstruct the research or the dissemination of its results.

Globalization and Multi-Sited Ethnography

As noted in Chapter 1, the impact of globalization is everywhere. Distant localities are becoming linked in such a way that forces and activities occurring thousands of miles away are shaping local events and situations, and vice versa. Connected by modern transportation, world trade, finance capital, transnational labor pools, and information superhighways, even the most geographically remote communities have become increasingly interdependent. Indeed, all of humanity now exists in what we refer to in this text as a *globalscape*—a worldwide interconnected landscape with multiple intertwining and overlapping peoples and cultures on the move.

One consequence of globalization is the formation of *diasporic* populations (*diaspora* is a Greek word, originally meaning "scattering"), living and working far from their original homeland. Some diasporic groups feel uprooted and fragmented, but others are able to transcend vast distances and stay in touch with family and friends through communication technologies. With Internet access to blogs and other sources of news, combined with e-mail, text messaging, Twitter, and a variety of social media platforms, geographically dispersed individuals spend more and more of their time in cyberspace (Appadurai, 1996). This electronically mediated environment enables people who are far from home to remain informed, to maintain their social networks, and even to hold onto a historical sense of ethnic identity that culturally distinguishes them from those with whom they share their daily routines in actual geographic space.

Globalization has given rise to a new trend in anthropological research and analysis known as **multi-sited ethnography**—the investigation and documentation of peoples and cultures embedded in the larger structures of a globalizing world, utilizing a range of methods in various locations of time and space. Engaged in such mobile ethnography, researchers seek to capture the emerging global dimension by following individual actors, organizations, objects, images, stories, conflicts, and even pathogens as they move about in various interrelated transnational situations and locations (Marcus, 1995; Robben & Sluka, 2007) Refugee communities around the world also fall into this category (**Figure 14.5**).

Among examples of multi-sited ethnographic research on a diasporic ethnic group is a recent study on transnational Han Chinese identities by Chinese American anthropologist Andrea Louie. Louie's fieldwork carried her to an array of locations in San Francisco, Hong Kong, and southern China—including her ancestral home in the Cantonese village Tiegang in Guangdong Province. Her paternal great-grandfather left the village in the 1840s, crossing the Pacific Ocean to work on railroad construction during the California Gold Rush. But other family members remained in their ancestral homeland. Here, Louie describes her research investigating Chinese identities from different and changing perspectives:

> My fieldwork on Chinese identities employed a type of mobile [ethnography] aimed at examining various parts of a "relationship" being forged anew across national boundaries that draws on metaphors of shared heritage and place. In my investigation of "Chineseness" I conducted participant observation and interviews in San Francisco with Chinese American participants of the In Search of Roots program,[1] as well as later in China when they visited their ancestral villages and participated in government-sponsored Youth Festivals. . . . I interviewed people in their homes, and apartments; in cafes, culture centers, and McDonald's restaurants; and in rural Chinese villages and on jet planes, focusing on various moments and contexts of interaction within which multiple and often discrepant discourses of Chineseness are brought together. (Louie, 2004, pp. 8–9)

Also emerging in multi-sited ethnography are greater interdisciplinary approaches to fieldwork, bringing in theoretical ideas and research methods from cultural studies, media studies, and mass communication. One example is the development of ethnographic studies of social networks, communicative practices, and other cultural expressions in cyberspace by means of digital visual and audio technologies. Known as **digital ethnography**, it is sometimes referred to as *cyberethnography* or *netnography* (Murthy, 2011).

Even in the fast-changing, globalizing world of the 21st century, core ethnographic research methods developed over a century ago continue to be relevant and revealing. New technologies have been added to the anthropologist's toolkit, but the hallmarks of our discipline—holistic research through fieldwork with participant observation—is still a valued and productive tradition. Having presented a sweeping historical overview of shifting anthropological research challenges and strategies, we turn now to the topic of research methods.

---

multi-sited ethnography The investigation and documentation of peoples and cultures embedded in the larger structures of a globalizing world, utilizing a range of methods in various locations of time and space.

digital ethnography An ethnographic study of social networks, communicative practices, and other cultural expressions in cyberspace by means of digital visual and audio technologies; also called *cyberethnography* or *netnography*.

---

[1] This program, run by organizations in Guangzhou and San Francisco, provides an opportunity for young adults (ages 17 to 25) of Cantonese descent to visit their ancestral villages in China.

VISUAL COUNTERPOINT

Figure 14.5 Multi-Sited Ethnography Anthropologist Catherine Besteman began fieldwork with Bantu communities in southern Somalia's Jubba Valley in the late 1980s, just before the outbreak of the civil war that ruined the country and forced many into exile. Since 2003, thousands of Somali Bantu have relocated to Lewiston, Maine, which has become an additional site for Besteman's ongoing research. Some of her undergraduate students at nearby Colby College participate in her work with these refugees. In the photo on the left, Besteman (in orange blouse) is interviewing in the Somalian village of Qardale. In the photo on the right, Besteman's students Elizabeth Powell and Nicole Mitchell are interviewing Iman Osman in his family's Lewiston apartment the year he graduated from high school. He and his family fled the war when he was just 4 years old, living in a refugee camp for a decade before finally coming to the United States.

Doing Ethnography

Every culture comprises underlying rules or standards that are rarely obvious. A major challenge to the anthropologist is to identify and analyze those rules. Fundamental to the effort is **ethnographic fieldwork**—extended on-location research to gather detailed and in-depth information on a society's customary ideas, values, and practices through participation in its collective social life.

Although the scope of cultural anthropology has expanded to include urban life in complex industrial and postindustrial societies, and even virtual communities in cyberspace, ethnographic methods developed for fieldwork in traditional small-scale societies continue to be central to anthropological research in all types of communities. The methodology still includes personal observation of and participation in the everyday activities of the community, along with interviews, mapping, collection of genealogical data, and recording of sounds and visual images. It all begins with selecting a research site and a research problem or question.

Site Selection and Research Question

Anthropologists usually work outside their own culture, society, or ethnic group, most often in a foreign country.

Although it has much to offer, anthropological study within one's own society may present special problems, as described by noted British anthropologist Sir Edmund Leach:

> Surprising though it may seem, fieldwork in a cultural context of which you already have intimate firsthand experience seems to be much more difficult than fieldwork which is approached from the naïve viewpoint of a total stranger. When anthropologists study facets of their own society their vision seems to become distorted by prejudices which derive from private rather than public experience. (Leach, 1982, p. 124)

Anthropologists doing studies in societies to which they belong are likely to be more successful if the researcher has first done work in some other culture. The more one learns of other cultures, the more one gains a fresh and more revealing perspective on one's own.

But wherever the site, research requires advance planning that usually includes obtaining funding and securing permission from the community to be studied

ethnographic fieldwork Extended on-location research to gather detailed and in-depth information on a society's customary ideas, values, and practices through participation in its collective social life.

(and, where mandated, permission from government officials as well). If possible, researchers make a preliminary trip to the site to make arrangements before moving there for more extended research.

After exploring the local conditions and circumstances, ethnographers have the opportunity to better define their specific research question or problem. For instance, what is the psychological impact of a new highway on members of a traditionally isolated farming community? Or how does the introduction of electronic media such as cell phones influence long-established gender relations in cultures with religious restrictions on social contact between men and women?

Preparatory Research

Before heading into the field, anthropologists do preparatory research. This includes delving into any existing written, visual, or sound information available about the people and place one has chosen to study. It may involve contacting and interviewing others who have some knowledge about or experience with the community, region, or country.

Because communication is key in ethnographic research, anthropologists need to learn the language used in the community selected for fieldwork. Many of the more than 6,000 languages currently spoken in the world have been recorded and written down, especially during the past century, so it is possible to learn some foreign languages prior to fieldwork. However, as in the early days of the discipline, some of today's anthropologists do research among peoples whose native languages have not yet been written down. In this case, the researcher may be able to find someone who is minimally bilingual to help him or her gain some proficiency with the language. Another possibility is to first learn an already recorded and closely related language, which provides some elementary communication skills during the early phase of the actual fieldwork.

Finally, anthropologists prepare for fieldwork by studying theoretical, historical, ethnographic, and other literature relevant to the research. For instance, anthropologists interested in understanding violence, both between and within groups, will read studies describing and theoretically explaining conflicts such as wars, insurgencies, raids, feuds, vengeance killings, and so on. Having delved into the existing literature, they may then formulate a theoretical framework and research question to guide them in their fieldwork. Such was the case when anthropologist Napoleon Chagnon applied sociobiological theory to his study of violence within Yanomamö Indian communities in South America's tropical rainforest, suggesting that males with an aggressive reputation as killers are reproductively more successful than those without such a status (Chagnon, 1988a).

Christopher Boehm took a different theoretical approach in his research on blood revenge among Slavic mountain people in Montenegro. He framed his research question in terms of the ecological function of this violent tradition because it regulated relations between groups competing for survival in a harsh environment with scarce natural resources (Boehm, 1987).

Participant Observation: Ethnographic Tools and Aids

Once in the field, anthropologists rely on *participant observation*—a research method in which one learns about a group's behaviors and beliefs through social involvement and personal observation within the community, as well as interviews and discussion with individual members of the group over an extended stay in the community (**Figure 14.6**). This work requires an ability to socially and psychologically adapt to a community with a different way of life. Keen personal observation skills are also essential, employing *all* the senses—sight, touch, smell, taste, and hearing—in order to perceive collective life in the other culture.

When participating in an unfamiliar culture, anthropologists are often helped by one or more generous individuals

Figure 14.6 Participant Observation The hallmark research methodology for anthropologists is participant observation—illustrated by this photo of anthropologist Julia Jean (*center*), who is both observing *and* participating in a Hindu ritual at a temple for the goddess Kamakhya in northeastern India.

in the village or neighborhood. They may also be taken in by a family, and through participation in the daily routine of a household, they will gradually become familiar with the community's basic shared cultural features.

Anthropologists may also formally enlist the assistance of **key consultants**—members of the society being studied who provide information to help researchers understand the meaning of what they observe. (Early anthropologists referred to such individuals as *informants*.) Just as parents guide a child toward proper behavior, so do these insiders help researchers unravel the mysteries of what at first is a strange, puzzling, and unpredictable world. To compensate local individuals for their help, fieldworkers may thank them for their time and expertise with goods, services, or cash.

Beyond the skills and resources noted previously, an anthropologist's most essential ethnographic tools in the field are notebooks, pen/pencil, camera, and sound and video recorders. Nowadays, most also use laptop computers equipped with data processing programs. And some field kits include GPS equipment, smartphones, and other modern handheld devices.

Although researchers may focus on a particular cultural aspect or issue, they will consider the culture as a whole for the sake of context. This holistic and integrative approach, a hallmark of anthropology, requires being tuned in to nearly countless details of daily life, both the ordinary and the extraordinary. By taking part in community life, anthropologists learn why and how events are organized and carried out. Through alert and sustained participation—carefully watching, questioning, listening, and analyzing over a period of time—they can usually identify, explain, and often predict a group's behavior.

Data Gathering: The Ethnographer's Approach

Information collected by ethnographers falls into two main categories: quantitative and qualitative data. **Quantitative data** consist of statistical or measurable information, such as population density, demographic composition of people and animals, and the number and size of houses; the hours worked per day; the types and quantities of crops grown; the amount of carbohydrates or animal protein consumed per individual; the quantity of wood, dung, or other kinds of fuel used to cook food or heat dwellings; the number of children born out of wedlock; the ratio of spouses born and raised within or outside the community; and so on.

Qualitative data include nonstatistical information about features such as settlement patterns, natural resources, social networks of kinship relations, customary beliefs and practices, personal life histories, and so on. Often, these unquantifiable data are the most important

part of ethnographic research because they capture the essence of a culture; this information provides us with deeper insights into the unique lives of different peoples, helping us truly understand what, why, and how they feel, think, and act in their own distinctive ways.

Taking Surveys

Unlike many other social scientists, anthropologists do not usually go into the field equipped with predetermined surveys or questionnaires. Those who use surveys usually do so after spending enough time on location to have gained the community's confidence and to know how to compose a questionnaire with categories that are culturally relevant.

Whether studying a community in geographic space or cyberspace, anthropologists who use surveys view them as one small part in a large research strategy that includes a considerable amount of qualitative data (**Figure 14.7**). They recognize that only by keeping an open mind while thoughtfully watching, listening, participating, and asking questions can they discover many aspects of a culture.

As fieldwork proceeds, anthropologists sort their complex impressions and observations into a meaningful whole, sometimes by formulating and testing limited or low-level hypotheses, but just as often by making use of imagination or intuition and following up on hunches. What is important is that the results are constantly checked for accuracy and consistency, for if the parts fail to fit together in a way that is internally coherent, it may be that a mistake has been made and further inquiry is necessary.

Two studies of a village in Peru illustrate the problem of gathering data through surveys alone. A sociologist conducted one study by surveying the villagers with a questionnaire and concluded that people in the village invariably worked together on one another's privately owned plots of land. By contrast, a cultural anthropologist who lived in the village for over a year (including the brief period when the sociologist did his study) witnessed that particular practice only once. The anthropologist's long-term participant observation revealed that although the idea of labor exchange relations was important to the people's sense of themselves, it was not a common economic practice (Chambers, 1995).

---

key consultant A member of the society being studied who provides information that helps researchers understand the meaning of what they observe; early anthropologists referred to such individuals as *informants*.

quantitative data Statistical or measurable information, such as demographic composition, the types and quantities of crops grown, or the ratio of spouses born and raised within or outside the community.

qualitative data Nonstatistical information such as personal life stories and customary beliefs and practices.

Courtesy of Jeffrey Snodgrass

Figure 14.7 Surveys in Cyberspace Since spring 2008, anthropologist Jeffrey Snodgrass has been studying videogaming. Conducting participant-observation research in and around the World of Warcraft (WoW), he has gathered information about this virtual community through interviewing and surveying its members. He has been particularly fascinated by players' relationships to their WoW avatars, the in-game graphical representations of their characters. Via avatars, gamers can temporarily separate or even dissociate from their actual-world persons and enter WoW's fantasyscape. Here Snodgrass (the pointy-eared Draenei shaman seated front left) and his virtual research team of graduate and undergraduate collaborators pose beneath WoW's Goblin Messiah.

The point here is that questionnaires all too easily embody the concepts and categories of the researcher, who is an outsider, rather than those of the people being studied. Even where this is not a problem, questionnaires tend to concentrate on what is measurable, answerable, and acceptable as a question, rather than probing the less obvious and more complex qualitative aspects of society or culture.

Moreover, for a host of reasons—fear, ignorance, hostility, hope of reward—people may give false, incomplete, or biased information (Sanjek, 1990). Keeping culture-bound ideas, which are often embedded in standardized questionnaires, out of research methods is an important point in all ethnographic research.

informal interview An unstructured, open-ended conversation in everyday life.
formal interview A structured question/answer session carefully notated as it occurs and based on prepared questions.

Interviewing

Asking questions is fundamental to ethnographic fieldwork and takes place in **informal interviews** (unstructured, open-ended conversations in everyday life) and **formal interviews** (structured question/answer sessions carefully notated as they occur and based on prepared questions). Informal interviews may be carried out at any time and in any place—on horseback, in a canoe, by a cooking fire, during ritual events, while walking through the community with a local inhabitant, and the list goes on. Such casual exchanges are essential, for it is often in these conversations that people share most freely. Moreover, questions put forth in formal interviews typically grow out of cultural knowledge and insights gained during informal ones.

Getting people to open up is an art born of a genuine interest in both the information and the person who is sharing it. It requires dropping all assumptions and cultivating the ability to *really* listen. It may even require a willingness to be the village idiot by asking simple questions to which the answers may seem obvious. Also, effective interviewers learn early on that numerous follow-up questions are vital given that first answers may mask truth rather than reveal it. Questions generally fall into one of two categories: broad, *open-ended questions* (Can you tell me about your childhood?) and *closed questions* seeking specific pieces of information (Where and when were you born?).

In ethnographic fieldwork, interviews are used to collect a vast range of cultural information: from life histories, genealogies, and myths to craft techniques and midwife practices to beliefs concerning everything from illness to food taboos. Genealogical data can be especially useful because they provide information about a range of social customs (such as cousin marriage), worldviews (such as ancestor worship), political relations (such as alliances), and economic arrangements (such as hunting or harvesting on clan-owned lands).

Researchers employ numerous **eliciting devices**—activities and objects used to draw out individuals and encourage them to recall and share information. There are countless examples of this: taking a walk with a local and asking about songs, legends, and place names linked to geographic features; sharing details about one's own family and neighborhood and inviting a telling in return; joining in a community activity and asking a local to explain the practice and why the participants are doing it; taking and sharing photographs of cultural objects or activities and asking locals to explain what they see in the pictures; presenting research findings to community members and documenting their responses.

Mapping

Many anthropologists have done fieldwork in remote places where there is little geographic documentation. Even if cartographers have mapped the region, standard maps seldom show geographic and spatial features that are culturally significant to the people living there. People inhabiting areas that form part of their ancestral homeland have a particular understanding of the area and their own names for local places. These native names may convey essential geographic information, describing the distinctive features of a locality such as its physical appearance, its specific dangers, or its precious resources.

Place names may derive from certain political realities such as headquarters, territorial boundaries, and so on. Others may make sense only in the cultural context of a local people's worldview as recounted in their myths, legends, songs, or other narrative traditions. Thus, to truly understand a place, some anthropologists make their own detailed geographic maps documenting culturally relevant geographic features in the landscape inhabited by the people they study (**Figure 14.8**).

Especially since the early 1970s, anthropologists have become involved in indigenous land use and occupancy studies for various reasons, including the documentation of traditional land claims. Researchers constructing individual map biographies may gather information from a variety of sources: local oral histories; early written descriptions of explorers, traders, missionaries, and other visitors; and data obtained from archaeological excavations.

One such ethnogeographic research project took place in northwestern Canada, during the planning stage of the building of the Alaska Highway natural gas pipeline. Because the line would cut directly though Native lands, local indigenous community leaders and federal officials insisted that a study be done to determine how the new construction would affect indigenous inhabitants. Canadian anthropologist Hugh Brody, one of the researchers in this ethnogeographic study, explained:

> These maps are the key to the studies and their greatest contribution. Hunters, trappers, fishermen, and berry-pickers mapped out all the land they had ever used in their lifetimes, encircling hunting areas species by species, marking gathering location and camping sites—everything their life on the land had entailed that could be marked on a map. (Brody, 1981, p. 147)

In addition to mapping the local place names and geographic features, anthropologists may also map out information relevant to the local subsistence, such as animal migration routes, favorite fishing areas, places where medicinal plants can be harvested or firewood cut, and so on.

Today, by means of the technology known as global positioning system (GPS), researchers can measure precise distances by triangulating the travel time of radio signals from various orbiting satellites. They can create maps that pinpoint human settlement locations and the layout of dwellings, gardens, public spaces, watering holes, pastures, surrounding mountains, rivers, lakes, seashores, islands, swamps, forests, deserts, and any other relevant feature in the regional environment.

To store, edit, analyze, integrate, and display this geographically referenced spatial information, some anthropologists use cartographic digital technology, known as geographic information systems (GIS). GIS makes it possible to map the geographic features and natural resources in a certain environment—and to link these data to ethnographic information about population density and distribution, social networks of kinship relations, seasonal patterns of land use, private or collective claims of ownership, travel routes, sources of water, and so on. With GIS

eliciting devices Activities and objects used to draw out individuals and encourage them to recall and share information.

Courtesy of the Projecto Etnoarqueológico de Amazona Meridional

Figure 14.8 Collecting GPS Data For anthropologist Michael Heckenberger, doing fieldwork among the Kuikuro people of the Upper Xingu River in the southern margins of the Amazon rainforest has become a collaborative undertaking. Together with other specialists on his research team, he has trained local tribespeople to help with the research project about their ancestral culture, which includes searching for the remains of ancient earthworks and mapping them. The photos above show trained local assistant Laquai Kuikuro collecting GPS data in a modern field of manioc—a primary dietary staple of indigenous Amazonian communities in Brazil—and later reviewing the downloaded data on a computer. On the right is a map showing GPS-charted indigenous earthworks in the Upper Xingu superimposed over a Landsat satellite image.

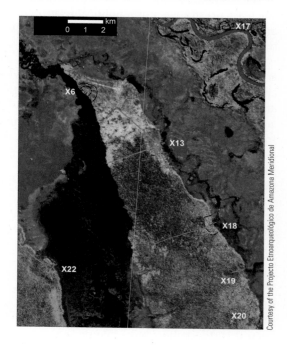

Courtesy of the Projecto Etnoarqueológico de Amazona Meridional

researchers can also integrate information about beliefs, myths, legends, songs, and other culturally relevant data associated with distinct locations. Moreover, they can create interactive inquiries for analysis of research data as well as natural and cultural resource management (Schoepfle, 2001).

Photographing and Filming

As noted previously, during fieldwork, most anthropologists use cameras, as well as notepads, computers, or sound recording devices to document their observations. Photography has been instrumental in anthropological research for more than a century. For instance, in the early 1880s, Franz Boas took photographs during his first fieldwork among the Inuit in the Canadian Arctic. And just a few years after the invention of the moving picture camera in 1894, anthropologists began filming people in action—recording traditional dances and other ethnographic subjects of interest.

As film technology developed, anthropologists turned increasingly to visual media for a wide range of cross-cultural research purposes. Some employed still photography in community surveys and elicitation techniques. Others took film cameras into the field to document the disappearing world of traditional foragers, herders, and farmers surviving in remote places. A few focused on

documenting traditional patterns of nonverbal communication such as body language and social space use for research purposes. Soon after the 1960 invention of the portable synchronous-sound camera, ethnographic filmmaking became increasingly important in producing a cross-cultural record of peoples all across the globe.

Since the digital revolution that began in the 1980s, we have been witnessing an explosive growth in visual media all across the world. It is not unusual for anthropologists to arrive in remote villages where at least a few native inhabitants take their own pictures or record their own stories and music. For researchers in the field, native-made audiovisual documents may represent a wealth of precious cultural information. The Anthropologists of Note feature details the long history of such equipment in anthropology.

ANTHROPOLOGISTS OF NOTE

Margaret Mead (1901–1978) • Gregory Bateson (1904–1980)

From 1936 to 1938 **Margaret Mead** and **Gregory Bateson** did collaborative ethnographic fieldwork in Bali. Bateson, Mead's husband at the time, was a British anthropologist trained by Alfred C. Haddon, who led the 1898 Torres Strait expedition and is credited with making the first ethnographic film in the field. During their stay in Bali, Bateson took about 25,000 photographs and shot 22,000 feet of motion picture

In 1938, after two years of fieldwork in Bali, Margaret Mead and Gregory Bateson began research in Papua New Guinea, where they staged this photograph of themselves to highlight the importance of cameras as part of the ethnographic toolkit. Note the camera on a tripod behind Mead and other cameras atop the desk.

film. Afterward, the couple coauthored the photographic ethnography *Balinese Character: A Photographic Analysis* (1942).

That same year, Bateson worked as an anthropological film analyst studying German motion pictures. Soon Mead and a few other anthropologists became involved in thematic analysis of foreign fictional films. She later compiled a number of such visual anthropology studies in a coedited volume titled *The Study of Culture at a Distance* (1953).

Mead became a tireless promoter of the scholarly use of ethnographic photography and film. In 1960, the year the portable sync-sound film camera was invented, Mead was serving as president of the American Anthropology Association. In her presidential address at the association's annual gathering, she pointed out what she saw as shortcomings in the discipline and urged anthropologists to use cameras more effectively.[a] Chiding her colleagues for not fully utilizing new technological developments, she complained that anthropology had come "to depend on words, and words, and words."

Mead's legacy is commemorated in numerous venues, including the Margaret Mead Film Festival hosted annually since 1977 by the American Museum of Natural History in New York City. Thus, it was fitting that during the Margaret Mead Centennial celebrations in 2001 the American Anthropological Association endorsed a landmark visual media policy statement urging academic committees to consider ethnographic visuals—and not just ethnographic writing—when evaluating scholarly output of academics up for hiring, promotion, and tenure.

---

[a]Mead, M. (1960). Anthropology among the sciences. *American Anthropologist 63*, 475–482.

Challenges of Ethnographic Fieldwork

Although ethnographic fieldwork offers a range of opportunities to gain better and deeper insight into the community being studied, it comes with a Pandora's box of challenges. At the least, it usually requires researchers to step out of their cultural comfort zone into an unknown world that is sometimes unsettling.

As touched upon in Chapter 1, anthropologists in the field are likely to face a wide array of challenges—physical, social, mental, political, and ethical. While they are handling these challenges, they must be fully engaged in work and social activities with the community. In addition, they are doing a host of other things, such as interviewing, taking copious notes, and analyzing data. In the following paragraphs we offer details on some of the most common personal struggles anthropologists face in the field.

Social Acceptance

Having decided where to do ethnographic research and what to focus on, anthropologists embark on the journey to their field site. Typically moving into a community with a culture unlike their own, most experience culture shock and loneliness at least during the initial stages of their work—work that requires them to establish social contacts with strangers who have little or no idea who they are, why they have come, or what they want from them. In short, a visiting anthropologist is as much a mystery to those she or he intends to study as the group is to the researcher.

Although there is no sure way of predicting how one will be received, it is certain that success in ethnographic fieldwork depends on mutual goodwill and the ability to develop friendships and other meaningful social relations. As New Zealand anthropologist Jeffrey Sluka notes, "The classic image of successful rapport and good fieldwork relations in cultural anthropology is that of the ethnographer who has been 'adopted' or named by the tribe or people he or she studies" (Sluka, 2007, p. 122).

Anthropologists adopted into networks of kinship relations not only gain social access and certain rights but also assume social obligations associated with their new kinship status. These relationships can be deep and enduring—as illustrated by Smithsonian anthropologist William Crocker's description of his 1991 return to the Canela tribal community after a twelve-year absence. He had lived among these Amazonian Indians in Brazil off and on for a total of sixty-six months from the 1950s through the 1970s (Figure 14.9). When he stepped out of the single-motor missionary plane that had brought him back in 1991, he was quickly surrounded by Canela:

> Once on the ground, I groped for names and
> terms of address while shaking many hands. Soon
> my Canela mother, Tutkhwey (dove-woman),
> pulled me over to the shade of a plane's wing and
> pushed me down to a mat on the ground. She put

both hands on my shoulders and, kneeling beside me, her head by mine, cried out words of mourning in a loud yodeling manner. Tears and phlegm dripped onto my shoulder and knees. According to a custom now abandoned by the younger women, she was crying for the loss of a grown daughter, Tsep-khwey (bat-woman), as well as for my return. (Crocker & Crocker, 2004, p. 1)

Since that 1991 reunion, Crocker has visited the Canela community every other year, always receiving a warm welcome and staying with locals. Although many anthropologists are successful in gaining social acceptance and even adoption status in communities where they do participant observation, they rarely go completely native and abandon their own homeland. Even after long stays in a community, and after learning to behave appropriately and communicate well, few become complete insiders.

Distrust and Political Tension

An anthropologist's fieldwork challenges include the possibility of getting caught in political rivalries and unwittingly used by factions within the community or being viewed with suspicion by government authorities who may interpret their systematic inquiries as the work of a spy. Anthropologist June Nash, for instance, has faced serious political and personal challenges doing fieldwork in various Latin American communities experiencing violent changes. As an outsider, she tried to avoid becoming embroiled in local conflicts but could not maintain her position as an impartial observer while researching a tin mining community in the Bolivian highlands. When

Figure 14.9 Social Acceptance in Fieldwork
Anthropologist William Crocker did fieldwork among Canela Indians in Brazil over several decades. He still visits the community regularly. In this 1964 photograph, a Canela woman (M~i~i- kw'ej, or Alligator Woman) gives him a traditional haircut while other members of the community look on. She is the wife of his adoptive Canela "brother" and therefore a "wife" to Crocker in Canela kinship terms. Among the Canela, it is improper for a mother, sister, or daughter to cut a man's hair.

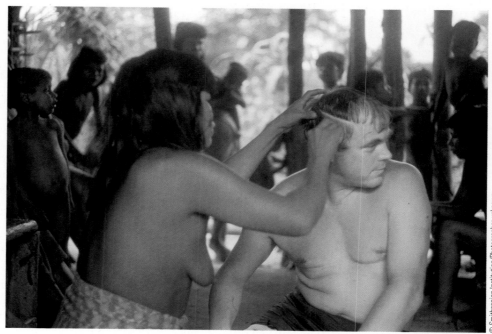

© Smithsonian Institution/Photographer unknown

the conflict between local miners and bosses controlling the armed forces became violent, Nash found herself in a revolutionary setting in which miners viewed her tape recorder as an instrument of espionage and suspected her of being a CIA agent (Nash, 1976).

All anthropologists face the overriding challenge of winning the trust that allows people to be themselves and share an unmasked version of their culture with a newcomer. Some do not succeed in meeting this challenge. So it was with anthropologist Lincoln Keiser in his difficult fieldwork in the remote town of Thull, situated in the Hindu Kush Mountains of northwestern Pakistan. Keiser ventured there to explore customary blood feuding among a Kohistani tribal community of 6,000 Muslims making their living by a mix of farming and herding in the rugged region. However, the people he had traveled so far to study did not appreciate his presence. As Keiser recounted, many of the fiercely independent tribesmen in this area, "where the AK-47 symbolizes the violent quality of male social relations," treated him with great disdain and suspicion, as a foreign "infidel":

> Throughout my stay in Thull, many people remained convinced I was a creature sent by the devil to harm the community. . . . [Doing fieldwork there] was a test I failed, for a *jirga* [political council] of my most vocal opponents ultimately forced me to leave Thull three months before I had planned. . . . Obviously, I have difficulty claiming the people of Thull as "my people" because so many of them never ceased to despise me. . . . Still, I learned from being hated. (Keiser, 1991, p. 103)

Gender, Age, Ideology, Ethnicity, and Skin Color

The challenges of Keiser's fieldwork stemmed in part from his non-Muslim religious identity, marking him as an outsider in the local community of the faithful. Gender, age, ethnicity, and skin color can also impact a researcher's access to a community. For instance, male ethnographers may face prohibitions or severe restrictions in interviewing women or observing certain women's activities. Similarly, a female researcher may not find ready reception among

males in communities with gender-segregation traditions. With respect to skin color, African American anthropologist Norris Brock-Johnson encountered social obstacles while doing fieldwork in the American Midwest, but his dark skin helped him gain "admission to the world of black Caribbean shipwrights" on the island of Bequia, where he studied traditional boatmaking (Robben, 2007, p. 61; see also Johnson, 1984).

Physical Danger

Ethnographic fieldwork in exotic places can be an adventure, but sometimes it presents physical danger. Although rare, some anthropologists have died in the field due to accident or illness. One dramatic example is that of American anthropologist Michelle Rosaldo. As a 37-year-old mother and university professor who had just published *Knowledge and Passion: Ilongot Notions of Self and Social Life* with Cambridge University Press, she returned to the Philippines for more fieldwork with the Ilongot. Trekking along a mountain trail on Luzon Island with her husband and fellow anthropologist, she slipped and fell to her death.

Another tragic accident involved Richard Condon, part of an American-Russian research team funded by the U.S. National Science Foundation for an anthropological study of health, population growth, and socialization in Alaska and the Russian Far East. In the late summer of 1995, he and three colleagues, along with five Yup'ik Eskimos, were traveling along the Bering Strait when their *umiak* ("skin-boat") flipped. Apparently, their boat had been attacked by a whale, wounded by an earlier party of seafaring Siberian Eskimo hunters. All nine men perished in the ice-cold water (Wenzel & McCartney, 1996).

Swedish anthropologist Anna Hedlund, currently researching non-state-armed groups in the Democratic Republic of Congo (DRC) in Africa, faces physical danger of a different sort. Living among rebels and investigating how they define and legitimize violence, she is surrounded by political tension and conflict (**Figure 14.10**).

Only a handful of anthropologists have been killed in the field. Among them is Raymond Kennedy, a Yale University professor who served as a U.S. military intelligence analyst in World War II. He specialized in Indonesia, a vast archipelago in Southeast Asia, composed of thousands of islands. His life came to an abrupt end in 1950 while he was finishing up a year of acculturation research. Recently independent after a brutal armed struggle that ended three centuries of Dutch colonial rule, the country was not yet stable. Kennedy was in his Jeep, traveling with a *Time Life* magazine photographer through beautiful mountainous terrain on the island of Java, when a band of guerrillas ambushed and executed them for reasons still not known (Embree, 1951; Price, 2011; "Two Americans are found slain," 1950).

Figure 14.10 Dangerous Anthropology Swedish anthropologist Anna Hedlund has done research in a range of politically tense and physically dangerous settings. Currently, she is working on the culture of non-state-armed groups in the DRC, focusing on how combatants define and legitimize violence. The work is based on extensive fieldwork in various military camps in the South Kivu province, eastern Congo. Here, we see her with combatants, pausing during a five-day trek to the rebel camp in the forest. Their faces have been blurred to protect their identities.

Subjectivity and Reflexivity

Whether working near home or abroad, when endeavoring to identify the rules that underlie each culture, ethnographers must grapple with the very real challenge of bias or subjectivity—his or her own and that of members in the community being studied. Researchers are expected to constantly check their own personal or cultural biases and assumptions as they work—and to present these self-reflections along with their observations. This practice of critical self-examination is known as *reflexivity*.

Because perceptions of reality may vary, an anthropologist must be extremely careful in describing a culture. To do so accurately, the researcher needs to seek out and consider three kinds of data:

1. The people's own understanding of their culture and the general rules they share: their ideal sense of the way their own society ought to be.
2. The extent to which people believe they are observing those rules: how they think they really behave.
3. The behavior that can be directly observed: what the anthropologist actually sees happening.

Clearly, the way people think they *should* behave, the way in which they think they *do* behave, and the way in which they *actually* behave may be distinctly different. By carefully examining and comparing these elements, anthropologists can draw up a set of rules that may explain the acceptable range of behavior within a culture.

Beyond the possibility of drawing false conclusions based on a group's ideal sense of itself, anthropologists run the risk of misinterpretation due to personal feelings and biases shaped by their own culture, as well as gender and age. It is important to recognize this challenge and make every effort to overcome it, for otherwise one may seriously misconstrue what one sees.

A case in point is the story of how male bias in the Polish culture in which Malinowski was raised caused him to ignore or miss significant factors in his pioneering study of the Trobrianders. Unlike today, when anthropologists receive special training before going into the field, Malinowski set out to do fieldwork in 1914 with little formal preparation. The following Original Study, written by anthropologist Annette Weiner, who ventured to the same islands almost sixty years later, illustrates how gender can impact one's research findings—both in terms of the bias that may affect a researcher's outlook and in terms of what native consultants may feel comfortable sharing with a particular researcher.

The Importance of Trobriand Women *BY ANNETTE B. WEINER*

Walking into a village at the beginning of fieldwork is entering a world without cultural guideposts. The task of learning values that others live by is never easy. The rigors of fieldwork involve listening and watching, learning a new language of speech and actions, and most of all, letting go of one's own cultural assumptions in order to understand the meanings others give to work, power, death, family, and friends. During my fieldwork in the Trobriand Islands of Papua New Guinea, I wrestled doggedly with each of these problems—and with the added challenge that I was working in the footsteps of a celebrated anthropological ancestor, Bronislaw Kasper Malinowski. . . .

In 1971, before my first trip to the Trobriands, I thought I understood many things about Trobriand customs and beliefs from having read Malinowski's exhaustive writings. Once there, however, I found that I had much more to discover. Finding significant differences in areas of importance, I gradually came to understand how he reached certain conclusions. . . .

My most significant point of departure from Malinowski's analyses was the attention I gave to women's productive work. In my original research plans, women were not the central focus of study, but on the first day I took up residence in a village I was taken by them to watch a distribution of their own wealth—bundles of banana leaves and banana fiber skirts—which they exchanged with other women in commemoration of someone who had recently died. Watching that event forced me to take women's economic roles more seriously than I would have from reading Malinowski's studies.

Although Malinowski noted the high status of Trobriand women, he attributed their importance to the fact that Trobrianders reckon descent through women. . . . Yet he never considered that this significance was underwritten by women's own wealth because he did not systematically investigate the women's productive activities. . . .

My taking seriously the importance of women's wealth not only brought women as the neglected half of society clearly into the ethnographic picture but also forced me to revise many of Malinowski's assumptions about Trobriand men. . . . For Malinowski, the basic relationships within a Trobriand family were guided by the matrilineal principle of "mother-right" and "father-love." A father was called "stranger" and had little authority over his own children. A woman's brother was the commanding figure and exercised control over his sister's sons. . . .

In my study of Trobriand women and men, a different configuration of reckoning descent through the maternal line emerged. A Trobriand father is not a "stranger" in Malinowski's definition, nor is he a powerless figure. The father is one of the most important persons in his child's life, and remains so even after his child grows up and marries. He gives his child many opportunities to gain things from his matrilineage, thereby adding to the available resources that he or she can draw upon.

At the same time, this giving creates obligations on the part of a man's children toward him that last even beyond his death. Thus, the roles that men and their children play in each other's lives are worked out through extensive cycles of exchanges, which define the strength of their relationships to each other and eventually benefit the other members of both their matrilineages. Central to these exchanges are women and their wealth.

. . . Only recently have anthropologists begun to understand the importance of taking women's work seriously. The "women's point of view" was largely ignored in the study of gender roles because anthropologists generally perceived women as living in the shadows of men—occupying the private rather than the public sectors of society, rearing children rather than engaging in economic or political pursuits.

In the Trobriand Islands, women's wealth consists of banana leaves and banana-fiber skirts, large quantities of which must be given away upon the death of a relative.

Adapted from Weiner, A. B. (1988). The Trobrianders of Papua New Guinea *(pp. 4–7). Reprinted by permission of Cengage Learning.*

Validation

As the Original Study makes clear, determining the accuracy of anthropological descriptions and conclusions can be difficult. In the natural sciences, one can replicate observations and experiments to try to establish the reliability of a researcher's conclusions. Thus, one can see for oneself if one's colleague has gotten it right. But validating ethnographic research is uniquely challenging because access to sites may be limited or barred altogether, due to a number of factors: insufficient funding, logistical difficulties in reaching the site, problems in obtaining permits, and changing cultural and environmental conditions. These factors mean that what could be observed in a certain context at a certain time cannot be observed at others. As a result, one researcher cannot easily confirm the reliability or completeness of another's account.

For this reason, anthropologists bear a heavy responsibility for factual reporting, including disclosing key issues related to their research: Why was a particular location selected as a research site and for which research objectives? What were the local conditions during fieldwork? Who provided the key information and major insights? How were data collected and recorded? Without such background information, it is difficult to judge the validity of the account and the soundness of the researcher's conclusions.

Putting It All Together: Completing an Ethnography

After collecting ethnographic information, the next challenge is to piece together all that has been gathered into a coherent whole that accurately describes the culture. Traditionally, ethnographies are detailed written descriptions composed of chapters on topics such as the circumstances and place of fieldwork itself; historical background; the community or group today; its natural environment; settlement patterns; subsistence practices; networks of kinship relations and other forms of social organization; marriage and sexuality; economic exchanges; political institutions; myths, sacred beliefs, and ceremonies; and current developments. These may be illustrated with photographs and accompanied by maps, kinship diagrams, and figures showing social and political organizational structures, settlement layout, floor plans of dwellings, seasonal cycles, and so on.

Sometimes ethnographic research is documented not only in writing but also with sound recordings and on film (**Figure 14.11**). Visual records may be used for documentation and illustration as well as for analysis or as a means of gathering additional information in interviews. Moreover, footage shot for the sake

Figure 14.11 Anthropologist-Filmmaker Hu Tai-Li An award-winning pioneer of ethnographic films in Taiwan, Tai-Li is a professor at National Chin-Hua University. She has directed and produced a half-dozen documentaries on a range of topics—including traditional rituals and music, development issues, and national and ethnic identity. Here she is filming Maleveq ("Five-Year Ceremony") rituals in the village of Kulalao, southern Taiwan. During this ceremony, lasting several days, indigenous Paiwan people celebrate their alliance with tribal ancestors and deities. Traditional belief holds that ancestral spirits attend this gathering; villagers beseech their blessings, welcoming them with special songs, dances, and food.

Courtesy of Hu Tai-Li

of documentation and research may be edited into a documentary film. Not unlike a written ethnography, such a film is a structured whole composed of numerous selected sequences, visual montage, juxtaposition of sound and visual image, and narrative sequencing, all coherently edited into an accurate visual representation of the ethnographic subject (Collier & Collier, 1986; El Guindi, 2004).

In recent years anthropologists have experimented with various digital media (Ginsburg, Abu-Lughod, & Larkin, 2009). With the emergence of digital technologies, the potential for anthropological research, interpretation, and presentation is greater than ever before. Digital recording devices provide ethnographers with a wealth of material to analyze and utilize toward building hypotheses. They also open the door to sharing findings in new, varied, and interactive ways in the far-reaching digitalized realm of the Internet. Digital ethnographers, having amassed a wealth of digital material while researching, are able to share their findings through a variety of outlets including DVDs, online photo essays, podcasts, and video blogs.

Ethnology: From Description to Interpretation and Theory

Largely descriptive in nature, ethnography provides the basic data needed for *ethnology*—the branch of cultural anthropology that makes cross-cultural comparisons and develops theories that explain why certain important differences or similarities occur between groups. As noted in Chapter 1, the end product of quality anthropological research is a coherent statement about culture or human nature that provides an explanatory framework for understanding the ideas and actions of the people being studied. In short, such an explanation or interpretation supported by a reliable body of data is a **theory**. As discussed in Chapter 1, theory is distinct from doctrine and dogma, which are assertions of opinions or beliefs formally handed down by an authority as indisputably true and accepted as a matter of faith.

Anthropologists do not claim that any one theory about culture is the absolute truth. Rather they judge or measure a theory's validity and soundness by varying degrees of probability; what is considered to be true is what is most probable. But although anthropologists are reluctant to make absolute statements about complex issues such as exactly how cultures function or change, they can and do provide fact-based evidence about whether assumptions have support or are unfounded and thus not true. Therefore, a *theory*, contrary to widespread misuse of the term, is much more than mere speculation; it is a critically examined explanation of observed reality.

Always open to future challenges born of new evidence or insights, scientific theory depends on demonstrable, fact-based evidence and repeated testing. So it is that, as our cross-cultural knowledge expands, the odds favor some anthropological theories over others. Old explanations or interpretations must sometimes be discarded as new theories based on better or more complete evidence are shown to be more effective or probable. Last but not least, theories also guide anthropologists in formulating new research questions and help them decide what data to collect and how to give meaning to their data.

Ethnology and the Comparative Method

A single instance of any phenomenon is generally insufficient for supporting a plausible hypothesis. Without some basis for comparison, the hypothesis grounded in a single case may be no more than a hunch born of a unique happenstance or particular historical coincidence. Theories in anthropology may be generated from worldwide cross-cultural or historical comparisons or even comparisons with other species. For instance, anthropologists may examine a global sample of societies in order to discover whether a hypothesis proposed to explain certain phenomena is supported by fact-based evidence. Of necessity, the cross-cultural researcher depends upon evidence gathered by other scholars as well as his or her own.

A key resource that makes this possible is the **Human Relations Area Files (HRAF)**, which is a vast collection of cross-indexed ethnographic, biocultural, and archaeological data catalogued by cultural characteristics and geographic location. This ever-growing data bank classifies more than 700 cultural characteristics and includes nearly 400 societies, past and present, from all around the world. Archived in about 300 libraries (on microfiche and/or online) and approaching a million pages of information, the HRAF facilitates comparative research on almost any cultural feature imaginable—warfare, subsistence practices, settlement patterns, marriage, rituals, and so on.

Among other things, anthropologists interested in finding explanations for certain social or cultural

---

theory A coherent statement that provides an explanatory framework for understanding; an explanation or interpretation supported by a reliable body of data.

Human Relations Area Files (HRAF) A vast collection of cross-indexed ethnographic, biocultural, and archaeological data catalogued by cultural characteristics and geographic location; archived in about 300 libraries on microfiche and/or online.

beliefs and practices can use the HRAF to test their hypotheses. For example, Peggy Reeves Sanday examined a sample of 156 societies drawn from the HRAF in an attempt to answer her comparative research questions concerning dominance and gender in different societies. Her study, published in 1981 (*Female Power and Male Dominance*), disproves the common misperception that women are universally subordinate to men, sheds light on the way men and women relate to each other, and ranks as a major landmark in the study of gender.

Cultural comparisons are not restricted to contemporary ethnographic data. Indeed, anthropologists frequently turn to archaeological or historical data to test hypotheses about cultural change. Cultural characteristics thought to be caused by certain specified conditions can be tested archaeologically by investigating similar situations where such conditions actually occurred. Also useful are data provided in *ethnohistories*, which are studies of cultures of the recent past through oral histories; accounts of explorers, missionaries, and traders; and analysis of records such as land titles, birth and death records, and other archival materials.

Anthropology's Theoretical Perspectives: A Brief Overview

Entire books have been written about each of anthropology's numerous theoretical perspectives. Here we offer a general overview to convey the scope of anthropological theories and their role in explaining and interpreting cultures.

In the previous chapter, we presented the barrel model of culture as a dynamic system of adaptation in which social structure, infrastructure, and superstructure intricately interact. Helping us to imagine culture as an integrated whole, this model allows us to think about something very complex by reducing it to a simplified scheme or basic design.

Although most anthropologists generally conceptualize culture as holistic and integrative, they may have very different takes on the relative significance of different elements that make up the whole and exactly how they relate to one another. We touch on these contrasting perspectives next.

idealist perspective A theoretical approach stressing the primacy of superstructure in cultural research and analysis.

materialist perspective A theoretical approach stressing the primacy of infrastructure (material conditions) in cultural research and analysis.

Idealist Perspective

When analyzing a culture, some argue that humans act primarily on the basis of their ideas, concepts, or symbolic representations. In their research and analysis, these anthropologists usually emphasize that to understand or explain why humans behave as they do, one must first get into other people's heads and try to understand how they imagine, think, feel, and speak about the world in which they live. Because of the primacy of the superstructure (ideas, values), this is known as an **idealist perspective** (not to be confused with idealism in the sense of fantasy or hopeful imagination).

Examples of idealist perspectives include psychological and cognitive anthropology (culture and personality), ethnoscience, structuralism, and postmodernism, as well as symbolic and interpretive anthropology. The latter approach is most famously associated with anthropologist Clifford Geertz, who viewed humans primarily as "symbolizing, conceptualizing, and meaning-seeking" creatures. Drawing on words from German historical sociologist Max Weber, Geertz described our species as "an animal suspended in webs of significance he himself has spun. I take culture to be those webs, and the analysis of it to be therefore not an experimental science in search of law but an interpretive one in search of meaning" (Geertz, 1973, p. 5).

Geertz developed an artful ethnographic research strategy in which a culturally significant event or social drama (for instance, a Balinese cockfight) is chosen for observation and analysis as a form of "deep play" that may provide essential cultural insights. Peeling back layer upon layer of socially constructed meanings, the anthropologist offers what Geertz called a "thick description" of the event in a detailed ethnographic narrative.

Materialist Perspective

Many other anthropologists hold a theoretical perspective in which they stress explaining culture by first analyzing the material conditions that they see as determining people's lives. They may begin their research with an inventory of available natural resources for food and shelter, the number of mouths to feed and bodies to keep warm, the tools used in making a living, and so on. Anthropologists who highlight such environmental or economic factors as primary in shaping cultures share a **materialist perspective**.

Examples of materialist theoretical approaches include Marxism, neo-evolutionism, cultural ecology, sociobiology, and cultural materialism. In cultural ecology, anthropologists focus primarily on the subsistence mechanisms in a culture that enable a group to successfully adapt to its natural environment. Building on cultural ecology, some anthropologists include considerations of political economy such as industrial production, capitalist markets, wage labor, and finance capital. A political economy perspective is closely associated with Marxist theory, which essentially explains major change in society as the result of growing conflicts between opposing social classes, namely those who possess property and those who do not.

One result of widening the scope—combining cultural ecology and political economy to take into account the emerging world systems of international production and trade relations—is known as *political ecology*. Closely related is *cultural materialism*, a theoretical research strategy identified with Marvin Harris (1979). Placing primary emphasis on the role of environment, demography, technology, and economy in determining a culture's mental and social conditions, he argues that anthropologists can best explain ideas, values, and beliefs as adaptations to economic and environmental conditions. Testing his cultural materialist principles against a number of "riddles of culture" ranging from food taboos and preferences to changes in American family structures, Harris's theoretical perspective provides us with numerous fascinating examples of biocultural connections. For instance, he argued that the real explanation as to why Jews and Muslims originally instituted a religious taboo on eating pork lies in the fact that pig farming threatened the integrity of the basic cultural and natural ecosystems of the Middle East. Linking this prohibition to population growth and massive deforestation in that region, Harris argued that the natural conditions appropriate for raising pigs became ever more scarce, and pork became even more of a tempting luxury. In short, in the Middle East "it was ecologically maladaptive to try to raise pigs in substantial numbers" (Harris, 1989, p. 44).

Other Perspectives

Not all anthropological perspectives fall neatly into idealist or materialist camps. For example, some give priority to social structure, focusing on this middle layer in our barrel model. Although it is difficult to pigeonhole various perspectives in this group, theoretical explanations worked out by pioneering French social thinkers like Émile Durkheim and his student Marcel Mauss influenced the development of several *structuralist* and *functionalist* theories. Primarily associated with British anthropologist Alfred Radcliffe-Brown and the Polish-born anthropologist Bronisław Malinowski in the mid-1900s, this approach focuses on the underlying patterns or structures of social relationships, attributing functions to cultural institutions in terms of the contributions they make toward maintaining a group's social order.

Beyond these three general groups, there are various other anthropological approaches. Some stress the importance of identifying general patterns or even discovering laws. Early anthropologists believed that

they could discover such laws by means of the theory of *unilinear cultural evolution* of universal human progress, beginning with what was then called "savagery," followed by "barbarism," and gradually making progress toward a condition of human perfection known as "high civilization"(Carneiro, 2003).

Although anthropologists have long abandoned such sweeping generalizations as unscientific and ethnocentric, some continued to search for universal laws in the general development of human cultures by focusing on technological development as measured in the growing capacity for energy capture per capita of the population. This theoretical perspective is sometimes called *neo-evolutionism*. Others seek to explain recurring patterns in human social behavior in terms of laws of natural selection by focusing on possible relationships with human genetics, a theoretical perspective identified with sociobiology. Yet others stress that broad generalizations are impossible because each culture is distinct and can only be understood as resulting from unique historical processes and circumstances. Some even go a step farther and focus on in-depth description and analysis of personal life histories of individual members in a group in order to reveal the work of a culture.

Beyond these cultural historical approaches, there are other theoretical perspectives that do not aim for laws or generalizations to explain culture. Theoretical perspectives that reject measuring and evaluating different cultures by means of some sort of universal standard, and stress that they can be explained or interpreted only in their own unique terms, are associated with the important anthropological principle known as *cultural relativism*, discussed in the previous chapter.

Ethical Responsibilities in Anthropological Research

As explained in this chapter, anthropologists obtain information about different peoples and their cultures through long-term, full-immersion fieldwork based on personal observation of and participation in the everyday activities of the community. Once they are admitted and allowed to stay, anthropologists are usually befriended and sometimes even adopted, gradually becoming familiar with the local social structures and cultural features and even with highly personal or politically sensitive details known only to trusted insiders.

Because the community is usually part of a larger and more powerful complex society, anthropological knowledge about how the locals live, what they own, what motivates them, and how they are organized has the potential to make the community vulnerable to exploitation and manipulation. In this context, it is good to be reminded of the ancient Latin maxim *scientia potentia est* ("knowledge is power"). In other words, anthropological knowledge may have far-reaching, and possibly negative, consequences for the peoples being studied.

This problematic relationship between knowledge and power is an uncomfortable one. Are there any rules that may guide anthropologists in their ethical decision making and help them judge right from wrong? This important issue is addressed in the code of ethics of the American Anthropological Association (discussed in Chapter 1). First formalized in 1971 and modified in its current form in 1998, this document outlines the various ethical responsibilities and moral obligations of anthropologists, including this central maxim: "Anthropological researchers must do everything in their power to ensure that their research does not harm the safety, dignity, or privacy of the people with whom they work, conduct research, or perform other professional activities."

The first step in this endeavor is to communicate in advance the nature, purpose, and potential impact of the planned study to individuals who provide information—and to obtain their informed consent or formal recorded agreement to participate in the research. But protecting the community one studies requires more than that; it demands constant vigilance and alertness. There are some situations in which this is particularly challenging—including working for a global business corporation, international bank, or government agency, such as the foreign service, police, or military (American Anthropological Association, 2007; González, 2009; McFate, 2007).

This challenge came to the fore again during the past decade when the U.S. government recruited social scientists, including anthropologists, to improve the military's ability to better understand the complexities of the "human terrain" in armed conflict environments such as Afghanistan and Iraq (**Figure 14.12**).

© Johann Spanner

Figure 14.12 Militarizing Anthropology Embedded in U.S. Army units, social scientists, including anthropologists, have conducted sociocultural assessments as part of the "human terrain system" (HTS). Designed to improve the military's ability to understand the complexities of the human terrain (civilian population) as it applied to operations in Iraq and Afghanistan, HTS has been part of a counterinsurgency strategy against regional insurgents since 2006. Anthropological involvement in the U.S. government's struggle for hearts and minds in war zones has been controversial since the mid-1960s.

Discussing the military application of anthropological theories and research methods, Australian linguist and counterinsurgency expert David Kilcullen argued:

> Conflict ethnography is key; to borrow a literary term, there is no substitute for a "close reading" of the environment. But it is a reading that resides in no book, but around you; in the terrain, the people, their social and cultural institutions, the way they act and think. You have to be a participant observer. And the key is to see beyond the surface differences between our societies and these environments (of which religious orientation is one key element) to the deeper social and cultural drivers of conflict,

drivers that locals would understand on their own terms. (Kilcullen, 2007)

Because anthropologists generally disapprove of politicizing ethnographic information and are committed to the ideal of "do no harm," the proposal of militarizing anthropology in arenas of violent conflict sparked intense debates due to ethical concerns that doing so may endanger local communities. It may not be possible to fully anticipate all the cross-cultural and long-term consequences—uses and abuses—of one's research findings. Navigating this ethical gray area is often difficult, but it is each anthropologist's responsibility to be aware of moral responsibilities, and to take every possible caution to ensure that one's research does not jeopardize the well-being of the people being studied.

CHAPTER CHECKLIST

What was the worldwide social context in which anthropology emerged as a discipline?

● Anthropology emerged during the heyday of colonialism (1870s–1930s). Europeans focused on the study of traditional peoples in overseas colonies they controlled, whereas North Americans focused primarily on their own countries' Native Indian and Eskimo communities.

● Expecting indigenous cultures to disappear through the impositions of colonialism, early anthropologists engaged in salvage ethnography (documenting endangered cultures), which now is known as urgent anthropology.

● In the 1930s, anthropologists began studying culture contact—how traditional cultures change when coming in contact with expanding capitalist societies. In the United States, this became known as acculturation.

● Applied anthropology—using anthropological knowledge and methods to solve practical problems in communities—came to the fore in the 1930s as dominant societies tried to understand traditional indigenous cultures in order to control them more effectively.

● The British government set up an anthropological research institute toward this end, and the United States established the Bureau of Indian Affairs to oversee federally recognized tribes on Indian reservations. The international Society of Applied Anthropology was founded in 1941.

How did ethnographic research approaches shift as a result of global conflict during World War II and the Cold War era that followed it?

● Some anthropologists turned their focus from small-scale traditional communities to modern state societies.

● Because ethnographic fieldwork was impossible in enemy societies and difficult in most other foreign countries during World War II, several anthropologists began researching cultures at a distance, developing national character studies through investigating film, literature, and newspapers.

In what ways has anthropology's scope expanded since the discipline began?

● Increasingly aware that a generalized understanding of human relations, ideas, and behavior depends upon knowledge of *all* cultures and peoples, anthropologists expanded their research to include complex, large-scale industrial societies organized in political states.

● During the Great Depression (1930s), some anthropologists worked in their own countries in settings ranging from factories to farming communities to suburban neighborhoods.

● In the 1930s, Hortense Powdermaker researched a racially segregated town in Mississippi, leading to her work in the 1940s on combating racism. She also spent a year researching the Hollywood film industry.

● Swiss anthropologist Alfred Métraux put together an international team of researchers to study contemporary race relations in Brazil, sponsored by UNESCO.

How have anthropologists attempted to solve the negative effects of massive cultural change imposed by elite cultures on powerless groups?

● In the 1950s anthropologists began studying peasants in order to understand the impact of complex state societies on traditional indigenous groups.

● Recognizing that their knowledge could be used to help people in ways defined by the people themselves, some anthropologists took up advocacy anthropology—research that is community based and politically involved.

● Anthropologists, such as Laura Nader, have urged studying up—ethnographic research in the world's centers of political and economic power to reveal how elites function in maintaining their positions.

How do anthropologists continue their work in an increasingly globalized context, and what methods are used in ethnographic research?

● Multi-sited ethnography investigates and documents peoples and cultures embedded in the larger structures of a globalizing world, utilizing a range of methods in various locations of time and space.

● Ethnography, a detailed description of a particular culture, relies upon fieldwork—extended on-location research to gather detailed and in-depth information on a society's customary ideas, values, and practices through participation in its collective social life.

● Participant observation is learning about a group's behaviors and beliefs through social involvement and personal observation with the community, as well as interviews and discussions with individual members of the group over an extended stay in the community.

● Key consultants (previously called informants) are individuals in the society being studied who provide information that helps the researcher understand what he or she observes.

● Ethnographers gather two types of data: Quantitative data consist of statistical or measurable information, such as population density; qualitative data describe features such as social networks of kinship relations, customary beliefs and practices, and personal life histories.

● Interviewing is either informal (unstructured, open-ended conversations in everyday life) or formal (structured question/answer sessions). Eliciting devices are activities and objects used to draw out individuals and encourage them to recall and share information.

● Ethnographic mapping goes beyond standard mapmaking to show geographic and spatial features that are culturally significant to the people living there, such as place names and stories about locations.

● Most anthropologists use cameras as well as notepads, computers, or sound recording devices to document their observations. Especially since the digital revolution in the 1980s, anthropologists carry digital recording equipment to the field and invite and train local members of the community to help with recording.

What challenges do ethnographers face?

● Culture shock and not being socially accepted by the society are common ethnographic difficulties. A major step toward being accepted and gaining access to information is being adopted into a network of kinship relations.

● Anthropologists must avoid getting involved in political rivalries and unwittingly used by factions within the community.

● An ethnographer's age, ideology, ethnicity, or skin color may block access to a community's individuals or ideas.

● Ethnographers may also be in physical danger through illness, accident, and occasional hostility.

● Ethnographers grapple with the challenge of bias or subjectivity—their own and that of members of the community being challenged.

● Validating ethnographic research is uniquely challenging because subsequent access to sites may be limited or barred altogether.

What is involved in producing an ethnographic study?

● Traditionally, ethnographies are written narratives, illustrated with photographs and accompanied by maps, kinship diagrams, and figures showing social and political organizational structures, settlement layout, seasonal cycles, and so on.

● Sometimes ethnographic research is documented not only in writing but also with sound recordings and on films.

What is involved in doing ethnology?

● Ethnography provides the basic data needed for ethnology—the branch of cultural anthropology that makes cross-cultural comparisons and develops theories that explain why certain important differences or similarities occur between groups. Theories—coherent statements providing explanations for these differences or similarities—are developed through ethnology.

● Ethnology relies on the comparative method. Theories in anthropology may be generated from worldwide cross-cultural or historical comparisons or even comparisons with other species.

● The Human Relations Area Files is a vast collection of cross-indexed ethnographic, biocultural, and archaeological data catalogued by cultural characteristics and geographic location.

What are the key theoretical perspectives in anthropology?

● Anthropology has many theoretical perspectives, but the two broadest categories are idealist and materialist.

● The idealist perspective stresses the primacy of superstructure in cultural research and analysis.

● The materialist perspective stresses the primacy of infrastructure (material conditions) in cultural research and analysis.

What are the ethical responsibilities in anthropological research?

● First formalized in 1971 and modified in its current form in 1998, the ethical code of the American Anthropological Association outlines the various ethnical responsibilities and moral obligations of anthropologists.

● The central maxim of the AAA ethics code is to ensure that anthropological research does not negatively impact the people being studied.

QUESTIONS FOR REFLECTION

1. In describing and interpreting human cultures, anthropologists have long relied on ethnographic fieldwork, including participant observation. What makes this research method uniquely challenging and effective? Of what use might the findings be for meeting the unique challenges of our globalizing world?

2. Early anthropologists engaged in salvage ethnography (urgent anthropology) to create a reliable record of indigenous cultures once widely expected to vanish. Although many indigenous communities did lose customary practices due to acculturation, descendants of those cultures can now turn to anthropological records to revitalize their ancestral ways of life. Do you think this is a good thing? Why or why not?

3. In our globalizing world, a growing number of anthropologists carry out multi-sited ethnography rather than conduct research in a single community. If you would do such a multi-sited research project, what would you focus on, and where would you conduct your actual participant observations and interviews?

4. If you were invited to "study up," on which cultural group would you focus? How would you go about getting access to that group for participant observation, and what serious obstacles might you encounter?

5. In light of professional ethics, what moral dilemmas might anthropologists face in choosing to advise a government in exploring or implementing a nonviolent solution to a military conflict? How is military anthropology different from other forms of applied anthropology, such as working for the Foreign Service, the World Bank, the Roman Catholic Church, or an international business corporation such as IBM and Intel?

ONLINE STUDY RESOURCES

CourseMate

Access chapter-specific learning tools, including learning objectives, practice quizzes, videos, flash cards, glossaries, and more in your Anthropology CourseMate.

Log into **www.cengagebrain.com** to access the resources your instructor has assigned and to purchase materials.

Challenge Issue

As social creatures dependent upon one another for survival, humans face the challenge of communicating clearly in a multiplicity of situations about countless things connected to our well-being. We do this with a variety of distinctive gestures, sounds, touches, and body postures. Our most sophisticated means of sharing large amounts of complex information is through language—a foundation stone of every human culture. Today, as shown in this photo of a street in Chinatown in Thailand's capital city of Bangkok, success in international trade and tourism depends on multilingual communication. Recognizing this challenge, Chinese merchants learned to survive in this particular foreign setting by commercially advertising in three distinctive scripts. Traders from Guangdong (Canton) and other Chinese coastal cities venturing overseas have a long tradition to build on, beginning with their ethnic enclave established in the Philippine seaport of Manila in 1594. Since then, they have formed bustling commercial centers in densely populated urban ghettos known as Chinatowns in major cities on every continent, from Amsterdam, Jakarta, and Johannesburg, to Lima, Melbourne, Mumbai, Nagasaki, San Francisco, and Toronto—just a few of the important cities in China's fast growing global trading empire.

Language and Communication

The human ability to communicate through language rests squarely on our biological makeup. We are "programmed" for language, be it through sounds or gestures. (Sign languages, such as the American Sign Language—ASL—used by the hearing impaired, are fully developed languages in their own right.) Beyond the cries of babies, which are not learned but which do communicate, humans must learn their language. So it is that a normal child from anywhere in the world readily acquires the language of his or her culture.

Language is a system of communication using sounds, gestures, or marks that are put together according to certain rules, resulting in meanings that are intelligible to all who share that language. These sounds, gestures, and marks are *symbols*—signs that are arbitrarily linked to something else and represent it in a meaningful way, as we discussed in a previous chapter. For example, the word *crying* is a symbol, a combination of sounds to which we assign the meaning of a particular action and which we can use to communicate that meaning, whether or not anyone around us is actually crying.

Signals, unlike culturally learned symbols, or meaningful signs, are instinctive sounds and gestures that have a natural or self-evident meaning. Screams, sighs, and coughs, for example, are signals that convey some kind of emotional or physical state. Throughout the animal kingdom, species communicate essential information by means of signals. Field studies as well as scientific experiments provide abundant scientific evidence that we cannot dismiss communication among nonhuman species as a set of simple instinctive reflexes or fixed action patterns.

Today, language experts debate how much credit to give to great apes and several other animals for their cognitive ability to attribute meaning to signs—that is, their capacity to communicate in symbols. Over the past

IN THIS CHAPTER YOU WILL LEARN TO

- Define *language* and distinguish between sign and symbol.
- Specify the three branches of linguistic anthropology.
- Observe cross-cultural differences in nonverbal means of communication.
- Trace the emergence of language, speech, and writing.
- Assess the close relationship between culture and language.
- Discuss the significance of literacy and telecommunication in today's world.

language A system of communication using sounds, gestures, or marks that are put together in meaningful ways according to a set of rules, resulting in meanings that are intelligible to all who share that language.

signals Instinctive sounds and gestures that have a natural or self-evident meaning.

few decades, researchers aiming to understand the biological basis, social use, and evolutionary development of language have investigated a fascinating array of animal communication systems, including dolphin whistles, whale songs, elephant rumbles, bee dances, and orangutan gestures. Some have studied language acquisition aptitude among apes by teaching them to communicate using ASL or "lexigrams" (symbols) on keyboard devices. Researchers must continue studying various systems of animal communication before we can fully understand how they relate to the development of much more complex human languages.

A remarkable example of the many scientific efforts under way on this subject is the case of Chantek, an orangutan who has learned some 150 gestures, many of which he puts together in innovative ways. Featured in the following Original Study, his story illustrates the creative process of language development and the capacity of a nonhuman primate to recognize symbols (see also Cartmill & Byrne, 2010).

ORIGINAL STUDY

Can Chantek Talk in Codes? *BY H. LYN WHITE MILES*

My foster son is a confused adolescent gang member who sometimes finds himself in trouble. Struggling with being different because he is defined as "the other," he often gets into trouble with the authorities. On one occasion, he was locked up and tried to escape—not to do any real harm but to have some fun. When I arrived to see what had happened, Chantek told me he was thirsty and angrily mentioned the "key man" who could set him free. In a few hesitant words, he recounted how he got "out" and how he "broke" some things. While fixing his gaze on the door, he asked, "Where are the keys?" When I explained that I didn't have them, he leaned on one arm, looked warily around, gestured toward the door, and whispered, "You—*secret* open?" He was asking me to assist in his second "escape" for the day.

Chantek (*left*) is now an adult male orangutan, as evidenced by his size and large cheek pads. Here we see him with Dumadi, an infant in his group at Zoo Atlanta.

My unusual foster son is an orangutan, Chantek, who belongs to the *Pongo pygmaeus* and not the *Homo sapiens* "gang." As such, he is defined as "the other" by Western society, which views humans as having dominion over other life forms. Chantek is an "enculturated orangutan" who for some time has played a key role in my primatology research on great ape language and cognition. During our time together at the University of Tennessee, Chattanooga, Chantek lived freely with me—not only learning sign language but also taking trips to the mall, parks, and a nearby lake. When in recent years he had to be moved to a nearby zoo, he encountered restrictions that he did not understand, and he quickly named the zookeeper "key man." Thus, his brief escape to forage for "cheese-meat-breads" (cheeseburgers).

Chantek acquired many symbolic processes of human language during his time at the university where he was surrounded by anthropology students using Orangutan Sign Language (OSL), a pidgin gestural communication based on American Sign Language.[a] His vocabulary included names for people, places, foods, actions, objects, animals, colors, pronouns, locations, attributes ("good," "hurt"), and emphasis ("more," "time-to-do"). His language ability was similar to the use of language by 2- to 3-year-old human children.[b] Building on his 150-sign vocabulary, Chantek also invented terms, such as "Dave-missing-finger" for an injured worker, "tomato-toothpaste" for ketchup, and "eye-drink" for contact lens solution. He even nicknamed himself "Tek" by touching his hand to his opposite shoulder, rather than the more cumbersome cheek-pad touch for "Chantek."

He created more complex meanings by combining his signs in new sequences such as asking me to secretly open the door—an association of words I had never used with him. He nuanced his communications with subtle modulations of meaning and could dissect the elements of his signs. In almost metaphorical ways, he signed "dog" for pictures of dogs, barking noises on the radio, and even strange orangutans on TV whom he called "orange dogs." He signed "break" before he broke and shared crackers and after he dismantled his toilet. He signed "bad" to himself before he grabbed a cat, when he bit into a radish, and when he sadly inspected a dead bird.

Chantek could play imitative games and also illustrated some of the functions of language such as displaced reference by talking about keys that were not present. He showed code switching by utilizing a different dialect, style, or register through whispering "secret" and making his signs very small in a tiny space hidden by his hairy long arms. We also used code switching when Chantek shifted from his intimate informal language with me to more formal communication when the keeper arrived, and Chantek signed he was "sorry," but with less than convincing articulation.

Chantek is a code switcher in another sense as well because he is a member of a small group of intelligent nonhumans who are "cultural hybrids" or "dual-cultured," meaning that he is a member of one species raised by another. His life journey has involved finding his way between two different worlds—his own orangutan gestural communication, leaf and stick tools, and navigation in his environment versus the world of human culture, technology, and language, as he learns to shade his meanings to fit the situation, play tic-tac-toe and computer games, and create stone tools and found art assemblage and jewelry.[c]

Significantly, Chantek engaged in deception by attempting his escape in the first place and by subtly lying about what had really happened. This phenomenon has been called the benchmark of language because it requires symbolically creating or assuming an alternate reality and "theory of mind." I learned that Chantek told at least three lies a week including signing "dirty" to go to the bathroom only to play with the knobs on the washing machine, or distracting my attention with words about dangerous "big cats" while he deceptively reached into my pocket for treats. Chantek even stole and pretended to swallow a pencil eraser and then lied by opening his mouth, signing "eat."

Early language research with apes focused on vocabulary lists and acquisition rates just to "prove" that apes could acquire some human symbols. The contest seemed to be whether human language was unique—and the answer always had to preserve our *Homo*-centric superiority. My anthropological work with Chantek has had the opportunity to focus on the development, functional use, and evolutionary significance of both natural ape and human communication, culture, and cognition. The issue is now more about how both apes and humans use communication and cultural traditions to meet our needs, to varying degrees. My anthropological approach looked at the development of communication in cultural context and explored how Chantek and I created a communication code together in what Andrew Lock called "the guided re-invention of language."[d] Analyzing my findings with those of earlier developmental studies of the cognitive and linguistic skills of nonhuman primates, I discovered that Chantek was far less imitative and more original in his communication because his human companions interrupted him less and allowed his inventive use of language more.

Chantek will live into his 50s or 60s, so there is still much more he can show us about the mind, culture, and language ability of orangutans. Given my own Native American and First Nations roots, I see his dual-cultured existence in terms of the Coast Salish tribal concept of "where different waters meet and are transformed." Chantek said this best by calling himself "orangutan person"—neither human nor natural ape but benefiting from the cultures of both. In fact, the Great Ape Project has proposed that apes might be legal persons who should have limited human rights.

However, in his zoo environment, administrators have had difficulty in doing code switching of their own. Among other things, they have discouraged Chantek's use of sign language, perhaps out of misguided efforts to restore him to a natural orangutan or fear that he will complain about the food or publicly sign "Chantek want go home." My vision is the creation of a Communication and Culture Center where intelligent and sentient animals like Chantek will have greater agency and learning opportunities than are currently provided and can explore their dual-cultured natures. Imagine enculturated apes making tools, communicating with us on the Internet, engaging in meaningful work, and inventing their own culture based on symbols. If we were to *really* listen to Chantek, what would he tell us?

Written expressly for this text, 2012.

---

[a]Miles, H. (1990). The cognitive foundations for reference in a signing orangutan. In S. Parker & K. Gibson (Eds.), *"Language" and intelligence in monkeys and apes: Comparative developmental perspectives* (pp. 511–539). Cambridge, UK: Cambridge University Press.

[b]Miles, H. (1999). Symbolic communication with and by great apes. In S. Parker, R. Mitchell, & H. Miles (Eds.), *The mentality of gorillas and orangutans: Comparative perspectives* (pp. 197–210). Cambridge, UK: Cambridge University Press.

[c]Miles, 1999.

[d]Lock, A. (1980). *The guided reinvention of language*. New York: Academic Press.

Although language studies such as the one involving Chantek reveal much about primate cognition, the fact remains that human culture is ultimately dependent on an elaborate system of communication far more complex than that of any other species—including our fellow primates. The reason for this is the sheer amount of knowledge that must be learned by each person from other individuals in order to fully participate in society, where almost everything is based on socially learned behavior. A significant amount of learning can and does take place in the absence of language by way of observation and imitation, guided by a limited number of meaningful signs or symbols. However, all known human cultures are so rich in content that they require communication systems that not only can give precise labels to various classes of phenomena but also permit people to think and talk about their own and others' experiences and expectations—past, present, and future.

The central and most highly developed human system of communication is language. Knowledge of the workings of language, then, is essential to a full understanding of what culture is about and how it operates.

Linguistic Research and the Nature of Language

Any human language—Chinese, English, Swahili, or whatever—is a means of transmitting information and sharing with others both collective and individual experiences. It is a system that enables us to translate our concerns, beliefs, and perceptions into symbols that can be understood and interpreted by others.

In spoken language, this is done by taking sounds—no language uses more than about fifty—and developing rules for putting them together in meaningful ways. Sign languages, such as American Sign Language, do the same, not with sound but by shaping and moving fingers, hands, and other body parts, along with making facial expressions, including mouthing. The vast array of languages in the world—some 6,000 or so distinctive ones—may well astound us by their complexity and great differences, yet language experts have found that each is fundamentally organized in similar ways.

The roots of **linguistics**—the systematic study of all aspects of language—trace back to the works of ancient language specialists in South Asia more than 2,000 years ago. The age of European exploration across the globe, from the late 1400s through the 1800s, set the stage for a great leap forward in the scientific study of language. Explorers, traders, missionaries, and other travelers accumulated information about a huge diversity of languages from all around the world. An estimated 12,000 languages still existed when they began their inquiries.

Linguists in the 19th century, including early anthropologists, made significant contributions in comparative research—discovering patterns, relationships, and systems in the sounds and structures of different languages and formulating laws and principles concerning language. In the past century, while still collecting data, researchers have made considerable progress in unraveling the reasoning process behind language construction, testing and working from new and improved theories (**Figure 15.1**).

Insofar as theories and facts of language are tested by independent researchers looking at the same data, it can now be said that we have a science of linguistics.

Figure 15.1 Linguistic Research in Samoa Italian-born American anthropologist Alessandro Duranti began researching Samoan language and culture about thirty-five years ago on Upolu—the second largest of nine volcanic islands comprising Samoa. Home to about 250,000 people, Samoa is among a wide scattering of islands in the Pacific, collectively known as Polynesia, and its language is one of about forty closely related Polynesian languages. Together, they form a small branch of the Oceanic language family, which includes about 450 languages spoken by just 2 million people inhabiting about 25,000 islands sprawled across the Pacific. Interested in political discourse and the language of agency, Duranti is seen here working with Salesa Asiata on grammatical patterns extracted from recorded conversations.

This science has three main branches: descriptive linguistics, historical linguistics, and a third branch that focuses on language in relation to social and cultural settings.

Descriptive Linguistics

How can an anthropologist, a trader, a missionary, a diplomat, or any other outsider research a foreign language that has not yet been described and analyzed, or for which there are no readily available written materials? There are hundreds of such undocumented languages in the world. Fortunately, effective methods have been developed to help with the task. Descriptive linguistics involves unraveling a language by recording, describing, and analyzing all of its features. It is a painstaking process, but it is ultimately rewarding in that it provides deeper understanding of a language—its structure, its unique linguistic repertoire (figures of speech, word plays, and so on), and its relationship to other languages.

The process of unlocking the underlying rules of a spoken language requires a trained ear and a thorough understanding of how multiple different speech sounds are produced. Without such know-how, it is extremely difficult to write out or make intelligent use of any data concerning a particular language. To satisfy this preliminary requirement, most people need special training in phonetics, discussed next.

Phonology

For a description and analysis of any language, one needs first an inventory of all its distinctive sounds. The systematic identification and description of the distinctive sounds in a language is known as **phonetics**. Rooted in the Greek word *phone* (meaning "sound"), phonetics is basic to **phonology**, the study of language sounds.

Some of the sounds used in other languages may seem very much like those of the researcher's own speech pattern, but others may be unfamiliar. For example, the *th* sound common in English does not exist in the Dutch language and is difficult for most Dutch speakers to pronounce, just as the *r* sound used in numerous languages is tough for Japanese speakers. And the unique "click" sounds used in Bushman languages in southern Africa are difficult for speakers of just about every other language.

While collecting speech sounds or utterances, the linguist works to isolate the **phonemes**—the smallest units of sound that make a difference in meaning. A process called the *minimal-pair test* may do this isolation and analysis. The researcher tries to find two short words that appear to be exactly alike except for one sound, such as *bit* and *pit* in English. If the substitution of *b* for *p* in this minimal pair makes a difference in meaning, as it does in English, then those two sounds have been identified as

distinct phonemes of the language and will require two different symbols to record.

As this example suggests, linguists distinguish many more phonemes (44) in English speech than the 26 letters used in the English alphabet. To transcribe different languages, which include many sounds foreign to English, linguists have developed an international phonetic alphabet: 107 letters, 52 diacritics (marks that change the sound value of the letter to which they are added), and four prosodic marks (designating rhythm, stress, and intonation). Beyond this linguistic standard, speech pathologists have developed additional letters and notations, enabling them to transcribe a range of far less common sounds.

Morphology, Syntax, and Grammar

While making and studying an inventory of distinctive sounds, linguists also look into **morphology**, the study of the patterns or rules of word formation in a language (including such things as rules concerning verb tense, pluralization, and compound words). They do this by marking out specific sounds and sound combinations that seem to have meaning. These are called **morphemes**—the smallest units of sound that carry a meaning in a language.

Morphemes are distinct from phonemes, which can alter meaning but have no meaning by themselves. For example, a linguist studying English in a North American farming community would soon learn that *cow* is a morpheme—a meaningful combination of the phonemes *c*, *o*, and *w*. Pointing to two of these animals, the linguist would elicit the word *cows* from local speakers. This would reveal yet another morpheme—the *s*—which can be added to the original morpheme to indicate plural.

The next step in unraveling a language is to identify its **syntax**—the patterns or rules by which morphemes are arranged into phrases and sentences. The **grammar** of the language will ultimately consist of all observations about its morphemes and syntax.

---

linguistics The modern scientific study of all aspects of language.

phonetics The systematic identification and description of distinctive speech sounds in a language.

phonology The study of language sounds.

phonemes The smallest units of sound that make a difference in meaning in a language.

morphology The study of the patterns or rules of word formation in a language, including the guidelines for verb tense, pluralization, and compound words.

morphemes The smallest units of sound that carry a meaning in language. They are distinct from phonemes, which can alter meaning but have no meaning by themselves.

syntax The patterns or rules by which words are arranged into phrases and sentences.

grammar The entire formal structure of a language, including morphology and syntax.

One of the strengths of modern descriptive linguistics is the objectivity of its methods. For example, English-speaking anthropologists who specialize in this will not approach a language with the idea that it must have nouns, verbs, prepositions, or any other of the form classes identifiable in English. Instead, they see what turns up in the language and attempt to describe it in terms of its own inner workings. This allows for unanticipated discoveries. For instance, unlike many other languages, English does not distinguish between feminine and masculine nouns. English speakers use the definite article *the* in front of any noun, whereas Spanish varies with gender and numbers, requiring four types of such definite articles: *la* (singular feminine), *el* (singular masculine), *las* (plural feminine), and *los* (plural masculine)—as in *las casas* (the houses) and *los jardines* (the gardens).

German speakers go one step further, utilizing three gendered articles in singular, but only one in plural: *die* (singular feminine), *der* (singular masculine), *das* (singular neuter), and *die* (plural, regardless of gender). For cultural historical reasons, Germans consider the house neuter, so they say *das Haus*, but concur with Spaniards that the garden is masculine. Some nouns, however, reverse gender in German–Spanish translation: the feminine sun (*die Sonne*) transgenders into a masculine *el sol*, and the masculine moon (*der Mond*) turns into a feminine *la luna*.

However, these language gender issues are not relevant everywhere. In the Andean highlands in South America, Quechua-speaking Indians are not concerned about whether nouns are gendered or neutral, for their language has no definite articles at all.

Historical Linguistics

Although descriptive linguistics focuses on all features of a particular language at any one moment in time, historical linguistics deals with the fact that languages change. In addition to deciphering "dead" languages that are no longer spoken, specialists in this field investigate relationships between earlier and later forms of the same language, study older languages to track the processes of change into modern ones, and examine interrelationships among older languages. For example, they attempt to sort out the development of Latin (spoken almost 1,500 years ago in southern Europe) into the Romance languages of Italian, Spanish, Portuguese, French, and Romanian by identifying natural shifts in the original language and

tracking modifications brought on by centuries of direct contact with Germanic-speaking invaders from northern Europe.

When focusing on long-term processes of change, historical linguists depend on written records of languages. They have achieved considerable success in working out the relationships among different languages, and these are reflected in schemes of classification. For example, English is one of approximately 140 languages classified in the larger Indo-European language family (**Figure 15.2**). A **language family** is a group of languages descended from a single ancestral language. This family is subdivided into some eleven subgroups (Germanic, Romance, and so on), indicating that there has been a long period (6,000 years or so) of **linguistic divergence** from an ancient unified language (reconstructed as Proto-Indo-European) into separate "daughter" languages. English is one of several languages in the Germanic subgroup (**Figure 15.3**), all of which are more closely related to one another than they are to the languages of any other subgroup of the Indo-European family.

Despite the differences between them, the languages of one subgroup share certain features when compared to those of another. As an illustration, the word for father in the Germanic languages always starts with an *f* or closely related *v* sound (Dutch *vader*, German *Vater*, Gothic *Fadar*). Among the Romance languages, by contrast, the comparable word always starts with a *p*: French *père*, Spanish and Italian *padre*—all derived from the Latin *pater*. The original Indo-European word for father was *p'tēr*, so in this case, the Romance languages have retained the earlier pronunciation, whereas the Germanic languages have diverged.

Historical linguists are not limited to the faraway past, for even modern languages are constantly transforming—adding new words, dropping others, or changing meaning. Studying them in their specific cultural context can help us understand the processes of change that may have led to linguistic divergence in the past.

Processes of Linguistic Divergence

One force for change is selective borrowing between languages. This is evident in the many French words present in the English language—and in the growing number of English words cropping up in languages all around the world due to globalization. Technological breakthroughs resulting in new equipment and products prompt linguistic shifts. For instance, the electronic revolution that brought us radio, television, and computers has created entirely new vocabularies. Over the last decade or so, Internet use has widened the meaning of a host of already existing English words—from *hacking* and *surfing* to *spam*. Entirely new words such as *blogging*, *vlogging*, and

language family A group of languages descended from a single ancestral language.
linguistic divergence The development of different languages from a single ancestral language.

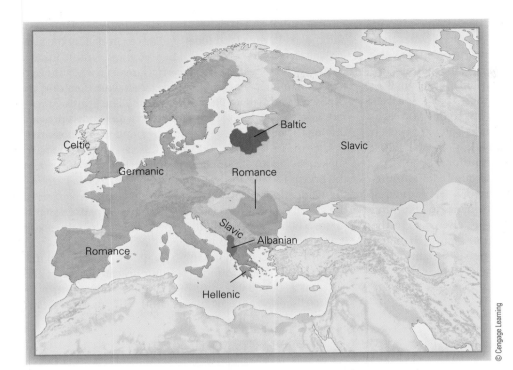

Figure 15.2 European Language Subgroups in Europe Not all languages spoken in Europe are part of the Indo-European family. For example, Basque—an isolated language also known as Euskara—is still spoken in the French–Spanish borderland. Moreover, languages spoken by Hungarians, Estonians, Finns, Komi (in northeast Russia), and Saami (in northern Scandinavia) belong to the Uralic language family.

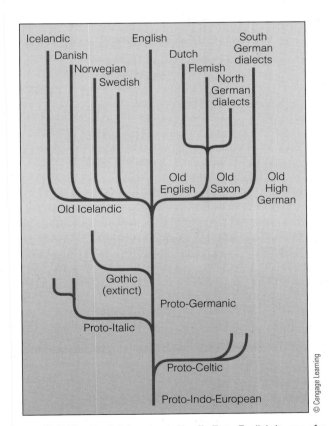

Figure 15.3 The English Language Family Tree English is one of a group of languages in the Germanic subgroup of the Indo-European family. This diagram shows its relationship to languages in the same subgroup. The root is an ancestral language originally spoken by early farmers and herders who spread north and west over Europe, bringing with them both their customs and their language.

netiquette have been coined, leading to the creation of Internet dictionaries such as netlingo.com.

There is also a tendency for any group within a larger society to create its own unique vocabulary, whether it is a street gang, sorority, religious group, prison inmates, or platoon of soldiers. By changing the meaning of existing words or inventing new ones, members of the in-group can communicate with fellow members while effectively excluding outsiders who may be within hearing range. Increasing professional specialization also contributes to coining new words and greatly expanding vocabularies. Finally, there seems to be a human tendency to admire the person who comes up with a new and clever idiom, a useful word, or a particularly stylish pronunciation. In other words, no language stands still.

Language Loss and Revival

Perhaps the most powerful force for linguistic change is the domination of one society over another, as demonstrated during 500 years of European colonialism. Such dominations persist today in many parts of the world, such as Taiwan's indigenous peoples being governed by Mandarin-speaking Chinese, Tarascan Indians by Spanish-speaking Mexicans, or Bushmen by English-speaking Namibians. In many cases, foreign political control has resulted in linguistic erosion or even complete disappearance, sometimes leaving only a faint trace in old, indigenous names for geographic features such as hills and rivers.

Over the last 500 years about half of the world's 12,000 or so languages have become extinct as a direct result of warfare, epidemics, and forced assimilation brought on by colonial powers and other aggressive outsiders. Other than the dominant languages today, very few people speak the remaining 6,000 languages, and these languages are losing speakers rapidly due to globalization. In fact, half of the remaining languages have fewer than 10,000 speakers each, and the other half are spoken by less than 1,000 each. Put another way, half of the world's languages are spoken by just 2 percent of the world's population (Crystal, 2002; see also Knight, Studdert-Kennedy, & Hurford, 2000).

In North America, only 150 of the original 300 indigenous languages still exist, and many of these surviving tongues are moving toward extinction at an alarming rate. Thousands of indigenous languages elsewhere in the world are also threatened. For example, fewer than ten people still speak N|uu, a "click" language traditionally spoken in South Africa's Kalahari Desert. N|uu is the only surviving member of the !Ui branch of the Tuu language family (previously called Southern Khoisan) (**Figure 15.4**).

Anthropologists predict that the number of languages still spoken in the world today will be cut in half by the year 2100, in large part because children born into ethnic minority groups no longer use the ancestral language when they go to school, migrate to cities, join the larger workforce, and are exposed to printed and electronic media. The printing press, radio, satellite television, Internet, and text messaging are driving the need for a shared language, and increasingly that is English. In the past 500 years, this language—originally spoken by about 2.5 million people living only in part of the British Isles in northwestern Europe—has spread around the world. Today, some 375 million people (5.4 percent of the global population) claim English as their native tongue. About a billion others (about 15 percent of humanity) speak it as a second or foreign language.

Although a common language allows people from different ethnic backgrounds to communicate, there is the risk that a global spread of one language may contribute to the disappearance of others. And with the extinction

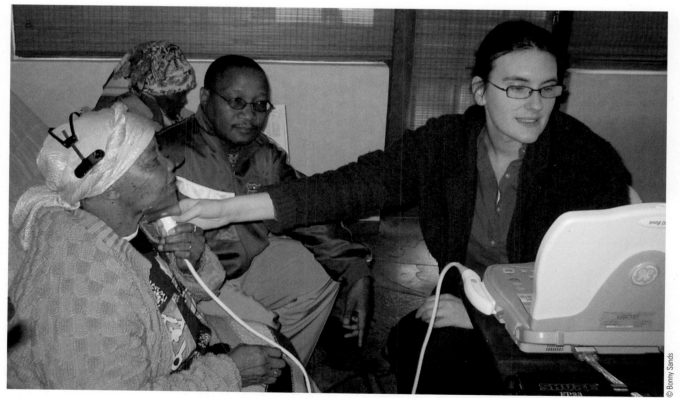

Figure 15.4 Modern Technology in Linguistic Analysis Several linguistic anthropologists are collaborating on field research with speakers of endangered Khoisan "click" languages such as N|uu in southern Africa. Using a portable ultrasound-imaging machine, they can capture the tongue movements of the click consonants. Here, U.S. linguist Johanna Brugman holds an ultrasound probe under the chin of one of the ten remaining N|uu speakers, Ouma Katrina Esau, who is helping to document how click sounds are made. Clicks are produced by creating suction within a cavity formed between the front and back parts of the tongue—except in the case of bilabial clicks in which the cavity is made between the lips and the back of the tongue. N|uu is one of only three languages remaining in the world that use bilabial clicks as consonants. The vertical bar in the word *N|uu* indicates a click sound.

© Bonny Sands

of each language, we lose "hundreds of generations of traditional knowledge encoded in these ancestral tongues"—a vast repository of knowledge about the natural world, plants, animals, ecosystems, and cultural traditions (Living Tongues, 2012).

A key issue in language preservation efforts today is the impact of electronic media such as the Internet, where content still exists in relatively few languages, and 84 percent of Internet users are native speakers of just ten of the world's 6,000 languages. In 2001, UNESCO established Initiative B@bel, which uses information and communication technologies to support linguistic and cultural diversity. Promoting multilingualism on the Internet, this initiative aims to bridge the digital divide—to make access to Internet content and services more equitable for users worldwide (**Figure 15.5**).

Sometimes, in reaction to a real or perceived threat of cultural dominance by powerful foreign societies, ethnic groups and even entire countries may seek to maintain or reclaim their unique identity by purging their vocabularies of "foreign" terms. Emerging as a significant force for linguistic change, such **linguistic nationalism** is particularly characteristic of the former colonial countries of Africa and Asia today. It is not limited to those countries, however, as one can see by periodic French attempts to purge their language of such Americanisms as *le hamburger*. Another example of this is France's decision to substitute the word *e-mail* with the government-approved term *couriel*.

For many ethnic minorities, efforts to counter the threat of linguistic extinction or to resurrect already extinct languages form part of their struggle to maintain a sense of cultural identity and dignity. A prime means by which powerful groups try to assert their dominance over minori-

ties living within their borders is to actively suppress their languages. Historically, examples of this include government-sanctioned efforts (1870s–1950s) to repress Native American cultures and fully absorb them into mainstream society. Government policies included taking Indian children away from their parents and putting them in boarding schools where only English was allowed, and students were often punished for speaking their traditional languages. Upon returning to their homes, many could no longer communicate with their own close relatives and neighbors.

Although now abolished, these institutions and the historical policies that shaped them did lasting damage to American Indian groups striving to maintain their cultural heritage. Especially over the past four decades, many of these besieged indigenous communities have been actively involved in language revitalization. Among numerous examples of this is the work of S. Neyooxet Greymorning, a Southern Arapaho, who developed ways to revive indigenous languages, including his own. Greymorning, a professor of anthropology and Native American studies at the University of Montana, tells his story in the Anthropology Applied feature.

Language in Its Social and Cultural Settings

Language is not simply a matter of combining sounds according to certain rules to come up with meaningful utterances. Individuals communicate with one another constantly—in households, in the street, on the job, and so on. People often vary in the ways they perform speech based on social context and cultural factors such as gender, age, class, and ethnicity. Moreover, what people choose to speak about, whisper, or keep secret in silence often reflects what is socially important or culturally meaningful in their community. For that reason, linguistic anthropologists also focus on the actual use of language in relation to its various distinctive social and cultural settings. This third branch of linguistic study falls into two categories: sociolinguistics and ethnolinguistics.

Sociolinguistics

Sociolinguistics, the study of the relationship between language and society, examines how social categories—such as age, gender, ethnicity, religion, occupation, and

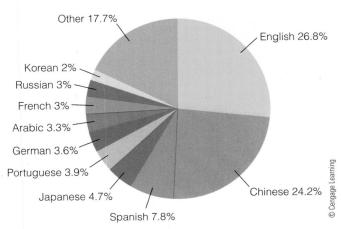

Figure 15.5 Language Use on the Internet Although the world's digital divide is diminishing, it is still dramatic. As illustrated here, over 80 percent of today's 2 billion Internet users are native speakers of just ten of the world's 6,000 languages. Among the fastest-growing Internet language groups today are Arabic, Chinese, and Russian. (Figures shown in pie chart are rounded.)

Data from http://www.internetworldstats.com. Figure from Haviland/Prins/Walrath/McBride, *The Essence of Anthropology*, 3E, Fig. 2.5, p. 45. © 2013 Cengage Learning.

Pie chart labels: Other 17.7%; English 26.8%; Korean 2%; Russian 3%; French 3%; Arabic 3.3%; German 3.6%; Portuguese 3.9%; Japanese 4.7%; Spanish 7.8%; Chinese 24.2%

© Cengage Learning

linguistic nationalism The attempt by ethnic minorities and even countries to proclaim independence by purging their language of foreign terms.

sociolinguistics The study of the relationship between language and society through examining how social categories—such as age, gender, ethnicity, religion, occupation, and class—influence the use and significance of distinctive styles of speech.

ANTHROPOLOGY APPLIED

When Bambi Spoke Arapaho: Preserving Indigenous Languages

By S. Neyooxet Greymorning

In life, there are experiences later recognized as defining moments. For me, a moment like that happened in my second year of college when some mysterious individual stood over me and asked, "What are you doing to help your people?" I remember getting up, going to the library, and walking along the stacks. Trailing my fingers over books, I randomly stopped and pulled one out. It was about the overall status of American Indian languages in the United States. Curious, I opened it, looked up Arapaho, and read that it was among the healthiest Native languages. Comforted by this, it didn't occur to me that a rapidly dwindling number of young Arapaho speakers was signaling the demise of my ancestral tongue. Years later when I told tribal Elder Francis Brown about this, he said, "The Elders called your name."

Perhaps they continued to call. When I went on to graduate school and studied anthropology, I felt driven to take almost every linguistic class available. By 1981, I understood that

to lose a language is to lose aspects of how a people make sense of themselves and the world they live in and the values that culturally and psychologically bind a people together shaping their identity. I decided to spend the summer on the Wind River Reservation in central Wyoming putting together an Arapaho dictionary. Then I learned that University of Massachusetts professor Dr. Zdeněk Salzmann, a Czech anthropologist who did linguistic work with the Arapaho, had the same idea. I called him, and he suggested we work together.

As a graduate student I dedicated myself to gaining the knowledge, skills, and experience that could contribute to revitalizing languages. Upon completing my doctorate, 1992, I was invited to direct a language and culture program on the Wind River Reservation where Arapaho language instruction had been introduced within the public school system in the late 1970s. By 1993, although Arapaho was taught from kindergarten to high school, my assessment revealed students were

able to say only a few basic phrases and vocabulary words having to do with food, animals, colors, and numbers—nothing near fluency and the goal of keeping Arapaho alive.

Recognizing the need for a different approach, I began laying the groundwork

Greymorning speaking about language revitalization.

---

class—influence the use and significance of distinctive styles of speech.

Language and Gender

As a major factor in personal and social identity, gender is often reflected in language use, so it is not surprising that numerous thought-provoking sociolinguistic topics fall under the category of language and gender. These include research on **gendered speech**—distinct male and female speech patterns, which vary across social and cultural settings. One of the first in-depth

studies in this genre explored the relationship of gender and power to explain why North American women exhibit less decisive speech styles than men. This early study and a subsequent wave of related scholarly works have produced new insights about language as a social speech "performance" in both private and public settings (Lakoff, 2004).

Gendered speech research also includes the study of distinct male and female syntax exhibited in various languages around the world, such as the Lakota language, still spoken at the Pine Ridge and Rosebud Indian reservations in South Dakota. When a Lakota woman asks someone, "How are you?" she says, "Tonik*thkahe*?" But when her brother poses the same question, he says, "Tonik*ukahwo*?" (**Figure 15.6**). As explained by

gendered speech Distinct male and female speech patterns, which vary across social and cultural settings.

to establish one of the first full-day language immersion preschools on a reservation: Hinono'eitiino'oowu'—the Arapaho Language Lodge. The aim was for language "providers" to speak only Arapaho and use a multifaceted approach that included not only word and phrase acquisition, but also response exercises, visual association, and interaction with videos and audio cassettes of songs.

I contacted Disney Studios and convinced them to allow us to translate *Bambi* into Arapaho as a learning aid.[a] *Bambi* seemed like a good choice because it echoed traditional stories in which animals speak, it was a story that most children on the reservation knew, and as the story unfolds Bambi uses simple childlike language as he learns to talk.

However, even a multifaceted approach that included Bambi speaking Arapaho was not turning the tide of language demise, so I began to think through the challenges with increased focus. From 1996 to 2002 I gradually developed a new approach, Accelerated Second Language Acquisition (ASLA©™). During 2003, using my children as language learners, I tested and honed ASLA into a workable methodology that helps retune the brain so people learn to visualize the language rather than continually translate back and forth in their minds between the language they know and the one they're learning.

To encourage language teachers on the reservation to adopt this approach, I modeled teaching Arapaho through ASLA at the University of Montana with remarkable results. Beyond efforts to help preserve Arapaho, I'm regularly asked to give ASLA workshops for others who are committed to Indigenous language revitalization. To date, I have had contact with over 1,200 individual language instructors from more than 60 different communities in the United States, Canada, and Australia, representing over 40 different languages.[b]

The challenge of preserving languages (and the keys to life that each one holds) is daunting. But something my uncle told me during a boyhood visit with him encourages me to be counted among those who keep trying. He woke me at dawn and took me to a pond. There was no wind, and the water was like glass. After instructing me to pick up a small stone, he said, "Now drop it in the pond and tell me what you see." Releasing the stone, I watched it make ever-widening circles on the water. "I want you to always remember," said my uncle, "that nothing is so small that it can't put something larger than itself into motion."

Written expressly for this text, 2010.

---

[a] See Greymorning, S. N. (2001). Reflections on the Arapaho Language Project or, when Bambi spoke Arapaho and other tales of Arapaho language revitalization efforts. In K. Hale & L. Hinton, *The green book of language revitalization in practice* (pp. 287–297). New York: Academic.

[b] For video examples of students of ASLA speaking Arapaho, plus written comments from language instructors and students about ASLA, go to www.nsilc.org.

Michael Two Horses, "Our language is gender-specific in the area of commands, queries, and a couple of other things."[1]

Social Dialects

Sociolinguists are also interested in **dialects**—varying forms of a language that reflect particular regions, occupations, or social classes and that are similar enough to be mutually intelligible. Technically, all dialects are languages—there is nothing partial or sublinguistic about them—and the point at which two different dialects become distinctly different languages is roughly the point at which speakers of one are almost totally unable to communicate with speakers of the other.

In the case of regional dialects, there is frequently a transitional territory, or perhaps a buffer zone, where features of both are found and understood. Distinguishing dialects from languages and revealing the relationship between power and language, the noted linguist–political activist Noam Chomsky often quoted the saying that a dialect is a language without an army[2] (Shook et al., 2004).

---

[1] Personal communication, April 2003.

[2] This saying is attributed to Yiddish linguist Max Weinreich.

dialects The varying forms of a language that reflect particular regions, occupations, or social classes and that are similar enough to be mutually intelligible.

Figure 15.6 Gendered Speech Howler Makers of the feature film *Dances with Wolves* aimed for cultural authenticity by casting Native American actors and hiring a female language coach to teach Lakota to those who did not know how to speak it. However, the lessons did not include the gendered speech aspect of Lakota—the fact that females and males follow different rules of syntax. So, when Native speakers of the language saw the film and realized that the actors portraying Lakota warriors were speaking like women, they snickered and then howled with laughter.

© Orion Pictures Corporation/Everett Collection

Such is the case in China, the world's most populous country with almost 1.4 billion inhabitants, almost all of whom speak Chinese. In fact, there are many Chinese languages, each consisting of many regional dialects. For instance, folk in Shanghai actually use a dialect of Wu Chinese spoken in the eastern region, whereas natives of Guangdong (Canton) speak a dialect of Yuehai, the major language of southwestern China. Migrants from the northern parts of the country, where numerous dialects of Mandarin Chinese are traditionally spoken, understand almost nothing of Wu or Yuehai because these Chinese languages are foreign to them. For this reason, almost all Chinese nationals today learn Standard Chinese, the country's official language, historically developed as a lingua franca based on a Mandarin dialect traditionally spoken in the country's capital city, Beijing.

Linguistic boundaries are not only geographic or territorial, but may also indicate or reflect social class, economic status, political rank, or ethnic identity. A classic example of the kind of dialect that may set one group apart from others within a single society is one spoken by many inner-city African Americans. Technically known as African American Vernacular English (AAVE), it has often been referred to as *black English* and *Ebonics*. Like any other dialect or language, AAVE is a highly structured mode of speech with patterned rules of sounds and sequences. Many of its distinctive features stem from the retention of sound patterns, grammatical rules concerning verbs, and even words of the West African languages spoken by the ancestors of present-day African Americans (Monaghan, Hinton, & Kephart, 1997).

In many societies where different dialects are spoken, individuals often become skilled at switching back and forth between them, depending on the situation in which they are speaking. Without being conscious of it, we all do the same thing when we switch from formality to informality in our speech, depending upon where we are and to whom we are talking. The process of changing from one language mode to another as the situation demands, whether from one language to another or from one dialect of a language to another, is known as **code switching**, the subject of several sociolinguistic studies. Fascinating new research on a distinct signing system known as Black ASL shows that code switching occurs even among those using sign language (McCaskill et al., 2012).

Ethnolinguistics

The study of the relationships between language and culture, and how they mutually influence and inform each other, is the domain of **ethnolinguistics**. In this type of research, anthropologists may investigate how a language reflects the culturally significant aspects of a people's traditional natural environment. For example, Aymara Indians living in the Bolivian highlands depend on the potato (or *luki*) as their major source of food, and their language has over 200 words for this vegetable, reflecting the many varieties they traditionally grow and the many different ways that they preserve and prepare it (**Figure 15.7**). Similarly, many people in the United States today possess a rich vocabulary allowing them to precisely

code switching The practice of changing from one mode of speech to another as the situation demands, whether from one language to another or from one dialect of a language to another.

ethnolinguistics A branch of linguistics that studies the relationships between language and culture and how they mutually influence and inform each other.

Figure 15.7
Linguistic Relativity
Aymara Indians living in the highlands of Bolivia and Peru in South America depend on the potato as their major source of food. Their language has over 200 words for this vegetable, reflecting the many varieties they traditionally grow and the many different ways they preserve and prepare it. This is an example of linguistic relativity.

© Kazuyoshi Namachi/Corbis

distinguish between many different types of cars, categorized by model, year, and manufacturer.

Another example concerns cultural categories of color: languages have different ways of dividing and naming the range of light in the electromagnetic spectrum visible to the naked human eye. In modern English we speak of black, red, orange, yellow, green, blue, indigo, violet, and white, as well as "invisible" colors such as ultraviolet and infrared. Other languages mark out different groupings on this continuum of hues. For instance, Indians in Mexico's northwestern mountains speaking Tarahumara have just one word for both green and blue—*siyoname.*

In the Hanunóo language, as spoken by the Mangyan on the Philippine island of Mindoro, there is no word for color. Instead, these tropical forest-dwellers value objects like textiles, beads, animals, feathers, plants, and fruit based on levels of brightness and saturation. Their classification can be reduced to just four terms: lightness (*malagti*), corresponding to white and other lightly tinted colors; darkness (*mabiru*), referring to black and dark-shaded versions of gray, blue, and green; wetness (*malatuy*), akin to fresh greenness; and dryness (*marara*), associated with "dried-out" reddish colors (Conklin, 1955).

The idea that the words and grammar of a language are directly linked to culture and affect how speakers of the language perceive and think about the world is known as **linguistic relativity**. This theoretical concept is associated with the pioneering ethnolinguistic research carried out by anthropologist Edward Sapir and his student Benjamin Whorf during the 1930s. Focusing on the interplay of language, thought, and culture, their research resulted in what is now known as the *Sapir-Whorf hypothesis*: the idea that each language provides particular

grooves of linguistic expression that predispose speakers of that language to perceive the world in a certain way.

Whorf gained many of these insights while translating English into Hopi, a North American Indian language still spoken in Arizona. Doing this work, he discovered that Hopi differs from English not only in vocabulary but also in terms of its grammatical categories such as nouns and verbs. For instance, Hopi use numbers for counting and measuring things that have physical existence, but they do not apply numbers in the same way to abstractions like time. They would have no problem translating an English sentence such as "I see fifteen sheep grazing on three acres of grassland," but an equally simple sentence such as "Three weeks ago, I enjoyed my fifteen minutes of fame" would require a much more complex translation into Hopi.

It is also of note that Hopi verbs express tenses differently than English verbs. Rather than marking past, present, and future, with *-ed*, *-ing*, or *will*, Hopi requires additional words to indicate if an event is completed, is still ongoing, or is expected to take place. So instead of saying, "Three strangers stayed for fifteen days in our village," a Hopi would say something like, "We remember three strangers stay in our village until the sixteenth day."

In addition, Hopi verbs do not express tense by their forms. Unlike English verbs that change form to indicate past, present, and future, Hopi verbs distinguish among a statement of fact (if the speaker actually witnesses a certain event), a statement of expectation, and a statement that

---

linguistic relativity The theoretical concept directly linking language and culture, holding that the words and grammar of a language affect how its speakers perceive and think about the world.

expresses regularity. For instance, when you ask an English-speaking athlete "Do you run?" he may answer "yes," when in fact he may at that moment be sitting in an armchair watching TV. A Hopi athlete asked the same question in his own language might respond "no" because in Hopi the statement of fact "he runs" translates as *wari* ("running occurs"), whereas the statement that expresses regularity—"he runs," such as on the track team—translates as *warikngwe* ("running occurs characteristically").

This shows that the Hopi language structures thinking and behavior with a focus on the present—on getting ready and carrying out what needs to be done right now. Whorf summed it up like this: "A characteristic of Hopi behavior is the emphasis on preparation. This includes announcing and getting ready for events well beforehand, elaborate precautions to insure persistence of desired conditions, and stress on good will as the preparer of good results" (Carroll, 1956, p. 148). Based on his research on the Hopi language and culture, Whorf developed his important theoretical insight "that the structure of the language one habitually uses influences the manner in which one understands his environment. The picture of the universe shifts from tongue to tongue" (Carroll, 1956, p. vi).

In the 1990s linguistic anthropologists devised new research strategies to actually test Sapir and Whorf's original hypothesis. One study found that speakers of Swedish and Finnish (neighboring peoples who speak radically different languages) working at similar jobs in similar regions under similar laws and regulations show significantly different rates of on-the-job accidents. The rates are substantially lower among the Swedish speakers. What emerges from comparison of the two languages is that Swedish (one of the Indo-European languages) emphasizes information about movement in three-dimensional space. Finnish (a Ural-Altaic language unrelated to Indo-European languages) emphasizes more static relations among coherent temporal entities. As a consequence, it seems that Finns organize the workplace in a way that favors the individual person over the temporal organization in the overall production process. This in turn leads to frequent production disruptions, haste, and (ultimately) accidents.

If language does mirror cultural reality, it would follow that changes in a culture will sooner or later be reflected in changes in the language. We see this happening all around the world today, including in the English language (Wolff & Holmes, 2011).

Language Versatility

In most societies throughout the world, it is not unusual for individuals to be fluent in two, three, or more languages. They succeed in this in large part because they experience training in multiple languages as children—not as high school or college students, which is the educational norm in the United States.

In some regions where groups speaking different languages coexist and interact, people often understand one another but may choose not to speak the other's language. Such is the case in the borderlands of northern Bolivia and southern Peru where Quechua-speaking and Aymara-speaking Indians are neighbors. When an Aymara farmer speaks to a Quechua herder in Aymara, the Quechua will reply in Quechua, and vice versa, each knowing that the other understands both languages even if speaking just one. The ability to comprehend two languages but express oneself in only one is known as *receptive* or *passive bilingualism*.

In the United States, perhaps reflecting the country's enormous size and power, many citizens are not interested in learning a second or foreign language. This is especially significant—and troubling—because the United States is not only one of the world's most ethnically diverse countries, but also the world's largest economy and heavily dependent on international trade relations. In our globalized world, being bilingual or multilingual may open doors of communication not only for trade but for work, diplomacy, art, and friendship. Ironically, reluctance to learn another language prevails in the United States despite the fact that the majority language in the Americas is not English but Spanish; Spanish is not only the majority language of the hemisphere but also the fastest-growing language in the United States.

Beyond Words: The Gesture–Call System

As efficient as they are at naming and talking about ideas, actions, and things, all languages are to some degree inadequate at communicating certain kinds of information that people need to know in order to fully understand what is being said. For this reason, human speech is always embedded within a gesture–call system of a type that we share with nonhuman primates.

The various sounds and gestures of this system serve to "key" speech, providing listeners with the appropriate frame for interpreting what a speaker is saying. Messages about human emotions and intentions are effectively communicated by this gesture–call system: Is the speaker happy, sad, mad, enthusiastic, tired, or in some other emotional state? Is he or she requesting information, denying something, reporting factually, or lying? Very little of this information is conveyed by spoken language alone. In fact, research shows that humans convey far more information through nonverbal means (tone of voice, body language) than through verbal means in their interactions and communications with each other (Poyatos, 2002).

Nonverbal Communication

The **gesture** component of the gesture–call system consists of facial expressions and body postures and motions that convey intended as well as subconscious messages. The study of such nonverbal signals is known as **kinesics**.

Humanity's repertoire of body language is enormous. This is evident if you consider just one aspect of it: the fact that a human being has about fifty facial muscles and is thereby capable of making more than 7,000 facial expressions! Thus, it should not be surprising to hear that at least 60 percent of our total communication takes place nonverbally.

Often, gestural messages complement spoken messages—for instance, nodding the head while affirming something verbally, raising eyebrows when asking a question, or using hands and fingers to illustrate or emphasize what is being talked about. However, nonverbal signals are sometimes at odds with verbal ones, and they have the power to override or undercut them. For example, a person may say the words "I love you" a thousand times to another, but if it is not true, the nonverbal signals will likely communicate that falseness.

Anthropologists paid little attention to the analysis of nonverbal communication prior to the 1950s, but since then a great deal of research has been devoted to this intriguing subject. Cross-cultural studies in this field have shown that there are many similarities around the world in such basic facial expressions as smiling, laughing, crying, and displaying shock or anger. The smirks, frowns, and gasps that we have inherited from our primate ancestry require little learning and are harder to fake than conventional or socially obtained gestures that are shared by members of a group, albeit not always consciously so.

Routine greetings are also similar around the world. Europeans, Balinese, Papuans, Samoans, Bushmen, and at least some South American Indians all smile and nod, and if the individuals are especially friendly, they will raise their eyebrows with a rapid movement, keeping them raised for a fraction of a second. By doing so, they signal a readiness for contact. The Japanese, however, suppress the eyebrow flash, regarding it as indecent. This example illustrates that there are important cross-cultural differences as well as similarities.

Another example can be found in gestural expressions for yes and no. In North America, one nods the head down then up for yes or shakes it left and right for no. The people of Sri Lanka also nod to answer yes to a factual question, but if asked to do something, a slow sideways movement of the head means yes. In Greece, the nodded head means yes, but no is indicated by jerking the head back so as to lift the face, usually with the eyes closed and the eyebrows raised.

Another aspect of body language has to do with social space: how people position themselves physically in relation to others. **Proxemics**, the cross-cultural study of social space, came to the fore through the work of anthropologist Edward Hall (1914–2009), who coined the term (Hall, 1963, 1990). As a young man in the 1930s, Hall worked with construction crews of Hopi and Navajo Indians, building roads and dams. After earning his doctorate, he worked with the U.S. State Department to develop the new field of intercultural communication at the Foreign Service Institute, and while training some 2,000 Foreign Service workers, his ideas about nonverbal communication began to crystallize.

Hall's research showed that people from different cultures have different frameworks for defining and organizing social space—the personal space they establish around their bodies, as well as the macrolevel sensibilities that shape cultural expectations about how streets, neighborhoods, and cities should be arranged. Among other things, Hall's investigation of personal space revealed that every culture has distinctive norms for closeness (**Figure 15.8**). You can see this for yourself if you are watching a foreign film, visiting another country, or taking part in a multicultural group. How close to one another do people stand when talking in the street or riding in a subway or elevator? Does the pattern match the one you are accustomed to in your own cultural corner?

Hall identified the range of cultural variation in four categories of proxemically relevant social spaces: intimate (0–18 inches), personal-casual (1½–4 feet), social-consultive (4–12 feet), and public distance (12 feet and beyond). Hall warned that different cultural definitions of socially accepted use of space within these categories can lead to serious miscommunication and misunderstanding in cross-cultural settings (Hall, 1990). His research has been fundamental for the present-day training of international businesspeople, diplomats, and others involved in intercultural work.

Paralanguage

The second component of the gesture–call system is **paralanguage**—specific voice effects that accompany speech and contribute to communication. These include vocalizations such as giggling, groaning, or sighing, as well as voice qualities such as volume, intensity, pitch, and tempo.

The importance of paralanguage is suggested by the comment, "It's not so much *what* was said as *how* it was said." Obviously, whispering or shouting can make a big difference in meaning, even though the uttered words would be the same when written down. Minor differences in pitch, tempo, and phrasing may seem less obvious, but they still impact how words are perceived. Studies show, for example, that even subliminal messages communicated

---

gestures Facial expressions and body postures and motions that convey intended as well as subconscious messages.

kinesics The study of nonverbal signals in body language including facial expressions and bodily postures and motions.

proxemics The cross-cultural study of people's perception and use of space.

paralanguage Voice effects that accompany language and convey meaning. These include vocalizations such as giggling, groaning, or sighing, as well as voice qualities such as pitch and tempo.

VISUAL COUNTERPOINT

Figure 15.8 Personal Space Across Cultures Cultures around the world have noticeably different attitudes concerning proxemics or personal space—how far apart people should be positioned in nonintimate social encounters. How does the gap between the U.S. businessmen pictured here compare with that of the robed men of Saudi Arabia?

below the threshold of conscious perception by seemingly minor differences in phrasing, tempo, length of answers, and the like are far more important in courtroom proceedings than even the most perceptive trial lawyer may have realized. Among other things, *how* a witness gives testimony alters the reception it gets from jurors and influences the witness's credibility (O'Barr & Conley, 1993).

Communication has changed radically over the past two decades with the rise of e-mail, text messaging, and Twitter. These technologies resemble the spontaneity and speed of face-to-face communication but lack the body signals and voice qualifiers that nuance what is being said (and hint at how it is being received). Studies show that the intended tone of e-mail messages is perceived correctly only 56 percent of the time. Misunderstood messages can quickly create problems and hostility. Because the risk of miscommunication with these technologies abounds, despite interpretation signals such as LOL (laugh out loud) or the smiley face ☺, certain sensitive exchanges are better made in person (Kruger et al., 2005).

Tonal Languages

There is enormous diversity in the ways languages are spoken. In addition to hundreds of vowels and consonants, sounds can be divided into tones—rises and falls in pitch that play a key role in distinguishing one word from another. About 70 percent of the world's languages are

tonal languages in which the various distinctive sound pitches of spoken words are not only an essential part of their pronunciation but are also key to their meaning.

Worldwide, at least one-third of the population speaks a tonal language, including many in Africa, Central America, and East Asia. For example, Mandarin Chinese has four contrasting tones: flat, rising, falling, and falling then rising. These tones are used to distinguish among normally stressed syllables that are otherwise identical. So, depending on intonation, *ba* can mean "to uproot," "to hold," "eight," or "a harrow" (farm tool) (Catford, 1988). Yuehai, the Chinese language spoken in Guangdong (Canton) and Hong Kong, uses six contrasting tones, and some Chinese dialects have as many as nine.

In nontonal languages such as English, tone can be used to convey an attitude or to change a statement into a question. But tone alone does not change the meaning of individual words as it does in Mandarin, where careless use of tones with the syllable *ma* could cause one to call someone's mother a horse!

Telecommunication: From Talking Drums to Whistled Speech

Even a very loud human voice has its natural limits beyond which our ears cannot pick up the sound. Of course, sounds carry farther in some environments than in others. For example, shouts across a lake or canyon are more easily heard than those passing through a thick forest.

---

tonal language A language in which the sound pitch of a spoken word is an essential part of its pronunciation and meaning.

Until the telecommunication inventions of the 19th century, acoustic space was limited by natural factors. Yet, long ago people found ways to expand their acoustic range, sounding information far beyond their loudest vocal reach. One example is the *talking drum*. Widespread among tonal-speaking peoples in West Africa, these large drums can transmit coded information that can be heard from as far away as 12 kilometers (7½ miles).

Another traditional telecommunication system used to expand acoustic space is **whistled speech**, or whistled language—an exchange of whistled words using a phonetic emulation of the sounds produced in spoken voice (Meyer, 2008; Meyer & Gautheron, 2006; Meyer, Meunier, & Dentel, 2007). Whistling sounds are generated by blowing, producing air vibrations at the mouth's aperture; the faster the air stream, the higher the noise. Whistled speech can be more effective across greater distances than shouted talk because it occurs at a higher pitch or frequency range.

Whistling techniques vary. Some involve both lips; others use lips and teeth or a retroflexed tongue with various finger combinations. Two-finger whistling can produce very loud sounds and in a ravine can be picked up by the human ear from as far away as 8 kilometers (5 miles).

Whistling lends itself to playing with melodies, and whistled speech may have developed from the whistling of purely musical phrases. Although its precise origins are not known, whistled speech still occurs in more than thirty languages around the world. It is found most often in communities that speak tonal languages, such as the Yupik-speaking Eskimos of St. Lawrence Island, who may have developed whistled speech to aid them when kayaking through dense fog or hunting in snow fields (**Figure 15.9**).

Although whistled speech tends to be an abridged form of everyday spoken language, its vocabulary can be considerable. In Silbo, for instance, traditionally used by Spanish-speaking inhabitants of La Gomera off the northwest African coast, islanders can whistle some 2,000 words. Like the talking drum, it is an endangered tradition—disappearing in part because the communities where the practice once thrived are no longer isolated or because the ancestral lifeways are vanishing or already gone. Moreover, the ever-expanding reach of mobile phones and other electronic telecommunication technologies have contributed to the demise of whistled language (Meyer & Gautheron, 2006).

The Origins of Language

Cultures all around the world have sacred stories or myths addressing the age-old question of the origins of human language. Anthropologists collecting these stories have often found that cultural groups tend to locate the place of origin in their own ancestral homelands and believe that the first humans also spoke their language.

© Rolex/Jacques Belat

Figure 15.9 Whistled Speech Occurring in about thirty languages around the world, whistled speech allows community members to exchange essential information in an abridged form of everyday spoken language. Here we see Elaine Kingeekuk, a Siberian Yupik speaker from St. Lawrence Island, Alaska, demonstrating whistled speech. A retired schoolteacher, she assists French linguist Julien Meyer in documenting her whistled language.

For example, ancient Israelites believed that it was Yahweh, the divine creator, who had given them Hebrew, the original tongue spoken in paradise. Later, when humans began building the high Tower of Babel to signify their own power and to link earth and heaven, Yahweh intervened. He created a confusion of tongues so that people could no longer understand one another, and he scattered them all across the face of the earth, leaving the massive tower unfinished (**Figure 15.10**).

Early scientific efforts to explain the origin of language suffered from a lack of solid data. Today, there is more scientific evidence, including genetic information, to work with—better knowledge of primate brains, new studies of primate communication, more information on the development of linguistic competence in children, more human fossils that can be used to tentatively reconstruct what ancient brains and vocal tracts were like, and a better understanding of the

whistled speech An exchange of whistled words using a phonetic emulation of the sounds produced in spoken voice; also known as *whistled language*.

© Scala/Art Resource

Figure 15.10 **The Tower of Babel** Described in the first book of the Bible, the Tower of Babel symbolizes an ancient West Asian myth about the origins of language diversity. According to this story, a united people speaking one language set out to build a tower to signify their power and link earth to heaven. Angered by their pride, their god Yahweh stopped the effort by confusing their languages and scattering them across the globe.

communication systems of fellow primates, as discussed in the Original Study about Chantek at the beginning of the chapter. Like humans, apes are capable of referring to events removed in time and space, a phenomenon known as **displacement** and one of the distinctive features of human language (Fouts & Waters, 2001).

Because there is continuity between gestural and spoken language, the latter could have emerged from the former through increasing emphasis on finely controlled movements of the mouth and throat. This scenario is consistent with the appearance of neurological structures underlying language in the earliest representatives of the genus *Homo* and steady enlargement of the human brain beginning as early as 2.5 million years ago. The soft tissues of the vocal tract related to speech are not preserved in the fossil record. But as outlined in the Biocultural Connection, a comparison of the vocal anatomy of chimps and humans allows paleoanthropologists to identify the anatomical differences responsible for human speech that appeared over the course of human evolution.

There are obvious advantages to spoken over gestural language for a species increasingly dependent on tool use for survival. To talk with your hands, you must stop whatever else you are doing with them; speech does not interfere with that. Other benefits include being able to talk in the dark, past opaque objects, or among speakers whose attention is diverted. Although we do not know precisely when the changeover to spoken language took place, all would agree that spoken languages are at least as old as the species *Homo sapiens*.

lifeways of early human ancestors. We still cannot conclusively prove how, when, and where human language first developed, but we can now theorize reasonably on the basis of more and better information.

The archaeological fossil and genetic records suggest that the archaic humans known as Neandertals (living from 28,000 to 125,000 years ago in Europe and western Asia) had the neurological and anatomical features necessary for speech. No skulls of the recently discovered Denisova hominin have been found, but genetic analysis suggests that these archaic humans ranging in Asia were close enough to Neandertals—their western "cousins" at the time—that they, too, shared that capacity. Fossilized brain casts from earlier members of the genus *Homo* provide evidence of specializations in the left hemisphere of the brain and associated with the development of language. The observation that the earliest stone tools were made predominantly by right-handed individuals also supports the idea that lateral specialization had occurred by this time.

Because human language is embedded within a gesture–call system of a type that we share with nonhuman primates (especially great apes), anthropologists have gained considerable insight into human language by observing the

From Speech to Writing

When anthropology developed as an academic discipline over a century ago, it concentrated its attention on small traditional communities that relied primarily on personal interaction and oral communication for survival. Cultures that depend on talking and listening often have rich traditions of storytelling and speechmaking, which play a central role in education, conflict resolution, political decision

displacement Referring to things and events removed in time and space.

BIOCULTURAL CONNECTION

The Biology of Human Speech

Although other primates have shown some capacity for language (a socially agreed upon code of communication), actual speech is unique to humans; this ability is linked to humans' distinct anatomical development of the vocal organs.

Of key importance are the positions of the human larynx (voice box) and the epiglottis. The larynx, situated in the respiratory tract between the pharynx (throat) and trachea (windpipe), contains the vocal cords. The epiglottis is the structure that separates the esophagus, or food pipe, from the windpipe as food passes from the mouth to the stomach. (See the figure for comparative diagrams of the anatomy of this region in apes and humans.)

As humans mature and develop the neurological and muscular coordination for speech, the larynx and epiglottis shift to a downward position. The human tongue bends at the back of the throat and is attached to the pharynx, the region of the throat where the food and airways share a common path. Sound occurs as air exhaled from the lungs passes over the vocal cords and causes them to vibrate.

Through continuous interactive movements of the tongue, pharynx, lips, and teeth, as well as nasal passages, the sounds are alternately modified to produce speech—the uniquely patterned sounds of a particular language. Based on longstanding socially learned patterns of speech, different languages stress certain distinctive types of sounds as significant and ignore others. For instance, languages belonging to the Iroquoian family, such as Mohawk, Seneca, and Cherokee, are among the few in the world that have no bilabial stops (*b* and *p* sounds). They also lack the labiodental spirants (*f* and *v* sounds), leaving the bilabial nasal *m* sound as the only consonant requiring lip articulation.

It takes many years of practice for people to master the muscular movements needed to produce the precise sounds of any particular language. But no human can produce the finely controlled speech sounds without a lowered position of the larynx and epiglottis.

BIOCULTURAL QUESTION
Sharing a capacity for speech, humans say and understand many thousands of words. Because macaws and other parrots also learn many words, do they have speech? And if so, do they actually think?

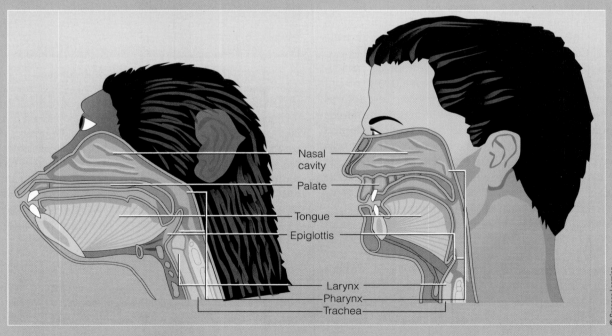

Nasal cavity
Palate
Tongue
Epiglottis
Larynx
Pharynx
Trachea

© Cengage Learning

A comparison of human and ape vocal organs.

making, spiritual or supernatural practices, and many other aspects of life.

Traditional orators (from the Latin *orare*, "to speak") are usually trained from the time they are young. They often enhance their extraordinary memorization skills through rhyme, rhythm, and melody. Orators may also employ special objects to help them remember—notched sticks, knotted strings, bands embroidered with shells, and so forth.

Traditional Iroquois Indian orators often performed their formal speeches with wampum belts made of hemp string with white and bluish-purple shell beads woven into distinctive patterns symbolizing important messages or agreements, including treaties with other nations (Figure 15.11).

Thousands of languages, past and present, have existed only in spoken form, but many others have been documented in visual graphic symbols of some sort. Over time, simplified pictures of things (pictographs) and ideas (ideographs) evolved into more stylized symbolic forms.

Although different peoples invented a variety of graphic styles, anthropologists distinguish an actual **writing system** as a set of visible or tactile signs used to represent units of language in a systematic way. Symbols carved into 8,600-year-old tortoise shells recently found in western China may represent the world's earliest evidence of elementary writing (Li et al., 2003).

A fully developed early writing system is Egyptian hieroglyphics, developed some 5,000 years ago and in use for about 3,500 years (Figure 15.12). Another very old system is *cuneiform*, an arrangement of wedge-shaped imprints developed primarily in Mesopotamia (southern Iraq), which lasted nearly as long. Cuneiform writing stands out among other early forms in that it led to the first phonetic writing system (that is, an **alphabet** or series of symbols representing the sounds of a language), ultimately spawning a wide array of alphabetic writing systems. About two millennia after these systems were established, others began to appear, developing independently in distant locations around the world (del Carmen Rodríguez Martínez et al., 2006).

Inscriptions discovered in Egypt's western desert suggest that our alphabet was invented almost 4,000 years ago by Semitic-speaking peoples in that region. Inscriptions carved into a natural limestone wall alongside hundreds of Egyptian hieroglyphs show that these Semites adopted a limited number of hieroglyphs as symbols for sounds in their own language. For instance, they took the glyph for ox and determined that it would stand for the sound at the start of the Semitic word for ox, which is *aleph*. (This symbol looks like the horned head of an ox—and like the letter *A* upside-down.) Likewise, they chose the Egyptian glyph for house to stand for the opening sound of the Semitic word for house, which is *beth*. (This symbol looks like a two-room house—and like the letter *B* tipped back.) The result was a writing system with characters based on a selection of Egyptian glyphs but representing sounds in early Semitic. Over the next thousand years, Semitic-speaking peoples inhabiting the eastern Mediterranean, including Phoenicians, adopted this system and developed the script into a more linear form (Himmelfarb, 2000).

Figure 15.11 **Mohawk Chief and Orator Hendrick Tejonihokarawa (c. 1660–c. 1735)** In 1710, Tejonihokarawa ("Open the Door") and three other American Indian tribal leaders from the Upper Hudson River in New York colony, sailed across the Atlantic on a diplomatic mission to the British royal court in London, where this portrait was painted. The wolf behind him indicates his clan affiliation, and the wampum belt he is holding carries a diplomatic message. Made of hemp string and shell beads (quahog and whelk shells), wampum designs were used to symbolize a variety of important messages or agreements, including treaties with other nations. (Painting is by the Dutch artist Johannes Verelst in 1710.)

Most of the alphabets used today descended from the Phoenician one. The Greeks adopted it about 2,800 years ago, modifying the characters to suit sounds in their own language. The word *alphabet* comes from the first two letters in the Greek writing system, *alpha* and *beta* (otherwise meaningless words in Greek). When Latin-speaking Romans expanded their empire throughout much of Europe, northern Africa, and western Asia, they used a modified Greek alphabet. From the 15th century onward, as European nations grew their trade networks and built colonial empires, the Latin alphabet spread far and wide, making it possible to mechanically reproduce writings in any human

---

writing system A set of visible or tactile signs used to represent units of language in a systematic way.

alphabet A series of symbols representing the sounds of a language arranged in a traditional order.

Figure 15.12 The Rosetta Stone This polished granitelike stele, inscribed with a royal decree in three scripts, was placed in an Egyptian temple over 2,200 years ago. The upper text is in Ancient Egyptian hieroglyphs, the middle portion is in late-Egyptian cursive script, and the lowest is in Ancient Greek. Rediscovered in 1799 by a French soldier in a military expedition to Egypt, and captured by the British two years later, this text provided the key to deciphering Egyptian hieroglyphs. It has been on display in the British Museum, London, since 1802.

language. Although other writing systems—such as Arabic, Chinese, Cyrillic, and Devanāgari—are used by perhaps half of literate humanity, digital media continue to expand the use of the Latin alphabet as a global writing system.

Literacy and Modern Telecommunication in Our Globalizing World

Thousands of years have passed since literacy first emerged, yet today one in five adults—775 million men and women—cannot read and write. Two-thirds of them are women, with rural women topping the list. (For example, about a third of India's more than 1.2 billion inhabitants cannot read and write.) Worldwide, 75 million children remain out of school, and millions more young people leave school without a level of literacy adequate for productive participation in their societies (UNESCO Institute for Statistics).

Illiteracy condemns already disadvantaged people to ongoing poverty—migrant rural workers, refugees, ethnic minorities, and those living in rural backlands and urban slums. Declaring literacy a human right, the United Nations established September 8 as International Literacy Day and proclaimed the period 2003 to 2012 as the Literacy Decade with the objective of extending literacy to all humanity. At this writing, surveys are under way to assess the results of this effort, but it is already clear that there are still many miles to go before reaching the goal of global literacy (United Nations Literacy Decade).

© Charles Sturge/Alamy

Figure 15.13 Telecommunications Worldwide The telecommunication revolution is reaching even the most remote places on earth thanks to satellite phones and cell phone towers powered by fossil fuel, the sun, or the wind. Those without phones of their own can often find mobile phone stands such as this one in Kampala, Uganda, in East Africa.

Although many people in the world still rely on others to write and read for them, the global telecommunication revolution has reached the most remote villagers on earth. The demand for mobile phones is high, even among the poor in rural backlands and urban slums—and they make long-distance communication possible without literacy (Figure 15.13).

At the end of 2011, there were 5.9 billion mobile phone subscriptions worldwide—equivalent to 87 percent of the population. In the developing world, mobile penetration was 79 percent, with Africa being the lowest region worldwide at 53 percent (International Telecommunication Union, 2012).

Many, including those who are illiterate, use these phones only for voice calls. But others also use them to download e-mails, exchange text messages, and explore the Internet. Beyond maintaining social networks, mobile phones are also used in everyday subsistence strategies. For example, they enable tens of millions of poor rural-dwellers in developing countries to locate the best prices for their produce—making it possible for growers to deal directly with district markets rather than going through intermediaries (Horst & Miller, 2006).

In today's fast-changing globalizing world, the mobile phone is more than a means of communication. It has become a survival tool—perhaps nowhere more so than in Saudi Arabia, which in 2012 ranked as the world's top "cellular nation," followed by Vietnam and Oman. On the move and surrounded by strangers, people use their mobiles to get and give information, to express their individuality, and to stay in touch—tweeting instead of whistling to avoid feeling lost in the global jungle.

CHAPTER CHECKLIST

What is *language*, and does the term apply only to humans?

● Language is a system of communication using sounds, gestures, or marks that are put together according to a set of rules. Through language people in every society are able to share their experiences, concerns, and beliefs, over the past and in the present, and to communicate these to the next generation. Language makes communication of infinite meanings possible to fellow speakers.

● Language experts debate about the cognitive ability of great apes and their capacity to attribute meaning to signs, even though these animals and many others have been found to communicate in remarkable ways. Several chimpanzees, gorillas, and orangutans have learned to use American Sign Language at the level of a 2- to 3-year-old human child.

What areas of language study or linguistics do anthropologists pursue?

● The three branches of language study in anthropology are descriptive linguistics, historical linguistics, and a third branch that focuses on language in relation to social and cultural settings.

● Descriptive linguists mark out and explain the features of a language at a particular time in its history. Their work includes phonology (the study of language sound patterns) and the investigation of grammar—all rules concerning morphemes (the smallest units of meaningful combinations of sounds) and syntax (the principles according to which phrases and sentences are built).

● Historical linguists investigate relationships between earlier and later forms of the same language—including identifying the forces behind the changes that have taken place in languages in the course of linguistic divergence. Their work provides a means of roughly dating certain migrations, invasions, and people's intercultural interactions.

● The third area of linguistic anthropology is the study of language as it relates to society and culture—research areas known as sociolinguistics and ethnolinguistics. Sociolinguists study the relationship between language and society, examining how social categories (such as age, gender, ethnicity, religion, occupation, and class) influence the use and significance of distinctive styles of speech. Ethnolinguists study the dynamic relationship between language and culture and how they mutually influence and inform each other.

How have languages evolved through time, and why have so many disappeared?

● All languages change—borrowing terms from other languages or inventing new words for new technologies or social realities. A major cause of language change is the domination of one society over another, which over the last 500 years led to the disappearance of about half of the world's 12,000 languages. A reaction to this loss and to the current far-reaching spread and domination of the English language is linguistic nationalism—purging foreign terms from a language's vocabulary and pressing for the revitalization of lost or threatened languages.

● Many of the world's languages have become extinct as a direct result of warfare, epidemics, and forced assimilation brought on by colonial powers and other aggressive outsiders. Other than the dominant languages in the world today, only very few people speak the remaining languages, and many of them are losing speakers rapidly due to globalization.

● A social dialect is the language of a group of people within a larger one, all of whom may speak more or less the same language.

Is language more than words?

● Human language is embedded in a gesture–call system inherited from our primate ancestors that serves to "key" speech, providing the appropriate frame for interpreting linguistic form.

● The gesture component consists of facial expressions and body postures and motions that convey intended as well as subconscious messages. The study of such nonverbal signals in body language is known as kinesics. Proxemics is the study of how people perceive and use space.

● The call component of the gesture–call system is represented by paralanguage, consisting of various voice qualities such as pitch and tempo and vocalizations such as giggling or sighing.

● About 70 percent of the world's languages are tonal, in which the musical pitch of a spoken word is an essential part of its pronunciation and meaning.

● Long before the telecommunication systems of the 19th and 20th centuries, people found ways to expand their acoustic range—including through talking drums and whistled speech.

What are the origins of spoken and written language, and how do modern telecommunication systems impact literacy around the world?

● Cultures around the world have sacred stories or myths about the origin of human languages.

● Language experts agree that spoken languages are at least as old as the species *Homo sapiens*.

● The first writing systems—Egyptian hieroglyphics and cuneiform—developed about 5,000 years ago. Recently discovered symbols carved into 8,600-year-old tortoise shells found in western China may represent the world's earliest evidence of elementary writing.

● The global telecom industry reaches into the most remote corners of the world, not only transforming how people communicate, but with whom and about what.

QUESTIONS FOR REFLECTION

1. In what ways do you feel prepared or unprepared to meet the challenge of communicating effectively in our increasingly globalized world?

2. Over the last 500 years, half of the world's 12,000 languages vanished. It is now estimated that about 30 languages per year will become extinct during the current century. Do you see this demise as positive or negative?

3. Applying the principle of linguistic relativity, how might your sense of self and the world around you be different if you had been raised in a Hopi-speaking community?

4. What distinguishes us from apes like Chantek the orangutan? What words might Chantek choose to tell us about his confined existence as a subject of scientific research?

5. How effective do you think digital codes like LOL (laugh out loud) and :-) (grin) are when e-mailing or texting? Given that so much of human communication and interaction is nonverbal, have your digital messages ever been misunderstood? If so, what do you think was at the root of the miscommunication, and how was it resolved?

ONLINE STUDY RESOURCES

CourseMate

Access chapter-specific learning tools, including learning objectives, practice quizzes, videos, flash cards, glossaries, and more in your Anthropology CourseMate.

Log into **www.cengagebrain.com** to access the resources your instructor has assigned and to purchase materials.

Challenge Issue

Every society faces the challenge of humanizing its children, teaching them the values, social codes, and skills that will enable them to become contributing members in the community. Most traditional communities raise children in ways that condition them for their future social status as adult men and women—making sure they have the appropriate appearance, apparel, attitude, and other culturally significant features that indicate gender differences. Here we see a Khanty mother braiding her daughter's hair. Her older girl watches a newborn in the cradle basket hanging from a rafter in their wooden house. They live in Yamal, a small fishing village on the northern Ob River in northwestern Siberia. Today, there are nearly 30,000 Khanty. They speak a language related to Hungarian, but most also know Russian because their sub-Arctic homeland was annexed by Russia centuries ago. Organized in male-dominated clans, some Khanty groups depend primarily on fishing, hunting, and fur trapping, whereas others are migratory reindeer breeders. The women teach their daughters and granddaughters to do women's work. Gaining power as they age, older women play an important role in Khanty spiritual life, including the naming of newborns. Following the belief that "children without teeth can talk with shamans," a clairvoyant female elder practices divination to discover which ancestor an infant embodies in order to reveal its name (Balzer, 1981).

Social Identity, Personality, and Gender

16

In 1690 English philosopher John Locke presented the *tabula rasa* theory in his book *An Essay Concerning Human Understanding.* This notion holds that a newborn human is like a blank slate, and what the individual becomes in life is written on the slate by his or her life experiences. The implication is that at birth all individuals are basically the same in their potential for character development and that their adult personalities are exclusively the products of their postnatal experiences, which differ from culture to culture.

Locke's idea offered high hopes for the all-embracing impact of intellectual and moral instruction on a child's character formation, but it missed the mark, as we now know, for it did not take into consideration genetic contributions to human behavior. Based on recent breakthroughs in human genetic research, anthropologists have come to recognize that an identifiable portion of our behavior is genetically influenced (Harpending & Cochran, 2002). This means that each person is born with a particular set of inherited tendencies that help mark out his or her adult personality. Although this genetic inheritance sets certain broad potentials and limitations, an individual's cultural environment, gender, social status, and unique life experiences, particularly in the early childhood years, also play a significant role in personality formation.

Because different cultures handle the raising and education of children in different ways, these practices and their effects on adult personalities are important subjects of anthropological inquiry. Such cross-cultural studies gave rise to the specialization of psychological anthropology and are the subjects of this chapter.

IN THIS CHAPTER YOU WILL LEARN TO

Assess the cultural forces that shape personality and social identity.

Explain how cultures are passed on and learned by offspring.

Distinguish between sex and gender from a cross-cultural perspective.

Illustrate the cultural relativity of normal and abnormal.

Identify culturally specific mental disorders.

Enculturation: The Self and Social Identity

From the moment of birth, a person faces multiple survival challenges. Obviously, newborns cannot take care of their own biological needs. Only in myths and romantic fantasies do we encounter stories about children successfully coming of age alone in the wilderness or accomplishing this feat having been raised by animals in the wild. Millions of children around the world have been fascinated by stories about Tarzan and the apes or the jungle boy Mowgli and the wolves. Moreover, young and old alike have been captivated by newspaper hoaxes about "wild" children, such as reports of a 10-year-old boy found running among gazelles in the Syrian Desert in 1946.

Fanciful imaginings aside, human children are biologically ill-equipped to survive without culture. This point has been driven home by several documented cases about feral children (*feral* comes from *fera*, which is Latin for "wild animal") who grew up deprived of human contact. None of them had a happy ending. For instance, there was nothing romantic about the girl Kamala, supposedly rescued from a wolf den in India in 1920: She moved about on all fours and could not feed herself. And everyone in Paris considered the naked "wild boy" captured in the woods outside Aveyron village in 1800 an incurable idiot.

Worse still is the true story of Genie, the "wild child" of Los Angeles, who spent her entire childhood in near total isolation. Imprisoned alone by her deranged father in a room with covered windows, she was infantile and emaciated when her nearly blind mother dragged the 13-year-old girl into a welfare office in 1970. Bounced back and forth between her mother, foster parents, and institutions, Genie never mastered the rudiments of language and now lives in a home for mentally disabled adults (Rymer, 1994). Clearly, the biological capacity for what we think of as human, which entails culture, must be nurtured to be realized.

Because culture is socially constructed and learned rather than biologically inherited, all societies must somehow ensure that culture is adequately transmitted from one generation to the next—a process we have already defined as *enculturation*. Because each group lives by a particular set of cultural rules, a child will have to learn the rules of his or her society in order to survive. Most of that learning takes place in the first few years when a child learns how to feel, think, speak, and ultimately act like an adult who embodies being Japanese, Kikuyu,

Lakota, Norwegian, or whatever ethnic or national group into which the child is born.

The first agents of enculturation in all societies are the members of the infant's household, especially the child's mother. (In fact, cultural factors are at work even before birth through what a pregnant mother eats, drinks, and inhales, as well as the sounds, rhythms, and activity patterns of her daily life.) Who the other members are depends on how households are structured in each particular society.

As the young person matures, individuals outside the household are brought into the enculturation process. These usually include other relatives and certainly the individual's peers. In some societies, professionals are brought into the process to provide formal instruction. In many societies children are allowed to learn through observation and participation, at their own speed.

Self-Awareness

Enculturation begins with the development of **self-awareness**—the ability to identify oneself as an individual creature, to reflect on oneself, and to evaluate oneself (**Figure 16.1**). Humans do not have this cognitive ability at birth, even though it is essential for their successful social functioning. It is self-awareness that permits one to take social responsibility for one's conduct, to learn how to react to others, and to assume a variety of roles in society. An important aspect of self-awareness is the attachment of positive value to one's self. Without this, individuals cannot be motivated to act to their advantage.

Self-awareness does not come all at once. In modern industrial and postindustrial societies, for example, self and nonself are not clearly distinguished until a child is about 2 years of age, lagging somewhat behind other cultures (Rochat, 2001). Self-awareness develops in concert with neuromotor development, which is known to proceed at a slower rate in infants from industrial societies than in infants in many, perhaps even most, small-scale farming or foraging communities. The reasons for this slower rate are not yet clear, although the amount of human contact and stimulation that infants receive seems to play an important role.

As noted earlier in this text, infants in the United States, for example, generally do not sleep with their parents, most often being put in rooms of their own. This is seen as an important step in making them into individuals, "owners" of themselves and their capacities. As a consequence, they do not experience the steady stream of personal stimuli, including smell, movement, and warmth, that they would if co-sleeping. Private sleeping also takes away the opportunity for frequent nursing through the night.

---

self-awareness The ability to identify oneself as an individual, to reflect on oneself, and to evaluate oneself.

Figure 16.1 Self-Awareness Recognizing herself in the mirror, this young girl has developed the self-awareness necessary to understand that she is a distinct individual. In modern industrial and postindustrial societies, self-awareness is typically established by about age 2—later than in other societies.

© Laura Dwight/Corbis

In the majority of the world's societies, infants routinely sleep with their parents, or at least their mothers. Also, they are carried or held most other times, usually in an upright position, often in the company of other people and amid various activities. The mother typically responds to a cry or "fuss" within seconds, usually offering the infant her breast.

So it is among traditional Ju/'hoansi (pronounced "zhutwasi") people of southern Africa's Kalahari Desert, whose infants breastfeed on demand in short frequent bouts—commonly nursing about four times an hour, for 1 or 2 minutes at a time. Overall, a 15-week-old Ju/'hoansi infant is in close contact with his or her mother about 70 percent of the time (compared to 20 percent for home-reared infants in the United States). Moreover, Ju/'hoansi babies usually have considerable contact with numerous other adults and children of all ages.

This steady stream of varied stimuli is significant, for studies show that stimulation plays a key role in the hardwiring of the brain; it is necessary for development of the neural circuitry. Looking at breastfeeding in particular, the longer children are breastfed, the better their overall health, the higher they will score on cognitive tests, and the lower the risk of obesity, allergies, and attention deficit hyperactivity disorder (Dettwyler, 1997). Because our biological heritage as primates has programmed us to

develop in response to social stimuli, it is not surprising that self-awareness and a variety of other beneficial qualities develop more rapidly in response to close contact with other humans.

Social Identity Through Personal Naming

Personal names are important devices for self-definition in all cultures. It is through naming that a social group acknowledges a child's birthright and establishes his or her social identity. Among the many cultural rules that exist in each society, those having to do with naming are unique because they individualize a person and at the same time identify one as a group member. Names often express and represent multiple aspects of one's group identity—ethnic, gender, religious, political, or even rank, class, or caste. Without a name, an individual is anonymous, has no social identity. For this reason, many cultures consider name selection to be an important issue and mark the naming of a child with a special event or ritual known as a **naming ceremony**.

---

naming ceremony A special event or ritual to mark the naming of a child.

Naming Practices Across Cultures

Worldwide, there are countless contrasting approaches to naming. For example, Aymara Indians in the Bolivian highland village of Laymi do not consider an infant truly human until they have given the child a name—and naming does not happen until the child begins to speak the Aymara language, typically around the age of 2. Once the child shows the ability to speak like a human, he or she is considered fit to be recognized as such with a proper name. The naming ceremony marks the toddler's social transition from a state of nature to culture and consequently to full acceptance into the Laymi community.

Unlike the Aymara, Icelanders name babies at birth. Following ancient custom, Icelandic infants receive their father's personal given name as their last name. The suffix *sen* is added to a boy's name and *dottir* to a girl's name. Thus, a brother and sister whose father is named Sven Olafsen would have the last names Svensen and Svendottir, respectively.

Although *patronyms* are common in Iceland, sometimes the mother's first name is chosen for her child's surname. Such *matronyms* (surnames based on mother's names) may be preferred for a boy or girl whose mother remains unmarried, is divorced, or simply prefers her own name identifying family status. This is the case with an Icelandic woman named Eva having a daughter named Gudrun Evasdottir and son Gunnar Evason. Matronymic traditions occur in several other parts of the world, including the Indonesian island of Sumatra, homeland of the Minangkabau. In this ethic group of several million people, children are members of their mother's clan, inheriting her family name.

Among the Netsilik Inuit in Arctic Canada, a mother experiencing a difficult delivery would call out the names of deceased people of admirable character. The name being called at the moment of birth is thought to enter the infant's body and help the delivery, and the child would bear that name thereafter. Inuit parents may also name their children for deceased relatives in the belief that the spiritual identification will help shape their character (Balikci, 1970).

It is common in numerous cultures for a person to receive a name soon after birth and then acquire new names during subsequent life phases. Navajo Indians from the southwestern United States name a child at birth, but traditionalists often give the baby an additional ancestral clan name soon after the child laughs for the first time. Among the Navajo, laughter is seen as the earliest expression of human language, a signal that life as a social being has started. Thus, it is an occasion for celebration, and the person who prompted that very first laugh invites family and close friends to a First Laugh Ceremony. At the gathering, the party sponsor places rock salt in the baby's hand and helps slide the salt all over the little one's body. Representing tears—of both

laughter and sadness—the salt is said to provide strength and protection, leading to a long, happy life. Then the ancestral name is given.[1]

In many cultures, a firstborn child's naming ceremony also marks a change in the parents' social status. This is reflected in what is known as *teknonymy* (from *teknon*, the Greek word for "child"), in which someone assumes an honorific name, usually derived from the oldest son, in place of (or alongside) his or her own given name. In Arab societies, such an honorific is known as *kunya*. For example, a young man who names his firstborn son Ishaq becomes known as Abu Ishaq ("Father of Isaac"), whereas his wife may assume the name Umm Ishaq ("Mother of Isaac"). Teknonymy occurs in societies in which only close relatives are permitted to address someone by his other personal name. If outsiders or inferiors do so, it may be regarded as inappropriate or disrespectful. Such a taboo exists among the Tuareg of the Sahara Desert in northern Africa, for example, where people prefer using the honorific name (**Figure 16.2**).

Naming and Identity Politics

Because names symbolically express and represent an individual's cultural self, they may gain particular significance in personal and collective identity politics. For instance, when an ethnic group or nation falls under the control of a more powerful and expanding neighboring group, its members may be forced to assimilate and give up their cultural identity. One early indicator may be that families belonging to the subjugated or overwhelmed group decide to abandon their own ancestral naming traditions. Such was the case when Russia expanded its empire into Siberia and colonized the Turkic-speaking Xakas. Within a few generations, most Xakas had Russian names (Butanayev, cited in Harrison, 2002).

The identity politics of personal naming practices can also be seen in North America. For example, American Indian families, whether they lived on or off their tribal reservations, came under pressure to forgo their cultural traditions, including their customary personal and family names. As part of the assimilation process, many agreed or were compelled to have their indigenous names translated into English. This was common practice in the 19th century, soon after the United States had annexed or conquered the Great Plains. An Osage named He-lo-ki-he, for instance, became Long Bow. Those who became Christian converts often adopted European names, at least for public identification and self-presentation. And so it was that No-pa-wal-la, another Osage tribesman, became known as Henry Pratt.

---

[1] Authors' participant observation at traditional Navajo First Laugh Ceremony of Wesley Bitsie-Baldwin; personal communication, LaVerne Bitsie-Baldwin and Anjanette Bitsie.

Figure 16.2 Tuareg Naming Ceremony Tuareg women gather around bowls of macaroni for a newborn's naming ceremony inside a tented home typical of those long used by these Sahara Desert nomads in northern Niger. For this special occasion, the women have smeared their hands and faces with indigo. Traditionally, Tuareg children are named on the eighth day after birth, and relatives come from near and far to participate and celebrate the arrival of a new member in their clan. The father and other male relatives gather outside for a Muslim religious ceremony, led by a *marabout*. This holy man offers a prayer and then ritually cuts the throat of a ram slaughtered for the feast. At that moment, the father publicly reveals his child's name, usually one taken from the Koran.

Name-change stories are also common among immigrants hoping to avoid racial discrimination or ethnic stigmatization. For instance, it was not uncommon for Jewish immigrants and their U.S.-born children trying to succeed in the entertainment industry to Americanize their names: Comedian Joan Molinsky became Joan Rivers and fashion designer Ralph Lifshitz became Ralph Lauren.

In identity politics, naming can also be a resistance strategy by a minority group asserting its cultural pride or even rights of self-determination against a dominant society. For instance, in the United States, African Americans with inherited Christian names that were imposed upon their enslaved ancestors have, in growing numbers, rejected those names. Many have also abandoned the faith tradition represented by those names to become members of the Nation of Islam (Black Muslims). An enduring example of this is champion boxer Cassius Clay, who converted to Islam in the mid-1960s. Rejecting his slave name, he became Muhammad Ali.

Self and the Behavioral Environment

The development of self-awareness requires basic orientations that structure the psychological fields in which the self acts. These include object orientation, spatial orientation, temporal orientation, and normative orientation.

Every individual must learn about a world of objects other than the self. Through this *object orientation*, each culture singles out for attention certain environmental features, while ignoring others or lumping them together into broad categories. A culture also explains the perceived environment. This is important, for a cultural explanation of one's surroundings imposes a measure of order and provides the individual with a sense of direction needed to act meaningfully and effectively.

Behind this lies a powerful psychological drive to reduce uncertainty—part of the common human need

VISUAL COUNTERPOINT

Figure 16.3 Spatial Orientation Traditionally, each culture provides its members with a comprehensive design for living, a master plan, to guide and instruct both individuals and the collective society for the environment they historically inhabit. Born and raised in the Arctic, Inuit and other Eskimos find many meaningful reference points in a region that appears endlessly empty and monotonous to outsiders. Without spatial orientation, one would soon be lost and surely perish. During the past few decades, the virtual environment of cyberspace has brought new challenges and opportunities to anyone with access to digital technology and the skills to navigate that electronic media world.

for a balanced and integrated perspective on the relevant universe. When confronted with ambiguity and uncertainty, people invariably strive to clarify and give structure to the situation; they do this in ways that their particular culture deems appropriate. Thus, our observations and explanations of the universe are largely culturally constructed and mediated symbolically through language. In fact, everything in the physical environment varies in the way it is perceived and experienced by humans. In short, we perceive the world around us through a cultural lens.

The behavioral environment in which the self acts also involves *spatial orientation*, or the ability to get from one object or place to another. Notably, when we speak of trying to "orient" ourselves, we are using an ancient word for *rising* that refers to the east, where the sun comes up. Traditionally, place names commonly contain references to significant geographic features in the landscape.

Finding your way to class, remembering where you left your car keys, directing someone to the nearest bus stop, maneuvering through airports, and traveling through deep underground networks in subway tunnels are examples of highly complex cognitive tasks based on spatial orientation and memory. So is an Inuit hunter's ability to kayak or sled long distances across vast Arctic water, ice, or snow—determining the route by means of a mental map, gauging his location by the position of the

sun in daytime, the stars at night, and even by the winds and smell of the air (**Figure 16.3**).

Technological revolutions in the 20th century have led to the invention of a newly created media environment, where we learn to orient ourselves in cyberspace. Without our spatial orientations, whether in natural or virtual reality, navigating through daily life would be impossible.

Temporal orientation, which gives people a sense of their place in time, is also part of the behavioral environment. Connecting past actions with those of the present and future provides a sense of self-continuity. This is the function of a calendar. Derived from the Latin word *kalendae*, which originally referred to a public announcement at the first day of a new month, or moon, such a chart gives people a framework for organizing their days, weeks, months, and even years. Just as the perceived environment of objects is organized in cultural terms, so too are time and space.

A final aspect of the behavioral environment is the *normative orientation*. Moral values, ideals, and principles, which are purely cultural in origin, are as much a part of the individual's behavioral environment as are trees, rivers, and mountains. Without them people would have nothing by which to gauge their own actions or those of others. Normative orientation includes, but is not limited to, standards that indicate what ranges of behavior are acceptable for males, females, and whichever additional gender roles exist in a particular society.

Culture and Personality

In the process of enculturation, each individual is introduced to a society's natural and human-made environment along with a collective body of ideas about the self and others. The result is a kind of internalized cultural master plan of the cosmos in which the individual will feel, think, and act as a social being. It is each person's particular guide of how to run the maze of life. When we speak of someone's personality, we are generalizing about that person's internalized map over time. Thus, personalities are products of enculturation, as experienced by individuals, each with his or her distinctive genetic makeup.

Personality does not lend itself to a formal definition, but for our purposes we may take it as the distinctive way a person thinks, feels, and behaves. Derived from the Latin word *persona*, meaning "mask," the term relates to the idea of learning to play one's role on the stage of daily life. Gradually, the mask, as it is placed on the face of a child, begins to shape that person until there is little sense of the mask as something superimposed. Instead it feels natural, as if one were born with it. The individual has successfully internalized the culture.

Personality Development: A Cross-Cultural Perspective on Gender

Although *what* one learns is important to personality development, most anthropologists assume that *how* one learns is no less important. Along with psychological theorists, anthropologists view childhood experiences as strongly influencing adult personality, and they are most interested in analyses that seek to prove, modify, or at least shed light on the cultural differences in shaping personality.

For example, the traditional ideal in Western societies has been for men to be tough, aggressive, assertive, dominant, and self-reliant, whereas women have been expected to be gentle, pliable, and caring. To many, these personality contrasts between male and female seem so natural that they are thought to be biologically grounded and therefore fundamental, unchangeable, and universal. But are they? Have anthropologists identified any psychological or personality characteristics that universally differentiate men and women?

U.S. anthropologist Margaret Mead is well known as a pioneer in the cross-cultural study of both personality and gender. In the early 1930s she studied three ethnic groups in Papua New Guinea—the Arapesh, the Mundugamor, and the Tchambuli. This comparative research suggested that whatever biological differences exist between men and women, they are extremely malleable. In short, she concluded, biology is not destiny. Mead found that among the Arapesh, relations between men and women were expected to be equal, with both genders exhibiting what most North Americans traditionally consider feminine traits (cooperative, nurturing, and gentle). She also discovered gender equality among the Mundugamor (now generally called Biwat); however, in that community both genders displayed supposedly masculine traits (individualistic, assertive, volatile, aggressive). Among the Tchambuli (now called Chambri), however, Mead found that women dominated men (Mead, 1960).

More recent anthropological research suggests that some of Mead's interpretations of gender roles were incorrect—for instance, Chambri women neither dominate Chambri men nor vice versa. Yet, overall her research generated new insights into the human condition, showing that male dominance is not genetically fixed in our human "nature." Instead, it is socially constructed in the context of particular cultural adaptations, and, consequently, alternative gender arrangements can be created. (See the Anthropologist of Note feature on page 406 about Mead's teacher, colleague, and close friend Ruth Benedict for her pathbreaking work on personality as a cultural construct.) Although biological influence in male–female behavior cannot be ruled out, it has nonetheless become clear that each culture provides different opportunities and has different expectations for ideal or acceptable behavior (Errington & Gewertz, 2001).

Childrearing and Gender among the Ju/'hoansi

To understand the importance of childrearing practices for the development of gender-related personality characteristics, consider the Ju/'hoansi Bushmen, native to the Kalahari Desert in the borderlands of Namibia and Botswana in southern Africa. Traditionally subsisting as nomadic hunter-gatherers (foragers), in the latter 20th century many Ju/'hoansi were forced to settle down—tending small herds of goats, planting gardens for their livelihood, and engaging in occasional wage labor on white-owned farms (Wyckoff-Baird, 2010).

Ju/'hoansi who traditionally forage for a living stress equality and do not tolerate dominance and aggressiveness in either gender. Males are as mild-mannered as females, and females are as energetic and self-reliant as males. By contrast, among the Ju/'hoansi who have recently settled in permanent villages, males and

---

personality The distinctive way a person thinks, feels, and behaves.

ANTHROPOLOGIST OF NOTE

Ruth Fulton Benedict (1887–1947)

Ruth Fulton Benedict came late to anthropology. After her graduation from Vassar College, she taught high school English, published poetry, and tried her hand at social work. At age 31, she began studying anthropology, first at the New School for Social Research in New York City and then at Columbia University. Having earned her doctorate under Franz Boas, she joined his department. One of her first students was Margaret Mead.

As Benedict herself once said, the main purpose of anthropology is "to make the world safe for human differences." In anthropology, she developed the idea that culture was a collective projection of the personality of those who created it. In her most famous book, *Patterns of Culture* (1934), she compared the cultures of three peoples—the Kwakiutl Indians of the coastal Pacific in Canada, the Zuni Indians of the Arizona desert in the United States, and the Melanesians of Dobu Island off the southern shore of Papua New Guinea. She held that each was comparable to a great work of art, with an internal coherence and consistency of its own.

Seeing the Kwakiutl as egocentric, individualistic, and ecstatic in their rituals, she labeled their cultural configuration "Dionysian" (named after the Greek god of wine and noisy feasting). The Zuni, whom she saw as living by the golden mean, wanting no part of excess or disruptive psychological states and distrusting of individualism, she characterized as "Apollonian" (named after the Greek god of poetry who exemplified beauty). The Dobuans, whose culture seemed to her magic-ridden, with everyone fearing and hating everyone else, she characterized as "paranoid."

Another theme of *Patterns of Culture* is that deviance should be understood as a conflict between an individual's

Ruth Benedict is known for her pioneering work on personality as a cultural construct.

personality and the norms of the culture to which the person belongs. Still in print today, *Patterns* has sold close to 2 million copies in a dozen languages. It had great influence on Mead during her cross-cultural gender studies among the Papuans in New Guinea.

Although *Patterns of Culture* still enjoys popularity in some nonanthropological circles, anthropologists have long since abandoned its approach as impressionistic. To compound the problem, Benedict's characterizations of cultures are misleading (the supposedly Apollonian Zunis, for example, indulge in such seemingly Dionysian practices as sword swallowing and walking over hot coals), and the use of value-laden terms such as *paranoid* prejudices others against the culture so labeled. Nonetheless, the book did have an enormous and valuable influence by focusing attention on the problem of the interrelation between culture and personality and by popularizing the reality of cultural variation.

females exhibit personality characteristics resembling those traditionally thought of as typically masculine and feminine in North America and other industrial societies.

Among the food foragers, each newborn child receives extensive personal care from his or her mother during the first few years of life, for the space between births is typically four to five years. This is not to say that mothers are constantly with their children. For instance, when women go to collect wild plant foods in the bush, they do not always take their offspring along. At such times, their fathers or other community adults supervise the children, one-third to one-half of whom are always found in camp on any given day. Because these include men as well as women, children are as much habituated to the male presence as to the female one.

Traditional Ju/'hoansi fathers spend much time with their offspring, interacting with them in nonauthoritarian ways (**Figure 16.4**). Although they may correct their children's behavior, so may women who neither defer to male authority nor use the threat of paternal punishment. Among these foragers, no one grows up to respect or fear male authority any more than female authority. In fact, instead of being punished by either parent, a child who misbehaves will simply be carried away and introduced to some other more agreeable activity.

Children of both sexes do equally little work. Instead, they spend much of their time in playgroups that include boys and girls of widely different ages. Older children, boys as well as girls, keep an eye out for the younger ones and do this spontaneously rather than as an assigned

© Anthony Bannister/Gallo Images/Corbis

Figure 16.4 Ju/'hoansi Parenting In traditional Ju/'hoansi society, fathers as well as mothers show great indulgence to children, who do not fear or respect male authority any more than female authority.

task. In short, Ju/'hoansi children in traditional foraging groups have few experiences that set one gender apart from the other.

But for those Ju/'hoansi who have been forced to abandon their traditional foraging life and who now reside in permanent settlements, the situation is very different. Women spend much of their time at home preparing food, doing other domestic chores, and tending the children. Men, meanwhile, spend many hours outside the household growing crops, raising animals, or doing wage labor. As a result, children are less habituated to their presence. This remoteness of the men, coupled with their more extensive knowledge of the outside world and their access to money, tends to strengthen male influence in the household.

Within these village households, gender typecasting begins early. As soon as girls are old enough, they are expected to attend to many of the needs of their younger siblings, thereby allowing their mothers more time to deal with other domestic tasks. This shapes and limits the behavior of girls, who cannot range as widely or explore as freely as they could without little brothers and sisters in tow. Boys, by contrast, have little to do with babies and toddlers, and when they are assigned work, it generally takes them away from the household. Thus, the space that village girls occupy becomes restricted, and they are trained in behaviors that promote passivity and nurturance, whereas village boys begin to learn the distant, controlling roles they will later play as adult men.

When comparing childrearing traditions in different cultures, we find that a group's economic organization

and the social relations in its subsistence practices impact the way a child is brought up, and this, in turn, affects the adult personality. Cross-cultural comparisons also show that there are alternative practices for raising children, which means that changing the societal conditions in which one's children grow up can alter significantly the way men and women act and interact.

With this in mind, we turn to a discussion about traditions of dependence and independence training. There are cultural variations within each of these types, and many societies exhibit a mixture of both styles.

Dependence Training

Some years after Margaret Mead's pioneering comparative research on gender, psychological anthropologists carried out a significant and wide-ranging series of cross-cultural studies on the effects of childrearing on personality. Among other things, their work showed that it is possible to identify three general patterns of childrearing. These patterns stem from a number of practices that, regardless of the reason for their existence, have the effect of emphasizing dependence on the one hand and independence on the other. For convenience, we will call these *dependence training, interdependence training,* and *independence training* (Whiting & Child, 1953).

Dependence training socializes people to think of themselves in terms of the larger whole. Its effect is to create community members whose idea of selfhood transcends individualism, promoting compliance in the performance of assigned tasks and keeping individuals within the group. This pattern is typically associated with extended families, which consist of several husband-wife-children units within the same household. It is most likely to be found in societies with an economy based on subsistence farming but also in foraging groups where several family groups may live together for at least part of the year. Big extended families are important because they provide the labor force necessary to till the soil, tend whatever flocks are kept, and carry out other part-time economic pursuits considered necessary for existence.

But built into these large families are potentially disruptive tensions. For example, important family decisions must be collectively accepted and followed. In addition, the in-marrying spouses—husbands and wives who come from other groups—must conform themselves to the group's will, something that may not be easy for them.

Dependence training helps to keep these potential problems under control and involves both supportive and corrective aspects. On the supportive side, parents are easygoing, and mothers yield to the desires of their young, particularly in the form of breastfeeding, which

---

dependence training Childrearing practices that foster compliance in the performance of assigned tasks and dependence on the domestic group, rather than reliance on oneself.

is provided on demand and continues for several years. Children may interpret such indulgence as a reward, one that reinforces that the family is the main agent in providing for children's needs. Also on the supportive side, at a relatively young age children are assigned a number of child-care and domestic tasks, all of which make significant and obvious contributions to the family's welfare. Thus, children learn early on that it is normal for family members to share and actively help one another.

On the corrective side, adults actively discourage selfish or aggressive behavior. Moreover, they tend to be insistent on overall obedience, which commonly inclines the individual toward being subordinate to the group. This combination of encouragement and discouragement in the socialization process teaches individuals to put the group's needs above their own—to be obedient, supportive, noncompetitive, and generally responsible, to stay within the fold and not do anything potentially disruptive. Indeed, a person's very definition of self comes from the individual being a part of a larger social whole rather than from his or her individual existence.

Interdependence among the Beng of West Africa

Recognizing that dependence training comes in many unique cultural variations, we now briefly turn to the Beng, a group of about 20,000 Mande-speaking farmers living in twenty-two villages in the tropical woodlands of Côte d'Ivoire, West Africa. Each family forms a large household, which includes the spirits of deceased ancestors. These spirits, known as *wru*, spend nights with their living relatives but depart at dawn for their invisible spirit village called *wrugbe*.

Believing in reincarnation, the Beng look upon infants not as new creatures but as reincarnated spirit ancestors gradually emerging from *wrugbe* back into everyday life. For this reason, Beng babies are embraced as profoundly spiritual beings who at first are only tentatively attached to life on earth. Their cries are interpreted as a longing for something from *wrugbe*, and good parents do everything within their power to make earthly life so comfortable and appealing that the babies will not be tempted to return there. This includes extensive grooming

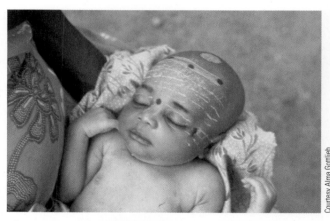

Figure 16.5 **Beng Baby, Côte d'Ivoire, West Africa** Beng people see babies as reincarnated ancestors with strong ties to the spirit world. To make sure these tiny "old souls" are not tempted to return to their *wrugbe*, or spirit village, they do everything possible to make earthly life appealing to them. This includes beautifying the child, as shown here, to help attract care from relatives and neighbors.

of the little ones to help attract additional care and love from relatives and neighbors (Figure 16.5). Held much of the day by an array of caregivers, Beng babies develop a broad variety of social ties and emotional attachments and appear generally free of stranger anxiety. Also, because they are thought to be living partly in the spirit world, these tiny "old souls" are allowed to determine their own sleeping and nursing schedules, and, notably, the biological mother is just one of many potential breastfeeders.

Having studied childrearing practices among these West African farmers, U.S. anthropologist Alma Gottlieb concludes that in Beng communities, the social goal is to promote *interdependence* rather than independence, in contrast to what is the normal practice in most North American families today. In short, Beng babies are made to feel "constantly cherished by as many people as possible," learning early on that individual security comes through the intertwining of lives, collectively sharing joys and burdens (Gottlieb, 2003, 2004, 2005).

Independence Training

Independence training fosters individual self-reliance and personal achievement. It is typically associated with societies in which a basic social unit consisting of parent(s) and offspring fends for itself. Independence training is particularly characteristic of mercantile (trading), industrial, and postindustrial societies where self-sufficiency and personal achievement are important traits for success, if not survival—especially for men, and increasingly for women.

This pattern also involves both encouragement and discouragement. On the negative side, a schedule, more than demand, dictates infant feeding. In North America, as noted previously, babies are rarely nursed for more

---

independence training Childrearing practices that foster independence, self-reliance, and personal achievement.

than a year. Many parents resort to an artificial nipple (pacifier) to satisfy the baby's sucking instincts—typically doing so to calm the child rather than out of an awareness that infants need sucking to strengthen and train coordination in the muscles used for feeding and speech.

North American parents are comparatively quick to start feeding infants baby food and even try to get them to feed themselves. Many are delighted if they can prop their infants up in the crib or playpen so that they can hold their own bottles. Moreover, as soon after birth as possible, children are commonly given their own private space, away from their parents. Collective responsibility is not pushed upon children; they are not usually given significant domestic tasks until later in childhood; and these are often carried out for personal benefit (such as to earn an allowance to spend as they wish) rather than as contributions to the family's welfare.

Displays of individual will, assertiveness, and even aggression are encouraged or at least tolerated to a greater degree than in cultures where dependence training is the rule. In schools, and even in the family, competition and winning are emphasized. Schools in the United States, for example, devote considerable resources to competitive sports. Competition is fostered within the classroom as well—overtly through practices such as spelling bees and awards and covertly through customs such as grading on a curve. In addition, there are various popularity contests, such as crowning a prom queen and king or holding an election to choose the classmate who is "best looking" or "most likely to succeed." Thus, by the time individuals have grown up in U.S. society, they have received a clear message: Life is about winning or losing, and losing is equal to failure (Turnbull, 1983b).

In sum, independence training is culturally adaptive in societies that emphasize individual achievement and in which members are expected to look out for their own interests. Its socialization patterns match cultural values and expectations increasingly prevalent in the spread of global capitalism.

One kind of training—independence, dependence, or a combination of both—is not inherently better or worse than any other. Compliant adults who are accepting of authority serve very well in a society that values cooperation and service toward the needs of the group. On the other hand, self-reliant, independent adults who are eager to explore new ways of doing things fit other societies that put a premium on individualism. Building on this basic cross-cultural comparison of childrearing practices, psychological anthropologists have greatly added to our increasingly sophisticated understanding of the complex relationship between culture and personality.

Group Personality

From the holistic perspective that anthropologists bring to the comparative study of childrearing, it is clear that these customary practices, personality development, and other aspects of culture are systemically interrelated. This insight has prompted research to explore whether whole societies might be analyzed in terms of particular personality types. Certainly, common sense suggests that personalities fitting for one culture may be less suitable for others. For example, an egocentric, aggressive personality would be out of place where modesty, self-denial, and sharing are the keys to success.

Unfortunately, common sense, like conventional wisdom in general, is not always the rule. Anthropologists asked themselves whether it would be possible to describe a group personality without falling into the trap of stereotyping. The answer is a qualified yes, especially with respect to traditional communities. The larger and more complex a society becomes, the greater its range in different personalities. In an abstract way, we may speak of a generalized *cultural personality* for a society, so long as we do not expect to find a uniformity of personalities within that society.

Consider, for example, the Yanomami Indians, who subsist on foraging and horticulture in the tropical forests of the Amazon. Commonly, Yanomami men strive to conform to a masculine ideal in their culture they call *waiteri*: being courageous, ferocious, humorous, and generous, all wrapped up into one heroic male personhood (Chagnon, 1990; Ramos, 1987). Yet, in their villages are men who are not so inclined and have quiet and somewhat retiring personalities. It is all too easy for an outsider to overlook these individuals when other, more "typical" Yanomami are in the front row, pushing and demanding attention (**Figure 16.6**).

Modal Personality

Obviously, any productive approach to the problem of group personality must recognize that each individual is unique to a degree in both genetic inheritance and life experiences, and it must leave room for a range of different personality types in any society. In addition, personality traits that may be regarded as appropriate in men may not be so regarded in women, and vice versa. Given these qualifiers, we may focus our attention on the **modal personality**, defined as those character traits that occur with the highest frequency in a social group and are therefore the most representative of its culture.

Modal personality is a statistical concept rather than the personality of an average person in a particular society. As such, it raises other questions for investigation: How do more complex societies organize diversity? How does diversity relate to cultural change? Such questions are easily missed if one associates a certain type of personality with one particular culture, as did some earlier anthropologists (see Ruth Benedict in the Anthropologist of Note). At the same time, modal personalities of different groups can still be compared.

modal personality Those character traits that occur with the highest frequency in a social group and are therefore the most representative of its culture.

Figure 16.6

***Waiteri*: Heroic Male Personhood** Yanomami Indians living in the Amazon rainforest of Venezuela show off as *waiteri* in a public performance befitting the traditional warrior ideal in their culture.

© N. Chagnon/Anthro-Photo

National Character

Several years ago, Italy's tourism minister publicly commented on "typical characteristics" of Germans, referring to them as "hyper-nationalistic blonds" and "beer-drinking slobs" holding "noisy burping contests" on Italy's beaches ("Italy–Germany verbal war hots up," 2003). Outraged (and proud of his country's excellent beer), Germany's chancellor canceled his planned vacation to Italy and demanded an official apology. Of course, many Germans think of Italians as dark-eyed, hot-blooded spaghetti eaters. To say so in public, however, might cause an uproar.

Unflattering stereotypes about foreigners are deeply rooted in cultural traditions everywhere. Many Japanese believe Koreans are stingy, crude, and aggressive, whereas many Koreans see the Japanese as cold and arrogant. Similarly, we all have in mind some image, perhaps not well defined, of the typical citizen of Mexico or England or China. And Americans traveling abroad may be insulted that others in the world hold the negative image of loud, brash, and arrogant Yankees. Although these are simply stereotypes, we might ask if these stereotypes have any basis in fact. In reality, does such a thing as *national character* exist?

Some anthropologists once thought that the answer might be yes, and they embarked on national character studies in the 1930s and 1940s, aiming to discover basic personality traits shared by the majority of the people of modern state societies. In what came to be

known as the *culture and personality* movement, their research emphasized childrearing practices and education as the factors theoretically responsible for such characteristics.

Early on it was recognized that the national character studies were flawed, mainly because they made generalizations based on limited data, relatively small samples of informants, and questionable assumptions about developmental psychology. These flaws notwithstanding, national character studies were important in that they helped change the anthropological focus from traditional small-scale communities of foragers, herders, and farmers in exotic places to people living in large-scale contemporary state societies. Moreover, they prompted new theoretical and methodological approaches to serious interdisciplinary group research (Beeman, 2000).

Core Values

An alternative approach to national character—one that allows for the fact that not all personalities will conform to cultural ideals—is that of Chinese American anthropologist Francis Hsu. His approach is to study **core values** (values especially promoted by a particular culture) and related personality traits. The Chinese, Hsu suggests, value kin ties and cooperation above all else. To them, mutual dependence is the very essence of personal relationships and has been for thousands of years (**Figure 16.7**). Compliance and subordination of one's

---

core values Those values especially promoted by a particular culture.

© Simon Kwong/Corbis

Figure 16.7 Core Values The collectively shared core values of Chinese culture promote the intergration of the individual into a larger group, as we see in this large gathering of Hong Kong residents practicing tai chi.

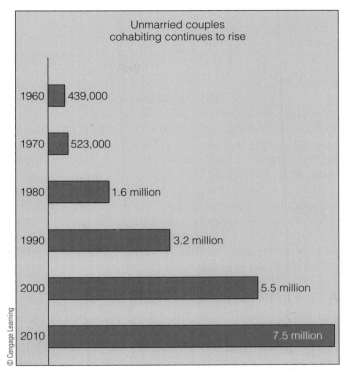

Unmarried couples
cohabiting continues to rise

1960	439,000
1970	523,000
1980	1.6 million
1990	3.2 million
2000	5.5 million
2010	7.5 million

© Cengage Learning

Figure 16.8 Cohabitation Rate in the United States The number of unmarried opposite-sex couples cohabiting in the United States continues to rise. These couples now make up 12 percent of all opposite-sex U.S. couples, married and unmarried.

Source: U.S. Census Bureau, 2010.

will to that of family and kin transcend all else, whereas self-reliance is neither promoted nor a source of pride.

Perhaps the core value held in highest esteem by North Americans of European descent is rugged individualism—traditionally for men but in recent decades for women as well. Each individual is supposed to be able to achieve anything he or she likes, given a willingness to work hard enough. From their earliest years, individuals are subjected to relentless pressures to excel, and as we have already noted, competition and winning are crucial to this. Undoubtedly, this contributes to the restlessness and drive seen as characteristic for much of North American society today—and increasingly common wherever people compete for survival, wealth, and power in the global market.

Also, to the degree that it motivates individuals to work hard and to go where the jobs are, this individualism fits well with the demands of a global market economy. Whereas individuals in Chinese traditional society are firmly bound into a larger group to which they have lifelong obligations, most urban North Americans and western Europeans live

isolated from relatives other than their young children and spouse—and even the commitment to marriage has lessened (**Figure 16.8**). Many people in western Europe, North America, and other industrial or postindustrial societies choose singlehood or cohabitation over marriage. Among those who do wed, many do so later in life, often prompted by the birth of a child. This growing individualism is also indicated by high divorce rates. In the United States those rates have leveled off since peaking in the 1980s, but more than 40 percent of U.S. marriages still fail (Morello, 2011; Natadecha-Sponsal, 1993; Noack, 2001).

Alternative Gender Models

As touched on earlier, the gender roles assigned to each sex vary from culture to culture and have an impact on personality formation. But what if the sex of an individual is not self-evident, as revealed in the following Original Study? Written when its author was an undergraduate student of philosophy at Bryn Mawr College in Pennsylvania, this narrative offers a compelling personal account of the emotional difficulties associated with intersexuality and gender ambiguity. For scholarly accounts of the issues presented here, readers may turn to several excellent books, including the one mentioned in this account (Roscoe, 1991).

The Blessed Curse *BY R. K. WILLIAMSON*

One morning not so long ago, a child was born. This birth, however, was no occasion for the customary celebration. Something was wrong: something very grave, very serious, very sinister. This child was born between sexes, an "intersexed" child. From the day of its birth, this child would be caught in a series of struggles involving virtually every aspect of its life. Things that required little thought under "ordinary" circumstances were, in this instance, extraordinarily difficult. Simple questions now had an air of complexity: "What is it, a girl or a boy?" "What do we name it?" "How shall we raise it?" "Who (or what) is to blame for this?"

A Foot in Both Worlds

The child referred to in the introductory paragraph is myself. As the great-granddaughter of a Cherokee woman, I was exposed to the Native American view of people who were born intersexed, and those who exhibited transgendered characteristics. This view sees such individuals in a very positive and affirming light. Yet my immediate family (mother, father, and brothers) were firmly fixed in a negative Christian Euramerican point of view. As a result, I was presented with two different and conflicting views of myself. This resulted in a lot of confusion within me about what I was, how I came to be born the way I was, and what my intersexuality meant in terms of my spirituality as well as my place in society.

I remember, even as a small child, getting mixed messages about my worth as a human being. My grandmother, in keeping with Native American ways, would tell me stories about my birth. She would tell me how she knew when I was born that I had a special place in life, given to me by God, the Great Spirit, and that I had been given "a great strength that girls never have, yet a gentle tenderness that boys never know" and that I was "too pretty and beautiful to be a boy only and too strong to be a girl only." She rejoiced at this "special gift" and taught me that it meant that the Great Spirit had "something important for me to do in this life." I remember how good I felt inside when she told me these things and how I soberly contemplated, even at the young age of 5, that I must be diligent and try to learn and carry out the purpose designed just for me by the Great Spirit.

My parents, however, were so repulsed by my intersexuality that they would never speak of it directly. They would just refer to it as "the work of Satan." To them, I was not at all blessed with a "special gift" from some

"Great Spirit," but was "cursed and given over to the Devil" by God. My father treated me with contempt, and my mother wavered between contempt and distant indifference. I was taken from one charismatic church to another in order to have the "demon of mixed sex" cast out of me. At some of these "deliverance" services I was even given a napkin to cough out the demon into!

In the end, no demon ever popped out of me. Still I grew up believing that there was something inherent within me that caused God to hate me, that my intersexuality was a punishment for this something, a mark of condemnation.

Whenever I stayed at my grandmother's house, my fears would be allayed, for she would once again remind me that I was fortunate to have been given this special gift. She was distraught that my parents were treating me cruelly and pleaded with them to let me live with her, but they would not let me stay at her home permanently. Nevertheless, they did let me spend a significant portion of my childhood with her. Had it not been for that, I might not have been able to survive the tremendous trials that awaited me in my walk through life.

A Personal Resolution

For me, the resolution to the dual message I was receiving was slow in coming, largely due to the fear and self-hatred instilled in me by Christianity. Eventually, though, the spirit wins out. I came to adopt my grandmother's teaching about my intersexuality. Through therapy, and a new, loving home environment, I was able to shed the constant fear of eternal punishment I felt for something I had no control over. After all, I did not create myself.

Because of my own experience, and drawing on the teaching of my grandmother, I am now able to see myself as a wondrous creation of the Great Spirit—but not only me. All creation is wondrous. There is a purpose for everyone in the gender spectrum. Each person's spirit is unique in her or his or her-his own way. It is only by living true to the nature that was bestowed upon us by the Great Spirit, in my view, that we are able to be at peace with ourselves and be in harmony with our neighbor. This, to me, is the Great Meaning and the Great Purpose.

Adapted from Williamson, R. K. (1995). The blessed curse: Spirituality and sexual difference as viewed by Euramerican and Native American cultures. The College News 18(4). Reprinted with permission of the author.

Intersexuality

The biological facts of human nature are not always as clear-cut as most people assume. At the level of chromosomes, biological sex is determined according to whether a person's 23rd chromosomal set is XX (female) or XY (male). Some of the genes on these chromosomes control sexual development. This standard biological package does not apply to all humans, and a considerable number are **intersexuals**—people who are born with reproductive organs, genitalia, and/or sex chromosomes that are not exclusively male or female. These individuals do not fit neatly into a binary gender standard (see Chase, 1998; Dreger, 1998; Fausto-Sterling, 1993).

For example, some people are born with a genetic disorder that results in them having only one X chromosome instead of the usual two. A person with this chromosomal complex, known as Turner syndrome, develops female external genitalia but has nonfunctional ovaries and is therefore infertile. Other individuals are born with the XY sex chromosomes of a male but have an abnormality on the X chromosome that affects the body's sensitivity to androgens (male hormones). This is known as androgen insensitivity syndrome (AIS). An adult XY person with complete AIS appears fully female with a normal clitoris, labia, and breasts. Internally, these individuals possess testes (up in the abdomen, rather than in their usual descended position in the scrotal sac), but they are otherwise born without a complete set of either male or female internal genital organs. They generally possess a short, blind-ended vagina.

There is a distinct category of intersexuality historically named after Hermaphrodites, a Greek god who was the son of Hermes (god of commerce and guide to the home of the dead) and Aphrodite (goddess of beauty and love). He became half-male and half-female when he fell in love with a nature goddess and both united in one single body. Today, most people knowledgeable on the subject reject the term *hermaphrodite* as stigmatizing and inaccurate. The Intersex Society of North America advocates describing these conditions as disorders of sexual development (DSD), which encourages clinicians to shift from focusing on gender and genitals to the exclusion of the real medical problems people with DSD face.

Intersexed individuals have both testicular and ovarian tissue. They may have a separate ovary and testis, but more commonly they have an *ovotestis*—a gonad containing both types of tissue. About 60 percent of intersexed people possess XX (female) sex chromosomes, and the remainder may have XY or a mosaic (a mixture). Their external genitalia may be ambiguous or female, and they may have a uterus or (more commonly) a hemi-uterus (half uterus) (Fausto-Sterling, 2003).

U.S. biologist Anne Fausto-Sterling, a specialist in this area, notes that the concept of intersexuality is rooted in an idealized biological world in which our species is perfectly divided into two kinds:

> That idealized story papers over [that] some women have facial hair, some men have none; some women speak with deep voices, some men veritably squeak. Less well known is the fact that on close inspection, absolute dimorphism disintegrates even at the level of basic biology. Chromosomes, hormones, the internal sex structures, the gonads and external genitalia all vary more than most people realize. Those born outside of the . . . dimorphic mold are called intersexuals. (Fausto-Sterling, 2003)

Intersexuality may be unusual but is not uncommon. In fact, about 1 percent of all humans are intersexed in some (not necessarily visible) way—in other words, well over 70 million people worldwide (Fausto-Sterling, 2003; Fausto-Sterling et al., 2000). Until recently, it was rarely discussed publicly in many societies (Figure 16.9). Since the mid-20th century, individuals with financial means in technologically advanced parts of the world have had the option of reconstructive surgery and hormonal treatments to alter such conditions. Many parents faced with raising a visibly intersexed child in a culture intolerant of such minorities have chosen this option. Obviously, a society's attitude toward these individuals can impact their personality—their fundamental sense of self and how they express it.

Transgenders

Mapping the sexual landscape, anthropologists have come to realize that gender bending exists in many cultures all around the world, playing a significant role in shaping behaviors and personalities. For example, indigenous communities in the U.S. Great Plains and Southwest created social space for alternatively gendered persons in their communities. Commonly identified today as **transgenders**, these are people who cross over or occupy an intermediate position in the binary male–female gender construction.

The Lakota of the northern Plains had a third-gender category of culturally accepted transgendered males who dressed as women and were thought to possess both male and female spirits. They called (and still call) these third-gender individuals *winkte*, applying the term to a male "who wants to be a woman." Thought to have special curing powers, *winktes* traditionally enjoyed considerable prestige in their communities. Among the neighboring Cheyenne, such a person was called *hemanah*, literally meaning "half-man, half-woman" (Medicine, 1994). The preferred term among most North American Indians today is *two-spirits* (Jacobs, 1994).

---

intersexuals People born with reproductive organs, genitalia, and/or sex chromosomes that are not exclusively male or female.

transgenders People who cross over or occupy an intermediate position in the binary male–female gender construction.

Rex Features via AP Images

Figure 16.9 Intersexuality in the Olympic Spotlight Caster Semenya is a South African middle-distance runner, born in 1991. At age 18, after winning the women's 800-meter race at the 2009 World Championships in Berlin, Semenya faced a global media storm with headlines such as "Gold Awarded amid Dispute over Runner's Sex." The International Association of Athletics Federations (IAAF) ordered biological testing that revealed that the runner has internal male sexual organs. After being withdrawn from international competitions, she was officially cleared by the IAAF in July 2010 and resumed her female athletic career. She ran in the 2011 World Championship and in the 2012 Summer Olympics, winning silver in both for the 800-meter event.

Such third-gender individuals are well known in Samoa, where males who take on the identity of females are referred to as *fa'afafines* ("the female way"). Becoming a *fa'afafine* is an accepted option for boys who prefer to dance, cook, clean house, and care for children and the elderly. In large families, it is not unusual to find two or three boys being raised as girls to take on domestic roles in their households (Holmes, 2000).

Transgenders cannot be simply lumped together as homosexuals. For example, the Tagalog-speaking people in the Philippines use the word *bakla* to refer to a man who views himself "as a male with a female heart." These individuals cross-dress on a daily basis, often becoming more "feminine" than Philippine women in their use of heavy makeup, in the clothing they wear, and in the way they walk. Like the Samoan *fa'afafines*, they are generally not sexually attracted to other *bakla* but are drawn to heterosexual men instead.

Another example is found among the Bugis, a Muslim ethnic group inhabiting Sulawesi Island in Indonesia and numbering more than 6 million. The Bugis acknowledge five genders: *oroané* (masculine male), *makunrai* (feminine female), *calabai* (feminine male), *calalai* (masculine female), and *bissu* (neither male nor female) (Davies, 2007). Representing and embodying all genders, *bissu* are traditionally high-ranking celibate intersexuals. Their name derives from the Bugis term for "clean" (*bessi*), and as such they serve as shamans, mediating between the human and the spirit world, inhabited by *dewata* (genderless spirits or gods). As one high-ranking Bugis, Angkong Petta Rala, explained in an interview, "*bissu* do not bleed, do not have breasts, and do not menstruate, therefore they are *clean* or *holy*" (Lathief, "Bissu: Imam-mam yang Menghibur," cited in Umar, 2008, pp. 7–8). Because traditional shamanism has no place in Islam theology, many Bugis view *bissu* as corrupted Muslims (Umar, 2008).

In addition, worldwide there are people who are gender variants: permanent or incidental transvestites (cross-dressers) without being homosexuals. Clearly, the cross-cultural sex and gender scheme is complex; the late 19th-century "homosexuality" and "heterosexuality" labels are inadequate to cover the full range of sex and gender diversity (Schilt & Westbrook, 2009).

Eunuchs

In addition to people who are intersexed or alternatively gendered, throughout history many boys and adult men have been subjected to neutering—crushing, cutting, or otherwise damaging their testicles. Commonly known as *castration*, this is an ancient and widespread cultural practice to transform someone's sexual status and thereby one's social identity.

Today, males sentenced as sex offenders in the United States and a growing number of European countries may request or be forced to undergo chemical castration, limiting or destroying their sex drive, not only as punishment but also as corrective treatment.

Historically, archaeological evidence from ancient Egypt, Iraq, Iran, and China suggests that castrating war captives may have begun several thousand years ago. Boys captured during war or slave-raiding expeditions were often castrated before being sold and shipped off to serve in foreign households, including royal courts. Castrated men were often put in charge of a ruler's harem, the women's quarters in a wealthy lord's household. In Europe, they became known as *eunuchs* (Greek for "guardian of the bed"), but in the Muslim world they were usually identified as *khādim*. In the 10th century, according to an early Kurdish historian, the caliph (ruler) of the Muslim empire in Baghdad had 11,000 *khādim*, 7,000 of whom were castrated black and 4,000 white slaves (Ayalon, 1999).

Eunuchs could rise to high status as priests and administrators, and some were even appointed to serve as military commanders as happened in the great Persian, Byzantine, and Chinese empires. Eunuchs served at the Chinese imperial court in Beijing for 2,000 years. During the Ming dynasty, the imperial household was said to include 20,000 of these castrated servants, some of whom achieved great prominence (Tsai, 1996). The last ruling emperor of China had about 1,500 eunuchs when he was forced to step down in 1912.

About the same time, the cultural institution of eunuchs also ended in Europe. Until then, a category of musical eunuchs, known as *castrati*, participated in operas and in Roman Catholic Church choirs, singing the female parts. Castrated before they reached puberty so as to retain their high voices, these selected boys were often orphaned or came from poor families. Without functioning testes to produce male sex hormones, physical development into manhood is aborted, so deeper voices—as well as body hair, semen production, and other usual male attributes—were not part of a castrati's biology.

In some cultures, there are also men who engage in self-castration or undergo voluntary castration. Early Christian monks in Egypt and neighboring regions voluntarily abstained from sexual relationships and sometimes castrated themselves for the sake of the kingdom of heaven. Such genital mutilation was also practiced among Coptic monks in Egypt and Ethiopia, until the early 20th century (Abbot, 2001).

One of the few places where there are still a substantial number of eunuchs—at least 500,000—is India. There, along with intersexuals and transgenders, they are known as *hijras*. Traditionally, *hijras* performed at important occasions such as births and marriages, but today many make a living, at least in part, as street performers (**Figure 16.10**).

Figure 16.10 Eunuchs in India These elegantly dressed street performers are eunuchs, part of a broad alternative gender category in India known as *hijras*. The exact number of eunuchs in India is unknown, but estimates range from 500,000 to 1 million. On the occasion pictured here, thousands of *hijras* from across the country gathered in the remote northern town of Rath—300 kilometers (185 miles) south of Lucknow, the capital of Uttar Pradesh state—for a convention to chart their collective agenda, including a more active role in politics.

Reuters

Collectively, these alternatively gendered individuals who are "neither man nor woman" are thought to number about 6 million in India alone (Nanda, 1999).

The Social Context of Sexual and Gender Identity

The cultural standards that define normal behavior for any society are determined by that society itself. Thus, what seems normal and acceptable (if not always popular) in one society is often considered abnormal and unacceptable—ridiculous, shameful, and sometimes even criminal—in another. For instance, according to a recent global report, state-sponsored homophobia (the irrational fear of humans with same-sex preferences) thrives in many countries, fueling aggressive intolerance. Worldwide, 78 out of 193 countries have laws criminalizing same-sex sexual acts between consenting adults. Most of these punish individuals found guilty with imprisonment, although five countries (Iran, Mauritania, Saudi Arabia, Sudan, Yemen—plus parts of Nigeria and Somalia) punish them with the death penalty (Itaborahy, 2012). Yet, as discussed earlier in this text, most countries do not have such laws and a growing number have passed legislation legalizing same-sex marriage.

The complexity, variability, and acceptability or unacceptability of sex and gender schemes across cultures is an important piece of the human puzzle—one that prods us to rethink social codes and the range of forces that shape personality as well as each society's definition of *normal* overall.

Normal and Abnormal Personality in Social Context

The boundaries that distinguish the normal from the abnormal vary across cultures and time, as do the standards of what is socially acceptable. In many cultures, individuals may stand out as "different" without being considered "abnormal" in the strictest sense of the word—and without suffering social rejection, ridicule, censure, condemnation, imprisonment, or some other penalty. Moreover, there are cultures that not only tolerate or accept a much wider range of diversity than others, but they may actually accord special status to the deviant or eccentric as unique, extraordinary, even sacred, as illustrated by the following example.

Sadhus: Holy Men in Hindu Culture

Ascetic Hindu monks in India and Nepal provide an ethnographic example of a culture in which abnormal individuals are socially accepted and even honored. These individuals, known as *sadhus*, illustrate the degree to which one's social identity and sense of personal self are cultural constructs. When a young Hindu man in India or Nepal decides to become a *sadhu*, he must transform his personal identity, change his sense of self, and leave his place in the social order. Detaching himself from the pursuit of earthly pleasures (*kama*) and power and wealth (*artha*), he makes a radical break with his family and friends and abandons the moral principles and rules of conduct prescribed for his caste (*dharma*). Symbolically expressing his death as a typical Hindu, he participates in his own funeral ceremony, followed by a ritual rebirth. As a born-again, he acquires a new identity as a *sadhu* and is initiated into a sect of religious mystics.

Surrendering all social, material, and even sexual attachments to normal human pleasures and delights, *sadhus* dedicate themselves to achieving spiritual union with the divine or universal soul. This is done through chanting sacred hymns or mystical prayer texts and yoga (an ascetic and mystic discipline involving prescribed postures and controlled breathing). The superhuman goal is to become liberated from the physical limits of the individual mortal self, including the cycle of life and death.

© Cengage Learning

The life of suffering chosen by *sadhus* may even include self-torture as a form of extreme penance. Naked or near naked ("sky-clad"), they spend most of their time around cremation grounds. On a regular basis they apply ashes to their body, face, and long, matted hair. Some pierce their tongue or cheeks with a long iron rod, stab a knife through their arm or leg, or stick their head into a small hole in the ground for hours on end. One subsect, known as *Aghori*, drink and eat from human skull bowls as a daily reminder of human mortality (**Figure 16.11**).

Most Hindus revere and sometimes even fear *sadhus*. Sightings are not uncommon because an estimated 5 million *sadhus* live in India and Nepal (Heitzman & Wordem,

Figure 16.11 *Sadhu* **Holy Man, India** This Shaivite *sadhu* of the *Aghori* subsect drinks from a human skull bowl, symbolizing human mortality. He is a srict follower of the Hindu god Shiva, whose image can be seen behind him.

2006; Kelly, 2006). Of course, if one of these bearded, long-haired, and nearly naked Hindu monks decided to practice his extreme yoga exercises and other sacred devotions in western Europe or North America, observers would consider such a holy man to be severely mentally disturbed.

Mental Disorders Across Time and Cultures

As the Hindu mystic monks in South Asia illustrate, no matter how extreme or bizarre certain behaviors might seem in a particular place and time, the abnormal is not always socially rejected. Moreover, the standards that define normal behavior may shift over time.

Such is the case with manic depression (now more properly called *bipolar disorder*) and attention deficit hyperactivity disorder (ADHD), both previously regarded as dreaded liabilities. In western Europe and North America, the manic and hyperactivity aspects of these conditions have gradually become viewed as assets in the quest for success. More and more, they are interpreted as indicative of "finely wired, exquisitely alert nervous systems" that make one highly sensitive to signs of change and able to fly from one thing to another, all the while exerting an intense energy and focused on the future. These are extolled as high virtues in the corporate world, where being considered "hyper" or "manic" is increasingly an expression of approval (Martin, 1999, 2009).

Just as social attitudes concerning a wide range of both psychological and physical differences change over time within a society, they also vary across cultures—as described in the Biocultural Connection on the next page.

Cultural Relativity and Abnormality

Does this suggest that normalcy is a meaningless concept when applied to personality? Within the context of a particular culture, the concept of normal personality is quite significant. Irving Hallowell, a major figure in the development of psychological anthropology, ironically observed that it is normal to share the delusions traditionally accepted by one's society. Abnormality involves

BIOCULTURAL CONNECTION

A Cross-Cultural Perspective on Psychosomatic Symptoms and Mental Health

Biomedicine, the dominant medical system of European and North American cultures, sometimes identifies physical ailments experienced by individuals as *psychosomatic*—a term derived from **psyche** ("mind") and *soma* ("body"). These ailments can be serious and painful, but because a precise physiological cause cannot be identified through scientific methods, the illness is viewed as something rooted in mental or emotional causes—and thus on some level not quite real.

Each culture possesses its own historically developed ideas about health, illness, and associated healing practices. Although biomedicine is based in modern Western traditions of science, it is also steeped in the cultural beliefs and practices of the societies within which it operates. Fundamentally informed by a dualistic mind–body model, biomedicine represents the human body as a complex machine with parts that can be manipulated by experts. This approach has resulted in spectacular treatments, such as antibiotics that have eradicated certain infectious diseases.

Today, the remarkable breakthroughs of biomedicine are spreading rapidly throughout the world, and people from cultures with different healing systems are moving into countries where biomedicine dominates. This makes treating illnesses defined by biomedicine as psychosomatic disorders all the more difficult.

Indicative of our biocultural complexity, psychological factors such as emotional stress, worry, and anxiety may stem from cultural contexts and result in increased physiological agitation like irregular heart pounding or palpitations, heightened blood pressure, headaches, stomach and intestinal problems, muscle pains and tensions, rashes, appetite loss, insomnia, fatigue, and a range of other troubles. Indeed, when individuals are unable to deal successfully with stressful situations in daily life and do not get the opportunity for adequate mental rest and relaxation, their natural immune systems may weaken, increasing their chances of getting a cold or some other infection. For people forced to adapt to a quickly changing way of life in their own country or immigrants adjusting to a foreign culture, these pressures may result in a range of disorders that are difficult to explain from the perspective of biomedicine.

Medical and psychological approaches developed in European and North American societies are often unsuccessful in dealing with these problems, for a number of reasons. For one, the various immigrant ethnic groups have different concepts of mind and body than do medical practitioners trained in biomedical Western medicine. Among many Caribbean peoples, for example, a widely held belief is that spiritual forces are active in the world and that they influence human identity and behavior. For someone with a psychosomatic problem, it is normal to seek help from a local *curandero* or *curandera* ("folk healer"), *a santiguadora* ("herbalist"), or even a *santéro* (a Santéria priest) rather than a medical doctor or psychiatrist. Not only does the client not understand the symbols of Western psychiatry, but a psychiatric visit is often too expensive and may imply that the person is *loco*.

During the past few decades, however, anthropologists have become increasingly involved in cross-cultural medical mediation, challenging negative biases and correcting misinformation about non-Western indigenous perceptions of mind–body connections. The inclusion of culturally appropriate healing approaches has gained acceptance among the Western medical and psychological establishment in Europe, North America, and many other parts of the world.

BIOCULTURAL QUESTION

Given the cross-cultural differences in concepts of mind and body, should authorities in a pluralistic society apply the same standards to faith healers as to medical doctors?

---

the development of a delusional system of which the culture does not approve. The individual, who is disturbed because he or she cannot adequately measure up to the norms of society and be happy, may be termed *neurotic*. When a person's delusional system is so different that it in no way reflects his or her society's norms, the individual may be termed *psychotic*.

If severe enough, culturally induced conflicts can produce psychosis and also determine its particular form. In a culture that encourages aggressiveness and suspicion, the insane person may be one who is passive and trusting. In a culture that encourages passivity and trust, the insane person may be the one who is aggressive and suspicious. Just as each society establishes its own norms, each individual is unique in his or her perceptions.

Although it is true that each particular culture defines what is and is not normal behavior, the situation is complicated by findings suggesting that major categories of mental disorders may be universal types of human affliction. Take, for example, schizophrenia—probably the most common of all psychoses and one that may be found in any culture, no matter how it is manifested. Individuals afflicted by schizophrenia experience distortions of reality that impair their ability to function adequately, so they often withdraw from the social world into their own psychological shell.

Although environmental factors play a role, evidence suggests that schizophrenia is caused by a biochemical disorder for which there is an inheritable tendency. One of its more severe forms is paranoid schizophrenia. Those suffering from it fear and mistrust nearly everyone. They hear voices that whisper dreadful things to them, and they are convinced that someone is "out to get them." Acting on this conviction, they engage in bizarre sorts of behaviors, which lead to their removal from society.

Culture-Bound Syndrome

A **culture-bound syndrome**, or *ethnic psychosis*, is a mental disorder specific to a particular cultural group (Simons & Hughes, 1985). A historical example is *windigo psychosis*, limited to northern Algonquian groups such as the Cree and Ojibwa. In their traditional belief systems, these Indians recognized the existence of cannibalistic monsters called windigos. Individuals afflicted by the psychosis developed the delusion that, falling under the control of these monsters, they were themselves transformed into windigos, with a craving for human flesh. As this happened, the psychotic individuals perceived people around them turning into edible animals—fat beavers, for instance. Although there are no known instances where sufferers of windigo psychosis actually devoured humans, they were acutely afraid of doing so, and people around them feared that they might.

Windigo psychosis may seem different from clinical cases of paranoid schizophrenia found in Euramerican cultures, but a closer look suggests otherwise. The disorder was merely being expressed in ways compatible with traditional northern Algonquian cultures. Ideas of persecution, instead of being directed toward other humans, were directed toward supernatural beings (the windigo monsters); cannibalistic panic replaced panic expressed in other forms.

Windigo behavior may seem exotic and dramatic, but psychotic individuals draw upon whatever imagery and symbolism their culture has to offer. For instance, the delusions of Irish schizophrenics draw upon the images and symbols of Irish Catholicism and feature Virgin and Savior motifs. In short, the underlying biomedical structure of the mental disorder may be the same in all cases, but its expression is culturally specific.

A Western example of a culture-bound syndrome is "hysteria," expressed by fainting spells, choking fits, and even seizures and blindness. Identified in industrializing societies of 19th-century Europe and North America, this disorder was particularly associated with young urban women in well-to-do social circles. In fact, the term invented for this "nervous disease" is derived from the Greek word meaning "uterus." Not only has the diagnosis of this disorder declined in the course of the 20th century, but the term itself was banished from the medical nomenclature (Gordon, 2000).

In more recent decades, we have seen the rise of two related culture-bound syndromes associated with consumer capitalism: *bulimia nervosa* and *anorexia nervosa*. Bulimia is characterized by frequent binge eating followed by vomiting or other frantic efforts to avoid gaining weight. Anorexia is an obsession to remain thin, evidenced in self-starvation that may result in death. This neurotic "fear of fatness" manifests itself in Western consumer societies where a growing percentage of the population is overweight or obese.

Bulimia and anorexia are primarily diagnosed in female adolescents who reside in a culture that exalts thinness, even as fast food and leisure snacking are more prevalent. With the globalization of consumer society's fat–thin contradiction, its associated psychological eating disorders are also crossing borders (Littlewood, 2004). Today, Japan is just behind the United States in deaths related to psychological eating disorders ("Eating disorders (most recent) by country," 2004).

Personal Identity and Mental Health in Globalizing Society

Anthropologists view childrearing, gender issues, social identity, and emotional and mental health issues in their cultural context; this perspective recognizes that each individual's unique personality, feelings of happiness, and overall sense of health are shaped or influenced by the particular culture within which the person is born and raised to function as a valued member of the community. These communities, however, are seldom stable.

As illustrated by the spread of consumer culture and its associated psychological disorders, people all across the world face sometimes bewildering challenges hurled at them by the forces of globalization. These forces impact how people raise their children, how their personalities are influenced, and how they maintain their individual and collective social, psychological, and mental health.

In the past few decades, medical and psychological anthropologists have made valuable contributions to improving health care, not only in so-called developing countries far away, but also in their own societies. However, mental health

---

culture-bound syndrome A mental disorder specific to a particular cultural group; also known as *ethnic psychosis*.

practices prevailing in Europe and North America remain ethnocentric when theorizing and treating psychological disorders—a problem reinforced by a reductionist biomedical mindset that largely ignores the role of cultural factors in the etiology, expression, course, and outcome of mental disorders. Furthermore, commercial pressures on the health-care establishment favor bioscience and pharmacotherapy, with drug companies providing a quick and cheap fix for the problem (Luhrmann, 2001).

Informed by cultural relativist views on normality and deviance, anthropological perspectives on identity, mental health, and psychiatric disorders are especially useful in pluralistic societies where people from different ethnic groups, each with a distinctive culture, coexist and interact. Intensified by globalization, this multi-ethnic convergence drives home the need for a medical pluralism providing multiple healing modalities suited for the cultural dynamics of the 21st century.

CHAPTER CHECKLIST

What is enculturation, and does it shape a person's personality and identity?

● Enculturation, the process by which individuals become members of their society, begins soon after birth. Its first agents are the members of an individual's household, and then it involves other members of society.

● For enculturation to proceed, a person must possess self-awareness, the ability to identify oneself as an individual, to reflect on oneself, and to evaluate oneself.

● A child's birthright and social identity are established through personal naming, a universal practice with numerous cross-cultural variations. A name is an important device for self-definition—without one, an individual has no identity, no self. Many cultures mark the naming of a child with a special ceremony.

● For self-awareness to emerge and function, four basic orientations are necessary to structure the behavioral environment in which the self acts: object orientation (learning about a world of objects other than the self), spatial orientation, temporal orientation, and normative orientation (an understanding of the values, ideals, and standards that constitute the behavioral environment).

How do a society's childrearing practices and concepts of sex and gender influence a person's behavior, personality, and identity?

● Gender behaviors and relations are malleable and vary cross-culturally. Each culture presents different opportunities and expectations concerning ideal or acceptable male–female behavior. In some cultures, male–female relations are based on equal status, with both genders expected to behave similarly. In others, male–female relations are based on inequality and are marked by different standards of expected behavior.

● Anthropological research demonstrates that gender dominance is a cultural construct and, consequently, that alternative male–female social arrangements can be created if so desired.

● Through cross-cultural studies psychological anthropologists have established the interrelation of personality, childrearing practices, and other aspects of culture.

● Dependence training, usually associated with traditional farming societies, stresses compliance in the performance of assigned tasks and dependence on the domestic group, rather than reliance on oneself.

● In contrast, independence training, typical of societies characterized by small, independent families, puts a premium on self-reliance, independent behavior, and personal achievement. Although a society may emphasize one sort of behavior over the other, it may not emphasize it to the same degree in both sexes.

● Some psychological anthropologists contend that childrearing practices have their roots in a society's customs for meeting the basic physical needs of its members and that these practices produce particular kinds of adult personalities.

● Intersexuals—individuals born with reproductive organs, genitalia, and/or sex chromosomes that are not exclusively male or female—do not fit neatly into either a male or female biological standard or into a binary gender standard. Numerous cultures have created social space for intersexuals, as well as transgenders—physically male or female persons who cross over or occupy an alternative social position in the binary male–female gender construction.

What determines cultural norms, and is there such a thing as group personality or national character?

● Early on, anthropologists worked on the problem of whether it is possible to delineate a group personality without falling into stereotyping. Each culture chooses, from the vast array of possibilities, those traits that it sees as normative or ideal. Individuals who conform to these traits are rewarded; the rest are not.

● The modal personality of a group is the body of character traits that occur with the highest frequency in a culturally bounded population. As a statistical concept, it opens up for investigation how societies organize the diverse personalities of their members, some of which conform more than others to the modal type.

● National character studies have focused on the modal characteristics of modern countries. Researchers have attempted to determine the childrearing practices and education that shape such a group personality.

● Many anthropologists believe national character theories are based on unscientific and overly generalized data; others focus on the core values promoted in particular societies, although recognizing that success in instilling these values in individuals may vary considerably.

● What is defined as *normal behavior* in any culture is determined by the culture itself; what may be acceptable or even admirable in one may not be so regarded in another. Abnormality involves developing personality traits not accepted by a culture.

Does culture play a role in a person's mental health?

● Culturally induced conflicts not only can produce psychological disturbance but can also determine the form of the disturbance. Similarly, mental disorders that have a biological cause, like schizophrenia, will be expressed by symptoms specific to the culture of the afflicted individual. Culture-bound syndromes, or ethnic psychoses, are mental disorders specific to a particular ethnic group.

● Multi-ethnic convergence, intensified by globalization, drives home the need for a medical pluralism providing multiple healing modalities suited for the cultural dynamics of the 21st century.

QUESTIONS FOR REFLECTION

1. Considering the cultural significance of naming ceremonies in so many societies, including among the Khanty profiled in this chapter's opening photo and Challenge Issue, what do you think motivated your parents when they named you? Does that have any influence on your sense of self?

2. Do you think that the type of childhood training you received shaped your personality? If so, would you continue that approach with your own children?

3. Margaret Mead's cross-cultural research on gender relations suggests that male dominance is a cultural construct and, consequently, that alternative gender arrangements can be created. Looking at your grandparents, parents, and siblings, do you see any changes in your own family? What about your own community? Do you think such changes are positive?

4. Given that over 70 million people in today's world are intersexed and that a very small fraction of these people have access to reconstructive surgery, what do you think of societies that have created cultural space for alternative gender options?

5. Do you know someone in your family, neighborhood, or school who is "abnormal"? What is the basis for that judgment, and do you think everyone shares that opinion? Can you imagine that personal habits you consider normal would be viewed as deviant in the past or in another country?

ONLINE STUDY RESOURCES

CourseMate

Access chapter-specific learning tools, including learning objectives, practice quizzes, videos, flash cards, glossaries, and more in your Anthropology CourseMate.

Log into **www.cengagebrain.com** to access the resources your instructor has assigned and to purchase materials.

© Keren Su/Corbis

Challenge Issue

Facing the challenge of getting food, fuel, shelter, and other necessities, humans must hunt, gather, produce, or otherwise obtain the means to satisfy such needs. During the span of human existence, this has been accomplished in a range of highly contrasting natural environments by different biological and cultural adaptations. Inventing and applying various technologies, humans have developed distinctive subsistence arrangements to harness energy and process required resources. Thus, we may find hunters in Namibia's desert, fishers in Norway, manioc planters in Brazil's rainforest, goat herders in Iran's mountains, steel-mill laborers in South Korea, computer techs in India's cities, and poultry farmers in rural Alabama. All human activities impact their environments, some radically transforming the landscape. Here we see peasant farmers practicing wet-rice cultivation on the mountainous slopes of southern China's Guangxi Province. They have carved out terraces to capture rainwater, prevent soil erosion, and increase food production.

Patterns of Subsistence

All living beings must satisfy certain basic needs to stay alive—including obtaining food, water, and shelter. Moreover, because these needs must be met on an ongoing basis, no creature could long survive if its relations with the environment were random and chaotic. People have a huge advantage over other animals in this regard. We have culture.

If the rains do not come and the hot sun turns grassland into desert, we may pump water from deep wells, quenching our thirst, irrigating the pastures, and feeding our grazing animals. Conversely, if the rains do not end and our pastures turn into marshlands, we may choose to build earth mounds for our villages or dig canals to drain flooded fields. And to keep our food supplies from rotting, we can preserve them by drying or roasting and keep them in safe storage places for protection and future use. When our tools fail or are inadequate, we may choose to replace them or invent better ones. And if our stomachs are incapable of digesting a particular food, we can prepare it by cooking.

We are, nonetheless, subject to similar basic needs and pressures as are all living creatures, and it is important to understand human survival from this point of view. The crucial concept that underlies such a perspective is adaptation: how humans adjust to and act upon the burdens and opportunities presented in daily life.

Adaptation

As discussed earlier in this book, *adaptation* is the process organisms undergo to achieve a beneficial adjustment to a particular environment. What makes human adaptation unique among all other species is our capacity to produce and reproduce culture, enabling us to creatively adapt to an extraordinary range of radically different environments. The biological underpinnings of this capacity include large brains and a long period of growth and development.

IN THIS CHAPTER YOU WILL LEARN TO

- Recognize the relationship between cultural adaptation and long-term cultural change.

- Distinguish between the different food-collecting and food-producing systems developed across the globe in the course of more than 40,000 years.

- Analyze the interrelationship of natural environment, technology, and social organization in cultures as systems of adaptation.

- Assess the significance of the Neolithic revolution in the context of cultural evolution.

- Explain the process of parallel evolution in contrast to convergent evolution.

- Critically discuss mass food production in the age of globalization.

How humans adjust to the burdens and opportunities presented in daily life is the basic concern of all cultures. As defined in a previous chapter, a people's *cultural adaptation* consists of a complex of ideas, activities, and technologies that enable them to survive and even thrive; in turn, that adaptation impacts their environment.

The process of adaptation establishes an ever-shifting balance between the needs of a population and the potential of its environment. This process can be illustrated by the Tsembaga people of Papua New Guinea, one of about twenty local groups of Maring speakers who support themselves chiefly through cultivating crops using simple hand tools such as digging sticks or hoes (Rappaport, 1969). Although the Tsembaga also raise pigs, they eat them only under conditions of illness, injury, warfare, or celebration. At such times the pigs are sacrificed to ancestral spirits, and their flesh is ritually consumed. (This guarantees a supply of high-quality protein when it is most needed.)

Traditionally, the Tsembaga and their neighbors are bound together in a unique cycle of pig sacrifices that serves to mark the end of hostilities between groups. Hostilities are periodically fueled by ecological pressures in which pigs play a significant role. Because they fulfill important functions in the community, pigs are rarely slaughtered. Extremely omnivorous eaters, they keep the village free of garbage and even human feces; moreover, they serve as status symbols for their owners who reserve them for important ritual feasts. But there are drawbacks to keeping the pigs alive and allowing them to multiply because their numbers grow quickly. Invading the village gardens, the hungry pigs eat the sweet potatoes and other crops, leaving almost nothing for their human owners. In short, they become a problem.

The need to expand food cultivation in order to feed the prestigious but pesky pigs puts a strain on the land best suited for farming. Sooner or later, fighting breaks out between the Tsembaga and their neighbors. Hostilities usually end after several weeks, followed by a pig feast ritual. For this event, the Tsembaga butcher and roast almost all of their pigs and feast heartily on them with invited allies. By means of this feast, the Tsembaga not only pay their debts to their allies and gain prestige, but also eliminate a major source of irritation and complaint between neighbors. Moreover, the feast leaves everyone well fed and physically strengthened as a result of the animal protein intake. Even without hostilities over scarce land, such large pig feasts have been held whenever the pig population has become unmanageable—every five to ten years, depending on the groups' success in growing crops and raising animals. Thus, the cycle of fighting and feasting keeps the ecological balance among humans, land, and animals.

Through their distinctive cultures, different human groups have managed to adapt to a very diverse range of natural environments—from Arctic snowfields to Polynesian coral islands, from the Sahara Desert to the Amazon rainforest. Adaptation occurs not only when humans make changes in their natural environment but also when they are biologically changed by their natural environment, as illustrated in this chapter's Biocultural Connection.

Adaptation and Environment

Adaptation involves both organisms and their environment. Organisms, including human beings, exist as members of a population; populations, in turn, must have the flexibility to cope with variability and change within the natural environment that sustains them. In biological terms, this flexibility means that different organisms within the population have somewhat differing genetic endowments. In cultural terms, it means that variation occurs among individual skills, knowledge, and personalities. Indeed, organisms and environments form dynamic interacting systems. And although environments do not determine culture, they do present certain possibilities and limitations: People might just as easily farm as fish, but we do not expect to find farmers in Siberia's frozen tundra or fishermen in the middle of North Africa's Sahara Desert.

Some anthropologists have adopted the ecologists' concept of **ecosystem**, defined as a system, or functioning whole, composed of both the natural environment and all the organisms living within it. The system is bound by the activities of the organisms, as well as by such physical processes as erosion and evaporation.

Adaptation in Cultural Evolution

Human groups adapt to their environments by means of their cultures. However, cultures may change over the course of time; they evolve. This is called **cultural evolution**. The process is sometimes confused with the idea of **progress**—the notion that humans are moving forward to a better, more advanced stage in their development toward perfection. Yet not all changes turn out to be positive in the long run, nor do they improve conditions

ecosystem A system, or a functioning whole, composed of both the natural environment and all the organisms living within it.

cultural evolution Cultural change over time—not to be confused with progress.

progress In anthropology, a relative concept signifying that a society or country is moving forward to a better, more advanced stage in its cultural development toward greater perfection.

© Cengage Learning

BIOCULTURAL CONNECTION

Surviving in the Andes: Aymara Adaptation to High Altitude

However adaptable we are as a species through our diverse cultures, some natural environments pose such extreme climatic challenges that the human body must make physical adaptations to successfully survive. The central Andean highlands of Bolivia offer an interesting example of complex biocultural interaction, where a biologically adapted human body type has emerged due to natural selection.

Known as the *altiplano*, this high plateau has an average elevation of 4,000 meters (13,000 feet). Many thousands of years ago, small groups of human foragers in the warm lowlands climbed up the mountain slopes in search of game and other food. The higher they moved, the harder it became to breathe due to decreasing molecular concentration, or partial pressure, of oxygen in the inspired air. However, upon reaching the cold and treeless highlands, they found herds of llamas and hardy food plants, including potatoes—reasons to stay. Eventually (about 4,000 years ago) their descendants domesticated both the llamas and the potatoes and developed a new way of life as high-altitude agropastoralists.

The llamas provided meat and hides, as well as milk and wool. And the potatoes, a rich source of carbohydrates, became their staple food. In the course of many centuries, the Aymara selectively cultivated more than 200 varieties of these tubers on small family-owned tracts of land. They boiled them fresh for immediate consumption and also freeze-dried and preserved them as *chuño*, which is the Aymara's major source of nutrition to this day.

Still surviving as highland subsistence farmers and herders, these Aymara Indians have adapted culturally and biologically to the cold and harsh conditions of Bolivia's altiplano. They live and go about their work at extremely high altitudes (up to 4,800 meters/ 15,600 feet), in which partial pressure

Aymara Indians, who survive as farmers and herders, move across the altiplano (high plateau) in Bolivia with their llamas.

of oxygen in the air is far lower than that to which most humans are biologically accustomed.

Experiencing a marked *hypoxia* (insufficient oxygenation of the blood), a person's normal physiological response to being active at such heights is quick and heavy breathing. Most outsiders visiting the altiplano typically need several days to acclimatize to these conditions. Going too high too quickly can cause *soroche* ("mountain sickness"), with physiological problems such as pulmonary hypertension, increased heart rates, shortness of breath, headaches, fever, lethargy, and nausea. These symptoms usually disappear when one becomes fully acclimated, but most people will still be quickly exhausted by otherwise normal physical exercise.

For the Aymara Indians whose ancestors have inhabited the altiplano for many thousands of years, the situation is different. Through generations of natural selection, their bodies have become biologically adapted to the low oxygen levels. Short-legged and barrel-chested, their small bodies have an unusually large thoracic volume compared to their tropical

lowland neighbors and most other humans. Remarkably, their expanded heart and lungs possess about 30 percent greater pulmonary diffusing capacity to oxygenate blood.

In short, the distinctly broad chests of the Aymara Indians are biological evidence of their adaptation to the low-oxygen atmosphere of a natural habitat in which they survive as high-altitude agropastoralists.

BIOCULTURAL QUESTION

If a group of Aymara Indians abandons their high-altitude homeland in the Bolivian altiplano and settles for a new life in the coastal lowlands, will their descendants still living in this low-altitude environment a dozen generations later have smaller chests?

For more information, see Baker, P. (Ed.). (1978). The biology of high altitude peoples. London: Cambridge University Press; Rupert, J. L., & Hochachka, P. W. (2001). The evidence for hereditary factors contributing to high altitude adaptation in Andean natives: A review. High Altitude Medicine & Biology 2 (2), 235–256.

Figure 17.1 Comanche Bison Hunt This depiction of a Comanche bison hunt was painted by artist George Catlin (1796–1872). Plains Indians such as the Comanche and Lakota developed similar cultures because they had to adapt to similar environmental conditions.

for every member of a society even in the short run. Complex, urban societies are not more highly evolved than those of food foragers. Rather, both are highly evolved but in quite different ways.

Cultural adaptation must also be understood from a long-term historical point of view. To fit into an ecosystem, humans (like all organisms) must have the potential to adjust to or become a part of it. A good example of this is the Comanche, whose known history begins in the highlands of southern Idaho (Wallace & Hoebel, 1952). Living in that harsh, arid region, these North American Indians traditionally subsisted on wild plants, small animals, and occasionally larger game. Their material equipment was simple and limited to what they (and their dogs) could carry or pull. The size of their groups was restricted, and what little social power could develop was in the hands of the shaman, who was a combination of healer and spiritual guide.

At some point in their nomadic history, the Comanche moved east onto the Great Plains, attracted by enormous bison herds. As much larger groups could be supported by the new and plentiful food supply, the Comanche needed a more complex political organization. Eventually, they acquired horses and guns from European and neighboring Indian traders. This enhanced their hunting capabilities

significantly and led to the emergence of powerful hunting chiefs (**Figure 17.1**).

The Comanche became raiders in order to get horses (which they did not breed for themselves), and their hunting chiefs evolved into war chiefs. The once materially unburdened and peaceful hunter-gatherers of the dry highlands became wealthy, and raiding became a way of life. In the late 18th and early 19th centuries, they dominated the southern Plains (now primarily Texas and Oklahoma). In moving from one regional environment to another and in adopting a new technology, the Comanche were able to take advantage of existing cultural capabilities to thrive in their new situation.

Sometimes societies that develop independently of one another find similar solutions to similar problems. For example, the Cheyenne Indians originally lived in the woodlands of the Great Lakes region where they cultivated crops and gathered wild rice, which fostered a distinct set of social, political, and religious practices. Then they moved to the Great Plains, where they became horse-riding bison hunters, taking up a form of Plains Indian culture resembling that of the Comanche, even though the cultural historical backgrounds of the two groups differed significantly. This is an example of **convergent evolution**—the development of similar cultural adaptations to similar environmental conditions by different peoples with different ancestral cultures.

Especially interesting is that the Cheyenne gave up crop cultivation completely and focused exclusively on hunting and gathering after their move into the vast grasslands of the northern High Plains. Contrary to the popular notion

convergent evolution In cultural evolution, the development of similar cultural adaptations to similar environmental conditions by different peoples with different ancestral cultures.

Figure 17.2 Stone Heads, Easter Island Few places have caused as much speculation as this tiny volcanic island, also known by the indigenous name of Rapa Nui. Isolated in the middle of the southern Pacific Ocean, it is one of the most remote and remarkable places on earth. Nearly 900 colossal stone statues, known as *moai*, punctuate the landscape. Towering up to 65 feet, they were made by the Rapanui people—Polynesian seafarers who settled there about 800 years ago. They greatly prospered and multiplied and then faced an ecosystemic collapse.

David Simchock/vagabondvistas.com

of evolution as a progressive movement toward increased manipulation of the environment, this ethnographic example shows that cultural historical changes in subsistence practices do not always shift from dependence on wild food to farming; changes may move in the other direction as well.

Related to the phenomenon of convergent evolution is **parallel evolution**, in which similar cultural adaptations to similar environmental conditions are achieved by peoples whose ancestral cultures were already somewhat alike. For example, the development of farming in Southwest Asia and Mesoamerica took place independently, as people in both regions, whose lifeways were already comparable, became dependent on a narrow range of plant foods that required human intervention for their protection and reproductive success. Both developed intensive forms of agriculture, built large cities, and created complex social and political organizations.

It is important to recognize that stability as well as change is involved in cultural adaptation and evolution; episodes of major adaptive change may be followed by long periods of relative stability in a cultural system. Moreover, not everybody benefits from change, especially if change is forced upon them. As history painfully demonstrates, all too often humans have made changes that have had disastrous results, leading to the deaths of countless people—not to mention other creatures—and to the destruction of the natural environment.

An Ecosystemic Collapse: The Tragic Case of Easter Island

Among the many examples of catastrophic environmental destruction is Easter Island in the southern Pacific, first settled about 800 years ago by Polynesian seafarers. Other Polynesians referred to this remote 163-square-kilometer (63-square-mile) island as Rapa Nui, and its inhabitants became known as Rapanui.

When the Rapanui arrived, 75 percent of the island was densely forested, primarily with jubaea palms. Clearing the woods for food gardens of taros, yams, and sweet potatoes, the Rapanui also raised domesticated chickens, hunted wild birds, fished the ocean, and gathered nuts, fruits, and seeds. They prospered, producing surpluses, growing dramatically in number; and they formed into a few dozen clans under a paramount chief, a sacred king.

Trees, felled for fuel and to build homes and fishing canoes, were also used as rollers for transporting huge stone statues, which became an extraordinary hallmark of Rapanui culture (**Figure 17.2**). However, over time, success turned to failure—evidently due to a collapse of the fragile ecosystem brought about by a combination of natural and cultural factors (Alfonso-Durraty, 2012).

Rats, which had come to the island with the settlers, contributed to the demise. Feasting on palm seeds and reproducing rapidly, the rat population soared and hindered the reseeding of the slow-growing trees. By the mid-1600s, the palm groves had disappeared, apparently done in by rats and human deforestation. As the forests disappeared, rich topsoil eroded, other indigenous and endemic plants became extinct, crop yields diminished, springs dried up, and flocks of migrant birds stopped coming to the island to roost. Moreover, from about 1600 to 1640, El Niño—a warming of water surface temperatures—decreased

parallel evolution In cultural evolution, the development of similar cultural adaptations to similar environmental conditions by peoples whose ancestral cultures were already somewhat alike.

biomass production, diminishing fish and other marine resources (Stenseth & Voje, 2009).

All of this led to periodic famine and chronic warfare between Rapanui rival factions. With their nearest neighbors over 2,500 kilometers (1,500 miles) to their west, they were truly an isolated people who had nowhere to go. By time Dutch seafarers arrived on Rapa Nui in 1722 (the name "Easter Island" was given by the Dutch explorers who landed there on Easter Sunday), its indigenous population had dropped to about 3,000. During the next two centuries, other foreigners added to the Rapanui's problems, bringing diseases and other miseries. These additional stressors nearly wiped the Rapanui from their treeless island, now covered by grass and volcanic rock (Métraux, 1957; Mieth & Bork, 2009).

Environmental destruction on a much more massive scale has occurred in many other parts of the world, especially in the course of the 20th century, ruining the lives of millions. Considering such collapses of ecosystems, we must avoid falling into the ethnocentric trap of equating change with progress or with seeing everything as adaptive.

Culture Areas

From early on, anthropologists recognized that ethnic groups living within the same broad habitat often share certain cultural traits. This reflects the fact that there is a fundamental relationship among their similar natural environment, available resources, and subsistence practices and that neighboring peoples are in contact and engage in exchange with one another.

Classifying groups according to their cultural traits, anthropologists have mapped geographic regions in which a number of societies have similar ways of life. Known as **culture areas**, such regions often correspond to ecological regions. In sub-Arctic North America, for example, migratory caribou herds graze across the vast tundra. For dozens of different groups that have made this area their home, these animals provide a major source of food as well as material for shelter and clothing. Adapting to more or less the same ecological resources in this sub-Arctic landscape, these groups have developed similar subsistence technologies and practices in the course of generations. Although they speak very different languages, they may all be said to form part of the same culture area.

Because of changes in the natural environment such as habitat destruction and the extinction of plant and animal species, culture areas are not always stable. Moreover, new species may be introduced, and technologies may be invented or adopted from more distant cultures. Such was the case with the indigenous culture area of the

culture area A geographic region in which a number of societies follow similar patterns of life.

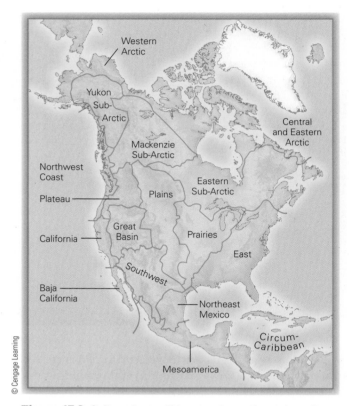

© Cengage Learning

Figure 17.3 Culture Areas This map shows the major culture areas that have been identified for North and Central America. Within each, there is an overall similarity of native cultures, as opposed to the differences that distinguish the cultures of one area from those of all others.

Great Plains in North America (**Figure 17.3**). For thousands of years, many indigenous groups with similar ways of life existed in this vast ecological area between the Mississippi River and the Rocky Mountains. Until the mid-1800s, when European immigrants invaded the region and almost completely annihilated the millions of free-ranging bison, these large grazing herds provided an obvious and practical source of food and materials for clothing and shelter.

The efficiency of indigenous groups in the southern grasslands increased greatly in the 1600s when they gained access to Spanish horses on the northern Mexican frontier and became mounted bison hunters. During the next century, the new horse complex spread northward to almost every indigenous group ranging in the Great Plains culture area. A total of thirty-one politically independent peoples, including the Cheyenne and Comanche just mentioned, reached a similar adaptation to this particular environment.

So it was that by the time Euramerican colonists invaded their vast hunting territories in the 19th century, the Indians of the Great Plains were all bison hunters, dependent on this animal for food, clothing, shelter, and bone tools. Each nation was organized into a number of warrior societies, and prestige came from hunting and fighting skills. Their villages were typically arranged in a distinctive circular pattern, and they shared many religious rituals, such as the Sun Dance.

During the 1870s and 1880s, railroads were built across the Great Plains, and mass slaughter of bison followed. More than 1 million of these animals were killed every year, mostly by non-Indians interested only in their hides and tongues (tongues were a luxury meat commodity, easily removed and compact to ship). With their herds almost exterminated, Indians of the Plains faced starvation, which made it impossible to effectively defend their homeland. This resulted in the near collapse of their traditional cultures from the 1890s onward.

Modes of Subsistence

Human societies all across the world have developed a cultural infrastructure that is compatible with the natural resources they have available to them and within the limitations of their various habitats. Each mode of subsistence involves not only resources but also the technology required to effectively capture and utilize them, as well as the kinds of work arrangements that are developed to best suit a society's needs. In the next few pages, we will discuss the major types of cultural infrastructure, beginning with the oldest and most universal mode of subsistence: food foraging.

Food-Foraging Societies

Before the domestication of food plants and animals, all people supported themselves through **food foraging**, a mode of subsistence involving some combination of hunting, fishing, and gathering wild plant foods. When food foragers had the earth to themselves, they had their pick of the best environments. But gradually, farming societies and, more recently, industrial and postindustrial societies (in which machines largely replaced human labor, hand tools, and animal power) appropriated the areas with rich soils and ample supplies of water. As a result, these expanding groups edged out the small foraging communities from their traditional habitats.

Today, at most a quarter of a million people—less than 0.004 percent of the world population of over 7 billion—still support themselves mainly as foragers. They are found only in the world's most marginal areas (frozen Arctic tundra, deserts, and inaccessible forests) and typically lead a migratory existence that makes it impractical to accumulate many material possessions. Because foraging cultures have nearly disappeared in areas having a natural abundance of food and fuel resources, anthropologists are necessarily cautious about making generalizations about the ancient human past based on in-depth studies of still-existing foraging groups that have adapted to more marginal habitats.

Present-day people who subsist by hunting, fishing, and wild plant collection are not following an ancient way of life because they do not know any better. Rather, they have been forced by circumstances into situations where foraging is the best means of survival or they simply prefer to live this way. In fact, foraging constitutes a rational response to particular ecological, economic, and sociopolitical realities. Moreover, for at least 2,000 years, hunters, fishers, and gatherers have met the demands for commodities such as furs, hides, feathers, ivory, pearls, fish, nuts, and honey within larger trading networks. Like everyone else, most food foragers are now part of a larger system with social, economic, and political relations extending far beyond regional, national, or even continental boundaries (**Figure 17.4**).

Characteristics of Food-Foraging Societies

Typically, foragers have ample and balanced diets and are less likely to experience severe famine than farmers. Their material possessions are limited, but so is their desire to amass things. Notably, they have plenty of leisure time for concentrating on family ties, social life, and spiritual development—apparently far more than people living in farming and industrial societies. Such findings clearly challenge the once widely held view that food foragers live a miserable existence. Among the few remaining food-foraging societies, there are some common features: mobility, small group size, flexible division of labor by gender, food sharing, egalitarianism, communal property, and rarity of warfare.

Mobility

Food foragers move as needed within a circumscribed region that is their home range to tap into naturally available food sources. Some groups, such as the Ju/'hoansi in the Kalahari Desert of southern Africa who depend on the reliable and highly drought-resistant mongongo nut, may keep to fairly fixed annual routes and cover only a restricted territory. Others, such as the traditional Shoshone in the western highlands of North America, had to cover a wider territory, their course determined by the local availability of the erratically productive pine nut.

A crucial factor in this mobility is availability of water. The distance between the food supply and the water must not be so great that more energy is required to fetch water than can be obtained from the food.

Small Group Size

Another characteristic of the food-foraging adaptation is the small size of local groups, typically fewer than a hundred people. No completely satisfactory explanation for this has been offered, but both ecological and social factors are involved. Among the ecological factors is the

food foraging A mode of subsistence involving some combination of hunting, fishing, and gathering of wild plant foods.

Figure 17.4 Remote but Not Isolated Peoples of the Kalahari Desert Human groups (including food foragers) do not exist in isolation except occasionally, and even then not for long. The bicycle this Bushman of southern Africa is riding is indicative of his links with the wider world, just as the wild tsama melons, bow, and quiver of arrows speak of his traditional hunter-gatherer life. For 2,000 years, Bushmen have been interacting regularly with neighboring farmers and pastoralists. Moreover, food foragers have supplied much of the commodities desired by the rest of the world, such as the elephant ivory used for keyboards on pianos so widely sought in 19th-century North America.

© Anthony Bannister; Gallo Images Corbis

carrying capacity of the land—the number of people that the available resources can support at a given level of food-getting techniques. This requires adjusting to seasonal and long-term changes in resource availability. Carrying capacity involves not only the immediate presence of food and water but also the tools and work necessary to secure them, as well as short- and long-term fluctuations in their availability.

In addition to seasonal or local adjustments, food foragers must make long-term adjustments to resources. Food-foraging populations usually stabilize at numbers well below the carrying capacity of their land. In fact, the home ranges of most food foragers can support from three to five times as many people as they typically do. In the long run, it may be more adaptive for a group to keep its numbers low rather than to expand indefinitely and risk destruction by a sudden and unexpected natural reduction in food resources. The population density of foraging groups surviving in marginal environments today rarely exceeds one person per square mile—a very low density.

How food-foraging peoples regulate population size relates to two things: how much body fat they accumulate and how they care for their children. Ovulation requires a certain minimum of body fat, and in traditional foraging societies this is not achieved until early adulthood. Hence, female reproductive maturity typically occurs between the early and mid-20s, and teenage pregnancies (at least successful ones) are virtually unknown (Frisch, 2002; Hrdy, 1999). Once a child is born, the mother nurses the child several

times each hour, even at night, and this continues over a period of four or five years. The constant stimulation of the mother's nipples suppresses the level of hormones that promote ovulation, making conception less likely, especially if work keeps the mother physically active, and she does not have a large store of body fat to draw on for energy (Konner & Worthman, 1980; Small, 1997). Continuing to nurse for several years, women give birth only at widely spaced intervals. Thus, the total number of offspring remains low but sufficient to maintain a stable population size (**Figure 17.5**).

Flexible Division of Labor by Gender

Division of labor exists in all human societies and is probably as old as human culture. Among food foragers, the hunting and butchering of large game as well as the processing of hard or tough raw materials are almost universally masculine occupations. By contrast, women's work in foraging societies usually focuses on collecting and processing a variety of plant foods, as well as other domestic chores that can be fit to the demands of breastfeeding and that are more compatible with pregnancy and childbirth.

Among food foragers today, the work of women is no less arduous than that of men. For example, Ju/'hoansi women may walk 12 miles a day to gather food, two or three times a week. They are carrying not only their children but also, on the return home, between 15 and 33 pounds of food. Still, they do not have to travel quite as far as do men on the hunt, and their work is usually less dangerous. Also, their tasks require less rapid mobility, do not need complete and undivided attention, and are readily resumed after interruption.

All of this is compatible with those biological differences that remain between the sexes. Certainly, women

---

carrying capacity The number of people that the available resources can support at a given level of food-getting techniques.

Although women in foraging societies commonly spend some time each day gathering plant foods, men rarely hunt on a daily basis (**Figure 17.6**). The amount of energy expended in hunting, especially in hot climates, is often greater than the energy return from the kill. Too much time spent searching out game might actually be counterproductive. Energy itself is derived primarily from plant carbohydrates, and it is usually the female gatherers who bring in the bulk of the calories. A certain amount of meat in the diet, though, guarantees high-quality protein that is less easily obtained from plant sources because meat contains exactly the right balance of all of the amino acids (the building blocks of protein) the human body requires. No one plant food does this, and in order to get by without meat people must hit on exactly the right combination of plants to provide the essential amino acids in the correct proportions.

Food Sharing

Another key feature of human social organization associated with food foraging is the sharing of food. Among the Ju/'hoansi, women have control over the food they collect and can share it with whomever they choose. Men, by contrast, are constrained by rules that specify how much meat is to be distributed and to whom. For the individual hunter, meat sharing is really a way of storing it for the future: His generosity, obligatory though it might be, gives him a claim on the future kills of other hunters. As a cultural trait, food sharing has the obvious survival value of distributing resources needed for subsistence.

Egalitarian Social Relations

A key characteristic of the food-foraging society is its egalitarianism. Because foragers are usually highly mobile and lack animal or mechanical transportation, they must be able to travel without many encumbrances, especially on food-getting expeditions. By necessity, the material goods they carry with them are limited to the barest essentials, which include implements for hunting, gathering, fishing, building, and cooking. (For example, the average weight of an individual's personal belongings among the Ju/'hoansi is just under 25 pounds.) In this context, it makes little sense for them to accumulate luxuries or surplus goods, and the fact that no one owns significantly more than another helps to limit status differences. Age and sex are usually the only sources of status differences.

It is important to realize that status differences by themselves do not constitute inequality, a point that is easily misunderstood especially when relations between men and women are concerned. In most traditional food-foraging societies, women did not and do not defer to men. To be sure, women may be excluded from some rituals in which men participate, but the reverse is also true.

Figure 17.5 Natural Birth Control Frequent nursing of children over four or five years acts to suppress ovulation among food foragers such as the Ju/'hoansi. As a consequence, women give birth to relatively few offspring at widely spaced intervals.

© Anthony Bannister, Gallo Images/Corbis

who are pregnant or who have infants to nurse cannot travel long distances in pursuit of game as easily as men can. By the same token, women may have preferred and been better at the less risky task of gathering.

But, saying that differing gender roles among food foragers is compatible with the biological differences between men and women is *not* saying that these roles are biologically determined. In fact, the division of labor by gender is often far less rigid among food foragers than it is in most other types of society. Thus, Ju/'hoansi males, when the occasion demands, willingly and without embarrassment gather wild plant foods, build huts, and collect water, even though all are regarded as women's work.

Notably, the food-gathering activities of women play a major role in the survival of their group: Research shows that contemporary food foragers may obtain up to 60 or 70 percent of their diet from plant foods, with perhaps some fish and shellfish also provided primarily by women (the exceptions tend to be food foragers living in Arctic regions, where plant foods are not available for much of the year).

VISUAL COUNTERPOINT

Figure 17.6 Ju/'hoansi Division of Labor Although food foragers such as the Ju/'hoansi Bushmen in southern African have a flexible division of labor, men usually do the hunting, whereas women prepare food. Both men and women gather wild foods such as ostrich eggs and edible plants—fruits, nuts, tubers. Here, Ju/'hoansi men return from a successful porcupine hunt, and women prepare a 3-pound ostrich egg omelet (equivalent to about two dozen chicken eggs). Traditionally, once the bird's large, hard shell has been emptied, it serves as a useful water container. If it shatters, pieces are fashioned into jewelry.

Moreover, the fruits of women's labor are controlled by them, not by men. Nor do women sacrifice their autonomy even in societies in which male hunting, rather than female gathering, brings in the bulk of the food.

Communal Property

Food foragers make no attempt to accumulate surplus foodstuffs, often an important source of status in agrarian societies. This does not mean that they live constantly on the verge of starvation because their environment is their natural storehouse. Except in the coldest climates (where a surplus must be set aside to see people through the long, lean winter season) or in times of acute ecological disaster, some food can almost always be found in a group's territory. Because food resources are typically shared and distributed equally throughout the group, no one achieves the wealth or status that hoarding might produce. In such a society, having more than others is a sign of deviance rather than a desirable characteristic.

The food forager's concept of territory contributes as much to social equality as it does to the equal distribution of resources. Most groups have home ranges within which access to resources is open to all members. What is available to one is available to all. If an Mbuti Pygmy hunter living in the forests of Central Africa discovers a honey tree, he has first rights; but when he has taken his share, others have a turn. In the unlikely possibility that he does not take advantage of his discovery, others will. No individual within the community privately owns the tree; the system is first come, first served. Therefore, knowledge of the existence of food resources circulates quickly throughout the entire group.

Rarity of Warfare

Although much has been written on the theoretical importance of hunting for shaping the supposedly competitive and aggressive nature of the human species, most anthropologists are unconvinced by these arguments. To be sure, warlike behavior on the part of food-foraging peoples is known, but such behavior is a relatively recent phenomenon in response to pressure from expansionist states. In the absence of such pressures, food-foraging peoples are remarkably nonaggressive and place more emphasis on peacefulness and cooperation than they do on violent competition.

How Technology Impacts Cultural Adaptations among Foragers

Like habitat, technology plays an important role in shaping the characteristics of the foraging life discussed previously. The mobility of food-foraging groups may depend on the availability of water, as among the Ju/'hoansi, or of game animals and other seasonal resources, as among the Mbuti in the Democratic Republic of Congo in Central Africa. Different hunting technologies and techniques may also play a part in determining movement, as well as population size and division of labor by gender.

Consider, for example, the Mbuti Pygmies in the Ituri tropical forest. All Mbuti bands hunt elephants with spears. However, for other game some of the bands use bows, and others use large nets. Those equipped with nets have a cooperative division of labor in which men, women, and children collaborate in driving antelope and other game into the net for the kill. Usually, this involves very long hours and movement over great distances as participants surround the animals and beat the woods noisily to chase the game in one direction toward the great nets. Because this sort of "beat-hunt" requires the cooperation of seven to thirty families, those using this method have relatively large camps.

Among Mbuti bow hunters, on the other hand, only men go after the game. These archers tend to stay closer to the village for shorter periods of time and live in smaller groups, typically of no more than six families. Although there is no significant difference in overall population density between net- and bow-hunting areas, archers generally harvest a greater diversity of animal species, including monkeys (Bailey & Aunger, 1989; Terashima, 1983).

Food-Producing Societies

Habitat and technology do not tell the whole story of how we humans feed ourselves. After the emergence of tool making, which enabled humans to consume significant amounts of meat as well as plant foods, the next truly momentous event in human history was the domestication of plants and animals. Over time, this achievement transformed cultural systems, with humans developing new economic arrangements, social structures, and ideological patterns based on plant cultivation, breeding and raising animals, or a mixture of both.

The transition from food foraging to food production first took place about 10,000 years ago in Southwest Asia (the Fertile Crescent, including the Jordan River Valley and neighboring regions in the Middle East). This was the beginning of the **Neolithic** or New Stone Age (from the Greek *neo* meaning "new" and *lith* meaning "stone") in which people possessed stone-based technologies and depended on domesticated plants and/or animals. Within the next few thousand years, similar early transitions to agricultural economies took place independently in other parts of the world where human groups began to raise and (later) alter wild cereal plants such as wheat, maize (corn), and rice; legumes such as beans; gourds such as squash; and tubers such as potatoes. Doing the same with a number of wild animal species ranging in their hunting

territories, they began to domesticate goats, sheep, pigs, cattle, and llamas (**Figure 17.7**).

Because these activities brought about a radical transformation in almost every aspect of their cultural systems, Australian-born archaeologist Gordon Childe introduced the term **Neolithic revolution** to refer to the profound cultural change associated with the early domestication of plants and animals. As humans became increasingly dependent on domesticated crops, they mostly gave up their mobile way of life and settled down to till the soil, sow, weed, protect, harvest, and safely store their crops. No longer on the move, they could build more permanent dwellings and began to make pottery for storage of water, food, and so on.

Just why this change came about is one of the important questions in anthropology. Because food production requires more work than food foraging, is more monotonous, and is often a less secure means of subsistence, it is unlikely that people became food producers voluntarily.

Initially, it appears that food production arose as a largely unintended byproduct of existing food management practices. Among many examples, we may consider the Paiute Indians, whose desert habitat in the western highlands of North America includes some oasis-like marshlands. These foragers discovered how to irrigate wild crops in their otherwise very dry homeland, thus increasing the quantity of wild seeds and bulbs to be harvested. Although their ecological intervention was very limited, it allowed them to settle down for longer periods in greater numbers than otherwise would have been possible.

Unlike the Paiute, who stopped just short of a Neolithic revolution, other groups elsewhere in the world continued to transform their landscapes in ways that favored the appearance of new varieties of particular plants and animals, which came to take on increasing importance for people's subsistence. Although probably at first accidental, it became a matter of necessity as growth outstripped people's ability to sustain themselves through food foraging. For them, food production became a subsistence option of last resort.

Producing Food in Gardens: Horticulture

With the advent of plant domestication, some societies took up **horticulture** (from the Latin *hortus*, meaning "garden") in which small communities of gardeners cultivate crops with simple hand tools, using neither irrigation

---

Neolithic The New Stone Age; a prehistoric period beginning about 10,000 years ago in which peoples possessed stone-based technologies and depended on domesticated plants and/or animals for subsistence.

Neolithic revolution The domestication of plants and animals by peoples with stone-based technologies, beginning about 10,000 years ago and leading to radical transformations in cultural systems; sometimes referred to as the *Neolithic transition*.

horticulture The cultivation of crops in food gardens, carried out with simple hand tools such as digging sticks and hoes.

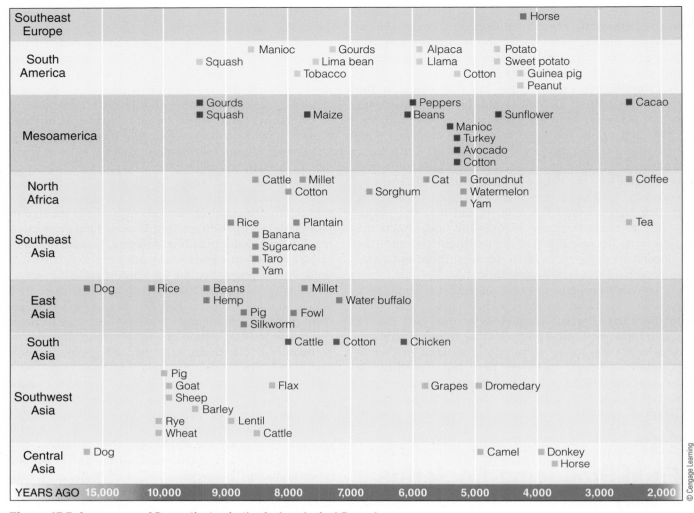

	15,000	10,000	9,000	8,000	7,000	6,000	5,000	4,000	3,000	2,000

Figure 17.7 Appearance of Domesticates in the Archaeological Record

nor the plow. Typically, horticulturists cultivate several varieties of food plants together in small, hand-cleared gardens. Because they do not typically fertilize the soil, they use a given garden plot for only a few years before abandoning it in favor of a new one. Often, horticulturists grow enough food for their subsistence, and occasionally they produce a modest surplus that can be used for other purposes such as intervillage feasts and exchange. Although their major food supplies may come from their gardens, many horticulturists will also hunt game, fish, and collect wild plant foods in the forest when need and opportunity arise.

One of the most widespread forms of horticulture, especially in the tropics, is **slash-and-burn cultivation**, or *swidden farming*, in which the natural vegetation is cut, the

slash is subsequently burned, and crops are then planted among the ashes. This is an ecologically sophisticated and sustainable way of raising food, especially in the tropics, when carried out under the right conditions: low population densities and adequate amounts of land. It mimics the diversity of the natural ecosystem, growing several different crops in the same field. Mixed together, the crops are less vulnerable to pests and plant diseases than a single crop.

Not only is the system ecologically sound, but it is far more energy efficient than modern farming methods used in developed countries such as the United States, where natural resources such as land and fuel are still relatively cheap and abundant, and many farms operate with financial support in the form of government subsidies or tax breaks. Whereas high-tech farming requires more energy input than it yields, slash-and-burn farming produces between 10 and 20 units of energy for every unit expended. A good example of how such a tropical food-gardening system works is provided by the Mekranoti Kayapo Indians of Brazil's Amazon forest, profiled in the following Original Study.

slash-and-burn cultivation An extensive form of horticulture in which the natural vegetation is cut, the slash is subsequently burned, and crops are then planted among the ashes; also known as *swidden farming*.

Gardens of the Mekranoti Kayapo

BY DENNIS WERNER

To plant a garden, Mekranoti men clear the forest and burn the debris. Then, in the ashes, men and women plant sweet potatoes, manioc, bananas, corn, pumpkins, papaya, sugar cane, pineapple, cotton, tobacco, and annatto, whose seeds yield achiote, the red dye used for painting ornaments and people's bodies. Because the Mekranoti don't bother with weeding, the forest gradually invades the garden. After the second year, only manioc, sweet potatoes, and bananas remain. And after three years or so there is usually nothing left but bananas. Except for a few tree species that require hundreds of years to grow, the area will look like the original forest twenty-five to thirty years later.

This gardening technique, known as slash-and-burn, is one of the most common in the world. At one time critics condemned it as wasteful and ecologically destructive, but today we know that, especially in the humid tropics, it may be one of the best gardening methods possible.

Continuous high temperatures encourage the growth of the microorganisms that cause rot, so organic matter quickly breaks down into simple minerals. The heavy rains dissolve these valuable nutrients and carry them deep into the soils, out of the reach of plants. The tropical forest maintains its richness because the heavy foliage shades the earth, cooling it and inhibiting the growth of the decomposers. A good deal of the rain is captured by leaves before ever reaching the ground.

When a tree falls in the forest and begins to rot, other plants quickly absorb the nutrients that are released. In contrast, with open-field agriculture, the sun heats the earth, the decomposers multiply, and the rains quickly leach the soils of their nutrients. In a few years a lush forest, if cleared for open one-crop agriculture, can be transformed into a barren wasteland.

A few months after the Mekranoti plant banana and papaya, these trees shade the soil, just as the larger forest trees do. The mixing of different kinds of plants in the same area means that minerals can be absorbed as soon as they are released; corn picks up nutrients very fast, whereas manioc is slow. Also, the small and temporary clearings mean that the forest can quickly reinvade its lost territory.

Because decomposers need moisture as well as warmth, the long Mekranoti dry season could alter this whole picture of soil ecology. But soil samples from recently burned Mekranoti fields and the adjacent forest floor showed that, as in most of the humid tropics, the high fertility of the Indians' garden plots comes from the trees that are burned there, not from the soil, as in temperate climates.

Getting a good burn is a tricky operation. Perhaps for this reason the more experienced and knowledgeable members of the community oversee its timing. If done too early, the rains will leach out the minerals in the ash before planting time. If too late, the debris will be too wet to burn properly. Then, insects and weeds that could plague the plants will not die and few minerals will be released into the soil. If the winds are too weak, the burn will not cover the entire plot. If they are too strong, the fire can get out of hand.

Shortly after burning the plots and clearing some of the charred debris, people begin the long job of planting, which takes up all of September and lasts into October. In the center of the circular garden plot the women dig holes and throw in a few pieces of sweet potatoes. After covering the tubers with dirt, they usually ask a male to stomp on the mound and make a ritual noise resembling a Bronx cheer—magic to ensure a large crop. Forming a large ring around the sweet potatoes, the Indians thrust pieces of manioc stems into the ground, one after the other. Once grown, these stems form a dense barrier around the sweet potato patch. Outside of the manioc ring, women plant yams, cotton, sugar cane, and annatto. An outermost circle of banana stalks and papaya trees is sowed by simply throwing the seeds on the ground, whereas corn, pumpkins, watermelons, and pineapple are planted throughout the garden; rapid growers, they are harvested long before the manioc matures.

When I lived with the Mekranoti, Western agronomists—accustomed to single-crop fields and a harvest that happens all at once—knew very little about slash-and-burn crop cultivation. Curious about the productivity of Mekranoti horticulture, I began measuring off areas of gardens to count how many manioc plants, ears of corn, or pumpkins were found there. The women thought it strange to see me struggling through the tangle of plants to measure off areas, 10 meters by 10 meters, placing string along the borders, and then counting what was inside. Sometimes I asked a woman to dig up all of the sweet potatoes within the marked-off area. My requests were bizarre, but they cooperated, holding on to the ends of the measuring tapes, or sending their children to help. For some plants, like bananas, I simply counted the number of clumps of stalks in the garden, and the number of banana bunches I could see growing in various clumps. By watching how long it took the bananas to grow, from the time I could see them until they were harvested, I could calculate a garden's total banana yield per year.

Combining the time allocation data with the garden productivities, I got an idea of how hard the Mekranoti need to work to survive. The data showed that for every hour of gardening one Mekranoti adult produces almost 18,000 kilocalories of food. (As a basis for comparison, people in the United States consume approximately 3,000 kilocalories of food per day.) As insurance against bad years, and in case they receive visitors from other villages, they grow far more produce than they need. But even so, they don't need to work very hard to survive. A look at the average amount of time adults spend on different tasks every week shows just how easygoing life in horticultural societies can be:

8.5 hours	Gardening
6.0 hours	Hunting
1.5 hours	Fishing
1.0 hour	Gathering wild foods
33.5 hours	All other jobs

Altogether, the Mekranoti need to work less than 51 hours a week, and this includes getting to and from work, cooking, repairing broken tools, and all of the other things we normally don't count as part of our work week.

Adapted from Werner, D. (1990). Amazon journey (pp. 105–112). Englewood Cliffs, NJ: Prentice-Hall.

Producing Food on Farms: Agriculture

In contrast to horticulture, **agriculture** (from the Latin *agri*, meaning "field") is growing food plants like grains, tubers, fruits, and vegetables in soil prepared and maintained for crop production. This form of more intensive food production involves using technologies other than hand tools, such as irrigation, fertilizers, and plows pulled by harnessed draft animals. In the developed countries of today's world, agriculture relies on fuel-powered tractors to produce food on large plots of land. But the ingenuity of some early agriculturalists is illustrated in this chapter's Anthropology Applied feature, highlighting an ecologically sound mountain-terracing and irrigation system established 1,000 years ago.

Among agriculturists, surplus crop cultivation is generally substantial—providing food not only for their own needs but also for those of various full-time specialists and nonproducing consumers. This surplus may be traded or sold for cash, or it may be coerced out of the farmers through taxes, rent, or tribute (forced gifts acknowledging submission or protection) paid to landowners or other dominant groups. These landowners and specialists—such as traders, carpenters, blacksmiths, sculptors, basketmakers, and stonecutters—typically reside in substantial towns or cities, where political power is centralized in the hands of a socially elite class. Dominated by more powerful groups and markets, much of what the farmers do is governed by political and economic forces over which they have little control.

Early food producers have developed several major crop complexes: two adapted to dry uplands and two to tropical wetlands. In the dry uplands of Southwest Asia, for example, farmers time their agricultural activities with the rhythm of the changing seasons, cultivating wheat, barley, oat, flax, rye, and millet. In the tropical wetlands of Southeast Asia, rice and tubers such as yams and taro are cultivated. In the Americas, people have adapted to natural environments similar to those of Africa and Eurasia but have cultivated their own indigenous plants. Typically, maize, beans, squash, and the potato are grown in drier areas, whereas manioc is extensively grown in the tropical wetlands.

Characteristics of Crop-Producing Societies

One of the most significant correlates of crop cultivation is the development of fixed settlements, in which farming families reside together near their cultivated fields. The task of food production lends itself to a different kind of social organization. Because the hard work of some members of the group could provide food for all, others become free to devote their time to inventing and manufacturing the equipment needed for a new sedentary way of life. Tools for digging and harvesting, pottery for storage and cooking, clothing made of woven textiles, and housing made of stone, wood, or sun-dried bricks all come out of the new settled living conditions and the altered division of labor.

The Neolithic revolution also brought important changes in social structure. At first, social relations were egalitarian and hardly different from those that prevailed among food foragers. As settlements grew, however, and large numbers of people had to share important resources such as land and water, a greater division of labor developed, and society became more complex in organization.

agriculture Intensive crop cultivation, employing plows, fertilizers, and/or irrigation.

Agricultural Development and the Anthropologist

Mountain terracing in Peru has counteracted erosion and provided irrigation for farmland.

Gaining insight into the traditional practices of indigenous peoples, anthropologists have often been impressed by the ingenuity of their knowledge. This awareness has spread beyond the profession to the Western public at large, giving birth to the popular notion that indigenous groups invariably live in some sort of blissful oneness with the environment. But this was never the message of anthropologists, who know that traditional people are only human, and like all human beings are capable of making mistakes. Just as we have much to learn from their successes, so too can we learn from their failures.

Archaeologist Ann Kendall is doing just this in the Patacancha Valley in the Andes Mountains of southern Peru. Kendall is director and founder of the Cusichaca Trust, near Oxford, England, a rural development organization that revives ancient farming practices. In the late 1980s, after working for ten years on archaeological excavations and rural development projects, she invited botanist Alex Chepstow-Lusty of Cambridge University to investigate climatic change and paleoecological data. His findings, along with Kendall's, provided evidence of intensive farming in the Patacancha Valley, beginning about 4,000 years ago. The research showed that over time

widespread clearing to establish and maintain farm plots, coupled with minimal terracing of the hillsides, had resulted in tremendous soil loss through erosion. By 1,900 years ago, soil degradation and a cooling climate had led to a dramatic reduction in farming. Then, about 1,000 years ago, farming was revived, this time with soil-sparing techniques.

Kendall's investigations have documented intensive irrigated-terrace construction over two periods of occupation, including Inca development of the area. It was a sophisticated system, devised to counteract erosion and achieve maximum agricultural production. The effort required workers to haul load after load of soil up from the valley floor. In addition, they planted alder trees to stabilize the soil and to provide both firewood and building materials.

So successful was this farming system by Inca times that the number of people living in the valley quadrupled to some 4,000, about the same as it is now. However, yet another reversal of fortune occurred when the Spanish took over Peru, and the terraces and trees here and elsewhere were allowed to deteriorate.

Armed with these research findings and information and insights gathered through interviews and meetings with locals, the Cusichaca Trust supported

the restoration of the terraces and 5.8 kilometers of canal. The effort relied on local labor working with traditional methods and materials—clay (with a cactus mix to keep it moist), stone, and soil. Local families have replanted 160 hectares of the renovated pre-conquest terraces with maize, potatoes, and wheat, and the plots are up to ten times more productive than they were.

Among other related accomplishments, twenty-one water systems have been installed, which reach more than 800 large families, and a traditional concept of home-based gardens has been adapted to introduce European-style vegetable gardens to improve diet and health and to facilitate market gardening. Since 1997, these projects have been under an independent local rural development organization known as ADESA.

The Cusichaca Trust has continued its pioneering work in areas of extreme poverty in Peru farther to the north, such as Apurimac and Ayacucho, using tried and tested traditional technology in the restoration of ancient canal and terrace systems.

For more background and current information, see Krajick, K. (1998). Greenfarming by the Incas? Science 281, 323; *and www. cusichaca.org.*

Mixed Farming: Crop Growing and Animal Breeding

As noted previously, indigenous food-producing cultures in the western hemisphere depended primarily on growing domesticated indigenous crops such as manioc, corn, and beans. With some exceptions—including the Aymara and Quechua, who traditionally also keep llamas and alpacas in their high-altitude homeland in the Andes Mountains of South America (see the Biocultural Connection)—American Indians obtained sufficient meat, fat, leather, and wool from wild game.

In contrast, Eurasian and African food-producing peoples often do not have an opportunity to obtain enough vitally important animal proteins from wild game, fish, or fowl. Many have developed a mixed subsistence strategy that combines crop cultivation with raising animals for food, labor, or trade.

Depending on cultural traditions, ecological circumstances, and animal habits, some species are kept in barns or fenced-off fields, whereas others may range freely in and around the settlement or designated pastures, albeit under supervision, branded or otherwise marked by their owners as private property. For instance, in some English farming communities (not unlike Papua villages in New Guinea) historically it was not unusual to find earmarked pigs freely roaming in the surrounding woodlands in search of acorns and any other food appealing to their omnivorous appetite.

Likewise, many ancient agricultural communities adapted to mountainous environments from the Alps to the Himalayas have traditionally herded livestock (cows, sheep, horses, and so on) in high summer pastures, leaving their narrow lowland valleys for alternative use—farming grains, keeping orchards, and growing vegetables and hay to feed animals in the winter. After the crop harvest, before the weather turns cold and snow covers the higher pastures, those who left the village to tend the herds bring the animals back to the valley and settle in for the winter season. **Figure 17.8** illustrates a contemporary instance of this "vertical" seasonal movement of herders and their livestock between high-altitude summer pastures and lowland valleys; this is an example of *transhumance* (*trans* means "across"; *humus* means "earth") (Cole & Wolf, 1999; see also Jones, 2005).

In contrast to transhumance, in which a number of men from the village annually move with their herds to seasonal pastures while other community members remain home in the settlement, there are also cultures in which the entire community migrates with the herds to their alternate grazing grounds—as described in the next section.

Herding Grazing Animals: Pastoralism

One of the more striking examples of human adaptation to the environment is **pastoralism**—breeding and managing large herds of domesticated herbivores (grazing and browsing animals), such as goats, sheep, cattle, horses, llamas, or camels. Unlike the forms of animal husbandry discussed previously, pastoralism is a specialized way of life centered on breeding and herding animals.

Figure 17.8 Transhumance Festival, Saint-Rémy-de-Provence, France At the end of spring, Saint-Rémy farmers drive their sheep from their nearby winter grazing grounds in the low hills of the Alpilles to the more distant high-altitude summer pastures in the Alps. Marking the move with a festival rich with tradition, the community gathers as shepherds parade several thousand sheep through the town.

Photograph by Guy Butters, guybutters.com

Dependent on livestock for daily survival, families in pastoral cultures own herds of grazing animals whose need for food and drink determines their everyday routines. When a dozen or more herding families join together, their collective herds may number in the thousands and sometimes even a few hundred thousand. Unlike crop cultivators who need to remain close to their fields, pastoral peoples do not usually establish permanent settlements because they must follow or drive their large herds to new pastures on a regular basis. Like their herds, most pastoralists must be mobile and have adjusted their way of life accordingly.

In environments that are too dry, cold, steep, or rocky for farming, nomadic pastoralism is an effective way of living, far more so than sheep or cattle ranching. One example of an environment that fits this description is the vast, arid grassland region that stretches eastward from North Africa through the Arabian Desert, across the plateau of Iran and into Turkistan and Mongolia. Today, in Africa and Asia alone, more than 21 million people are pastoralists, still migrating with their herds. These nomadic groups regard movement as a natural part of life.

Case Study: Bakhtiari Herders in the Zagros Mountains

Counted among the world's pastoral groups are the Bakhtiari, a fiercely independent people with a way of life uniquely adapted to the seasonal fluctuations of the unforgiving Zagros Mountains of western Iran (Barth, 1962; Coon, 1958; Salzman, 1967). For many thousands of years, Bakhtiari life has revolved around the seasonal migrations needed to provide good grazing lands for herds of goats and fat-tailed sheep—hazardous journeys as long as 200 miles, over mountains as high as 12,000 feet, and through deep chasms and churning watercourses.

Each fall, before the harsh winter comes to the mountains, these nomads load their tents and other belongings on donkeys and drive their flocks down to the warm plains that border western Iraq. Here the grazing land is excellent and well watered during the winter months. In the spring, when the low-lying pastures dry up, they return to the mountain valleys, where a new crop of grass is sprouting. For this trek, they split into five groups, each composed of some 5,000 individuals and 50,000 animals.

The return trip north is especially dangerous because the mountain snows are melting, and the gorges are full of turbulent, ice-cold water rushing down from the mountain peaks. This long trek is further burdened by the newborn spring lambs and goat kids. Where the watercourses are not very deep, the nomads ford them. The Bakhtiari cross deep channels, including one river that is a half-mile wide, with the help of inflatable goatskin rafts, on which they place infants and elderly or infirm family members, as well as lambs and kids. Men swim alongside the rafts, pushing them through the icy water. If they work from dawn to dusk, the nomads can get all of the people and animals across the river in five days. Dozens of animals drown each day.

In the mountain passes, where a biting wind numbs the skin and brings tears to the eyes, the Bakhtiari trek a rugged slippery trail. Climbing the steep escarpments is dangerous, and often the stronger men must carry their children and the baby goats on their shoulders as they make their way over the ice and snow to the lush mountain valley that is their destination.

The journey is familiar but not predictable. It can take weeks because the flocks travel slowly and need constant attention. Men and older boys walk the route, driving the sheep and goats as they go. Women and children usually ride atop donkeys, along with the tents and other equipment (**Figure 17.9**).

Reaching their destination, the Bakhtiari set up tents—traditionally cloth shelters woven by the women. The tents are a fine example of adaptation to a changing environment. Made of black goat-hair, they retain heat and repel water during the winter and keep out heat during the summer. These portable homes are easy to erect, take down, and transport. Inside, the furnishings are sparse and functional, but also artful. Heavy felt pads or elaborate wool rugs, also woven by the women, cover the ground, and pressed against the inside walls of the tent are stacks of blankets, goatskin containers, copper utensils, clay jugs, and bags of grain.

Central to Bakhtiari subsistence, sheep and goats provide milk, cheese, butter, meat, hides, and wool. Women and girls spend considerable time spinning wool into yarn—sometimes doing so while riding atop donkeys on the less difficult parts of their migration. They use the yarn to make not only rugs and tents, but also clothing, storage bags, and other essentials. With men owning and controlling the animals, which are of primary importance in Bakhtiari life, women generally have less economic and political power than their fathers, brothers, or husbands, but they are by no means without influence.

---

pastoralism The breeding and managing of migratory herds of domesticated grazing animals, such as goats, sheep, cattle, llamas, and camels.

Figure 17.9 Bakhtiari Pastoralists In the Zagros Mountains region of Iran, pastoral nomads follow seasonal pastures, migrating vast distances with their huge herds of goats and sheep over rugged terrain that includes perilously steep, snowy passes and fast ice-cold rivers.

The Bakhtiari live in the political state of Iran but have their own traditional system of justice, including laws and a penal code. They are governed by tribal leaders, or *khans*, men who are elected or inherit their office. Most Bakhtiari *khans* grew wealthy when oil was discovered in their homeland around the start of the 20th century, and many of them are well educated, having attended Iranian or foreign universities.

Despite this, and although some of them own houses in cities, the *khans* spend much of their lives among their people in the mountains. Such prominence of men in both economic and political affairs is common among pastoral nomads; theirs is very much a man's world. That said, elderly Bakhtiari women eventually may gain a good deal of power. And some women of all ages today are gaining a measure of economic control by selling their beautiful handmade rugs to traders, which brings in cash to their households.

Although pastoral nomads like the Bakhtiari depend on their herds to meet their basic daily needs, they also trade surplus animals, leather, and wool (and various crafts such as woven rugs) with farmers or merchants. In exchange they receive crops and valued commodities such as flour, dried fruit, spices, tea, metal knives, pots and

kettles, cotton or linen textiles, guns, and (more recently) lightweight plastic containers, sheets, and so on. In other words, there are many ties that connect them to surrounding agricultural and industrial societies.

Intensive Agriculture: Urbanization and Peasantry

With the intensification of agriculture, some farming settlements grew into towns and even cities (**Figure 17.10**). Urbanization created greater complexity—labor specialization, the formation of elite groups, public management, taxation, and policing. For food and fuel, urbanized populations depended on what was produced or foraged in surrounding areas. Thus, the urban ruling class sought to widen its territorial power and political control over rural populations.

Once a powerful group managed to dominate a community of farmers, it also imposed its rules—forcing them to work harder and obliging them to make payments in farm produce or labor services as fees for land use and protection and/or as acknowledgment of submission. Burdened by taxes to feed those repressing them, these farmers were left with little for their own families and lost their independence. Subjected to an ever-more dominant group, they became **peasants**. These small-scale producers

peasant A small-scale producer of crops or livestock living on land self-owned or rented in exchange for labor, crops, or money and exploited by more powerful groups in a complex society.

Figure 17.10 **Locations of Major Early Civilizations** The Native civilizations of the western hemisphere developed wholly independently of those in Africa and Eurasia. Chinese civilizations may have developed independently of those that arose early in Mesopotamia, the Nile Valley, and the Indus Valley.

of crops or livestock live on land self-owned or rented in exchange for labor, crops, or money and are usually exploited by more powerful groups in a complex society (Wolf, 1966).

And so it continues in many parts of the world today. No matter how hard they work, peasants typically possess too little land of their own to go beyond meeting the most basic needs of their families. Unable to produce enough of a surplus to sell for cash, they rarely have capital to buy the laborsaving equipment that could increase their production. Most peasants remain stuck in poverty, struggling to make ends meet. Meanwhile, big landowners and wealthy merchants have the means to expand their holdings and to invest in new machinery that leads to increased productivity and profitability.

Industrial Food Production

Until about 200 years ago, human societies all across the world had developed cultural infrastructures based on foraging, horticulture, agriculture, or pastoralism. This changed with the invention of the steam engine in England, which brought about an industrial revolution that quickly spread to other parts of the globe. Replacing animal and human labor, as well as hand tools, new machines were invented, first powered by steam, then by biofuels (coal, gas, oil), sharply increasing factory production and boosting mass transportation. Throughout the 1800s and 1900s, this resulted in large-scale **industrial societies**. Technological inventions utilizing electricity and (since the 1940s) nuclear energy brought about more dramatic changes in social and economic organization on a worldwide scale.

Modern industrial technologies have transformed food production. In contrast to traditional farms and plantations, which historically depended on human labor (often forced) and on animal power in many places, modern agriculture depends on newly invented laborsaving

devices such as tractors, combines, milk machines, and so on. With large machines plowing, seeding, weeding, mowing, and harvesting crops, the need for farmhands and other rural workers is sharply diminished. This has also happened with livestock—in particular, hogs, cattle, and poultry.

Industrial food production may be defined as large-scale businesses involved in mass food production, processing, and marketing that primarily rely on laborsaving machines. It has had far-reaching economic, social, and political consequences, not all of which are readily recognized as related and intertwined. Today, large food-producing corporations own enormous tracts of land on which they mass-produce tons of mechanically harvested crops or raise huge numbers of meat animals. Crops and animals alike are harvested, processed, packed, and shipped with ever-greater efficiency to supermarkets to feed largely urban masses. Profits are considerable, especially for corporate owners and shareholders.

Although meat, poultry, and other agricultural products are relatively cheap and thus affordable, industrial food production by agribusiness has often been a disaster for millions of peasants and small farmers. Even medium-sized farms growing corn, wheat, or potatoes or raising cows, hogs, and chickens can rarely compete without government subsidies. For that reason, the number of family-owned farms in western Europe and North America has dramatically declined in the past few decades. This process has led to huge drops in many rural populations, decimating many farming communities.

For the family farms that have managed to survive, there is seldom enough income to cover the costs of a large household, including education, health care, farm and household insurance, and taxes. This situation forces individuals to seek money-earning opportunities elsewhere, often far away. Ironically, some hire on as cheap wage laborers in poultry- or meat-packing plants where working conditions are distasteful and often dangerous.

Maximizing profits, agribusinesses are constantly streamlining food production and seeking ways to reduce labor costs by trimming the number of workers, minimizing employee benefits, and driving down wages. Pushing for market expansion beyond regional or even national boundaries, the largest among them have gone global. In the United States, for example, the poultry industry, which requires vast quantities of corn and soy to feed the fast-growing roosters known as "broilers," now has

industrial society A society in which human labor, hand tools, and animal power are largely replaced by machines, with an economy primarily based on big factories.

industrial food production Large-scale businesses involved in mass food production, processing, and marketing, which primarily rely on labor-saving machines.

Figure 17.11 Chicken Harvester Chickens ready for butchering are usually grabbed by their feet, stuffed in crates, and trucked off to the slaughterhouse. But some farmers use mechanical harvesters. Moving through a chicken barn, a harvester can pick up about 200 birds in 30 seconds. Once full, it places the birds in holding containers. From there, the chickens are mechanically transferred to a packing unit, which automatically counts them and places them into drawers that are stacked, loaded onto a truck, and transported to a processing plant. There the chickens are mass-killed, cut up, and packaged.

© Anglia Autoflow Ltd.

a worldwide market in addition to growing domestic demand.

During the past half century, per capita consumption of chicken in the United States has increased tenfold to about 85 pounds per year. Considerably cheaper than pork or beef, it now represents nearly half of all meat eaten. Even so, U.S. consumption does not begin to match U.S. production, given that the United States is the world's largest producer of chicken meat—some 36 billion pounds per year.

Most large-scale poultry farmers raise these broilers in enclosed "chicken houses." Each building is big enough to hold about 23,000 birds until they reach the butchering size (about 5 or 6 pounds), which takes just seven weeks (Figure 17.11). Chicken farms are located primarily in the southeastern states where there is ready access to corn and soy feed. The country's biggest broiler processing plant, located in Carthage, Mississippi, and owned by Tyson Foods, is capable of slaughtering almost 2.5 million chickens per week.

The $55 billion U.S. poultry business exports billions of tons of chicken annually to dozens of countries around the world. Nearly a quarter of its frozen chicken meat goes to Russia (over 900,000 tons composed of more than a billion chicken legs). Another 400,000 tons go to China (primarily chicken feet, more than 1.2 billion of them). See this chapter's Globalscape for more about chicken farming.

Today's industrial food production and global marketing complex, involving a network of interlinked distribution centers, is made possible by an electronic-digital revolution that began in the late 20th century and that continues today primarily in parts of North America, western Europe, Japan, and a few other wealthy countries. The economies of these regions are increasingly based on the research and development of knowledge and technologies, as well as on providing information, services, and finance capital on a global scale (Ritzer, 2007).

New subsistence strategies over the past few centuries that use technological inventions to more effectively harness energy are commonly valued as progress. Yet, as discussed in this chapter, not all innovations turn out to be positive in the long run, nor do they improve the quality of life for every member of a society even in the short run.

A few thousand generations ago, our anatomically modern human ancestors emerged in Africa. They multiplied and dispersed, ultimately occupying every continent on earth. Adjusting as they went, each of these migrating groups developed its own cultural repertoire of ideas and practices to secure food, fuel, and safety for themselves and their offspring. Measured in terms of population growth, geographic expansion, and technological know-how, *Homo sapiens* has been enormously successful in adapting itself to a wide range of different natural environments and developing the means required to satisfy its needs. As long as the collective needs of a population remain within its means, the group can be said to enjoy a degree of relative abundance or affluence. However, when the needs of a group exceed the available means, the group will face shortages or scarcity.

Globalscape

AP Images/J. Scott Applewhite

© Bill Ling/Getty Images

Chicken Out: Bush's Legs or Phoenix Talons?

Every evening in Moscow, Russians can be found enjoying a traditional dinner that may begin with *borscht* (beet soup) and *smetana* (sour cream), followed by a main course of *kotleta po-kievski* (boneless fried chicken breast)—or, if the budget is a bit tight, *nozhki busha* (chicken legs), baked, fried, or roasted—served with cabbage and potatoes.

Foreign visitors may recognize the breast entrée as chicken Kiev but may be baffled to learn that the specialty *nozhki busha* translates as "Bush's legs." That is because these big meaty legs are imported from the United States and first appeared on Russian menus when the Soviet Union collapsed in 1991, during George W. Bush's presidency (1989–1993). At the time, the Russian economy was dismal, and few people could afford beef or pork. Even chicken legs were too expensive for ordinary Russians. To help the transition to a capitalist democracy, the U.S. government promoted the advantages of free markets and global trade. What better propaganda than cheap chicken—especially because the American preference for white meat resulted in a surplus of the dark-meat legs. And

so it was that the U.S. poultry industry entered the Russian market. Today, Russia imports more U.S. chicken than it produces on its own farms, especially legs—over a billion!

What happens with a typical 6-pound broiler chicken butchered by a Mexican immigrant working for minimum wage in a Mississippi poultry plant? As we have seen, its legs are served up in Moscow, and its breasts end up on U.S. dining tables or on the menus of international airlines. And the rest of the bird? One of its frozen wings goes into a giant container shipped to Korea; the other to West Africa. The offal (neck, heart, liver, and guts) is transported to Jamaica, where it is boiled and dished up in soup. The excess fat gets converted into biodiesel fuel at an experimental refinery in Texas. And what about its cute yellow feet? They are exported to Shanghai, deep-fried, stewed, and served up as a delicacy called *fèngzhuâ*, or Phoenix talons, last seen being nibbled on by a visiting New York banker.

Global Twister

What happens to the feathers?

Because abundance and shortage are based on the relationship between means and needs, affluence and scarcity are relative concepts. And for that reason, anthropologists tend to be cautious about the uncritical use of the term *progress* as applied to economic development. Although there is no question that millions of people do enjoy a life of health and abundance, perhaps more so than their own ancestors, a few billion must work harder and longer hours to put food on the table, and many hundreds of millions more live in poverty, are malnourished, and die too young. For them, the notion of human progress does not match their reality.

CHAPTER CHECKLIST

What are cultural adaptation and cultural evolution?

● Cultural adaptation is the complex of ideas, activities, and technologies that enable people to survive in a certain environment and in turn to impact the environment.

● Adaptation includes both organisms and their environment; an ecosystem is a functioning whole composed of the natural environment and all the organisms living in it.

● Cultural evolution—the changing of cultures over time—should not be confused with the idea of progress—the notion that humans are moving forward to a better, more advanced stage in their development toward perfection.

● Easter Island is a tragic example of catastrophic environmental destruction.

● Convergent evolution is the development of similar cultural adaptations to similar environmental conditions by different peoples with different ancestral cultures. Parallel evolution is the same phenomenon, but it emerges with peoples whose ancestral cultures were already similar.

What are the major subsistence strategies and the characteristics of the societies that practice them?

● The oldest and most universal mode of subsistence or adaptation among humans is food foraging. It requires people to move their residence according to changing food sources. Local group size is kept small, possibly because small numbers fit the land's capacity to sustain the group.

● A habitat rich in natural resources can sustain more people than marginal lands that are home to the world's few surviving foragers. Another characteristic of food-foraging societies is egalitarianism.

● The shift from food foraging to food production, known as the Neolithic revolution, began about 10,000 years ago.

● Horticulture is the cultivation of crops in gardens using simple hand tools. A common horticulture practice is slash-and-burn cultivation in which the natural vegetation is cut, the slash is burned, and crops are planted among the ashes.

● Agriculture, a more complex activity, involves growing crops on farms with irrigation, fertilizers, and/or animal-powered plows. Crop-producing societies led to fixed settlements, new technologies, and altered division of labor.

● Mixed farming involves a combination of crop growing and animal breeding; it may occur in mountainous environments where farmers practice transhumance, moving their livestock between high-altitude summer pastures and lowland valleys.

● Pastoralism is a subsistence mode that relies on breeding and managing large herds of domesticated herbivores, such as cattle, sheep, and goats. Pastoralists are usually nomadic, moving as needed to provide animals with pasture and water.

● Intensive agriculture led to urbanization and peasantry. Farm settlements grew into towns and cities, and social complexity expanded to include labor specialization, elite classes, public management, taxation, and policing.

● Industrial food production features large-scale businesses involved in mass food production, processing, and marketing, and relying on laborsaving machines. It is rooted in the industrial revolution, which began 200 years ago with the invention of the steam engine. Human labor, animal power, and hand tools replaced machines and resulted in massive cultural change in many societies.

● Today's industrial food production and global marketing complex, involving a network of interlinked distribution centers, are made possible by an electronic-digital revolution that began in the late 20th century.

QUESTIONS FOR REFLECTION

1. In capturing essential natural resources, humans often modify their environments. Have you seen any examples of landscapes radically transformed for economic reasons? Who do you think benefits or loses most?

2. What was so radical about the domestication of plants and animals that led to it being referred to as the Neolithic *revolution*? Can you think of any equally radical changes in subsistence practices going on in the world today?

3. Consider the ideas of change and progress in light of the agricultural development project described in the Anthropology Applied feature. Come up with your own definition of *progress* that goes beyond the standard idea of technological and material advancement.

4. Technological development in industrial societies often results in highly productive machines effectively replacing animal and human workers. Think of a useful mechanical device and consider its benefits and costs, not only to you but also to others.

5. When buying a chicken breast sandwich in a deli, try to imagine where the food that fed your particular bird was cultivated; where the chicken was cooped up; how, where, and by whom it was slaughtered and packaged. And finally, while enjoying that breast stuck between slices of bread, ask yourself who might be chewing on the bird's feet somewhere on the other side of the world.

ONLINE STUDY RESOURCES

CourseMate

Access chapter-specific learning tools, including learning objectives, practice quizzes, videos, flash cards, glossaries, and more in your Anthropology CourseMate.

Log into **www.cengagebrain.com** to access the resources your instructor has assigned and to purchase materials.

Challenge Issue

All humans face the challenge of securing resources needed for immediate and long-term survival. Whatever we lack, we may seek to get through exchange or trade. In today's capitalist societies, people can exchange almost anything of value without ever actually meeting in person. But the market in traditional societies is a real location where people personally meet to exchange goods at designated times. So it is at this market just outside Keren, a mountain city in Eritrea, a small country in northeastern Africa. Situated at a crossroads between the Red Sea and the vast desert in the interior, this strategically important city is an agricultural center surrounded by small farms. On Mondays, people gather here to purchase and peddle everything from spices and household utensils to fruits, vegetables, firewood, and roofing materials. On the outer edge of this sprawling market, turbaned farmers of the local Bilen tribe trade with nomadic herders of the region's Tigre tribe, buying or selling camels, cattle, sheep, goats, and mules. All around the world, at marketplaces like this one, people from different places forge and affirm social networks of friends, neighbors, and allies needed for their safety and well-being.

Economic Systems

18

An **economic system** is an organized arrangement for producing, distributing, and consuming goods. Because people, in pursuing a particular means of subsistence, necessarily produce, distribute, and consume things, our discussion of subsistence patterns in the previous chapter obviously involved economic matters. Yet economic systems encompass much more than we have covered so far.

Economic Anthropology

Although anthropologists have adopted theories and concepts from economists, theoretical principles derived from the study of capitalist market economies have limited applicability to economic systems in societies that are not industrialized and in which people do not produce and exchange goods for private profit. This is because, in these non-state societies, the economic sphere of behavior is not separate from the social, political, and religious spheres, and thus is not completely free to follow its own purely economic logic.

Although economic behavior and institutions can be analyzed in strictly economic terms, doing so ignores the crucial noneconomic considerations that impact the way things are in real life. To explain how the schedule of wants or demands of a given society is balanced against the supply of goods and services available, anthropologists introduce a noneconomic variable: culture. As a case in point, we may look briefly at yam production among the Trobriand Islanders, who inhabit a group of coral islands that lie in the southern Pacific Ocean off the eastern tip of New Guinea (Weiner, 1988).

Case Study: The Yam Complex in Trobriand Culture

Trobriand men spend a great deal of their time and energy raising yams—not for themselves or their own households, but to give to

economic system An organized arrangement for producing, distributing, and consuming goods.

- Explain why the anthropological variable of culture is important in understanding noncapitalist economies.

- Distinguish various economic arrangements for producing, distributing, and consuming goods.

- Compare forms of gift exchange, redistribution, and trade.

- Analyze how leveling mechanisms actually work in different cultures.

- Describe the role of money in market economies.

- Summarize the impact of global markets on local communities.

others, normally their sisters and married daughters. The purpose of cultivating these starchy edible roots is not to provision the households that receive them because most of what people eat they grow for themselves in gardens where they plant taro, sweet potatoes, tapioca, greens, beans, and squash, as well as breadfruit and banana trees. The reason a man gives yams to a woman is to show his support for her husband and to enhance his own influence.

Once received by the woman, the gift yams are loaded into her husband's yam house, symbolizing his worth as a man of power and influence in his community (**Figure 18.1**). He may use some of these yams to purchase a variety of things, including arm shells, shell necklaces and earrings, betel nuts, pigs, chickens, and locally produced goods such as wooden bowls, combs, floor mats, lime pots, and even magic spells. He may use some yams to fulfill social obligations. For instance, a man is expected to present yams to the relatives of his daughter's husband when she marries and again when death befalls a member of the husband's family.

Finally, any man who aspires to high status and power is expected to show his worth by organizing a yam competition, during which he gives away huge quantities of yams to invited guests. As anthropologist Annette Weiner explains: "A yam house, then, is like a bank account; when full, a man is wealthy and powerful. Until yams are cooked or they rot, they may circulate as limited currency. That is why, once harvested, the usage of yams for daily food is avoided as much as possible" (Weiner, 1988, p. 86).

By giving yams to his sister or daughter, a man not only expresses his confidence in the woman's husband, but also makes the latter indebted to him. Although the recipient rewards the gardener and his helpers by throwing a feast, at which they are fed cooked yams, taro, and—what everyone especially looks forward to—ample pieces of pork, this in no way pays off the debt. The debt can be repaid only in women's wealth, which consists of bundles of banana leaves and skirts made of the same material dyed red.

Although the banana leaf bundles are of no utilitarian value, extensive labor is invested in their production, and large quantities of them, along with skirts, are regarded as essential for paying off all the members of other family

Figure 18.1 **A Trobriand Yam Storage House** Trobriand Island men devote a great deal of time and energy to raising yams, not for themselves but to give to others. These yams, which have been raised by men related through marriage to a chief, are about to be loaded into the chief's yam house.

groups who were close to a recently deceased relative in life and who assisted with the funeral. Also, the wealth and vitality of the dead person's family group are measured by the quality and quantity of the bundles and skirts so distributed.

Because a man has received yams from his wife's brother, he is obligated to provide his wife with yams for purchasing the necessary bundles and skirts, beyond those she has produced, to help with payments following the death of a member of her family. Because deaths are unpredictable and can occur at any time, a man must have yams available for his wife when she needs them. This, and the fact that she may require all of his yams, acts as an effective check on a man's wealth.

Like people the world over, the Trobriand Islanders assign meanings to objects that make those objects worth far more than their cost in labor or materials. Yams, for example, establish long-term relationships that lead to other advantages, such as access to land, protection, assistance, and other kinds of wealth.

Thus, yam exchanges are as much social and political transactions as they are economic ones. Banana leaf bundles and skirts, for their part, are symbolic of the political status of families and of their immortality. In their distribution, which is related to rituals associated with death, we see how men in Trobriand society are ultimately dependent on women and their valuables. Looked at in terms of modern capitalist economics, these activities appear meaningless, but viewed in terms of traditional Trobriand values and concerns, they make a great deal of sense.

Production and Its Resources

In every society, particular customs and rules govern the kinds of work done, who does the work, attitudes toward the work, how it is accomplished, and who controls the resources necessary to produce desired goods, knowledge, and services. The primary resources in any culture are raw materials, technology, and labor. The rules directing the use of these are embedded in a people's culture and determine the way the economy operates within any given natural environment.

Land and Water Resources

All societies regulate allocation of valuable natural resources—especially land and water. Food foragers must determine who will hunt game and gather plants in their home range and where these activities take place. Groups that rely on fishing or growing crops need to make similar decisions concerning who will carry out which task on which stretch of water or land. Farmers must have some means of determining title to land and access to water supplies for irrigation. Pastoralists require a system that determines rights to watering places and grazing land, as well as the right of access to land where they move their herds.

In Western capitalist societies, a system of private ownership of land and rights to natural resources generally prevails. Although elaborate laws have been enacted to regulate the buying, owning, and selling of land and water resources, if individuals wish to reallocate

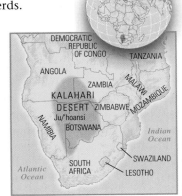

valuable farmland to some other purpose, for instance, they generally can.

In traditional nonindustrial societies, land is often controlled by kinship groups such as the family or band rather than by individuals. For example, among the Ju/'hoansi of the Kalahari Desert, each band of ten to thirty people lives on roughly 250 square miles of land, which they consider to be their territory—their own country. These territories are not defined by boundaries but in terms of waterholes that are located within them (**Figure 18.2**). The land is said to be owned by those who have lived the longest in the band, usually a group of brothers and sisters or cousins. Their concept of landholding, however, is not something easily translated into modern Western terms of private ownership. Within their traditional worldview, no part of their homeland can be sold for money or traded away for goods. Outsiders must ask permission to enter the territory, but denying the request would be unthinkable.

Territorial boundaries tend to be vaguely defined, and to avoid friction foragers may designate part of their territory as a buffer zone between them and their neighbors. The adaptive value of such a "no man's land" is obvious: The size of band territories, as well as the size of the bands, can adjust to keep in balance with availability of resources in any given place. Such adjustment would be more difficult under a system of individual ownership of clearly bounded land.

Among some African and Asian rural societies, a tributary system of land ownership prevails. All land is said to belong to the head chief, who allocates it to various subchiefs, who in turn distribute it to family groups. Then the family group leaders assign individual plots to each farmer. Just as in traditional Europe, these men owe allegiance to the subchiefs (or nobles) and the head chief (or king). The people who work the land must pay tribute (like rent or taxes) in the form of products or special services, such as fighting for the king when necessary.

These people do not really own the land; rather, it is a kind of lease. Yet, as long as the land is kept in use, rights to such use will pass to their heirs. No user, however, can give away, sell, or otherwise dispose of a plot of land without approval from the elder of the family group. When an individual no longer uses the allocated land, it reverts to the head of the large family group, who reallocates it to some other group member. The important operative principle here is that the system extends the individual's right to use land for an indefinite period, but the land is not "owned" outright. This serves to maintain the integrity of valuable farmland as such, preventing its loss through subdivision and conversion to other uses.

Technology Resources

All societies have some means of creating and allocating tools that are used to produce goods, as well as traditions for passing them on to succeeding generations. A society's

Figure 18.2 Core Features as Territory Markers Food foragers, like the Ju/'hoansi of the Kalahari Desert in southern Africa, define their territories on the basis of core features such as waterholes.

technology—the number and types of tools employed, combined with knowledge about how to make and use them—is directly related to the lifestyles of its members. Food foragers and pastoral nomads who are frequently on the move are apt to have fewer and more portable tools than more settled peoples such as sedentary farmers. Thus, the average weight of an individual's personal belongings among the Ju/'hoansi is just under 25 pounds, limited to the barest essentials such as implements for hunting, gathering, fishing, building, and cooking. Pastoral nomads, aided by pack animals, typically have more material possessions than foragers, but still fewer than people who live in permanent settlements.

Food foragers make and use a variety of tools, many ingenious in their effectiveness. Some of these they make for their individual use, but codes of generosity are such that a person may not refuse to give or loan what is requested. Tools may be given or loaned to others in exchange for the products resulting from their use. For example, a Ju/'hoansi who gives his arrows to another hunter has a right to a share of any animals the hunter kills. Game is considered to belong to the man whose arrow killed it, even when he is not present on the hunt. In this context, it makes little sense for them to accumulate luxuries or surplus goods, and the fact that no one owns significantly more than another helps to limit status differences.

Among horticulturalists, the axe, digging stick, hoe, and containers are important tools. The person who makes a tool has first rights to it, but when he or she is not using it, any family member may ask to use it, and the request is rarely denied. Refusal would cause people to treat the tool owner with scorn for this singular lack of concern for others. If a relative helps raise the crop traded for a particular tool, that relative becomes part owner of the implement, and it may not be traded or given away without his or her permission.

In permanently settled agricultural communities, tools and other productive goods are more complex, heavier, and costlier to make. In such settings, individual ownership tends to be more absolute, as are the conditions under which people may borrow and use such equipment. It is

technology Tools and other material equipment, together with the knowledge of how to make and use them.

easy to replace a knife lost by a relative during palm cultivation but much more difficult to replace an iron plow or a diesel-fueled harvesting machine. Rights to the ownership of complex tools are more rigidly applied; generally, the person who has manufactured or purchased such equipment is considered the sole owner and decides who may use it and under which conditions, including compensation.

Labor Resources and Patterns

In addition to raw materials and technology, labor is a key resource in any economic system. A look around the world reveals many different labor patterns, but two features are almost always present in human cultures: a basic division of labor by gender and by age.

Division of Labor by Gender

Anthropologists have studied extensively the social division of labor by gender in cultures of all sorts. Whether men or women do a particular job varies from group to group, but typically work has been and often continues to be divided into the tasks of either one or the other. For example, the practices most commonly regarded as women's work have tended to be those that can be carried out near home and that are easily resumed after interruption. The tasks historically regarded as men's work have tended to be those requiring physical strength, rapid mobilization of high bursts of energy, frequent travel at some distance from home, and assumption of high levels of risk and danger.

Figure 18.3 **Women's Work?** These Hmong women in Vietnam are carrying heavy firewood, even though this work may be considered inappropriate for women in some cultures. For villagers living in the rural areas of developing countries all around the world, firewood is used as a source of energy for preparing meals—and women are usually the ones who collect and haul it.

Many exceptions occur, however, as in societies where women regularly carry burdensome loads or put in long hours of hard work cultivating crops in the fields (**Figure 18.3**). In some societies, women perform almost three-fourths of all work, and in several societies they have served as warriors. For example, in the 19th-century West African kingdom of Dahomey (now called Benin), thousands of women served in the armed forces of the Dahomean king, and some considered the women to be better fighters than their male counterparts. Also, there are references to female warriors in ancient Ireland,

and archaeological evidence indicates their presence among Vikings.

During World War II in the early 1940s, some 58,000 Soviet Russian women engaged in frontline combat defending their homeland against German invaders, and during the Vietnam War in the 1960s and early 1970s, North Vietnamese women fought in mixed-gender communist army units. Today, women serve in the military of most countries, but only Canada, Denmark, France, Germany, and a few others permit them to join combat units.

Instead of looking for key biological factors to explain the social division of labor, a more useful strategy is to examine the kinds of work that men and women do in the context of specific societies to see how they relate to other cultural and historical factors. Researchers find a continuum of patterns, ranging from flexible integration of men and women to rigid segregation by gender (Sanday, 1981).

The *flexible/integrated pattern* is exemplified by the Ju/'hoansi we just discussed and is seen most often among food foragers (as well as in communities in which crops are traditionally cultivated primarily for family consumption). In such societies, men and women perform up to 35 percent of activities with approximately equal participation, and tasks deemed especially appropriate for one gender may be performed by the other without loss of face, as the situation warrants. Where these practices prevail, boys and girls grow up in much the same way, learn to value cooperation over competition, and become equally habituated to adult men and women, who interact with one another on a relatively equal basis.

Societies following a *segregated pattern* define almost all work as either masculine or feminine, so men and women rarely engage in joint efforts of any kind. In such societies, it is inconceivable that someone would even think of doing something considered the work of the opposite sex. This pattern is frequently seen in pastoral nomadic, intensive agricultural, and industrial societies, where men's work keeps them outside the home for much of the time. Typically, men in such societies are expected to be tough, aggressive, and competitive—and this often involves assertions of male superiority, and hence authority, over women. Historically, societies segregated by gender often have imposed their control on societies featuring integration, upsetting the egalitarian nature of the latter.

In the third pattern of labor division by gender, sometimes called the *dual sex configuration*, men and women carry out their work separately, as in societies segregated by gender, but the relationship between them is one of balanced complementarity rather than inequality. Although each gender manages its own affairs, the interests of both men and women are represented at all levels. Thus, as in integrated societies, neither gender exerts dominance over the other. The pattern may be seen among certain American Indian peoples with economies based upon subsistence farming, as well as among several West African kingdoms, including that of the aforementioned Dahomeans.

In postindustrial societies, the division of labor by gender becomes blurred and even irrelevant, resembling the flexible/integrated pattern of traditional foragers briefly discussed previously. Although gender preferences and discrimination in the workplace exist in societies

making the economic transition, cultural ideas more fitting agricultural or industrial societies predictably change in due time, adjusting to postindustrial challenges and opportunities.

Division of Labor by Age

Division of labor according to age is also typical of human societies. Among the Ju/'hoansi, for example, children are not expected to contribute significantly to subsistence until they reach their late teens. Indeed, until they possess adult levels of strength and endurance, many "bush" foods are tough for them to gather. Until that point, youngsters contribute primarily by taking care of their littlest siblings while grownups deal with subsistence needs.

Although elderly Ju/'hoansi will usually do some foraging for themselves, they are not expected to contribute much food. By virtue of their advanced age, they have memories of customary practices and events that happened far in the past. Thus, they are repositories of accumulated wisdom—the libraries of a nonliterate people—and are able to suggest solutions to problems younger adults have never before had to face. Considered useful for their knowledge, they are far from being unproductive members of society.

In some food-foraging societies, women do continue to make a significant contribution to provisioning in their later years. Among the Hadza of East Africa, the input of older women is critical to their daughters when they have new infants to nurse. The energy costs of lactation, along with the tasks of holding, carrying, and nursing an infant, all encumber the mother's foraging efficiency. Those most immediately affected by this are a woman's weaned children not yet old enough to forage effectively for themselves. The problem is solved by the foraging efforts of grandmothers (Hawkes, O'Connell, & Blurton Jones, 1997).

In many traditional farming societies, children as well as older people may make a greater contribution to the economy in terms of work and responsibility than is common in industrial or postindustrial societies. In most peasant communities across the globe, children not only look after their younger brothers and sisters but also help with housework, in the barn, or in the fields. By age 7 or so, boys begin to help out, weed the fields, bring in crops, care for small animals, or catch some fish and small game. By that same age, girls begin contributing to the work of the household. Soon, they are constantly busy with an array of chores—helping prepare food, fetching wood and water, sweeping, selling goods at local markets, and so forth (Vogt, 1990).

Children also work in many industrial societies, where poor and often large families depend on every possible contribution to the household. There, however, economic necessity may easily lead to the exploitation of children as cheap labor on farms, in mines, and in factories. Child

institutionalized child labor. However, they still import vast quantities of goods available at bargain prices because they are made by poorly paid children—items ranging from rugs and carpets to clothing, toys, and soccer balls (Smith, 2008).

Cooperative Labor

Cooperative work groups can be found everywhere—in foraging as well as food-producing and in nonindustrial as well as industrial societies. Often, if the effort involves the whole community, a festive spirit permeates the work.

For example, in many rural parts of sub-Saharan Africa, work parties begin with the display of a pot of beer to be consumed after the tasks have been finished. Home-brewed from millet, their major cereal crop, the beer is not really payment for the work; indeed, the labor involved is worth far more than the beer consumed. Rather, together enjoying the low-alcohol but highly nutritious beverage is more of a symbolic activity to celebrate the spirit of friendship and mutual support. Recompense comes as individuals sooner or later participate in work parties for others. In areas all around the world, farmers traditionally help one another during harvest and haying seasons, often sharing major pieces of equipment.

In most human societies, the basic unit within which work takes place is the household. Traditionally—and still in many parts of the world—it is both a unit of production and consumption, where work as well as meals and domestic comfort are shared. In industrial societies these two economic spheres are now usually separated. This development is the result, in part, of task specialization.

Figure 18.4 **Child Labor in India** Many of the soccer balls that children play with in the United States and Europe are handstitched by children in India, most working in factories under brutal conditions for pennies a day. After past scandals about soccer ball factories using child labor, many companies started adding labels stating that the balls were not made with child labor—but those labels are often sewn on the balls by children as young as 6 years old.

Bachpan Bachao Andolan

labor has become a matter of increasing concern as large capitalist corporations rely more and more on the low-cost production of food and goods in the world's poorer countries. Today, some 215 million child laborers (under age 14) are at work, almost all in developing economies where their families depend on the extra income they bring home. Many enter the labor force when they are only 6 or 7 years old, working full-time, from dawn to dusk, for extremely low wages ("New ILO global report on child labor," 2010) (**Figure 18.4**).

Many wealthy industrialized societies in Europe and North America long ago passed laws officially prohibiting

Task Specialization

In contemporary industrial and postindustrial societies, there is a great diversity of specialized tasks to be performed, and no individual can even begin to know all of those customarily seen as fitting for his or her age and gender. However, although specialization continues to increase, modern technologies are making labor divisions based on gender less relevant. By contrast, in small-scale foraging and traditional crop-cultivating societies, in which division of labor typically occurs along lines of age and gender, each person has knowledge and competence in all aspects of work appropriate to his or her age and gender. Yet, even in these nonindustrial societies there is a measure of specialization.

An example of task specialization can be found among the Afar people of the Danakil Depression in the borderlands of Eritrea and Ethiopia, one of the lowest and hottest places on earth (Nesbitt, 1935). The desolate landscape features sulfur fields, smoking fissures, volcanic tremors, and vast salt plains. Since ancient times, groups of Afar men periodically mine the salt, hacking blocks from the plain's crust. The work is backbreaking, all the more so with temperatures soaring to 140 degrees Fahrenheit.

Along with the physical strength required for such work under the most trying conditions, successful mining demands specialized planning and organization skills for getting to and from the worksite. Pack camels have to be fed in advance because importing sufficient fodder for them interferes with their ability to carry out salt (**Figure 18.5**). Food and water, packed by Afar women at the desert's edge, must be carried in for the miners, typically numbering thirty to forty per group. Travel is arranged for nighttime to avoid the scorching sun (Mesghinna, 1966; O'Mahoney, 1970).

In the past few decades, we have seen the emergence of new forms of task specialization in an international division of labor and in response to global markets of supply and demand. Many of these specializations are linked to tourism, now one of the largest industries in the world. Estimates vary, but in 2011 the industry employed some 260 million people and generated about $6 trillion—9 percent of the total value of goods and services produced worldwide (World Travel & Tourism Council, 2012). Some communities that still hold onto a natural habitat with a wealth of plant and animal life are able to tap into a specialized niche known as *ecotourism*, as detailed in this chapter's Anthropology Applied feature.

Figure 18.5 **Task Specialization: Mining Salt in Ethiopia** Scorching hot and dry, the Danakil Desert in northeastern Africa lies some 370 feet below sea level—remains of what was once part of the Red Sea—with enormous salt flats. Afar nomads come here periodically to quarry this rock salt. Using camels, they haul the heavy slabs to the interior highlands for trade.

ANTHROPOLOGY APPLIED

Global Ecotourism and Local Indigenous Culture in Bolivia

By Amanda Stronza

We traveled in a small fleet of motorized canoes. As the sun dipped behind the trees one steamy afternoon in April 2002, we turned the last few bends of the Tuichi River and arrived at our destination, the Chalalán Ecolodge of northern Bolivia. Our group included eighteen indigenous leaders from various parts of the Amazon rainforest, a handful of regional tour operators, conservationists, environmental journalists, and me—an applied anthropologist studying the effects of ecotourism on local livelihoods, cultural traditions, and resource use. We had been navigating for nine hours through lowland rainforest to visit one of the first indigenous, community-run ecotourism lodges in the world.

As we wended our way, combing the riverbanks for caimans, capybaras, tapirs, and jaguars, our conversations meandered too. Mostly, the indigenous leaders shared stories of how ecotourism had affected their own forests and communities. They spoke of tourists who brought both opportunities and conflicts, and of their own efforts to balance conservation and development. They compared notes on wildlife in their regions, the kinds of visitors they had attracted, the profits they'd earned, the new skills they had gained, and the challenges they were facing as they sought to protect their lands and cultural traditions while

also engaging with the global tourism industry.

Having studied ecotourism in the Amazon since 1993, I felt honored to be on board participating in these discussions. With support from the Critical Ecosystem Partnership Fund, I had the opportunity that year—the International Year of Ecotourism—to assemble leaders from three indigenous ecotourism projects in South America. All three were partnerships between local communities and private tour companies or nongovernmental organizations. For example, the lodge we were visiting, Chalalán, came about through a partnership between the Quechua-Tacana community of San José de Uchupiamonas, Bolivia, and two global organizations, Conservation International and the Inter-American Development Bank. Much of the $1,450,000 invested in Chalalán went toward preparing community members to assume full ownership and management of the lodge within five years. After a successful transfer in 2001, the lodge now belonged to San José's 600-member Quechua-Tacana community.

The indigenous leaders who gathered for this trip had keen, firsthand knowledge about the costs and benefits ecotourism can bring. They were former hunters, now leading tourists as birding and wildlife guides; small farmers and artisans making traditional handicrafts to sell to visitors; river-savvy fishermen supplementing their incomes by driving tour boats; and local leaders whose intimate knowledge of their communities helped them manage their own tour companies. Among them was Chalalán's general manager Guido Mamani, who recounted the benefits Chalalán had brought to the Tacana of San José. "Ten years ago," he recalled, "people were leaving San José because there were few ways to make a living. Today, they are returning because of pride in the success of Chalalán. Now, they

see opportunity here." As a result of their renewed pride in their mix of Quechua and Tacana histories, the community has begun hosting tourists for cultural tours in San José. "We want to give tourists presentations about the community and our customs," Mamani explained, "including our legends, dances, traditional music, the coca leaves, the traditional meals. We want to show our culture through special walks focusing on medicinal and other useful plants."

Mamani and the other indigenous ecotourism leaders characterized the success of their lodges in three ways: economic, social, and environmental. Chalalán, for example, counted its economic success in terms of employment and new income. It directly employs eighteen to twenty-four people at a time, and additional families supply farm produce and native fruits to the lodge. With artisans selling handicrafts to tourists, the community has gained regional fame for its wooden carved masks. The social benefits of Chalalán include new resources for education, health care, and communication. With their profits from tourism, the community built a school, a clinic, and a potable water system. They also purchased an antenna, solar panels, and a satellite dish to connect with the world from their remote forests along the Tuichi River.

Beyond these sorts of material improvements, ecotourism has catalyzed symbolic changes for the people of San José. "We have new solidarity in our cultural traditions," one woman noted, "and now we want to show who we are to the outside world." These experiences of Chalalán and similar projects suggest that ecotourism may be more than just a conservation and development idea—it may also be a source of pride, empowerment, and strengthened cultural identity among indigenous peoples.

Written expressly for this text, 2011.

Distribution and Exchange

In societies without a money economy, the rewards for labor are usually direct. The workers in a family group consume what they harvest, eat what the hunter or gatherer brings home, and use the tools they themselves make. But even where no formal medium of exchange such as money exists, some distribution of goods takes place. Anthropologists often classify the cultural systems of distributing material goods into three modes: reciprocity, redistribution, and market exchange (Polanyi, 1968).

Reciprocity

Reciprocity refers to the exchange of goods and services, of roughly equal value, between two parties. This may involve gift giving. Notably, individuals or groups in most cultures like to think that the main point of the transaction is the gift itself, yet what actually matters are the social ties that are created or reinforced between givers and receivers. Because reciprocity is about a relationship between the self and others, gift giving is seldom really selfless. The overriding, if unconscious, motives of gift giving are to establish or reaffirm a social relationship, fulfill social obligations, and perhaps gain a bit of prestige in the process.

Cultural traditions dictate the specific manner and occasion of exchange. For example, when indigenous hunters in Australia kill a kangaroo, the meat is divided among the hunters' families and other relatives. Each person in the camp gets a particular share, the size and part depending on the nature of the person's kinship tie to the hunters.

Such obligatory sharing of food reinforces community bonds and ensures that everyone eats. By giving away part of a kill, the hunters get social credit for a similar amount of food in the future.

Reciprocity falls into several categories. The Australian food distribution example just noted constitutes an example of **generalized reciprocity**—exchange in which the value of what is given is not calculated, nor is the time of repayment specified (**Figure 18.6**). Gift giving, in the unselfish sense, also falls into this category. So, too, does the act of a kindhearted soul who stops to help a stranded motorist or someone else in distress and refuses payment with the admonition: "Pass it on to the next person in need."

Most generalized reciprocity, however, occurs among close kin or people who otherwise have very close ties with one another. Within such circles of intimacy, people give to others when they have the means and can count on receiving from others in time of need. Typically, participants will not consider such exchanges in economic terms but will couch them explicitly in terms of family and friendship social relations.

Exchanges that occur within a group of relatives or between friends generally take the form of generalized or balanced reciprocity. In **balanced reciprocity**, the giving and receiving, as well as the time involved, are quite specific: Someone has a direct obligation to reciprocate promptly in equal value in order for the social relationship to continue. Examples of balanced reciprocity in contemporary North American society include customary practices such as hosting a baby shower for young friends expecting their first baby, giving presents at birthdays and various other culturally prescribed special occasions,

Figure 18.6

Generalized Reciprocity among the Ju/'hoansi These Ju/'hoansi men are cutting up meat that will be shared by others in the camp. Food distribution practices of such food foragers are an example of generalized reciprocity.

© Stan Washburn/Anthro-Photo

and buying drinks when it is one's turn at a gathering of friends and associates.

Giving, receiving, and sharing as so far described constitute a form of social security or insurance. A family contributes to others when they have the means and can count on receiving from others in time of need.

Negative reciprocity is a third form of exchange, in which the aim is to get something for as little as possible. The parties involved have opposing interests and are not usually closely related; they may be strangers or even enemies. Often such exchanges are neither fair nor balanced, and they are not expected to be. This type of reciprocity may involve hard bargaining, manipulation, or outright cheating. An extreme form of negative reciprocity is to take something by force, although realizing that one's victim may seek compensation or retribution for losses.

Sometimes elements of negative as well as balanced reciprocity are present in an exchange. Such is often the case with political fundraising in the United States, in which big contributors expect their generosity will buy influence with a candidate, resulting in benefits of equal value. The politician may seek to do as little as possible in return, but not so little as to jeopardize future donations. Those who accept too much or who give too much in return risk legal repercussions.

Trade and Barter

Trade refers to a transaction in which two or more people are involved in an exchange of something—a quantity of food, fuel, clothing, jewelry, animals, or money, for example—for something else of equal value. In such a transaction, the value of the trade goods can be fixed by previous agreements or negotiated on the spot by the trading partners.

When there is no money involved and the parties negotiate a direct exchange of one trade good for another, the transaction is considered a *barter*. In barter, arguing about the price and terms of the deal may well be in the form of negative reciprocity, with each party aiming to get the better end of the deal. Relative value is calculated, and despite an outward show of indifference, sharp dealing is generally the rule, when compared to the more balanced nature of exchanges within a group.

One interesting mechanism for facilitating exchange between potentially adversarial groups is **silent trade** in which no verbal communication takes place. In fact, it may involve no actual face-to-face contact at all. Such cases have often characterized the dealings between food-foraging peoples and their food-producing neighbors— such as the Mbuti Pygmy of Congo's Ituri forest, who trade bushmeat for plantains and other crops grown by Bantu villagers on small farms. It works like this: People from the forest leave trade goods in a clearing, then retreat and wait. Agriculturalists come to the spot, survey the goods, leave what they think is a fair exchange of their own wares, and then leave. The forest people return, and if satisfied with the offer, take it with them. If not, they

leave it untouched, signifying that they expect more. In this way, for 2,000 or so years, foragers have supplied various commodities in demand to a wider economy (Turnbull, 1961; Wilkie & Curran, 1993).

Silent trade may occur due to lack of a common language. A more probable explanation is that it helps control situations of distrust and potential conflict— maintaining peace by preventing direct contact. Another possibility that does not exclude the others is that it makes exchange possible when problems of status might make verbal communication unthinkable. In any event, silent trade provides for the exchange of goods between groups despite potential barriers.

Kula Ring: Gift Giving and Trading in the South Pacific

Balanced reciprocity can take more complicated forms, whereby mutual gift giving serves to facilitate social interaction, smoothing relations between traders wanting to do business. One classic ethnographic example of balanced reciprocity between trading partners seeking to be friends and do business at the same time is the **Kula ring** in the southwestern Pacific Ocean. This practice was first described by anthropologist Bronislaw Malinowski and involves thousands of seafarers going to great lengths to establish and maintain good trade relations; this centuries-old ceremonial exchange system continues to this day (Malinowski, 1961; Weiner, 1988).

Kula participants are men of influence who travel to islands within the Trobriand ring to exchange prestige items—red shell necklaces (*soulava*), which are circulated around the ring of islands in a clockwise direction, and white shell armbands (*mwali*), which are carried in the opposite direction (**Figure 18.7**). Each man in the Kula is linked to partners on the islands that neighbor his own. To a partner residing on an island in the clockwise direction, he offers a *soulava* and receives in return a *mwali*. He makes the reverse exchange of a *mwali* for a *soulava* to a partner living in the counterclockwise direction. Each of these trade partners eventually passes on the object to a Kula partner farther along the chain of islands.

reciprocity The exchange of goods and services, of approximately equal value, between two parties.

generalized reciprocity A mode of exchange in which the value of the gift is not calculated, nor is the time of repayment specified.

balanced reciprocity A mode of exchange in which the giving and the receiving are specific as to the value of the goods or services and the time of their delivery.

negative reciprocity A mode of exchange in which the aim is to get something for as little as possible. Neither fair nor balanced, it may involve hard bargaining, manipulation, outright cheating, or theft.

silent trade Exchange of goods between mutually distrusting ethnic groups so as to avoid direct personal contact.

Kula ring A mode of balanced reciprocity that reinforces trade and social relations among the seafaring Melanesians who inhabit a large ring of islands in the southwestern Pacific Ocean.

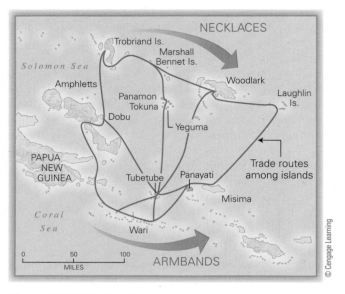

Figure 18.7 Kula Ring The ceremonial gift exchanges of shell necklaces and armbands in the Kula ring encourage trade and barter throughout the Melanesian islands.

Soulava and *mwali* are ranked according to their size, their color, how finely they are polished, and their particular histories. Some of them are so famous that they create a sensation when they appear in a village.

Traditionally, men make their Kula journeys in elaborately carved dugout canoes, sailing and paddling these boats, which are 6 to 7.5 meters (20 to 25 feet) long, across open waters to shores some 100 kilometers (about 60 miles) or more away (**Figure 18.8**). The adventure is often dangerous and may take men away from their homes for several weeks, sometimes even months. Although men on Kula voyages may use the opportunity to trade for practical goods, acquiring such items is not always the reason for these voyages—nor is Kula exchange a necessary part of regular trade expeditions.

Perhaps the best way to view the Kula is as an indigenous insurance policy in an economy fraught with danger and uncertainty. It establishes and reinforces social partnerships among traders doing business on distant shores, ensuring a welcome reception from people who have similar vested interests. This ceremonial exchange

Figure 18.8 Kula Boat In Melanesia, men of influence paddle and sail within a large ring of islands in the southwestern Pacific off the eastern coast of Papua New Guinea to participate in the ceremonial trading of Kula shells, which smoothes trade relations and builds personal prestige.

network does more than simply enhance the trade of foods and other goods essential for survival. Melanesians participating in the Kula ring have no doubt that their social position has to do with the company they keep, the circles in which they move. They derive their social prestige from the reputations of their partners and the valuables that they circulate. By giving and receiving armbands and necklaces that accumulate the histories of their travels and the names of those who have possessed them, men proclaim their individual fame and talent, gaining considerable influence for themselves in the process.

Like other forms of currency, *soulava* and *mwali* must flow from hand to hand; once they stop flowing, they may lose their value. A man who takes these valuables out of their interisland circuit invites criticism. Not only might he lose prestige or social capital as a man of influence, but he might become a target of sorcery for unraveling the cultural fabric that holds the islands together as a functioning social and economic order.

As this example from the South Pacific illustrates, the potential tension between trading partners may be resolved or lessened by participation in a ritual of balanced reciprocity. As an elaborate complex of ceremony, political relationships, economic exchange, travel, magic, and social integration, the Kula ring illustrates the inseparability of economic matters from the rest of culture. Although perhaps difficult to recognize, this is just as true in modern industrial societies as it is in traditional Trobriand society—as is evident when heads of state engage in ceremonial gift exchanges at official visits.

Redistribution

Redistribution is a form of exchange in which goods flow into a central place where they are sorted, counted, and reallocated. In societies with a sufficient surplus to support some sort of government, goods in the form of gifts, tribute, taxes, and the spoils of war are gathered into storehouses controlled by a chief or some other leader. From there they are handed out again. The leadership has three motives in redistributing this income: The first is to gain or maintain a position of power through a display of wealth and generosity; the second is to assure those who support the leadership an adequate standard of living by providing them with desired goods; and the third is to establish alliances with leaders of other groups by hosting them at lavish parties and giving them valuable goods.

The redistribution system of the ancient Inca empire in the Andean highlands of South America was one of the most efficient the world has ever known, both in the collection of tribute (obligatory contributions or gifts in the form of crops, goods, and services) and in its methods of administrative control (Mason, 1957). Administrators kept inventories of resources and a census of the population, which at its peak reached 6 million. Each craft specialist had to produce a specific quota of goods from materials supplied by overseers. Required labor was used for some agricultural and mining work. Unpaid labor was also used in a program of public works that included a remarkable system of roads and bridges throughout the mountainous terrain, aqueducts that guaranteed a supply of water, temples for worship, and storehouses that held surplus food for times of famine.

Careful accounts were kept of income and expenditures. A central administration, regulated by the Inca emperor and his relatives, had the responsibility for ensuring that production was maintained and that commodities were distributed. Holding power over this command economy, the ruling elite lived in great luxury, but sufficient goods were redistributed to the common people to ensure that no one would be left in dire need or face the indignity of pauperism.

Taxes imposed by central governments of countries all around the world today are one form of redistribution—required payments typically based on a percentage of one's income and property value. Typically, a portion of the taxes goes toward supporting the government itself whereas the rest is redistributed either in cash (such as welfare payments and government loans or subsidies to businesses) or in the form of services (such as military defense, law enforcement, food and drug inspection, schools, highway construction, and the like). Tax codes vary greatly among countries. In many European countries, wealthy citizens are taxed at a considerably higher percentage of their income than are U.S. citizens.

Spending Wealth to Gain Prestige

In societies where people devote most of their time to subsistence activities, gradations of wealth are small, kept that way through various cultural mechanisms and systems of reciprocity that serve to spread quite fairly what little wealth exists.

It is a different situation in ranked societies where substantial surpluses are produced, and the gap between the have-nots and the have-lots can be considerable. In these societies, showy display for social prestige—known as **conspicuous consumption**—is a strong motivator for the distribution of wealth. In industrial and postindustrial societies, excessive efforts to impress others with one's wealth or status play a prominent role. The display of symbolic prestige items particular to these societies—designer clothes, expensive jewelry, mansions, luxury cars, private planes—fits neatly into an economy based on consumer wants.

---

redistribution A mode of exchange in which goods flow into a central place, where they are sorted, counted, and reallocated.

conspicuous consumption A showy display of wealth for social prestige.

AP Images/Daily Sitka Sentinel/James Poulson

Figure 18.9 Potlatch Today Among Native Americans living along the Pacific Northwest coast of North America, one gains prestige by giving away valuables at the potlatch feast. Here we see Tlingit clan members dressed in traditional Chilkat and Raven's Tail robes during a recent potlatch in Sitka, Alaska.

A form of conspicuous consumption also occurs in some crop-cultivating and foraging societies. Various American Indian groups living along the Pacific Northwest coast—including the Tlingit, Haida, and Kwakwaka'wakw (Kwakiutl)—illustrate this through potlatches. A **potlatch** is a ceremonial event in which a village chief publicly gives away stockpiled food and other goods that signify wealth (**Figure 18.9**). (The term comes from the Chinook Indian word *patshatl*, which means "gift.")

Traditionally, a chief whose village had built up enough surplus to host such a feast for other villages in the region would give away large piles of sea otter furs, dried salmon, blankets, and other valuables while making boastful speeches about his generosity, greatness, and glorious ancestors. While other chiefs became indebted to him, he reaped the glory of successful and generous leadership and saw his prestige rise. In the future, his own

village might face shortages, and he would find himself on the receiving end of a potlatch. Should that happen, he would have to listen to the self-serving and pompous speeches of rival chiefs. Obliged to receive, he would temporarily lose prestige and status.

In extreme displays of wealth, chiefs even destroyed some of their precious possessions. This occurred with some frequency in the second half of the 19th century, after European contact triggered a process of cultural change that included new trade wealth. Outsiders might view such grandiose displays as wasteful to the extreme. However, these extravagant giveaway ceremonies have played an ecologically adaptive role in a coastal region where villages alternately faced periods of scarcity and abundance and relied upon alliances and trade relations with one another for long-term survival. The potlatch provided a ceremonial opportunity to strategically redistribute surplus food and goods among allied villages in response to periodic fluctuations in fortune.

A strategy that features this sort of accumulation of surplus goods for the express purpose of displaying wealth and giving it away to raise one's status is known

---

potlatch On the northwestern coast of North America, an indigenous ceremonial event in which a village chief publicly gives away stockpiled food and other goods that signify wealth.

as a **prestige economy.** In contrast to conspicuous consumption in industrial and postindustrial societies, the emphasis is not on amassing goods that then become unavailable to others. Instead, it is on gaining wealth in order to give it away for the sake of prestige and status.

Leveling Mechanisms

The potlatch is an example of a **leveling mechanism**— a cultural obligation compelling prosperous members of a community to give away goods, host public feasts, provide free service, or otherwise demonstrate generosity so that no one permanently accumulates significantly more wealth than anyone else. With leveling mechanisms at work, greater wealth brings greater social pressure to spend and give generously. In exchange for such demonstrated altruism, a person not only increases his or her social standing in the community, but may also keep disruptive envy at bay.

Underscoring the value of collective well-being over individual self-interest, leveling mechanisms are important for the long-term survival of traditional communities. The potlatch is just one example of many cultural varieties of leveling mechanism. By pressuring members into sharing their wealth in their own community rather than hoarding it or privately investing it elsewhere, leveling mechanisms do more than keep resources in circulation. They also reduce social tensions among relatives, neighbors, and others in the community, promoting a collective sense of togetherness. An added practical benefit is that they ensure that necessary services within the society are performed.

Market Exchange

To an economist, **market exchange** has to do with the buying and selling of goods and services, with prices set by rules of supply and demand. Personal loyalties and moral values are not supposed to play a role, but they often do. Because the actual location of the transaction is not always relevant in today's world, we must distinguish between the *marketplace* and *market exchange*.

Marketplace and Market Exchange

Typically, until well into the 20th century, market exchange was carried out in specific localities or *marketplaces*. This is still the case in much of the nonindustrial world and even in numerous centuries-old European and Asian towns and cities. In food-producing societies, marketplaces overseen by a centralized political authority provide the opportunity for farmers, pastoralists, or peasants in the surrounding rural territories to exchange some of their livestock and produce for needed items manufactured in factories or in the workshops of craft specialists

living (usually) in towns and cities. Thus, markets require some sort of complex division of labor as well as centralized political organization.

The traditional market is local, specific, and contained— like the one pictured at the beginning of this chapter. Prices are typically set on the basis of face-to-face bargaining rather than by unseen forces wholly removed from the transaction itself. Notably, sales do not necessarily involve money; instead, goods may be directly exchanged through some form of barter among the specific individuals involved.

In industrializing and industrial societies, many market transactions still take place in a specific identifiable location—including international trade fairs such as the mammoth semiannual Canton Trade Fair in Guangzhou, China. In the spring of 2012, 24,000 Chinese enterprises participated in the event, along with 520 companies from 44 foreign countries. Combined, they offered more than 150,000 products and generated more than $36 million in sales among 210,000 buyers from 213 countries ("111th Canton Fair," 2012).

It is increasingly common for people living in technologically wired parts of the world to buy and sell everything from cattle to cars without ever being in the same city, let alone the same space. For example, think of Internet companies such as eBay and Craigslist on which all buying and selling occur electronically and irrespective of geographic distance. When people talk about a market in today's industrial or postindustrial world, the particular geographic location where something is bought or sold is often not important at all.

The faceless market exchanges that take place in industrial and postindustrial societies stand in stark contrast to experiences in the marketplaces of nonindustrial societies, which involve much of the excitement of a fair. Traditional exchange centers are colorful places where a host of sights, sounds, and smells awaken the senses. Typically, vendors and/or their family members produced the goods they are selling, thereby personalizing the transactions. Dancers and musicians may perform, and feasting and fighting may mark the end of the day. In these markets social relationships and personal interactions are key elements, and noneconomic activities may overshadow economic ones. In short, such markets are gathering places where people renew friendships, see

---

prestige economy The creation of a surplus for the express purpose of displaying wealth and giving it away to raise one's status.

leveling mechanism A cultural obligation compelling prosperous members of a community to give away goods, host public feasts, provide free service, or otherwise demonstrate generosity so that no one permanently accumulates significantly more wealth than anyone else.

market exchange The buying and selling of goods and services, with prices set by rules of supply and demand.

VISUAL COUNTERPOINT

© Jack Kurtz/The Image Works

© Miles Ertman/Masterfile

Figure 18.10 **Going to Market** In many societies, particularly in developing countries, the market is an important focus of social as well as economic activity, as shown in the photo on the right of a crowded outdoor marketplace in Aswan, Egypt. In contrast, the packer pictured on the left works at an Amazon.com distribution center in Fernley, Nevada, preparing orders purchased on the Internet. With online shopping, people buy and sell with no social interaction whatsoever.

relatives, gossip, and keep up with the world, while procuring needed goods they cannot produce for themselves (Plattner, 1989) (**Figure 18.10**).

Money as Means of Exchange

Although there have been marketplaces without money of any sort, money does facilitate trade. **Money** may be defined as something used to make payments for other goods and services as well as to measure their value. Its critical attributes are durability, transportability, divisibility, recognizability, and interchangeability. Items that have been used as money in various societies include salt, shells, precious stones, special beads, livestock, and valuable metals, such as iron, copper, silver, and gold. As revealed in this chapter's Biocultural Connection, cacao beans were also used as money—and more.

About 5,000 years ago, merchants and others in Mesopotamia (a vast area between the Tigris and Euphrates Rivers, encompassing much of present-day Iraq and neighboring border areas) began using pieces of precious metal such as silver in their transactions. Once they agreed on the value of these pieces as a means of exchange (money),

more complex commercial developments followed. As the means of exchange were standardized in terms of value, it became easier to accumulate, lend, or borrow money for specified amounts and periods of time against payment of interest. Gradually, some merchants began to do business with money itself, and they became bankers.

As the use of money became widespread, the metal units were adapted to long-term use, easy storage, and long-distance transportation. In many cultures, such pieces of iron, copper, or silver were cast as miniature models of especially valuable implements like sword blades, axes, or spades. But some 2,600 years ago in the ancient kingdom of Lydia (southwestern Turkey), they were molded into small, flat discs conforming to different sizes and weights (Davies, 2005). Over the next few centuries, metal coins were also standardized in terms of the metal's purity and value, such as 100 units of copper = 10 units of silver = 1 unit of gold.

By about 2,000 years ago, the commercial use of such coins was spreading throughout much of Europe and becoming increasingly common in parts of Asia and Africa, especially along trade routes and in urban centers. Thus, money set into motion radical economic changes in many traditional societies and introduced what has been called *merchant capitalism* in many parts of the world (Wolf, 1982).

money A means of exchange used to make payments for other goods and services as well as to measure their value.

BIOCULTURAL CONNECTION

Cacao: The Love Bean in the Money Tree

Several thousand years ago Indians in the tropical lowlands of southern Mexico discovered how to produce a hot brew from ground, roasted beans. They collected these beans from melon-shaped fruit pods growing in trees identified by today's scientists as *Theobroma cacao*. By adding honey, vanilla, and some flowers for flavoring, they produced a beverage that made them feel good and believed that these beans were gifts from their gods.

Soon, cacao beans became part of long-distance trade networks and appeared in the Mexican highlands, where the Aztec elite adopted this drink brewed from *cacahuatl*, calling it "*chocolatl*." In fact, these beans were so highly valued that Aztecs also used them as money. When Spanish invaders conquered Guatemala and Mexico in the 1520s, they adopted the region's practice of using cacao beans as currency inside their new colony. They also embraced the custom of drinking chocolate, which they introduced to Europe, where it became a luxury drink as well as a medicine.[a]

In the next 500 years, chocolate developed into a $14 billion global business, with the United States as the top importer of cacao beans or cacao products. Women buy 75 percent of the chocolate products, and on Valentine's Day more than $1 billion worth of chocolate is sold.

What is it about chocolate that makes it a natural love drug? Other than carbohydrates, minerals, and vitamins, it contains about 300 chemicals, including some with mood-altering effects. For instance, cacao beans contain several chemical components that trigger feelings of pleasure in the human brain. In addition to tryptophan, which increases serotonin levels, chocolate also contains phenylethylamine, an amphetamine-like substance that stimulates the body's own dopamine and has slight antidepressant effects. Chocolate contains anandamide (*anan* means "bliss" in Sanskrit), a messenger molecule that triggers the brain's pleasure center. Also naturally produced in the brain, anandamide's mood-enhancing effect is the same as that obtained from marijuana leaves.[b] Finally, chocolate also contains a mild stimulant called theobromine ("food of god"), which stimulates the brain's production of natural opiates, reducing pain and increasing feelings of satisfaction and even euphoria.

These chemicals help explain why the last Aztec ruler Montezuma drank so much chocolate. A Spanish eyewitness, who visited his royal palace in the Aztec capital in 1519, later reported that Montezuma's servants sometimes brought their powerful lord

in cups of pure gold a drink made from the cocoa-plant, which they said he took before visiting his wives. . . . I saw them bring in a good fifty large jugs of this chocolate, all frothed up, of which he would drink a little. They always served it with great reverence.[c]

BIOCULTURAL QUESTION

Viewed as a divine gift by Mexican Indians, chocolate stimulates our brain's pleasure center. Why would women buy this natural love drug in much greater quantities than men?

---

[a]For an excellent cultural history of chocolate, see Coe, S. D., & Coe, M. D. (1996). *The true history of chocolate*. New York: Thames and Hudson; Grivetti, L. E. (2005). From aphrodisiac to health food: A cultural history of chocolate. *Karger Gazette* (68).

[b]Personal communication, Lawrence C. Davis, Kansas State University.

[c]del Castillo, B. D. (1963). *The conquest of New Spain* (pp. 226–227) (translation and introduction by J. M. Cohen). New York: Penguin.

Local Economies and Global Capitalism

Imposing market production schemes on other societies and ignoring cultural differences can have unintended negative economic consequences, especially in this era of globalization. For example, it has led prosperous countries to impose inappropriate development schemes in parts of the world that they regard as economically underdeveloped. Typically, these schemes focus on increasing the target country's gross national product through large-scale production that all too often boosts the well-being of a few but results in poverty, poor health, discontent, and a host of other ills for many (**Figure 18.11**).

Among many examples of this scenario is the global production of soy, which has increased greatly in many parts of the world. Of particular note is Paraguay, where big landowners, in cooperation with large agribusinesses (most of which are owned by neighboring Brazilians), produce genetically modified seeds, developed and marketed by foreign companies, especially the U.S.-based multinational

Figure 18.11 Protesting the World Trade Organization Founded in 1995 to regulate international trade, the World Trade Organization (WTO) has often been accused of favoring rich countries over poor ones. Public gatherings to protest its policies have been and continue to be common worldwide—particularly in developing countries with large numbers of subsistence farmers struggling to hold onto their livelihoods in the face of globalizing agribusiness. This crowd of protesters gathered during an informal meeting of trade officials from thirty-five countries hosted by India in its capital city, New Delhi, in 2009. Headquartered in Geneva, the WTO has 155 member countries.

corporation Monsanto. Although these landowners and agribusinesses possess just 1 percent of the total number of Paraguayan farms, they own almost 80 percent of the country's agricultural land. Exporting the soy, they make hefty profits because production costs are low, and international demand is high for cattle feed and biofuel.

But the victims of progress are the poor—hundreds of thousands of small farmers, landless peasants, rural laborers, and their families. Traditionally growing much of their own food (plus a bit extra for the local market) on small plots, many of them have been edged out and forced to work for hunger wages or to migrate to the city, or even abroad, in order to survive. Those who stay face malnutrition and other hardships because they lack enough fertile land to feed their families and do not earn enough to buy basic foodstuffs (Fogel & Riquelme, 2005).

Because every culture is an integrated system (as illustrated by the barrel model presented in the chapter on

culture), a shift in the infrastructure, or economic base, impacts interlinked elements of the society's social structure and superstructure. As the ethnographic examples of the potlatch and the Kula ring show, economic activities in traditional cultures are intricately intertwined with social and political relations, and may even involve spiritual elements. Agribusinesses and other large-scale economic operations or development schemes that do not take such structural complexities into consideration may have unforeseen harmful consequences for a society.

Fortunately, there is now a growing awareness on the part of development officials that future projects are unlikely to succeed without the expertise that anthropologists can bring to bear. And, in some parts of the world anthropologists with indigenous roots are leading the way in shaping development agendas that build on rather than destroy tradition—as relayed in this chapter's Anthropologist of Note about Rosita Worl, a Tlingit from Juneau, Alaska.

ANTHROPOLOGIST OF NOTE

Rosita Worl

Alaskan anthropologist **Rosita Worl,** whose Tlingit names are Yeidiklats'akw and Kaa hani, belongs to the Thunderbird Clan from the ancient village of Klukwan in southeastern Alaska. During her growing-up years by the Chilkat River, elders taught her to speak loudly so her words could be heard above the sound of crashing water. And her mother, a cannery union organizer, took her along to meetings.

As a university student, Worl led a public protest for the first time—successfully challenging a development scheme in Juneau detrimental to local Tlingit. When she decided to

Tlingit anthropologist Rosita Worl is president of the Sealaska Heritage Institute and a board member of the Alaska Federation of Natives.

David Sheakley, Sealaska Heritage Institute

pursue her anthropology doctorate at Harvard, she did so with a strong sense of purpose: "You have to be analytical about your culture," she says. "At one time, before coming into contact with other societies, we were just able to live our culture, but now we have to be able to keep it intact while integrating it into modern institutions. We have to be able to communicate our cultural values to others and understand how those modern institutions impact those values."

Worl's graduate studies included fieldwork among the Inupiat of Alaska's North Slope region—research that resulted in her becoming a spokesperson at state, national, and international levels for the protection of whaling practices and the indigenous subsistence lifestyle. For over three decades now, she has fought to safeguard traditional rights to natural resources essential for survival, for current and future generations, including her own children and grandchildren.

A recognized leader in sustainable, culturally informed economic development, Worl has held several major positions at the Sealaska Corporation, a large Native-owned business enterprise with almost 18,000 shareholders primarily of Tlingit and neighboring Haida and Tsimshian descent. Created under the 1971 Alaska Native Claims Settlement Act, Sealaska is now the largest private landholder in southeastern Alaska. Its subsidiaries collectively employ over a thousand people and include timber harvesting,

marketing wood products, land and forest resource management, construction, and information technology. Putting the holistic perspective and analytical tools of anthropology into practice, Worl has spearheaded efforts to incorporate the cultural values of southeast Alaska Natives into Sealaska—including shareholding opportunities for employees.

Currently, Worl serves as president of Sealaska Heritage Institute, a Native nonprofit organization that seeks to perpetuate and enhance Tlingit, Haida, and Tsimshian cultures, including language preservation and revitalization. Also on the faculty of the University of Alaska Southeast, she has written extensively about indigenous Alaska for academic and general audiences. She founded the journal *Alaska Native News* to educate Native Alaskans on a range of issues and is deeply involved in the implementation of the 1990 Native American Graves Protection and Repatriation Act.

Sought for her knowledge and expertise, Worl has served on the board of directors of the Smithsonian Institution's National Museum of the American Indian, as well as Cultural Survival, Inc. She has earned many honors for her work, including the American Anthropological Association's Solon T. Kimball Award for Public and Applied Anthropology, received in 2008 in recognition of her exemplary career in applying anthropology to public life in Alaska and beyond.

Informal Economy and the Escape from State Bureaucracy

Powerful business corporations promote their profit-making agendas through slogans such as "free trade," "free markets," and "free enterprise." But the commercial

success of such enterprises, foreign or domestic, does not come without a price, and all too often that price is paid by still-surviving indigenous foragers, small farmers, herders, fishermen, local artisans such as weavers and carpenters, and so on. From their viewpoint, such slogans of freedom have the ring of "savage capitalism," a term now commonly used in Latin America to describe a world order in which the powerless are often condemned to poverty and misery.

Many of these powerful corporations are successful, at least in part because they manage to avoid the taxes imposed on smaller businesses. The same is often true for the wealthy, who have special access to loopholes and other opportunities to reduce or eliminate taxes that others are obliged to pay. Some of those less privileged, though, have found creative ways to avoid paying taxes and to "beat the system." The system, in this case, refers to the managing bureaucracy in a state-organized society politically controlled by an elected or appointed governing elite.

State bureaucracies seek to manage and control economic activities for regulation and taxation purposes. However, they do not always succeed in these efforts for a variety of reasons: insufficient government resources; underpaid, unskilled, or unmotivated inspectors and administrators; and a culture of corruption. In state-organized societies where large numbers of people habitually avoid bureaucratic regulators seeking to monitor and tax their activities, there is a separate, undocumented economic system known as the **informal economy**—a network of producing and circulating marketable commodities, labor, and services that for various reasons escapes government control (enumeration, regulation, or other types of public monitoring or auditing).

This informal sector may encompass a range of activities: house cleaning, child care, gardening, repair or construction work, making and selling alcoholic beverages, street peddling, money lending, begging, prostitution, gambling, drug dealing, pick-pocketing, and labor by illegal foreign workers, to mention just a few.

These off-the-books activities, including fraud and trade in stolen or smuggled goods on the black market, have existed for a long time but generally have been dismissed by economists as of marginal importance. Yet, in many countries of the world, the informal economy is, in fact, more important than the formal economy and may involve more than half the labor force and up to 40 percent of a country's gross national product (GNP). In many places, large numbers of under- and unemployed people who have only limited access to the formal economic sector in effect improvise, "getting by" on scant resources. Meanwhile, more affluent members of society may dodge various regulations in order to maximize returns and/or to vent their frustrations at their perceived loss of self-determination in the face of increasing government regulation.

Many adult men and women from poor regions in the world seek cash-earning opportunities abroad when they cannot find a paying job within their own country. For multiple reasons such as visa requirements, most laborers who cross international borders legally get temporary work permits as "guest workers" but are not immigrants in that foreign country.

North Africa and Southwest Asia are cheap foreign labor reservoirs for the wealthy industrialized countries of western Europe, whereas Latin America and the Caribbean provide workers for the United States, which draws more migrant laborers than any other country in the world. These workers often send *remittances* (a portion of their earnings) to their families back in their home village or town abroad. The World Bank (2012) estimates that $351 billion in remittances flowed to developing countries in 2011. The top recipients of officially recorded remittances that year were India ($58 billion), China ($57 billion), Mexico ($24 billion), and the Philippines ($23 billion).

For a very poor country such as Jamaica, the total annual inflow of remittances (nearly $2.2 billion in 2011) comprises about 15 percent of that Caribbean island's income. Over a quarter of Jamaicans receive remittances from relatives working abroad, and the average value of such cash transfers for a typical Jamaican household is higher than the average per capita gross domestic product (GDP) in that island nation. For a specific example, see this chapter's Globalscape.

Now that globalization is connecting national, regional, and local markets in which natural resources, commodities, and human labor are bought and sold, people everywhere in the world face new economic opportunities and confront new challenges. Not only are natural environments more quickly and radically transformed by means of new powerful technologies, but long-established subsistence practices, economic arrangements, social organizations, and associated ideas, beliefs, and values are also under enormous pressure.

---

informal economy A network of producing and circulating marketable commodities, labor, and services that for various reasons escapes government control.

Globalscape

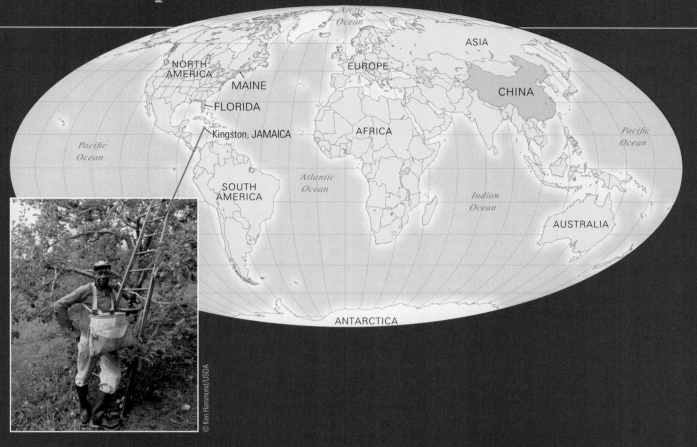

© Ken Hammond/USDA

How Much for a Red Delicious?

Each fall, about 600 Jamaicans migrate to Maine for the apple harvest.[a] While plucking the trees with speed and skill, they listen to reggae music that reminds them of home. Calling each other "brother," they go by nicknames like "Rasta." Most are poor peasants from mountain villages in the Caribbean where they grow yams. But their villages do not produce enough to feed their families, so they go elsewhere to earn cash.

Before leaving Jamaica, they must cut their dreadlocks and shave their beards. Screened and contracted by a labor recruiter in Kingston, they receive a temporary foreign farm workers visa from the U.S. embassy and then fly to Miami. Traveling northward by bus, many work on tobacco farms en route to Maine's orchards (and in Florida's sugar cane fields on the way home). Earning the minimum hourly wage as regulated by the federal H-2A program for "temporary agricultural workers," they work seven days a week, up to ten hours daily. Orchard owners value these foreigners because they are twice as productive as local pickers. Moreover, handpicked apples

graded "extra fancy" earn farmers eight times the price of apples destined for processing.

While in the United States, the Jamaicans remain quite isolated, trying to save as much as they can to send more money home. Just before leaving the country, Rasta and his "brothers" buy things like a television, refrigerator, clothes, and shoes to take home as gifts or as goods to be resold for profit. Lately, their cash-earning opportunities in Maine have been disappearing due to a tide of cheaper illegal workers and a diminished demand for U.S.-grown apples due to increasing Chinese competition.

Although rural labor conditions for seasonal migrant workers in the United States have been likened to indentured service (causing some critics to call the federal H-2A program "rent-a-slave"), for Jamaicans like Rasta, it is an opportunity to escape from the dismal poverty on their Caribbean island.

Global Twister

When you take a big bite from your next apple, think of a brother like Rasta. What do you think is "fair value" anyway?

---

[a]See Rathke, L. (1989). To Maine for apples. *Salt Magazine 9* (4), 24–47.

CHAPTER CHECKLIST

What is an economic system, relative to subsistence?

● An economic system is an organized arrangement for producing, distributing, and consuming goods. Each society allocates natural resources (especially land, water, and fuel), technology, and labor according to its own priorities.

● In food-foraging societies, core features of the region may mark a group's territory. This provides flexibility because the size of a group and its territories can be adjusted according to the availability of resources in any particular place.

● The technology of a people (the tools they use and the knowledge about them) is related to their mode of subsistence. All societies have some means of creating and allocating the tools used to produce goods.

● Labor is a major productive resource, and the allotment of work is commonly governed by rules according to gender and age. Cross-culturally, only a few broad generalizations can be made covering the kinds of work performed by men and women.

● A more productive strategy is to examine the kinds of work that men and women do in the context of specific societies to see how it relates to other cultural and historical factors.

● The cooperation of many people working together is a typical feature of both nonindustrial and industrial societies. Task specialization is important even in societies with very simple technologies.

How are goods distributed?

● The processes of distribution may be distinguished as reciprocity, redistribution, and market exchange.

● Reciprocity, the exchange of goods and services of roughly equal value, comes in three forms: generalized (in which the value is not calculated, nor the time of repayment specified); balanced (in which one has an obligation to reciprocate promptly); and negative (in which the aim is to get something for as little as possible).

● A classic ethnographic example of balanced reciprocity between trading partners seeking to maintain social ties while also doing business is the Kula ring among islanders of the southwestern Pacific Ocean. The Kula ring involves both balanced reciprocity and sharp trading.

● *Trade* refers to a transaction in which two or more people are involved in an exchange of something for something else of equal value. Such exchanges have elements of reciprocity but involve a greater calculation of the relative value of goods exchanged.

● Barter is a form of trade in which no money is involved, and the parties negotiate a direct exchange of one trade good for another. It may well be in the form of negative reciprocity, as each party aims to get the better end of the deal.

● Redistribution requires a strong, centralized political organization. A government assesses a tax or tribute on each citizen to support its activities, leaders, and religious elite and then redistributes the rest, usually in the form of public services. The system of tax collection and delivery of government services and subsidies in the United States is a form of redistribution.

● Conspicuous consumption, or display for social prestige, is a motivating force in societies that produce a surplus of goods. The prestige comes from publicly giving away one's valuables, as in the potlatch ceremony, which is also an example of a leveling mechanism.

What is market exchange, and where is the marketplace?

● In nonindustrial societies, the marketplace is usually a specific site where people exchange produce, livestock, and material items they have made. It also functions as a place to socialize and get news.

● Although market exchanges may take place through bartering and other forms of reciprocity, money (something used to make payments for goods and services as well as to measure their value) makes market exchange more efficient.

● In state-organized societies with market economies, the informal sector—composed of economic activities set up to avoid official scrutiny and regulation—may be more important than the formal sector. The informal economy includes remittances (earnings) that migrant laborers working abroad send to their families back in their home village or town.

How does global capitalism impact local economies?

● When powerful countries impose market production schemes on other societies, the impact can be negative— as in the global production of soy in Paraguay where big landowners in cooperation with large agribusinesses have edged out small farmers and landless peasants.

● Increasingly, development officials are utilizing the expertise that anthropologists provide in planning their projects.

QUESTIONS FOR REFLECTION

1. Imagine a global banking crisis in which the capitalist economy based on money, interest, and credit has collapsed. How long do you think it would take for a market to develop like the one in Keren, Eritrea, shown in the chapter opening photograph? Which goods do you think would have exchange value in your culture, and what would you do to get those goods in fair trade?

2. Consider the differences between the three varieties of reciprocity. What role does each play in your own experience as a member of a family, local community, and wider society?

3. As the potlatch ceremony shows, prestige may be gained by giving away wealth. Does such a prestige-building mechanism exist in your own society? If so, how does it work?

4. When shopping for groceries in a supermarket, think of this chapter's Globalscape and try to imagine the great chain of human hands involved in getting something as simple as a nice red apple from a distant orchard to your mouth. How many people do you think handled the fruit to get it to you?

5. Economic relations in traditional cultures are usually wrapped up in social, political, and even spiritual issues. Can you think of any examples in your own society in which the economic sphere is inextricably intertwined with other structures in the cultural system?

ONLINE STUDY RESOURCES

CourseMate

Access chapter-specific learning tools, including learning objectives, practice quizzes, videos, flash cards, glossaries, and more in your Anthropology CourseMate.

Log into **www.cengagebrain.com** to access the resources your instructor has assigned and to purchase materials.

SAM PANTHAKY/AFP/Getty Images

Challenge Issue

Worldwide, humans face the challenge of managing sexual relations and forging social alliances essential to the survival of individuals and their offspring. Adapting to particular natural environments and distinct economic and political challenges, each group establishes its own social arrangements in terms of childrearing tasks, gender relations, household and family structures, and residence patterns. Because marriage and family play a fundamental role in any society, wedding rituals are especially significant. Whether private or public, sacred or secular, weddings reveal, confirm, and underscore important cultural values. Symbolically rich, they usually feature certain speech rituals, plus prescribed apparel, postures and gestures, food and drink, songs and dances passed down through generations. Here we see a Muslim bride in Gujarat, western India, surrounded by female relatives and friends on the eve before her wedding. Their hands are beautifully decorated with traditional designs created with dye made from the crushed leaves of the tropical henna tree. Known as *mehndi*, this temporary body art is an age-old custom among Muslims and Hindus in parts of southern Asia, as well as northern Africa. Often the groom's name is hidden within elegant designs of flowers and vines that symbolize love, fertility, and protection. A bride's *mehndi* evening, traditionally held at her parents' home, is a lively female-only gathering with special food, singing, and lovemaking instructions, along with hand painting.

Sex, Marriage, and Family

19

Unlike individuals raised in traditional Muslim families, such as the bride featured in this chapter's opening photo, young people in the Trobriand Islands of the South Pacific traditionally enjoy great sexual freedom. By age 7 or 8, children begin playing erotic games and imitating adult seductive attitudes. Within another four or five years, they start pursuing sexual partners in earnest—experimenting erotically with a variety of individuals.

Because attracting sexual partners ranks high among young Trobrianders, they spend a great deal of time beautifying themselves (**Figure 19.1**). Their daily conversations are loaded with sexual hints, and they employ magical spells as well as small gifts to entice a prospective sex partner to the beach at night or to the house in which boys sleep apart from their parents. Girls, too, sleep apart from their parents, so youths have considerable freedom in arranging their erotic adventures. Boys and girls play this game as equals, with neither having an advantage over the other (Weiner, 1988).

By the time Trobrianders are in their mid-teens, meetings between lovers may take up most of the night, and love affairs are apt to last for several months. Ultimately, a young islander begins to meet the same partner again and again, rejecting the advances of others. When the couple is ready, they appear together one morning outside the young man's house as a way of announcing their intention to be married.

Until the latter part of the 20th century, the Trobriand attitude toward adolescent sexuality was in marked contrast to that of most Western cultures in Europe and North America, where individuals were not supposed to have sexual relations before or outside of marriage. Since then, practices in much of the

IN THIS CHAPTER YOU WILL LEARN TO

- Discuss how different cultures permit or restrict sexual relations.

- Distinguish several marriage forms and understand their determinants and functions.

- Contrast family and household forms across cultures.

- Explain a range of marital residence patterns.

- Weigh the impact of globalization and reproductive technology on marriage and family.

© Hideo Haga/HAGA/The Image Works

Figure 19.1 Sex Appeal among the Trobrianders To attract lovers, young Trobriand women and men must look as attractive and seductive as possible. This young woman's beauty has been enhanced by face painting and adornments given to her by her father.

modern industrialized world have converged toward those of the Trobrianders, even though the traditional ideal of premarital sexual abstinence has not been abandoned entirely and is upheld in many traditional Christian, Muslim, and similarly conservative families.

Control of Sexual Relations

In the absence of effective birth control, the usual outcome of sexual activity between fertile individuals of the opposite sex is that, sooner or later, the woman becomes pregnant. Given the intricate array of social responsibilities involved in rearing the children that are born of sexual relations—and the potential for conflict resulting from unregulated sexual competition—it is not surprising

that all societies have cultural rules that seek to regulate those relations, although those rules vary considerably across cultures.

For instance, in some societies, sexual intercourse during pregnancy is taboo, whereas in others it is looked upon positively as something that promotes the growth of the fetus. And although some cultures sharply condemn same-sex acts or relations, many others are indifferent and do not even have a special term to distinguish homosexuality as significant in its own right. In several cultures same-sex acts are not only accepted but even prescribed.

Such is the case in some Papua societies in New Guinea, for example, where certain prescribed male-to-male sexual acts are part of initiation rituals required of all boys to become respected adult men (Kirkpatrick, 2000). In those cultures, people traditionally see the transmission of semen from sexually mature males to younger boys, through oral sex, as vital for building up the strength needed to protect against the supposedly debilitating effects of adult heterosexual intercourse (Herdt, 1993).

Despite longstanding culture-based opposition to homosexuality in many areas of the world, this sexual orientation exists within the wider range of human sexual relations, emotional attractions, and social identities, and it is far from uncommon (**Figure 19.2**). Homosexuality is found in diverse contexts—from lifelong loving relationships to casual sexual encounters, and from being fully open to being utterly private and secretive. During the past few decades, public denigration and condemnation of homosexuality have diminished in numerous countries, and same-sex relationships have become a publicly accepted part of the cosmopolitan lifestyle in metropolitan centers from Amsterdam to Paris and Rio de Janeiro to San Francisco. As recently as 2009, India decriminalized homosexuality, followed by several other countries (Timmons & Kumar, 2009). Clearly, the social rules and cultural meanings of all sexual behavior are subject to great variability not only across cultures but also across time.

Marriage and the Regulation of Sexual Relations

As noted previously, in much of Europe and North America the traditional ideal was (and in some communities still is) that all sexual activities outside of marriage were disapproved or even forbidden. Individuals were expected to establish a family through marriage, by which one gains an exclusive right of sexual access to another person. The main purpose of sexual intercourse was not erotic pleasure but reproduction.

Recognizing the potential risks of unregulated sexual relations, including unplanned pregnancies by a man other than the lawful husband, these societies often criminalized extramarital affairs as adultery. Reinforcing public awareness of the moral rules, authorities could turn sexual

VISUAL COUNTERPOINT

Figure 19.2 Expressions of Same-Sex Affection Although same-sex relationships have existed for thousands of years and are permitted in many parts of the world, homosexuals in sexually restrictive societies are shamed and shunned, and may be beaten, flogged, banished, imprisoned, or even murdered. Even in societies that have become less restrictive, public displays of same-sex affection (between men in particular) are often looked upon as distasteful or even disgusting. One nationwide exception in the United States is the sports arena where athletes freely hug each other, and may even pat each other on the behind or leap into each other's arms without bringing their sexual orientation into question. Attitudes are shifting all around the globe, however, as evident in this photo of two just-wed Argentinean men kissing after receiving their official marriage license on November 16, 2009—the first in Latin America. This Buenos Aires couple sought a license not only because they love each other, but also because they wanted the shared health insurance policy, inheritance rights, and other privileges married couples in their country traditionally enjoy.

transgressions into a public spectacle of shame, torture, or even death. According to strict religious law—historically shared by Jews, Christians, and Muslims alike—adultery was punishable by death. The Bible demands that both wrongdoers, having placed themselves outside the moral community, be stoned to death outside the town entrance (Deuteronomy 22:24 and Leviticus 20:10).

Many centuries later, among European Christian colonists in 17th- and 18th-century New England, a woman's participation in adultery remained a serious crime. Although it did not lead to stoning, women so accused were shunned by the community and could be imprisoned.

Such restrictions remain (or are sometimes reinstated) in those traditional Muslim societies in northern Africa and western Asia where age-old Shariah law regulates social behavior in strict accordance with religious standards of morality.

For example, in a Taliban-controlled village in northern Afghanistan, conservative mullahs (priests) found a young couple guilty of adultery, proclaiming it an offense prohibited by God. Buried waist-deep in holes outside the village, the 23-year-old married woman and her 28-year-old lover were stoned to death in the summer of 2010,

a brutal spectacle attended by hundreds of villagers and filmed on a mobile phone (Amnesty International, 2010). Turning legal transgressions into a public display, authorities reinforce awareness of the rules of social conduct, even if a sentence is ultimately dropped or changed.

A side effect of such restrictive rules of sexual behavior is that they may contribute to limiting the spread of sexually transmitted diseases. For instance, the global epidemic of HIV/AIDS has had dramatically less impact in northern Africa's Muslim countries than in the non-Muslim states of sub-Saharan Africa. Statistics vividly illustrate the impact of religious and cultural prohibitions (although other factors may also be involved): The reported percentage of adults infected by the virus is 0.1 percent in Algeria, Morocco, and Tunisia, in contrast to some 17 percent in South Africa, 25 percent in Botswana, and 26 percent in Swaziland (Gray, 2004; UNAIDS, 2009).

Notably, because sexuality is a taboo topic in Muslim societies, many may not seek appropriate counseling, testing, and treatment for HIV/AIDS. For this reason, the actual infection rate may be somewhat higher than reported in these figures (Hasnain, 2005). Communities devastated by this sexually transmitted disease not only confront a serious public health problem but also face a cultural challenge in that they must create a new public awareness and adjust attitudes about sexual pleasure so that they do not endanger their collective well-being.

Yet most cultures in the world do not sharply regulate an individual's sexual practices. Indeed, a majority of all cultures are considered sexually permissive or semipermissive (the former having few or no restrictions on sexual experimentation before marriage, the latter allowing some experimentation but less openly). A minority of known societies—about 15 percent—have rules requiring that sexual involvement take place only within marriage.

This brings us to an anthropological definition of **marriage**—a culturally sanctioned union between two or more people that establishes certain rights and obligations between the people, between them and their children, and between them and their in-laws. Such marriage rights and obligations most often include, but are not limited to, sex, labor, property, childrearing, exchange, and status. Thus defined, marriage is universal. Notably, our definition of *marriage* refers to "people" rather than "a man and a woman" because in some countries same-sex marriages are socially acceptable and allowed by law, even though opposite-sex marriages are far more common. We will return to this point later in the chapter.

In many cultures, marriage is considered the central and most important social institution. In such cultures, people will spend considerable time and energy on maintaining marriage as an institution. They may do so in various ways, including highlighting the ritual moment when the wedding takes place, festively memorializing the event at designated times such as anniversaries, and making it difficult to divorce.

In some societies, however, marriage is a relatively marginal institution and is not considered central to the establishment and maintenance of family life and society. For instance, marriage has lost much of its traditional significance in wealthy northwestern European nations, in part due to changes in the political economy, more balanced gender relations, and shared public benefits of these capitalist welfare states.

Sexual and Marriage Practices among the Nayar

The relative unimportance of marriage as the major defining institution for establishing a family is not unique to wealthy European nations. For instance, historically, marriage has been of marginal significance in the family life of the Nayar of Kerala in southwestern India. A landowning

warrior caste, corporations made up of kinsmen related in the female line traditionally hold their estates. These blood relatives live together in a large household, with the eldest male serving as manager.

Like Trobriand Islanders, the Nayar are a sexually permissive culture. A classic anthropological study describes three transactions related to traditional Nayar sexual and marriage practices, many of which have changed since the mid-1900s (Goodenough, 1970; Gough, 1959). The first, occurring shortly before a girl experiences her first menstruation, involves a ceremony that joins her with a "ritual husband." This union does not necessarily involve sexual relations and lasts only a few days. Neither individual has any further obligation, but when the girl becomes a woman, she and her children typically participate in ritual mourning for the man when he dies. This temporary union establishes the girl as an adult ready for motherhood and eligible for sexual activity with men approved by her household.

The second transaction takes place when a young Nayar woman enters into a continuing sexual liaison with a man approved by her family. This is a formal relationship that requires the man to present her with gifts three times each year until the relationship is terminated. In return, the man can spend nights with her. Despite ongoing sexual privileges, however, this "visiting husband" has no economic obligations to her, nor is her home regarded as his home. In fact, she may have the same arrangement with more than one man at the same time. Regardless of the number of men with whom she is involved, this second transaction, the Nayar version of marriage, clearly specifies who has sexual rights to whom and includes rules that deter conflicts between the men.

If a Nayar woman becomes pregnant, one of the men with whom she has a relationship (who may or may not be the biological father) must formally acknowledge paternity by presenting gifts to the woman and the midwife. This establishes the child's birthrights—as does birth registration in Western societies. Once a man has ritually acknowledged fatherhood by gift giving, he may continue to take interest in the child, but he has no further obligations. Support and education for the child are the responsibility of the mother and her brothers, with whom she and her offspring live.

Indeed, unlike most other cultural groups in the world, the traditional Nayar household includes only the mother,

marriage A culturally sanctioned union between two or more people that establishes certain rights and obligations between the people, between them and their children, and between them and their in-laws. Such marriage rights and obligations most often include, but are not limited to, sex, labor, property, childrearing, exchange, and status.

Figure 19.3 Charles Darwin and His First-Cousin Wife, Emma Wedgewood Before proposing, Charles made a "pros and cons" list about marrying Emma. It said nothing about their
close familial relationship. Rather, the concerns of this famous English naturalist centered on
the question of whether supporting a wife and children would compromise his scientific career.
Ultimately, the idea of a "constant companion (& friend in old age)" won out. During their three-
month engagement he wrote to her: "I think you will humanize me, & soon teach me there is
greater happiness, than building theories, & accumulating facts in silence & solitude." Bonds
of real affection linked the couple throughout their long lives.

her children, and her other biological or blood relatives,
technically known as **consanguineal kin**. It does not
include any of the "husbands" or other people related
through marriage—technically known as **affinal kin**.
In other words, sisters and their offspring all live together
with their brothers and their mother and her brothers.
Historically, this arrangement addressed the need for security in a cultural group in which warfare was common.

Among the Nayar, sexual relations are forbidden
between consanguineal relatives and thus are permitted
only with individuals who live in other households. This
brings us to another human universal: the incest taboo.

Incest Taboo

Just as marriage in its various forms is found in all cultures, so is the **incest taboo**—the prohibition of sexual
contact between certain close relatives. But what is defined
as "close" is not the same in all cultures. Moreover, such
definitions may be subject to change over time. Although
the scope and details of the taboo vary across cultures and
time, almost all societies past and present strongly forbid
sexual relations at least between parents and children and
nearly always between siblings. In some societies the taboo

extends to other close relatives, such as cousins, and even
some relatives linked through marriage (**Figure 19.3**).

Anthropologists have long been fascinated by the
incest taboo and have proposed several explanations for
its cross-cultural existence and variation. The simplest
explanation is that our species has an "instinctive" repulsion for incest. It has been documented that human beings
raised together have less sexual attraction for one another.
However, by itself this "familiarity breeds contempt"
argument may simply substitute the result for the cause.
The incest taboo ensures that children and their parents,
who are constantly in close contact, avoid regarding one
another as sexual objects. Besides this, if an instinctive
horror of incest exists, how do we account for the far from
rare violations of the incest taboo? In the United States,
for instance, over 10 percent of children under 18 years of
age have been involved in incestuous relations (U.S. Dept.
of Health and Human Services, 2005; Whelehan, 1985).

consanguineal kin Biologically related relatives, commonly referred
to as blood relatives.

affinal kin People related through marriage.

incest taboo The prohibition of sexual relations between closely
related individuals.

Moreover, so-called instinctive repulsion does not explain institutionalized incest, such as a requirement that the divine ruler of the Inca empire in ancient Peru be married to his own (half) sister. Sharing the same father, both siblings belonged to the political dynasty that derived its sacred right to rule the empire from Inti, its ancestral Sun God. And by virtue of this royal lineage's godly origin, their children could claim the same sacred political status as their human-divine father and mother. Ancient emperors in Egypt also practiced such religiously prescribed incest based on a similar claim to godly status.

Early students of genetics argued that the incest taboo prevents the harmful effects of inbreeding. Although this is so, it is also true that, as with domestic animals, inbreeding can increase desired characteristics as well as detrimental ones. Furthermore, undesirable effects will show up sooner with inbreeding, so whatever genes are responsible for them are quickly eliminated from the population. That said, a preference for a genetically different mate does tend to maintain a higher level of genetic diversity within a population, and in evolution this variation works to a species' advantage. Without genetic diversity a species cannot adapt biologically to environmental change.

The inbreeding or biological-avoidance theory of incest can be challenged on several fronts. For instance, detailed census records made in Roman Egypt about 2,000 years ago show that brother–sister marriages were not uncommon among ordinary members of the farming class, and we have no evidence for linking this cultural practice to any biological imperatives (Leavitt, 1990). To the contrary, some anthropologists have argued that the incest taboo exists as a cultural means to preserve the stability and integrity of the family, which is essential to maintaining social order. Sexual relations between family members other than the husband and wife would introduce competition, destroying the harmony of a social unit fundamental to societal order.

Endogamy and Exogamy

Whatever its cause, the utility of the incest taboo can be seen by examining its effects on social structure. Closely related to prohibitions against incest are cultural rules against **endogamy** (from Greek *endon*, "within," and *gamos*, "marriage"), or marriage within a particular group of individuals (cousins and in-laws, for example). If the group is defined as one's immediate family alone, then societies generally prohibit or at least discourage endogamy, thereby promoting **exogamy** (*exo* is Greek for "outside"), or marriage outside the group. Yet, a

society that practices exogamy at one level may practice endogamy at another. Among the Trobriand Islanders, for example, each individual has to marry outside of his or her own clan and lineage (exogamy). However, because eligible sex partners are to be found within one's own community, village endogamy is commonly practiced.

Since the early 20th century, restrictions on close-kin marriages have increased in Europe and other parts of the world. Because of this, worldwide migrations by peoples from countries in which such marriages remain customary may lead to cross-cultural problems. British anthropologist Adam Kuper recently discussed this issue based on research with Muslim immigrant families from Pakistan. (Notably, Kuper's own paternal grandparents, Baltic Jews who immigrated to South Africa, were first cousins.) According to Kuper,

> In Pakistan, and in the Pakistani diaspora, a preference is commonly expressed for marriage within the extended family or *birādarī*. . . . Perhaps unexpectedly, the rate of cousin marriage among Pakistani immigrants to Britain is higher than the rate in rural Pakistan. And the rate of cousin marriage is particularly high among younger British Pakistanis. Around a third of the marriages of the immigrant generation were with first cousins, but well over half the marriages of the British-born generation are with first cousins. This is a consequence of British immigration regulations. . . . It is very difficult to enter Britain unless one is married to a British citizen. In most cousin marriages, one partner immigrates to Britain from Pakistan. Alison Shaw found that 90 per cent of the first-cousin marriages in her sample of British Pakistanis in Oxford involved one spouse who came directly from Pakistan. . . . (Kuper, 2008, p. 731)

Kuper notes that although health risks to offspring of such close-kin marriages are "rather low," and generally "within the limits of acceptability," research by geneticists does indicate that "the risk of birth defects or infant mortality is roughly doubled for the children of first cousins." However, he adds, in western Europe this debate is not just about medical risks, but also about immigration and cultural friction: "Father's brother's daughter marriage is taken to be a defining feature of Islamic culture, and it is blamed not only for overloading the health service but also for resistance to integration and cultural stagnation. It is also associated with patriarchy, the suppression of women, and forced marriages" (Kuper 2008, p. 731).

In the United States, laws against first-cousin marriages exist in thirty-one states, and there is a general assumption nationwide that these laws are rooted in genetics (Ottenheimer, 1996). (See a discussion of U.S. marriage prohibitions in the Biocultural Connection.)

---

endogamy Marriage within a particular group or category of individuals.

exogamy Marriage outside a particular group or category of individuals.

BIOCULTURAL CONNECTION

Marriage Prohibitions in the United States

By Martin Ottenheimer

In the United States, every state has laws prohibiting the marriage of some relatives. Every state forbids parent–child and sibling marriages, but there is considerable variation in prohibitions concerning more distant relatives. For example, although the majority of states ban marriage between first cousins, nineteen states allow it and others permit it under certain conditions. Notably, the United States is the only country in the Western world that has prohibitions against first-cousin marriage.

Many people in the United States believe that laws forbidding marriage between family members exist because parents who are too close biologically run the risk of producing children with mental and physical defects. Convinced that first cousins fall within this "too close" category, they believe laws against first-cousin marriage were established to protect families from the effects of harmful genes.

There are two major problems with this belief: First, cousin prohibitions were enacted in the United States long before the discovery of the genetic mechanisms of disease. Second, genetic research has shown that offspring of first-cousin couples do not have any significantly greater risk of

negative results than offspring of very distantly related parents.

Why, then, do some North Americans maintain this belief? To answer this question, it helps to know that laws against first-cousin marriage first appeared in the United States right after the mid-1800s when evolutionary models of human behavior became fashionable. In particular, a pre-Darwinian model that explained social evolution as dependent upon biological factors gained popularity. It supposed that "progress from savagery to civilization" was possible when humans ceased inbreeding. Cousin marriage was thought to be characteristic of savagery, the lowest form of human social life, and it was believed to inhibit the intellectual and social development of humans. It became associated with "primitive" behavior and dreaded as a threat to a civilized America.

Thus, a powerful myth emerged in American popular culture, which has since become embedded in law. That myth is held and defended to this day, sometimes with great emotion despite being based on a discredited social evolutionary theory and contradicted by the results of modern genetic research.

Recently, a group of geneticists published the result of a study of consanguineous unions, estimating that there is "about a 1.7–2.8% increased risk for congenital defects above the population background risk."[a] Not only is this a high estimate, it is also well within the bounds of the margin of statistical error. But even so, it is a lower risk than that associated with offspring from women over the age of 40—who are not forbidden by the government to marry or bear children.

BIOCULTURAL QUESTION

What do you think is the underlying cultural logic that makes some societies traditionally forbid first cousins from marrying each other, whereas others, equally unfamiliar with genetics, accept or even prefer such marriages?

Written expressly for this text, 2005; revised and updated, 2011.

---

[a]Bennett, R. L., et al. (2002, April). Genetic counseling and screening of consanguineous couples and their offspring: Recommendations of the National Society of Genetic Counselors. *Journal of Genetic Counseling 11* (2), 97–119.

Early anthropologists suggested that our ancestors discovered the advantage of intermarriage as a means of creating bonds of friendship. French anthropologist Claude Lévi-Strauss (see the Anthropologist of Note) elaborated on this idea. He saw exogamy as a form of intergroup social exchange in which "wife-giving" and "wife-taking" (or, as happens in communities with female-headed households, husband-giving and husband-taking) created alliances between distinct communities. By extending the social network, potential enemies turn into relatives who may provide support in times of hardship or violent conflict.

Building on the theory advanced by Lévi-Strauss, other anthropologists have proposed that exogamy is an

important means of creating and maintaining political alliances and promoting trade between groups, thereby ensuring mutual protection and access to needed goods and resources not otherwise available. Forging wider kinship networks, exogamy also functions to integrate distinctive groups and thus potentially reduces violent conflict.

Distinction Between Marriage and Mating

In contrast to mating, which occurs when individuals join for purposes of sexual relations, marriage is a socially

ANTHROPOLOGIST OF NOTE

Claude Lévi-Strauss (1908–2009)

Claude Lévi-Strauss lived to be 100. When he died, he was the most celebrated anthropologist in the world. Born in Belgium, where his father briefly worked as a portrait painter, he grew up in Paris. As a boy during World War I, Claude lived with his grandfather, a rabbi of Versailles.

He studied law and philosophy at the Sorbonne, married a young anthropologist named Dina Dreyfus, and became a philosophy teacher. In 1935, the couple ventured across the ocean to Brazil's University of São Paulo, where his wife taught anthropology and he sociology. Influenced by 18th-century romantic philosopher Rousseau and fascinated by historical accounts of Brazilian Indians, he preferred ethnographic research and lectured on tribal social organizations.

In 1937, he and Dina organized an expedition into the Amazon forest, visiting Bororo and other tribal villages and collecting artifacts for museums. In 1938, they made another journey and researched recently contacted Nambikwara Indians. Back in Paris together in 1939, their marriage dissolved. That same year, the Second World War erupted, and the French army mobilized its soldiers, including Lévi-Strauss.

A year after Nazi Germany conquered France in 1940, Lévi-Strauss escaped to New York City, where he became an anthropology professor at the New School for Social Research. Teaching courses on South American Indians during the war years, he befriended other European exiles, including the linguist Roman Jakobson, who pioneered the structural analysis of language.

Renowned French anthropologist Claude Lévi-Strauss at age 100 in his home library.

After the war, Lévi-Strauss became French cultural consul in the United States, based in New York. Maintaining ties with the academic community, including anthropologist Margaret Mead, he completed his two-part doctoral thesis: *The Elementary Structures of Kinship* and *The Family and Social Life of the Nambikwara Indians*. Theoretically influenced by Jakobson's structural linguistics, his thesis analyzed the logical structures underlying the social relations of kin-ordered societies.

Building on Marcel Mauss's 1925 study of gift exchange as a means to build or maintain a social relationship, he applied the concept of reciprocity to kinship, arguing that marriage is based on the exchange relationship between kin-groups of "wife-givers" and "wife-takers." Returning to France in late 1947, he became associate director of the ethnographic museum in Paris and successfully defended his thesis at the Sorbonne. His structural analysis was recognized as a pioneering study in kinship and marriage.

In 1949, Lévi-Strauss joined an international body of experts invited by UNESCO to discuss and define the *race concept*, a disputed term associated with discrimination and genocide. Three years later, he authored *Race and History*, a book that became instrumental in UNESCO's worldwide campaign against racism and ethnocentrism. By then, he had become an anthropology professor at the École Pratique des Hautes Études in Paris. Continuing his prolific writing, he published *Tristes Tropiques* (1955). This memoir about his ethnographic adventures among Amazonian Indians won him international fame. His next book, *Structural Anthropology* (1963), also became a classic. It presented his theoretical perspective that the human mind produces logical structures, classifying reality in terms of binary oppositions (such as light–dark, good–evil, nature–culture, and male–female) and that all humans share a mental demand for order expressed in a drive toward classification.

In 1959, Lévi-Strauss was appointed to a chair in social anthropology at the Collège de France and founded his own institute there. Specializing in the comparative study of religion, he undertook a massive comparative study and structural analysis of myths, resulting in a series of instantaneously classic books. In 1973, he was elected to the centuries-old Académie Française, a prestigious institution with just forty members known as "immortals." Countless other honors from around the world followed.

Now, survived by his wife, Monique, and two sons, he lies in a small rural cemetery in Burgundy, near his old mansion, where he liked to reflect on the human condition.

binding and culturally recognized relationship. Only marriage is backed by social, political, and ideological factors that regulate sexual relations as well as reproductive rights

and obligations. Even among the Nayar in India, discussed previously, where traditionally marriage seems to have involved little other than a sexual relationship, a woman's husband is legally obligated to provide her with gifts at specified intervals. Additionally, Nayar woman may not legally have sex with a man to whom she is not married.

Thus, although mating is biological, marriage is cultural. This is evident when we consider the various forms of marriage around the world.

Forms of Marriage

Within societies, and all the more so across cultures, we see contrasts in the constructs and contracts of marriage. Indeed, as is evident in the definition of *marriage* given previously, this institution comes in various forms—and these forms are distinct in terms of the number and gender of spouses involved.

Monogamy

Monogamy—marriage in which both partners have just one spouse—is the most common form of marriage worldwide. In North America and most of Europe, it is the only legally recognized form of marriage. In these places, not only are other forms prohibited, but systems of inheritance, whereby property and wealth are transferred from one generation to the next, are based on the institution of monogamous marriage. In some parts of the world (including Europe and North America) where divorce rates are high and people who have been divorced remarry, an increasingly common form of marriage is **serial monogamy**, whereby an individual marries a series of partners in succession.

Polygamy

Monogamy is the most common marriage form worldwide, but it is not the most culturally preferred. That distinction goes to **polygamy** (one individual having multiple spouses) and specifically to **polygyny**, in which a man is married to more than one woman (*gyne* is Greek for "woman" and "wife"). Favored in about 80 to 85 percent of the world's cultures, polygyny is commonly practiced in parts of Asia and much of sub-Saharan Africa (Lloyd, 2005).

Although polygyny is the favored marriage form in these places, monogamy exceeds it, but for economic rather than moral or legal reasons. In many polygynous societies, in which a groom is usually expected to compensate a bride's family in cash or kind, a man must be fairly wealthy to be able to afford more than one wife. Multiple surveys of twenty-five sub-Saharan African countries where polygyny is common show that it declined by about half between the 1970s and 2001. This dramatic decline has many reasons, one of which is related to families making an economic transition from traditional farming and herding to wage labor in cities. Nonetheless, polygyny remains highly significant with an overall average of 25 percent of married women in such unions (Lloyd, 2005).

Polygyny is particularly common in traditional food-producing societies that support themselves by herding grazing animals or growing crops and in which women do the bulk of cultivation. Under these conditions, women are valued both as workers and as childbearers. Because the labor of wives in polygynous households generates wealth and little support is required from husbands, the wives have a strong bargaining position within the household. Often, they have considerable freedom of movement and some economic independence through the sale of crafts or crops. Wealth-generating polygyny is found in its fullest elaboration in parts of sub-Saharan Africa and southwestern Asia, though it is known elsewhere as well (White, 1988).

In societies practicing wealth-generating polygyny, most men and women do enter into polygynous marriages, although some are able to do so earlier in life than others. This is made possible by a female-biased sex ratio and/or a mean age at marriage for females that is significantly below that for males. In fact, this marriage pattern is frequently found in societies in which violence, including war, is common and many young males lose their lives in fighting. Their high combat mortality results in a population in which women outnumber men.

By contrast, in societies in which men are more heavily involved in productive work, generally only a small minority of marriages are polygynous. Under these circumstances, women are more dependent on men for support, so they are valued as childbearers more than for the work they do. This is commonly the case in pastoral nomadic societies in which men are the primary owners and tenders of livestock. This makes women especially vulnerable if they prove incapable of bearing children, which is one reason a man may seek another wife.

Another reason for a man to take on secondary wives is to demonstrate his high position in society. But where men do most of the productive work, they must work extremely hard to support more than one wife, and few actually do so. Usually, it is the exceptional hunter or male shaman ("medicine man") in a food-foraging society or a particularly wealthy man in a horticultural, agricultural, or pastoral society who is most apt to practice polygyny. When he does, it is usually of the *sororal* type, with the co-wives being sisters. Having lived their lives together before marriage, the sisters continue to do so with their husband, instead of occupying separate dwellings of their own.

Polygyny also occurs in a few places in Europe. For example, English laws concerning marriage changed in 1972 to accommodate immigrants who traditionally prac-

monogamy A marriage form in which both partners have just one spouse.

serial monogamy A marriage form in which a man or a woman marries or lives with a series of partners in succession.

polygamy A marriage form in which one individual has multiple spouses at the same time; from the Greek words *poly* ("many") and *gamos* ("marriage").

polygyny A marriage form in which a man is married to two or more women at the same time; a form of polygamy.

ticed polygyny. Since that time polygamous marriages have been legal in England for some specific religious minorities, including Muslims and Sephardic Jews. According to one family law specialist, the real impetus behind this law change was a growing concern that "destitute immigrant wives, abandoned by their husbands, [were] overburdening the welfare state" (Cretney, 2003, pp. 72–73).

It is estimated that about 100,000 people currently live in polygamous households in the United States. Of these, about 20,000 are Mormons belonging to the Fundamentalist Church of Jesus Christ of Latter-Day Saints, many of whom reside in the Utah–Arizona border towns of Hildale and Colorado City (Figure 19.4). They hold on to a 19th-century Mormon doctrine that plural marriage brings exaltation in heaven—even though the practice was officially declared illegal in the United States in 1862 and was renounced in 1890 by the Church of Jesus Christ of Latter-Day Saints, the mainstream Mormon church headquartered in Salt Lake City.

A small but growing number of other Christian fundamentalists groups in the United States also practice polygamy, but most polygamists in the country are immigrants (both Muslim and non-Muslim) originating from Asian and African countries in which the practice is traditionally embedded and legal. Polygamous households are also growing among Black Muslim orthodox households in several major U.S. cities (McDermott, 2011; Schilling, 2012).

Despite its illegality and concerns that the practice can jeopardize the rights and well-being of young women, regional law enforcement officials have adopted a "live and let live" attitude toward religious-based polygyny in their region. Women involved in the practice are sometimes outspoken in defending it. One woman—a lawyer and one of nine co-wives—expresses her attitude toward polygyny as follows:

> I see it as the ideal way for a woman to have a career and children. In our family, the women can help each other care for the children. Women in monogamous relationships don't have that luxury. As I see it, if this lifestyle didn't already exist, it would have to be invented to accommodate career women. (Johnson, 1991, p. A22)

In some societies, if a man dies, leaving behind a wife and children, it is customary that one of his brothers marries the widowed sister-in-law. But this obligation does not preclude the brother having another wife then or in the future. This custom, called the *levirate* (from the Latin *levir*, which means "husband's brother"), provides security for the widow (and her children). A related marriage tradition is the *sororate* (Latin *soror* means "sister"), in which a man has the right to marry a sister (usually younger) of his deceased wife. In some societies, the sororate also applies to a man who has married a woman who is unable to bear children. This practice entitles a man to a replacement wife from his in-laws. In societies that have the levirate and sororate—customary in many traditional foraging, farming, and herding cultures—the in-law relationship between the two families is maintained even after the spouse's death and secures an established alliance between two groups.

VISUAL COUNTERPOINT

Figure 19.4 Polygamous Marriages An American Christian polygamist with his three wives and children stand in front of their dormitory-style home in Utah (*left*), and a Baranarana man of Upper Guinea poses with his two wives and children (*right*). Although this marriage form is legally prohibited in the United States, perhaps as many as 100,000 Americans live in polygamous households today.

Although monogamy and polygyny are the most common forms of marriage in the world today, other forms do occur. **Polyandry**, the marriage of one woman to two or more men simultaneously, is known in only a few societies. The rarity of polyandry could be due to longer life expectancy for women or to slightly lower female infant mortality, either of which might produce a society with a surplus of women.

Fewer than a dozen societies are known to have favored this form of marriage, but they involve people as widely separated from one another as the Marquesan Islanders of Polynesia and Tibetans in Asia (Figure 19.5). In Tibet, where inheritance is in the male line and arable land is limited, the marriage of brothers to a single woman (*fraternal polyandry*) keeps the land together by preventing it from being repeatedly subdivided among sons from one generation to the next. Unlike monogamy, it also holds down population growth, thereby avoiding increased pressures on resources. Finally, among Tibetans who practice a mixed economy of farming, herding, and trading in the Trans Himalayas, fraternal polyandry provides the household with an adequate pool of male labor for all three subsistence activities (Levine & Silk, 1997).

Figure 19.5 **Polyandrous Marriage** Polyandry—marriage between one woman and two or more men—occurs in fewer than a dozen societies, including among the Nyinba people living in northwest Nepal's Nyinba Valley in the Humla district near Tibet. Pictured here, from right: the older husband Chhonchanab with first daughter Dralma, the wife Shilangma, the younger husband KaliBahadur, and the second daughter Tsering.

Other Forms of Marriage

Notable among several other marriage forms is **group marriage**. Also known as *co-marriage*, this is a rare arrangement in which several men and women have sexual access to one another. Until a few decades ago, Inupiat Eskimos in northern Alaska, for instance, engaged in "spouse exchange" (*nuliaqatigiit*) between non-kin, with two conjugal husband–wife couples being united by shared sexual access. Highly institutionalized arrangements, these intimate relationships implied ties of mutual aid and support across territorial boundaries and were expected to last throughout the lifetime of the participants (Chance, 1990). The ties between the couples were so strong that their children retained a recognized relationship to one another (Spencer, 1984).

There are also arrangements anthropologists categorize as **fictive marriage**—marriage by proxy to the symbols of someone not physically present in order to establish a social status for a spouse and heirs. One major reason for such a marriage is to control rights to property in the next generation.

Various types of fictive marriages exist in different parts of the world. In the United States, for example, proxy marriage ceremonies accommodate physically separated partners, such as seafarers, prisoners, and military personnel deployed abroad.

In several traditional African societies—most famously among Nuer cattle herders of southern Sudan—a woman may marry a man who has died without heirs. In such situations the deceased man's brother may become his stand-in, or proxy, and marry a woman on his behalf. As in the case

of the marriage custom of the sororate discussed previously, the biological offspring will be considered as having been fathered by the dead man's spirit. Recognized as his legitimate children, they are his rightful heirs. Because such spouses are absent in the flesh yet believed to exist in spirit form, anthropologists refer to these fictive unions as *ghost marriages* (Evans-Pritchard, 1951).

Choice of Spouse

The Western romantic ideal that an individual should be free to marry whomever he or she chooses is certainly not universally embraced. In many societies, marriage and the establishment of a family are considered far too important to be left to the desires of young people. The individual relationship of two people who are expected to spend their lives together and raise their children together is viewed as incidental to the more serious matter of allying two families through the marriage bond. Marriage involves a transfer of rights between families, including rights to property and rights over children, as well as sexual rights. Thus, marriages tend to be arranged for the economic and political advantage of the family unit.

Although arranged marriages are rare in North American society, they do occur. Among ethnic minorities, they may

polyandry A marriage form in which a woman is married to two or more men at one time; a form of polygamy.

group marriage A marriage form in which several men and women have sexual access to one another; also called *co-marriage*.

fictive marriage A marriage form in which a proxy is used as a symbol of someone not physically present to establish the social status of a spouse and heirs.

serve to preserve traditional values that people fear might otherwise be lost. Among families of wealth and power, marriages may be orchestrated by segregating their children in private schools and carefully steering them toward appropriate spouses. The following Original Study illustrates how marriages may be arranged in cultures in which such traditional practices remain commonplace.

Arranging Marriage in India

BY SERENA NANDA

Six years after my first field trip to India, I returned to do research among the middle class in Bombay, a modern, sophisticated city. Planning to include a study of arranged marriages in my project, I thought I might even participate in arranging one myself. An opportunity presented itself almost immediately. A friend from my previous Indian trip was in the process of arranging for the marriage of her eldest son. Because my friend's family was eminently respectable and the boy himself personable, well educated, and nice looking, I was sure that by the end of my year's fieldwork, we would have found a match.

The basic rule seems to be that a family's reputation is most important. It is understood that matches would be arranged only within the same caste and general social class, although some crossing of subcastes is permissible if the class positions of the bride's and groom's families are similar. Although dowry is now prohibited by law in India, extensive gift exchanges took place with every marriage. Even when the boy's family does not "make demands," every girl's family nevertheless feels the obligation to give the traditional gifts—to the girl, to the boy, and to the boy's family. Particularly when the couple would be living in the joint family—that is, with the boy's parents and his married brothers and their families, as well as with unmarried siblings, which is still very common even among the urban, upper-middle class in India—the girl's parents are anxious to establish smooth relations between their family and that of the boy. Offering the proper gifts, even when not called "dowry," is often an important factor in influencing the relationship between the bride's and groom's families and perhaps, also, the treatment of the bride in her new home.

In a society where divorce is still a scandal and the divorce rate is exceedingly low, an arranged marriage is the beginning of a lifetime relationship not just between the bride and groom but between their families as well. Thus, although a girl's looks are important, her character is even more so because she is being judged as a prospective daughter-in-law as much as a prospective bride. . . .

My friend is a highly esteemed wife, mother, and daughter-in-law. She is religious, soft-spoken, modest, and deferential. She rarely gossips and never quarrels, two qualities highly desirable in a woman. A family that has the reputation for gossip and conflict among its womenfolk will not find it easy to get good wives for their sons. . . .

Originally from North India, my friend's family had lived for forty years in Bombay, where her husband owned a business. The family had delayed in seeking a match for their eldest son because he had been an air force pilot for several years, stationed in such remote places that it had seemed fruitless to try to find a girl who would be willing to accompany him. In their social class, a military career, despite its economic security, has little prestige and is considered a drawback in finding a suitable bride. . . .

The son had recently left the military and joined his father's business. Because he was a college graduate, modern, and well traveled, from such a good family, and, I thought, quite handsome, it seemed to me that he, or rather his family, was in a position to pick and choose. I said as much to my friend. Although she agreed that there were many advantages on their side, she also said, "We must keep in mind that my son is both short and dark; these are drawbacks in finding the right match." . . .

An important source of contacts in trying to arrange her son's marriage was my friend's social club in Bombay. Many of the women had daughters of the right age, and some had already expressed an interest in my friend's son. I was most enthusiastic about the possibilities of one particular family who had five daughters, all of whom were pretty, demure, and well educated. Their mother had told my friend, "You can have your pick for your son, whichever one of my daughters appeals to you most." I saw a match in sight. "Surely," I said to my friend, "we will find one there. Let's go visit and make our choice." But my friend did not seem to share my enthusiasm.

When I kept pressing for an explanation of her reluctance, she admitted, "See, Serena, here is the problem. The family has so many daughters, how will they be able to provide nicely for any of them? . . . Because this is our eldest son, it's best if we marry him to a girl who is the only daughter, then the wedding will truly be a gala affair." I argued that surely the quality of the girls themselves made up for any deficiency in the elaborateness of the wedding. My friend admitted this point but still seemed reluctant to proceed.

Is there something else," I asked her, "some factor I have missed?" "Well," she finally said, "there is one other thing. They have one daughter already married and living in Bombay. The mother is always complaining to me that the girl's in-laws don't let her visit her own family often

What she said was true and I promised myself to be more patient. I had really hoped and expected that the match would be made before my year in India was up. But it was not to be. When I left India my friend seemed no further along in finding a suitable match for her son than when I had arrived.

Two years later, I returned to India and still my friend had not found a girl for her son. By this time, he was close to 30, and I think she was a little worried. Because she knew I had friends all over India, and I was going to be there for a year, she asked me to "help her in this work" and keep an eye out for someone suitable. . . .

enough. So it makes me wonder, will she be that kind of mother who always wants her daughter at her own home? This will prevent the girl from adjusting to our house. It is not a good thing." And so, this family of five daughters was dropped as a possibility.

Somewhat disappointed, I nevertheless respected my friend's reasoning and geared up for the next prospect. This was also the daughter of a woman in my friend's social club. There was clear interest in this family and I could see why. The family's reputation was excellent; in fact, they came from a subcaste slightly higher than my friend's own. The girl, an only daughter, was pretty and well educated and had a brother studying in the United States. Yet, after expressing an interest to me in this family, all talk of them suddenly died down and the search began elsewhere.

"What happened to that girl as a prospect?" I asked one day. "You never mention her anymore. She is so pretty and so educated, what did you find wrong?"

"She is too educated. We've decided against it. My husband's father saw the girl on the bus the other day and thought her forward. A girl who 'roams about' the city by herself is not the girl for our family." My disappointment this time was even greater, as I thought the son would have liked the girl very much. . . . I learned that if the family of the girl has even a slightly higher social status than the family of the boy, the bride may think herself too good for them, and this too will cause problems. . . .

After one more candidate, who my friend decided was not attractive enough for her son, almost six months had passed, and I had become anxious. My friend laughed at my impatience: "You Americans want everything done so quickly. You get married quickly and then just as quickly get divorced. Here we take marriage more seriously. If a mistake is made we have not only ruined the life of our son or daughter, but we have spoiled the reputation of our family as well. And that will make it much harder for their brothers and sisters to get married. So we must be very careful."

It was almost at the end of my year's stay in India that I met a family with a marriageable daughter whom I felt might be a good possibility for my friend's son. . . . This new family had a successful business in a medium-sized city in central India and were from the same subcaste as my friend. The daughter was pretty and chic; in fact, she had studied fashion design in college. Her parents would not allow her to go off by herself to any of the major cities in India where she could make a career, but they had compromised with her wish to work by allowing her to run a small dress-making boutique from their home. In spite of her desire to have a career, the daughter was both modest and home-loving and had had a traditional, sheltered upbringing.

I mentioned the possibility of a match with my friend's son. The girl's parents were most interested. Although their daughter was not eager to marry just yet, the idea of living in Bombay—a sophisticated, extremely fashion-conscious city where she could continue her education in clothing design—was a great inducement. I gave the girl's father my friend's address.

Returning to Bombay on my way to New York, I told my friend of this newly discovered possibility. She seemed to feel there was potential but, in spite of my urging, would not make any moves herself. She rather preferred to wait for the girl's family to call upon them.

A year later I received a letter from my friend. The family had visited, and her daughter and their daughter had become very good friends. During that year, the two girls had frequently visited each other. I thought things looked promising.

Last week I received an invitation to a wedding: My friend's son and the girl were getting married. Because I had found the match, my presence was particularly requested at the wedding. I was thrilled. Success at last! As I prepared to leave for India, I began thinking, "Now, my friend's younger son, who do I know who has a nice girl for him . . . ?"

Adapted from Nanda, S. (1992). Arranging a marriage in India. In P. R. De Vita (Ed.). The naked anthropologist (pp. 139–143). Belmont, CA: Wadsworth.

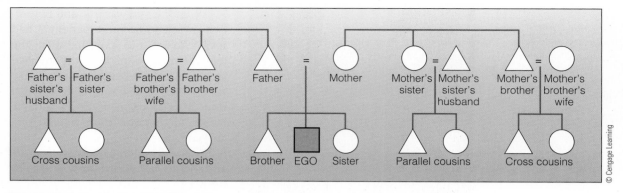

Figure 19.6 **Kinship Relationships** Anthropologists use diagrams of this sort to illustrate kinship relationships. This one shows the distinction between cross cousins and parallel cousins. In such diagrams, males are always shown with triangles, females with circles, marital ties with an equal sign (=), sibling relationships with a horizontal line, and parent–child relationships with a vertical line. Terms are given from the perspective of the individual labeled EGO, who can be male or female.

Cousin Marriage

Although cousin marriage is prohibited in some societies, certain cousins are the preferred marriage partners in others. A **parallel cousin** is the child of a father's brother or a mother's sister (Figure 19.6). In some societies, the preferred spouse for a man is his father's brother's daughter (or, from the woman's point of view, her father's brother's son). This is known as *patrilateral parallel-cousin marriage.*

Although not obligatory, such marriages have been favored historically among Arabs, the ancient Israelites, and the ancient Greeks. All of these societies are (or were) hierarchical in nature—that is, some people are ranked higher than others because they have more power and property—and although male dominance and descent are emphasized, daughters as well as sons inherit property of value. Thus, when a man marries his father's brother's daughter (or a woman marries her father's brother's son), property is retained within the single male line of descent. Generally, in these societies the greater the property, the more this form of parallel-cousin marriage is apt to occur.

A **cross cousin** is the child of a mother's brother or a father's sister (see Figure 19.6). Some societies favor *matrilateral cross-cousin marriage*—marriage of a man to his mother's brother's daughter or a woman to her father's sister's son. This preference exists among food foragers (such as the Aborigines of Australia) and some farming cultures (including various peoples of southern India). Among food foragers, who inherit relatively little in the way of property, such marriages help establish and maintain ties of solidarity between social groups. In agricultural societies, however, the transmission of property is an important determinant. In societies that trace descent exclusively in the female line, for instance, property and other important rights usually pass from a man to his sister's son; under cross-cousin marriage, the sister's son is also the man's daughter's husband.

Same-Sex Marriage

As noted earlier in this chapter, our definition of *marriage* refers to a union between "people" rather than "a man and a woman" because in some societies same-sex marriages are socially acceptable and officially allowed by law. Marriages between individuals of the same sex may provide a way of dealing with problems for which opposite-sex marriage offers no satisfactory solution. This is the case with woman–woman marriage, a practice permitted in many societies of sub-Saharan Africa, although in none does it involve more than a small minority of all women.

Details differ from one society to another, but woman–woman marriages among the Nandi of western Kenya may be taken as representative of such practices in Africa (Oboler, 1980). The Nandi are a pastoral people who also do considerable farming. Control of most significant property and the primary means of production—livestock and land—is exclusively in the hands of men and may be transmitted only to their male heirs, usually their sons. Because polygyny is the preferred form of marriage, a man's property is

---

parallel cousin The child of a father's brother or a mother's sister.
cross cousin The child of a mother's brother or a father's sister.

Figure 19.7 Same-Sex Marriage in the United States Tory receives a celebratory kiss from her father alongside her new spouse, Monica, at their wedding in Connecticut, where same-sex marriage became legal in 2008.

normally divided equally among his wives for their sons to inherit. Within the household, each wife has her own home in which she lives with her children, but all are under the authority of the husband, who is a remote and aloof figure within the family. In such situations, the position of a woman who bears no sons is difficult; not only does she not help perpetuate her husband's male line—a major concern among the Nandi—but also she has no one to inherit the proper share of her husband's property.

To get around these problems, a woman of advanced age who bore no sons may become a female husband by marrying a young woman. The purpose of this arrangement is for the young wife to provide the male heirs her female husband could not. To accomplish this, the woman's wife enters into a sexual relationship with a man other than her female husband's male husband; usually it is one of his male relatives. No other obligations exist between this woman and her male sex partner, and her female husband is recognized as the social and legal father of any children born under these conditions.

In keeping with her role as female husband, this woman is expected to abandon her female gender identity and, ideally, dress and behave as a man. In practice, the ideal is not completely achieved, for the habits of a lifetime are difficult to reverse. Generally, it is in the context of domestic activities, which are most highly symbolic of female identity, that female husbands most completely assume a male identity.

The individuals in woman–woman marriages enjoy several advantages. By assuming male identity, a barren or sonless woman raises her status considerably and even achieves near equality with men, who otherwise occupy a far more favored position in Nandi society than women. A woman who marries a female husband is usually one who is unable to make a good marriage, often because she (the female husband's wife) has lost face as a consequence of premarital pregnancy. By marrying a female husband, she too raises her status and also secures legitimacy for her children. Moreover, a female husband is usually less harsh and demanding, spends more time with her, and allows her a greater say in decision making than a male husband does. The one thing she may not do is engage in sexual activity with her marriage partner. In fact, female husbands are expected to abandon sexual activity altogether, including with their male husbands to whom they remain married even though the women now have their own wives.

In contrast to woman–woman marriages among the Nandi are same-sex marriages that include sexual activity between partners. Over the past decade, the legal recognition of such unions has become a matter of vigorous debate in some parts of the world. Nearly a dozen countries—Argentina, Belgium, Canada, Denmark, Iceland, the Netherlands, Norway, Portugal, South Africa, Spain, and Sweden—have legalized same-sex marriages. In the United States, such marriages are now legal in nine states, as well as the District of Columbia (**Figure 19.7**).

The issue of same-sex marriage remains unsettled in many parts of the world, with official policies sometimes swinging back and forth—evidence of the fact that cultures are dynamic and capable of change. In addition, close to a dozen U.S. states and about two dozen countries around the world recognize *civil unions* (also known as *civil* or *domestic partnerships*), which offer a varying range of marriage benefits.

Among the arguments most commonly marshaled by opponents of same-sex unions is the claim that marriage has always been between males and females—but as we have just seen, this is not true. Same-sex marriages have been documented not only for a number of societies in Africa but in other parts of the world as well (Kuefler, 2007). As among the Nandi, they provide acceptable positions in society for individuals who might otherwise be marginalized.

Marriage and Economic Exchange

Marriages in many human societies are formalized by some sort of economic exchange. This may take the form of a gift exchange known as **bridewealth** (sometimes called *bride-price*), which involves payments of money or valuable goods to a bride's parents or other close kin.

This usually happens in patrilineal societies in which the bride will become a member of the household in which her husband grew up; this household will benefit from her labor as well as from the offspring she produces. Thus, her family must be compensated for their loss.

Bride-price not a simple buying and selling of women; rather, it can contribute to the bride's household (through purchases of jewelry or furnishings) or can help finance an elaborate and costly wedding celebration. It also enhances the stability of the marriage because it usually must be refunded if the couple separates. Other forms of compensation are an exchange of women between families—"My son will marry your daughter if your son will marry my daughter." Yet another is **bride service**, a period of time during which the groom works for the bride's family.

In a number of societies, especially those with an agriculturally based economy, women often bring a dowry with them at marriage. A **dowry** is a woman's share of parental property that, instead of passing to her upon her parents' death, is given to her at the time of her marriage (**Figure 19.8**). This does not mean that she retains control of this property after marriage. In some European and Asian countries, for example, a woman's property traditionally falls exclusively under her husband's control. Having benefited by what she has brought to the marriage, however, he is obligated to look out for her future

Figure 19.8 Dowries in Traditional Farming Societies In some societies, when a woman marries she receives her share of the family inheritance (her dowry), which she brings to her new family (unlike bride-price, which passes from the groom's family to the bride's family). Shown here are Slovakian women in a traditional farming village each carrying a trousseau (*výbava nevesty*)—consisting of the bride's clothes, linen, bedding, and other objects of her dowry—in a festive procession to her new home. Traditionally, the bride keeps her finer linen in a beautifully carved or painted dowry chest. In addition, her birth family contributes some livestock, land, or other form of wealth, which Slovaks call *veno*, to the new household. Held in her name, this property provides the woman with a measure of independence from her husband.

© John Eastcott/Yva Momatiuk/Woodfin Camp & Associates

well-being, including her security after his death. In the United States today, a form of dowry persists with the custom of the bride's family paying the wedding expenses.

One of the functions of dowry is to ensure a woman's support in widowhood (or after divorce), an important consideration for societies in which men carry out the bulk of productive work, and women are valued for their reproductive potential rather than for the work they do. In such societies, women incapable of bearing children are especially vulnerable, but the dowry they bring with them at marriage helps protect them against desertion. Another function of dowry is to reflect the economic status of the woman in societies in which differences in wealth are important. It also permits women, with the aid of their parents and kin, to compete through dowry for desirable (that is, wealthy) husbands.

Divorce

Like marriage, divorce in most societies is a matter of great concern to the couple's families because it impacts not only the individuals dissolving their marital relationship but also offspring, in-laws, other relatives, and sometimes entire communities. Indeed, divorce may have social, political, and economic consequences far beyond the breakup of a couple and their household.

Across cultures, divorce arrangements can be made for a variety of reasons and with varying degrees of difficulty. Among the Gusii farmers of western Kenya, for instance, sterility and impotence are grounds for a divorce. Among certain aboriginal peoples in northern Canada and Chenchu foragers in central India, divorce is traditionally discouraged after children are born; couples usually are urged by their families to accept their differences. By contrast, in the southwestern United States, a traditional Hopi Indian woman in Arizona could divorce her husband at any time merely by placing his belongings outside the door to indicate he is no longer welcome. Among the most common reasons for divorce across cultures are infidelity, sterility, cruelty, and desertion (Betzig, 1989; Goodwin, 1999).

In most non-Western societies, a divorced woman quickly remarries, thus adult unmarried women are rare. In many societies, economic considerations are often the strongest motivation to wed. On the island of New Guinea, a man does not marry because of sexual needs, which he can readily satisfy out of wedlock, but because there it is important to have a female partner to carry out tasks that traditionally fall to women—making pots and cooking his meals, fabricating nets, and weeding his plantings. Likewise, women in communities that depend on males for their fighting abilities need husbands who are raised to be able warriors as well as good hunters.

Although divorce rates may be high in various parts of the world, they have become so high in Western industrial and postindustrial societies that many worry about the future of what they view as traditional and familiar forms of marriage and the family. It is interesting to note that although divorce was next to impossible in Western societies between 1000 and 1800, in those centuries few marriages lasted more than about ten or twenty years, due to high mortality rates caused in part by inadequate health care and poor medical expertise (Stone, 2005). For instance, women dying in childbirth ended many marriages. With increased longevity, separation by death has diminished, and separation by legal action has grown. In the United States divorce rates have leveled off since peaking in the 1980s, but over 40 percent of marriages still do not survive (Morello, 2011).

Family and Household

Dependence on group living for survival is a basic human characteristic. We have inherited this from primate ancestors, although we have developed it in our own distinctly human way—through culture. No matter how each culture defines what constitutes a family, this social unit forms the basic cooperative structure that ensures an individual's primary needs and provides the necessary care for children to develop as healthy and productive members of the group and thereby ensure its future.

Comparative historical and cross-cultural studies reveal a wide variety of family patterns, and these patterns may change over time. Thus, the definition of **family** is necessarily broad: two or more people related by blood, marriage, or adoption. The family may take many forms, ranging from a single parent with one or more children, to a married couple or polygamous spouses with offspring, to several generations of parents and their children.

In all known cultures, past and present, gender plays at least some role in determining the division of labor. An effective way to facilitate economic cooperation between men and women and simultaneously provide for a close bond between mother and child is by establishing residential groups that include adults of both sexes. The differing nature of male and female roles, as defined by different cultures, makes it advantageous in many cultures for a child to have an adult of the same sex available to serve as a proper model for the appropriate adult role. The presence of adult men and women in the same residential group provides for this. The men, however, need not be the women's

---

bridewealth The money or valuable goods paid by the groom or his family to the bride's family upon marriage; also called *bride-price*.

bride service A designated period of time when the groom works for the bride's family.

dowry A payment at the time of a woman's marriage that comes from her inheritance, made to either her or her husband.

family Two or more people related by blood, marriage, or adoption. The family may take many forms, ranging from a single parent with one or more children, to a married couple or polygamous spouses with or without offspring, to several generations of parents and their children.

Figure 19.9 Household Versus Family Households can include many individuals not related to one another biologically or through marriage, as is seen in this royal household celebration at the Yoruba palace in Oyo, Nigeria. Commonly in societies with nobility, the royal family lives with many others not related to the ruler.

husbands. In some societies they are the women's brothers—as in the case of the Nayar, discussed earlier in this chapter, among whom sisters and their children live together with their brothers and their mother and her brothers.

For purposes of cross-cultural comparison, anthropologists define the **household** as a domestic unit of one or more persons living in one residence. In the vast majority of human societies, most households are made up of family members, but they may also include nonrelatives, such as servants. However, there are many other arrangements.

For instance, among the Mundurucu Indians, a horticultural people living in the center of Brazil's Amazon rainforest, married men and women are members of separate households, meeting periodically for sexual activity. At age 13, boys join their fathers in the men's house. Meanwhile, their sisters continue to live with their mothers and the younger boys in two or three houses grouped around the men's house. Thus, the men's house constitutes one household inhabited by adult males and their sexually mature sons, and the women's houses are inhabited by adult women and prepubescent boys and girls.

An array of other domestic arrangements can be found in other parts of the world, including situations in which coresidents of a household are not related biologically or by marriage—such as the service personnel in an elaborate royal household, apprentices in the household of craft specialists, low-status clients in the household of rich and powerful patrons, or groups of children being raised by paired teams of adult male and female community members in an Israeli kibbutz (a collectively owned and operated agricultural settlement). So it is that *family* and *household* are not always synonymous (Figure 19.9).

Forms of the Family

To discuss the various forms families take in response to particular social, historical, and ecological circumstances, we must first distinguish between a **conjugal family** (in Latin *conjugere* means "to join together"), which is formed on the basis of marital ties, and a **consanguineal family** (based on the Latin word *consanguineus*, literally meaning "of the same blood"), which consists of related women, their brothers, and the women's offspring.

Consanguineal families are not common, but there are more examples than the classic case of the Nayar described earlier in the chapter. Among these are the Musuo of southwestern China and the Tory Islanders—a Roman Catholic, Gaelic-speaking fishing people living off the coast of Ireland. Typically, Tory Islanders do not marry until they are in their late 20s or early 30s. By then, commented one local woman,

> It's too late to break up arrangements that you have already known for a long time. . . . You know, I have my sisters and brothers to look after, why should I leave home to go live with a husband? After all, he's got his sisters and his brothers looking after him. (Fox, 1981)

Notably, because the community numbers but a few hundred people, husbands and wives are within easy commuting distance of each other.

According to a cross-cultural survey of family types in 192 cultures around the world, the extended family is most common, present in nearly half of those cultures, compared

household A domestic unit of one or more persons living in one residence. Other than family members, a household may include nonrelatives, such as servants.

conjugal family A family established through marriage.

consanguineal family A family of blood relatives, consisting of related women, their brothers, and the women's offspring.

nuclear family A group consisting of one or two parents and dependent offspring, which may include a stepparent, stepsiblings, and adopted children. Until recently this term referred only to the mother, father, and child(ren) unit.

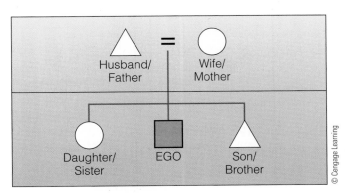

Figure 19.10 The Nuclear Family This diagram shows the relationships in a traditional nuclear family, a form that is common but declining in North America and much of Europe.

to the nuclear family at 25 percent, and polygamy at 22 percent (Winick, 1970). Each of these is discussed next.

The Nuclear Family

The smallest family unit is the **nuclear family**, made up of one or two parents and dependent offspring, which may include a stepparent, stepsiblings, and adopted children (Figure 19.10). Until recently, the term *nuclear family* referred solely to the mother, father, and child(ren) unit—the family form that most North Americans, Europeans, and many others regard as the normal or natural nucleus of larger family units. In the United States, traditional mother, father, child(ren) nuclear family households reached their highest frequency around 1950, when 60 percent of all households conformed to this model (Stacey, 1990). Today, such families make up about 20 percent of U.S. households, and the term *nuclear family* is used to cover the social reality of several types of small parent–child units, including single parents with children and same-sex couples with children (Irvine, 1999; U.S. Census Bureau, 2010).

Industrialization and market capitalism have played a historical role in shaping the nuclear family most of us are familiar with today. One reason for this is that factories, mining and transportation companies, warehouses, shops, and other businesses generally pay individual wage earners

only for the jobs they are hired to do. Whether these workers are single, married, divorced, or have siblings or children is really not a concern to the profit-seeking companies. Because jobs may come and go, individual wage earners must remain mobile to adapt to the labor markets. And because few wage earners have the financial resources to support large numbers of relatives without incomes of their own, industrial or postindustrial societies do not favor the continuance of larger extended families (discussed below), which are standard in most societies traditionally dependent on pastoral nomadism, agriculture, or horticulture.

Interestingly, the nuclear family is also likely to be prominent in traditional foraging societies such as that of the Eskimo people who live in the barren Arctic environments of eastern Siberia (Russia), Alaska, Greenland, and Canada (where Eskimos are now known as Inuit) (Figure 19.11). In the winter the traditional Inuit husband and wife, with their children, roam the vast Arctic Canadian snowscape in their quest for food. The husband hunts and makes shelters. The wife cooks, is responsible for the children, and makes the clothing and keeps it in good repair. One of a wife's traditional chores is to chew her husband's boots to soften the leather for the next day so that he can resume his quest for game. The wife and her children could not survive without the husband, and life for a man is unimaginable without a wife.

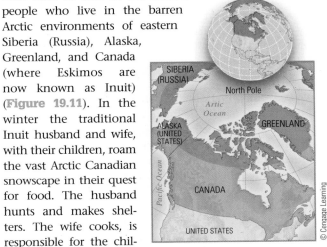

Similar to nuclear families in industrial societies, those living under especially harsh environmental conditions must be prepared to fend for themselves. Such isolation comes with its own set of challenges, including the difficulties of rearing children without multigenerational support

Figure 19.11 Nuclear Families in the Canadian Arctic Among Inuit people in Canada who still hunt for much of their food, nuclear families, such as the one shown here, are typical. Their isolation from other relatives is usually temporary. Much of the time they are found in groups of at least a few related families.

Figure 19.12 Extended Family Households In many Maya communities, sons bring their wives to live in houses built on the edges of a small open plaza, on one edge of which their father's house already stands. Numerous household activities are carried out on this plaza—children play while adults do some productive work or socialize with guests. The head of the family is the sons' father, who makes most of the important decisions. All members of the family work together for the common good and deal with outsiders as a single unit.

© Joe Cavanaugh/DDB Stock

and a lack of familial care for the elderly. Nonetheless, this form of family is well adapted to a mode of subsistence that requires a high degree of geographic mobility. For the Inuit in Canada, this mobility permits the hunt for food; for other North Americans, the hunt for jobs and improved social status require a mobile form of family unit.

The Extended Family

When two or more closely related nuclear families cluster together in a large domestic group, they form a unit known as the **extended family**. This larger family unit, common in traditional horticultural, agricultural, and pastoral societies around the world, typically consists of siblings with their spouses and offspring, and often their parents. All of these kin, some related by blood and some by marriage, live and work together for the common good and deal with outsiders as a single unit. Extended family households exist in many parts of the world, including among the Maya of Central America and Mexico (Vogt, 1990) (Figure 19.12).

Because members of the younger generation bring their husbands or wives to live in the family, extended families have continuity through time. As older members die off, new members are born into the family. Extended families have built into them particular challenges. Among these are difficulties that the in-marrying individual is likely to have in adjusting to the spouse's family.

Nontraditional Families and Nonfamily Households

In North America and parts of Europe, increasing numbers of people live in nonfamily households, either alone or with people who are not relatives. In fact, about one-third of households in the United States fall into this category (Figure 19.13). Many others live as members of what are often called *nontraditional families.*

Increasingly common are *cohabitation* households, made up of unmarried couples. Since 1960, such households have increased dramatically in number especially among young couples in their 20s and early 30s in North America and parts of Europe. In Norway, for example, over half of all live births now occur outside marriage. One reason for this is that Norwegian couples who have lived together for at least two years and who have children have many of the same rights and obligations as their married counterparts (Noack, 2001). For many, however, cohabitation represents a relatively short-term domestic arrangement because most cohabiting couples either marry or separate within two years (Forste, 2008).

Cohabitation breakup has contributed to the growing number of *single-parent* households—as have increases in divorce, sexual activity outside marriage, declining marriage rates among women of childbearing age, and the number of women preferring single motherhood. In the United States, more than a third of all births occur outside of marriage (Stein & St. George, 2009). The percentage of U.S. single-parent households has grown to nearly 10 percent, whereas the number composed of married couples with children has dropped to about 20 percent. Although single-parent households account for about 10 percent of all U.S. households, they are home to 30 percent of all children (under 18 years of age) in the country (U.S. Census Bureau, 2010).

In the vast majority of cases, a child in a single-parent household lives with the mother. Single-parent households headed by women are neither new nor restricted to industrial or postindustrial societies. They have been studied for a long time in Caribbean countries, where men historically have been exploited as a cheap source of labor for sugar, coffee, or banana plantations. In more recent decades, many of these men are now also working as temporary migrant laborers in foreign countries, primarily in the United States—often living in temporary households composed of fellow laborers.

extended family Two or more closely related nuclear families clustered together in a large domestic group.

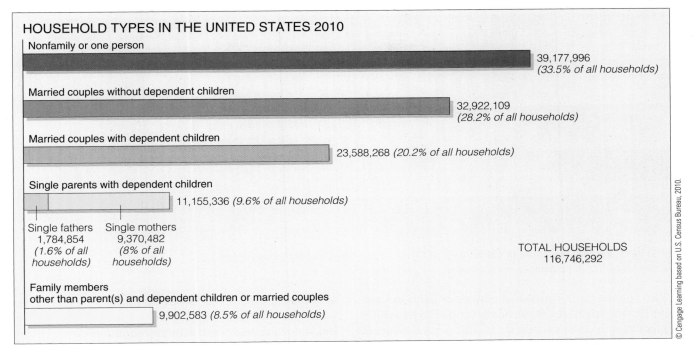

HOUSEHOLD TYPES IN THE UNITED STATES 2010

Nonfamily or one person
39,177,996
(33.5% of all households)

Married couples without dependent children
32,922,109
(28.2% of all households)

Married couples with dependent children
23,588,268 *(20.2% of all households)*

Single parents with dependent children
11,155,336 *(9.6% of all households)*

Single fathers
1,784,854
(1.6% of all households)

Single mothers
9,370,482
(8% of all households)

TOTAL HOUSEHOLDS
116,746,292

Family members
other than parent(s) and dependent children or married couples
9,902,583 *(8.5% of all households)*

© Cengage Learning based on U.S. Census Bureau, 2010.

Figure 19.13 Various Kinds of U.S. Households What has been traditionally considered the most prevalent household type, married couples with dependent children, is now only about 20 percent of the total number of households.

Also significant today are the high numbers of *blended families*. These are families composed of a married couple together raising children from previous unions.

Residence Patterns

When some form of conjugal or extended family is the norm, family exogamy requires that either the husband or wife, if not both, must move to a new household upon marriage. There are several common patterns of residence that a newly married couple may adopt—the prime determinant being ecological circumstances, although other factors enter in as well. Thus, postmarital residence arrangements, far from being arbitrary, are adaptive in character.

Patrilocal residence is a pattern in which a married couple lives in the husband's father's place of residence. This arrangement is most often found in cultural situations in which men play a predominant role in subsistence, particularly if they own property that can be accumulated; when polygyny is customary; when warfare is prominent enough to make cooperation among men especially important; and when an elaborate political organization exists in which men wield authority. These conditions are most often found together in societies that rely on animal husbandry and/or intensive agriculture for subsistence. Where patrilocal residence is customary, the bride often must move to a different band or community. In such cases, her parents' family is not only losing the services of a useful family member, but they are losing her potential offspring as well. Hence, usually there is some kind of compensation to her family, most commonly bride-price.

Matrilocal residence, in which a married couple lives in the wife's mother's place of residence, is likely if cultural ecological circumstances make the role of the woman predominant for subsistence. It is found most often in horticultural societies in which political organization is relatively uncentralized and cooperation among women is important. The Hopi Indians provide one example. Although it is the Hopi men who do the farming, the women control access to land and "own" the harvest. Men are not even allowed in the granaries. Under matrilocal residence, men usually do not move very far from the family in which they were raised, so they are available to help out there from time to time. Therefore, marriage usually does not involve compensation to the groom's family. Less common, but also found in matrilineal societies, is *avunculocal residence*, in which the couple lives with the husband's mother's brother.

In **neolocal residence**, a married couple forms a household in a separate location. This occurs when the independence of the nuclear family is emphasized. In industrial societies such as the United States—in which most economic activity occurs outside rather than inside the family, and it is important for individuals to be able to move where jobs can be found—neolocal residence is better suited than any of the other patterns.

patrilocal residence A residence pattern in which a married couple lives in the husband's father's place of residence.
matrilocal residence A residence pattern in which a married couple lives in the wife's mother's place of residence.
neolocal residence A residence pattern in which a married couple establishes its household in a location apart from either the husband's or the wife's relatives.

© Edward Burtynsky

Figure 19.14 **Factory Dormitory in China** Many of China's 114 million migrant laborers work in factories and live in dormitories such as this.

Also noteworthy is **ambilocal residence** (*ambi* in Latin means "both"). In this arrangement, the couple can join either the groom's or the bride's family, living wherever the resources are best or their presence is most needed or appreciated. This flexible pattern is particularly common among food-foraging peoples—if resources are scarce in the territory of the husband's family group, the couple may join the wife's relatives for more readily available food supplies in their domain.

Marriage, Family, and Household in Our Globalized and Technologized World

Large-scale immigration, modern technology, and multiple other factors in the emerging political economy of global capitalism also impact the cross-cultural mosaic of marriage, family, and household. For instance, electronic and digital communication by way of fiber-optic cables and satellites has transformed how individuals express sexual attraction and engage in romantic courtship.

Today, local, cross-cultural, and transnational love relations bloom via the Internet. Numerous online companies provide dating and matchmaking services, permitting individuals to post personal profiles and search for romantic partners or future spouses in a secured Internet setting. Such services also appeal to individuals in ethnic or religious diasporas seeking others with compatible personal, ethnic, or religious backgrounds. Indian matrimonial websites, for instance, are now also used for purposes of arranged marriages, allowing parents to upload a video profile of their child, screen potential suitors, and settle on the right match.

Social media also permit the pursuit of traditionally prohibited relationships through clandestine text messaging

of forbidden desires and tabooed intimacies—for example, across castes in India and between young unmarried men and women in traditional Muslim communities.

Adoption and New Reproductive Technologies

Although it has not been uncommon for childless couples in many cultures throughout human history to adopt children, including orphans and even captives, today it is a transnational practice for adults from industrial and postindustrial countries to travel across the world in search of children to adopt, regardless of their ethnic heritage (see the Globalscape). Also increasingly common is open adoption, which makes it possible for a child to have a relationship with both the biological and the adoptive parents.

Among other contributing factors to today's diversity of families and households are *new reproductive technologies* (NRTs), including various forms of *in vitro fertilization* (IVF) in which an egg is fertilized in a laboratory. The embryo is then transferred to the uterus to begin a pregnancy or is frozen for future use. In cases of IVF with a surrogate mother using donor egg and sperm, a newborn essentially has five parents: the birth parents who provided the egg and sperm, the surrogate mother who carried the baby, and the parents who will raise the baby.

Migrant Workforces

Also of note in terms of new residential patterns is the ever-growing number of households composed of temporary and migrant workers. Today, China alone has 114 million of them, mostly young people who left the peasant villages of their childhood and traveled to fast-growing cities to work in factories, shops, and restaurants. Some pile into apartments with friends or coworkers; others live in factory dormitories—new, single-generation households that stand in stark contrast to the multigenerational extended family households in which they were raised (**Figure 19.14**).

ambilocal residence A residence pattern in which a married couple may choose either matrilocal or patrilocal residence.

Globalscape

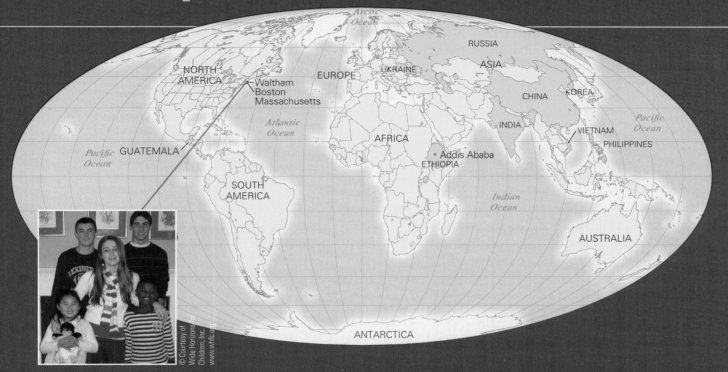

© Courtesy of
Wide Horizons for
Children, Inc.
www.whfc.org

Transnational Child Exchange?

Settling into her seat for the flight to Boston, Kathryn cradled the sleepy head of her newly adopted son, Mesay. As the plane lifted away from African soil and presented a sweeping view of Ethiopia's capital, tears slid down her cheeks. Were the tears for Ethiopia's loss of a boy, a boy's loss of Ethiopia, or her profound joy for the gift of adoption?

Child exchange is a universal phenomenon, taking place across the world and throughout human history. Just as *marriage* and *kinship* mean different things in different cultures, so does *child exchange*, referred to in the English language as *adoption*. In some cultures, adoption is rare, whereas in others, such as in Polynesian communities in the Pacific Islands, it is very common. For instance, in a small village in Tahiti it was found that over 25 percent of children were raised by adoptive parents.

A cross-cultural understanding of adoption is vital now that child exchange has become part of the global flow, especially from poor countries in Africa, Latin America, Southeast Asia, and eastern Europe, to affluent countries in North America and western Europe. The global exchange of children initially involved war orphans after World War II. In recent decades, extreme poverty has become a major factor, as mothers confronting serious deprivation may feel forced to abandon, give away, or sometimes sell their children. Whether brokered by government or nongovernmental agencies, by for-profit or nonprofit enterprises, global child exchange has become a big business—legal and illegal, moral and amoral, happifying and horrifying. This is especially true in poor countries where most workers earn less than a dollar a day, and a foreign adoption nets $12,000 to $35,000 in broker fees.

Since the early 1970s, about 500,000 foreign children have been adopted into families in the United States alone. A nearly equal number ended up in other wealthy countries. The global flow to the United States peaked in 2004 when nearly 23,000 arrived—most from China (30%), Russia (25%), Guatemala (14%), and Korea (7%), with 5,500 flown in from other poor countries such as India, Philippines, Ukraine, and Vietnam. Statistics vary and shift according to adoption rules. Some countries have shut the door on foreign adoptions due to accusations of exporting or even selling children. Others restrict or prohibit it for religious reasons. Sudan, for example, forbids foreign adoption of Muslim children and automatically classifies religiously unidentified orphans as Muslim.

A country that does not discriminate on the basis of religion is its neighbor Ethiopia, which has gained popularity as an infant-provider country. One of six U.S. agencies officially approved to do foreign adoptions from Ethiopia is Wide Horizons for Children in Waltham, Massachusetts, which has placed many Ethiopian children with U.S. families. Among them is Mesay (pictured in the family photo above), now settled into his new life with Kathryn, her husband, and their four other children, including a sister about his age, adopted from China as an infant.

Global Twister

How do you compare a European or North American woman who accepts a surrogate pregnancy fee of $115,000 to $150,000 to cover the costs of bearing a child for someone else to a Third World mother living in poverty, who decides to give up her child for adoption for a price?

Similar scenes are repeated all around the world as individuals in this transient workforce set up house together far away from home in order to make a living.

Although many countries have passed legislation intended to provide migrants with protections concerning housing, as well as work conditions and pay (such as the 1983 Migrant and Seasonal Agricultural Worker Protection Act in the United States), living conditions for these workers are often miserable (Chang, 2005).

As the various ethnographic examples in this chapter illustrate, our species has invented a wide variety of marriage, family, and household forms, each in correspondence with related features in the social structure and conforming to the larger cultural system. In the face of new challenges, we explore and tinker in search of solutions, sometimes finding completely new forms and other times returning to time-tested patterns of more traditional varieties.

CHAPTER CHECKLIST

How do different cultures permit or restrict sexual relations?

Every society has rules and customs concerning sexual relations, marriage, household and family structures, and childrearing practices, all of which play important roles in establishing and maintaining the social alliances and continuity that help ensure a society's overall well-being.

A majority of cultures are sexually permissive and do not sharply regulate personal sexual practices. Others are restrictive and explicitly prohibit all sexual activity outside of marriage. Of these, a few punish adultery by imprisonment, social exclusion, or even death, as traditionally prescribed by some religious laws.

Incest taboos forbid marriage and sexual relations between certain close relatives—usually between parent–child and siblings at a minimum. A truly convincing explanation of the incest taboo has yet to be advanced, but it is related to the practices of endogamy (marrying within a group of individuals) and exogamy (marrying outside a group).

What is marriage?

Marriage is a culturally sanctioned union between two or more people that establishes certain rights and obligations between them, them and their children, and them and their in-laws.

Marriage falls into several broad categories. Monogamy, having one spouse, is the most common form of marriage. Serial monogamy, in which a man or woman marries a series of partners, has become common among Europeans and North Americans.

Polygamy, in which one individual has multiple spouses, comes in two forms: polygyny and polyandry. A man must have a certain amount of wealth to be able to afford polygyny (marriage to more than one wife at the same time). Yet in societies where women do most of the productive work, polygyny may serve as a means of generating wealth for a household. Although few marriages in a given society may be polygynous, it is an appropriate and even preferred form of marriage in the majority of the world's societies.

Because few communities have a surplus of men, polyandry (the custom of a woman having several husbands) is uncommon. Also rare is group marriage, in which several men and several women have sexual access to one another.

In Western industrial and postindustrial countries, marriages are generally based on ideals of romantic love. In non-Western societies, economic considerations are of major concern in arranging marriages, and marriage serves to bind two families as allies.

Preferred marriage partners in many societies are particular cross cousins (mother's brother's daughter if a man; father's sister's son if a woman) or, less commonly, parallel cousins on the paternal side (father's brother's son or daughter). Cross-cousin marriage is a means of maintaining and reinforcing solidarity between related groups.

Some societies support same-sex marriages. For example, woman–woman marriages as practiced in some African cultures provide a socially approved way to deal with problems for which heterosexual marriages offer no satisfactory solution. In recent years, several countries and some U.S. states have legalized same-sex marriage.

In many human societies, marriages are formalized by economic exchange—such as a reciprocal gift exchange between the bride's and groom's relatives. More common is bridewealth, the payment of money or other valuables from the groom's to the bride's kin.

Bride service occurs when the groom is expected to work for a period of time for the bride's family. A dowry is the payment of a woman's inheritance at the time of marriage to her or to her husband. Its purpose is to ensure support for women in societies where men do most of the productive work, and women are valued primarily for their reproductive potential.

Divorce is possible in all societies. Although reasons and frequency vary, the most common reasons for divorce across cultures are infidelity, sterility, cruelty, and desertion.

How do family and household differ, and what is the relationship between them?

The family may take many forms, ranging from a single parent with one or more children, to a married couple or polygamous spouses with or without offspring, to several generations of parents and their children.

A family is distinct from a household, which is a domestic unit of one or more persons living in one residence. Other than family members, a household may include nonrelatives, such as servants. In the vast majority of human societies, most households are made up of families or parts of families, but there are many other household arrangements.

The most basic domestic unit is the nuclear family—a group consisting of one or more parents and dependent offspring, which may include a stepparent, stepsiblings, and adopted children. Until recently, the term referred solely to the mother, father, and child(ren) unit.

This family form is common in the industrial and postindustrial countries of North America and Europe and also in societies, such as the Inuit, that live in harsh environments. It is well suited to the mobility required both in food-foraging groups and in industrial societies where job changes are frequent.

The extended family consists of several closely related nuclear families living and often working together in a single household.

What kinds of marital residence patterns exist across cultures?

Three common residence patterns are patrilocal (in which a married couple lives in the locality of the husband's father's place of residence), matrilocal (living in the locality of the wife's mother's place of residence), and neolocal (living in a locality apart from the husband's or wife's parents).

In North America and parts of Europe, increasing numbers of people live in nonfamily households, either alone or with nonrelatives. This includes the fast-growing category of unmarried couples who cohabitate. There are many others living in nontraditional families, including single-parent households and blended families.

How do globalization and technology impact marriage and family?

New reproductive technologies, surrogacy, and international adoptions are adding new dimensions to familial relationships.

Another phenomenon changing the makeup of households and families worldwide is the ever-growing population of temporary and migrant workers.

QUESTIONS FOR REFLECTION

1. According to Hindu and Muslim tradition in South Asia and North Africa, a bride's *mehndi* evening is a lively female-only gathering with special food, singing, and lovemaking instructions, along with hand painting. Does your culture have similar gender-segregated pre-wedding events? If so, what is the purpose of such a celebration?

2. Members of traditional communities in countries where the state is either weak or absent depend on consanguineal and affinal relatives to help meet the basic challenges of survival. In such traditional societies, why would it be risky to choose marriage partners exclusively on the basis of romantic love? Can you imagine other factors playing a role if the long-term survival of your community is at stake?

3. Although most women in Europe and North America probably view polygyny as a marriage practice exclusively benefiting men, women in cultures where such marriages are traditional may stress more positive aspects of sharing a husband with several co-wives. Are there conditions under which you think polygyny could be considered relatively beneficial for women?

4. Many children in Europe and North America are raised in single-parent households. In contrast to the United States, where most children living with their unmarried mothers grow up in economically disadvantaged households, relatively few children raised by unmarried mothers in Norway face poverty. Why do you think that is?

5. Why do you think your own culture has historically prescribed restrictive rules about sexual relations, not only with respect to heterosexual contact outside marriage but also condemning same-sex relations? Do you expect economic and social changes in a society will further change ideas and attitudes toward sex and marriage? And if so, will they become more or less restrictive?

ONLINE STUDY RESOURCES

CourseMate

Access chapter-specific learning tools, including learning objectives, practice quizzes, videos, flash cards, glossaries, and more in your Anthropology CourseMate.

Log into **www.cengagebrain.com** to access the resources your instructor has assigned and to purchase materials.

© Harald E. L. Prins

Challenge Issue

All humans face the challenge of creating and maintaining a social network that reaches beyond the capabilities of close relatives or a single household to provide security and support. On a basic level that network is arranged by kinship, extending to more distantly related individuals who claim descent from the same ancestor. For many traditional peoples around the world, including Scottish highlanders, large kin-groups called clans have been important. There are several dozen Scottish clans, with members often sharing the same surname. Pictured here is the opening parade of the international Clan Grant summer games in Spey Valley, Scotland. Like members of other clans, the Grants publicly show their collective identity by wearing kilts and shawls with the distinct tartan (plaid) of their clan. Over several centuries, thousands of Scots were deported, fled, or emigrated from their homelands, settling overseas, especially in Australia, Canada, and the United States. Many, including people from Clan Grant, married into North American Indian tribes. Today, their widely scattered offspring can be found across the globe, including among Cherokee, Cree, or Muskogee Indians. Aided by the Internet, many seek to reestablish social ties of shared descent, traveling long distances to clan gatherings to celebrate their cultural heritage with traditional dancing, piping, games, and food. Cherokees attended the Clan Grant gathering shown here.

Kinship and Descent

All societies rely on some form of family and household organization to meet basic human needs: securing food, fuel, and shelter; protecting against danger; coordinating work; regulating sexual activities; and organizing childrearing. Although they may be efficient and flexible, the family and household organizations of many societies may not be sufficient to handle all the challenges they confront. For example, members of one independent local group often need some means of interacting with people outside their immediate circle for defense against natural disasters or outside aggressors. A wider circle may also be necessary in forming a cooperative workforce for tasks that require more participants than close relatives alone can provide.

Humans have come up with many ways to widen their circles of support to meet such challenges. One is through a formal political system, with personnel to make and enforce laws, keep the peace, allocate scarce resources, and perform other regulatory and societal functions. But the predominant way to build this support in societies that are not organized as political states—especially foraging, crop-growing, and herding societies—is by means of **kinship**, a network of relatives into which individuals are born and married, and with whom they cooperate based on customarily prescribed rights and obligations. The more that individuals become enmeshed in larger networks, as happens in political states, the less they depend on kinship for survival. Still, as explained in this chapter, kinship is fundamental in the organization of any society, past and present.

Descent Groups

A common way of organizing a society along kinship lines is by creating what anthropologists call descent groups. Found in many societies, a **descent group** is any kin-group whose members share a direct line of descent from a real (historical) or fictional common ancestor. Members of such a group trace their shared connections back to such an

kinship A network of relatives into which individuals are born and married, and with whom they cooperate based on customarily prescribed rights and obligations.

descent group Any kin-group whose members share a direct line of descent from a real (historical) or fictional common ancestor.

IN THIS CHAPTER YOU WILL LEARN TO

- Explain how kinship is the basis of social organization in every culture.

- Apply kinship terminology as a cross-cultural code for analyzing social networks.

- Contrast cultures in which ancestry is traced through foremothers, forefathers, or both.

- Distinguish the characteristics of lineages and clans from those of kindreds.

- Identify three kinship terminology systems and the significance of their distinct classifications of close relatives for family attitudes and behavior.

- Interpret totemism as a cultural phenomenon.

- Discuss the significance of kinship in the contexts of adoption and new reproductive technologies.

BIOCULTURAL CONNECTION

Maori Origins: Ancestral Genes and Mythical Canoes

Anthropologists have been fascinated to find that the oral traditions of Maori people in New Zealand fit quite well with scientific findings. New Zealand, an island country whose dramatic geography served as the setting for the *Lord of the Rings* film trilogy, lies in a remote corner of the Pacific Ocean about 1,900 kilometers (1,200 miles) southeast of Australia. Named by Dutch seafarers who landed on its shores in 1642, it was claimed by the British as a colony about 150 years later. Maori, the country's indigenous people, fought back but were outgunned, outnumbered, and forced to lay down their arms in the early 1870s. Today, nearly 600,000 of New Zealand's 4.1 million citizens claim some Maori ancestry.

Maori have an age-old legend about how they came to Aotearoa ("Land of the Long White Cloud"), their name for New Zealand: More than twenty-five generations ago, their Polynesian ancestors arrived in a great fleet of sailing canoes from Hawaiki, their mythical homeland sometimes identified with Tahiti where the native language closely resembles their own. According to chants and genealogies passed down through the ages, this fleet consisted of at least seven (perhaps up to thirteen) seafaring canoes. Estimated to weigh about 5 tons, each of these large dugouts had a single claw-shaped sail and carried 50 to 120 people, plus food supplies, plants, and animals.

As described by Maori anthropologist Te Rangi Hiroa (Peter Buck), the seafaring skills of these voyagers enabled them to navigate by currents, winds, and stars across vast ocean expanses.[a] Perhaps escaping warfare and tribute payments in Hawaiki, they probably made the 5-week-long voyage around 1350 AD, although there were earlier and later canoes as well.

Traditional Maori society is organized into about thirty different *iwis* ("tribes"), grouped into thirteen *wakas* ("canoes"), each with its own traditional territory. Today, prior to giving a formal talk, Maori still introduce themselves by identifying their *iwi*, their *waka*, and the major sacred places of their ancestral territory. Their genealogy connects them to their tribe's founding ancestor who was a crewmember or perhaps even a chief in one of the giant canoes mentioned in the legend of the Great Fleet.[b]

Maori oral traditions about their origins mesh with scientific data based on anthropological and more recent genetic research. Study by outsiders can be controversial because Maori equate an individual's genes to his or her genealogy, which belongs to one's *iwi* or ancestral community. Considered sacred and entrusted to the tribal elders, genealogy is traditionally surrounded by *tapu* ("sacred prohibitions").[c] The Maori term for genealogy is *whakapapa* ("to set layer upon layer"), which is also a word for gene. This Maori term captures something of the original *genous*, the Greek word for "begetting offspring." Another Maori word for *gene* is *ira tangata* ("life spirit of mortals"), and for them, a gene has *mauri* (a "life force"). Given these spiritual associations, genetic investigations of Maori human DNA could not proceed until the Maori themselves became actively involved in the research.

Together with other researchers, Maori geneticist Adele Whyte has examined sex-linked genetic markers, namely mitochondrial DNA in women and Y chromosomes in men.[d] She recently calculated that the number of Polynesian females required to found New Zealand's Maori population ranged between 170 and 230 women. If the original fleet sailing to Aotearoa consisted of seven large canoes, it probably carried a total of about 600 people (men, women, and children).

ancestor through a chain of parent–child links. The addition of a few culturally meaningful obligations and taboos helps hold the structured social group together.

Although many important functions of the descent group are taken over by other institutions when a society becomes politically organized as a state, elements of such kin-ordered groups (kin-groups) may continue. We see this with many traditional indigenous societies that have become part of larger state societies yet endure as distinctive kin-ordered communities. So it is with the Maori of New Zealand, featured in this chapter's Biocultural Connection. Retaining key elements of their traditional social structure, they are still organized in about thirty large descent groups known as *iwi* ("tribes"), which form part of larger social and territorial units known as *waka* ("canoes").

Descent group membership must be sharply defined in order to operate effectively in a kin-ordered society. If membership is allowed to overlap, it is unclear where someone's primary loyalty belongs, especially when different descent groups have conflicting interests. Membership can be determined in a number of ways. The most common way is what anthropologists refer to as *unilineal descent*.

The canoes the ancient Maori used probably looked similar to this contemporary Maori sea canoe.

A comparison of the DNA of Maori with that of Polynesians across the Pacific Ocean and peoples from Southeast Asia reveals a genetic map of ancient Maori migration routes. Mitochondrial DNA, which is passed along virtually unchanged from mothers to their children, provides a genetic clock linking today's Polynesians to southern Taiwan's indigenous coastal peoples, showing that female ancestors originally set out from that island off the southeastern coast of China about 6,000 years ago.[e] In the next few thousand years, they migrated by way of the Philippines and then hopped south and east from island to island. Adding to their gene pool in the course of later generations, Melanesian males from New Guinea and elsewhere joined the migrating bands before arriving in Aotearoa.

In short, Maori cultural traditions in New Zealand are generally substantiated by anthropological as well as molecular biological data.

BIOCULTURAL QUESTION

Why do you think the Maori view genealogy as sacred and attach certain prohibitions to it?

[a]Buck, P. H. (1938). *Vikings of the Pacific.* Chicago: University Press of Chicago.

[b]Hanson, A. (1989). The making of the Maori: Culture invention and its logic. *American Anthropologist 91* (4), 890–902.

[c]Mead, A. T. P. (1996). Genealogy, sacredness, and the commodities market. *Cultural Survival Quarterly 20* (2).

[d]Whyte, A. L. H. (2005). Human evolution in Polynesia. *Human Biology 77* (2), 157–177.

[e]"Gene study suggests Polynesians came from Taiwan." (2005, July 4). Reuters.

Unilineal Descent

Unilineal descent (sometimes called *unilateral descent*) establishes group membership based on descent traced exclusively through either the male *or* the female line of ancestry.

Traditionally, unilineal descent groups are common in many parts of the world. Each newborn becomes part of a specific descent group, traced through the female line (by **matrilineal descent**) or through the male line (by **patrilineal descent**). In matrilineal societies females are culturally recognized as socially significant because they are considered responsible for the descent group's continued existence. In patrilineal societies, this responsibility falls on the male members

unilineal descent Descent traced exclusively through either the male or the female line of ancestry to establish group membership.
matrilineal descent Descent traced exclusively through the female line of ancestry to establish group membership.
patrilineal descent Descent traced exclusively through the male line of ancestry to establish group membership.

of the descent group, thereby enhancing their social importance.

The two major forms of a unilineal descent group (be it patrilineal or matrilineal) are the lineage and the clan. A **lineage** is a unilineal kin-group descended from a common ancestor or founder who lived four to six generations ago and in which relationships among members can be exactly stated in genealogical terms. A **clan** is an extended unilineal kin-group, often consisting of several lineages, whose members claim common descent from a remote ancestor, usually legendary or mythological.

Patrilineal Descent and Organization

Patrilineal descent is the more widespread of the two unilineal descent systems. Through forefathers, members of a patrilineal group trace their descent from a common ancestor (**Figure 20.1**). Brothers and sisters belong to the descent group of their father's father, their father, their father's siblings, and their father's brother's children. A man's son and daughter also trace their descent back through the male line to their common ancestor. In the typical patrilineal group, authority over the children rests with the father or his elder brother. A woman belongs to the same descent group as her father and his brothers, but her children do not because they are born into her husband's descent group.

Patrilineal kinship organization is traditionally embedded in many cultures worldwide and often endures despite radical political and economic changes. So it is among the Han, China's ethnic majority. Even after the 1949 communist revolution that radically changed Chinese society, remnants of the old patrilineal clan system persist—especially in rural areas.

Patrilineal Descent among Han Chinese

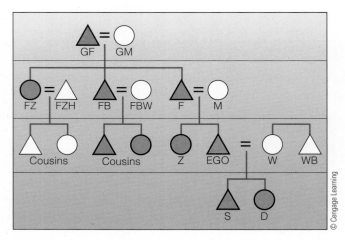

For a few thousand years the basic unit for economic cooperation among the Han Chinese was the large extended family, typically including aged parents and their sons, their sons' wives, and their sons' children (Hsiaotung, 1939). With patrilocal residence, Han children grew up in a

Figure 20.1 **Tracing Patrilineal Descent** Only the individuals symbolized by a filled-in circle or triangle are in the same descent group as EGO (the central person from whom the degree of each kinship relationship is traced). The abbreviation F stands for father, B for brother, H for husband, S for son, M for mother, Z for sister, W for wife, D for daughter, and G for grand.

household dominated by their father and his male relatives. The father was a source of discipline, and children customarily maintained a respectful social distance.

With brothers and their sons being part of the same household, a Han boy's paternal uncle was like a second father. He was treated with the same obedience and respect as the father, and his sons were like brothers. Accordingly, the Han kinship term for one's own father is also used for the father's brother, and the term for a brother is used for the father's brother's sons. When extended families became too large and unwieldy, one or more sons established separate households—but the tie to their household of birth remained strong.

Although family membership was and is important for each Han individual, the traditional primary social unit is the lineage, or in Han terms, the *tsu*. Each *tsu* is a corporate kin-group whose members trace their ancestry back about five generations exclusively through the male line to a common ancestor. A woman belongs to her father's *tsu*, but traditionally, for all practical purposes, she was absorbed by the *tsu* of her husband, with whom she lived after marriage.

The *tsu* could be counted on to help its members economically, and it functioned as a legal body, passing judgment on misbehaving members. People affiliated with the same *tsu* came together on ceremonial occasions, including weddings, funerals, and rituals honoring their ancestors. Recently deceased ancestors, up to about three generations back, were given offerings of food and paper money on the anniversaries of their births and deaths, whereas more distant ancestors were collectively worshiped five times a year. Each *tsu*

lineage A unilineal kin-group descended from a common ancestor or founder who lived four to six generations ago and in which relationships among members can be exactly stated in genealogical terms.

clan An extended unilineal kin-group, often consisting of several lineages, whose members claim common descent from a remote ancestor, usually legendary or mythological.

Figure 20.2 An Ancestral Temple in Zhejiang Province, China Among the Han, the ethnic majority in China, almost all ancestral temples, or clan houses, are dedicated to male forebears, reflecting the country's long-established patrilineal rules of descent and cultural values. Clan members affirm their place in the kin-group by making offerings to the ancestors in special temples such as the one pictured here, located in a family home.

maintained its own shrine for storage of ancestral tablets on which the names of all members were recorded (**Figure 20.2**).

Just as families periodically split up into new ones, larger descent groups periodically splintered along the lines of their main family branches. Causes for splits included disputes among brothers over management of landholdings and suspicion of unfair division of profits. Even after such fissions, a new *tsu* continued to recognize and honor its lineage tie to the old *tsu*. Thus, over many generations, a whole hierarchy of descent groups came into being, with all persons having the same surname considering themselves to be members of a great patrilineal clan. With this came the rule that individuals bearing the same clan surname could not marry each other. This marriage rule is still widely practiced today.

Traditionally, owing obedience and respect to their fathers and older patrilineal relatives, Han children had to marry whomever their parents chose for them. Sons were required to care for their elderly parents and to fulfill ceremonial obligations to them after their death. In turn, inheritance passed from fathers to sons, with an extra share going to the eldest because he ordinarily made the greatest contribution to the household.

Han women, by contrast, had no claims on their families' heritable property. Once married, a woman was in effect cast off by her own *tsu* in order to produce children for her husband's family and *tsu*. Yet, members of her birth *tsu* retained some interest in her after her departure. For example, her mother would assist her in the birth of her children, and her brothers or some other male relative might intervene if her husband or other members of his family treated her badly.

Although *tsu* bonds have weakened in communist China, some of the obligations and attitudes of the traditional corporate kin-group persist today. At a minimum, contemporary Han Chinese maintain the traditions of children obeying and respecting their fathers and older patrilineal relatives.

As the Han example suggests, a patrilineal society is very much a man's world. No matter how needed and valued women may be, they find themselves in a difficult position. Far from resigning themselves to a subordinate position, however, they actively work the system to their own advantage as best they can.

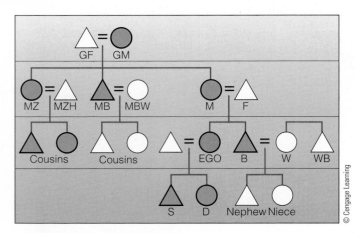

Figure 20.3 Tracing Matrilineal Descent This diagram can be compared with patrilineal descent in Figure 20.1. The two patterns are virtually mirror images. Note that a man cannot transmit descent to his own children.

Matrilineal Descent and Organization

Matrilineal descent is traced exclusively through the female line (**Figure 20.3**), just as patrilineal descent is through the male line. However, the matrilineal pattern differs from the patrilineal in that it does not automatically confer gender authority. For example, among the Mosuo, one of several matrilineal ethnic minorities in southwestern China, property passes through the female line, women are often heads of their households, and they are usually the ones making the business decisions. Yet, political power tends to be in the hands of males (Mathieu, 2003) (**Figure 20.4**).

Similar arrangements exist across the globe in a wide range of matrilineal societies in which women have considerable power without holding exclusive authority in the descent group. Typically, power is shared with the brothers, rather than the husbands, of the women through whom descent is traced. Apparently, a function of matrilineal systems is to provide continuous female solidarity within the female work group.

Matrilineal systems are usually found in horticultural societies in which women perform much of the work in the house and nearby gardens. Matrilineal descent in part prevails because women's labor as crop cultivators is vital to the society.

In a matrilineal system, brothers and sisters belong to the descent group of the mother, the mother's mother, the mother's siblings, and the mother's sisters' children.

Figure 20.4 Matrilineal Family among the Mosuo Unlike the Han, the ethnic majority in China who are patrilineal, several ethnic minorities in southwestern China are matrilineal, including the Mosuo. The women in the Mosuo family shown here are blood relatives of one another, and the men are their brothers. Mosuo husbands live apart from their wives, in the households of their sisters.

Thus, every male belongs to the same descent group as his mother, and a man's own children belong to his wife's descent group, not his.

Although not true of all matrilineal systems, a common feature is the relative weakness of the social tie between wife and husband. A woman's husband lacks authority in the household they share. Her brother, and not the husband-father, distributes goods, organizes work, settles disputes, supervises rituals, and administers inheritance and succession rules. Meanwhile, her husband fulfills the same role in his own sister's household. Furthermore, his sister's son rather than his son inherits his property and status. Thus, brothers and sisters maintain lifelong ties with one another, whereas marital ties may be severed. In matrilineal societies, unsatisfactory marriages are more easily ended than in patrilineal societies.

Matrilineal Descent among Hopi Indians

Among the Hopi Indians, a farming people whose ancestors have lived for many centuries in *pueblos* ("villages") in the desert lands of northeastern Arizona, society is divided into a number of clans based strictly on matrilineal descent (Connelly, 1979).

At birth, every Hopi is assigned to his or her mother's clan. This affiliation is so important that, in a very real sense, a person has no social identity in the community apart from it. Two or more clans together constitute larger supra-clan units, which anthropologists refer to as *phratries* (discussed later in this chapter).

Phratries and clans are the major kinship units in Hopi culture, but the basic functional social units consist of lineages, and there are several in each village. A senior woman (usually the eldest) heads each Hopi lineage, with her brother or mother's brother keeping the sacred "medicine bundle" (objects of spiritual power considered essential for peoples' well-being) and playing an active role in running lineage affairs. The senior woman is no mere figurehead. She may act as mediator to help resolve disputes among group members. Also, although her brother and mother's brother have the right to offer her advice and criticism, they are equally obligated to listen to what she has to say, and she does not yield her authority to them.

Most female authority, however, is exerted within the household, and here men clearly take second place. These households consist of the women of the lineage with their husbands and unmarried sons, all of whom used to live in sets of adjacent rooms in single large buildings. Today, nuclear families often live (frequently with a maternal relative or two) in separate houses, but motorized vehicles enable related households to maintain close contact and cooperation as before.

Hopi lineages function as landholding corporations, allocating land for the support of member households. "Outsiders," the husbands of the women whose lineage owns the land, farm these lands, and the harvest belongs to these women. Thus, Hopi men spend their lives laboring for their wives' lineages, and in return they are given food and shelter.

Sons learn from their fathers how to farm, yet a man has no real authority over his son. This is because a man's own children belong to his wife's lineage whereas his sister's children form part of his. When parents have difficulty with an unruly child, the mother's brother is called upon to mete out discipline. A man's loyalties are therefore divided between his wife's household on the one hand and his sisters' on the other. According to tradition, if a man is perceived as being an unsatisfactory husband, his wife merely has to place his personal belongings outside the door, and the marriage is over.

In addition to their economic and legal functions, lineages play a role in Hopi ceremonial activities. A lineage owns a special house where the matrilineal clan's religious paraphernalia are stored and cared for by the "clan mother." Together with her brother, the clan's "big uncle," she helps manage ceremonial activities (**Figure 20.5**).

Other Forms of Descent

Among Samoan Islanders (and many other cultures in the Pacific as well as in Southeast Asia), a person has the option of affiliating with either the mother's or the father's descent group. Known as *ambilineal descent*, such a kin-ordered system provides a measure of flexibility. However, this flexibility also introduces a possibility of dispute and conflict as unilineal groups compete for members. This problem does not arise under *double descent*, or double unilineal descent, a rare system in which descent is matrilineal for some purposes and patrilineal for others.

Generally, where double descent is traced, the matrilineal and patrilineal groups take action in different spheres of society. For example, among the Yakö of eastern Nigeria, property is divided into both patrilineal and matrilineal possessions (Forde, 1968). The patrilineage owns perpetually productive resources, such as land, whereas the matrilineage owns consumable property, such as livestock. The legally weaker matriline is somewhat more important in religious matters than the patriline. Through double descent, a Yakö might inherit grazing lands from the father's patrilineal group and certain ritual privileges from the mother's matrilineal group.

Finally, when descent derives equally from the mother's and father's families, anthropologists use the term

Bilateral descent exists in various foraging cultures and is also common in many contemporary state societies with agricultural, industrial, or postindustrial economies. For example, although most people in Europe, Australia, and Latin America typically inherit their father's family name (indicative of a culture's history in which patrilineal descent is the norm), they usually consider themselves as much a member of their mother's as their father's family.

Descent Within the Larger Cultural System

There is a close relationship between the descent system and a cultural system's infrastructure. Generally, patrilineal descent predominates when male labor is considered of prime importance, as among pastoralists and agriculturalists. As already noted, matrilineal descent predominates mainly among horticulturalists in societies in which female work in subsistence is especially important. Numerous matrilineal societies are found in southern Asia, one of the world's earliest cradles of food production. They are also prominent in parts of indigenous North America, South America's tropical lowlands, and parts of Africa.

In many societies an individual has no legal or political status except as a lineage member. Citizenship is derived from lineage membership and legal status depends on it, so political powers are derived from it as well. Because lineage endures after the deaths of members with new members continually born into it, it has a continuing existence that enables it to act like a corporation, as in owning property, organizing productive activities, distributing goods and labor power, assigning status, and regulating relations with other groups. As a repository of religious traditions, the descent group solidifies social cohesion. Ancestor worship, for example, is often a powerful force acting to enhance group solidarity. Thus, a lineage is a strong, effective base of social organization.

Whatever form of descent predominates, the kin of both mother and father are important components of the social structure in all societies. Just because descent may be traced patrilineally, this does not mean that matrilineal relatives are necessarily unimportant. It simply means that, for purposes of group membership, the mother's relatives are excluded. Similarly, under matrilineal descent, the father's relatives are excluded for purposes of group membership.

By way of example, among the matrilineal Trobriand Islanders in the southern Pacific, discussed in previous chapters, children belong to their mother's descent groups, yet fathers play an important role in their upbringing. Upon marriage, the bride and groom's paternal relatives contribute to the exchange of gifts, and, throughout life, a man may expect his paternal kin to help him improve his economic and political position in society. Eventually, sons may expect to inherit personal property from their fathers.

© Anders Ryman/Corbis

Figure 20.5 Matrilineal Clan Ceremonial Life Like their Hopi neighbors, White Mountain Apaches (pictured here) are organized into matrilineal clans. Closely related through the maternal line, small groups of Apache Indian women traditionally live and work together, farming on stream banks in the Arizona mountains and gathering wild foods in ancestral territories. They trace their ancestry to *Is dzán naadleeshe'* ("Changing Woman"), a mythological founding mother. This photo shows three generations in prayer during a traditional puberty ceremony known as *na'ii'ees* ("getting her ready"), also called a Sunrise Dance. During this event that marks a girl's transition into womanhood, the sacred power of her clan's founding mother ritually passes to her.

bilateral descent. In such a system individuals trace descent through both of their parents' ancestors. We recognize bilateral descent when individuals apply the same genealogical terms to identify similarly related individuals on both sides of the family. For instance, when they speak of a "grandmother" or "grandfather," no indication is given as to whether these relatives are on the paternal or maternal side of the family.

bilateral descent Descent traced equally through father and mother's ancestors; associating each individual with blood relatives on both sides of the family.

As a traditional institution in a kin-ordered society, the descent group often endures in state-organized societies in which political institutions are ineffective or weakly developed. Such is the case in many countries of the world today, especially in remote mountainous or desert villages difficult to reach by state authorities.

Because the ideas, values, and practices associated with traditional descent groups may be deeply embedded, such cultural patterns often endure in *diasporic communities* among immigrants who have relocated from their ancestral homelands and retain distinct identities as ethnic minority groups in their new host countries. In such situations, it is not uncommon for people to seek familiar, kin-ordered cultural solutions to challenges faced in unfamiliar state-organized settings. We see an example of this in the following Original Study on honor killing in the Netherlands.

ORIGINAL STUDY

Honor Killings in the Netherlands

BY CLEMENTINE VAN ECK

When I first told my anthropology professors I wanted to write my dissertation on honor killing among Turkish immigrants in the Netherlands, they told me no way. It was the mid-1990s, and everyone seemed to feel that writing negative things about struggling immigrants was discriminatory. Better to choose a subject that would help them deal with the challenges of settling in Dutch society, such as the problems they experienced as foreigners in school or at work. But I was quite determined to investigate this issue and finally found a professor who shared my interest—Dr. Anton Blok. He himself was specialized in Italian mafia,[a] so was quite used to violence of the cultural sort.

Before getting into some of the details of my research, I need to set the stage. Until the 1960s, the Netherlands was a relatively homogeneous society (despite its colonial past). The major differences among its people were not ethnic but religious, namely their distinct ties to Catholicism or Protestantism (of various kinds). The country's population makeup began to change dramatically after the economic boom of the 1960s created a need for cheap labor and led to an influx of migrants from poor areas in Mediterranean countries seeking wage-earning opportunities.

These newcomers came not as immigrants but as "guest laborers" (*gastarbeiders*) expected to return to their countries of origin, including Italy, Yugoslavia, Turkey, and Morocco. Although many did go back home, numerous others did not. In contrast to most of the guest workers from southern European nations, those from Turkey and Morocco are mainly Muslim. And unlike southern European workers who stayed on as immigrants and successfully assimilated into Dutch society, many of the Muslim newcomers formed isolated, diasporic communities.

During the past several decades, these communities have expanded in size and are concentrated in certain areas of various cities. Today, the Turkish population in the Netherlands is about 350,000. Most of them have become Dutch citizens, but they maintain some key cultural features of their historical "honor-and-shame" traditions. And this is what is at stake when we are dealing with the problem of honor killing.

Anthropologists have identified honor-and-shame traditions in many parts of the world, especially in remote traditional herding and farming societies where the power of the political state is either absent or ineffective. People in such areas, my professor, Dr. Blok, explained,

cannot depend on stable centers of political control for the protection of life and patrimony. In the absence of effective state control, they have to rely on their own forces—on various forms of self-help. These conditions . . . put a premium on self-assertive qualities in men, involving the readiness and capacity to use physical force in order to guarantee the immunity of life and property, including women as the most precious and vulnerable part of the patrimony of men. The extremes of this sense of honour are reached when even merely glancing at a woman is felt as an affront, an incursion into a male domain, touching off a violent response.[b]

Beyond serving as a means of social control in isolated areas, honor-and-shame traditions may be used in situations where state mechanisms are alien to a certain group of people, as among some Turkish and Moroccan migrants in the Netherlands. Focusing on the latter, I tried to make sense of certain cultural practices that often baffle indigenous Dutch citizens accustomed to a highly organized bureaucratic state in which our personal security and justice are effectively managed by social workers, police, courts, and so on. Most of all, I wanted to understand honor killings.

Honor killings are murders in the form of a ritual, and they are carried out to purify tarnished honor—specifically honor having to do with something Turks refer to as *namus*. Both men and women possess *namus*. For women and girls *namus* means chastity, whereas for men it means having chaste family members. A man is therefore dependent for his *namus* on the conduct of the womenfolk in his family. This means in effect that women and girls must not have illicit contact with a member of the opposite sex and must avoid becoming the subject of gossip because gossip alone can impugn *namus*. The victim of an honor killing can be the girl or woman who tarnished her honor, or the man who did this to her (usually her boyfriend). The girl or woman is killed by her family members, the man is killed by the family of the girl/woman whose honor he has violated.

As I was wrapping up my PhD in 2000, Dutch society still did not seem quite ready to acknowledge the phenomenon of honor killing. That year a Kurdish boy whose parents were born in Turkey tried to shoot the boyfriend of his sister. Because the attempt took place in a high school and resulted in injury to several students and a teacher, authorities focused on the issue of school safety rather than on the cultural reasons behind the murder attempt.

A shift in government and public awareness of honor killing took place in 2004. That year three Muslim Turkish women were killed by their former husbands on the street. Coming in quick succession, one after the other, these murders did not escape the attention of government officials or the media. Finally, honor killing was on the national agenda. In November of that year I was appointed as cultural anthropologist at the Dutch police force in The Hague district and began working with law enforcers on honor killing cases there (and soon in other areas of the country).

On November 2, 2004, the day I gave an opening speech about honor killings to colleagues at my new job, a radical Muslim migrant from Morocco shot the famous Dutch author and film director Theo van Gogh, well known for his critical, often mocking, views on Islam. Although his murder was not an honor killing, it had key elements of that cleansing ritual: It occurred in a public place (on the street) in front of many people, the victim had to die (injury would not suffice), the killer used many shots (or knife thrusts), the killing was planned (it was not the product of a sudden outburst), and the killer had no remorse.

Let me tell you about a recent and quite typical case. On a Friday evening the local police in an eastern Dutch community called in the help of our police team. A 17-year-old Turkish girl had run away to the family home of her Dutch boyfriend, also 17. Her father, who had discovered that this boy had a police record, telephoned his parents and asked them to send the daughter home. The parents tried to calm him down and told him his daughter was safe at their house. But as he saw it, she was in the most unsafe place in the world, for she was with the boy she loved. This could only mean that her virginity was in jeopardy and therefore the *namus* of the whole family.

My colleagues and I concluded that the girl had to be taken out of her boyfriend's home that same night: The father knew the place, he did not want the boy as a son-in-law, and he believed his daughter was not mature enough to make a decision about something as important as marriage. ("Just having a boyfriend" was not allowed. You either marry or you do not have a boyfriend, at least not an obvious one.) Because of my honor killing research, I was well aware of similar situations that ended in honor killings. To leave the girl where she was would invite disaster.

After we persuaded the prosecutor that intervention was necessary, the girl was taken from her boyfriend's house and brought to a guarded shelter to prevent her from fleeing back to him the next day. This is anthropology-in-action. You cannot always just wait and see what will happen (although I admit that as a scholar this is very tempting); you have to take responsibility and take action if you are convinced that a human life is at stake.

When I took up the study of cultural anthropology, I did so just because it intrigued me. I never imagined that what I learned might become really useful. So, what I would like to say to anthropology students is: Never give up on an interesting subject. One day it might just matter that you have become an expert in that area. At this moment I am analyzing all kinds of threatening cases and drawing up genealogies of the families involved—all in the effort to deepen our understanding of and help prevent honor killings.

Written expressly for this text, 2011.

---

[a]Blok, A. (1974). *The mafia of a Sicilian village 1860–1960*. New York: Harper & Row.

[b]Blok, A. (1981). Rams and billy-goats: A key to the Mediterranean code of honour. *Man, New Series 16 (3)*, 427–440. See also Van Eck, C. (2003). *Purified by blood: Honour killings amongst Turks in the Netherlands*. Amsterdam: Amsterdam University Press.

Lineage Exogamy

A common characteristic of lineages is *exogamy*. As defined in the previous chapter, this means that lineage members must find their marriage partners in other lineages. One advantage of exogamy is that competition for desirable spouses within the group is curbed, promoting the group's internal cohesiveness. Lineage exogamy means that each marriage is more than a union between two individuals; it is also a new alliance between lineages. This helps to maintain them as components of larger social systems. Finally, lineage exogamy promotes open communication within a society, facilitating the diffusion of knowledge and exchange of goods and services from one lineage to another.

In contemporary North American Indian communities, kinship and descent still play an essential role in tribal membership—as illustrated in this chapter's Anthropology Applied.

ANTHROPOLOGY APPLIED

Resolving a Native American Tribal Membership Dispute

By Harald E. L. Prins

In autumn 1998, I received a call from the tribal chief of the Aroostook band of Micmacs in northern Maine asking for help in resolving a bitter tribal membership dispute. The conflict centered on the fact that several hundred individuals had become tribal members without proper certification of their Micmac kinship status. Traditionalists in the community argued that their tribe's organization was being taken over by "non-Indians." With the formal status of so many members in question, the tribal administration could not properly determine who was entitled to benefit from the available health, housing, and education programs. After some hostile confrontations between the factions, tribal elders requested a formal inquiry into the membership controversy, and I was called in as a neutral party with a long history of working with the band.

My involvement as an advocacy anthropologist began in 1981 when these Micmacs (also spelled Mi'kmaq) first employed me, along with Bunny McBride, to help them achieve U.S. government recognition of their Indian

status. At the time, the Micmacs formed a poor and landless community not yet officially recognized as a tribe. During that decade, we helped the band define its political strategies, which included petitioning for federal recognition of their Indian status; claiming their traditional rights to hunt, trap, and fish; and even demanding return of lost ancestral lands.

To generate popular support for the effort, I coproduced a film about the community (*Our Lives in Our Hands*, 1986). Most important, we gathered oral histories and detailed archival documentation to address kinship issues and other government criteria for tribal recognition. The latter included important genealogical records showing that most Micmac adults in the region were at least "half-blood" (having two of their grandparents officially recorded as Indians).

Based on this evidence, we effectively argued that Aroostook Micmacs could claim aboriginal title to lands in the region. Also, we were able to convince politicians in Washington, DC, to introduce a special bill to acknowledge their tribal status and settle their land claims. When formal hearings were held in 1990, I testified in the U.S. Senate as an expert witness for the Micmacs. The following year, the Aroostook Band of Micmacs Settlement Act became federal law. This made the band eligible for the financial assistance (health, housing, education, and child welfare) and economic development loans that are available to all federally recognized tribes

in the United States. Moreover, the law provided the band with funding to buy a 5,000-acre territorial base in Maine.

Flush with federal funding and rapidly expanding its activities, the 500-member band became overwhelmed by complex bureaucratic regulations now governing their existence. Without formally established ground rules determining who could apply for tribal membership, and overlooking federally imposed regulations, hundreds of new names were rather casually added to its tribal rolls.

By 1997, the Aroostook band population had ballooned to almost 1,200 members, and Micmac traditionalists were questioning the legitimacy of many whose names had been added to the band roster. With mounting tension threatening to destroy the band, the tribal chief invited me to evaluate critically the membership claims of more than half the tribe. In early 1999, I reviewed the kinship records submitted by hundreds of individuals whose membership on the tribal rolls was in question. Several months later, I offered my final report to the Micmac community.

After traditional prayers, sweetgrass burning, drumming, and a traditional meal of salmon and moose, I formally presented my findings. Based on the official criteria, about 100 lineal descendants of the original members and just over 150 newcomers met the minimum required qualifications for membership; several hundred others would have to be removed from the tribal roster. After singing, drumming, and closing prayers, the Micmac gathering dispersed.

Today, the band numbers about 850 members and is doing well. It has purchased several tracts of land (collectively over 600 acres), including a small residential reservation near Presque Isle, now home to about 200 Micmacs. Also located here are new tribal administration offices, a health clinic, and a cultural center.

© Donald Sanipass

The Sanipass-Lafford family cluster in Chapman, Maine, represent a traditional Micmac residential kin-group. Such extended families typically include grandchildren and bilaterally related family members such as in-laws, uncles, and aunts. Taken from the Sanipass family album, this picture shows a handful of members in the mid-1980s: Marline Sanipass Morey with two of her nephews and uncles.

From Lineage to Clan

In the course of time, as generation succeeds generation and new members are born into the lineage, the kin-group's membership may become too large to manage or may outgrow the lineage's resources. When this happens, as we have seen with the Chinese *tsu*, **fission** occurs; that is, the original lineage splits into new, smaller lineages. Usually, the members of the new lineages continue to recognize their original relationship to one another. The result of this process is the appearance of a larger kind of descent group: the clan.

As already noted, a *clan*—typically consisting of several lineages—is an extended unilineal descent group whose members claim common descent from a distant ancestor (usually legendary or mythological) but are unable to trace the precise genealogical links back to that ancestor. This stems from the great genealogical depth of the clan, whose founding ancestor lived so far in the past that the links must be assumed rather than known in detail. A clan differs from a lineage in another respect: It lacks the residential unity that is generally (although not always) characteristic of a lineage's core members.

As with the lineage, descent may be patrilineal, matrilineal, or ambilineal. Hopi Indians are an example of matrilineal clans (*matriclans*), whereas Han Chinese and Scottish highlanders, pictured in this chapter's opening, provide examples of patrilineal clans (*patriclans*). Tracing descent exclusively through men from a founding paternal ancestor, Scottish highland clans are often identified with the prefix "Mac" or "Mc" (from an old Celtic word meaning "son of"), such as MacDonald, McGregor, and Maclean.

Because clan membership is often dispersed rather than localized, it usually does not involve a shared holding of tangible property. Instead, it involves collective participation in ceremonial and political matters. Only on special occasions will the membership gather together for specific purposes.

However, clans may handle important integrative functions. Like lineages, they may regulate marriage through exogamy. Because of their dispersed membership, clans give individuals the right of entry into associated local groups no matter where they are. Members usually are expected to give protection and hospitality to others in the clan. Traditionally, this more encompassing kinship construct facilitated free travel of clan members to multiple member villages.

Lacking the residential unity of lineages, clans frequently depend on symbols—of animals, plants, natural forces, colors, and special objects—to provide members with solidarity and a ready means of identification. These symbols, called *totems*, often are associated with the clan's

mythical origin and reinforce for clan members an awareness of common descent.

The word *totem* comes from the Ojibwa American Indian word *ototeman*, meaning "he is a relative of mine." **Totemism** was defined by British anthropologist A. R. Radcliffe-Brown (1931) as a set of customary beliefs and practices that set up a special system of relations between the society and important plants, animals, and other natural objects. Totemism varies among cultures. For example, Aborigines in central Australia such as the Arunta believe that each clan descends from a mythological spirit animal. Native Americans in northwest Canada such as the Tsimshian on the Pacific Coast also use totemic animals to designate their exogamous matrilineal clans but do not claim these creatures are mythological clan ancestors.

Among these coastal Indians, individuals inherit their lineage affiliations from their mothers. As such, every Tsimshian forms part of a matrilineal "house group," a corporate kin-group known as a *waap* (the plural is *wuwaap*). Typically, each village consists of about twenty such houses, ranked according to importance. Each Tsimshian house group forms part of a larger exogamous matrilineal clan, of which there are four. An animal symbolically represents these clans: Blackfish (Killer Whale), Wolf, Eagle, and Raven. Carvings of these crest animals, coupled with several other animal and human images symbolically marking the mythology and history of the lineage and validating its claims and privileges, are displayed on monumental red-cedar *totem poles* standing upright in front of the large wooden dwellings inhabited by the *wuwaap* (Anderson, 2006) (**Figure 20.6**).

We can see a reductive variation of totemism in contemporary industrial and postindustrial societies in which sports teams are often given the names of such powerful wild animals as bears, lions, and wildcats. In the United States, this extends to the Democratic Party's donkey and the Republican Party's elephant, and to the Elks, the Lions, and other fraternal and social organizations. These animal emblems, or mascots, however, do not involve the notion of biological descent and the strong sense of kinship that they symbolize for clans, nor are they linked with the traditional ritual observances associated with clan totems.

Phratries and Moieties

Larger kinds of descent groups are phratries and moieties (**Figure 20.7**). A **phratry** (after the Greek word for "brotherhood") is a unilineal descent group composed of at least two clans that supposedly share a common ancestry, whether or not they really do. Like individuals in the clan, phratry members cannot trace precisely their descent links to a common ancestor, although they firmly believe such an ancestor existed. For example, there are nine phratries in Hopi society, and within each phratry member clans are expected to support one another and observe strict exogamy. Because people from all nine phratries can be found living in any given Hopi village,

---

fission In kinship studies, the splitting of a descent group into two or more new descent groups.

totemism The belief that people are related to particular animals, plants, or natural objects by virtue of descent from common ancestral spirits.

phratry A unilineal descent group composed of at least two clans that supposedly share a common ancestry, whether or not they really do.

Figure 20.6 **Tshimshian People Raising a Totem Pole** The tradition of erecting totem poles to commemorate special events endures in several Native American communities in the Pacific Northwest. Carved from tall cedar trees, these spectacular monuments display a clan or lineage's ceremonial property and are prominently positioned as posts in the front of a house, as markers at gravesites, and at other places of significance. Often depicting legendary ancestors and mythological animals, the painted carvings symbolically represent a descent group's cultural status and associated privileges in the community. Noted carver David Boxley, a member of the Eagle clan, gifted this pole to the community.

marriage partners can usually be found in one's home community. This same dispersal of membership provides individuals with rights of entry into villages other than their own.

If the entire society is divided into only two major descent groups, whether they are equivalent to clans or phratries, each group is called a **moiety** (after the French word *moitié*, for "half"). Members of the moiety believe themselves to share a common ancestor but cannot prove it through definitive genealogical links. As a rule, the feelings of kinship among members of lineages and clans are stronger than those of members of phratries and moieties.

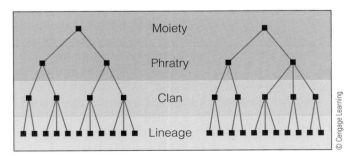

Figure 20.7 **Descent Groups** This diagram shows the organizational hierarchy of moieties, phratries, clans, and lineages. Each moiety is subdivided into phratries, each phratry is subdivided into clans, and each clan is subdivided into lineages.

This may be due to the much larger size and more diffuse nature of the latter groups.

Because feelings of kinship are often weaker between people from different clans, the moiety system is a cultural invention that binds clan-based communities into a social network of obligatory giving and receiving. By institutionalizing reciprocity between groups of clans, the moiety system joins together families who otherwise would not be sufficiently invested in maintaining the commonwealth.

Like lineages and clans, phratries and moieties are often exogamous, and so are bound together by marriages between their members. And like clans, they provide members rights of access to other communities. In a community that does not include one's clan members, one's phratry members are still there to turn to for hospitality. Finally, moieties may perform reciprocal services for one another. Among them, individuals look to members of the opposite "half" in their community for the necessary mourning rituals when a member of their own moiety dies. Such interdependence between moieties serves to maintain the cohesion of the entire society.

The principle of institutionalized reciprocity between groups of matrilineal clans organized into two equal

moiety Each group, usually consisting of several clans, that results from a division of a society into two halves on the basis of descent.

Figure 20.8 Village Life in Moieties Many Amazonian Indians in South America's tropical woodlands traditionally live in circular villages socially divided into moieties. Here we see the Canela Indians' Escalvado village as it was in 1970. The village is 300 meters (165 feet) wide. The community's "upper" moiety meets in the western part. Nearly all of the 1,800 members of the Canela tribe reside in the village during festival seasons, but otherwise they are largely dispersed into their smaller, farm-centered circular villages. (Behind the larger-circle village is a smaller abandoned village where part of the tribe lived before uniting under one chief. Missionaries built the landing strip that runs through it.)

© Ray Roberts Brown/Smithsonian Institution

halves, or moieties, is beautifully illustrated in the circular settlement pattern of many traditional Indian villages in the tropical forest of South America's Amazon region (**Figure 20.8**). Dwellings located in half of the village are those of clans belonging to one exogamous moiety, and those on the opposite side are the dwellings of clans belonging to the other. Because their clans are often matrilineal, the institutionalized rules of reciprocity in this kin-ordered community traditionally require that a woman marry a man from a clan house on the opposite side of the village, who then moves into her ancestral clan house. Their son, however, will one day have to find a wife from his father's original moiety and will have to move to his father's mother's side of the village. In this way, the moiety system of institutionalized reciprocity functions like a social "zipper" between clans engaged in a repetitive cycle of exchange relations.

Bilateral Kinship and the Kindred

Important as patrilineal or matrilineal descent groups are in many cultures, such kin-groups do not exist in every society. In some, we encounter another type of extended family group known as the **kindred**—a grouping of blood relatives based on bilateral descent. The kindred includes

all relatives with whom **EGO** shares at least one grandparent, great-grandparent, or even great-great-grandparent, on his or her father's *and* mother's side. Thus, depending on how many generations back one reckons, someone's kindred may include the entire direct-line offspring of his or her eight great-grandparents, or sometimes even sixteen great-great-grandparents (**Figure 20.9**).

In societies in which small domestic units (nuclear families or single-parent households) are of primary importance, bilateral kinship and kindred organization are likely to result. This can be seen in modern industrial and postindustrial societies, in emerging market economies in the developing world, and in still-existing food-foraging societies throughout the world.

Most Europeans and peoples of European descent in other parts of the world are familiar with the kindred: Those who belong to it are simply referred to as "relatives." It typically includes those blood relatives on both sides of the family who are seen on important occasions, such as family weddings, reunions, and funerals. In Ireland, Puerto Rico, or the United States, for example, nearly everyone can identify the members of their kindred up to grandparents (or even great-grandparents) and to their first cousins, nephews, and nieces. Some can even identify second cousins in their kindred, but few can go beyond that.

In traditional societies with bilateral descent, kindreds play a significant role in a variety of situations. Kindred members ("next of kin") may be called upon to seek justice or revenge for harm done to someone in the group. They might raise bail, serve as witnesses, or help compensate a victim's family. If blood money (financial reparation for the loss of a murdered relative) is involved, kindred members would be entitled to a share of it. In such societies, a trading or raiding party may be composed of a kindred, with the

kindred A grouping of blood relatives based on bilateral descent. Includes all relatives with whom EGO shares at least one grandparent, great-grandparent, or even great-great-grandparent, on his or her father's *and* mother's side.

EGO In kinship studies, the central person from whom the degree of each kinship relationship is traced.

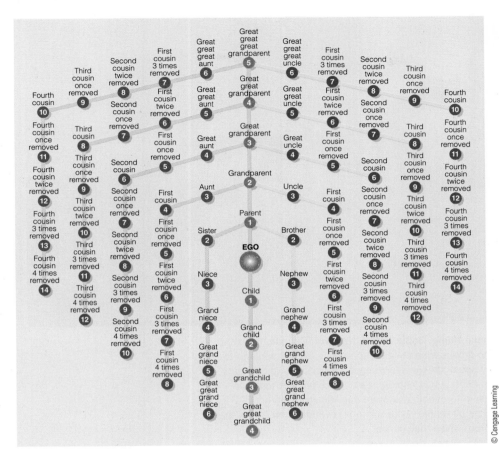

Figure 20.9 EGO and His or Her Kindred The kindred designates a person's exact degree of blood relatedness to other members of the family. This determines not only one's social obligations toward relatives, but also one's rights. For instance, when a wealthy widowed great-aunt without children dies without a will, specific surviving members of her kindred will be legally entitled to inherit from her.

© Cengage Learning

group coming together to perform a particular function, share in the results, and then disband. The kindred may also act as a ceremonial group for initiations and other rites of passage. Finally, kindreds may play a role in regulating marriage through exogamy.

Because kindreds are EGO-centered, each is unique, except among full siblings. Beyond being in the middle of one's own kindred, a person belongs to several kindreds centered on other individuals with memberships that overlap to various degrees. Thus, each person can turn to his or her own kindred for aid, or may be called upon by others, by virtue of being a member of their kindreds.

Kinship Terminology and Kinship Groups

A system of organizing people who are relatives into different kinds of groups—whether kindreds, lineages, or clans—influences how relatives are labeled. Kinship terminology systems vary considerably across cultures, reflecting the positions individuals occupy within their respective societies and helping to differentiate one relative from another. Distinguishing factors include gender, generational differences, or genealogical differences. In the various systems of kinship terminology, any one of these factors may be emphasized at the expense of others.

By looking at the terms a particular society uses for their relatives, an anthropologist can determine the structure of kin-groups, discern the most important relationships, and sometimes interpret the prevailing attitudes concerning various relationships. For instance, a number of languages use the same term to identify a brother and a cousin, and others have a single word for cousin, niece, and nephew. Some cultures find it useful to distinguish the eldest brother from his younger brothers and have different words for them. And unlike English, many languages distinguish between an aunt who is a mother's sister and one who is a father's sister.

Regardless of the factors emphasized, all kinship terminologies accomplish two important tasks. First, they classify similar kinds of individuals into single specific categories; second, they separate different kinds of individuals into distinct categories. Generally, two or more kin are merged under the same term when the individuals have more or less the same rights and obligations with respect to the person referring to them as such. This is the case among most English-speaking North Americans, for instance, when someone refers to a mother's sister and a father's sister both as an aunt. As far as the speaker is concerned, both relatives possess a similar status.

Several different systems of kinship terminology result from the application of the previously discussed principles—including the Eskimo, Hawaiian, Iroquois, Crow, Omaha, Sudanese, Kariera, and Aranda systems, each named after the ethnographic example first or best described by anthropologists. The last five of these

Figure 20.10 **Inuit Family at Outpost Camp Home, Baffin Island, Nunavut, Canada** The Inuit in Canada are one of several large Eskimo groups inhabiting Arctic regions from Greenland to Alaska and eastern Siberia. Although they speak different languages and dialects, they share a traditional way of life primarily based on hunting and fishing in which the nuclear family is the primary social unit. As such, their kinship terminology system specifically identifies EGO's mother, father, brother, and sister and lumps all other relatives into a few broad categories that do not distinguish the side of the family from which they derive.

systems are fascinating in their complexity and are found among only a few of the world's societies. However, to illustrate some of the basic principles involved, we will focus our attention on the first three systems.

The Eskimo System

The Eskimo system, which is comparatively rare among all the world's systems, is the one used by most contemporary Europeans, Australians, and North Americans. It is also used by a number of indigenous food-foraging peoples, including Arctic peoples such as the Inuit and other Eskimos—hence the name (**Figure 20.10**).

Sometimes referred to as the *lineal system*, the **Eskimo system** emphasizes the nuclear family by specifically identifying mother, father, brother, and sister while lumping together all other relatives into a few large categories (**Figure 20.11**). For example, the father is distinguished from the father's brother (uncle), but the father's brother is not distinguished from the mother's brother (both are called uncle). The mother's sister and father's sister are treated similarly, both called aunt. In addition, all the sons

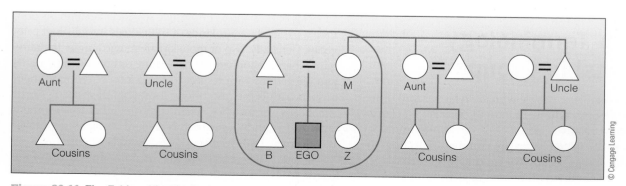

Figure 20.11 **The Eskimo Kinship System** Kinship terminology in this system emphasizes the nuclear family (circled). EGO's father and mother are distinguished from EGO's aunts and uncles, and siblings are distinguished from cousins.

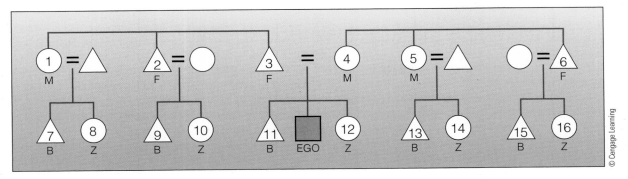

Figure 20.12 **The Hawaiian Kinship System** In this kinship system the men numbered 2 and 6 are called by the same term as father (3); the women numbered 1 and 5 are called by the same term as mother (4). All cousins of EGO's own generation (7 through 16) are considered brothers (B) and sisters (Z).

and daughters of aunts and uncles are called cousin, thereby making a generational distinction but without indicating the side of the family to which they belong or even their gender.

Unlike other terminologies, the Eskimo system provides separate and distinct terms for nuclear family members. This is probably because the Eskimo system is generally found in bilateral societies where the dominant kin-group is the kindred, in which only immediate family members are important in day-to-day affairs. This is especially true of modern European and North American societies, in which many families are independent—living apart from and not directly involved with other relatives except on special occasions. Thus, most North Americans (and others) generally distinguish between their closest kin (parents and siblings) but lump together (as aunts, uncles, cousins) other kin on both sides of the family.

The Hawaiian System

The **Hawaiian system** of kinship terminology, common (as its name implies) in Hawaii and other islands in the central Pacific Ocean but found elsewhere as well, is the least complex system in that it uses only a few terms. The Hawaiian system is also called the *generational system* because all relatives of the same generation and sex are referred to by the same term (**Figure 20.12**). For example, in one's parents' generation, the term used to refer to one's father is used as well for the father's brother and mother's brother. Similarly, one's mother, mother's sister, and father's sister are all grouped together under a single term. In EGO's generation, male and female cousins are distinguished by gender and are equated with brothers and sisters.

The Hawaiian system reflects the absence of strong unilineal descent, and members on both the father's and the mother's sides are viewed as more or less equal. The siblings of EGO's father and mother are all recognized as being similar relations and are merged under a single term appropriate for their gender. In like manner, the children belonging to

the siblings of EGO's parents are related to EGO in the same way as are the brother and sister. Falling under the incest taboo, they are ruled out as potential marriage partners.

The Iroquois System

In the **Iroquois system** of kinship terminology, the father and father's brother are referred to by a single term, as are the mother and mother's sister; however, the father's sister and mother's brother are given separate terms (**Figure 20.13**). In one's own generation, brothers, sisters, and parallel cousins (offspring of parental siblings of the same sex—that is, the children of the mother's sister or father's brother) of the same sex are referred to by the same terms, which is logical enough considering that they are the offspring of people who are classified in the same category as EGO's actual mother and father. Cross cousins (offspring of parental siblings of opposite sex—that is, the children of the mother's brother or father's sister) are distinguished by terms that set them apart from all other kin. In fact, cross cousins are often preferred as spouses, for marriage to them reaffirms alliances between related lineages or clans.

Iroquois terminology, named for the Iroquois Indians of North America's woodlands, is in fact very widespread and is usually found with unilineal descent groups. It was, for example, the terminology in use until recently in rural Chinese society.

Eskimo system Kinship reckoning in which the nuclear family is emphasized by specifically identifying the mother, father, brother, and sister, while lumping together all other relatives into broad categories such as uncle, aunt, and cousin; also known as a *lineal system*.

Hawaiian system Kinship reckoning in which all relatives of the same sex and generation are referred to by the same term: also known as the *generational system*.

Iroquois system Kinship reckoning in which a father and father's brother are referred to by a single term, as are a mother and mother's sister, but a father's sister and mother's brother are given separate terms. Parallel cousins are classified with brothers and sisters, whereas cross cousins are classified separately but not equated with relatives of some other generation.

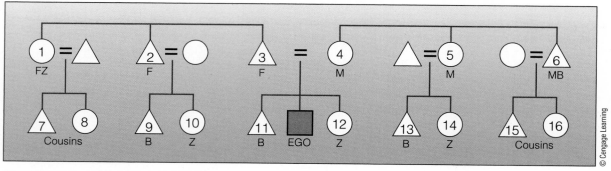

Figure 20.13 The Iroquois Kinship System According to the Iroquois system of kinship terminology, EGO's father's brother (2) is called by the same term as the father (3); the mother's sister (5) is called by the same term as the mother (4); but the people numbered 1 and 6 are each referred to by a distinct term. Those people numbered 9 through 14 are all considered siblings, but 7, 8, 15, and 16 are considered cousins.

Making Relatives

In every culture—from kin-ordered foraging, herding, or farming communities to state-organized capitalist societies—people have developed ideas about the status of relatives. These ideas concern how someone becomes one of "us"—whether by birth, paternal recognition, or some other means. And although many languages may stress the biological, as the English term *blood relative* demonstrates, what ultimately matters is the culturally defined social status of a person who is recognized as kin, with all the specific rights and obligations that come with being a daughter, son, brother, or sister to someone else in that kin-group. That is what "being related" is all about and what gives it symbolic meaning with practical consequences. Each kin term marks out a specific set of rights and obligations for individuals socially identified by such a cultural label. In state societies governed by law, these rights may even be legally spelled out in detail.

Fictive Kin by Ritual Adoption

One example of making relatives of individuals who are not biologically related is adoption—as discussed in the previous chapter's Globalscape on the transnational adoption of children. Adoption is a longstanding and widespread cultural practice in many societies all across the world.

Historically, families and clans facing exceptional challenges to their survival sometimes went to war to obtain human captives from other societies—sometimes young men, but usually women and children. These captives would then be adopted. This occurred among Iroquois Indians in northeastern America. In the 17th and 18th centuries, they often incorporated specially selected war captives and other valued strangers, including European

colonists, into their kin-groups in order to make up for population losses due to warfare and disease. As soon as these newcomers were ceremonially naturalized, they acquired essentially the same birthright status as those actually born into one of the families and were henceforth identified by the same kin term as the member being replaced.

Today, it is still not uncommon in traditional societies, especially in kin-ordered communities, for the head of a clan or family to adopt an outsider, especially when such an individual is valued as a contributing member because of unique skills or contacts with the outside world. Anthropologists may be adopted in this way, as noted in our fieldwork chapter, when they are conducting long-term participant observation in a culture in which such ritual incorporation into a kin-group is customary. As outsiders committed to learning the language and culture, anthropologists may also offer valuable services in return, bringing useful gifts such as steel axes or machetes. As adopted members of a family or clan, such out/insiders provide a useful link with powerful external forces, including international organizations with a mission to protect human rights.

Becoming a godparent is a form of ritual adoption traditionally practiced in many parts of Europe—and spreading to other parts of the world through European colonization or settlement. Generally, this involves the parent(s) of a newborn child inviting another adult, whether already a relative or not, to sponsor their child when he or she is baptized and formally named. This creates a spiritual relationship in which the godfather and godmother assume co-responsibility for the child's wellbeing. (Figure 20.14).

One of the many variations of this institution is *compadrazgo*, or "coparenthood." Especially common in Latin America, *compadrazgo* involves a child's father and/or mother and godfather and/or godmother becoming linked to each other through the ritual of a Roman

Figure 20.14 Godparents at Baby's Baptism In addition to being born into a family, people may gain relatives through adoption. Godparenting is a form of ritual adoption in which a person accepts certain lasting obligations toward someone else's child. Typically, it includes sponsoring the child's baptism ceremony, indicating a spiritual relationship. Here we see Cardinal Timothy Dolan, Archbishop of New York, baptizing a little girl held by her mother. Standing behind her, the baby's father smiles proudly while Father Dolan sprinkles blessed water on the child's head, symbolizing spiritual purification and admission into the Roman Catholic Church. Also looking on with joy are the father's brother and mother's sister. As the designated godfather and godmother, they assume responsibility for their godchild's faith and upbringing. Although the child's parents each chose a sibling for this important role, they could have selected anyone in good standing with the church.

Catholic baptism; they thereby agree to certain mutual rights and obligations. In *compadrazgo*, the main emphasis is placed not on the child–godparent relationship but on the fictive kinship between the child's parents and the sponsor who becomes a ritual coparent, or *compadre*. Historically common in South Europe and Latin America, such quasi-kinship is

> a pact for mutual support between the two *compadres*, co-parents, involved. Such a pact can be entered into between two *compadres* who are each other's equals in social and economic standing. Very often, however, it is formed between people, of whom one is wealthier, of higher social standing and more powerful politically than the other. (Wolf & Hansen, 1972, pp. 131–132)

Kinship and New Reproductive Technologies

Today's advances in reproductive technologies also pose new opportunities for kin-making. As defined in the previous chapter, *new reproductive technologies (NRTs)* are alternative means of reproduction such as surrogate motherhood and in vitro fertilization. Since 1978, when the world's first test-tube baby was created, thousands of babies have been created outside the womb, without sexual intercourse—and all kinds of new technologies have become part of the reproductive repertoire.

These technologies have opened up a mind-boggling array of reproductive possibilities and social relations. For example, if a child is conceived from a donor egg, implanted in another woman's womb, to be raised by yet another woman, who is the child's mother? To complicate matters even further, the egg may have been fertilized by sperm from a donor not married to, or in a sexual relationship with, any of these women. Indeed, it has been suggested that about a dozen different modern kin-type categories are embraced in the concepts of mother and father in today's changing societies (Stone, 2005).

Clearly, NRTs challenge previously held notions of parenthood and kinship. They force us to rethink what being biologically related to others really means. Moreover, they drive home the point that the human capacity for securing relatives is not only impressive and ingenious but also fascinating.

CHAPTER CHECKLIST

What is kinship, and what role does it play in social organization?

● Kinship is a network of relatives into which individuals are born and married, and with whom they cooperate based on customarily prescribed rights and obligations.

● In nonindustrial societies, kin-groups commonly deal with challenges that families and households cannot handle alone—challenges involving defense, resource allocation, and the need for cooperative labor. As societies become larger and more complex, formal political systems take over many of these matters.

What is a descent group, and what are its various forms?

● A descent group is any kin-group whose members share a direct line of descent from a real (historical) or fictional common ancestor.

● Unilineal descent establishes kin-group membership exclusively through the male or female line. Patrilineal descent is traced through the male line, and matrilineal is traced through the female line. In all societies the kin of both mother and father are important elements in the social structure, regardless of how descent group membership is defined. However, unlike the patrilineal pattern, matrilineal descent does not automatically confer gender authority.

● There is a close relationship between the descent system and a cultural system's infrastructure. Generally, patrilineal descent predominates when male labor is considered of prime importance, as it is among pastoralists and agriculturalists. Matrilineal descent predominates mainly among horticulturalists when female work in subsistence is especially important.

● The two major forms of a unilineal descent group (patrilineal or matrilineal) are the lineage and the clan. A lineage is a unilineal kin-group descended from a common ancestor or founder who lived four to six generations ago and in which relationships among members can be exactly stated in genealogical terms. A clan is an extended unilineal kin-group, often consisting of several lineages, whose members claim common descent from a remote ancestor, usually legendary or mythological.

● Double descent is a rare system in which descent is matrilineal for some purposes and patrilineal for others. Ambilineal descent provides a measure of flexibility in that an individual has the option of affiliating with either the mother's or father's descent group. Bilateral descent describes descent deriving from both the mother's and father's families equally.

What role does descent play within the larger cultural system?

● Lineages are commonly exogamous (meaning that members must marry outside the lineage). This avoids

sexual competition within the group. In addition, marriage of a group member represents an alliance of two lineages. Lineage exogamy also serves to maintain open communication within a society and fosters the exchange of information among lineages.

● Unlike lineages, clan residence is usually dispersed rather than localized. In the absence of residential unity, totems (symbols from nature that remind members of their common ancestry) often reinforce clan identification.

● A phratry is a unilineal descent group of two or more clans that supposedly share a common ancestry. When a society is divided into two halves, each half consisting of one or more clans, these two major descent groups are called moieties.

● In a bilateral descent system, individuals are affiliated equally with the mother's and father's families. Such a large group is socially impractical and is usually reduced to a small circle of paternal and maternal relatives called the kindred. A kindred is never the same for any two people except siblings. Bilateral kinship and kindred organization predominate in societies where nuclear families are common.

What does kinship terminology reveal about human relations?

● Kinship terminology varies across cultures. The terms people use for their relatives can reveal the structure of kinship groups, the importance of certain relationships, and prevailing attitudes about specific kin. Some languages use the same term to identify a brother and a cousin, suggesting that these kin are of equal importance to an individual. Kin merged under the same term have the same basic rights and obligations with respect to the person referring to them as such.

● The Hawaiian system is the simplest system of kinship terminology, with all relatives of the same generation and gender referred to by the same term.

● The Eskimo system, also used by English-speaking North Americans and many others, emphasizes the nuclear family and merges all other relatives in a given generation into a few large, generally undifferentiated categories.

● In the Iroquois system, a single term is used for a father and his brother and another for a mother and her sister. Parallel cousins are equated with brothers and sisters but distinguished from cross cousins.

● Adoption and the practice of godparenting establish additional kin categories.

● New reproductive technologies separating conception from sexual intercourse and eggs from wombs challenge traditional notions of kinship and gender and create new social categories.

QUESTIONS FOR REFLECTION

1. Thousands of Scots and people of Scottish descent from across the globe travel annually to traditional events known as the gathering of the clans. Do you care about your own distant relatives or ancestors, and what will you pass on from your cultural heritage to the next generation?

2. People in modern industrial and postindustrial societies generally treasure ideas of personal freedom, individuality, and privacy as essential to their happiness. Considering the social functions of kinship relations in traditional non-state societies, why do you think that such ideas may be considered unsociable and even dangerously selfish?

3. In some North American Indian languages, the English word for loneliness is translated as "I have no relatives." What does that tell you about the importance of kinship in traditional cultures?

4. Do you use a networking platform such as Facebook or Twitter to stay in touch with relatives, friends, schoolmates, or colleagues? Where are these individuals in your digital social network geographically located? How often do you see them in real space, and is your interaction with them different in person than online?

5. One reason anthropologists are so interested in understanding a culture's kinship terminology system is that it offers a quick but crucially important insight into a group's social structure. Why do you think this is especially true for traditional communities of foragers, herders, and farmers but is less so for urban neighborhoods in industrial and postindustrial societies?

ONLINE STUDY RESOURCES

CourseMate

Access chapter-specific learning tools, including learning objectives, practice quizzes, videos, flash cards, glossaries, and more in your Anthropology CourseMate.

Log into **www.cengagebrain.com** to access the resources your instructor has assigned and to purchase materials.

Challenge Issue

Beyond ties of kinship and household, people extend their social networks to cope with multiple challenges of human survival. They form groups based on shared identities, interests, or objectives, with memberships that may be compulsory or voluntary. Together, individuals interact, collaborate, and overcome obstacles. Collective action strengthens ties that bind but also reduces tensions that divide. In playing games, including sports, people show off superior mental or physical skills within and between groups but also reveal or act out some of their culture's core values. Many sports have their origins in warfare, with rivals demonstrating skills and endurance. Here we see Afghan horsemen playing a traditional sport, in which sometimes up to 200 riders fiercely compete for possession of a headless body of a goat. For this reason, the region's Tajik and Pashtun refer to their national sport as *buzkashi* ("goat-grabbing"). Players from rival teams pick up and carry the carcass around a marker at one end of the field and then throw it into the scoring circle at the opposite end. Competing for glory and prize money on special holidays, all the players—and spectators— in these gender-segregated cultures are male.

Grouping by Gender, Age, Common Interest, and Social Status

IN THIS CHAPTER YOU WILL LEARN TO

- Explain how social groups are formed based on age and gender, with anthropological examples of each.

- Identify different types of common-interest groups, noting their function in expanding an individual's social network beyond relatives, friends, and neighbors.

- Distinguish between egalitarian and stratified societies, with examples of each.

- Compare open-class and closed-class societies, with cultural anthropological details of each.

- Evaluate the structural similarities and differences between class, caste, and race in a stratified society.

- Recognize the challenges and opportunities of social mobility in different types of societies.

Anthropologists have given considerable attention to kinship and marriage, which operate as organizing principles in all societies and are usually the prime basis of social order in stateless societies. Yet, because ties of kinship and household are not always sufficient to handle all the challenges of human survival, people also form groups based on gender, age, common interest, and social status.

Grouping by Gender

As shown in preceding chapters, division of labor along gender lines occurs in all human societies. In some cultures, many tasks that men and women undertake may be shared, or people may perform work normally assigned to the opposite sex without loss of face. In others, however, men and women are rigidly segregated in what they do. Such is the case in many maritime cultures, where seafarers aboard fishing, whaling, and trading ships are usually men. For instance, we find temporary all-male communities aboard ships of coastal Basque fishermen in northwestern Spain, Yupik Eskimo whalers in Alaska, and Swahili merchants sailing along the East African coast. These seafarers commonly leave their wives, mothers, and daughters behind in their home ports, sometimes for months at a time.

Clearly demarcated grouping by gender also occurs in many traditional horticultural societies. For instance, among the Mundurucu Indians of Brazil's Amazon rainforest, men and women work, eat, and sleep separately. From age 13 onward, males live together in one large house, whereas women, girls, and preteen boys occupy two or three houses grouped around the men's house: Men associate with men, and women with women.

Figure 21.1 Sacred Trumpets of the Amazon Gender-based groups are common among the Mundurucu and numerous other Amazonian Indian nations such as the Yawalapiti pictured here, who live on the Tuatuari River in Brazil's upper Xingu region. Gender issues are symbolically worked out in their mythologies and ceremonial dances. One common theme concerns ownership of the sacred trumpets, which represent spiritual power. The tribesmen zealously guard these trumpets, and only men are allowed to play them. Traditionally, women were even forbidden to see them.

© Reuters/Corbis

Among the Mundurucu, relations between the sexes are not harmonious but rather are in opposition. According to their belief, sex roles were once reversed. Women ruled over men and controlled the sacred trumpets that are the symbols of power and represent the reproductive capacities of women. But because women could not hunt, they could not supply the meat demanded by the ancient spirits that possessed the trumpets. This enabled the men to take the trumpets from the women, establishing their dominance in the process. Ever since, the trumpets have been carefully guarded and hidden in the men's house, and traditionally women were prohibited from even seeing them (**Figure 21.1**).

Thus, Mundurucu men express fear and envy toward women and seek to control them by force. For their part, the women neither like nor accept a submissive status, and even though men occupy all formal positions of political and religious leadership, women are autonomous in the economic realm.

Alongside notable differences, there are also interesting similarities between the Mundurucu beliefs and those of traditional European and North American cultures. For example, many 19th-century European and U.S. intellectuals held to the idea that patriarchy (rule by men) had replaced an earlier state of matriarchy (rule by women). Moreover, the idea that men may use force to control women is deeply embedded in Judaic, Christian, and Muslim traditions. Although gender inequality has largely been erased in many parts of the world, gender-based groups persist for purposes of mutual support, religious worship, sports, and entertainment.

Grouping by Age

Like gender, grouping by age is based on human biology and as such is a cultural universal. All human societies recognize a number of life stages. The demarcation and duration of these stages vary across cultures, but each one provides distinctive social roles and comes with certain cultural features such as specific patterns of activity, attitudes, obligations, and prohibitions.

In many cultures, the social position of an individual in a specific life stage is also marked by a distinctive outward appearance in terms of dress, hairstyle, body paint, tattoos, insignia, or some other symbolic distinction. Typically, these stages are designed to help the transition from one age to another, to teach needed skills, or to lend economic assistance. Often they are taken as the basis for the formation of organized groups.

In North America today, for instance, a child's first friends are usually children of his or her own age. Starting preschool or kindergarten with age-mates, children typically move through a dozen or more years in the educational system together. At specified ages they are allowed to see certain movies, drive cars, and do things reserved for adults, such as voting, drinking alcoholic beverages, and serving in the military. Ultimately, North Americans retire from their paid jobs at a specified age and, increasingly, spend the final years of their lives in retirement communities, segregated from the rest of society. In the course of their life cycle, they are referred to by a series of labels, including "babies," "teenagers," "adults," "middle-agers," and "senior citizens"—whether they like it or not and for no other reason than the number of years they have lived.

Age classification also plays a significant role in non-Western societies that, at a minimum, mark distinctions among immature, mature, and older people whose physical powers are waning. In these societies old age often has profound significance, bringing with it the period of greatest respect (for women it may mean the first social equality with men). Rarely are the elderly shunted aside or abandoned. Even the Inuit of the Canadian Arctic, who are often cited as a migratory people who literally abandon their old and infirm relatives, do so only in truly desperate circumstances, when the traveling group's physical survival is at stake. In all oral tradition societies, elders are the repositories of accumulated wisdom for their people. Recognized as such and no longer expected to carry out many subsistence activities, they play a major role in passing on cultural knowledge to their grandchildren.

As a result of improvements in health care, medical technology, and other factors reducing mortality, more and more people live longer today than in previous generations, especially in wealthy societies. In the United States, for example, the average life expectancy rose from about 49 in 1900 to 68 in 1950 and reached just above 77 in 2000. Generally, women live longer than men, but the gap has widened from less than two years a century ago to more than five today, with American women now enjoying an average life expectancy of about 80 years. Japanese women hold the record for the world's longest life expectancy, with an average life span of about 86.5, whereas Japanese men average about six years less.

With the rise in average life expectancy, people not only grow older but also grow in numbers. For instance, the number of U.S. senior citizens 65 years and older is expected to swell from about 40 million to 70 million (20 percent of the overall U.S. population) within the next two decades. Consequently, health and welfare costs for the elderly will continue to rise, a social and financial burden shared with Japan and many other rapidly aging societies (U.S. Census Bureau, Statistical Abstract, 2012).

Institutions of Age Grouping

An organized category of people with membership on the basis of age is known as an **age grade**. Entry into and transfer out of age grades may be accomplished individually, either by a biological distinction, such as puberty, or by a socially recognized status, such as marriage or childbirth.

Members of an age grade may have much in common—engaging in similar activities and sharing the same orientation and aspirations. In many cultures, a specific time is established for ritually moving from a younger to an older grade. An example of this is the traditional Jewish ceremony of the *bar mitzvah* (a Hebrew term meaning "son of the commandment"), marking that a 13-year-old boy has reached the age of religious duty and responsibility.

Bat mitzvah, "daughter of the commandment," is the term for the equivalent ritual for a girl.

Although members of senior groups commonly expect deference from and acknowledge certain responsibilities to their juniors, this does not necessarily mean that one grade is seen as better, or worse, or even more important than another. There can be standardized competition (opposition) between age grades, such as that traditionally between first-year and second-year students on U.S. college campuses.

In addition to age grades, some societies feature age sets (sometimes referred to as *age classes*). An **age set** is a formally established group of people born during a certain time span who move together through the series of age-grade categories. Members of an age set usually remain closely associated throughout their lives. This is akin to but distinct from the broad and informal North American practice of identifying generation clusters composed of all individuals born within a particular time frame—such as baby boomers (1946–1964), Gen-Xers (1961–1981), and the Millennial or Internet generation (1982–2000) (year spans approximate).

The notion of an age set implies strong feelings of loyalty and mutual support. Because such groups may possess property, songs, shield designs, and rituals and are internally organized for collective decision making and leadership, age sets are distinct from simple age grades.

Age Grouping in East Africa

Although age is a criterion for group membership in many parts of the world, its most varied and elaborate use is found in several pastoral groups in East Africa, such as the Maasai, Samburu, and Tiriki in Kenya (Sangree, 1965). In Tiriki society, each boy born within a fifteen-year period joins a particular age set. Seven named age sets exist, but only one is open for membership at a time. When it closes, the next one opens. And so it continues until the passage of 105 years (7 times 15), when the first set's membership is gone due to death, and it opens once again to take in new recruits.

Members of Tiriki age sets remain together for life as they move through four successive age grades. Advancement in age grades occurs at fifteen-year intervals, coinciding with the closing of the oldest age set and the opening of a new one. Each age group has its own particular duties and responsibilities. Traditionally, the first age grade, the Warriors, served as guardians of the country, and members

---

age grade An organized category of people based on age; every individual passes through a series of such categories over his or her lifetime.

age set A formally established group of people born during a certain time span who move together through the series of age-grade categories; sometimes called *age class*.

Figure 21.2 Maasai Warrior Age-Grade Ceremony Like the Tiriki and some other pastoralists in East Africa, the Maasai form age sets—established groups of people born during a similar time span who move together through the series of age-grade categories. The opening parade, shown here, of the elaborate *eunoto* ceremony begins the coming of age of *morans* ("Warriors") for Maasai subclans of western Kenya. At the end of the ceremony, these men will be in the next age grade—junior adults—ready to marry and start families. Members of the same age set, they were initiated together into the Warrior age grade as teenagers. They spent their Warrior years raiding cattle (an old tradition that is now illegal but nonetheless still practiced) and protecting their community homes and animal enclosures (from wild animals and other cattle raiders). The *eunoto* ceremony includes a ritual in which mothers shave the heads of the Warriors, marking the end of many freedoms and the passage to manhood.

gained renown through fighting (**Figure 21.2**). Under British colonial rule, however, this traditional function largely fell by the wayside with the decline of intergroup raiding and warfare; individual members of this age grade may now find excitement and adventure by leaving their community for extended employment or study elsewhere.

The next age grade, the Elder Warriors, had few specialized tasks in earlier days beyond learning skills they would need later on by assuming an increasing share of administrative activities. For example, they would chair the postfuneral gatherings held to settle property claims after someone's death. Traditionally, Elder Warriors also served as envoys between elders of different communities. Nowadays, they hold nearly all of the administrative and executive roles opened up by the creation and growth of a centralized Tiriki administrative bureaucracy.

Judicial Elders, the third age grade, traditionally handled most tasks connected with the administration and settlement of local disputes. Today, they still serve as the local judiciary body.

Members of the Ritual Elders, the senior age grade, used to preside over the priestly functions of ancestral shrine observances on the household level, at subclan meetings, at semiannual community appeals, and at rites of initiation into the various age grades. They also were credited with access to special magical powers. With the decline of ancestor worship over the past several decades, many of these traditional functions have been lost, and no new ones have arisen to take their places. Nonetheless, Ritual Elders continue to hold the most important positions in the initiation ceremonies, and their power as sorcerers and expungers of witchcraft is still recognized.

Grouping by Common Interest

The rise of urban, industrialized societies in which individuals are often separated from their kin has led to a proliferation of **common-interest associations**— associations that result from an act of joining and are

VISUAL COUNTERPOINT

© Todd Gipstein/Corbis

© Leo Uehara

Figure 21.3 **Common-Interest Associations** The range of common-interest associations is astounding, as suggested by these photos of Shriners and Yakuza gang members. The Shriners (*left*), capped in tasseled red fezzes, are a secret fraternal order of middle-class males committed to "fun, fellowship, and service." Founded in the United States in 1870, the group was named after the Ancient Arabic Order of Nobles of the Mystic Shrine. Today, it is an international organization with 200 chapters across North and South America, Europe, and Southeast Asia. Much older than the Shriners, the Yakuza is a Japanese crime syndicate, whose members sport elaborate and visually specific tattoos with samurai images. Its 100,000 or so members, organized in three major associations, refer to their groups as "chivalrous organizations" (*ninkyō dantai*), claiming to be redistributing wealth through crime. Operating in the Japanese underworld as well as abroad, the Yakuza resembles the mafia historically based in Sicily.

based on sharing particular activities, objectives, values, or beliefs (**Figure 21.3**). Some are rooted in common ethnic, religious, or regional background. Such associations help people meet a range of needs from companionship to safe work conditions to learning a new language and customs upon moving from one country to another.

Common-interest associations are also found in many traditional societies, and there is some evidence that they arose with the emergence of the first horticultural villages. Notably, associations in traditional societies may be just as complex and highly organized as those found in industrialized countries.

Kinds of Common-Interest Associations

The variety of common-interest associations is astonishing. In the United States, they include sport, hobby, and civic service clubs; religious and spiritual organizations; political parties; labor unions; environmental

organizations; urban gangs; private militias; immigrant groups; academic organizations such as the American Anthropological Association; women's and men's clubs of all sorts—the list goes on and on. Their goals may include the pursuit of friendship, recreation, and the promotion of certain values, as well as governing, seeking peace on a local or global scale, and defending economic interests.

Some associations aim to preserve traditional songs, history, language, moral beliefs, and other customs among members of various ethnic minorities. So it is among many immigrant groups from Africa who live in major cities around the world, including in the United States. Today, some 250,000 African-born immigrants live in the New York metropolitan area. The city's largest African group hails from Ghana, a former British colony in West

common-interest association An association that results from an act of joining based on sharing particular activities, objectives, values, or beliefs, sometimes rooted in common ethnic, religious, or regional background.

VISUAL COUNTERPOINT

Todd Heisler/The New York Times/Redux

Dave Sanders/The New York Times/Redux

Figure 21.4 Induction of an Ashanti Chief in New York City Nearly a quarter-million African-born immigrants live in New York City, and more come from Ghana than from any other country on that continent. Many are part of Ghana's Ashanti ethnic group and are members of the Asanteman Association of the USA and its New York branch. They swear allegiance to their traditional king in Ghana (the *Asantehene*) and elect a local chief, who carries the title of *Asantefuohene*. New York's newest Ashanti chief, formally addressed as *Nana Okokyeredom Owoahene Acheampong Tieku*, works in the Bronx as an accountant and goes by the name Michael. The king sent a high-ranking chief from Ghana for his 2012 swearing-in ceremony.

Africa. Using electronic media, Ghanaians manage to maintain regular contact with relatives, friends, and others back home. Many of them are Ashanti, a large ethnic group historically powerful as an independent nation politically organized since the 1670s as a kingdom with a confederation of 37 paramount chiefdoms. Known as *Asanteman*, this kingdom is governed to this day by a ruler who carries the royal title of *Asantehene* and resides in the royal palace of his ancestors. His sacred power is symbolized by the "golden stool," believed to have floated down from heaven into the lap of his forefather and containing the spirit-soul (*sunsum*) of the Ashanti nation. The current

king is a British-educated business executive with international professional experience.

For purposes of mutual support and to maintain their cultural identity in the diaspora, Ashanti migrants in New York City formed the Asanteman Association of the USA in 1982, which now has numerous branches across country. Members swear allegiance to their king in Ghana and elect local chiefs in the cities where they now live (**Figure 21.4**).

The following Original Study provides a detailed example of how another ethnic minority group establishes a sense of traditional community, even within modern cities, by means of symbolic geographic boundary markers.

ORIGINAL STUDY

The Jewish *Eruv*: Symbolic Place in Public Space *BY SUSAN LEES*

Cultural anthropologists are interested in how a geographic space becomes a culturally meaningful *place*—an area that we may think of as "our territory" or that we designate for one particular purpose or another, such as pasturing animals, playing sports, gardening, or worshiping. As in a baseball diamond, there are certain boundaries to such places. We may mark them off with lines or

symbols not readily comprehensible to outsiders, who may not understand what makes a "foul ball" until we explain the rules and the symbols.

At times, different cultural groups may occupy the same geographic space, but each will see and divide it differently in terms that are meaningful only within their group. We see this on maps where international borders cut through traditional tribal or ethnic group territories, as with the Yupik Eskimos of Alaska and Siberia. And we see it in various urban communities that may divide up their city spaces in ways perceptible only to themselves.

An example can be found among Orthodox Jews who ritually define the boundaries of their communities for the purpose of Sabbath observance: Once a week, on the seventh day religiously reserved for worship and obligatory rest, the area enclosed by the boundaries becomes, by definition, a single shared symbolic domain. This symbolically enclosed space is called an *eruv*, which means "combination" of public and private space—that is, the private spaces of the household and the public areas of the sidewalks, streets, and perhaps parks are combined on the Sabbath as one big communal household.

The purpose of the *eruv* for Orthodox communities is to accommodate one of the many Sabbath prohibitions on religiously defined "work": the work of "carrying" objects from a private domain to a public one, or vice versa, or carrying objects for any distance in a public domain. On the Sabbath, if there is an *eruv*, observant Jews may carry within the entire *eruv* enclosure as if they were in their own homes. For instance, they are permitted to push a baby stroller or a wheelchair within the ritually enclosed neighborhood. This makes it possible for whole families—including small children and disabled individuals—to attend religious services in the synagogue or to socialize with one another and still be faithful to traditional law.

Historically, *eruv* boundaries were in fact the walls of houses and courtyards and city walls within which communities were enclosed. But today, where there are no walls, communities sometimes erect thin strings or wires, or sometimes just use wires already there on utility poles (such as phone or electricity wires) to demarcate the boundaries. These are known to members of the community but usually are invisible to outsiders because they are part of the urban landscape anyway.

I was first drawn to the subject of the *eruv* three decades ago, when I leafed through my mother's copy of the Code of Jewish Law still found in many Jewish households. Much of this text concerns rules about observing the Sabbath.

As an anthropologist, I was intrigued by explanations given for certain practices because they heightened awareness of the uniqueness of Jewish identity in a world where temptations to assimilate with the larger, dominant culture were strong. Most of all, the *eruv* captured my interest because it seemed to create, not just prohibit something. It transformed a group of diverse urban households into one common household, not just a community but a real "private" home. The symbolic "walls" around this collective domain were erected not to keep others out but to enclose its members and thus erase the actual walls of each individual household.

The ritual that creates an *eruv* requires that one member take a loaf of bread and make other members co-owners of that loaf; the symbolism of a household is shared ownership (not consumption) of this most symbolically meaningful food. The boundaries of the *eruv* "household" they co-inhabit must be contiguous, broken only by symbolic doorways through which they can pass as if through doorways of their individual homes. As long as the contiguity is maintained, they can extend the *eruv* to incorporate hundreds or even thousands of other houses. It occurred to me then that in a highly urbanized mass society of mostly strangers, this symbolic unification of sometimes widely separated Jewish households was an extraordinary thing.

The majority of North American Jews who are members of religious congregations belong to Reform synagogues (the other major groups are Conservative and Orthodox), and American Reform Judaism officially abandoned the *eruv* as a Sabbath practice in 1846. When I first became interested in the subject, there were rather few *eruvin* anywhere.

But in the early 1970s, on the heels of the 1960s civil rights movement in the United States, a shift in Jewish identity issues occurred, and some younger generation Jews began to turn to traditional practices that distinguished them from mainstream society and more assimilated Jews. It was in this context that a proliferation of new *eruvin* occurred in both urban and suburban contexts. Meanwhile, some Jews resisted this expression of difference, and within the wider Jewish community there was considerable strife over the question of the "authenticity" of the beliefs and practices of more assimilated Jews.

This map illustrates the *eruv* boundaries in Washington, DC—one of many symbolically enclosed spaces created by Orthodox Jews in cities around the world.

Most *eruvin* have been established without conflict, but a handful have been highly controversial. In my research, I was interested to find that Jews are among the principal parties on both sides of *eruv* conflicts. Opponents of the *eruv* appear to fear the creation, or re-creation, of ghettos of inassimilable Jews who neither conform to nor respect the ideals of the dominant or mainstream culture—who appear "foreign" in appearance and practices. Thus, the *eruv* conflict appears on one level to be an argument among Jews adhering to different beliefs about how they should live in modern society with other groups and among themselves. Interestingly, when Jewish religious leaders were first developing the laws of the *eruv* more than 2,000 years ago, this problem of how Jews could maintain a communal identity while living as a diasporic group (dispersed from their ancestral homeland) was among their primary concerns.

The *eruv* is one symbolic device to reinforce community as neighborhood—to establish a meaningful place for a distinct group in a diverse society. Ethnic church parishes often have done the same for other urban groups. Neighborhood identities like these can be the basis for disputes about exclusivity, but they can also ease the maintenance of cultural traditions and humanize life in the city.

Written expressly for this text, 2008.

Men's and Women's Associations

In some societies women have not established formal common-interest associations to the extent that men have, either because women are restricted by their male-dominated culture or because women are absorbed on the domestic front with a host of activities compatible with childrearing. Moreover, some functions of men's associations—such as military combat duties—often are culturally defined as fit only for adult males or are repugnant to women. Still, as cross-cultural research makes clear, women often play important roles in associations of their own as well as in those in which men predominate. Notably, an ever-expanding feminist movement has directly or indirectly inspired and promoted the formation of professional organizations for women.

Throughout Africa, women's social clubs complement the men's and are linked to a variety of economic and social matters. These clubs provide information on economic opportunities, offer mutual support, and give spiritual counseling; they are also concerned with educating women, with promoting craftworks, and with charitable and wealth-generating activities. Increasingly, women's clubs are devoted to politics. In Sierra Leone, dancing societies have developed under urban conditions into complex organizations with a set of new objectives. The resulting dancing *compin* (Krio for "company") is composed of young women (along with men) performing plays based on traditional music and dances and raising money for various mutual benefit causes (Little, 1973; Steady, 2001).

In rural areas all around the world, women's craft associations and cooperatives are increasingly common and economically productive. Many are enhanced through Internet marketing opportunities, which make it possible for the cooperatives to sell directly to buyers in far-off places, especially Western markets. Others take advantage of the ever-growing number of tourists looking for adventure in travel to remote areas **(Figure 21.5)**.

Women's rights organizations, consciousness-raising groups, and professional clubs are examples of some of the

Figure 21.5 Women's Weaving Cooperative in Peru
Established in a small Andean highland village about halfway between Pisac and the ancient Inca royal capital Cuzco, this co-op is committed to spinning, dying, and weaving wool from llamas and alpacas as women here have done for many generations—completely by hand using only natural materials and dyes. Most of the men in Ccaccaccollo, Peru, work as carriers for tourists hiking the Inca Trail.

associations arising directly or indirectly out of feminist movements. These groups cover the entire range of association formation, from simple friendship and support groups to associations centered on politics, sports, the arts, spirituality, charity, and economic endeavors—on a national and even international scale. One example of a global female youth movement is the World Association of Girl Guides and Girl Scouts. Founded in England in 1928, this association supports young-female scouting organizations with a total membership of over 10 million girls and young women in 145 countries.

A far-reaching example on the economic front is India's Self-Employed Women's Association (SEWA), founded in 1972 and headquartered in the northwestern city of Ahmedabad. With over a half-million members, it is India's single largest union of informal sector workers. Notably, 94 percent of the country's female labor force is in this sector. Working with more than 200 cooperatives and thousands of individual artisans and small-scale farmers from poor rural areas, SEWA has helped to establish supportive services vital to helping women achieve the goals of full employment and self-reliance—services such as savings and credit, health care, child care, insurance, legal aid, capacity building, and communication services. SEWA's Trade Facilitation Centre has grown into a global network aimed at making women's voices and contributions significant factors in world trade decisions.

Associations in the Digital Age

Despite the diversity and vitality of common-interest associations, some social analysts have noted a recent decline in participation in all sorts of these groups, at least in North America. Those who have observed this trend see it as part of a more general drop in civic participation.

People are spending less time socializing face-to-face with others. Instead, millions spend their time with an ever-growing array of electronic and/or digital devices, communicating with others, entertaining themselves, and shopping.

Whether accessed by computer or mobile phone, social networking platforms—such as Facebook (with nearly 1 billion subscribers worldwide in 2012), Gmail (425 million users), Twitter (500 million active users), and Chinese weibo/microblog sites (over 300 million users)—enable individuals to text message and exchange images with "friends," continually update their personal or other information, and engage in microblogging.

In the United States, teenagers text message on average more than 60 times a day—a figure probably not much different from that of their age-mates in Japan, Australia, and other technologically advanced societies. A new study shows that texting

> far surpasses the frequency with which [U.S. teens] pick other forms of *daily* communication, including phone calling by cell phone (39% do that with others every day), face-to-face socializing outside of school (35%), social network site messaging (29%), instant messaging (22%), talking on landlines (19%) and emailing (6%). (Lenhart, 2012)

People in societies all across the globe now have direct access to an ever-expanding range of relatively cheap digital communication tools—especially mobile phones. As noted in the chapter on language and communication, by the end of 2011 there were 5.9 billion mobile phone subscriptions worldwide, and close to 90 percent of the world's population is within mobile coverage (**Figure 21.6**) (International Telecommunication Union, 2012).

Figure 21.6 Constant Communication High-speed wireless networks in affluent Japan, as in many other parts of the world, make it possible for people to continually tap into information and exchange messages and images by means of portable computers or, increasingly, web-enabled mobile telephones. For Japanese commuters, who spend hours staring at tiny screens on their mobiles while riding the world's most extensive network of subways and commuter trains, microblogging is especially popular.

David Sacks/Getty Images

Excluding time spent texting or talking on phones, U.S. children ages 8 to 18 spend more than 7½ hours a day using entertainment media. About 2 hours of this daily media consumption occurs on mobile devices—such as cell phones or handheld video game players. Another hour consists of "old" content—TV or music—delivered through new pathways on a computer (Rideout, Foehr, & Roberts, 2010).

These technologies are now also used by office managers, city mayors, law enforcers, physicians, and school principals for purposes of quick communication and have become instrumental in the functioning of many social groups. Importantly, in highly mobile societies and globally interconnected cultures, these new social media make it possible to build and expand social networks regardless of geographic distance and across international boundaries.

Grouping by Social Status in Stratified Societies

Social stratification is a common and powerful structuring force in many of the world's societies. Basically, **stratified societies** are those in which people are hierarchically divided and ranked into social strata, or layers, and do not share equally in the basic resources that support income, status, and power. Members of the bottom strata typically have fewer resources, lower prestige, and less power than those in top-ranked strata. In addition, they usually face greater or more oppressive restrictions and obligations and must work harder for far less material reward and social recognition.

In short, social stratification amounts to culturally institutionalized inequality. In the United States, certain ethnic (or racial) minorities—in particular Hispanic, African American, and American Indian groups—are among those who have been historically marginalized, posing a challenge for individuals born into these low-ranked strata to move up the social ladder. As profiled in this chapter's Anthropology Applied feature, their needs are often ignored in development efforts.

stratified societies Societies in which people are hierarchically divided and ranked into social strata, or layers, and do not share equally in the basic resources that support income, status, and power.
egalitarian societies Societies in which people have about the same rank and share equally in the basic resources that support income, status, and power.
social class A category of individuals in a stratified society who enjoy equal or nearly equal prestige according to the hierarchical system of evaluation.
caste A closed social class in a stratified society in which membership is determined by birth and fixed for life.

Stratified societies stand in sharp contrast to **egalitarian societies**, in which everyone has about equal rank and power and about the same access to basic resources. In these societies, social values of communal sharing are culturally emphasized and approved; wealth hoarding and elitist pretensions are despised, belittled, or ridiculed. As we saw in earlier chapters, foraging societies are characteristically egalitarian, although there are some exceptions.

Social Class and Caste

A **social class** may be defined as a category of individuals in a stratified society who enjoy equal or nearly equal prestige according to the system of evaluation. The qualification "nearly equal" is important because a certain amount of inequality may occur even within a given class. Class distinctions are not always clear-cut and obvious in societies that have a wide and continuous range of differential privileges.

A **caste** is a closed social class in a stratified society in which membership is determined by birth and fixed for life. The opposite of the principle that all humans are born equal, the caste system is based on the principle that humans are born and remain unequal until death. Castes are strongly endogamous, and offspring are automatically members of their parents' caste.

The Traditional Hindu Caste System

The classic ethnographic example of a caste system is the traditional Hindu caste system of India (also found in other parts of Asia), which encompasses a complex ranking of social groups on the basis of "ritual purity." Each of some 2,000 different castes considers itself as a distinct community higher or lower than other castes, although their particular ranking varies across geographic regions and over time.

The different castes are associated with specific occupations and customs, such as food habits and styles of dress, along with rituals involving notions of purity and pollution. Ritual pollution is the result of contact such as touching, accepting food from, or having sex with a member of a lower caste. To remain pure, traditional Hindus are taught to follow the ritual

ANTHROPOLOGY APPLIED

Anthropologists and Social Impact Assessment

Anthropologists frequently do a type of policy research called a *social impact assessment*, which entails collecting data about a community or neighborhood for planners of development projects. Such an assessment seeks to determine a project's effect by determining how and upon whom its impact will fall and whether the impact is likely to be positive or negative.

In the United States, any project requiring a federal permit or license or using federal funds by law must be preceded by a social impact assessment as part of the environmental review process. Examples of such projects include highway construction, urban renewal, water diversion schemes, and land reclamation. Often, such projects are sited so that their impact falls most heavily on neighborhoods or communities inhabited by people in low socioeconomic strata—sometimes because the projects are viewed as a way of improving the lives of poor people and sometimes because the poor people have less political power to block these proposals.

As an illustration of this kind of work, anthropologist Sue Ellen Jacobs was hired to do a social impact assessment of a water diversion project in New Mexico planned by the Bureau of Land Reclamation in cooperation with the Bureau of Indian Affairs. This project

proposed construction of a diversion dam and an extensive canal system for irrigation on the Rio Grande. The project would affect twenty-two communities primarily inhabited by Hispanic Americans, as well as two Indian pueblos. Unemployment was high in the region, and the project was seen as a way to promote urbanization, which theoretically would be associated with industrial development and would also bring new land into production for intensive agriculture.

What the planners failed to take into account was that both the Hispanic and Indian populations were heavily committed to farming for household consumption (with some surpluses raised for the market), using a system of irrigation canals that had been established for 300 years. These canals are maintained by elected supervisors familiar with the communities and knowledgeable about water laws, ditch management, and sustainable crop production. Such individuals can resolve conflicts concerning water allocation and land use, among other issues. Under the proposed project, this system was to be given up in favor of one in which fewer people would control larger tracts of land and water allocation would be in the hands of a government technocrat. One of the

strongest measures of local government would be lost.

Not surprisingly, Jacobs discovered widespread community opposition to this project, and her report helped convince Congress that any positive impact was far outweighed by negative effects. One of the major objections to the construction project was that it would obliterate the centuries-old irrigation system. Project planners did not seem to recognize the antiquity and cultural significance of these traditional irrigation structures, referring to them as "temporary diversion structures." The fact that the old dams associated with the ditches were attached to local descent groups was simply not acknowledged in the government documents.

Beyond infringing on local control, the project threatened the community with a range of negative side effects: problems linked to population growth and relocation, a loss of fishing and other river-related resources, and new health hazards, including increased threat of drowning, insect breeding, and airborne dust.

Based in part on Van Willigen, J. (1986). Applied anthropology (p. 169). South Hadley, MA: Bergin & Garvey. See also Van Willigen, J. (2002). Applied anthropology: An Introduction. Westport, CT: Bergin & Garvey.

path of duty, or *dharma*, of the specific caste into which they are born, and to avoid everyone and everything considered taboo to their caste. For this reason, castes are always endogamous. Differences in caste rankings are traditionally justified by the religious doctrine of the transmigration of the soul or *karma*—a belief that one's status in this life is determined by one's deeds in previous lifetimes.

All of these castes, or *jatis*, are organized into four ranked orders, or *varnas* (literally meaning "colors"), distinguished partly by occupation and ranked in order of descending religious status of purity (Figure 21.7). The religious foundation for this social hierarchy is found in a 2,000-year-old sacred text known as the Laws

of Manu, which traditional Hindus consider to be the highest authority on their cultural institutions. It defines the Brahmans as the purest and therefore highest *varna*.

As priests and lawgivers, Brahmans represent the world of religion and learning. Next come the fighters and rulers, known as the Kshatriyas. Below them are the Vaisyas (merchants and traders), who are engaged in commercial, agricultural, and pastoral pursuits. At the bottom are the Sudras (artisans and laborers), an order required to serve the other three *varnas* and who also make a living by handicrafts. Members born into these four *varnas* are believed to have been reincarnated from a morally correct earlier life in a lower-ranked order.

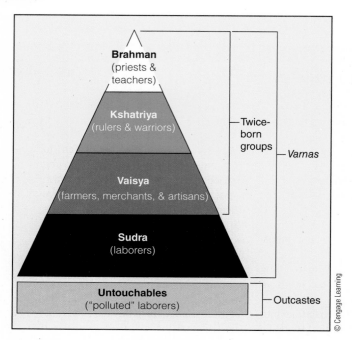

Figure 21.7 The Hindu Caste System Hindu castes are organized into four "grades of being" called *varnas* ("colors") that determine what members are permitted to do, touch, or eat; where they live; how they dress; and who they can marry. The highest-ranking order Brahman is associated with the color white, below which are Kshatriya (red) and Vaisya (brown). Below these three are Sudra (black), who make a living as laborers. Lower still are the "polluted" laborers, the Untouchables, who are charged with cleaning the streets and with the collection and disposal of garbage, animal carcasses, and sewage.

Falling outside the *varna* system is a fifth category of degraded individuals. These outcastes, known as Untouchables or as *Dalits* (a Sanskrit name meaning "crushed" or "suppressed"), are tasked with doing the dirty work in society—collecting garbage, removing animal carcasses, cleaning streets, and disposing of dung, sewage, and other refuse (Figure 21.8). Brahmans and members of other *varnas* avoid direct contact with Untouchables, believing that touching or accepting food from them would result in ritual pollution. Commonly associated with filth, outcastes constitute a large pool of cheap labor at the beck and call of those controlling economic and political affairs. In an effort to bestow some dignity on these poverty-stricken victims of the caste system, Hindu nationalist leader Mahatma Gandhi renamed them *harijan* or "children of God."

Although India's national constitution of 1950 sought to abolish the caste system, the traditional hierarchy remains deeply entrenched in Hindu culture and is still widespread throughout southern Asia, especially in rural India. In what has been called India's hidden apartheid, entire villages in many Indian states remain completely segregated by caste.

Untouchables represent about 15 percent of India's population—nearly 170 million people—and must endure social isolation, humiliation, and discrimination based exclusively on their birth status. Even their shadows are seen as polluting. They may not cross the line dividing their part of the village from that occupied by higher castes, may not drink water from public wells, and may not visit the same temples as the higher castes. Their children are still often made to sit at the back of classrooms, and in rural areas some are denied access to education altogether. However, over the past half century, Untouchables, in concert with the lowest-ranking Sudra castes, have built a civil rights movement—described later in this chapter (Office of the United Nations Higher Commissioner for Human Rights, 2007).

Similar castelike situations are found in other places in the world. In Bolivia, Ecuador, and several other South and Central American countries, for example, the wealthy upper class remains almost exclusively white and rarely intermarries with people of American Indian or African descent. In contrast, the lower class of working poor in those countries is primarily made up of American Indian, black, or mixed-race laborers and peasants.

Likewise, most European stratified societies were historically organized in closed social classes known as *estates*—ranked as clergy, nobility, and citizens—each with distinctive political rights (privileges). Titles and forms of address hierarchically identified these estates, and they were publicly distinguished by dress and codes of behavior. Not unlike the lowest castes in the Hindu caste system, a large underclass of millions of serfs ranked at the bottom of the European hierarchy. Prohibited from owning land or a business, *serfs* could not vote and did not enjoy the rights of free citizens. Often dirt poor, they worked on large farms and houses owned by the elite. Unlike slaves, they could not be traded as personal property of their masters, but they were restricted in their right to free movement and required their master's consent to marry.

Serfdom existed for many centuries in much of Europe. Russia was that continent's last country to abolish this system in 1861—just two years before slavery was abolished in the United States. It was several more decades before the slave system officially ended in Brazil, China, and other countries.

Historical Racial Segregation in South Africa and the United States

Other than social class, caste, and estate, the hierarchy in a stratified society may be based on ethnic origin or skin color. For instance, dark-skinned individuals culturally classified as colored or black may encounter social rules excluding them from certain jobs or neighborhoods and making it difficult if not impossible to befriend or marry someone with a lighter skin color. (As discussed earlier in

Figure 21.8 **Doing the Dirty Work** Rubbish picking is a task traditionally performed by Dalits (Untouchables) in the hierarchical caste system of Indian society. These pickers in Mysore, Karnataka, India, may sometimes be joined by a roaming holy cow.

our text, the terms *race, black*, and *white* are purely social constructions, with no basis in biology. For simplicity, we use them here without quotation marks.)

One of the best-known historical examples of a pluralistic country with social stratification based on the notion of race is South Africa. From 1948 to 1992, a minority of 4.5 million people of European descent sought to protect its power and "racial purity" by means of a repressive regime of racial segregation and discrimination against 25 million indigenous black Africans. Known as *apartheid* (an Afrikaans-Dutch term meaning "segregation" or "separation"), this white superiority ideology officially relegated indigenous dark-skinned Africans to a low-ranking stratum. Similar to the Hindu caste system with its concepts of ritual purity and pollution, South African whites feared pollution of their purity through direct personal contact with blacks (**Figure 21.9**).

Until the mid-20th century, institutionalized racial segregation officially prevailed in the United States, where the country's ruling upper class was historically comprised exclusively of individuals of European (Caucasian or white) descent. For generations, it was against the law for whites to marry blacks or American Indians. Even after black slavery was abolished in the United States in 1863, such interracial mixing prohibitions remained in force in many states from Maine to Florida. Today, despite significant steps toward equality since enactment of civil rights laws in the 1960s that officially prohibited race-based segregation and race-based discrimination, American blacks

as a racial minority (with notable individual exceptions) still rank lower in terms of wealth and health (Boshara, 2003; Kennickell, 2003).

Indicators of Social Status

Social classes are manifested in various ways, including *symbolic indicators*. For example, in the United States certain activities and possessions are indicative of class: occupation (a garbage collector has a different class status than a medical specialist); wealth (rich people are generally in a higher social class than poor people); dress ("white collar" versus "blue collar"); form of recreation (people in the upper class are expected to play golf rather than shoot pool down at the pool hall—but they can shoot pool at home or in a club); residential location (people in the upper class do not ordinarily live in slums); kind of car; and so on. All sorts of status symbols are indicative of class position, including measures such as the number of bathrooms in a person's house. That said, class rankings do not fully correlate with economic status or pay scales. The local garbage collector or unionized car-factory laborer typically makes more money than an average college professor with a doctorate.

Symbolic indicators involve factors of lifestyle, but differences in life chances may also signal differences in class standing. Life is apt to be easier for members of an upper class as opposed to a lower class. This shows up in a tendency for lower infant mortality and longer life

Figure 21.9 Apartheid in South Africa During South Africa's apartheid regime (1948–1992), the white minority of European descent imposed strict racial segregation in that country, which not only dictated where blacks were allowed to live or work, but also prohibited who they could marry, where they could worship and socialize, and even where they could swim.

Courtesy of the United Nations

expectancy for the upper class. There is also a tendency for greater physical stature and better overall health among people of the upper class—the result of healthier diet and protection from serious illness in their growing-up years (see the Biocultural Connection).

Maintaining Stratification

In any system of stratification, those who dominate proclaim their supposedly superior status by means of a powerful ideology, commonly asserting it through intimidation or propaganda (in the form of gossip, media, religious doctrine, and so forth) that presents their position as normal, natural, divinely guided, or at least well deserved. So it is with certain religious ideologies that effectively assert that the social order is divinely fixed and therefore not to be questioned. With the aid of culturally institutionalized thought structures, religious and otherwise, those in power hope that members of the lower classes will thereby "know their place" and not contest their domination by the chosen elite. If, however, this domination is contested, the elite usually control the power of the state and use its institutions to protect their privileged position.

In India, for example, Hindu belief in reincarnation and an incorruptible supernatural power that assigns people to a particular caste position, as a reward or punishment for the deeds and misdeeds of past lives, justifies one's position in this life. If, however, individuals faithfully perform the duties appropriate to their caste in this lifetime, then they can expect to be reborn into a higher caste in a future

existence. Thus, in the minds of orthodox Hindus, one's caste position is something earned rather than the accident of birth that outside observers might assume.

In contrast to India's traditional caste system, which explicitly recognizes and legitimizes disparity among people, the principle of human equality is fundamental to the American worldview. This founding principle prevails despite the U.S. history of racial and gender discrimination and its stark differences in wealth, status, and power.

Social Mobility

Most stratified societies offer at least some **social mobility**—an upward or downward change in one's social class position. The prospects of improving status and wealth help to ease the strains inherent in any system of inequality.

Social mobility is most common in societies made up of independent nuclear families in which the individual is closely tied to fewer people, especially when neolocal residence is the norm, and it is assumed that individuals will leave their family of birth when they become adults. In such social settings—through hard work, occupational success, opportune marriage, and dissociation from the lower-class family in which they grew up—individuals can more easily move up in status and rank.

In societies in which the extended family or lineage is the usual form, upward social mobility is hampered because each individual is strongly tied to many relatives (both close and more distant); those climbing the social ladder are culturally obliged to leave none in the kin-group behind. In all likelihood, many relatives of the highly successful Côte d'Ivoire soccer players described in this chapter's Globalscape (page 534) have collectively experienced upward mobility through their kinship ties to these newly wealthy athletes.

social mobility An upward or downward change in one's social class position in a stratified society.

BIOCULTURAL CONNECTION

African Burial Ground Project

By Michael Blakey

In 1991, construction workers in lower Manhattan unearthed what turned out to be part of a six-acre burial ground containing remains of an estimated 15,000 enslaved African captives brought to New York in the 17th and 18th centuries to build the city and provide the labor for its thriving economy. The discovery sparked controversy as the African American public held protests and prayer vigils to stop the part of a federal building project that nearly destroyed the site. In 1993, the site was designated a National Historic Landmark, which opened the door to researching and protecting the site.

As a biological anthropologist and African American, I had a unique opportunity to work together with the descendant African American community to develop a plan that included both extensive biocultural research and the humane retention of the sacred nature of the site, ultimately through reburial and the creation of a fitting memorial. The research also involved archaeological and historical studies that used a broad African diasporic context for

understanding the lifetime experiences of these people who were enslaved and buried in New York.

Studying a sample population of 419 individuals from the burial ground, our team used an exhaustive range of skeletal biological methods, producing a database containing more than 200,000 observations of genetics, morphology, age, sex, growth and development, muscle development, trauma, nutrition, and disease. The bones revealed an unmistakable link between biology and culture: physical wear and tear of an entire community brought on by the social institution of slavery.

We now know, based on this study, that life for Africans in colonial New York was characterized by poor nutrition, grueling physical labor that enlarged and often tore muscles, and death rates that were unusually high for 15- to 25-year-olds. Many of these young adults died soon after arriving on slaving ships. Few Africans lived past 40 years of age, and less than 2 percent lived beyond 55. Church records show strikingly different mor-

tality trends for the Europeans of New York: About eight times as many English as Africans lived past 55 years of age, and mortality in adolescence and the early 20s was relatively low.

Skeletal research also showed that those Africans who died as children and were most likely to have been born in New York exhibited stunted and disrupted growth and exposure to high levels of lead pollution—unlike those who had been born in Africa (and were distinguishable because they had filed teeth). Fertility was very low among enslaved women in New York, and infant mortality was high. In these respects, this northern colonial city was very similar to South Carolina and the Caribbean to which its economy was tied—regions where conditions for African captives were among the harshest.

Individuals in this deeply troubling burial ground came from warring African states including Calibar, Asante, Benin, Dahomey, Congo, Madagascar, and many others—states that wrestled with the European demand for human slaves. They resisted their enslavement through rebellion, and they resisted their dehumanization by carefully burying their dead and preserving what they could of their cultures.

BIOCULTURAL QUESTION

Although few will question that slavery is an inhuman system of labor exploitation, was it economically rational for slave owners to mistreat their "human chattel," as indicated by the poor health, low fertility, and high mortality of African slaves in colonial New York?

Adapted from Blakey, M. (2003). African Burial Ground Project. Revised and updated by the author for the 12th edition of this textbook. See also Blakey, M. (May, 2010). African Burial Ground Project: Paradigm for cooperation? Museum International 62 (1-2), 61–68.

The excavation site of the African Burial Ground in Lower Manhattan in New York City now features a distinctive memorial that commemorates the story of this important historical archaeological project. Now a national monument, the site is managed by the National Park Service.

© A. J. Giordano/Corbis SABA

Globalscape

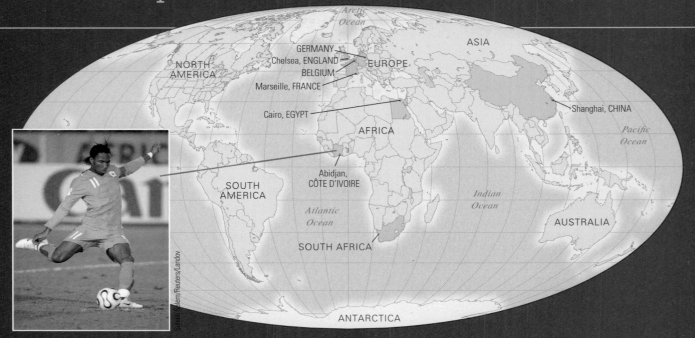

Suhaib Salem/Reuters/Landov

Playing Football for Pay and Peace?

The world's most popular sport is football (called *soccer* in the United States), with countless amateur and professional clubs and associations on every continent. The game originated in the British Isles, where youth at schools and adults with money and leisure time competed for championships—a luxury out of reach for the working class.

This changed about 150 years ago, when tournaments turned into commercial spectacles with clubs earning revenues from ticket and advertising sales. Initially opposed by upper-class traditionalists defending the sport as a healthy and character-building activity for amateurs (*amator*, Latin for "lover"), the emergence of professional clubs made it possible for athletes from the British working class to play for pay.

Today, most professionals playing for the world's top football clubs are young millionaires such as Didier Drogba (pictured here), who plays for China's Shanghai Shenhua and for his own country—the Côte d'Ivoire national team, nicknamed "the Elephants." Born in Abidjan, the major city in this former French West African colony, Drogba is a southerner belonging to the Bete, one of the country's sixty-five ethnic groups. Recruited at an early age for a Belgian club and becoming a powerful striker, he was drafted by a French club in Marseille for $8 million. Chosen French Player of the Year in 2004, after just one season, he signed with England's champion team, Chelsea, for a record $42-million multi-year contract (not counting endorsements).

By the time Drogba left Chelsea for Shanghai in 2012, he had scored more goals for Chelsea than any other foreign player and was that team's fourth highest goal scorer of all time. His new salary in China, some $300,000 a week, makes him one of the world's highest paid footballers.

With the average Ivoirian earning less than $1,000 per year, it is not surprising that athletic talents like Drogba venture across the globe for fortune and fame. In fact, all members of the Côte d'Ivoire national football team normally play abroad, most for wealthy European clubs. Meanwhile, their home country has been wracked by a brutal civil war pitting southern ethnic groups against northern ones.

Ninety percent of Côte d'Ivoire's foreign exchange earnings come from cocoa beans. As a world-renowned sports star, Drogba began appearing in ads promoting the international sale of Ivoirian chocolate. He also began to promote peace: During the 2006 World Cup games in Germany, enthusiastically watched on television by millions of fellow Ivoirians back home, team captain Drogba and his teammates (representing both southern and northern Côte d'Ivoire) pleaded that the unity of the Elephants in the stadium should inspire fellow Ivoirians to settle their conflict and reunite as a country. In 2007, a peace agreement was signed after Drogba helped move the Elephants' African Cup of Nations qualifier match to the rebel stronghold of Bouake, where warring leaders found themselves celebrating their national team together.

Fighting broke out again in early February 2011 over contested political elections. Soon thereafter, Drogba joined the Truth, Reconciliation, and Dialogue Commission as a representative—his eye still on the goal of bringing lasting peace to his home nation. Meanwhile, Côte d'Ivoire and over 200 other countries have entered qualification rounds for the 2014 World Cup, hosted by Brazil. Once again, Drogba will captain his country's national team, exhibiting the unity he wishes for his country.

Global Twister

How realistic is Drogba's idea that a national multi-ethnic soccer team can help unite his country's rival factions in a lasting way?

Figure 21.10 **Dinner Time in Tent City, Sacramento, California** Stratified societies are hierarchically structured into social classes that can be closed, like Hindu castes in traditional India, or open, as in the United States and most other industrialized societies based on capitalist economies. Either way, people ranking at the bottom of the social order tend to be powerless and poor. The open-class system of the United States allows individuals to move upward in social rank and become one of the have-lots, but they may also slide down the social ladder and end up as have-nots. Today, almost 40 million American women, men, and children (over 13 percent) are officially classified as "in poverty." About 3.5 million of these poor periodically experience being homeless in any given year, and about 150,000 are chronically homeless. A disproportionate number (40 percent) is African American, but most are Americans of European descent. Homelessness is growing due to a worsening global economy that has spiked unemployment and home foreclosures and contributed to the fiscal crises of many U.S. cities and the state of California.

Societies that permit a great deal of upward and downward mobility are referred to as *open-class societies*—although the openness is apt to be less in practice than members hope or believe. In the United States, despite its rags-to-riches ideology, most mobility involves a move up or down only a notch; if this continues in a family over several generations, however, it may add up to a major change. Nonetheless, U.S. society makes much of the relatively rare examples of great upward mobility consistent with its cultural values and tends to overlook the numerous cases of little or no upward (not to mention downward) mobility (**Figure 21.10**).

Caste societies exemplify *closed-class societies* because of their severe institutionalized limits on social mobility. Yet, even the Hindu caste system, with its guiding ideology that all social hierarchies within it are eternally fixed, has a degree of flexibility and mobility. Although individuals cannot move up or down the caste hierarchy, whole groups can do so depending on claims they assert for higher ranking and on how well they can convince or manipulate others into acknowledging their claims.

During the past half century, political activism has stirred among members of India's vast underclass of Dalits or Untouchables. Historically discriminated against and economically exploited, they now number about 250 million scattered all across this massive South Asian country of 1.2 billion people. A growing political force, Dalits are now organizing themselves on local, regional, and even national levels. Their movement for civil rights is facilitated by increased access to digital communication technology.

Within the vast underclass of Dalits, women and children are especially vulnerable, barely surviving at the very bottom of Indian society. In recent years, however, Dalit women in many parts of India have joined hands with the intention of claiming social justice. Perhaps best known among them is a group in India's northern province of Uttar Pradesh who vigorously protest government discrimination and official corruption and strive to create opportunities for women. Dressed in vibrant pink saris and wielding traditional Indian fighting sticks known as *lathi*, they are the Gulabi ("Pink")

Figure 21.11 The Gulabi Gang
Sometimes referred to as "pink vigilantes," these poor rural women are part of a movement challenging their country's repressive status quo. Most of them are Dalits (Untouchables). Dressed in pink saris (*gulabi* means "pink" in Hindi), they demand justice by shaming and intimidating abusive men as well as corrupt officials who deny them equal access to water, farming supplies, and other resources.

Gang (**Figure 21.11**). They demand justice—shaming and intimidating abusive men and corrupt officials who deny them equal access to water, farming supplies, and other resources. As one of these "pink vigilantes" puts it, "On my own I have no rights, but together, as the Gulabi Gang, we have power" (Dunbar, 2008).

The Dalit women's movement in India illustrates that even long-established and culturally entrenched hierarchical orders are not immune to challenge, reform, or revolution.

Great disparities in wealth, power, and privilege may persist and even grow in many parts of the world, but there are notable social changes in the opposite direction. In the course of the 19th century, slavery was abolished and declared illegal nearly everywhere in the world. And in the last century, civil rights, women's rights, and other human rights movements resulted in social and legal reforms, as well as changes in ideas and values regarding hierarchical social orders in many countries.

CHAPTER CHECKLIST

Beyond kinship, what kinds of groups do humans form and why?

● Because ties of kinship and household are not always sufficient to handle all the challenges of human survival, people also form groups based on gender, age, common interest, and social status.

● Grouping by gender separates men and women to varying degrees in different societies; in some they may be together much of the time, whereas in others they may spend much of their time apart, even to the extreme of eating and sleeping separately.

● Age grouping is another form of association that may augment or replace kinship grouping. An age grade is a category of people organized by age.

● Some societies also have age sets, which are composed of individuals who are initiated into an age grade at the same time and move together through a series of life stages. The most varied use of age grouping is found in African societies south of the Sahara. Among the Maasai of East Africa, for example, age sets pass through four successive age grades.

● Common-interest associations are linked with rapid social change and urbanization. They have increasingly assumed the roles formerly played by kinship or age groups. In urban areas they help new arrivals cope with the changes demanded by the move.

● Common-interest associations also are seen in traditional societies, and their roots may be found in the first horticultural villages.

● The Internet has lessened face-to-face interaction while opening up new forms of virtual communication through social media.

What is a stratified society, and what are the possibilities and limitations of upward and downward social mobility?

● A stratified society is divided into two or more categories of people who do not share equally in basic resources that support income, status, and power. Societies may be stratified by gender, age, social class, or caste.

● A social class is comprised of individuals who enjoy equal or nearly equal prestige according to a society's system of evaluation. Class distinctions are not always clear-cut and obvious in societies that have a wide and continuous range of differential privileges. Social classes can be expressed through symbolic indicators like activities and possessions that mark class position.

● A caste is a closed social class in which membership is determined by birth and fixed for life. The traditional Hindu caste system of India (also found in some other parts of Asia) is the classic ethnographic example of this system, which encompasses a complex ranking of some 2,000 castes associated with specific occupations and customs, including food habits and styles of dress and rituals involving notions of purity and pollution. These castes are organized into four basic orders or *varnas*.

● The hierarchy in a stratified society may also be based on ethnic origin or skin color. One example of stratification based on the notion of race is found in South Africa where people of European descent maintained power through apartheid—a repressive regime of racial segregation and discrimination against indigenous black Africans from 1948 to 1992.

● Caste societies exemplify closed-class societies because of their severe institutionalized limits on social mobility; yet even in these systems there is some flexibility through group action, as seen in the Dalit movement in India.

● Open-class societies are those with the easiest mobility, although the move is usually limited to one rung up or down the social ladder. The degree of mobility is related to social factors such as access to higher education or the prevailing type of family organization. When the extended family is the norm, mobility tends to be severely limited. The independent nuclear family makes mobility easier.

QUESTIONS FOR REFLECTION

1. Soon after domesticating wild horses more than 5,000 years ago, tribesmen in Central Asia herded their flocks of sheep and goats on horseback. Highly mobile, they also launched swift surprise attacks on enemies. This tradition is reflected in *buzkashi*, Afghanistan's national sport. Which core values do you think are reflected or expressed in the sport most popular in your own country?

2. When young adults leave their parental home to go to college or find employment in a distant part of the country, they face the challenge of establishing new social relationships—ones that are not based on kinship but on common interest. To which common-interest associations do you belong and why?

3. Do you use social media to stay in touch with relatives, friends, schoolmates, or colleagues? Where are these individuals in your cyberspace network geographically located? How often do you see them in real space, and is your interaction with them different in person than online?

4. Do you think that members of an upper class or caste in a socially stratified system have a greater vested interest in the idea of law and order than those forced to exist on the bottom of such societies? Why or why not?

5. Slavery in the United States was officially abolished in 1863. Almost a century later, race-based segregation was officially outlawed in the United States, about the same time as caste-based discrimination of Untouchables was constitutionally outlawed in India. Do you think that these laws have ended discrimination against historically repressed groups? If not, what do you think is required to end social injustice?

ONLINE STUDY RESOURCES

CourseMate

Access chapter-specific learning tools, including learning objectives, practice quizzes, videos, flash cards, glossaries, and more in your Anthropology CourseMate.

Log into **www.cengagebrain.com** to access the resources your instructor has assigned and to purchase materials.

© Nigel Dickinson

Challenge Issue

Maintaining peace and order is a daily challenge in every society, especially when different ethnic and religious communities coexist under the same political umbrella. Such is the case in Kano territory situated in the savannahs of northern Nigeria. For hundreds of years an independent domain occupied by Hausa and Fulani peoples, Kano is historically ruled by an emir who now governs according to Shariah, a moral and legal code based on what traditional Muslims accept as God's infallible law. The emirate endured under British colonial rule and has continued as a state in Nigeria, a multi-ethnic and religiously diverse republic since 1960. Here we see Kano's emir, Alhaji Ado Bayero (dressed in white), in a *durbar*, which is a military parade held annually in a festival ending the Muslim holy month of Ramadan. Regional chiefs who head cavalry regiments surround the emir, showcasing their horsemanship in a public display of loyalty. Pious and wealthy, this emir has promoted modern economic development and embraced Western education. In recent years, however, an extremist sect has broken the peace in his emirate, asserting that pure Islam has been corrupted by Westernization. Calling themselves *Boko Haram* ("Western education is sinful"), these militants have launched *jihad* ("holy war") to create a Muslim fundamentalist state.

Politics, Power, War, and Peace

In all societies, from the largest to the smallest, people face the challenge of maintaining social order, securing safety, protecting property, resolving conflicts, and much more. This involves mobilizing, contesting, and controlling power. All human relations entail a degree of **power**, which refers to the ability of individuals or groups to impose their will upon others and make them do things even against their own wants or wishes.

Ranging from persuasion to violence, power drives politics—a term that derives from the Greek word *polis*, referring to a self-governing "city." Many definitions have been proposed, but one of the most famous is that **politics** is the process determining who gets what, when, and how (Lasswell, 1990). In the political process, coalitions of individuals and groups defend or dispute an established economic, social, or ideological order as they fight or negotiate with rival factions and foreign neighbors. Political organization takes many forms, of which the state is just one.

Ironically, the political ties that facilitate much-needed human coexistence and cooperation also create the dynamics that may lead to social tension and sometimes to violent conflict within and between groups. We see this in a wide range of situations, from riots to rebellions to revolutions. Therefore, every society must have ways and means for resolving internal conflicts and preventing a breakdown of its social order. Moreover, each society must possess the capacity to deal with neighboring societies in peaceful or troubled times.

Today, state governments and international political coalitions play a central role in maintaining social order across the globe. Despite the predominance of state societies, there are many groups in which political organization consists of flexible and informal kinship systems. Between these two polarities of kin-ordered and state-organized political systems lies a world of variety.

power The ability of individuals or groups to impose their will upon others and make them do things even against their own wants or wishes.

politics The process determining who gets what, when, and how.

IN THIS CHAPTER YOU WILL LEARN TO

- Analyze how the issue of power is crucially important in every society.
- Recognize the difference between authority and coercion.
- Distinguish and discuss types of political organization and leadership.
- Determine how politics, economics, and maintenance of (in)equality are linked.
- Contrast systems of justice and conflict resolution across cultures.
- Recognize causes of warfare past and present.
- Identify the role of ideology in justifying aggression versus nonviolent resistance.
- Evaluate the importance of diplomacy and treaties in restoring and maintaining peace.

Systems of Political Organization

The term **political organization** refers to the way power is accumulated, arranged, executed, and structurally embedded in society, whether in organizing a whale hunt, managing irrigated farmlands, collecting taxes, or raising a military force. In short, it is the means through which a society creates and maintains social order. It assumes a variety of forms among the peoples of the world, but anthropologists have simplified this complex subject by identifying four basic kinds of political systems: bands, tribes, chiefdoms, and states (**Figure 22.1**). The first two are uncentralized systems; the latter two are centralized.

Uncentralized Political Systems

Until recently, many non-Western peoples have had neither chiefs with established rights and duties nor any fixed form of government, as those who live in modern states understand the term. Instead, marriage and kinship have formed their principal means of social organization. The economies of these societies are primarily of a subsistence type, and populations are typically small.

Leaders do not have real power to force compliance with the society's customs or rules, but if individuals do not conform, they may become targets of scorn and gossip or even be banished. Important decisions are usually made in a collective manner by agreement among adults. Dissenting members may decide to act with

TYPES OF POLITICAL ORGANIZATION

The symbol → indicates that the attribute varies between less and more complex societies of that type.

	BAND	TRIBE	CHIEFDOM	STATE
MEMBERSHIP				
Number of people	Dozens and up	Hundreds and up	Thousands and up	Tens of thousands and up
Settlement pattern	Mobile	Mobile or fixed: 1 or more villages	Fixed: 2 or more villages	Fixed: Many villages and cities
Basis of relationships	Kin	Kin, descent groups	Kin, rank, and residence	Class and residence
Ethnicities and languages	1	1	1	1 or more
GOVERNMENT				
Decision making, leadership	Egalitarian	Egalitarian or Big Man	Centralized, hereditary	Centralized
Bureaucracy	None	None	None, or 1 or 2 levels	Many levels
Monopoly of force and information	No	No	No → Yes	Yes
Conflict resolution	Informal	Informal	Centralized	Laws, judges
Hierarchy of settlement	No	No	No → Paramount village or head town	Capital
ECONOMY				
Food production	No	No → Yes	Yes → Intensive	Intensive
Labor specialization	No	No	No → Yes	Yes
Exchanges	Reciprocal	Reciprocal	Redistributive (tribute)	Redistributive (taxes)
Control of land	Band	Descent group	Chief	Various
SOCIETY				
Stratified	No	No	Yes, ranked by kin	Yes, by class or caste
Slavery	No	No	Some, small-scale	Some, large-scale
Luxury goods for elite	No	No	Yes	Yes
Public architecture	No	No	No → Yes	Yes
Indigenous literacy	No	No	No → Some	Often

© Cengage Learning

Figure 22.1 Four Types of Political Systems This figure outlines the four basic types of political systems: bands, tribes, chiefdoms, and states. Bands and tribes are uncentralized political organizations; chiefdoms and states are centralized.

the majority, or they may choose to adopt some other course of action, including leaving the group.

This egalitarian form of political organization provides great flexibility, which in many situations offers an adaptive advantage. Because power in these kin-ordered communities is shared, with nobody exercising exclusive control over collective resources or public affairs, individuals typically enjoy much more freedom than those who are part of larger and more complex political systems.

Bands

The **band** is a relatively small and loosely organized kin-ordered group that inhabits a common territory and that may split periodically into smaller family groups that are politically and economically independent. Typically, bands are found among food foragers and other small-scale migratory communities in which people organize into politically autonomous extended family groups that usually camp together as long as environmental and subsistence circumstances are favorable. Bands periodically break up into smaller groups to forage for food or visit other relatives. The band is the oldest form of political organization because all humans were once food foragers and remained so until the development of farming and pastoralism over the past 10,000 years.

Given their foraging mode of subsistence, band population densities are usually less than one person per square mile. Because bands are egalitarian and small, numbering at most a few hundred people, there is no real need for formal, centralized political systems. Everyone is related to—and knows on a personal basis—everyone else with whom dealings are required, so there is high value placed on getting along. Conflicts that do arise are usually settled informally through gossip, ridicule, direct negotiation, or mediation. When negotiation or mediation is used, the focus is on reaching a solution considered fair by all concerned parties, rather than on conforming to some abstract law or rule.

Decisions affecting a band are made with the participation of all its adult members, with an emphasis on achieving consensus—a collective agreement—rather than a simple majority. Individuals become leaders by virtue of their abilities and serve in that capacity only as long as they retain the confidence of the community. They cannot coerce others to abide by their decisions. A leader who exceeds what people are willing to accept quickly loses followers.

An example of the informal nature of band leadership is found among the Ju/'hoansi Bushmen of the Kalahari Desert, mentioned in earlier chapters. Each Ju/'hoansi band is composed of a group of families that live together, linked through kinship ties to one another and to the headman (or, less often, headwoman). The head, called the *kxau*, or "owner," is the focal point for the band's claims on the territory through which it traditionally

Figure 22.2 **Band Leadership** Toma Tsamkxao was the headman of a Ju/'hoansi band. Lightly armed, he led his migratory community of hunters and gatherers in the Kalahari Desert. They ranged the region freely much as their ancestors did for almost 40,000 years. About half a century ago, outsiders imposed radical changes on Bushmen bands. Some, guided by wise leaders like Tsamkxao, survived the upheaval and now subsist on a mix of livestock and crop farming, crafts and tourism, and some traditional foraging.

ranges as a migratory community (**Figure 22.2**). He or she does not personally own the land and natural resources but symbolically represents the ancestral rights of band members to them. If the head leaves the area to live elsewhere, people turn to someone else to lead them.

When local resources are no longer adequate to sustain a band, the leader coordinates and leads the move, selecting the new campsite. Except for the privilege of having first choice of a spot for his or her own fire, the leader of the band has few unique rewards or duties. For example, a Ju/'hoansi head is not a judge and does not punish other band members. Troublemakers and wrongdoers are judged and held accountable by public opinion, usually expressed by gossip, which can play an important role in curbing socially unacceptable behavior.

Through gossip—talking behind someone's back and spreading rumors about behavior considered disruptive, shameful, or ridiculous—people accomplish several

political organization The way power, as the capacity to do something, is accumulated, arranged, executed, and structurally embedded in society; the means through which a society creates and maintains social order and reduces social disorder.

band A relatively small and loosely organized kin-ordered group that inhabits a specific territory and that may split periodically into smaller extended family groups that are politically and economically independent.

objectives while avoiding the potential disruption of open confrontation. First, gossip underscores and reinforces the cultural standards of those who abide by the unwritten rules of proper conduct. At the same time, the gossip discredits those who violate standards of socially acceptable behavior. Furthermore, because gossip can damage a person's reputation and is often fueled by hidden jealousy or a secret desire to retaliate against someone considered too accomplished or successful, it may function as a leveling mechanism to reduce a real or perceived threat of an individual becoming too dominant.

Another prime technique in small-scale societies for resolving disputes, or even avoiding them in the first place, is mobility. Those unable to get along with others of their group may feel pressured to move to a different group in which existing kinship ties give them rights of entry.

Tribes

The second type of uncentralized authority system is the tribe. In anthropology, the term **tribe** refers to a wide range of kin-ordered groups that are politically integrated by some unifying factor and whose members share a common ancestry, identity, culture, language, and territory.

Typically, a tribe has an economy based on some form of crop cultivation or livestock raising. Tribes develop when a number of culturally related bands come together, peacefully settle disputes, participate in periodic visiting and communal feasting, and intermarry for purposes of economic exchange and/or collective self-defense against common enemies. For this reason, tribal membership is usually larger than band membership. Moreover, tribal population densities generally far exceed that of migratory bands and may be as high as 250 people per square mile. Greater population density introduces a new set of problems, as opportunities for bickering, begging, adultery, and theft increase markedly, especially among people living in permanent villages.

Each tribe consists of one or more self-supporting and self-governing local community (including smaller kin-groups earlier discussed as bands) that may then form alliances with others for various purposes. As in the band, political organization in the tribe is informal and temporary. Whenever a situation requiring political integration of all or several groups within the tribe arises—perhaps for defense, to carry out a raid, to pool resources in times of scarcity, or to capitalize on a windfall that must be distributed quickly before it spoils—groups come together to deal with the situation in a cooperative manner. When the problem is satisfactorily solved, each group then resumes autonomy.

In many tribal societies, the organizing unit and seat of political authority is the clan, composed of people who consider themselves descended from a common ancestor. Within the clan, elders or headmen and/or headwomen regulate members' affairs and represent their clan in interactions with other clans. As a group, the elders of all the clans may form a council that acts within the community or for the community in dealings with outsiders. Because clan members usually do not all live together in a single community, clan organization facilitates joint action with members of related communities when necessary.

Leadership in tribal societies is also relatively informal, as is evident in a wide array of past and present examples. Among these is the Big Man common in Melanesia, including New Guinea and other islands in the South Pacific. Heading up localized descent groups or a territorial group, the Big Man combines a measure of interest in his community's welfare with a great deal of cunning and calculation for his own personal gain. His power is personal, for he holds no political office in any formal sense, nor is he elected. His prestige as a political leader is the result of strategic acts that raise him above most other tribe members and that attract loyal followers who benefit from or depend on his success.

The Kapauku in the west central highlands of New Guinea typify this form of political organization. Among these Papua, the Big Man is called the *tonowi* ("rich one"). To achieve this status, one must be male, wealthy, generous, and eloquent. Physical bravery and an ability to deal with the supernatural are also common *tonowi* characteristics, but they are not essential (**Figure 22.3**).

A Kapauku Big Man functions as the headman of the village unit in a wide variety of situations within and beyond the community. He represents his group in dealing with outsiders and other villages and acts as negotiator and/or judge when disputes break out among his followers. As a *tonowi*, he acquires political power through giving loans. Villagers comply with his requests because they are in his debt (often interest-free), and they do not want to have to repay their loans. Those who have not yet borrowed from him may wish to do so in the future, so they, too, want to keep his goodwill. A *tonowi* who refuses to lend money to fellow villagers may be shunned, ridiculed, and, in extreme cases, even killed by a group of warriors. Such unfavorable reactions ensure that individual economic wealth is dispersed throughout the community.

A Big Man gains further support from his relatives and from taking into his household young male apprentices

---

tribe In anthropology, the term for a range of kin-ordered groups that are politically integrated by some unifying factor and whose members share a common ancestry, identity, culture, language, and territory.

of East Africa (discussed in the previous chapter), the Warrior age grade guards the village and grazing lands, whereas Judicial Elders resolve disputes. The oldest age grade, the Ritual Elders, advise on matters involving the well-being of all the Tiriki people. With the tribe's political affairs in the hands of the various age grades and their officers, this type of organization enables the largely independent kin-groups to solve conflicts and sometimes avoid feuding between the lineages.

The Pashtun, a large ethnic group with tribes on both sides of the border between Afghanistan and Pakistan, provide another example of decentralized political organization. Periodically, groups of male elders, each representing their kinfolk, gather to deal with collective challenges. In such a political assembly, known as a *jirga*, these Pashtun tribal leaders make joint decisions by consensus—from settling disputes, working out treaties, and resolving trade issues to establishing law and order in their war-torn homelands (**Figure 22.4**).

Centralized Political Systems

Political authority is not centralized in bands and tribes, but this changes when populations grow, individuals specialize, division of labor increases, and surplus is exchanged in expanding trade networks. This process creates opportunities for some enterprising individuals or groups to gain control at the expense of others. In such increasingly complex societies, political authority and power are concentrated in a single individual (the chief) or in a body of individuals (the state). In centralized systems, political organization relies more heavily on institutionalized power, authority, and even coercion.

Chiefdoms

A **chiefdom** is a politically organized territory centrally ruled by a chief heading a kin-based society with prestige ranking and a redistributive economy. Rank in such a hierarchical political system is determined by the closeness of one's relationship to the chief. Those closest are officially superior and receive deferential treatment from those of lower status. The office of the chief is usually for life and often hereditary. Typically, it passes from a man to his younger brother, a son, or his sister's son, depending on whether descent is traced patrilineally or matrilineally.

Unlike the headman or headwoman in bands and tribes, the leader of a chiefdom is generally a true authority figure with the power to command, settle disputes, punish, and reward. This chief serves to maintain peace and order within and between allied communities.

Chiefdoms have a recognized hierarchy consisting of major and minor authorities that control major and

Figure 22.3 Big Man from West Papua, New Guinea Wearing his official regalia, the *tonowi* is recognizable among fellow Kapauku and neighboring Papua highlanders as a man of wealth and power.

© George Holton/Photo Researchers, Inc.

who receive business training along with food and shelter. He also gives them a loan that enables them to marry when the apprenticeship ends. In return, they act as messengers and bodyguards. After leaving, they remain tied to the *tonowi* by bonds of affection and gratitude.

Because a Big Man's wealth comes from his success at breeding pigs (the focus of the entire Kapauku economy, as described in the chapter on patterns of subsistence), it is not uncommon for a *tonowi* to lose his fortune rapidly due to poor management or simple bad luck with his pigs. Thus, the Kapauku political structure shifts frequently: As one man loses wealth and consequently power, another gains it and becomes a *tonowi*. These changes prevent any single Big Man from holding political power for too long.

Political Integration Beyond the Kin-Group

Age sets, age grades, and common-interest groups discussed in the previous chapter are among the political integration mechanisms used by tribal societies. Cutting across territorial and kin-groupings, these organizations link members from different lineages and clans. For example, among the Tiriki

---

chiefdom A politically organized society in which several neighboring communities inhabiting a territory are united under a single ruler.

Figure 22.4 Gathering of Tribal Leaders In traditional kin-ordered societies such as tribes, political power is neither centralized nor monopolized. Instead, social networks of extended families, lineages, or clans share political power. As shown in this photo of tribal elders attending a *Loya Jirga* ("Grand Assembly") in Afghanistan's capital city of Kabul, Pashtun leaders gather periodically to discuss and resolve conflicts and other collective challenges.

© Asia File/Alamy

minor subdivisions. Such an arrangement is a chain of command, linking leaders at every level, with each owing personal loyalty to the chief. It serves to bind groups in the heartland to the chief's headquarters, whether it is a large tent, wood house, or stone hall. Although leaders of chiefdoms are almost always male, in some cultures a politically astute wife, sister, or single daughter of a deceased chief could inherit this powerful position as well.

Chiefs usually control the economic activities of those who fall under their political rule. Typically, chiefdoms involve redistributive systems, and the chief has control over surplus goods and perhaps even over the community's labor force. Thus, he (and sometimes she) may demand a share of the harvested crop from farmers, which may then be redistributed throughout the domain. Similarly, manpower may be periodically drafted to form battle groups, build fortifications, dig irrigation works, or construct ceremonial sites.

The chief may also amass a great amount of personal wealth and pass it on to offspring. Land, cattle, and luxury goods produced by specialists can be collected by the chief and become part of the power base. Moreover, high-ranking families of the chiefdom may engage in the same practice and use their possessions as evidence of superior social status.

Traditionally, chiefdoms have been unstable, with lesser chiefs trying to take power from higher-ranking chiefs, or rival chiefs vying for supreme power as paramount chiefs. In precolonial Hawaii, for example, where war was the way to gain territory and maintain power, great chiefs set out to conquer each other in an effort to become paramount chief of all the islands. When one chief defeated another, the loser and all his nobles were dispossessed of their property and lucky to escape alive. The new paramount chief then appointed his own supporters to positions of political power.

Among the many symbols indicating their supreme political rank, paramount chiefs carry a title of renown

not only recognized in their own domain but beyond. In English, the title *paramount chief* is often translated as "king." This covers a range of political authority figures— from the high-ranking ruler elected by an alliance of chiefs to the leader of a politically centralized society historically divided in chiefdoms. As such, indigenous royal titles— *malku* in Aymara for rulers in the Andean highlands of Bolivia; *raja* in Hindi for those in India; *gyalpo* in Tibetan for Himalayan rulers in Sikkim and Bhutan; *emir* or *sultan*, both Arabic, for rulers throughout Islamic Asia and North Africa; and *vorst* or *fürst* in Germanic Europe—are all translated as "king." Historically, the Indian subcontinent alone numbered 565 princely states, both large and small.

The political distinction between a paramount chiefdom, princely state, or kingdom by whatever name cannot be sharply drawn. As an intermediary form of political organization between tribes and states, most chiefdoms, paramount chiefdoms, and kingdoms have disappeared in the course of time. However, many hundreds still exist in parts of Asia and Africa, for example—albeit no longer as politically independent or sovereign domains. Subordinated to the state as a more powerful political system, those that endure do so as an enclosed territorial division such as a district or province, with its traditional rulers and their successors remaining in office, although with reduced authority.

Due to their wealth and prestige, and holding onto traditional titles and other high-status symbols, high-ranking chiefs and kings (or queens) are often well positioned to successfully adapt to the new order. Especially in pluralistic states with an ineffective or otherwise challenged centralized government, regional political rulers such as traditional paramount chiefs, emirs, and kings may (re)gain power and claim greater independence.

Such is the case with chiefs among the Kpelle, the largest ethnic group in Liberia, a pluralistic West African country

Figure 22.5 Paramount Chiefs and International Diplomacy In a special diplomatic ceremony commemorating the bilateral relationship between Liberia and China and expressing appreciation for China's economic investment and financial aid in his domain, Paramount Chief Moses Galakrumah of the Kpelle chiefdom of Panta, Bong County, appointed the Chinese ambassador Zhou Yuxiao as honorary paramount chief. Together with Chief Elder Togba Gbonpelee, he briefed his high-ranking Chinese guest on the history of the Panta chiefdom and dressed China's senior envoy in a traditional Kpelle robe, along with a wooden sword and staff—symbols of power and bravery.

inhabited by about 30 ethnic groups. Traditionally, the Kpelle are politically divided in several independent paramount chiefdoms, each comprising an alliance of smaller chiefdoms. Whereas the Kpelle inhabit territories in Liberia's eastern interior, African Americans from the United States, including former slaves, colonized its coastal region. Aided by the American Colonization Society, these black settlers founded the Republic of Liberia in 1847, naming its capital Monrovia in honor of U.S. president James Monroe. Since then, these Americo-Liberians have dominated the country's political economy. However, they never fully succeeded in centralizing political power. This left traditional paramount chiefs among the Kpelle and their neighbors largely in control of regional affairs as salaried state officials, mediating between the inhabitants in their districts (traditional chiefdoms) and the central government.

Today, many Kpelle are rice farmers, but they also engage in wage labor. Their paramount chief, like those of other ethnic groups, receives government commissions on taxes and court fees collected within his district, plus a commission for providing laborers for Liberia's numerous foreign-owned mines and rubber plantations. He also gets a stipulated amount of rice from each farming household and gifts from people who approach him for favors. Moreover, he has the authority to settle disputes, and people compensate him for that as well.

In keeping with his high social status, a Kpelle chief has at his disposal uniformed messengers, a literate clerk, and the symbols of wealth: several wives, embroidered gowns, and freedom from manual labor. After a devastating civil war (1989–2003), Liberia's government has tried to rebuild the pluralistic country's economy by decentralizing some of its governing power, granting the traditional chiefs more political, legal, and administrative control. Some now even participate in international diplomacy for their country (**Figure 22.5**).

States

The **state** is a politically organized territory occupied by a class-stratified society with a centralized government and definite boundaries. The most formal of political systems, it is organized and directed by a government that has the capacity and authority to manage and tax its subjects, make laws and maintain order, and use military force to defend or expand its territories. Two of the smallest states today measure less than 2.5 square kilometers (1 square mile), whereas the largest covers about 17 million square kilometers (6.6 million square miles).

---

state A political institution established to manage and defend a complex, socially stratified society occupying a defined territory.

Often states are ruled by coalitions of well-connected and wealthy individuals or groups that have accumulated and fought over power. Possessing the resources (including money, weapons, and manpower), these ruling elites exercise power through institutions, such as a government and its bureaucracy, which allow them to arrange and rearrange a society's social and economic order.

A large population in a state-organized society requires increased food production and wider distribution networks. Together, these lead to a transformation of the landscape by way of irrigation and terracing, carefully managed crop rotation cycles, intensive competition for clearly demarcated lands and roads, and enough farmers and other rural workers to support market systems and a specialized urban sector.

Under such conditions, corporate groups that stress exclusive membership multiply rapidly, ethnic differentiation and ethnocentrism become more pronounced, and the potential for social conflict increases dramatically. Given these circumstances, state institutions—which minimally involve a bureaucracy, a military, and (often) an official religion—provide the means for numerous and diverse groups to function together as an integrated whole.

An important aspect of the state is its delegation of authority to maintain order within and outside its borders. Police, foreign ministries, war ministries, and other bureaucracies function to control and punish disruptive acts of crime, dissension, and rebellion. By such agencies the state asserts authority impersonally and in a consistent, predictable manner. Throughout history, neighboring states have often had conflicts over territorial boundaries (**Figure 22.6**).

States first began to emerge over 5,000 years ago. Often unstable, many have disappeared in the course of history, some temporarily and others forever. Some were annexed by other states, and others collapsed or fragmented into smaller political units. Although some present-day states are very old—such as Japan, which has endured as a state for almost 1,500 years—few are older than the United States, an independent country since 1783.

A key distinction to make at this point is between state and nation. A **nation** is a people who share a collective identity based on a common culture, language, territorial base, and history (Clay, 1996). Today, there are roughly 5,000 nations (including tribes and ethnic groups) throughout the world, many of which have existed since before recorded history. By contrast, there are about 200 independent states in the world today, most of which did not exist before the end of World War II (1945).

As these numbers imply, nation and state do not always coincide, as they do, for example, in Iceland, Japan, and Swaziland. In fact, about 75 percent of the world's states are *pluralistic societies*, defined in an earlier chapter as societies in which two or more ethnic groups or nationalities are politically organized into one territorial state but maintain their cultural differences (Van den Berghe, 1992). Typically, smaller nations (including tribes) and other groups find themselves at the mercy of one or more powerful nations or ethnic groups gaining political control over the state.

Frequently facing discrimination or repression, some minority nations seek to improve their political position by seceding and founding an independent state. In splitting the state's territory, they usually encounter stiff opposition with sometimes violent confrontations. So it is

Figure 22.6 Territorial Boundaries
After the British empire pulled out of South Asia over 60 years ago, that subcontinent erupted in warfare between Muslims and Hindus. The region was then carved up along religious lines into Pakistan and India. Since then, these countries have fought three wars against each other. The tense political relations between these nuclear-armed rivals are symbolically displayed in the military border-closing ritual at Wagah. Every evening, Pakistani Pathan guards, wearing black uniforms and fantailed headgear of the same color, face India's border guards, dressed in khaki uniforms and hats adorned with scarlet fantails. Brandishing rifles and parading in goosestep, they greet each other, lock gates, and lower their national flags.

© Reuters/Corbis

with the Tuareg, a nomadic Berber nation of Muslim herders and traders whose ancestral homeland stretches across a vast expanse of the Sahara Desert carved up by North African states such as Mali, Niger, Libya, and Algeria.

The Kurds are another nation whose ancestral homeland of about 200,000 square kilometers (77,000 square miles) has been subdivided. Like the Tuareg, many Kurds are willing to fight for political autonomy or even national independence, but they are forced to accept their minority status in the neighboring modern states of Turkey, Iraq, and Iran. With a population of about 27 million, they are much more numerous than Australians, for example. In fact, the total population of the four Scandinavian countries—Denmark, Finland, Norway, and Sweden—is less than that of the Kurds (**Figure 22.7**).

Forming a new nation state is a political challenge, and many ethnic groups or national minorities have had to take up arms and fight for their independence. Such has been the case in the violent breakup of Serb-dominated Yugoslavia, which was split into six smaller states between 1989 and 1992. However, some of these newly formed republics still have ethnic minorities. In southeast Serbia, for example, Albanian-speaking Kosovars fought a war of independence in 1999. The government of Serbia, dominated by Serbian-speaking Christians, later granted Kosovo autonomous status as a province. In 2008, Kosovars unilaterally declared their province an independent nation state, a status not (yet) internationally recognized.

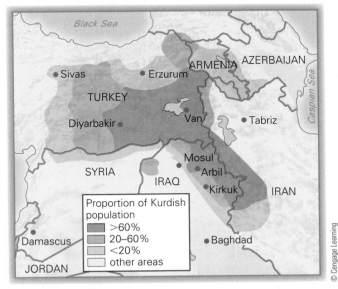

Figure 22.7 The Kurd Nation Across State Borders
The Kurds—most of whom live in Turkey, Iran, and Iraq—are an example of a nation without a state. With a population of about 27 million, they are much more numerous than Australians, for example. In fact, the total population of the four Scandinavian countries—Denmark, Finland, Norway, and Sweden—is less than that of the Kurds, who have no independent country of their own.

Political Systems and the Question of Authority

Whatever a society's political system, it must find some way to obtain and retain the people's allegiance. In uncentralized systems, in which every adult participates in all decision making, loyalty and cooperation are freely given because each person is considered a part of the political system. However, as the group grows larger and the organization becomes more formal, the problem of obtaining and keeping public support becomes greater.

Centralized political systems may rely upon coercion as a means of social control. This, however, can be risky because the large numbers of personnel needed to apply force may themselves become a political power. Also, the emphasis on force typically creates resentment and may lessen cooperation. Thus, police states are generally short-lived; most societies choose less extreme forms of social coercion. In the United States, this is reflected in the increasing emphasis placed on *cultural* controls, discussed later in this chapter. Laura Nader (see the Anthropologist of Note) is well known for her anthropological research concerning issues of power, including cultural control.

Also basic to the political process is the concept of **authority**, claiming and exercising power as justified by law or custom of tradition. Unlike **coercion**, which imposes obedience or submission by force or intimidation, authority is based on the socially accepted rules or codified laws binding people together as a society. Without these rules and laws, however different in each culture, political rule lacks *legitimacy* and will be interpreted and perhaps openly challenged as unjust and wrong, opening the door to forced removal.

In a *monarchy*—a state headed by a single ruler—political authority can be based on different sources of legitimacy, including divine will, birthright in a royal lineage, or an election held among free citizens or a wealthy upper class (nobles). In a *theocracy*—a state ruled by a priestly elite headed by a supreme priest claiming holy or even divine status—legitimacy is embedded in sacred doctrine. In an *aristocracy*, on the other hand, the ruling noble elite claims legitimacy traditionally rooted in a ritual mixture of high-status ancestry and class endogamy, military dominance, economic wealth, and ceremonial capital.

Finally, in a *democracy* rulers claim legitimacy based on the idea that they act as representatives of the free citizens who elected them into office with the mandate to act on

---

nation A people who share a collective identity based on a common culture, language, territorial base, and history.

authority Claiming and exercising power as justified by law or custom of tradition.

coercion Imposition of obedience or submission by force or intimidation.

ANTHROPOLOGIST OF NOTE

Laura Nader (b. 1930)

Laura Nader has stood out among her peers from the start of her career in 1960, when she became the first woman faculty member in the anthropology department at the University of California, Berkeley.

Nader and her three siblings grew up in Winsted, Connecticut, children of immigrants from Lebanon. As she recalls, "My dad left Lebanon for political reasons, and when he came to the land of the free, he took it seriously. So we were raised to believe that you should be involved in public issues." They were also taught to question assumptions.

Laura Nader, a cultural anthropology professor at the University of California, Berkeley, specializes in law, dispute resolution, and controlling processes.

Both Nader and her younger brother Ralph have made careers of doing this. She is an anthropologist noted for her cross-cultural research on law, justice, and social control and their connection to power structures. He is a consumer advocate and frequent U.S. presidential candidate who is a watchdog on issues of public health and the safety and quality of life.

Laura Nader's undergraduate studies included a study-abroad year in Mexico. Later, while earning her doctorate in anthropology at Radcliffe College, she returned to Mexico to do fieldwork in a Zapotec Indian peasant village in the Sierra Madre Mountains of Oaxaca. Reflecting on this and subsequent research, she says,

In the 1950s, when I went to southern Mexico, I was studying how the Zapotec organize their

lives, what they do with their problems, what they do when they go to court. And when I came back to this country, I started looking at American equivalents, at how Americans solve their consumer and service complaints.

Nader's first decade of teaching at Berkeley coincided with the Vietnam War, an era when the campus was in a perpetual state of turmoil with students demonstrating for peace and civil rights. Becoming a scholar-activist, she called upon colleagues to "study up" and do research on the world's power elite. "The study of man," she wrote in 1972, "is confronted with an unprecedented situation: Never before have a few, by their actions and inactions, had the power of life and death over so many members of the species."

To date, the results of Nader's own research have appeared in over a hundred publications. Among these are her numerous books, including *Naked Science—Anthropological Inquiry into Boundaries, Power, and Knowledge* (1996) and *The Life of the Law: Anthropological Projects* (2002).

Playing a leading role in the development of the anthropology of law, Nader has taken on specialists in the fields of law, children's issues, nuclear energy, and science (including her own profession), critically questioning the basic assumptions ("central dogmas") under which these experts operate. She presses her students to do the same—to think critically, question authority, and break free from the "controlling processes" of the power elite. In 2000, Nader accepted one of the highest honors of the American Anthropological Association—an invitation to give the distinguished lecture at its annual gathering.

Adapted from "Interview with Laura Nader." (2000, November). California Monthly.

---

the basis of collectively approved rules in the form of law. A democracy may have a king or queen as symbolic head. With an elected president as titular head, such a state is usually identified as a *republic*.

For example, as noted in this chapter's opening, the authority of the current emir of Kano in Nigeria is based on his royal ancestry and political-religious tradition. Like his predecessors, he is the son of an emir, was formally appointed by a group of high-ranking chiefs serving as "king makers," and was confirmed by the Nigerian state as his uncle's successor to the throne in 1963.

The emir's authority is also based on religion because Islam remains the basis of an emir's historic right as the

spiritual-political head of about 8 million Muslim subjects in his domain. As emir, he plays an active role as patron of Islamic scholarship. And because he made the pilgrimage to the sacred site of Mecca, he bears the honorific title *Alhaji*.

Beyond the legitimacy of his claim to rulership, the current emir's authority is also based on his personal achievements as an internationally educated diplomat, politician, and successful businessman whose great personal wealth gained him a reputation for generosity.

For purposes of symbolic display of his authority, the emir hosts *durbars* ("parades") celebrating his emirate's cultural heritage at public festivals in which his followers demonstrate their personal loyalty to him as their *sarki* ("king"). Finally, indicative of his prestige, the current emir has four wives (allowed by Islam) and about 60 concubines residing in his harem at the 800-year-old royal palace (Nast, 2005; Shea, 2007).

Politics and Religion

Clearly, as suggested in our discussion of the emirate of Kano, where Shariah (Islamic law) was instituted in 2000, politics is often intricately intertwined with religion. Frequently, it is religion that legitimizes the political order and leadership. Religious beliefs may influence or provide authoritative approval to customary rules and laws. For instance, acts that people believe to be sinful, such as murder, are often illegal as well.

In both industrial and nonindustrial societies, belief in the supernatural is important and is reflected in people's political institutions. Medieval Christian Europe well exemplifies the effect of religion on politics: Holy wars were fought over the smallest matter; labor was mobilized to build immense cathedrals in honor of the Virgin Mary and other saints; kings and queens ruled by "divine right," and they asked for the blessing of the pope (who claimed spiritual authority and political supremacy as head of the Roman Catholic Church) in all important ventures, marital or martial.

In Japan, until the mid-20th century, people were taught to believe they were subjects of a sacred king to be obeyed and worshiped as a divine ruler—not unlike the god-kings heading the ancient Egyptian, Inca, and Aztec empires. After defeat in World War II in 1945, Japan came under American military occupation for a number of years. As dictated by the U.S. government, their emperor was allowed to remain in office as a leader of his conquered nation, albeit no longer as a god.

Modern Iran was proclaimed an Islamic republic in the 1979 revolution that toppled the authoritarian regime of the shah; its first head of state, Ayatollah Ruhollah Khomeini, was titled the most holy of all Shiite Muslim holy men. As the highest-ranking religious and political authority of the country, he was pronounced its supreme leader, a position he held until his death ten years later. Since then, Iran has remained a theocratic republic with a high-ranking Shiite Muslim cleric, or grand ayatollah, as its most powerful authority. The country's democratically elected parliament and president are subordinate to the ayatollah (**Figure 22.8**).

VISUAL COUNTERPOINT

© Reuters/Corbis

© K. Prose/Pressnet/Tophan/The Image Works

Figure 22.8 Church and State in Iran and Great Britain In contrast to countries such as the United States, where religion and state are constitutionally separated, countries such as Iran and Great Britain permit a much closer relationship between political and religious affairs. For instance, since 1989, a grand ayatollah named Ali Khamenei has held the title of Supreme Leader of the Islamic Republic of Iran, serving as the country's highest-ranking religious and political authority. In England, Queen Elizabeth is not only her country's nominal head of state but also the Supreme Governor of the Church of England, which entitles her to appoint the Anglican bishops in that state.

The fact that the president of the United States takes the oath of office by swearing on a Bible is another instance of the use of religion to legitimize political power, as is the phrase "one nation, under God" in the Pledge of Allegiance. U.S. coins are etched with the phrase "In God We Trust," many governmental meetings begin with a prayer or an invocation, and the expression "so help me God" is routinely used in legal proceedings. Despite an official separation of church and state, religious legitimization of government lingers. Similarly, for her coronation in 1953, Queen Elizabeth II placed her right hand on a Bible and kissed the sacred book when she signed the oath.

Politics and Gender

Historically, irrespective of cultural configuration or type of political organization, women have held important positions of political leadership far less often than men. But there have been many significant exceptions, including some female chiefs *heading* Algonquian Indian communities in southern New England in the 17th century and among the Taino, Timucua, Caddo, and other early American Indian chiefdoms in the Caribbean and southeastern United States. Traditionally, there were also female rulers of Polynesian chiefdoms and kingdoms in the Pacific, including Tonga, Samoa, and Hawaii. Moreover, there were numerous powerful queens heading monarchies and even empires in Asia, Africa, and Europe during the past few thousand years (Linnekin, 1990; Ralston & Thomas, 1987; Trocolli, 2005).

Perhaps the most notable example among historical female rulers is Queen Victoria, the long-reigning queen of England, Scotland, Wales, and Ireland. Also recognized as monarch in a host of colonies all over the world, Victoria even acquired the title Empress of India. Ruling the British empire from 1837 until 1901, she was perhaps the world's wealthiest and most powerful leader. Her great-great-granddaughter Queen Elizabeth II has ruled nearly as long. Elizabeth ascended to the royal throne as sovereign head of Great Britain upon the death of her father, King George VI. With her coronation the following year, she became the symbolic head of the Commonwealth, an inter-governmental organization of fifty-four independent states (almost all former British colonies), collectively promoting free trade, rule of law, human rights, and world peace.

High-profile female leadership is becoming more common, and in most contemporary societies women have gained the same political rights and opportunities as men. In recent years, a growing number of women have been elected as presidents, chancellors, or prime ministers. Countries with elected female heads of state now or in recent years include Argentina, Australia, Brazil, Chile, Costa Rica, Germany, India, Indonesia, Ireland, Liberia, Norway, Pakistan, the Philippines, Sri Lanka, and Thailand. Others lead political opposition parties, sometimes heading mass movements. Among the latter is Aung San Suu Kyi in Myanmar (Burma), profiled toward the end of this chapter.

Although there have been and continue to be many societies in which women have lower visibility in the political arena, that does not necessarily indicate that they lack power in political affairs. For example, among the six allied Iroquois Indian nations in northeastern America, only men were appointed to serve as high-ranking chiefs on the confederacy's great council; however, they were completely beholden to women, for only their "clan mothers" could select candidates to this high political office. Moreover, women actively lobbied the men on the councils, and the clan mothers had the right to depose a chief representing their clan whenever it suited them.

As for women having more visible roles in traditional societies, one example is the dual-sex government system of the Igbo in Nigeria, West Africa. Among the Igbo, each political unit traditionally had separate political institutions for men and women, so that both genders had an autonomous sphere of authority as well as an area of shared responsibility (Okonjo, 1976). At the head of each political unit was a male *obi*, considered the head of government although he presided over only the male community, and a female *omu*, the acknowledged mother of the whole community but in practice concerned with the female section. Unlike a queen (though both she and the *obi* were crowned), the *omu* was neither the *obi*'s wife nor the previous *obi*'s daughter.

Just as the *obi* had a council of dignitaries to advise him and act as a check against any arbitrary exercise of power, a council of women served the *omu*. The duties of the *omu* and her advisors involved tasks such as establishing rules and regulations for the community market (marketing was a woman's activity) and hearing cases involving women brought to her from throughout the town or village. If such cases also involved men, then she and her council would cooperate with the *obi* and his council.

In the Igbo system, women managed their own affairs. They had the right to enforce their decisions and rules with sanctions similar to those employed by men, including strikes, boycotts, and "sitting on" someone, including a man:

> To "sit on" or "make war on" a man involved gathering at his compound, sometimes late at night, dancing, singing scurrilous songs which detailed the women's grievances against him and often called his manhood into question, banging on his hut with the pestles women used for pounding yams, and perhaps . . . roughing him up a bit. A man might be sanctioned in this way for mistreating his wife, for violating the women's market rules, or for letting his cows eat the women's crops. The women would stay at his hut throughout the day, and late into the night if necessary, until he repented and promised to mend his ways. (Van Allen, 1997, p. 450)

When the British imposed colonial rule on the Igbo in the late 1800s, they failed to recognize the autonomy and power of the women. This is ironic because, as noted earlier, the long-reigning and powerful head of the British empire at the time was Queen Victoria. Nevertheless, British colonial administrators introduced reforms that destroyed traditional arrangements of female autonomy and power. As a result, Igbo women lost much of their traditional equality and became politically subordinate to men.

Cultural Controls in Maintaining Order

Every culture has various forms of **cultural control** to ensure that individuals or groups conduct themselves in ways that support the social order. People who challenge or disturb the order face negative consequences. We may distinguish between internal and external forms of cultural control.

As discussed in an earlier chapter, individuals born and raised in a particular society undergo a process of enculturation during which ideas, values, and associated structures of emotion are internalized, impacting their thoughts, feelings, and behavior. The internalization of cultural control leads to what we know as **self-control**—a person's capacity to manage his or her spontaneous feelings and to restrain impulsive behavior.

The second form of cultural control is external, as it is based on historically developed or politically imposed rules of order enforced by others in society. This external form is **social control**, which authorities in ranked or stratified societies such as chiefdoms and states maintain by various means of persuasion and coercion, including intimidation, threats, and financial or physical punishment.

Internalized Control

Developed during the enculturation process and deeply embedded in our consciousness, self-control may be motivated by ideas or emotions associated with positive cultural values such as self-denial for the common good. For example, many cultures honor traditions of charity, self-sacrifice, or other good deeds. Performed out of a desire to help those in need, such acts of kindness or generosity may spring from a spiritual or religious worldview.

Self-control may also be motivated by negative ideas and associated emotions such as a fear of misfortune or bad luck—concepts that are culturally relative and variable. As an example, we may look at Wape hunters in Papua New Guinea. Traditionally, Wape hunters believe that the spirits of their deceased ancestors roam the woods claimed by their lineage, protect them from enemy invaders, and assist them in the hunt by driving wild game their way (Mitchell, 1973). Moreover, they believe that ancestral spirits punish anyone who has wronged them or their descendants by preventing wrongdoers from finding game or hitting their mark. Like the devout Christian who avoids sinning for fear of hell, the Wape hunter fears some sort of supernatural punishment for wrongdoing, even though no one in his village may be aware of his bad deed. For the Wape, then, successful hunting depends upon avoiding quarrels and maintaining tranquility within the community so as not to antagonize anybody's deceased ancestor.

Externalized Control: Sanctions

Because internalized controls are not wholly sufficient even in bands and tribes, every society develops externalized social controls, known as **sanctions**, designed to

---

cultural control Control through beliefs and values deeply internalized in the minds of individuals.

self-control A person's capacity to manage her or his spontaneous feelings, restraining impulsive behavior.

social control External control through open coercion.

sanction An externalized social control designed to encourage conformity to social norms.

encourage conformity to social standards of acceptable behavior. Operating within social groups of all sizes and involving a mix of cultural and social controls, sanctions may vary significantly within a given society, but they fall into one of two categories: positive or negative.

Positive sanctions consist of incentives to conform, such as awards, titles, promotions, and other demonstrations of recognized approval. Negative sanctions consist of threats such as shaming, fining, flogging, branding, banishing, jailing, and even killing for violating the standards.

For sanctions to be effective, they must be applied consistently, and they must be generally known among members of the society. Even if some individuals are not convinced of the advantages of social conformity, they are still more likely to obey society's rules than to accept the consequences of not doing so.

Sanctions may be formal or informal, depending on whether a legal statute is involved. In the United States, the man who goes shirtless in shorts to a church service may be subject to a variety of informal sanctions, ranging from disapproving glances from the clergy to the chuckling of other parishioners. If, however, he were to show up without any clothing at all, he would be subject to the formal negative sanction of arrest for indecent exposure. Only in the second instance would he have been guilty of breaking the **law**—formal rules of conduct that, when violated, effectuate negative sanctions.

Cultural Control: Witchcraft

In societies with or without centralized political systems, witchcraft sometimes functions as an agent of cultural control and involves both self-control and social controls. An individual will think twice before offending a neighbor if convinced that the neighbor could retaliate by resorting to black magic. Similarly, individuals may not wish to be accused of practicing witchcraft, and so they behave with greater circumspection.

Among the Azande of South Sudan, people who think they have been bewitched may consult an oracle, who, after performing the appropriate mystical rites, may establish or confirm the identity of the offending witch (Evans-Pritchard, 1937). Confronted with this evidence, the witch will usually agree to cooperate in order to avoid any additional trouble. Should the victim die, the relatives of the deceased may choose to make magic against the witch, ultimately accepting the death of some villager as evidence of both guilt and the efficacy of their magic.

For the Azande, witchcraft provides not only a sanction against antisocial behavior but also a means of dealing with natural hostilities and death. No one wishes to be thought of as a witch, and surely no one wishes to be victimized by one. By institutionalizing their emotional responses, the Azande successfully maintain social order.

Holding Trials, Settling Disputes, and Punishing Crimes

Among traditional Inuit in northern Canada, the customary way of settling a dispute is through a *song duel* in which the individuals insult each other through songs specially composed for the occasion. Although society does not intervene, spectators represent its interests, and their applause determines the outcome. If, however, social harmony cannot be restored—and that is the goal, rather than assigning and punishing guilt—one or the other disputant may move to another band. Ultimately, there is no binding legal authority (**Figure 22.9**).

By contrast, in Western societies someone who commits an offense against another person may become subject to a series of complex legal proceedings. In criminal cases the primary concern is to assign and punish guilt rather than to help out the victim. The offender will be arrested by the police; tried before a judge and perhaps a jury; and, depending on the severity of the crime, may be fined, imprisoned, or even executed. Rarely does the victim receive restitution or compensation. Throughout this chain of events, the accused party is dealt with by police, judges, jurors, and jailers, who may have no personal acquaintance whatsoever with the plaintiff or the defendant.

The judge's work is difficult and complex. In addition to sifting through evidence presented in a courtroom trial, he or she must consider a wide range of norms, values, and earlier rulings to arrive at a decision that is considered just, not only by the disputing parties but by the public and other judges as well.

Traditionally, in numerous politically centralized societies, incorruptible supernatural, or at least nonhuman, powers are thought to make judgments through a *trial by ordeal*. For example, among the Kpelle of Liberia discussed earlier in this chapter, when guilt is in doubt a licensed "ordeal operator" may apply a hot knife to a suspect's leg. If the leg is burned, the suspect is guilty; if not, innocence is assumed. But the operator does not merely heat the knife and apply it. After massaging the suspect's legs and determining the knife is hot enough, the operator then strokes his own leg with it without being burned, demonstrating

---

law Formal rules of conduct that, when violated, effectuate negative sanctions.

Figure 22.9 Inuit Song Duel Among Inuit of northern Canada, the traditional way of settling a dispute in the community is through a song duel, in which the individuals insult each other in songs composed for the occasion. The applause of onlookers determines the winner, and the affair is considered closed; no further action is expected.

that the innocent will escape injury. The knife is then applied to the suspect.

Up to this point—consciously or unconsciously—the operator has read the suspect's nonverbal cues: gestures, the degree of muscular tension, amount of perspiration, and so forth. From this the operator can judge whether the anxiety the accused exhibits indicates probable guilt; in effect, a psychological stress evaluation has been made. As the knife is applied, it is manipulated to either burn or not burn the suspect, once this judgment has been made. The operator does this manipulation easily by controlling how long the knife is in the fire, as well as the pressure and angle at which it is pressed against the leg (Gibbs, 1983).

The use of the lie detector (polygraph) in the United States is a similar example of assessing guilt, although the guiding ideology is scientific rather than metaphysical. This nonhuman agency is thought to establish objectively who is lying and who is not, but in reality the polygraph operator cannot just "read" the needles of the machine. He or she must judge whether they are registering a high level of anxiety brought on by the testing situation, as opposed to the stress of guilt. Thus, the polygraph operator has much in common with the Kpelle ordeal operator.

Although state societies make a clear distinction between offenses against an individual and those against the state, in non-state societies such as bands and tribes all offenses are viewed as transgressions against individuals or kin-groups (families, lineages, clans, and so on). Disputes between individuals or kin-groups may seriously disrupt the social order, especially in small groups where the disputants, though small in absolute numbers, may be a large percentage of the total population. For example, although the Inuit traditionally have no effective domestic or economic unit beyond the family, a dispute between two people will interfere with the ability of members of separate families to come to one another's aid when necessary and is consequently a matter of wider social concern. Through collectively evaluating the situation and determining who is right or wrong, community members focus on restoring social harmony rather than punishing an offender.

Punitive justice, such as imprisonment, may be the most common approach to justice in state societies, but it has not proven to be an effective way of changing criminal behavior. As a result, indigenous communities in Canada have successfully urged their federal government to reform justice services to make them more consistent with indigenous values and traditions (Criminal Code of Canada, §718.2e). In particular, they have pressed for restorative justice techniques such as the Talking Circle, traditionally used in various forms by several Native American groups. For this, parties involved in a conflict come together in a circle with equal opportunity to express their views—one at a time, free of interruption. Usually, a "talking stick" (or an eagle feather or some other symbolic object) is held by whoever is speaking to signal that she or he has the right to talk at that moment, and others have the responsibility to listen.

In North America over the past four decades there has been significant movement away from the courts in favor of outside negotiation and mediation to resolve a wide variety of disputes. Many jurists see this as a means to clear overloaded court dockets so as to concentrate on more important cases. Leaders in the field of dispute resolution today are finding effective ways to bring about balanced resolutions to conflict. An example of this approach is examined in the Anthropology Applied feature.

ANTHROPOLOGY APPLIED

William Ury: Dispute Resolution and the Anthropologist

In an era when disputes quickly escalate into violence, conflict management is of growing importance. A world leader in this profession is anthropologist William L. Ury, an independent negotiations specialist who has wide-ranging experience working out conflicts—from family feuds to boardroom battles to ethnic wars.

In his first year at graduate school, Ury began looking for ways to apply anthropology to practical problems, including conflicts of all dimensions. He wrote a paper about the role of anthropology in peacemaking and on a whim sent it to Roger Fisher, a law professor noted for his work in negotiation and world affairs. Fisher, in turn, invited the young graduate student to coauthor a kind of how-to book for international mediators. The book they researched and wrote together turned out to have a far wider audience because it presented basic principles of negotiation that could be applied to household spats, manager–employee conflicts, or international crises. Titled *Getting to Yes: Negotiating Agreement Without Giving In*, it sold millions of copies, was translated into twenty-one languages, and earned the nickname "the negotiator's bible."

While working on *Getting to Yes*, Ury and Fisher cofounded the Program on Negotiation (PON) at Harvard Law School, pulling together an interdisciplinary group of academics interested in new approaches to and applications of the negotiation process. Today, this applied research center is a multi-university consortium that trains mediators, businesspeople, and government officials in negotiation skills. It has four key goals: (1) design, implement, and evaluate better dispute resolution practices; (2) promote collaboration among practitioners and scholars; (3) develop education programs and materials for instruction in negotiation and dispute resolution; (4) increase public awareness and understanding of successful conflict resolution efforts.

In 1982, Ury earned his doctorate in anthropology from Harvard with a dissertation titled "Talk Out or Walk Out: The Role and Control of Conflict in a Kentucky Coal Mine." Afterward, he taught for several years while maintaining a leadership role at PON. In particular, he devoted himself to PON's Global Negotiation Project (initially known as the Project on Avoiding War). Today, having left his teaching post at Harvard, Ury continues to serve as director of the Global Negotiation Project, writing, consulting, and running regular workshops on dealing with difficult people and situations.

Utilizing a cross-cultural perspective sharpened through years of anthropological research, he has specialized in ethnic and secessionist disputes, including those between white and black South Africans, Serbs and Croats, Turks and Kurds, Catholics and Protestants in Northern Ireland, and Russians and Chechens in the former Soviet Union.

Among the most effective tools in Ury's applied anthropology work are the books he continues to write on dispute resolution—from his 1993 *Getting Past No* to his 2007 title, *The Power of a Positive No*. His 1999 book, *Getting to Peace: Transforming Conflict at Home, at Work, and in the World*, he examines what he calls the "third side," which is the role that the surrounding community can play in preventing, resolving, and containing destructive conflict between two parties.[a]

Like others in this field, Ury aims to create a culture of negotiation in a world where adversarial, win-lose attitudes are out of step with the increasingly interdependent relations among people. In writing and action, he challenges entrenched ideas that violence and war are inevitable, offering convincing evidence that human beings have as much inherent potential for cooperation and coexistence as they do for violence conflict. Certain that violence is a choice, Ury says, "Conflict is not going to end, but violence can."[b]

---

[a]Pease, T. (2000, Spring). Taking the third side. *Andover Bulletin*. Ury also covers this topic in his 2010 talk for the noted TED series: www.ted.com/talks/william_ury.html

[b]Ury, W. L. (2002, Winter). A global immune system. *Andover Bulletin*; see also www.pon.harvard.edu/

Violent Conflict and Warfare

Although the regulation of a society's internal affairs is an important function of any political system, it is by no means the sole function. Another is the management of its external affairs—relations not just among different states but among different bands, lineages, clans, or whatever the largest autonomous political unit may be. And just as force, threatened or actual, may be used to maintain or restore order within a society, such powerful pressures are also used in the conduct of external affairs.

Humans have a grim track record when it comes to violence. Far more lethal than spontaneous and individual outbursts of aggression, organized violence in the form of war is responsible for enormous destruction of life and property. In the past 5,000 years or so, some 14,000 wars have been fought, resulting in many hundreds of millions of casualties. In the 20th century alone, an estimated 150 million people lost their lives due to human violence.

The scope of violent conflict is wide, ranging from individual fights, local feuds, raids, and piracy (see the Globalscape), to rebellions, insurgencies, guerrillas, and formally declared wars fought by professional armed forces.

Globalscape

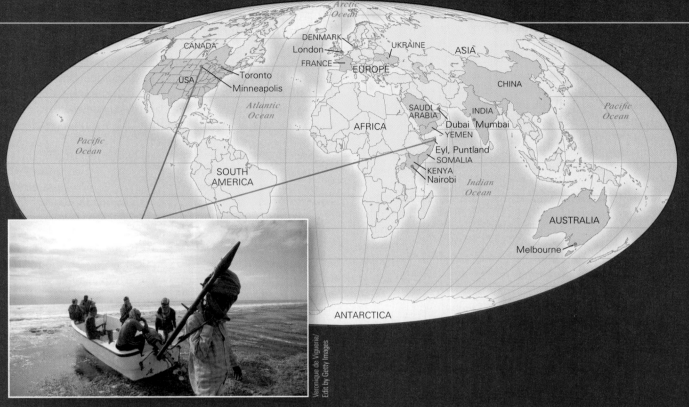

Veronique de Viguerie/
Edit by Getty Images

Pirate Pursuits in Puntland?

Abshir Boya, a towering Somali pirate, is active in coastal waters off the Horn of Africa, which juts deep into the Arabian Sea. He lives in the old fishing port of Eyl in Puntland, an autonomous territory in Somalia. By 2009, Eyl had become a pirate haven, holding a dozen hijacked foreign ships and their multinational crews.

Like Boyah, most of the few hundred other pirates based in Puntland are Darod clansmen pressed out of their traditional fisheries by foreign commercial fleets polluting their coasts and depleting their fish stocks. Since 1991, Somalia has been splintered by rebellions, clan rivalries, and armed foreign interventions. It no longer has a centralized power system maintaining law and order for its citizens, who survive on an average annual income of $600. With a national economy in tatters, Boyah and his clansmen spied the wealth passing through the Arabian Sea and decided to grab a share.

Bankrolled by emigrated Somali investors living in cities such as Melbourne, Dubai, Nairobi, London, Toronto, and Minneapolis, pirate gangs are equipped with radios, cell phones, and GPS, plus semi-automatic pistols, assault rifles, and rocket-propelled grenade launchers bought in Yemen. Speeding across open sea in skiffs, they chase cargo ships, oil tankers, and cruise ships from around the world, including the United States, Canada, Denmark, France, Saudi Arabia, India, and China.

Some pirate captains have banked success, including Boyah, who claims to have led over twenty-five hijackings. Ship owners pay huge ransoms—31 of them in 2011, averaging $5 million each. Somali sea bandits—about a thousand in total—are obliged to pay their backers and share earnings with many poor relatives in their large clans. Notably, ransoms represented only about 2 percent of piracy costs for shippers in 2011. Insurance companies covering the ships took in $635 million, and private armed security forces earned $530 million. About 30 countries spent a total of $1.3 billion on military operations. These and numerous other antipiracy expenses totaled nearly $7 billion.[a]

At their peak of success in 2009, Somali pirates held dozens of captured ships and nearly a thousand seamen. By mid-2012, those numbers were down to about a dozen vessels and several hundred crew, due to an increase in foreign naval patrols and prosecutions. Earlier that year, the European Union toughened its antipiracy mandate to allow forces patrolling the Indian Ocean to attack bases in Somalia. Numerous Somali pirates have been killed or captured.

Criminal prosecution of piracy in international waters is problematic due to questions over jurisdiction. Despite these questions, many pirates are now in jails in half a dozen foreign countries.

[a]One Earth Future Foundation. (2012). *The economic cost of Somali piracy 2011.* http://oceansbeyondpiracy.org/sites/default/files/economic_cost_of_piracy_2011_summary.pdf (retrieved August 28, 2012)

Global Twister

What is justice for Somali fishermen pressed into piracy?

Why War?

In addition to the varying scales and methods of warfare, there are different motives, strategic objectives, and political or moral justifications for it. Some societies engage in defensive wars only and avoid armed confrontations with others unless seriously threatened or actually attacked. Others initiate aggressive wars to pursue particular strategic goals, including material benefits in the form of precious resources such as oil, as well as territorial expansion or control over trade routes. Although competition for scarce resources may turn violent and lead to war, aggressive wars may also be waged for ideological reasons, such as spreading one's worldview or religion and defeating "evil" and "wrongdoers" elsewhere.

Beyond such explanations for warfare, is there something in our genetic makeup that makes it inevitable? Some argue that males of the human species are naturally aggressive. As evidence they point to aggressive group behavior exhibited by chimpanzees in Tanzania, where researchers observed one group systematically destroy another and take over their territory. Also, they cite the "fierce" behavior of people such as the Yanomami Indians who inhabit the Amazon rainforest on either side of the border between Brazil and Venezuela. These tropical horticulturalists and foragers have been described as living in a chronic state of war, and some scientists suggest this exemplifies the way all humans once behaved.

Occasionally, archaeologists have discovered spear points made of stone embedded in ancient human skeletons. Also, there is ample evidence that armed conflicts in the form of deadly feuds and raids have long existed in stateless societies such as foraging bands, horticultural villagers, or nomadic herders. However, warfare among humans is likely to be specific to a situation rather than an unavoidable expression of genetic predisposition for violent behavior (see this chapter's Biocultural Connection).

Moreover, war is not a universal phenomenon because in various parts of the world there are societies that do not practice warfare as we know it. Examples include people as diverse as the Ju/'hoansi Bushmen and Pygmy peoples of southern Africa, the Arapesh of New Guinea, and the Jain of India, as well as the Amish of North America. Among societies that do practice warfare, levels of violence may differ dramatically.

Evolution of Warfare

We have ample reason to suppose that war—not to be confused with more limited forms of deadly violence such as raids—has become a problem only in the last 10,000 years, since the invention of food-production techniques and especially since the formation of centralized states 5,000 years ago. It has reached crisis proportions in the past 200 years, with the invention of modern weaponry and increased direction of violence against civilian populations.

War, as most of us think of it, is a relatively recent phenomenon. Among food foragers, with their uncentralized political systems, violence may erupt sporadically, but warfare was all but unknown until recent times. Because territorial boundaries and membership among food-foraging bands are usually fluid and loosely defined, a man who hunts with one band today may hunt with a neighboring band next month. This renders warfare impractical.

So, too, does the systematic exchange of marriage partners among food-foraging groups, which makes it likely that someone in each band will have a sibling, parent, or cousin in a neighboring band. Moreover, the absence of a food surplus among foragers makes prolonged combat difficult. In sum, where populations are small, food surpluses are absent, property ownership is minimal, and state organization does not exist, the likelihood of organized violence by one group against another is small (Knauft, 1991).

Despite the traditional view of the gardener or farmer as a gentle tiller of the soil, it is among such people, along with pastoralists, that warfare becomes prominent. One reason may be that food-producing peoples have a far greater tendency to grow in population; in contrast, populations of food foragers are generally maintained well below *carrying capacity*—the number of people that the available resources can support at a given level of food-getting techniques. This population growth, if unchecked, can lead to resource depletion—a problem commonly solved by seizing the resources of others.

In addition, the commitment to a fixed piece of land inherent in farming makes such societies somewhat less fluid in their membership than those of food foragers. Instead of marrying distantly, farmers marry locally, depriving them of long-distance kin networks. In rigidly matrilocal or patrilocal societies, each new generation is bound to the same territory, no matter how small it may be or how large the group trying to live within it.

The availability of unoccupied lands may not serve as a sufficient detriment to the outbreak of war. Among slash-and-burn farmers, for example, competition for land cleared of old-growth forest frequently leads to hostility and armed conflict. The centralization of political control and the possession of valuable property among farming people provide many more incentives for warfare.

A conflict may quickly escalate and lead to a fight, sometimes with lethal consequences. Launching an armed raid or invasion into enemy territory requires considerable planning and organization. Violent confrontations involving chiefdoms and, even more so, states increased in scale

BIOCULTURAL CONNECTION

Sex, Gender, and Human Violence

At the start of the 21st century, war and violence are no longer the strictly male domains that they were in many societies in the past. War has become embedded in civilian life in many parts of the world, and it impacts the daily lives of women and children. Moreover, women now serve in the military forces of several states, although their participation in combat is often limited. Some female soldiers in the United States argue that gender should not limit their participation in combat as they consider themselves as strong, capable, and well trained as their male counterparts. Others believe that biologically based sex differences make war a particularly male domain.

Scientists have long argued that males are more suited to combat because natural selection has made them on average larger and stronger than females. Darwin first proposed this idea, known as sexual selection, in the 19th century. At that time he theorized that physical specializations in animal species—such as horns, vibrant plumage, and, in the case of humans, intelligence and tool use—demonstrate selection acting upon males to aid in the competition for mates. In these scenarios, male reproductive success is thought to be optimized through a strategy of "spreading seed"—in other words, by being sexually active with as many females as possible.

Females, on the other hand, are considered gatekeepers who optimize their reproductive success through caring for individual offspring. According to this theory of sexual selection, in species where male–male competition is high, males will be considerably larger than females, and aggression will serve males well. In monogamous species, males and females will be of similar sizes.

Primatologist Richard Wrangham has taken the idea of sexual selection even further. In his book *Demonic Males*, he explores the idea that both male aggression and patriarchy have an evolutionary basis. He states that humans, like our close cousin the chimpanzee, are "party gang" species characterized by strong bonds among groups of males who have dominion over an expandable territory. These features "suffice to account for natural selection's ugly legacy, the tendency to look for killing opportunities when hostile neighbors meet."[a] Violence, in turn, generates a male-dominated social order: "Patriarchy comes from biology in the sense that it emerges from men's temperaments out of their evolutionarily derived efforts to control women and at the same time have solidarity with fellow males in competition against outsiders."[b] Although Wrangham allows that evolutionary forces have shaped women as well, he suggests that females' evolutionary interests cannot be met without cooperation with males.

Feminist scholars have pointed out that these scientific models are gendered in that they incorporate the norms derived from the scientists' culture. Darwin's original model of sexual selection incorporated the Victorian gender norms of the passive female and active male. Primatologist Laura Fedigan suggests that in Darwinian models women evolved in positive directions only by a coattails process whereby females were "pulled along" toward improved biological states by virtue of the progress of the genes they shared with males.[c] Wrangham's revised, more recent *Demonic Males* theory is similarly shaped by culture. It incorporates the dominant world order (military states) and the gender norms (aggressive males) it values. In both cases, the putatively scientific theory has created a natural basis for a series of social conventions.

This does not mean that biological differences between the sexes cannot be studied in the natural world. Instead, scientists studying sex differences must be especially sensitive to how they may project cultural beliefs onto nature. Meanwhile, the attitudes of some women soldiers continue to challenge generalizations regarding "military specialization" by gender.

BIOCULTURAL QUESTION

All across the world, males are far more likely to serve as warriors than females and, consequently, are far more likely to lose their lives on the battlefield. Do you think that there is any structural relationship between high male combat mortality rates and polgyny as the preferred marriage type in most traditional cultures?

---

[a]Wrangham, R., & Peterson, D. (1996). *Demonic males* (p. 168). Boston: Houghton Mifflin.

[b]Ibid., p. 125.

[c]Fedigan, L. M. (1986). The changing role of women in models of human evolution. *Annual Review of Anthropology 15*, 25–66.

and resulted in ever-growing numbers of casualties on the battlefield. The escalation of violence in the political evolution, which led to the formation of the earliest kingdoms and empires 4,000 to 5,000 years ago, continued into the 21st century, the deadliest in human history.

Before the development of tribes and chiefdoms, autonomous bands could field only a few dozen warriors for short periods of fighting. Today, rulers of states recruit thousands, even millions, maintaining fighters on a full-time basis as professional soldiers.

For illustration purposes, consider three famous battles: In the 1815 Battle of Waterloo that ended Napoleon's rule of the French empire, some 150,000 soldiers and 45,000 horses engaged in combat south of Brussels on a battlefield under 8 square kilometers (3 square miles in size). Within just nine hours, 45,000 men and 34,000 horses lay dead or wounded. During World War II, the Battle of Stalingrad, fought from the fall of 1942 into January 1943, claimed about 1.5 million casualties. At the end of the war, only 5,000 out of 300,000 German soldiers returned from Russia alive. In the Battle of Hsupeng (also known as the Huaihai Campaign) ending the Chinese civil war in early 1949, more than 2 million troops fought on a flat plain of 7,600 square miles, with almost 700,000 casualties (including captives).

The evolution of warfare is also driven by new inventions in military technology, with weapons becoming increasingly complex and effective—from slings, clubs, spears, and arrows to machine guns, supersonic jet fighters, atomic bombs, high-energy laser beams, computer viruses, and pilotless drones (**Figure 22.10**). In modern warfare, casualties are not just civilians but also *children*, and they far outnumber the casualty rate of soldiers.

Almost a century ago, tens of thousands of soldiers on the French-German frontline in World War I experienced chemical warfare for the first time in human history. Although other poison gases had been used a few years earlier, troops in the trenches in 1917 were attacked by mustard gas—a chemical poison that causes blindness, large blisters on exposed skin, and (if inhaled)

Figure 22.10 Drone Pilot Operator From his computer console at a military command post in New York State, this U.S. Attack Wing airman remotely operates a drone aircraft in support of American ground troops battling enemies in tribal territories of Afghanistan and neighboring Pakistan. Equipped with Hellfire missiles, his drone surveys the terrain with powerful cameras beaming live video via satellite. Drones can be thought of as modern versions of dangerous spirits magically directed by invisible warlords. U.S. forces have used Predator drones since 1995, targeting enemies primarily in Muslim insurgencies across western Asia and North Africa. During that same period, the entertainment industry has provided opportunities for "child soldiers" across the globe to play telewarfare video games in arcades or at home.

Heather Ainsworth/The New York Times/Redux

bleeding and blistering in the mouth, throat, and lungs. The development of weapons of mass destruction has been horrendously effective.

Today, the chemical, biological, and nuclear weapon arsenals stockpiled by many states are sufficient to wipe out all life on the planet, many times over. Because dangerous poisons, such as the anthrax bacterium or the nerve gas Sarin, are cheap and easy to produce, non-state groups, including terrorists, also seek to acquire to them, if only to threaten to use them against more powerful opponents.

Ideologies of Aggression

Whatever may be possible in terms of military technology, it takes ideas and motivation to turn humans into killers, and that stems from culture. Justifications for war are embedded in a society's *worldview*—the collective body of ideas that members of a culture generally share concerning the ultimate shape and substance of their reality. It is said that war is dehumanizing; that ideological process usually begins with degrading opponents to a lower status as barbaric, evil, ugly, worthless, or otherwise inferior. Having thus dehumanized their opponents, humans conjure justifications for slaughter and pillage, often raping vanquished women, mutilating enemy bodies for trophies, and turning captives into slaves.

Ultimately, war also dehumanizes the aggressor. Recalling his experiences in trench warfare in which he was wounded in the summer of 1917, a German combat veteran wrote: "We have become wild beasts. . . . We have lost all feeling for one another [and] plunge again into the horror . . . madly savage and raging; we will kill, for they are still our mortal enemies [and] if we don't destroy them, they will destroy us" (Remarque, 1929, pp. 113–116).

No matter how extreme and negative the emotions may be when confronting the enemy, warriors are usually physically and mentally trained for combat. In preparing and conditioning young men (and sometimes women) for the battlefield, they are indoctrinated by an ideology justifying war, which may come wrapped in magic and other metaphysics.

There are all too many examples of how religious and ideological justifications for war are embedded in a society's worldview. They range from the Christian Crusades directed against Muslims in Palestine and surrounding Islamic territories about 700 to 900 years ago to the more recent *jihad* waged by Islamic fundamentalists in southwestern Asia and North Africa. The latter include militant extremists, such as Al-Qaeda and Jemaah Islamiyah, aiming to restore "pure" Islam, topple regimes that promote or tolerate religious corruption, and expel all infidels (nonbelievers) from ancestral soil. The following example from East Africa provides a more detailed look.

A Crusade in Uganda: The Rise and Fall of a Militant Christian Cult

Once described as the Pearl of Africa, Uganda is a pluralistic country with about 34 million inhabitants divided into more than a dozen ethnic groups, including the Acholi. During the colonial period, British missionaries converted a large majority of Ugandans to Christianity.

Since gaining independence in 1962, Uganda has suffered numerous regional insurgencies, civil wars, and interethnic clashes, resulting in death or displacement for millions. During the 1981–1986 Ugandan Bush War, Acholi soldiers fought with the losing faction, suffering huge losses and humiliation.

By 1986, many Acholi Christians believed the apocalypse described in the Bible's Book of Revelation was upon them. One such Acholi was Alice Auma, a 30-year-old woman who had been married and divorced twice for being barren. Alice found inspiration in the biblical promise of a "new earth" free of suffering and death. Through a vision she believed was divine, she learned that a holy messenger had chosen her as his spirit-medium. Sometimes this powerful spirit took possession of Alice. She named him *Lakwena*—the Acholi word for "apostle" or "messenger from God"—and claimed that he commanded the heavenly force of 144,000 redeemed men described in Revelation.

In 1986, spiritually empowered by Lakwena, Alice became a *nebi* (Acholi translation for a "biblical prophet"). At séances, she gave herself over to *malaika* (Swahili for "angels"), who filled her with power to heal people diagnosed as victims of evil spirits. Gaining a reputation as a witchdoctor, she became known as Alice Lakwena. Her patients included many Acholi soldiers who believed they were possessed by *cen*—the polluting spirits of killed enemies seeking revenge. To keep their soul and body clean, Alice ordered them to abstain from alcohol and sex.

Feeling divinely directed to liberate her homeland from evil and found a Christian theocracy based on the Ten Commandments, Alice recruited 8,000 Acholi and other northern warriors for a crusade to free Uganda from all enemies of God. She called her militant cult the Holy

Spirit Mobile Force. In late 1987, supernaturally aided by Lakwena and his phantom army of 144,000, Alice led 7,000 of her warriors southward, aiming to capture Uganda's capital city, Kampala.

Filled with *malaika*, Alice's troops marched in cross-shaped battle formations, carrying Bibles and singing hymns. They had smeared their bodies with holy oil extracted from wild shea nuts, assured it would shield them from bullets. They were armed with rifles, plus magic sticks and stones blessed to explode when hurled at the enemy. In the first few battles, they scored victories when terrified government troops ran away. But 80 kilometers east of Kampala, the Holy Spirit Mobile Force was massacred, mowed down in a barrage of mortar attacks and machine-gun fire. Convinced that bullets could not pierce the purified, Alice interpreted this defeat as evidence that evil spirits had gained control over many in her own army. Abandoning the battlefield, she escaped into Kenya where she died in a refugee camp twenty years later.

Hundreds of Holy Spirit warriors who survived the ordeal joined other rebel groups, including the Lord's Resistance Army (LRA) formed by Joseph Kony, an Acholi witchdoctor. A former Roman Catholic altar boy related to Alice, Kony adopted some of her spiritual repertoire in founding a militant cult based on a mixture of indigenized Christian and Muslim beliefs and practices. After growing to a force of 4,000 warriors, his insurgency degenerated into a murderous campaign based on terror tactics. The LRA also kidnapped many thousands of children, indoctrinating them to become merciless fighters (**Figure 22.11**).

By 2006, LRA troops had dwindled to about 600, and the Uganda army had forced them across the border into the Democratic Republic of Congo. The rebels hid out in Garamba National Park—a vast wilderness inhabited by elephants, giraffes, hippos, rare white rhinoceroses, and many other animals.

Since then, despite peace talk efforts, Kony's soldiers continue to carry out periodic raids. For instance, in a June 2008 foray into South Sudan, they forcibly added some 1,000 new recruits, including hundreds of abducted children. In air and ground military offensives throughout the following six months, Ugandan soldiers attacked rebel camps in the Garamba forest, killing more than 150 LRA troops, capturing another 50 (including several low-level commanders), and rescuing many of the kidnapped children and other forced recruits. The LRA retaliated with killing raids, capturing replacement recruits, including more children.

In the past few years, nearly half a million people have fled their villages for fear of attack—not only in the Democratic Republic of Congo, but also in neighboring

Helen Margaret Giovanello

Figure 22.11 Young Acholi Soldier in the Lord's Resistance Army After Alice Lakwena's crusade ended in a bloodbath, her relative Joseph Kony adopted some of her ideas, forming the Lord's Resistance Army (LRA). Unlike Alice, he often forced children into service. In 2006 he and his fighters, including the armed teenager pictured here, retreated into the Democratic Republic of Congo's vast Garamba National Park and staged raids from there. Wanted for war crimes and accused of being a demon, Kony remains in hiding.

Sudan and the Central African Republic. Kony, the rebel army's charismatic Christian cult leader, remains at large, still believing in his divinely guided insurgency (Allen, 2006; Behrend, 1999; Finnström, 2008).

Genocide

As these cross-cultural examples of violent conflict indicate, warfare often involves a complex dynamic of economic, political, and ideological interests. Such is especially the case when violence escalates into **genocide**—the physical extermination of one people by another, either as a deliberate act or as the accidental outcome of activities

---

genocide The physical extermination of one people by another, either as a deliberate act or as the accidental outcome of activities carried out by one people with little regard for their impact on others.

carried out by one people with little regard for their impact on others.

The most widely known act of genocide in recent history was the attempt of the Nazis during World War II to wipe out European Jews and Roma (Gypsies) in the name of racial superiority and improvement of the human species. Reference to this mass extermination as *the* Holocaust—as if it were unique—tends to blind us to the fact that genocide is an age-old and ongoing phenomenon, with many examples from across the globe and throughout human history. In North America, for example, European settlers massacred numerous indigenous communities from the 1500s up until the late 1800s in California.

One of the most infamous 19th-century acts of genocide was the systematic killing of the indigenous inhabitants of Tasmania, a large island about the size of Ireland and located just south of Australia. Collectively known as Palawa, they subsisted as hunter-gatherers probably not unlike their ancestors who migrated there almost 40,000 years ago. European seafarers first came ashore in 1642 but made no contact.

About 160 years later, the British claimed the remote island and designated it as a penal colony for exiled prisoners. Then numbering about 5,000, the Palawa were divided into several regional ethnic groups speaking different languages. Armed with spears, Palawa warriors defending their families and hunting territories were no match for the invaders equipped with firearms. On December 1, 1826, the island newspaper *Colonial Times* declared:

SELF DEFENSE IS THE FIRST LAW OF NATURE. THE GOVERNMENT MUST REMOVE THE NATIVES—IF NOT, THEY WILL BE HUNTED DOWN LIKE WILD BEASTS, AND DESTROYED!

Soon, slaughter and newly introduced diseases led to Palawa extinction, and the island was fully secured for British sheep farmers and the commercial wool industry. In 1876, the last full-blooded Tasmanian was carried to her grave. A similar tragedy unfolded in Tierra del Fuego, a large island on the tip of the South American continent, where British sheep farmers drove off the indigenous Selk'nam, who are also extinct.

Among numerous more contemporary examples of genocide, Khmer Rouge soldiers in Cambodia killed 1.7 million fellow citizens, or 20 percent of that country's population, between 1975 and 1979. During the next decade, government-sponsored terrorism against indigenous communities in Guatemala reached its height, and Saddam Hussein's government used poison gas against the Kurdish ethnic minority in northern Iraq. In 1994, Hutus in the African country of Rwanda slaughtered about 800 million of their Tutsi neighbors ("Leave none to tell the story: Genocide in Rwanda," 2004). Estimates vary, but during the 20th century as many as 83 million people died of genocide (White, 2001). The horrors continue in the current century with, among others, the genocidal campaign against the non-Arab black peoples in the Darfur desert region of western Sudan.

Armed Conflicts Today

Currently, there are several dozen wars raging around the globe. They occur not only *between* states but also *within* pluralistic countries where interethnic conflicts abound and/or where the political leadership and government bureaucracy are corrupt, repressive, ineffective, or without popular support (**Figure 22.12**).

Notably, many armies around the world recruit not only adult men but also women and children. Experts estimate that some 250,000 child soldiers, many as young as 12, are participating in armed conflicts around the world, especially in Africa. Among the notorious examples is the Lord's Resistance Army mentioned previously, which reportedly kidnapped over 60,000 children to train as fierce fighters ("Child soldiers global report 2008," 2009; UN Dispatch, 2006).

The following examples offer some specific data on wars from the last decade of the 20th century to today. In the 1990s, about 2.5 million people died, and many millions more became refugees due to fighting in South Sudan, leading to that region's secession and political independence as a new state in 2011. And since warfare erupted in the eastern region of the Democratic Republic of Congo in 1998, almost 6 million people have died, and millions more have been forced to flee their home villages. Involving eight African states and about twenty-five armed forces, this gruesome war with mass murder and mass rape is known as Africa's World War.

Foreign military intervention is also a hallmark of long-lasting wars in regions that are strategically important or that are rich in natural resources, including Afghanistan and Iraq. In addition to many hundreds of thousands of fatalities in these countries, primarily among noncombatants (children, women, elderly), there has been massive destruction of roads, bridges, buildings, and livelihoods. Without a political leadership capable of effectively governing these pluralistic countries, providing security, and maintaining law and order, both war-torn countries seem doomed to be failed states.

Beyond these wars, there are numerous so-called low-intensity wars involving guerrilla organizations, rebel armies, resistance movements, terrorist cells, and a host of other armed groups engaged in violent conflict with official state-controlled armed forces. Every year, confrontations result in hundreds of hot spots and violent flashpoints, most of which are never reported in Western news media.

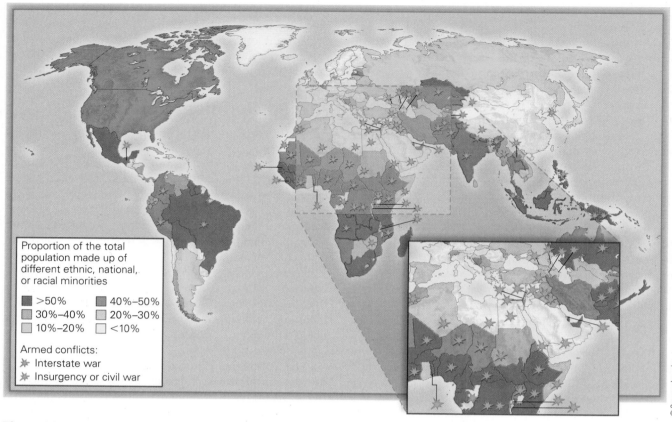

Figure 22.12 Ethnic Groups and Violent Conflict In pluralistic societies in which two or more ethnic groups or nationalities form part of the same political state, violent conflict between neighboring groups is not uncommon.

Proportion of the total population made up of different ethnic, national, or racial minorities

- >50%
- 40%–50%
- 30%–40%
- 20%–30%
- 10%–20%
- <10%

Armed conflicts:
- ✳ Interstate war
- ✳ Insurgency or civil war

© Cengage Learning

Peace Through Diplomacy

The resolution of conflicts within and between groups by nonviolent means is a vital part of this chapter's discussion. Throughout history, people have tried to prevent conflicts from escalating into violence, just as they have endeavored to end existing violence and restore peaceful relations. For this to succeed, politically organized groups designate high-ranking trusted individuals to discuss a mutually acceptable agreement to secure peace. Authorized as representatives acting on behalf of their tribal elders, chief, king, or other sovereign head, these envoys usually carry evidence of their official status and mission as envoys or diplomats (from the Greek *diploma*, originally meaning "folded paper").

Diplomatic evidence may be in the form of a written document, marked by a signature, seal, or some other sign representing the authorizing government. In different cultures across the globe, a wide range of ceremonial artifacts have been used in diplomatic protocol—such as special shell-beaded belts (*wampum*) presented by Iroquois chiefs and long-stemmed tobacco pipes smoked by Lakota leaders and numerous other Plains Indian peoples.

Thus equipped, delegates participate in formal rituals brokering terms of agreement, including mutually binding rules to prevent or end conflict and live in friendship and peace. These terms so negotiated may secure rights of access or claims to tracts of disputed land, water, other natural resources, safe passage across territorial boundaries for trade or pilgrimages to sacred sites, and a host of other issues setting rules to maintain order and avoid conflict.

A formally binding agreement between two or more groups that are independent and politically self-governing (such as tribes, chiefdoms, and states) is a contract known as a **treaty**. Determining issues of war and peace and influencing the survival and well-being of multitudes, treatymaking is ritually concluded with a ceremonial performance. When the rules as formulated in a treaty are ignored or violated, the pact of friendship is broken. With relations chilling or turning hostile, war may follow.

treaty A contract or formally binding agreement between two or more groups that are independent and self-governing political groups such as tribes, chiefdoms, and states.

Figure 22.13 West Papua Independence Movement Lani tribal leader Benny Wenda (center in red shirt) became a political prisoner in Indonesia due to his role in West Papua's struggle for independence from Indonesia. He escaped while awaiting trial. Fearing for his life and expecting no justice from a legal system that denied Papua indigenous rights, he went into exile and was granted asylum by the British government in 2002. Lobbying for his country's peaceful transition to independence, Wenda launched the International Parliamentarians for West Papua (IPWP) at the British Parliament in London, on October 15, 2008. Here we see Wenda and other West Papuans with several British Parliamentarians in the House of Commons. Standing next to Wenda is IPWP's chairman, Andrew Smith, a Member of Parliament (MP) from Oxford. This cross-party group of politicians supporting self-determination for the people of West Papua has grown to almost 100 parliamentarians. A former Labour Party cabinet minister, Smith also chairs Britain's All Party Parliamentary Group for West Papua, which meets regularly.

Treaties between two sovereign parties are known as *bilateral* treaties, and these have been made for many thousands of years. International treaties are more recent, involving many neighboring states on a continent or, since the past century, across the globe. Today, many indigenous nations who could not resist more powerful states claiming political control or ownership over their ancestral lands are appealing to international organizations for support in their struggle against repression, respect for their human rights and cultural freedom, and restoration of their political rights of self-determination in their homeland.

Throughout the world today, there are politically repressed ethnic and religious groups as well as indigenous peoples who struggle for freedom and self-determination. Among them are tribal peoples of West Papua, New Guinea, many of whom remained isolated from the outside world until half a century ago. Those living in remote highland villages had little knowledge of the expansionist strategy guiding neighboring Indonesia into politically annexing their homeland in 1963. Soon thereafter, frustrated in their political desire for independence, indigenous activists founded the Free Papua Movement. Since then, Indonesian military and police have brutally repressed Papua freedom fighters, threatening, imprisoning, and killing thousands; thousands more have been driven into hiding in the forested mountains or into exile abroad. One exiled West Papua leader, Benny Wenda, now lives in England; from there he continues the struggle for his country's independence through international organizations and diplomatic channels (**Figure 22.13**).

Politics of Nonviolent Resistance

There are other options for resolving major political conflicts besides fighting with deadly weapons or international diplomacy. In 1947, India and Pakistan gained political independence from their British colonial overlords in part due to a nonviolent resistance movement led by Mohandas Gandhi.

Born into the Vaisya caste in Gujarat, in 1869, Gandhi was the son of a high-ranking district official. In 1888, he sailed to London, where he completed his law studies. Failing to establish himself as a lawyer in India, the 23-year-old accepted a position in Johannesburg, South Africa. There, like fellow dark-skinned Indians, he experienced racist discrimination.

Making a decision to fight colonial repression and injustice, Gandhi built a movement founded on the concept of *satyagraha*, which he conceived while serving as a legal advisor for Indian traders and laborers working in British South Africa in 1906. The term is based on the Sanskrit words *satya* ("truth"), implying love, and *agraha* ("firmness"). As he described it, applying *satyagraha* to the pursuit of truth required weaning one's opponent from the error of injustice

> by patience and sympathy. . . . And patience means self-suffering. So the doctrine came to mean vindication of truth, not by infliction of suffering on the opponent, but on one's own self. . . . A satyagrahi enjoys a degree of freedom not possible for others, for he becomes a truly fearless person. Once his

mind is rid of fear, he will never agree to be another's slave. (Gandhi, 1999, vol. 19 p. 220 & vol. 8 p. 151)

Returning to India in 1915, Gandhi mobilized the first of many mass protests against colonial injustices applying *satyagraha* as a "weapon of the strong" that "admits no violence under any circumstance" (Gandhi, 1999).

The journey toward independence was long and full of losses for Gandhi and his *satyagrahis*, but they emerged victorious in 1947. Tragically, six months later, as Gandhi strove to maintain peace between religious factions, a Hindu extremist assassinated the 79-year-old hero.

Gandhi's triumphant example lives on. Among the many current examples of nonviolent resistance is the popular mass movement to end the military grip on power in Myanmar, formerly known as Burma. It is led by Aung San Suu Kyi, an Oxford University–trained political leader raised in the Buddhist tradition like most of her followers. She is the daughter of a freedom fighter who led the country in its struggle to end British colonial rule; her father was assassinated six months before independence in 1947.

In 1988, Suu Kyi founded the National League for Democracy (NLD) as a coordinating

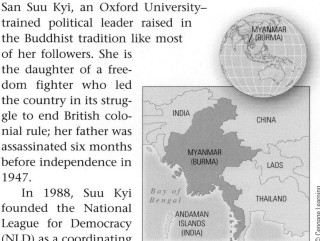

Figure 22.14 **Ethnic Minorities from Myanmar Cheering for Aung San Suu Kyi** Having fled war and repression, these refugees have been living in the large Mae La camp in Thailand, 10 kilometers from the border of their home country in Myanmar. For them and many others, Suu Kyi's picture is an icon of democracy, freedom, and hope.

body for nonviolent resistance. Two years later, after winning a majority of the national votes and gaining 81 percent of the seats in the Myanmar Parliament, she was placed under house arrest and isolated from the public, as well as from her husband and two children. Refusing to compromise her principles and accept exile, she endured in solitude and periodically went on hunger strikes. She became one of the world's most prominent political prisoners and was awarded the Nobel Peace Prize and many other international honors for her courageous human rights activism.

In 2011, having been confined for fifteen of the previous twenty-one years and widowed, she finally regained her freedom and resumed her public role as head of the opposition movement. Six months later, her NLD Party won almost all of the vacant seats in the House of Representatives, with Suu Kyi taking her long-denied seat in Parliament. She used her first speech in Parliament to call for laws protecting the rights of her country's impoverished and repressed ethnic minorities, including the Kachin, Karen, and Shan peoples who have long fought for their freedom as indigenous nations (**Figure 22.14**).

Throughout the world, liberation, civil rights, and pro-democracy movements have successfully applied the politics of nonviolent action in their struggles against political repression, racist discrimination, and dictatorships (Sharp, 1973, 2010; Stolberg, 2011).

As the cross-cultural examples featured in this chapter show, the political challenges of maintaining order and resolving conflicts are complex, involving economic, political, and ideological factors. Military technology has led to the launching of ever-more effective killing machines operating in factories of death. The challenge of eliminating human violence has never been greater than it is in today's world—nor has the cost of *not* finding a way to do so. Throughout history and across the globe, individuals and groups have created, adopted, and applied ways to avoid and resolve conflicts by means of nonviolence. As we will see in the next chapter, the search for peace and harmony crosses political and chronological boundaries and is among the challenges humans engage through religion and spirituality.

CHAPTER CHECKLIST

What is power, and why is it a crucially important issue in every society?

● Power is the ability of individuals or groups to impose their will upon others and make them do things even against their own wants and wishes. Ranging from persuasion to violence, power drives politics—the process of determining who gets what, when, and how.

● A society's political organization establishes how power is accumulated, arranged, executed, and structurally embedded in that society.

What are the different types of political organization in uncentralized societies?

● The band is a relatively small (a few hundred people at most) and loosely organized kin-ordered group that inhabits a common territory and that may split into smaller extended family groups that are politically and economically independent.

● Typically, bands are found among food foragers and other nomadic societies in which people organize into politically autonomous family groups that usually camp together as long as environmental and subsistence circumstances are favorable. Political organization in bands is democratic, and informal control is exerted by public opinion in the form of gossip and ridicule. Leaders of bands are usually older men whose personal authority lasts only as long as members approve of their leadership.

● In anthropology, a tribe is a kin-ordered group politically integrated by a unifying factor; its members share a common ancestry, identity, culture, language, and territory. With an economy usually based on crop cultivation or herding, the tribe's population is larger than that of the band, although family units within the tribe are still relatively autonomous and egalitarian. Political organization is transitory, and leaders have no coercive means of maintaining authority.

● In many tribal societies the organizing political unit is the clan, composed of people who consider themselves descended from a common ancestor. Clan elders may regulate affairs and represent their group in relations with other clans. Another type of tribal leadership is the Big Man, who builds up his wealth and political power until he must be reckoned with as a leader.

What are the different types of political organization in centralized societies?

● A chiefdom is a politically organized territory centrally ruled by a chief heading a kin-based society with prestige ranking and a redistributive economy. Rank in such a hierarchical political system is determined by the closeness of one's relationship to the chief. The chief may accumulate great personal wealth, enhancing his power base, which he may pass on to his heirs. The office of the chief is usually for life and often hereditary.

⬤ Traditionally, chiefdoms have been unstable, with lesser chiefs trying to take power from higher-ranking chiefs, or rival chiefs vying with one another for supreme power as paramount chiefs.

⬤ Hundreds of chiefdoms still exist but no longer as politically independent or sovereign domains. One example is the Kpelle of Liberia, West Africa.

⬤ The most centralized political organization is the state—a politically organized territory occupied by a class-stratified society with a centralized government and definite boundaries. It is organized and directed by a government that has the capacity and authority to manage and tax its subjects, make laws and maintain order, and use military force to defend or expand its territories.

⬤ States began to emerge over 5,000 years ago. They are inherently unstable and transitory and differ from nations, which are communities of people who share a collective identity based on a common culture, language, territorial base, and history.

⬤ Nation and state do not always coincide.

How do political organizations establish authority?

⬤ Authority—claiming and exercising power as justified by law or custom of tradition—is basic to the political process. Unlike coercion, which imposes obedience by force or intimidation, authority is based on the socially accepted rules or codified laws binding people together as a society.

⬤ In a monarchy—a state headed by a single ruler—legitimacy may be based on divine will, birthright, or election by the elite class. In a theocracy—a state ruled by a priestly elite headed by a supreme priest—legitimacy is embedded in sacred doctrine. In an aristocracy, it is claimed through a combination of ancestry, class endogamy, military dominance, and economic wealth.

⬤ Most governments use some measure of ideology, including religion, to legitimize political power.

⬤ Historically, far fewer women than men have held important positions of political leadership, but there are notable exceptions. Lower visibility in politics does not necessarily indicate that women lack political power. Today, a growing number of women have been elected as president, chancellor, or prime minister.

How do political systems maintain social order?

⬤ Every culture has internal and external forms of cultural control. Internalized controls, self-imposed by enculturated individuals who share beliefs and values about what is proper and what is not, lead to self-control. Such control may also be motivated by fear of misfortune or supernatural punishment for wrongdoing.

⬤ Externalized controls, maintained by authorities in ranked societies through persuasion or coercion, comprise social control. They come in the form of sanctions. Positive sanctions are rewards by others, whereas negative sanctions include threat of imprisonment, fines, corporal punishment, or loss of face. Sanctions are either formal, including actual laws, or informal, involving norms.

⬤ In societies with or without centralized political systems, witchcraft may function as an agent of cultural control and involves both self-control and social controls.

⬤ Law is formal rules of conduct that, when violated, lead to negative sanctions. In centralized political systems, this authority rests with the government and court system, whereas uncentralized societies give this authority directly to the injured party.

⬤ In contrast to bands, tribes, and chiefdoms, state societies distinguish between offenses against the state and those against an individual.

⬤ Punitive justice (such as imprisonment) stands in contrast to restorative justice.

What role do violence and warfare play in societies' efforts to regulate external affairs and conflicts?

⬤ To regulate external affairs, societies may resort to the threat or use of force—from individual fights, local feuds, raids, and piracy to rebellions, insurgencies, guerrillas, and formally declared wars fought by professional armed forces.

⬤ Some societies engage in defensive wars only, avoiding armed confrontations unless seriously threatened or attacked. Others initiate aggressive wars for material or ideological objectives. Over the past 5,000 years, humans have fought some 14,000 wars resulting in many hundreds of millions of casualties.

⬤ Warfare among humans is likely to be situation specific rather than an unavoidable expression of genetic predisposition for violent behavior. There are some societies that do not practice warfare as we know it—such as the Jain of India and Pygmy peoples of southern Africa.

⬤ War—not to be confused with more limited forms of deadly violence such as raids—has become a problem only in the last 10,000 years, since the invention of food-production techniques and especially since the formation of centralized states 5,000 years ago. It has reached crisis proportions in the past 200 years, intensified by modern weaponry.

⬤ Justifications for war are embedded in a society's worldview—the collective body of ideas that members of a culture generally share concerning the ultimate shape and substance of their reality. Examples of this range from the Christian Crusades against Muslims about 700 to 900 years ago to the more recent *jihad* waged by Islamic fundamentalists in Southwest Asia and North Africa.

Genocide is the physical extermination of one people by another, either as a deliberate act or as the accidental outcome of activities carried out by one people with little regard for the impact on others. There are many historic examples of this, such as England wiping out the indigenous population of Tasmania in the 19th century in order to secure the large island for its own sheep farmers and commercial wool industry. During the 20th century, about 83 million people have died of genocide.

There are several dozen wars raging in the world today. Some are wars between states, and others are wars within pluralistic states where interethnic conflicts abound and/or where the political leadership and government bureaucracy are corrupt, repressive, ineffective, or without popular support.

What nonviolent approaches do humans use to resolve conflicts?

Throughout history, people have used diplomacy to prevent conflicts from escalating into violence.

Treaties are formally binding agreements between two or more groups that are independent and self-governing political groups such as tribes, chiefdoms, and states.

In 1947, India and Pakistan gained political independence from their British colonial overlords in part due to a nonviolent resistance movement led by Mohandas Gandhi.

A present-day example of nonviolent resistance is the popular mass movement to end the military grip on power in Myanmar led by Aung San Suu Kyi.

QUESTIONS FOR REFLECTION

1. In Nigeria, a large pluralistic society with many ethnic groups and tribes, the northern half is predominantly Muslim and governed by Shariah law. What do you think of a government like the emirate of Kano that does not keep politics and religion separate? Can you imagine your own country being governed by a ruler combining spiritual and political leadership?

2. Do you think there is a relationship between a profitable arms industry, promoting military dominance, and the pursuit of war as a means of solving conflicts? If so, what is the role of an ideology that asserts national and/or religious righteousness?

3. If political organization functions to impose or maintain order and to resolve conflicts, why do you think that the government in a country such as yours is so interested in legitimizing its power? What happens when a government loses such legitimacy?

4. When your own government declares war against another country, on which basis does it seek to justify its decision to send soldiers into battle?

5. Do you think nonviolent resistance is effective as a tactic challenging social or political injustice? Can you imagine a situation in which such protest is not only effective but would also be legitimate? If so, on what grounds?

ONLINE STUDY RESOURCES

CourseMate

Access chapter-specific learning tools, including learning objectives, practice quizzes, videos, flash cards, glossaries, and more in your Anthropology CourseMate.

Log into **www.cengagebrain.com** to access the resources your instructor has assigned and to purchase materials.

Challenge Issue

As self-aware and self-reflecting beings, humans face emotional and intellectual challenges born of the need to make sense of our place in the universe. We puzzle over truly big questions about time and space and wrestle with existential questions about our own fate, life, and death. For countless generations, our species has creatively engaged in such reflections on the unknown, the mysterious, the supernatural. We do this in sacred narratives and rituals—prayers, chants, dances, prostrations, burnings, and sacrificial offerings—the cornerstones of many religions. Here we see Christian pilgrims walking toward the shrine of the Virgin of Guadalupe, the patron saint of Mexico. For centuries, Nahuatl-speaking Mexican Indians have referred to this brown-skinned Saint Mary, the virgin mother of Jesus Christ, as Tonantzin ("Our Revered Mother"), their traditional name for an ancient Aztec earth and fertility goddess. Believers claim she manifested herself in a blaze of light to an Aztec youth in 1531, a decade after the Spanish destruction of the Aztec empire. Representing purity, hope, and motherly love, she embodies a longing for a world of social justice and interethnic tolerance. Annually, her shrine in Mexico City attracts more than 6 million devotees, making it one of the largest pilgrimage sites on earth.

Spirituality, Religion, and Shamanism

Religions play an important role in determining cultural identity in many societies across the globe, sometimes overruling other major identity markers such as kinship, social class, and ethnicity or nationality. From an anthropological point of view, spirituality and religion are part of a cultural system's *superstructure*, earlier defined as the collective body of ideas, beliefs, and values by which members of a culture make sense of the world and their place in it. In contrast to theology or other disciplines, anthropology examines the entirety of shared concepts concerning the ultimate shape and substance of reality in terms of a people's **worldview**.

Notably, just 16 percent of the world's population is categorized as nonreligious (**Figure 23.1**). A small minority in that category is atheist, a broad label covering a range of worldviews, including individually held spiritual beliefs that do not fit any formally institutionalized religion.

As touched on in earlier chapters, and here discussed in greater detail, the superstructure of cultural systems is intricately connected with the infrastructure and social structure. Guided by our barrel model, we therefore expect adaptations in the superstructure when there are technological, economic, social, and/or political changes. Based on that principle, worldwide transformations in the ideological landscape are to be anticipated as an integral component of globalization. Reviewing world history for the past few thousand years, scholars recognize radical transformations in religious and spiritual beliefs and rituals everywhere. Taking the long view, we discover that, like political states discussed in the previous chapter, most religions we know today are, in fact, not that old. And even those that appear to be old are quite different from when they began.

In this chapter we offer a cross-cultural review and comparative historical perspective on a wide range of spiritual traditions and religions. We explain how societies have developed worldviews concerning the non-ordinary, mysterious, transcendental, supernatural, or metaphysical—cultural superstructures with particular repertoires of spiritual beliefs, ritual practices, and religious institutions, often considered sacred or holy.

worldview The collective body of ideas that members of a culture generally share concerning the ultimate shape and substance of their reality.

IN THIS CHAPTER YOU WILL LEARN TO

- Articulate how religion is related to other parts of a cultural system.

- Distinguish a cross-cultural variety of supernatural beings and spiritual forces.

- Compare different types of rituals and their functions in society.

- Describe how religions legitimize spiritual leadership.

- Recognize why places become sacred sites and turn into pilgrimage destinations.

- Explain beliefs in evil magic, or witchcraft, linking this to fear and social control.

- Interpret why shamanic healing is thought to be effective.

- Analyze the connection between cultural upheaval and new religious movements.

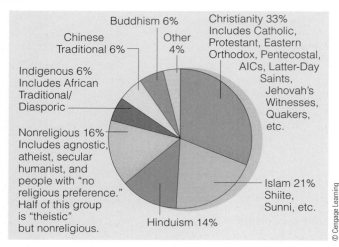

Buddhism 6%

Chinese Traditional 6%

Other 4%

Christianity 33% Includes Catholic, Protestant, Eastern Orthodox, Pentecostal, AICs, Latter-Day Saints, Jehovah's Witnesses, Quakers, etc.

Indigenous 6% Includes African Traditional/ Diasporic

Nonreligious 16% Includes agnostic, atheist, secular humanist, and people with "no religious preference." Half of this group is "theistic" but nonreligious.

Islam 21% Shiite, Sunni, etc.

Hinduism 14%

© Cengage Learning

Figure 23.1 Major Religions of the World This chart shows the world's major religions with percentages of their adherents. The total adds up to more than 100 percent due to rounding. Two have enormous followings: Christianity, with almost 2.2 billion adherents (half of whom are Roman Catholic), and Islam, with about 1.7 billion (an overwhelming majority of whom are Sunnis). Within both religions are numerous major and minor divisions, splits, and sects.

Sources: adherents.com; Pew Research Center, 2011.

Roles of Spirituality and Religion

Among people in all societies, particular spiritual or religious beliefs and practices fulfill individual and collective psychological and emotional needs. They reduce anxiety by providing an orderly view of the universe and answers to existential questions, including those concerning suffering and death. They provide a path by which people transcend the burdens of mortal existence and attain, if only momentarily, hope and relief.

Spiritual or religious beliefs and practices also serve numerous cultural purposes. For instance, a religion held in common by a group of people reinforces community values and provides moral guidelines for personal conduct. It also offers narratives and rituals used to confirm a social hierarchy and sanction political power; conversely, it may allow for narratives *countering* the legitimacy of powerholders, even providing justifications and rituals to resist and challenge them. Last but not least, people often turn to religion or spirituality in the hope of reaching a specific goal, such as restoring health, securing a harvest, ending violence, or being rescued from danger (**Figure 23.2**).

Figure 23.2 Bugi Sailors Praying, Indonesia The Bugi of Sulawesi (Celebes) are famous for their oceangoing schooners. For generations, these Indonesian seafarers have plied the waters between Malaysia and Australia, transporting spices and other freight. Life at sea is risky—sudden storms, piracy, and other mishaps—and sailors pray for safety. This prayerful Bugi gathering in Jakarta on Java Island took place on a holiday ending Ramadan, the Islamic month of fasting. During that time Muslims refrain from eating, drinking liquids, smoking, and sexual activities, from sunrise to sunset. This taboo serves to purify thought and build restraint for Allah's sake.

Anthropologists recognize that not everyone believes in a supernatural force or entity, but they also agree that there is no known culture that does not provide some set of ideas about existence beyond ordinary and empirically verifiable reality, or—for lack of a better word—ideas concerning the supernatural or metaphysical. Because such ideas serve cultural purposes and fulfill emotional and psychological needs, it makes sense that spirituality and religion developed tens of thousands of years ago and spread across the globe.

In the wake of major technological inventions and new discoveries since the 1600s, European intellectuals predicted that magic, myth, and religion would be replaced by empirical research, proven facts, and scientific theories. They expected that as science progressed, beliefs and rituals based on what they argued to be ignorance and superstition would gradually disappear. Some even forecasted the end of religion altogether. But to date, and despite tremendous scientific achievements, that has not occurred. In many places, the opposite trend seems to prevail, in particular where radical technological, social, and economic transformations destabilize the long-established cultural order, challenge deeply embedded worldviews, and leave people feeling insecure and threatened. Confronted by sweeping changes over which people have little or no control, many turn to religion and spirituality.

Anthropological Approach to Spirituality and Religion

Worldwide, people are inspired and guided by strongly held ideas about the supernatural, putting into practice what they deeply believe to be true or right. It is not the responsibility of anthropologists to pass judgment on the metaphysical truth of any particular faith system, but it is their challenge to show how each embodies a number of revealing facts about humanity and the particular cultural superstructure, or worldview, within which these religious or spiritual beliefs are ideologically embedded.

Based on a cross-cultural and comparative historical perspective on worldviews, we define **religion** as an organized system of ideas about the spiritual sphere or the supernatural, along with associated ceremonial practices by which people try to interpret and/or influence aspects of the universe otherwise beyond their access or control. Similar to religion, **spirituality** is concerned with the sacred, as distinguished from ordinary reality, but it is often individual rather than collective and

does not require a formal institution. Both indicate that many aspects of the human experience are thought to be beyond natural or scientific explanation.

Because no culture, including those of modern industrial and postindustrial societies, has achieved complete certainty in controlling existing or future conditions and circumstances of human life, spirituality and/or religion continue to play a role in all known cultures. However, considerable variability exists globally (**Figure 23.3**).

At one end of the anthropological spectrum are food-foraging peoples, whose technological ability to control their natural environment is limited. Broadly speaking, they hold that nature is pregnant with the spiritual. Embedded and manifested in all aspects of their culture, spirituality permeates their daily activities—from food hunting or gathering to making fires, building homes, and conversations about life before or after death. It also mirrors and confirms the egalitarian nature of social relations in their societies, in that individuals do not plead with high-ranking deities for aid the way members of stratified societies more typically do. Their holistic worldview is often referred to as *naturalistic*, an imprecise but workable term.

At the other end of our spectrum are state societies with commercial or industrial economies, sophisticated technologies, and social stratification based on a complex division of labor. There, high-ranking social groups typically seek to control and manage the construction of a society's worldview as an ideological means of legitimizing and reinforcing their vested interests in its hierarchical structure. Usually featuring a ranked order of supernatural beings—for instance, God and (in some religions) the angels, saints, or other holy figures—it simultaneously reflects and reinforces the stratified system in which it is embedded. In such societies, religion tends to be less integrated into everyday activities, and its practice is usually confined to specific times, occasions, and locations.

Religions provide a powerful ideology justifying inequality in a state society, but may also inspire subordinated peoples to envision an alternative social order freeing them from exploitation, repression, and humiliation. Thus, religiously motivated social movements have challenged political establishments.

---

religion An organized system of ideas about the spiritual sphere or the supernatural, along with associated ceremonial practices by which people try to interpret and/or influence aspects of the universe otherwise beyond their control.

spirituality Concern with the sacred, as distinguished from material matters. In contrast to religion, spirituality is often individual rather than collective and does not require a distinctive format or traditional organization.

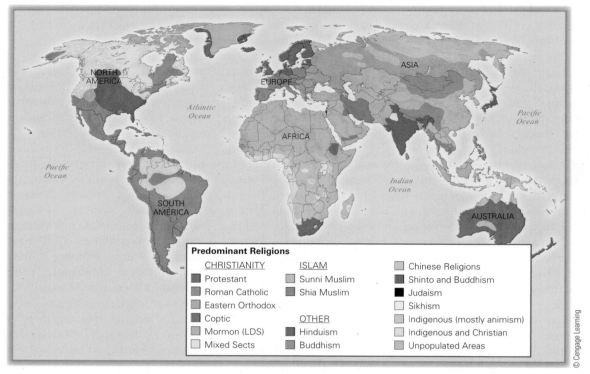

Figure 23.3 Global Distribution of Predominant Religions This map depicts only the global distribution of major religions, indicating where they predominate. In some areas, the mixture of different religions is such that no single faith is shared by most of that region's inhabitants. Not detailed enough to show pockets with significant numbers of a particular faith, it also omits many religions that are dispersed or eclipsed by others—including several worldwide ones such as Ahmadiyya (a Muslim sect, with 10 million adherents); Jehovah's Witnesses (a Christian sect with 7 million adherents); and Bahá'í (with 6 million adherents, emphasizing the spiritual unity of all mankind and recognizing divine messengers from various religions).

Myth and the Mapping of a Sacred Worldview

Because much remains beyond human capacity to actually observe and explain based on obvious or empirical evidence alone, people have creatively worked out narratives explaining the fundamentals of human existence—where we and everything in our world came from, why we are here, and where we are going. Describing a worldview, these narratives are referred to as **myths** (*mythos*, Greek for "word," "speech") and play a fundamental role in religious and spiritual beliefs. Mapping a people's *cosmology*—their understanding of the universe, its form and working—myths are believed to be true, even sacred, by those subscribing to the particular worldview engendering such narratives.

Typically, a myth features supernatural forces or beings engaged in extraordinary or miraculous performances. It may offer a morality play, providing an ethical code for its audience and guidelines for human behavior. For example, the Puranas (a body of religious texts, including cosmological myths, considered sacred by Buddhists and Hindus) are rich in such material. So are the Bible, Koran, and Torah, each held sacred in distinct but historically related religions originating in Southwest Asia. We will discuss myths further within the context of art in the next chapter, but here it is important to underscore that these stories, whether orally transmitted or in writing, have been passed on from generation to generation and inform believers with a sacred map of the cosmos or universe and their place in it.

Supernatural Beings and Spiritual Forces

A hallmark of religion is belief in spiritual forces and supernatural beings. Attempting to control by religious means what cannot be controlled in other ways, humans turn to prayer, sacrifice, and other religious or spiritual rituals. Their actions presuppose the existence of spiritual forces that can

---

myth A sacred narrative that explains the fundamentals of human existence—where we and everything in our world came from, why we are here, and where we are going.

© The Art Gallery Collection/Alamy

Figure 23.4 Judeo-Christian God Giving Life to Adam The patriarchal nature of traditional Euramerican society is depicted on the ceiling of the Sistine Chapel in Rome, Italy. The image of a supreme male diety creating the first man, named Adam ("human being"), is culturally articulated and ideologically justified by its Judeo-Christian theology. Afterward, according to this biblical story, the first woman, named Eve, is formed from Adam's rib.

be tapped into, or supernatural beings interested in human affairs and available for aid. In many cultures, these supernatural forces or spiritual beings are associated with unique geographic locations valued as sacred sites—extraordinary rocks, lakes, wells, waterfalls, mountains, and so forth.

Supernatural beings can be divided into three categories: deities (gods and goddesses), ancestral spirits, and other sorts of spirit beings. Although the variety of deities and spirits recognized by the world's cultures is tremendous, it is possible to make certain generalizations about them.

Gods and Goddesses

Not all religions *anthropomorphize* the divine, but many do. Symbolically constructing a divine order that mirrors a society's gender structure, many religions recognize male and female deities. Gods and goddesses, or divinities, are the great and more remote supernatural beings. Generally speaking, cultures that subordinate women to men attribute masculine gender to the more powerful gods or supreme deity. For instance, in traditional Christian religions believers speak of God as a father who had a divine son born from a human mother but do not entertain thoughts of God as a mother or as a divine daughter (Figure 23.4). Such male-privileging religions developed in many societies traditionally based on the herding of animals or intensive agriculture, frequent warfare, and politics controlled by men.

Goddesses, by contrast, are likely to be prominent in societies where women play a significant role in the economy and enjoy relative equality with men. Such societies are most often those that depend on crop cultivation traditionally carried out solely or mostly by women. Typically, these may feature fertility and earth goddesses.

Some religions recognize deities represented as male–female combinations. For example, one of the Greek gods, also recognized in the Roman empire, was Hermaphroditus, the beautiful two-sexed son of Hermes (alias Mercury) and Venus (alias Aphrodite). A similar third-gender divinity is recognized by Hindus worshiping Ardhanarishvara ("the Lord who is half woman").

If a religion recognizes only one supremely powerful divinity as creator and master of the universe, we speak of **monotheism**. If it acknowledges more than one divinity, each governing a particular domain, we label it **polytheism**. Gods and goddesses of ancient Greece illustrate the latter: Zeus ruled the sky, Poseidon the sea, and Hades the underworld and the dead. In addition to these three brothers, Greek mythology features a host of other deities, both male and female, each similarly concerned with specific aspects of life and the universe. Athena and Nike, for instance, were goddesses of war and victory, respectively. A **pantheon**, or the collection of gods and goddesses such as those of the Greeks, is common in many religions, today most famously in Hinduism.

Because states typically have grown through conquest, often their pantheons have expanded, with local deities of conquered peoples being incorporated into the official state pantheon. A frequent feature of pantheons is the presence of a supreme deity, who may be all but totally ignored by humans. Aztecs of the Mexican highlands, for instance, recognized a supreme duo to whom they paid little attention. Assuming this divine pair was unlikely to be interested in ordinary humans, they devoted themselves to lesser deities thought to be more directly concerned with human affairs.

Ancestral Spirits

Beliefs in ancestral spirits support the concept that human beings consist of intertwined components: body/matter (physical) and mind/soul (spiritual). This dualistic concept carries with it the possibility of a spirit being freed from the body—through dream, trance, or death—and even having a separate existence. Frequently, where a belief in

monotheism The belief in only one supremely powerful divinity as creator and master of the universe.

polytheism The belief in multiple gods and/or goddesses, as contrasted with monotheism—the belief in one god or goddess.

pantheon All the gods and goddesses of a people.

ancestral spirits exists, these nonphysical beings are seen as retaining an active interest and membership in society.

Beliefs in ancestral spirits are found in many parts of the world, especially among people having unilineal descent systems with their associated ancestor orientation. In several African cultures, the concept is highly elaborate, and people believe ancestral spirits behave much like humans. They are able to feel hot, cold, and pain and may even die a second death by drowning or burning. Because spirits sometimes participate in family and lineage events, seats will be provided for them, even though they are invisible. If spirits are annoyed, they may send sickness or death. Eventually, they are reborn as new members of their lineage, so adults need to observe infants closely to determine just who has been reborn.

Ancestor spirits also play an important role in the patrilineal society of traditional China. Giving birth to sons is historically regarded as an obligation to the ancestors because boys inherit their father's ancestral duties. For the gift of life, a boy is forever indebted to his parents, owing them obedience, deference, and a comfortable old age. Even after their death, he has to provide for them in the spirit world, placing food, money, and incense on ancestral altars on the anniversaries of their births and deaths.

Other Types of Supernatural Beings and Spiritual Forces

Animism

One widespread concept concerning supernatural beings is **animism**, a belief that nature is enlivened or energized by distinct personalized spirit beings separable from physical bodies or the material substance they inhabit. Spirits such as souls and ghosts are thought to dwell in humans, animals, and plants, as well as human-made artifacts and natural features such as stones, mountains, and wells; for animists, the world is filled with particular spirits.

These spirit beings are a highly diverse lot. Less remote than gods and goddesses, they may be benevolent, malevolent, or just plain neutral. Involved in people's daily affairs, they also may be awesome, terrifying, lovable, or mischievous. Because they may be pleased or irritated by human actions, people are obliged to be concerned about them.

Animism is typical of those who see themselves as being a part of nature rather than superior to it (Figure 23.5). This includes most food foragers and food gardeners, among others. Deities, if they are believed to exist at all in such societies, may be seen as having created the world and perhaps making it fit to live in; but in animism, spirits are the ones to beseech when ill, the ones to help or hinder the shaman, and the ones whom the ordinary hunter may meet when off in the wilderness.

Animatism

Although supernatural power is often thought of as being vested in spirit beings, it does not have to be. Such is the case with **animatism**—the belief that nature is enlivened or energized by an impersonal force or supernatural energy, which may make itself manifest in any special place, thing, or living creature. This basic concept, which probably developed well before the first transition from food foraging to food production 10,000 years ago, is still present in many societies around the

Figure 23.5 Inuit Food Ritual Inuit of Arctic Canada refer to spirit beings as *anirniit* (singular *anirniq*, meaning "breath") and still obey certain taboos and perform rituals when killing game animals and dividing the meat. This is to avoid offending the animal's spirit (which remains alive and may take revenge on the hunter). Today, most Inuit are Christians, and their concept of *anirniq* is akin to "soul." But traditional food rituals continue. In this photo, Inuit at Baffin Island pray before a shared Easter feast of fish and seal meat.

world today. For example, in China it appears in the form of a concept known as *qi* (or *ch'i*), which may be translated as "vital energy." Inuit people in Arctic Canada think of this force in terms of a "cosmic breath-soul" they call *sila*. In northeastern America, Algonquian-speaking indigenous peoples refer to impersonal spirit power as *manitou*.

One of the best-studied examples of animatism can be found in the Pacific where Oceanic peoples inhabiting hundreds of islands share a concept they refer to as *mana*. Not unlike the idea of a cosmic energy passing into and through everything, affecting living and nonliving matter alike, *mana* is probably best defined as "supernaturally conferred potency" (Keesing, 1992, p. 236)—similar to "the force" in the *Star Wars* films. Traditional Maori, Tahitians, Tongans, and other Oceanic peoples typically attribute success (identified by actual achievements such as triumph in combat, bountiful harvest, abundant fish or game, and so on) to *mana*—and see it as proof of *mana*. In short, this metaphysical concept rests on pragmatic evidence.

Animism (a belief in distinct spirit beings) and animatism (which lacks particular substance or individual form) are not mutually exclusive and are often found in the same culture. This is the case among the Inuit pictured in Figure 23.5, who believe in spirit beings known as *anirniit* as well as in the impersonal spirit power they call *sila* (Merkur, 1983).

In many religious traditions, certain geographic places are thought to be spiritually significant or are held sacred for various reasons, including ideas here discussed in terms of animism and animatism. Typically, such sites are rivers, lakes, waterfalls, islands, forests, caves, and—especially—mountains. We revisit the topic of sacred sites later in the chapter.

Religious Specialists

Most cultures include individuals who guide others in their spiritual search and ritual practices. Thought to be inspired, enlightened, or even holy, they command respect for their skills in contacting and influencing spiritual beings and manipulating or connecting to supernatural forces. Often, they display unique personality traits that make them particularly well suited to perform these tasks for which they have undergone special training.

Priests and Priestesses

In societies with resources to support a full-time religious specialist, a **priest or priestess** will be authorized to perform sacred rituals and mediate between fellow humans and supernatural powers, divine spirits, or deities. In many societies, they are familiar figures known by official titles such as *lama, kahuna, imam, priest, minister, rabbi, swami,* or *copa pitào*. How they dress, what they eat, where they live, and numerous other indicators may distinguish them from others in society and symbolically indicate their special status.

Reserving exclusive rights to exercise spiritual power, groups of priests and/or priestesses bond together in an effort to monopolize the means of sacred practice. This includes controlling holy sites of worship, supervising prescribed rituals, and maintaining possession of regalia, relics, statues, images, texts, and other representations of holiness. In so doing, they also create, promote, and maintain the ideological sources needed to symbolically construct the religious authority from which they derive their legitimacy.

When deities are identified in masculine terms, it is not surprising that the most important religious leadership positions are reserved for men. Such is the case in Judaism, Islam, as well as the Roman Catholic Church, the latter of which has always been headed by a male pope and his all-male council, the College of Cardinals.

Female religious specialists are likely to be found only in societies in which women are acknowledged to significantly contribute to the economy, and gods and goddesses are both recognized (Lehman, 2002). Also, all around the world women fully devoted to a religious life have formed their own gender-segregated institutions such as all-female convents headed by an abbess. Such nunneries not only exist in countries with longstanding Christian traditions, but were also founded in the Himalayas and many other Buddhist regions in southern and eastern Asia, including Taiwan, as described by American anthropologist Hillary Crane in the Biocultural Connection on the next page.

Spiritual Lineages: Legitimizing Religious Leadership

As with political institutions discussed in the previous chapter, religious organizations are maintained by rules that define ideological boundaries, establish membership criteria, and regulate continuity of legitimate leadership in the faith community. And, like other institutions, religions have always been challenged by changes. Even in a highly stable cultural system, every generation must deal with natural transitions in the life cycle, including death

---

animism The belief that nature is enlivened or energized by distinct personalized spirit beings separable from bodies.

animatism The belief that nature is enlivened or energized by an impersonal spiritual force or supernatural energy, which may make itself manifest in any special place, thing, or living creature.

priest or priestess A full-time religious specialist formally recognized for his or her role in guiding the religious practices of others and for contacting and influencing supernatural powers.

BIOCULTURAL CONNECTION

Change Your Karma and Change Your Sex?

By Hillary Crane

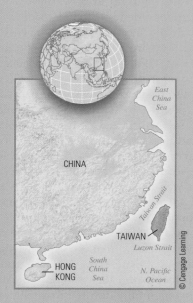

As Mahayana Buddhists, Taiwanese Chan (Zen) monastics believe that all humans are able to reach enlightenment and be released from reincarnation. But they believe it is easier for some because of the situation into which they are born—for example, if one is born in a country where Buddhism is practiced, in a family that teaches proper behavior, or with exceptional mental or physical gifts.

Chan monastics view contrasting human circumstances as the result of the karma accrued in previous lives. They believe certain behavior—such as diligently practicing Buddhism—improves karma and the chances of attaining spiritual goals in this lifetime or coming back

in a better birth. Other behavior—such as killing a living being, eating meat, desiring or becoming attached to things or people—accrues bad karma.

One way karma manifests itself is in one's sex. Taiwanese Buddhists believe that being born female makes it harder to attain spiritual goals. This idea comes, in part, from the inferior status of women in Taiwan and the belief that their "complicated bodies" and monthly menstruation cycles can distract them. Moreover, they believe, women are more enmeshed in their families than men, and their emotional ties keep them focused on worldly rather than spiritual tasks.

Taiwanese Buddhists who decide to become monks and nuns must break from their families to enter a monastery. Because women are thought to be more attached to their families than are men, leaving home is seen as a particularly big step for nuns and a sign that they are more like men than most women. In fact, a nun's character is considered masculine, unlike the frightened, indecisive, and emotional traits usually associated with women in Taiwan. When they leave home nuns even stop referring to themselves as women and call one another *shixiong* ("dharma brother"). They use this linguistic change to signal that they identify themselves as men and to remind one another to behave like men, particularly like the monks at the temple.

Monastics also reduce their attachments to worldly things like music and food. Nuns usually emphasize forsaking food and eat as little as possible. Their appearance, already quite masculine because they shave their heads and wear loose, gray clothing, becomes even more so when they lose weight—particularly in their hips, breasts, and thighs. Also, after becoming monastics, they often experience a slowing or stopping of their menses. Although these physical changes can be attributed to change in diet and lifestyle, the nuns point to them as signs they are becoming men, making progress toward their spiritual goals, and improving their karma.

BIOCULTURAL QUESTION

The Zen Buddhist ideal of enlightenment, realized when the soul is released from reincarnation, prescribes an extreme ascetic lifestyle for nuns that makes them physically incapable of biological reproduction. Do you think that their infertility allows these female monastics to emotionally adapt to a way of life that denies them motherhood?

Written expressly for this text, 2008. For a more detailed treatment of this topic, see Crane, H. (2001). Men in spirit: The masculinization of Taiwanese Buddhist nuns. Ph.D dissertation, Brown University.

---

of religious leaders. In many religions, spiritual leadership is thought to be vested in divine authority, representing or even embodying the divine itself. How do religions secure legitimate successors and avoid disruption and confusion?

Several major religions follow a principle of leadership in which divine authority is passed down from a spiritual founding figure, such as a prophet or saint, to a chain of successors who derive legitimacy as religious leaders from their status in such a lineage. Here identified as **spiritual lineage**, this principle has been worked out in numerous cross-cultural variations over the course of thousands of years. It not only applies to leadership of entire religions but to segmental divisions of religions, such as sects and orders.

spiritual lineage A principle of leadership in which divine authority is passed down from a spiritual founding figure, such as a prophet or saint, to a chain of successors.

Whereas kings in traditional political dynasties derive legitimacy from their ancestral blood lineage, religious leaders obtain it from their spiritual line of descent as specified in each particular religious tradition. The longer these lineages have existed, the greater their opportunities for building up a fund of symbolic capital—ideas and rituals, including sacred gestures, dances, songs, and texts. This fund also includes regalia, paintings, statues, and sacred architecture such as shrines, tombs, and temples, along with the land on which they stand. Thus, some religious leaders and their followers have accumulated a considerable amount of material wealth utilized in the exercise of religious authority, in addition to the immaterial holdings of traditional knowledge and sacred rituals.

Here, to illustrate the cross-cultural range of spiritual lineages, we distinguish four major forms. First, in some religions, spiritual leaders or high-ranking priests claim divine authority based on recognized biological descent from a common ancestor believed to have been a prophet, saint, or otherwise sacred, holy, or even divine being. Such is the case with *kohanim*, high-ranking Israelite priests, claiming patrilineal descent from the legendary high priest Aaron believed to have lived about 3,500 years ago.

In other religions, leaders personally groom, train, and appoint a spiritual heir, a successor tasked with guarding and continuing the spiritual legacy of the order or sect as established by its founder. For example, a sect of Muslim mystics known as Sufi is widely dispersed across Asia and North Africa and historically divided into many dozens of orders, or brotherhoods. Each brotherhood is headed by a master teacher, known by an honorific title such as *sheikh*. The sheikh derives his spiritual authority from his position in a *silsila* (Arabic, meaning "chain"), named after a founding saint who originally laid down a particular method of prayer and ritual practiced by followers seeking oneness with God (Abun-Nasr, 2007; Anjum, 2006).

A third form of legitimizing the authority of a religious leader is by election. In such cases, a group of leading elders comes together in a ritual gathering at a traditionally designated location and chooses one of their own to succeed the deceased leader. One of the best-known examples in world history is the election of a pope by a group of cardinals— "princes" of the Roman Catholic Church who proclaim the new pope to be the divinely ordained spiritual heir of St. Peter, Vicar of Christ. Believed by 1.2 billion Christians to hold the sacred key to heaven, the pope is traditionally addressed as "Holy Father." The current Pope Benedict XVI is the 265th holder of this nearly 2,000-year-old religious office.

A fourth and final example of spiritual lineage is found in Tibetan Buddhism, divided into four major orders or schools. Each has its own monasteries, monks of various ranks from novice to lama, and a wealth of ancient texts, ritual practices, meditations, and other sacred knowledge passed on largely by oral tradition. Highest in rank among the monks are reincarnated saints. These are individuals who, fully emanating the divine Buddha spirit, achieved enlightenment during their lifetime; led by compassion, they chose to give up *nirvana* ("eternal bliss") after death to return to life on earth. To fulfill this role, such a saintly person must be recognized. Toward this end, a select group of high-ranking lamas guided by omens seeks out a newborn boy believed to be a *tulku* ("emanated incarnation") of a recently deceased saintly lama in their spiritual lineage. Once they find the little boy, they ritually induct and enthrone him and begin grooming him for his designated spiritual leadership position in the Buddhist order (**Figure 23.6**).

Of about 500 *tulku* lineages in Tibetan Buddhism, the most famous is the Dalai Lama ("teacher who is spiritually as deep as the ocean"). This illustrious lineage traces its origins to a high-ranking monk named Gendun Drup (1391–1474), thought to have embodied the Buddha spirit of compassion. A few years after the death of the thirteenth Dalai Lama in 1933, high-ranking monks from his order identified a 2-year-old boy in a small farming village as his reincarnated "wisdom mind." Renaming him Tenzin Gyatso, they later enthroned the little *tulku* as His Holiness, the fourteenth Dalai Lama— the highest-ranking political and spiritual position among Tibetan Buddhists for centuries.

Shamans

Societies without religious professionals have existed far longer than those that have them. Although lacking full-time specialists, they have always included individuals considered capable of connecting with supernatural beings and forces—individuals such as shamans. That capacity, partially based on learned techniques, is also based on personality and particular emotional experiences that could be described as "mystical." Supplied with spiritual knowledge in the form of a vision or some other extraordinary revelation, they are believed to be supernaturally empowered to heal the sick, change the weather, control the movements of animals, and foretell the future. As they perfect these and related skills, they may combine the role of a diviner and a healer, becoming a shaman.

Originally, the word *shaman* referred to medical-religious specialists, or spiritual guides, among the Tungus and other Siberian pastoral nomads with animist beliefs. By means of various techniques such as fasting, drumming, chanting, or dancing, as well as hallucinogenic mushrooms (*fly agaric*), these shamans enter into a trance. In this waking dream state, they experience visions of an alternate reality inhabited by spirit beings such as guardian animal spirits who may assist with healing. Similar spiritual practices exist in many indigenous cultures outside Siberia, especially in the Americas. For that reason, the term *shaman* is frequently applied to a variety of part-time spiritual leaders, diviners, and traditional healers active in many other parts of the world (Kehoe, 2000).

VISUAL COUNTERPOINT

Figure 23.6 Buddhist Lama Dilgo Khyentsé Rinpoche and His Reincarnation Dilgo Khyentsé Yangsi Rinpoche There are many spiritual lineages in Tibetan Buddhism not as well known as that of the Dalai Lama. The monk on the left is a reincarnation of a Buddhist master identified as the first Khyentsé ("Compassionate Wisdom"). In 1832 at age 12, the first Khyentsé was recognized as the combined incarnation of an 8th-century Tibetan religious king and a profoundly learned Buddhist master. Renamed Jamyang Khyentsé Wangpo and receiving intensive training, he was ordained throne-holder of a major Tibetan monastery and became a living saint. Dying in 1892, he reincarnated in 1910 as a little boy—a *tulku* renamed Dilgo Khyentsé Rinpoche (*Rinpoche*, a title given to *tulkus*, means "Precious One"). Before Dilgo Khyentsé passed away at the Shechen Monastery in Nepal at age 81, he gave subtle indications concerning how and where his "wisdom mind" would be reincarnated. After his death, another high-ranking lama in his order, who had been his close friend and disciple, had visions and dreams. Guided by these instructions, a search party identified a boy born in Nepal in the summer of 1993 as his reincarnation. The boy (*right*) was renamed Dilgo Khyentsé Yangsi in 1996. With his legitimate status in this *tulku* lineage confirmed by the Dalai Lama, the young monk was enthroned at his predecessor's monastery the following year.

Anthropologist Michael Harner (see Anthropologist of Note feature), a modern-day shamanic practitioner famous for his participant observation among Shuar (or Jivaro) Indian shamans in the Amazon rainforest, defined a **shaman** as someone who at will enters an altered state of consciousness "to contact and utilize an ordinarily hidden reality in order to acquire knowledge, power, and to help other persons. The shaman has at least one, and usually more, 'spirits' in his or her personal service" (Harner, 1980, p. 20).

shaman A person who at will enters an altered state of consciousness to contact and utilize an ordinarily hidden reality in order to acquire knowledge, power, and to help others.

Shamanic Experience

Someone may become a shaman by passing through stages of learning and practical experience, often involving psychological and emotional ordeals brought about by isolation, fasting, physical torture, sensory deprivation, and/or *hallucination* (Latin, for "mental wandering"). Hallucinations may occur when one is in a trance state; they can come about spontaneously, but they can also be induced by drumming or consuming mind-altering drugs such as psychoactive vines or mushrooms.

Because shamanism is rooted in altered states of consciousness and the human nervous system universally produces these trance states, individuals experience

ANTHROPOLOGIST OF NOTE

Michael J. Harner (b. 1929)

A world-renowned expert on shamanism, American anthropologist **Michael Harner** studied at the University of California, Berkeley. Starting out in archaeology and collaborating with Alfred Kroeber on Mohave pottery research, he later switched to ethnography. Intrigued by the Jívaro, legendary for shrinking human heads, he ventured into eastern Ecuador's tropical forest in 1956, at age 27. For nearly a year, he lived among these Amazonian Indians, now better known as Shuar. They still subsisted on food gardens and by hunting and gathering; they fiercely guarded their freedom and launched raids on enemy tribes.

Holding an animistic worldview, the Shuar distinguish between what Harner has identified as ordinary and non-ordinary realities. They believe that supernatural forces govern daily life and that spirit beings can be perceived and engaged only by shamans capable of entering non-ordinary reality. They access this reality by drinking *natema*, a bitter brew made from a jungle vine known as *ayahuasca* ("vine of the soul"). As they told Harner, drinking this hallucinogenic potion, shamans enter an altered state of consciousness in which they perceive and

engage what they believe are the "true" forces governing sickness and health, life and death.

Harner returned to the Upper Amazon in 1960 for more ethnographic fieldwork, this time among the Conibo in eastern Peru. Seeking greater insight on *ayahuasca's* psychological impact on the native cosmology, he drank the magic brew. Passing through the door of perception into the shamanic view of reality, he found himself in a world beyond his "wildest dreams": a supernatural landscape inhabited by spirit beings. Singing incredibly beautiful music, they began to carry his soul away and he felt he was dying. Coming out of this experience, and later ones with Conibo shamans, Harner realized that anthropologists had seriously underestimated the powerful influence hallucinogenic drugs had on Amazonian Indian ideologies and practices.

In 1963, Harner earned his doctorate at UC Berkeley, and the next year went back to Shuar country for additional shamanic experience. In 1966, having taught at UC Berkeley and served as associate director of the Lowie Museum of Anthropology, he became a visiting professor at Yale and Columbia Universities. In 1969, he did fieldwork among a neighboring Jivaroan-speaking tribe, the Achuara, and the following year joined the graduate faculty of the New School for Social Research in New York City. Over the next few years he published his monograph, *The Jívaro: People of the Sacred Waterfalls*, an edited volume titled *Hallucinogens and Shamanism*, and numerous academic articles.

Continuing cross-cultural research on shamanism, Harner became interested in drumming as an alternative means of achieving what he now identifies as SSC (shamanic state of consciousness). Learning and using this method of monotonous percussive sound ("sonic driving"), he began offering training workshops and in 1979 founded the Center for Shamanic Studies. A year later, he published *The Way of the Shaman*, a groundbreaking book now translated into a dozen languages.

Collaborating with his wife, clinical psychologist Sandra Harner, he established the Foundation for Shamanic Studies, a nonprofit charitable and educational organization dedicated to the preservation, study, and transmission of shamanic knowledge. Its Urgent Assistance program supports the survival of shamanic healing knowledge among such indigenous peoples as the Canadian Inuit, Scandinavian Sámi, and Tuvans of central Asia and Siberia.

Since resigning from his university professorship in 1987, this anthropologist has been fully devoted to shamanic studies and healing practice, training others, including physicians, psychotherapists, and other health care professionals. The Foundation's faculty assists him in this work.

In his most recent book, *Cave and Cosmos: Shamanic Encounters with Spirits and Heavens* (2013), Harner recounts and compares experiences of shamanic "ascension" and offers instructions on his core-shamanism techniques.

© 2011 France Viana

Michael Harner—anthropologist, shaman, and founder of the Foundation for Shamanic Studies in Mill Valley, California.

Figure 23.7 Traditional Shaman in Mongolia This female shaman in Mongolia, bordering Siberia, uses a drum crafted from the wood of a tree struck by lightning and covered with leather made from a female red deer. It is believed that when the shaman goes into a trance, her drum transforms into a magical steed that carries her into the dark sky of her ancestors.

similarly structured visual, auditory, somatic (touch), olfactory (smell), and gustatory (taste) hallucinations. The widespread occurrence of shamanism and the remarkable similarities among shamanic traditions everywhere are consequences of this universal neurological inheritance. But the meanings ascribed to sensations experienced in altered states and made of their content are culturally determined; hence, despite their overall similarities, indigenous traditions typically vary in particular details (Figure 23.7).

Shamans can be contrasted with priests and priestesses in that the latter serve dieties of the society. As agents of divine beings, priests and priestesses order believers what to think and do, whereas shamans may challenge or negotiate with the spirits. In return for services rendered, shamans may collect a fee—money, fresh meat, or some other valuable. In some cases, shamans are rewarded by the prestige that comes as a result of a healing or some other extraordinary feat.

Shamanic Healing

Shamana are essentially spiritual go-betweens who acts on behalf of some human client, often to bring about healing or to foretell a future event. Typically, they enter a trance state, experience the sensation of traveling to the alternate world, and see and interact with spirit beings. Shamans try to impose their will upon these spirits, an inherently dangerous contest, considering the superhuman powers that spirits are thought to possess.

An example of this can be seen in the trance dances of the Ju/'hoansi Bushmen of Africa's Kalahari Desert. Traditional Ju/'hoansi belief holds that illness and misfortune are caused by invisible arrows shot by spirits.

The arrows can be removed by healers, those who possess the powerful healing force called *n/um* (the Ju/'hoansi equivalent of *mana*). Some healers can activate *n/um* by solo singing or instrument playing, but more often this is accomplished through the medicinal curing ceremony or trance dance (Figure 23.8).

Acting on behalf of a client or patient, a shaman may put on a dramatic performance; such an artful

Figure 23.8 Ju/'hoansi Shaman Healer and Helper in Trance Dance Ju/'hoansi shamans may find their way into a trance by dancing around a fire to the pulsating sound of melodies sung by women. Eventually, sometimes after several hours, "the music, the strenuous dancing, the smoke, the heat of the fire, and the healers' intense concentration cause their *n/um* to heat up. When it comes to a boil, trance is achieved. At that moment, the *n/um* becomes available as a powerful healing force to serve the entire community. In trance, a healer lays hands on and ritually cures everyone sitting around the fire" (Shostak, 2000, pp. 259–260).

demonstration of spiritual power assures members of the community that prevailing upon supernatural powers and spirits otherwise beyond human control can bring about invulnerability from attack, success at love, or the return of health.

The precise effects of the shamanic treatment are not known, but its psychological and emotional impact is thought to contribute to the patient's recovery. For healing to occur, the shaman needs to be convinced of the effectiveness of his or her spiritual powers and techniques. Likewise, the patient must see the shaman as a genuine healing master using appropriate techniques. Finally, to close the triangle's "magic field," the community within which the shaman operates on the patient must view the healing ceremony and its practitioner as potentially effective and beneficial. From an anthropological perspective, shamanic healings can be understood by means of a three-cornered model: the *shamanic complex* (Figure 23.9). This triangle is created by the interrelationship of the shaman, the patient, and the community to which both belong.

Shamanic healing ceremonies involve social-psychological dynamics also present in Western medical treatments. Consider, for example, the *placebo effect*—the beneficial result a patient experiences after a particular treatment, due to the person's expectations concerning the treatment rather than from the treatment itself. Notably, some people involved in modern medicine work collaboratively with practitioners of traditional belief systems toward the healing of various illnesses (Harner & Harner, 2000; Offiong, 1999).

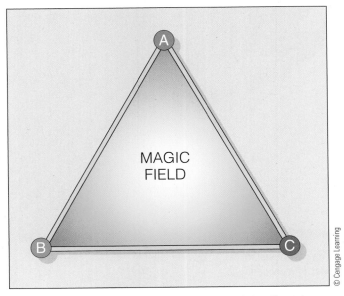

Figure 23.9 The Shamanic Complex Shamanic healing takes place within a "magic field" created when the shaman (A) and patient (B), as well as their community (C), are all convinced that the shaman is a genuine healing master using appropriate techniques that are effective and beneficial. Similar psychological processes are involved in Western medical treatments.

Ritual Performances

Rituals are culturally prescribed symbolic acts or procedures designed to guide members of a community in an orderly way through personal and collective transitions. Relieving anxiety and tensions in crises, rituals provide symbolic means of reinforcing a group's social bonds. Not all of them concern the sacred (consider, for example, college graduation ceremonies in North America). But those that do are ideologically linked to beliefs in the supernatural, playing a crucial role as spirituality or religion in action.

Anthropologists have classified several different types of ritual. These include rituals of purification, rites of passage, rites of intensification, and magical rituals, including witchcraft.

Rites of Purification: Taboo and Cleansing Ceremonies

In many religious and spiritual traditions, rituals have been developed to symbolically restore one's place in the cosmic order, removing "dirt," washing "impurity," and making "clean" in body, mind, and soul. Anthropologists specializing in comparative religion have been intrigued by the cross-cultural variation in cultural categories classifying certain animals, plants, objects, or acts as unclean or dirty and others as dangerous.

In every society, people follow certain culturally prescribed rules about what is dirty or filthy, or whichever term symbolically represents pollution—rules that say what they cannot eat, drink, touch, talk, or even think about. For instance, many millions of Hindus eat pork but avoid beef because they regard the cow as a sacred animal. On the other hand, many millions of Muslims consume beef but avoid pork because in Islam swine is considered unclean. In the words of British anthropologist Mary Douglas, "Dirt offends against order. Eliminating it is not a negative movement, but a positive effort to organise the environment" (1966, pp. 2–3).

Culturally prescribed avoidances involving ritual prohibitions are known as **taboo**, a term derived from the Polynesian word *tabu* (or *tapu*). Among Pacific Islanders it refers to something that has supernatural power and is to be avoided. It can apply to an object (such as food), a person (such as a high-ranking noble), or a place (a shrine or temple). Especially applied to blood and anything associated with sickness and death, taboos are

---

ritual A culturally prescribed symbolic act or procedure designed to guide members of a community in an orderly way through personal and collective transitions.

taboo Culturally prescribed avoidances involving ritual prohibitions, which, if not observed, lead to supernatural punishment.

taken very seriously. When a taboo is violated, believers expect supernatural punishment will follow. This penalty may come in magical form as misfortune—an unlucky accident, resulting in loss, sickness, or death. It is also possible that the taboo breaker will be punished by designated members in the community and may be ordered to undergo a purification ritual and make a sacrifice. Sometimes, the ultimate sacrifice is demanded, and the offender is executed.

For complex historical reasons of their own, some societies stress taboos much more than others. For instance, as discussed in the previous chapter, the traditional hierarchy in the Hindu caste society is religiously reinforced by strict rules against ritual pollution that govern the lives of members of the different *varnas*.

Whether someone has violated a taboo, or is otherwise no longer clean, many cultures have developed **rites of purification** to establish or restore purity. These may involve one person, but many are group or community ceremonial affairs. As symbolic acts, purification rituals are filled with spiritual or religious meaning. They impact participants emotionally and psychologically (restoring a sense of inner peace and cosmic harmony), as well as socially, such as by establishing or restoring harmony within their family, community, or some other group.

A cross-cultural comparison of these spiritual or religious ceremonies shows that the four elements of water, air, fire, and/or earth have been used in a wide range of rituals for thousands of years all across the globe. For instance, cleansing by water is very common in many forms of baptism, hot steam is used in sweat lodges, burning fragrant organic matter (such as plant leaves or resins) is used in smoking and smudging ceremonies. The human body and mind may also be subjected to rituals of internal purification by means of prayer, meditation, chanting, fasting, or dancing (**Figure 23.10**).

Figure 23.10 A Sufi *Sema* (Prayer Dance) in Aleppo, Syria Sufism, a mystical Muslim movement that emerged a thousand years ago, emphasizes the surrender of individual ego and attachment to worldly things in order to be receptive to God's grace. Known as "whirling dervishes," these Sufi dancers are part of the Mevlevi brotherhood, a spiritual lineage founded by the Persian Sufi master (*mawlana*) Jalal ad-Din ar-Rumi in the 13th century. According to Mevlevi tradition, during the *sema* the soul is freed from earthly ties and is able to jubilantly commune with the divine. (*Dervish* literally means "doorway" and is thought to be an entrance from the material world to the spiritual.) The felt hat represents personal ego's tombstone, and the wide skirt symbolizes its shroud.

Rites of Passage

Rites of passage are rituals marking important ceremonial moments when members of a society move from one distinctive social stage in life to another, such as birth, marriage, and death. When crossing the boundary (*limen*) between such stages, people briefly cease to be part of the stage left behind and have not yet become integrated into the next. Like travelers passing through a border area between two countries not controlled by either of them, they are neither here nor there. Guiding people through such uncertain transit zones, rituals associated with changing social status unfold in three phases: *separation* (pre-liminary), *transition* (liminary), and *incorporation* (post-liminary).

Phase one is the ceremonial removal of the individual from everyday society, phase two a period of ritual isolation, and phase three the formal return and readmission back into society in his or her new status (Van Gennep, 1960). Because certain transitions in the human life cycle are crucially important to the individual as well as to the social order of the community, these rituals may involve a religious specialist, such as a priest or priestess.

This sequence of phases occurs in a great array of rites of passage all around the world—from wedding ceremonies marking the transition from single to married status to ceremonies identifying the transference of religious leadership in a spiritual lineage to a designated heir to ceremonies initiating new members into a distinctive group. An example of the latter, described in an earlier chapter, is when young Maasai men in East Africa's grasslands move into the Warrior age grade; they are removed from their families and ritually initiated by circumcision, returning weeks later as *moranes*, armed warriors with a distinctive hairstyle and dress.

Likewise, when Mende girls in West Africa's savannahs begin menstruating, they are ritually prepared for womanhood. Separated from family, they spend weeks in seclusion. Discarding their childhood clothes, they learn the moral and practical responsibilities of motherhood from senior women. Believing circumcision enhances a girl's reproductive potential, these elders are tasked with removing each girl's clitoris (considered a female version of a penis). A good deal of singing, dancing, storytelling, and food accompany the ordeal and the training, which produces a strong sense of sisterhood. The girls emerge from their initiation as women in knowledgeable control of their sexuality, eligible for marriage and childbearing.

Rites of Intensification

Rites of intensification are rituals that take place during a crisis in the life of the group and serve to bind individuals together. Whatever the precise nature of the crisis—a drought that threatens crops, the sudden appearance of an enemy war party, the onset of an epidemic—mass ceremonies are performed to ease the sense of danger.

Figure 23.11 Hindu Cremation Ceremony in Bali, Indonesia Balinese people deal with death by turning what could be a painful emotional experience of grief and loss into a joyous celebration of life's progressive continuity through rebirth in a future existence. As a social reminder of Hindu caste differences, the family of a deceased relative uses this ceremony to display wealth and social rank. Funeral pyres built for members of a noble or royal family on the island are duly impressive.

This unites people in a common effort so that fear and confusion yield to collective action and a degree of optimism. The balance in the relations of all concerned is restored to normal, and the community's values are celebrated and affirmed.

An individual's death might be regarded as the ultimate crisis or point of separation in that person's life, but it is, as well, a point of separation for the entire group, particularly if the group is small. A member of the community has been removed, so its composition has been seriously altered. The survivors, therefore, must readjust and restore balance. They also need to reconcile themselves to the loss of someone to whom they were emotionally tied. As such, a funerary ceremony is an example of an intensification ritual that permits the surviving family and community to express in nondisruptive ways their emotional upset over the death while providing for social readjustment (**Figure 23.11**).

rite of purification A symbolic act carried out by an individual or a group to establish or restore purity when someone has violated a taboo or is otherwise unclean.

rite of passage A ritual that marks an important ceremonial moment when members of a society move from one distinctive social stage in life to another, such as birth, marriage, and death. It features three phases: separation, transition, and incorporation.

rite of intensification A ritual that takes place during a crisis in the life of the group and serves to bind individuals together.

Rites of intensification do not have to be limited to times of overt crisis. In regions where human activities change in accordance with seasonal climatic shifts, these rites take the form of annual ceremonies. They are particularly common among horticultural and agricultural peoples. Ritually articulating traditional ideas about the role of the supernatural in the cyclical return of rain, the light and warmth of the sun, and other factors of nature vital to healthy and bountiful crops, these ceremonies are staged to correspond with the crucially important planting and harvesting seasons. A similar cultural linkage between the annual subsistence cycle and the ceremonial calendar with its rites of intensification can be found in societies based on seasonal fishing and herding or hunting of migratory animals.

Magical Rituals

People in many cultures believe that supernatural powers can be compelled to act in certain ways for good or evil purposes by recourse to specified formulas. In short, they believe in **magic** and carry out magical rituals to ensure positive ends such as good crops, fertility of livestock, replenishment of hunted game, prevention of accidents, healing of illness, protection against injury, promise of victory, and the defeat of enemies, real or imagined. In traditional societies many of these rituals rely on *fetishes*—objects believed to possess magical powers (**Figure 23.12**).

Magical rituals are also popular in wealthy industrialized societies. Individuals commonly seek "good luck" when the outcome is in doubt or beyond one's influence—from lighting a votive candle for someone going through a hard time, to wearing lucky boxers on a hot date, to the curious gesturing baseball pitchers perform on the mound.

Anthropologists distinguish between two fundamental principles of magic. The first principle—that like produces like—is identified as **imitative magic** or *sympathetic magic*. In Myanmar (Burma) in Southeast Asia, for example, a rejected lover might engage a sorcerer to make an image of his would-be love. If this image were tossed into water, to the accompaniment of certain charms, it was expected that the girl would go mad and suffer a fate similar to that of her image.

The second principle is that of **contagious magic**—the idea that things or persons once in contact can influence each other after the contact is broken. The most

Figure 23.12 **Congolese Fetish** This 100-year-old carving from the Democratic Republic of Congo is a *nkondi*, with supernatural power coming in part from magic herbs hidden inside by a diviner. Such fetishes are traditionally used to identify wrongdoers, including thieves and witches responsible for mishaps, diseases, or death. A *nkondi* is activated by provocations (such as hammering nails into it) or invocations urging magic punishment of the suspects.

common example of contagious magic is the permanent relationship between an individual and any part of his or her body, such as hair, fingernails, or teeth. For instance, the Basutos of Lesotho in southern Africa were careful to conceal their extracted teeth to make sure they did not fall into the hands of certain mythical beings who could harm the owners of the teeth by working magic on them. Related to this is the custom in Western societies of treasuring things that have been touched by special people. Such items range from a saint's relics to possessions of other admired or idolized individuals, from rock stars to sports heroes to spiritual gurus.

magic Specific formulas and actions used to compel supernatural powers to act in certain ways for good or evil purposes.

imitative magic Magic based on the principle that like produces like; sometimes called *sympathetic magic*.

contagious magic Magic based on the principle that things or persons once in contact can influence each other after the contact is broken.

Figure 23.13 Assessing Ch'i Energy Feng shui master R. D. Chin determines the *ch'i* of a new office space in a Manhattan skyscraper, one side of which faces the city's central *ch'i* point—the Empire State Building. The consultant is planning the space, with the location of stairways and the CEO's office to be determined.

Divination: Omens and Oracles

Designed to access or influence supernatural powers, magical rituals have also been developed to prepare for the uncertain future—for the unseen and for the not yet present. Fears of pending dangers—for example, storms, attacks, betrayals, diseases, and death—call for precautionary measures, such as what to avoid and where to go. How does one find and interpret the signs, or *omens*, foretelling the future? The answer, as developed in many cultures, is through **divination**, a magical ritual designed to discover what is unknowable by ordinary means, in particular signs predicting fate or destiny.

Various ancient methods of divination exist, including *geomancy* (from Greek, *geo* for "earth" and *manteia* for "divination"), a technique traditionally considered sacred and practiced by shamans, prophets, fortunetellers, or other oracles in communication with supernatural forces. Skilled to interpret omens, a diviner practicing geomancy may toss a handful of sand or pebbles, for example, and then analyze its random patterns, searching for information hidden to ordinary people. Other divination methods include decoding flame or smoke patterns in a fire (*pyromancy*), wind and cloud formation in the air (*aeromancy*), or colors, ripples, and whirls in water (*hydromancy*).

Whereas Mongolian and Chinese shamans traditionally use an animal shoulder blade (*scapulamancy*) for divination purposes, Aymara *yachajs* ("possessors of knowledge") in the Andean highlands may probe sacred coca leaves or the convoluted pile of intestines of a slaughtered guinea pig for omens. Much better known, of course, is the divination technique involving palm reading (*chiromancy*), perhaps most famously practiced by female Gypsy fortunetellers. So-called mediums are popular, too, also in the United States, where many people believe them to be capable of contacting spirits of deceased relatives ready to pass on messages from beyond by means of an ancient ritual method known as *necromancy*.

Believed to possess knowledge hidden from ordinary people, diviners are feared in many cultures. However, they are also in high demand among those who believe in diviners' capacity to predict the future, and those believers may seek consultation before undertaking something important or risky. An example of this is *feng shui*, an ancient Chinese divination technique. Literally translated as "wind-water," its traditional Chinese characters signify "tao of heaven and earth." In the past few decades, this method has grown in popularity in North America as well, in particular in California, where homebuilders and buyers frequently hire feng shui consultants to help them design or redesign homes and offices to conform to the principle of *qi* or *ch'i* ("vital energy") (Figure 23.13).

In some religious traditions, including Christianity, fortunetelling and other divination rituals have long been viewed with suspicion, and in many places these practices have been prohibited. Especially when performed by individuals functioning in other religious or spiritual traditions believed to be false or worse, divination is condemned as evil magic, sorcery, or witchcraft.

Witchcraft: Anxiety and Fears of Evil Magic

Magical rituals intended to cause misfortune or inflict harm are often referred to as sorcery, or **witchcraft**, believed to be practiced by individuals embodying evil

divination A magical procedure or spiritual ritual designed to discern what is not knowable by ordinary means, such as foretelling the future by interpreting omens.
witchcraft Magical rituals intended to cause misfortune or inflict harm.

spirit power or those collaborating with malevolent supernatural beings. In contrast to magic-working experts inclined to do good, these individuals inspire awe, or even fear. Historically, such dangerous magic-working individuals are known in English under a variety of names such as *wizard, sorcerer*, or simply *witch*—imprecise terms often used interchangeably. This is also true for other languages using a variety of terms like *brujo* (Spanish), *uwisin* (Shuar), *umthakathi* (Zulu), *mchawi* (Swahili), and *wu* (Chinese).

Fear of witches is especially prevalent during periods of uncertainty and transition. When mysterious illnesses, devastating droughts, accidental deaths, economic uncertainties, and other upheavals disturb the cultural order, confusion may result in a surge of suspicion and a focus on disliked, unsociable, isolated individuals. Especially in patrilineal or patrilocal communities, the accused is often an older woman, typically single or widowed and without children. For instance, about 80 percent of the estimated 50,000 "witches" tried, tortured, and killed in Europe in the 16th and 17th centuries were female. Among matrilineal and matrilocal groups, however, people tend to think of witches as male.

Not all people suspected of mysterious malevolence are prosecuted, let alone executed, but witchcraft accusations clearly function as a social control mechanism, horribly reinforcing the moral code. Fear of being accused of being a witch encourages individuals to suppress as best they can those personality traits that are looked upon with disapproval. A belief in witchcraft thus serves as a broad control on what is believed to be antisocial behavior (Behringer, 2004).

Navajo Skin-Walkers

Beliefs in evil magic are widespread and take many forms. One interesting example comes from the Navajo, Native Americans historically surviving as sheepherders and small-scale irrigation farmers in the vast deserts of Arizona and New Mexico. The Navajo have a substantial repertoire of sacred rituals for healing victims of sorcery, all related to accusations of evil magic.

Among Navajos, who live in a residence group organized around a head woman, traditional belief holds that a person suffering from severe anxiety disorder, repetitive nightmares, or delusions is a victim of sorcery. The idea is that a ghost or some other evil spirit, traveling under cover of darkness, is responsible. And

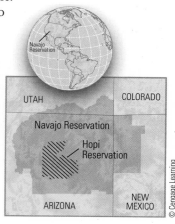

according to the Navajo, the suspect is a powerful sorcerer, almost always a man, probably someone who has killed a relative and committed incest.

These dangerous Navajo sorcerers, resembling the werewolf of European folklore and the *nagual* in rural Mexico, are believed to be able to change themselves into animal form. Referred to as a *'ánt'įįhnii* ("skin-walker"), such a sorcerer stealthily goes to a secluded spot, such as a cave at night. There, he transforms into a coyote or wolf. Disguised in animal form, he emerges and runs fast toward his victim, bringing on *'ánt'į* ("the curse"). Having completed his accursed mission, the skin-walker swiftly returns to his hideaway, transforms again into human form, and slips back into his home before dawn (Kluckhohn, 1944; Selinger, 2007).

Sacred Sites: Saints, Shrines, and Miracles

Sacred sites are typically positioned in a transitional, or *liminary*, zone between the natural and supernatural, the secular and spiritual, earth and heaven. Reaching high into the sky, mountaintops are often considered to be magical places, shrouded in mystery. For instance, the Japanese view the snowcapped perfect volcanic cone of Mount Fuji ("Ever-Lasting Life") as a sacred place. Ancient Greeks considered Mount Olympus to be the mythological abode of Zeus, the king of all their gods. Likewise, Kikuyu view Mount Kenya as the earthly dwelling place of their creator god Ngai.

Some sites become sacred because they are places where ordinary human beings experienced something extraordinary—heard a divine voice or saw a guardian spirit, patron saint, or archangel. Often a site is declared sacred because believers associate it with a miracle-working mystic, saint, prophet, or other holy person. The tombs of such individuals often turn into shrines (*scrinium*, Latin for "round box" or "container," holding relics). For example, stories of miraculous events and special powers emanating from Muslim tombs are common wherever Sufism, a far-reaching mystical branch of Islam, is popular (Gladney, 2004).

Based on the principle of contagious magic, any material substance physically linked to a miraculous event or individual may itself become revered as holy or sacred. This may include bones, fingernails, hair, or any other body part believed to have belonged to a saint, or something the person wore, possessed, or simply touched. All these things may be treasured as holy relics and safeguarded in a shrine, inspiring the faithful.

Burial sites of saints often gain such importance that people feel inspired to construct a very large shrine for the saint's entombment; termed a *mausoleum*, some of these are large enough for the interment of lesser saints and pious individuals desiring proximity to the sacred saint after death. However large or small, shrines are religious focal points for prayer, meditation, and sacrifice.

Figure 23.14 Pilgrims at Mount Kailash in Tibet Rising 6,700 meters (over 22,000 feet), this mountain has been sacred for many generations to Buddhists and Hindus, as well as Jains and followers of Bön (Tibet's indigenous religion). Every year a few thousand pilgrims make the tortuous 52-kilometer (32-mile) trek around it, some of them by crawling the entire distance.

© Alexander van der Made

Pilgrimages: Devotion in Motion

Every year, many millions of devotees of many religions—including Buddhism, Christianity, Hinduism, Islam, and their many branches—walk, climb, or even crawl to a sacred or holy site. Whether it is a saint's tomb, a mountain, lake, river, waterfall, or some other particular place believed to be metaphysically significant, *pilgrims* (from Latin *peregrinus*, meaning "wanderer") travel there seeking enlightenment, proving their devotion, and/or hoping to experience a miracle.

On their sacred journey, pilgrims participate in a religious drama, performing ritually prescribed acts such as prayers, chants, or prostrations. A devotion in motion, the **pilgrimage** demands personal sacrifices from the travelers. Enjoying little comfort, they may suffer from thirst and hunger, heat and cold, pain and fear while on the road, sometimes for many days or even months. Pilgrims often travel through unfamiliar territories where they may run into problems, including robbery, kidnapping, starvation, and even death. To identify their status as spiritually inspired travelers, some wear special clothes, shave their heads, carry amulets, chant prayers, or perform other prescribed rituals along the way.

One of the most challenging pilgrimages is the climb up the slopes of a mountain range in the Himalayas where Mount Kailash rises 6,700 meters (over 22,000

feet). Located in western Tibet, this black, snowcapped mountain stands out boldly in a dramatic landscape sacred to Hindus and Buddhists, as well as Jains and Bönpos (**Figure 23.14**). The latter, who practice an ancient Tibetan shamanic religion, refer to this hallowed mountain as Tisé ("Water Peak") because it is the source of four sacred rivers. For Hindus, it is the holy abode of Lord Shiva, the destroyer of ignorance and illusion and the divine source of yoga. Jains view Kailash as the sacred place where their divine cultural hero Rishabha ("Bull")—an incarnation of Lord Vishnu—first achieved full enlightenment. Finally, Tibetan Buddhists revere it as Gangs Rinpoche ("Snow Lord") and believe it to be the abode of Khorlo Demchok ("Circle of Bliss")—a wrathful deity who uses his power to destroy the three major obstacles to enlightenment: anger, greed, and ignorance.

For all four of these religious traditions, climbing to the summit of this holy mountain is taboo. So, pilgrims demonstrate their devotion by means of a ritual encirclement, or circumambulation—clockwise by Buddhists and Hindus, and in reverse by Jains and Bönpos. The rugged, 52-kilometer (32-mile) trek is seen

---

pilgrimage A devotion in motion. Traveling, often on foot, to a sacred or holy site to reach for enlightenment, prove devotion, and/or experience a miracle.

as a sacred ritual that removes sins and brings good fortune. Each year thousands follow the ancient tradition of encircling the mountain on foot. The most devout pilgrims turn their circumambulation into a sacrificial ordeal: Prostrating their bodies full length, they extend their hands forward and make a mark on the ground with their fingers; then they rise, pray, crawl ahead on hands and knees to the mark, and then repeat the process again and again.

One of the world's largest pilgrimages is the *hajj*—a performance of piety now made by 1.8 million Muslims traveling to Mecca in Saudi Arabia each year from all across the globe. The largest contingent of hajjis—about 300,000 a year—comes from Indonesia. One of the five pillars of Islam, the hajj brings all of these pilgrims together for collective prayers and other sacred rituals at the Kaaba in Mecca, their religion's holiest site.

Christianity, originating in what was an eastern province of the Roman empire about 2,000 years ago, has created a sacred landscape dotted with dozens of major pilgrimage sites in Southwest Asia and Europe. As in other ancient religions, these sites are symbolically associated with miracles and legendary holy men and women. For example, for nearly a millennium Christian pilgrims from all over Europe have made the long and difficult journey to Santiago de Compostela. Tens of thousands travel to this Spanish seaport each year—most by foot, some by bicycle, and a few on horseback like their medieval counterparts. About 180,000 pilgrims walk the final 100 kilometers to the old cathedral with the shrine containing the sacred remains of the apostle Saint James venerated as Santiago (Santo-Iago) since the Middle Ages and recognized as the official patron saint of Spain. Many more Roman Catholics make pilgrimages to shrines devoted to Saint Mary, as described following.

Female Saints: Divine Protection for the Weak

Many religions consider the divine order primarily or exclusively as masculine, as noted earlier. Ideologically reproducing the hierarchical social order dominated by men, this arrangement reflects the worldview of traditional cultures that revere male deities, prophets, and saints in officially sponsored cults and devotions. But religions are not monolithic, and some provide flexible spiritual space for alternatives, such as Christian cults devoted to female saints such as Mary, the virgin mother of Jesus Christ, the son of God.

More powerful than the pope in Rome, Mary has been loved and adored as a holy mother residing in heaven. Worldwide, Roman Catholic multitudes look up to her for divine protection. Like other Christian saints, she is thought to perform miracles and to be capable of physically manifesting herself at places and times of her choosing. Through the centuries, many believers claim to have witnessed such holy moments, some officially reporting the miracle. Typically, these believers are young members of the underclass—herders, peasants, or fishermen, for example. Beyond stories about the female saint manifesting herself to such low-status rural folk, the discovery of sacred relics (such as a drowned or buried statue representing Mary) may also generate excitement and hope in difficult times.

Stories and relics religiously associated with miracles performed by saints such as the Virgin Mary quickly attract popular attention and turn into myths. Inspired or led by individuals claiming divine authority based on immediate revelation, devotees typically build a shrine to commemorate the encounter or to safeguard the sacred relic. Developing outside the power structure of established religious institutions, these local devotions may turn into popular cults. Difficult if not impossible to stop, these cults may spawn mass movements, leading church authorities to consider whether to formally approve of the cult and take control of the Marian (Saint Mary) devotion. Sanctioned by the church or not, these shrines attract pilgrims in search of divine forgiveness, protection, healing, and compassionate love.

Among the best known Marian pilgrimage sites are the ones in Lourdes (France) and Fatima (Portugal), along with the Mexican shrine dedicated to the brown-skinned Virgin of Guadalupe detailed in the next section.

Black Madonnas and Brown-Skinned Virgin Mothers

As folk-based popular religious movements, Saint Mary cults not only developed across Europe, but also in Latin America, the Philippines, and other parts of the world historically colonized and dominated by Roman Catholics originating from Europe. The religious ideas and rituals of Catholicism changed many indigenous cultures—and were also changed by them. Of particular interest in this shifting religious landscape are Black Madonnas: brown or dark-colored clay or wooden statues, or painted images, representing the virgin mother. One of the many Black Madonna statues is enshrined in Aparecida, Brazil, where a popular cult emerged in her honor in the mid-18th century and now attracts over 10 million pilgrims annually.

Another popular devotion involving brown-skinned Saint Mary concerns the Virgin of Guadalupe, highlighted in this chapter's opening photo. As mentioned there, this Mexican cult originated in 1531, a decade after the Aztec Indian empire had been conquered by a Spanish army. That year, a recently converted young

Figure 23.15 Virgin of Guadalupe Pilgrim, Mexico City On December 9, 1531, Saint Mary appeared to Mexican Indian Juan Diego, a recent Christian convert, as he passed by Tepeyac Hill in what is now Mexico City. At the site of this encounter, the Basilica of Our Lady of Guadalupe was built with a shrine containing sacred evidence of this miraculous apparition. Pictured here is a weary pilgrim, sleeping alongside images of the virgin outside the basilica.

AP Images/Marco Ugarte

Aztec Christian named Juan Diego proclaimed a remarkable encounter with a holy woman who appeared to him in a blaze of light. Speaking his native Nahuatl tongue, she identified herself as the virgin mother and asked that a shrine be built in her honor. After their miraculous meeting, he discovered her image mysteriously imprinted on the inside of his simple white-hemp *tilma* ("cloak"). Seen as divine proof of Mary's manifestation, this sacred relic was soon enshrined in the chapel built in her honor at the foot of the hill where she appeared—now part of Mexico City.

A few decades later, a powerful Spanish bishop imposing religious order in the Mexican colony became aware of the emerging brown-virgin cult and saw it as an ideological means of unifying and controlling a racially divided population. Eventually, in 1780 church authorities officially declared her patron saint of Mexico, even promoting her to the title of Empress of the Americas in 1945. In 2002, nearly 500 years after Juan Diego's mystical encounter started this Marian devotion, Pope John Paul II canonized him before a crowd of 12 million. Diego became the first Native American to be declared a Roman Catholic saint. Today, most of the 6 million pilgrims who visit the Virgin of Guadalupe's shrine each year to see the sacred *tilma* relic discovered by Diego are mestizo or indigenous Mexicans (Figure 23.15).

Desecration: Ruining Sacred Sites

Although popular shrines are destinations for believers from near and far, they are also potential targets of **desecration**. By means of such ideologically inspired violation of a sacred site, enemies aim to inflict harm, if only symbolically, on people judged to have impure, false, or evil beliefs and ritual practices. Desecrations have occurred across the globe for thousands of years, as evidenced in archaeological sites and recorded in oral traditions or historical documents.

For example, during the Protestant Reformation in the 16th and 17th centuries, Christian Protestant iconoclasts campaigning against idolatry in the Netherlands and England destroyed untold numbers of ancient Roman Catholic statues and other treasures kept in sacred shrines. More recently, in Afghanistan, Taliban religious authorities shattered two huge 1,500-year-old statues they considered to be idols. Carved into the side of a sandstone cliff in the high mountain valley of Bamiyan, one of them, representing a celestial wisdom Buddha ("the enlightened one") stood 55 meters (180 feet) high; the other, representing Siddhartha Gautama, the founder of Buddhism himself, rose to 37 meters (121 feet). In 2001, the Taliban obliterated both monuments with artillery and dynamite.

Destruction in the name of religion is not unique to Christian or Muslim puritans, as militant Hindus and others also engage in similar desecrations. All of this pales in comparison with China's Cultural Revolution in the 1960s, when masses of activists, swept up in state-sponsored antireligious fervor, went on a rampage destroying religious monuments, sculptures, carvings, and paintings, as well as a large number of age-old sacred shrines.

desecration Ideologically inspired violation of a sacred site intended to inflict harm, if only symbolically, on people judged to have impure, false, or even evil beliefs and ritual practices.

Cultural Dynamics in the Superstructure: Religious and Spiritual Change

New technologies, improved means of transportation, internationalization of production and labor markets, and worldwide movements of ideas and practices all contribute to challenging and even destabilizing long-established cultural systems and associated worldviews. Reacting to these challenges and radical upheavals, people often turn to the supernatural to allay the anxiety of a world going awry.

The need to find deeper meaning in life and to make sense of an increasingly complex, uncharted, confusing, and sometimes frightening existence drives humans to continue their explorations—religious and spiritual, as well as scientific. Some people bundle or devise their own spiritual beliefs and rituals. Others form or join new spiritual movements.

Reactionary religious movements are also on the rise in culturally destabilized societies. Typically, these call for a radical return to traditional foundations prescribed in sacred texts and narrowly interpreted by conservative spiritual leaders. Examples include Islamic fundamentalism in countries such as Afghanistan, Egypt, and Iran; Jewish fundamentalism in Israel and the United States; and Hindu fundamentalism in India. Christian fundamentalism is represented in the dramatic growth of evangelical denominations in the United States, Latin America, and sub-Saharan Africa.

Revitalization Movements

No anthropological consideration of religion is complete without some mention of **revitalization movements**—movements for radical cultural reform in response to widespread social disruption and collective feelings of great stress and despair.

As deliberate efforts to construct a more satisfying culture, revitalization movements aim to reform not just the religious sphere of activity but may also impact an entire cultural system. Many such movements developed in indigenous societies where European colonial exploitation caused enormous upheaval. They also occurred in 16th-century Europe—as evidenced in the emergence of Puritans, Mennonites, and other Protestant groups when traditional societies faced radical transformations triggered by early capitalism and other

forces. Likewise, revitalization movements emerged in response to the industrial revolution triggering similar radical transformations in agrarian societies in the 19th century, not only in Europe but also in the northeastern United States, where Mormonism, Jehovah's Witnesses, Seventh-Day Adventists, and others began as Christian revitalization movements.

Revitalization movements can be found in many religions. One of the best known among Muslims is Ahmadiyya, founded in South Asia during British colonial rule in the late 19th century when Christian missionaries were actively proselytizing in predominantly Hindu, Muslim, or Sikh communities. Known as Ahmadis, followers of this Muslim sect number about 10 million across the globe. They believe that Allah (God) sent Mirza Ghulam Ahmad (1835–1908) as a prophet, a divinely ordained reformer (*mujjaddid*) like Muhammad. As the long-awaited Messiah, he embodied the second coming of the Christ, sent to bring about, by peaceful means, the final triumph of Islam as the only true religion for humanity, end all religious strife, and restore divinely guided morality, justice, and peace.

Recent U.S. revitalization movements also include the revival or introduction of traditional American Indian ceremonies such as the sweat lodge now common on many tribal reservations in North America, as well as the spectacular Sun Dance ceremony held each summer at various reservations in the Great Plains. Similar cultural revivals of "spiritual neo-traditions" are on the rise in many parts of the world, including Europe (Prins, 1994). Tens of thousands of people in Great Britain, attracted to a naturalistic worldview, now practice forms of "ecospiritualism" (Prins, 1996, p. 206), which often involves a revival of the ancient pre-Christian Celtic tradition of Druidry (Figure 23.16).

A similar nature-centered revival of pre-Christian beliefs and rituals is under way in Germanic-speaking parts of northern Europe, such as among Asatru in Scandinavia. Seeking a sacred relationship with nature, they worship the earth, elements of the sky, and forces such as thunder, as well as spirits they believe arise from sacred places like mountains and rivers. Similar tradition-based ecospiritual movements are developing throughout the industrialized world, including the United States.

Syncretic Religions

In Africa, during and following the period of foreign colonization and missionization, indigenous groups resisted or creatively revised Christian teachings and formed culturally appropriate religious movements. During the past century, thousands of indigenous Christian churches have been founded in Africa. These churches are often born of alternative theological interpretations and new divinely inspired revelations. They also originate from disapproval

---

revitalization movements Social movements for radical cultural reform in response to widespread social disruption and collective feelings of great stress and despair.

Figure 23.16 Stonehenge, Wiltshire County, England In 2010, the neo-tradition of Druidry was officially recognized as a religion in Great Britain. Stonehenge, a 4,500-year-old Neolithic site, is one of its sacred centers. With 10,000 followers, modern Druidry is rooted in the pre-Christian tradition of the Celtic peoples indigenous to the British Isles.

by foreign missionaries concerning the preservation of traditional beliefs and rituals culturally associated with animism, ancestor worship, and spirit possession, as well as kinship and marriage.

Today, the African continent is as religiously and spiritually diverse as ever. Although at least 40 percent of the population is Christian, and more than another 40 percent is Muslim, myriad African indigenous religions persist and are often merged with Christianity or Islam.

Syncretic Religions Across the Atlantic: Vodou in Haiti

In almost four centuries of trans-Atlantic slave trading, African captives stolen from hundreds of towns and villages from Mauretania south to Angola and beyond were shipped without material belongings to labor on cotton, sugar, coffee, and tobacco plantations from Virginia to Brazil. Ripped from family and community, individual slaves clung to some of their ancestral beliefs and knowledge of rituals.

Sharing a life of forced labor, slaves from different ethnic, linguistic, and religious backgrounds formed small communities, pooled remembered religious ideas and rituals, and creatively forged a spiritual repertoire of their own. Founded on a mix of Yoruba and other African beliefs and practices, their emerging religions also incorporated Christian features, including terminology from the languages of slave-owning colonists. In some cases,

elements from a region's indigenous American cultures were also included.

Such creative blending of indigenous and foreign beliefs and practices into new cultural forms illustrates what anthropologists define as **syncretism**. Especially after slavery was abolished in the course of the 1800s, these syncretic spiritual repertoires developed into Afro-Caribbean religions such as Vodou in Haiti and Santería in Cuba, which resemble Candomblé in Brazil. All of these religions are spreading as adherents freely migrate across borders (Fernández Olmos & Paravisini-Gebert, 2003).

Vodou emerged in Haiti in the early 1800s after this small tropical country in the Caribbean Sea won its independence from France in a decade-long slave revolt. The name means "divine spirit" in the language of the Fon, a large ethnic group in Benin and southwestern Nigeria. Providing an escape from the indignities of poverty and hopelessness, Vodou was developed by ex-slaves speaking French-based Creole. Now mostly poor black peasants, they are nominal Roman Catholics who, like their African ancestors across the Atlantic, believe in spirit possession.

Vodou rituals center on the worship of what Haitians refer to as *loas*—also known by Creole terms such as *anges* ("angels"), *saints* ("saints"), or simply as *mystères* ("mysteries"). This tradition is essentially based on a belief in

syncretism The creative blending of indigenous and foreign beliefs and practices into new cultural forms.

Figure 23.17 **Haitian Women in a Vodou Bathing Ritual** In mid-July every year, thousands of Haitian pilgrims journey to a sacred waterfall in the mountains north of Port-au-Prince, Haiti, in reverence to a Black Madonna known as Our Lady of Carmel. This Marian devotion is ritually associated with a major *loa*, or Vodou spirit, named Erzulie Dantor, who mysteriously appeared on a palm tree at this waterfall about 150 years ago. Since then, an important devotional activity is bathing in this sacred water, a deeply spiritual experience in which Vodou practitioners like these women enter a trance filled with divine grace.

a reciprocal relationship between the spirits of the living and those of the dead, representing multiple expressions of the divine. Spirits of deceased ancestors and other relatives can be summoned by means of drumming in a temple. Dancing to the beat, worshipers enter into trance. This is when a person's spirit temporarily vacates the human body, replaced by a *loa* from the spirit world who takes possession—the moment of divine grace (**Figure 23.17**).

Religious Pluralism and Secularization

Although Christianity in Europe is losing ground as a result of Islam's rise, a much more substantial decline is due to **secularization.** In this process of cultural change, a population tends toward a nonreligious worldview, ignoring or rejecting institutionalized spiritual beliefs and rituals. Over the last few decades, growing numbers of western Europeans have declared themselves to be without religion.

Secularization is especially noteworthy in a prosperous capitalist country like Germany, which has been for many centuries predominantly Lutheran and Roman Catholic. Today, almost 40 percent of Germans identify themselves as nonreligious, compared to a mere 4 percent forty years ago. In contrast, religion is becoming *more* important in many parts of eastern Europe where atheism was communist state ideology for several generations in the 20th century.

Secularization also takes place in other wealthy industrialized countries. In the United States, for example, 20 percent of all adults are religiously unaffiliated—and the figure jumps to about 35 percent among adults under 30. Their ranks include more than 13 million self-described atheists and agnostics—nearly 6 percent of the U.S. public (Pew Research Center, 2012). As in other large countries, there are regional contrasts, with the secularization trend among New Englanders far outpacing several areas in the southeastern United States, where 80 to 85 percent claim that religion plays an important role in their lives.

With over 2,000 distinctive faiths, the U.S. religious landscape is highly diversified, and the country has given birth to many new religions, a few of which have gone global. Moreover, in the past few decades, Asian immigrant groups have greatly added to the religious diversification in North America as well as in Europe. In response, even global finance business is adapting to the changing ideological landscape, as illustrated in this Original Study on Shariah-compliant banking.

secularization A process of cultural change in which a population tends toward a nonreligious worldview, ignoring or rejecting institutionalized spiritual beliefs and rituals.

ORIGINAL STUDY

Sacred Law in Global Capitalism BY BILL MAURER

I will never forget my introduction to Islamic banking. It happened at a 1998 conference when I happened into a darkened room where the founder of an Islamic investment firm was showing a clip from the old Hollywood classic movie, *It's a Wonderful Life.* On the screen, George Bailey, played by Jimmy Stewart, faces an anxious crowd of Bedford Falls citizens, who have rushed into his Building and Loan, passbooks in hand, desperate to get their money. There is about to be a run on the bank.

One of the townspeople says he wants his money, *now.* George protests, "But you're thinking of this place all wrong—as if I had the money back in a safe. The money's not *here.* Why, your money's in Joe's house that's right next to yours, and in the Kennedy house, and Mrs. Macklin's house, and in a hundred others. You're lending them the money to build and then they're gonna pay it back to you as best they can. . . . Now, we can get through this thing all right. We've got to stick together, though. We've got to have faith in each other." The people cry, "I've got doctor's bills to pay!" "Can't feed my kids on faith!"

Then Mary, George's newlywed bride, shouts from behind the counter, "I've got two thousand dollars!" and holds up a wad of bills. It is the money for their honeymoon. George chimes in, "This'll tide us over until the bank reopens tomorrow." He proceeds to disburse money based on people's stated needs ("Could I have $17.50?" one woman asks meekly) and guaranteed only by his trust in them.

Seconds before six o'clock, the last client leaves. George has just two dollars left. He, Mary, his Uncle Billy, and two cousins count down the seconds and then lock the doors. They have managed to stay in business for one more day. They place the two remaining dollars in a tray, and George offers a toast: "To Mama Dollar and to Papa Dollar, and if you want this old Building and Loan to stay in business you better have a family real quick." "I wish they were rabbits," says Cousin Tilly.

At this point in the film, the conference host paused the video and said, "This is the first *lariba* movie." A murmur went through the crowd. No one quite knew what he meant. Most of the audience was Muslim; this was a Christmas movie. What was our host trying to say?

I now know that *lariba* is Arabic for "no increase." The Koran invokes the term *riba* (increase) twenty times, and the term is often translated as interest or usury (excessive interest). Islamic banking and finance aim to avoid *riba* through profit-and-loss sharing, leasing, or other forms of equity- or asset-based financing.

We are all aware of the recent global financial crisis, which led to the collapse of major corporations, the nationalization of big banks and car companies, massive unemployment, and unnerving insecurity for many people in the United States and around the world. One of the leading causes of the crisis was the marketing of debt to people who probably could not repay, and the packaging of those debts into complicated financial instruments that were supposed to curb risk but instead increased it.

What, you might ask, does anthropology have to contribute to the study of the financial markets, money, and the wider economy? Quite a lot, actually. Among other things, anthropologists have repeatedly demonstrated that economic decisions thought to be purely rational and self-interested are actually deeply embedded in social relationships, cultural values, and religious beliefs.

Take securitized debt instruments, for example—loans like mortgages, chopped up and rebundled together into salable commodities. When they started to go sour, many commentators blamed the instruments' complexity and called for a return to an economy based on real things instead of abstract tradable debt. However, we know from our research across the globe that peoples in different cultures do not always differentiate the real from the abstract in the same way. A person's reputation might be deemed more solid and real than a piece of gold. And a piece of gold has real value only because people agree to it as a convention.

After that 1998 conference, I began my study of global Islamic banking, including the efforts of American Muslims to create a new kind of "Islamic" mortgage that enables devout Muslims to buy a home in accordance with Islam's prohibition of interest. Instead of financing a home purchase with interest-bearing debt, Islamic alternatives rely on either leasing contracts (a sort of rent-to-own arrangement where the bank owns the house and the purchaser buys out the bank's share over time) or a partnership arrangement (like a joint business venture). Rather than having debt and interest at the center of the mortgage, as in a conventional loan, the house itself and its fair market rental value are at the center. The purchaser buys out the bank's share over time. At the center is the asset—the real thing—not the debt.

Of course, there is no reason why a joint partnership to own a piece of property is any more "real" or less "abstract" than bundling together debt. It depends on one's point of view, and one's precommitments to certain values—prohibiting interest and sharing risk, for example, or distributing risk onto others. In Islamic finance, the former is seen as "Shariah compliant," or in accord with Islamic law; and the latter, as unjust because it offloads one's own share of risk onto others.

Palani Mohan /The New York Times/Redux

Until the early 1990s, millions of Muslims throughout the world had few investment opportunities due to the ethics derived from Shariah law. Since then, hundreds of Islamic financial institutions have emerged in over fifty countries. Big American and European banks, including Citibank, have also entered the Islamic banking business in order to tap into the rising oil wealth. Today, Shariah-compliant banks manage well over $750 billion globally. Here we see three Muslim women in Kuala Lumpur, Malaysia.

At the same time, Islamic mortgages often require relatively large down payments; this excludes poorer people from achieving the American dream of homeownership. So, we need to ask ourselves whether the virtues of adherence to the precepts of one's religion outweigh broader social goals of financial inclusion.

Global Islamic banking today owes much to the immigration of Middle Eastern and South Asian students and professionals to the United States and western Europe since the 1970s, and the consolidation of large U.S.–Muslim organizations. The oil boom in the Middle East during the 1970s, which sparked renewed interest in Islamic banking in many Muslim-majority countries, also encouraged the development of a loosely knit interconnected network of Muslim international businessmen, who, working for oil and chemical companies as well as financial firms, gained experience in Western regulatory and business environments.

Islamic home financing expanded greatly after the 2001 terrorist attack on New York's World Trade Center and the Pentagon; these attacks sent shockwaves through the capitalist world system dominated by Wall Street. First of all, Americans in general, Muslims included, took their money out of the stock market after the attack and started investing in real estate, buoyed by low interest rates and feeding the speculative real estate bubble. Second, Islamic mutual funds had been able to maintain their "Islamicity" in part by contributing a portion of their profits to charity in order to religiously "cleanse" the funds; however, as charities came under governmental suspicion for terrorist money laundering, many Muslims withdrew their investments from these funds. Third, home financing, American Muslims told me, is the cornerstone of the "American dream," and they were eager to demonstrate their commitment to that dream.

People involved in Islamic banking and finance are continually engaged in an effort to define precisely what their field is. Is *riba* simply Arabic for "interest," or does *riba* refer only to "excessive interest" or usury? Does the prohibition say something about justice, or does it moralize about proper market relationships? Like any aspect of culture—economy included—Islamic banking is always a field of debate. And more debate, not less, may help us all to find just, peaceful, and profitable ways out of the various catastrophes we continually make for ourselves, as we create the abstractions and realities that mutually determine our lives together.

Written expressly for this text, 2010.

In this cross-cultural survey of religion and spirituality, we explored and contrasted numerous worldviews with their symbolic constructs of the universe and our place in it. Made and remade in the course of history, all of these ideological systems reflect human wonderings and ponderings—about life and death, health and illness, past and future, real time and dream time, the known and unknown. Dynamic and inherently complex as the superstructure of a cultural system, a worldview provides imaginative answers, even as it creates mysteries of its own. Whatever its symbolic substance or form, it plays a powerful role in social bonding and control, forging ideological ties that bind and divide.

Religions, as explained and illustrated in this chapter, are not just about spiritual beliefs and rituals, however important these may be. They are also fundamental in the symbolic construction of social identities—the ways in which billions of people see themselves—and motivate people to act or not act in prescribed ways. Performing religion or spirituality, individually or collectively, people not only express what they feel and think but also *who* they are. By tradition or choice, this provides them with another identity marker, beyond features such as gender, speech, kinship, place, or status. Given the cultural variations and historical changes, different markers are stressed or recognized as socially significant.

The cultural upheavals triggered by globalization have made the anthropological study of religion not only fascinating but crucial in our efforts to better understand our species in all its creative and destructive cultural capacity.

CHAPTER CHECKLIST

What are religion and spirituality, and what role do they play in a cultural system?

● Religion is an organized system of ideas about the spiritual sphere or the supernatural, and it is a key part of every culture's worldview. Religion consists of beliefs and practices by which people try to interpret and/or influence aspects of the universe otherwise beyond their control.

● Like religion, spirituality is concerned with sacred matters, but it is often individual rather than collective and does not require a distinctive format or traditional organization.

● Among food-foraging peoples, religion is intertwined in everyday life. As societies become more complex, religion may be restricted to particular occasions.

● Spiritual and religious beliefs and practices fulfill numerous psychological and emotional needs, such as reducing anxiety by providing an orderly view of the universe and answering existential questions, including those concerning suffering and death.

● Myths are narratives that explain the fundamentals of human existence—where we and everything in our world came from, why we are here, and where we are going.

● A traditional religion reinforces group norms and provides moral sanctions for individual conduct. Its narratives and rituals confirm the existing social order, but it may also provide vehicles for challenging that order. People often turn to religion or spirituality in the hope of reaching a specific goal such as restoring health.

What types of supernatural beings and forces are included in the worldview of humans?

● Religion is characterized by a belief in supernatural beings and forces, which can be appealed to for aid through prayer, sacrifice, and other rituals. Supernatural beings may be grouped into three categories: major deities (gods and goddesses), ancestral spirits, and other sorts of spirit beings.

● Gods and goddesses are great but remote beings that control the universe. Whether people recognize gods, goddesses, or both has to do with how men and women relate to each other in everyday life.

● Monotheism holds that there is one supreme divinity; polytheism acknowledges more than one deity.

● Belief in ancestral spirits is based on the dualistic idea that human beings consist of a body and a soul, or vital spirit. Freed from the body at death, the spirit continues to participate in human affairs. This belief is characteristic of descent-based groups with their associated ancestor orientation.

● Animism, the belief that nature is animated (enlivened) by distinct personalized spirit beings separable from bodies, is common among peoples who see themselves as part of nature rather than superior to it.

● Animatism, sometimes found alongside animism, is a belief that nature is energized by an impersonal spiritual force—as in the Chinese concept of *ch'i*.

What are the different types of religious specialists?

● Priests and priestesses are full-time religious specialists authorized to perform sacred rituals and mediate with supernatural powers on behalf of others.

● Priests and priestesses typically hold their position by way of spiritual lineage in which divine authority is passed down from a spiritual founder to a chain of successors.

● There are four major forms of spiritual lineage: biological descent, training and appointment by religious leaders, election, and recognition of a reincarnated saint.

● Shamans are individuals skilled at entering an altered state of consciousness to contact and utilize an ordinarily hidden reality in order to acquire knowledge and supernatural power to help other people. Their special powers have come to them through some personal experience.

What are religious rituals and rites, and what purposes do they serve?

● A religious ritual is a culturally symbolic act or procedure designed to guide members of a community in an orderly way through personal and collective transitions. It is religion in action—the means through which people relate to the supernatural.

● Rites of purification are rituals performed to establish or restore purity when someone has violated a taboo or is otherwise unclean.

● Rites of passage are rituals marking an important stage in an individual's life cycle, such as birth, marriage, and death. They feature three phases: separation, transition, and incorporation.

● Rites of intensification are rituals that ease anxiety and bind people together when they face a collective crisis or change.

What are magic, divination, and witchcraft?

● People in many cultures believe in magic: the idea that supernatural powers can be compelled to act in certain ways for good or evil purposes through specified formulas.

● Many societies have magical rituals to ensure good fortune. Magic is considered to be both imitative (like produces like) and contagious.

● Divination is a magical procedure or spiritual ritual designed to find out what is not knowable by ordinary means, particularly through signs foretelling fate or destiny. Examples include geomancy and chiromancy (palmistry).

● Witchcraft—magical rituals intended to cause misfortune or inflict harm and often referred to as sorcery—is believed to be practiced by people who embody evil spirit power or collaborate with malevolent supernatural beings.

● Belief in witchcraft is widespread, takes many forms, and is especially common during periods of uncertainty.

What are sacred sites and pilgrimages?

● Sacred sites come in many forms. Some are places where ordinary people experienced something extraordinary. Others are associated with a holy person, including shrines or burial sites. Exceptional natural places, especially mountaintops, are often considered magical or sacred.

● A pilgrimage is a devotion in motion—a journey, often on foot, to a sacred site by individuals reaching for enlightenment, proving devotion, and/or hoping to experience a miracle. Among the largest pilgrimages is the hajj made by 1.8 million Muslims traveling to Mecca in Saudi Arabia each year from all around the world.

● Many pilgrimages center on cults of the Virgin Mary. These include Black Madonnas—dark-colored clay or wooden statues or painted images representing the virgin mother. One of them, the Virgin of Guadalupe in Mexico City, draws 6 million pilgrims annually.

● Sacred sites are potential targets of desecration—ideological violation of a sacred site aimed at harming, if only symbolically, people judged to have impure, false, or evil beliefs and ritual practices.

What are revitalization movements, and how are they connected to social upheaval?

● Revitalization movements, which can happen in any culture, arise when people seek radical cultural reform in response to widespread social disruption and collective feelings of anxiety and despair.

● Revitalization movements are not restricted to indigenous peoples historically dominated by colonial powers. They include the 19th-century rise of Mormonism in the United States and ecospiritualism in many Western nations, such as the rise of Druidry in England.

● The revival of traditional American Indian ceremonies such as the sweat lodge and Sun Dance ceremony are other revitalization examples.

● Syncretism, the creative blending of indigenous and foreign beliefs and practices into new cultural forms, can be found worldwide. This includes the practice of Vodou among former slaves in Haiti, which features elements of Roman Catholicism and traditional African beliefs such as spirit possession.

What is secularization?

● Secularization is a process of cultural change in which a population tends toward a nonreligious worldview, ignoring or rejecting institutionalized spiritual beliefs and rituals.

● Fairly common in wealthy countries, secularization has become especially prevalent in western Europe.

QUESTIONS FOR REFLECTION

1. There is more to culture than making survival possible, as humans also search for meaning in the universe and their place in it. Many put their faith in spirit forces, supernatural beings, or deities, seeking existential answers and praying for protection and support. Christian pilgrims in Mexico put their faith in a holy mother figure in heaven. Does your worldview provide you with the same or a similar spiritual support in times of hardship or suffering?

2. People in every culture experience anxiety, fear, and social tension, and many attribute accidents, illnesses, or other misfortunes to evil magic practiced by malevolent individuals such as witches or sorcerers. Do you believe people really possess such supernatural powers to inflict harm?

3. Do the basic dynamics of the shamanic complex also apply to preachers or priests in modern churches and medical doctors working in modern hospitals? Can you think of some similarities among the shaman, preacher, and medical doctor in terms of their respective fields of operation?

4. Graduation is a rite of passage, also known as commencement or convocation, when a high-ranking university official presents students who have completed their studies an academic degree. Can you identify the three phases in this ceremony?

5. Revitalization movements occur in reaction to the upheavals caused by rapid colonization and modernization. Do you think that the rise of religious fundamentalism among Christians, Muslims, Jews, and Hindus is a response to such upheavals as well?

ONLINE STUDY RESOURCES

CourseMate

Access chapter-specific learning tools, including learning objectives, practice quizzes, videos, flash cards, glossaries, and more in your Anthropology CourseMate.

Log into **www.cengagebrain.com** to access the resources your instructor has assigned and to purchase materials.

Challenge Issue

Humans in all cultures face the challenge of creatively articulating ideas and emotions concerning themselves and the world around them. Across the globe, people have developed art forms—musical, visual, verbal, movement, and so on—that symbolically express meanings and messages. Art may be individual and personal. It may also communicate, stimulate, and reinforce experiences and feelings of collective cultural identity. So it is with this group of Amazonian Indians in traditional ceremonial paint and dress. Their heads are crowned with colorful radiating feathers that represent the universe. Their faces and bodies are painted with black and red designs that convey strength—the black dye made of charcoal and *genipap* fruit juice, the red of crushed *urucu* seeds. And they carry age-old tribal weapons—clubs, spears, bows, and arrows. What is not traditional is their transportation. These Kayapo warriors are riding in a rented Brazilian bus to a town on the lower Xingu River to stage a political protest. With dance, song, oratory, and body ornamentation, they are demonstrating against a $17 billion hydropower project, the third largest in the world. For two decades they have held artful protests to halt the building of a dam that threatens the health and cultural traditions of the Kayapo, along with those of other Xingu River tribes.

The Arts

Humans in all cultures throughout time have expressed feelings and ideas about themselves and the world around them through **art**—the creative use of the human imagination to aesthetically interpret, express, and engage life, modifying experienced reality in the process. Art comes in many forms, including visual, verbal, musical, and motion—sometimes in combination and in an ever-expanding array of formats made possible by the continual emergence of new technologies. Most societies, past and present, have used art to symbolically express almost every part of their culture, including ideas about religion, kinship, and ethnic identity.

From an anthropological perspective, the photo that opens this chapter is far more than a curious image of traditionally painted, feathered, and armed Kayapo Indians traveling to a protest rally in a modern bus. Their intended event is an illustration of **performance art**—a creatively expressed promotion of ideas by artful means dramatically staged to challenge opinion and/or provoke purposeful action. In Kayapo culture, dancing combined with the singing of warrior chants is a traditional variation of this art form—as it is in many societies all across the globe. Through this particular performance, dramatically and artfully staged as a public spectacle in an electronic media environment, they expected to reach a global audience of millions and win widespread support for their political struggle against an overpowering opponent (Conklin, 1997; Prins, 2002). Although demonstrations by Kayapo and neighboring tribes of the Xingu River have drawn international attention, the dam is now being built and will soon flood 400 square kilometers (150 square miles) of tropical forest and destroy their habitat.

Despite daily evidence of political (and commercial) uses of art, most people living in the industrialized corners of the world think of the arts almost exclusively as an aesthetic pleasure for personal or shared enjoyment. From this "art for art's sake" perspective, art appears to be confined to a distinctive cultural domain, quite apart from political, economic, religious, and otherwise pragmatic or ideological activities. But in most traditional cultures, art is almost always deeply embedded, so much so that many of these cultures do not have a distinctive term for it.

art The creative use of the human imagination to aesthetically interpret, express, and engage life, modifying experienced reality in the process.

performance art A creatively expressed promotion of ideas by artful means dramatically staged to challenge opinion and/or provoke purposeful action.

IN THIS CHAPTER YOU WILL LEARN TO

- Define *art* and examine how it is intertwined with other parts of a cultural system.

- Summarize anthropology's cross-cultural and comparative historical perspective on art.

- Identify different types of art, each with specific anthropological examples.

- Recognize how art expresses worldview and analyze its functions in the context of religion and shamanism.

- Explain and give examples of the relationship between art and cultural identity.

- Analyze how art has become a commodity in a market economy, and critically evaluate what that means in a globalized environment of rapid change.

For instance, commenting on beautiful ivory figurines carved by Aivilik Inuit (Eskimo hunters in Arctic Canada), anthropologist Edmund Carpenter observes: "No word meaning 'art' occurs in Aivilik, nor does 'artist.' . . . Art to the Aivilik is an act, not an object; a ritual, not a possession. . . . They are more interested in the creative activity than in the product of that activity [and do not differentiate between] works of art and utilitarian objects: but the two are usually one (Carpenter, 1959, n.p.). Carpenter elaborates:

> When we look at [Eskimo] art & see the particular shape of it, we are only looking at its after-life. Its real life is the movement by which it got to be that shape. Eskimo often discard carvings immediately after making them. (Carpenter, 1968, pp. 69–74; see also Prins & McBride, 2012)

In many cultures, the "real life" of some artful objects begins with death because they are made not to please or be admired by the living, but to accompany people who have passed on to an afterlife. We see an example of this in exquisite objects discovered in the ancient tomb of the young Egyptian Tutankhamen. Museumgoers in today's world have flocked to King Tut exhibitions. Yet, the objects on display were not created for human eyes, but rather to guarantee the eternal life of the divine pharaoh and to protect him from evil forces that might enter his body and gain control over it. Symbols of worldview, they were deeply embedded in the culture.

Similarly, we may listen to the singing of a sea chantey purely for aesthetic pleasure, as a form of entertainment. But, in the era of sailing by wind power alone, sea chanteys served very useful and practical purposes. They set the appropriate rhythm for the performance of specific shipboard tasks such as hoisting or reefing sails, and the same qualities that make them pleasurable to listen to today served to coordinate these tasks and to relieve boredom.

Such intricate links between art and other aspects of life are common in human societies around the world. This can also be seen in the way that art has been incorporated into everyday, functional objects—from utensils, pottery, and baskets used to serve, carry, or store food to carpets and mats woven by nomadic herders to cover the ground inside their portable tent dwellings. Designs painted on or woven or carved into such objects typically express ideas, values, and objects that have meaning to an entire community (**Figure 24.1**).

All of this goes to show that artful expression is as basic to human beings as talking and is by no means limited to a unique category of individuals specialized as artists. For example, all human beings adorn their

VISUAL COUNTERPOINT

Figure 24.1 Functional and Aesthetic Art On the left is a wooden spoon used by the Dan people of Côte d'Ivoire in West Africa, carver unknown. On the right is a bronze sculpture, *Spoon Woman*, created by the Italian artist Alberto Giacometti in 1926. Both may be beautiful, but one is functional and the other purely aesthetic. Usually, traditional utilitarian objects, no matter how exquisite, are identified only in terms of the "primitive" or "tribal" cultures in which they were made. In contrast, "works of art," created for the sake of art itself, are typically tied to the name of the person who made them. How curious it is that this great modern piece credited to the famous Giacometti was inspired by an elegant functional object made by a now-nameless West African.

Dan peoples, Liberia, Cote d'Ivoire, Ceremonial Ladle. Wood, Height 20-1/2 × Width 4-3/4 × Depth 3-1/4 inches. Indiana University Art Museum, Bloomington,63.221. Photograph by: Michael Cavanagh and Kevin Montague

Giraudon/Art Resource. N.Y. © 2012 Alberto Giacometti Estate/Licensed VAGA and Artists Rights Society (ARS), New York, NY

bodies in certain ways and by doing so make a statement about who they are, both as individuals and as members of society. Similarly, people in all cultures tell stories in which they express their values, hopes, and concerns and in the process reveal much about themselves and the nature of the world as they see it.

In short, all peoples engage in artistic expression. And, they have been doing this in countless ways for more than 40,000 years—from carving mammoth ivory figures, to fashioning and playing vulture wing bone flutes, to painting animals on ancient rock walls, to digital music jamming on iPhones. Far from being a luxury to be afforded or appreciated by a minority of sophisticated experts or frivolous lovers of art, creativity is a necessary activity in which everyone participates in one way or another.

Whether a particular work of art is intended to be appreciated purely for beauty or to serve some practical purpose, it requires the same special combination of symbolic representation of form and expression of feeling that constitute the creative imagination. Because human creativity and the ability to symbolize are universal, art is an important subject for anthropological study.

The Anthropological Study of Art

Anthropologists have found that art often reflects a society's collective ideas, values, and concerns. Indeed, through the cross-cultural study of art, we may discover much about different worldviews and religious beliefs, as well as political ideas, social values, kinship structures, economic relations, and historical memory.

In approaching art as a cultural phenomenon, anthropologists have the pleasant task of cataloguing, photographing, recording, describing, and analyzing all possible forms of imaginative activity in any particular culture. An enormous variety of forms and modes of artistic expression exists in the world. Because people everywhere continue to create and develop in ever-new ways, there is no end to the interesting process of collecting and describing the world's ornaments, ceremonial masks, body decorations, clothing variations, blanket and rug designs, pottery and basket styles, monuments, architectural embellishments, legends, work songs, dances, and other art forms—many of them rich with religious symbolism.

To study and analyze art, anthropologists employ a combination of aesthetic, narrative, and interpretive approaches. The distinctions among these methods can be illustrated through a famous work of Western art, Leonardo da Vinci's painting *The Last Supper*, showing Jesus Christ and his apostles on their last night together

before his arrest and crucifixion. A non-Christian viewing this late 15th-century mural in Italy will see thirteen people at a table, apparently enjoying a meal. Although one of the men clutches a bag of money and appears to have knocked over a dish of salt, nothing else in the scene seems out of the ordinary.

Aesthetically, our non-Christian observer may admire the way the composition fits the space available, how the attitudes of the men are depicted, and the means by which the artist conveys a sense of movement. As narrative, the painting may be seen as a record of customs, table manners, dress, and architecture. But to interpret this picture—to perceive its real meaning—the viewer must be aware that in Christian symbolic culture money traditionally represents the root of all evil, and spilling the salt suggests impending disaster. But even this is not enough; to fully understand this work of art, one must know something of the beliefs of Christianity. And if one wishes to understand other renditions of the Last Supper made by artists in other corners of the world, it is necessary to bring insights about those cultures into the equation as well (**Figure 24.2**). In other words, moving to the interpretive level of studying art requires knowledge of the symbols and beliefs of the people responsible for the art (Lewis-Williams, 1990).

A good way to deepen our insight into the relationship between art and the rest of culture is to examine critically some of the generalizations that have already been made about specific art forms. Because it is impossible to cover all art forms in the space of a single chapter, we will concentrate on just a few—visual, verbal, and musical—in that order.

Visual Art

For many people, the first thing that springs to mind in connection with the word *art* is some sort of visual image, be it a painting, drawing, sketch, or whatever. Created primarily for visual perception, **visual art** ranges from etchings and paintings on various surfaces (including the human body) to sculptures and weavings made with an array of materials.

In many parts of the world, people have been making pictures in one way or another for a very long time—etching in bone; engraving in rock; painting on cave walls and rock surfaces; carving and painting on wood, gourds, and clay pots; or painting on textiles, bark cloth, animal hide, or even their own bodies. Some form of visual art is a part of every historically known human culture, and extraordinary examples have been found at prehistoric sites dating back almost 45,000 years.

---

visual art Art created primarily for visual perception, ranging from etchings and paintings on various surfaces (including the human body) to sculptures and weavings made with an array of materials.

Courtesy of Erin Erkun

Figure 24.2 *The Last Supper* **by Marcos Zapata (c. 1710–1773)** To interpret this painting, one must know about Christianity and the artist's cultural background. It depicts the final meal shared by a spiritual leader and his twelve followers the eve before his execution, an event commemorated by Christians for nearly 2,000 years. For centuries, artists in many societies have imagined this event in paintings, often copying from others before them. This artist was an indigenous painter living in Cuzco, once capital of the Inca empire and long colonized by Spaniards. Baptized as a Christian, he was influenced by European imagery but made cultural adjustments so fellow Andean Indians coming to the church would understand its significance. Directly looking at us is St. Peter, showing his sacred key to heaven. At the center of the table sits Jesus, foretelling his death as a sacrifice, promising he will resurrect and return as the Messiah. However, instead of a sheep lamb, Zapata painted a roasted *cui* (*Cavia porcellus*) on the platter. Traditionally eaten by Andean highlanders, this domesticated guinea pig has long been used for sacrificial and divining purposes; it is a culturally relevant substitute for the sacrificial lamb, a traditional Israelite symbol representing their divine rescue from slavery in Egypt. He also substituted red wine with *chicha*, an indigenous beer made of fermented maize.

Symbolism in Visual Art

As a type of symbolic expression, visual art may be representational (imitating closely the forms of nature) or abstract (drawing from natural forms but representing only their basic patterns or arrangements). In some of the Indian art of North America's northwest coast, for example, animal figures may be so highly stylized as to be difficult for an outsider to identify. Although the art appears abstract, the artist has created it based on nature, even though he or she has exaggerated and deliberately transformed various shapes to express a particular feeling toward the animals. Because artists do these exaggerations and transformations according to the aesthetic principles of their Indian culture, their meanings are understood not just by the artist but by other members of the community as well.

This collective understanding of symbols is a hallmark in traditional art. Unlike modern Western art, which is judged in large part on its creative originality and the unique vision of an individual artist, traditional art is all about community and shared symbolism. Consider, for example, symbols related to kinship. As discussed in earlier chapters, small-scale traditional societies—hunter-gatherers, nomadic herders, slash-and-burn horticulturists—are profoundly interested in kinship relations. In such societies, kinship may be symbolically expressed in stylized motifs and colorful designs etched or painted on human skin, animal hides or bones, pottery, wood, rocks, or almost any other surface imaginable. To cultural outsiders these designs appear to be purely decorative, ornamental, or

VISUAL COUNTERPOINT

Figure 24.3 **Kinship Symbolism in Art** In the figure at left, the top row shows the stylized human figures that are the basic bricks used in the construction of genealogical patterns. The bottom row shows how these basic figures are linked arm-and-leg with diagonally adjacent figures to depict descent. For thousands of years people all over the world have linked such figures together, creating the familiar geometric patterns that we see in countless art forms—from pottery to sculpture to weavings—patterns that informed eyes recognize as genealogical. Pictured in the figure on the right are traditional wooden shields with kinship designs made by Asmat people in West Papua.

abstract, but they can actually be decoded in terms of genealogical iconography primarily illustrating social relations of marriage and descent (Prins, 1998; Schuster & Carpenter, 1996) **(Figure 24.3)**.

Shared symbolism has also been fundamental to the traditional visual art of tattooing—although that is changing in some parts of the world, as discussed in the following Original Study.

ORIGINAL STUDY

The Modern Tattoo Community *BY MARGO DEMELLO*

As an anthropology graduate student in the early 1990s, I had no idea what (or, more accurately, whom) to study for my field research. Working as an animal advocate, I had a house full of creatures to care for, which left me in no position for long-term travel to a far-off field site.

Then one of my professors suggested a topic that was literally under my nose—tattooing. I myself had several tattoos and spent quite a bit of time with other tattooed people, including my husband, who had just become a professional tattooist.

Early on in my research, I, along with my husband, strove to find a way to "join" what is known as the "tattoo community," finding that it was not as friendly and open as we had imagined it to be. As an anthropologist, I came to see that the sense of exclusion we felt reflected the fact that we were on the lower rungs of a highly stratified social group in which an artist's status is based on such features as class, geography, and professional and artistic credentials,

and a "fan" might be judged on the type and extent of his or her tattoos, the artist(s) who created them, the level of media coverage achieved, and more. This awareness led to one of the major focuses of my work: how class and status increasingly came to define this once working-class art form.

Ultimately, I spent almost five years studying and writing about tattooing, finding my "community" wherever tattooed people talked about themselves and each other—within the pages of tattoo magazines and mainstream newspapers, on Internet newsgroups, and at tattoo-oriented events across the country. I spent countless hours in tattoo shops watching the artists work; I collected what I call "tattoo narratives," which are often elaborate, sometimes spiritual, stories that people tell about their tattoos; and I followed the careers of seminal artists. I even learned to tattoo a bit myself, placing a few particularly ugly images on my patient husband's body.

Tattoos are created by inserting ink or some other pigment through the epidermis (outer skin) into the dermis (the second layer of skin) through the use of needles. They may be beautiful as designs in and of themselves, but they can also express a multitude of meanings about the wearer and his or her place within the social group. Whether used in an overt punitive fashion (as in the tattooing of slaves or prisoners) or to mark clan or cult membership, religious or tribal affiliation, social status, or marital position, tattoos have historically been a social sign. They have long been one of the simplest ways of establishing humans as social beings. In fact, tattooing is one of the most persistent and universal forms of body art and may date back as far as the Upper Paleolithic era (10,000–40,000 years ago).

Tattoos as signs derive their communicative power from more than a simple sign-to-meaning correspondence: They also communicate through color, style, manner of execution, and location on the body. Traditionally inscribed on easily viewable parts of the body, tattoos were designed to be "read" by others and were part of a collectively understood system of inscription. However, for many middle-class North Americans today tattoos are more about private statement than public sign, and these individuals, especially women, tend to favor smaller tattoos in private spots.

The process by which tattooing has expanded in the United States from a working-class folk art into a more widespread and often refined aesthetic practice is related to a number of shifts in North American culture that occurred during the 1970s and 1980s. This time period saw the introduction of finely trained artists into tattooing, bringing with them radically different backgrounds and artistic sensibilities to draw from. More and more middle-class men and women began getting tattooed, attracted by the expanded artistic choices and the new, more spiritual context of body decoration.

Tattoos have been partially transformed into fine art by a process of redefinition and framing based on formal qualities (that is, the skill of the artist, the iconic content of the tattoo, the style in which the tattoo is executed, and so on) and ideological qualities (the discourses that surround "artistic" tattoos, discourses that point to some higher reality on which the tattoo is based). When it is judged that a tattoo has certain formal artistic qualities as well as expresses a higher, often spiritual, reality, then it is seen as art.

Although it may seem as though tattoos are not good candidates to be defined as art, due to their lack of permanence (the body, after all, ages and dies) and their seeming inability to be displayed within a gallery setting, modern tattoo art shows get around these problems by photographing tattoos and displaying them in a way that showcases the "art" and often minimizes the body. By both literally and figuratively "framing" tattoos in a museum or gallery setting, or within an art book, the tattoo is removed from its social function and remade into art.

The basic working-class American tattoo designs (such as "Mother" or "Donna" inscribed alongside a heart) have been relegated to the bottom rung of today's tattoo hierarchy in the United States. Such tattoos are now seen by middle-class artists and fans as too literal, too transparently obvious, and too grounded in everyday experience and social life to qualify as art.

The modern, artistic tattoos that have increasingly gained favor are less "readable" and no longer have an easily recognizable function. Often derived from foreign (or "exotic") cultures (such as Polynesia) and custom-drawn for the wearer, they tend to eliminate the social aspect in favor of the highly individualistic. Some are purely decorative, and those that are intended to signify meaning often do so only for the individual or those in his or her intimate circle.

© RossParry.co.uk

While serving in Afghanistan, British soldier Shaun Clark vowed to have the name of every British troop killed there tattooed on his body to honor their sacrifice. By the time he sat down in the tattooist's chair to fulfill his promise in 2009, that number had reached 232, and it took nearly five hours to inscribe all the names on his back. Adding new names each Remembrance Day (November 12), the count has reached nearly 400 and spread to one of his legs.

Tattoos in the United States have traveled a long way from the tattoo of old: brought to North America by way of British Captain James Cook's 18th-century explorations of the Pacific, moving, over time, from a mark of affiliation to a highly individual statement of personal identity, losing and regaining function, meaning, and content along the way. In our increasingly global world, tattoo designs and motifs move swiftly and easily across cultural boundaries. As this happens, their original, communal meanings are often lost—but they are not meaningless. An animal crest tattoo traditionally worn by Indians on the northwest coast of North America to signify clan membership may now be worn by a non-Native in Boston as an artful, often private, sign of rebellion against Western "coat and tie" consumer culture.

Written expressly for this text, 2005. For more on this topic, see DeMello, M. (2000). *Bodies of inscription: A cultural history of the modern tattoo community.* Durham, NC: Duke University Press.

Rock Art from Southern Africa

Rock art—paintings and engravings made on the faces of rock outcrops and on the interior walls of rock shelters—is one of the world's oldest art traditions, dating back at least 40,000 years. Bushmen in southern Africa practiced this art continually from 27,000 years ago (perhaps earlier) until the beginning of the 20th century when European colonization led to the demise of their societies. Their art depicted humans and animals in highly sophisticated ways, sometimes in static poses but often in highly animated scenes. It also featured what appear to be abstract signs—dots, zigzags, nested curves, and the like. Until fairly recently, non-Bushmen were puzzled by the significance of these abstract features, as well as by the fact that new pictures were often created directly over existing images.

Because Bushmen rock art, especially the paintings, are generally seen as beautiful and pleasurable to look at, it is not surprising that the specialists who first studied them took the aesthetic approach, analyzing how things were depicted. Investigating the various colored pigments, they found that the Bushmen had used charcoal and specularite (hematite mineral) for black; silica, china clay, and gypsum for white; and ferric oxide for red and reddish-brown hues—and that they had mixed the colors with fat, blood, and perhaps water. The paint had been applied to the rough rock with great skill. Indeed, the effectiveness of the line and the way shading was used to suggest the contours of the animals' bodies elicit admiration, as does the realistic rendering of details such as the twist of an eland's horns or the black line running along its back.

Specialists also analyze the narrative quality of Bushmen rock art, investigating *what* it depicts. Certainly, aspects of Bushmen life are shown, as in several hunting scenes of men among animals—especially eland, which they believed possessed supernatural powers (**Figure 24.4**). Often the men are outfitted with spears or bows, arrows, and quivers. Some depictions show hunting nets and also fish traps. Women are also portrayed—identifiable by

Figure 24.4 Rock Art by Bushmen in Southern Africa Bushmen created rock paintings and engravings depicting animals they believed possessed great supernatural powers, especially the eland. Many of these renderings also featured trance dancing, sometimes showing shamans magically transforming into birds, appearing elongated and weightless as if in flight or water—imagery based on altered states of consciousness experienced in trance.

their visible sexual characteristics and the stone-weighted digging sticks they carry.

In addition to aesthetic and narrative approaches, researchers study rock art from an interpretive angle—looking at it in light of contemporary ethnographic research among modern-day Bushmen communities. Doing so, we see that certain designs relate to the shamanic trance dance. These often include fly whisks (used to extract invisible arrows of sickness) and designs of hand-clapping women surrounding dancing men whose bodies are bent forward in the distinctive posture caused by the cramping of abdominal muscles as they go into trance. The designs also show dancers' arms outstretched behind their backs, which present-day Bushmen do to catch more *n/um* (supernatural power).

However, for a more complete interpretation of this scene, anthropologists have to go beyond ethnographic observation and description of the trance dance and learn about altered states of consciousness. Laboratory research shows that humans typically move through three stages when entering a trance. In the first stage, the nervous system generates images of luminous, pulsating, revolving, and constantly shifting geometric patterns known as *entoptic phenomena*—similar to images seen during a migraine headache. Usually, these include dots, zigzags, grids, filigrees, nested curves, and parallel lines, often in a spiral pattern.

In the second stage, the brain tries to make sense of these abstract forms (a process known as *construal*). Here, cultural influences come into play, so a trancing Bushman in southern Africa's Kalahari is likely to construe a grid pattern as markings on the skin of a giraffe, nested curves as a honeycomb (honey is a delicacy in the region), and so forth. An American police officer in New York or a Chinese priest in Shanghai would construe the patterns in very different ways.

During the third and deepest trance stage, people tend to feel as if they are at one with their visions, passing into a rotating tunnel or vortex. Typically, the tunnel has latticelike sides in which *iconic images* of animals, humans, and monsters appear, merging with the entoptic forms of the early trance stages. Because these iconic images are culture specific, individuals usually see things that have high significance within their culture. Thus, Bushmen often see the eland, a massive antelope they believe carries supernatural powers for making rain. One of the things shamans try to do in trance is to "capture" these envisioned elands ("rain animals") for purposes of making rain.

All of this helps us understand why elands are so prominent in Bushmen rock art. Moreover, it reveals the significance of the zigzags, dots, grids, and so forth that are so often a part of the compositions. It also leads to an understanding of other puzzling features of the art. For example, the third trance stage includes sensations such as being stretched out or elongated, weightlessness as in flight or in the water, and difficulty breathing as when under water. Hence we find depictions in the art of humans who appear to be abnormally long, as well as individuals who appear to be swimming or flying.

Another well-documented trance phenomenon is the sensation of being transformed into some sort of animal. Such experiences are triggered in the deepest stage of trance if the individual sees or thinks of an animal. This sensation accounts for the part human–part animal (*therianthrope*) images in the art.

Finally, we are able to comprehend the layering of one work of art over another with the interpretative approach; not only are the visions seen in trance commonly superimposed on one another as they rotate and move, but if the trancer stares at a painting or engraving of an earlier vision, the new one will appear as if projected on the old.

The interpretive approach makes clear, then, that the rock art of southern Africa—even in the case of compositions that otherwise might appear to be scenes of everyday life—is intimately connected with the practices and beliefs of shamanism. After shamans came out of trance and reflected on their visions, they painted or engraved their recollections on the rock faces. But these were more than records of important visions; they had their own innate power, owing to their supposed supernatural origin. This being so, when the need arose for a new trance experience, it might be held where the old vision was recorded to draw power from it.

A similar interpretive analysis is needed to fully understand the art of Huichol Indians living in Mexico, as profiled in this chapter's Biocultural Connection feature.

Verbal Art

Verbal art is creative word use on display that includes stories, myths, legends, tales, poetry, metaphor, rhyme, chants, drama, cant, proverbs, jokes, puns, riddles, and tongue twisters.

In the 19th century, when the industrial revolution triggered a series of radical changes in the national cultural fabric of state societies, the pressures of modernization were also transforming the way of life in traditional communities of peasants and other rural peoples. Although many folk communities still preserved

---

verbal art Creative word use on display that includes stories, myths, legends, tales, poetry, metaphor, rhyme, chants, drama, cant, proverbs, jokes, puns, riddles, and tongue twisters.

BIOCULTURAL CONNECTION

Peyote Art: Divine Visions among the Huichol

For generations, Huichol Indians living in Mexico's mountainous western Sierra Madre region have created art remarkable for its vibrant colors. They are especially noted for their spectacular beadwork and embroidery. Although many people far and wide appreciate the intricate beauty of Huichol art, most are probably unaware that the colorful designs express a religious worldview tied to the chemical substance of a sacred plant: a small cactus "button" known as peyote (*Lophophora williamsii*).[a]

Among the many Huichol gods and goddesses, all addressed in kinship terms, is Our Grandfather Fire. His principal spirit helper is Our Elder Brother Deer, a messenger between the gods and humans. Serving the Huichol as their spiritual guide, this divine deer is also the peyote cactus itself. Huichol Indians refer to peyote as *yawéi hikuri*, the "divine flesh of Elder Brother Deer." Guided by their shamans on a pilgrimage to harvest peyote, they "hunt" this "deer" in Wirikúta, the sacred desert highlands where their ancestor deities dwell. Having found and "shot" the first cactus button with an arrow, they gather many more, later to be consumed in fresh, dried, or liquid form.

Huichol artist Olivia Carrillo makes peyote-inspired art in Real de Catorce, a town in the mountains of central Mexico. About an hour's horseback ride away from the Huichol sacred mountain Wirikúta, the town is located in the peyote heartland.

Participating in a holy communion with the creator god, Huichol shamans consume peyote (the divine flesh) as a sacrament. Doing so, they enter into an ecstatic trance. With the help of peyote, their spiritual guide, they become hawks or eagles soaring high in the sky. Having visions extending far across the world, they interact directly with their gods and seek advice on behalf of those who need help in dealing with illness and other misfortunes.

From a chemical point of view, peyote contains a psychotropic substance identified by scientists as an alkaloid. By consuming some of this toxic

organic substance, the Huichol move into an altered state of consciousness. In this dreamlike psychological state, which is also profoundly emotional, they experience religiously inspired, brilliantly colored visions from their spirit world.

These are reflected in Huichol art, such as the piece pictured here in which a stylized peyote button and deer have been rendered in rainbow-hued beadwork by Huichol artist Olivia Carrillo, who lives in the peyote heartland of central Mexico. The sacred cactus, with its flower- or starlike shape, is the most prominent symbolic design in Huichol art, beaded onto fabric and objects of all kinds or embroidered on clothing.

BIOCULTURAL QUESTION

In Huichol Indian art we often find vibrantly colored peyote buttons, articulating shamanic visions induced by this psychotropic cactus. What was it that inspired traditional European artists to paint Christian holy men and women with a halo—a silver- or gold-colored ring around or above their heads?

---

[a]Schaeffer, S. B., & Furst, P. T. (Eds.). (1996). *People of the peyote: Huichol Indian history, religion, and survival.* Albuquerque: University of New Mexico Press.

---

their own unique historical heritage, their distinctive local customs—including legends, songs, dances, dress, and crafts—began to disappear without a trace. Alarmed about these vanishing traditions, some amateur scholars and professional academics began collecting the unwritten popular stories (and other artistic traditions) of rural peoples. They coined the word **folklore** to distinguish between "folk art" and the "fine art" of the elite. Today, many linguists and anthropologists prefer to speak of a

culture's oral traditions and verbal arts rather than its folklore and folktales, recognizing that the distinction between folk art and fine art is a projection imposed by Western elites.

---

folklore A term coined by 19th-century scholars studying the unwritten stories and other artistic traditions of rural peoples to distinguish between "folk art" and the "fine art" of the literate elite.

Generally, the narratives that make up the verbal arts have been divided into several basic and recurring categories, including myth, legend, and tale.

Myth

As discussed in the previous chapter, the term **myth** comes from the Greek word *mythos*, meaning "speech" or "story." It is a narrative that explains the fundamentals of human existence—where we and everything in our world came from, why we are here, and where we are going. A myth provides a rationale for religious beliefs and practices and sets cultural standards for proper behavior. A typical creation or origin myth, traditional with the western Abenaki Indians of northwestern New England and southern Quebec, is as follows:

> In the beginning, *Tabaldak*, "The Owner," created all living things but one—the spirit being who was to accomplish the final transformation of the earth. *Tabaldak* made man and woman out of a piece of stone, but he didn't like the result, their hearts being cold and hard. So, he broke them up, and their remains today can be seen in the many stones that litter the landscape of the Abenaki homeland. Then *Tabaldak* tried again, this time using living wood, and from this came all later Abenakis. Like the trees from which the wood came, these people were rooted in the earth and could dance as gracefully as trees swaying in the wind.
>
> The one living thing not created by *Tabaldak* was *Odzihózo*, "He Makes Himself from Something." This transformer created himself out of dust, but he wasn't able to accomplish it all at once. At first, he managed only his head, body, and arms; the legs came later, growing slowly as legs do on a tadpole. Not waiting until his legs were grown, he set out to transform the shape of the earth. He dragged his body about with his hands, gouging channels that became the rivers. To make the mountains, he piled dirt up with his hands. Once his legs grew, *Odzihózo's* task was made easier; by merely extending his legs, he made the tributaries of the main stream. . . .
>
> The last work he made was Lake Champlain and liked it so well that he climbed onto a rock in Burlington Bay and changed himself into stone so he could sit there and enjoy his masterpiece through the ages. He is still there and he is still given offerings of tobacco as Abenakis pass this way. The Abenaki call the rock *Odzihózo*, since it is the Transformer himself. (Haviland & Power, 1994)

myth A sacred narrative that explains the fundamentals of human existence—where we and everything in our world came from, why we are here, and where we are going.

legend A story about a memorable event or figure handed down by tradition and told as true but without historical evidence.

Such a myth, insofar as it is believed, accepted, and perpetuated in a culture, expresses part of a people's traditional worldview. This Abenaki myth accounts for the existence of rivers, mountains, lakes, and other features of the landscape (such as Odzihózo Rock pictured in Figure 24.5), as well as of humans and all other living things. It also sanctions particular attitudes and behaviors. The myth is a product of creative imagination and is a work of art, as well as potentially a religious statement.

Extrapolating from the details of this particular Abenaki myth, we may conclude that these people recognize a kinship among all living things; after all, they were all part of the same creation, and even humans were made from living wood. This idea of closeness among all living things led the Abenaki to show special respect to the animals they hunted in order to sustain their own lives. For example, before eating meat, they placed an offering of grease on the fire to thank Tabaldak.

A characteristic of myths, including this one, is that they simplify and explain the unknown in terms of the known. The analysis of myths has been carried to great lengths, becoming a field of study almost unto itself. Myth making is an extremely significant kind of human creativity, and studying the myth-making process and its results can offer valuable insight into the way people perceive and think about their world.

Legend

A **legend** is a story about a memorable event or figure handed down by tradition and told as true but without historical evidence. Legends commonly consist of pseudo-historical narratives that account for the deeds of heroes, the movements of peoples, and the establishment of local customs, typically with a mixture of realism and the supernatural or extraordinary. As stories, they are not necessarily believed or disbelieved, but they usually serve to entertain as well as to instruct and to inspire or bolster pride in family, community, or nation. Legends all around the world tell us something about the cultures in which they are found.

A noteworthy example of a popular legend is that American Indians at Cape Cod welcomed the English Pilgrims who came to the "New World" seeking religious freedom—generously sharing their food and helping the newcomers survive their first winter. Gaining acceptance in the 19th century, this romantic first-arrival story is often told during Thanksgiving, an important national holiday in the United States. For Native Americans, it is a false representation of what actually happened almost 400 years ago—the beginning of a foreign invasion and violent dispossession of their ancestral homeland. Thus, many Native Americans do not celebrate Thanksgiving Day.

To a degree, in literate societies the function of legends has been taken over by history. The trouble is that history does not always tell people what they want to hear about

© Ray Brown

Figure 24.5 **Odzihózo Rock, Lake Champlain, Burlington, Vermont** This small granite island is featured in the creation myth of Abenaki Indians, the original inhabitants of this region. For untold generations, they have referred to it as Odzihózo after the mythical transformer who laid out the river channels and lake basins in northeastern North America.

themselves, or, conversely, it tells them things that they would prefer not to hear. By projecting their culture's hopes and expectations onto the record of the past, they seize upon and even exaggerate some past events while ignoring or giving scant attention to others. Although this often takes place unconsciously, so strong is the motivation to transform history into legend that states have even gone so far as to deliberately rewrite it.

An **epic** is a long, dramatic narrative, recounting the celebrated deeds of a historic or legendary hero, often sung or recited in poetic language. In parts of western and Central Africa, people hold remarkably elaborate and formalized recitations of extremely long legends, lasting several hours and even days. These long narratives have been described as veritable encyclopedias of a culture's most diverse aspects, with direct and indirect statements about history, institutions, relationships, values, and ideas. Epics are typically found in nonliterate societies with some form of state political organization; they serve to transmit and preserve a culture's legal and political precedents and practices.

Legends may incorporate mythological details, especially when they make an appeal to the supernatural, and are therefore not always clearly distinct from myth. Legends may also incorporate proverbs and

incidental tales and thus be related to other forms of verbal art as well.

For the anthropologist, the secular and apparently realistic portions of legends, whether long or short, carry particular significance because of the clues they provide as to what constitutes a culture's approved or ideal ethical behavior. The subject matter of legends is essentially problem solving and mentoring, and the content is likely to include physical and psychological trials of many kinds. Certain questions may be answered explicitly or implicitly: In what circumstances, if any, does the culture permit homicide? What kinds of behavior are considered heroic or cowardly? Does the culture stress forgiveness over retaliation as an admirable trait?

Tale

A third type of creative narrative, the **tale**, is recognized as fiction that is for entertainment but may also draw a moral or teach a practical lesson. Consider this brief

epic A long, dramatic narrative, recounting the celebrated deeds of a historic or legendary hero, often sung or recited in poetic language.

tale A creative narrative that is recognized as fiction for entertainment but may also draw a moral or teach a practical lesson.

© Inspirits/www.inspirits.net

Figure 24.6 Father, Son, and Donkey in China A Uyghur father prepares his donkey cart together with his son to transport fruits to the market. A scene such as this may bring to mind the internationally popular "Father, Son, and Donkey" tale. Told in different versions, this tale conveys a basic motif or story situation—father and son trying in vain to please everyone. (The cart, basket, and saddle blanket are examples of functional art.)

summary of a tale from Ghana in West Africa, known as "Father, Son, and Donkey" (Figure 24.6):

A father and his son farmed their corn, sold it, and spent part of the profit on a donkey. When the hot season came, they harvested their yams and prepared to take them to storage, using their donkey. The father mounted the donkey and they all three proceeded on their way until they met some people. "What? You lazy man!" the people said to the father. "You let your young son walk barefoot on this hot ground while you ride on a donkey? For shame!" The father yielded his place to the son, and they proceeded until they came to an old woman. "What? You useless boy!" said the old woman. "You ride on the donkey and let your poor father walk barefoot on this hot ground? For shame!" The son dismounted, and both father and son walked on the road, leading the donkey behind them until they came to an old man. "What? You foolish people!" said the old man. "You have a donkey and you walk barefoot on the hot ground instead of riding?" And so it goes. Listen: When you are doing something and other people come along, just keep on doing what you like.

This is precisely the kind of tale that is of special interest in traditional folklore studies. It is an internationally popular "numbskull" tale. Versions of it have been recorded in India, Southwest Asia, southern and western Europe, and North America, as well as in West Africa. It is classified or catalogued as exhibiting a basic **motif** or story situation—father and son trying to please everyone—one of the many thousands that have been found to recur in tales around the world. Despite variations in detail, every version follows the same basic structure in the sequence of events, sometimes called the syntax of the tale: A peasant father and son work together, a beast of burden is purchased, the three set out on a short excursion, the father rides and is criticized, the son rides and is criticized, both walk and are criticized, and a conclusion is drawn.

Tales of this sort (not to mention myths and legends) that are found to have wide geographic distribution raise some questions: Where did they originate? Did the story arise only once and then pass from one culture to another (diffusion)? Or did the stories arise independently (independent invention) in response to like causes in similar settings, or perhaps as a consequence of inherited mental preferences and images deeply embedded in the evolutionary construction of the human brain? Or is it merely that there are logical limits to the structure of stories, so that, by coincidence, different cultures are bound to come up with similar motifs and syntax (Gould, 2000)?

A surprisingly large number of motifs in European and African tales are traceable to ancient sources in India, evidence of diffusion of tales. Of course, purely local tales also exist. Within any particular culture, anthropologists usually can categorize local types of tales: animal, human experience, trickster, dilemma, ghost, moral, scatological, nonsense tales, and so on. In West Africa, for example, there is a remarkable prevalence of stories with animal protagonists. Many were carried to the slaveholding areas of the Americas; the Uncle Remus stories about Brer Rabbit and Brer Fox may be part of this tradition.

The significance of tales for the anthropologist rests partly in this matter of their distribution. They provide evidence of either cultural contacts or cultural isolation and of limits of influence and cultural cohesion.

Anthropologists are interested, however, in more than these questions of distribution. Like legends, tales very often illustrate local solutions to universal human ethical problems, and in some sense they state a moral philosophy. Anthropologists recognize that regardless of where the tale of the father, the son, and the donkey originated, the fact that it is told in West Africa suggests that it states something valid for that culture. The tale's lesson of a necessary degree of self-confidence in the face of arbitrary social criticism is therefore something that can be found in the culture's values and beliefs.

motif A story situation in a tale.

© Anthro-Photo

Figure 24.7 Bedouin Women Singing and Making Bread The *ghinnawas* or "little songs" of the Awlad 'Ali Bedouins in Egypt punctuate conversations carried out while the people perform everyday chores. Through these songs, they can express what otherwise are taboo subjects.

Other Verbal Art

Myths, legends, and tales, prominent as they are in anthropological studies, in many cultures turn out to be no more important than many other verbal arts. In the culture of the Awlad 'Ali Bedouins of Egypt's western desert, for example, poetry is a lively and active verbal art, especially as a vehicle for personal expression and private communication. These Bedouins use two forms of poetry. One is the elaborately structured and heroic poems men chant or recite only on ceremonial occasions and in specific public contexts. The other is the *ghinnawas* or "little songs" that punctuate everyday conversations, especially of women. Simple in structure, these deal with personal matters and feelings more appropriate to informal social situations, and older men regard them as the unimportant productions of women and youths (Figure 24.7).

Despite this official devaluation in the male-dominated Bedouin society, "little songs" play a vital part in people's daily lives. In these poems individuals are shielded from the consequences of making statements and expressing sentiments that contravene the moral system. Paradoxically, by sharing these "immoral" sentiments only with intimates and veiling them in impersonal traditional formulas, those who recite them demonstrate

that they have a certain control, which actually enhances their moral standing. As is often true of folklore in general, the "little songs" of the Awlad 'Ali provide a culturally appropriate outlet for otherwise taboo thoughts or opinions (Abu-Lughod, 1986). The same is true for disaster jokes or comedic satire in numerous contemporary societies.

In all cultures the words of songs constitute a kind of poetry. Poetry and stories recited with gesture, movement, and props become drama. Drama combined with dance, music, and spectacle becomes a public celebration. The more we look at the individual arts, the clearer it becomes that they often are interrelated and interdependent. The verbal arts are, in fact, simply differing manifestations of the same creative imagination that produces music and the other arts.

Musical Art

Evidence of humans making music reaches far back in time. Archaeologists have found flutes and whistles (resembling today's recorders) made from the bones of mammoths and birds and dating back at least 42,000 years (Higham et al., 2012). And historically known food-foraging peoples were not without music. In the Kalahari Desert, for example, a Ju/'hoansi hunter off by himself would play a tune on his bow simply to help pass the time. (Long before anyone thought of beating swords into plowshares, some genius discovered that bows could be used not just to kill but to make music as well.) In northern New England, Abenaki shamans used cedar flutes to call game, lure enemies, and attract women. In addition, shamans would use a drum—over which two rawhide strings were stretched to produce a buzzing sound, representing singing—to allow communication with the spirit world.

The study of music in specific cultural settings, or **ethnomusicology**, began in the 19th century with the collection of folk songs and has developed into a specialized subfield of anthropological study. Ethnomusicologists look at music within its cultural context and from a comparative and relativistic perspective (Nettl, 2005). Early ethnomusicologists focused primarily on non-Western musical traditions in tribal cultures. Today, some also study folk music or music played and enjoyed in different ethnic communities within industrialized modern states.

Music is a form of communication that includes a nonverbal auditory component. The information it transmits is often abstract and emotional rather than concrete and objective, and different listeners experience it in a variety of ways. Such factors make it difficult to construct a definition that satisfies across cultures. Broadly speaking, **music** may be defined as an art form whose medium is sound and silence; a form of communication that includes a nonverbal auditory component with elements of tonality, rhythm, pitch, and timbre.

In general, human music is said to differ from natural sounds—the songs of birds, wolves, and whales, for example—by being almost everywhere perceived in terms of a repertoire of tones at fixed or regular intervals: in other words, a scale. Scale systems and their modifications make up what is known as *tonality* in music. These vary cross-culturally, so it is not surprising that something that sounds musical to one group of people may come across as noise to another.

Humans make closed systems out of a formless range of possible sounds by dividing the distance between a tone and its first overtone or sympathetic vibration (which always has exactly twice as many vibrations as the basic tone) into a series of measured steps. In the Western or European system, the distance between the basic tone and the first overtone is called

the *octave*; it consists of seven steps—five whole tones and two semitones. The whole tones are further divided into semitones, collectively resulting in a twelve-tone musical scale. Interestingly, some birds pitch their songs to the same scale as Western music (Gray et al., 2001), perhaps influencing the way these people developed their scale.

One of the most common alternatives to the semitonal system is the *pentatonic* (five-tone) system, which divides the octave into five nearly equidistant tones. Such scales may be found all over the world, including in much European folk music. Arabic and Persian music have smaller units of a third of a tone with seventeen and twenty-four steps in the octave. Even quarter-tone scales are used in large parts of South Asia, North Africa, and the Middle East with subtleties of shading that are nearly indistinguishable to most Western ears. Thus, even when Westerners can hear what sounds like melody and rhythm in these systems, for many the total result may sound peculiar or "out of tune."

Pitch is the quality of a sound governed by the rate of vibrations producing it—in other words, the degree of highness or lowness of a tone. *Timbre*, another element of music, is the characteristic quality of sound produced by a particular instrument or voice—also known as *tone color*. It is what distinguishes one musical sound from another, even when they have the same pitch and loudness. For example, a violin and a flute playing the same note equally loud have a different timbre.

Another organizing factor in music is *rhythm*. Involving tempo, stress, and measured repetition, it may be more important than tonality. One reason for this may be our constant exposure to natural pulses, such as our own heartbeat and patterns of breathing and walking. Even before we are born, we are exposed to our mother's heartbeat and to the rhythms of her movements, and as infants we experience rhythmic touching, petting, stroking, and rocking (Dissanayake, 2000).

The rhythms of traditional European music are most often measured into recurrent patterns of two, three, and four beats, with combinations of weak and strong beats to mark the division and form patterns. Non-European music is likely to move in patterns of five, seven, or eleven beats, with complex arrangements of internal beats and sometimes *polyrhythms*: one instrument or singer using a pattern of three beats, for example, whereas another uses a pattern of five or seven. Polyrhythms are frequent in the drum music of West Africa, which shows remarkable precision in the overlapping of rhythmic lines (**Figure 24.8**). Non-European music also may contain *shifting rhythms*: a pattern of three beats, for example, followed by a pattern of two or five beats with little or no regular

---

ethnomusicology The study of a society's music in terms of its cultural setting.

music Broadly speaking, an art form whose medium is sound and silence; a form of communication that includes a nonverbal auditory component with elements of tonality, pitch, rhythm, and timbre.

Figure 24.8 Senegalese Musician Zale Seck Like so many other cultural elements, musical instruments and styles of playing and singing now circulate around the globe, as do the artists themselves. One such example is West African musician Saliou "Zale" Seck, known for his "funky crisscrossing rhythms." A member of the Lébou tribe, *Zale* was born in the old fishing town of Yoff, just north of Senegal's capital city of Dakar. He performs Wolof percussive music on a traditional skin-covered *djembe* (hand drum) and *sabar* (played with one hand and a stick). Coming from a long line of *griots* (oral historians-traditional storytellers), he transmits his people's memory through lyrics of love and humanity. Fluent in French (his country was a French colony for many years), Zale has toured Europe and played on radio and television in France. Recently, Zale relocated to the French-speaking Canadian city of Quebec to further pursue his musical career.

recurrence or repetition of any one pattern, although the patterns are fixed and identifiable as units.

Melody involves both tonality and rhythm. It is a rhythmical succession of musical tones organized as a distinct phrase or sequence of phrases.

The Functions of Art

Art in all its many forms has countless functions beyond adding beauty and entertainment to everyday life. For anthropologists and others seeking to understand cultures beyond their own, art offers insights into a culture's worldview, giving clues about everything from gender and kinship relations to religious beliefs, political ideas, and historical memory.

For those within a society, art may serve to display social status, spiritual identity, and political power. An example of this can be seen in the totem poles of Indians living along North America's northwest coast. Erected in front of the homes of chiefs, these poles are inscribed with symbols that are visual reminders of the social hierarchy. Similarly, art is used to mark kinship ties, as seen in Scottish tartans designed to identify clan affiliation. It can also affirm group solidarity and identity beyond kinship lines, as evidenced in national emblems such as the dragon (Bhutan), bald eagle (United States), maple leaf (Canada), crescent moon (Turkey), and cedar tree (Lebanon) that typically appear on coins and government buildings.

Sometimes art is employed to express political themes and influence events, as in the counter-culture rock and folk music of the 1960s in the United States. Other times it is used to transmit traditional culture and ancestral ties, as in epic poems passed down from generation to generation. Myths, another verbal art form, may offer basic explanations about the world and set cultural standards for right behavior.

As an activity or behavior that contributes to human well-being and that helps give shape and significance to life, art is often intricately intertwined with religion and spirituality. In fact, in elaborate ceremonies involving ornamentation, masks, costumes, songs, dances, and effigies, it is not easy to say precisely where art stops and religion begins. Shamans drum to help create a trance state, Buddhist monks chant to focus their meditation, Christians sing hymns to praise God. Also, since ancient times, rituals and symbols concerning death have been infused with artistry—from evocative funereal music and beautiful sacred objects buried with a body to detailed mummy portraits in ancient Egypt. Today, in some parts of the world, artisans create coffins that are so creative that they find their way into museums as art (see the Globalscape feature, next page).

Furthermore, music, dance, and other arts may be used, like magic, to "enchant"—to take advantage of the emotional or psychological predispositions of another person or group so as to cause them to perceive reality in a way favorable to the interests of the enchanter. Often art is created to honor or beseech the aid of a deity, an ancestral spirit, or an animal spirit. Indeed, the arts may be used to manipulate a seemingly inexhaustible list of human passions, including desire, terror, wonder, love, fantasy, and vanity. Marketing specialists are well aware of this, which is why they routinely employ certain music and images in their advertising—as do promoters of political, ideological, charitable, or other causes.

Art in all its varied forms is used in a vast number of ways for a great array of purposes. To simplify our discussion of its numerous functions, we will consider a particular art form as embedded in a cultural system: music.

Globalscape

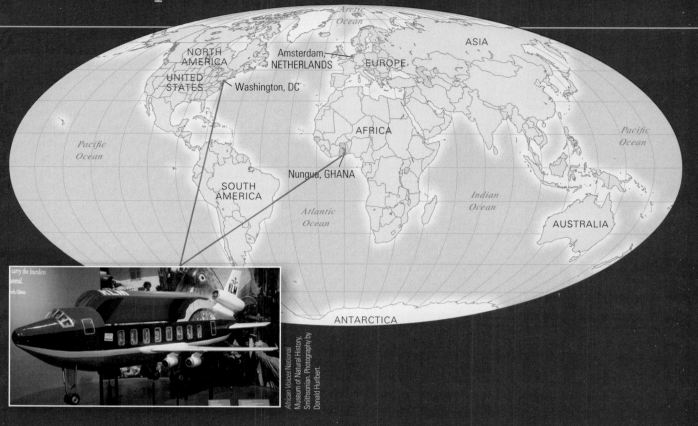

NORTH AMERICA
UNITED STATES
Washington, DC
Pacific Ocean
SOUTH AMERICA
Atlantic Ocean
Amsterdam, NETHERLANDS
EUROPE
ASIA
AFRICA
Nungua, GHANA
Arctic Ocean
Indian Ocean
Pacific Ocean
AUSTRALIA
ANTARCTICA

African Voices National Museum of Natural History, Smithsonian. Photography by Donald Hurlbert.

Do Coffins Fly?

In his workshop in Nungua, Ghana, master carpenter Paa Joe makes unique painted wooden coffins for his clients in his Ga society and beyond. Some are spectacular, representing richly colored tropical fish or even luxury cars, such as Mercedes-Benz. Celebrating the life accomplishments of the deceased, these designer coffins show off the family's prominent status and wealth.

As a collective expression of culturally shared ideas about the afterlife, a Ga funeral ceremony reminds the mourners of important values embodied in the departed individual. Seeing the deceased off on a journey to the afterlife, Ga mourners call out praises to this person, and some may even pour schnapps on the coffin. Henceforth, the deceased will continue to be ritually honored as an ancestor by descendants.

The 747 jumbo jet coffin pictured here confers upon the deceased the prestige and mystique of air travel. Its colors, blue and white, are those of the KLM Royal Dutch Airline, a long-time provider of air service between this West African country and the rest of the world. Its creator, Paa Joe, began working at age 15 for his cousin Kane Quaye, a carpenter known for designer coffins. Later, Joe started his own workshop and soon began receiving orders from other parts of the world—not only from individuals but also from museums. Using wood, enamel paint, satin, and Christmas wrapping paper, Joe created this KLM airplane coffin in 1997 for the Smithsonian National Museum of Natural History in Washington, DC, where millions of visitors from all over the globe now admire this Ghanian funereal ritual object.

Global Twister

When the Smithsonian Museum purchased one of Paa Joe's remarkable coffins for public display, did this West African funereal ritual object transform into a work of art?

Based on script for African Voices exhibition at NMNH, Smithsonian, courtesy of Dr. Mari Jo Arnoldi.

The Functions of Music

Music is a powerful identifier. Many marginalized groups have used it for purposes of self-identification—as a means of building group solidarity and distinguishing themselves from the dominant culture and sometimes as a channel for direct social and political commentary. Examples of this range from ethnic groups sponsoring music festivals to rock bands such as Britain's Rolling Stones, Coldplay, and Radiohead to North American rap artists Kanye West, Eminem, and Jay-Z. Music plays an important role in Native American potlatches and powwows where American Indian groups gather to reaffirm and celebrate their ethnic identities. And Scottish gatherings would not be Scottish without the sound of the highland bagpipes and the fiddle.

This power of music to shape identity has had varying consequences. The English understood that the bagpipes created a strong sense of identity among the highland regiments of the British army and encouraged it within certain bounds, even as they suppressed piping in Scotland itself under the Disarming Act. Over time, the British military piping tradition was assimilated into the Scottish piping tradition and so was accepted and spread by Scottish pipers. As a result, much of the supposedly Scottish piping one hears today consists of marches written within the conventions of the musical tradition of England, though shaped to fit the physical constraints of the instrument. Less often heard is the "classical" music known in Scottish Gaelic as Pibroch ("pipering") or, as some prefer to call traditional pipe music, Ceòl Mòr ("great music"). This more traditional Scottish pipe music has been revived over the past century and is now often romantically associated with rising cultural pride and nationalist sentiment.

The English adoption of the highland bagpipe into Scottish regiments is an instance of those in authority employing music to further a political agenda. So, too, in Ireland, Comhaltas Ceoltoiri Eireann (the Society of the Musicians of Ireland) has promoted the collection and performance of traditional Irish music. And in Brittany and Galicia, music is playing an important role in attempts to revive the spirits of the indigenous Celtic cultures in these regions of France and Spain.

The social function of music is most obvious in songs because these contain verbal text. Like other verbal forms, songs often express a group's values, beliefs, and concerns, but they do so with an increased formalism resulting from adherence to the systematic rules or conventions of pitch, rhythm, timbre, and musical genre. For this reason, music plays an important part in the cultural preservation and revitalization efforts of indigenous peoples around the world whose traditions were repressed or nearly exterminated through colonialism.

Work songs have played an important part in manual labor, serving to coordinate efforts in heavy or dangerous labor (such as weighing anchor and furling sail on ships), to synchronize axe or hammer strokes, and to pass time and relieve tedium as with oyster-shucking songs (**Figure 24.9**). Songs also have been used to soothe babies to sleep, to charm animals into giving more milk, to keep witchcraft at bay, and to advertise goods. Songs may serve social and political purposes, spreading particular ideas swiftly and effectively by giving them a special form involving poetic language and rhythm and by attaching a pleasing and appropriate tune, be it solemn or light.

Figure 24.9 Laborers in Mali, West Africa, Working to the Beat of a Drum The drumming helps to set the pace of work, unify the workforce, and relieve boredom.

ANTHROPOLOGY APPLIED

Bringing Back the Past

By Jennifer Sapiel Neptune

Near the turn of the 20th century, a young Penobscot woman sat for a photograph, wearing a very old and elaborately beaded ceremonial chief's collar. She was the daughter of Joseph and Elizabeth Nicola and the descendant of a long line of tribal leaders. Her name was Florence Nicola, and she would go on to live a long life, marry Leo Shay, raise a family, and be remembered as a fine basketmaker and dedicated advocate for our tribe. Her efforts brought increased educational opportunities, the right for Native people in the state of Maine to vote in state and federal elections, and the first bridge that would connect our small village of Indian Island in the Penobscot River to the mainland.

Now, over one hundred years later, the photograph has resurfaced and found its way back to her son, Charles Shay. Charles brought the photograph of his mother to our tribal historian who recognized the collar as one he had seen in the book *Penobscot Man* by Frank G. Speck, and he was then able to trace it to the collections of the Smithsonian Institution's Museum of the American Indian.

In the late part of the 19th century the idea of the "vanishing Indian" took hold in anthropology—leading to a specialized field known as "salvage ethnography," which sought to save traditional knowledge, life ways, and material culture. Collecting examples of material culture to be sold into museum collections had become a business for some—which was how the collar Florence wore in the photograph came to be purchased by George Heye sometime before 1905 and

Penobscot artist and cultural anthropologist Jennifer Neptune hugs tribal elder Charles Shay after giving him the traditional collar he commissioned. Modeled after a collar owned by his ancestors and now in the Smithsonian Institution's National Museum of the American Indian, the piece took Neptune more than 300 hours to make.

In the United States there are numerous examples of marginalized social and ethnic groups attempting to gain a larger audience and more compassion for their plight through song. The clearest example may be African Americans, whose ancestors were captured and carried across the Atlantic Ocean to be sold as slaves. Out of their experience emerged spirituals and, ultimately, gospel, jazz, blues, rock and roll, and rap. These forms all found their way into the North American mainstream and beyond. Even neoclassical composers such as Francis Poulenc (French), Antonín Dvořák (Czech), and many others were influenced by African American jazz. In short, music of a marginalized group of former slaves eventually captivated the entire world.

In the 1950s and 1960s performers such as Pete Seeger and Joan Baez gained great visibility when supporting civil and human rights causes in the United States. Both performers' celebrity status led to the broader dissemination of their social and political beliefs.

In Australia, certain ceremonial songs of the Aborigines have taken on a new legal function, as they are being introduced into court as evidence of early settlement patterns. These songs recount ancient adventures of mythic ancestors who lived in "Dreamtime" and created waterholes, mountains, valleys, and other significant features in the landscape. The ancestors' tracks are known as *songlines*, and through ceremonial songs countless generations of Aborigines have passed on sacred ecological knowledge.

This oral tradition helps Aborigines to claim extensive indigenous land ownership, thus allowing them greater authority to use the land, as well as to negotiate and profit from the sale of natural resources. This had been impossible before. The British, upon their annexation of Australia, declared the land ownerless (*Terra Nullius*). Although the Aborigines had preserved their records of ownership in song and story, these were not admissible in the British courts.

then joined the collections of the museum. I have always found it ironic that we as a people and culture did not vanish, but during this time many of our tribes' most precious material objects did.

As a teenager I spent a lot of time in the library at the University of Maine looking through photographs in books of Penobscot beadwork, appliqué ribbon work, basketry, and carvings that were now in museums all over the world. I dreamed of being able to visit these objects, to study them up close, and to be able to find a way to bring them back into our world. It was for this reason that I went into anthropology, to learn how to research and write about my own culture. I started doing reproductions of the old beadwork designs, became a basket-maker, consulted on museum exhibitions, sold my own artwork, and worked with the Maine Indian Basketmakers Alliance promoting the work of basketmakers and artists from the four tribes in Maine.

In the spring of 2006 Charles showed me the photograph of his mother and asked me if I could make a reproduction of the collar for him.

As I worked on the collar, I was struck by how so much had changed since the late 18th century when the original collar was made. Back then the wool, silk ribbon, and beads its maker used had come by ship, horse, and foot from trade or treaty annuities; my materials were ordered over the Internet and came by UPS and FedEx. She worked by the light of the sun or fire; I worked mostly in the evenings with electric lights. Her world had northern forests still untouched by logging and filled with caribou and wolves; my world had airplanes, cars, and motorboats.

As I worked some more, I thought about what had stayed the same. We had lived and watched the sun rise and set on the same island our ancestors had for over 7,000 years. I wondered if we had stitched the same prayers into our work and if we used the same medicinal plants to soothe our aching hands and shoulders at the end of the day.

There are no words that can express how gratifying it was to hand over the finished collar to Charles—and to have played a part in returning to him, his family, and our tribe a part our history.

One hundred years ago when the collar left my community, anthropology seemed to be about taking objects, stories, and information away. As an anthropologist and artist I believe that I have a responsibility to use what I have learned to give back to my community. I have been so fortunate to be able to have spent time in museum collections visiting objects that most of my own people will never have the opportunity to see. What I learned from my time with the collar was that the objects that left still have a relationship with us today; they have a story that wants to be told, and they are waiting for someone to listen.

Written expressly for this text, 2011.

In the early 1970s, however, the Aborigines exposed the injustice of the situation, and the Australian government began responding in a more favorable, if still limited, fashion, granting the claims of traditional ownership to groups in the Northern Territory. Gradually, more Aboriginal land rights and sacred sites are being recognized; evidence of native ownership includes recordings of Aborigine songs indicative of traditional patterns of settlement, travel, and land use (Koch, 1997).

Music gives basic human ideas a concrete form, made memorable and attractive with melody and rhythm. Whether a song's content is didactic, satiric, inspirational, religious, political, or purely emotional, the formless has been given form, and feelings hard to express in words alone are communicated in a symbolic and notable way that can be repeated and shared. This, in turn, shapes and gives meaning to the community.

Art, Globalization, and Cultural Survival

Clearly, there is more to art than meets the eye or ear (not to mention the nose and tongue—consider how burning incense or tobacco is part of the artfulness of sacred ceremonies, and imagine the cross-cultural array of smells and tastes in the cooking arts). In fact, art is such a significant part of culture that many endangered indigenous groups around the world—those whose lifeways have been threatened first by colonialism and now by globalization—are using aesthetic expressions as part of a cultural survival strategy (see Anthropology Applied feature, above).

Many have found that a traditional art form—a dance, a song, a dress, a basket, a carving, or anything that is distinctly beautiful and well-made or performed—can serve as a powerful symbol that conveys the vital

VISUAL COUNTERPOINT

Figure 24.10 **Traditional Maori War Dance Globalized** In cultures all across the world, people are not only concerned with making a living, but also with defending themselves against hostile outsiders. Those traditionally sent off to battle rely on their strength and weapons, but they may also boost their collective fighting spirits and intimidate and inspire fear in their rivals through musical rituals. Some of these traditional war rituals have been preserved and adapted for performance in theater or competitive male team sports. One spectacular example is the *haka*, a war dance (and song) originally performed by Maori warriors in New Zealand and now performed by rival rugby and football teams from many Pacific Islander nations. The photo on the left shows Maori dancers performing the *haka* on stage; on the right we see the Texas Trinity Trojans high school football team perform *haka* on the field. The Trojans have several outstanding players from Tonga, a large group of islands south of Samoa. Their families migrated to the United States for employment opportunities but maintain close contact and frequently visit home. For the Tongans and their teammates in Texas, jointly performing the *haka* minutes before the game gives them pride in their heritage and inspires them to win. Among the first college football players from the Pacific to act out the war dance before a game were Samoan athletes at Kansas State University in the early 1980s.

message: "We're still here, and we're still a culturally distinct people with our own particular beliefs and values."

Among many examples is the *haka*, a traditional war dance (and song) that Maori warriors in New Zealand did before battle. A century ago, New Zealand's national rugby team began performing the *haka* before every match. The tradition spread to other teams all across New Zealand, then to other Pacific Islanders, and even to the U.S. mainland (**Figure 24.10**).

Throughout the world there are countless examples of art playing a role in the struggle for cultural preservation and indigenous rights. You've seen a small sampling in this chapter, starting with the opening photograph of Amazonian Indians en route to stage a political protest with performance art composed of songs, dances, traditional weapons, body paint, and feather headdresses—one image suggesting the remarkable range of art and the roles it plays in human lives.

CHAPTER CHECKLIST

Why do anthropologists study art?

● Anthropologists have found that art often reflects a society's worldview.

● From myths, songs, dances, paintings, carvings, and other art forms, anthropologists may learn how a people imagine their reality and understand themselves and other beings around them.

● Through the cross-cultural study of art and creativity, we discover much about different

worldviews, religious beliefs, political ideas, social values, kinship structures, economic relations, and historical memory.

What is art?

● Art is the creative use of the human imagination to aesthetically interpret, express, and engage life, modifying experienced reality in the process. It comes in many forms, including performance, visual, verbal, and musical.

● Performance art is a creatively expressed promotion of ideas by artful means dramatically staged to challenge opinion and/or provoke purposeful action.

● Visual art, created primarily for visual perception, ranges from etchings and paintings on various surfaces (including the human body) to sculptures and weavings made with an array of materials. Key approaches in analyzing visual art are aesthetic, narrative, and interpretive.

● Verbal art is creative word use on display that includes stories, fairytales, myths, legends, proverbs, chants, poetry, metaphor, rhyme, drama, cant, jokes, puns, riddles, and tongue twisters.

How are myths, legends, and tales different from one another?

● A myth is a short story about how the cosmos came about, including the factors that are responsible for the way it is and the significant features of the worldview. An example is the Abenaki Indian creation story of Tabaldak and Odzihózo.

● A legend is a story about a memorable event or figure handed down by tradition and told as true but without historical evidence. A noteworthy example is the American Thanksgiving legend about English Pilgrims and American Indians.

● A tale is a creative narrative that is recognized as fiction for entertainment but may also draw a moral or teach a practical lesson. One example is the "Father, Son, and Donkey" story, told in different versions around the world.

What are music and ethnomusicology?

● Ethnomusicology, the study of a society's music in terms of its cultural setting, began in the 19th century with the collection of folk songs from non-Western musical traditions. Today, it includes music played in ethnic communities within industrialized modern states.

● Music is difficult to define in a way that satisfies across cultures. Broadly speaking, it as an art form whose medium is sound and silence or a form of communication that includes a nonverbal auditory component with elements of tonality, rhythm, pitch, and timbre.

What are the functions of art?

● Art in all its many forms has countless functions beyond providing aesthetic pleasure. Myths, for example, may offer basic explanations about the world and set cultural standards for right behavior.

● The verbal arts generally transmit and preserve a culture's customs and values. Songs, too, may do this within the structures imposed by musical form.

● Any art form, to the degree that it is characteristic of a particular society, may contribute to the cohesiveness or solidarity of that society. Yet, art may also express political themes and be used to influence events and create social change.

● Often art is created for religious purposes, to honor or beseech the aid of a divine power, a sacred being, an ancestral spirit, or an animal spirit.

QUESTIONS FOR REFLECTION

1. In this chapter's opening photograph, you saw indigenous activists, colorfully painted and with feathered headdresses, on their way to an important protest rally. If your livelihood was seriously threatened and you wanted to try to avoid violent confrontation, would you contemplate performance art as a means of political action? If so, how and by means of which art form?

2. All across the world and throughout human history, people have creatively expressed ideas and feelings through art, whether in music, dance, imagery, or sculpture. Do you know any specific forms of art originally created for and performed by your own community? Do these art forms have any cultural meaning or social function?

3. Among the Maori in New Zealand, tattooing is a traditional form of skin art, and their tattoo designs are typically based on cultural symbols understood by all members in the community. Are the tattoo designs in your culture based on traditional motifs that have a shared symbolic meaning?

4. Because kinship relations are important in small-scale traditional societies, these relationships are often symbolically represented in artistic designs and motifs. What are some of the major concerns in your society, and are these concerns reflected in any of your culture's art forms?

5. Many museums and private collectors in Europe and North America are interested in so-called tribal art, such as African statues or American Indian masks originally used in sacred rituals. Are there sacred objects such as paintings or carvings in your religion that might also be collected, bought, or sold as art?

ONLINE STUDY RESOURCES

CourseMate

Access chapter-specific learning tools, including learning objectives, practice quizzes, videos, flash cards, glossaries, and more in your Anthropology CourseMate.

Log into **www.cengagebrain.com** to access the resources your instructor has assigned and to purchase materials.

Challenge Issue

Environmental, demographic, technological, and other changes challenge cultures to adjust at an ever-faster pace. Some peoples confront change on their own terms, welcoming new ideas, products, and practices as improvements. But the price of "progress" is seldom fair. Often it comes at the expense of groups whose well-being is not served. Among these are 7,000 reindeer-herding Nenets in northwest Siberia. Well adapted to this sub-Arctic environment, they depend on reindeer meat and hides, supplemented by hunting, trapping, fishing, and berry gathering. As needed, they sell or butcher their animals, exchanging surplus meat, hides, and antlers for cash. In summer they encamp on the barrens of Yamal Peninsula. Each fall, before snow covers the mosses and grasses, they journey 1,000 kilometers south for wintering. Now, Russia's global energy corporation Gazprom is upending their lives, extracting natural gas from deep under the vast frozen tundra where Nenets and their animals have ranged for generations. Constructing drilling towers, pumping stations, pipelines, as well as new towns, asphalt roads, bridges, and railways, it has transformed the region. For Gazprom, selling almost half of its gas abroad, the value of this peninsula is measured in huge profits, with financial concerns far outweighing wilderness preservation or indigenous self-determination.

Processes of Cultural Change

Anthropologists are interested not only in describing cultures and explaining how they are structured as systems of adaptation, but also in understanding why and how cultures change. Because systems generally work to maintain stability, cultures are often fairly steady and remain so unless there is a critical shift in one or more significant factors such as natural environment, demographics, technology, markets—or in people's perceptions of the various conditions to which they are adapted.

Archaeological studies reveal how elements of a culture may persist for long periods. In Australia, for example, the cultures of indigenous inhabitants remained relatively consistent over many thousands of years because they successfully adapted to comparatively minor fluctuations in their social conditions and natural environments, making changes from time to time in tools, utensils, and other material support.

Although stability may be a striking feature of many traditional cultures, all cultures are capable of adapting to changing conditions—climatic, economic, political, or ideological. However, not all change is positive or adaptive, and not all cultures are equally well equipped for making the necessary adjustments in a timely fashion. In a stable society, change may occur gently and gradually, without altering in any fundamental way the culture's underlying structures. So it was in much of Brazil or Canada, for example, prior to the European invasion five centuries ago.

Sometimes, though, the pace of change increases dramatically. This is what happened during the industrial revolution, beginning with England, when its agriculture-based society transformed into a machine-based manufacturing society within a few generations beginning in the 1770s. Such changes may disrupt to the point of destabilizing or even breaking down a cultural system. The modern world is full of such examples of radical changes, from the political-economic disintegration of the former Soviet Union and the dramatic capitalist transformation of communist China to the devastation by global corporations of indigenous communities inhabiting remote regions from the cold Arctic tundra to the hot Amazonian jungle.

IN THIS CHAPTER YOU WILL LEARN TO

- Analyze why and how cultural systems change.

- Identify the key mechanisms of cultural change, providing examples.

- Explain the consequences of unequal power in culture contact.

- Compare directed and undirected change.

- Recognize and discuss reactions to repressive change.

- Assess the importance of self-determination in successful cultural change.

- Connect modernization ideology to international resource exploitation and global markets.

Cultural Change and the Relativity of Progress

The dynamic processes involved in cultural change are manifold, including accidental discoveries, deliberate inventions, and borrowing from other peoples who introduce or force new commodities, technologies, and practices.

Change imposed upon one group by another continues in much of the world today as culture contact intensifies between societies unequal in power. Among those who have the power to drive and direct change in their favor, it is typically referred to as "progress," which literally translates as "to move forward"—that is, in a positive direction. But *progress* is a relative term that implies improvement as defined by the people who profit or otherwise benefit from the changes set into motion. In other words, progress is in the eye of the beholder because not everyone benefits from change. In fact, countless peoples (including traditional foraging, herding, and peasant communities in many parts of the world) have become the victims of progress, seeing their lives destroyed by powerful others focused on plucking almost all of the fruits for themselves.

In recent decades, growing numbers of anthropologists have focused on the historical impact international market expansionism has had on rural and urban communities around the world, radically challenging, altering, or even destroying their traditional cultures. One of the first and most prominent among these scholars was Eric Wolf, an Austria-born U.S. anthropologist who personally experienced the global havoc and upheaval of the 20th century (see Anthropologist of Note).

Mechanisms of Change

Some of the major mechanisms involved in cultural change are innovation, diffusion, and cultural loss. These types of change are typically voluntary and are not imposed on a population by outside forces.

Innovation

A major factor in cultural change, innovation is any new idea, method, or device that gains widespread acceptance in society. **Primary innovation** is the creation, invention, or chance discovery of a completely new idea, method, or device. A **secondary innovation** is a deliberate application or modification of an existing idea, method, or device.

---

primary innovation The creation, invention, or chance discovery of a completely new idea, method, or device.
secondary innovation The deliberate application or modification of an existing idea, method, or device.

What makes people come up with, and accept, an innovation? The most obvious incentive is reflected in the age-old proverb "Necessity is the mother of invention." We see this in an early prehistoric example of a primary innovation: the spear-thrower (also known as *atlatl*, its Aztec Indian name). Invented at least 15,000 years ago by big game hunters who needed more effective technology to ensure success and safety, this device made it possible to hurl a dart or javelin with much greater thrust. Using it increased a projectile's distance some 60 percent and delivered much more force upon impact. Equipped with this new technology, a hunter boosted his effective kill range and gained competitive advantage. Much later examples of primary innovation are the wheel, the alphabet, the concept of zero, the telescope, and the steam engine (an 18th-century invention that spawned the industrial revolution), to mention just a few major inventions.

Although many innovations are the result of inventive designs and experimentation, others may initially come about through accidental discoveries. These may gain acceptance and spawn innovations within their particular cultural contexts. For example, over a million years ago *Homo erectus* discovered that pieces of burning wood or hot coal remained after fires ignited by lightning burned down trees. Then they figured out that these remnants could be used to kindle a fire at a time and location of their choosing. Accordingly, they collected hot coals and kept them alive in a portable container, occasionally feeding them with some fuel, until it was time to build the next campfire.

A few hundred thousand years later, archaic *Homo sapiens* came up with a primary innovation when they discovered how to create fire by friction—rotating a wooden stick on a fireboard to produce the ember that could spark a fire in a pile of dry grass, leaves, or bark. The bow drill, a secondary innovation invented in Eurasia during the Upper Paleolithic, improved upon its predecessor, enabling a firemaker to more effectively maintain the speed and pressure needed to create enough friction to ignite the tinder. The bow drill turned out to have alternative uses, such as boring narrow holes in bone, ivory, and stone.

Another firemaking method—producing sparks by striking a flint against pyrite (iron sulfide)—led to further breakthroughs: In the early Iron Age, about 3,000 years ago, some individuals discovered that a small piece of portable high-carbon iron was a more effective striking surface than pyrite stone. This method remained in use until edged out by a new friction device invented in France at the beginning of the 19th century—the match, a small wooden stick, tipped with gelatin-coated phosphate or sulfur ("brimstone").

An innovation must be reasonably consistent with a society's needs, values, and goals in order to gain acceptance. Take, for instance, the invention of wheel-and-axle technology. About 1,500 years ago, indigenous peoples in Mesoamerica came up with the concept. But instead of building wagons to be pulled by trained dogs or human captives, they created wheeled animal effigies, most often representing dogs but

ANTHROPOLOGIST OF NOTE

Eric R. Wolf (1923–1999)

Like the millions of peasants about whom he wrote, **Eric Wolf** personally experienced radical upheaval in his life due to powerful outside political forces. A war refugee in his teens, he survived the battlefields and mass murders of Nazi-occupied Europe. Driven by the inequities and atrocities he witnessed during World War II, he turned to anthropology to sort through issues of power. Viewing anthropology as the most scientific of the humanities and the most humane of the sciences, he became famous for his comparative historical studies on peasants, power, and the transforming impact of capitalism on traditional nations.

Wolf's life began in Austria shortly after the First World War. During that terrible conflict, his Austrian father had been a prisoner of war in Siberia, where he met Wolf's mother, a Russian exile. When peace returned, the couple married and settled in Vienna, where Eric was born in 1923. Growing up in Austria's capital and then (because of his father's job) in Sudetenland in what is now the Czech Republic, young Eric enjoyed a life of relative ease. He relished summers spent in the Alps among local peasants in exotic costumes, and he drank in his mother's tales about her father's adventures with Siberian nomads.

Life changed for Eric in 1938 when Adolf Hitler grabbed power in Germany, annexed Austria and Sudetenland, and threatened Jews like the Wolfs. Seeking security for their 15-year-old son, Eric's parents sent him to high school in England. In 1940, a year after World War II broke out, British authorities believed invasion was imminent and ordered aliens, including Eric, into an internment camp. There he met other refugees from Nazi-occupied Europe and had his first exposure to Marxist theories. Soon he left England for New York City and enrolled at Queens College, where Professor Hortense Powdermaker, a former student of Malinowski, introduced him to anthropology.

1994 Photograph by Michael Macdonald, EWLS (Eric Wolf's Last Student) and "staunch banner carrier for Wolfian anthropology" (Wolf 12/25/1998)

Born in Austria, Eric Wolf became an American anthropologist famous for his pioneering research on peasant societies.

In 1943, the 20-year-old refugee enlisted in the U.S. Army's 10th Mountain Division. Fighting in the mountains of Tuscany, Italy, he won a Silver Star for combat bravery. At the war's end, Wolf returned to New York and studied anthropology under Julian Steward and Ruth Benedict at Columbia University. After earning his doctorate in 1951 based on fieldwork in Puerto Rico, he did extensive research on Mexican peasants.

In 1961, he became a professor at the University of Michigan. A prolific writer, Wolf gained tremendous recognition for his fourth book, *Peasant Wars of the Twentieth Century*, first published during the height of the Vietnam War. Protesting that war, he headed a newly founded ethics committee in the American Anthropological Association and helped expose counterinsurgency uses of anthropological research in Southeast Asia.

From 1971 onward, Wolf held a distinguished professorship at Lehman College of the City University of New York (CUNY), where his classes were filled with working-class students of all ethnic backgrounds, including many who took the anthropology courses he taught in Spanish. In addition, he taught at the Graduate Center (CUNY). Among his many publications, is his award-winning book, *Europe and the People Without History* (1982). In 1990, he received a MacArthur "genius" prize. In his final publications, he explored how ideas and power are connected though the medium of culture.

---

also jaguars, monkeys, and other mammals, and left it at that. On the other side of the Atlantic, this same technology—discovered a few thousand years earlier—led to major secondary innovations resulting in a series of radical cultural changes in transportation technology, ultimately resulting in motorized vehicles such as cars, trains, and planes.

A culture's internal dynamics may encourage particular innovative tendencies, even as they may discourage or suppress others. Force of habit tends to obstruct ready acceptance of the new or unfamiliar because people typically stick with what they are used to rather than adopt something strange that requires adjustment on their part.

Obstacles to change are often ideologically embedded in religious traditions. Consider, for instance, early rejections of scientific insights about the earth's position in the universe. Polish mathematician and astronomer Nicolaus Copernicus discovered that the earth rotates around the sun and published his new *heliocentric* theory in 1534, just before he died. In the early 1600s, the Italian physicist and mathematician Galileo Galilei verified this controversial theory by means of a much-improved telescope. In 1633, not long after publishing and defending his findings, he was tried for heresy because his observational astronomy ran counter to the dogma of the Roman Catholic Church, which was

Pedro Ugarte/AFP/Getty Images

Figure 25.1 Bagpipers, Royal Army Marching Band of Bhutan Unlike neighboring India, Bhutan remained independent from British colonial rule. This small Himalayan kingdom, known to the Bhutanese as Drukyul ("land of the dragons"), is generally averse to foreign cultural influences. However, the Drukpa ("dragon people") have selectively embraced a few innovations, including the Scottish bagpipes, which found their way here via India during the colonial era. Wearing traditional dress, bagpipers in the royal band play imported instruments, producing a droning sound similar to age-old sacred trumpets played by Buddhist monks in this region. They and other Drukpa musicians lead the way for singing the national anthem Druk Tsendhen ("the thunder dragon kingdom"), honoring the fifth traditional Druk Gyalpo ("dragon king"), who serves as head of this Buddhist state.

firmly based on a *geocentric* worldview as revealed in sacred texts. Facing a death sentence, Galileo recanted and was condemned to life under house arrest. In 1758, after numerous additional scientific breakthroughs challenged Catholic dogma, heliocentric books were removed from the forbidden list of that powerful international institution.

Diffusion

The spread of certain ideas, customs, or practices from one culture to another is known as **diffusion**. So common is cross-cultural borrowing that U.S. anthropologist Ralph Linton suggested that it accounts for as much as 90 percent of any culture's content.

People are creative about their borrowing, however, picking and choosing from multiple possibilities and sources. Usually, their selections are limited to those compatible with the existing culture. An example is the inclusion of bagpipes in the marching band of the royal army of Bhutan. Traditionally played by Scottish Highland regiments when marching into combat and in official ceremonies, this musical instrument features one double-reed pipe operated by finger stops and three drone pipes. All the pipes are sounded by air forced with the left arm from a leather bag kept filled by the player's breath. The bagpipe's drone sounds resemble those of Bhutan's traditional sacred trumpets played in ancient Buddhist religious ceremonies in this small Himalayan kingdom (**Figure 25.1**).

The extent of cultural borrowing can be surprising. Consider, for example, paper, the compass, and gunpowder. All three of these innovations were invented in China long before Europeans became aware of them about 700 years ago. Accepting these foreign artifacts, Europeans

diffusion The spread of certain ideas, customs, or practices from one culture to another.

Figure 25.2 Making Corn Mush in Italy Having spread from the tropics of the Mexican highlands to much of the rest of North and South America, corn diffused rapidly to the rest of the world after Italian explorer Christopher Columbus first crossed the Atlantic in 1492. A long-time favorite dish in Italy is polenta (a thick mush made of cornmeal). Here we see it being made the traditional way: boiled in a big copper cauldron over a fire of hot coals and then spread out and cooled to firmness on a wooden or stone slab. In recent years, polenta has become a favored menu item in many chic American restaurants.

© Hubert Stadler/Corbis

and others analyzed and improved them where needed. Such is the case with the mixture of sulfur, charcoal, and potassium nitrate the Chinese used for fireworks and portable hand cannons. Soon after learning about it, Europeans, Koreans, and Arabs adopted and adapted this primitive artillery and gunpowder, triggering a revolution in traditional warfare from the 1300s onward. Two centuries later, Europeans introduced firearms to the Americas. Within decades, indigenous groups such as the Mi'kmaq in the Gulf of Maine began using them in their raids, transforming warfare as they had known it for generations.

America's indigenous peoples not only adopted weapons and other foreign trade goods, but also shared numerous inventions and discoveries their ancestors had made in the course of many centuries. Of special note is the range of domestic plants developed ("invented") by the Indians—potatoes, beans, tomatoes, peanuts, avocados, manioc, chili peppers, squash, chocolate, sweet potatoes, and corn ("maize"), to name a few—all of which now furnish a major portion of the world's food supply. In fact, American Indians are recognized as primary contributors to the world's varied cuisine and credited with developing the largest array of nutritious foods (Weatherford, 1988).

Diffusion of a Global Staple Food: Maize

Particularly significant among the domesticated plants diffusing from the Americas is corn, also known as *maize* (derived from a Caribbean Indian word *maíz*). The English originally referred to this Native American cereal plant as "Indian corn." First cultivated by indigenous peoples in the Mexican highlands over 7,000 years ago, this food crop diffused to much of the rest of North, Central, and South America over the next few millennia.

In 1493, the explorer Columbus returned from America to Spain with a sampling of maize. First planted in kitchen gardens in Andalusia, in the course of several decades maize spread to other parts of Spain and Portugal. From there it diffused southwest, reaching France and northern Italy by the late 1530s. Producing more calories per acre than traditional European crops, it was initially grown as green fodder to feed pigs and other livestock. However, forced by poverty and famine, peasants and other poor folk in southern Europe accepted this new food as cornmeal cakes or thick porridge (**Figure 25.2**). Portuguese traders introduced maize to western Africa and across the Indian Ocean to South Asia from where it spread to China before the mid-1500s.

Diffusing across the globe, maize has become one of the world's major staple foods and has been culturally incorporated under many different names. This dietary revolution not only altered people's lives but is also responsible for enormous population growth, especially since the 18th century (Braudel, 1979). Today, a greater weight of maize is produced each year than rice, wheat, or any other grain—about 800 million tons, with over half of the global production taking place in the United States and China.

In recent years, an enormous quantity of maize has been grown for biomass fuel, such as ethanol, as an alternative to nonrenewable fossil fuels such as oil. Moreover, the production of genetically engineered maize (manipulated with herbicide or drought-resistant genes) has been gaining ground, especially in the United States and many developing countries, but this practice is resisted by European farmers and consumers.

Diffusion of a Global Measurement System: Metrics

Another remarkable example of diffusion—breaking through multiple language barriers and long-held local traditions—is the metric system used for measuring length, weight, capacity, currency, and temperature. Based on a classification in

Figure 25.3 Camel Mobile Library Providing books and reading materials to the Somali-speaking nomads in the remote Garissa and the Wajir areas in its northeastern districts, Kenya's National Library Association challenges the region's 85 percent illiteracy rate. The program consists of three teams, each with three male camels capable of traveling routes impassable even for 4-wheel drive vehicles. One camel is loaded with two boxes containing 200 books, one transports the library tent, and a third carries miscellaneous items needed for the program.

which standard units of measurement are multiplied or divided by 10 in order to produce larger or smaller units, this rational system has simplified calculations and is practical on many levels of accounting and management.

A Dutch engineer first proposed the use of decimal fractions for measures, weights, and currency in everyday life. Three centuries later, in 1795, soon after the revolution that toppled the royal regime, the French First Republic adopted the metric system as its official system of measurement. Then, with French military expansion under Napoleon in the early 19th century, the system was forced upon conquered neighboring countries—standardizing a bewildering array of regional and local measurement systems on the European continent.

By 1900, about forty countries had adopted the metric system. It continued to spread during the 20th century, despite initial reluctance or even resistance in some countries, such as Great Britain. Since the early 1970s, that country and most of its former colonies have fully transitioned to metric. British law now defines each "Imperial unit" in terms of the metric equivalent (although many older Britons still hold on to traditional measurements such as inches, feet, and miles in daily life). Today, at least officially, the metric system is almost universal, with the exception of just seven countries including Myanmar (Burma), Liberia, and, most notably, the United States (Cardarelli, 2003; Vera, 2011).

Cultural Loss

Most often people look at cultural change as an accumulation of innovations. Frequently, however, the acceptance of a new innovation results in **cultural loss**—the

cultural loss The abandonment of an existing practice or trait.

abandonment of an existing practice or trait. For example, in ancient times chariots and carts were used widely in northern Africa and southwestern Asia, but wheeled vehicles virtually disappeared from Morocco to Afghanistan about 1,500 years ago. Camels replaced them, not because of some reversion to the past but because camels used as pack animals worked better. The old Roman empire roads had deteriorated, and these sturdy animals traveled well with or without roads. Their endurance, longevity, and ability to ford rivers and traverse rough ground made pack camels admirably suited for the region. Plus, they were economical in terms of labor: A wagon required a man for every two draft animals, but a single person could manage up to six pack camels.

Reflecting on Westerners' surprise over this rejection of a cultural innovation, U.S. paleontologist Stephen Jay Gould commented that

> Wheels have come to symbolize in our culture . . . intelligent exploitation and technological progress. . . . The success of camels reemphasizes a fundamental theme. . . . Adaptation, be it biological or cultural, represents a better fit to specific, local environments, not an inevitable stage in a ladder of progress. Wheels were a formidable invention, and their uses are manifold. . . . But camels may work better in some circumstances. Wheels, like wings, fins, and brains, are exquisite devices for certain purposes, not signs of intrinsic superiority. (Gould, 1983, p. 159)

Gould's point remains relevant in many remote and hot desert regions, where camels are still the favored and most reliable form of transportation for many purposes (Figure 25.3).

Often overlooked is another facet of losing apparently useful traits: loss without replacement. An example of this is the historical absence of boats among the indigenous

Figure 25.4 **Protesting Acculturation** Until a few decades ago, these Aché Indians survived as traditional hunters and gatherers in the deep tropical forest of eastern Paraguay. Not unlike the Ju/'hoansi of southern Africa, they were organized in small migratory bands and rarely had contact with outsiders. Armed with spears and bows and arrows, they could not defend their homeland against large numbers of foreign invaders equipped with chainsaws, bulldozers, and firearms. Massacres and foreign diseases, coupled with massive deforestation of their hunting territories, almost annihilated these people in the 1950s and 1960s. Since then, they have been exposed to intensive acculturation. Here we see the breakup of an Aché encampment in the middle of Asunción, Paraguay's capital city, where they lived during many weeks of protest against government policies.

inhabitants of the Canary Islands, a group of small islands isolated off North Africa's Atlantic coastline. The ancestors of these people must have had boats because without them they could never have transported themselves and their domestic livestock to the islands in the first place. Later, without boats, they had no way to communicate with other islands or with the mainland. This loss of something useful came about due to the islands' lack of stone suitable for making polished stone axes, which in turn limited the islanders' carpentry (Coon, 1954).

Repressive Change

Innovation, diffusion, and cultural loss all may take place among peoples who are free to decide for themselves what changes they will or will not accept. However, people do not always have the liberty to make their own choices. Frequently, they are forced to make changes they would not willingly make, usually in the course of conquest and colonialism. A direct outcome in many cases is repressive change to a culture, which anthropologists call *acculturation*. The most radical form of repressive change is ethnocide.

Acculturation and Ethnocide

Acculturation is the massive cultural change that occurs in a society when it experiences intensive firsthand contact with a more powerful society. It always involves an element of force—either directly, as in conquests, or indirectly, as in the implicit or explicit threat that force will be used if people refuse to make the demanded changes. Other variables include degree of cultural difference; circumstances, intensity, frequency, and hostility of contact; relative status of the agents of contact; who is dominant and who is submissive; and whether the nature of the flow is reciprocal or nonreciprocal. *Acculturation* and *diffusion* are not equivalent terms; one culture can borrow from another without being in the least forced into change (**Figure 25.4**).

In the course of cultural contact, any number of things may happen. Merger or fusion occurs when two cultures lose their separate identities and form a single culture, as historically expressed by the melting pot ideology of English-speaking, Protestant Euramerican culture in the United States. Sometimes, though, one of the cultures loses its autonomy

---

acculturation The massive cultural change that occurs in a society when it experiences intensive firsthand contact with a more powerful society.

but retains its identity as a subculture in the form of a caste, class, or ethnic group. This is typical of conquest or slavery situations. The United States provides examples of these phenomena, despite its melting pot ideology; we need look no further than the nearest American Indian reservation.

Acculturation may occur as a result of military conquest, political and economic expansion, or massive invasion and breaking up of cultural structures by dominant newcomers who know or care little about the traditional beliefs and practices of the people they seek to control. Under the sway of powerful outsiders—and unable to effectively resist imposed changes and obstructed in carrying out many of their own social, religious, and economic activities—subordinated groups are forced into new social and cultural practices that tend to isolate individuals and destroy the integrity of their traditional communities. In virtually all parts of the world today, people are faced with the tragedy of forced removal from their traditional homelands, as entire communities are uprooted to make way for hydroelectric projects, grazing lands for cattle, mining operations, or highway construction.

Ethnocide, the violent eradication of an ethnic group's collective cultural identity as a distinctive people, occurs when a dominant society deliberately sets out to destroy another society's cultural heritage. This may take place when a powerful nation aggressively expands its territorial control by annexing neighboring peoples and their territories, incorporating the conquered groups as subjects. A policy of ethnocide typically includes forbidding a subjugated nation's ancestral language, criminalizing their traditional customs, destroying their religion and demolishing sacred places and practices, breaking up their social organizations, and dispossessing or removing the survivors from their homelands—in essence, stopping short of physical extermination while removing all traces of their unique culture.

Tibet provides one tragic example of ethnocide. The Chinese communist army in 1950 invaded Tibet and subsequently initiated ethnocidal policies by means of systematic attacks against traditional Tibetan culture. Seeking to stamp out deeply rooted religious beliefs and practices, the communists ordered the demolition of most Buddhist temples and monasteries. Following a mass uprising, hundreds of thousands of Tibetans were killed or forced into exile abroad. Trying to annihilate Tibetan identity, China sought to turn the surviving Tibetans into political subjects who would culturally identify themselves as Chinese nationals (Smith, 2009). There have been dramatic demonstrations against Chinese rule. In 2011 and 2012, at least fifty Tibetans protested by setting themselves on fire (Gladstone, 2012).

Ethnocide may also take place when so many carriers of a culture die that those who manage to survive become refugees, living among peoples of different cultures. Examples of this may be seen in many parts of the world today.

ethnocide The violent eradication of an ethnic group's collective cultural identity as a distinctive people; occurs when a dominant society deliberately sets out to destroy another society's cultural heritage.

Ethnocide in Amazonia: Yąnomami

A particularly well-documented case of ethnocide occurred in South America's Amazon rainforest in 1968, when developers hired killers to wipe out several Indian groups, using arsenic, dynamite, and machine guns from light planes. To this day, violence continues to haunt indigenous peoples inhabiting this vast tropical forest. Most of these groups are besieged by outsiders aggressively penetrating their homelands in search of precious resources and, in the process, destroying their way of life.

Ethnocide in the Amazon is especially well documented for the Yąnomami Indians of the Upper Orinoco drainage. With a current population of about 24,000 (9,000 living in Brazil and 15,000 across the border in Venezuela), these hunters and food gardeners occupy about 18 million hectares. They reside in about 125 autonomous villages, each inhabited by 30 to 300 people living collectively in large circular dwellings known as *shabonos*.

Almost completely isolated from the outside world until the mid-1900s, the Yąnomami did experience cultural change prior to first contact with foreign traders and Christian missionaries. Evidence for this was in their gardens, where they planted nonindigenous food crops—plantains and bananas, both originating in Africa—acquired through exchange. This adoption increased gardening productivity, triggering population growth and, so it seems, more raids in intervillage conflicts.

Through trading and raiding, the Yąnomami also acquired iron tools, especially machetes and axes. Having these, along with newly introduced firearms, their internal conflicts became increasingly violent. According to some anthropologists, a condition of endemic warfare ensued, with violence becoming the cause of death for perhaps nearly a third of adult men.

Cultural change accelerated when foreign missionaries and traders became a permanent presence on their frontiers beginning in the 1950s. Despite their fierce reputation, the Yąnomami soon became victims of repeated assaults by gold miners, cattle ranchers, and other foreigners seeking to capitalize on their natural resources.

In the late 1960s, a measles epidemic killed hundreds of Yąnomami. Without microbiological knowledge of bacteria and viruses, these Amazonian Indians traditionally attribute illness and death to evil magic, or sorcery, and this demands that surviving relatives seek revenge.

Threats to Yąnomami survival multiplied in the 1980s, when many thousands of Brazilian loggers and *garimpeiros* ("gold miners") invaded their lands, attacking villagers defending their territories (Turner, 1991). Miners also illegally crossed into Venezuela, spreading the violence. The Brazilian state, considering legalizing large-scale logging and mining in indigenous territories, stepped up its military presence in these borderlands, sending troops, building barracks, and expanding airstrips in the Yąnomami heartland. Huge stretches of forest were torched to build mining camps. Dozens of planes flew in daily, transporting personnel, equipment, and fuel.

Miners, loggers, and soldiers lured Yąnomami women with commodities, infecting them with sexually transmitted diseases that spread quickly into the indigenous communities. On top of prostitution, the invaders introduced alcoholism. Processing the ore, miners also polluted the rivers with mercury, poisoning fish and other creatures, including the Yąnomami. Within the decade, 20 percent of the Yąnomami died, and 70 percent of their ancestral lands in Brazil were illegally expropriated.

A campaign against this ethnocide, led by the Committee for the Creation of Yąnomami Park and Survival International, forced the Brazilian government to protect indigenous territories and expel the miners. Creating a Yąnomami Park (in fact, a reservation) in 1992, the Brazilian state slowed but failed to stop the ethnocide and *ecocide* (environmental destruction) because *garimpeiros* crossed the border into Venezuela where they continued massacring Yąnomami men, women, and children.

In the mid-1990s, after years of pressure by the Inter-American Commission on Human Rights, Venezuelan state authorities finally agreed to protect the Yąnomami in the remote borderlands and to provide some basic health care to reduce alarming mortality rates. To this day, Amazonian Indians such as the Yąnomami are forced to live in a climate of fear, with violent intimidation, physical threats, and occasional killings, aggravated by poor health, low life expectancy, and discrimination, challenging their survival as an indigenous people.

In such difficult times, spiritual leaders are especially important. Among these is Davi Kopenawa, a shaman from the Yąnomami village of Watoriketheri (**Figure 25.5**). He and other shamans—traditionally skilled in contacting dangerous spirits in order to cure the sick and seek revenge against enemies—now confront the deadly forces of ethnocide and ecocide. Recognized as a spokesperson for the Yąnomami in Brazil, Kopenawa has gained an international reputation as a political activist. He uses his extraordinary powers in defense of his Amazonian homeland, negotiating with powerful foreign institutions, corporations, and nongovernmental organizations in a heroic effort to stop the relentless destruction of Brazil's indigenous peoples, cultures, and environment (Conklin, 2002; Kopenawa & Albert, 2010).

Directed Change

Although the process of acculturation often unfolds without planning, powerful elites may devise and enforce programs of cultural change, directing immigrant or subordinated groups into learning and accepting dominant society's cultural beliefs and practices. So it was with the Ju/'hoansi of southern Africa. Rounded up by government officials in the early 1960s, these Bushmen were confined to a reservation in Tsumkwe where they could not possibly provide for their own needs. The government supplied them with rations, but these were insufficient to meet basic nutritional needs.

Figure 25.5 **Yąnomami Shaman and Political Activist Davi Kopenawa** Traditionally, Yąnomami shamans such as Davi Kopenawa, seen here surrounded by women and children standing in front of their *shabono*, cure the sick by contacting the spirit world. Known as *shabori*, they apply their skills in negotiating extraordinary challenges with *hekura* ("dangerous spirits"). Today, those challenges include ethnocide and ecocide. Yąnomami rely on shamans such as Kopenawa to use their remarkable powers when negotiating with strangers representing powerful foreign institutions, corporations, and nongovernmental organizations in an effort to prevent further harm to their communities.

© Fiona Watson/Survival

In poor health and prevented from developing meaningful alternatives to traditional activities, the Ju/'hoansi became embittered and depressed, and their death rate came to exceed the birthrate. Within the next few years, however, surviving Ju/'hoansi began to take matters into their own hands. They returned to waterholes in their traditional homeland, where, assisted by anthropologists and others concerned with their welfare, they are trying to sustain themselves by raising livestock. Whether this will succeed remains to be seen because there are still many obstacles to overcome.

One byproduct of colonial dealings with indigenous peoples has been the growth of applied anthropology, which was originally focused on advising government programs of directed cultural change and solving practical problems through anthropological techniques and knowledge. For example, in the United States, the Bureau of American Ethnology was founded in 1876 to gather reliable data the government might use to formulate Indian policies. At the time, anthropologists were convinced of the practicality of their discipline, and many who did ethnographic work among Indians devoted a great deal of time, energy, and money to assisting their informants, whose interests were frequently at risk.

In the 20th century, the scope and intent of applied anthropology expanded. In the first part of that century, the applied work of Franz Boas—who almost singlehandedly trained an entire generation of anthropologists in the United States—proved instrumental in reforming the country's immigration policies. With impressive statistical data based on comparative skull measurements and related physical anthropological studies, this German Jewish immigrant challenged popular race theories of the day. He demonstrated that theories privileging non-Jewish immigrants from western Europe and discrimination against Jews and others deemed undesirable were based not on fact but on deeply rooted racial prejudice.

In the 1930s, anthropologists with clearly pragmatic objectives did a number of studies in industrial and other institutional settings in the United States. With World War II came increased involvement in colonial administration beyond U.S. borders, especially in the Pacific, by American officers trained in anthropology. The rapid postwar recovery of Japan was due in no small measure to the influence of anthropologists in structuring the U.S. occupation. Anthropologists continue to play an active role today in administering U.S. trust territories in the Pacific.

All too often, however, states and other powerful institutions directly intervening in the affairs of different ethnic groups or foreign societies fail to seek professional advice from anthropologists who possess relevant cross-cultural expertise and deeper insights. Such failures have contributed to a host of avoidable errors in planning and executing nation-building programs in ethnically divided countries such as Iraq and Afghanistan, both of which are now devastated by war and violence.

Today, applied anthropologists are in growing demand in the field of international development because of their specialized knowledge of social structure, value systems, and the functional interrelatedness of cultures targeted for development. Those working in this arena face a particular challenge: As anthropologists, they are bound to respect other peoples' dignity and cultural integrity, yet they are asked for advice on how to change certain aspects of those cultures. If the people themselves request the change, there is no difficulty, but typically the change is requested from outsiders. Supposedly, the proposed change is for the good of the targeted population, yet members of that community do not always see it that way. The extent to which applied anthropologists should go in advising outsiders how to manipulate people to embrace the changes proposed for them is a serious ethical question, especially when it concerns people without the power to resist.

In direct response to such critical questions concerning the application and benefits of anthropological research, an alternative type of practical anthropology has emerged during the last half century. Known by a variety of names—including action anthropology and committed, engaged, involved, and advocacy anthropology—this involves community-based research and action in collaboration and solidarity with indigenous societies, ethnic minorities, and other besieged or repressed groups. In sum, not only are the practical applications of anthropology necessary, but there is a growing demand for anthropologically informed pragmatic solutions.

Reactions to Change

The reactions of indigenous peoples to the changes outsiders have thrust upon them have varied considerably. Some have responded by moving to the nearest available forest, desert, or other remote place in hopes of being left alone. In Brazil, a number of communities once located near the coast took this option a few hundred years ago and were successful until the great push to develop the Amazon forest began in the 1960s. Others, like many Indians of North America, took up arms to fight back but were ultimately forced to sign treaties and surrender much of their ancestral land, after which they were reduced to an impoverished underclass in their own territories. Today, they continue to fight through nonviolent means to retain their identities as distinct peoples and to regain control over natural resources on their lands.

Resisting **assimilation**, a process of cultural absorption of an ethnic minority by a dominant society, people often seek emotional comfort from **tradition**—customary ideas

---

assimilation Cultural absorption of an ethnic minority by a dominant society.

tradition Customary ideas and practices passed on from generation to generation, which in a modernizing society may form an obstacle to new ways of doing things.

and practices passed on from generation to generation, which in a modernizing society may form an obstacle to new ways of doing things. Traditions play an important role in a cultural process identified as **accommodation**. In anthropology, this refers to an adaptation process by which a people modifies its traditional culture in response to pressures by a dominant society so as to preserve its distinctive ethnic identity and resist assimilation (Prins, 1996). In pursuit of such an accommodation strategy, ethnic groups may try to retain their distinctive identities by maintaining cultural boundaries such as holding onto traditional language, festive ceremonies, customary dress, ritual songs and dances, unique food, and so on. Later in this chapter we discuss two ethnographic examples of accommodation.

Syncretism

When people are able to hold on to some of their traditions in the face of powerful outside domination, the result may be *syncretism*—defined in an earlier chapter as the creative blending of indigenous and foreign beliefs or practices into new cultural forms. Not unlike hybrids in the animal or plant worlds, these new forms take shape in a dynamic process of cultural adaptation in which groups gradually negotiate a collective response to new challenges in their social environment. Vodou, practiced in Haiti and described in a previous chapter, is one of many examples of religious syncretism. But syncretism also occurs in other cultural domains, including art and fashion, architecture, marriage rituals, warfare, and even sports.

An intriguing illustration of this can be found among the Trobriand Islanders of the southern Pacific, whose cultural practices we looked at in earlier chapters. Yams are to Trobrianders what reindeer are for the Nenets—the staple of their subsistence, the wealth of their economy, and the core of their culture. These edible tubers (*Dioscorea batatas*, often confused with sweet potatoes) may grow longer than 1.5 meters (5 feet) and weigh over 65 kilograms (150 pounds). After women harvest the crop, everyone celebrates. The major event in their traditional July and August harvest festivals is a *kayasa*, a ritual competition in which rival village chiefs show off their *kuvi*—colossal yams over 3.5 meters (12 feet) long. Centered on these huge tubers, the *kayasa* ceremony involves dancing and ritual fighting between neighboring communities. The chief hosting the event is always declared the winner.

When Trobrianders were under colonial rule, British administrators as well as Christian protestant missionaries and teachers took notice of the *kayasa* ceremony. They found it scandalous for its erotic displays of "wild" dancing, accompanied by chanting and shouting—suggestive of sexual intercourse, body parts, and so on. A Methodist missionary set about "civilizing" these tropical islanders by teaching cricket at the mission school. He hoped this gentlemanly sport would replace Trobriand rivalry and fighting, encouraging comportment in dress, sportsmanship, and ultimately religion.

But that is not what happened. Although the Trobrianders took to the sport, they "rubbished" the British rules. Making cricket their own, they played in traditional battle dress and incorporated battle magic and erotic dancing into the game. They modified the British style of pitching, making it resemble the old Trobriand way of throwing a spear. And following the game, they held massive feasts, where wealth was displayed to enhance their prestige (**Figure 25.6**).

Cricket, in its altered form, has been made to serve traditional systems of prestige and exchange. Exuberance and pride are displayed by everyone associated with the sport, and the players are as much concerned with conveying the full meaning of who they are as with scoring runs. From the sensual dressing in preparation for the game to the team chanting songs full of sexual metaphors to the erotic dancing between the innings, it is clear that each participant is playing for his own importance, for the fame of his team, and for the hundreds who watch the playful spectacle.

Revitalization Movements

In contrast to cultural changes that are invited or initiated by peoples themselves, those that are imposed or experienced as disruptive may be resisted or rejected. Such a reaction may lead to a *reform* movement or take on a more extreme character as a *revitalization movement*. As noted in the chapter on religion and spirituality, such radical movements develop in response to widespread social disruption and collective feelings of anxiety and despair. They are often, but not always, religiously or spiritually based. Some revitalization movements take on an armed revolutionary character, as did the Taliban in Afghanistan. When primary ties of culture, social relationships, and activities are broken, and meaningless activity is imposed by outside forces, individuals and groups characteristically react by rejecting newly introduced cultural elements and reclaiming historical roots and traditional identity, along with a measure of spiritual imagination.

Anthropologists recognize a sequence common to the revitalization process. First is the normal state of society, in which stress is not too great, and sufficient cultural means exist to satisfy needs. Next comes a phase

accommodation In anthropology, refers to an adaptation process by which a people resists assimilation by modifying its traditional culture in response to pressures by a dominant society in order to preserve its distinctive ethnic identity.

Figure 25.6 Syncretism: Trobriand Cricket Indigenous peoples have reacted to colonialism in many different ways. When British missionaries pressed Trobriand Islanders of Melanesia to celebrate their regular yam harvests with a game of "civilized" cricket rather than traditional "wild" erotic dances, Trobrianders responded by transforming the staid British sport into an exuberant event that featured sexual chants and dances between innings. This is an example of syncretism—the creative blending of indigenous and foreign beliefs and practices into new cultural forms.

© Wolfgang Kaehler/Corbis

of cultural upheaval, triggered by foreign invasion, domination, and exploitation, leading to growing frustration and stress brought about by cultural upheaval. The third phase is marked by a deepening of the crisis in which normal means of resolving social and psychological tensions are inadequate or fail. The decline may trigger a radical response in the form of a collective effort to restore, or revitalize, the culture. During this phase, a prophet or some other spiritual leader inspired by supernatural visions or guidance attracts a following, leading to a cult sometimes spiraling into a religious movement (Wallace, 1970).

Cargo Cults

One particular historical example of a revitalization movement is the **cargo cult**—a spiritual movement (especially noted in Melanesia in the Southwest Pacific) in reaction to disruptive contact with Western capitalism; the cult promises resurrection of deceased relatives, destruction or enslavement of white foreigners, and the magical arrival of utopian riches.

Indigenous Melanesians referred to the white man's wealth as "cargo" (pidgin English for European trade goods transported by ships or airplanes). In times of great social stress, native prophets emerged, predicting that the time of suffering would come to an end and a new paradise on earth would soon arrive. Their deceased

ancestors would return to life, and the rich white man would magically disappear—swallowed by an earthquake or swept away by a huge wave. However, the valued Western trade goods would be left for the prophets and their cult followers, who performed rituals to hasten this supernatural redistribution of wealth (see Lindstrom, 1993; Worsley, 1957).

A Contemporary Indigenous Revitalization Movement: Qullasuyu

In contrast to Melanesia's cargo cults, which were intensive and passing, a revitalization movement may also gain political state support and change a society's cultural institutions. One example of this is now taking place in Bolivia. In this pluralistic South American country, most citizens are of indigenous descent and still speak an ancestral home language other than Spanish. The two most common are Aymara and Quechua, spoken by people inhabiting what was historically known as Qullasuyu, the southeastern district of Tawantinsuyu (*Quechua* means "union of four districts"), the indigenous name for the ancient Inca empire.

Following the December 2005 election of President Evo Morales, Bolivia's indigenous revitalization movement has enjoyed that country's government support. The son of an Aymara father and Quechua mother, this socialist head of state was previously a militant peasant leader representing masses of migrant farmers growing coca in the subtropical lowlands. Since the 1980s, he had risen to prominence as an agrarian trade union leader promoting indigenous farmers' rights. The day before his presidential inauguration in January 2006, his unique

cargo cult A spiritual movement (especially noted in Melanesia) in reaction to disruptive contact with Western capitalism, promising resurrection of deceased relatives, destruction or enslavement of white foreigners, and the magical arrival of utopian riches.

Figure 25.7 Celebrating Aymara New Year Aymara Indians mark the new year by participating in a sunrise ceremony at the sacred ruins of Tiwanaku near the shore of Lake Titicaca. Signifying the beginning of 5515 (on the Aymara calendar) at dawn in mid-June 2007, they celebrated the event at the northern solstice—an astronomical event when the sun reaches its lowest excursion relative to the equator on the celestial sphere. Their hands raised to catch the first morning rays, these Bolivians participate in a Qullasuyu revitalization movement that for many includes a return to precolonial indigenous beliefs and rituals, such as worship of the sun as the supreme reigning sky deity.

stance as the country's first indigenous president was publicly recognized at a special ceremony held at the famous archaeological site of Tiwanaku. Standing there, flanked by *amautas* ("spiritual leaders"), Morales was vested with the neotraditional indigenous royal title of *apu mallku* ("condor king") of Qullasuyu.

Situated between La Paz and Lake Titicaca, Tiwanaku is unequaled in cultural significance as the ceremonial center of Bolivia's indigenous revitalization movement. Long abandoned, its enormous temple complex with its large pyramid, Akapana, was the capital of an ancient civilization that endured for many centuries before mysteriously collapsing about a thousand years ago. Because its inhabitants left no written records, their language remains unknown, which means Aymara and Quechua peoples can share this archaeological site symbolically representing their proud cultural heritages. Vesting these ruins with political and spiritual meaning as a sacred monument, they feel inspired to reclaim indigenous autonomy and to reject the foreign culture imposed on them during almost 500 years of colonial domination and capitalist exploitation.

In 2007, pursuing his revitalization agenda, President Morales chose Tiwanaku for an official event celebrating the adoption of the United Nations Declaration for the Rights of Indigenous Peoples. Two years later, the seven-colored *wiphala* representing Qullasuyu became Bolivia's

official co-flag. It now flies alongside the country's long-established red, yellow, and green national banner (Van Cott, 2008; Yates, 2011).

After four years in office, doubling as *apu mallku* and president, Morales was reelected. Again, his 2010 indigenous head-of-state celebration was conducted on top of Tiwanaku's pyramid ruin mound, Akapana. As before, spiritual leaders in spectacular neotraditional dress stood at his side while multitudes of Aymara and Quechua watched with a spirit of admiration and celebration.

Beyond restoring, preserving, and protecting indigenous cultural sites, customs, and so on, the revitalization movement in Bolivia involves a reclamation of precolonial sacred rituals, such as the worship of indigenous earth and sky deities, in particular the sun and moon (**Figure 25.7**). Informed by an animistic worldview, the movement seeks to restore a more harmonious relationship among communities of humans, animals, and plants, as well as the rest of the natural environment—recognizing all as part of one large ecosystem, a living "Mother Earth," traditionally held sacred as Pachamama. Formalizing this, in 2010 Bolivia's Plurinational Legislative Assembly passed the *Ley de Derechos de la Madre Tierra* ("The Law of the Rights of Mother Earth"), granting all of nature equal rights to humans (Estado Plurinacional de Bolivia, 2010).

Rebellion and Revolution

As briefly noted with respect to the Taliban in Afghanistan, when the scale of discontent within a society reaches a critical level, the possibilities are high for a violent reaction such as a rebellion or **insurgency**—organized armed resistance by a group of rebels to an established government or authority in power. For instance, there have been many peasant insurgencies around the world in the course of history. Historically, such uprisings are triggered by repressive regimes that impose new taxes on already struggling small farmers unable to feed their families under such levels of exploitation (Wolf, 1999b).

One recent example is the Zapatista Maya Indian insurgency in southern Mexico, which began in the mid-1990s and has not yet been resolved. This uprising involves thousands of poor Indian farmers whose livelihoods have been threatened by disruptive changes imposed on them; their human rights under the Mexican constitution have never been fully implemented (**Figure 25.8**).

In contrast to insurgencies, which have rather limited objectives, a **revolution**—a radical change in a society or culture—involves a more dramatic transformation. Revolutions occur when the level of discontent in a society is very high. In the political arena, revolution involves the forced overthrow of the existing government and the establishment of a completely new one.

Such was the case when Muslim fundamentalists in Iran toppled the imperial regime of the shah in 1979 and replaced him with Ayatollah Khomeini, a high-ranking Shiite Muslim religious leader. Returning to his homeland from exile and becoming Iran's new leader, he instituted a new social and political order based on Islamic fundamentalist principles.

The question of why revolutions erupt, as well as why they frequently fail to live up to the expectations of the people initiating them, is uncertain. It is clear, however, that the colonial policies of countries such as Britain, France, Spain, Portugal, and the United States during the 19th and early 20th centuries have created a worldwide situation in which revolution is nearly inevitable. Despite the political independence most colonies have gained since World War II, powerful countries continue to exploit many of these "underdeveloped" countries for their natural resources and cheap labor, causing a deep resentment of rulers beholden to foreign

powers. Further discontent has been caused as governing elites in newly independent states try to assert their control over peoples living within their boundaries. By virtue of a common ancestry, possession of distinct cultures, persistent occupation of their own territories, and traditions of self-determination, the peoples they aim to control identify themselves as distinct nations and refuse to recognize the legitimacy of what they regard as a foreign government.

Thus, in many former colonies, large numbers of people have taken up arms to resist annexation and absorption by imposed state governments run by people of other nationalities. As they attempt to make their multi-ethnic states into unified countries, ruling elites of one nationality set about stripping the peoples of other nations within their states of their lands, resources, and particular cultural identities. The phenomenon is so common that Belgian sociologist Pierre van den Berghe has renamed what modern states refer to as "nation building" as, in fact, "nation killing" (Van den Berghe, 1992).

One of the most important facts of our time is that the vast majority of the distinct peoples of the world have never consented to rule by the governments of states within which they find themselves living (Nietschmann, 1987). In many newly emerging countries, such peoples feel they have no other option than to take up weapons in armed protest and fight.

Apart from rebellions against authoritarian regimes, such as in the Chinese, French, and Russian revolutions, many uprisings in modern times have been insurgencies against political rule imposed by foreign powers. Such resistance usually takes the form of national independence movements that wage campaigns of armed defiance against colonial or imperial dominance. The Mexican war of liberation against Spain in the early 1800s and the Algerian struggle for independence from France in the 1950s are relevant examples.

Of the hundreds of armed conflicts in the world today, almost all are in the economically poor countries of Africa, Asia, and Latin America, many of which were at one time under European colonial domination. Of these wars, the majority are between the state and one or more nations or ethnic groups within the state's borders. These groups are seeking to maintain or regain control of their personal lives, communities, lands, and resources in the face of what they regard as repression or subjugation by a foreign power.

Revolutions do not always accomplish what they set out to do. One of the stated goals of the 1949 Chinese communist revolution, for example, was to liberate women from the oppression of a strongly patriarchal society in which a woman owed lifelong obedience to a male relative—first her father, later her husband, and, after his death, her oldest son. Although changes were

---

insurgency An organized armed resistance or violent uprising to an established government or authority in power; also known as *rebellion*.

revolution Radical change in a society or culture. In the political arena, it involves the forced overthrow of the existing government and establishment of a completely new one.

Matias Recart/AFP/Getty Images

Figure 25.8 Zapatista Revolutionary Movement On New Year's Day 1994, when the North American Free Trade Agreement (NAFTA) went into effect, 3,000 armed peasants belonging to the Zapatista revolutionary movement invaded towns in southern Mexico. Mostly Maya Indians, they declared war on the Mexican government, claiming that globalization was destroying their rural communities. Strong Internet presence helped them build an international network of political support. Now committed to nonviolent resistance to Mexican state control, Zapatistas have created thirty-two self-governing municipalities and established their own local health, justice, and education services. These municipalities are grouped in five regional zones, called *caracoles* (conch shell), referring to Maya sacred cosmology as mythological upholders of the sky. The *caracoles* consist of various Maya ethnic groups—Cho'l, Mam, Tojolabal, Tzeltal, Tzotzil, and Zoque—each headed by a representative council.

and continue to be made, the transformation overall has been frustrated by the cultural lens through which the revolutionaries viewed their work. A tradition of deeply rooted patriarchy extending back at least 2,200 years is not easily overcome and has influenced many of the decisions made by communist China's leaders since the revolution.

Despite the current rapid changes taking place in China's expanding urban areas, in many rural parts of the country a woman's life is still largely determined by her relationship to a man—be it her father, husband, or son—rather than by her own efforts or failures. Moreover, many rural women face official local policies that identify their primary roles as wives and mothers. When they do work outside the house, it is generally at jobs with low pay, low status, and no benefits (**Figure 25.9**).

Women's no-wage home labor (and low-wage outside labor) for their husbands' households have been essential to China's economic expansion, which relies on the allocation of labor by the heads of patrilineal households (Liu, 2007).

In part due to China's one-child rule resulting in a shortage of marriage partners for men, rural women face the threat of being abducted for wives and workers. In 2000, after an outbreak of "bride-napping" during the previous decade, government authorities cracked down on the practice. Tens of thousands of women and girls were freed, but the practice continues ("Bartered brides," 2009; "China to execute bride traffickers," 2000; U.S. Department of State, 2007).

Facing obstacles that many rural Chinese women feel are insurmountable, more than 1 million of them

Figure 25.9 Rural Women Removing Chips From Computer Boards, Guiyu, China Since the late 1980s, e-waste from developed countries has been imported to China and broken down at Guiyu. The city comprises 21 villages with 5,500 family workshops handling e-waste and being exposed to carcinogens.

attempt suicide each year—typically by swallowing pesticides or fertilizer. Of these, 150,000 die. Rural China is the only place on earth where more women kill themselves than men (Pearson et al., 2002).

The situation of rural women in China shows that the undermining of revolutionary goals, if it occurs, is not necessarily by political opponents. Rather, it may be a consequence of the revolutionaries' own traditional cultural background. In rural China, that includes patrilineal exogamy, patrilocality, and a patriarchal conservatism in which female labor is controlled by male heads of families. As long as these traditional views continue to hold sway, women will be seen as commodities.

Revolution is a relatively recent phenomenon, occurring only during the past 5,000 years or so. The reason is that rebellion requires a centralized political authority to rebel against, and states did not exist before 5,000 years ago. In kin-ordered societies organized as tribes and bands, without a centralized government, there could be no rebellion or political revolution.

Modernization

One of the most frequently used terms to describe social and cultural changes as they are occurring today is **modernization**. This is most clearly defined as an all-encompassing and global process of political and socioeconomic change, whereby developing societies acquire some of the cultural characteristics common to Western industrial societies.

Derived from the Latin word *modo* ("just now"), modernization literally refers to something "in the present time." The dominant idea behind this concept is that "becoming modern" is becoming like European, North American, and other wealthy industrial or postindustrial societies, with the clear implication that not to do so is to be stuck in the past—backward, inferior, and needing to be improved. It is unfortunate that the term *modernization* continues to be so widely used, but because it is, we need to recognize its problematic one-sidedness, even as we continue to use it.

The process of modernization may be best understood as consisting of five subprocesses, all interrelated and with no fixed order of appearance:

- *Technological development*: In the course of modernization, traditional knowledge and techniques give way to the application of scientific knowledge and techniques borrowed mainly from the industrialized West.
- *Agricultural development*: This is represented by a shift in emphasis from subsistence farming to commercial farming. Instead of raising crops and livestock for their own use, people turn with growing frequency to the production of cash crops, with increased reliance on a cash economy and on global markets for selling farm products and purchasing goods.
- *Urbanization*: This subprocess is marked particularly by population movements from rural settlements into cities.

---

modernization The process of political and socioeconomic change, whereby developing societies acquire some of the cultural characteristics of Western industrial societies.

- *Industrialization*: Here human and animal power become less important, and greater emphasis is placed on material forms of energy—especially fossil fuels—to drive machines.
- *Telecommunication*: The fifth and most recent subprocess involves electronic and digital media processing and sharing of news, commodity prices, fashions, and entertainment, as well as political and religious opinions. Information is widely dispersed to a mass audience, far across national borders.

As modernization proceeds, other changes are likely to follow. In the political realm, political parties and some sort of electoral apparatus frequently appear, along with the development of an administrative bureaucracy. In formal education, institutional learning opportunities expand, literacy increases, and an indigenous educated elite develops. Many long-held rights and duties connected with kinship are altered, if not eliminated, especially when distant relatives are concerned. If social stratification is a factor, social mobility increases as ascribed status becomes less important and personal achievement counts for more.

Finally, as traditional beliefs and practices are undermined, formalized religion becomes less important in many areas of thought and behavior. As discussed in the chapter on religion, this may turn into a growing trend toward a nonreligious worldview with people ignoring or rejecting institutionalized spiritual beliefs and rituals. Known as *secularization*, this process is especially noteworthy in highly organized capitalist states like Germany, for many centuries predominantly Lutheran and Roman Catholic. Now, almost 40 percent of Germans identify themselves as nonreligious, an increase from less than 4 percent just forty years ago.

Secularization is also taking place in other western European countries, as well as in other parts of the world. However, in places in which the state is weak and unbridled capitalism has dramatically increased insecurity among the exploited and impoverished masses, the opposite may result, with a reactionary trend toward a more spiritual or even religious worldview. This phenomenon is evident in many eastern European, Asian, and African countries—discussed in the chapter on religion.

Indigenous Accommodation to Modernization

A closer examination of traditional cultures that have felt the impact of modernization will help to illustrate some of the problems such cultures have encountered. Earlier in this chapter, we noted that ethnic groups, unable to resist changes but unwilling to surrender their distinctive cultural heritage and identity, may pursue a strategy of accommodation. Many have done so, but with variable success. Here we offer two ethnographic examples: the Sámi people living in the Arctic and sub-Arctic tundra of northwest Russia and Scandinavia and the Shuar Indians of Ecuador.

Sámi Herders: The Snowmobile Revolution and Its Unintended Consequences

Until about half a century ago, Sámi reindeer herders in Scandinavia's Arctic tundra lived much like the Nenets featured in this chapter's opening photo. In the 1960s, however, they purchased snowmobiles, expecting motorized transportation to make herding physically easier and economically more advantageous. But that is not what happened.

Given the high cost of buying, maintaining, and fueling the machines, Sámi herders faced a sharp rise in their need for money. To obtain cash, men began going outside their communities for wage labor more than just occasionally, as had previously been the case. Moreover, once snowmobiles were introduced, the familiar, prolonged, and largely peaceful relationship between herder and beast changed into a noisy, traumatic one. The humans that reindeer encountered came speeding out of the woods on noisy, smelly machines that invariably chased the animals, often for long distances. Instead of helping the reindeer in their winter food quest, aiding does with their calves, and protecting the herd from predators, the men appeared only periodically, either to slaughter or to castrate the animals (**Figure 25.10**).

The reindeer became wary of people, resulting in de-domestication, with reindeer scattering and running off to less accessible areas. In addition, snowmobile harassment seemed to adversely affect birthing and the survival of calves. For example, within a decade the average size of the family herd among the Sámi in Finland had dropped from fifty to twelve—a number that is not economically viable. The financial cost of mechanized herding and the decline in domesticated herd size have led many Sámi to abandon herding altogether (Pelto, 1973). Today, only about 10 percent of Sámi in Finland are full-time herders, and they vie with outside economic institutions such as forestry and tourism for access to and use of land (Williams, 2003). Their situation is echoed among Sámi across Scandinavia (Wheelersburg, 1987).

Figure 25.10 **Sámi Reindeer Herding** In the 1960s, Sámi reindeer herders in Scandinavia's Arctic tundra adopted newly invented snowmobiles, convinced that these machines would make traditional herding physically easier and economically more advantageous. As it turned out, the financial cost of mechanized herding and the decline in domesticated herd size caused many to abandon herding altogether. Here, a herder tries to lasso one of his reindeer.

Shuar Cattle Farmers: An Indigenous Experiment in Amazon's Tropical Forest

In contrast to the Sámi in northern Europe, the Shuar Indians of Ecuador's tropical forest deliberately avoided modernization until it was inevitable. Historically better known as Jivaro, these Amazonian Indians subsisted on hunting wild game and cultivating food gardens, periodically clearing small patches of forest by slash-and-burn. In 1964, threatened with the loss of their land base as more and more Ecuadoran colonists intruded into their territory, leaders from the many, widely scattered Shuar communities came together and founded a fully independent ethnic organization—the Shuar Federation—to take control of their own future.

Recognized by Ecuador's government, the group is officially dedicated to promoting the social, economic, and cultural advancement of the growing Shuar population. Through their association, the Shuar took control of their own education, using their own language and mostly Shuar teachers; they established their own

bilingual radio station and a bilingual newspaper; and they participated in coordinating their own economic development efforts with official government agencies. Perhaps most important, the alliance provided a means for dealing with the pressing problem of land control.

Ecuador's government categorized almost all tropical woodlands in the Upper Amazon as *tierra baldía* ("empty land") because, although indigenous people lived there in widely scattered communities, most of their ancestral hunting land remained undeveloped wilderness that lacked legal documentation of ownership. With many thousands of young mestizo (mixed Indian European ancestry) farmers in Ecuador's highland valleys unable to feed their growing families, officials encouraged them to resettle in the Oriente, the "Wild East" of Ecuador. In the 1960s, it comprised almost half of the country's territory, but only about 2.5 percent of its total population. Accordingly, roads and bridges were constructed, enabling mestizos to claim title to "free" land and also providing them with access to the national market and export. Further capitalizing on its "empty lands," the state began selling concessions to the foreign or domestic logging, oil, and mining companies extracting its natural resources.

Besieged by development, and without legally recognized title to their ancestral lands, the Shuar Federation attracted financial assistance and expert advice through foreign aid agencies and turned large tracts of woodland into pasture for cattle ranching. By the early 1970s, it had secured title to almost 100,000 hectares of communal land and established a cattle herd of more than 15,000 head. Beyond supplementing the traditional Shuar diet of wild game and produce from slash-and-burn gardens, cattle provided them with something to sell—a means of earning cash to pay for commodities, health care, and so on.

Because Shuar turned to cattle primarily to secure legal title to their lands, it is not surprising that many switched to other income sources when alternatives opened up as a result of roads now connecting them to the rest of the country. In recent decades, many Shuar have largely abandoned cattle grazing, even allowing a reforestation of pasture lands. Instead, now that their title is officially documented, they have turned to growing labor-intensive cash crops, not only fruits, plantain, and manioc, but also coffee and cacao for sale to urban consumers or for export (Rudel, Bates, & Machinguiashi, 2002).

The strategy of accommodation pursued by the Shuar shows that sometimes positive results can occur when indigenous peoples are free to determine their own destinies even in the face of intense outside pressures. Tragically, until recently, few have had that option. Nevertheless, like the Shuar, some groups have resourcefully resisted the outside forces of destruction arrayed against them. Some receive help from anthropologists, as discussed in this chapter's Anthropology Applied feature.

Globalization in the "Underdeveloped" World

Throughout the so-called underdeveloped world, in Africa, Asia, Latin America, and elsewhere, whole countries are in the throes of radical political and economic change and overall cultural transformation. In fact, inventions and major advances in industrial production, mass transportation, and communication and information technologies are transforming societies in Europe and North America as well. As discussed in Chapter 1, this worldwide process of accelerated modernization interconnecting all parts of the earth in one vast interrelated and all-encompassing system is known as *globalization*, evidenced in global movements of natural resources, trade goods, human labor, finance capital, information, and infectious diseases.

All around the globe we are witnessing the removal of economic activities—or at least their control—from the family and community setting. And we are seeing the altered structure of the family in the face of the changing labor market: young children relying increasingly on parents alone for affection and support, instead of depending on their entire extended family; parental authority generally declining; schools replacing the family as the primary educational unit; couples dealing with the difficulties of commuter marriages as they pursue jobs in different cities or even countries; old people spending their last days in nursing homes and assisted living facilities rather than with family members; and the list goes on.

In many societies, this modernization process is now happening very fast, often without the necessary time to adjust. Changes that took generations to accomplish in Europe and North America are attempted within the span of a single generation in developing countries. In the process cultures frequently face unforeseen disruptions and a rapid erosion of dearly held values they had no intention of giving up. Anthropologists doing fieldwork in distant communities throughout the world witness how these traditional cultures have been impacted, and often destroyed, by powerful global forces.

Commonly, the burden of modernization in developing countries falls most heavily on women. For example, the commercialization of agriculture often involves land reforms that overlook or ignore women's traditional land rights. This reduces their control of and access to resources at the same time that mechanization of food production and processing drastically reduces their opportunities for employment. As a consequence, women are confined more and more to traditional domestic tasks, which are increasingly devalued as commercial production becomes the dominant concern.

Moreover, the domestic workload tends to increase because men are less available to help out; tasks such as fuel gathering and water collection are made more difficult as common land and resources come to be privately owned and as woodlands are reserved for commercial exploitation. As well, the growing of nonfood crops for the world market—such as cotton and sisal or luxury crops such as tea, coffee, and cacao (the source of chocolate)—makes households vulnerable to wide price fluctuations. As a result, people cannot afford the high-quality diet that subsistence farming provided, and they become malnourished. In short, with modernization, women frequently find themselves in an increasingly inferior position. As their workload increases, the value assigned to the work they do declines, as does their relative educational status, not to mention their health and nutrition.

Most anthropologists, based on their fieldwork experience, recognize that new roads, harbors, railways, and airstrips impact the earth's remaining wilderness—such as tropical forests, arid deserts, and Arctic tundra. These developments have costs. We opened this chapter with a photo of a Russian energy corporation now exploiting the natural gas fields deep below the encampments of Nenet reindeer herders. Like the Shuar and countless other peoples, Nenets confront outsiders bringing about radical changes they often do not want

ANTHROPOLOGY APPLIED

Development Anthropology and Dams

Over a 35-year career in scholarly and applied work, Michael M. Horowitz, president and executive director of the Institute for Development Anthropology (IDA) and distinguished professor of anthropology at the State University of New York at Binghamton, has made pioneering contributions to applied anthropology. His work has focused on achieving equitable economic growth, environmental sustainability, conflict resolution, and participatory government in the former colonial world.

Since cofounding IDA in 1976, Horowitz has been its principal leader. He has played a key role in bringing anthropology forward as an applied science in international development organizations such as the World Bank, the United Nations Fund for Women, and the U.S. Agency for International Development (USAID), as well as nongovernmental organizations (NGOs) such as Oxfam. He has mentored several generations of young scholars and professionals—paying particular attention to those from developing countries—encouraging the application of anthropology's comparative and holistic methodologies and theories to empower low-income majorities in the so-called underdeveloped world.

Horowitz's work with pastoralists and floodplain dwellers has had substantial positive impact on the well-being of small producers and landholders in developing countries. A clear example of this is the impact of his work on the lives and livelihoods of people living downstream of a hydropower dam in West Africa. Beginning in the 1980s, he and his IDA team carried out rigorous anthropological research along the Senegal River. Their study showed that traditional, pre-dam,

Visible from space, China's Three Gorges Dam is the world's largest and most powerful hydroelectric dam. With a length of about 2,300 meters (7,700 feet) and a height of 185 meters (330 feet), it controls the Yangtze, the world's third largest river. After fifteen years of construction with a price tag of $22 billion, it became operational in 2009. The dam was built to provide a clean energy alternative to coal and to control flooding along the Yangtze River. However, it has been controversial since its inception because it has flooded ancient archaeological and cultural sites, displacing more than 1.4 million people, and it has caused significant ecological changes, including risks of landslides that threaten some 4 million people. Unlike the dam described in this Anthropology Applied feature, not one social scientist was consulted in the planning and assessment phase of Three Gorges Dam.

flood-recession farming yielded better results than irrigated agriculture and was better for the environment.

This finding influenced decisions made by these countries and affiliated NGOs to manage the system with a controlled release from the Manatali Dam in Mali in order to reproduce as nearly as possible the pre-dam flow system. Horowitz's long-term field research demonstrated that seasonal flooding would provide economic, environmental, and sociocultural benefits for nearly a million small producers.

The work carried out by Horowitz and his IDA colleagues on the Senegal River Basin Monitoring Activity (SRBMA) was a breakthrough in the concepts of resettlement and river management, and it continues to influence development policy, not only in Africa, but also in Southeast Asia.

Based in part on Young, W. C. (2000). Kimball Award winner. Anthropology News 41 (8), 29; and updated in 2003 with personal communication from the Institute for Development Anthropology.

and cannot stop, challenging them to a degree that often exceeds their coping capability. Meanwhile, powerful groups with interests in capitalizing on cheap natural and human resources wherever available justify their relentless expansion, arguing that modernization is both inevitable

and good for everyone, in particular for "primitive" and "underdeveloped" peoples who ought to be given opportunities to prosper and become wealthy just like themselves. For a serious look at the consequences of these changes, see the Biocultural Connection feature.

BIOCULTURAL CONNECTION

Studying the Emergence of New Diseases

Since the Neolithic, people have had to cope with a host of new diseases that began as a consequence of changes in human behavior. Recently, this has become a renewed source of concern following the resurgence of infectious diseases and the spread of a host of new and lethal diseases.[a]

More than thirty diseases new to medicine have emerged in the past three decades. Perhaps the best known of these is AIDS, which has become a top killer among infectious diseases. Since 1981, more than 30 million people have died of AIDS, and today some 34 million people around the world are living with AIDS/HIV.[b] But there are others—like Ebola hemorrhagic fever, which causes victims to bleed to death; other hemorrhagic fevers like dengue fever, Lassa fever, and hantavirus; invasive streptococcus A, which consumes the victims' flesh; Legionnaire's disease; and Lyme disease.

Although it is not clear what has sparked the appearance and spread of these new diseases, one theory is that some are the result of human activities. In particular, road construction and the intrusion of people into remote ecological settings, such as rainforests, along with worldwide shipping and airplane traffic, allow viruses and other infectious microbes to spread rapidly to large numbers of people. It is now generally accepted that the HIV virus responsible for AIDS transferred to humans from chimpanzees in the tropical forests of the Democratic Republic of Congo (DRC) as a consequence of hunting and butchering these animals for food. For the first thirty years, few people were affected; it was not until people began congregating in quickly growing cities like Kinshasa that conditions were ripe for an epidemic.

Most of the "new" viruses that have suddenly afflicted humans are in fact old ones present in animals—such as monkeys (monkey pox), rodents (hantavirus), deer (Lyme disease), and insects (West Nile virus). What is different is that something has enabled them to jump from their animal hosts to humans.

In the DRC, civil war created a situation in which villagers in the central part of the country were faced with starvation. Their response was to increase the hunting of animals, including monkeys, squirrels, and rats that carry a disease called monkey pox. Related to smallpox, the disease transfers easily to humans, resulting in the largest outbreak of this disease ever seen among humans. This outbreak has been even more serious because of an apparently new strain of the infection, enabling it to spread from person to person, instead of only from an animal host.[c]

Large-scale habitat disturbance is an obvious explanation for such disease transfers. In another part of the world, medical anthropologist Carol Jenkins (1945–2008) conducted early health-related research among various ethnic groups in Papua New Guinea (PNG) from 1982 to 1995. Aiming to understand the interplay between ecological disturbance and the emergence of new diseases, she tracked the health of local people in the wake of a massive logging operation. Her work provided valuable insights, such as clarifying how the disease organisms spread from animal hosts to humans.

Jenkins's research in PNG was unique because baseline health data on local people was gathered before the environment was disturbed. Researchers, many trained by Jenkins, continue to build on and draw conclusions from her studies.

The importance of such investigations is obvious: In an era of globalization, as air travel allows diseases to spread worldwide, we need a fuller understanding of how pathogens interact with their hosts if we are to devise effective preventive and therapeutic strategies to deal with them.

BIOCULTURAL QUESTION

Because often new viruses and bacteria spread rapidly, what do you think of government-funded research and development of killer diseases for purposes of biological warfare?

---

[a]Gibbons, A. (1993). Where are new diseases born? *Science 261*, 680–681.

[b]"HIV & AIDS Information from avert.org." www.avert.org.

[c]Cohen, J. (1997). Is an old virus up to new tricks? *Science 277*, 312–313.

This worldview overlooks the fact that the standard of living for the middle and upper classes in wealthy or industrialized countries is based on a consumption rate of nonrenewable resources whereby a small fraction of the world's population uses the vast majority of these natural resources. Unfortunately, despite rosy predictions about a better future, hundreds of millions of people in our world remain trapped in a wretched reality, struggling against poverty, hunger, poor health, and other dangers. In the next and final chapter of this book, we further explore the underlying structures and deeper causes of these problems and look at the role anthropology can and does play in helping to meet these challenges.

CHAPTER CHECKLIST

Why and how do cultural systems change?

● Although stability may be a striking feature of many traditional cultures, all cultures are capable of adapting to changing conditions—climatic, economic, political, or ideological.

● Dynamic processes involved in cultural change are manifold, including accidental discoveries, deliberate inventions to solve some perceived problem, and borrowing from other peoples who introduce—or force—new commodities, technologies, and practices.

● *Progress* is a relative term that implies improvement as defined by the people who benefit from the changes.

What are the mechanisms of voluntary cultural change?

● Major mechanisms involved in voluntary cultural change are innovation, diffusion, and cultural loss.

● Innovation is any new idea, method, or device that gains widespread acceptance in society. A primary innovation is the creation, invention, or discovery of a new idea, method, or device. A secondary innovation is a deliberate application or modification of these innovations.

● A culture's internal dynamics may encourage certain innovative tendencies while discouraging others. Force of habit may obstruct the acceptance of an innovation.

● Diffusion, the spread of certain ideas, customs, or practices from one culture to another, may account for up to 90 percent of a culture's content. Many domestic food plants developed by American Indians spread around the world, including corn, also known as maize. Typically, people borrow only those cultural elements that are compatible with their own.

● Cultural loss involves the abandonment of some practice or trait.

What is repressive change?

● Frequently, changes are forced upon one group by another, usually in the course of conquest and colonialism.

● Acculturation is the massive cultural change that occurs in a society when it experiences intensive first-hand contact with a more powerful society. It may occur as a result of military conquest, political and economic expansion, or the substantial influx of dominant new-comers.

● Ethnocide is the violent eradication of an ethnic group's collective cultural identity as a distinctive people.

It occurs when a dominant society deliberately sets out to destroy another society's cultural heritage. Among many examples is the experience of Yąnomami Indians of the Amazon forest in Brazil and Venezuela.

What is directed change?

● Although the process of acculturation often unfolds without planning, powerful elites may devise and enforce programs of cultural change, directing immigrant or sub-ordinated groups into learning and accepting a dominant society's cultural beliefs and practices.

● Applied anthropology—the application of anthropological insights and methods to solving practical problems—arose as anthropologists sought to provide colonial administrators with a better understanding of native cultures, either to better control them or to avoid their serious disruption.

● An alternative type of practical anthropology emerged in the latter 20th century. Known by various names including *action anthropology*, it involves community-based research and action in collaboration with indigenous societies, ethnic minorities, and other besieged or repressed groups. A serious ethical issue for applied anthropologists is how far they should go in trying to change the ways of other peoples.

How do people react to repressive change?

● Reactions of indigenous peoples to imposed changes vary considerably. Some have retreated to inaccessible places in hopes of being left alone, whereas others have lapsed into apathy.

● Some, like the Trobriand Islanders, have reasserted their traditional culture's values by modifying foreign practices to conform to indigenous values, a phenomenon known as syncretism.

● If a culture's values are widely out of step with the reality of their daily lives, revitalization movements may arise.

● One example of a revitalization movement is the cargo cult (especially noted in Melanesia in the southwest Pacific) in reaction to disruptive contact with Western capitalism. A more recent example is the indigenous revitalization movement in Bolivia, led by the country's Aymara Indian president, Evo Morales.

● When the scale of discontent within a society is high, violent reaction such as rebellion or insurgency (organized armed resistance to the established government or authority in power) is likely. And if the level of dissatisfaction rises even higher, it may lead to revolution—a radical change in a society or culture. In the political arena, *revolution* refers to the forced overthrow of an existing government and the establishment of a new one.

What are modernization and self-determination?

● *Modernization* refers to an all-encompassing and global process of political and socioeconomic change, whereby developing societies acquire some of the cultural characteristics common to Western industrial societies.

● The process of modernizations consists of five subprocesses: technological development, agricultural development, urbanization, industrialization, and telecommunication. Other changes follow in the areas of political organization, education, social organization, and religion. As traditional beliefs and practices are undermined, secularization may rise.

● Self-determination is deeply valued by traditional cultures feeling the impact of modernization and other cultural changes.

● Attempting to claim self-determination does not guarantee success. Sámi reindeer herders living in northern Scandinavia discovered this when they adopted snowmobiles and faced a dramatic decline in the size of their herds. In contrast, Shuar Indians in the Amazon who subsisted on wild game and forest gardens increased their social and economic security when they turned to raising cattle as a means of securing legal title to their lands.

QUESTIONS FOR REFLECTION

1. Reflecting on the plight of Nenet reindeer herders in northwest Siberia, do you think it ethical to criticize global energy companies for measuring the value of wilderness areas in profits if you benefit from the resulting lower cost to fill your gas tank, fly across the country, or heat your home?

2. In this chapter we discussed diffusion and the fact that as much as 90 percent of any culture's content is borrowed. Take a close look at your own community and try to identify how many things you eat, wear, or use that were first cultivated, domesticated, historically invented, or manufactured in your own culture. Then try to figure out the culture or country of origin of all the rest. Feel free to use a detailed world atlas, which itself was invented in what is now Belgium.

3. When hearing or reading about insurgencies or violent uprisings in the news, have you ever wondered why people are willing to risk their lives to bring about change? What do you think accounts for that level of commitment?

4. When societies become involved in the modernizing process, all levels of their cultural systems are affected by these changes. Do you think that people are fully aware of the long-term consequences of the changes they themselves may have welcomed? Can you come up with any examples of unforeseen changes in your own community or neighborhood?

5. Globalization radically challenges most of us to adjust at an ever-faster pace within increasingly complex transnational settings. Do you feel that these changes are good for everyone?

ONLINE STUDY RESOURCES

CourseMate

Access chapter-specific learning tools, including learning objectives, practice quizzes, videos, flash cards, glossaries, and more in your Anthropology CourseMate.

Log into **www.cengagebrain.com** to access the resources your instructor has assigned and to purchase materials.

Challenge Issue

For at least 10,000 years, humans have met the challenges of survival by adapting to their natural environment and transforming it to fit their needs. They have turned deserts, forests, swamps, and mountainsides into pastures, farmlands, and industrial centers, creating opportunities (and sometimes unanticipated challenges) for an ever-growing population. Since the beginning of the industrial revolution about two centuries ago, the human population grew from 1 billion to well over 7 billion—half now living and working in urban areas. With the launching of the first telecommunication satellites in the 1950s, followed by the Internet in the 1960s, personal computers in the 1970s, and the World Wide Web in the 1990s, the digital revolution has accelerated the globalization process. Spinning webs of interconnectivity, people everywhere are adapting to new media environments. Using social media, a few billion humans weave in and out of cyberspace on a daily basis for work, news, entertainment, politics, and social networking. In China, cyber cafés known as 网吧 (wangba) can be found in most cities. This is one of hundreds in Beijing, the capital city.

Global Challenges, Local Responses, and the Role of Anthropology

In early 2012, the population of our species reached 7 billion—a historic milestone for humanity but hardly cause for celebration. In the course of a few thousand generations, our ancestors have met the challenges of survival not only by adapting to changing climates and different natural environments but also by transforming them to fit the needs of an ever-growing population. They turned deserts, forests, swamps, and mountainsides into pastures, farmlands, and, more recently, industrial centers.

Billions of people are now connected by means of electronic, fiber-optic, and digital telecommunication technology. About a thousand operational satellites orbit the earth—revolving between 250 and 22,500 miles (400 and 35,000 kilometers) above the surface. Nearly 560 of these are designated specifically for telecommunication, whereas others serve military, scientific, and weather forecasting purposes. Also included among these are twenty-four global positioning satellites (GPS), orbiting at 10,600 miles (16,000 kilometers) above earth. Wireless telecommunication technology by means of mass-produced, lightweight, and mobile electronic equipment—telephone, television, and computer all wrapped in one little machine—now constantly and instantly links billions of people across the globe.

With the exception of a few isolated communities, people from all corners of the world are connected to one another, directly or indirectly. Because globalization seems unstoppable, we are compelled to ask: How can the thousands of different societies that have existed for centuries, if not millennia, maintain their distinctive cultural identities and deal successfully with the multiple challenges hurled at them?

Cultural Revolutions: From *Terra Incognita* to Google Earth

It is difficult to imagine that just five centuries ago, much of the earth was still unmapped *terra incognita*. That does not mean that people had no knowledge of foreign cultures: Long-distance migrations and journeys by traders, raiders, and pilgrims have been part of human history for millennia. But these explorations were not accurately documented and summarized in a comprehensive format. And so it was that Norse voyages to Canada's northeast coast more than a thousand years ago and Chinese naval expeditions (equipped with compass) to eastern Africa in the early 1400s had little or no impact on our geographic understanding of the world.

This changed soon after Christopher Columbus first crossed the Atlantic Ocean in 1492 and Ferdinand Magellan's expedition completed the first circumnavigation of the globe in 1522. News of their discoveries of foreign lands, peoples, and natural resources spread quickly by means of the recently invented movable-type printing press. Geographic information improved, and cartographers began printing more accurate maps, leading to the publication of the first world atlas in Antwerp in 1570. Not long afterward, observational astronomy verified that the earth is not the center of the universe.

Just over two centuries ago, the invention of steam engines and other machinery launched the industrial revolution, with large-scale factory production and an expanding transportation network of steam-powered trains and ships. The invention of electrical generators and the incandescent lightbulb in the mid-1800s radically transformed patterns of human behavior within a few generations. The speed of change accelerated with the introduction of gasoline- or petrol-fueled internal combustion engines in the 1870s, which led to automobiles, followed by airplanes a few decades later—part of the mass travel and transportation revolution of the 20th century. That period also brought major innovations in telecommunications technology—from print media to telegraph, camera, telephone, radio, television, communications satellites, and the Internet—making it possible to exchange more information with more people faster and over greater distances.

Of note in this fast process of radical cultural change is the discovery of nuclear fission in the late 1930s. During World War II (1939–1945), the United States developed enriched uranium, built the world's first nuclear reactor to breed plutonium, and produced the first nuclear weapons. In 1945, its warplanes dropped atomic bombs on the citizens of Hiroshima and Nagasaki, forcing the Japanese enemy into unconditional surrender.

Today, more than thirty countries operate hundreds of nuclear power reactors generating heat and electricity. Of these, nine have stockpiled nuclear weapons, collectively owning an arsenal estimated at about 20,000 warheads capable of destroying human civilization many times over. Nuclear energy may have benefited many societies, but some accidents have been disastrous. In 2011, a massive, earthquake-induced tsunami flooded Japan's Fukushima nuclear power plant, resulting in a meltdown. Radioactive fallout contaminated a 20-kilometer (12-mile) zone, forcing the long-term (perhaps permanent) evacuation of 100,000 citizens.

All of these technological inventions have transformed the ways we humans live—and how we perceive our place and destiny in the universe. In 1969, American astronauts landed on the moon. Three years later, on an aborted lunar trip, they took the first full-view photo of earth (**Figure 26.1**). This image had a profound impact on humanity, igniting the environmental movement and the idea of "One Earth, One World" (World Commission on Environment & Development, 1987).

About a dozen years before this photograph was taken, the United States had secretly launched its first strategic reconnaissance satellite for photographic surveillance of the earth's surface. During the Cold War with Russia and its communist allies (1947–1989), technological improvements led to an eye-in-the-sky investigation system known as Keyhole. Specializing in geospatial data visualization applications, a CIA-funded company created EarthViewer 3D in 2001. Three years later, Google, a U.S.-based megacorporation providing Internet-related products and services, acquired the technology, which

Figure 26.1 First Full-View Photo of Earth This famous "Blue Marble" shot represents the first photograph in which our planet is in full view. The crew took the picture on December 7, 1972, as *Apollo 17* left earth's orbit for the moon. With the sun at their backs, the crew had a perfectly lit view of the blue planet.

NASA Johnson Space Center

made this virtual globe, map, and geographic information program commercially available to the public.

Today, we inhabit a planet that is under constant surveillance from satellites relentlessly orbiting high above us. And we now take for granted that we can freely download detailed photographs of almost any spot on the face of the earth.

The ever-growing interconnectedness of our species is evident in the global flow of humans, their products, and their ideas—made possible by modern mass transportation and telecommunications media. This has resulted in many external similarities across cultures, spawning speculations that humanity's future will feature a single homogenous global culture. Already, peoples worldwide increasingly enjoy much of the same entertainment, watch and listen to the many of the same world news stories, often eat the same fast

foods, wear the same types of clothing, play the same sports, dance to the same music, and communicate in the same few dominant languages. The continuation of such trends, so this thinking goes, would mean that North Americans who travel a hundred years from now to Botswana, Colombia, or Denmark would find the local inhabitants living in a manner similar or even identical to theirs.

Certainly, it is striking—the extent to which such items as Western-style fast food, soft drinks, clothing, music, and movies have spread to virtually all parts of the globe. Among many examples is the U.S.-based global corporation McDonald's—the world's largest fast-food chain. With 33,500 restaurants in almost 120 countries, McDonald's serves about 60 million customers a day (McDonald's, 2012) (**Figure 26.2**). Famous for its Big Mac

Patrick Baz/AFP/Getty Images

Figure 26.2 McDonald's, Riyadh, Saudi Arabia A U.S.-based company founded in 1955, McDonald's is the leading global food service retailer with more than 33,500 restaurants in nearly 120 countries. Its Golden Arches have become an internationally recognized symbol for fast-service fries, chicken, hamburgers, salads, and milkshakes. Many of these restaurants are franchises owned and operated by local businesspeople who are members of the same society as most of their customers. Success depends not only on quality fast food and quick service, but also on respecting cultural food taboos. In India, home to nearly a billion Hindus who obey a taboo on beef, the Big Mac is made with lamb or chicken and is known as a Maharaja Mac. Beef burgers are not a problem in Saudi Arabia, where the first McDonald's franchise opened in 1993. Operated by Arab Muslims, there are now a hundred McDonald's in that nation, including this one in the capital city of Riyadh, where men and women are gender segregated in different lines and dining areas.

hamburger, it has become emblematic of what is often perceived as the homogenization of the world's different cultures in the age of globalization, sometimes referred to as the "McDonaldization" of societies (Ritzer, 1983).

Yet, as we look at reactionary movements—including the rise of religious fundamentalism, nationalism, and ethnic identity politics around the world—the forecast of a single global culture appears unrealistic. If a single homogenous global culture is not in the making, what is?

Global Integration Processes

For more than a century now, integration processes have been pursued on a worldwide scale, albeit with mixed success. One of the first international organizations was the Red Cross, followed by the International Olympic Games (**Figure 26.3**). The need for global integration became all the more urgent in the wake of the Second World War, which ended with atomic bombs and resulted in the ruination of hundreds of cities and the deaths of 55 million people. Recognizing the urgency of international cooperation, the world's most powerful states instituted the World Bank and the International Monetary Fund in 1944. To prevent perpetual war, they also formed the United Nations (UN) in 1945, soon followed by a number of global nongovernmental organizations (NGOs) such as the UN Education and Science Organization (UNESCO), World Health Organization (WHO), and later the World Trade Organization (WTO). Likewise, global humanitarian aid organizations formed, such as Amnesty International and Doctors Without Borders.

In addition, countries all around the world have developed mass tourism industries that connect people in other ways. Tourism is a $1.1 trillion industry in which an estimated 900 million international tourists travel per year. The industry generates over $3 billion in receipts daily.

Such global integration mechanisms connect people all around the world, and they play a constructive role in maintaining a world system. Notably, however, they do not produce a global transnational culture.

Figure 26.3 2012 Olympics, London, England The Olympics are unique among the many strands in today's global web. Inspired by the ancient Greek sporting event held at Olympia 2,000 years ago, the games have become a global spectacle, with thousands of athletes from all around the world competing in a different country every four years. In today's world—where powerful states have conquered and destroyed many smaller nations and tens of millions have been killed in warfare worldwide—this global sports gathering is a crucial ritual, celebrating international peace in a friendly rivalry for medals and prestige.

REUTERS/Gary Hershorn/Landov

Pluralistic Societies and Multiculturalism

As described in the chapter on politics, ethnic groups or nations have organized as independent states for about 5,000 years. Many expanded—often by means of military conquest—and as republics, kingdoms, or empires engaged in nation-building projects, pressing subject or allied peoples into cultural assimilation. Other neighboring ethnic groups joined together, confederating into one political union or territorial state. In such *pluralistic societies*, each member group maintains its distinctive language and cultural heritage.

Today, there are a number of other forms of political integration among neighboring ethnic groups, such as the twenty-seven countries that collectively established the European Union. These countries achieved this unification despite the hindrances of linguistic differences, distinctive cultural traditions, bureaucratic red tape, and (most recently) a sovereign debt crisis.

One way of curbing divisive pressures inherent in pluralistic societies is to officially adopt a public policy of **multiculturalism** based on mutual respect and tolerance for cultural differences. In contrast to state policies of assimilation in which a dominant ethnic group uses its power to impose its own culture as the standard, policies of multiculturalism assert the value of different cultures coexisting within a country, stressing reciprocal responsibility of all citizens to accept the rights of others to freely express their views and values. An example of long-established multiculturalism may be seen in states such as Switzerland, where peoples speaking German, French, Italian, and Romansh coexist under the same government.

Cultural pluralism is more common than multiculturalism, but several multi-ethnic countries have recently changed their cultural assimilation policies. One example of a country moving toward multiculturalism is the United States, which now has over 120 different ethnic groups within its borders, in addition to hundreds of federally recognized American Indian groups. Another is Australia with over a hundred ethnic groups and eighty languages spoken within its territorial boundaries. Many European countries are seeing similar shifts, as millions of foreign immigrants have settled there during the past few decades.

Such changes are never easy and often spark protests. As a consequence of swings of majority opinion in the political electorate, some governments stop pursuing multiculturalism, focusing instead on cultural assimilation and social integration of immigrant minorities.

Pluralistic Societies and Fragmentation

Pluralistic societies, in virtually all parts of the world, show a tendency to fragment, usually along major linguistic, religious, or ethno-nationalist divisions. Because of this trend, some predict a world in which ethnic groups will become increasingly nationalistic rather than united in response to globalization, each group stressing its unique cultural heritage and emphasizing differences with neighboring groups. This *devolution* inclination is evident in numerous nationalist movements today—including separatist movements of the Scots in the United Kingdom (Britain), the Kurds in Turkey and Iraq, and the Karen in Myanmar (Burma). In the United States, indigenous nations, such as the Mohawk of Akwesasne, continue to seek greater political self-determination on their tribal territories.

When states with extensive territories lack adequate transportation and communication networks or major unifying cultural forces (such as a common religion or national language), it is more likely that separatist intentions will be realized. One recent example is the political breakup of the Soviet Union in 1991 into about a dozen independent republics—Russia, Armenia, Belarus, Estonia, Ukraine, Moldova, and Georgia, among others. A year after Moldova's independence, this pluralistic society fragmented even further when its border region, Transnistria, broke away and formed a sovereign republic with limited recognition. And in 2008, about seventeen years after Georgia gained its own independence as an internationally recognized state, this multi-ethnic republic diminished in size when two of its ethnically distinct regions, South Ossetia and Abkhazia, officially split after years of separatist pressure. More recently, in July 2011 Sudan in northeastern Africa officially split along an ethnic, religious, and geographic fault line, producing international recognition of the Republic of South Sudan as the 193rd member state of the United Nations.

Global Migrations: Refugees, Migrants, and Diasporic Communities

Throughout history, challenges such as famine, poverty, and violent threats by dangerous neighbors have forced people to move—often scattering members of an ethnic group. People also move for other reasons, including economic opportunity and political or religious freedom. Whether forced or free, **migration**—mobility in geographic space, involving temporary or permanent change in usual place of residence—has always had a significant effect on world social geography, contributing to cultural change and development, to the diffusion of ideas and innovations, and to the complex mixture of peoples and cultures found in the world today.

---

multiculturalism The public policy for managing cultural diversity in a multi-ethnic society, officially stressing mutual respect and tolerance for cultural differences within a country's borders.

migration Mobility in geographic space, involving temporary or permanent change in usual place of residence. Internal migration is movement within countries; external migration is movement to a foreign country.

Internal migration occurs when people move within the boundaries of their country, shifting their usual residence from one civil division to another. Typically, migrants leave their farms, villages, and small towns in the rural backlands and move to cities to find greater economic opportunity, escape from poverty and starvation, and possibly avoid armed conflict in their home region. *External migration* is movement from one country to another (**Figure 26.4**). Such migration may be voluntary (people seeking better conditions and opportunities abroad), but all too often it may be involuntary. People who are taken as slaves or prisoners, or who have been driven from their homelands by war, political unrest, religious persecution, or environmental disasters, are involuntary migrants.

Every year, a few million people migrate to wealthy countries in search of wage labor and a better future for themselves and their offspring. Although most cross international borders as legal immigrants, seeking work permits and ultimately citizenship in their new homeland, many migrants are illegal and do not enjoy crucial rights and benefits. Beyond the masses of migrants, nearly 45 million refugees can be found in almost half of the world's countries. Some 15 million refugees have been forced outside their countries, most of them suffering in makeshift camps where they cannot make a living (UN Refugee Agency, 2011).

Migrants and refugees often face great challenges as poor newcomers in host societies—all the more so because they may encounter racism and discrimination. As a consequence, many newcomers form or join communities of people who have come from the same part of the world. Modern transportation and telecommunication technology make it possible for these *diasporic communities*, which exist all across the globe, to remain in contact with relatives and friends who have settled elsewhere, as well as with their country of origin. Indicative of this aspect of globalization is that today about 200 million people (almost 3 percent of the world's population) live outside their countries of birth—not as refugees or immigrants but as *transnationals* who earn their living in one country as they remain citizens of another.

Over the past few decades, mass migration across international borders has dramatically changed the ethnic composition of affluent societies in Australia, western Europe, and North America. For example, today, the number of foreign-born people residing in the United States far exceeds that of the 38 million native-born African Americans. Most of these immigrants come from Latin

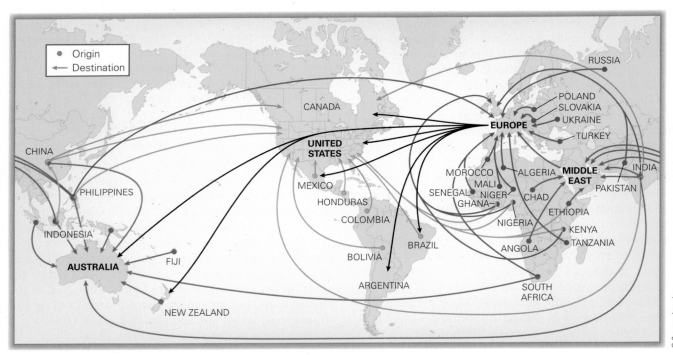

Figure 26.4 Migrating for Work In our globalized world, nearly 215 million people have moved across international borders for better income-earning opportunities. They include farm and meat plant laborers, cleaners, cab drivers, construction workers, servers in the tourism industry, as well as shopkeepers, nurses, doctors, engineers, and computer specialists. Not shown here is the international flow of 15 million refugees, over half from Asian and African countries. Unlike migrants who choose to move in hopes of improving their lives, refugees are forced to flee to save their lives or preserve their freedom.

America, including 13 million from Mexico alone. As the largest and fastest-growing group of immigrants in the United States, these immigrants are settled primarily in California and Texas, where many form Spanish-speaking ethnic enclaves.

In addition, the United States is now home to over 25 million immigrants from Asian countries (such as China and India) and sub-Saharan African countries (such as Nigeria and Ethiopia). Over the past three decades, the number of African immigrants self-identifying as "black" has rapidly increased from 65,000 to more than 1.1 million—and that figure continues to grow. Black immigrants from the Caribbean now number 1.7 million, but their rate of increase is slowing down. Collectively, these many millions of new immigrants contribute to the ever-changing multicultural fabric of U.S. society (Capps, McCabe, & Fix, 2012).

Meanwhile, on the other side of the Atlantic, millions of foreign migrants are radically changing European societies and cultures. For instance, almost 20 percent (about 12 million) of the people living in France today are foreign-born immigrants and their offspring, primarily originating from former colonial territories in West Africa and Southeast Asia. Islam is now the second-largest religion in France with about 6 million adherents. Likewise, England is now home to over 1.5 million South Asians, plus another 1.3 million people of African descent, also hailing predominantly from the former British colonies.

About 3.5 million people of Turkish origin now reside in western Germany, not counting a few million other foreign-born immigrants and their offspring. Initially needed as cheap unskilled laborers, Turks were hired as "guest workers" in highly industrialized urban areas. Because most of them remained, the authorities instituted a family reunification policy, which resulted in hundreds of thousands of Turkish relatives entering the country. Even after several decades in Germany, most German Turks do not possess citizenship and have not become culturally integrated into German society. Turkish, spoken by Germany's largest ethnic minority, has become that country's second language.

As a consequence of millions of foreign immigrants, Europe's native-born or *autochtonous* (from the Greek *auto*, "self," and *khton*, "soil") populations are currently wrestling with their national identities in a period of rapid change. With their concerns compounded by economic insecurity, social tensions are on the rise, and so are racism and xenophobia, directed especially against foreign-born Muslims who do not assimilate.

Although migrants frequently experience hostility, hardship, disappointment, and sometimes failure in their new countries, those who remain trapped in their troubled lands of origin often face worse challenges: malnutrition, hunger, chronic disease, and violence. By means of telecommunications technology, including the Internet and mobile phones, millions of foreign migrants today remain in touch with relatives and friends in their homeland communities, not only to gain news but also for emotional and financial support. Worldwide, electronic transfers to developing countries total some $351 billion per year (World Bank, 2012). Remittances, however, have declined due to the global recession, causing real hardship in the impoverished communities that have come to depend on the support.

Migrants and Xenophobia: Violent Conflict in Assam

Migrants moving to areas traditionally inhabited by other ethnic groups may run into hostile opposition, especially when they compete for scarce resources, pose a threat to security, or are otherwise unwelcome as newcomers. As such, they may be targeted for a hate-mongering campaign. Such **xenophobia**—fear or hatred of strangers or anything foreign—is especially inflammatory when social tensions rise in times of economic insecurity, challenging collective health and well-being. Under such circumstances, space for intercultural tolerance narrows; instead of blurring social boundaries, these divisions become more sharply defined, emphasizing ethnic differences over human commonalities.

This situation is evident when attitudes toward foreign laborers and recent immigrants grow so intensely negative that it does not take much to ignite brutal violence. In the summer of 2012, for example, xenophobia erupted into interethnic violence in Assam, northeast India, as the Bodos, an indigenous Buddhist mountain people, clashed with Bengali-speaking Muslim immigrants over scarce farmland. Within a few weeks, dozens of people from both sides had been killed, and many more were wounded. Nearly 400 settlements in disputed areas were abandoned, as about 400,000 Bengalis packed up what they could carry and fled. This population is now dispersed in 270 refugee camps (**Figure 26.5**).

Migrants, Urbanization, and Slums

Most migrants are poor and begin their new lives in expanding urban areas. During the past fifty years, the world's urban population has more than tripled. Today, for the first time in world history, a majority of our species now resides in urban areas—over 3.5 billion people. Just two centuries ago, at the start of the industrial revolution, only about 3 percent of the world's population lived in cities.

Until 1950, the largest city in the world was London. Although briefly overtaken by New York, the current urban frontrunner has long been Tokyo, now counting 37 million inhabitants. Cities have not only grown in size but also in number. Today, there are almost 500 cities with populations exceeding 1 million. Of these more than

---

xenophobia Fear or hatred of strangers or anything foreign.

AP Images

Figure 26.5 Migrants on the Run Bengali Muslims—newcomers to villages in India's northeast state of Assam—leave their homes following ethnic clashes with the indigenous Bodos in which many people were killed and dozens of homes were burned to the ground. Government troops sent to quell communal clashes over land rights were ordered to shoot suspected rioters on sight.

twenty-five are megacities, each with populations over 10 million. Urban areas are gaining about 67 million people per year—about 1.3 million every week. As the global population grows, the number of big cities will increase substantially, with the majority located in coastal areas of developing countries.

Historically, cities grow primarily as a result of migration by masses of people escaping rural poverty or seeking economic opportunity. Many of these migrants have little or no education, lack technical skills, and have little or nothing to offer other than selling their labor power. Girls and young women, in particular, may be forced into sexual labor as prostitutes, risking their health, safety, and general well-being. Their expectations crushed by harsh reality, and far away from their home regions, migrants often find themselves condemned to a life in squalor in crowded shanty towns or slums, with limited access to clean water, waste disposal, and electricity.

One of the main concentrations of urban poor on the planet today can be found in Lagos, Nigeria's commercial capital and Africa's largest city. In just four decades, its population has exploded from less than 1.4 million in 1970 to perhaps 21 million today. Unable to manage the enormous influx of migrants and their offspring, the city now features huge overcrowded slums where two-thirds of the city's inhabitants reside.

Lagos is not unique: Unplanned, makeshift, urban squatter settlements are burgeoning around the globe. For instance, about half of the 11 million inhabitants of Manila, capital of the Philippines, now live in slums (**Figure 26.6**).

Worldwide, about 1 billion people currently reside in slums, and the number is rapidly growing. They face similar challenges as they struggle to survive in places of urban squalor variously known as *villas miserias, ghettos, barrios, favelas, bidons, chalis, kampungs, aashwa'i*, or *mabanda*. About 60 percent of these slum-dwellers live in Asia, 20 percent in Africa, 13 percent in Latin America and the Caribbean, and only 6 percent in Europe. Remarkably, in sub-Saharan Africa, 72 percent of the urban population lives in slums—a higher proportion than anywhere else in the world (Birch & Wachter, 2011; United Nations Human Settlements Program, 2003).

© Francis R. Malasig/epa/Corbis

Figure 26.6 Slum in Manila Half of the inhabitants of Manila, the capital of the Philippines, live in slums such as this.

Structural Power in the Age of Globalization

How did our species manage to construct such a world—so interconnected and so unfairly arranged between millions of have-lots and billions of have-nots? A simple question, but difficult to answer. Part of the explanation, most scholars will agree, lies in a new form of expansive international capitalism as it emerged since the mid-1900s. Operating under the banner of globalization, it builds on earlier cultural structures of worldwide trade networks, and it is the successor to a system of colonialism in which a handful of powerful, mainly European, capitalist states ruled and exploited foreign nations inhabiting distant territories.

Enormously complex and turbulent, globalization is a dynamically structured process in which individuals, business corporations, and political institutions actively rearrange and restructure the political field to their own competitive advantage, vying for increasingly scarce natural resources, cheap labor, new commercial markets, and ever-larger profits. This restructuring occurs in a vast arena spanning the entire globe. Doing this requires a great deal of power.

As discussed in the chapter on politics, *power* refers to the ability of individuals or groups to impose their will upon others and make them do things even against their own wants or wishes. Power plays a major role in coordinating and regulating the collective behavior toward law and order within and beyond a particular community or society.

There are different levels of power within societies, as well as among societies. Anthropologist Eric Wolf pointed out the importance of understanding a macro level of power that he referred to as **structural power**—power that organizes and orchestrates the systemic interaction within and among societies, directing economic and political forces on the one hand and ideological forces that shape public ideas, values, and beliefs on the other (Wolf, 1999a). The concept of structural power applies not only to regional political organizations such as chiefdoms or states, but also captures the complex new cultural formations currently restructuring and transfiguring societies and environments everywhere on earth.

Joseph Nye—a Harvard University political scientist and former assistant secretary of defense in the U.S. government—refers to these two major interacting forces in the worldwide arena as "hard power" and "soft power" (Nye, 2002).

---

structural power Power that organizes and orchestrates the systemic interaction within and among societies, directing economic and political forces on the one hand and ideological forces that shape public ideas, values, and beliefs on the other.

Figure 26.7 Global Military Spending by Country In 2011, world military spending reached $1.55 trillion, with the United States accounting for more than 44 percent of the total. (Expenditures are rounded to the nearest billion.)

Source: Stockholm International Peace Research Institute, 2012.

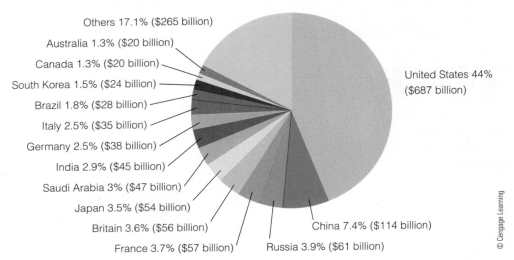

Percentage of Global Military Spending by Country in *Billions* of Dollars

- Others 17.1% ($265 billion)
- Australia 1.3% ($20 billion)
- Canada 1.3% ($20 billion)
- South Korea 1.5% ($24 billion)
- Brazil 1.8% ($28 billion)
- Italy 2.5% ($35 billion)
- Germany 2.5% ($38 billion)
- India 2.9% ($45 billion)
- Saudi Arabia 3% ($47 billion)
- Japan 3.5% ($54 billion)
- Britain 3.6% ($56 billion)
- France 3.7% ($57 billion)
- Russia 3.9% ($61 billion)
- China 7.4% ($114 billion)
- United States 44% ($687 billion)

© Cengage Learning

Hard power is the kind of coercive power that is backed up by economic and military force. **Soft power** coopts rather than coerces, pressing others through attraction and persuasion to change their ideas, beliefs, values, and behaviors. Propaganda is a form of soft power, although the exercise of ideological influence (the global struggle for hearts and minds) also operates through more subtle means, such as foreign aid, international diplomacy, news media, sports, entertainment, museum exhibits, and academic exchanges.

Military Hard Power

Today, the United States has more hard power at its disposal than any of its allies or rivals worldwide. It is the global leader in military expenditure, spending $687 billion in 2011, followed by China ($114 billion). As the world's still dominant superpower, the United States is responsible for about 44 percent of the $1.55 trillion spent on arms worldwide (**Figure 26.7**).

Moreover, although there are seven other states with nuclear-weapon capability (Britain, France, and China, as well as Israel, India, Pakistan, and North Korea, collectively possessing about 900 active nuclear warheads), Russia and the United States have by far the largest nuclear arsenals at their disposal. Russia has about 4,500 operational warheads, plus several thousand nonoperational warheads. The United States possesses about 5,100 warheads and 3,500 that are retired and awaiting dismantlement (Arms Control Association, 2012).

In addition to military might, hard power involves using economic strength as a political instrument of coercion or intimidation in the global structuring process. Among other things, this means that economic size and productivity, technological capability, and finance capital may be brought to bear on the global market, forcing less powerful states to weaken the systems protecting their workers, natural resources, and local markets.

As the world's largest economy and leading exporter, the United States has long pushed for free trade for its corporations doing business on a global scale. Sometimes it uses military power to impose changes on a foreign political landscape by means of armed interventions or full-scale invasions.

In the past century, the world's wealthiest and most powerful countries—including the United States, Germany, Russia, China, Japan, Britain, and France—have engaged in such belligerence. For this reason, many others view these heavily armed behemoths with suspicion, even as potential threats, apt to use overwhelming military force in order to benefit their own interests, from fruit to fuel, microchips to automobiles, and phones to satellites.

Home to more global corporations than any other country, the United States endeavors to protect its interests by investing in what it refers to as a "global security environment." However, through maneuvering toward this strategic objective, the nuclear-armed superpower often confronts opposition from (potentially) hostile rivals such as Russia and China, contesting its ambitions for worldwide supremacy. Moreover, numerous other countries, unable to afford expensive weapons systems or blocked from developing or acquiring them, have invested in biological or chemical weaponry. Still others, including relatively powerless political groups, have resorted to insurgencies, guerrilla tactics, or terrorism.

Economic Hard Power

Global corporations, rare before the latter half of the 20th century, now are a far-reaching economic and political force in the world. Modern-day business giants such as Shell, Toyota, and General Electric are actually clusters of several corporations joined by ties of common ownership and responsive to a common management strategy. Usually tightly controlled by a head office in one country, megacorporations organize

hard power Power that coerces others and that is backed up by economic and military force.

soft power Power that coopts rather than coerces, pressing others through attraction and persuasion to change their ideas, beliefs, values, and behaviors.

and integrate production across the international boundaries of different countries for interests formulated in corporate boardrooms, regardless of whether these are consistent with the interests of people in the countries in which they operate. Megacorporations are the products of the technological revolution, for without mass transportation, sophisticated data processing equipment, and telecommunication they could not conduct or manage their transnational capitalist operations.

Although typically thought of as responding impersonally to outside market forces, megacorporations are in fact controlled by an ever-shrinking number of wealthy capitalists who benefit directly from their operations. Unlike political leaders, the world's largest individual stockholders and most powerful corporate directors are virtually unknown to the general public. For that matter,

most people cannot even name the world's ten leading global corporations, which include Walmart, Shell, and Toyota. Each of the top ten business giants currently generates annual revenues well over $200 billion, and three of them top the $400 billion mark (**Figure 26.8**).

So great is the power of large businesses operating all across the globe that they increasingly thwart the wishes of national governments or international organizations such as the United Nations, Red Cross, and the International Court of Justice. Because megacorporations restrict information about their operations, it can be difficult for governments to make informed policy decisions. It took years for the U.S. Congress to extract information from tobacco companies so that it could make decisions about tobacco legislation, and it is nearly as slow-going today getting energy and media companies to provide data needed for regulatory purposes.

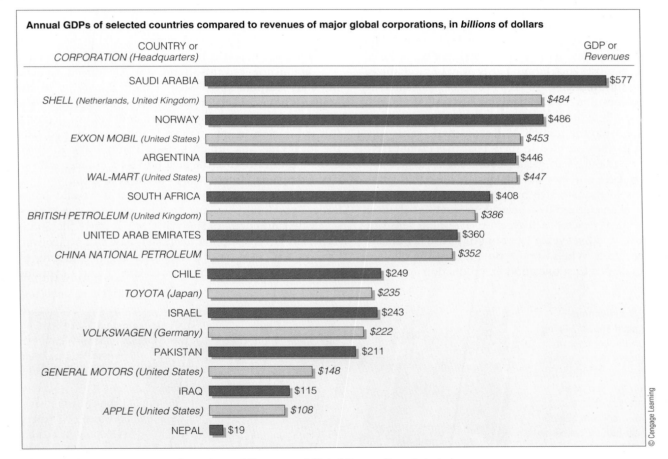

Annual GDPs of selected countries compared to revenues of major global corporations, in *billions* of dollars

COUNTRY or CORPORATION (Headquarters)	GDP or Revenues
SAUDI ARABIA	$577
SHELL (Netherlands, United Kingdom)	$484
NORWAY	$486
EXXON MOBIL (United States)	$453
ARGENTINA	$446
WAL-MART (United States)	$447
SOUTH AFRICA	$408
BRITISH PETROLEUM (United Kingdom)	$386
UNITED ARAB EMIRATES	$360
CHINA NATIONAL PETROLEUM	$352
CHILE	$249
TOYOTA (Japan)	$235
ISRAEL	$243
VOLKSWAGEN (Germany)	$222
PAKISTAN	$211
GENERAL MOTORS (United States)	$148
IRAQ	$115
APPLE (United States)	$108
NEPAL	$19

© Cengage Learning

Figure 26.8 GDPs of Selected Countries and Revenues of Global Corporations In today's consumer-driven world, it is not uncommon for the yearly revenues of large multinational corporations to equal and even exceed the total value of all goods and services produced within many countries per year, known as a country's gross domestic product (GDP). This graph shows the annual GDPs of selected countries alongside the annual revenues of leading global corporations. Notably, revenues of each of the top three corporations exceeded the GDPs of 171 of the world's 195 countries. Not shown here are the countries with the highest and lowest GDPs. Half have GDPs below $30 billion, a third below $10 billion, and about a quarter below $5 billion. Only 15 countries surpass $1 trillion, including the United States at just over $15 trillion, with China in second place at about $7 trillion. Note that GDP says nothing about the unequal distribution of wealth within a country.

Source: Based on the Global 500 list of corporate revenues and the World Development Indicators database, 2012.

Beyond this information problem, global corporations have repeatedly shown they can overrule foreign policy decisions. Although some might see this as a hopeful trend for getting beyond ethnocentric motivations, it raises the unsettling issue of whether the global arena should be controlled by immense powerful private corporations interested only in financial profits. According to a recent study that diagrammed the interrelationships of more than 43,000 corporations, 147 companies control nearly 40 percent of the monetary value of all transnational corporations. Of the top fifty of these companies, most are involved in banking, financial services, and insurance (Ehrenberg, 2011; Vitali, Glattfelder, & Battiston, 2011).

Global corporations are changing the shape of the world and the lives of individuals everywhere, including those they employ. In the never-ending search for cheap labor, these megacorporations have returned to a practice once common in the textile mills of 19th-century Britain and New England but now on a much larger scale. More than ever before, they have come to favor women for low-skilled assembly jobs. In so-called underdeveloped countries, as subsistence farming gives way to mechanized agriculture for production of crops for export, women are less able to contribute to their families' survival. Along with the devaluation of domestic work, this pressures women to seek jobs outside the household to contribute to its support. Because most women in these countries do not have the time or resources to get an education or to develop special job skills, only low-paying jobs are open to them.

Faceless relations between producers and consumers, which are characterized by a grossly unequal distribution of power, have exacted a high cost: a terrible sense of indifference, apathy, even a loss of faith in the dehumanized system itself. When workers do not trust their bosses and bosses do not trust one another, production and trade relations on every level are damaged. This alienation may ultimately lead to a systemic breakdown (Blacksmith & Harter, 2011; Gurchiek, 2012).

With production, trading, and banking operations on a global scale, the breakdown in one part of the system may trigger a worldwide chain reaction of failures. This is what occurred with the global financial crisis in 2008, sparked by the bankruptcy of a handful of mismanaged Wall Street firms—a crisis with worldwide ramifications not yet resolved (Ribeiro, 2009).

Globalization does more than create a worldwide arena in which megacorporations reap megaprofits. It also wreaks havoc in many traditional cultures, destroying their natural habitats and disrupting their long-established social organization. Consider, for example, how international investors have turned to precious metals like gold and silver in response to current financial crises and economic uncertainty. In recent years, a sharply growing international demand for silver bullion sent prices skyrocketing from an average of $4.60 per ounce in 2002 to over $35.00 per ounce in 2011—the highest price in over two decades.

Capitalizing on this trend, the U.S.-based General Minerals Corporation (GMC) bought the rights to the Mallku Khota concession in Bolivia in 2003. One of the world's largest undeveloped silver and indium deposits, this concession in the Andean highlands is named after the local Quechua Indian peasant community. In 2004, GMC began exploring the area under its Bolivian subsidiary, Compañía Minera Mallku Khota (CMMK).

In 2006, the same year political activist and leftist leader Evo Morales became the first indigenous person to be elected president of Bolivia, GMC formed the South American Silver Corporation (SAC). Based in Vancouver, Canada, SAC took over CMMK and began operating in Mallku Khota. Exploration showed that the area contains

Figure 26.9 Indigenous Protest Against Global Mining Company In the summer of 2012, members of indigenous communities from Bolivia's Mallku Khota region traveled nearly 300 kilometers to the capital city of La Paz for a political demonstration. Their protest concerned foreign mining operations on their lands. Several Quechua activists were killed during the protest.

AP Images/Juan Karita

over 370 million ounces of silver (plus some 1,600 tons of indium and more than 2,000 tons of gallium), with an estimated (after-tax) net value of $1.54 billion. Expecting to produce more than 13 million ounces of silver per year, as well as 80 tons of indium and 15 tons of gallium, the corporation projected a 15-year mine-life.

Plans began to unravel when Mallku Khota began protesting that the company would ruin their land. After local Quechua activists took five miners hostage, clashes with police followed, and several Quechua were killed during a protest demonstration in La Paz in the summer of 2012 (**Figure 26.9**). A few weeks later, before actual mining operations had started, Bolivia's government expropriated the Mallku Khota project.

Now that the concession has been nationalized, the state-owned mining company may seek an Asian investment partner, several of which are already active in Bolivia (but are based on China, Japan, and South Korea). Will the Bolivian government make sure its indigenous population reaps some benefits from this company developed on their lands? Or will this be another example of the global trend of economic inequality in which the poor become poorer and the rich richer?

Soft Power: A Global Media Environment

In addition to reliance on military and economic hard power in the global quest for dominance and profit, competing states and corporations utilize the ideological persuasion of soft power as transmitted through electronic and digital media, communication satellites, and other information technology. One of the major tasks of soft power is to sell the general idea of globalization as something positive and progressive (as "freedom," "free trade," "free market") and to frame or brand anything that opposes capitalism in negative terms.

Global mass media corporations like Cable News Network (CNN) possess enormous soft power. This U.S.-based private company produces and distributes news and other information through transnational cable and satellite networks, as well as websites. With bureaus in over thirty countries, its twenty-four-hour news coverage is available to more than 1.5 billion people all over the world. Like other media giants, such as BBC and Al Jazeera, CNN not only reports news but also selects the visual imagery and determines what to stress or repress. By means of their tremendous soft power, these corporations influence public perception and action ("hearts and minds").

The far-reaching capabilities of modern electronic and digital technologies have led to the creation of a global media environment that plays a major role in how individuals and even societies view themselves and their place in the world. Together with radio and television, the Internet is now the dominant means of mass communication around the world. The global flow of information made possible by fiber-optic cables, cell towers, and communication satellites orbiting the earth is almost entirely digital-electronic, taking place in a new boundless cultural space that has been called a "global mediascape"(Appadurai, 1990).

In recent years, the power of corporations has become all the greater through media expansion. Over the past two decades, a global commercial media system has developed, dominated by a few megacorporations (such as General Electric, Time Warner, and Disney), most based in the United States. Control of television, Internet, and other media, as well as the advertising industry, gives global corporations enormous influence on the ideas and behavior of hundreds of millions of ordinary people across the world (**Figure 26.10**).

Social Media: Parties with Cookies

Social media, spawned by the Internet, is used for multiple purposes—from popular entertainment to political action. Among countless examples is the *flash mob* in which individuals, responding to a signal, briefly come together at a designated spot in a public space for a joint performance and then disperse.

Figure 26.10 Global Branding The poorest people in the world often wear clothing discarded by those who are better off—and people from all walks of life can be found wearing clothes with corporate logos, as demonstrated by this Maká Indian woman in Paraguay. The power wielded by big business (such as the Disney media corporation) is illustrated by the fact that corporations influence consumers to pay for clothing and countless other goods that advertise corporate products.

The first successful American mob took place in New York City at the department store Macy's, where some 150 mobbers entered the store in search of a "love rug." A year later, groups in seventy-six cities across thirty-two countries participated in a mob marking the one-year anniversary of the Macy's event (Delio, 2004).

Originally devoted to silly stagings, flash mobs now range from playful and bizarre to artful and political. Using tools such as Twitter and Facebook, the principle of flash mobs has been applied to organize street protests and political rallies, as in the wave of antigovernment protests of the Arab Spring in North Africa and beyond.

Many others—from government agencies, banks, and businesses to actors, academics, and politicians—value and use social media for their own particular reasons. For example, Facebook users—which, according to the company, number more than a billion—include companies, organizations, and institutions in addition to individuals (Vance, 2012). Harnessing soft power for purposes of influencing public opinion, moving capital, selling music, or gaining prestige, for example, they use the same modern connectivity tools for direct communication. As such, these social media can be manipulated for propaganda, public opinion making, government surveillance, personal data mining, and deception for political and military purposes. That brings us to the subject of structural violence.

Problems of Structural Violence

Structural power and its associated concepts of hard and soft power enable us to better understand the global arena in which local communities throughout the world are now compelled to operate and the unequal distribution of wealth, health, and power in today's world. When structural power undermines the well-being of individuals or groups, we speak of **structural violence**—physical and/or psychological harm (including repression, environmental destruction, poverty, hunger, illness, and premature death) caused by impersonal, exploitative, and unjust social, political, and economic systems (Farmer, 1996).

The Universal Declaration of Human Rights, officially adopted by all members of the United Nations in 1948, provides a useful baseline for identifying structural violence. Anthropologists played a key role in drafting this important document, which begins with the statement that "recognition of the inherent dignity and of the equal and inalienable rights of all members of the human family is the foundation of freedom, justice, and peace in the world" (United Nations, Universal Declaration of Human Rights).

Generally speaking, structural violence concerns the impersonal systemic violation of the human rights of individuals and communities to a healthy, peaceful, and dignified life.

Although human rights abuses are nothing new, globalization has enormously expanded and intensified structural violence and its countless manifestations—including the cultural destruction already indicated, as well as widespread poverty; overpopulation; hunger, obesity, and malnutrition; and pollution and global warming.

Poverty

In 1960 the average income for the twenty wealthiest countries in the world was fifteen times that of the twenty poorest countries. Today, it is thirty times higher (World Bank, 2012a). Notably, these broad-stroke figures fail to indicate that some of the world's poorest countries have a small number of very rich citizens and that some very wealthy countries include many poor inhabitants. In fact, the income disparity between rich and poor *within* most countries has been widening in recent years—as evident in the *Gini income inequality index* annually posted by the United Nations. The Gini index ranges from 0 to 100, with 0 corresponding to perfect equality (everyone has the same income) and 100 corresponding to perfect inequality (one person has all the income, and everyone else has zero income).

For example, in communist China, home to about 1.3 billion of the world's 7 billion people, income disparity has skyrocketed. Reaching a Gini index of 51.6, it now surpasses that of the world's leading capitalist country, the United States, where the gap has widened to 47.4—higher than any other wealthy industrialized country. Income distribution is far more equal in most of Europe, and the smallest rich–poor gap in the world is in Norway (25.6). Countries with the greatest income inequality are clustered in southern Africa and Latin America, with the largest gap in South Africa (63.6). Income disparity in India stands at 39.9 (Hodgson, 2012).

Measured on a global scale, the chasm between have-lots and have-nots has reached stratospheric proportions:

- The richest 20 percent of the world's population enjoys more than 80 percent of global income, compared to the poorest 20 percent, which has a mere 1 percent.
- The richest 1 percent of the world's population has the same combined income as the bottom 56 percent.
- Forty percent of all people on the planet live on less than $2 per day (Ortiz & Cummins, 2011).

These statistics represent a gross inequity that poses a radical challenge for achieving global security and well-being. The situation would be even worse without the efforts of individuals, organizations, and institutions dedicated to narrowing the insupportable gap between the world's wealthiest and poorest peoples. Among those was anthropologist Ann Dunham—the mother of the forty-fourth president of the United States, Barack Obama. She is featured in this chapter's Anthropology Applied.

---

structural violence Physical and/or psychological harm (including repression, environmental destruction, poverty, hunger, illness, and premature death) caused by impersonal, exploitative, and unjust social, political, and economic systems.

Anthropologist S. Ann Dunham, Mother of a U.S. President

By Nancy I. Cooper

As our plane descended over the island of Java, the most spectacular sight of my life came into view: a full-blown eruption of Merapi volcano billowing clouds of ash straight up into the sky. On the lower slopes of this exploding "mountain of fire" (*gunung api*) hundreds of thousands of people would have to flee their homes and farms. My thoughts were with them—and with my friend Ann Dunham. She had researched and worked with rural people in this region as an applied anthropologist before her untimely death at age fifty-two in 1995. I had known her while doing my own research here on Indonesia's most populated island. I was returning to meet some of the people she had known.

Stanley Ann Dunham's life started out ordinary enough in an American working-class family from Kansas. They lived in several states before settling in the ethnically diverse state of Hawai'i. As a teen Ann thrived there, embracing the common humanity in cultural differences. At the University of Hawai'i in Honolulu, she met and married an economics student from Kenya, East Africa. In 1961, she gave birth to his namesake, Barack Obama Jr., who would grow up to be the forty-fourth president of the United States. The marriage was short-lived, and Ann became a single parent.

While studying anthropology, Ann met and married Lolo Soetoro, a geography student from Java. In 1967 she and her young son joined him in Jakarta, Indonesia's capital city. Befriending local boys, "Barry" happily roamed nearby fields among goats and water buffalo. Ann gave birth to daughter Maya and became interested in hand-made crafts like basketry, ceramics, and leatherwork, trying her own hand at weaving and batik. This interest grew into concern about the welfare of small enterprises embedded within larger, more powerful economic systems.

Soon, Ann began working as a consultant, hired by what became a long list of mostly foreign aid and economic development organizations. At the Ford Foundation's Southeast Asia regional office in Jakarta, for example, she oversaw grants in the Women and Employment branch and collaborated on a study of rural women in the outlying islands of Indonesia. In the 1980s, as a cottage industries development consultant with the Agricultural Development Bank of Pakistan, she arranged credit for low-income handicraft castes in the Punjab, including blacksmiths.

Next, Ann became a research coordinator (funded by USAID and the World Bank) at Bank Rakyat Indonesia, helping implement a microcredit project for owners of small rural businesses. Today, this bank has one of the largest microfinance programs in the world, and microcredit is widely recognized as a significant means of lessening poverty. In between appointments, Ann returned to Hawai'i to settle her children in school and continue her own studies. She also did a brief stint with Women's World Banking based in New York City.

The data Ann and her research teams collected during these years, combined with her anthropological fieldwork, culminated in her 1992 doctoral dissertation on peasant blacksmithing, published by Duke University Press in 2009.[a] In both words and action, Ann argued against Western modernization theories that insisted that all developing economies must go through the same stages Western capitalist economies experienced in order to succeed in the global market environment. Recognizing the disturbing effects that rapid modernization often has on indigenous populations with colonial histories, she refuted such damaging notions and sought ways to solve the real challenges of emerging economies with sensitivity and analytical prowess.

Ann Dunham's contributions were formally recognized fifteen years after her death when she was awarded Indonesia's highest civilian honor. Accepting the prize on behalf of his mother from President Susilo Bambang Yudhoyono, President Obama said, "In honoring her, you honor the spirit that led her to travel into villages throughout the country."

I felt that spirit as I traveled through Java's limestone hills where we had worked years earlier. Word spread quickly through the village of Kajar that Ann's friend was visiting, and I was greeted warmly. I sat with the family of the late owner of the blacksmithing cooperative featured in Ann's book, swapping stories about her and looking at photos she had taken of them and fellow villagers. And I spent long hours visiting with blacksmiths as they hammered hot scrap metal into useful tools.

All too soon, it was time to leave. Volcanic ash had shut down the airport where I had landed, so I left the region by rail. As the train pulled away from the station, images of blacksmithing and new friends danced in my head, along with renewed memories of an engaged anthropologist whose work changed people's lives for the better.

Written expressly for this text, 2011.

Ann Dunham turns the wheel of an agricultural machine in Pakistan in 1987.

Provided by Nancy Cooper, Anthropology Dept., University of Hawaii

----

[a]Ann died before having an opportunity to revise her dissertation for publication, as she had planned; Alice G. Dewey, her advisor, and I, her fellow graduate student, carried it to completion at the request of Ann's daughter, Maya.

Overpopulation

In 1750, 1 billion people lived on earth. Over the next two centuries our numbers climbed to nearly 2.5 billion. And between 1950 and 2000, the world population soared above 6 billion. Today, the world's population is over 7 billion, with one-third of our species residing in just two countries: China and India. Such staggering increases are highly significant because population growth increases the scale of hunger and pollution—and the many troubles tied to them. Although controlling population growth does not eliminate the other difficulties, we are unlikely to be able to solve them unless population growth is stopped or even reversed.

Despite progress in population control, the number of humans on earth continues to grow overall. Projections are extremely tricky, given variables such as war, famine, and infectious diseases, but current estimates suggest that global population will surge to 9 billion by 2050 (Kaiser, 2011). The severity of the situation becomes clear with the realization that the present world population can be sustained only by using up nonrenewable resources such as oil.

Hunger, Obesity, and Malnutrition

As frequently dramatized in media reports, hundreds of millions of people face hunger on a regular basis, leading to a variety of health problems, premature death, and other forms of suffering. Today, over a quarter of the world's countries do not produce enough food to feed their populations, and they cannot afford to import what is needed.

Hunger is caused not only by drought and pests, but also by violent ethnic, religious, or political conflicts that displace families. During the 20th century, 44 million people died due to human-made famine (The Hunger Project, 2011; White, 2001). For example, in several sub-Saharan African countries plagued by chronic civil strife, it has been almost impossible to raise and harvest crops because hordes of hungry refugees, roaming militias, and underpaid soldiers constantly raid the fields (**Figure 26.11**).

Beyond violent political, ethnic, or religious conflicts that uproot families from their traditional food sources,

ABACAUSA/Polaris

Figure 26.11 World's Largest Refugee Camp In Somalia, Africa, extended drought and years of civil war have caused chronic famine and chased huge numbers of people out of the country. Nearly 500,000 are stuck in this vast camp in Dadaab, Kenya, near the Somalia border. It was established in 1991 to provide food and shelter for up to 90,000 refugees fleeing the war, but two decades of ongoing conflict and natural disasters in Somalia have generated a continuous flow of Somalis into the camp. Housing more than five times the number for which it was originally built, the camp is jammed and resources are inadequate. Moreover, situated on a flood plain, it is inaccessible for extended periods during the rainy season, making the delivery of life-saving food, water, and health care unreliable.

famine is fueled by a global food production and distribution system geared to satisfy the demands of the world's most powerful countries. For example, in Africa, Asia, and Latin America, millions of acres once devoted to subsistence farming have been given over to the raising of cash crops for export. This has enriched members of elite social classes in these parts of the world, while satisfying the appetites of people in developed countries for coffee, tea, chocolate, bananas, and beef. Small-scale farmers who used to till the land for their own food needs have been relocated—either to urban areas, where all too often there is no employment for them, or to areas ecologically unsuited for farming.

Also of note, governments of the wealthiest capitalist states in North America and western Europe spend between $100 billion and $300 billion annually on agricultural subsidies given primarily to large farmers and agricultural corporations. Small farmers in poor countries cannot compete with subsidized agribusinesses that are selling mass-produced and often genetically engineered crops. Many small farmers have been forced to quit farming, leave their villages, and seek work in cities or as migrant workers abroad.

Today, about 1 billion people in the world experience chronic hunger. A majority (almost 650 million) of these people live in Asia and the Pacific islands. Next comes sub-Saharan Africa with about 265 million, followed by the Middle East and North Africa with 53 million, and another 15 million in the world's wealthy countries (Food and Agriculture Organization of the United Nations, 2009). Of particular note, every year famine claims the lives of some 6 million children ages 5 and under, and those who survive it often suffer physical and mental impairment (The Hunger Project, 2011; Swaminathan, 2000).

Most of the world's hungry are victims of structural violence. This is because the increasing rate of starvation is due not only to environmental calamities, but to human actions ranging from warfare to massive job cuts, growing poverty rates, and the collapse of local markets caused by foreign imports.

Ironically, although many millions are starving in some parts of the world, many millions of others are overeating—literally eating themselves to death. In fact, the number of overfed people now exceeds those who are underfed. According to the World Watch Institute in Washington, DC, more than 1.1 billion people worldwide are now overweight. Over 350 million of these are obese, but still often malnourished in that their diets lack certain nutrients. Evaluating the mortality risk associated with obesity, health-care workers use a body mass index (BMI), indicating human body fat based on a person's weight and height. A BMI of 18.5 to 25 indicates optimal weight, whereas moderately obese individuals measure between 30 and 35, severely obese from 35 to 40, and morbidly obese even higher than that.

Seriously concerned about the sharp rise in associated health problems (including stroke, diabetes, cancer,

and heart disease), the World Health Organization classifies obesity as a global epidemic. Overeating is particularly unhealthy for individuals living in societies where machines have eased the physical burdens of work and other human activities, which helps explain why more than half of the people in some industrial and post-industrial countries are overweight.

However, the obesity epidemic is not due solely to excessive eating and lack of physical activity. A key ingredient is the high sugar and fat content of mass-marketed foods. Thus, in Japan, where food habits differ significantly from those in the United States, obesity plagues just over 3 percent of the population, compared to the U.S. rate of 36 percent among adults and 17 percent among those ages 2 to 19. In fact, U.S. obesity figures have doubled over the past three decades, placing it at the top of the obesity chart among wealthy industrialized countries. Obesity rates differ between men and women, higher and lower income groups, and various ethnic groups. The highest U.S. rate is among African American women, half of whom suffer from obesity. Due to the high rates of childhood obesity, current U.S. youth are the first generation not expected to outlive their parents (Centers for Disease Control and Prevention, 2012).

The problem has become a serious concern even in some developing countries, especially where people have switched to a diet based on processed or canned fast food. The highest rates of obesity in the world can now be found among island nations in the Pacific Ocean, such as Nauru, Fiji, Samoa, and Tonga. Nauru, formerly known as Pleasant Island, tops the list.

Traditionally, Nauruans valued food as a symbol of well-being and social pride, considered fat to be a sign of beauty, and associated large body size with strength and prosperity (Pollock, 1995). In the days when Nauruans still depended largely on fishing and gathering for most of their food, obesity was not a medical problem. So, what happened?

Only 21 square kilometers (8 square miles) in size, Nauru is composed of sedimentary rock that contains vast deposits of phosphates—raw material used to make fertilizer. In the early 1900s, foreign companies descended upon this lush tropical island and over the next six decades mined more than 34 million tons of rock. Most of it was shipped to Australia, where it was processed and used to enrich vast stretches of farmland. Nauru, stripped of fertile soil and vegetation, became a cratered wasteland (Nazzal-Batayneh, 2005).

Compensating the indigenous inhabitants for the destruction of their small paradise, mining companies provided families with royalties. With cash in hand, and increasingly less access to traditional foods such as coconut, pandanus fruit, and fish, islanders purchased imported processed foods high in sugar and fat. Today, phosphate wealth has disappeared, but the junk food diet remains, and 80 percent of the indigenous population of this small island republic in Micronesia has become obese; almost half of Nauruans ages 55 to 64 now have diabetes, and large numbers are ill and dying from diseases once rare among Pacific Islanders (**Figure 26.12**).

Pollution and Global Warming

Pollution is another key aspect of structural violence brought on by the world's most powerful countries, which are also the greatest producers and consumers of energy. During the past 200 years, global cultural development has relied on burning increasing quantities of fossil fuels (coal, oil, and gas), with dire results: Massive deforestation and desertification, along with severe air, water, and soil pollution, now threaten all life on earth.

In addition, fossil fuel use has dramatically increased carbon dioxide levels, trapping more heat in the earth's atmosphere. Most atmospheric scientists believe that the efficiency of the atmosphere in retaining heat—the greenhouse effect—is being enhanced by increased carbon dioxide, methane, and other gases produced by industrial and agricultural activities. The result, global warming, threatens to dramatically alter climates in all parts of the world.

Rising temperatures are causing more and greater storms, droughts, and heat waves, devastating populations in vulnerable areas. And if the massive meltdown of Arctic ice continues, rising sea levels will inundate low coastal

Figure 26.12 Structural Violence and Obesity On the South Pacific island of Nauru, the world's smallest independent republic, about 80 percent of the 14,000 inhabitants are now classified as obese. Averaging 35 BMI, this island nation in Micronesia also has the world's highest rate of diabetes. Their small tropical paradise stripped bare by phosphate mining companies, these indigenous peoples have become dependent on junk food. Many are now ill and dying from diseases historically uncommon among Oceanic peoples.

areas worldwide. Entire islands may soon disappear, including thousands of villages and even large cities. Experts also predict that global warming will lead to an expansion of the geographic ranges of tropical diseases and increase the incidence of respiratory illnesses due to additional smog caused by warmer temperatures. Also, they expect an increase in deaths due to heat waves, as witnessed in Europe (70,000 deaths in 2003) and Russia (55,000 deaths in 2010) (Parry, 2011).

Especially since the industrial revolution about two centuries ago, societies have experienced the negative effects of environmental degradation. Much of this ruin is caused by ever-increasing amounts of non-biodegradable waste and toxic emissions into the soil, water, and air. Until very recently, this pollution was officially tolerated for the sake of maximizing profits that primarily benefit select individuals, groups, and societies. Today, industries in many parts of the world are producing highly toxic waste at unprecedented rates. Pollutants such as various oxides of nitrogen or sulfur cause the development of acid precipitation, which damages soil, vegetation, and wildlife. Air pollution in the form of smog is often dangerous for human health.

Moreover, poisonous smokestack gases are clearly implicated in acid rain, which is damaging lakes and forests all over northeastern North America. Air containing water vapor with a high acid content is, of course, harmful to the lungs, but there is a greater health hazard involved. As groundwater and surface water become more acidic, the solubility of lead, cadmium, mercury, and aluminum, all of them toxic, rises sharply. For instance, for 17 percent of the world's farmland, the aluminum contamination is high enough to be toxic to plants—and has been linked to senile dementia, Alzheimer's, and Parkinson's disease, three major health problems in industrial countries.

Finding their way into the world's oceans, toxic substances also create hazards for seafood consumers. For instance, Canadian Inuit face health problems related to eating fish and sea mammals that feed in waters contaminated by industrial chemical waste such as polychlorinated biphenyls (PCBs) (see the Biocultural Connection). Also of great concern are harmful chemicals in plastics used for water bottles, baby bottles, and can linings. Environmental poisoning affects peoples all across the globe.

Structural violence also manifests itself in the shifting of manufacturing and hazardous waste disposal from developed to developing countries. In the late 1980s, a tightening of environmental regulations in industrialized countries led to a dramatic rise in the cost of hazardous waste disposal. Seeking cheaper ways to get rid of the wastes, "toxic traders" began shipping hazardous waste to eastern Europe and especially to poor and underdeveloped countries in western Africa—thereby passing on the health risks of poisonous cargo to the world's poorest people (see the Globalscape).

Toxic Breast Milk Threatens Arctic Culture

Asked to picture the Inuit people inhabiting the Arctic coasts of Canada, Greenland, and Labrador, you are likely to envision them dressed in fur parkas and moving across a pristine, snow-covered landscape on dogsleds—perhaps coming home from hunting seal, walrus, or whale.

Such imaginings are still true—except for the pristine part. Although Inuit live nearer to the North Pole than to any city, factory, or farm, they are not isolated from the pollutants of modern society. Chemicals originating in the cities and farms of North America, Europe, and Asia travel thousands of miles to Inuit territories via winds, rivers, and ocean currents. These toxins have a long life in the Arctic, breaking down very slowly due to icy temperatures and low sunlight. Ingested by zooplankton, the chemicals spread through the seafood chain as one species consumes another. The result is alarming levels of pesticides, mercury, and industrial chemicals in Arctic animals—and in the Inuit people who rely on fishing and hunting for food.

Of particular note are toxic chemicals known as PCBs (polychlorinated biphenyls), used widely over several decades for numerous purposes, such as industrial lubricants, insulating materials, and paint stabilizers. Research shows a widespread presence of PCBs in the breast milk of women around the globe. But nowhere on earth is the concentration higher than among the Inuit—on average seven times that of nursing mothers in Canada's biggest cities.[a]

PCBs have been linked to a wide range of health problems—from liver damage to weakened immune systems to cancer. Studies of children exposed to PCBs in the womb and through breast milk show impaired learning and memory functions.

Beyond having a destructive impact on the health of humans (and other animal species), PCBs are impacting the economy, social organization, and psychological well-being of Arctic peoples. Nowhere is this truer than among the 450 Inuit living on Broughton Island, near Canada's Baffin Island. Here, word of skyrocketing PCB levels cost the community its valuable market for Arctic char fish. Other Inuits refer to them as "PCB people," and it is said that Inuit men now avoid marrying women from the island.[b]

Inuit people, who have no real alternatives for affordable food, soundly reject the suggestion that the answer to these problems is a change of diet. Abandoning the consumption of traditional seafood would destroy a 4,000-year-old culture based on hunting and fishing. Countless aspects of traditional Inuit culture—from worldview and social arrangements to vocabularies and myths—are linked to Arctic animals and the skills it takes to rely on them for food and so many other things. As one Inuit put it: "Our foods do more than nourish our bodies. They feed our souls. When I eat Inuit foods, I know who I am."[c]

The manufacture of PCBs is now banned in many Western countries (including the United States), and PCB levels are gradually declining worldwide. However, because of their persistence (and widespread presence in remnant industrial goods such as fluorescent lighting fixtures and electrical appliances), they are still the highest-concentration toxins in breast milk, even among mothers born after the ban.

Furthermore, even as PCBs decline, other commercial chemicals are finding their way northward. To date, about 200 hazardous compounds originating in industrialized regions have been detected in the bodies of Arctic peoples.[d] Global warming is fueling the problem, because as glaciers and snow melt, long-stored toxins are released.

BIOCULTURAL QUESTION

Because corporations are able to profit from large-scale and long-distance commercial activities, we should not be surprised that their operations may also cause serious damage to fellow humans in remote natural environments. What do you think of the profiteering of structural violence?

[a]Colborn, T., Dumanoski, D., & Myers, J. P. (1997). *Our stolen future* (pp. 107–108). New York: Plume/Penguin.

[b]Arctic Monitoring Assessment Project (AMAP). (2003). *AMAP assessment 2002: Human health in the Arctic* (pp. xii–xiii, 22–23). Oslo: AMAP.

[c]Ingmar Egede, quoted in Cone, M. (2005). *Silent snow: The slow poisoning of the Arctic* (p. 1). New York: Grove.

[d]Additional sources: Johansen, B. E. (2002). The Inuit's struggle with dioxins and other organic pollutants. *American Indian Quarterly* 26 (3), 479–490; Natural Resources Defense Council. (2005, March 25). Healthy milk, healthy baby: Chemical pollution and mother's milk. www.NRDC.org; Williams, F. (2005, January 9). Toxic breast milk? *New York Times Magazine*.

Can this Inuit woman trust her breast milk?

© B & C Alexander/Photo Researchers, Inc.

Globalscape

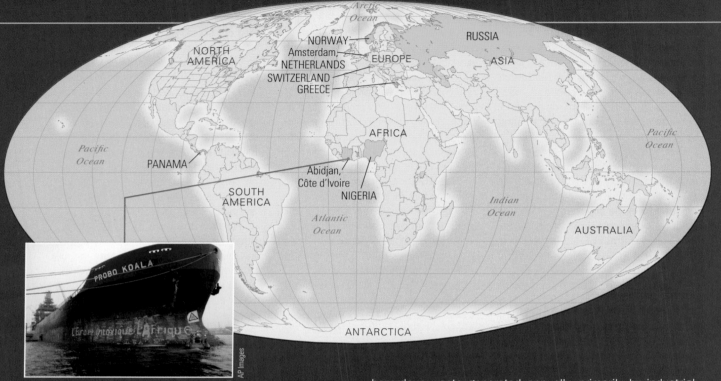

AP Images

Probo Koala's Dirty Secrets?

One day in 2006, the *Probo Koala* unloaded a cargo of processed fuel in Nigeria, West Africa. Then the tanker sailed to Amsterdam where a Dutch treatment plant was to process its 400 tons of leftover toxic sludge. Navigating the oceans under the Panamanian flag, this ship's all-Russian crew serves under a Greek captain. Managed and operated by a Greek maritime company, the ship's registered owner is based in Norway. For this journey, it was chartered by a Dutch subsidiary of Trafigura, a global multibillion-dollar company headquartered in Switzerland that specializes in transporting oil and mineral products.

When port authorities in Amsterdam discovered that the *Probo Koala*'s captain had underreported the poison levels in his cargo, the cost of treating the waste jumped to $600,000. Unwilling to pay the higher fee, the captain ordered his ship back to West Africa in search of a cheap place to dispose of the waste. Finding unscrupulous businessmen and corrupt officials in Côte d'Ivoire, he negotiated a dumping fee of about $18,000. Deposited in open-air waste pits on the edge of Abidjan (population 5 million), the substance gave off toxic gas that burned lungs and skin and caused severe headaches and vomiting—killing seventeen people and injuring at least 30,000.

The *Probo Koala* forms part of a profitable global business network capitalizing on the more than 350 million tons of

hazardous waste generated annually, primarily by industrial societies. Although most of this waste is now properly disposed, some companies avoid environmental regulations and high treatment costs within Europe and North America, seeking cheap (possibly illegal) options, including dumping at sea. Many millions of tons of hazardous waste are transported across the oceans to underdeveloped countries.

In a 2009 out-of-court settlement, Trafigura agreed to pay a total of $43,000 to cover all claims. Many saw settlement as a slap on the hand that in no way matched the gravity of the crime. Convinced that Trafigura knew the toxicity and illegality of the dump, Greenpeace and Amnesty International carried out a three-year investigation on the incident. Released in the fall of 2012, the report calls for Trafigura to face a criminal trial in the United Kingdom and criticizes the lack of international regulations for preventing and dealing with toxic dumping activities.

Meanwhile, Trafigura has paid nearly $500 million in legal and reparation costs, but there are indications that the authorities in Côte d'Ivoire have failed to redistribute compensation to the victims of the dumping. Greenpeace and Amnesty International are calling for freedom from toxic waste dumping to be a human right, which would allow victims of large- and small-scale dumping to seek legal redress more easily, in national and international courts.[a]

Global Twister

Although hazardous waste dumping by the *Probo Koala* resulted in the arrest of several African businessmen in Côte d'Ivoire, should the other participants in this global crime be judged and punished? If so, under which laws?

---

[a] Harvey, F. (2012, September 24). Trafigura lessons have not been learned, report warns. *The Guardian*. www.guardian.co.uk/environment/2012/sep/25/trafigura-lessons-toxic-waste-dumping (retrieved October 3, 2012)

Energy Consumption Per Person, by country, 2009.

Figure 26.13 Global Energy Consumption North Americans have long been among the world's highest energy consumers, contributing significantly to carbon dioxide (CO_2) emissions, the major cause of global warming. Today, their consumption rate is about twice that of Europe and some ten times higher than the average in Africa. The United States alone accounts for 16 percent of CO_2 emissions worldwide. Other top emitters are the European Union (11 percent), India (6 percent), Russia (5 percent), and Japan (4 percent). But all are topped by China, which in recent years has soared to 29 percent. (These figures and this map do not take climate into account; for that, see Sivak & Schoettle, 2012.)

Source: Energy Consumption per Person, by Country, 2009, from *BURN: An Energy Journal.*
Reprinted by permission.

When toxic trading became public knowledge, international outrage about the poisoning of soil, air, and water in these poor countries led to the Basel Convention, an international agreement to prohibit the export of hazardous wastes and minimize their generation. Today, the scope of the convention is severely limited by the fact that the United States, the largest toxic residue producer in the world, has not ratified the agreement (Basel Action Network, 2010). Moreover, unscrupulous entrepreneurs and corrupt government officials in these destitute countries have found ways to circumvent the treaty obligations.

From the latter 19th century to the end of the 20th, a small number of wealthy countries (primarily in western Europe and North America) reaped many economic benefits of early industrialization and global trade—and became responsible for an estimated two-thirds of the atmospheric buildup of heat-trapping carbon dioxide (CO_2), the major cause of global warming. By contrast, all of Africa—a huge continent about the size of Canada, Europe, and the United States, combined—was responsible for less than 3 percent of the global CO_2 emissions in the past hundred years.

Today, measuring the inequality in human terms, each person in the United States adds, on average, 17.2 metric tons of CO_2 a year to the atmosphere, compared to less than 2 tons per capita in Africa. In recent years, CO_2 emissions have diminished slightly in the United States and a bit more in Europe, where they now stand at 7.5 tons. Meanwhile, China, the world's most populous country, has become the top emitter, mainly due to dramatic and rapid economic growth. There, since 2002, CO_2 emissions have jumped 150 percent to 7.2 tons per capita.

Globally, CO_2 emissions from the consumption of energy are about 4.5 tons per person—and rising (Olivier, Janssens-Maenhout, & Peters, 2012; Sivak & Schoettle, 2012) (**Figure 26.13**). According to U.S. botanist Peter Raven, "If everyone lived like Americans, you'd need three planet earths . . . to sustain that level of consumption" (quoted in Becker, 2004, p. 90).

Yet, millions of peasants, herders, fishermen, and other folk inhabiting the world's developing countries in Africa, Asia, and Latin America find themselves paying for the progress enjoyed by societies that have reaped the benefits of industrialization for several generations. They now suffer from global-induced droughts and floods, but they lack the capital to effectively deal with them.

Reactions to Globalization

No matter how effectively a dominant state or corporation combines its hard and soft power, globalization does run into opposition. Pockets of resistance exist within the wealthy industrial and postindustrial states as well as elsewhere in the world. This resistance may be manifested in the rise of traditionalism and revitalization movements—efforts to return to life as it was (or how people think it was) before the familiar order became unhinged and people became unsettled. Some of these reactionary movements may take the form of resurgent ethno-nationalism or religious fundamentalist movements. Others may find expression in alternative grass-roots movements—from radical environmental groups to peace groups to the more recently formed ecotarian movement that focuses on selecting food based on the ecological impact of its production and transportation.

Although it is true that states and big corporations have expanded their power and influence through electronic communication technologies, it is also true that these same technologies present opportunities to those who traditionally have been powerless. They provide a means of distributing information and promoting activities that are distinct from or in opposition to those of dominant society.

One striking case of a cultural reaction to globalization is the Taliban, a group of Muslim religious fundamentalists in Afghanistan. The *Taliban* (the Pashto word for "students," specifically of Islam) helped to force the Russian army out of their country and end the subsequent civil war; then they rose to power in the 1990s and imposed a radical version of traditional Islamic law (Shariah) in an effort to create an Islamic republic based on strict religious values.

In the United States, there has been a similar, though less radical, reaction against modernity. "Born again" and other fundamentalist citizens seek to shape or transform not only their towns but also states and even the entire country by electing politicians committed to forging a national culture based on what they see as American patriotism, English-only legislation, and traditional Christian values (Harding, 2001).

Ethnic Minorities and Indigenous Peoples: Struggles for Human Rights

Throughout this book, we have discussed a wide range of cultures all across the globe. Many of our examples involve peoples who see themselves as members of distinct nations by virtue of their birth and their cultural and territorial heritage—nations over whom peoples of some other ethnic background have tried to assert political control. An estimated 5,000 such national groups exist in the world today, compared to just under 200 internationally recognized countries. Although some of these national or ethnic groups are very small in population and area—100 or so people living on a few acres—many others are quite large. The Karen people inhabiting southern and southeastern Myanmar (Burma), for example, number between 4.5 to 5 million, exceeding the population of nearly half of the countries in the world. And Kurds, living in Turkey, Iran, and Iraq, number about 30 million.

The reactions of groups to forced annexation and domination by state regimes controlled by other nations range from the nonviolence of the Sámi in Scandinavia or the Maori of New Zealand to bloody fights for national independence by Basque separatists in Spain, Karen in eastern Myanmar, Chechens in southern Russia, or Palestinians in the Middle East. In pursuit of self-determination, national autonomy, independence, or another political objective, many struggles have been going on for years or even decades.

Since the mid-1900s, global institutions such as the United Nations have tried to address the problem of discrimination, repression, and crimes against humanity—in particular, genocide. For example, even though it often fails to act on it, the General Assembly's 1966 Covenant of Human Rights states unequivocally:

> In those states in which ethnic, religious or linguistic minorities exist, persons belonging to such minorities shall not be denied the rights, in community with the other members of their group, to enjoy their own culture, to profess and practice their own religion or to use their own language. (Bodley, 2008, p. 122)

This covenant applies not only to minority groups, but also to indigenous peoples, who comprise about 5 percent of the world's population.

Nearly all indigenous groups are relatively small nations. Typically, they have suffered repression or discrimination by ethnically different, more powerful, and almost always more heavily populated groups that have gained control over their ancestral homelands. In the early 1970s, indigenous peoples began to organize self-determination movements, resisting acculturation and challenging violations of their human rights. Joining forces across international borders, they established the World Council of Indigenous Peoples in 1975.

In 2007, after many years of popular media campaigns, political lobbying, and diplomatic pressure by hundreds of indigenous leaders and other activists all around the globe, the UN General Assembly finally adopted the Declaration on the Rights of Indigenous Peoples (**Figure 26.14**). A foundational document in the global

Figure 26.14 **Worldwide Indigenous Peoples Conference** In 1982 the United Nations Sub-Commission on the Promotion and Protection of Human Rights established a Working Group on Indigenous Populations (WGIP). Eleven years later WGIP completed a draft of the Declaration on the Rights of Indigenous Peoples, ratified in 2007. And in 2012, 2,000 delegates attended the UN Permanent Forum for Indigenous Issues session in New York.

human rights struggle, it contains some 150 articles urging respect for indigenous cultural heritage, calling for official recognition of indigenous land titles and rights of self-determination, and demanding an end to all forms of oppression and discrimination as a principle of international law.

Anthropology's Role in Meeting the Challenges of Globalization

Globalization triggers worldwide changes, but different peoples and cultures are not necessarily changing in the same fashion or in the same direction. Worldwide, it places some individuals, groups, or regions in a favorable position to take advantage of new opportunities, but confronts others with pain and no gain. As repeatedly noted in this textbook, globalization is a complex and dynamic process with a vast

range of national, regional, and even local cultural reactions and adjustments. With thousands of years of world history as our guide, we can see that the ongoing process of cultural deconstruction and reconstruction, now involving more than 7 billion humans crowding the earth's surface, is neither orderly nor peaceful and will never be so.

Today, many of the cultures studied by the earliest anthropologists more than a century ago have changed profoundly in response to powerful outside influences and internal dynamics. Others have disappeared as a result of deadly epidemics, violent conflicts, acculturation, ethnocide, or genocide. All too often, the only detailed records we now possess of these altered and vanished cultures are those that some visiting anthropologist was able to document before it was too late.

But anthropologists do much more than try to preserve precious information about distinctive peoples and cultures, past and present. As chronicled in the pages of this book, they also attempt to explain why our bodies and cultures are similar or different, why and how they

ANTHROPOLOGIST OF NOTE

Paul Farmer (b. 1959)

Medical anthropologist **Paul Farmer**—doctor, Harvard professor, world-renowned infectious disease specialist, and recipient of a MacArthur "genius" grant—grew up in a trailer park in Florida without running water.[a] Admitted to Duke University on scholarship, he majored in anthropology and labored alongside poor Haitian farmworkers in North Carolina's tobacco fields. After getting his BA in 1982, he spent a year in Haiti and found his life's calling: to diagnose and cure infectious diseases and transform health care on a global scale by focusing on the world's poorest communities. Returning to the United States, Farmer earned both an MD and a PhD in anthropology from Harvard in 1990.

While still a graduate student, Farmer returned frequently to Haiti and became increasingly involved in health issues in the area of Cange, a remote village in the destitute Central Plateau region. There,

Medical anthropologist Paul Farmer with patients in Haiti.

he formed a group called Zanmi Lasante (Haitian Kreyol for "Partners in Health"). A handful of other American activists joined him in the endeavor, including his fellow anthropologist and Harvard Medical School friend, Jim Yong Kim, who became president of the World Bank three decades later.

In 1985, the Zanmi Lasante group established a clinic with financial support from a Boston philanthropist. Two years later they founded the Boston-based Partners in Health (PIH) foundation to support their growing endeavor to help the poorest of the poor deal with infectious diseases, especially AIDS and tuberculosis.

The endeavor includes research (ethnographic as well as medical) needed to carry the work forward with a clear vision. As an applied anthropologist aiming to ease human suffering, Farmer bases his activism on holistic and interpretive ethnographic analysis that includes "a historical understanding of the large-scale social and economic structures in which affliction is embedded."[b] Issues of structural violence are fundamental in his research and practice. Noting that social and economic inequalities "have powerfully sculpted not only the [demographic] distribution of infectious diseases but also the course of health outcomes among the afflicted," he concludes, "inequality itself constitutes our modern plague."[c]

Since its founding, Zanmi Lasante has expanded its one-room clinic to a multiservice health complex that includes a primary school, an infirmary, a surgery wing, a training program for health outreach workers, a 104-bed hospital, a women's clinic, and a pediatric care facility. Moreover, it has

pioneered the treatment of multidrug-resistant tuberculosis and HIV in Haiti. Partners in Health, now funded by a wide range of organizations, has expanded its reach to include Lesotho, Malawi, and Rwanda in Africa, as well as Peru, Mexico, Russia, and the United States. The foundation's reach continues to grow, fueled by Farmer's passionate conviction that health is a human right.

In concert with his active and extensive work with PIH around the globe, Farmer is a professor of medical anthropology in Harvard University's Department of Social Medicine. He also maintains an active practice in infectious diseases and is chief of the Division of Social Medicine and Health Inequalities at Brigham and Women's Hospital in Boston. Among numerous honors, he has received the Margaret Mead Award from the American Anthropological Association and is the subject of the Pulitzer Prize–winning book by Tracy Kidder (see footnote below).

[a]This profile draws from numerous sources, including: Kidder, T. (2003). *Mountains beyond mountains: The quest of Dr. Paul Farmer, a man who would cure the world.* New York: Random House.

[b]Farmer, P. (2004, June). An anthropology of structural violence. *Current Anthropology 45,* 3, 305–325; see also Farmer, P. (1996). On suffering and structural violence: A view from below. *Daedalus 125* (1), 261–283.

[c]Farmer, P. (2001). *Infections and inequalities: The modern plagues* (p. 15). Berkeley: University of California Press.

did or did not change. Moreover, they try to identify the particular knowledge and insights that each culture holds concerning the human condition—including contrasting views about the place of human beings in the world, how natural resources are used and treated, and how one relates to fellow humans and other species.

Anthropologists are trained to understand and explain economic, social, political, ideological, biological, and environmental features and processes as parts of interrelated dynamic systems. Theoretical concepts, such as structural power and structural violence, reveal the complex and significant interconnections between remote and seemingly unrelated factors and processes.

A holistic and integrative perspective, as developed and tested by several generations of anthropologists in the course of more than a century of cross-cultural research in all parts of the world, has become essential to our understanding of such troubling problems as ethnocide, overpopulation, poverty, food shortages, environmental destruction, and disease in the age of globalization. The value of this perspective has been confirmed by international organizations that now employ anthropologists for their professional insights. For example, after a series of ill-conceived and mismanaged development projects that harmed more than helped local populations, the World Bank contracted dozens of anthropologists for projects all around the world. In fact, Jim Yong Kim, a Korean American physician with a doctorate in anthropology, now heads this powerful global institution. Other international organizations—as well as some global corporations, news media, and state government and intelligence agencies—also employ anthropologists.

There have always been anthropologists who reach beyond studying different cultures to assist besieged groups struggling to survive in today's rapidly changing world. In so doing, they put into practice their own knowledge about humankind—knowledge deepened through the comparative perspective of anthropology, which is cross-culturally, historically, and biologically informed. Counted among these applied anthropologists are Ann Dunham, profiled earlier in this chapter, and Paul Farmer, a world-renowned medical doctor, anthropologist, and human rights activist (see the Anthropologist of Note).

An interdisciplinary profession straddling the arts, sciences, and humanities, anthropology has a remarkable record of contributing important knowledge about our own species and all its stunning complexity and amazing variety. Anthropology's distinct holistic approach has helped to solve practical problems on local and global levels—and continues to do so today. More relevant than ever, it offers vital insight toward a cross-cultural understanding of globalization and its highly diverse local impact.

Most of the unique individuals drawn to this discipline are inspired by the old but still valid idea that anthropology must aim to live up to its longstanding ideal as the most liberating of the sciences. As stated by the famous anthropologist Margaret Mead, "Never doubt that a small group of committed people can change the world; indeed it is the only thing that ever has."

CHAPTER CHECKLIST

What does our world look like today?

● Since the industrial revolution began 200 years ago, modern technology has radically increased production, transportation, and communication worldwide, and the human population has grown to more than 7 billion— half living and working in urban areas.

● With the launching of the first telecommunication satellites in the mid-1950s, followed by the Internet in the 1960s, personal computers in the 1970s, and the World Wide Web in the 1990s, the digital revolution has accelerated the globalization process. Using social media, a few billion humans weave in and out of cyberspace on a daily basis.

● The growing interconnectedness of our species is evident in the global flow of humans, their products, and their ideas—made possible by modern mass transportation and telecommunications media. This has resulted in many external similarities across cultures, spawning speculation that humanity's future will feature a single homogenous global culture. This is sometimes referred to as the "McDonaldization" of societies.

● Beyond fashion, food, film, and other cultural overlaps, global integrative processes include the Olympic Games, the United Nations, the World Health Organization, as well as humanitarian aid organizations such as the Red Cross and Amnesty International.

● Anthropologists are skeptical that a global culture or political system is emerging; comparative historical and cross-cultural research shows the persistence of distinctive worldviews and the tendency of large multi-ethnic states to come apart.

What are pluralistic societies and multiculturalism?

● In pluralistic societies two or more ethnic groups or nationalities are politically organized into one territorial state. Ethnic tension is common in such states and sometimes turns violent, which can lead to formal separation.

● To manage cultural diversity within such societies, some countries have adopted multiculturalism, which is an official public policy of mutual respect and tolerance for cultural differences.

● An example of long-established multiculturalism may be seen in states such as Switzerland, where people speaking German, French, Italian, and Romansh coexist under the same government.

Is fragmentation common in pluralistic societies?

● Pluralistic societies, in virtually all parts of the world, show a tendency to fragment, usually along major linguistic, religious, or ethno-nationalist divisions.

● Especially when state territories are extensive and lack adequate transportation and communication networks, as well as major unifying cultural forces such as a common religion or national language, separatist intentions may be realized.

● Throughout history, challenges such as famine, poverty, and violent threats by dangerous neighbors have forced people to move—often scattering members of an ethnic group.

● Migration—voluntary or involuntary—is mobility in geographic space, involving temporary or permanent change in usual place of residence. It may be internal (within the boundaries of one's country) or external (from one country to another).

● Every year several million people migrate to wealthy countries in search of wage labor and a better future. In addition 45 million refugees can be found in almost half of the world's countries.

● Migrants moving to areas traditionally inhabited by other ethnic groups may face xenophobia—fear or hatred of strangers.

● Most migrants begin their new lives in expanding urban areas. Today, 1 billion people live in slums.

What is structural power?

● *Structural power* refers to the global forces that direct economic and political institutions and shape public ideas and values. It comes in two forms: hard power, which is coercive and is backed up by economic and military force, and soft power, which coopts through ideological persuasion.

● The most powerful country in the world today remains the United States, home to more global corporations than any other state. Responsible for 44 percent of the world's $1.55 trillion military expenditures, it engages in military interventions around the world to defend or benefit its corporate interests.

● Cutting across international boundaries, global corporations are a powerful force for worldwide integration despite the political, linguistic, religious, and other cultural differences that separate people. Their power and wealth often exceeds that of national governments.

● Major players in the globalization process, these megacorporations influence the ideas and behavior of people worldwide. In pursuit of wealth and power, states and corporations now compete for increasingly scarce natural resources, cheap labor, new commercial markets, and ever-larger profits in a huge political arena spanning the entire globe.

● Competing states and corporations utilize the ideological persuasion of soft power (as transmitted through electronic and digital media, communication satellites, and other information technology) to sell the general idea of globalization as something positive and to frame or brand anything that opposes capitalism in negative terms.

● The far-reaching capabilities of modern communication technologies have led to the creation of a new global media environment that plays a major role in how individuals and even societies view themselves and their place in the world.

● Although providing megaprofits for large corporations, globalization often wreaks havoc in many traditional cultures and disrupts long-established social organization. This engenders worldwide resistance against superpower domination—and with that an emerging world system that is inherently unstable, vulnerable, and unpredictable.

How has the globalization of structural power led to an increase in structural violence?

● One result of globalization is the expansion and intensification of structural violence—physical and/or psychological harm (including repression, cultural and environmental destruction, poverty, hunger and obesity, illness, and premature death) caused by impersonal, exploitative, and unjust social, political, and economic systems.

● Structural violence is a systemic violation of the human rights of individuals and communities to a healthy, peaceful, and dignified life as defined by the Universal Declaration of Human Rights adopted by members of the United Nations in 1948.

● Reactions against the structural violence of globalization include the rise of traditionalism and revitalization movements—efforts to return to life as it was (or how people think it was) before the familiar order became unhinged and people became unsettled. These may take the form of resurgent ethno-nationalism or religious fundamentalist movements.

How might anthropological know-how help counter structural violence?

● Some dramatic changes in cultural values and motivations, as well as in social institutions and the types of technologies we employ, are required if humans are going to realize a sustainable future for generations to come. The shortsighted emphasis on consumerism and individual self-interest characteristic of the world's affluent countries needs to be abandoned in favor of a more balanced social and environmental ethic.

● Anthropologists have a contribution to make in bringing about this shift. They are well versed in the dangers of culture-bound thinking, and they bring a holistic biocultural and comparative historical perspective to the

challenge of understanding and balancing the needs and desires of local communities in the age of globalization.

● Inspired by human rights ideals, there have always been "applied" anthropologists who reach beyond studying different cultures to assist besieged groups struggling to survive in today's rapidly changing world.

QUESTIONS FOR REFLECTION

1. Since the launching of the first satellites into orbit and the start of the Internet, the telecommunications revolution has changed how humans interact, entertain, work, and even make and maintain friendships. Can you imagine a world in which cyberspace is militarized and social media are suppressed and dismantled? How would you and your friends adjust to that new reality?

2. Reflecting on the human condition past and present, and the challenges facing your own family in the age of globalization, do you imagine the future in terms of continued progress? How do you measure that, and by which cultural standard?

3. Considering the relationship between structural power and structural violence, does your own lifestyle—in terms of buying clothes and food, driving cars, and so on—reflect or have an effect on the globalization process?

4. In the global mediascape, television viewers and Internet users are not only consumers of news and entertainment but are also exposed to soft power. Can you think of an example of soft power in your daily life? And at which point does such influence turn into propaganda or manipulation?

5. When you hear or read about Muslim religious fundamentalists in western Asia or northern Africa strongly defending their traditional beliefs and practices, or even aggressively rejecting modern changes imported from the United States or Europe, do you recognize similar reactionary movements in your own country? What fuels such reactions?

ONLINE STUDY RESOURCES

CourseMate

Access chapter-specific learning tools, including learning objectives, practice quizzes, videos, flash cards, glossaries, and more in your Anthropology CourseMate.

Log into **www.cengagebrain.com** to access the resources your instructor has assigned and to purchase materials.

Glossary

abduction Movement away from the midline of the body or from the center of the hand or foot.

absolute dating In archaeology and paleoanthropology, dating archaeological or fossil materials in units of absolute time using scientific properties such as rates of decay of radioactive elements; also known as *chronometric dating*.

acclimatization Long-term physiological adjustments made in order to attain equilibrium with a specific environmental stimulus.

accommodation In anthropology, refers to an adaptation process by which a people resists assimilation by modifying its traditional culture in response to pressures by a dominant society in order to preserve its distinctive ethnic identity.

acculturation The massive cultural change that occurs in a society when it experiences intensive firsthand contact with a more powerful society.

Acheulean tool tradition The prevalent style of stone tools associated with *Homo erectus* remains and represented by the hand-axe.

action theory The theory that self-serving actions by forceful leaders play a role in civilization's emergence.

adaptation A series of beneficial adjustments to a particular environment.

adaptive radiation The rapid diversification of an evolving population as it adapts to a variety of available niches.

adduction Movement toward the midline of the body or to the center of the hand or foot.

adjudication A mediation with an unbiased third party making the ultimate decision.

advocacy anthropology Research that is community based and politically involved.

affiliative Behaving in a manner that tends to promote social cohesion.

affinal kin People related through marriage.

age grade An organized category of people based on age; every individual passes through a series of such categories over his or her lifetime.

age set A formally established group of people born during a certain time span who move together through the series of age-grade categories; sometimes called *age class*.

agriculture Intensive crop cultivation, employing plows, fertilizers, and/or irrigation.

alleles Alternate forms of a single gene.

Allen's rule The tendency for the bodies of mammals living in cold climates to have shorter appendages (arms and legs) than members of the same species living in warm climates.

alphabet A series of symbols representing the sounds of a language arranged in a traditional order.

altruism Concern for the welfare of others expressed as increased risk undertaken by individuals for the good of the group.

ambilocal residence A residence pattern in which a married couple may choose either matrilocal or patrilocal residence.

anagenesis A sustained directional shift in a population's average characteristics.

analogies In biology, structures possessed by different organisms that are superficially similar due to similar function but that do not share a common developmental pathway or structure.

ancestral Characteristics that define a group of organisms that are due to shared ancestry.

animatism The belief that nature is enlivened or energized by an impersonal spiritual force or supernatural energy, which may make itself manifest in any special place, thing, or living creature.

animism The belief that nature is enlivened or energized by distinct personalized spirit beings separable from bodies.

anthropoids The suborder of primates that includes New World monkeys, Old World monkeys, and apes (including humans).

anthropology The study of humankind in all times and places.

applied anthropology The use of anthropological knowledge and methods to solve practical problems, often for a specific client.

arboreal Living in the trees.

arboreal hypothesis A theory for primate evolution that proposes that life in the trees was responsible for enhanced visual acuity and manual dexterity in primates.

archaeology The study of cultures through the recovery and analysis of material remains and environmental data.

Archaic cultures The term used to refer to Mesolithic cultures in the Americas.

archaic *Homo sapiens* A loosely defined group within the genus *Homo* that "lumpers" use for fossils with the combination of large brain size and ancestral features on the skull.

Ardipithecus One of the earliest genera of bipeds that lived in eastern Africa. *Ardipithecus* is actually divided into two species: the older, *Ardipithecus kadabba*, which dates to between 5.2 and 5.8 million years ago, and the younger, *Ardipithecus ramidus*, which dates to around 4.4 million years ago.

art The creative use of the human imagination to aesthetically interpret, express, and engage life, modifying experienced reality in the process.

artifact Any object fashioned or altered by humans.

assimilation Cultural absorption of an ethnic minority by a dominant society.

Aurignacian tradition Toolmaking tradition in Europe and western Asia at the beginning of the Upper Paleolithic.

Australopithecus The genus including several species of early bipeds from southern and eastern Africa living between about 1.1 and 4.3 million years ago, one of whom was directly ancestral to humans.

Australopithecus sebida A newly identified species of South African gracile australopithecine dated precisely to between 1.97 and 1.98 million years ago, with derived *Homo*-like characteristics in the hands and pelvis.

authority Claiming and exercising power as justified by law or custom of tradition.

balanced reciprocity A mode of exchange in which the giving and the receiving are specific as to the value of the goods or services and the time of their delivery.

band A relatively small and loosely organized kin-ordered group that inhabits a specific territory and that may split periodically into smaller extended family groups that are politically and economically independent.

Bergmann's rule The tendency for the bodies of mammals living in cold climates to be shorter and rounder than members of the same species living in warm climates.

bilateral descent Descent traced equally through father and mother's ancestors; associating each individual with blood relatives on both sides of the family.

binocular vision Vision with increased depth perception from two eyes set next to each other, allowing their visual fields to overlap.

bioarchaeology The archaeological study of human remains—bones, skulls, teeth, and sometimes hair, dried skin, or other tissue—to determine the influences of culture and environment on human biological variation.

biocultural An approach that focuses on the interaction of biology and culture.

biological anthropology The systematic study of humans as biological organisms; also known as *physical anthropology*.

bipedalism A special form of locomotion, distinguishing humans and their ancestors from the African great apes, in which the organism walks upright on two feet; also called *bipedality*.

blade technique A method of stone tool manufacture in which long, parallel-sided flakes are struck off the edges of a specially prepared core.

brachiation Moving from branch to branch using the arms, with the body hanging suspended below.

bride-price The money or valuable goods paid by the groom or his family to the bride's family upon marriage; also called *bridewealth*.

bride service A designated period of time when the groom works for the bride's family.

bridewealth The money or valuable goods paid by the groom or his family to the bride's family upon marriage; also called *bride-price*.

Bronze Age In the Old World, the period marked by the production of tools and ornaments of bronze; began about 5,000 years ago in China, the Mediterranean, and Southwest Asia, and about 500 years earlier in Southeast Asia.

burin A stone tool with chisel-like edges used for working bone, horn, antler, and ivory.

cargo cult A spiritual movement (especially noted in Melanesia) in reaction to disruptive contact with Western capitalism, promising resurrection of deceased relatives, destruction or enslavement of white foreigners, and the magical arrival of utopian riches.

carrying capacity The number of people that the available resources can support at a given level of food-getting techniques.

cartography The craft of making maps of remote regions.

caste A closed social class in a stratified society in which membership is determined by birth and fixed for life.

catarrhines The primate infraorder that includes Old World monkeys, apes, and humans.

chiefdom A politically organized society in which several neighboring communities inhabiting a territory are united under a single ruler.

chromatid One half of the X shape of chromosomes visible once replication is complete. Sister chromatids are exact copies of each other.

chromosomes In the cell nucleus, the structures visible during cellular division containing long strands of DNA combined with a protein.

chronometric dating In archaeology and paleoanthropology, dating archaeological or fossil materials in units of absolute time using scientific properties such as rates of decay of radioactive elements; also known as *absolute dating*.

civil disobedience Refusal to obey civil laws in an effort to induce change in governmental policy or legislation, characterized by the use of passive resistance or other nonviolent means.

civilization In anthropology, societies in which large numbers of people live in cities, are socially stratified, and are governed by a ruling elite working through centrally organized political systems called states.

clade A taxonomic grouping that contains a single common ancestor and all of its descendants.

cladogenesis Speciation through a branching mechanism whereby an ancestral population gives rise to two or more descendant populations.

clan An extended unilineal kin-group, often consisting of several lineages, whose members claim common descent from a remote ancestor, usually legendary or mythological.

clavicle The collarbone connecting the sternum (breastbone) with the scapula (shoulder blade).

clines The gradual changes in the frequency of an allele or trait over space.

code switching The practice of changing from one mode of speech to another as the situation demands, whether from one language to another or from one dialect of a language to another.

codon Three-base sequence of a gene that specifies a particular amino acid for inclusion in a protein.

coercion Imposition of obedience or submission by force or intimidation.

cognitive capacity A broad concept including intelligence, educability, concept formation, self-awareness, self-evaluation, attention span, sensitivity in discrimination, and creativity.

co-marriage A marriage form in which several men and women have sexual access to one another; also called *group marriage*.

common-interest association An association that results from the act of joining, based on sharing particular activities, objectives, values, or beliefs, sometimes rooted in common ethnic, religious, or regional background.

community In primatology, a unit of primate social organization composed of fifty or more individuals who collectively inhabit a large geographic area.

conjugal family A family established through marriage.

consanguineal family A family of blood relatives, consisting of related women, their brothers, and the women's offspring.

consanguineal kin Biologically related relatives, commonly referred to as blood relatives.

conspicuous consumption A showy display of wealth for social prestige.

contagious magic Magic based on the principle that things or persons once in contact can influence each other after the contact is broken.

continental drift According to the theory of plate tectonics, the movement of continents embedded in underlying plates on the earth's surface in relation to one another over the history of life on earth.

convergent evolution In biological evolution, a process by which unrelated populations develop similarities to one another due to similar function rather than shared ancestry.

convergent evolution In cultural evolution, the development of similar cultural adaptations to similar environmental conditions by different peoples with different ancestral cultures.

coprolites Preserved fecal material providing evidence of the diet and health of past organisms.

core values Those values especially promoted by a particular culture.

cranium The braincase of the skull.

Cro-Magnons Europeans of the Upper Paleolithic after about 36,000 years ago.

cross cousin The child of a mother's brother or a father's sister.

cultural adaptation A complex of ideas, technologies, and activities that enables people to survive and even thrive in their environment.

cultural anthropology The study of patterns in human behavior, thought, and emotions, focusing on humans as culture-producing and culture-reproducing creatures. Also known as *social* or *sociocultural anthropology*.

cultural control Control through beliefs and values deeply internalized in the minds of individuals.

cultural evolution Cultural change over time—not to be confused with progress.

cultural loss The abandonment of an existing practice or trait.

cultural relativism The idea that one must suspend judgment of other people's practices in order to understand them in their own cultural terms.

cultural resource management A branch of archaeology concerned with survey and/or excavation of archaeological and historical remains that might be threatened by construction or development; also involved with policy surrounding protection of cultural resources.

culture A society's shared and socially transmitted ideas, values, emotions, and perceptions, which are used to make sense of experience and generate behavior and are reflected in that behavior.

culture area A geographic region in which a number of societies follow similar patterns of life.

culture-bound A perspective that produces theories about the world and reality that are based on the assumptions and values from the researcher's own culture.

culture-bound syndrome A mental disorder specific to a particular ethnic group; also known as *ethnic psychosis*.

culture shock In fieldwork, the anthropologist's personal disorientation and anxiety that may result in depression.

datum point The starting point or reference for a grid system.

demographics Population characteristics such as the number of individuals of each age and sex.

dendrochronology In archaeology and paleoanthropology, a technique of chronometric dating based on the number of rings of growth found in tree trunks.

Denisovans A newly discovered group of archaic *Homo sapiens* from southern Siberia dated to between 30,000 and 50,000 years ago.

dental formula The number of each tooth type (incisors, canines, premolars, and molars) on one half of each jaw. Unlike other mammals, primates possess equal numbers on their upper and lower jaws so the dental formula for the species is a single series of numbers.

dependence training Childrearing practices that foster compliance in the performance of assigned tasks and dependence on the domestic group, rather than reliance on oneself.

derived Characteristics that define a group of organisms and that did not exist in ancestral populations.

descent group Any kin-group whose members share a direct line of descent from a real (historical) or fictional common ancestor.

desecration Ideologically inspired violation of a sacred site intended to inflict harm, if only symbolically, on people judged to have impure, false, or even evil beliefs and ritual practices.

developmental adaptation A permanent phenotypic variation derived from interaction between genes and the environment during the period of growth and development.

dialects The varying forms of a language that reflect particular regions, occupations, or social classes and that are similar enough to be mutually intelligible.

diastema A space between the canines and other teeth allowing the large projecting canines to fit within the jaw.

diffusion The spread of certain ideas, customs, or practices from one culture to another.

digital ethnography An ethnographic study of social networks, communicative practices, and other cultural expressions in cyberspace by means of digital visual and audio technologies; also called *cyberethnography* or *netnography*.

discourse An extended communication on a particular subject.

disease A specific pathology; a physical or biological abnormality.

displacement Referring to things and events removed in time and space.

diurnal Active during the day and at rest at night.

divination A magical procedure or spiritual ritual designed to discern what is not knowable by ordinary means, such as foretelling the future by interpreting omens.

DNA (deoxyribonucleic acid) The genetic material consisting of a complex molecule whose base structure directs the synthesis of proteins.

doctrine An assertion of opinion or belief formally handed down by an authority as true and indisputable.

domestication An evolutionary process whereby humans modify, intentionally or unintentionally, the genetic makeup of a population of wild plants or animals, sometimes to the extent that members of the population are unable to survive and/or reproduce without human assistance.

dominance hierarchy An observed ranking system in primate societies, ordering individuals from high (alpha) to low standing corresponding to predictable behavioral interactions including domination.

dominant In genetics, a term to describe the ability of an allele for a trait to mask the presence of a recessive allele.

dowry A payment at the time of a woman's marriage that comes from her inheritance, made to either her or her husband.

ecological niche A species' way of life considered in the full context of its environment including factors such as diet, activity, terrain, vegetation, predators, prey, and climate.

economic system An organized arrangement for producing, distributing, and consuming goods.

ecosystem A system, or a functioning whole, composed of both the natural environment and all the organisms living within it.

egalitarian societies Societies in which people have about the same rank and share equally in the basic resources that support income, status, and power.

EGO In kinship studies, the central person from whom the degree of each kinship relationship is traced.

eliciting devices Activities and objects used to draw out individuals and encourage them to recall and share information.

empirical Research based on observations of the world rather than on intuition or faith.

enculturation The process by which a society's culture is passed on from one generation to the next and individuals become members of their society.

endemic The public health term for a disease that is widespread in a population.

endocast A cast of the inside of a skull; used to help determine the size and shape of the brain.

endogamy Marriage within a particular group or category of individuals.

entoptic phenomena Bright pulsating forms that are generated by the central nervous system and seen in states of trance.

enzymes Proteins that initiate and direct chemical reactions.

epic A long, dramatic narrative, recounting the celebrated deeds of a historic or legendary hero, often sung or recited in poetic language.

epicanthic eyefold A fold of skin at the inner corner of the eye that covers the true corner of the eye; common in Asiatic populations.

Eskimo system Kinship reckoning in which the nuclear family is emphasized by specifically identifying the mother, father, brother, and sister, while lumping together all other relatives into broad categories such as uncle, aunt, and cousin; also known as a *lineal system*.

estrus In some primate females, the time of sexual receptivity during which ovulation is visibly displayed.

ethnic group People who collectively and publicly identify themselves as a distinct group based on shared cultural features such as common origin, language, customs, and traditional beliefs.

ethnicity This term, rooted in the Greek word *ethnikos* ("nation") and related to *ethnos* ("custom"), is the expression for the set of cultural ideas held by an ethnic group.

ethnic psychosis A mental disorder specific to a particular ethnic group; also known as *culture-bound syndrome*.

ethnocentrism The belief that the ways of one's own culture are the only proper ones.

ethnocide The violent eradication of an ethnic group's collective cultural identity as a distinctive people; occurs when a dominant society deliberately sets out to destroy another society's cultural heritage.

ethnographic fieldwork Extended on-location research to gather detailed and in-depth information on a society's customary ideas, values, and practices through participation in its collective social life.

ethnography A detailed description of a particular culture primarily based on fieldwork.

ethnolinguistics A branch of linguistics that studies the relationships between language and culture and how they mutually influence and inform each other.

ethnology The study and analysis of different cultures from a comparative or historical point of view, utilizing ethnographic accounts and developing anthropological theories that help explain why certain important differences or similarities occur among groups.

ethnomusicology The study of a society's music in terms of its cultural setting.

Eve hypothesis The theory that modern humans are all derived from one single population of archaic *Homo sapiens* who migrated out of Africa after 100,000 years ago, replacing all other archaic forms due to their superior cultural capabilities; also known as the *recent African origins hypothesis* or the *out of Africa hypothesis.*

evolution The changes in allele frequencies in populations; also known as *microevolution.*

evolutionary medicine An approach to human sickness and health combining principles of evolutionary theory and human evolutionary history.

exogamy Marriage outside the group.

experimental archaeology The recreation of ancient lifeways by modern paleoanthropologists and archaeologists in order to test hypotheses, interpretations, and assumptions about the past.

extended family Two or more closely related nuclear families clustered together into a large domestic group.

family Two or more people related by blood, marriage, or adoption. The family may take many forms, ranging from a single parent with one or more children, to a married couple or polygamous spouses with or without offspring, to several generations of parents and their children.

fictive marriage A marriage form in which a proxy is used as a symbol of someone not physically present to establish the social status of a spouse and heirs.

fieldwork The term anthropologists use for on-location research.

fission In kinship studies, the splitting of a descent group into two or more new descent groups.

flotation An archaeological technique employed to recover very tiny objects by immersion of soil samples in water to separate heavy from light particles.

fluorine dating In archaeology or paleoanthropology, a technique for relative dating based on the fact that the amount of fluorine in bones is proportional to their age.

folklore A term coined by 19th-century scholars studying the unwritten stories and other artistic traditions of rural peoples to distinguish between "folk art" and the "fine art" of the literate elite.

food foraging A mode of subsistence involving some combination of hunting, fishing, and gathering of wild plant foods.

foramen magnum A large opening in the skull through which the spinal cord passes and connects to the brain.

forensic anthropology The identification of human skeletal remains for legal purposes.

formal interview A structured question/answer session, carefully notated as it occurs and based on prepared questions.

fossil The preserved remains of past life forms.

founder effects A particular form of genetic drift deriving from a small founding population not possessing all the alleles present in the original population.

fovea centralis A shallow pit in the retina of the eye that enables an animal to focus on an object while maintaining visual contact with its surroundings.

gender The cultural elaborations and meanings assigned to the biological differentiation between the sexes.

gendered speech Distinct male and female speech patterns that vary across social and cultural settings.

gene flow The introduction of alleles from the gene pool of one population into that of another.

gene pool All the genetic variants possessed by members of a population.

generalized reciprocity A mode of exchange in which the value of the gift is not calculated, nor is the time of repayment specified.

genes The portions of DNA molecules that direct the synthesis of specific proteins.

genetic adaptations Discrete genetic changes built into the allele frequencies of populations or microevolutionary change brought about by natural selection.

genetic code The sequence of three bases (a codon) that specifies the sequence of amino acids in protein synthesis.

genetic drift The chance fluctuations of allele frequencies in the gene pool of a population.

genocide The physical extermination of one people by another, either as a deliberate act or as the accidental outcome of activities carried out by one people with little regard for their impact on others.

genome The complete structure sequence of DNA for a species.

genotype The alleles possessed for a particular trait.

genus (genera) In the system of plant and animal classification, a group of like species.

gestures Facial expressions and body postures and motions that convey intended as well as subconscious messages.

globalization Worldwide interconnectedness, evidenced in rapid global movement of natural resources, trade goods, human labor, finance capital, information, and infectious diseases.

gracile australopithecines Members of the genus *Australopithecus* possessing a more lightly built chewing apparatus; likely had a diet that included more meat than that of the robust *australopithecines*; best represented by the South African species *A. africanus.*

grade A general level of biological organization seen among a group of species; useful for constructing evolutionary relationships.

grammar The entire formal structure of a language, including morphology and syntax.

grave goods Items such as utensils, figurines, and personal possessions, symbolically placed in the grave for the deceased person's use in the afterlife.

grid system A system for recording data in three dimensions from an archaeological excavation.

grooming The ritual cleaning of another animal's coat to remove parasites and other matter.

group marriage A marriage form in which several men and women have sexual access to one another; also called *co-marriage.*

haplorhines The subdivision within the primate order based on shared genetic characteristics; includes tarsiers, New World monkeys, Old World monkeys, and apes (including humans).

hard power Power that coerces others and that is backed up by economic or military force.

Hardy-Weinberg principle The concept that demonstrates algebraically that the percentages of individuals that are homozygous for the dominant allele, homozygous for the recessive allele, and heterozygous should remain constant from one generation to the next, provided that certain specified conditions are met.

Hawaiian system Kinship reckoning in which all relatives of the same sex and generation are referred to by the same term; also known as the *generational system.*

health disparity A difference in the health status between the wealthy elite and the poor in stratified societies.

hemoglobin The protein that carries oxygen in red blood cells.

heterozygous Refers to a chromosome pair that bears different alleles for a single gene.

historical archaeology The archaeological study of places for which written records exist.

holistic perspective A fundamental principle of anthropology: The various parts of human culture and biology must be viewed in the broadest possible context in order to understand their interconnections and interdependence.

homeotherm An animal that maintains a relatively constant body temperature despite environmental fluctuations.

home range The geographic area within which a group of primates usually moves.

hominid African hominoid family that includes humans and their ancestors. Some scientists, recognizing the close relationship of humans, chimps, bonobos, and gorillas, use the term *hominid* to refer to all African hominoids. They then divide the hominid family into two subfamilies: the Paninae (chimps, bonobos, and gorillas) and the Homininae (humans and their ancestors).

hominin The taxonomic subfamily or tribe within the primates that includes humans and our ancestors.

hominoid The taxonomic division superfamily within the Old World primates that includes gibbons, siamangs, orangutans, gorillas, chimpanzees, bonobos, and humans.

Homo The genus of bipeds that appeared 2.5 million years ago, characterized by increased brain size compared to earlier bipeds. The genus is divided into various species based on features such as brain size, skull shape, and cultural capabilities.

Homo erectus "Upright human." A species within the genus *Homo* first appearing just after 2 million years ago in Africa and ultimately spreading throughout the Old World.

Homo habilis "Handy human." The first fossil members of the genus *Homo* appearing 2.5 million years ago, with larger brains and smaller faces than australopithecines.

homologies In biology, structures possessed by two different organisms that arise in similar fashion and pass through similar stages during embryonic development, although they may have different functions.

homozygous Refers to a chromosome pair that bears identical alleles for a single gene.

horticulture The cultivation of crops in food gardens, carried out with simple hand tools such as digging sticks and hoes.

household A domestic unit of one or more persons living in the same residence. Other than family members, a household may include nonrelatives, such as servants.

Human Relations Area Files (HRAF) A vast collection of cross-indexed ethnographic, biocultural, and archaeological data catalogued by cultural characteristics and geographic location; archived in about 300 libraries on microfiche and/or online.

hunting response A cyclic expansion and contraction of the blood vessels of the limbs that balances releasing enough heat to prevent frostbite with maintaining heat in the body core.

hydraulic theory The theory that explains civilization's emergence as the result of the construction of elaborate irrigation systems, the functioning of which required full-time managers whose control blossomed into the first governing body and elite social class; also known as *irrigation theory*.

hypoglossal canal The opening in the skull that accommodates the tongue-controlling hypoglossal nerve.

hypothesis A tentative explanation of the relationships between certain phenomena.

hypoxia The reduced availability of oxygen at the cellular level.

idealist perspective A theoretical approach stressing the primacy of superstructure in cultural research and analysis.

illness The meanings and elaborations given to a particular physical state.

imitative magic Magic based on the principle that like produces like; sometimes called *sympathetic magic*.

incest taboo The prohibition of sexual relations between closely related individuals.

incorporation In a rite of passage, reincorporation of a temporarily removed individual into society in his or her new status.

independence training Childrearing practices that promote independence, self-reliance, and personal achievement.

industrial food production Large-scale businesses involved in mass food production, processing, and marketing, which primarily rely on labor-saving machines.

industrial society A society in which human labor, hand tools, and animal power are largely replaced by machines, with an economy primarily based on big factories.

informal economy A network of producing and circulating marketable commodities, labor, and services that for various reasons escape government control.

informal interview An unstructured, open-ended conversation in everyday life.

informed consent A formal recorded agreement between the subject and the researcher to participate in the research.

infrastructure The economic foundation of a society, including its subsistence practices and the tools and other material equipment used to make a living.

innovation Any new idea, method, or device that gains widespread acceptance in society.

insurgency An organized armed resistance or violent uprising to an established government or authority in power; also known as *rebellion*.

intersexuals People born with reproductive organs, genitalia, and/or sex chromosomes that are not exclusively male or female.

irrigation theory The theory that explains civilization's emergence as the result of the construction of elaborate irrigation systems, the functioning of which required full-time managers whose control blossomed into the first governing body and elite social class; also known as *hydraulic theory*.

Iroquois system Kinship reckoning in which a father and a father's brother are referred to by a single term, as are a mother and mother's sister, but a father's sister and mother's brother are given separate terms. Parallel cousins are classified with brothers and sisters, while cross cousins are classified separately but not equated with relatives of some other generation.

ischial callosities Hardened, nerveless pads on the buttocks that allow baboons and other primates to sit for long periods of time.

isotherm An animal whose body temperature rises or falls according to the temperature of the surrounding environment.

karyotype The array of chromosomes found inside a single cell.

Kenyanthropus platyops A proposed genus and species of biped contemporary with early australopithecines; may not be a separate genus.

key consultant A member of the society being studied who provides information that helps researchers understand the meaning of what they observe. Early anthropologists referred to such individuals as *informants*.

kindred A grouping of blood relatives based on bilateral descent. Includes all relatives with whom EGO shares at least one grandparent, great-grandparent, or even great-great-grandparent on his or her father's *and* mother's side.

kinesics The study of nonverbal signals in body language including facial expressions and bodily postures and motions.

kinship A network of relatives into which individuals are born and married, and with whom they cooperate based on customarily prescribed rights and obligations.

k-selected Reproduction involving the production of relatively few offspring with high parental investment in each.

Kula ring A mode of balanced reciprocity that reinforces trade and social relations among the seafaring Melanesians who inhabit a large ring of islands in the southwestern Pacific Ocean.

lactase An enzyme in the small intestine that enables humans to assimilate lactose.

lactose A sugar that is the primary constituent of fresh milk.

language A system of communication using sounds, gestures, or marks that are put together according to certain rules, resulting in meanings that are intelligible to all who share that language.

language family A group of languages descended from a single ancestral language.

law Formal rules of conduct that, when violated, effectuate negative sanctions.

law of competitive exclusion When two closely related species compete for the same niche, one will out-compete the other, bringing about the latter's extinction.

law of independent assortment The Mendelian principle that genes controlling different traits are inherited independently of one another.

law of segregation The Mendelian principle that variants of genes for a particular trait retain their separate identities through the generations.

legend A story about a memorable event or figure handed down by tradition and told as true but without historical evidence.

legitimacy In politics, the right of political leaders to govern—to hold, use, and allocate power—based on the values a particular society embraces.

Levalloisian technique Toolmaking technique by which three or four long triangular flakes are detached from a specially prepared core; developed by members of the genus *Homo* transitional from *H. erectus* to *H. sapiens*.

leveling mechanism A cultural obligation compelling prosperous members of a community to give away goods, host public feasts, provide free service, or otherwise demonstrate generosity so that no one permanently accumulates significantly more wealth than anyone else.

lineage A unilineal kin-group descended from a common ancestor or founder who lived four to six generations ago, and in which relationships among members can be exactly stated in genealogical terms.

linguistic anthropology The study of human languages—looking at their structure, history, and relation to social and cultural contexts.

linguistic divergence The development of different languages from a single ancestral language.

linguistic nationalism The attempt by ethnic minorities and even countries to proclaim independence by purging their language of foreign terms.

linguistic relativity The theoretical concept directly linking language and culture, holding that the words and grammar of a language affect how its speakers perceive and think about the world.

linguistics The modern scientific study of all aspects of language.

Lower Paleolithic The first part of the Old Stone Age beginning with the earliest Oldowan tools spanning from about 200,000 or 250,000 to 2.6 million years ago.

macroevolution Evolution above the species level or leading to the formation of new species.

magic Specific formulas and actions used to compel supernatural powers to act in certain ways for good or evil purposes.

mammals The class of vertebrate animals distinguished by bodies covered with hair or fur, self-regulating temperature, and in females, milk-producing mammary glands.

market exchange The buying and selling of goods and services, with prices set by rules of supply and demand.

marriage A culturally sanctioned union between two or more people that establishes certain rights and obligations between the people, between them and their children, and between them and their in-laws. Such marriage rights and obligations most often include, but are not limited to, sex, labor, property, childrearing, exchange, and status.

marrow The fatty nutritious tissue inside of long bones where blood cells are produced.

material culture The durable aspects of culture such as tools, structures, and art.

materialist perspective A theoretical approach stressing the primacy of infrastructure (material conditions) in cultural research and analysis.

matrilineal descent Descent traced exclusively through the female line of ancestry to establish group membership.

matrilocal residence A residence pattern in which a married couple lives in the wife's mother's place of residence.

mediation The settlement of a dispute through negotiation assisted by an unbiased third party.

medical anthropology A specialization in anthropology that brings theoretical and applied approaches from cultural and biological anthropology to the study of human health and disease.

medical pluralism The practice of multiple medical systems, each with its own techniques and beliefs, in a single society.

medical system A patterned set of ideas and practices relating to illness.

meiosis A kind of cell division that produces the sex cells, each of which has half the number of chromosomes found in other cells of the organism.

melanin A dark pigment produced in the outer layer of the skin that protects against damaging ultraviolet solar radiation.

menarche First menstruation in the maturation of a human female.

menopause The cessation of menstrual cycles.

Mesoamerica The region extending from central Mexico to northern Central America.

Mesolithic The Middle Stone Age of Europe, Asia, and Africa beginning about 12,000 years ago.

metabolic rate The rate at which bodies burn energy (food) to function.

microevolution The changes in allele frequencies in populations; also known as *evolution*.

microlith A small blade of flint or similar stone, several of which were hafted together in wooden handles to make tools; widespread in the Mesolithic.

middens A refuse or garbage disposal area in an archaeological site.

Middle Paleolithic The middle part of the Old Stone Age characterized by the development of the Mousterian tool tradition and the earlier Levalloisian techniques.

migration Mobility in geographic space, involving temporary or permanent change in usual place of residence; internal migration is movement within countries; external migration is movement to a foreign country.

mitosis A kind of cell division that produces new cells having exactly the same number of chromosome pairs, and hence copies of genes, as the parent cell.

modal personality Those character traits that occur with the highest frequency in a social group and are therefore the most representative of its culture.

modernization The process of political and socioeconomic change, whereby developing societies acquire some of the cultural characteristics of Western industrial societies.

moiety Each group, usually consisting of several clans, that results from a division of a society into two halves on the basis of descent.

molecular anthropology The anthropological study of genes and genetic relationships, which contributes significantly to our understanding of human evolution, adaptation, and diversity.

molecular clock The hypothesis that dates of divergences among related species can be calculated through an examination of the genetic mutations that have accrued since the divergence.

money A means of exchange used to make payments for other goods and services as well as to measure their value.

monogamous In primatology, mating for life with a single individual of the opposite sex.

monogamy A marriage form in which both partners have just one spouse.

monotheism The belief in only one supremely powerful divinity as creator and master of the universe.

morphemes The smallest units of sound that carry a meaning in language. They are distinct from phonemes, which can alter meaning but have no meaning by themselves.

morphology The study of the patterns or rules of word formation in a language, including the guidelines for verb tense, pluralization, and compound words.

motif A story situation in a tale.

Mousterian tool tradition The tool industry of the Neandertals and their contemporaries of Europe, Southwest Asia, and North Africa from 40,000 to 125,000 years ago.

multiculturalism The public policy for managing cultural diversity in a multi-ethnic society, officially stressing mutual respect and tolerance for cultural differences within a country's borders.

multiregional hypothesis The hypothesis that modern humans originated through a process of simultaneous local transition from *Homo erectus* to *Homo sapiens* throughout the inhabited world.

multi-sited ethnography The investigation and documentation of peoples and cultures embedded in the larger structures of a globalizing world, utilizing a range of methods in various locations of time and space.

music Broadly speaking, an art form whose medium is sound and silence; a form of communication that includes a non-verbal auditory component with elements of pitch, rhythm, and timbre.

mutation The chance alteration of genetic material that produces new variation.

myth A sacred narrative that explains the fundamentals of human existence—where we and everything in our world came from, why we are here, and where we are going.

naming ceremony A special event or ritual to mark the naming of a child.

natal group The group or the community an animal has inhabited since birth.

nation A people who share a collective identity based on a common culture, language, territorial base, and history.

Natufian culture A Mesolithic culture from the lands that are now Israel, Lebanon, and western Syria, between about 10,200 and 12,500 years ago.

natural selection The evolutionary process through which factors in the environment exert pressure, favoring some individuals over others to produce the next generation.

Neandertals A distinct group within the genus *Homo* inhabiting Europe and Southwest Asia from approximately 30,000 to 125,000 years ago.

negative reciprocity A mode of exchange in which the aim is to get something for as little as possible. Neither fair nor balanced, it may involve hard bargaining, manipulation, outright cheating, or theft.

negotiation The use of direct argument and compromise by the parties to a dispute to arrive voluntarily at a mutually satisfactory agreement.

Neolithic The New Stone Age; a prehistoric period beginning about 10,000 years ago in which peoples possessed stone-based technologies and depended on domesticated crops and/or animals for subsistence.

Neolithic revolution The domestication of plants and animals by peoples with stone-based technologies, beginning about 10,000 years ago and leading to radical transformations in cultural systems; sometimes referred to as the *Neolithic transition.*

neolocal residence A residence pattern in which a married couple establishes its household in a location apart from either the husband's or the wife's relatives.

new reproductive technologies (NRTs) Alternative means of reproduction such as surrogate motherhood and in vitro fertilization.

nocturnal Active at night and at rest during the day.

notochord A rodlike structure of cartilage that, in vertebrates, is replaced by the vertebral column.

nuclear family A group consisting of one or two parents and dependent offspring, which may include a stepparent, stepsiblings, and adopted children. Until recently this term referred only to the mother, father, and child(ren) unit.

Oldowan tool tradition The first stone tool industry, beginning between 2.5 and 2.6 million years ago.

Old Stone Age A period of time beginning with the earliest Oldowan tools, spanning from about 200,000 to 2.6 million years ago; also known as the *Lower Paleolithic.*

opposable Having the ability to bring the thumb or big toe in contact with the tips of the other digits on the same hand or foot in order to grasp objects.

out of Africa hypothesis The theory that modern humans are all derived from one single population of archaic *Homo sapiens* who migrated out of Africa after 100,000 years ago, replacing all other archaic forms due to their superior cultural capabilities; also known as the *recent African origins hypothesis* or the *Eve hypothesis.*

ovulation The moment when an egg released from an ovary into the womb is receptive for fertilization.

paleoanthropology The anthropological study of biological changes through time (evolution) to understand the origins and predecessors of the present human species.

Paleoindians The earliest inhabitants of North America.

palynology In archaeology and paleoanthropology, a technique of relative dating based on changes in fossil pollen over time.

pantheon All the gods and goddesses of a people.

paralanguage Voice effects that accompany language and convey meaning. These include vocalizations such as giggling, groaning, or sighing, as well as voice qualities such as pitch and tempo.

parallel cousin The child of a father's brother or a mother's sister.

parallel evolution In cultural evolution, the development of similar cultural adaptations to similar environmental conditions by peoples whose ancestral cultures are already somewhat alike.

participant observation In ethnography, the technique of learning a people's culture through social participation and personal observation within the community being studied, as well as interviews and discussion with individual members of the group over an extended period of time.

pastoralism The breeding and managing of migratory herds of domesticated grazing animals, such as goats, sheep, cattle, llamas, and camels.

patrilineal descent Descent traced exclusively through the male line of ancestry to establish group membership.

patrilocal residence A residence pattern in which a married couple lives in the husband's father's place of residence.

peasant A small-scale producer of crops or livestock living on land self-owned or rented in exchange for labor, crops, or money and exploited by more powerful groups in a complex society.

percussion method A technique of stone tool manufacture performed by striking the raw material with a hammerstone or by striking raw material against a stone anvil to remove flakes.

performance art A creatively expressed promotion of ideas by artful means dramatically staged to challenge opinion and/or provoke purposeful action.

personality The distinctive way a person thinks, feels, and behaves.

phenotype The observable or testable appearance of an organism that may or may not reflect a particular genotype due to the variable expression of dominant and recessive alleles.

phonemes The smallest units of sound that make a difference in meaning in a language.

phonetics The systematic identification and description of distinctive speech sounds in a language.

phonology The study of language sounds.

phratry A unilineal descent group composed of at least two clans that supposedly share a common ancestry, whether or not they really do.

physical anthropology The systematic study of humans as biological organisms; also known as *biological anthropology.*

physiological adaptation A short-term physiological change in response to a specific environmental stimulus. An immediate short-term response is not very efficient and is gradually replaced by a longer-term response; see *acclimatization.*

pilgrimage A devotion in motion. Traveling, often on foot, to a sacred or holy site to reach for enlightenment, prove devotion, and/or experience a miracle.

platyrrhines The primate infraorder that includes New World monkeys.

pluralistic society A society in which two or more ethnic groups or nationalities are politically organized into one territorial state but maintain their cultural differences.

political organization The way power, as the capacity to do something, is accumulated, arranged, executed, and structurally embedded in society; the means through which a society creates and maintains social order and reduces social disorder.

politics The process determining who gets what, when, and how.

polyandry A marriage form in which a woman is married to two or more men at one time; a form of polygamy.

polygamy A marriage form in which one individual has multiple spouses at the same time; from the Greek words *poly* ("many") and *gamos* ("marriage").

polygenetic inheritance Two or more genes contributing to the phenotypic expression of a single characteristic.

polygyny A marriage form in which a man is married to two or more women at the same time; a form of polygamy.

polymerase chain reaction (PCR) A technique for amplifying or creating multiple copies of fragments of DNA so that it can be studied in the laboratory.

polymorphic Describing species with alternative forms (alleles) of particular genes.

polytheism The belief in multiple gods and/or goddesses, as contrasted with monotheism—the belief in one god or goddess.

polytypic Describing the expression of genetic variants in different frequencies in different populations of a species.

population In biology, a group of similar individuals that can and do interbreed.

postindustrial society A society with an economy based on research and development of new knowledge and technologies, as well as providing information, services, and finance capital on a global scale.

potassium-argon dating In archaeology and paleoanthropology, a technique of chronometric dating that measures the ratio of radioactive potassium to argon in volcanic debris associated with human remains.

potlatch On the northwestern coast of North America, an indigenous ceremonial event in which a village chief publicly gives away stockpiled food and other goods that signify wealth.

power The ability of individuals or groups to impose their will upon others and make them do things even against their own wants or wishes.

preadapted Possessing characteristics that, by chance, are advantageous in future environmental conditions.

prehensile Having the ability to grasp.

prehistory A conventional term used to refer to the period of time before the appearance of written records; does not deny the existence of history, merely of *written* history.

pressure flaking A technique of stone tool manufacture in which a bone, antler, or wooden tool is used to press, rather than strike off, small flakes from a piece of flint or similar stone.

prestige economy The creation of a surplus for the express purpose of displaying wealth and giving it away to raise one's status.

priest or priestess A full-time religious specialist formally recognized for his or her role in guiding the religious practices of others and for contacting and influencing supernatural powers.

primary innovation The creation, invention, or chance discovery of a completely new idea, method, or device.

primates The group of mammals that includes lemurs, lorises, tarsiers, monkeys, apes, and humans.

primatology The study of living and fossil primates.

prion An infectious protein lacking any genetic material but capable of causing the reorganization and destruction of other proteins.

progress In anthropology, a relative concept signifying that a society or country is moving forward to a better, more advanced stage in its cultural development toward greater perfection.

projection In cartography, refers to the system of intersecting lines (of longitude and latitude) by which part or all of the globe is represented on a flat surface.

prosimians The suborder of primates that includes lemurs, lorises, and tarsiers.

proxemics The cross-cultural study of people's perception and use of space.

punctuated equilibria A model of macroevolutionary change that suggests evolution occurs via long periods of stability or stasis punctuated by periods of rapid change.

qualitative data Nonstatistical information such as personal life stories and customary beliefs and practices.

quantitative data Statistical or measurable information, such as demographic composition, the types and quantities of crops grown, or the ratio of spouses born and raised within or outside the community.

race In biology, the taxonomic category of subspecies that is not applicable to humans because the division of humans into discrete types does not represent the true nature of human biological variation. In some societies race is an important social category.

racism A doctrine of superiority by which one group justifies the dehumanization of others based on their distinctive physical characteristics.

radiocarbon dating In archaeology and paleoanthropology, a technique of chronometric dating based on measuring the amount of radioactive carbon (^{14}C) left in organic materials found in archaeological sites.

rebellion Organized armed resistance to an established government or authority in power; also known as *insurgency*.

recent African origins hypothesis The theory that modern humans are all derived from one single population of archaic *Homo sapiens* who migrated out of Africa after 100,000 years ago, replacing all other archaic forms due to their superior cultural capabilities; also known as the *Eve hypothesis* or the *out of Africa hypothesis*.

recessive In genetics, a term to describe the inability of an allele for a trait to mask the presence of a dominant allele.

reciprocity The exchange of goods and services, of approximately equal value, between two parties.

reconciliation In primatology, a friendly reunion between former opponents not long after a conflict.

redistribution A mode of exchange in which goods flow into a central place, where they are sorted, counted, and reallocated.

relative dating In archaeology and paleoanthropology, designating an event, object, or fossil as being older or younger than another by noting the position in the earth, by measuring the amount of chemicals contained in fossil bones and artifacts, or by identifying its association with other plant, animal, or cultural remains.

religion An organized system of ideas about the spiritual sphere or the supernatural, along with associated ceremonial practices by which people try to interpret and/or influence aspects of the universe otherwise beyond their control.

reproductive success The relative production of fertile offspring by a genotype. In practical terms, the number of offspring produced by individual members of a population is tallied and compared to that of others.

revitalization movements Social movements for radical cultural reform in response to widespread social disruption and collective feelings of great stress and despair.

revolution Radical change in a society or culture. In the political arena, it involves the forced overthrow of an existing government and establishment of a completely new one.

ribosomes Structures in the cell where translation occurs.

rifting In geology, the process by which a rift, or a long narrow zone of faulting, results when two geological plates come together.

rite of intensification A ritual that takes place during a crisis in the life of the group and serves to bind individuals together.

rite of passage A ritual that marks an important ceremonial moment when members of a society move from one distinctive social stage in life to another, such as birth, marriage, and death. It features three phases: separation, transition, and incorporation.

rite of purification A symbolic act carried out by an individual or a group to establish or restore purity when someone has violated a taboo or is otherwise metaphorically unclean.

ritual A culturally prescribed symbolic act or procedure designed to guide members of a community in an orderly way through personal and collective transitions.

RNA (ribonucleic acid) Similar to DNA but with uracil substituted for the base thymine. Transcribes and carries instructions from DNA from the nucleus to the ribosomes, where it directs protein synthesis. Some simple life forms contain RNA only.

robust australopithecines Several species within the genus *Australopithecus*, who lived from about 1 to 2.5 million years ago in eastern and southern Africa; known for the rugged nature of their chewing apparatus (large back teeth, large chewing muscles, and a bony ridge on their skull tops to allow for these large muscles).

r-selected Reproduction involving the production of large numbers of offspring with relatively low parental investment in each.

sagittal crest A crest running from front to back on the top of the skull along the midline to provide a surface of bone for the attachment of the large temporal muscles for chewing.

Sahul The greater Australian landmass including Australia, New Guinea, and Tasmania. At times of maximum glaciation and low sea levels, these areas were continuous.

sanction An externalized social control designed to encourage conformity to social norms.

savannah Semi-arid plains environment as in eastern Africa.

scapula The shoulder blade.

secondary innovation The deliberate application or modification of an existing idea, method, or device.

secularization A process of cultural change in which a population tends toward a nonreligious worldview, ignoring or rejecting institutionalized spiritual beliefs and rituals.

secular trend A physical difference among related people from distinct generations that allows anthropologists to make inferences about environmental effects on growth and development.

self-awareness The ability to identify oneself as an individual, to reflect on oneself, and to evaluate oneself.

self-control A person's capacity to manage her or his spontaneous feelings, restraining impulsive behavior.

separation In a rite of passage, the temporary ritual removal of the individual from society.

serial monogamy A marriage form in which a man or a woman marries or lives with a series of partners in succession.

seriation In archaeology and paleoanthropology, a technique for relative dating based on putting groups of objects into a sequence in relation to one another.

sexual dimorphism Within a single species, differences between males and females in the shape or size of a feature not directly related to reproduction, such as body size or canine tooth shape and size.

shaman A person who at will enters an altered state of consciousness to contact and utilize an ordinarily hidden reality in order to acquire knowledge, power, and to help others.

sickle-cell anemia An inherited form of anemia produced by a mutation in the hemoglobin protein that causes the red blood cells to assume a sickle shape.

signals Instinctive sounds and gestures that have a natural or self-evident meaning.

silent trade A process for the exchange of goods between mutually distrusting ethnic groups so as to avoid direct personal contact.

slash-and-burn cultivation An extensive form of horticulture in which the natural vegetation is cut, the slash is subsequently burned, and crops are then planted among the ashes; also known as *swidden farming*.

social class A category of individuals in a stratified society who enjoy equal or nearly equal prestige according to the hierarchical system of evaluation.

social control External control through open coercion.

social mobility An upward or downward change in one's social class position in a stratified society.

social structure The rule-governed relationships—with all their rights and obligations—that hold members of a society together. This includes households, families, associations, and power relations, including politics.

society An organized group or groups of interdependent people who generally share a common territory, language, and culture and who act together for collective survival and well-being.

sociolinguistics The study of the relationship between language and society through examining how social categories—such as age, gender, ethnicity, religion, occupation, and class—influence the use and significance of distinctive styles of speech.

soft power Power that coopts rather than coerces, pressing others through attraction and persuasion to change their ideas, beliefs, values, and behaviors.

soil marks The stains that show up on the surface of recently plowed fields that reveal an archaeological site.

speciation The process of forming new species.

species The smallest working units in biological classificatory systems; reproductively isolated populations or groups of populations capable of interbreeding to produce fertile offspring.

spirituality Concern with the sacred, as distinguished from material matters. In contrast to religion, spirituality is often individual rather than collective and does not require a distinctive format or traditional organization.

spiritual lineage A principle of leadership in which divine authority is passed down from a spiritual founding figure, such as a prophet or saint, to a chain of successors.

stabilizing selection Natural selection acting to promote stability rather than change in a population's gene pool.

state A political institution established to manage and defend a complex, socially stratified society occupying a defined territory.

stereoscopic vision Complete three-dimensional vision, or depth perception, from binocular vision and nerve connections that run from each eye to both sides of the brain, allowing nerve cells to integrate the images derived from each eye.

stratified In archaeology, a term describing sites where the remains lie in layers, one upon another.

stratified societies Societies in which people are hierarchically divided and ranked into social strata, or layers, and do not share equally in basic resources that support income, status, and power.

stratigraphy In archaeology and paleoanthropology, the most reliable method of relative dating by means of strata.

strepsirhines The subdivision within the primate order based on shared genetic characteristics; includes lemurs and lorises.

structural power Power that organizes and orchestrates the systemic interaction within and among societies, directing economic and political forces on the one hand and ideological forces that shape public ideas, values, and beliefs on the other.

structural violence Physical and/or psychological harm (including repression, environmental destruction, poverty, hunger, illness, and premature death) caused by impersonal, exploitative, and unjust social, political, and economic systems.

subculture A distinctive set of ideas, values, and behavior patterns by which a group within a larger society operates, while still sharing common standards with that larger society.

Sunda The combined landmass of the contemporary islands of Java, Sumatra, Borneo, and Bali that was continuous with mainland Southeast Asia at times of low sea levels corresponding to maximum glaciation.

superstructure A society's shared sense of identity and worldview. The collective body of ideas, beliefs, and values by which members of a society make sense of the world—its shape, challenges, and opportunities—and understand their place in it. This includes religion and national ideology.

suspensory hanging apparatus The broad powerful shoulder joints and muscles found in all the hominoids, allowing these large-bodied primates to hang suspended below the tree branches.

swidden farming An extensive form of horticulture in which the natural vegetation is cut, the slash is subsequently burned, and crops are then planted among the ashes; also known as *slash-and-burn cultivation*.

symbol A sound, gesture, mark, or other sign that is arbitrarily linked to something else and represents it in a meaningful way.

sympathetic magic Magic based on the principle that like produces like; also known as *imitative magic*.

syncretism The creative blending of indigenous and foreign beliefs and practices into new cultural forms.

syntax The patterns or rules by which words are arranged into phrases and sentences.

taboo Culturally prescribed avoidances involving ritual prohibitions, which, if not observed, lead to supernatural punishment.

tale A creative narrative that is recognized as fiction for entertainment but may also draw a moral or teach a practical lesson.

taxonomy The science of classification.

technology Tools and other material equipment, together with the knowledge of how to make and use them.

tertiary scavenger In a food chain, the third animal group (second to scavenge) to obtain meat from a kill made by a predator.

theory A coherent statement that provides an explanatory framework for understanding; an explanation or interpretation supported by a reliable body of data.

thrifty genotype Human genotype that permits efficient storage of fat to draw on in times of food shortage and conservation of glucose and nitrogen.

tonal language A language in which the sound pitch of a spoken word is an essential part of its pronunciation and meaning.

tool An object used to facilitate some task or activity. Although toolmaking involves intentional modification of the material of which it is made, tool use may involve objects either modified for some particular purpose or completely unmodified.

totemism The belief that people are related to particular animals, plants, or natural objects by virtue of descent from common ancestral spirits.

tradition Customary ideas and practices passed on from generation to generation, which in a modernizing society may form an obstacle to new ways of doing things.

transcription The process of conversion of instructions from DNA into RNA.

transgenders People who cross over or occupy an intermediate position in the binary male–female gender construction.

transition In a rite of passage, temporary isolation of the individual following separation and prior to incorporation into society.

translation The process of conversion of RNA instructions into proteins.

treaty A contract or formally binding agreement between two or more groups that are independent and self-governing political groups such as tribes, chiefdoms, and states.

tribe In anthropology, the term for a range of kin-ordered groups that are politically integrated by some unifying factor and whose members share a common ancestry, identity, culture, language, and territory.

unilineal descent Descent traced exclusively through either the male or the female line of ancestry to establish group membership.

Upper Paleolithic The last part (10,000 to 40,000 years ago) of the Old Stone Age, featuring tool industries characterized by long, slim blades and an explosion of creative symbolic forms.

urgent anthropology Ethnographic research that documents endangered cultures; also known as *salvage ethnography*.

vegeculture The cultivation of domesticated root crops, such as yams, manioc, and taro together in a single field, generally by planting cuttings instead of seeds.

verbal art Creative word use on display that includes stories, fairytales, myths, legends, proverbs, chants, poetry, metaphor, rhyme, drama, cant, jokes, puns, riddles, and tongue twisters.

vertebrates Animals with a backbone, including fish, amphibians, reptiles, birds, and mammals.

visual art Art created primarily for visual perception, ranging from etchings and paintings on various surfaces (including the human body) to sculptures and weavings made with an array of materials.

visual predation hypothesis A theory for primate evolution that proposes that hunting behavior in tree-dwelling primates was responsible for their enhanced visual acuity and manual dexterity.

whistled speech An exchange of whistled words using a phonetic emulation of the sounds produced in spoken voice; also known as whistled language.

witchcraft Magical rituals intended to cause misfortune or inflict harm.

worldview The collective body of ideas that members of a culture generally share concerning the ultimate shape and substance of their reality.

writing system A set of visible or tactile signs used to represent units of language in a systematic way.

xenophobia Fear or hatred of strangers or anything foreign.

References

Abbot, E. (2001). *A history of celibacy.* Cambridge, MA: Da Capo Press.

Abu-Lughod, L. (1986). *Veiled sentiments: Honor and poetry in a Bedouin society.* Berkeley: University of California Press.

Abun-Nasr, J. M. (2007). *Muslim communities of grace: The Sufi brotherhoods in Islamic religious life.* New York: Columbia University Press.

Adams, R. M. (2001). Scale and complexity in archaic states. *Latin American Antiquity 11,* 188.

adherents.com.

Aguirre Beltrán, G. (1974). Applied anthropology in Mexico. *Human Organization 33* (1), 1–6.

Alfonso-Durraty, M. (2012). Personal communication.

Allen, J. S., & Cheer, S. M. (1996). The non-thrifty genotype. *Current Anthropology 37,* 831–842.

Allen, T. (2006). *Trial justice: The International Criminal Court and the Lord's Resistance Army.* London & New York: Zed Books/International African Institute.

Alvard, M. S., & Kuznar, L. (2001). Deferred harvest: The transition from hunting to animal husbandry. *American Anthropologist 103* (2), 295–311.

Amábile-Cuevas, C. F., & Chicurel, M. E. (1993). Horizontal gene transfer. *American Scientist 81,* 338.

Ambrose, S. H. (2001). Paleolithic technology and human evolution. *Science 291,* 1748–1753.

American Anthropological Association. (1998). Statement on "race." www.aaanet.org/stmts/racepp. htm (retrieved August 1, 2012)

American Anthropological Association. (2007). Executive board statement on the Human Terrain System Project. www.aaanet.org/about/ policies/statements/human-terrain-system-statement.cfm

Amnesty International. (2010, August 16). Afghan couple stoned to death by Taleban. www.amnesty.org/ en/news-and-updates/afghan-couple-stoned-death-taleban-2010-08-16 (retrieved October 6, 2012)

Amnesty International. (2012). Death penalty in 2011. www.amnesty.org/en/ death-penalty (retrieved September 5, 2012)

Anderson, M. S. (2006). *The Allied Tribes Tsimshian of north coastal British Columbia: Social organization, economy and trade.* Unpublished PhD dissertation. http://faculty.arts.ubc.ca/menzies/ documents/anderson.pdf

Andrews, L. B., & Nelkin, D. (1996). The Bell Curve: A statement. *Science 271,* 13.

Anjum, T. (2006). Sufism in history and its relationship with power. *Islamic Studies 45* (2), 221–268.

Appadurai, A. (1990). Disjuncture and difference in the global cultural economy. *Public Culture 2,* 1–24.

Appadurai, A. (1996). *Modernity at large: Cultural dimensions of globalization.* Minneapolis: University of Minnesota Press.

Arctic Monitoring Assessment Project. (2003). *AMAP assessment 2002: Human health in the Arctic* (pp. xii–xiii, 22–23). Oslo: AMAP.

Arms Control Association. (2012). Nuclear weapons: Who has what at a glance. www.armscontrol.org/fact-sheets/Nuclearweaponswhohaswhat (retrieved October 1, 2012)

Arnold, F., Kishor, S., & Roy, T. K. (2002). Sex-selective abortions in India. *Population and Development Review 28* (4), 759–785.

Aureli, F., & de Waal, F. B. M. (2000). *Natural conflict resolution.* Berkeley: University of California Press.

Ayalon, D. (1999). *Eunuchs, caliphs, and sultans: A study in power relationships.* Jerusalem: Mangess Press.

Babiker, M. A., et al. (1996). Unnecessary deprivation of common food items in glucose-6-phosphate dehydrogenase deficiency. *Annals of Saudi Arabia 16* (4), 462–463.

Bailey, R. C., & Aunger, R. (1989). Net hunters vs. archers: Variations in women's subsistence strategies in the Ituri forest. *Human Ecology 17,* 273–297.

Baker, P. (Ed.). (1978). *The biology of high altitude peoples.* London: Cambridge University Press.

Balikci, A. (1970). *The Netsilik Eskimo.* Garden City, NY: Natural History Press.

Balter, M. (1998). Why settle down? The mystery of communities. *Science 282,* 1442–1444.

Balter, M. (1999). A long season puts Çatalhöyük in context. *Science 286,* 890–891.

Balter, M. (2001). In search of the first Europeans. *Science 291,* 1724.

Balter, M. (2001a). Did plaster hold Neolithic society together? *Science 294,* 2278–2281.

Balzer, M. M. (1981). Rituals of gender identity: Markers of Siberian Khanty ethnicity, status, and belief. *American Anthropologist 83* (4), 850–867.

Barkai, R., & Liran, R. (2008). Midsummer sunset at Neolithic Jericho. *Time and Mind: The Journal of Archaeology, Consciousness, and Culture 1* (3), 273–284.

Barnouw, V. (1985). *Culture and personality* (4th ed.). Homewood, IL: Dorsey Press.

Barr, R. G. (1997, October). The crying game. *Natural History,* 47.

Barrett, L., et al. (2004). Habitual cave use and thermoregulation in chacma baboons (*Papio hamadryas ursinus*). *Journal of Human Evolution 46* (2), 215–222.

"Bartered brides." (2009, March 12). *Economist.* www.economist.com/ node/13278577 (retrieved October 31, 2012)

Barth, F. (1962). Nomadism in the mountain and plateau areas of South West Asia. *The problems of the arid zone* (pp. 341–355). Paris: UNESCO.

Basel Action Network. (2010). Country status: Waste trade ban agreements. http://ban.org/country_status/ country_status_chart.html (retrieved November 3, 2012)

Bates, D. G. (2001). *Human adaptive strategies: Ecology, culture, and politics* (2nd ed.). Boston: Allen & Bacon.

Bateson, G., & Mead, M. (1942). *Balinese character: A photographic analysis.* New York: New York Academy of Sciences.

Becker, J. (2004, March). China's growing pains. *National Geographic,* 68–95.

Beeman, W. O. (2000). Introduction: Margaret Mead, cultural studies, and international understanding. In M. Mead & R. Métraux (Eds.), *The study of culture at a distance* (pp. xiv–xxxi). New York & Oxford, UK: Berghahn Books.

Behrend, H. (1999). *Alice Lakwena and the Holy Spirits: War in northern Uganda 1986–97.* Oxford, UK: James Currey.

Behringer, W. (2004). *Witches and witch-hunts: A global history.* Cambridge, UK: Polity Press.

Bekoff, M., et al. (Eds.). (2002). *The cognitive animal: Empirical and theoretical perspectives on animal cognition.* Cambridge, MA: MIT Press.

Benedict, R. (1934). *Patterns of culture.* Boston: Houghton Mifflin.

Bennett, R. L., et al. (2002, April). Genetic counseling and screening of consanguineous couples and their offspring: Recommendations of the National Society of Genetic Counselors. *Journal of Genetic Counseling 11* (2), 97–119.

Bernard, H. R. (2006). *Research methods in anthropology: Qualitative and quantitative approaches* (4th ed.). Walnut Creek, CA: AltaMira Press.

Betzig, L. (1989). Causes of conjugal dissolution: A cross-cultural study. *Current Anthropology 30,* 654–676.

Birch, E. L., & Wachter, S. M. (Eds.). (2011). *Global urbanization.* Philadelphia: University of Pennsylvania Press.

Birdsell, J. H. (1977). The recalibration of a paradigm for the first peopling of Greater Australia. In J. Allen, J. Golson, & R. Jones (Eds.), *Sunda and Sahul: Prehistoric studies in Southeast Asia, Melanesia, and Australia* (pp. 113–167). New York: Academic Press.

Blackless, M., et al. (2000). How sexually dimorphic are we? Review and synthesis. *American Journal of Human Biology 12,* 151–166.

Blacksmith, N., & Harter, J. (2011, October 28). Majority of American workers not engaged in their jobs. *Gallup Wellbeing.* www.gallup.com/poll/150383/Majority-American-Workers-Not-Engaged-Jobs.aspx (retrieved October 1, 2012)

Blakey, M. (2003, October 29). Personal communication. *African Burial Ground Project.* Department of Anthropology, College of William & Mary.

Blakey, M. (2010, May). African Burial Ground Project: Paradigm for cooperation? *Museum International 62* (1-2), 61–68.

Blok, A. (1974). *The mafia of a Sicilian village 1860–1960.* New York: Harper & Row.

Blok, A. (1981). Rams and billy-goats: A key to the Mediterranean code of honour. *Man, New Series 16* (3), 427–440.

Blom, A., et al. (2004). Behavioral responses of gorillas to habituation in the Dzanga-Ndoki National Park, Central African Republic. *International Journal of Primatology 25,* 179–196.

Blumberg, R. L. (1991). *Gender, family, and the economy: The triple overlap.* Newbury Park, CA: Sage.

Blumenbach, J. F. (1795). *On the natural variety of mankind.* Germany: University of Göttingen.

Boas, F. (1909, May 28). Race problems in America. *Science 29* (752), 839–849.

Bodley, J. H. (2007). *Anthropology and contemporary human problems* (5th ed.). Lanham, MD: AltaMira Press.

Bodley, J. H. (2008). *Victims of progress* (5th ed.). Lanham, MD: AltaMira Press.

Boehm, C. (1987). *Blood revenge.* Philadelphia: University of Pennsylvania Press.

Boehm, C. (2000). The evolution of moral communities. *School of American Research, 2000 Annual Report,* 7.

Bogucki, P. (1999). *The origins of human society.* Oxford, UK: Blackwell Press.

Bongaarts, J. (1998). Demographic consequences of declining fertility. *Science 182,* 419.

Boshara, R. (2003, January/February). Wealth inequality: The $6,000 solution. *Atlantic Monthly 291,* 91.

Boškovic, A. (Ed.). (2009). *Other people's anthropologies: Ethnographic practice on the margins.* Oxford, UK: Berghahn Books.

Brace, C. L. (2000). *Evolution in an anthropological view.* Walnut Creek, CA: AltaMira Press.

Bradford, P. V., & Blume, H. (1992). *Ota Benga: The Pygmy in the zoo.* New York: St. Martin's Press.

Braudel, F. (1979). *The structures of everyday life: Civilization and capitalism 15th–18th century* (vol. 1, pp. 163–167). New York: Harper & Row.

Brettell, C. B., & Sargent, C. F. (Eds.). (2000). *Gender in cross-cultural perspective* (3rd ed.). Upper Saddle River, NJ: Prentice-Hall.

Brody, H. (1981). *Maps and dreams.* New York: Pantheon.

Broecker, W. S. (1992, April). Global warming on trial. *Natural History,* 14.

Brunet, M., et al. (2002). A new hominid from the Upper Miocene of Chad, Central Africa. *Nature 418,* 145–151.

Buck, P. H. (1938). *Vikings of the Pacific.* Chicago: University Press of Chicago.

Capps, R., McCabe, K., & Fix, M. (2012). *Diverse streams: Black African migration to the United States.* Washington, DC: Migration Policy Institute. www.migrationpolicy.org/pubs/CBI-AfricanMigration.pdf (retrieved September 30, 2012)

Carbonell, E., et al. (2008). The first hominin of Europe. *Nature 452* (7186), 465–469.

Cardarelli, F. (2003). *Encyclopedia of scientific units, weights, and measures. Their SI equivalences and origins.* London: Springer.

Carneiro, R. L. (1970). A theory of the origin of the state. *Science 169,* 733–738.

Carneiro, R. L. (2003). *Evolutionism in cultural anthropology: A critical history.* Boulder, CO: Westview Press.

Caroulis, J. (1996). Food for thought. *Pennsylvania Gazette 95* (3), 16.

Carpenter, E. S. (1959). *Eskimo.* Toronto: University of Toronto Press.

Carpenter, E. S. (1968). We wed ourselves to the mystery: A study of tribal art. *Explorations 22,* 66–74.

Carroll, J. B. (Ed.). (1956). *Language, thought and reality: Selected writings of Benjamin Lee Whorf.* Cambridge, MA: MIT Press.

Cartmill, E. A., & Byrne, R. W. (2010) Semantics of orangutan gesture: Determining structure and meaning through form and use. *Animal Cognition.* doi: 10.1007/s10071-010-0328-7

Cartmill, M. (1998). The gift of gab. *Discover 19* (11), 64.

Carpenter, E. S. (1959). *Eskimo.* Toronto: University of Toronto Press.

Carpenter, E. S. (1968). We wed ourselves to the mystery: A study of tribal art. *Explorations 22,* 66–74.

Cashdan, E. (2008). Waist-to-hip ratio across cultures: Trade-offs between androgen- and estrogen-dependent traits. *Current Anthropology 49* (6).

Catford, J. C. (1988). *A practical introduction to phonetics.* Oxford, UK: Clarendon Press.

Centers for Disease Control and Prevention. (2012). Overweight and obesity. www.cdc.gov/obesity/index.html (retrieved November 8, 2012)

Chagnon, N. A. (1988a). Life histories, blood revenge, and warfare in a tribal population. *Science 239,* 935–992.

Chagnon, N. A. (1988b). *Yanomamö: The fierce people* (3rd ed.). New York: Holt, Rinehart & Winston.

Chagnon, N. A. (1990). On Yanomamö violence: Reply to Albert. *Current Anthropology 31* (2), 49–53.

Chambers, R. (1995). *Rural development: Putting the last first.* Englewood Cliffs, NJ: Prentice-Hall.

Chan, J. W. C., & Vernon, P. E. (1988). Individual differences among the peoples of China. In J. W. Berry (Ed.), *Human abilities in cultural context* (pp. 340–357). Cambridge, UK: Cambridge University Press.

Chance, N. A. (1990). *The Iñupiat and Arctic Alaska: An ethnography of development.* New York: Harcourt.

Chang, L. (2005, June 9). A migrant worker sees rural home in new light. *Wall Street Journal.*

Chase, C. (1998). Hermaphrodites with attitude. *Gay and Lesbian Quarterly 4* (2), 189–211.

Chatty, D. (1996). *Mobile pastoralists: Development planning and social change in Oman.* New York: Columbia University Press.

Chicurel, M. (2001). Can organisms speed their own evolution? *Science 292,* 1824–1827.

"Child soldiers global report 2008." (2009). Despite progress, efforts to end the recruitment and use of child soldiers are too little and too late for many children. www.childsoldiersglobalreport.org/ (retrieved August 28, 2012)

"China to execute bride traffickers." (2000, October 20). *BBC News*.http://news.bbc.co.uk/2/hi/asia-pacific/981675.stm (retrieved October 31, 2012)

Claeson, B. (1994). The privatization of justice: An ethnography of control. In L. Nader (Ed.), *Essays on controlling processes* (pp. 32–64). *Kroeber Anthropological Society Papers* (no. 77). Berkeley: University of California Press.

Clark, E. E. (1966). *Indian legends of the Pacific Northwest.* Berkeley: University of California Press.

Clark, G. A. (2002). Neandertal archaeology: Implications for our origins. *American Anthropologist 104* (1), 50–67.

Clarke, R. J., & Tobias, P. V. (1995). Sterkfontein Member 2 foot bones of the oldest South African hominid. *Science 269,* 521–524.

Clay, J. W. (1996). What's a nation? In W. A. Haviland & R. J. Gordon (Eds.), *Talking about people* (2nd ed., pp. 188–189). Mountain View, CA: Mayfield.

Coco, L. E. (1994). Silicone breast implants in America: A choice of the official breast? In L. Nader (Ed.), *Essays on controlling processes* (pp. 103–132). *Kroeber Anthropological Society Papers* (no. 77). Berkeley: University of California Press.

Coe, S. D., & Coe, M. D. (1996). *The true history of chocolate.* New York: Thames & Hudson.

Cohen, J. (1997). Is an old virus up to new tricks? *Science 277,* 312–313.

Cohen, J. (2009). Out of Mexico? Scientists ponder swine flu's origin. *Science 324* (5928), 700–702.

Cohen, M. N., & Armelagos, G. J. (1984a). *Paleopathology at the origins of agriculture.* Orlando: Academic Press.

Cohen, M. N., & Armelagos, G. J. (1984b). Paleopathology at the origins of agriculture: Editors' summation. In *Paleopathology at the origins of agriculture.* Orlando: Academic Press.

Colborn, T., Dumanoski, D., & Myers, J. P. (1996). Hormonal sabotage. *Natural History 3,* 45–46.

Colborn, T., Dumanoski, D., & Myers, J. P. (1997). *Our stolen future.* New York: Plume/Penguin Books.

Cole, J. W., & Wolf, E. R. (1999). *The hidden frontier: Ecology and ethnicity in an alpine valley* (with a new introduction). Berkeley: University of California Press.

Collier, J., & Collier, M. (1986). *Visual anthropology: Photography as a research method.* Albuquerque: University of New Mexico Press.

Collins, B. (2005). *The trouble with poetry.* New York: Random House.

Conard, N. J. (2009). A female figurine from the basal Aurignacian deposits of Hohle Fels Cave in southwestern Germany. *Nature 459* (7244), 248.

Cone, M. (2005). *Silent snow: The slow poisoning of the Arctic.* New York: Grove Press.

Conklin, B. (1997). Body paint, feathers, and VCRs: Aesthetics and authenticity in Amazonian activism. *American Ethnologist 24* (4), 711–737.

Conklin, B. A. (2002). Shamans versus pirates in the Amazonian treasure chest. *American Anthropologist 104* (4), 1050–1061.

Conklin, H. C. (1955). Hanunóo color categories. *Southwestern Journal of Anthropology 11,* 339–344.

Connelly, J. C. (1979). Hopi social organization. In A. Ortiz (Ed.), *Handbook of North American Indians: Southwest* (vol. 9, pp. 539–553). Washington, DC: Smithsonian Institution.

Coon, C. S. (1954). *The story of man.* New York: Knopf.

Coon, C. S. (1958). *Caravan: The story of the Middle East.* New York: Holt, Rinehart & Winston.

Coon, C. S. (1962). *The origins of races.* New York: Knopf.

Copeland, S. R., et al. (2011, June 2). Strontium isotope evidence for landscape use by early hominins. *Nature 474,* 76–78. doi: 10.1038/nature10149

Coppa, A., et al. (2006). Early Neolithic tradition of dentistry. *Nature 440,* 755–756.

Crane, H. (2001). *Men in spirit: The masculinization of Taiwanese Buddhist nuns.* PhD dissertation, Brown University.

Cretney, S. (2003). *Family law in the twentieth century: A history.* New York: Oxford University Press.

Criminal Code of Canada, § 718.2(e).

Crocker, W. A., & Crocker, J. (2004). *The Canela: Kinship, ritual, and sex in an Amazonian tribe.* Belmont, CA: Wadsworth.

Crystal, D. (2002). *Language death.* Cambridge, UK: Cambridge University Press.

Culotta, E., & Koshland, D. E., Jr. (1994). DNA repair works its way to the top. *Science 266,* 1926.

D'Adesky, A.-C. (2004). *Moving mountains: the race to treat global AIDS.* New York: Verso.

Dalton, R. (2009). Fossil primate challenges Ida's place: Controversial German specimen is related to lemurs, not humans, analysis of an Egyptian find suggests. *Nature 461,* 1040.

Darwin, C. (1859). *On the origin of species.* New York: Atheneum.

Darwin, C. (1871). *The descent of man and selection in relation to sex.* New York: Random House (Modern Library).

Darwin, C. (1887). *Autobiography.* Reprinted in *The life and letters of Charles Darwin* (1902). F. Darwin (Ed.), London: John Murray.

Davies, G. (2005). *A history of money from the earliest times to present day* (3rd ed.). Cardiff, UK: University of Wales Press.

Davies, S. G. (2007). *Challenging gender norms: Five genders among the Bugis in Indonesia.* Belmont, CA: Thomson Wadsworth.

Deetz, J. (1977). *In small things forgotten: The archaeology of early American life.* Garden City, NY: Doubleday/Anchor.

de la Torre, S., & Snowden, C. T. (2009). Dialects in pygmy marmosets? Population variation in call structure. *American Journal of Primatology 71* (5), 333–342.

del Carmen Rodríguez Martínez, M., et al. (2006). Oldest writing in the New World. *Science 313* (5793), 1610–1614.

del Castillo, B. D. (1963). *The conquest of New Spain* (translation and introduction by J. M. Cohen). New York: Penguin Books.

Delio, M. (2004). Global chaos, just for fun. *Wired.* www.wired.com/culture/lifestyle/news/2004/06/63872 (retrieved October 1, 2012)

DeMello, M. (2000). *Bodies of inscription: A cultural history of the modern tattoo community.* Durham, NC: Duke University Press.

DeSilva, J. M. (2009). Functional morphology of the ankle and the likelihood of climbing in early hominins. *Proceeding of the National Academy of Sciences, USA 106,* 6567–6572.

Dettwyler, K. A. (1994). *Dancing skeletons: Life and death in West Africa.* Prospect Heights, IL: Waveland Press.

Dettwyler, K. A. (1997, October). When to wean. *Natural History,* 49.

de Waal, F. B. M. (2000). Primates: A natural heritage of conflict resolution. *Science 28,* 586–590.

de Waal, F. B. M. (2001). Sing the song of evolution. *Natural History 110* (8), 77.

de Waal, F. B. M., Kano, T., & Parish, A. R. (1998). Comments. *Current Anthropology 39,* 408, 413.

Diamond, J. (1996). Empire of uniformity. *Discover 17* (3), 83–84.

Diamond, J. (1997). *Guns, germs, and steel.* New York: Norton.

Diamond, J. (1998). Ants, crops, and history. *Science 281,* 1974–1975.

Diamond, J. (2005). *Collapse: How societies choose to fail or succeed.* New York: Viking/Penguin Books.

Dissanayake, E. (2000). Birth of the arts. *Natural History 109* (10), 89.

Dorit, R. (1997). Molecular evolution and scientific inquiry, misperceived. *American Scientist 85,* 475.

Douglas, M. (1966). *Purity and danger: An analysis of concepts of pollution and taboo.* London: Routledge & Kegan Paul.

Dreger, A. D. (1998, May/June). "Ambiguous sex" or ambivalent medicine? *Hastings Center Report 28* (3), 2435. http://alicedreger.com/ambivalent_medicine_files/Dreger%20HCR%201998%20Ambiguous%20Sex.pdf

Dunbar, P. (2008, January 19). The pink vigilantes: The Indian women fighting for women's rights. *Mail Online.* www.dailymail.co.uk/news/article-509318/The-pink-vigilantes-The-Indian-women-fighting-womens-rights.html (retrieved August 26, 2012)

Dunham, S. A. (2009). *Surviving against the odds: Village industry in Indonesia.* Durham, NC: Duke University Press.

Durant, J. C. (2000, April 23). Everybody into the gene pool. *New York Times Book Review,* 11.

"Eating disorders (most recent) by country." (2004). *Nationmaster.com.* www.nationmaster.com/graph/mor_eat_dis-mortality-eating-disorders (retrieved August 1, 2012)

Eaton, S. B., Konner, M., & Shostak, M. (1988). Stone-agers in the fast lane: Chronic degenerative diseases in evolutionary perspective. *American Journal of Medicine 84* (4), 739–749.

Egan, T. (1999, February 28). The persistence of polygamy. *New York Times Magazine,* 52.

Ehrenberg, R. (2011, September 24). Financial world dominated by a few deep pockets. *Science News 180* (7). 13. www.sciencenews.org (retrieved October 1, 2012)

Ehrlich, P. R., & Ehrlich, A. H. (2008). *The dominant animal: Human evolution and the environment.* Washington, DC: Island Press.

El Guindi, F. (2004). *Visual anthropology: Essential method and theory.* Walnut Creek, CA: AltaMira Press.

Ellison, P. T. (2003). *On fertile ground: A natural history of human reproduction.* Cambridge, MA: Harvard University Press.

Embree, J. F. (1951). Raymond Kennedy, 1906–50. *Far Eastern Quarterly 10* (2), 170–172.

Erickson, C. L. (2001). Pre-Columbian Fish Farming in the Amazon. *Expedition 43* (3), 7–8.

Erickson, P. A., & Murphy, L. D. (2003). *A history of anthropological theory* (2nd ed.). Peterborough, Ontario: Broadview Press.

Errington, F. K., & Gewertz, D. B. (2001). *Cultural alternatives and a feminist anthropology: An analysis of culturally constructed gender interests in Papua New Guinea.* Cambridge, UK, & New York: Cambridge University Press.

Esber, G. S., Jr. (1987). Designing Apache houses with Apaches. In R. M. Wulff & S. J. Fiske (Eds.), *Anthropological praxis: Translating knowledge into action* (pp. 187–196). Boulder, CO: Westview Press.

Estado Plurinacional de Bolivia. (2010). *Anteproyecto de Ley de la Madre Tierra por las Organizaciones Sociales del Pacto de Unidad.* www.redunitas .org/NINA_Anteproyectode%20 ley%20madre%20tierra.pdf (retrieved September 23, 2012)

Evans-Pritchard, E. E. (1937). *Witchcraft, oracles, and magic among the Azande.* London: Oxford University Press.

Evans-Pritchard, E. E. (1951). *Kinship and marriage among the Nuer.* New York: Oxford University Press.

Fagan, B. M. (1995). *People of the earth* (8th ed., p. 19). New York: HarperCollins.

Farmer, P. (1996). On suffering and structural violence: A view from below. *Daedalus 125* (1), 261–283.

Farmer, P. (2001). *Infections and inequalities: The modern plagues.* Berkeley: University of California Press.

Farmer, P. (2004, June). An anthropology of structural violence. *Current Anthropology 45,* 3.

Fausto-Sterling, A. (1993, March/April). The five sexes: Why male and female are not enough. *The Sciences 33* (2), 20–24.

Fausto-Sterling, A. (2003, August 2). Personal e-mail communication.

Fausto-Sterling, A., et al. (2000). How sexually dimorphic are we? Review and synthesis. *American Journal of Human Biology 12,* 151–166.

Fedigan, L. M. (1986). The changing role of women in models of human evolution. *Annual Review of Anthropology 15,* 25–56.

Fedigan, L. M. (1992). *Primate paradigms: Sex roles and social bonds.* Chicago: University of Chicago Press.

Fernandez-Carriba, S., & Loeches, A. (2001). Fruit smearing by captive chimpanzees: A newly observed food-processing behavior. *Current Anthropology 42,* 143–147.

Fernández Olmos, M., & Paravisini-Gebert, L. (2003). *Creole religion of the Caribbean: An introduction from Vodou and Santeria to Obeah and Espiritismo.* New York: New York University Press.

Ferrie, H. (1997). An interview with C. Loring Brace. *Current Anthropology 38,* 851–869.

Field, L. W. (2004). Beyond "applied" anthropology. In T. Biolsi (Ed.), *A companion to the anthropology of American Indians* (pp. 472–479). Oxford, UK: Blackwell Press.

Finnström, S. (2008). *Living with bad surroundings: War, history, and everyday moments in northern Uganda.* Durham, NC: Duke University Press.

Fisher, R., & Ury, W. L. (1991). *Getting to yes: Negotiating agreement without giving in* (2nd ed.). Boston: Houghton Mifflin.

Fogel, R., & Riquelme, M. A. (2005). *Enclave sojero. Merma de soberania y pobreza.* Asuncion: Centro de Estudios Rurales Interdisciplinarias.

Folger, T. (1993). The naked and the bipedal. *Discover 14* (11), 34–35.

Food and Agriculture Organization of the United Nations. (2009, June 19). 1.02 billion people hungry: One sixth of humanity undernourished—more than ever before. www.fao.org/news/story/en/ item/20568/icode/ (retrieved October 3, 2012)

Ford, A. The BRASS/El Pilar Program. www.marc.ucsb.edu/elpilar/ (retrieved October 3, 2012)

Forde, C. D. (1968). Double descent among the Yakö. In P. Bohannan & J. Middleton (Eds.), *Kinship and social organization* (pp. 179–191). Garden City, NY: Natural History Press.

Forste, R. (2008). *Prelude to marriage, or alternative to marriage? A social demographic look at cohabitation in the U.S.* Working paper. Social Science Electronic Publishing. http://papers.ssrn.com/ sol3/papers.cfm?abstract_id=269172 (retrieved August 18, 2012)

Fouts, R. S., & Waters, G. (2001). Chimpanzee sign language and Darwinian continuity: Evidence for a neurology continuity of language. *Neurological Research 23,* 787–794.

Fowke, K. R., Nagelkerke, N. J., Kimani, J., Simonsen, J. N., Anzala, A. O., Bwayo, J. J., MacDonald, K. S., Ngugi, E. N., & Plummer, F. A. (1996). Resistance to HIV-1 infection among persistently seronegative prostitutes in Nairobi, Kenya. *Lancet 348* (9038), 1347–1351.

Fox, R. (1968). *Encounter with anthropology.* New York: Dell.

Fox, R. (1981, December 3). [Interview]. Coast Telecourses, Inc., Los Angeles.

Franzen, J. L., et al. (2009). Complete primate skeleton from the middle Eocene of Messel in Germany: Morphology and paleobiology. *PLoS One 4* (5), e5723.

Frisch, R. (2002). *Female fertility and the body fat connection.* Chicago: University of Chicago Press.

Gandhi, M. K. (Ed.). (1999). *The collected works of Mahatma Gandhi* (vols. 8 & 19). New Delhi: Publications Division, Government of India.

Gebo, D. L., Dagosto, D., Beard, K. C., & Tao, Q. (2001). Middle Eocene primate tarsals from China: Implications for haplorhine evolution. *American Journal of Physical Anthropology 116,* 83–107.

Geertz, C. (1973). *The interpretation of culture.* London: Hutchinson.

"Gene study suggests Polynesians came from Taiwan." (2005, July 4). Reuters.

Gero, J. M., & Conkey, M. W. (Eds.). (1991). *Engendered archaeology: Women and prehistory.* New York: Wiley-Blackwell.

Gibbons, A. (1993). Where are new diseases born? *Science 261,* 680–681.

Gibbons, A. (1997). Ideas on human origins evolve at anthropology gathering. *Science 276,* 535–536.

Gibbons, A. (1998). Ancient island tools suggest *Homo erectus* was a seafarer. *Science 279,* 1635.

Gibbons, A. (2001). The riddle of coexistence. *Science 291,* 1726.

Gibbons, A. (2001a). Studying humans—and their cousins and parasites. *Science 292,* 627.

Gibbs, J. L., Jr. (1983). [Interview]. *Faces of culture: Program 18.* Fountain Valley, CA: Coast Telecourses.

Ginsburg, F. D., Abu-Lughod, L., & Larkin, B. (Eds.). (2009). *Media worlds: Anthropology on new terrain.* Berkeley: University of California Press.

Gladney, D. C. (2004). *Dislocating China: Muslims, minorities and other subaltern subjects.* London: Hurst.

Gladstone, R. (2012, August 27). China: 2 Tibetan teenagers set themselves on fire. *nytimes.com.* www.nytimes .com/2012/08/28/world/asia/2-tibetan-teenagers-set-themselves-on-fire-in-china.html (retrieved September 21, 2012)

"Global 500: Our annual ranking of the world's largest corporations." (2012). *CNN Money.* http:// money.cnn.com/magazines/fortune/ global500/2012/full_list/index.html (retrieved October 1, 2012)

Goldsmith, M. L. (2005). Habituating primates for field study: Ethical considerations for great apes. In T. Turner (Ed.), *Biological anthropology and ethics: From repatriation to genetic identity* (pp. 49–64). New York: SUNY Press.

Goldsmith, M. L., Glick, J., & Ngabirano, E. (2006). Gorillas living on the edge: Literally and figuratively. In N. E. Newton-Fisher, et al. (Eds.), *Primates of western Uganda* (pp. 405–422). New York: Springer.

González, R. J. (2009). *American counterinsurgency: Human science and the human terrain.* Chicago: University of Chicago Press.

Goodall, J. (1986). *The chimpanzees of Gombe: Patterns of behavior.* Cambridge, MA: Belknap Press.

Goodall, J. (1990). *Through a window: My thirty years with the chimpanzees of Gombe.* Boston: Houghton Mifflin.

Goodenough, W. H. (1970). *Description and comparison in cultural anthropology.* Chicago: Aldine.

Goodman, M., et al. (1994). Molecular evidence on primate phylogeny from DNA sequences. *American Journal of Physical Anthropology 94,* 7.

Goodwin, R. (1999). *Personal relationships across cultures.* New York: Routledge.

Gordon, R. (2000). *Eating disorders: Anatomy of a social epidemic* (2nd ed.). New York: Wiley-Blackwell.

Gordon, R., Lyons, H., & Lyons, A. (Eds.). (2010). *Fifty key anthropologists.* New York: Routledge.

Gottlieb, A. (2003). *The afterlife is where we come from: The culture of infancy in West Africa.* Chicago: University of Chicago Press.

Gottlieb, A. (2004). Babies as ancestors, babies as spirits: The culture of infancy in West Africa. *Expedition 46* (3), 13–21.

Gottlieb, A. (2005). Non-Western approaches to spiritual development among infants and young children: A case study from West Africa. In P. L. Benson et al. (Eds.), *The handbook of spiritual development in childhood and adolescence* (pp. 150–162). Thousand Oaks, CA: Sage.

Gough, K. (1959). The Nayars and the definition of marriage. *Journal of the Royal Anthropological Institute of Great Britain and Ireland 89,* 23–34.

Gould, S. J. (1983). *Hen's teeth and horses' toes.* New York: Norton.

Gould, S. J. (1989). *Wonderful life.* New York: Norton.

Gould, S. J. (1991). *Bully for brontosaurus.* New York: Norton.

Gould, S. J. (1991a). *The flamingo's smile: Reflections in natural history.* New York: Norton.

Gould, S. J. (1994). The geometer of race. *Discover 15* (11), 65–69.

Gould, S. J. (2000). The narthex of San Marco and the pangenetic paradigm. *Natural History 109* (6), 29.

Grant, M. (1916). The passing of the great race. New York: Scribner.

Gray, P. B. (2004, May). HIV and Islam: Is HIV prevalence lower among Muslims? *Social Science & Medicine 58* (9), 1751–1756.

Gray, P. M., et al. (2001). The music of nature and the nature of music. *Science 291*, 52.

Green, R. E., et al. (2010, May 7). A draft sequence of the Neandertal genome. *Science 328* (5979), 710–722.

Greymorning, S. N. (2001). Reflections on the Arapaho Language Project or, when Bambi spoke Arapaho and other tales of Arapaho language revitalization efforts. In K. Hale & L. Hinton, *The green book of language revitalization in practice* (pp. 287–297). New York: Academic Press.

Griffin, D., & Fitzpatrick, D. (2009, September 1). Donor says he got thousands for his kidney. *CNNWorld.com.* http://articles.cnn.com/2009-09-01/world/blackmarket.organs_1_kidney-transplants-kidney-donor-kidney-specialist?_s=PM:WORLD (retrieved June 10, 2012)

Grivetti, L. E. (2005). From aphrodisiac to health food: A cultural history of chocolate. *Karger Gazette* (68).

Guillette, E. A., et al. (1998, June). An anthropological approach to the evaluation of preschool children exposed to pesticides in Mexico. *Environmental Health Perspectives 106*, 347.

Gurchiek, K. (2012). Survey finds significant erosion in engagement around the world. *Society for Human Resource Management.* www.weknownext.com/workforce/survey-finds-significant-erosion-in-engagement-around-globe (retrieved October 1, 2012)

Haglund, W. D., Conner, M., & Scott, D. D. (2001). The archaeology of contemporary mass graves. *Historical Archaeology 35* (1), 57–69.

Hahn, R. A. (1992). The state of federal health statistics on racial and ethnic groups. *Journal of the American Medical Association 267* (2), 268–271.

Hale, C. (2004). *Himmler's crusade: The true story of the 1938 Nazi expedition into Tibet.* New York: Bantam.

Hall, E. T. (1963). A system for the notation of proxemic behavior. *American Anthropologist 65*, 1003–1026.

Hall, E. T. (1990). *The hidden dimension.* New York: Anchor.

Handwerk, B. (2005, March 8). King Tut not murdered violently, CT scans show. *National Geographic News*, 2.

Hanson, A. (1989). The making of the Maori: Culture invention and its logic. *American Anthropologist 91* (4), 890–902.

Harcourt-Smith, W. E. H., & Aiello, L. C. (2004). Fossils, feet and the evolution of human bipedal locomotion. *Journal of Anatomy 204*, 412.

Harding, S. F. (2001). *The book of Jerry Falwell: Fundamentalist language and politics.* Princeton, NJ: Princeton University Press.

Hare, B., Brown, M., Williamson, C., & Tomasello, M. (2002). The domestication of social cognition in dogs. *Science 298* (5598). 1634–1636.

Harner, M. J. (Ed.). (1973). *Hallucinogens and shamanism.* New York: Oxford University Press.

Harner, M. J. (1980). *The way of the shaman: A guide to power and healing.* San Francisco: Harper & Row.

Harner, M. J. (1984). *The Jivaro: People of the sacred waterfalls.* Berkeley: University of California Press.

Harner, M. J. (2013). *Cave and cosmos: Shamanic encounters with spirits and heavens.* Berkeley: North Atlantic Books.

Harner, M. J., & Harner, S. (2000). Core practices in the shamanic treatment of illness. *Shamanism 13* (1&2), 19–30.

Harpending, H., & Cochran, G. (2002). In our genes. *Proceedings of the National Academy of Sciences, USA 99* (1), 10–12.

Harris, M. (1979). *Cultural materialism: The struggle for a science of culture.* New York: Random House.

Harris, M. (1989). *Cows, pigs, wars, and witches: The riddles of culture.* New York: Vintage/Random House.

Harrison, K. D. (2002). Naming practices and ethnic identity in Tuva. *Proceedings of the Chicago Linguistics Society 35* (2).

Hart, D. (2006, April 21). Humans as prey. *Chronicle of Higher Education.*

Hart, D., & Sussman, R. W. (2005). *Man the hunted: Primates, predators, and human evolution.* Boulder, CO: Westview Press.

Harvey, F. (2012, September 24). Trafigura lessons have not been learned, report warns. *The Guardian.* www.guardian.co.uk/environment/2012/sep/25/trafigura-lessons-toxic-waste-dumping (retrieved October 3, 2012)

Hasnain, M. (2005, October 27). Cultural approach to HIV/AIDS harm reduction in Muslim countries. *Harm Reduction Journal 2*, 23.

Haviland, W. A. (2002). Settlement, society and demography at Tikal. In J. Sabloff (Ed.), *Tikal.* Santa Fe: School of American Research.

Haviland, W. A., & Power, M. W. (1994). *The original Vermonters: Native inhabitants, past and present* (2nd ed.). Hanover, NH: University Press of New England.

Hawkes, K., O'Connell, J. F., & Blurton Jones, N. G. (1997). Hadza women's time allocation, offspring, provisioning, and the evolution of long postmenopausal life spans. *Current Anthropology 38*, 551–577.

Hawks, J. (2009). Ankles of the Australopithecines. *John Hawks Weblog.* http://johnhawks.net/weblog/reviews/early_hominids/anatomy/desilva-2009-chimpanzee-climbing-talus.html (retrieved July 5, 2012)

Heita, K. (1999). Imanishi's world view. *Journal of Japanese Trade and Industry 18* (2), 15.

Heitzman, J., & Wordem, R. L. (Eds.). (2006). *India: A country study* (sect. 2, 5th ed.). Washington, DC: Federal Research Division, Library of Congress.

Helman, C. B. (2003). *Culture, health, and illness: An introduction for health professionals.* New York: Butterworth Heinemann Medical.

Henry, S., & Porter, D. (2011, October 27). Levy Izhak Rosenbaum pleads guilty to selling black market kidneys. *Huffingtonpost.com.* www.huffingtonpost.com/2011/10/27/levy-izhak-rosenbaum-plea_n_1035624.html (retrieved June 10, 2012)

Henshilwood, C. S., d'Errico, F., van Niekerk, K. L., Coquinot, Y., Jacobs, Z., Lauritzen, S.-E., Menu, M., & Garcia-Moreno. R. (2011). A 100,000-year-old ochre-processing workshop at Blombos Cave, South Africa. *Science 334* (6053), 219. doi:10.1126/science.1211535

Herdt, G. H. (1993). Semen transactions in Sambia culture. In D. N. Suggs & A. W. Mirade (Eds.), *Culture and human sexuality* (pp. 298–327). Pacific Grove, CA: Brooks/Cole.

Herrnstein, R. J., & Murray, C. (1994). *The bell curve.* New York: Free Press.

Higham, T., et al. (2012). Testing models for the beginnings of the Aurignacian and the advent of figurative art and music: The radiocarbon chronology of Geißenklösterle. *Journal of Human Evolution 62* (6), 664–676.

Himmelfarb, E. J. (2000, January/February). First alphabet found in Egypt. Newsbrief. *Archaeology 53* (1).

Hitchcock, R. K., & Enghoff, M. (2004). *Capacity-building of first people of the Kalahari, Botswana: An evaluation.* Copenhagen: International Work Group for Indigenous Affairs.

"HIV & AIDS information from avert.org." www.avert.org.

Hodgson, A. (2012). Special report: Income inequality rising across the globe. *Euromonitor International.* http://blog.euromonitor.com/2012/03/special-report-income-inequality-rising-across-the-globe.html (retrieved October 1, 2012)

Hole, F., & Heizer, R. F. (1969). *An introduction to prehistoric archeology.* New York: Holt, Rinehart & Winston.

Holmes, L. D. (2000). "Paradise Bent" (film review). *American Anthropologist 102* (3), 604–605.

Horst, H., & Miller, D. (2006). *The cell phone: An anthropology of communication.* New York: Berg.

Hostetler, J. A., & Huntington, G. E. (1992). *Amish children: Education in the family, school, and community* (2nd ed.). New York: Harcourt, Brace & Jovanovich.

Hrdy, S. B. (1999). Body fat and birth control. *Natural History 108* (8), 88.

Hsiaotung, F. (1939). *Peasant life in China.* London: Kegan Paul.

The Hunger Project. (2011). www.thp.org (retrieved October 1, 2012)

Ingmanson, E. J. (1998). Comment. *Current Anthropology 39*, 409.

Inoue, S., & Matsuzawa, T. (2007). Working memory of numerals in chimpanzees. *Current Biology 17*, 23, 1004–1005.

International Telecommunication Union. (2012). 2011 ICT facts and figures. www.itu.int/ITU-D/ict/facts/2011/material/ICTFactsFigures2011.pdf (retrieved June 4, 2012)

Internet World Stats: Usage and Population Statistics. www.internetworldstats.com (retrieved June 4, 2012) "Interview with Laura Nader." (2000, November). *California Monthly.*

Irvine, M. (1999, November 24). Mom-and-pop houses grow rare. *Burlington Free Press.*

Itaborahy, P. L. (2012). State-sponsored homophobia: A world survey of laws criminalising same-sex sexual activity between consenting adults. Brussels: International Lesbian, Gay, Bisexual, Trans and Intersex Association. http://old.ilga.org/Statehomophobia/ILGA_State_Sponsored_Homophobia_2012.pdf

"Italy–German verbal war hots up." (2003, July 9). Reuters. *Deccan Herald.* http://archive.deccanherald.com/deccanherald/july09/f4.asp (retrieved July 31, 2012)

Jacobs, S. E. (1994). Native American two-spirits. *Anthropology Newsletter 35* (8), 7.

Jacoby, R., & Glauberman, N. (Eds.). (1995). *The Bell Curve debate.* New York: Random House.

Jane Goodall Institute. www.janegoodall.org/janes-story (retrieved June 15, 2012)

Johansen, B. E. (2002). The Inuit's struggle with dioxins and other organic pollutants. *American Indian Quarterly 26* (3), 479–490.

Johnson, D. (1991, April 9). Polygamists emerge from secrecy, seeking not just peace but respect. *New York Times*, A22.

Johnson, N. B. (1984). Sex, color, and rites of passage in ethnographic research. *Human Organization 43* (2), 108–120.

Jolly, A. (1991). Thinking like a vervet. *Science 251*, 574.

Jones, S. (2005). Transhumance re-examined. *Journal of the Royal Anthropological Institute 11* (4), 841–842.

Kaiser, J. (1994). A new theory of insect wing origins takes off. *Science 266*, 363.

Kaiser, J. (2011, May 4). 10 billion plus: Why world population projections were too low. *Science Insider.* http://news.sciencemag.org/scienceinsider/2011/05/10-billion-plus-why-world-population.html (retrieved October 1, 2012)

Kaplan, M. (2007, May 31). Upright orangutans point way to walking. Published online: *Nature*, doi:10.1038/news070528–8.

Kaplan, M. (2008, August 5). Almost half of primate species face extinction. *Nature.* doi:10.1038/news.2008.1013 (retrieved June 23, 2012)

Karavanić, I., & Smith, F. H. (2000). More on the Neanderthal problem: The Vindija case. *Current Anthropology 41*, 839.

Kaw, E. (1993). Medicalization of racial features: Asian American women and cosmetic surgery. *Medical Anthropology Quarterly 7* (1), 74–89.

Kay, R. F., Fleagle, J. G., & Simons, E. L. (1981). A revision of the Oligocene apes of the Fayum Province, Egypt. *American Journal of Physical Anthropology 55*, 293–322.

Keesing, R. M. (1992). Some problems in the study of Oceanic religion. *Anthropologica 34* (2), 231–246.

Kehoe, A. (2000). *Shamans and religion: An anthropological exploration in critical thinking.* Prospect Heights, IL: Waveland Press.

Keiser, L. (1991). *Friend by day, enemy by night: Organized vengeance in a Kohistani community.* Fort Worth: Holt, Rinehart & Winston.

Kelly, T. L. (2006). *Sadhus, the great renouncers.* Photography exhibit, Indigo Gallery, Naxal, Kathmandu, Nepal. www.asianart.com/exhibitions/sadhus/index.html (retrieved August 1, 2012)

Kennickell, A. B. (2003, November). *A rolling tide: Changes in the distribution of wealth in the U.S. 1989–2001.* Washington, DC: Federal Reserve Board/Levy Economics Institute.

Kibii, J. M., et al. (2011, September 9). A partial pelvis of *Australopithecus sebida. Science 333* (6048), 1407–1411.

Kidder, T. (2003). *Mountains beyond mountains: The quest of Dr. Paul Farmer, a man who would cure the world.* New York: Random House.

Kilcullen, D. (2007, May 12). Religion and insurgency. *Small Wars Journal.* http://smallwarsjournal.com/blog/religion-and-insurgency (retrieved August 1, 2012)

King, J. (2010, July 28). Reducing the crack and powder cocaine sentencing disparity should also reduce racial disparities in sentences and prisons. *NACDL news release.* www.nacdl.org/newsreleases.aspx?id=19533 (retrieved August 2, 2012)

Kirkpatrick, R. C. (2000). The evolution of human homosexual behavior. *Current Anthropology 41*, 384.

Kitchen, A., Miyamoto, M. M., & Mulligan, C. J. (2008). A three-stage colonization model for the peopling of the Americas. *PLoS One 3* (2), e1596. doi:10.1371/journal.pone.0001596

Kluckhohn, C. (1944). Navajo witchcraft. *Papers of the Peabody Museum of American Archaeology and Ethnology 22* (2).

Knauft, B. (1991). Violence and sociality in human evolution. *Current Anthropology 32*, 391–409.

Knight, C., Studdert-Kennedy, M., & Hurford, J. (Eds.). (2000). *The evolutionary emergence of language: Social function and the origins of linguistic form.* Cambridge, UK: Cambridge University Press.

Koch, G. (1997). Songs, land rights, and archives in Australia. *Cultural Survival Quarterly 20* (4).

Komai, T., & Fukuoka, G. (1934, October). Post-natal growth disparity in monozygotic twins. *Journal of Heredity 25*, 423–430.

Konner, M., & Worthman, C. (1980). Nursing frequency, gonadal function, and birth spacing among !Kung hunter-gatherers. *Science 207*, 788–791.

Kopenawa, D., & Albert, B. (2010). *La chute du ciel: Paroles d'un chaman Yanomami.* Paris: Terre Humaine, Plon.

Krajick, K. (1998). Greenfarming by the Incas? *Science 281*, 323.

Kraybill, D. B. (2001). *The riddle of Amish culture.* Baltimore: Johns Hopkins University Press.

Kruger, J., et al. (2005, December). Egocentrism over e-mail: Can people communicate as well as they think? *Journal of Personality and Social Psychology 89* (6), 925–936.

Kuefler, M. (2007). The marriage revolution in late antiquity: The Theodosian Code and later Roman marriage law. *Journal of Family History 32* (4), 343–370.

Kunzig, R. (1999). A tale of two obsessed archaeologists, one ancient city and nagging doubts about whether science can ever hope to reveal the past. *Discover 20* (5), 84–92.

Kuper, A. (2008). Changing the subject—about cousin marriage, among other things. *Journal of the Royal Anthropological Institute 14* (4), 717–735.

LaFont, S. (Ed.). (2003). *Constructing sexualities: Readings in sexuality, gender, and culture.* Upper Saddle River, NJ: Prentice-Hall.

Lai, C. S. L., et al. (2001). A forkhead-domain gene is mutated in severe speech and language disorder. *Nature 413*, 519–523.

Lakoff, R. T. (2004). *Language and woman's place.* M. Bucholtz (Ed.). New York: Oxford University Press.

Lampl, M., Velhuis, J. D., & Johnson, M. L. (1992). Saltation and stasis: A model of human growth. *Science 258* (5083), 801–803.

Landau, M. (1991). *Narratives of human evolution.* New Haven, CT, and London: Yale University Press.

Lasswell, H. D. (1990). *Politics: Who gets what, when, how.* Gloucester, MA: Peter Smith.

Lawler, A. (2001). Writing gets a rewrite. *Science 292*, 2419.

Leach, E. (1982). *Social anthropology.* Glasgow: Fontana Paperbacks.

Leakey, M. G., Spoor, F., Brown, F. H., Gathogo, P. N., Kiare, C., Leakey, L. N., & McDougal, I. (2001). New hominin genus from eastern Africa shows diverse middle Pliocene lineages. *Nature 410*, 433–440.

"Leave none to tell the story: Genocide in Rwanda." (2004). www.hrw.org/legacy/reports/1999/rwanda/ (retrieved August 28, 2012)

Leavitt, G. C. (1990). Sociobiological explanations of incest avoidance: A critical review of evidential claims. *American Anthropologist 92*, 982.

Leclerc-Madlala, S. (2002). Bodies and politics: Healing rituals in the democratic South Africa. In V. Faure (Ed.), *Les cahiers de l'IFAS*, no. 2. Johannesburg: The French Institute.

Lee, R. B., & Daly, R. H. (1999). *The Cambridge encyclopedia of hunters and gatherers.* New York: Cambridge University Press.

Lehman, E. C., Jr. (2002, Fall). Women's path into the ministry. *Pulpit & Pew Research Reports 1*, 4.

Lenhart, A. (2012, March 19). Teens, smartphones & texting. *Pew Internet &*

American Life Project. http://pewinternet.org/Reports/2012/Teens-and-smartphones.aspx (retrieved August 23, 2012)

Lestel, D. (1998). How chimpanzees have domesticated humans. *Anthropology Today 12* (3).

Leth, P. M. (2007). The use of CT scanning in forensic autopsy. *Forensic Science, Medicine, and Pathology 3* (1), 65–69.

Levine, N. E., & Silk, J. B. (1997). Why polyandry fails. *Current Anthropology 38,* 375–398.

Levine, R. A. (2007). Ethnographic studies of childhood: A historical overview. *American Anthropologist 109* (2), 247–260.

Lévi-Strauss, C. (1952). *Race and history.* Paris: UNESCO.

Lévi-Strauss, C. (1955). *Tristes tropiques.* Paris: Librarie Plon.

Lévi-Strauss, C. (1963). The sorcerer and his magic. In *Structural anthropology.* New York: Basic Books. (orig. 1958)

Lewin, R. (1993). Paleolithic paint job. *Discover 14* (7), 64–70.

Lewis-Williams, J. D. (1990). *Discovering southern African rock art.* Cape Town & Johannesburg: David Philip.

Lewontin, R. C. (1972). The apportionment of human diversity. In T. Dobzhansky et al. (Eds.), *Evolutionary biology* (pp. 381–398). New York: Plenum Press.

Lewontin, R. C., Rose, S., & Kamin, L. J. (1984). *Not in our genes.* New York: Pantheon.

Li, X., Harbottle, G., Zhang, J., & Wang, C. (2003). The earliest writing? Sign use in the seventh millennium BC at Jiahu, Henan Province, China. *Antiquity 77,* 31–44.

Lindenbaum, S. (1978). *Kuru sorcery: Disease and danger in the New Guinea highlands.* New York: McGraw-Hill.

Lindstrom, L. (1993). *Cargo cult: Strange stories of desire from Melanesia and beyond.* Honolulu: University of Hawaii Press.

Linnekin, J. (1990). *Sacred queens and women of consequence: Rank, gender, and colonialism in the Hawaiian Islands.* Ann Arbor: University of Michigan Press.

Little, K. L. (1973). African women in town: An aspect of Africa's social revolution (pp. 58–62). New York: Cambridge University Press.

Littlewood, R. (2004). Commentary: Globalization, culture, body image, and eating disorders. *Culture, Medicine, and Psychiatry 28* (4), 597–602.

Liu, J. (2007). *Gender and work in urban China: Women workers of the unlucky generation.* London: Routledge.

Living Tongues. www.livingtongues.org (retrieved June 4, 2012)

Lloyd, C. B. (Ed.). (2005). *Growing up global: The changing transitions to adulthood in developing countries.* Washington, DC: National Academies Press.

Lock, A. (1980). *The guided reinvention of language.* New York: Academic Press.

Lock, M. (2001). *Twice dead: Organ transplants and the reinvention of death.* Berkeley: University of California Press.

Louie, A. (2004). *Chineseness across borders: Renegotiating Chinese identities in China and the United States.* Durham and London: Duke University Press.

Luhrmann, T. M. (2001). *Of two minds: An anthropologist looks at American psychiatry.* New York: Vintage.

Lurie, N. O. (1973). Action anthropology and the American Indian. In *Anthropology and the American Indian: A symposium.* San Francisco: Indian Historical Press.

Maggioncalda, A. N., & Sapolsky, R. M. (2002). Disturbing behaviors of the orangutan. *Scientific American 286* (6), 60–65.

Mair, L. (1957). *An introduction to social anthropology.* London: Oxford University Press.

Malinowski, B. (1945). *The dynamics of culture change.* New Haven, CT: Yale University Press.

Malinowski, B. (1961). *Argonauts of the western Pacific.* New York: Dutton.

Mann, C. C. (2002). The real dirt on rainforest fertility. *Science 297,* 920–923.

Mann, C. C. (2005). *1491: New revelations of the Americas before Columbus.* New York: Knopf.

Marcus, G. (1995). Ethnography in/of the world system: The emergence of multi-sited ethnography. *Annual Review of Anthropology 24,* 95–117.

Marcus, J., & Flannery, K. V. (1996). *Zapotec civilization: How urban society evolved in Mexico's Oaxaca Valley.* New York: Thames & Hudson.

Marks, J. (2000, May 12). 98% alike (what our similarity to apes tells us about our understanding of genetics). *Chronicle of Higher Education,* B7.

Marks, J. (2008a). Caveat emptor: Genealogy for sale. *Newsletter of the ESRC Genomics Network 7,* 22–23.

Marks, J. (2008b). Race: Past, present, and future. In B. Koenig, S. Lee, & S. Richardson (Eds.), *Revisiting race in a genomic age* (pp. 21–38). New Brunswick, NJ: Rutgers University Press.

Marshack, A. (1989). Evolution of the human capacity: The symbolic evidence. *Yearbook of physical anthropology* (vol. 32, pp. 1–34). New York: Alan R. Liss.

Marshall, E. (2001). Preclovis sites fight for acceptance. *Science 291,* 1732.

Martin, E. (1994). *Flexible bodies: Tracking immunity in American culture from the days of polio to the age of AIDS.* Boston: Beacon Press.

Martin, E. (1999). Flexible survivors. *Anthropology News 40* (6), 5–7.

Martin, E. (2009). *Bipolar expeditions: Mania and depression in American culture.* Princeton, NJ: Princeton University Press.

Martorell, R. (1988). Body size, adaptation, and function. *GDP,* 335–347.

Mason, J. A. (1957). *The ancient civilizations of Peru.* Baltimore: Penguin Books.

Mathieu, C. (2003). *A history and anthropological study of the ancient kingdoms of the Sino-Tibetan borderland—Naxi and Mosuo.* New York: Mellen.

Max Planck Institute of Evolutionary Anthropology. (2012). Denisova genome. Public data set: http://aws.amazon.com/datasets/2357 (retrieved July 19, 2012)

McCaskill, C., Lucas, C., Bayley, R., & Hill, J. (2012). *The hidden treasure of Black ASL: Its history and structure* (with contributions from J. C. Hill,

R. Dummet-King, P. Baldwin, & R. Hogue). Washington, DC: Gallaudet University Press.

McDermott, L. (1996). Self-representation in Upper Paleolithic female figurines. *Current Anthropology 37,* 227–276.

McDermott, R. (2011, April 1). Polygamy: More common than you think. *Wall Street Journal.* http://online.wsj.com/article/SB10001424052748703806304576234551596322690.html (retrieved October 7, 2012)

McDonald's. (2012). www.aboutmcdonalds.com (retrieved September 29, 2012)

McElroy, A., & Townsend, P. K. (2003). *Medical anthropology in ecological perspective.* Boulder, CO: Westview Press.

McFate, M. (2007). *Role and effectiveness of socio-cultural knowledge for counterinsurgency.* Alexandria, VA: Institute for Defense Analysis.

McGrew, W. C. (2000). Dental care in chimps. *Science 288,* 1747.

McHenry, H. M., & Jones, A. L. (2006). Hallucial convergence in early hominids. *Journal of Human Evolution 50,* 534–539.

McKenna, J. J., Ball, H., & Gettler, L. T. (2007). Mother–infant cosleeping, breastfeeding and SIDS: What biological anthropology has discovered about normal infant sleep and pediatric sleep medicine. *Yearbook of Physical Anthropology 50,* 133–161.

McKenna, J. J., & McDade, T. (2005, June). Why babies should never sleep alone: A review of the co-sleeping controversy in relation to SIDS, bedsharing, and breastfeeding. *Pediatric Respiratory Reviews 6* (2), 134–152.

Mead, A. T. P. (1996). Genealogy, sacredness, and the commodities market. *Cultural Survival Quarterly 20* (2).

Mead, M. (1960). Anthropology among the sciences. *American Anthropologist 63,* 475–482.

Mead, M. (1963). *Sex and temperament in three primitive societies* (3rd ed.). New York: Morrow. (orig. 1935)

Mead, M., & Métraux, R. (Eds.). (1953). *The study of culture at a distance.* Chicago: University of Chicago Press.

"Media frenzy." (2009, May 27). Editorial. *Nature 459,* 484.

Medicine, B. (1994). Gender. In M. B. Davis (Ed.), *Native America in the twentieth century.* New York: Garland.

Mellars, P. (2009). Archaeology: Origins of the female image. *Nature 459,* 176–177.

Merkur, D. (1983). Breath-soul and wind owner: The many and the one in Inuit religion. *American Indian Quarterly 7* (3), 23–39.

Mesghinna, H. M. (1966). Salt mining in Enderta. *Journal of Ethiopian Studies 4* (2).

Métraux, A. (1957). *Easter Island: A stone-age civilization of the Pacific.* New York: Oxford University Press.

Meyer, J. (2008). Typology and acoustic strategies of whistled languages: Phonetic comparison and perceptual cues of whistled vowels. *Journal of the International Phonetic Association 38,* 69–94.

Meyer, J., & Gautheron, B. (2006). Whistled speech and whistled languages. In K. Brown (Ed.), *Encyclopedia of language & linguistics* (2nd ed., vol. 13, pp. 573–576). Oxford, UK: Elsevier.

Meyer, J., Meunier, F., & Dentel, L. (2007). Identification of natural whistled vowels by non-whistlers. *Proceedings of Interspeech 2007*. Antwerp, Belgium.

Mieth, A., & Bork, H.-R. (2009). Humans, climate or introduced rats—which is to blame for the woodland destruction on prehistoric Rapa Nui (Easter Island)? *Journal of Archaeological Science*. doi:10.1016/j.jas.2009.10.006

Miles, H. (1990). The cognitive foundations for reference in a signing orangutan. In S. Parker & K. Gibson (Eds.), *"Language" and intelligence in monkeys and apes: Comparative developmental perspectives* (pp. 511–539). Cambridge, UK: Cambridge University Press.

Miles, H. (1993). Language and the orangutan: The "old person" of the forest. In P. Cavalieri & P. Singer (Eds.), *The great ape project* (pp. 45–50). New York: St. Martin's Press.

Miles, H. (1999). Symbolic communication with and by great apes. In S. Parker, R. Mitchell, & H. Miles (Eds.), *The mentality of gorillas and orangutans: Comparative perspectives* (pp. 197–210). Cambridge, UK: Cambridge University Press.

Mitchell, W. E. (1973, December). A new weapon stirs up old ghosts. *Natural History Magazine*, 77–84.

Monaghan, L., Hinton, L., & Kephart, R. (1997). Can't teach a dog to be a cat? The dialogue on Ebonics. *Anthropology Newsletter 38* (3), 1, 8, 9.

Montagu, A. (1998). *Man's most dangerous myth: The fallacy of race* (6th ed.). Lanham, MD: Rowman & Littlefield.

Moore, J. (1998). Comment. *Current Anthropology 39*, 412.

Morello, C. (2011, May 18). Number of long-lasting marriages in U.S. has risen, Census Bureau reports. *Washington Post*.

Murthy, D. (2011). Emergent digital ethnographic methods for social research. In S. N. Hesse-Biber (Ed.), *The handbook of emergent technologies in social research* (pp. 158–179). New York: Oxford University Press.

Mydens, S. (2001, August 12). He's not hairy, he's my brother. *New York Times*. www.nytimes.com/2001/08/12/weekinreview/ideas-trends-he-s-not-hairy-he-s-my-brother.html (retrieved June 25, 2012)

Nabhan, G. P. (2004). *Why some like it hot: Food, genes, and cultural diversity*. Washington, DC: Island Press.

Nader, L. (Ed.). (1996). *Naked science: Anthropological inquiry into boundaries, power, and knowledge*. New York: Routledge.

Nader, L. (1997). Controlling processes: Tracing the dynamics of power. *Current Anthropology 38*, 715–717.

Nader, L. (2002). *The life of the law: Anthropological projects*. Berkeley: University of California Press.

Nanda, S. (1992). Arranging a marriage in India. In P. R. DeVita (Ed.), *The naked anthropologist* (pp. 139–143). Belmont, CA: Wadsworth.

Nanda, S. (1999). *Neither man nor woman: The hijras of India*. Belmont, CA: Wadsworth.

Nash, J. (1976). Ethnology in a revolutionary setting. In M. A. Rynkiewich & J. P. Spradley (Eds.), *Ethics and anthropology: Dilemmas in fieldwork*. New York: Wiley.

Nast, H. J. (2005). *Concubines and power: Five hundred years in a northern Nigerian palace*. Minneapolis: University of Minnesota Press.

Natadecha-Sponsal, P. (1993). The young, the rich and the famous: Individualism as an American cultural value. In P. R. DeVita & J. D. Armstrong (Eds.), *Distant mirrors: America as a foreign culture* (pp. 46–53). Belmont, CA: Wadsworth.

Natural Resources Defense Council. (2005, March 25). Healthy milk, healthy baby: Chemical pollution and mother's milk. www.nrdc.org/breastmilk/ (retrieved October 3, 2012)

Nazzal-Batayneh, M. (2005). Nauru: An environment destroyed and international law. www.lawanddevelopment.org/articles/nauru.html (retrieved October 3, 2012)

Nesbitt, L. M. (1935). *Hell-hole of creation*. New York: Knopf.

Nettle, B. (2005). *The study of ethnomusicology: Thirty-one issues and concepts*. Chicago: University of Illinois Press.

"New ILO global report on child labor." (2010, May 8). International Labour Organization. www.ilocarib.org.tt/index.php?option=com_content&view=article&id=1363:new-ilo-global-report-on-child-labour&catid=214:2010-news&Itemid=1209 (retrieved August 7, 2012)

Nichols, J. (2008). Language spread rates as indicators of glacial-age peopling of the Americas. *Current Anthropology 49* (6), 1109–1117.

Nietschmann, B. (1987). The third world war. *Cultural Survival Quarterly 11* (3), 1–16.

Noack, T. (2001). Cohabitation in Norway: An accepted and gradually more regulated way of living. *International Journal of Law, Policy, and the Family 15* (1), 102–117.

Normile, D. (1998). Habitat seen as playing larger role in shaping behavior. *Science 279*, 1454.

Nunney, L. (1998). Are we selfish because we are nice, or are we nice because we are selfish? *Science 281*, 1619.

Nye, J. (2002). *The paradox of American power: Why the world's only superpower can't go it alone*. New York: Oxford University Press.

O'Barr, W. M., & Conley, J. M. (1993). When a juror watches a lawyer. In W. A. Haviland & R. J. Gordon (Eds.), *Talking about people* (2nd. ed., pp. 42–45). Mountain View, CA: Mayfield.

Oboler, R. S. (1980). Is the female husband a man? Woman/woman marriage among the Nandi of Kenya. *Ethnology 19*, 69–88.

O'Carroll, E. (2008, June 27). Spain to grant some human rights to apes. *Christian Science Monitor*.

Office of the United Nations Higher Commissioner for Human Rights, Committee on the Elimination of Racial Discrimination, India. (2007, March). Consideration of state reports. www2.ohchr.org/english/bodies/cerd/cerds70.htm (retrieved August 25, 2012)

Offiong, D. A. (1999). Traditional healers in the Nigerian health care delivery system and the debate over integrating traditional and scientific medicine. *Anthropological Quarterly 72* (3), 118–130.

Okonjo, K. (1976). The dual-sex political system in operation: Igbo women and community politics in midwestern Nigeria. In N. Hafkin & E. Bay (Eds.), *Women in Africa*. Stanford, CA: Stanford University Press.

Olivier, J. G. L., Janssens-Maenhout, G., & Peters, J. A. H. W. (2012). *Trends in global CO_2 emissions*. The Hague: PBL Netherlands Environmental Assessment Agency. http://edgar.jrc.ec.europa.eu/CO2REPORT2012.pdf (retrieved November 7, 2012)

O'Mahoney, K. (1970). The salt trade. *Journal of Ethiopian Studies 8* (2).

One Earth Future Foundation. (2012). *The economic cost of Somali piracy 2011*. http://oceansbeyondpiracy.org/sites/default/files/economic_cost_of_piracy_2011_summary.pdf (retrieved August 28)

"111th Canton Fair." (2012). *Live Trading News*. www.livetradingnews.com/111th-canton-fair-74669.htm#.UCKSrcgsAch (retrieved August 8, 2012)

Ortiz, I., & Cummins, M. (2011). Global inequality: Beyond the bottom billion—A rapid review of income distribution in 141 countries. *UNICEF*. www.unicef.org/socialpolicy/index_58230.html (retrieved October 1, 2012)

Otte, M. (2000). On the suggested bone flute from Slovenia. *Current Anthropology 41*, 271.

Ottenheimer, M. (1996). *Forbidden relatives: The American myth of cousin marriage*. Champaign: University of Illinois Press.

Paredes, J. A., & Purdum, E. D. (1990). "Bye, bye Ted. . .". *Anthropology Today 6* (2), 9.

Parés, J. M., et al. (2000). On the age of hominid fossils at the Sima de los Huesos, Sierra de Atapuerca, Spain: Paleomagnetic evidence. *American Journal of Physical Anthropology 111*, 451–461.

Parish, A. (1998). Comment. *Current Anthropology 39*, 414.

Parnell, R. (1999). Gorilla exposé. *Natural History 108* (8), 43.

Parry, W. (2011, March 17). Recent heat waves likely warmest since 1500 in Europe. www.livescience.com/13296-european-russia-heat-waves-climate-change.html (retrieved November 8, 2012)

Patterson, F. G. P., & Gordon, W. (2002). Twenty-seven years of Project Koko and Michael. In B. Galdikas et al. (Eds.), *All apes great and small: Chimpanzees, bonobos, and gorillas* (vol. 1, pp. 165–176). New York: Kluwer Academic.

Pearson, V., Phillips, M. R., He, F., & Ji, H. (2002). Attempted suicide among young rural women in the People's Republic of China: Possibilities for prevention. *Suicide and Life-Threatening Behavior 32* (4), 359–369.

Pease, T. (2000, Spring). Taking the third side. *Andover Bulletin*.

Pelto, P. J. (1973). *The snowmobile revolution: Technology and social change in the Arctic.* Menlo Park, CA: Cummings.

Pew Research Center, Pew Forum on Religion & Public Life. (2011). The future of the global Muslim population: Projections for 2010–2030. www.pewforum.org/The-Future-of-the-Global-Muslim-Population.aspx (retrieved September 17, 2012)

Pew Research Center, Pew Forum on Religion & Public Life. (2012, October 9). "Nones" on the rise: One-in-five adults have no religious affiliation. www.pewforum.org/Unaffiliated/nones-on-the-rise.aspx#_ftn3 (retrieved October 23, 2012)

Pickering, R., et al. (2011). *Australopithecus sediba* at 1.977 ma and implications for the origins of the genus *Homo. Science 333 (6048),* 1421–1423.

Pike, A. W. G., et al. (2012). U-series dating of Paleolithic art in 11 caves in Spain. *Science 336,* 1409–1413.

Pink, S. (2001). *Doing visual ethnography: Images, media, and representation in research.* Thousand Oaks, CA: Sage.

Plattner, S. (1989). Markets and market places. In S. Plattner (Ed.), *Economic anthropology.* Stanford, CA: Stanford University Press.

Pohl, M. E. D., Pope, K. O., & von Nagy, C. (2002). Olmec origins of Mesoamerican writing. *Science 298,* 1984–1987.

Polanyi, K. (1968). The economy as instituted process. In E. E. LeClair Jr. & H. K. Schneider (Eds.), *Economic anthropology: Readings in theory and analysis* (pp. 127–138). New York: Holt, Rinehart & Winston.

Pollan, M. (2001). *The botany of desire: A plant's-eye view of the world.* New York: Random House.

Pollan, M. (2008). *In defense of food: An eater's manifesto.* New York: Penguin Books.

Pollock, N. J. (1995). Social fattening patterns in the Pacific—the positive side of obesity. A Nauru case study. In I. DeGarine & N. J. Pollock (Eds.), *Social aspects of obesity* (pp. 87–109). London: Routledge.

Pospisil, L. (1963). *The Kapauku Papuans of West New Guinea.* New York: Holt, Rinehart & Winston.

Powdermaker, H. (1939). *After freedom: A cultural study in the Deep South.* New York: Viking.

Power, M. G. (1995). Gombe revisited: Are chimpanzees violent and hierarchical in the "free" state? *General Anthropology 2* (1), 5–9.

Poyatos, F. (2002). *Nonverbal communication across disciplines* (3 vols.). Amsterdam: John Benjamins.

"President Obama descends from the first African enslaved for life in America." (2012, July). *Ancestry.com.* www.ancestry.com/obama (retrieved August 10, 2012)

Price, D. H. (2011). How the CIA and Pentagon harnessed anthropological research during the Second World War and Cold War with little critical notice. *Journal of Anthropological Research 67* (3), 333–356.

Prins, H. E. L. (1994). Neo-traditions in Native communities: Sweat lodge and Sun Dance among the Micmac today, In W. Cowan (Ed.), *Proceedings of the 25th Algonquian conference* (pp. 383–394). Ottawa: Carleton University Press.

Prins, H. E. L. (1996). *The Mi'kmaq: Resistance, accommodation, and cultural survival.* New York: Harcourt Brace.

Prins, H. E. L. (1998). Book review of Schuster, C., & Carpenter, E. *American Anthropologist 100* (3), 841.

Prins, H. E. L. (2002). Visual media and the primitivist perplex: Colonial fantasies and indigenous imagination in North America. In F. Ginsburg, L. Abu-Lughod, & B. Larkin (Eds.), *Media worlds: Anthropology on new terrain* (pp. 58–74). Berkeley: University of California Press.

Prins, H. E. L., & Krebs, E. (2006). Toward a land without evil: Alfred Métraux as UNESCO anthropologist 1948–1962. In *60 years of UNESCO history. Proceedings of the international symposium in Paris, 16–18 November 2005.* Paris: UNESCO.

Prins, H. E. L., & McBride, B. (2012). Upside down: Arctic realities & indigenous art (museum review essay). *American Anthropologist 114* (2), 359–364.

Pruetz, J. D., & Bertolani, P. (2007, March 6). Savanna chimpanzees, *Pan troglodytes verus,* hunt with tools. *Current Biology 17,* 412–417.

Quinn, N. (2005). Universals of child rearing. *Anthropological Theory 5,* 475–514.

Radcliffe-Brown, A. R. (1931). Social organization of Australian tribes. *Oceana Monographs 1,* 29.

Radelet, M. L., & Lacock, T. L. (2009). Do executions lower homicide rates? The views of leading criminologists. *Journal of Criminal Law and Criminology 99* (2), 489.

Ralston, C., & Thomas, N. (Eds.). (1987). Sanctity and power: Gender in Polynesian history. *Journal of Pacific History* (special issue) *22* (3–4).

Ramos, A. R. (1987). Reflecting on the Yanomami: Ethnographic images and the pursuit of the exotic. *Current Anthropology 2* (3), 284–304.

Rapp, R. (1999). *Testing women, testing the fetus: The social impact of amniocentesis in America (The Anthropology of Everyday Life).* New York: Routledge.

Rappaport, R. A. (1969). Ritual regulation of environmental relations among a New Guinea people. In A. P. Vayda (Ed.), *Environment and cultural behavior* (pp. 181–201). Garden City, NY: Natural History Press.

Rasmussen, M., et al. (2011). An aboriginal Australian genome reveals separate human dispersals into Asia, *Science 334* (6052), 94–98. doi: 10.1126/science.1211177

Rathje, W., & Murphy, C. (2001). *Rubbish!: The archaeology of garbage.* Tucson: University of Arizona Press.

Rathke, L. (1989). To Maine for apples. *Salt Magazine 9* (4), 24–47.

Recer, P. (1998, February 16). Apes shown to communicate in the wild. *Burlington Free Press,* 12A.

Reich, D., et al. (2010, December 23). Genetic history of an archaic hominin group from Denisova Cave in Siberia. *Nature 468,* 1053–1060.

Reich, D., et al. (2012). Reconstructing Native American population history. *Nature.* doi: 10.1038/nature11258

Relethford, J. H. (2001). Absence of regional affinities of Neandertal DNA with living humans does not reject multiregional evolution. *American Journal of Physical Anthropology 115,* 95–98.

Relethford, J. H., & Harpending, H. C. (1994). Craniometric variation, genetic theory, and modern human origins. *American Journal of Physical Anthropology 95,* 249–270.

Remarque, E. M. (1929). *All quiet on the western front.* Boston: Little, Brown.

Reynolds, V. (1994). Primates in the field, primates in the lab. *Anthropology Today 10* (2), 4.

Ribeiro, G. L. (2009). Non-hegemonic globalizations: Alternative transnational processes and agents. *Anthropological Theory 9* (3), 297–329.

Rice, P. (2000). Paleoanthropology 2000—part 1. *General Anthropology 7* (1), 11.

Rideout, V. J., Foehr, U. G., & Roberts, D. F. (2010, January). *Generation M2: Media in the lives of 8- to18-year-olds.* A Kaiser Family Foundation Study. Menlo Park, CA: Henry J. Kaiser Family Foundation. www.kff.org/entmedia/upload/8010.pdf (retrieved August 25, 2012)

Ridley, M. (1999). *Genome: The autobiography of a species in 23 chapters.* New York: HarperCollins.

Rightmire, G. P. (1998). Evidence from facial morphology for similarity of Asian and African representatives of *Homo erectus. American Journal of Physical Anthropology 106,* 61–85.

Ritzer, G. (1983). The McDonaldization of society, *Journal of American Culture 6* (1), 100–107.

Ritzer, G. (2007). *The coming of post-industrial society* (2nd ed.). New York: McGraw-Hill.

Robben, A. C. G. M. (2007). Fieldwork identity: Introduction. In A. C. G. M. Robben & J. A. Sluka (Eds.), *Ethnographic fieldwork: An anthropological reader.* Malden, MA: Blackwell Press.

Robben, A. C. G. M., & Sluka, J. A. (Eds.). (2007). *Ethnographic fieldwork: An anthropological reader.* Malden, MA: Blackwell Press.

Rochat, P. (2001). Origins of self-concept. In G. Bremner & A. Fogel (Eds.), *Blackwell handbook of infant development* (pp. 191–212). Malden, MA: Blackwell Press.

Rogers, J. (1994). Levels of the genealogical hierarchy and the problem of hominoid phylogeny. *American Journal of Physical Anthropology 94,* 81–88.

Romer, A. S. (1945). *Vertebrate paleontology.* Chicago: University of Chicago Press.

Roosevelt, A. C. (1984). Population, health, and the evolution of subsistence: Conclusions from the conference. In M. N. Cohen & G. J. Armelagos (Eds.), *Paleopathology at the origins of agriculture* (pp. 572–574). Orlando: Academic Press.

Rosaldo, M. Z. (1980). *Knowledge and passion: Ilongot notions of self & social life* (Cambridge Studies in Cultural Systems). New York: Cambridge University Press.

Roscoe, W. (1991). *Zuni man-woman.* Albuquerque: University of New Mexico Press.

Rose, S. (2009). Darwin 200: Should scientists study race and IQ? NO: Science and society do not benefit. *Nature 457,* 786–788.

Rudel, T. K., Bates, D., & Machinguiashi, R. (2002). Ecologically noble Amerindians? Cattle ranching and cash cropping among Shuar and colonists in Ecuador. *Latin American Research Review 37* (1), 144–159.

Rupert, J. L., & Hochachka, P. W. (2001). The evidence for hereditary factors contributing to high altitude adaptation in Andean natives: A review. *High Altitude Medicine & Biology 2* (2), 235–256.

Rymer, R. (1994). *Genie: A scientific tragedy.* New York: HarperCollins.

Sacks, O. (1998). *Island of the colorblind.* New York: Knopf.

Sahlins, M. (1972). *Stone Age economics.* Chicago: Aldine.

Salzman, P. C. (1967). Political organization among nomadic peoples. *Proceedings of the American Philosophical Society 111,* 115–131.

Sanday, P. R. (1975). On the causes of IQ differences between groups and implications for social policy. In M. F. A. Montagu (Ed.), *Race and IQ* (pp. 232–238). New York: Oxford University Press.

Sanday, P. R. (1981). *Female power and male dominance: On the origins of sexual inequality.* Cambridge, UK: Cambridge University Press.

Sangree, W. H. (1965). The Bantu Tiriki of western Kenya. In J. L. Gibbs Jr. (Ed.), *Peoples of Africa* (pp. 69–72). New York: Holt, Rinehart & Winston.

Sanjek, R. (1990). On ethnographic validity. In R. Sanjek (Ed.), *Field notes.* Ithaca, NY: Cornell University Press.

Sapolsky, R. (2002). *A primate's memoir: Love, death, and baboons in East Africa.* New York: Vintage.

Savage-Rumbaugh, S., & Lewin, R. (1994). *Kanzi: The ape at the brink of the human mind.* New York: Wiley.

Sawert, H. (2002, October 11–12). *TB and poverty in the context of global TB control.* World Health Organization. Satellite Symposium on TB & Poverty. www.stoptb.org/assets/documents/resources/publications/acsm/H.RightsReport2001.pdf

Schaeffer, S. B., & Furst, P. T. (Eds.). (1996). *People of the peyote: Huichol Indian history, religion, and survival.* Albuquerque: University of New Mexico Press.

Schilling, C. (2012, August 20). Love, American style: Polygamy gets sizzle. *WorldNetDaily.* www.wnd.com/2012/08/love-american-style-polygamy-gets-sizzle/ (retrieved October 7, 2012)

Schilt, K., & Westbrook, L. (2009, August). Doing gender, doing heteronormativity: "Gender normals," transgender people, and the social maintenance of heterosexuality. *Gender & Society 23* (4), 440–464.

Schoepfle, M. (2001). Ethnographic resource inventory and the National Park Service. *Cultural Resource Management 5,* 1–7.

Schuster, C., & Carpenter, E. (1996). *Patterns that connect: Social symbolism in ancient and tribal art.* New York: Abrams.

Scully, T. (2008). Online anthropology draws protest from aboriginal group. *Nature 453,* 1155. doi:10.1038/4531155a.

Seiffert, E. R., et al. (2009). Convergent evolution of anthropoid-like adaptations in Eocene adapiform primates. *Nature 461,* 1118–1121.

Selinger, B. (2007). The Navajo, psychosis, Lacan, and Derrida. *Texas Studies in Literature and Language 49* (1), 64–100.

Semenov, S. A. (1964). *Prehistoric technology.* New York: Barnes & Noble.

Senut, B., et al. (2001). First hominid from the Miocene (Lukeino formation, Kenya). *C. R. Academy of Science, Paris 332,* 137–144.

Seyfarth, R. M., Cheney, D. L., & Marler, P. (1980). Vervet monkey alarm calls: Semantic communication in a free-ranging primate. *Animal Behavior 28* (4), 1070–1094.

Seyfarth, R. M., et al. (1980). Monkey responses to three different alarm calls: Evidence for predator classification and semantic communication. *Science 210,* 801–803.

Sharp, G. (1973). *The politics of nonviolent action.* Boston: Extending Horizons Books, Porter Sargent Publishers.

Sharp, G. (2010). *From dictatorship to democracy: A conceptual framework for liberation* (4th ed.). East Boston: Einstein Institution.

Sharpe, K., & Van Gelder, L. (2006). Evidence of cave marking by Paleolithic children. *Antiquity 80* (310), 937–947.

Shea, P. J. (2007). Excellent legacies of Abo Bayero. In A. U. Adamu (Ed.), *Chieftaincy and security in Nigeria: Past, present, and future* (pp. i–vi). http://ibrahimshekarau.com/downloads/videos1/books/12.pdf (retrieved August 26, 2012)

Sheets, P. D. (1993). Dawn of a New Stone Age in eye surgery. In R. J. Sharer & W. Ashmore (Eds.), *Archaeology: Discovering our past.* Palo Alto, CA: Mayfield.

Shi, L. (2009). Little quilted vests to warm parents' hearts: Redefining the gendered practice of filial piety in rural north-eastern China. *China Quarterly 198,* 348–363.

Shook, J. R., et al. (Eds.). (2004). *Dictionary of modern American philosophers, 1860–1960.* Bristol, UK: Thoemmes Press.

Shostak, M. (2000). *Nisa: The life and words of a !Kung woman.* Cambridge, MA: Harvard University Press.

Shreeve, J. (1994). Terms of estrangement. *Discover 15* (11), 60.

Shreeve, J. (1995). *The Neandertal enigma: Solving the mystery of modern human origins.* New York: William Morrow.

Silverstein, J. (2012). Bonds beyond blood: DNA testing and refugee family resettlement. *Anthropology News 53* (4), 11.

Simons, E. L., et al. (2009, July 22). Outrage at high price paid for a fossil. Correspondence. *Nature 460,* 456.

Simons, R. C., & Hughes, C. C. (Eds.). (1985). *The culture-bound syndromes: Folk illnesses of psychiatric and anthropological interest.* New York: Springer.

Simpson, S. (1995, April). Whispers from the ice. *Alaska,* 23–28.

Simpson, S. W., et al. (2008). A female *Homo erectus* pelvis from Gona, Ethiopia. *Science 322* (5904), 1089–1092.

Sivak, M., & Schoettle, B. (2012). Accounting for climate in ranking countries' carbon dioxide emissions. *American Scientist.* www.americanscientist.org/issues/id.15839,y.0,no.,content.true,page.3,css.print/issue.aspx (retrieved November 7, 2012)

Sluka, J. A. (2007). Fieldwork relations and rapport: Introduction. In A. C. G. M. Robben & J. A. Sluka (Eds.), *Ethnographic fieldwork: An anthropological reader.* Malden, MA: Blackwell Press.

Small, M. F. (1997). Making connections. *American Scientist 85,* 503.

Small, M. F. (2008, August 15). Why red is such a potent color. *Live Science.* www.livescience.com/5043-red-potent-color.html (retrieved June 20, 2012)

Small, M. F. (2009, May 15). Why "Ida" inspires navel-gazing at our ancestry. *Live Science.* www.livescience.come/history/090520-hn-ida.html

Smedley, A. (2007). *Race in North America: Origin and evolution of a worldview.* Boulder, CO: Westview Press.

Smith, M. D. (2008, September 16). Indian child labor exploited in production of soccer balls. *Huffington Post.* www.aolnews.com/2008/09/16/indian-child-labor-exploited-in-production-of-soccer-balls/ (retrieved August 7, 2012)

Smith, W. W. (2009). *China's Tibet: Autonomy or assimilation?* Lanham, MD: Rowman & Littlefield.

Songok, E. M., Luo, M., Liang, B., Mclaren, P., Kaefer, N., Apidi, W., Boucher, G., Kimani, J., Wachihi, C., Sekaly, R., Fowke, K., Ball, B. T., & Plummer, F. A. (2012). Microarray analysis of HIV resistant female sex workers reveal a gene expression signature pattern reminiscent of a lowered immune activation state. *PLoS One 7* (1), e30048.

Spencer, R. F. (1984). North Alaska Coast Eskimo. In D. Damas (Ed.), *Arctic: Handbook of North American Indians* (vol. 5, pp. 320–337). Washington, DC: Smithsonian Institution Press.

Springen, K. (2008, September 15). What it means to be a woman: How women around the world cope with infertility. *Newsweek.com.* www.thedailybeast.com/newsweek/2008/09/14/what-it-means-to-be-a-woman.html (retrieved June 12, 2012)

Stacey, J. (1990). *Brave new families.* New York: Basic Books.

Steady, F. C. (2001). *Women and the Amistad connection, Sierra Leone Krio Society.* Rochester, VT: Schenkman.

Stedman, H. H., et al. (2004). Myosin gene mutation correlates with anatomical changes in the human lineage. *Nature 428,* 415–418.

Stein, R., & St. George, D. (2009, May 13). Babies increasingly born to unwed mothers. *Washington Post.*

Stenseth, N. C., & Voje, K. L. (2009). Easter Island: Climate change might have contributed to past cultural and societal changes. *Climate Research 39*, 111–114.

Stockholm International Peace Research Institute. (2012). www.sipri.org/ (retrieved November 8, 2012)

Stolberg, S. G. (2011, February 16). Shy U.S. intellectual created play-book used in a revolution. *New York Times*. www.nytimes.com/2011/02/17/world/middleeast/17sharp.html?pagewanted=all (retrieved August 28, 2012)

Stone, L. (2005). *Kinship and gender: An introduction* (3rd ed.). Boulder, CO: Westview Press.

Strier, K. (1993, March). Menu for a monkey. *Natural History*, 42.

Strum, S., & Mitchell, W. (1987). Baboon models and muddles. In W. Kinsey (Ed.), *The evolution of human behavior: Primate models*. Albany: SUNY Press.

Suárez-Orozoco, M. M., Spindler, G., & Spindler, L. (1994). *The making of psychological anthropology, II*. Fort Worth: Harcourt Brace.

Swaminathan, M. S. (2000). Science in response to basic human needs. *Science 287*, 425.

Tamm, E., et al. (2007). Beringian standstill and spread of Native American frontiers. *PLoS One 2* (9), e829. doi: 10.1371/journal.pone.0000829

Tapper, M. (1999). *In the blood: Sickle-cell anemia and the politics of race*. Philadelphia: University of Pennsylvania Press.

Terashima, H. (1983). Mota and other hunting activities of the Mbuti archers: A socio-ecological study of subsistence technology. *African Studies Monograph* (Kyoto), 71–85.

Thomas, E. M. (1994). *The tribe of the tiger: Cats and their culture*. New York: Simon & Schuster.

Thompson, K. (2012, July 30). Obama's purported link to early American slave is latest twist in family tree. *Washington Post*. www.washingtonpost.com/politics/purported-obama-link-to-first-american-slave-is-latest-twist-in-presidents-family-tree/2012/07/30/gJQAYuG1KX_story.html?hpid=z4 (retrieved August 10, 2012)

Thomson, K. S. (1997). Natural selection and evolution's smoking gun. *American Scientist 85*, 516.

Thorpe, S. K. S., Holder, R. L., & Crompton, R. H. (2007). Origin of human bipedalism as an adaptation for locomotion on flexible branches. *Science 316*, 1328–1331.

Timmons, H., & Kumar, H. (2009, July 3). Indian court overturns gay sex ban. *New York Times*.

Toth, N., et al. (1993). Pan the tool-maker: Investigations in the stone tool-making and tool-using capabilities of a bonobo (*Pan paniscus*). *Journal of Archaeological Science 20* (1), 81–91.

Tracy, J. L., & Matsumoto, D. (2008). The spontaneous expression of pride and shame: Evidence for biologically innate nonverbal displays. *Proceedings of the National Academy of Sciences 105* (33), 11655–11660.

Trevathan, W., Smith, E. O., & McKenna, J. J. (Eds.). (1999). *Evolutionary medicine*. London: Oxford University Press.

Trifonov, V., Khiabanian, H., Greenbaum, B., & Rabadan, R. (2009). The origin of the recent swine influenza A (H1N1) virus infecting humans. *Eurosurveillance 14* (17). www.eurosurveillance.org/ViewArticle.aspx?ArticleId=19193 (retrieved July 16, 2012)

Trocolli, R. (2005). *Elite status and gender: Women leaders in chiefdom societies of the Southeastern U.S.* PhD dissertation, University of Florida.

Trouillot, M. R. (1996). Culture, color, and politics in Haiti. In S. Gregory & R. Sanjek (Eds.), *Race*. New Brunswick, NJ: Rutgers University Press.

Tsai, S.-S. H. (1996). *The eunuchs in the Ming dynasty*. Albany: SUNY Press.

Turnbull, C. M. (1961). *The forest people*. New York: Simon & Schuster.

Turnbull, C. M. (1983a). *Mbuti Pygmies: Change and adaptation*. New York: Holt, Rinehart & Winston.

Turnbull, C. M. (1983b). *The human cycle*. New York: Simon & Schuster.

Turner, T. (1991). Major shift in Brazilian Yanomami policy. *Anthropology Newsletter 32* (5), 1, 46.

"Two Americans are found slain on Jeep journey in Central Java." (1950, April 29). *New York Times*.

Tylor, E. B. (1871). *Primitive culture: Researches into the development of mythology, philosophy, religion, language, art and customs*. London: Murray.

Umar, U. (2008). *Dancing with spirits: Negotiating bissu subjectivity through Adat*. MA thesis, Department of Religious Studies. University of Colorado, Boulder. Ann Arbor, MI: ProQuest.

UNAIDS. (2009). *2009 AIDS epidemic update*. www.unaids.org/en/dataanalysis/epidemiology/2009aidsepidemicupdate/ (retrieved June 28, 2012)

UN Dispatch. (2006, July 26). Study estimates 250,000 active child soldiers. www.undispatch.com/study-estimates-250000-active-child-soldiers (retrieved August 28, 2012)

UNESCO Decade for Literacy. www.unesco.org/new/en/education/themes/education-building-blocks/literacy/un-literacy-decade/

UNESCO Institute for Statistics. The official source of literacy data. www.uis.unesco.org/literacy/Pages/default.aspx?SPSLanguage=EN (retrieved June 4, 2012)

United Nations Declaration on the Rights of Indigenous Peoples. (2007). www.un.org/esa/socdev/unpfii/documents/DRIPS_en.pdf (retrieved November 8, 2012)

United Nations Human Settlements Programme. (2003). *The challenge of slums: Global report on human settlement*. London: Earthscan Publications.

United Nations Literacy Decade (2003–2012). UNESCO. www.unesco.org/new/en/education/themes/education-building-blocks/literacy/un-literacy-decade (retrieved June 4, 2012)

United Nations, Universal Declaration of Human Rights. www.un.org/en/documents/udhr/index.shtml (retrieved October 1, 2012)

UN Refugee Agency. (2011, June 20). World Refugee Day: UNHCR report finds 80 per cent of world's refugees in developing countries. www.unhcr.org/4dfb66ef9.html (retrieved September 30, 2012)

Ury, W. L. (1982). *Talk out or walk out: The role and control of conflict in a Kentucky coal mine*. PhD dissertation, Harvard University Press.

Ury, W. L. (1993). *Getting past no: Negotiating your way from confrontation*. New York: Bantam.

Ury, W. L. (1999). *Getting to peace: Transforming conflict at home, at work, and in the world*. New York: Viking.

Ury, W. L. (2002, Winter). A global immune system. *Andover Bulletin*.

Ury, W. L. (2007). *The power of a positive no*. New York: Bantam.

U.S. Census Bureau. (2010). Families and living arrangements. www.census.gov/hhes/families/ (retrieved August 19, 2012)

U.S. Census Bureau, Statistical Abstract. (2012). Births, deaths, marriages, and divorces: Life expectancy. www.census.gov/compendia/statab/cats/births_deaths_marriages_divorces/life_expectancy.html (retrieved August 23, 2012)

U.S. Department of Health and Human Services, Administration on Children, Youth, and Families. (2005). *Child maltreatment 2003*. Washington, DC: U.S. Government Printing Office.

U.S. Department of State, Diplomacy in Action. (2007). China. www.state.gov/j/drl/rls/hrrpt/2007/100518.htm (retrieved October 31, 2012)

Van Allen, J. (1997). Sitting on a man: Colonialism and the lost political institutions of Igbo women. In R. Grinker & C. Steiner (Eds.), *Perspectives on Africa*. Boston: Blackwell Press.

Vance, A. (2012, October 4). Facebook: The making of 1 billion users. *Businessweek.com*. www.businessweek.com/articles/2012-10-04/facebook-the-making-of-1-billion-users (retrieved November 8, 2012)

Van Cott, D. L. (2008). *Radical democracy in the Andes*. Cambridge, UK: Cambridge University Press.

Van den Berghe, P. (1992). The modern state: Nation builder or nation killer? *International Journal of Group Tensions 22* (3), 191–208.

Van Eck, C. (2003). *Purified by blood: Honour killings amongst Turks in the Netherlands*. Amsterdam: Amsterdam University Press.

Van Gennep, A. (1960). *The rites of passage*. Translated by M. Vizedom & G. L. Caffee. Chicago: University of Chicago Press. (orig. 1909)

Van Willigen, J. (1986). *Applied anthropology*. South Hadley, MA: Bergin & Garvey.

Van Willigen, J. (2002). *Applied anthropology: An Introduction*. Westport, CT: Bergin & Garvey.

Vera, H. (2011). *The social life of measures: Metrication in the United States and Mexico, 1789–2004*, PhD dissertation, Sociology and Historical Studies, New School for Social Research.

Vidya, R. (2002). Karnataka's unabating kidney trade. *Frontline.* www.frontlineonnet .com/fl1907/19070610.htm (retrieved June 10, 2012)

Vitali, S., Glattfelder, J. B., & Battiston, S. (2011). The network of global corporate control. *PloS One 6* (10), e25995. doi:10.1371/journal. pone.0025995

Vogt, E. Z. (1990). *The Zinacantecos of Mexico: A modern Maya way of life* (2nd ed.). Fort Worth: Holt, Rinehart & Winston.

Wallace, A. F. C. (1970). *Culture and personality* (2nd ed.). New York: Random House.

Wallace, E., & Hoebel, E. A. (1952). *The Comanches.* Norman: University of Oklahoma Press.

Washington, H. (2006) *Medical apartheid: The dark history of medical experimentation on black Americans from colonial times to the present*, New York: Anchor.

Weatherford, J. (1988). *Indian givers: How the Indians of the Americas transformed the world.* New York: Ballantine.

Weaver, T. (2002). Gonzalo Aguirre Beltrán: Applied anthropology and indigenous policy. In *The dynamics of applied anthropology in the twentieth century: The Malinowski award papers* (pp. 34–37). Oklahoma City: Society for Applied Anthropology.

Weiner, A. B. (1988). *The Trobrianders of Papua New Guinea.* New York: Holt, Rinehart & Winston.

Wells, S. (2002). *The journey of man: A genetic odyssey.* Princeton, NJ: Princeton University Press.

Wenzel, G. W., & McCartney, A. P. (1996, September). Richard Guy Condon (1952–1995). *Arctic 49* (3), 319–320.

Werner, D. (1990). *Amazon journey.* Englewood Cliffs, NJ: Prentice-Hall.

Wheelersburg, R. P. (1987). New transportation technology among Swedish Sámi reindeer herders. *Arctic Anthropology 24* (2), 99–116.

Whelehan, P. (1985). Review of incest, a biosocial view. *American Anthropologist 87*, 678.

White, D. R. (1988). Rethinking polygyny: Co-wives, codes, and cultural systems. *Current Anthropology 29*, 529–572.

White, M. (2001). *Historical atlas of the twentieth century.* http://users.erols.com/ mwhite28/20centry.htm (retrieved August 28, 2012)

White, T., Asfaw, B., Degusta, D., Gilbert, H., Richards, G., Suwa, G., & Howell, F. C. (2003). Pleistocene *Homo sapiens* from the Middle Awash, Ethiopia. *Nature 423*, 742–747.

White, T. D. (2003). Early hominids— diversity or distortion? *Science 299*, 1994–1997.

White, T. D., & Toth, N. (2000). Cutmarks on a Plio-Pleistocene hominid from Sterkfontein, South Africa. *American Journal of Physical Anthropology 111*, 579–584.

White, T. D., et al. (2009, October). *Ardipithecus ramidus* and the paleobiology of early hominoids. *Science 326* (5949), 64, 75–86.

Whiting, J. W. M., & Child, I. L. (1953). *Child training and personality: A cross-cultural study.* New Haven, CT: Yale University Press.

Whyte, A. L. H. (2005). Human evolution in Polynesia. *Human Biology 77* (2), 157–177.

"Why the stories are told," Aunty Beryl Carmichael. *Aboriginal culture: Dreamtime stories.* www.rmwebed.com .au/HSIE/y10/abc/dreamtime/dreamtime .htm (retrieved August 28, 2012)

Wiley, A. S. (2004). *An ecology of high-altitude infancy: A biocultural perspective.* Cambridge, UK: Cambridge University Press.

Wilkie, D. S., & Curran, B. (1993). Historical trends in forager and farmer exchange in the Ituri rainforest of northeastern Zaire. *Human Ecology 21* (4), 389–417.

Williams, F. (2005, January 9). Toxic breast milk? *New York Times Magazine.*

Williams, S. (2003). Tradition and change in the sub-Arctic: Sámi reindeer herding in the modern era. *Scandinavian Studies 75* (2), 228–256.

Williamson, R. K. (1995). The blessed curse: Spirituality and sexual difference as viewed by Euramerican and Native American cultures. *The College News 18* (4).

Wills, C. (1994). The skin we're in. *Discover 15* (11), 79.

Winick, C. (Ed.). (1970). *Dictionary of anthropology.* Totowa, NJ: Littlefield, Adams.

Wolf, E. R. (1966). *Peasants.* Englewood Cliffs, NJ: Prentice-Hall.

Wolf, E. R. (1982). *Europe and the people without history.* Berkeley: University of California Press.

Wolf, E. R. (1999a). *Envisioning power: Ideologies of dominance and crisis.* Berkeley: University of California Press.

Wolf, E. R. (1999b). *Peasant wars of the twentieth century* (2nd ed.). Norman: University of Oklahoma Press.

Wolf, E. R., & Hansen, E. C. (1972). *The human condition in Latin America.* New York: Oxford University Press.

Wolf, E. R., & Trager, G. I. (1971). Hortense Powdermaker: 1900–1970. *American Anthropologist 73* (3), 784.

Wolff, P., & Holmes, K. J. (2011). Linguistic relativity. *WIRE's Cognitive Science 2*, 253–265.

Wolpoff, M., & Caspari, R. (1997). *Race and human evolution.* New York: Simon & Schuster.

Woodford, M. H., Butynski, T. M., & Karesh W. (2002). Habituating the great apes: The disease risks. *Oryx 36*, 153–160.

World Bank. (2012). Migration and remittances. *WorldBank.org.* http://web .worldbank.org/WBSITE/EXTERNAL/ NEWS/0,,contentMDK:20648762~pa gePK:64257043~piPK:437376~theSite PK:4607,00.html (retrieved October 1, 2012)

World Bank. (2012a). Poverty. www .worldbank.org/en/topic/poverty (retrieved October 1, 2012)

World Commission on Environment & Development. (1987). Our common future. A/42/427. www.un-documents.net/ocf-ov.htm (retrieved September 29, 2012)

World Development Indicators Database. (2012, September 18). Gross domestic product, 2011. *Worldbank .org.* http://databank.worldbank.org/ databank/download/GDP.pdf (retrieved October 1, 2012)

World Health Organization, Preamble to the Constitution. (1948). www.who.int/about/definition/ en/print.html

World Health Organization. (2012, June). Children: Reducing mortality. Fact sheet no. 178. www.who.int/ mediacentre/factsheets/fs178/en/index .html (retrieved August 11, 2012)

World Travel & Tourism Council. (2012). Annual report, 2011. www .wttc.org

World Watch Institute. www .worldwatch.org/

Worsley, P. (1957). *The trumpet shall sound: A study of "cargo" cults in Melanesia.* London: Macgibbon & Kee.

Wrangham, R., & Peterson, D. (1996). *Demonic males.* Boston: Houghton Mifflin.

Wu, X., & Poirier, F. E. (1995). *Human evolution in China.* New York: Oxford University Press.

Wyckoff-Baird, B. (2010, March 19). Indicators from Ju/'hoan Bushmen in Namibia. *Cultural Survival.* www .culturalsurvival.org/ourpublications/ csq/article/indicators-juhoan-bushmen-namibia (retrieved October 2, 2012)

Yates, D. (2011). *Archaeological practice and political change: Transitions and transformations in the use of the past in nationalist, neoliberal and indigenous Bolivia.* PhD dissertation, Department of Archaeology, Cambridge, UK: University of Cambridge.

Young, W. C. (2000). Kimball award winner. *Anthropology News 41* (8), 29.

Zeder, M. A., & Hesse, B. (2000). The initial domestication of goats (*Capra hircus*) in the Zagros Mountains 10,000 years ago. *Science 287*, 2254–2257.

Zeresenay, A., et al. (2006). A juvenile early hominin skeleton from Dikika, Ethiopia. *Nature 443*, 296–301.

Zilhão, J. (2000). Fate of the Neandertals. *Archaeology 53* (4), 30.

Zimmer, C. (2009, September 21). The secrets inside your dog's mind. *Time .com.* www.time.com/time/magazine/ article/0,9171,1921614-1,00.html (retrieved July 16, 2012)

Bibliography

Abbot, E. (2001). *A history of celibacy.* Cambridge, MA: Da Capo Press.

Abu-Lughod, L. (1986). *Veiled sentiments: Honor and poetry in a Bedouin society.* Berkeley: University of California Press.

Abun-Nasr, J. M. (2007). *Muslim communities of grace: The Sufi brotherhoods in Islamic religious life.* New York: Columbia University Press.

Adams, R. E. W. (1977). *Prehistoric Mesoamerica.* Boston: Little, Brown.

Adams, R. M. (1966). *The evolution of urban society.* Chicago: Aldine.

Adams, R. M. (2001). Scale and complexity in archaic states. *Latin American Antiquity 11,* 188.

adherents.com.

Adler, S. (1959). Darwin's illness. *Nature,* 1102–1103.

Aguirre Beltrán, G. (1974). Applied anthropology in Mexico. *Human Organization 33* (1), 1–6.

Alfonso-Durraty, M. (2012). Personal communication.

Allen, J. S., & Cheer, S. M. (1996). The non-thrifty genotype. *Current Anthropology 37,* 831–842.

Allen, T. (2006). *Trial justice: The International Criminal Court and the Lord's Resistance Army.* London & New York: Zed Books/International African Institute.

Alper, J. S., et al. (Eds.). (2002). *The double-edged helix: Social implications of genetics in a diverse society.* Baltimore: Johns Hopkins University Press.

Alvard, M. S., & Kuznar, L. (2001). Deferred harvest: The transition from hunting to animal husbandry. *American Anthropologist 103* (2), 295–311.

Amábile-Cuevas, C. F., & Chicurel, M. E. (1993). Horizontal gene transfer. *American Scientist 81,* 338.

Ambrose, S. H. (2001). Paleolithic technology and human evolution. *Science 291,* 1748–1753.

American Anthropological Association. (1998). Statement on "race." www.aaanet.org/stmts/racepp.htm (retrieved August 1, 2012)

American Anthropological Association. (2007). Executive board statement on the Human Terrain System Project. www.aaanet.org/about/policies/statements/human-terrain-system-statement.cfm

Amnesty International. (2010, August 16). Afghan couple stoned to death by Taleban. www.amnesty.org/en/news-and-updates/afghan-couple-stoned-death-taleban-2010-08-16 (retrieved October 6, 2012)

Amnesty International. (2012). Death penalty in 2011. www.amnesty.org/en/death-penalty (retrieved September 5, 2012)

Anderson, M. S. (2006). *The Allied Tribes Tsimshian of north coastal British Columbia: Social organization, economy and trade.* Unpublished PhD dissertation. http://faculty.arts.ubc.ca/menzies/documents/anderson.pdf

Anderson, S. (2010, February). The polygamists. *National Geographic,* 36, 39. http://ngm.nationalgeographic.com/2010/02/polygamists/anderson-text (retrieved September 6, 2011)

Andrews, L. B., & Nelkin, D. (1996). *The Bell Curve*: A statement. *Science 271,* 13.

Anjum, T. (2006). Sufism in history and its relationship with power. *Islamic Studies 45* (2), 221–268.

Anthony, D. (2007). *The horse, the wheel, and language.* Princeton, NJ: Princeton University Press.

Appadurai, A. (1990). Disjuncture and difference in the global cultural economy. *Public Culture 2,* 1–24.

Appadurai, A. (1996). *Modernity at large: Cultural dimensions of globalization.* Minneapolis: University of Minnesota Press.

Appenzeller, T. (1998). Art: Evolution or revolution? *Science 282,* 1451–1454.

Arctic Monitoring Assessment Project. (2003). *AMAP assessment 2002: Human health in the Arctic* (pp. xii–xiii, 22–23). Oslo: AMAP.

Arms Control Association. (2012). Nuclear weapons: Who has what at a glance. www.armscontrol.org/factsheets/Nuclearweaponswhohaswhat (retrieved October 1, 2012)

Armstrong, D. F., Stokoe, W. C., & Wilcox, S. E. (1993). Signs of the origin of syntax. *Current Anthropology 34,* 349–368.

Arnold, F., Kishor, S., & Roy, T. K. (2002). Sex-selective abortions in India. *Population and Development Review 28* (4), 759–785.

Ashmore, W. (Ed.). (1981). *Lowland Maya settlement patterns.* Albuquerque: University of New Mexico Press.

Aureli, F., & de Waal, F. B. M. (2000). *Natural conflict resolution.* Berkeley: University of California Press.

Ayalon, D. (1999). *Eunuchs, caliphs, and sultans: A study in power relationships.* Jerusalem: Mangess Press.

Babiker, M. A., et al. (1996). Unnecessary deprivation of common food items in glucose-6-phosphate dehydrogenase deficiency. *Annals of Saudi Arabia 16* (4), 462–463.

Bailey, R. C., & Aunger, R. (1989). Net hunters vs. archers: Variations in women's subsistence strategies in the Ituri forest. *Human Ecology 17,* 273–297.

Baker, P. (Ed.). (1978). *The biology of high altitude peoples.* London: Cambridge University Press.

Balikci, A. (1970). *The Netsilik Eskimo.* Garden City, NY: Natural History Press.

Balter, M. (1998). Why settle down? The mystery of communities. *Science 282,* 1442–1444.

Balter, M. (1999). A long season puts Çatalhöyük in context. *Science 286,* 890–891.

Balter, M. (2001). Did plaster hold Neolithic society together? *Science 294,* 2278–2281.

Balter, M. (2001). In search of the first Europeans. *Science 291,* 1724.

Balzer, M. M. (1981). Rituals of gender identity: Markers of Siberian Khanty ethnicity, status, and belief. *American Anthropologist 83* (4), 850–867.

Barham, L. S. (1998). Possible early pigment use in South-Central Africa. *Current Anthropology 39,* 703–710.

Barkai, R., & Liran, R. (2008). Midsummer sunset at Neolithic Jericho. *Time and Mind: The Journal of Archaeology, Consciousness, and Culture 1* (3), 273–284.

Barnard, A. (1995). Monboddo's *Orang Outang* and the definition of man. In R. Corbey & B. Theunissen (Eds.), *Ape, man, apeman: Changing views since 1600* (pp. 71–85). Leiden: Department of Prehistory, Leiden University.

Barnouw, V. (1985). *Culture and personality* (4th ed.). Homewood, IL: Dorsey Press.

Barr, R. G. (1997, October). The crying game. *Natural History,* 47.

Barrett, L., et al. (2004). Habitual cave use and thermoregulation in chacma baboons (*Papio hamadryas ursinus*). *Journal of Human Evolution 46* (2), 215–222.

"Bartered brides." (2009, March 12). *Economist.* www.economist.com/node/13278577 (retrieved October 31, 2012)

Barth, F. (1962). Nomadism in the mountain and plateau areas of South West Asia. *The problems of the arid zone* (pp. 341–355). Paris: UNESCO.

694

Bar-Yosef, O. (1986). The walls of Jericho: An alternative interpretation. *Current Anthropology 27,* 160.

Bar-Yosef, O., Vandermeesch, B., Arensburg, B., Belfer-Cohen, A., Goldberg, P., Laville, H., Meignen, L., Rak, Y., Speth, J. D., Tchernov, E., Tillier, A-M., & Weiner, S. (1992). The excavations in Kebara Cave, Mt. Carmel. *Current Anthropology 33,* 497–550.

Basel Action Network. (2010). Country status: Waste trade ban agreements. http://ban.org/country_status/country_status_chart.html (retrieved November 3, 2012)

Bates, D. G. (2001). *Human adaptive strategies: Ecology, culture, and politics* (2nd ed.). Boston: Allen & Bacon.

Bateson, G., & Mead, M. (1942). *Balinese character: A photographic analysis.* New York: New York Academy of Sciences.

Becker, J. (2004, March). China's growing pains. *National Geographic,* 68–95.

Bednarik, R. G. (1995). Concept-mediated marking in the Lower Paleolithic. *Current Anthropology 36,* 606.

Beeman, W. O. (2000). Introduction: Margaret Mead, cultural studies, and international understanding. In M. Mead & R. Métraux (Eds.), *The study of culture at a distance* (pp. xiv–xxxi). New York & Oxford, UK: Berghahn Books.

Behrend, H. (1999). *Alice Lakwena and the Holy Spirits: War in northern Uganda 1986–97.* Oxford, UK: James Currey.

Behrend, H., & Luig, U. (Eds.). (2000). *Spirit possession, modernity, and power in Africa.* Madison: University of Wisconsin Press.

Behrensmeyer, A. K., Todd, N. E., Potts, R., & McBrinn, G. E. (1997). Late Pliocene faunal turnover in the Turkana basin, Kenya, and Ethiopia. *Science 278,* 1589–1594.

Behringer, W. (2004). *Witches and witch-hunts: A global history.* Cambridge, UK: Polity Press.

Bekoff, M., et al. (Eds.). (2002). *The cognitive animal: Empirical and theoretical perspectives on animal cognition.* Cambridge, MA: MIT Press.

Bell, D. (1997). Defining marriage and legitimacy. *Current Anthropology 38,* 241.

Belshaw, C. S. (1958). The significance of modern cults in Melanesian development. In W. Lessa & E. Z. Vogt (Eds.), *Reader in comparative religion: An anthropological approach.* New York: Harper & Row.

Benedict, R. (1959). *Patterns of culture.* New York: New American Library.

Bennett, R. L., et al. (2002, April). Genetic counseling and screening of consanguineous couples and their offspring: Recommendations of the National Society of Genetic Counselors. *Journal of Genetic Counseling 11* (2), 97–119.

Berdan, F. F. (1982). *The Aztecs of Central Mexico.* New York: Holt, Rinehart & Winston.

Bergendorff, S. (2009). *Simple lives, cultural complexity: Rethinking culture in terms of complexity theory.* Lanham, MD: Rowman & Littlefield.

Bermúdez de Castro, J. M., Arsuaga, J. L., Cabonell, E., Rosas, A., Martinez, I., & Mosquera, M. (1997). A hominid from the lower Pleistocene of Atapuerca, Spain: Possible ancestor to Neandertals and modern humans. *Science 276,* 1392–1395.

Bernal, I. (1969). *The Olmec world.* Berkeley: University of California Press.

Bernard, H. R. (2006). *Research methods in anthropology: Qualitative and quantitative approaches* (4th ed.). Walnut Creek, CA: AltaMira Press.

Bernardi, B. (1985). *Age class systems: Social institutions and policies based on age.* New York: Cambridge University Press.

Bernstein, R. E., et al. (1984). Darwin's illness: Chagas' disease resurgens. *Journal of the Royal Society of Medicine 77,* 608–609.

Berra, T. M. (1990). *Evolution and the myth of creationism.* Stanford, CA: Stanford University Press.

Berreman, G. D. (1968). Caste: The concept of caste. *International encyclopedia of the social sciences* (vol. 2, pp. 333–338). New York: Macmillan.

Betzig, L. (1989). Causes of conjugal dissolution: A cross-cultural study. *Current Anthropology 30,* 654–676.

Bicchieri, M. G. (Ed.). (1972). *Hunters and gatherers today: A socioeconomic study of eleven such cultures in the twentieth century.* New York: Holt, Rinehart & Winston.

Binford, L. R. (1972). *An archaeological perspective.* New York: Seminar Press.

Binford, L. R., & Chuan, K. H. (1985). Taphonomy at a distance: Zhoukoudian, the cave home of Beijing man? *Current Anthropology 26,* 413–442.

Birch, E. L., & Wachter, S. M. (Eds.). (2011). *Global urbanization.* Philadelphia: University of Pennsylvania Press.

Birdsell, J. H. (1977). The recalibration of a paradigm for the first peopling of Greater Australia. In J. Allen, J. Golson, & R. Jones (Eds.), *Sunda and Sahul: Prehistoric studies in Southeast Asia, Melanesia, and Australia* (pp. 113–167). New York: Academic Press.

Blackless, M., et al. (2000). How sexually dimorphic are we? Review and synthesis. *American Journal of Human Biology 12,* 151–166.

Blacksmith, N., & Harter, J. (2011, October 28). Majority of American workers not engaged in their jobs. *Gallup Wellbeing.* www.gallup.com/poll/150383/Majority-American-Workers-Not-Engaged-Jobs.aspx (retrieved October 1, 2012)

Blakey, M. (2003, October 29). Personal communication. *African Burial Ground Project.* Department of Anthropology, College of William & Mary.

Blakey, M. (May, 2010). African Burial Ground Project: Paradigm for cooperation? *Museum International 62* (1–2), 61–68.

Blok, A. (1974). *The mafia of a Sicilian village 1860–1960.* New York: Harper & Row.

Blok, A. (1981). Rams and billy-goats: A key to the Mediterranean code of honour. *Man, New Series 16* (3), 427–440.

Blom, A., et al. (2004). Behavioral responses of gorillas to habituation in the Dzanga-Ndoki National Park, Central African Republic. *International Journal of Primatology 25,* 179–196.

Blumberg, R. L. (1991). *Gender, family, and the economy: The triple overlap.* Newbury Park, CA: Sage.

Blumer, M. A., & Byrne, R. (1991). The ecological genetics and domestication and the origins of agriculture. *Current Anthropology 32,* 30.

Boas, F. (1909, May 28). Race problems in America. *Science 29* (752), 839–849.

Boas, F. (1962). *Primitive art.* Gloucester, MA: Peter Smith.

Boas, F. (1966). *Race, language and culture.* New York: Free Press.

Bodley, J. H. (2007). *Anthropology and contemporary human problems* (5th ed.). Lanham, MD: AltaMira Press.

Bodley, J. H. (2008). *Victims of progress* (5th ed.). Lanham, MD: AltaMira Press.

Boehm, C. (1987). *Blood revenge.* Philadelphia: University of Pennsylvania Press.

Boehm, C. (2000). The evolution of moral communities. *School of American Research, 2000 Annual Report,* 7.

Bogucki, P. (1999). *The origins of human society.* Oxford, UK: Blackwell Press.

Bohannan, P. (Ed.). (1967). *Law and warfare: Studies in the anthropology of conflict.* Garden City, NY: Natural History Press.

Bohannan, P., & Middleton, J. (Eds.). (1968). *Kinship and social organization.* Garden City, NY: Natural History Press.

Bohannan, P., & Middleton, J. (Eds.). (1968). *Marriage, family, and residence.* Garden City, NY: Natural History Press.

Bolinger, D. (1968). *Aspects of language.* New York: Harcourt.

Bongaarts, J. (1998). Demographic consequences of declining fertility. *Science 182,* 419.

Bonvillain, N. (2007). *Language, culture, and communication: The meaning of messages* (5th ed.). Upper Saddle River, NJ: Prentice-Hall.

Bordes, F. (1972). *A tale of two caves.* New York: Harper & Row.

Bornstein, M. H. (1975). The influence of visual perception on culture. *American Anthropologist 77* (4), 774–798.

Boshara, R. (2003, January/February). Wealth inequality: The $6,000 solution. *Atlantic Monthly 291,* 91.

Boškovic, A. (Ed.). (2009). *Other people's anthropologies: Ethnographic practice on the margins.* Oxford, UK: Berghahn Books.

Bowen, J. R. (2004). *Religions in practice: An approach to the anthropology of religion* (3rd ed.). Boston: Allyn & Bacon.

Bowie, F. (2006). *The anthropology of religion* (2nd ed.). Malden, MA: Blackwell Press.

Brace, C. L. (1981). Tales of the phylogenetic woods: The evolution and significance of phylogenetic trees. *American Journal of Physical Anthropology 56,* 411–429.

Brace, C. L. (1997). Cro-Magnons "R" us? *Anthropology Newsletter 38* (8), 1.

Brace, C. L. (2000). *Evolution in an anthropological view.* Walnut Creek, CA: AltaMira Press.

Brace, C. L., Nelson, H., & Korn, N. (1979). *Atlas of human evolution* (2nd ed.). New York: Holt, Rinehart & Winston.

Bradfield, R. M. (1998). *A natural history of associations* (2nd ed.). New York: International Universities Press.

Bradford, P. V., & Blume, H. (1992). *Ota Benga: The Pygmy in the zoo.* New York: St. Martin's Press.

Braidwood, R. J. (1960). The agricultural revolution. *Scientific American 203,* 130–141.

Braidwood, R. J. (1975). *Prehistoric men* (8th ed.). Glenview, IL: Scott, Foresman.

Brain, C. K. (1968). Who killed the Swartkrans ape-men? *South African Museums Association Bulletin 9,* 127–139.

Brain, C. K. (1969). The contribution of Namib Desert Hottentots to an understanding of australopithecine bone accumulations. *Scientific Papers of the Namib Desert Research Station,* 13.

Branda, R. F., & Eatoil, J. W. (1978). Skin color and photolysis: An evolutionary hypothesis. *Science 201,* 625–626.

Braudel, F. (1979). *The structures of everyday life: Civilization and capitalism 15th–18th century* (vol. 1, pp. 163–167). New York: Harper & Row.

Brettell, C. B., & Sargent, C. F. (Eds.). (2000). *Gender in cross-cultural perspective* (3rd ed.). Upper Saddle River, NJ: Prentice-Hall.

Brew, J. O. (1968). *One hundred years of anthropology.* Cambridge, MA: Harvard University Press.

Brody, H. (1997). *Maps and dreams.* Long Grove, IL: Waveland Press.

Broecker, W. S. (1992, April). Global warming on trial. *Natural History,* 14.

Brothwell, D. R., & Higgs, E. (Eds.). (1969). *Science in archaeology* (rev. ed.). London: Thames & Hudson.

Brown, B., Walker, A., Ward, C. V., & Leakey, R. E. (1993). New *Australopithecus boisei* calvaria from East Lake Turkana, Kenya. *American Journal of Physical Anthropology 91,* 137–159.

Brown, D. E. (1991). *Human universals.* New York: McGraw-Hill.

Brown, P., et al. (2004). A new small-bodied hominin from the Late Pleistocene of Flores, Indonesia. *Nature 431,* 1055–1061.

Brunet, M., et al. (2002). A new hominid from the Upper Miocene of Chad, Central Africa. *Nature 418,* 145–151.

Buck, P. H. (1938). *Vikings of the Pacific.* Chicago: University Press of Chicago.

Buckland, T. J. (Ed.). (2007). *Dancing from past to present: Nation, culture, identities.* Madison: University of Wisconsin Press.

Burling, R. (1970). *Man's many voices: Language in its cultural context.* New York: Holt, Rinehart & Winston.

Burling, R. (1993). Primate calls, human language, and nonverbal communication. *Current Anthropology 34,* 25–53.

Butynski, T. M. (2001). Africa's great apes. In B. Beck et al. (Eds.), *Great apes and humans: The ethics of coexistence* (pp. 3–56). Washington, DC: Smithsonian Institution Press.

Byers, D. S. (Ed.). (1967). *The prehistory of the Tehuacan Valley: Environment and subsistence* (vol. 1). Austin: University of Texas Press.

Cachel, S. (1997). Dietary shifts and the European Upper Paleolithic transition. *Current Anthropology 38,* 590.

Callaway, E. (2007, December 3). Chimp beats students at computer game. *Nature.* doi:10.1038/news.2007.317

Capps, R., McCabe, K., & Fix, M. (2012). *Diverse streams: Black African migration to the United States.* Washington, DC: Migration Policy Institute. www.migrationpolicy.org/pubs/CBI-AfricanMigration.pdf (retrieved September 30, 2012)

Carbonell, E., et al. (2008). The first hominin of Europe. *Nature 452* (7186), 465–469.

Cardarelli, F. (2003). *Encyclopedia of scientific units, weights, and measures. Their SI equivalents and origins.* London: Springer.

Carneiro, R. L. (1970). A theory of the origin of the state. *Science 169,* 733–738.

Carneiro, R. L. (2003). *Evolutionism in cultural anthropology: A critical history.* Boulder, CO: Westview Press.

Caroulis, J. (1996). Food for thought. *Pennsylvania Gazette 95* (3), 16.

Carpenter, E. S. (1959). *Eskimo.* Toronto: University of Toronto Press.

Carpenter, E. S. (1968). We wed ourselves to the mystery: A study of tribal art. *Explorations 22,* 66–74.

Carroll, J. B. (Ed.). (1956). *Language, thought and reality: Selected writings of Benjamin Lee Whorf.* Cambridge, MA: MIT Press.

Carroll, S. B. (2005). *Endless forms most beautiful: The new science of evo devo.* New York: Norton.

Cartmill, E. A., & Byrne, R. W. (2010) Semantics of orangutan gesture: Determining structure and meaning through form and use. *Animal Cognition.* doi: 10.1007/s10071-010-0328-7

Cartmill, M. (1998). The gift of gab. *Discover 19* (11), 64.

Cashdan, E. (1989). Hunters and gatherers: Economic behavior in bands. In S. Plattner (Ed.), *Economic anthropology* (pp. 21–48). Stanford, CA: Stanford University Press.

Cashdan, E. (2008). Waist-to-hip ratio across cultures: Trade-offs between androgen- and estrogen-dependent traits. *Current Anthropology 49* (6).

Catford, J. C. (1988). *A practical introduction to phonetics.* Oxford, UK: Clarendon Press.

Cavalieri, P., & Singer, P. (1994). *The Great Ape Project: Equality beyond humanity.* New York: St. Martin's.

Cavalli-Sforza, L. L. (1977). *Elements of human genetics.* Menlo Park, CA: W. A. Benjamin.

Centers for Disease Control and Prevention. (2009). Differences in prevalence of obesity among black, white, and Hispanic adults—United States, 2006–2008. *Morbidity and Mortality Weekly Report 58* (27), 740–744.

Chagnon, N. A. (1988). Life histories, blood revenge, and warfare in a tribal population. *Science 239,* 935–992.

Chagnon, N. A. (1988). *Yanomamö: The fierce people* (3rd ed.). New York: Holt, Rinehart & Winston.

Chagnon, N. A. (1990). On Yanomamö violence: Reply to Albert. *Current Anthropology 31* (2), 49–53.

Chagnon, N. A., & Irons, W. (Eds.). (1979). *Evolutionary biology and human social behavior.* North Scituate, MA: Duxbury Press.

Chambers, R. (1995). *Rural development: Putting the last first.* Englewood Cliffs, NJ: Prentice-Hall.

Chan, J. W. C., & Vernon, P. E. (1988). Individual differences among the peoples of China. In J. W. Berry (Ed.), *Human abilities in cultural context* (pp. 340–357). Cambridge, UK: Cambridge University Press.

Chance, N. A. (1990). *The Iñupiat and Arctic Alaska: An ethnography of development.* New York: Harcourt.

Chang, K. C. (Ed.). (1968). *Settlement archaeology.* Palo Alto, CA: National Press.

Chang, L. (2005, June 9). A migrant worker sees rural home in new light. *Wall Street Journal.*

Chase, C. (1998). Hermaphrodites with attitude. *Gay and Lesbian Quarterly 4* (2), 189–211.

Chatty, D. (1996). *Mobile pastoralists: Development planning and social change in Oman.* New York: Columbia University Press.

Cheater, A. (2005). *The anthropology of power.* London: Routledge.

Cheney, D. L., & Seyfarth, R. M. (2007). *Baboon metaphysics: The evolution of a social mind.* Chicago: University of Chicago Press.

Chicurel, M. (2001). Can organisms speed their own evolution? *Science 292,* 1824–1827.

"Child soldiers global report 2008." (2009). Despite progress, efforts to end the recruitment and use of child soldiers are too little and too late for many children. www.childsoldiersglobalreport.org/ (retrieved August 28, 2012)

Childe, V. G. (1951). *Man makes himself.* New York: New American Library. (orig. 1936)

Childe, V. G. (1954). *What happened in history.* Baltimore: Penguin Books.

"China to execute bride traffickers." (2000, October 20). *BBC News.* http://news.bbc.co.uk/2/hi/asia-pacific/981675.stm (retrieved October 31, 2012)

Cigno, A. (1994). *Economics of the family.* New York: Oxford University Press.

Ciochon, R. L., & Fleagle, J. G. (Eds.). (1987). *Primate evolution and human origins.* Hawthorne, NY: Aldine.

Ciochon, R. L., & Fleagle, J. G. (1993). *The human evolution source book.* Englewood Cliffs, NJ: Prentice-Hall.

Claeson, B. (1994). The privatization of justice: An ethnography of control. In L. Nader (Ed.), *Essays on controlling processes* (pp. 32–64). *Kroeber Anthropological Society Papers* (no. 77). Berkeley: University of California Press.

Clark, E. E. (1966). *Indian legends of the Pacific Northwest.* Berkeley: University of California Press.

Clark, G. (1967). *The Stone Age hunters.* New York: McGraw-Hill.

Clark, G. (1972). *Starr Carr: A case study in bioarchaeology.* Reading, MA: Addison-Wesley.

Clark, G. A. (1997). Neandertal genetics. *Science 277,* 1024.

Clark, G. A. (2002). Neandertal archaeology: Implications for our origins. *American Anthropologist 104* (1), 50–67.

Clark, J. G. D. (1962). *Prehistoric Europe: The economic basis.* Stanford, CA: Stanford University Press.

Clark, W. E. L. (1960). *The antecedents of man.* Chicago: Quadrangle Books.

Clark, W. E. L. (1966). *History of the primates* (5th ed.). Chicago: University of Chicago Press.

Clark, W. E. L. (1967). *Man-apes or apemen? The story of discoveries in Africa.* New York: Holt, Rinehart & Winston.

Clarke, R. J. (1998). First ever discovery of a well preserved skull and associated skeleton of *Australopithecus. South African Journal of Science 94,* 460–464.

Clarke, R. J., & Tobias, P. V. (1995). Sterkfontein member 2 foot bones of the oldest South African hominid. *Science 269,* 521–524.

Clay, J. W. (1996). What's a nation? In W. A. Haviland & R. J. Gordon (Eds.), *Talking about people* (2nd ed., pp. 188–189). Mountain View, CA: Mayfield.

Clough, S. B., & Cole, C. W. (1952). *Economic history of Europe* (3rd ed.). Lexington, MA: Heath.

Coco, L. E. (1994). Silicone breast implants in America: A choice of the official breast? In L. Nader (Ed.), *Essays on controlling processes* (pp. 103–132). *Kroeber Anthropological Society Papers* (no. 77). Berkeley: University of California Press.

Coe, S. D. (1994). *America's first cuisines.* Austin: University of Texas Press.

Coe, W. R. (1967). *Tikal: A handbook of the ancient Maya ruins.* Philadelphia: University of Pennsylvania Museum.

Coe, S. D., & Coe, M. D. (1996). *The true history of chocolate.* New York: Thames & Hudson.

Coe, W. R., & Haviland, W. A. (1982). *Introduction to the archaeology of Tikal.* Philadelphia: University Museum.

Cohen, J. (1997). Is an old virus up to new tricks? *Science 277,* 312–313.

Cohen, J. (2009). Out of Mexico? Scientists ponder swine flu's origin. *Science 324* (5928), 700–702.

Cohen, M. N. (1977). *The food crisis in prehistory.* New Haven, CT: Yale University Press.

Cohen, M. N. (1995). Anthropology and race: The Bell Curve phenomenon. *General Anthropology 2* (1), 1–4.

Cohen, M. N. (1998). *Culture of intolerance: Chauvinism, class, and racism in the United States.* New Haven, CT: Yale University Press.

Cohen, M. N., & Armelagos, G. J. (1984). *Paleopathology at the origins of agriculture.* Orlando: Academic Press.

Cohen, M. N., & Armelagos, G. J. (1984). Paleopathology at the origins of agriculture: Editors' summation. In *Paleopathology at the origins of agriculture.* Orlando: Academic Press.

Colborn, T., Dumanoski, D., & Myers, J. P. (1996). Hormonal sabotage. *Natural History 3,* 45–46.

Colborn, T., Dumanoski, D., & Myers, J. P. (1997). *Our stolen future.* New York: Plume/Penguin Books.

Cole, J. W., & Wolf, E. R. (1999). *The hidden frontier: Ecology and ethnicity in an alpine valley* (with a new introduction). Berkeley: University of California Press.

Collier, J., & Collier, M. (1986). *Visual anthropology: Photography as a research method.* Albuquerque: University of New Mexico Press.

Collier, J., Rosaldo, M. Z., & Yanagisako, S. (1982). Is there a family? New anthropological views. In B. Thorne & M. Yalom (Eds.), *Rethinking the family: Some feminist questions* (pp. 25–39). New York: Longman.

Collier, J. F., & Yanagisako, S. J. (Eds.). (1987). *Gender and kinship: Essays toward a unified analysis.* Stanford, CA: Stanford University Press.

Collins, B. (2005). *The trouble with poetry.* New York: Random House.

Conard, N. J. (2009). A female figurine from the basal Aurignacian deposits of Hohle Fels Cave in southwestern Germany. *Nature 459* (7244), 248.

Cone, M. (2005). *Silent snow: The slow poisoning of the Arctic.* New York: Grove Press.

Conklin, B. (1997). Body paint, feathers, and VCRs: Aesthetics and authenticity in Amazonian activism. *American Ethnologist 24* (4), 711–737.

Conklin, B. A. (2002). Shamans versus pirates in the Amazonian treasure chest. *American Anthropologist 104* (4), 1050–1061.

Conklin, H. C. (1955). Hanunóo color categories. *Southwestern Journal of Anthropology 11,* 339–344.

Connelly, J. C. (1979). Hopi social organization. In A. Ortiz (Ed.), *Handbook of North American Indians: Southwest* (vol. 9, pp. 539–553). Washington, DC: Smithsonian Institution Press.

Conner, M. (1996). The archaeology of contemporary mass graves. *SAA Bulletin 14* (4), 6, 31.

Conroy, G. C. (1997). *Reconstructing human origins: A modern synthesis.* New York: Norton.

Coon, C. S. (1962). *The origins of races.* New York: Knopf.

Coon, C. S., Garn, S. N., & Birdsell, J. (1950). *Races: A study of the problems of race formation in man.* Springfield, IL: Thomas.

Coontz, S. (2005). *Marriage, a history: From obedience to intimacy, or how love conquered marriage.* New York: Viking Adult.

Cooper, A., Poinar, H. N., Pääbo, S., Radovci, C. J., Debénath, A., Caparros, M., Barroso-Ruiz, C., Bertranpetit, J., Nielsen-March, C., Hedges, R. E. M., & Sykes, B. (1997). Neanderthal genetics. *Science 277,* 1021–1024.

Copeland, S. R., et al. (2011, June 2). Strontium isotope evidence for landscape use by early hominins. *Nature 474,* 76–78. doi: 10.1038/nature10149

Coppa, A., et al. (2006). Early Neolithic tradition of dentistry. *Nature 440,* 755–756.

Coppens, Y., Howell, F. C., Isaac, G. L., & Leakey, R. E. F. (Eds.). (1976). *Earliest man and environments in the Lake Rudolf Basin: Stratigraphy, paleoecology, and evolution.* Chicago: University of Chicago Press.

Corbey, R. (1995). Introduction: Missing links, or the ape's place in nature. In R. Corbey & B. Theunissen (Eds.), *Ape, man, apeman: Changing views since 1600* (p. 1). Leiden: Department of Prehistory, Leiden University.

Cornwell, T. (1995, November 10). Skeleton staff. *Times Higher Education,* 20.

Corruccini, R. S. (1992). Metrical reconsideration of the Skhul IV and IX and Border Cave I crania in the context of modern human origins. *American Journal of Physical Anthropology 87,* 433–445.

Cottrell, L. (1963). *The lost pharaohs.* New York: Grosset & Dunlap.

Courlander, H. (1971). *The fourth world of the Hopis.* New York: Crown.

Cowgill, G. L. (1997). State and society at Teotihuacan, Mexico. *Annual Review of Anthropology 26,* 129–161.

Crane, H. (2001). *Men in spirit: The masculinization of Taiwanese Buddhist nuns.* PhD dissertation, Brown University.

Cretney, S. (2003). *Family law in the twentieth century: A history.* New York: Oxford University Press.

Criminal Code of Canada, § 718.2(e).

Crocker, W. A., & Crocker, J. (2004). *The Canela: Kinship, ritual, and sex in an Amazonian tribe.* Belmont, CA: Wadsworth.

Crystal, D. (2002). *Language death.* Cambridge, UK: Cambridge University Press.

Culbert, T. P. (Ed.). (1973). *The Classic Maya collapse.* Albuquerque: University of New Mexico Press.

Culotta, E. (1995). New hominid crowds the field. *Science 269,* 918.

Culotta, E., & Koshland, D. E., Jr. (1994). DNA repair works its way to the top. *Science 266,* 1926.

D'Adesky, A.-C. (2004). *Moving mountains: The race to treat global AIDS.* New York: Verso.

Dalton, G. (1971). *Traditional tribal and peasant economics: An introductory survey of economic anthropology.* Reading, MA: Addison-Wesley.

Dalton, R. (2009). Fossil primate challenges Ida's place: Controversial German specimen is related to lemurs, not humans, analysis of an Egyptian find suggests. *Nature 461,* 1040.

Daniel, G. (1970). *The first civilizations: The archaeology of their origins.* New York: Apollo Editions.

Daniel, G. (1975). *A hundred and fifty years of archaeology* (2nd ed.). London: Duckworth.

Darwin, C. (1859). *On the origin of species.* New York: Atheneum.

Darwin, C. (1871). *The descent of man and selection in relation to sex.* New York: Random House (Modern Library).

Darwin, C. (1887). *Autobiography.* Reprinted in *The life and letters of Charles Darwin* (1902). F. Darwin (Ed.), London: John Murray.

Davenport, W. (1959). Linear descent and descent groups. *American Anthropologist 61,* 557–573.

Davies, G. (2005). *A history of money from the earliest times to present day* (3rd ed.). Cardiff, UK: University of Wales Press.

Davies, J. B., et al. (2007). *The world distribution of household wealth.* Santa Cruz: University of California, Mapping Global Inequalities, Center for Global, International, and Regional Studies.

Davies, S. G. (2007). *Challenging gender norms: Five genders among the Bugis in Indonesia.* Belmont, CA: Thomson Wadsworth.

"A decade of CSQ." (1991, Winter). *Cultural Survival Quarterly 15*(4), entire issue.

Deetz, J. (1967). *Invitation to archaeology.* New York: Doubleday.

Deetz, J. (1977). *In small things forgotten: The archaeology of early American life.* Garden City, NY: Doubleday/Anchor.

de la Torre, S., & Snowden, C. T. (2009). Dialects in pygmy marmosets? Population variation in call structure. *American Journal of Primatology 71* (5), 333–342.

del Carmen Rodríguez Martínez, M., et al. (2006). Oldest writing in the New World. *Science 313* (5793), 1610–1614.

del Castillo, B. D. (1963). *The conquest of New Spain* (translation and introduction by J. M. Cohen). New York: Penguin Books.

Delio, M. (2004). Global chaos, just for fun. *Wired.* www.wired.com/culture/lifestyle/news/2004/06/63872 (retrieved October 1, 2012)

DeMello, M. (2000). *Bodies of inscription: A cultural history of the modern tattoo community.* Durham, NC: Duke University Press.

De Mott, B. (1990). *The imperial middle: Why Americans can't think straight about class.* New York: Morrow.

d'Errico, F., Zilhão, J., Julien, M., Baffier, D., & Pelegrin, J. (1998). Neandertal acculturation in Western Europe? *Current Anthropology 39*, 521.

DeSilva, J. M. (2009). Functional morphology of the ankle and the likelihood of climbing in early hominins. *Proceeding of the National Academy of Sciences, USA 106*, 6567–6572.

Desowitz, R. S. (1987). *New Guinea tapeworm and Jewish grandmothers.* New York: Norton.

Dettwyler, K. A. (1994). *Dancing skeletons: Life and death in West Africa.* Prospect Heights, IL: Waveland Press.

Dettwyler, K. A. (1997, October). When to wean. *Natural History,* 49.

de Villiers, J., & de Villiers, P. (1978). *Language acquisition.* Cambridge, MA: Harvard University Press.

DeVore, I. (Ed.). (1965). *Primate behavior: Field studies of monkeys and apes.* New York: Holt, Rinehart & Winston.

de Waal, F. B. M. (1996). *Good natured: The origins of right and wrong in humans and other animals.* Cambridge, MA: Harvard University Press.

de Waal, F. B. M. (2000). Primates—A natural heritage of conflict resolution. *Science 28*, 586–590.

de Waal, F. B. M. (2001). *The ape and the sushi master.* New York: Basic Books.

de Waal, F. B. M. (2001). Sing the song of evolution. *Natural History 110* (8), 77.

de Waal, F. B. M. (2003). *My family album: Thirty years of primate photography.* Berkeley: University of California Press.

de Waal, F. B. M., & Johanowicz, D. L. (1993). Modification of reconciliation behavior through social experience: An experiment with two macaque species. *Child Development 64*, 897–908.

de Waal, F. B. M., Kano, T., & Parish, A. R. (1998). Comments. *Current Anthropology 39*, 408, 413.

de Waal, F. B. M., & Lanting, F. (1998). *Bonobo: The forgotten ape.* Berkeley: University of California Press.

Diamond, J. (1994). How Africa became black. *Discover 15* (2), 72–81.

Diamond, J. (1994). Race without color. *Discover 15* (11), 83–89.

Diamond, J. (1996). Empire of uniformity. *Discover 17* (3), 83–84.

Diamond, J. (1997). *Guns, germs, and steel.* New York: Norton.

Diamond, J. (1998). Ants, crops, and history. *Science 281*, 1974–1975.

Diamond, J. (2005). *Collapse: How societies choose to fail or succeed.* New York: Viking/Penguin Books.

Dissanayake, E. (2000). Birth of the arts. *Natural History 109* (10), 89.

Dixon, J. E., Cann, J. R., & Renfrew, C. (1968). Obsidian and the origins of trade. *Scientific American 218*, 38–46.

Dobyns, H. F., Doughty, P. L., & Lasswell, H. D. (Eds.). (1971). *Peasants, power, and applied social change.* London: Sage.

Dobzhansky, T. (1962). *Mankind evolving.* New Haven, CT: Yale University Press.

Dorit, R. (1997). Molecular evolution and scientific inquiry, misperceived. *American Scientist 85*, 475.

Douglas, M. (1966). *Purity and danger: An analysis of concepts of pollution and taboo.* London: Routledge & Kegan Paul.

Dozier, E. (1970). *The Pueblo Indians of North America.* New York: Holt, Rinehart & Winston.

Draper, P. (1975). !Kung women: Contrasts in sexual egalitarianism in foraging and sedentary contexts. In R. Reiter (Ed.), *Toward an anthropology of women* (pp. 77–109). New York: Monthly Review Press.

Dreger, A. D. (1998, May/June). "Ambiguous sex" or ambivalent medicine? *Hastings Center Report 28* (3), 2435. http://alicedreger.com/ambivalent _medicine_files/Dreger%20HCR%20 1998%20Ambiguous%20Sex.pdf

Drewnowski, A., & Specter, S. E. (2004). Poverty and obesity: The role of energy density and energy costs. *American Journal of Clinical Nutrition 79* (1), 6–16.

Driver, H. (1964). *Indians of North America.* Chicago: University of Chicago Press.

Dubois, C. (1944). *The people of Alor.* Minneapolis: University of Minnesota Press.

Dubos, R. (1968). *So human an animal.* New York: Scribner.

Dunbar, P. (2008, January 19). The pink vigilantes: The Indian women fighting for women's rights. *Mail Online.* www .dailymail.co.uk/news/article-509318/ The-pink-vigilantes-The-Indian-women- fighting-womens-rights.html (retrieved August 26, 2012)

Dundes, A. (1980). *Interpreting folklore.* Bloomington: Indiana University Press.

Dunham, S. A. (2009). *Surviving against the odds: Village industry in Indonesia.* Durham, NC: Duke University Press.

Durant, J. C. (2000, April 23). Everybody into the gene pool. *New York Times Book Review,* 11.

Duranti, A. (2001). Linguistic anthropology: History, ideas, and issues. In A. Duranti (Ed.), *Linguistic anthropology: A reader* (pp. 1–38). Oxford: Blackwell Press.

Durkheim, E. (1964). *The division of labor in society.* New York: Free Press.

Durkheim, E. (1965). *The elementary forms of the religious life.* New York: Free Press.

"Eating disorders (most recent) by country." (2004). *Nationmaster.com.* www.nationmaster.com/graph/mor_eat_ dis-mortality-eating-disorders (retrieved August 1, 2012)

Eaton, S. B., Konner, M., & Shostak, M. (1988). Stone-agers in the fast lane: Chronic degenerative diseases in evolutionary perspective. *American Journal of Medicine 84* (4), 739–749.

Edey, M. A., & Johannson, D. (1989). *Blueprints: Solving the mystery of evolution.* Boston: Little, Brown.

Edwards, J. (Ed.). (1999). *Technologies of procreation: Kinship in the age of assisted conception.* New York: Routledge.

Edwards, S. W. (1978). Nonutilitarian activities on the Lower Paleolithic: A look at the two kinds of evidence. *Current Anthropology 19* (1), 135–137.

Egan, T. (1999, February 28). The persistence of polygamy. *New York Times Magazine,* 52.

Egede, I. Quoted in Cone, M. (2005). *Silent snow: The slow poisoning of the Arctic.* New York: Grove Press.

Eggan, F. (1954). Social anthropology and the method of controlled comparison. *American Anthropologist 56,* 743–763.

Ehrenberg, R. (2011, September 24). Financial world dominated by a few deep pockets. *Science News 180* (7). 13. www.sciencenews.org (retrieved October 1, 2012)

Ehrlich, P. R., & Ehrlich, A. H. (2008). *The dominant animal: Human evolution and the environment.* Washington, DC: Island Press.

Eiseley, L. (1958). *Darwin's century: Evolution and the men who discovered it.* New York: Doubleday.

Eisenstadt, S. N. (1956). *From generation to generation: Age groups and social structure.* New York: Free Press.

El Guindi, F. (2004). *Visual anthropology: Essential method and theory.* Walnut Creek, CA: AltaMira Press.

Elkin, A. P. (1964). *The Australian Aborigines.* Garden City, NY: Doubleday/ Anchor.

Ellis, C. (2006). *A dancing people: Powwow culture on the southern plains.* Lawrence: University Press of Kansas.

Ellison, P. T. (2003). *On fertile ground: A natural history of human reproduction.* Cambridge, MA: Harvard University Press.

Embree, J. F. (1951). Raymond Kennedy, 1906–50. *Far Eastern Quarterly 10* (2), 170–172.

Enard, W., et al. (2002). Molecular evolution of FOXP2, a gene involved in speech and language. *Nature 418*, 869–872.

Erickson, C. L. (2001). Pre-Columbian Fish Farming in the Amazon. *Expedition 43* (3), 7–8.

Erickson, P. A., & Murphy, L. D. (2003). *A history of anthropological theory* (2nd ed.). Peterborough, Ontario: Broadview Press.

Errington, F. K., & Gewertz, D. B. (2001). *Cultural alternatives and a feminist anthropology: An analysis of culturally constructed gender interests in Papua New Guinea.* Cambridge, UK, & New York: Cambridge University Press.

Ervin-Tripp, S. (1973). *Language acquisition and communicative choice.* Stanford, CA: Stanford University Press.

Esber, G. S., Jr. (1987). Designing Apache houses with Apaches. In R. M. Wulff & S. J. Fiske (Eds.), *Anthropological praxis: Translating knowledge into action* (pp. 187–196). Boulder, CO: Westview Press.

Essoungou, A-M. (2010, April). Africa's displaced people: Out of the shadows. *Africa Renewal, 6.*

Estado Plurinacional de Bolivia. (2010). *Anteproyecto de Ley de la Madre Tierra por las Organizaciones Sociales del Pacto de Unidad.* www.redunitas .org/NINA_Anteproyectode%20 ley%20madre%20tierra.pdf (retrieved September 23, 2012)

Evans, W. (1968). *Communication in the animal world.* New York: Crowell.

Evans-Pritchard, E. E. (1937). *Witchcraft, oracles, and magic among the Azande.* London: Oxford University Press.

Evans-Pritchard, E. E. (1951). *Kinship and marriage among the Nuer.* New York: Oxford University Press.

Evans-Pritchard, E. E. (1968). *The Nuer: A description of the modes of livelihood and political institutions of a Nilotic people.* London: Oxford University Press.

Fagan, B. (2001). *The seventy great mysteries of the ancient world.* New York: Thames & Hudson.

Fagan, B. M. (1995). *People of the earth* (8th ed.). New York: HarperCollins.

Fagan, B. M. (1995). The quest for the past. In L. L. Hasten (Ed.), *Annual editions 95/96: Archaeology* (p. 10). Guilford, CT: Dushkin.

Fagan, B. M. (1999). *Archaeology: A brief introduction* (7th ed.). New York: Longman.

Fagan, B. M. (2000). *Ancient lives: An introduction to archaeology.* Englewood Cliffs, NJ: Prentice-Hall.

Fagan, B. M., Beck, C., & Silberman, N. A. (1998). *The Oxford companion to archaeology.* New York: Oxford University Press.

Falk, D. (1975). Comparative anatomy of the larynx in man and the chimpanzee: Implications for language in Neanderthal. *American Journal of Physical Anthropology 43* (1), 123–132.

Falk, D. (1989). Ape-like endocast of "Ape Man Taung." *American Journal of Physical Anthropology 80*, 335–339.

Falk, D. (1993). A good brain is hard to cool. *Natural History 102* (8), 65.

Falk, D. (1993). Hominid paleoneurology. In R. L. Ciochon & J. G. Fleagle (Eds.), *The human evolution source book.* Englewood Cliffs, NJ: Prentice-Hall.

Falk, D. (2004). *Braindance: New discoveries about human origins and brain evolution* (revised and updated). Gainesville: University Press of Florida.

Falk, D., et al. (2005). The brain of LB1, *Homo floresiensis. Science 308*, 242–245.

Farmer, P. (1992). *AIDS and accusation: Haiti and the geography of blame.* Berkeley: University of California Press.

Farmer, P. (1996). On suffering and structural violence: A view from below. *Daedalus 125* (1), 261–283.

Farmer, P. (2001). *Infections and inequalities: The modern plagues.* Berkeley: University of California Press.

Farmer, P. (2003). *Pathologies of power: Health, human rights, and the new war on the poor.* Berkeley: University of California Press.

Farmer, P. (2004, June). An anthropology of structural violence. *Current Anthropology 45*, 3.

Fausto-Sterling, A. (1993, March/April). The five sexes: Why male and female are not enough. *The Sciences 33* (2), 20–24.

Fausto-Sterling, A. (2000, July/August). The five sexes revisited. *The Sciences 40* (4), 19–24.

Fausto-Sterling, A. (2003, August 2). Personal e-mail communication.

Fausto-Sterling, A., et al. (2000). How sexually dimorphic are we? Review and synthesis. *American Journal of Human Biology 12*, 151–166.

Feder, K. L. (2008). *Frauds, myths, and mysteries: Science and pseudoscience in archaeology* (6th ed.). New York: McGraw-Hill.

Fedigan, L. M. (1986). The changing role of women in models of human evolution. *Annual Review of Anthropology 15*, 25–56.

Fedigan, L. M. (1992). *Primate paradigms: Sex roles and social bonds.* Chicago: University of Chicago Press.

Fernandez-Carriba, S., & Loeches, A. (2001). Fruit smearing by captive chimpanzees: A newly observed food-processing behavior. *Current Anthropology 42*, 143–147.

Fernández Olmos, M., & Paravisini-Gebert, L. (2003). *Creole religion of the Caribbean: An introduction from Vodou and Santeria to Obeah and Espiritismo.* New York: New York University Press.

Ferrie, H. (1997). An interview with C. Loring Brace. *Current Anthropology 38*, 851–869.

Field, L. W. (2004). Beyond "applied" anthropology. In T. Biolsi (Ed.), *A companion to the anthropology of American Indians* (pp. 472–479). Oxford, UK: Blackwell Press.

Finkler, K. (2000). *Experiencing the new genetics: Family and kinship on the medical frontier.* Philadelphia: University of Pennsylvania Press.

Finnström, S. (2008). *Living with bad surroundings: War, history, and everyday moments in northern Uganda.* Durham, NC: Duke University Press.

Firth, R. (1946). *Malay fishermen: Their peasant economy.* London: Kegan Paul.

Firth, R. (1952). *Elements of social organization.* London: Watts.

Firth, R. (1957). *Man and culture: An evaluation of Bronislaw Malinowski.* London: Routledge.

Firth, R. (Ed.). (1967). *Themes in economic anthropology.* London: Tavistock.

Fisher, R., & Ury, W. L. (1991). *Getting to yes: Negotiating agreement without giving in* (2nd ed.). Boston: Houghton Mifflin.

Flannery, K. V. (1973). The origins of agriculture. In B. J. Siegel, A. R. Beals, & S. A. Tyler (Eds.), *Annual review of anthropology* (vol. 2, pp. 271–310). Palo Alto, CA: Annual Reviews.

Flannery, K. V. (Ed.). (1976). *The Mesoamerican village.* New York: Seminar Press.

Fleagle, J. (1998). *Primate adaptation and evolution.* New York: Academic Press.

Fogel, R., & Riquelme, M. A. (2005). *Enclave sojero. Merma de soberania y pobreza.* Asuncion: Centro de Estudios Rurales Interdisciplinarias.

Folger, T. (1993). The naked and the bipedal. *Discover 14* (11), 34–35.

Food and Agriculture Organization of the United Nations. (2009, June 19). 1.02 billion people hungry: One sixth of humanity undernourished—more than ever before. www.fao.org/ news/story/en/item/20568/icode/ (retrieved October 3, 2012)

Forbes, J. D. (1964). *The Indian in America's past.* Englewood Cliffs, NJ: Prentice-Hall.

Ford, A. The BRASS/El Pilar Program. www.marc.ucsb.edu/elpilar/ (retrieved October 3, 2012)

Forde, C. D. (1968). Double descent among the Yakö. In P. Bohannan & J. Middleton (Eds.), *Kinship and social organization* (pp. 179–191). Garden City, NY: Natural History Press.

Forste, R. (2008). *Prelude to marriage, or alternative to marriage? A social demographic look at cohabitation in the U.S.* Working paper. Social Science Electronic Publishing. http://papers.ssrn.com/ sol3/papers.cfm?abstract_id=269172 (retrieved August 18, 2012)

Fortes, M. (1950). Kinship and marriage among the Ashanti. In A. R. Radcliffe-Brown & C. D. Forde (Eds.), *African systems of kinship and marriage.* London: Oxford University Press.

Fortes, M. (1969). *Kinship and the social order: The legacy of Lewis Henry Morgan.* Chicago: Aldine.

Fortes, M., & Evans-Prichard, E. E. (Eds.). (1962). *African political systems.* London: Oxford University Press. (orig. 1940)

Fossey, D. (1983). *Gorillas in the mist.* Burlington, MA: Houghton Mifflin.

Foster, G. M. (1955). Peasant society and the image of the limited good. *American Anthropologist 67*, 293–315.

Fouts, R. S., & Waters, G. (2001). Chimpanzee sign language and Darwinian continuity: Evidence for a neurology continuity of language. *Neurological Research 23*, 787–794.

Fowke, K. R., Nagelkerke, N. J., Kimani, J., Simonsen, J. N., Anzala, A. O., Bwayo, J. J., MacDonald, K. S., Ngugi, E. N., & Plummer, F. A. (1996). Resistance to HIV-1 infection among persistently seronegative prostitutes in Nairobi, Kenya. *Lancet 348* (9038), 1347–1351.

Fox, R. (1967). *Kinship and marriage in an anthropological perspective.* Baltimore: Penguin Books.

Fox, R. (1968). *Encounter with anthropology.* New York: Dell.

Fox, R. (1981, December 3). [Interview]. Coast Telecourses, Inc., Los Angeles.

Frake, C. (1961). The diagnosis of disease among the Subanun of Mindinao. *American Anthropologist 63,* 113–132.

Frake, C. O. (1992). Lessons of the Mayan sky. In A. F. Aveni (Ed.), *The sky in Mayan literature* (pp. 274–291). New York: Oxford University Press.

Frankfort, H. (1968). *The birth of civilization in the Near East.* New York: Barnes & Noble.

Franzen, J. L., et al. (2009). Complete primate skeleton from the middle Eocene of Messel in Germany: Morphology and paleobiology. *PLoS One 4* (5), e5723.

Fraser, D. (1962). *Primitive art.* New York: Doubleday.

Fraser, D. (Ed.). (1966). *The many faces of primitive art: A critical anthology.* Englewood Cliffs, NJ: Prentice-Hall.

Frayer, D. W. (1981). Body size, weapon use, and natural selection in the European Upper Paleolithic and Mesolithic. *American Anthropologist 83,* 57–73.

Frazer, J. G. (1961, reissue). *The new golden bough.* New York: Doubleday/Anchor.

Freeman, L. G. (1992). *Ambrona and Torralba: New evidence and interpretation.* Paper presented at the 91st Annual Meeting, American Anthropological Association.

Fried, M. (1967). *The evolution of political society: An essay in political anthropology.* New York: Random House.

Fried, M., Harris, M., & Murphy, R. (1968). *War: The anthropology of armed conflict and aggression.* Garden City, NY: Natural History Press.

Friedl, E. (1975). *Women and men: An anthropologist's view.* New York: Holt, Rinehart & Winston.

Friedman, J. (Ed.). (2003). *Globalization, the state, and violence.* Walnut Creek, CA: AltaMira Press.

Frisch, R. (2002). *Female fertility and the body fat connection.* Chicago: University of Chicago Press.

Frye, D. P. (2000). Conflict management in cross-cultural perspective. In F. Aureli & F. B. M. de Waal, *Natural conflict resolution* (pp. 334–351). Berkeley: University of California Press.

Galdikas, B. (1995). *Reflections on Eden: My years with the orangutans of Borneo.* New York: Little, Brown.

Gamble, C. (1986). *The Paleolithic settlement of Europe.* Cambridge, UK: Cambridge University Press.

Gandhi, M. K. (Ed.). (1999). *The collected works of Mahatma Gandhi* (vols. 8 & 19). New Delhi: Publications Division, Government of India.

Garn, S. M. (1970). *Human races* (3rd ed.). Springfield, IL: Thomas.

Gebo, D. L., Dagosto, D., Beard, K. C., & Tao, Q. (2001). Middle Eocene primate tarsals from China: Implications for haplorhine evolution. *American Journal of Physical Anthropology 116,* 83–107.

Geertz, C. (1963). *Agricultural involution: The process of ecological change in Indonesia.* Berkeley: University of California Press.

Geertz, C. (1973). *The interpretation of culture.* London: Hutchinson.

Geertz, C. (2004). Religion as a cultural system. In M. Banton (Ed.), *Anthropological approaches to the study of religion* (pp. 1–46). London: Routledge.

"Gene study suggests Polynesians came from Taiwan." (2005, July 4). Reuters.

Gero, J. M., & Conkey, M. W. (Eds.). (1991). *Engendered archaeology: Women and prehistory.* New York: Wiley-Blackwell.

Gettleman, J. (2011, July 9). South Sudan, the newest nation, is full of hope and problems. *New York Times.* www.post-gazette.com/pg/11190/1159402-82-0.stm (retrieved August 22, 2011).

Gibbons, A. (1993). Where are new diseases born? *Science 261,* 680–681.

Gibbons, A. (1997). Ideas on human origins evolve at anthropology gathering. *Science 276,* 535–536.

Gibbons, A. (1998). Ancient island tools suggest *Homo erectus* was a seafarer. *Science 279,* 1635.

Gibbons, A. (2001). The riddle of coexistence. *Science 291,* 1726.

Gibbons, A. (2001). Studying humans—and their cousins and parasites. *Science 292,* 627.

Gibbs, J. L., Jr. (1965). The Kpelle of Liberia. In J. L. Gibbs Jr. (Ed.), *Peoples of Africa* (pp. 216–218). New York: Holt, Rinehart & Winston.

Gibbs, J. L., Jr. (1983). [Interview]. *Faces of culture: Program 18.* Fountain Valley, CA: Coast Telecourses.

Gierstorfer, C. (2007). Peaceful primates, violent acts. *Nature 447,* 7.

Gilley, B. J. (2007). *Becoming two-spirit: Gay identity and social acceptance in Indian Country.* Lincoln: University of Nebraska Press.

Ginsburg, F. D., Abu-Lughod, L., & Larkin, B. (Eds.). (2009). *Media worlds: Anthropology on new terrain.* Berkeley: University of California Press.

Gladney, D. C. (2004). *Dislocating China: Muslims, minorities and other subaltern subjects.* London: Hurst.

Gladstone, R. (2012, August 27). China: 2 Tibetan teenagers set themselves on fire. *nytimes.com.* www.nytimes.com/2012/08/28/world/asia/2-tibetan-teenagers-set-themselves-on-fire-in-china.html (retrieved September 21, 2012)

Gleason, H. A., Jr. (1966). *An introduction to descriptive linguistics* (rev. ed.). New York: Holt, Rinehart & Winston.

Gledhill, J. (2000). *Power and its disguises: Anthropological perspectives on politics* (2nd ed.). Boulder, CO: Pluto Press.

"Global 500: Our annual ranking of the world's largest corporations." (2012). *CNN Money.* http://money.cnn.com/magazines/fortune/global500/2012/full_list/index.html (retrieved October 1, 2012)

Goldsmith, M. L. (2005). Habituating primates for field study: Ethical considerations for great apes. In T. Turner (Ed.), *Biological anthropology and ethics: From repatriation to genetic identity* (pp. 49–64). New York: SUNY Press.

Goldsmith, M. L., Glick, J., & Ngabirano, E. (2006). Gorillas living on the edge: Literally and figuratively. In N. E. Newton-Fisher, et al. (Eds.), *Primates of western Uganda* (pp. 405–422). New York: Springer.

Gonzalez, J. (2002, January 11). Tracking Africa's fast-growing indigenous churches on DVD. *UA News.* http://uanews.org/node/5799 (retrieved September 16, 2011)

González, R. J. (2009). *American counter-insurgency: Human science and the human terrain.* Chicago: University of Chicago Press.

Goodall, J. (1986). *The chimpanzees of Gombe: Patterns of behavior.* Cambridge, MA: Belknap Press.

Goodall, J. (1990). *Through a window: My thirty years with the chimpanzees of Gombe.* Boston: Houghton Mifflin.

Goodall, J. (2000). *Reason for hope: A spiritual journey.* New York: Warner Books.

Goodenough, W. (Ed.). (1964). *Explorations in cultural anthropology: Essays in honor of George Murdock.* New York: McGraw-Hill.

Goodenough, W. H. (1970). *Description and comparison in cultural anthropology.* Chicago: Aldine.

Goodenough, W. H. (1990). Evolution of the human capacity for beliefs. *American Anthropologist 92,* 601.

Goodman, A., & Armelagos, G. J. (1985). Death and disease at Dr. Dickson's mounds. *Natural History 94* (9), 12–18.

Goodman, M., et al. (1994). Molecular evidence on primate phylogeny from DNA sequences. *American Journal of Physical Anthropology 94,* 7.

Goodwin, R. (1999). *Personal relationships across cultures.* New York: Routledge.

Goody, J. (1969). *Comparative studies in kinship.* Stanford, CA: Stanford University Press.

Goody, J. (1976). *Production and reproduction: A comparative study of the domestic domain.* Cambridge, UK: Cambridge University Press.

Goody, J. (1983). *The development of the family and marriage in Europe.* Cambridge, MA: Cambridge University Press.

Gordon, R. (2000). *Eating disorders: Anatomy of a social epidemic* (2nd ed.). New York: Wiley-Blackwell.

Gordon, R., Lyons, H., & Lyons, A. (Eds.). (2010). *Fifty key anthropologists.* New York: Routledge.

Gordon, R. J. (1992). *The Bushman myth: The making of a Namibian underclass.* Boulder, CO: Westview Press.

Gordon, R. J., & Megitt, M. J. (1985). *Law and order in the New Guinea highlands.* Hanover, NH: University Press of New England.

Gottlieb, A. (2003). *The afterlife is where we come from: The culture of infancy in West Africa.* Chicago: University of Chicago Press.

Gottlieb, A. (2004). Babies as ancestors, babies as spirits: The culture of infancy in West Africa. *Expedition 46* (3), 13–21.

Gottlieb, A. (2005). Non-Western approaches to spiritual development among infants and young children: A case study from West Africa. In P. L. Benson et al. (Eds.), *The handbook of spiritual development in childhood and adolescence* (pp. 150–162). Thousand Oaks, CA: Sage.

Gough, K. (1959). The Nayars and the definition of marriage. *Journal of the Royal Anthropological Institute of Great Britain and Ireland 89,* 23–34.

Gould, S. J. (1983). *Hen's teeth and horses' toes.* New York: Norton.

Gould, S. J. (1989). *Wonderful life.* New York: Norton.

Gould, S. J. (1991). *Bully for brontosaurus.* New York: Norton.

Gould, S. J. (1991). *The flamingo's smile: Reflections in natural history.* New York: Norton.

Gould, S. J. (1994). The geometer of race. *Discover 15* (11), 65–69.

Gould, S. J. (1996). *Full house: The spread of excellence from Plato to Darwin.* New York: Harmony Books.

Gould, S. J. (1996). *The mismeasure of man* (2nd ed.). New York: Norton. [ep]

Gould, S. J. (1997). *Questioning the millennium.* New York: Crown.

Gould, S. J. (2000). The narthex of San Marco and the pangenetic paradigm. *Natural History 109* (6), 29.

Gould, S. J. (2000). What does the dreaded "E" word mean anyway? *Natural History 109* (1), 34–36.

Graves, J. L. (2001). *The emperor's new clothes: Biological theories of race at the millennium.* New Brunswick, NJ: Rutgers University Press.

Gray, P. B. (2004, May). HIV and Islam: Is HIV prevalence lower among Muslims? *Social Science & Medicine 58* (9), 1751–1756.

Gray, P. M., et al. (2001). The music of nature and the nature of music. *Science 291,* 52.

Green, R. E., et al. (2010, May 7). A draft sequence of the Neandertal genome. *Science 328* (5979), 710–722.

Greymorning, S. N. (2001). Reflections on the Arapaho Language Project or, when Bambi spoke Arapaho and other tales of Arapaho language revitalization efforts. In K. Hale & L. Hinton, *The green book of language revitalization in practice* (pp. 287–297). New York: Academic Press.

Griffin, D., & Fitzpatrick, D. (2009, September 1). Donor says he got thousands for his kidney. *CNNWorld.com.* http://articles.cnn.com/2009-09-01/world/blackmarket.organs_1_kidney-transplants-kidney-donor-kidney-specialist?_s=PM:WORLD (retrieved June 10, 2012)

Grine, F. E. (1993). Australopithecine taxonomy and phylogeny: Historical background and recent interpretation. In R. L. Ciochon & J. G. Fleagle (Eds.), *The human evolution source book.* Englewood Cliffs, NJ: Prentice-Hall.

Grivetti, L. E. (2005). From aphrodisiac to health food: A cultural history of chocolate. *Karger Gazette* (68).

Grossman, J. (2002, April 8). Should the law be kinder to kissin' cousins? A genetic report should cause a rethinking of incest laws. *Find Law.* http://writ.news.findlaw.com/grossman/20020408.html (retrieved August 13, 2012)

Grün, R., & Thorne, A. (1997). Dating the Ngandong humans. *Science 276,* 1575.

Guillette, E. A., et al. (1998, June). An anthropological approach to the evaluation of preschool children exposed to pesticides in Mexico. *Environmental Health Perspectives 106,* 347.

Gurchiek, K. (2012). Survey finds significant erosion in engagement around the world. *Society for Human Resource Management.* www.weknownext.com/workforce/survey-finds-significant-erosion-in-engagement-around-globe (retrieved October 1, 2012)

Guthrie, S. (1993). *Faces in the clouds: A new theory of religions.* New York: Oxford University Press.

Gutin, J. A. (1995). Do Kenya tools root birth of modern thought in Africa? *Science 270,* 1118–1119.

Hager, L. (1989). *The evolution of sex differences in the hominid bony pelvis.* PhD dissertation. University of California, Berkeley.

Haglund, W. D., Conner, M., & Scott, D. D. (2001). The archaeology of contemporary mass graves. *Historical Archaeology 35* (1), 57–69.

Hahn, R. A. (1992). The state of federal health statistics on racial and ethnic groups. *Journal of the American Medical Association 267* (2), 268–271.

Hale, C. (2004). *Himmler's crusade: The true story of the 1938 Nazi expedition into Tibet.* New York: Bantam.

Hall, E. T. (1959). *The silent language.* Garden City, NY: Doubleday/Anchor.

Hall, E. T. (1963). A system for the notation of proxemic behavior. *American Anthropologist 65,* 1003–1026.

Hall, E. T. (1990). *The hidden dimension.* New York: Anchor.

Halverson, J. (1980). Review of the book *Altamira revisited and other essays on early art. American Antiquity 54,* 883.

Hamblin, D. J., & the Editors of Time-Life. (1973). *The first cities.* New York: Time-Life.

Hamburg, D. A., & McGown, E. R. (Eds.). (1979). *The great apes.* Menlo Park, CA: Cummings.

Hammond, D. (1972). *Associations.* Reading, MA: Addison-Wesley.

Handwerk, B. (2005, March 8). King Tut not murdered violently, CT scans show. *National Geographic News,* 2.

Hanson, A. (1989). The making of the Maori: Culture invention and its logic. *American Anthropologist 91* (4), 890–902.

Harcourt-Smith, W. E. H., & Aiello, L. C. (2004). Fossils, feet and the evolution of human bipedal locomotion. *Journal of Anatomy 204,* 403–416.

Harding, S. F. (2001). *The book of Jerry Falwell: Fundamentalist language and politics.* Princeton, NJ: Princeton University Press.

Hare, B., Brown, M., Williamson, C., & Tomasello, M. (2002). The domestication of social cognition in dogs. *Science 298* (5598). 1634–1636.

Harlow, H. F. (1962). Social deprivation in monkeys. *Scientific American 206,* 1–10.

Harner, M. J. (Ed.). (1973). *Hallucinogens and shamanism.* New York: Oxford University Press.

Harner, M. J. (1980). *The way of the shaman: A guide to power and healing.* San Francisco: Harper & Row.

Harner, M. J. (1984). *The Jivaro: People of the sacred waterfalls.* Berkeley: University of California Press.

Harner, M. J. (2013). *Cave and cosmos: Shamanic encounters with spirits and heavens.* Berkeley: North Atlantic Books.

Harner, M. J., & Harner, S. (2000). Core practices in the shamanic treatment of illness. *Shamanism 13* (1&2), 19–30.

Harpending, H., & Cochran, G. (2002). In our genes. *Proceedings of the National Academy of Sciences USA 99* (1), 10–12.

Harpending, J. H., & Harpending, H. C. (1995). Ancient differences in population can mimic a recent African origin of modern humans. *Current Anthropology 36,* 667–674.

Harris, M. (1968). *The rise of anthropological theory: A history of theories of culture.* New York: Crowell.

Harris, M. (1979). *Cultural materialism: The struggle for a science of culture.* New York: Random House.

Harris, M. (1989). *Cows, pigs, wars, and witches: The riddles of culture.* New York: Vintage/Random House.

Harrison, G. G. (1975). Primary adult lactase deficiency: A problem in anthropological genetics. *American Anthropologist 77,* 815–819.

Harrison, K. D. (2002). Naming practices and ethnic identity in Tuva. *Proceedings of the Chicago Linguistics Society 35* (2).

Hart, D. (2006, April 21). Humans as prey. *Chronicle of Higher Education.*

Hart, D., & Sussman, R. W. (2005). *Man the hunted: Primates, predators, and human evolution.* Boulder, CO: Westview Press.

Hartwig, W. C. (2002). *The primate fossil record.* New York: Cambridge University Press.

Hartwig, W. C., & Doneski, K. (1998). Evolution of the hominid hand and toolmaking behavior. *American Journal of Physical Anthropology 106,* 401–402.

Harvey, F. (2012, September 24). Trafigura lessons have not been learned, report warns. *The Guardian.* www.guardian.co.uk/environment/2012/sep/25/trafigura-lessons-toxic-waste-dumping (retrieved October 3, 2012)

Hasnain, M. (2005, October 27). Cultural approach to HIV/AIDS harm reduction in Muslim countries. *Harm Reduction Journal 2,* 23.

Hatcher, E. P. (1985). *Art as culture, an introduction to the anthropology of art.* New York: University Press of America.

Haviland, W. (1967). Stature at Tikal, Guatemala: Implications for ancient Maya, demography, and social organization. *American Antiquity 32,* 316–325.

Haviland, W. (1970). Tikal, Guatemala and Mesoamerican urbanism. *World Archaeology 2*, 186–198.

Haviland, W. A. (1972). A new look at Classic Maya social organization at Tikal. *Ceramica de Cultura Maya 8*, 1–16.

Haviland, W. A. (1974). Farming, seafaring and bilocal residence on the coast of Maine. *Man in the Northeast 6*, 31–44.

Haviland, W. A. (1975). The ancient Maya and the evolution of urban society. *University of Northern Colorado Museum of Anthropology*, Miscellaneous Series, 37.

Haviland, W. A. (1997). The rise and fall of sexual inequality: Death and gender at Tikal, Guatemala. *Ancient Mesoamerica 8*, 1–12.

Haviland, W. A. (2002). Settlement, society and demography at Tikal. In J. Sabloff (Ed.), *Tikal*. Santa Fe: School of American Research.

Haviland, W. A. (2003). *Tikal, Guatemala: A Maya way to urbanism*. Paper prepared for Third INAH/Penn State Conference on Mesoamerican Urbanism.

Haviland, W. A., & Moholy-Nagy, H. (1992). Distinguishing the high and mighty from the hoi polloi at Tikal, Guatemala. In A. F. Chase & D. Z. Chase (Eds.), *Mesoamerican elites: An archaeological assessment*. Norman: Oklahoma University Press.

Haviland, W. A., & Power, M. W. (1994). *The original Vermonters: Native inhabitants, past and present* (2nd ed.). Hanover, NH: University Press of New England.

Haviland, W. A., et al. (1985). *Excavations in small residential groups of Tikal: Groups 4F-1 and 4F-2*. Philadelphia: University Museum.

Hawkes, K., O'Connell, J. F., & Blurton Jones, N. G. (1997). Hadza women's time allocation, offspring provisioning, and the evolution of long postmenopausal life spans. *Current Anthropology 38*, 551–577.

Hawks, J. (2009). Ankles of the Australopithecines. *John Hawks Weblog.* http://johnhawks.net/weblog/reviews/early_hominids/anatomy/desilva-2009-chimpanzee-climbing-talus.html (retrieved July 5, 2012)

Hazardous waste trafficking. (2011). www.choike.org/2009/eng/informes/informes/1157.html (retrieved September 19, 2011)

Heilbroner, R. L., & Thurow, L. C. (1981). *The economic problem* (6th ed.). Englewood Cliffs, NJ: Prentice-Hall.

Heita, K. (1999). Imanishi's world view. *Journal of Japanese Trade and Industry 18* (2), 15.

Heitzman, J., & Wordem, R. L. (Eds.). (2006). *India: A country study* (sect. 2, 5th ed.). Washington, DC: Federal Research Division, Library of Congress.

Helm, J. (1962). The ecological approach in anthropology. *American Journal of Sociology 67*, 630–649.

Helman, C. B. (2007). *Culture, health, and illness: An introduction for health professionals* (5th ed.). New York: Trans-Atlantic Publications.

Henry, D. O., et al. (2004). Human behavioral organization in the Middle Paleolithic: Were Neandertals different? *American Anthropologist 107* (1), 17–31.

Henry, J. (1965). *Culture against man.* New York: Vintage.

Henry, S., & Porter, D. (2011, October 27). Levy Izhak Rosenbaum pleads guilty to selling black market kidneys. *Huffingtonpost.com.* www.huffingtonpost.com/2011/10/27/levy-izhak-rosenbaum-plea_n_1035624.html (retrieved June 10, 2012)

Henshilwood, C. S., d'Errico, F., van Niekerk, K. L., Coquinot, Y., Jacobs, Z., Lauritzen, S.-E., Menu, M., & Garcia-Moreno. R. (2011). A 100,000-year-old ochre-processing workshop at Blombos Cave, South Africa. *Science 334* (6053), 219. doi:10.1126/science.1211535

Herdt, G. (Ed.). (1996). *Third sex, third gender: Beyond sexual dimorphism in culture and history.* New York: Zone.

Herdt, G. H. (1993). Semen transactions in Sambia culture. In D. N. Suggs & A. W. Mirade (Eds.), *Culture and human sexuality* (pp. 298–327). Pacific Grove, CA: Brooks/Cole.

Herskovits, M. J. (1952). *Economic anthropology: A study in comparative economics* (2nd ed.). New York: Knopf.

Herskovits, M. J. (1964). *Cultural dynamics.* New York: Knopf.

Hertz, N. (2001). *The silent takeover: Global capitalism and the death of democracy.* New York: Arrow Books.

Hewes, G. W. (1973). Primate communication and the gestural origin of language. *Current Anthropology 14*, 5–24.

Higham, T., et al. (2012). Testing models for the beginnings of the Aurignacian and the advent of figurative art and music: The radiocarbon chronology of Geißenklösterle. *Journal of Human Evolution 62* (6), 664–676.

Himmelfarb, E. J. (2000, January/February). First alphabet found in Egypt. Newsbrief. *Archaeology 53* (1).

Hitchcock, R. K., & Enghoff, M. (2004). *Capacity-building of first people of the Kalahari, Botswana: An evaluation.* Copenhagen: International Work Group for Indigenous Affairs.

"HIV & AIDS information from avert.org." www.avert.org.

Hobaiter, C., & Byrne, R. W. (2011, July). The gestural repertoire of the wild chimpanzee. *Animal Cognition 14* (4).

Hodgen, M. (1964). *Early anthropology in the sixteenth and seventeenth centuries.* Philadelphia: University of Pennsylvania Press.

Hodgson, A. (2012). Special report: Income inequality rising across the globe. *Euromonitor International.* http://blog.euromonitor.com/2012/03/special-report-income-inequality-rising-across-the-globe.html (retrieved October 1, 2012)

Hoebel, E. A. (1958). *Man in the primitive world: An introduction to anthropology.* New York: McGraw-Hill.

Hoebel, E. A. (1960). *The Cheyennes: Indians of the Great Plains.* New York: Holt, Rinehart & Winston.

Hoebel, E. A. (1972). *Anthropology: The study of man* (4th ed.). New York: McGraw-Hill.

Holden, C. (1999). Ancient child burial uncovered in Portugal. *Science 283*, 169.

Hole, F. (1966). Investigating the origins of Mesopotamian civilization. *Science 153*, 605–611.

Hole, F., & Heizer, R. F. (1969). *An introduction to prehistoric archeology.* New York: Holt, Rinehart & Winston.

Holloway, R. L. (1980). The O. H. 7 (Olduvai Gorge, Tanzania) hominid partial brain endocast revisited. *American Journal of Physical Anthropology 53*, 267–274.

Holloway, R. L. (1981). The Indonesian *Homo erectus* brain endocast revisited. *American Journal of Physical Anthropology 55*, 503–521.

Holloway, R. L. (1981). Volumetric and asymmetry determinations on recent hominid endocasts: Spy I and II, Djebel Jhroud 1, and the Salb *Homo erectus* specimens, with some notes on Neanderthal brain size. *American Journal of Physical Anthropology 55*, 385–393.

Holloway, R. L., & de LaCoste-Lareymondie, M. C. (1982). Brain endocast asymmetry in pongids and hominids: Some preliminary findings on the paleontology of cerebral dominance. *American Journal of Physical Anthropology 58*, 101–110.

Holmes, L. D. (2000). "Paradise Bent" (film review). *American Anthropologist 102* (3), 604–605.

Holy, L. (1996). *Anthropological perspectives on kinship.* London: Pluto.

Hopkin, M. (2007, February 22). Chimps make spears to catch dinner. *Nature.* doi:10.1038/news070219–11

Horst, H., & Miller, D. (2006). *The cell phone: An anthropology of communication.* New York: Berg.

Hostetler, J. A., & Huntington, G. E. (1992). *Amish children: Education in the family, school, and community* (2nd ed.). New York: Harcourt, Brace & Jovanovich.

Houle, A. (1999). The origin of platyrrhines: An evaluation of the Antarctic scenario and the floating island model. *American Journal of Physical Anthropology 109*, 554–556.

Howell, F. C. (1970). *Early man.* New York: Time-Life.

Hrdy, S. B. (1999). Body fat and birth control. *Natural History 108* (8), 88.

Hsiaotung, F. (1939). *Peasant life in China.* London: Kegan Paul.

Hsu, F. L. (1961). *Psychological anthropology: Approaches to culture and personality.* Homewood, IL: Dorsey Press.

Human Rights Watch and the Center for Human Rights and Global Justice. (2007). Hidden apartheid: Caste discrimination against India's "Untouchables." www.chrgj.org/docs/IndiaCERDShadowReport.pdf (retrieved September 15, 2011)

The Hunger Project. (2011). www.thp.org (retrieved October 1, 2012)

Hutter, M. (Ed.). (2003). *The family experience: A reader in cultural diversity* (4th ed.). Boston: Allyn & Bacon.

Hymes, D. (1964). *Language in culture and society: A reader in linguistics and anthropology.* New York: Harper & Row.

Hymes, D. (Ed.). (1972). *Reinventing anthropology.* New York: Pantheon.

Hymes, D. (1974). *Foundations in sociolinguistics: An ethnographic approach.* Philadelphia: University of Pennsylvania Press.

Inda, J. X., & Rosaldo, R. (Eds). (2001). *The anthropology of globalization: A reader.* Malden, MA, and Oxford, UK: Blackwell Press.

Ingmanson, E. J. (1998). Comment. *Current Anthropology 39,* 409.

Inkeles, A., & Levinson, D. J. (1954). National character: The study of modal personality and socio-cultural systems. In G. Lindzey (Ed.), *Handbook of social psychology.* Reading, MA: Addison-Wesley.

Inoue, S., & Matsuzawa, T. (2007). Working memory of numerals in chimpanzees. *Current Biology 17,* 23, 1004–1005.

International Lesbian, Gay, Bisexual, Trans, and Intersex Association (ILGA). (2009). *The 2009 report on state-sponsored homophobia.*

International Telecommunication Union. (2012). 2011 ICT facts and figures. www.itu.int/ITU-D/ict/facts/2011/material/ICTFactsFigures2011.pdf (retrieved June 4, 2012)

International Union for Conservation of Nature and Natural Resources (IUCN). www.iucn.org/ (retrieved June 2012)

Internet World Stats: Usage and Population Statistics. www.internetworldstats.com (retrieved June 4, 2012) "Interview with Laura Nader." (2000, November). *California Monthly.*

Irvine, M. (1999, November 24). Mom-and-pop houses grow rare. *Burlington Free Press.*

Itaborahy, P. L. (2012). State-sponsored homophobia: A world survey of laws criminalising same-sex sexual activity between consenting adults. Brussels: International Lesbian, Gay, Bisexual, Trans and Intersex Association. http://old.ilga.org/Statehomophobia/ILGA_State_Sponsored_Homophobia_2012.pdf

"Italy–German verbal war hots up." (2003, July 9). Reuters. *Deccan Herald.* http://archive.deccanherald.com/deccanherald/july09/f4.asp (retrieved July 31, 2012)

Jacobs, S. E. (1994). Native American two-spirits. *Anthropology Newsletter 35* (8), 7.

Jacoby, R., & Glauberman, N. (Eds.). (1995). *The Bell Curve debate.* New York: Random House.

Jane Goodall Institute. www.janegoodall.org/janes-story (retrieved June 15, 2012)

Jennings, F. (1976). *The invasion of America.* New York: Norton.

Jennings, J. D. (1974). *Prehistory of North America* (2nd ed.). New York: McGraw-Hill.

Johansen, B. E. (2002). The Inuit's struggle with dioxins and other organic pollutants. *American Indian Quarterly 26* (3), 479–490.

Johanson, D., & Shreeve, J. (1989). *Lucy's child: The discovery of a human ancestor.* New York: Avon.

Johanson, D. C., & Edey, M. (1981). *Lucy, the beginnings of humankind.* New York: Simon & Schuster.

Johanson, D. C., Edgar, B., & Brill, D. (1996). *From Lucy to language.* New York: Simon & Schuster.

Johanson, D. C., & White, T. D. (1979). A systematic assessment of early African hominids. *Science 203,* 321–330.

Johanson, D. C., & Wong, K. (2009). *Lucy's legacy: The quest for human origins.* New York: Harmony.

John, V. (1971). Whose is the failure? In C. L. Brace, G. R. Gamble, & J. T. Bond (Eds.), *Race and intelligence.* Washington, DC: American Anthropological Association.

Johnson, D. (1991, April 9). Polygamists emerge from secrecy, seeking not just peace but respect. *New York Times,* A22.

Johnson, N. B. (1984). Sex, color, and rites of passage in ethnographic research. *Human Organization 43* (2), 108–120.

Jolly, A. (1985). *The evolution of primate behavior* (2nd ed.). New York: Macmillan.

Jolly, A. (1991). Thinking like a vervet. *Science 251,* 574.

Jolly, C. J. (1970). The seed eaters: A new model of hominid differentiation based on a baboon analogy. *Man 5,* 5–26.

Jolly, C. J., & Plog, F. (1986). *Physical anthropology and archaeology* (4th ed.). New York: Knopf.

Jones, S. (2005). Transhumance re-examined. *Journal of the Royal Anthropological Institute 11* (4), 841–842.

Jones, S., Martin, R., & Pilbeam, D. (1992). *Cambridge encyclopedia of human evolution.* New York: Cambridge University Press.

Joukowsky, M. A. (1980). *A complete field manual of archeology: Tools and techniques of fieldwork for archaeologists.* Englewood Cliffs, NJ: Prentice-Hall.

Joyce, C. (1991). *Witnesses from the grave: The stories bones tell.* Boston: Little, Brown.

Kaiser, J. (1994). A new theory of insect wing origins takes off. *Science 266,* 363.

Kaiser, J. (2011, May 4). 10 billion plus: Why world population projections were too low. *Science Insider.* http://news.sciencemag.org/scienceinsider/2011/05/10-billion-plus-why-world-population.html (retrieved October 1, 2012)

Kalwet, H. (1988). *Dreamtime and inner space: The world of the shaman.* New York: Random House.

Kaplan, D. (1972). *Culture theory.* Englewood Cliffs, NJ: Prentice-Hall.

Kaplan, D. (2000). The darker side of the original affluent society. *Journal of Anthropological Research 53* (3), 301–324.

Kaplan, M. (2007, May 31). Upright orangutans point way to walking. *Nature.* doi:10.1038/news070528–8.

Kaplan, M. (2008, August 5). Almost half of primate species face extinction. *Nature.* doi:10.1038/news.2008.1013 (retrieved June 23, 2012)

Karavanić, I., & Smith, F. H. (2000). More on the Neanderthal problem: The Vindija case. *Current Anthropology 41,* 839.

Kaw, E. (1993). Medicalization of racial features: Asian American women and cosmetic surgery. *Medical Anthropology Quarterly 7* (1), 74–89.

Kay, R. F., Fleagle, J. G., & Simons, E. L. (1981). A revision of the Oligocene apes of the Fayum Province, Egypt. *American Journal of Physical Anthropology 55,* 293–322.

Kay, R. F., Ross, C., & Williams, B. A. (1997). Anthropoid origins. *Science 275,* 797–804.

Kedia, S., & Van Willigen, J. (2005). *Applied anthropology: Domains of application.* New York: Praeger.

Keen, B. (1971). *The Aztec image in western thought.* New Brunswick, NJ: Rutgers University Press.

Keesing. R. M. (1992). Some problems in the study of Oceanic religion. *Anthropologica 34* (2), 231–246.

Kehoe, A. (2000). *Shamans and religion: An anthropological exploration in critical thinking.* Prospect Heights, IL: Waveland Press.

Keiser, L. (1991). *Friend by day, enemy by night: Organized vengeance in a Kohistani community.* Fort Worth: Holt, Rinehart & Winston.

Kelly, R. L., & Thomas, D. H. (2012). *Archaeology* (6th ed.). Belmont, CA. Wadsworth.

Kelly, T. L. (2006). *Sadhus, the great renouncers.* Photography exhibit, Indigo Gallery, Naxal, Kathmandu, Nepal. www.asianart.com/exhibitions/sadhus/index.html (retrieved August 1, 2012)

Kennickell, A. B. (2003, November). *A rolling tide: Changes in the distribution of wealth in the U.S. 1989–2001.* Washington, DC: Federal Reserve Board/Levy Economics Institute.

Kenyon, K. (1957). *Digging up Jericho.* London: Ben.

Kertzer, D. I. (1989). *Ritual, politics, and power.* New Haven, CT: Yale University Press.

Key, M. R. (1975). *Paralanguage and kinesics: Nonverbal communication.* Metuchen, NJ: Scarecrow Press.

Kibii, J. M., et al. (2011, September 9). A partial pelvis of *Australopithecus sebida. Science 333* (6048), 1407–1411.

Kidder, T. (2003). *Mountains beyond mountains: The quest of Dr. Paul Farmer, a man who would cure the world.* New York: Random House.

Kilcullen, D. (2007, May 12). Religion and insurgency. *Small Wars Journal.* http://smallwarsjournal.com/blog/religion-and-insurgency (retrieved August 1, 2012)

King, J. (2010, July 28). Reducing the crack and powder cocaine sentencing disparity should also reduce racial disparities in sentences and prisons. *NACDL news release.* www.nacdl.org/newsreleases.aspx?id=19533 (retrieved August 2, 2012)

Kirkpatrick, R. C. (2000). The evolution of human homosexual behavior. *Current Anthropology 41,* 384.

Kitchen, A., Miyamoto, M. M., & Mulligan, C. J. (2008). A three-stage colonization model for the peopling of the Americas. *PLoS One 3* (2), e1596. doi:10.1371/journal.pone.0001596

Kleinman, A. (1976). Concepts and a model for the comparison of medical systems as cultural systems. *Social Science and Medicine 12* (2B), 85–95.

Kluckhohn, C. (1944). Navajo witchcraft. *Papers of the Peabody Museum of American Archaeology and Ethnology 22* (2).

Kluckhohn, C. (1970). *Mirror for man.* Greenwich, CT: Fawcett.

Knauft, B. (1991). Violence and sociality in human evolution. *Current Anthropology 32*, 391–409.

Knight, C., Studdert-Kennedy, M., & Hurford, J. (Eds.). (2000). *The evolutionary emergence of language: Social function and the origins of linguistic form.* Cambridge, UK: Cambridge University Press.

Koch, G. (1997). Songs, land rights, and archives in Australia. *Cultural Survival Quarterly 20* (4).

Komai, T., & Fukuoka, G. (1934, October). Post-natal growth disparity in monozygotic twins. *Journal of Heredity 25*, 423–430.

Konner, M., & Worthman, C. (1980). Nursing frequency, gonadal function, and birth spacing among !Kung hunter-gatherers. *Science 207*, 788–791.

Kopenawa, D., & Albert, B. (2010). *La chute du ciel: Paroles d'un chaman Yanomami.* Paris: Terre Humaine, Plon.

Koufos, G. (1993). Mandible of *Ouranopithecus macedoniensis* (hominidae: primates) from a new late Miocene locality in Macedonia (Greece). *American Journal of Physical Anthropology 91*, 225–234.

Krader, L. (1968). *Formation of the state.* Englewood Cliffs, NJ: Prentice-Hall.

Krajick, K. (1998). Greenfarming by the Incas? *Science 281*, 323.

Kramer, P. A. (1998). The costs of human locomotion: Maternal investment in child transport. *American Journal of Physical Anthropology 107*, 71–85.

Kraybill, D. B. (2001). *The riddle of Amish culture.* Baltimore: Johns Hopkins University Press.

Kroeber, A. (1958). Totem and taboo: An ethnologic psycho-analysis. In W. Lessa & E. Z. Vogt (Eds.), *Reader in comparative religion: An anthropological approach.* New York: Harper & Row.

Kroeber, A. L. (1939). Cultural and natural areas of native North America. In *American archaeology and ethnology* (vol. 38). Berkeley: University of California Press.

Kroeber, A. L. (1963). *Anthropology: Cultural processes and patterns.* New York: Harcourt.

Kroeber, A. L., & Kluckhohn, C. (1952). *Culture: A critical review of concepts and definitions.* Cambridge, MA: Harvard University Press.

Kruger, J., et al. (2005, December). Egocentrism over e-mail: Can people communicate as well as they think? *Journal of Personality and Social Psychology 89* (6), 925–936.

Kuefler, M. (2007). The marriage revolution in late antiquity: The Theodosian Code and later Roman marriage law. *Journal of Family History 32* (4), 343–370.

Kuhn, T. (1968). *The structure of scientific revolutions.* Chicago: University of Chicago Press.

Kummer, H. (1971). *Primate societies: Group techniques of ecological adaptation.* Chicago: Aldine.

Kunzig, R. (1999). A tale of two obsessed archaeologists, one ancient city and nagging doubts about whether science can ever hope to reveal the past. *Discover 20* (5), 84–92.

Kuper, A. (2008). Changing the subject—about cousin marriage, among other things. *Journal of the Royal Anthropological Institute 14* (4), 717–735.

Kuper, H. (1965). The Swazi of Swaziland. In J. L. Gibbs (Ed.), *Peoples of Africa* (pp. 479–511). New York: Holt, Rinehart & Winston.

Kurtz, D. V. (2001). *Political anthropology: Paradigms and power.* Boulder, CO: Westview Press.

Kushner, G. (1969). *Anthropology of complex societies.* Stanford, CA: Stanford University Press.

LaFont, S. (Ed.). (2003). *Constructing sexualities: Readings in sexuality, gender, and culture.* Upper Saddle River, NJ: Prentice-Hall.

Lai, C. S. L., et al. (2001). A forkhead-domain gene is mutated in severe speech and language disorder. *Nature 413*, 519–523.

Lakoff, R. T. (2004). *Language and woman's place.* M. Bucholtz (Ed.). New York: Oxford University Press.

Lambek, M. (2002). *A reader in the anthropology of religion.* London: Blackwell Press.

Lampe, F. P. (2010). The anthropology of Christianity: Context, contestation, rupture, and continuity. *Reviews in Anthropology 39* (1), 66–88.

Lampl, M., Velhuis, J. D., & Johnson, M. L. (1992). Saltation and stasis: A model of human growth. *Science 258* (5083), 801–803.

Lancaster, J. B. (1975). *Primate behavior and the emergence of human culture.* New York: Holt, Rinehart & Winston.

Landau, M. (1991). *Narratives of human evolution.* New Haven, CT, & London: Yale University Press.

Lang, I. A., et al. (2008). Association of urinary bisphenol A concentration with medical disorders and laboratory abnormalities in adults. *Journal of the American Medical Association 300* (11), 1303–1310.

Lanning, E. P. (1967). *Peru before the Incas.* Englewood Cliffs, NJ: Prentice-Hall.

Larsen, C. S., Matter, R. M., & Gebo, D. L. (1998). *Human origins: The fossil record.* Long Grove, IL: Waveland Press.

Larsen, J. (2006, July 28). Setting the record straight: More than 52,000 Europeans died from heat in summer 2003. *Earth Policy Institute.* www .earth-policy.org/plan_b_updates/2006/update56 (retrieved October 3, 2012)

Lasswell, H. D. (1990). *Politics: Who gets what, when, how.* Gloucester, MA: Peter Smith.

Lawler, A. (2001). Writing gets a rewrite. *Science 292*, 2419.

Layton, R. (1991). *The anthropology of art* (2nd ed.). Cambridge, UK: Cambridge University Press.

Leach, E. (1962). The determinants of differential cross-cousin marriage. *Man 62*, 238.

Leach, E. (1962). On certain unconsidered aspects of double descent systems. *Man 214*, 13–34.

Leach, E. (1982). *Social anthropology.* Glasgow: Fontana Paperbacks.

Leacock, E. (1981). *Myths of male dominance: Collected articles on women cross culturally.* New York: Monthly Review Press.

Leakey, L. S. B. (1965). *Olduvai Gorge, 1951–1961* (vol. 1). London: Cambridge University Press.

Leakey, L. S. B. (1967). Development of aggression as a factor in early man and prehuman evolution. In C. Clements & D. Lundsley (Eds.), *Aggression and defense.* Los Angeles: University of California Press.

Leakey, L. S. B., Tobias, P. B., & Napier, J. R. (1964). A new species of the genus *Homo* from Olduvai Gorge. *Nature 202*, 7–9.

Leakey, M. D. (1971). *Olduvai Gorge: Excavations in Beds I and II. 1960–1963.* London & New York: Cambridge University Press.

Leakey, M. G., Spoor, F., Brown, F. H., Gathogo, P. N., Kiare, C., Leakey, L. N., & McDougal, I. (2001). New hominin genus from eastern Africa shows diverse middle Pliocene lineages. *Nature 410*, 433–440.

"Leave none to tell the story: Genocide in Rwanda." (2004). www .hrw.org/legacy/reports/1999/rwanda/ (retrieved August 28, 2012)

Leavitt, G. C. (1990). Sociobiological explanations of incest avoidance: A critical review of evidential claims. *American Anthropologist 92*, 982.

Leclerc-Madlala, S. (2002). Bodies and politics: Healing rituals in the democratic South Africa. In V. Faure (Ed.), *Les cahiers de l'IFAS,* no. 2. Johannesburg: The French Institute.

Lee, R. B. (1993). *The Dobe Ju/'hoansi.* Fort Worth: Harcourt Brace.

Lee, R. B., & Daly, R. H. (1999). *The Cambridge encyclopedia of hunters and gatherers.* New York: Cambridge University Press.

Lee, R. B., & DeVore, I. (Eds.). (1968). *Man the hunter.* Chicago: Aldine.

Leeds, A., & Vayda, A. P. (Eds.). (1965). *Man, culture and animals: The role of animals in human ecological adjustments.* Washington, DC: American Association for the Advancement of Science.

Lees, R. (1953). The basis of glottochronology. *Language 29*, 113–127.

Lehman, E. C., Jr. (2002, Fall). Women's path into the ministry. *Pulpit & Pew Research Reports 1*, 4.

Lehmann, A. C., & Myers, J. E. (Eds.). (1993). *Magic, witchcraft and religion: An anthropological study of the supernatural* (3rd ed.). Mountain View, CA: Mayfield.

Lehmann, W. P. (1973). *Historical linguistics: An introduction* (2nd ed.). New York: Holt, Rinehart & Winston.

Leigh, S. R., & Park, P. B. (1998). Evolution of human growth prolongation. *American Journal of Physical Anthropology 107*, 331–350.

LeMay, M. (1975). The language capability of Neanderthal man. *American Journal of Physical Anthropology 43* (1), 9–14.

Lenhart, A. (2012, March 19). Teens, smartphones & texting. *Pew Internet & American Life Project.* http://pewinternet .org/Reports/2012/Teens-and-smartphones .aspx (retrieved August 23, 2012)

Lenski, G. (1966). *Power and privilege: A theory of social stratification.* New York: McGraw-Hill.

Leroi-Gourhan, A. (1968). The evolution of Paleolithic art. *Scientific American 218*, 58ff.

Lestel, D. (1998). How chimpanzees have domesticated humans. *Anthropology Today 12* (3).

Leth, P. M. (2007). The use of CT scanning in forensic autopsy. *Forensic Science, Medicine, and Pathology 3* (1), 65–69.

Lett, J. (1987). *The human enterprise: A critical introduction to anthropological theory.* Boulder, CO: Westview Press.

Levine, N. E., & Silk, J. B. (1997). Why polyandry fails. *Current Anthropology 38*, 375–398.

Levine, R. (1973). *Culture, behavior and personality.* Chicago: Aldine.

Levine, R. A. (2007). Ethnographic studies of childhood: A historical overview. *American Anthropologist 109* (2), 247–260.

Lévi-Strauss, C. (1952). *Race and history.* Paris: UNESCO.

Lévi-Strauss, C. (1955). *Tristes tropiques.* Paris: Librarie Plon.

Lévi-Strauss, C. (1963). The sorcerer and his magic. In *Structural anthropology.* New York: Basic Books. (orig. 1958)

Lewellen, T. C. (2002). *The anthropology of globalization: Cultural anthropology enters the 21st century.* Westport, CT: Greenwood Publishing Group/Bergin & Garvey.

Lewin, R. (1983). Is the orangutan a living fossil? *Science 222*, 1223.

Lewin, R. (1985). Tooth enamel tells a complex story. *Science 228*, 707.

Lewin, R. (1986). New fossil upsets human family. *Science 233*, 720–721.

Lewin, R. (1987). Debate over emergence of human tooth pattern. *Science 235*, 749.

Lewin, R. (1987). The earliest "humans" were more like apes. *Science 236*, 1062–1063.

Lewin, R. (1987). Four legs bad, two legs good. *Science 235*, 969.

Lewin, R. (1987). Why is ape tool use so confusing? *Science 236*, 776–777.

Lewin, R. (1988). Molecular clocks turn a quarter century. *Science 235*, 969–971.

Lewin, R. (1993). Paleolithic paint job. *Discover 14* (7), 64–70.

Lewis, I. M. (1965). Problems in the comparative study of unilineal descent. In M. Banton (Ed.), *The relevance of models for social organization.* London: Tavistock.

Lewis-Williams, J. D. (1990). *Discovering southern African rock art.* Cape Town & Johannesburg: David Philip.

Lewis-Williams, J. D., & Dowson, T. A. (1988). Signs of all times: Entoptic phenomena in Upper Paleolithic art. *Current Anthropology 29*, 201–245.

Lewis-Williams, J. D., & Dowson, T. A. (1993). On vision and power in the Neolithic: Evidence from the decorated monuments. *Current Anthropology 34*, 55–65.

Lewis-Williams, J. D., Dowson, T. A., & Deacon, J. (1993). Rock art and changing perceptions of Southern Africa's past: Ezeljagdspoort reviewed. *Antiquity 67*, 273–291.

Lewontin, R. C. (1972). The apportionment of human diversity. In T. Dobzhansky et al. (Eds.), *Evolutionary biology* (pp. 381–398). New York: Plenum Press.

Lewontin, R. C., Rose, S., & Kamin, L. J. (1984). *Not in our genes.* New York: Pantheon.

Li, X., Harbottle, G., Zhang, J., & Wang, C. (2003). The earliest writing? Sign use in the seventh millennium bc at Jiahu, Henan Province, China. *Antiquity 77*, 31–44.

Lieberman, P. (2006). *Toward an evolutionary biology of language.* Cambridge, MA: Belknap Press.

Lindenbaum, S. (1978). *Kuru sorcery: Disease and danger in the New Guinea highlands.* New York: McGraw-Hill.

Lindstrom, L. (1993). *Cargo cult: Strange stories of desire from Melanesia and beyond.* Honolulu: University of Hawaii Press.

Linnekin, J. (1990). *Sacred queens and women of consequence: Rank, gender, and colonialism in the Hawaiian Islands.* Ann Arbor: University of Michigan Press.

Little, K. (1964). The role of voluntary associations in West African urbanization. In P. van den Berghe (Ed.), *Africa: social problems of change and conflict.* San Francisco: Chandler.

Little, K. L. (1973). *African women in town: An aspect of Africa's social revolution* (pp. 58–62). New York: Cambridge University Press.

Littlewood, R. (2004). Commentary: Globalization, culture, body image, and eating disorders. *Culture, Medicine, and Psychiatry 28* (4), 597–602.

Liu, J. (2007). *Gender and work in urban China: Women workers of the unlucky generation.* London: Routledge.

Livingstone, F. B. (1973). The distribution of abnormal hemoglobin genes and their significance for human evolution. In C. Loring Brace & J. Metress (Eds.), *Man in evolutionary perspective.* New York: Wiley.

Living Tongues. www.livingtongues.org (retrieved June 4, 2012)

Lloyd, C. B. (Ed.). (2005). *Growing up global: The changing transitions to adulthood in developing countries.* Washington, DC: National Academies Press.

Lochhead, C. (2004, February 5). Court says same-sex marriage is a right *.San Francisco Chronicle.*

Lock, A. (1980). *The guided reinvention of language.* New York: Academic Press.

Lock, M. (2001). *Twice dead: Organ transplants and the reinvention of death.* Berkeley: University of California Press.

Lorenzo, C., Carretero, J. M., Arsuaga, J. L., Gracia, A., & Martinez, I. (1998). Intrapopulational body size variation and cranial capacity variation in middle Pleistocene humans: The Sima de los Huesos sample (Sierra de Atapuerca, Spain). *American Journal of Physical Anthropology 106*, 19–33.

Loubser, J. H. N. (2003). *Archaeology: The comic.* Lanham, MD: AltaMira Press.

Louie, A. (2004). *Chineseness across borders: Renegotiating Chinese identities in China and the United States.* Durham & London: Duke University Press.

Lovejoy, C. O. (1981). Origin of man. *Science 211* (4480), 341–350.

Lowie, R. H. (1948). *Social organization.* New York: Holt, Rinehart & Winston.

Lowie, R. H. (1956). *Crow Indians.* New York: Holt, Rinehart & Winston. (orig. 1935)

Lowie, R. H. (1966). *Culture and ethnology.* New York: Basic Books.

Lucy, J. A. (1997). Linguistic relativity. *Annual Review of Anthropology 26*, 291–312.

Luhrmann, T. M. (2001). *Of two minds: An anthropologist looks at American psychiatry.* New York: Vintage.

Lurie, N. O. (1973). Action anthropology and the American Indian. In *Anthropology and the American Indian: A symposium.* San Francisco: Indian Historical Press.

MacCormack, C. P. (1977). Biological events and cultural control. *Signs 3*, 93–100.

MacLarnon, A. M., & Hewitt, G. P. (1999). The evolution of human speech: The role of enhanced breathing control. *American Journal of Physical Anthropology 109*, 341–363.

MacNeish, R. S. (1992). *The origins of agriculture and settled life.* Norman: University of Oklahoma Press.

Maggioncalda, A. N., & Sapolsky, R. M. (2002). Disturbing behaviors of the orangutan. *Scientific American 286* (6), 60–65.

Mair, L. (1957). *An introduction to social anthropology.* London: Oxford University Press.

Mair, L. (1969). *Witchcraft.* New York: McGraw-Hill.

Mair, L. (1971). *Marriage.* Baltimore: Penguin Books.

Malefijt, A. D. W. (1969). *Religion and culture: An introduction to anthropology of religion.* London: Macmillan.

Malinowski, B. (1945). *The dynamics of culture change.* New Haven, CT: Yale University Press.

Malinowski, B. (1961). *Argonauts of the western Pacific.* New York: Dutton.

Mann, A., Lampl, M., & Monge, J. (1990). Patterns of ontogeny in human evolution: Evidence from dental development. *Yearbook of Physical Anthropology 33*, 111–150.

Mann, C. C. (2002). The real dirt on rainforest fertility. *Science 297*, 920–923.

Mann, C. C. (2005). *1491: New revelations of the Americas before Columbus.* New York: Knopf.

Marcus, G. (1995). Ethnography in/of the world system: The emergence of multi-sited ethnography. *Annual Review of Anthropology 24*, 95–117.

Marcus, J., & Flannery, K. V. (1996). *Zapotec civilization: How urban society evolved in Mexico's Oaxaca Valley.* New York: Thames & Hudson.

Marks, J. (1995). *Human biodiversity: Genes, race, and history.* Hawthorne, NY: Aldine.

Marks, J. (2000, April 8). A feckless quest for the basketball gene. *New York Times.*

Marks, J. (2000, May 12). 98% alike (what our similarity to apes tells us about our understanding of genetics). *Chronicle of Higher Education*, B7.

Marks, J. (2002). *What it means to be 98 percent chimpanzee: Apes, people, and their genes.* Berkeley: University of California Press.

Marks, J. (2008). Caveat emptor: Genealogy for sale. *Newsletter of the ESRC Genomics Network 7*, 22–23.

Marks, J. (2008). Race: Past, present, and future. In B. Koenig, S. Lee, & S. Richardson (Eds.), *Revisiting race in a genomic age* (pp. 21–38). New Brunswick, NJ: Rutgers University Press.

Marks, J. (2009). *Why I am not a scientist: Anthropology and modern knowledge.* Berkeley: University of California Press.

Marsella, A. J., & White, G. (1982). *Cultural conceptions of mental health and therapy.* New York: Springer.

Marshack, A. (1972). *The roots of civilization: A study in prehistoric cognition: The origins of art, symbol and notation.* New York: McGraw-Hill.

Marshack, A. (1976). Some implications of the Paleolithic symbolic evidence for the origin of language. *Current Anthropology 17* (2), 274–282.

Marshack, A. (1989). Evolution of the human capacity: The symbolic evidence. *Yearbook of physical anthropology* (vol. 32, pp. 1–34). New York: Alan R. Liss.

Marshall, E. (2001). Preclovis sites fight for acceptance. *Science 291*, 1732.

Marshall, L. (1961). Sharing, talking and giving: Relief of social tensions among !Kung Bushmen. *Africa 31*, 231–249.

Martin, E. (1994). *Flexible bodies: Tracking immunity in American culture from the days of polio to the age of AIDS.* Boston: Beacon Press.

Martin, E. (1999). Flexible survivors. *Anthropology News 40* (6), 5–7.

Martin, E. (2009). *Bipolar expeditions: Mania and depression in American culture.* Princeton, NJ: Princeton University Press.

Martorell, R. (1988). Body size, adaptation, and function. *GDP*, 335–347.

Mascia-Lees, F. E., & Black, N. J. (2000). *Gender and anthropology.* Prospect Heights, IL: Waveland Press.

Mason, J. A. (1957). *The ancient civilizations of Peru.* Baltimore: Penguin Books.

Mathieu, C. (2003). *A history and anthropological study of the ancient kingdoms of the Sino-Tibetan borderland—Naxi and Mosuo.* New York: Mellen.

Matson, F. R. (Ed.). (1965). *Ceramics and man.* New York: Viking Fund Publications in Anthropology, no. 41.

Mauss, M. (2000). *The gift: The form and reason for exchange in archaic society* (translation by W. D. Halls and foreword by M. Douglas). New York: Norton.

Max Planck Institute of Evolutionary Anthropology. (2012). Denisova genome. Public data set: http://aws.amazon.com/datasets/ 2357 (retrieved July 19, 2012)

Maybury-Lewis, D. (1960). Parallel descent and the Apinaye anomaly. *Southwestern Journal of Anthropology 16*, 191–216.

Maybury-Lewis, D. (1984). *The prospects for plural societies. 1982 Proceedings of the American Ethnological Society.* Washington, DC: American Ethnological Society.

Maybury-Lewis, D. (2001). *Indigenous peoples, ethnic groups, and the state* (2nd ed.). Boston: Allyn & Bacon.

Mayr, E., & Diamond, J. (2002). *What evolution is.* New York: Basic Books.

McCaskill, C., Lucas, C., Bayley, R., & Hill, J. (2012). *The hidden treasure of Black ASL: Its history and structure* (with contributions from J. C. Hill, R. Dummet-King, P. Baldwin, & R. Hogue). Washington, DC: Gallaudet University Press.

McCorriston, J., & Hole, F. (1991). The ecology of seasonal stress and the origins of agriculture in the Near East. *American Anthropologist 93*, 46–69.

McDermott, L. (1996). Self-representation in Upper Paleolithic female figurines. *Current Anthropology 37*, 227–276.

McDermott, R. (2011, April 1). Polygamy: More common than you think. *Wall Street Journal.* http://online. wsj.com/article/SB100014240527487 03806304576234551596322690.html (retrieved October 7, 2012)

McDonald's. (2012). www.aboutmcdonalds .com (retrieved September 29, 2012)

McElroy, A., & Townsend, P. K. (2003). *Medical anthropology in ecological perspective.* Boulder, CO: Westview Press.

McFate, M. (2007). *Role and effectiveness of socio-cultural knowledge for counterinsurgency.* Alexandria, VA: Institute for Defense Analysis.

McGrew, W. C. (2000). Dental care in chimps. *Science 288*, 1747.

McHenry, H. (1975). Fossils and the mosaic nature of human evolution. *Science 190*, 425–431.

McHenry, H. M. (1992). Body size and proportions in early hominids. *American Journal of Physical Anthropology 87*, 407–431.

McHenry, H. M., & Jones, A. L. (2006). Hallucial convergence in early hominids. *Journal of Human Evolution 50*, 534–539.

McKenna, J. (1999). Co-sleeping and SIDS. In W. Trevathan, E. O. Smith, & J. J. McKenna (Eds.), *Evolutionary medicine.* London: Oxford University Press.

McKenna, J. J. (2002, September–October). Breastfeeding and bedsharing. *Mothering*, 28–37.

McKenna, J. J., Ball, H., & Gettler, L. T. (2007). Mother–infant cosleeping, breastfeeding and SIDS: What biological anthropology has discovered about normal infant sleep and pediatric sleep medicine. *Yearbook of Physical Anthropology 50*, 133–161.

McKenna, J. J., & McDade, T. (2005, June). Why babies should never sleep alone: A review of the co-sleeping controversy in relation to SIDS, bedsharing, and breastfeeding. *Pediatric Respiratory Reviews 6* (2), 134–152.

McNeil, W. (1992). *Plagues and people.* New York: Anchor.

Mead, A. T. P. (1996). Genealogy, sacredness, and the commodities market. *Cultural Survival Quarterly 20* (2).

Mead, M. (1928). *Coming of age in Samoa.* New York: Morrow.

Mead, M. (1960). Anthropology among the sciences. *American Anthropologist 63*, 475–482.

Mead, M. (1963). *Sex and temperament in three primitive societies.* New York: New American Library. (orig. 1935)

Mead, M. (1970). *Culture and commitment.* Garden City, NY: Natural History Press, Universe Books.

Mead, M., & Métraux, R. (Eds.). (1953). *The study of culture at a distance.* Chicago: University of Chicago Press.

"Media frenzy." (2009, May 27). Editorial. *Nature 459*, 484.

Medicine, B. (1994). Gender. In M. B. Davis (Ed.), *Native America in the twentieth century.* New York: Garland.

Melaart, J. (1967). *Catal Hüyük: A Neolithic town in Anatolia.* London: Thames & Hudson.

Mellars, P. (1989). Major issues in the emergence of modern humans. *Current Anthropology 30*, 356–357.

Mellars, P. (2009). Archaeology: Origins of the female image. *Nature 459*, 176–177.

Merkur, D. (1983). Breath-soul and wind owner: The many and the one in Inuit religion. *American Indian Quarterly 7* (3), 23–39.

Merrell, D. J. (1962). *Evolution and genetics: The modern theory of genetics.* New York: Holt, Rinehart & Winston.

Merriam, A. P. (1964). *The anthropology of music.* Chicago: Northwestern University Press.

Merzenich, H., Zeeb, H., & Blettner, M. (2010). Decreasing sperm quality: A global problem? *BMC Public Health.* doi: 10.1186/1471-2458-10-24

Mesghinna, H. M. (1966). Salt mining in Enderta. *Journal of Ethiopian Studies 4* (2).

Métraux, A. (1957). *Easter Island: A stone-age civilization of the Pacific.* New York: Oxford University Press.

Meyer, J. (2008). Typology and acoustic strategies of whistled languages: Phonetic comparison and perceptual cues of whistled vowels. *Journal of the International Phonetic Association 38*, 69–94.

Meyer, J., & Gautheron, B. (2006). Whistled speech and whistled languages. In K. Brown (Ed.), *Encyclopedia of language & linguistics* (2nd ed., vol. 13, pp. 573–576). Oxford, UK: Elsevier.

Meyer, J., Meunier, F., & Dentel, L. (2007). Identification of natural whistled vowels by non-whistlers. *Proceedings of Interspeech 2007.* Antwerp, Belgium.

Michaels, J. W. (1973). *Dating methods in archaeology.* New York: Seminar Press.

Mieth, A., & Bork, H.-R. (2009). Humans, climate or introduced rats—which is to blame for the woodland destruction on prehistoric Rapa Nui (Easter Island)? *Journal of Archaeological Science.* doi:10.1016/j.jas.2009.10.006

Miles, H. (1983). Two-way communication with apes and the evolution of language. In E. de Grollier (Ed.), *Glossogenetics: The origin and evolution of language* (pp. 201–210). Paris: Harwood Academic Publishers.

Miles, H. (1986). How can I tell a lie? Apes, language and the problem of deception. In R. Mitchell & N. Thompson (Eds.), *Deception: Perspectives on human and nonhuman deceit* (pp. 145–266). Albany: SUNY Press.

Miles, H. (1990). The cognitive foundations for reference in a signing orangutan. In S. Parker & K. Gibson (Eds.), *"Language" and intelligence in monkeys and apes: Comparative developmental perspectives* (pp. 511–539). Cambridge, UK: Cambridge University Press.

Miles, H (1993). Language and the orangutan: The "old person" of the forest. In P. Cavalieri & P. Singer (Eds.), *The great ape project* (pp. 45–50). New York: St. Martin's Press.

Miles, H. (1994). ME CHANTEK: The development of self-awareness in a signing orangutan. In S. Parker, R. Mitchell, & M. Boccia (Eds.), *Self-awareness in monkeys and apes: Developmental Perspectives* (pp. 254–272). Cambridge, UK: Cambridge University Press.

Miles, H. (1999). Symbolic communication with and by great apes. In S. Parker, R. Mitchell, & H. Miles (Eds.), *The mentality of gorillas and orangutans: Comparative perspectives* (pp. 197–210). Cambridge, UK: Cambridge University Press.

Miles, H. (2003). Personhood. In J. Goodall et al. (Eds.). *The Great Ape Project Census: Recognition for the uncounted* (introduction by P. Singer, pp. 239–244). Portland, OR: Great Ape Project Books.

Miles, H., & Roberts, W. (1998). Methodologies, not method for primate theory of mind. *Behavioral and Brain Sciences 21* (1), 126.

Millon, R. (1973). *Urbanization of Teotihuacán, Mexico: The Teotihuacán map* (vol. 1, part 1). Austin: University of Texas Press.

Mintz, S. (1996). A taste of history. In W. A. Haviland & R. J. Gordon (Eds.), *Talking about people* (2nd ed., pp. 81–82). Mountain View, CA: Mayfield.

Minugh-Purvis, N. (1992). The inhabitants of Ice Age Europe. *Expedition 34* (3), 33–34.

Mitchell, R., & Miles, H. (1993). Apes have mimetic culture. *Behavioral and Brain Sciences 16* (4), 768.

Mitchell, W. E. (1973, December). A new weapon stirs up old ghosts. *Natural History Magazine*, 77–84.

Modell, J. (1994). *Kinship with strangers: Adoption and interpretations of kinship in American culture.* Berkeley: University of California Press.

Molnar, S. (1992). *Human variation: Races, types and ethnic groups* (3rd ed.). Englewood Cliffs, NJ: Prentice-Hall.

Monaghan, L., Hinton, L., & Kephart, R. (1997). Can't teach a dog to be a cat? The dialogue on Ebonics. *Anthropology Newsletter 38* (3), 1, 8, 9.

Montagu, A. (1964). *The concept of race.* London: Macmillan.

Montagu, A. (1975). *Race and IQ.* New York: Oxford University Press.

Montagu, A. (1998). *Man's most dangerous myth: The fallacy of race* (6th ed.). Lanham, MD: Rowman & Littlefield.

Moore, J. (1998). Comment. *Current Anthropology 39*, 412.

Morello, C. (2011, May 18). Number of long-lasting marriages in U.S. has risen, Census Bureau reports. *Washington Post.*

Morgan, L. H. (1877). *Ancient society.* New York: World Publishing.

Morphy, H., & Perkins, M. (Eds.). (2006). *Anthropology of art: A reader.* Boston: Blackwell Press.

Murdock, G. P. (1965). *Social structure.* New York: Free Press.

Murdock, G. P. (1971). How culture changes. In H. L. Shapiro (Ed.), *Man, culture and society* (2nd ed.). New York: Oxford University Press.

Murthy, D. (2011). Emergent digital ethnographic methods for social research. In S. N. Hesse-Biber (Ed.), *The handbook of emergent technologies in social research* (pp. 158–179). New York: Oxford University Press.

Mydens, S. (2001, August 12). He's not hairy, he's my brother. *New York Times.* www.nytimes.com/2001/08/12/weekinreview/ideas-trends-he-s-not-hairy-he-s-my-brother.html (retrieved June 25, 2012)

Nabhan, G. P. (2004). *Why some like it hot: Food, genes, and cultural diversity.* Washington, DC: Island Press.

Nader, L. (Ed.). (1969). *Law in culture and society.* Chicago: Aldine.

Nader, L. (Ed.). (1981). *No access to law: Alternatives to the American judicial system.* New York: Academic Press.

Nader, L. (Ed.). (1996). *Naked science: Anthropological inquiry into boundaries, power, and knowledge.* New York: Routledge.

Nader, L. (1997). Controlling processes: Tracing the dynamics of power. *Current Anthropology 38*, 715–717.

Nader, L. (2002). *The life of the law: Anthropological projects.* Berkeley: University of California Press.

Nanda, S. (1992). Arranging a marriage in India. In P. R. DeVita (Ed.), *The naked anthropologist* (pp. 139–143). Belmont, CA: Wadsworth.

Nanda, S. (1999). *Neither man nor woman: The hijras of India.* Belmont, CA: Wadsworth.

Nash, J. (1976). Ethnology in a revolutionary setting. In M. A. Rynkiewich & J. P. Spradley (Eds.), *Ethics and anthropology: Dilemmas in fieldwork.* New York: Wiley.

Nast, H. J. (2005). *Concubines and power: Five hundred years in a northern Nigerian palace.* Minneapolis: University of Minnesota Press.

Natadecha-Sponsal, P. (1993). The young, the rich and the famous: Individualism as an American cultural value. In P. R. DeVita & J. D. Armstrong (Eds.), *Distant mirrors: America as a foreign culture* (pp. 46–53). Belmont, CA: Wadsworth.

Natural Resources Defense Council. (2005, March 25). *Healthy milk, healthy baby: Chemical pollution and mother's milk.* www.nrdc.org/breastmilk/ (retrieved October 3, 2012)

Nazzal-Batayneh, M. (2005). Nauru: An environment destroyed and international law. www.lawanddevelopment.org/articles/nauru.html (retrieved October 3, 2012)

Neer, R. M. (1975). The evolutionary significance of vitamin D, skin pigment, and ultraviolet light. *American Journal of Physical Anthropology 43*, 409–416.

Nesbitt, L. M. (1935). *Hell-hole of creation.* New York: Knopf.

Nettle, B. (2005). *The study of ethnomusicology: Thirty-one issues and concepts.* Chicago: University of Illinois Press.

"New ILO global report on child labor." (2010, May 8). International Labour Organization. www.ilocarib.org.tt/index.php?option=com_content&view=article&id=1363:new-ilo-global-report-on-child-labour&catid=214:2010-news&Itemid=1209 (retrieved August 7, 2012)

Nichols, J. (2008). Language spread rates as indicators of glacial-age peopling of the Americas. *Current Anthropology 49* (6), 1109–1117.

Nietschmann, B. (1987). The third world war. *Cultural Survival Quarterly 11* (3), 1–16.

Noack, T. (2001). Cohabitation in Norway: An accepted and gradually more regulated way of living. *International Journal of Law, Policy, and the Family 15* (1), 102–117.

Norbeck, E., Price-Williams, D., & McCord, W. (Eds.). (1968). *The study of personality: An interdisciplinary appraisal.* New York: Holt, Rinehart & Winston.

Normile, D. (1998). Habitat seen as playing larger role in shaping behavior. *Science 279*, 1454.

Nunney, L. (1998). Are we selfish because we are nice, or are we nice because we are selfish? *Science 281*, 1619.

Nye, J. (2002). *The paradox of American power: Why the world's only superpower can't go it alone.* New York: Oxford University Press.

Oakley, K. P. (1964). *Man the toolmaker.* Chicago: University of Chicago Press.

O'Barr, W. M., & Conley, J. M. (1993). When a juror watches a lawyer. In W. A. Haviland & R. J. Gordon (Eds.), *Talking about people* (2nd. ed., pp. 42–45). Mountain View, CA: Mayfield.

Oboler, R. S. (1980). Is the female husband a man? Woman/woman marriage among the Nandi of Kenya. *Ethnology 19*, 69–88.

O'Carroll, E. (2008, June 27). Spain to grant some human rights to apes. *Christian Science Monitor.*

Office of the United Nations Higher Commissioner for Human Rights, Committee on the Elimination of Racial Discrimination, India. (2007, March). Consideration of state reports. www2.ohchr.org/english/bodies/cerd/cerds70.htm (retrieved August 25, 2012)

Offiong, D. (1985). Witchcraft among the Ibibio of Nigeria. In A. C. Lehmann & J. E. Myers (Eds.), *Magic, witchcraft, and religion* (pp. 152–165). Palo Alto, CA: Mayfield.

Offiong, D. A. (1999). Traditional healers in the Nigerian health care delivery system and the debate over integrating traditional and scientific medicine. *Anthropological Quarterly 72* (3), 118–130.

Okonjo, K. (1976). The dual-sex political system in operation: Igbo women and community politics in midwestern Nigeria. In N. Hafkin & E. Bay (Eds.), *Women in Africa.* Stanford, CA: Stanford University Press.

O'Mahoney, K. (1970). The salt trade. *Journal of Ethiopian Studies 8* (2).

One Earth Future Foundation. (2012). *The economic cost of Somali piracy 2011.* http://oceansbeyondpiracy.org/ sites/default/files/economic_cost_of_ piracy_2011_summary.pdf (retrieved August 28)

"111th Canton Fair." (2012). *Live Trading News.* www.livetradingnews. com/111th-canton-fair-74669.htm#. UCKSrcgsAch (retrieved August 8, 2012)

Ong, A. (1999). *Flexible citizenship: The cultural logics of transnationality.* Durham, NC: Duke University Press.

Ortiz, A. (1969). *The Tewa world.* Chicago: University of Chicago Press.

Ortiz, I., & Cummins, M. (2011). Global inequality: Beyond the bottom billion—A rapid review of income distribution in 141 countries. *UNICEF.* www.unicef.org/socialpolicy/ index_58230.html (retrieved October 1, 2012)

Oswalt, W. H. (1972). *Other peoples other customs: World ethnography and its history.* New York: Holt, Rinehart & Winston.

Otte, M. (2000). On the suggested bone flute from Slovenia. *Current Anthropology 41,* 271.

Otten, C. M. (1971). *Anthropology and art: Readings in cross-cultural aesthetics.* Garden City, NY: Natural History Press.

Ottenheimer, M. (1996). *Forbidden relatives: The American myth of cousin marriage.* Champaign: University of Illinois Press.

Paredes, J. A., & Purdum, E. D. (1990). "Bye, bye Ted. . .". *Anthropology Today 6* (2), 9.

Parés, J. M., et al. (2000). On the age of hominid fossils at the Sima de los Huesos, Sierra de Atapuerca, Spain: Paleomagnetic evidence. *American Journal of Physical Anthropology 111,* 451–461.

Parish, A. (1998). Comment. *Current Anthropology 39,* 414.

Parkin, R. (1997). *Kinship: An introduction to basic concepts.* Cambridge, MA: Blackwell Press.

Parnell, R. (1999). Gorilla exposé. *Natural History 108* (8), 43.

Patterson, F., & Linden, E. (1981). *The education of Koko.* New York: Holt, Rinehart & Winston.

Patterson, F., Miles, H., & Savage-Rumbaugh, E. (2003). *Maui Ape Preserve (MAP): The Ape Consortium for Global Research, Education and Conservation.* Woodside, CA: The Gorilla Foundation-koko.org.

Patterson, F. G. P., & Gordon, W. (2002). Twenty-seven years of Project Koko and Michael. In B. Galdikas et al. (Eds.), *All apes great and small: Chimpanzees, bonobos, and gorillas* (vol. 1, pp. 165–176). New York: Kluwer Academic.

Patterson, T. C. (1981). *Archeology: The evolution of ancient societies.* Englewood Cliffs, NJ: Prentice-Hall.

Peacock, J. L. (2002). *The anthropological lens: Harsh light, soft focus* (2nd ed.). New York: Cambridge University Press.

Pearson, V., Phillips, M. R., He, F. , & Ji, H. (2002). Attempted suicide among young rural women in the People's Republic of China: Possibilities for prevention. *Suicide and Life-Threatening Behavior 32* (4), 359–369.

Pease, T. (2000, Spring). Taking the third side. *Andover Bulletin.*

Pelto, G. H., Goodman, A. H., & Dufour, D. L. (Eds.). (2000). *Nutritional anthropology: Biocultural perspectives on food and nutrition.* Mountain View, CA: Mayfield.

Pelto, P. J. (1973). *The snowmobile revolution: Technology and social change in the Arctic.* Menlo Park, CA: Cummings.

Penniman, T. K. (1965). *A hundred years of anthropology.* London: Duckworth.

Pennisi, E. (1999). Genetic study shakes up out of Africa theory. *Science 283,* 1828.

Peters, C. R. (1979). Toward an ecological model of African Plio-Pleistocene hominid adaptations. *American Anthropologist 81* (2), 261–278.

Petersen, J. B., Neuves, E., & Heckenberger, M. J. (2001). Gift from the past: *Terra preta* and prehistoric American occupation in Amazonia. In C. McEwan & C. Barreo (Eds.), *Unknown Amazon* (pp. 86–105). London: British Museum Press.

Peterson, F. L. (1962). *Ancient Mexico: An introduction to the pre-Hispanic cultures.* New York: Capricorn Books.

Pew Research Center, Pew Forum on Religion & Public Life. (2011). The future of the global Muslim population: Projections for 2010–2030. www .pewforum.org/The-Future-of-the-Global-Muslim-Population.aspx (retrieved September 17, 2012)

Pew Research Center, Pew Forum on Religion & Public Life. (2012, October 9). "Nones" on the rise: One-in-five adults have no religious affiliation. www.pewforum.org/Unaffiliated/ nones-on-the-rise.aspx#_ftn3 (retrieved October 23, 2012)

Pfeiffer, J. E. (1985). *The creative explosion.* Ithaca, NY: Cornell University Press.

Pickering, R., et al. (2011). *Australopithecus sediba* at 1.977 ma and implications for the origins of the genus *Homo. Science 333* (6048), 1421–1423.

Piddocke, S. (1965). The potlatch system of the southern Kwakiutl: A new perspective. *Southwestern Journal of Anthropology 21,* 244–264.

Piggott, S. (1965). *Ancient Europe.* Chicago: Aldine.

Pike, A. W. G., et al. (2012). U-series dating of Paleolithic art in 11 caves in Spain. *Science 336,* 1409–1413.

Pilbeam, D. (1987). Rethinking human origins. In *Primate evolution and human origins.* Hawthorne, NY: Aldine.

Pilbeam, D., & Gould, S. J. (1974). Size and scaling in human evolution. *Science 186,* 892–901.

Pimentel, D. (1991). Response. *Science 252,* 358.

Pink, S. (2001). *Doing visual ethnography: Images, media, and representation in research.* Thousand Oaks, CA: Sage.

Pinker, S. (1994). *The language instinct: How the mind creates language.* New York: William Morrow.

Piperno, D. R., & Fritz, G. J. (1994). On the emergence of agriculture in the new world. *Current Anthropology 35,* 637–643.

Plattner, S. (Ed.). (1989). *Economic anthropology.* Stanford, CA: Stanford University Press.

Plattner, S. (1989). Markets and market places. In S. Plattner (Ed.), *Economic anthropology.* Stanford, CA: Stanford University Press.

Pohl, M. E. D., Pope, K. O., & von Nagy, C. (2002). Olmec origins of Mesoamerican writing. *Science 298,* 1984–1987.

Polanyi, K. (1968). The economy as instituted process. In E. E. LeClair Jr. & H. K. Schneider (Eds.), *Economic anthropology: Readings in theory and analysis* (pp. 127–138). New York: Holt, Rinehart & Winston.

Pollan, M. (2001). *The botany of desire: A plant's-eye view of the world.* New York: Random House.

Pollan, M. (2008). *In defense of food: An eater's manifesto.* New York: Penguin Books.

Pollock, N. J. (1995). Social fattening patterns in the Pacific—the positive side of obesity. A Nauru case study. In I. DeGarine & N. J. Pollock (Eds.), *Social aspects of obesity* (pp. 87–109). London: Routledge.

Pope, G. G. (1989). Bamboo and human evolution. *Natural History 10,* 56.

Pope, G. G. (1992). Craniofacial evidence for the origin of modern humans in China. *Yearbook of Physical Anthropology 35,* 291.

Pospisil, L. (1963). *The Kapauku Papuans of West New Guinea.* New York: Holt, Rinehart & Winston.

Pospisil, L. (1971). *Anthropology of law: A comparative theory.* New York: Harper & Row.

Powdermaker, H. (1939). *After freedom: A cultural study in the Deep South.* New York: Viking.

Power, M. G. (1995). Gombe revisted: Are chimpanzees violent and hierarchical in the "free" state? *General Anthropology 2* (1), 5–9.

Poyatos, F. (2002). *Nonverbal communication across disciplines* (3 vols.). Amsterdam: John Benjamins.

Premack, A. J., & Premack, D. (1972). Teaching language to an ape. *Scientific American 277* (4), 92–99.

"President Obama descends from the first African enslaved for life in America." (2012, July). *Ancestry. com.* www.ancestry.com/obama (retrieved August 10, 2012)

Price, D. H. (2011). How the CIA and Pentagon harnessed anthropological research during the Second World War and Cold War with little critical notice. *Journal of Anthropological Research 67* (3), 333–356.

Price, T. D., & Feinman, G. M. (Eds.). (1995). *Foundations of social inequality.* New York: Plenum Press.

Pringle, H. (1997). Ice Age communities may be earliest known net hunters. *Science 277,* 1203–1204.

Pringle, H. (1998). The slow birth of agriculture. *Science 282,* 1446–1449.

Prins, H. E. L. (1994). Neo-traditions in Native communities: Sweat lodge and Sun Dance among the Micmac today. In W. Cowan (Ed.), *Proceedings of the 25th Algonquian conference* (pp. 383–394). Ottawa: Carleton University Press.

Prins, H. E. L. (1996). *The Mi'kmaq: Resistance, accommodation, and cultural survival.* New York: Harcourt Brace.

Prins, H. E. L. (1998). Book review of Schuster, C., & Carpenter, E. *American Anthropologist 100* (3), 841.

Prins, H. E. L. (2002). Visual media and the primitivist perplex: Colonial fantasies and indigenous imagination in North America. In F. Ginsburg, L. Abu-Lughod, & B. Larkin (Eds.), *Media worlds: Anthropology on new terrain* (pp. 58–74). Berkeley: University of California Press.

Prins, H. E. L., & Krebs, E. (2006). Toward a land without evil: Alfred Métraux as UNESCO anthropologist 1948–1962. In *60 years of UNESCO history. Proceedings of the international symposium in Paris, 16–18 November 2005.* Paris: UNESCO.

Prins, H. E. L., & McBride, B. (2012). Upside down: Arctic realities & indigenous art (museum review essay). *American Anthropologist 114* (2), 359–364.

Profet, M. (1991). The function of allergy: Immunological defense against toxins. *Quarterly Review of Biology 66* (1), 23–62.

Profet, M. (1995). *Protecting your baby to be.* New York: Addison-Wesley.

Pruetz, J. D., & Bertolani, P. (2007, March 6). Savanna chimpanzees, *Pan troglodytes verus*, hunt with tools. *Current Biology 17*, 412–417.

Puleston, D. E. (1983). *The settlement survey of Tikal.* Philadelphia: University Museum.

Quinn, N. (2005). Universals of child rearing. *Anthropological Theory 5*, 475–514.

Radcliffe-Brown, A. R. (1931). Social organization of Australian tribes. *Oceana Monographs 1*, 29.

Radcliffe-Brown, A. R., & Forde, C. D. (Eds.). (1950). *African systems of kinship and marriage.* London: Oxford University Press.

Radelet, M. L., & Lacock, T. L. (2009). Do executions lower homicide rates? The views of leading criminologists. *Journal of Criminal Law and Criminology 99* (2), 489.

Radin, P. (1923). The Winnebago tribe. In *37th annual report of the Bureau of American Ethnology, 1915–1916* (pp. 33–550). Washington, DC: U.S. Government Printing Office.

Ralston, C., & Thomas, N. (Eds.). (1987). Sanctity and power: Gender in Polynesian history. *Journal of Pacific History* (special issue) *22* (3–4).

Ramos, A. R. (1987). Reflecting on the Yanomami: Ethnographic images and the pursuit of the exotic. *Current Anthropology 2* (3), 284–304.

Rapp, R. (1999). *Testing women, testing the fetus: The social impact of amniocentesis in America (The Anthropology of Everyday Life).* New York: Routledge.

Rappaport, R. A. (1969). Ritual regulation of environmental relations among a New Guinea people. In A. P. Vayda (Ed.), *Environment and cultural behavior* (pp. 181–201). Garden City, NY: Natural History Press.

Rappaport, R. A. (1984). *Pigs for the ancestors* (enl. ed.). New Haven, CT: Yale University Press.

Rappaport, R. A. (1999). *Holiness and humanity: Ritual in the making of religious life.* New York: Cambridge University Press.

Rasmussen, M., et al. (2011). An aboriginal Australian genome reveals separate human dispersals into Asia, *Science 334* (6052), 94–98. doi: 10.1126/science.1211177

Rathje, W., & Murphy, C. (2001). *Rubbish!: The archaeology of garbage.* Tucson: University of Arizona Press.

Rathje, W. L. (1974). The garbage project: A new way of looking at the problems of archaeology. *Archaeology 27*, 236–241.

Rathje, W. L. (1993). Rubbish! In W. A. Haviland & R. J. Gordon (Eds.), *Talking about people: Readings in contemporary cultural anthropology.* Mountain View, CA: Mayfield.

Rathke, L. (1989). To Maine for apples. *Salt Magazine 9* (4), 24–47.

Read, C. E. (1973). *The role of faunal analysis in reconstructing human behavior: A Mousterian example.* Paper presented at the meetings of the California Academy of Sciences, Long Beach.

Read-Martin, C. E., & Read, D. W. (1975). Australopithecine scavenging and human evolution: An approach from faunal analysis. *Current Anthropology 16* (3), 359–368.

Recer, P. (1998, February 16). Apes shown to communicate in the wild. *Burlington Free Press*, 12A.

Redfield, R. (1953). *The primitive world and its transformations.* Ithaca, NY: Cornell University Press.

Redman, C. L. (1978). *The rise of civilization: From early farmers to urban society in the ancient Near East.* San Francisco: Freeman.

Reich, D., et al. (2010, December 23). Genetic history of an archaic hominin group from Denisova Cave in Siberia. *Nature 468*, 1053–1060.

Reich, D., et al. (2012). Reconstructing Native American population history. *Nature.* doi: 10.1038/nature11258

Reid, J. J., Schiffer, M. B., & Rathje, W. L. (1975). Behavioral archaeology: Four strategies. *American Anthropologist 77*, 864–869.

Reiter, R. (Ed.). (1975). *Toward an anthropology of women.* New York: Monthly Review Press.

Relethford, J. H. (2001). Absence of regional affinities of Neandertal DNA with living humans does not reject multiregional evolution. *American Journal of Physical Anthropology 115*, 95–98.

Relethford, J. H., & Harpending, H. C. (1994). Craniometric variation, genetic theory, and modern human origins. *American Journal of Physical Anthropology 95*, 249–270.

Remarque, E. M. (1929). *All quiet on the western front.* Boston: Little, Brown.

Renfrew, C. (1973). *Before civilization: The radiocarbon revolution and prehistoric Europe.* London: Jonathan Cape.

Reynolds, V. (1994). Primates in the field, primates in the lab. *Anthropology Today 10* (2), 4.

Ribeiro, G. L. (2009). Non-hegemonic globalizations: Alternative transnational processes and agents. *Anthropological Theory 9* (3), 297–329.

Rice, D. S., & Prudence, M. (1984). Lessons from the Maya. *Latin American Research Review 19* (3), 7–34.

Rice, P. (2000). Paleoanthropology 2000—part 1. *General Anthropology 7* (1), 11.

Richmond, B. G., Fleagle, J. K., & Swisher III, C. C. (1998). First hominoid elbow from the Miocene of Ethiopia and the evolution of the Catarrhine elbow. *American Journal of Physical Anthropology 105*, 257–277.

Richter, C. A., et al. (2007). In vivo effects of bisphenol A in laboratory rodent studies. *Reproductive Toxicology 24* (2), 199–224.

Rideout, V. J., Foehr, U. G., & Roberts, D. F. (2010, January). *Generation M²: Media in the lives of 8- to 18-year-olds. A Kaiser Family Foundation Study.* Menlo Park, CA: Henry J. Kaiser Family Foundation. www.kff.org/entmedia/upload/8010.pdf (retrieved August 25, 2012)

Ridley, M. (1999). *Genome: The autobiography of a species in 23 chapters.* New York: HarperCollins.

Rightmire, G. P. (1990). *The evolution of* Homo erectus: *Comparative anatomical studies of an extinct human species.* Cambridge, UK: Cambridge University Press.

Rightmire, G. P. (1998). Evidence from facial morphology for similarity of Asian and African representatives of *Homo erectus. American Journal of Physical Anthropology 106*, 61–85.

Rindos, D. (1984). *The origins of agriculture: An evolutionary perspective.* Orlando: Academic Press.

Ritzer, G. (1983). The McDonaldization of society, *Journal of American Culture 6* (1), 100–107.

Ritzer, G. (2007). *The coming of postindustrial society* (2nd ed.). New York: McGraw-Hill.

Robben, A. C. G. M. (2007). Fieldwork identity: Introduction. In A. C. G. M. Robben & J. A. Sluka (Eds.), *Ethnographic fieldwork: An anthropological reader.* Malden, MA: Blackwell Press.

Robben, A. C. G. M., & Sluka, J. A. (Eds.). (2007). *Ethnographic fieldwork: An anthropological reader.* Malden, MA: Blackwell Press.

Rochat, P. (2001). Origins of self-concept. In G. Bremner & A. Fogel (Eds.), *Blackwell handbook of infant development* (pp. 191–212). Malden, MA: Blackwell Press.

Rogers, J. (1994). Levels of the genealogical hierarchy and the problem of hominoid phylogeny. *American Journal of Physical Anthropology 94*, 81–88.

Romer, A. S. (1945). *Vertebrate paleontology.* Chicago: University of Chicago Press.

Roosevelt, A. C. (1984). Population, health, and the evolution of subsistence: Conclusions from the conference. In M. N. Cohen & G. J. Armelagos (Eds.), *Paleopathology at the origins of agriculture* (pp. 572–574). Orlando: Academic Press.

Rosaldo, M. Z. (1980). *Knowledge and passion: Ilongot notions of self & social life (Cambridge Studies in Cultural Systems).* New York: Cambridge University Press.

Rosas, A., & Bermúdez de Castro, J. M. (1998). On the taxonomic affinities of the Dmanisi mandible (Georgia). *American Journal of Physical Anthropology 107,* 145–162.

Roscoe, P. B. (1995). The perils of "positivism" in cultural anthropology. *American Anthropologist 97,* 497.

Roscoe, W. (1991). *Zuni man-woman.* Albuquerque: University of New Mexico Press.

Rose, S. (2009). Darwin 200: Should scientists study race and IQ? NO: Science and society do not benefit. *Nature 457,* 786–788.

Rowe, M., & Mittermeier, R. A. (1996). *The pictorial guide to the living primates.* East Hampton, NY Pogonias.

Rowe, T. (1988). New issues for phylogenetics. *Science 239,* 1183–1184.

Rudel, T. K., Bates, D., & Machinguiashi, R. (2002). Ecologically noble Amerindians? Cattle ranching and cash cropping among Shuar and colonists in Ecuador. *Latin American Research Review 37* (1), 144–159.

Ruhlen, M. (1994). *The origin of language: Tracing the evolution of the mother tongue.* New York: Wiley.

Rupert, J. L., & Hochachka, P. W. (2001). The evidence for hereditary factors contributing to high altitude adaptation in Andean natives: A review. *High Altitude Medicine & Biology 2* (2), 235–256.

Russon, A., & Miles, H. (1995, November). Cultured orangutans: Culture beyond humans. In H. Miles (Chair), *Do apes have culture?* Annual meeting of the American Anthropological Association, Washington, DC.

Ruvolo, M. (1994). Molecular evolutionary processes and conflicting gene trees: The hominoid case. *American Journal of Physical Anthropology 94,* 89–113.

Rymer, R. (1994). *Genie: A scientific tragedy.* New York: HarperCollins.

Sabloff, J. A. (1997). *The cities of ancient Mexico* (rev. ed.). New York: Thames & Hudson.

Sabloff, J. A., & Lambert-Karlovsky, C. C. (1973). *Ancient civilization and trade.* Albuquerque: University of New Mexico Press.

Sabloff, J. A., & Lambert-Karlovsky, C. C. (Eds.). (1974). *The rise and fall of civilizations, modern archaeological approaches to ancient cultures.* Menlo Park, CA: Cummings.

Sachs, E., Rosenfeld, B., Lhewa, D., Rasmussen, A., & Keller, A. (2008). Entering exile: Trauma, mental health, and coping among Tibetan refugees arriving in Dharamsala, India. *Journal of Traumatic Stress 21* (2), 199–208.

Sacks, O. (1998). *Island of the colorblind.* New York: Knopf.

Sahlins, M. (1961). The segmentary lineage: An organization of predatory expansion. *American Anthropologist 63,* 322–343.

Sahlins, M. (1968). *Tribesmen.* Englewood Cliffs, NJ: Prentice-Hall.

Sahlins, M. (1972). *Stone Age economics.* Chicago: Aldine.

Salzman, P. C. (1967). Political organization among nomadic peoples. *Proceedings of the American Philosophical Society 111,* 115–131.

Sanday, P. R. (1975). On the causes of IQ differences between groups and implications for social policy. In M. F. A. Montagu (Ed.), *Race and IQ* (pp. 232–238). New York: Oxford University Press.

Sanday, P. R. (1981). *Female power and male dominance: On the origins of sexual inequality.* Cambridge, UK: Cambridge University Press.

Sanday, P. R. (2002). *Women at the center: Life in a modern matriarchy.* Ithaca, NY: Cornell University Press.

Sangree, W. H. (1965). The Bantu Tiriki of western Kenya. In J. L. Gibbs Jr. (Ed.), *Peoples of Africa* (pp. 69–72). New York: Holt, Rinehart & Winston.

Sanjek, R. (1990). On ethnographic validity. In R. Sanjek (Ed.), *Field notes.* Ithaca, NY: Cornell University Press.

Sapir, E. (1921). *Language.* New York: Harcourt.

Sapolsky, R. (2002). *A primate's memoir: Love, death, and baboons in East Africa.* New York: Vintage.

Savage-Rumbaugh, S., & Lewin, R. (1994). *Kanzi: The ape at the brink of the human mind.* New York: Wiley.

Sawert, H. (2002, October 11–12). *TB and poverty in the context of global TB control.* World Health Organization. Satellite Symposium on TB & Poverty. www.stoptb.org/assets/documents/ resources/publications/acsm/H. RightsReport2001.pdf

Scarr-Salapatek, S. (1971). Unknowns in the IQ equation. *Science 174,* 1223–1228.

Schaeffer, S. B., & Furst, P. T. (Eds.). (1996). *People of the peyote: Huichol Indian history, religion, and survival.* Albuquerque: University of New Mexico Press.

Schaller, G. B. (1971). *The year of the gorilla.* New York: Ballantine.

Scheflen, A. E. (1972). *Body language and the social order.* Englewood Cliffs, NJ: Prentice-Hall.

Schepartz, L. A. (1993). Language and human origins. *Yearbook of Physical Anthropology 36,* 91–126.

Scheper-Hughes, N. (2003, May 10). Keeping an eye on the global traffic in human organs. *Lancet 361* (9369), 1645–1648.

Schilling, C. (2012, August 20). Love, American style: Polygamy gets sizzle. *WorldNetDaily.* www.wnd.com/2012/08/ love-american-style-polygamy-gets-sizzle/ (retrieved October 7, 2012)

Schilt, K., & Westbrook, L. (2009, August). Doing gender, doing heteronormativity: "Gender normals," transgender people, and the social maintenance of heterosexuality. *Gender & Society 23* (4), 440–464.

Schoepfle, M. (2001). Ethnographic resource inventory and the National Park Service. *Cultural Resource Management 5,* 1–7.

Schrire, C. (Ed.). (1984). *Past and present in hunter-gatherer studies.* Orlando: Academic Press.

Schusky, E. L. (1975). *Variation in kinship.* New York: Holt, Rinehart & Winston.

Schusky, E. L. (1983). *Manual for kinship analysis* (2nd ed.). Lanham, MD: University Press of America.

Schuster, C., & Carpenter, E. (1996). *Patterns that connect: Social symbolism in ancient and tribal art.* New York: Abrams.

Schwartz, J. H. (1984). Hominoid evolution: A review and a reassessment. *Current Anthropology 25* (5), 655–672.

Scully, T. (2008). Online anthropology draws protest from aboriginal group. *Nature 453,* 1155. doi:10.1038/4531155a

Scupin, R. (Ed.). (2000). *Religion and culture: An anthropological focus.* Upper Saddle River, NJ: Prentice-Hall.

Seeger, A. (2004). *Why Suyá sing: A musical anthropology.* Champaign: University of Illinois Press.

Seiffert, E. R., et al. (2009). Convergent evolution of anthropoid-like adaptations in Eocene adapiform primates. *Nature 461,* 1118–1121.

Selinger, B. (2007). The Navajo, psychosis, Lacan, and Derrida. *Texas Studies in Literature and Language 49* (1), 64–100.

Sellen, D. W., & Mace, R. (1997). Fertility and mode of subsistence: A phylogenetic analysis. *Current Anthropology 38,* 886.

Semenov, S. A. (1964). *Prehistoric technology.* New York: Barnes & Noble.

Senut, B., et al. (2001). First hominid from the Miocene (Lukeino formation, Kenya). *C. R. Academy of Science, Paris 332,* 137–144.

Seyfarth, R. M., Cheney, D. L., & Marler, P. (1980). Vervet monkey alarm calls: Semantic communication in a free-ranging primate. *Animal Behavior 28* (4), 1070–1094.

Seyfarth, R. M., et al. (1980). Monkey responses to three different alarm calls: Evidence for predator classification and semantic communication. *Science 210,* 801–803.

Shapiro, H. (Ed.). (1971). *Man, culture and society* (2nd. ed.). New York: Oxford University Press.

Sharer, R. J., & Ashmore, W. (2007). *Archaeology: Discovering our past* (4th ed.). New York: McGraw-Hill.

Sharp, G. (1973). *The politics of nonviolent action.* Boston: Extending Horizons Books, Porter Sargent Publishers.

Sharp, G. (2010). *From dictatorship to democracy: A conceptual framework for liberation* (4th ed.). East Boston: Einstein Institution.

Sharpe, K., & Van Gelder, L. (2006). Evidence of cave marking by Paleolithic children. *Antiquity 80* (310), 937–947.

Shea, P. J. (2007). Excellent legacies of Abo Bayero. In A. U. Adamu (Ed.), *Chieftaincy and security in Nigeria: Past, present, and future* (pp. i–vi). http:// ibrahimshekarau.com/downloads/ videos1/books/12.pdf (retrieved August 26, 2012)

Sheets, P. D. (1993). Dawn of a new Stone Age in eye surgery. In R. J. Sharer & W. Ashmore. *Archaeology: Discovering our past* (2nd ed.). Palo Alto, CA: Mayfield.

Sherzer, J. (2002). *Speech play and verbal art.* Austin: University of Texas Press.

Shi, L. (2009). Little quilted vests to warm parents' hearts: Redefining the gendered practice of filial piety in rural north-eastern China. *China Quarterly 198*, 348–363.

Shipman, P. (1993). *Life history of a fossil: An introduction to taphonomy and paleoecology.* Cambridge, MA: Harvard University Press.

Shook, J. R., et al. (Eds.). (2004). *Dictionary of modern American philosophers, 1860–1960.* Bristol, UK: Thoemmes Press.

Shostak, M. (2000). *Nisa: The life and words of a !Kung woman.* Cambridge, MA: Harvard University Press.

Shreeve, J. (1994). Terms of estrangement. *Discover 15* (11), 60.

Shreeve, J. (1995). *The Neandertal enigma: Solving the mystery of modern human origins.* New York: William Morrow.

Shuey, A. M. (1966). *The testing of Negro intelligence.* New York: Social Science Press.

Sillen, A., & Brain, C. K. (1990). Old flame. *Natural History 4,* 10.

Silverstein, J. (2012). Bonds beyond blood: DNA testing and refugee family resettlement. *Anthropology News 53* (4), 11.

Simons, E. L. (1972). *Primate evolution.* New York: Macmillan.

Simons, E. L. (1989). Human origins. *Science 245,* 1349.

Simons, E. L., et al. (2009, July 22). Outrage at high price paid for a fossil. Correspondence. *Nature 460,* 456.

Simons, R. C., & Hughes, C. C. (Eds.). (1985). *The culture-bound syndromes: Folk illnesses of psychiatric and anthropological interest.* New York: Springer.

Simpson, G. G. (1949). *The meaning of evolution.* New Haven, CT: Yale University Press.

Simpson, S. (1995, April). Whispers from the ice. *Alaska,* 23–28.

Simpson, S. W., et al. (2008). A female *Homo erectus* pelvis from Gona, Ethiopia. *Science 322* (5904), 1089–1092.

Skelton, R. R., McHenry, H. M., & Drawhorn, G. M. (1986). Phylogenetic analysis of early hominids. *Current Anthropology 27,* 21–43.

Skolnick, A., & Skolnick, J. (Eds.). (2001). *Family in transition* (11th ed.). Boston: Allyn & Bacon.

Sluka, J. A. (2007). Fieldwork relations and rapport: Introduction. In A. C. G. M. Robben & J. A. Sluka (Eds.), *Ethnographic fieldwork: An anthropological reader.* Malden, MA: Blackwell Press.

Small, M. F. (1997). Making connections. *American Scientist 85,* 503.

Small, M. F. (2008, August 15). Why red is such a potent color. *Live Science.* www.livescience.com/5043-red-potent-color.html (retrieved June 20, 2012)

Small, M. F. (2009, May 15). Why "Ida" inspires navel-gazing at our ancestry. *Live Science.* www.livescience.come/history/090520-hn-ida.html

Smedley, A. (2007). *Race in North America: Origin and evolution of a worldview.* Boulder, CO: Westview Press.

Smith, B. D. (1977). Archaeological inference and inductive confirmation. *American Anthropologist 79* (3), 598–617.

Smith, B. H. (1994). Patterns of dental development in *Homo, Australopithecus, Pan,* and *gorilla. American Journal of Physical Anthropology 94,* 307–325.

Smith, M. D. (2008, September 16). Indian child labor exploited in production of soccer balls. *Huffington Post.* www.aolnews.com/2008/09/16/indian-child-labor-exploited-in-production-of-soccer-balls/ (retrieved August 7, 2012)

Smith, P. E. L. (1976). *Food production and its consequences* (2nd ed.). Menlo Park, CA: Cummings.

Smith, W. W. (2009). *China's Tibet: Autonomy or assimilation?* Lanham, MD: Rowman & Littlefield.

Smuts, B. (1987). What are friends for? *Natural History 96* (2), 36–44.

Snowden, C. T. (1990). Language capabilities of nonhuman animals. *Yearbook of Physical Anthropology 33,* 215–243.

Songok, E. M., Luo, M., Liang, B., Mclaren, P., Kaefer, N., Apidi, W., Boucher, G., Kimani, J., Wachihi, C., Sekaly, R., Fowke, K., Ball, B. T., & Plummer, F. A. (2012). Microarray analysis of HIV resistant female sex workers reveal a gene expression signature pattern reminiscent of a lowered immune activation state. *PLoS One 7* (1), e30048.

Spencer, R. F. (1984). North Alaska Coast Eskimo. In D. Damas (Ed.), *Arctic: Handbook of North American Indians* (vol. 5, pp. 320–337). Washington, DC: Smithsonian Institution Press.

Spindler, G., & Stockard, J. E. (Eds.). (2006). Globalization and change in fifteen cultures. Belmont, CA: Wadsworth.

Spradley, J. P. (1979). *The ethnographic interview.* New York: Holt, Rinehart & Winston.

Spradley, J. P. (1980). *Participant observation.* New York: Holt, Rinehart & Winston.

Springen, K. (2008, September 15). What it means to be a woman: How women around the world cope with infertility. *Newsweek.com.* www.thedailybeast.com/newsweek/2008/09/14/what-it-means-to-be-a-woman.html (retrieved June 12, 2012)

Stacey, J. (1990). *Brave new families.* New York: Basic Books.

Stahl, A. B. (1984). Hominid dietary selection before fire. *Current Anthropology 25,* 151–168.

Stanford, C. B. (1998). The social behavior of chimpanzees and bonobos: Empirical evidence and shifting assumptions. *Current Anthropology 39,* 399–420.

Stanford, C. B. (2001). *Chimpanzee and red colobus: The ecology of predator and prey.* Cambridge, MA: Harvard University Press.

Stanley, S. M. (1979). *Macroevolution.* San Francisco: Freeman.

Stannard, D. E. (1992). *American holocaust.* Oxford, UK: Oxford University Press.

Steady, F. C. (2001). *Women and the Amistad connection, Sierra Leone Krio Society.* Rochester, VT: Schenkman.

Steady, F. C. (2005). *Women and collective action in Africa.* New York: Palgrave Macmillan.

Stedman, H. H., et al. (2004). Myosin gene mutation correlates with anatomical changes in the human lineage. *Nature 428,* 415–418.

Stein, R., & St. George, D. (2009, May 13). Babies increasingly born to unwed mothers. *Washington Post.*

Stenseth, N. C., & Voje, K. L. (2009). Easter Island: Climate change might have contributed to past cultural and societal changes. *Climate Research 39,* 111–114.

Steward, J. H. (1972). *Theory of culture change: The methodology of multilinear evolution.* Urbana: University of Illinois Press.

Stiles, D. (1979). Early Acheulean and developed Oldowan. *Current Anthropology 20* (1), 126–129.

Stiles, D. (1992). The hunter-gatherer "revisionist" debate. *Anthropology Today 8* (2), 13–17.

Stockard, J. E. (2002). *Marriage in culture: Practice and meaning across diverse societies.* Fort Worth: Harcourt College.

Stocking, G. W., Jr. (1968). *Race, culture and evolution: Essays in the history of anthropology.* New York: Free Press.

Stolberg, S. G. (2011, February 16). Shy U.S. intellectual created playbook used in a revolution. *New York Times.* www.nytimes.com/2011/02/17/world/middleeast/17sharp.html?pagewanted=all (retrieved August 28, 2012)

Stone, L. (2005). *Kinship and gender: An introduction* (3rd ed.). Boulder, CO: Westview Press.

Stone, R. (1995). If the mercury soars, so may health hazards. *Science 267,* 958.

Strier, K. (1993, March). Menu for a monkey. *Natural History,* 42.

Stringer, C. B., & McKie, R. (1996). *African exodus: The origins of modern humanity.* London: Jonathan Cape.

Strum, S., & Mitchell, W. (1987). Baboon models and muddles. In W. Kinsey (Ed.), *The evolution of human behavior: Primate models.* Albany: SUNY Press.

Stuart-MacAdam, P., & Dettwyler, K. A. (Eds.). (1995). *Breastfeeding: Biocultural perspectives.* New York: Aldine.

Suárez-Orozoco, M. M., Spindler, G., & Spindler, L. (1994). *The making of psychological anthropology, II.* Fort Worth: Harcourt Brace.

Suwa, G., Kono, R. T., Katoh, S., Asfaw, B., & Beyene, Y. (2007, August 23). A new species of great ape from the late Miocene epoch in Ethiopia. *Nature 448,* 921–924. Published online: doi:10.1038/nature06113.

Swadesh, M. (1959). Linguistics as an instrument of prehistory. *Southwestern Journal of Anthropology 15,* 20–35.

Swaminathan, M. S. (2000). Science in response to basic human needs. *Science 287,* 425.

Swartz, M. J., Turner, V. W., & Tuden, A. (1966). *Political anthropology.* Chicago: Aldine.

Swisher III, C. C., Curtis, G. H., Jacob, T., Getty, A. G., & Widiasmoro, A. S. (1994). Age of the earliest known hominids in Java, Indonesia. *Science 263,* 1118–1121.

Tamm, E., et al. (2007). Beringian standstill and spread of Native American frontiers. *PLoS One 2* (9), e829. doi: 10.1371/journal/pone.0000829

Tannen, D. (1990). *You just don't understand: Women and men in conversation.* New York: Morrow.

Tapper, M. (1999). *In the blood: Sickle-cell anemia and the politics of race.* Philadelphia: University of Pennsylvania Press.

Tattersall, I., & Schwartz, J. H. (1999). Hominids and hybrids: The place of Neanderthals in human evolution. *Proceedings of the National Academy of Science 96* (13), 7117–7119.

Tax, S. (Ed.). (1962). *Anthropology today: Selections.* Chicago: University of Chicago Press.

Taylor, G. (2000). *Castration: Abbreviated history of western manhood.* New York: Routledge.

Tedlock, B. (2005). *The woman in the shaman's body: Reclaiming the feminine in religion and medicine.* New York: Random House.

Templeton, A. R. (1994). Eve: Hypothesis compatibility versus hypothesis testing. *American Anthropologist 96* (1), 141–147.

Templeton, A. R. (1995). The "Eve" hypothesis: A genetic critique and reanalysis. *American Anthropologist 95* (1), 51–72.

Templeton, A. R. (1996). Gene lineages and human evolution. *Science 272,* 1363–1364.

Terashima, H. (1983). Mota and other hunting activities of the Mbuti archers: A socio-ecological study of subsistence technology. *African Studies Monograph* (Kyoto), 71–85.

Thomas, E. M. (1994). *The tribe of the tiger: Cats and their culture.* New York: Simon & Schuster.

Thompson, K. (2012, July 30). Obama's purported link to early American slave is latest twist in family tree. *Washington Post.* www.washingtonpost.com/ politics/purported-obama-link-to-first-american-slave-is-latest-twist-in-presidents-family-tree/2012/07/30/gJQAYuG1KX_story.html?hpid=z4 (retrieved August 10, 2012)

Thomson, K. S. (1997). Natural selection and evolution's smoking gun. *American Scientist 85,* 516.

Thorne, A. G., & Wolpoff, M. D. H. (1981). Regional continuity in Australasian Pleistocene hominid evolution. *American Journal of Physical Anthropology 55,* 337–349.

Thornhill, N. Quoted in Haviland, W. A., & Gordon, R. J. (Eds.). (1993). *Talking about people* (p. 127). Mountain View, CA: Mayfield.

Thorpe, S. K. S., Holder, R. L., & Crompton, R. H. (2007). Origin of human bipedalism as an adaptation for locomotion on flexible branches. *Science 316,* 1328–1331.

Timmons, H., & Kumar, H. (2009, July 3). Indian court overturns gay sex ban. *New York Times.*

Tobias, P. V., & von Königswald, G. H. R. (1964). A comparison between the Olduvai hominines and those of Java and some implications for hominid phylogeny. *Nature 204,* 515–518.

Toth, N., et al. (1993). Pan the toolmaker: Investigations in the stone tool-making and tool-using capabilities of a bonobo (*Pan paniscus*). *Journal of Archaeological Science 20* (1), 81–91.

Tracy, J. L., & Matsumoto, D. (2008). The spontaneous expression of pride and shame: Evidence for biologically innate nonverbal displays. *Proceedings of the National Academy of Sciences 105* (33), 11655–11660.

Trevathan, W., Smith, E. O., & McKenna, J. J. (Eds.). (1999). *Evolutionary medicine.* London: Oxford University Press.

Trevor-Roper, H. (1992). Invention of tradition: The highland tradition of Scotland. In E. Hobsbawm & T. Ranger (Eds.), *The invention of tradition* (ch. 2). Cambridge, UK: Cambridge University Press.

Trifonov, V., Khiabanian, H., Greenbaum, B., & Rabadan, R. (2009). The origin of the recent swine influenza A (H1N1) virus infecting humans. *Eurosurveillance 14* (17). www.eurosurveillance.org/ViewArticle.aspx?ArticleId=19193 (retrieved July 16, 2012)

Trinkaus, E. (1986). The Neanderthals and modern human origins. *Annual Review of Anthropology 15,* 197.

Trinkaus, E., & Shipman, P. (1992). *The Neandertals: Changing the image of mankind.* New York: Knopf.

Trocolli, R. (2005). *Elite status and gender: Women leaders in chiefdom societies of the Southeastern U.S.* PhD dissertation, University of Florida.

Trouillot, M. R. (1996). Culture, color, and politics in Haiti. In S. Gregory & R. Sanjek (Eds.), *Race.* New Brunswick, NJ: Rutgers University Press.

Trouillot, M. R. (2003). *Global transformations: Anthropology and the modern world.* New York: Palgrave Macmillan.

Tsai, S.-S. H. (1996). *The eunuchs in the Ming dynasty.* Albany: SUNY Press.

Tumin, M. M. (1967). *Social stratification: The forms and functions of inequality.* Englewood Cliffs, NJ: Prentice-Hall.

Turnbull, C. M. (1961). *The forest people.* New York: Simon & Schuster.

Turnbull, C. M. (1983). *The human cycle.* New York: Simon & Schuster.

Turnbull, C. M. (1983). *Mbuti Pygmies: Change and adaptation.* New York: Holt, Rinehart & Winston.

Turner, T. (1991). Major shift in Brazilian Yanomami policy. *Anthropology Newsletter 32* (5), 1, 46.

Turner, V. W. (1957). *Schism and continuity in an African society.* Manchester, UK: University Press.

Turner, V. W. (1969). *The ritual process.* Chicago: Aldine.

"Two Americans are found slain on Jeep journey in Central Java." (1950, April 29). *New York Times.*

Tylor, E. B. (1871). *Primitive culture: Researches into the development of mythology, philosophy, religion, language, art and customs.* London: Murray.

Tylor, E. B. (1931). Animism. In V. F. Calverton (Ed.), *The making of man: An outline of anthropology.* New York: Modern Library.

Ucko, P. J., & Rosenfeld, A. (1967). *Paleolithic cave art.* New York: McGraw-Hill.

Ucko, P. J., Tringham, R., & Dimbleby, G. W. (Eds.). (1972). *Man, settlement, and urbanism.* London: Duckworth.

Umar, U. (2008). *Dancing with spirits: Negotiating bissu subjectivity through Adat.* MA thesis, Department of Religious Studies. University of Colorado, Boulder. Ann Arbor, MI: ProQuest.

UNAIDS. (2009). *2009 AIDS epidemic update.* www.unaids.org/en/dataanalysis/epidemiology/2009aidsepidemicupdate/ (retrieved June 28, 2012)

UN Dispatch. (2006, July 26). Study estimates 250,000 active child soldiers. www.undispatch.com/study-estimates-250000-active-child-soldiers (retrieved August 28, 2012)

UNESCO Decade for Literacy. www.unesco.org/new/en/education/themes/education-building-blocks/literacy/un-literacy-decade/

UNESCO Institute for Statistics. The official source of literacy data. www.uis.unesco.org/literacy/Pages/default.aspx?SPSLanguage=EN (retrieved June 4, 2012)

UNICEF. (2011, February 23). Child protection from violence, exploitation, and abuse. www.unicef.org/protection/index_childlabour.html (retrieved September 15, 2011)

United Nations Human Settlements Program. (2003). *The challenge of slums: Global report on human settlement.* London: Earthscan Publications.

United Nations Literacy Decade (2003–2012). UNESCO. www.unesco.org/new/en/education/themes/education-building-blocks/literacy/un-literacy-decade (retrieved June 4, 2012)

United Nations, Universal Declaration of Human Rights. www.un.org/en/documents/udhr/index.shtml (retrieved October 1, 2012)

UN Refugee Agency. (2011, June 20). World Refugee Day: UNHCR report finds 80 per cent of world's refugees in developing countries. www.unhcr.org/4dfb66ef9.html (retrieved September 30, 2012)

Ury, W. L. (1982). *Talk out or walk out: The role and control of conflict in a Kentucky coal mine.* PhD dissertation, Harvard University Press.

Ury, W. L. (1993). *Getting past no: Negotiating your way from confrontation.* New York: Bantam.

Ury, W. L. (1999). *Getting to peace: Transforming conflict at home, at work, and in the world.* New York: Viking.

Ury, W. L. (2002, Winter). A global immune system. *Andover Bulletin.*

Ury, W. L. (Ed.). (2002). *Must we fight? From the battlefield to the schoolyard—A new perspective on violent conflict and its prevention.* Hoboken, NJ: Jossey-Bass.

Ury, W. L. (2007). *The power of a positive no.* New York: Bantam.

U.S. Census Bureau. (2010). Families and living arrangements. www.census.gov/hhes/families/ (retrieved August 19, 2012)

U.S. Census Bureau, Statistical Abstract. (2012). Births, deaths, marriages, and divorces: Life expectancy. www.census.gov/compendia/statab/cats/births_deaths_marriages_divorces/life_expectancy.html (retrieved August 23, 2012)

U.S. Department of Health and Human Services, Administration on Children, Youth, and Families. (2005). *Child maltreatment 2003.* Washington, DC: U.S. Government Printing Office.

U.S. Department of State, Diplomacy in Action. (2007). China. www.state.gov/j/drl/rls/hrrpt/2007/100518.htm (retrieved October 31, 2012)

U.S. Senate Special Committee on Aging. http://aging.senate.gov/ (retrieved August 23, 2012)

Van Allen, J. (1997). Sitting on a man: Colonialism and the lost political institutions of Igbo women. In R. Grinker & C. Steiner (Eds.), *Perspectives on Africa.* Boston: Blackwell Press.

Van Cott, D. L. (2008). *Radical democracy in the Andes.* Cambridge, UK: Cambridge University Press.

Van den Berghe, P. (1992). The modern state: Nation builder or nation killer? *International Journal of Group Tensions 22* (3), 191–208.

Van Eck, C. (2003). *Purified by blood: Honour killings amongst Turks in the Netherlands.* Amsterdam: Amsterdam University Press.

Van Gennep, A. (1960). *The rites of passage.* Translated by M. Vizedom & G. L. Caffee. Chicago: University of Chicago Press. (orig. 1909)

Van Tilberg, J. A. (1994). *Easter Island archaeology, ecology, and culture.* London: British Museum Press.

Van Willigen, J. (1986). *Applied anthropology.* South Hadley, MA: Bergin & Garvey.

Van Willigen, J. (2002). *Applied anthropology: An introduction.* Westport, CT: Bergin & Garvey.

Vera, H. (2011). *The social life of measures: Metrication in the United States and Mexico, 1789–2004,* PhD dissertation, Sociology and Historical Studies, New School for Social Research.

Vidya, R. (2002). Karnataka's unabating kidney trade. *Frontline.* www.frontlineonnet .com/fl1907/19070610.htm (retrieved June 10, 2012)

Vincent, J. (1979). On the special division of labor, population, and the origins of agriculture. *Current Anthropology 20* (2), 422–425.

Vincent, J. (2002). *The anthropology of politics: A reader in ethnography, theory, and critique.* Boston: Blackwell Press.

Vitali, S., Glattfelder, J. B., & Battiston, S. (2011). The network of global corporate control. *PloS One 6* (10), e25995. doi:10.1371/journal .pone.0025995

Voget, F. W. (1975). *A history of ethnology.* New York, Holt, Rinehart & Winston.

Vogt, E. Z. (1990). *The Zinacantecos of Mexico: A modern Maya way of life* (2nd ed.). Fort Worth: Holt, Rinehart & Winston.

vom Saal, F. S., & Myers, J. P. (2008). Bisphenol A and risk of metabolic disorders. *Journal of the American Medical Association 300* (11), 1353–1355.

Wagner, P. L. (1960). *A history of ethnology.* New York: Holt, Rinehart & Winston.

Wallace, A. F. C. (1956). Revitalization movements. *American Anthropologist 58,* 264–281.

Wallace, A. F. C. (1966). *Religion: An anthropological view.* New York: Random House.

Wallace, A. F. C. (1970). *Culture and personality* (2nd ed.). New York: Random House.

Wallace, E., & Hoebel, E. A. (1952). *The Comanches.* Norman: University of Oklahoma Press.

Walrath, D. (2006). Gender, genes, and the evolution of human birth. In P. L. Geller & M. K. Stockett (Eds.), *Feminist anthropology: Past, present, and future.* Philadelphia: University of Pennsylvania Press.

Washburn, S. L., & Moore, R. (1980). *Ape into human: A study of human evolution* (2nd ed.). Boston: Little, Brown.

Washington, H. (2006) *Medical apartheid: The dark history of medical experimentation on black Americans from colonial times to the present,* New York: Anchor.

Weatherford, J. (1988). *Indian givers: How the Indians of the Americas transformed the world.* New York: Ballantine.

Weaver, M. P. (1972). *The Aztecs, Maya and their predecessors.* New York: Seminar Press.

Weaver, T. (2002). Gonzalo Aguirre Beltrán: Applied anthropology and indigenous policy. In *The dynamics of applied anthropology in the twentieth century: The Malinowski award papers* (pp. 34–37). Oklahoma City: Society for Applied Anthropology.

Weiner, A. B. (1977). Review of Trobriand cricket: An ingenious response to colonialism. *American Anthropologist 79,* 506.

Weiner, A. B. (1988). *The Trobrianders of Papua New Guinea.* New York: Holt, Rinehart & Winston.

Weiner, J. S. (1955). *The Piltdown forgery.* Oxford, UK: Oxford University Press.

Weiss, M. L., & Mann, A. E. (1990). *Human biology and behavior* (5th ed.). Boston: Little, Brown.

Wells, S. (2002). *The journey of man: A genetic odyssey.* Princeton, NJ: Princeton University Press.

Wenzel, G. W., & McCartney, A. P. (1996, September). Richard Guy Condon (1952–1995). *Arctic 49* (3), 319–320.

Werner, D. (1990). *Amazon journey.* Englewood Cliffs, NJ: Prentice-Hall.

Wernick, R., & the Editors of Time-Life. (1973). *The monument builders.* New York: Time-Life.

Wheeler, P. (1993). Human ancestors walked tall, stayed cool. *Natural History 102* (8), 65–66.

Wheelersburg, R. P. (1987). New transportation technology among Swedish Sámi reindeer herders. *Arctic Anthropology 24* (2), 99–116.

Whelehan, P. (1985). Review of incest, a biosocial view. *American Anthropologist 87,* 678.

White, D. R. (1988). Rethinking polygyny: Co-wives, codes, and cultural systems. *Current Anthropology 29,* 529–572.

White, L. (1949). *The science of culture: A study of man and civilization.* New York: Farrar, Strauss.

White, L. (1959). *The evolution of culture: The development of civilization to the fall of Rome.* New York: McGraw-Hill.

White, M. (2001). *Historical atlas of the twentieth century.* http://users.erols.com/ mwhite28/20centry.htm (retrieved August 28, 2012)

White, R. (1992). The earliest images: Ice Age "art" in Europe. *Expedition 34* (3), 37–51.

White, T., Asfaw, B., Degusta, D., Gilbert, H., Richards, G., Suwa, G., & Howell, F. C. (2003). Pleistocene *Homo sapiens* from the Middle Awash, Ethiopia. *Nature 423,* 742–747.

White, T. D. (1979). Evolutionary implications of Pliocene hominid footprints. *Science 208,* 175–176.

White, T. D. (2003). Early hominids—diversity or distortion? *Science 299,* 1994–1997.

White, T. D., & Toth, N. (2000). Cutmarks on a Plio-Pleistocene hominid from Sterkfontein, South Africa. *American Journal of Physical Anthropology 111,* 579–584.

White, T. D., et al. (2009, October). *Ardipithecus ramidus* and the paleobiology of early hominoids. *Science 326* (5949), 64, 75–86.

Whitehead, N. L., & Ferguson, R. B. (Eds.). (1992). *War in the tribal zone.* Santa Fe: School of American Research Press.

Whitehead, N. L., & Ferguson, R. B. (1993, November). Deceptive stereotypes about tribal warfare. *Chronicle of Higher Education,* A48.

Whiting, B. B. (Ed.). (1963). *Six cultures: Studies of child rearing.* New York: Wiley.

Whiting, J. W. M., & Child, I. L. (1953). *Child training and personality: A cross-cultural study.* New Haven, CT: Yale University Press.

Whiting, J. W. M., Sodergem, J. A., & Stigler, S. M. (1982). Winter temperature as a constraint to the migration of preindustrial peoples. *American Anthropologist 84,* 289.

Whorf, B. (1946). The Hopi language, Toreva dialect. In *Linguistic structures of Native America.* New York: Viking Fund.

Whyte, A. L. H. (2005). Human evolution in Polynesia. *Human Biology 77* (2), 157–177.

"Why the stories are told," Aunty Beryl Carmichael. *Aboriginal culture: Dreamtime stories.* www.rmwebed.com. au/HSIE/y10/abc/dreamtime/dreamtime.htm (retrieved August 28, 2012)

Wiley, A. S. (2004). *An ecology of high-altitude infancy: A biocultural perspective.* Cambridge, UK: Cambridge University Press.

Wilk, R. R. (1996). *Economics and culture: An introduction to economic anthropology.* Boulder, CO: Westview Press.

Wilkie, D. S., & Curran, B. (1993). Historical trends in forager and farmer exchange in the Ituri rainforest of northeastern Zaire. *Human Ecology 21* (4), 389–417.

Willey, G. R. (1966). *An introduction to American archaeology: North America* (vol. 1). Englewood Cliffs, NJ: Prentice-Hall.

Willey, G. R. (1971). *An introduction to American archaeology: South America* (vol. 2). Englewood Cliffs, NJ: Prentice-Hall.

Williams, F. (2005, January 9). Toxic breast milk? *New York Times Magazine.*

Williams, S. (2003). Tradition and change in the sub-Arctic: Sámi reindeer herding in the modern era. *Scandinavian Studies 75* (2), 228–256.

Williamson, R. K. (1995). The blessed curse: Spirituality and sexual difference as viewed by Euro-American and Native American cultures. *The College News 18* (4).

Wills, C. (1994). The skin we're in. *Discover 15* (11), 79.

Wilson, A. K., & Sarich, V. M. (1969). A molecular time scale for human evolution. *Proceedings of the National Academy of Science 63,* 1089–1093.

Wingert, P. (1965). *Primitive art: Its tradition and styles.* New York: World.

Winick, C. (Ed.). (1970). *Dictionary of anthropology.* Totowa, NJ: Littlefield, Adams.

Wirsing, R. L. (1985). The health of traditional societies and the effects of acculturation. *Current Anthropology 26* (3), 303–322.

Wittfogel, K. A. (1957). *Oriental despotism, a comparative study of total power.* New Haven, CT: Yale University Press.

Wolf, E. R. (1966). *Peasants.* Englewood Cliffs, NJ: Prentice-Hall.

Wolf, E. R. (1982). *Europe and the people without history.* Berkeley: University of California Press.

Wolf, E. R. (1999). *Envisioning power: Ideologies of dominance and crisis.* Berkeley: University of California Press.

Wolf, E. R. (1999). *Peasant wars of the twentieth century* (2nd ed.). Norman: University of Oklahoma Press.

Wolf, E. R., & Hansen, E. C. (1972). *The human condition in Latin America.* New York: Oxford University Press.

Wolf, E. R., & Trager, G. I. (1971). Hortense Powdermaker: 1900–1970. *American Anthropologist 73* (3), 784.

Wolf, M. (1972). *Women and the family in rural Taiwan.* Stanford, CA: Stanford University Press.

Wolf, M. (1985). *Revolution postponed: Women in contemporary China.* Stanford, CA: Stanford University Press.

Wolff, P., & Holmes, K. J. (2011). Linguistic relativity. *WIRE's Cognitive Science 2,* 253–265.

Wolpoff, M. (1996). *Australopithecus:* A new look at an old ancestor. *General Anthropology 3* (1), 2.

Wolpoff, M., & Caspari, R. (1997). *Race and human evolution.* New York: Simon & Schuster.

Wolpoff, M. H. (1977). Review of earliest man in the Lake Rudolf Basin. *American Anthropologist 79,* 708–711.

Wolpoff, M. H. (1982). *Ramapithecus* and hominid origins. *Current Anthropology 23,* 501–522.

Wolpoff, M. H. (1993). Evolution in *Homo erectus:* The question of stasis. In R. L. Ciochon & J. G. Fleagle (Eds.),

The human evolution source book. Englewood Cliffs, NJ: Prentice-Hall.

Wolpoff, M. H. (1993). Multiregional evolution: The fossil alternative to Eden. In R. L. Ciochon & J. G. Fleagle (Eds.), *The human evolution source book.* Englewood Cliffs, NJ: Prentice-Hall.

Wolpoff, M. H., Wu, X. Z., & Thorne, A. G. (1984). Modern *Homo sapiens* origins: A general theory of hominid evolution involving fossil evidence from east Asia. In F. H. Smith & F. Spencer (Eds.), *The origins of modern humans* (pp. 411–483). New York: Alan R. Liss.

Wood, B., & Aiello, L. C. (1998). Taxonomic and functional implications of mandibular scaling in early hominines. *American Journal of Physical Anthropology 105,* 523–538.

Wood, B., Wood, C., & Konigsberg, L. (1994). *Paranthropus boisei:* An example of evolutionary stasis? *American Journal of Physical Anthropology 95,* 117–136.

Woodford, M. H., Butynski, T. M., & Karesh W. (2002). Habituating the great apes: The disease risks. *Oryx 36,* 153–160.

Woodward, V. (1992). *Human heredity and society.* St. Paul, MN: West.

Woolfson, P. (1972). Language, thought, and culture. In V. P. Clark, P. A. Escholz, & A. F. Rosa (Eds.), *Language.* New York: St. Martin's Press.

World Bank. (2012). Migration and remittances. *WorldBank.org.* http://web .worldbank.org/WBSITE/EXTERNAL/ NEWS/0,,contentMDK:20648762~pa gePK:64257043~piPK:437376~theSite PK:4607,00.html (retrieved October 1, 2012)

World Bank. (2012). Poverty. http:// www.worldbank.org/en/topic/poverty (retrieved October 1, 2012)

World Commission on Environment & Development. (1987). Our common future. A/42/427. www.un-documents.net/ocf-ov.htm (retrieved September 29, 2012)

World Development Indicators Database. (2012, September 18). Gross domestic product, 2011. *Worldbank.org.* http://databank .worldbank.org/databank/download/ GDP.pdf (retrieved October 1, 2012)

World Health Organization, Preamble to the Constitution. (1948). www.who.int/about/definition/ en/print.html

World Health Organization. (2004). *Statistical information system.* www.who .int/whosis/en/ (retrieved September 2, 2011)

World Health Organization. (2010, February). *Female genital mutilation.* Fact sheet no. 241. www.who.int/mediacentre/ factsheets/fs241/en/ (retrieved September 16, 2011)

World Health Organization. (2012, June). Children: Reducing mortality. Fact sheet no. 178. www.who.int/ mediacentre/factsheets/fs178/en/index .html (retrieved August 11, 2012)

World Travel & Tourism Council. (2012). Annual report, 2011. www .wttc.org

Worsley, P. (1957). *The trumpet shall sound: A study of "cargo" cults in Melanesia.* London: Macgibbon & Kee.

Worsley, P. (1959, May). Cargo cults. *Scientific American 200,* 117–128.

Wrangham, R., & Peterson, D. (1996). *Demonic males.* Boston: Houghton Mifflin. [ep]

Wright, R. M. (1997). Violence on Indian day in Brazil 1997: Symbol of the past and future. *Cultural Survival Quarterly 21* (2), 47–49.

Wu, X., & Poirier, F. E. (1995). *Human evolution in China.* New York: Oxford University Press.

Wulff, R. M., & Fiske, S. J. (1987). *Anthropological praxis: Translating knowledge into action.* Boulder, CO: Westview Press.

Wyckoff-Baird, B. (2010, March 19). Indicators from Ju/'hoan Bushmen in Namibia. *Cultural Survival.* www .culturalsurvival.org/ourpublications/ csq/article/indicators-juhoan-bushmen-namibia (retrieved October 2, 2012)

Yates, D. (2011). *Archaeological practice and political change: Transitions and transformations in the use of the past in nationalist, neoliberal and indigenous Bolivia.* PhD dissertation, Department of Archaeology, Cambridge, UK: University of Cambridge.

Young, A. (1981). The creation of medical knowledge: Some problems in interpretation. *Social Science and Medicine 17,* 1205–1211.

Young, W. C. (2000). Kimball award winner. *Anthropology News 41* (8), 29.

Zeder, M. A., & Hesse, B. (2000). The initial domestication of goats (*Capra hircus*) in the Zagros Mountains 10,000 years ago. *Science 287,* 2254–2257.

Zeresenay, A., et al. (2006). A juvenile early hominin skeleton from Dikika, Ethiopia. *Nature 443,* 296–301.

Zilhão, J. (2000). Fate of the Neandertals. *Archaeology 53* (4), 30.

Zimmer, C. (1999). New date for the dawn of dream time. *Science 284,* 1243.

Zimmer, C. (2005). *Smithsonian intimate guide to human origins.* New York: HarperCollins.

Zimmer, C. (2009, September 21). The secrets inside your dog's mind. *Time .com.* www.time.com/time/magazine/ article/0,9171,1921614-1,00.html (retrieved July 16, 2012)

Zohary, D., & Hopf, M. (1993). *Domestication of plants in the Old World* (2nd ed.). Oxford, UK: Clarendon Press.

Index